Advance praise for *Who Built America?*

"*Who Built America?* stands out from other textbooks in the clarity of its focus. The labor theme serves as an excellent framework, allowing the authors to synthesize most of the events in the standard chronology of history while still providing a distinctive perspective."
— Lawrence A. Peskin, *Morgan State University*

"*Who Built America?* is a textbook of remarkable scope and diversity, with the narrative drive of a good novel. This is how it should be."
— Betty Mitchell, *University of Massachusetts, Dartmouth*

"A history of American society must begin and end with its people and *Who Built America?* excels at this."
— Gordon Harvey, *University of Louisiana, Monroe*

"The new subheadings in the table of contents are a wonderful addition. Students need a way to organize material, and these subdivisions make the chapters easier to follow."
— Diane Barnes, *Youngstown State University*

"The visual materials in *Who Built America?* have always been terrific. The pictures, for example, are often unique to this text, while one sees the same things over and over in others. *WBA?*'s successful search for materials on working people in particular make it especially captivating for students in search of a fresh perspective on the American past."
— Jama Lazerow, *Wheelock College*

Who Built America?

THIRD EDITION

Volume Two
Since 1877

American Social History Project
The City University of New York

Roy Rosenzweig
George Mason University

Nelson Lichtenstein
University of California, Santa Barbara

Visual Editors: Joshua Brown, Graduate Center, City University of New York, and David Jaffee, Bard Graduate Center for Studies in The Decorative Arts, Design, and Culture

Executive Editor: Stephen Brier, Graduate Center, City University of New York

Supervising Editor: Pennee Bender, Graduate Center, City University of New York

Based on previous editions authored by: Joshua Freeman, Stephen Brier, David Bensman, Susan Porter Benson, David Brundage, Bret Eynon, Bruce Levine, Bryan Palmer, and Susan Strasser

Who Built America?

Working People and the Nation's History

THIRD EDITION

Volume Two
Since 1877

BEDFORD / ST. MARTIN'S

BOSTON ✦ NEW YORK

For Bedford/St. Martin's

Publisher for History: Mary V. Dougherty
Director of Development for History: Jane Knetzger
Executive Developmental Editor for History: William J. Lombardo
Developmental Editor: Shannon Hunt
Production Editors: Deborah Baker and Annette Pagliaro Sweeney
Production Supervisor: Jennifer Peterson
Executive Marketing Manager: Jenna Bookin Barry
Editorial Assistants: Holly Dye and Adrianne Hiltz
Production Assistants: Lindsay DiGianvittorio and Katherine Caruana
Copyeditor: Barbara Willette
Text and Cover Design: Joyce Weston
Indexer: James O'Brien
Cover Art: Photo courtesy of Kheel Center for Labor-Management and Archives, School of Industrial and Labor Relations, Cornell University
Cartography: Mapping Specialists Limited
Composition: Pine Tree Composition
Printing and Binding: R. R. Donnelley & Sons Company

President: Joan E. Feinberg
Editorial Director: Denise B. Wydra
Director of Marketing: Karen Melton Soeltz
Director of Editing, Design, and Production: Marcia Cohen
Managing Editor: Elizabeth M. Schaaf

Library of Congress Control Number: 2007934299

Manufactured in the United States of America.

2   1   0   9   8

f   e   d   c

For information, write: Bedford/St. Martin's, 75 Arlington Street, Boston, MA 02116 (617-399-4000)

ISBN-10: 0-312-44691-8 (Vol. One)   ISBN-10: 0-312-44692-6 (Vol. Two)
ISBN-13: 978-0-312-44691-8   ISBN-13: 978-0-312-44692-5

For Roy Rosenzweig (1950–2007), trusted friend and collaborator, world-class historian, and coauthor and coeditor, who was with us every step of the way for the past twenty-five years and who helped us understand that to recover a meaningful past, we needed to give voice to ordinary people, embrace innovation in all its forms, and possess, as he always did, a great sense of humor.

Preface

Who built the seven towers of Thebes?
The books are filled with the names of kings.
Was it kings who hauled the craggy blocks of stone? . . .
In the evening when the Chinese wall was finished,
Where did the masons go? . . .

> —Bertolt Brecht, "Questions from a
> Worker Who Reads" (1935)

WHO BUILT AMERICA? surveys the nation's past from an important but often neglected perspective: the transformations wrought by the changing nature and forms of work and the role that working people played in the making of modern America. In an age when globalizing economies, profound technological changes, and ever more remote exercises of power are altering the nature of life and labor, *Who Built America?*'s distinctive interpretation of the nation's past is more necessary than ever. Not merely a documentation of the country's presidents, politics, and wars, *Who Built America?* focuses on the fundamental social and economic conflicts that have shaped U.S. history and challenges the notion that the vast majority of America's citizens have always been united in a broad consensus about the nation's basic values and shared in its extraordinary prosperity. This emphasis puts the history of the workplace, community, family, gender roles, race, and ethnicity at the center of the more familiar textbook narrative of politics and economic development; in doing so, it renders more intelligible the beliefs and actions of the nation's economic, political, and intellectual elites. By taking up the central questions of how the nation's work has changed and how workers have changed the nation, *Who Built America?* offers an indispensable guide to the historical developments that have brought us to the present day.

Approach

We have defined the category of "working people" broadly. Throughout much of its history, the nation's actual workforce embraced a wide spectrum of people laboring in very different conditions and settings. Answering the question "Who built America?" therefore requires attention not only to wage-earning industrial employees but also to indentured servants, slaves, tenant farmers, sharecroppers, independent farm families, artisans, small proprietors, day laborers, clerks, domestic workers, outworkers, service and technical workers, and women and children performing unpaid family labor—in short, the great majority of the American population at every phase of the country's development.

This book grew out of the now four-decades-old effort to reinterpret American history from the bottom up—drawing on studies of workers, women, consumers, farmers, African Americans, and immigrants—that has helped transform our understanding of the past. The American Social History Project (ASHP) was founded in 1981 at the City University of New York by Herbert Gutman (a pioneer of what was then the "new social history") and Stephen Brier to bring this history to the broadest possible audience. In addition to this book, ASHP has produced over the past quarter-century a wide range of accessible educational materials in print, video, and digital media and worked closely with college, high school, and adult and labor education teachers to help them use these resources effectively in their classrooms.

Who Built America?, now in its third edition, retains its distinctive interpretation and strong point of view. We continue to tackle controversial issues and offer opinions that are sometimes critical of celebrated figures or dominant beliefs. Our view is that readers would rather encounter a clearly stated perspective, even if they disagree with it, than bland platitudes about the past.

Organization and Coverage

This volume of *Who Built America?* is divided into three parts. Its principal theme is the increasing significance of global industrial capitalism and wage labor for the nation's economy, social relations, domestic politics, foreign policy, and intellectual life since 1877 and the corresponding growth and transformation of the American working class. A prologue sets the stage for this story by recapitulating the story of Reconstruction and the 1877 railroad strikes, which are also covered in the first volume. Each part is preceded by a brief essay that lays out the events, changes, and ideas covered in the chapters to come. These essays help students to think synthetically and thematically about the material.

- Part One considers the years between the great railroad strikes of 1877 and the outbreak of war in Europe in 1914, exploring industrial capitalism's Gilded Age growth and the resulting rise of mass movements of protest, including the labor movement, Populism, and socialism. It also covers U.S. overseas expansion, the increasing racism and segregationist legislation that rolled back gains achieved by African Americans in the Reconstruction era, the massive wave of immigration from eastern and southern Europe that transformed the nation's cities after 1900, the dramatic changes in popular culture and everyday life in the early twentieth century, and the progressive movement that emerged in response to the nation's growing political and economic crisis.

- Part Two surveys the two world wars and the turbulent decades between them. It examines the unparalleled growth and power of U.S. political and economic institutions, and the continued recomposition of the American working class through a vast internal migration of Americans, white and black, from the rural South. Tracing the dramatic impact of the Great Depression, this part details working people's unprecedented mobilization, that gave birth to the industrial union movement and an expansive sense of citizenship and empowerment for millions of working Americans. This new political engagement helped sustain the partial welfare state created by Franklin Roosevelt's New Deal and America's entry into and ultimate victory in World War II.

- Part Three examines life in post–World War II America, as U.S. military and economic ascendancy and tensions with the Soviet Union defined the Cold War era. It explores the triumph, decline, and continued struggles of the labor movement and the changing working-class experience as new waves of immigrants arrived after 1965. Highlighting the birth of the civil rights movement that transformed America's political culture and moral values and gave rise to a host of new social movements, Part Three covers U.S. involvement in Vietnam, the subsequent rise of the New Right, and the continued conflicts over gender and race. Moving into the twenty-first century, this part's final chapters consider economic globalization, America's war on terror, and the increasing divide between the nation's wealthy and the poor and middle classes.

New to This Edition and Distinctive Features

The most visible change in the third edition is a reorganized chapter structure that makes *Who Built America?* work better as a textbook. Each chapter now has several main sections with subsections, enabling students to navigate the chapters more efficiently. New outlines at the beginning of each chapter show coverage at a glance. All section headings have been revised for clarity, all chapter and section introductions have been strengthened to help students focus on key ideas, and each chapter ends with a conclusion that reinforces the main points and eases the transition to the next chapter. Detailed timelines (Years in Review) are provided at the end of each chapter to ensure that key events are not lost in the narrative flow and to facilitate review. For instructors and students seeking to explore topics in greater depth, there is also at the end of each chapter a list of Additional Readings that encompass the topics covered in that chapter.

Just as important, for this edition we have taken into account the vast outpouring of recent scholarship to explore more deeply the histories of Spanish-speaking peoples, women, popular culture, new technologies, and developments in the American Southwest and Far West. At the same time, we have linked these histories both to changing class and racial dynamics in the broader society and to the decisions made by economic and political elites. We have also expanded discussions of the global context which defined American labor and politics. Where new historical evidence has come to light, we have modified our interpretation. Volume Two ends with an entirely new chapter — "America's World After 9/11" — that examines the social history and impact of September 11, 2001; the realities exposed and questions raised by the catastrophic effects of Hurricane Katrina; the effects of globalization on America's working people; and the continuing war in Iraq.

In response to user feedback, this edition of *Who Built America?* also contains more "Voices" in each chapter — excerpts from letters, diaries, autobiographies, poems, songs, journalism, fiction, official testimony, oral histories, and other historical documents. These primary sources convey the experiences and beliefs of working people who lived through the events recounted in the text and offer instructors additional opportunities for assignments and discussions. In the interest of clarity, we have modernized some of the spelling, punctuation, and usage in these records.

Visual Program

The drawings, paintings, prints, cartoons, photographs, objects, and other visual media that we have selected to illustrate *Who Built America?* supplement the book's themes and narrative, showing the people, places, and events discussed in the text. In this new edition, we have included examples of material culture — from implements used in the workshop or office to furniture used in the home — to show how everyday objects embodied significant changes in social life. But in keeping with our approach in the first two editions of the book, our illustrations also address subjects not included in the narrative; they offer perspectives on the past that were often not articulated in the written record or were conveyed in a wholly different way from "the word" via visual media. Throughout U.S. history, ideas, experiences, events, and conditions were recorded and expressed in evocative and provocative images and objects that Americans treated with as much seriousness and enjoyment as they did text. Sometimes tainted by racism or chauvinism and marked by invidious caricatures, Americans challenged these images as part of their larger longstanding struggles to achieve equality. In short, images mattered, and the illustrations and captions in each chapter of *Who Built America?* offer readers a parallel narrative that, in juxtaposition to the text, demonstrates how different visual media interpreted and thus helped shape beliefs about the people, events, and ideas of the time.

Supplements

NEW   Computerized Test Bank for *Who Built America?* Written by Steven H. Jaffe, Ph.D. (Volume 1), and John Spencer of Ursinus College (Volume 2), the new Test Bank for *Who Built America?* offers multiple-choice, short answer, and essay questions for each chapter, providing opportunities for ongoing assessments and cumulative exams.

NEW   Instructor's Resource CD-ROM. Includes PowerPoint presentations built around chapter outlines, maps, figures, and selected images from the textbook, plus JPEG versions of all maps and figures and selected images.

NEW   Book Companion Site at bedfordstmartins.com/whobuiltamerica The companion Web site gathers all the electronic resources for *Who Built America?* at a single Web address, providing convenient links to assignment and research materials such as the libraries at Make History and the resources provided by the American Social History Project/Center for Media and Learning.

Acknowledgments

Despite the major changes implemented by the authors and editors of this edition, the narrative of *Who Built America?* rests heavily on the labors of the authors of the previous two editions: David Bensman, Susan Porter Benson, Stephen Brier, Joshua Brown, David Brundage, Bret Eynon, Joshua Freeman, Bruce Levine, Nelson Lichtenstein, Bryan Palmer, and Susan Strasser. We want to note with regret the passing of Susan Porter Benson, who was one of the original authors and contributors to the American Social History Project. In addition, we want to thank the many people who helped to bring forth this edition, especially our colleagues at Bedford/ St. Martin's: Joan Feinberg, Mary Dougherty, Jane Knetzger, William

Lombardo, Donna Dennison, Shelby Disario, Jenna Bookin Barry, Patricia Rossi, Shannon Hunt, Amy Leathe, Holly Dye, Adrianne Hiltz, Elizabeth Schaaf, Annette Pagliaro Sweeney, and Deborah Baker.

Elizabeth Shermer, a graduate student at the University of California, Santa Barbara, proved invaluable as a researcher and editor for the portions of Volume Two written by Nelson Lichtenstein. We are deeply grateful to Jim O'Brien for his superb work on the index. We thank Jeannette Gabriel, Tom Harbison, Madeleine Lopez, Vernon Lucas, Karl Hagstrom Miller, Leah Potter, Tabitha Tally, and Andrea Ades Vásquez for research and advice. We especially thank Will Menaker for research assistance and help in locating and captioning illustrations. We reiterate our sincere thanks to the many people who helped on the first two editions (and are acknowledged in those volumes). And we thank Lynn Hunt for her abiding faith in and commitment to the American Social History Project.

To the following colleagues who gave us encouragement and valuable feedback at various stages during the preparation of this edition, we are most grateful: Gregg Andrews, Texas State University, San Marcos; Jay Antle, Johnson County Community College; Diane Barnes, Youngstown State University; Michael Botson, Houston Community College; Tracy Campbell, University of Kentucky; Robert Cassanello, University of Central Florida; Elizabeth Clement, University of Utah; Gregory Dorr, University of Alabama; Laurence Gross, University of Massachusetts Lowell; Gordon Harvey, University of Louisiana at Monroe; Robert Harmon, Elgin Community College; Martin Halpern, Henderson State University; Patricia Knol, Triton College; Jama Lazerow, Wheelock College; Norman Markowitz, Rutgers University; Betty Mitchell, University of Massachusetts Dartmouth; Jason Newman, Cosumnes River College; Greg O'Brien, University of Southern Mississippi; Lawrence Peskin, Morgan State University; Dona Reaser, Columbus State Community College; Steve Rosswurm, Lake Forest College; Victor Silverman, Pomona College; Ashley Sousa, West Valley College; and Steve Stein, University of Memphis.

Finally, we would be remiss if we ended our acknowledgments without noting the role of the late Herbert Gutman (1929–1985) in creating the American Social History Project, which gave birth to this book, and in shaping the generation of historical scholarship on which it is based. Our collective and individual debts to Herb are immeasurable. We hope that this new edition of *Who Built America?* meets the high standards he set for himself throughout his rich but too brief career.

Contents

2. Community and Conflict: Working People Respond to Industrial Capitalism, 1877–1893 76

3. From Depression to Expansion: Industrial Capitalism Triumphs at Home and Abroad, 1893–1900 124

Part Three. Cold War America—And After, 1946–2007   552

13. Economic Adversity Transforms the Nation, 1973–1989   682

About the Authors and Editors

Nelson Lichtenstein is Professor of History at the University of California, Santa Barbara, where he directs the Center for the Study of Work, Labor and Democracy. He is the author of *Labor's War at Home: The CIO in World War II* (1982, 2003), *Walter Reuther: The Most Dangerous Man in Detroit* (1997), and *State of the Union: A Century of American Labor* (2002), which won the Philip Taft Prize in Labor History. He has held fellowships from the Guggenheim and Rockefeller Foundations and often writes for *New Labor Forum, Dissent,* and *The Los Angeles Times.* His edited books include *Industrial Democracy in America: The Ambiguous Promise* (1993), *Wal-Mart: The Face of Twenty-First-Century Capitalism* (2006), *American Capitalism: Social Thought and Political Economy in the Twentieth Century* (2006), and *Major Problems in the History of American Workers* (2003).

Roy Rosenzweig was Mark and Barbara Fried Professor of History and New Media at George Mason University, where he founded the Center for History and New Media (http://chnm.gmu.edu), and served as its director until his death in October 2007. Roy was the author, coauthor, and coeditor of numerous books, including *The Park and the People: A History of Central Park; The Presence of the Past: Popular Uses of History in American Life; Eight Hours for What We Will: Workers and Leisure in an Industrial City, 1870–1920; History Museums in the United States: A Critical Assessment; Presenting the Past: Essays on History and the Public;* and *Digital History: A Guide to Gathering, Presenting, and Preserving the Past on the Web.* He was co-creator of the CD-ROM *Who Built America?,* which won the James Harvey Robinson Prize of the American Historical Association for its "outstanding contribution to the teaching and learning of history," as well as the Web sites *History Mat-*

ters and *World History Matters,* which won the same prize. He was also the recipient of the Richard W. Lyman Award for "outstanding achievement in the use of information technology to advance scholarship and teaching in the humanities."

Stephen Brier, Executive Editor, cofounded the American Social History Project in 1981 with the late Herbert Gutman and served as its Executive Director until 1998. He was the supervising editor and coauthor of the first edition of the *Who Built America?* textbook and executive editor of the second edition. He also coauthored the two *Who Built America?* CD-ROMs and was the executive producer of ASHP's award-winning *Who Built America?* video series and the Web site *History Matters: The U.S. Survey Course on the Web.* Dr. Brier is the Vice President for Information Technology and External Programs, the codirector of the New Media Lab, and the coordinator of the doctoral Certificate Program in Interactive Technology and Pedagogy at the Graduate Center of the City University of New York. He has written numerous scholarly and popular articles on race, class, and ethnicity in U.S. labor history and on the educational impact of instructional media and information technology.

Joshua Brown, Visual Editor, is the Executive Director of the American Social History Project/ Center for Media and Learning and Professor of History at the Graduate Center of the City University of New York. He was visual editor of the first edition of *Who Built America?* and also coauthored the accompanying CD-ROMs and video documentary series. He has served as executive producer on many digital and Web projects, including *Liberty, Equality, Fraternity: Exploring the French Revolution, History Matters: The U.S. Survey Course on the Web, The Lost*

Museum: Exploring Antebellum American Life and Culture, and *The September 11 Digital Archive*. Brown is author of *Beyond the Lines: Pictorial Reporting, Everyday Life, and the Crisis of Gilded Age America* (2002), coauthor (with Eric Foner) of *Forever Free: The Story of Emancipation and Reconstruction* (2005), and coeditor of *History from South Africa: Alternative Visions and Practices* (1991), as well as numerous essays and reviews on the history of U.S. visual culture. He serves on the editorial boards of *Common-place*, *Labor*, and the *Encyclopedia of American Studies* and is a member of the American Antiquarian Society. His cartoons and illustrations appear regularly in academic and popular publications in print and online.

Pennee Bender, Supervising Editor, is the Associate Director and a Media Producer with the American Social History Project/Center for Media and Learning at the Graduate Center of the City University of New York. She was a co-creator of the Web site *History Matters: The U.S. Survey Course on the Web* and of two CD-ROMs: *Who Built America? From the Great War of 1914 to the Dawn of the Atomic Age* and *Liberty, Equality, Fraternity: Exploring the French Revolution*. She also served as Web producer of *The Lost Museum: Exploring Antebellum American Life and Culture* and *What Exit: New Jersey and Its Turnpike*. Her film and video credits include *Savage Acts: Wars, Fairs, and Empire; Heaven Will Protect the Working Girl; The West Bank: Whose Promised Land; Bitter Cane; Missing Persons/Personas Ausentes;* and *Labor Produces*. She has a Ph.D. in U.S. history from New York University and teaches working women's history at the Cornell Institute for Industrial and Labor Relations.

Ellen Noonan, Supervising Editor, works as a director of education programs and a media producer at the American Social History Project/Center for Media and Learning at the Graduate Center of the City University of New York. While with ASHP/CML, she has helped to conceptualize and write for the Web sites *History Matters: The U.S. Survey Course on the Web, The Lost Museum: Exploring Antebellum American Life and Culture*, and *The September 11 Digital Archive*. She has also designed and implemented faculty development programs serving hundreds of New York City public school social studies teachers. She served as Managing Editor and member of the Editorial Collective of *Radical History Review*, and she received her Ph.D. in U.S. History from New York University.

David Jaffee teaches American material culture at the Bard Graduate Center or Studies in the Decorative Arts, Design, and Culture. He is the author of *People of the Wachusett: Greater New England in History and Memory, 1630–1860* (1999) and is completing a book titled *Craftsmen and Consumers in Early America, 1760–1860*. He has also written many essays on artists and artisans in early America as well as on the use of new media in the history classroom. He was the project director of two NEH grants at the City College of New York to develop multimedia resources for the teaching of U.S. history. He has been the recipient of various fellowships from organizations including the Metropolitan Museum of Art, the Winterthur Museum, and the Huntington Library.

Who Built America?

THIRD EDITION

Volume Two
Since 1877

Prologue

From the Civil War
to the Great Uprising of Labor:
Reconstructing the Nation

1865–1877

"Railroad Riot"

The Sixth Regiment of the Maryland National Guard fire on railroad strikers and sympathizers in the streets of Baltimore during the July 1877 "Great Uprising." *Frank Leslie's Illustrated Newspaper,* August 4, 1877 — American Social History Project.

SHORTLY AFTER THE CONFEDERATE capital of Richmond, Virginia, fell to Union troops in April 1865, an ex-slave, whose name is recorded only as Cyrus, decided he would no longer work in the fields. Emma Mordecai, the mistress of Rosewood plantation where Cyrus lived, questioned him about his refusal. Cyrus responded with a radically new interpretation of the relationship between former slaves and their former masters. He rejected a regime under which "it seems like we 'uns do all the work and [only] gets a part." Now, he continued, "there ain't going to be no more Master and Mistress, Miss Emma. All is equal. I done hear it from the courthouse steps. . . . All the land belongs to the Yankees now, and they gonna divide it among the colored people. Besides, the kitchen of the big house is my share. I help build it."

Cyrus's eloquent response to Miss Emma raised a fundamental question: whether those who had "built" America would share in the fruits of their labor. Such questions would echo through not only the dozen years that followed the end of the Civil War, but also the century and beyond, from Reconstruction's end to the new millennium — the period covered in this volume of *Who Built America?* For those who are beginning the story with Volume 2, this prologue briefly summarizes some of the key developments in the dozen years following the end of the Civil War that are the subject of the last chapter of Volume 1. It focuses particularly on matters of labor and politics and especially on three key events: Reconstruction, the Centennial celebration of 1876, and the great railroad strikes of 1877.

Reconstruction: America's Unfinished Revolution

The South's defeat in 1865 settled two major debates: Would the union survive? Would America remain half slave and half free? But other political disputes went unresolved. Who would hold economic and political power in the South in the war's aftermath? How would the land be worked and how would labor be organized? What would freedom mean for the four million former slaves? The answers to these momentous questions would define the era known as Reconstruction.

African Americans Act on Freedom   African Americans' unceasing efforts to secure economic, political, and familial rights made them central players in the Reconstruction drama. Ex-slaves expressed their newfound freedom in diverse ways. For some, it was as specific and personal as the decision to take a new name; for others, it was as fundamental as uniting their family in a single household. Freedom meant dressing as one pleased, perhaps wearing a colorful shirt or hat. It was also refusing to be deferential to one's former owner. Soon after the Confederacy's final defeat, freedpeople in Richmond, Virginia, for example, held meetings without securing white permission, and they walked in Capitol Square, an area that had previously been reserved for white residents, refusing to yield the sidewalks to approaching white men and women.

Freedom also meant that thousands of freed slaves could travel unrestricted and search for loved ones who had been sold away or displaced under slavery or during the war's upheavals. Thousands of freedmen and women placed advertisements in newspapers searching for family members. Former slaves hastened to formalize long-standing relationships, officially registering and solemnizing their marriages as a way to restore their rights to family life. For the first time, many freedpeople set up households in which men could take their place as head of the family, women could refuse full-time fieldwork, and parents could protect their children. When white planters tried to retain African American children as laborers under the guise of apprenticeships, freedpeople fought them in court and often won. These households served as one base for constructing new social and political relations in the post-emancipation period.

The first years after emancipation also saw a tremendous upsurge in African American demands for education and control over their churches. Freedpeople built schools and hired black teachers. They also challenged white domination of biracial congregations and founded their own churches, such as the African Methodist Episcopal (AME) Church. These independent churches became the moral and cultural centers of African American life, and their preachers—along with schoolteachers and

The Great Labor Question from a Southern Point of View

An 1865 cartoon in the northern Republican magazine *Harper's Weekly* contrasts the idle planter with the industrious former slave. "My boy," the planter says hypocritically, "we've toiled and taken care of you long enough — now you've got to work!" *Harper's Weekly,* July 29, 1865 — American Social History Project.

ex-soldiers — emerged as community leaders. The churches often hosted political meetings, including dozens of conventions, meetings, and rallies at which freedmen raised demands for full civil equality, including, for example, access to education and the right to bear arms, vote, and serve on juries.

The newly free Americans saw land ownership as the key to realizing their independence and ensuring their freedom. Many believed that they were entitled to land in return for their years of unpaid labor, which had created the wealth of the cotton South and the industrialized North. "Our wives, our children, our husbands, have been sold over and over again to purchase the lands we now locates upon; for that reason we have a divine right to use the land," declared freedman Bayley Wyat in protesting the eviction of African Americans from land assigned to them by Union troops during the war. Wyat and others knew all too well that without land, they would remain fundamentally subservient to the economic power of their former owners. "Every colored man will be a slave, and feel himself a slave," one soldier argued, "until he can raise his own bale of cotton and put his own mark upon it and say this is mine."

Many southern blacks trusted the federal government, acting through the Freedmen's Bureau (which Congress had set up just before the end of the war), to help them achieve economic self-sufficiency. The bureau's 900 agents and officials, many of them idealistic Union army officers, did much to aid the freedpeople with education and medical care in the war's aftermath. And although the Freedmen's Bureau adopted extremely coercive labor policies throughout the South, the freedpeople continued to turn to bureau agents to protest brutality, harsh working conditions, and the hostility and inattention of local courts and police.

The struggles over the meaning of emancipation generated constant conflicts between black and white southerners. The enduring power of white southerners set boundaries on black freedom. These boundaries were especially narrow in rural areas still dominated by whites, who reacted badly to any assertion of personal freedom by former slaves. During the first year of freedom, countless incidents of violence were directed against freed slaves for simply expressing their personal independence.

Plantation owners especially opposed black southerners' efforts to secure land. Planters and freedpeople alike understood that black landownership would destroy white control of labor in the South and would lead to the collapse of the plantation economy. If even a few independent black farmers succeeded, concluded one Mississippi planter, "all the others will be dissatisfied with their wages no matter how good they may be and thus our whole labor system is bound to be upset." To maintain control, planters looked to their state governments. The struggle over the meaning and extent of freedom for African Americans would now shift to the political arena.

Presidential Reconstruction and Its Critics   By the end of 1865, former supporters and leaders of the Confederacy again controlled state governments. The lenient pardoning policies of President Andrew Johnson enabled these men to reassert their dominance. Johnson, a tailor from Tennessee, had been the only southerner who chose to remain in his seat in the U.S. Senate after his home state seceded from the Union. His reward for that decision was selection as Lincoln's running mate in 1864, and he became president when Lincoln was assassinated in April 1865. As president, Johnson believed that only the planters possessed the experience, prestige, and power to control the volatile black population and that the planters were therefore the best hope for the South's future. In May 1865, Johnson offered total amnesty to white southerners who would swear basic loyalty to the Union. He allowed the Confederate states to be rapidly readmitted to the

Pardoned
President Andrew Johnson pardons former Confederates in the White House. Stanley Fox, *Harper's Weekly*, October 14, 1865 — American Social History Project.

Union as long as they ratified the Thirteenth Amendment abolishing slavery, repudiated the Confederate debt, and nullified the ordinances of secession. Once they had complied, they could organize state elections and reestablish governments, a process that was completed in nearly all southern states by the fall of 1865. For Johnson, Reconstruction was now complete.

The fall elections returned many ex-Confederates to office, and they immediately passed legislation favoring the interests of planters. In particular, the Black Codes, a series of rigid labor-control laws, defined the status of newly freed African Americans as landless agricultural laborers with no bargaining power and restricted mobility. A freedman who was found to be without "lawful employment," for example, could be arrested. The laws attempted to ensure that planters would have an ongoing immobile and dependent supply of cheap labor and to keep African Americans in a subordinate status. Some laws barred blacks from handling guns or possessing alcohol; others required that they be off city streets by a specific hour.

Authorities never fully enforced the Black Codes, largely because of labor scarcity and the opposition of African American workers and Freedmen's Bureau agents. Nonetheless, their passage enraged Radical Republicans, a group of congressmen whose political roots lay in the antebellum antislavery movement. Led by Representative Thaddeus Stevens of Pennsylvania and Senator Charles Sumner of Massachusetts, the Radicals sought a vast increase in federal power to obtain new rights for the freedpeople and to revolutionize social conditions in the South. Although Republicans held a three-to-one majority in Congress, most were moderates. But even they were profoundly disturbed by the Black Codes and by the restored power and influence of the ex-Confederate leaders who had passed these laws. In December 1865, moderates joined Radicals in refusing to seat the newly elected southern congressional representatives. This action initiated a confrontation with President Johnson and, in the process, transformed the meaning and nature of Reconstruction.

One of the first steps in this transformation occurred in early 1866, when Congress passed a civil rights bill that conferred U.S. citizenship on the freedpeople, granted them "full and equal benefit of all laws," and gave federal courts the power to defend the rights of these new citizens from interference by state governments. This bill nullified the Supreme Court's 1857 *Dred Scott* decision (which had denied citizenship to African Americans), expanded the powers of the federal courts, marked a dramatic break from the deeply rooted American tradition of states' rights, and placed the federal government squarely on the side of extending citizenship and defending individual rights. An outraged President Johnson vetoed the legislation as an unconstitutional infringement of states' rights. But the Republican Congress overrode Johnson's veto in April 1866, the first time in U.S.

history that a major piece of legislation was passed over a president's objection. Three months later, Congress also overrode Johnson's veto of a bill to extend the life and power of the Freedmen's Bureau.

The Radicals in Congress sought an even more sweeping approach. Stevens and Sumner envisioned not just civil rights for African Americans, but a total transformation of southern society. Echoing the demands of freedpeople, Stevens called in 1866 for confiscating the land of the planters and distributing it among the ex-slaves. "The whole fabric of southern society must be changed," he proclaimed, "and never can it be done if this opportunity is lost." The best the Radicals could achieve, however, was the Fourteenth Amendment, which passed both houses of Congress in June 1866 and was then sent to the states for ratification. When finally approved in 1868, the Fourteenth Amendment granted full citizenship to African Americans and prohibited states from denying them "equal protection of the laws." This dramatically transformed the constitutional balance of power. Previously, Americans had viewed states as the guardians of the rights of their citizens against the power of the federal government. Now the roles were reversed.

President Johnson issued an appeal to southern legislatures to reject the new amendment. Encouraged by Johnson's position, all southern states but one (ironically, Tennessee) refused to ratify the Fourteenth Amendment. The Union had won the war but now appeared to be losing the peace. The fall 1866 congressional elections thus became a referendum on the Fourteenth Amendment and on Johnson's opposition to extending Reconstruction. As voters considered the issues, increasing antiblack violence spread through the South. In Memphis in May and in New Orleans in July, local authorities stood by or actively participated as white southerners slaughtered African Americans. In the wake of this racist brutality, Republicans scored a landslide victory in the November 1866 elections, and the biggest winners among them were the Radicals.

Radical Reconstruction   The Republican mandate encouraged the Radicals to present an even bolder agenda, which became known as Radical Reconstruction. The centerpiece of this agenda, the Reconstruction Act of March 1867, passed over President Johnson's veto, and it divided the former confederate states into five military districts. Each state was required to hold a constitutional convention and to draft a new state constitution. African Americans, protected by federal troops, would participate in the conventions, and the new constitutions would include provisions for black suffrage. The act also required newly elected state legislatures to ratify the Fourteenth Amendment as a condition for their readmission to the Union. The guarantee of black voting rights seemed to many Americans to represent the final stage of sweeping political revolution.

Passage of the Reconstruction Act in March 1867 undercut the political and economic power of the planter class and fostered political activity among freedpeople. A massive and unprecedented movement of freedpeople into the political arena soon followed. Black southerners created Union (or Loyal) Leagues, which helped to build schools and churches. The leagues also organized militia companies to defend communities from white violence and called strikes and boycotts for better wages and fairer labor contracts. They even organized a number of local chapters on an interracial basis.

In the fall of 1867, southerners began electing delegates to the state constitutional conventions. Freedpeople participated in astonishing numbers. Women joined in local meetings to select candidates. Between 70 and 90 percent of eligible black males voted in every state in the South, and they elected 265 African Americans as delegates. For the first time in American history, blacks and whites met together to prepare constitutions under which they would be governed. The constitutions that they produced were among the most progressive in the nation. They created social-welfare agencies, reformed the criminal law, and more equitably distributed the burden of taxation. Most important, the constitutions guaranteed civil and political rights to both black and white Americans.

The intensity and extent of black political participation transformed southern politics. After 1867, the southern Republican party, with heavy support from African Americans, dominated all the new state governments. Although they represented an actual majority only in South Carolina's legislature, black Americans captured a total of six hundred legislative seats in southern states. Between 1868 and 1876, southern states elected fourteen black representatives to the U.S. Congress, two black U.S. senators, and six black lieutenant governors. In addition, thousands of African Americans served local southern communities as supervisors, voter registrars, aldermen, mayors, magistrates, sheriffs and deputies, postal clerks, members of local school boards, and justices of the peace.

White allies were essential to black political success. With African Americans in a majority only in South Carolina and Mississippi, the Republican Party needed to develop a coalition that included some white support. White "carpetbaggers"—northerners who traveled to the South with inexpensive suitcases made of carpet to participate in Reconstruction— were perhaps most visible, but the "scalawags," the native white southerners who supported the Republican Party, were most critical to Republican successes in the South. Most scalawags were poor yeoman farmers from the southern mountains who had long resented the large planters' monopoly on land, labor, and political power. Most of the Republican Party's southern adherents, then, were poor people, black and white, with a strong hostility to the planter aristocracy.

Electioneering in the South
A *Harper's Weekly* engraving captured freedpeople actively engaged in the 1868 election campaign. W. L. Sheppard, *Harper's Weekly,* July 25, 1868 — American Social History Project.

During their period in power—from two years in Tennessee to eight in South Carolina—the Republican governments made important economic and legal gains for black and white working people. They created a public school system where none had existed before. These schools, though segregated by race and better in the cities than in the countryside, were nonetheless a symbol of real progress. By 1876, about half of all southern children were enrolled in school—a vast increase, since few Southern communities had tax-supported public schools before the Civil War. Several Radical governments also passed laws banning racial discrimination in public accommodations, notably streetcars, restaurants, and hotels.

New laws helped landless agricultural laborers, both black and white. Radical Republicans passed lien laws that gave farm laborers a first claim on crops if their employers went bankrupt. And the repeal of the notorious Black Codes enabled some people to achieve their dream of land ownership. By 1876, 14,000 African American families in South Carolina (about one-seventh of the state's black population) had acquired homesteads, as had a handful of white families.

Freedpeople now negotiated a new kind of compromise with planters on how the land would be worked and who would reap its bounty. Rather than working in gangs for wages, individual families now tended small plots independently, renting land from planters for cash or, more commonly, for a fixed share of the year's crop. By 1870, "sharecropping" had become the dominant form of black agricultural labor, especially in the vast cotton lands. The system was a far cry from the freedpeople's first objective, which was to own land, and it became connected to a credit system that drastically reduced workers' economic freedom later in the century. But in the short run, sharecropping freed black workers from the highly regimented gang-labor system, allowing them a good deal of control and autonomy over their work, their time, and their family arrangements.

These very real economic and legal gains did not occur without cost. The southern Republican Party experienced constant tensions within the fragile coalition that was its base. Large increases in state spending on schools and social programs, combined with the ongoing promotion of transportation and industry, led to tremendous hikes in taxes. This tax burden fell increasingly not only on wealthy planters, but also on poor whites who owned little property. Revelations of political corruption among Republican officials (e.g., bribery of state officials by railroads looking for government aid) compounded the growing disaffection of white voters.

The End of Reconstruction   The Republican Party's loss of political power and influence among its white constituents was clear in 1869, when Tennessee and Virginia became the first states to return to conservative Democratic control. This political retreat — a process that conservatives called "redemption" — could not have happened without a sharp change in northern public opinion and the movement of the northern Republican Party away from the original goals of Radical Reconstruction.

Ordinary northerners had only a limited commitment to the political and civil rights of African Americans, and after 1867, Democrats defeated Republicans in a number of northern states. Many northern politicians claimed that they were simply worn out by the long military battles of the Civil War and the political battles that followed. With the removal of the most overt signs of southern intransigence, their support for further change weakened. Waning enthusiasm for Reconstruction was evident in the failure to drive Andrew Johnson from office after his impeachment by the House of Representatives in 1868; the U.S. Senate failed by one vote to remove Johnson from office for his efforts to undermine Reconstruction.

Moderate Republican leaders who came to power in the late 1860s were willing to abandon southern blacks in order to cultivate northern business support. That support depended on revitalizing the southern economy and retreating from the social and political experimentation that had defined Reconstruction's early years. Northern politicians were now prepared to leave the fate of the South, economically if not yet politically, in the hands of the former slave owners. Northern Republicans therefore began removing federal troops from the region, leaving large planters free to "redeem" the South as they saw fit.

The presence of black voters stood as the remaining major obstacle to the return of conservative rule. The large planters first tried to limit freedpeople's political activities by using economic power to threaten them with loss of employment. When economic pressure proved unsuccessful, the planters turned to more violent methods of intimidation. The Ku Klux Klan provided their most effective weapon. Founded by Confederate veterans in Tennessee in 1866, the Klan grew rapidly after the advent of Radical Reconstruction. Many of its rank-and-file members were poor men, but its leaders tended to be prominent planters and their sons. The Klan was in essence the paramilitary arm of the southern Democratic Party, systematically employing violence against freedpeople and their organizations. Klan night riders terrorized individual freedmen who refused to work for their employers or complained about low wages. They targeted black Civil War veterans and freedpeople who had succeeded in breaking out of the plantation system. Hooded Klansmen broke up meetings; threatened, shot, and lynched Radical and Union League leaders; and drove black voters away from the polls all across the South. Such targeted violence profoundly affected postwar politics in the South. Even though African Americans fought back valiantly, the Klan succeeded in destroying Republican organizations and demoralizing entire communities of freedpeople.

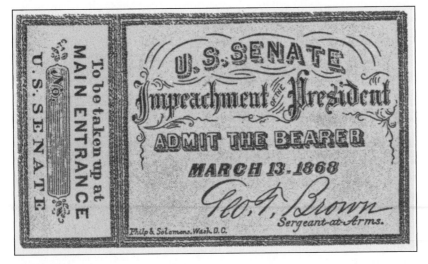

Political Theater

A ticket of admission to watch the Andrew Johnson impeachment proceedings. General Collections, Library of Congress.

In the face of such incredible violence, Congress finally acted. In 1869, it approved the Fifteenth Amendment to the U.S. Constitution. The amendment (ratified in 1870) stated that the states could not deny or abridge the right to vote "on account of race, color, or previous condition of servitude." (The notable absence of "sex" from this list kept women from voting.) It did allow numerous "nonracial" means of limiting suffrage; southern states would later introduce poll (voting) taxes and literacy tests to restrict black voting. Nevertheless, the Fifteenth Amendment demonstrated that moderate Republicans were not yet willing to stand by and allow their party in the South to be terrorized and destroyed by violence.

In March 1871, a series of grisly events shook the nation and galvanized Congress to take further action. In the small town of Meridian, Mississippi, Klansmen and their supporters had brutally murdered thirty African Americans. Congress appointed a committee to investigate. Aghast at the tales of carnage they heard, members of Congress passed a series of enforcement acts imposing harsh penalties on those who used organized terrorism for political purposes. The Ku Klux Klan Act, for example, made certain crimes against a citizen's rights punishable under federal, not state, law. President Ulysses S. Grant, who had been a victorious Union army general before being elected president in 1868, declared martial law in parts of South Carolina and dispatched U.S. Army troops to the area in 1871. The U.S. attorney general indicted and tried hundreds of Klansmen in South Carolina, North Carolina, and Mississippi. The federal government had broken the Klan's back, at least temporarily.

But 1872 marked the beginning of the end of the federal presence in the South. Groups similar to the Klan multiplied, using violence and intimidation to achieve Democratic victories. The Democrats assumed, correctly, as it turned out, that neither Congress nor the president would again act decisively to prevent political violence and fraud in the South.

The economic panic of 1873, which launched a severe nationwide depression that would last more than five years, exacerbated the political retreat. Across the South, the depression drove many black landowners and renters back into the ranks of laborers, sharply reduced wage levels, and eventually helped to transform sharecropping into a system of peonage that bound laborers to creditors (landowners and merchants) through their debts. In the North, the depression encouraged businessmen to abandon the last remnants of Reconstruction. White working people, focusing their attention on immediate problems in their own workplaces and communities and still unconvinced by arguments for racial equality, also turned away from the radical Republicanism of the mid-1860s.

Only federal intervention could have prevented the renewed violence that reinstalled white Democratic regimes throughout the South. But President Grant's administration, which had acted forcefully against the Klan in 1871, turned down requests for federal troops in 1875. The North no longer seemed outraged by political violence directed against freedpeople.

Capitalizing on this weariness, Northern Democrats scored important victories in the 1874 elections and subsequently took control of the House of Representatives. Thus, beginning in 1875, Democrats increasingly challenged Republican dominance in Washington, D.C., as they rebuilt their party from the shambles of the war. The revived Democratic Party united most of the South, and it attracted a growing number of workingmen in northern industrial areas by attacking the increasing concentration of wealth and corruption in politics.

In the 1876 presidential election, the Democrats seemed on the verge of victory. Their candidate, Samuel J. Tilden, captured a majority of the popular vote and appeared to have won in the electoral college as well. But Republicans, backing Rutherford B. Hayes, disputed the returns in Louisiana, South Carolina, and Florida and threw the election into question. Nearly three months of wrangling and intrigue followed, accompanied

Terror

Members of the Ku Klux Klan of Moore City, North Carolina, prepare to execute a victim in August 1871. *Frank Leslie's Illustrated Newspaper,* October 7, 1871 — American Social History Project.

not only by growing panic in the business community, but also by widespread fear of renewed war between North and South.

In late February 1877, only a few weeks before the new president was to be inaugurated, pressure from businessmen and politicians forced a resolution to the conflict. In the Compromise of 1877, the Democrats yielded the presidency to Hayes. In exchange, they received a share of federal appointments (including the appointment of at least one southerner to Hayes's cabinet), federal assistance to southern railroads, and the by then largely symbolic final removal of federal troops from the southern states. The agreement cleared the way for the removal of African Americans from national and local politics and the collapse of the Republican Party in the South. A key figure in securing the compromise was the Democratic iron magnate Abram Hewitt. A journalist described Hewitt as a man "with one hand upon his heart and the other hand in his pocket." Hewitt, speaking for himself and for other businessmen who were coming to believe that they could best achieve their goals by supporting both parties, announced, "I would prefer four years of Hayes's administration to four years of civil war." The compromise to resolve the disputed election of 1876 thus brought the end of Reconstruction and what one historian has aptly dubbed "reunion and reaction."

The Centennial and the Other America

The year that resulted in the hotly contested presidential election also marked a venerable anniversary for the United States that seemingly provided an opportunity for celebration. The republic had survived for a century since declaring its independence from England. Although only a decade had passed since the end of the bloody Civil War, some Americans believed that their country deserved a spectacular birthday party—a centennial celebration that would display the nation's achievements in industry, science, agriculture, and the arts. Designed to meet these heady expectations, the Centennial Exposition opened on 450 expansive acres in Philadelphia's Fairmount Park on May 10, 1876. Ten million people, from every state and more than thirty countries, flocked to the party over the next six months.

The major exhibition buildings were gigantic. In this still largely rural nation, Agricultural Hall covered more than ten acres. Inside, visitors marveled at the latest mowing and reaping machines. But the centerpiece of the Exposition was the 700-ton, 40-foot-high Corliss Double Walking-Beam Engine, which generated 1,400 horsepower, enough to drive all the other machines in the enormous hall. Powered by a steam boiler in an adjacent building and running almost silently, the engine was an awesome creation, representing in the beauty of its motion, design, and power the very essence of the new industrial age.

Some Americans, however, were less enthralled by the sights, grandeur, pomp, and sense of marvel of the Centennial Exposition. They viewed it less as a celebration of the nation's achievements than as a diversion from hard and bitter daily reality. Neglected and sometimes stifled by the lavish festivities, these "other Americans"—women, African Americans, American Indians, and workers—raised issues that would resonate far into the future.

The Centennial's Women's Pavilion, for example, was fraught with division. Paid for with contributions from across the country, the pavilion presented visitors with crafts, inventions, and institutions established and conducted by women. But to many observers, the displays seemed no more than curiosities, a glimpse of a quaint and separate world. The National Woman's Suffrage Association—as if announcing the division between the pavilion planners who espoused the private, "domestic" sphere and the advocates who demanded a wider role for women in American society—held its founding meeting in New York City on the same day that the Women's Pavilion opened in Philadelphia. And at the Centennial's July Fourth ceremonies, feminists Elizabeth Cady Stanton and Susan B. Anthony disrupted the proceedings to read a Woman's Declaration of Independence. "We cannot forget, even in this glad hour," it proclaimed "that while all men of every race, and clime, and condition, have been invested with the full rights of citizenship under our hospitable flag, all women still suffer the degradation of disfranchisement."

But if women's participation was limited, that of African Americans was virtually nonexistent. African American women, who had helped to raise funds for the Centennial, found no place in the Women's Pavilion. The crews that constructed the Centennial buildings included no black workers, and visitors saw African Americans doing only menial tasks or performing in the Southern Restaurant, where (as a guidebook described it) "a band of old-time plantation 'darkies' . . . sing their quaint melodies and strum the banjo." This pervasive racism manifested itself again during the Centennial's opening ceremonies. Frederick Douglass—escaped slave, militant aboli-

The Great Corliss Engine
The Corliss Engine was one of the main attractions when the Centennial Exposition opened in May 1876. President Ulysses Grant and Emperor Dom Pedro II of Brazil ventured into Machinery Hall to see the largest steam engine in the world start up (as depicted in this illustration). Moments later, hundreds of machines sprang into motion throughout the fairgrounds, powered by the 1,400-horsepower giant. The Corliss Engine served as a symbol of the fair — as an object of national pride, exemplifying the triumph of industrialism over craft production. *Frank Leslie's Illustrated Newspaper,* May 20, 1876 — American Social History Project.

The Freed Slave
African Americans were generally unwelcome at the 1876 Centennial Exposition. But one exhibit attracted the interest of black visitors to the Philadelphia fairgrounds: a statue by an Austrian sculptor commemorating emancipation. Fernando Miranda, *Frank Leslie's Illustrated Newspaper*, August 5, 1876 — American Social History Project.

tionist, and acknowledged leader of the nation's African Americans—had been invited to sit on the opening-day speakers' platform, although he was not given an opportunity to speak. A policeman, convinced that no black man belonged among the invited dignitaries, barred Douglass's way until a U.S. senator finally intervened on his behalf.

Even America's Indian population played a more pronounced—if not more popular—role than that of African Americans. The Smithsonian Institution had mounted a massive Centennial exhibit of Indian artifacts, replete with pottery, tepees, totem poles, and life-size costumed mannequins. But in July 1876, news reached the Centennial that belied this notion of Indians as a "museum people": the military victory of Sioux and Cheyenne warriors at the Battle of Little Big Horn in Dakota Territory, where General George Custer and more than 200 U.S. Army soldiers perished. Many white visitors viewing the material artifacts of destroyed Indian cultures shared the feelings of novelist William Dean Howells, who wrote, "The red man, as he appears in effigy and in photograph in this collection, is a hideous demon, whose malign traits can hardly inspire any emotion softer than abhorrence."

The Great Uprising of Labor

Some employers arranged excursions to the Centennial as a way of easing workers' growing discontent with the ravages of industrial capitalism. Railroad and coal-mining firms enthusiastically organized such trips, hoping that they would soothe the bitterness Irish mining families felt over the suppression of the recent "Long Strike" in eastern Pennsylvania and the destruction of their union. The Philadelphia and Reading Coal and Iron Company sent 1,100 men, women, and children from the Pennsylvania mines on an all-expense-paid trip to the Centennial. But the free trips could not conceal the deep—often bloody—rifts between capital and labor. As the miners visited the exposition in the spring of 1876, twenty fellow miners charged with being members of a secret, prolabor society called the Molly Maguires were being tried, found guilty of murder, and sentenced to death in a Schuylkill County courtroom less than 100 miles away.

A much greater challenge to the vision of industrial progress hallowed by the Centennial developed just a few short months later. A massive railroad strike, the first truly national strike in the country's history, sym-bolized a turning point in U.S. history. Although the strike failed in the short run, it marked the birth of a working-class movement that was far broader and more powerful than anything seen before.

"The Great Uprising" of 1877, as the press called it, was brought on by the hard times of the 1873 depression, then in its fourth year. Railroad work-ers had suffered one wage reduction after another since the onset of the depression. On July 16, 1877, Baltimore and Ohio (B&O) workers in Mar-tinsburg, West Virginia, staged a spontaneous strike in response to yet another wage cut. Three days later, as the strike intensified, President Rutherford B. Hayes ordered federal troops into West Virginia to protect the B&O and the nation from "insurrection."

The use of federal troops in a domestic labor dispute incited popular anger across the country. In Baltimore, the Maryland state militia fired on huge crowds of workers, leaving eleven dead and forty wounded. Work stoppages rapidly spread north and west along the railroad lines to Pennsyl-

July 22, 1877
The scorched interior of the Pennsylvania Railroad upper roundhouse the day after the battle between Philadelphia militia and Pittsburgh strikers. S. V. Albee, *The Railroad War* — Paul Dickson Collection.

vania, where in Pittsburgh, the strike reached its most dramatic climax. Because many Pittsburgh citizens sympathized with the railroad workers, the Pennsylvania Railroad sought help from the state militia, based in Philadelphia. But when the troops reached Pittsburgh on July 21, 1877, a large and angry crowd of strikers and sympathizers met them. Unnerved by the reception, the soldiers suddenly thrust their bayonets. Crowd members threw rocks, and the troops answered with a volley of rifle fire, killing twenty Pittsburgh citizens, including a woman and three small children.

News of the deaths spread quickly. Pittsburgh residents, including thousands of workers from nearby mills, mines, and factories, converged on the Pennsylvania Railroad yards. By dawn, they had set fire to the railroad roundhouse, where the militiamen had retreated. Twenty more Pittsburgh residents and five soldiers lay dead at the end of the ensuing gun battle.

In the next few days, the strike spread across the Midwest. Workers— skilled and unskilled—took over entire towns, shutting down work until employers met their demands. The same railroad and telegraph lines that had unified the nation and laid the groundwork for the full emergence of industrial capitalism now linked and unified workers' protests. Without any central organization (most national unions were defunct as a result of the depression), the conflict spawned local committees, many led by radicals, that provided unity and direction to the strike. In Chicago, for example, the conflict quickly became a citywide general strike. Open class warfare featured running battles between police and strikers and vigilante groups among businessmen and professionals mobilized against the workers. In St. Louis, thousands of workers participated in a general strike that, although largely peaceful, shut down virtually all of the city's industries while government officials fled. Black workers took an active role in that strike, closing down canneries and docks. When an African American steamboat worker, addressing a crowd of white workers, asked, "Will you stand to us regardless of color?" the crowd responded, "We will! We will! We will!" Racism prevailed in other strikes, however, particularly in the Far West. In San Francisco, a crowd that had gathered to discuss strike action ended up rampaging through the city's Chinese neighborhoods, killing several residents and burning buildings.

Conclusion: The Continuing Struggle over Who Built America and Who Deserves Its Rewards

Participants in the Great Uprising of 1877 directed their anger mainly against the railroads and the unchecked corporate power they typified, not against capitalism as a whole. Working people in 1877 were seeking to set limits on the system's unbridled economic power and (like the former slave Cyrus in 1865) to assert workers' right to an equitable share of the economic

PUBLISHED BY CURRIER & IVES   Copyright 1876, by Currier & Ives, N.Y.   125 NASSAU ST. NEW YORK

bounty they helped to produce. Despite the nationwide mobilization of workers, the strikers failed in the face of the massive power of the railroads and their allies in state and national government. But no matter which side Americans had supported in the strike, few who surveyed the death and destruction left in its wake could find solace—let alone take pride—in the memory of the unmitigated industrial progress that had been celebrated at the Centennial a short year before.

The Great Uprising demonstrated that the United States was not immune to the class-based conflict that had plagued Europe since the birth of industrial capitalism. That conflict would intensify at critical moments over the coming years, but it would never recur in quite the way it had in the summer of 1877. The chapters that follow detail the changing divisions that dominated American life in the years after the end of Reconstruction and the great railroad strike. First and foremost among these divisions was the conflict between capital and labor. But the chapters also chronicle the struggles of women, African Americans, American Indians, and European, Latino, Asian, and Caribbean immigrants as they attempted to achieve

1876 — *On Guard*

Even as Americans celebrated the Centennial, they remained uneasy about the nation's future. In 1876, few could ignore the effects of three years of economic depression. But as this Currier and Ives print indicated, many Americans blamed the nation's problems on agitators and ideas from abroad. Currier and Ives, 1876, lithograph — Prints and Photographs Division, Library of Congress.

greater rights and inclusion in American society. Working people repeatedly asserted their right to share in what they perceived as the egalitarian promise of the American Revolution. These claims to a "republican" heritage and invocations of working for the common good were often counterpoised against an emphasis on the sanctity of private property and an acquisitive individualism espoused by wealthy elites and their publicists. The struggles between these contrasting world views were played out in an international arena increasingly dominated by the United States but also fundamentally shaped by the American people's experience of war, economic dislocation, and ideological conflict. In the process, working people like Cyrus who "helped build" America would repeatedly ask whether they would receive an equal share of its bounty.

Part One

Monopoly and Upheaval

1877–1914

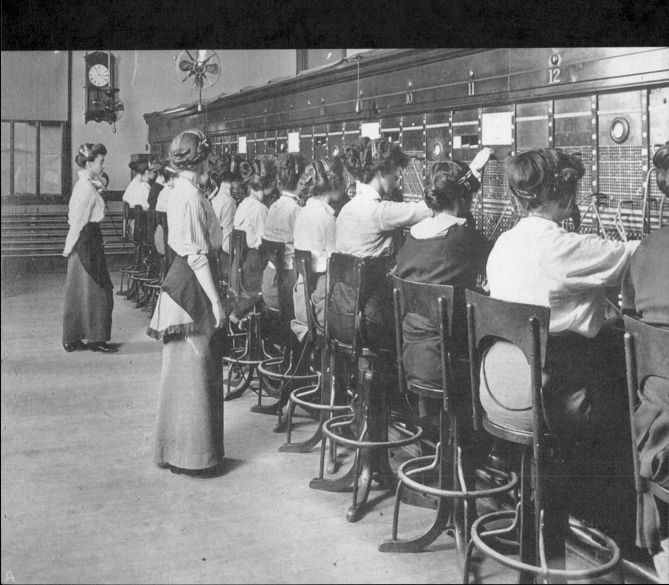

*T*HE GREAT RAILROAD strikes of the summer of 1877, as the young labor leader Samuel Gompers noted, sounded an alarm that heralded a new era of conflict and division in the nation. Issues of slavery and emancipation had preoccupied Americans' minds during the previous decades, as the bloody Civil War led to Reconstruction — a time when the freedpeople in the post–Civil War South not only gained their freedom but also secured U.S. citizenship, the right to vote and hold elective office, access to education, and some modest measure of economic and religious independence. However, in the early months of 1877, the newly installed administration of Republican president Rutherford B. Hayes agreed to withdraw the few remaining federal troops that were keeping order in the southern states in exchange for Democratic party support for Hayes's contested election. As Reconstruction crumbled, industrial capitalism flourished, and the nation's working men and women fought to find a place for themselves amid the extraordinary economic, political, and social changes of the next four decades.

The United States became the world's most powerful industrial nation during the years between the end of Reconstruction and the beginning of World War I, boasting massive manufacturing enterprises and unprecedented productivity. In this same period, the nation launched a war with Spain that resulted in U.S. domination of Puerto Rico, the Philippines, Cuba, and Hawaii. The face of America also changed, as millions of immigrants from Europe, Asia, and Latin America poured into the United States after 1900, feeding industrial capitalism's seemingly insatiable appetite for new workers. Urban America took modern form and shape as the populations of New York and Chicago swelled beyond a million residents each and contemporary transportation, sanitation, and safety systems came into being. New consumer products, new means of mass distribution, and new forms of recreation reshaped everyday life in the city and the countryside.

U.S. capitalism enabled the growth of economic monopoly, unimaginable individual wealth, and unbridled political power. It also made many Americans—as well as the millions of other individuals who lived and worked under U.S. control in the Caribbean, Latin America, Asia, and the islands in the Pacific Ocean—dependent on wages or on market relations.

Americans were sharply divided on the meaning of the changes in their nation. On one side stood industrial capitalists and their political and intellectual supporters. They justified capitalists' newly won wealth and power with an ideology that celebrated acquisitive individualism, free markets, and the "survival of the fittest." On the other side stood the working men and women whose labor powered the system—African Americans, native-born white Americans, and European, Latin American, Caribbean, and Asian immigrants. They embraced the ideal of collectivity and the power of mutual rather than individual action to blunt the devastating impact of industrial capitalism on their work, family life, and communities. Of course, many Americans—small business owners, machine politicians, white-collar workers—did not entirely agree with either position, siding with industrial capitalists in some circumstances and with working people in others. And working people themselves were often divided along lines of race, gender, ethnicity, religion, and region.

As the dizzying growth of industrial capitalism transformed people and communities, cultures of collectivity arose. From those bases, working people launched a series of violent class wars that were unprecedented in the nation's history. They carved the names and dates of individual battles into the public consciousness: Haymarket (1886), Homestead and Coeur D'Alene (1892), Pullman (1894), Lawrence (1912), Paterson (1913), and Ludlow (1914). Radical ideologies embraced by workers craving change, including populism, feminism, anarchism, and socialism, animated many of these conflicts. By 1900, many of the most fundamental challenges to industrial capitalism in the Gilded Age—the Knights of Labor and the Populists, in particular—had been beaten back.

At the same time, this heady brew of labor struggle, political unrest, and a spate of tragic factory fires and coal mine explosions fostered a belief, shared by workers, middle-class professionals, and even some business leaders, that someone needed to take action against the problems caused by capitalist excesses. This conviction drove a series of reform movements, often spearheaded by women, which collectively came to be known as progressivism. Progressivism articulated a modern notion that government should play a central role in regulating the nation's social, economic, and political ills. Reformers successfully addressed some of the issues facing the nation: child labor, factory safety, tainted food and drugs, political corruption, and unchecked economic monopoly. Women pushed harder than ever for their right to vote. But the progressive movement did little for African Americans, who saw only regression from the gains they had won during Reconstruction.

As war loomed over Europe, the particular concerns that gave rise to progressivism would increasingly take a back seat to concern over the spreading international crisis. Nonetheless, progressive reform inaugurated a new era in U.S. politics, one in which the federal government took some small steps toward its now familiar role as guarantor of economic stability and the basic safety and health of its citizens.

1

Progress and Poverty: Industrial Capitalism in the Gilded Age

1877–1893

The Ironworkers' Noontime
Few painters chose industrial work as a subject in the late nineteenth century, because its conditions seemed inappropriate for a medium that tended to highlight noble and aesthetic themes. Thomas Anshutz's painting, completed around 1880, is therefore an unusual work, realistically portraying the weariness of skilled ironworkers at a nail factory in Wheeling, West Virginia, while also celebrating the workers' strength and pride in their craft. Thomas Pollock Anshutz, 1880, oil on canvas, 17⅛ × 24 inches — The Fine Arts Museums of San Francisco, Gift of Mr. and Mrs. John D. Rockefeller 3rd.

The NORTH'S VICTORY in the Civil War inaugurated a period of extraordinary growth and consolidation for the American economy. With the nation's political boundaries restored, northern manufacturers regained access to southern markets, and dramatic industrial development brought the United States into a new era. Within fifteen years of the war's end, Andrew Carnegie built his first steel plant, John D. Rockefeller organized Standard Oil, and Alexander Graham Bell began manufacturing telephones. By 1893, the United States was the world's leading industrial power, producing more than the combined total of its three largest competitors: England, France, and Germany. Leading entrepreneurs such as Carnegie and Rockefeller became unimaginably wealthy. The ostentatious display of wealth combined with cultural superficiality and political corruption inspired Mark Twain and Charles Dudley Warner to dub the era "the Gilded Age" in a novel by that name.

The nation's postwar economic growth owed much to its abundant natural resources: rich farmland provided food for a growing urban workforce, and extensive coal, iron, and mineral deposits supplied raw materials to mills and factories. During and immediately after the war, Republicans — backed by powerful iron manufacturers and coal mine owners — had passed laws to stimulate industrial growth, enabling wealthy investors and industrialists to exploit the nation's resources. High import tariffs protected American industry from foreign competition, and federal loans and huge land grants encouraged railroad expansion. Although their legislation served the wealthy, Republicans paid lip service to the key role of labor in the expanding economy. That combination of probusiness legislation and proworker rhetoric helped to ensure the party's political dominance in the postwar decades.

The phenomenal growth of the American economy in the nineteenth century also had a dark underside, which a short, red-haired newspaperman named Henry George experienced firsthand. George lost his job as a printer in the depression of 1857. He then launched a successful, crusading San Francisco newspaper, only to see it wiped out in the panic of 1873. In the aftermath of the epochal railroad strikes of 1877, George redirected his crusading spirit toward writing a book that would expose what he saw as the fundamental paradox of his day: the persistence of horrifying poverty amid stunning economic progress. In 1880, George moved from California to New York to promote his newly published book and to look for work. Like George, post–Civil War Americans lived under a single, national economic system that shaped the lives of everyone, East and West, North and South—albeit not always in the same ways. And as the title of his book, *Progress and Poverty*, indicated, this tidal wave of industrial capitalism brought devastation to the lives of millions even as it made the United States a global economic power. "The 'tramp' comes with the locomotive," he wrote in burning indignation, "and the almshouses and prisons are as surely the marks of 'material progress' as are costly dwellings, rich warehouses, and magnificent churches."

The Industrialization of America

The railroads provided both the model and the engine for this industrial transformation. But the railroads and other giant industrial enterprises that spread across the nation in these years moved at a fitful pace dictated by an unstable economy, which punctuated the boom years with periods of dark depression. Despite this unevenness, the larger outlines of an unprecedented process of change could be glimpsed—from agriculture to industry, from household and artisan to factory production, from water and animal power to fossil fuels, from country to city, from economic independence to wage dependency, from the homeland of one's ancestors to a strange new land. How one experienced this new urban-industrial world depended on your class, race, gender, ethnicity, region, and age. As Henry George knew all too well, America's working people not only built America, but also paid the price for the economic transformation of the late nineteenth century.

Building a Railroad System in an Unstable Economy   The explosion of industrial growth depended on the dramatic expansion of the railroads. In 1869, workers for the Union Pacific and Central Pacific completed the transcontinental link. The 125,000 miles of track that would be laid in the next twenty-five years would give the United States the most extensive transportation system in the world, promoting economic development across the continent (Map 1.1).

Laying those thousands of miles of track was hard, dirty work. All over the country, bosses recruited workers, oversaw their work, and organized the camps where they lived. Irish immigrants filled the ranks of the early railroad workforce. Chinese work gangs predominated in western railroad work during the 1860s and 1870s. Japanese firms provided laborers to northwestern railroads. In the Southwest, agents recruited laborers in Mexican border towns and turned them over to railroad contractors. In West Virginia and Virginia, Italians brought in by New York *padrones* (bosses) did the work; farther south, white bosses patrolled as young African Americans laid track.

Railroad systems required new kinds of organization and coordination as well as new tracks. Railroad executives were the first modern salaried business managers, employees with little or no financial interest in the companies they served. Even before the Civil War, these managers had developed entirely new kinds of accounting procedures, reporting practices, and channels of authority that enabled their organizations to operate across broad geographic expanses. In the 1870s and 1880s, they had to devise uniform

MAP 1.1 Railroads Span the Nation, 1870–1890

The completion of the transcontinental railroad in 1869 marked the start rather than the finish of the railroad construction boom. In the next two decades, the nation's railroad network almost tripled in size. By 1890, the United States had 164,000 miles of railroad track and the most extensive transportation network in the world. But the system continued to grow, and it reached a peak of 254,000 miles in 1964.

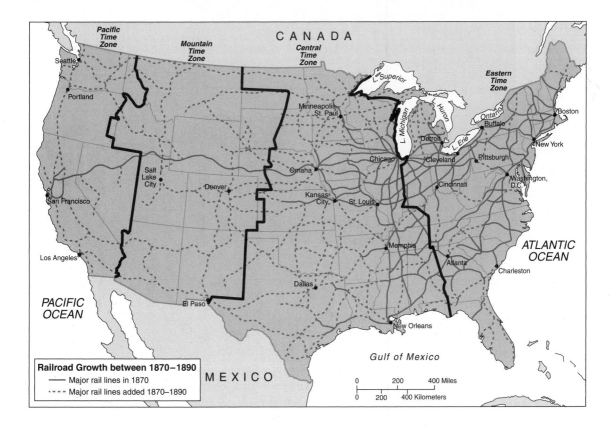

Railroad Growth between 1870–1890
— Major rail lines in 1870
- - - Major rail lines added 1870–1890

Railroad Time, Standard Time
This E. Howard Wall Regulator clock hung in the offices of the Baltimore & Ohio Railroad. Railroads spurred standardization in several facets of industrial life: rail equipment, business organization, and train schedules. Until 1883, Americans followed solar time, each locality setting clocks at noon on the basis of when the sun reached its highest point. However, each railroad maintained a single time across its entire line, leading to discrepancies in the schedules of competing lines as well as in localities across the continent. In 1883, a group of railroad superintendents instituted the new system of standard time with four time zones across the continental United States. Wall Regulator, c. 1880, E. Howard Clock Co., Boston, Massachusetts—National Museum of American History, Smithsonian Institution.

standards and procedures that would allow cars loaded with manufactured products to move freely from one rail line to another.

Railroads operated on a chaotic system of local and regional times, each set by the sun. A passenger might arrive in New York at 1:30 Pittsburgh time and still catch a train leaving that city at 1:15 New York time. To bring order out of this chaos, in 1883, the railroads adopted the four standard time zones that are still used today. Three years later, the railroads finally implemented a standard track gauge, which enabled cars to switch easily from one rail line to another. Then the biggest railroads helped to shape the Interstate Commerce Act of 1887, which codified accounting methods so that goods could move unhindered across the country.

The effects of the railroads' expansion rippled throughout the nation. Small producers who had once dominated local markets—for example, a Cincinnati maker of iron stoves—faced more distant competition. Industries feeding the railroads' enormous demands for iron, steel, stone, and lumber also expanded. In 1882, nine-tenths of the nation's steel went into rails, and about a quarter of its annual timber production went into crossties. And because railroads enabled producers to sell to consumers across the continent, manufacturers produced larger quantities and experimented with new, large-scale production processes. The Bessemer converter, which transformed raw iron into steel at a relatively low cost, helped to increase steel output, which was ten times greater in 1892 than in 1877. Other basic industries grew, too; the output of copper multiplied by seven and that of crude oil by four during the same years.

Despite an expanding market, America's late-nineteenth-century economy was profoundly unstable. The cost of building the railroads was unprecedented. Pursuing huge commissions and profits from every aspect of the business, investment bankers acted as agents for railroads seeking capital, as brokers for investors, as members of the railroads' boards of directors, and as investors of their own firms' money. The firm of Jay Cooke, one of the chief railroad speculators, became overextended in a time of unregulated credit and collapsed in 1873. It was so large, so central to railroad financing, and so tied to prominent politicians that its failure triggered a financial panic. The New York Stock Exchange closed for a week, and across the country, banks failed as people scrambled to get their money out.

Then followed five years of the most severe depression America had seen. One million workers lost their jobs; many faced starvation, and others tramped the land seeking relief and employment. Railroad building virtually stopped. Nearly 50,000 firms closed their doors. An upswing in the late 1870s brought a brief return to prosperity, but industrial expansion was again undercut by another (but less devastating) depression lasting from 1882 to 1885 (Figure 1.1).

The "business cycle," this boom-and-bust pattern of alternating rapid growth and sharp depression, characterized rapidly developing industrial capitalism. Even during an economic boom, few wage workers—even the highly skilled—could count on full-time, year-round work. Businessmen faced similar uncertainty. Those who avoided outright failure grappled with a long-term decline in the prices of manufactured goods; from 1866 to 1890, average prices for products dropped by over half. This decline affected nearly every sector of the economy, slashing both profits and wages.

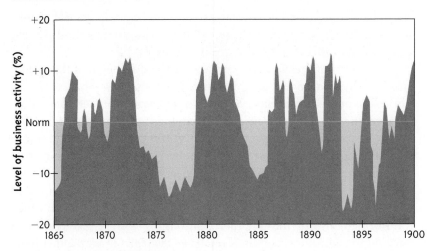

FIGURE 1.1   An Unstable Economy

The late nineteenth century was an era of explosive growth and devastating depression. The boom-and-bust cycle of industrial capitalism resulted in three major depressions—those of 1873–1879, 1882–1885, and 1893–1897—and shrouded the so-called Gilded Age.

Rapid growth, cutthroat competition, and plummeting prices went hand in hand. Railroad companies had to pay high fixed costs to maintain equipment and track as well as substantial interest on the bonds that had financed their construction. Given these strong incentives to continue operations, managers dropped rates to rock bottom. Over the last thirty years of the nineteenth century, freight prices fell by 70 percent, severely squeezing railroad profits. As railroad rates plummeted, so did wholesale prices because transportation costs made up such a large share of the final cost of manufactured goods. The new industrial system held out the hope of material plenty, but it was anything but predictable.

The Emergence of Urban-Industrial Life   As railroads and industries developed, citizens from all walks of life became increasingly dependent on the financial ups and downs of companies representing huge concentrations of money and power. Americans found their accustomed ways of living and working overturned. In just over thirty years of industrial growth, a modern working class and a new business elite had emerged in a nation that had once been dominated by farmers, merchants, and small-town artisans. Wide-scale poverty emerged at the same time; the human misery that had horrified American observers of English industrialization now scarred the United States. "We are fast drifting to that condition of society which preceded the downfall of [ancient] Sparta, Macedonia, Athens, and Rome," wrote a railroad carpenter in the late 1870s, "where a few were very rich, and the many very poor."

"Tramps' Terror"

To some Americans, the unemployed who wandered the country in search of work during the 1870s posed a threat to order and safety. The "tramp menace," many argued, required a repressive response, and advertisements like this exploited the pervasive fear. *Frank Leslie's Illustrated Newspaper*, April 7, 1877—American Social History Project.

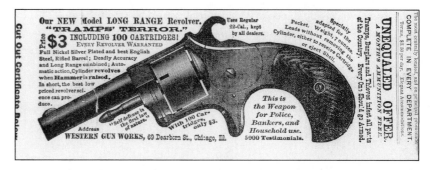

With industrialization came a transition from household and artisan to factory production, a change that affected the daily lives of most Americans. By the eve of the Civil War, most people were buying and wearing manufactured textiles instead of weaving homespun. By the 1890s, many other consumer goods were factory-made — not only long-standing craft products such as soap and furniture, but also items that nobody had ever made by hand, such as kerosene lamps and sewing machines.

The change from home to factory production went along with a fundamental shift from agriculture to industry. Before the Civil War, eight out of ten Americans lived in rural areas. But the balance shifted over the next decades as farm machinery dramatically increased productivity. Fewer farmers could feed more industrial workers. Manufacturing grew dramatically; the number of factory laborers almost tripled between 1860 and 1890 and nearly doubled again by 1910 (Figure 1.2).

The shift from agriculture to industry also accelerated the decline of self-employment and the rise of wage work. In 1860, half of American workers were self-employed, and the other half earned wages. Many still believed that hard work and individual sacrifice would pave the way to economic independence. Industrial growth after the Civil War frustrated these hopes, and by 1900, two-thirds of the American workers depended on wages. Writing in the 1880s, Joseph Buchanan, a Colorado printer, recalled that an industrious and economical worker could have bought a little business in the 1860s. "Today the opportunity to start in his business for himself has been thrust from him by the greedy hand of the great manufacturers. . . . The man who can rise from the wage condition in these days must catch a windfall from his uncle or [find] a bank unlocked."

Industrialization after the Civil War involved another profound transformation: from water power and animal power to fossil fuels. Coal had been used extensively since the 1840s, but its use expanded exponentially during the decades after the war, as did that of the newer fuels, oil and gas. No longer did Americans rely on oxen and mules or rushing streams powering water mills for energy needs. Instead, they extracted energy sources from the earth, using expensive technologies, and shipped them long distances by rail. Mining companies ravaged the land they exploited, and fossil fuels polluted the air as they burned.

Manufacturers using coal and steam no longer had to locate factories alongside rivers and could instead choose sites for their access to railroads, raw materials, consumer markets, and a ready supply of workers. Industrial growth therefore centered in cities, which grew twice as fast as the nation's population as a whole. In 1860, only New York, Philadelphia, and Brooklyn had more than 250,000 inhabitants. Thirty years later, eleven cities surpassed that size, and Philadelphia, Chicago, and New York each topped one million. "We cannot all live in cities," newspaper editor Horace Greeley mused, "yet nearly all seem determined to do so." The modern American city that emerged during these decades offered such essential urban services as professional fire and police forces, sewers and garbage disposal, large hospitals, and public transportation systems.

The big cities housed both great wealth and foul slums. Rapid expansion bred overcrowding and squalor in unplumbed tenements, while businessmen's mansions boasted marble floors and mother-of-pearl washbasins. But between these extremes were skilled workers and members of a distinctive new middle socioeconomic stratum. Middle-class Americans were generally descended from families that had lived in America for generations or had immigrated from the British Isles; they worked as self-employed businesspeople, as professionals, or in the office jobs created by expanding corporations. They lived in growing suburban neighborhoods, joined there by the best-paid skilled workers and their families, who moved to escape the noise and dirt of downtown industrial districts.

The new, giant business and government organizations produced most of the new office jobs. Before 1880, only a handful of large firms, such as Western Union and Montgomery Ward, operated on a national scale. By 1890, however, a number of industrial enterprises had begun to sell such products as cigarettes, soap, matches, oatmeal, and other processed foods to a national market. This required not only expanded productive capacity, but also bigger office staffs. Bureaucracies developed similarly in national government to perform tasks such as processing the mounting numbers of patent applications and the pension claims of Civil War veterans and their widows and children.

Both national companies and government bureaucracies created new kinds of work that was mechanized during the 1880s by the typewriter, which produced letters and memoranda three times faster than writing with

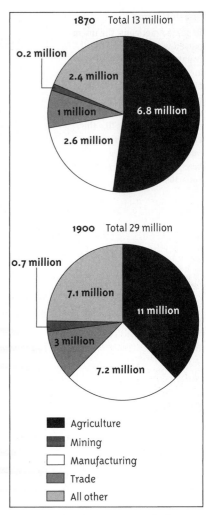

FIGURE 1.2 From Agriculture to Industry: A Changing Workforce

As the nation industrialized between 1870 and 1900, the labor force more than doubled, largely through immigration. The biggest increases came in manufacturing, which almost tripled.

Bandit's Roost

Great disparities between wealth and poverty accompanied the rapid expansion of U.S. cities. Reformer Jacob Riis's photographs starkly portrayed "how the other half lives" to the audiences who attended his lantern-slide shows or saw engraved versions in newspapers. But, as is evident in this photograph of an alley on New York's Lower East Side, Riis often posed and framed his subjects in ways that were meant to arouse not only sympathy but also fear and distaste among viewers. Dr. Henry Piffard or Richard Hoe Lawrence (for Jacob Riis), 1888—Jacob A. Riis Collection, Museum of the City of New York.

pen and ink. The typewriter, combined with the growing demand for clerical labor, transformed the office from an all-male preserve to a hierarchy in which men dictated and women served. By 1890, almost one-third of students in business schools were women, mostly enrolled in stenography and typing courses.

A great wave of immigration also reshaped American society during the late nineteenth century. The largest worldwide population movement in human history brought 10 million immigrants to the United States between 1860 and 1890. In the 1880s alone, 5.25 million people entered, as many as had arrived during the first six decades of the century. They came primarily from Ireland, Germany, and Britain, as they had before the Civil War, but people from all points of the compass now joined them. From Scandinavia, Italy, China, and the Austro-Hungarian Empire came hundreds of thousands of men to work on American farms and railroads and in American factories. Increasingly, in the 1880s and 1890s, immigrants came from eastern and southern Europe.

Immigrants crowded the large cities. By 1880, nearly nine of every ten Chicagoans were first- or second-generation immigrants. These new Americans especially dominated the urban industrial workforce; approximately one of every three industrial workers in the late nineteenth century had immigrated to the United States. As a clergyman observed of Chicago, "Not every foreigner is a workingman, but in the cities, at least, it may almost be said that every workingman is a foreigner."

They participated in a global labor market, sensitive to the potential for employment in both their native lands and their adopted one. Matthias Dorgathen, for example, was one of 1,700 miners who journeyed to North America from the Ruhr district of Germany in 1881 when mines there cut wages and laid off workers. Those leaving their homelands adjusted their plans according to the ups and downs of the U.S. business cycle; immigration fell sharply during the American depressions of 1873–1878 and 1882–1885, and it rose during the boom period of the late 1880s. The catalysts for going to America varied from group to group. Rural poverty and political instability sent more than 2 million Chinese in search of better opportunities in Southeast Asia, Peru, Hawaii, and the Caribbean in the second half of the nineteenth century; more than 300,000 came to the United States. Rapid population growth and a major agricultural depression had forced off the land most of the 1.5 million men and women who left Ireland for America between the Civil War and 1890. Emigrants from more developed countries such as Great Britain and Germany fled a long European industrial depression that was triggered in part by competition from the United States.

As American demand for industrial labor soared, railroad and steamship companies sought out this much-needed labor force, advertising the glories of American life throughout Europe and China. But the stories told by friends and family already in America proved more convincing. Pioneering immigrants kept in touch with their Old World families and communities and sponsored those who chose to follow. The success of Francesco Barone, a prosperous Buffalo saloonkeeper, inspired 8,000 people to move from Barone's home village in Sicily to his adopted city; he assisted many of them directly.

These intertwined processes of industrialization, bureaucratization, urbanization, and immigration had begun before the Civil War, but they accelerated sharply in the 1870s and 1880s. The tentacles of urban-industrial life reached far into the countryside, drawing everybody into a market economy that was no longer local or face-to-face. A family who lived in a Nebraska sod hut and ordered a dishpan from a Montgomery Ward catalogue paid for it with money from the sale of their grain. How much they got for the grain depended on decisions made in eastern corporate headquarters and on the weather in other grain-growing areas around the globe.

The Making of an Industrial Working Class   A diverse and stratified working class emerged as part of industrial capitalism's post–Civil War growth. Race and ethnicity, skill levels, gender, and age separated working people. Even in the same family, men and women, adults and children encountered very different employment opportunities. Skilled workers made up one-sixth of the workforce. They were typically white men from families that had long been resident in the United States, but some were immigrants and children of immigrants from England, Ireland, and Germany. These skilled, proud, and relatively well-paid craftsmen—the "labor aristocracy"—dominated such trades as carpentry.

Because workers usually secured jobs through family and friends, many trades took on a decidedly ethnic character. The sons of Irish immigrants tended to work as plumbers, carpenters, and bricklayers. Germans controlled furniture making, brewing, and baking. The English, Welsh, and Scots—who had emigrated from the center of the world's first industrial

Cigars and the News

While his fellow workers make cigars, one craftsman reads aloud from a newspaper. This arrangement, in which cigar makers pooled their wages to cover the pay of the designated reader, indicates how some skilled trades maintained pre-industrial customs even as their work became subdivided and mechanized. Lewis Hine, 1909— International Museum of Photography at George Eastman House.

revolution—filled the ranks of skilled machinists, metalworkers, and miners.

Skilled workers enjoyed high wages because employers relied on their knowledge and paid a premium for it. Late-nineteenth-century entrepreneurs excelled at amassing the wherewithal to build factories but depended on skilled workers to run them. Craft skills therefore gave workers some measure of power and control over daily conditions on the job.

Late-nineteenth-century skilled workers embraced ideals of craft unity and collective action in the same way that capitalists celebrated individualism and profitability. Some skilled workers unionized, and some joined radical groups to fulfill collective ideals. But no more than one-third of the workers in any nineteenth-century trade belonged to unions, and skilled craftsmen generally stayed away from radical movements. As long as they could earn a good living and keep their employers' respect, most craft workers wanted neither trouble on the job nor social upheaval. Their power rested as much on their skills, knowledge, and workplace relationships as on the strength of their formal organizations or any larger social vision.

Unskilled laborers could not as readily control their working conditions. New immigrants, African Americans, and impoverished women and children of all races and nationalities compelled by financial circumstances to take any available work filled the ranks of the unskilled. African American men did menial labor for wages, serving as gardeners, coach drivers, and doormen; women were confined largely to domestic service. Mexican American men labored on the railroads and in the expanding mining industries of Colorado, New Mexico, and Arizona; their wives and children worked southwestern farmlands that their ancestors had occupied for generations.

Wages varied directly with an occupational group's power and social status. Men typically received at least 50 percent more than women. White workers commanded wages that were significantly higher than those paid to African Americans, Mexican Americans, and Chinese Americans. Skilled craftsmen earned much more than the unskilled. The best-paid craftsmen (a locomotive engineer or a glassblower, for example) could bring home more than $800 a year in the 1880s, whereas an unskilled textile worker's family had to survive on $350.

Even skilled workers had reason to worry. The proportion of skilled jobs in the labor market was declining as industry mechanized. Oscar

Ameringer, a teenager newly arrived in Cincinnati, brought with him cabinetmaking skills he had learned from his father in Germany. But Ameringer's skills meant little in the furniture factories of the United States. "The work was monotonous, the hours of drudgery ten a day, my wages a dollar," he later wrote. Workers frequently lost time because of injury or illness. And all workers faced the burden of unemployment during the troughs of the business cycle. In 1878, at the end of the five-year depression, well over half a million working people remained unemployed. Employment picked up, but by the mid-1880s, as many as two million were again out of work.

But low wages actually bought more goods over time. While wages remained fairly steady from 1870 until the end of the century, virtually everything became less expensive. The food that cost $1.00 in 1870 sold for just 78 cents a decade later—an enormous benefit to working-class families, who generally spent half their income on food. Thus, "real" wages, adjusted for changes in the cost of living, actually rose slowly. Nevertheless, most unskilled workers remained in poverty during this period, and many families had to send more than one family member out to work. The number of women and children in the labor force more than doubled between 1870 and 1890.

In the 1870s and 1880s, one in every six or seven paid workers was a woman. English-speaking white women could take advantage of two rapidly growing "white-collar" (a reference to the white shirts that were once standard for office workers) occupations: retail selling and office work. But in general, the women who most often worked outside their homes— African American and immigrant women—had the worst economic prospects. Except for African American women, who worked for wages throughout their lives, female workers were almost all young and unmarried. Still, by 1890, a small but growing minority—almost one in every seven female wage earners—was married.

Women's employment outside the home aroused controversy, especially in middle-class families. But even working-class men argued for a "family wage" that would make it possible for women to avoid wage work outside the home. Some wondered whether a woman who worked could be truly respectable. Others contended that women worked just for "pin money," in order "to decorate themselves beyond their needs and station." Employers often used this argument to justify paying women less than men and laying women off first during hard times. Persistent questions about the legitimacy of women's paid work dragged down female workers' earnings. As one Iowa shoe saleswoman complained in 1886, "I don't get the salary the men clerks do, although this day I am six hundred sales ahead! Call this justice? But I have to grin and bear it, because I am so unfortunate as to be a woman."

The Slaves of the Sweaters
A New York immigrant tailor's family returns from a contractor, carrying material to be sewn into garments back home. Scenes of urban poverty, such as this one depicted in an 1890 engraving, were featured in illustrated newspapers. Photography and individual "art" prints, however, tended to celebrate the city, with depopulated images focusing on the "grand style" architecture of new buildings or constructing distant bird's-eye views of ideal urban landscapes. William A. Rogers, *Harper's Weekly*, April 26, 1890—American Social History Project.

Most women who could afford to stay at home did so. Employment was hazardous to women's health: the death rate of women wage-earners was twice that of other women. Many predominantly female occupations, such as domestic service and "home work"—work paid by the piece done in tenement residences—demanded extraordinarily long hours. And some women faced sexual exploitation and abuse by male bosses and coworkers. At best, wage-earning women suffered the same hardships as men—periodic unemployment, long hours, and dangerous conditions—with even lower pay. And in an era of rigid gender roles, women worked a "second shift" at home, performing household labor in homes that were not equipped with running water or electricity.

Children's labor helped to sustain millions of working-class families. During the last thirty years of the nineteenth century, about one in six children between the ages of ten and fifteen years held jobs. They toiled for meager wages in textile mills, tobacco-processing plants, and print shops. They roamed the streets as newsboys, bootblacks, and scrap collectors. In southern cotton mills, their year-round workdays lasted twelve hours, and they sometimes worked the night shift. Their lack of schooling meant that they would have few opportunities beyond factory work. A few states (particularly in New England) prohibited child labor and required school attendance, but the laws were loosely enforced and easily ignored by desperate parents and greedy employers.

Although divided by skill, ethnicity, race, gender, and age, working people in the late nineteenth century had much in common. They worked long hours—typically ten-hour days, six days a week. More and more workers also encountered the impersonality of the large factory, the sense of being an anonymous cog in a big wheel. Between 1870 and 1900, the average workforce in cotton mills and tobacco factories doubled.

Many employers sought ways to raise profits by reducing workers' already paltry wages. Some cut wages; others required workers to bear part of the costs associated with their tasks. Clothing manufacturers required employees to buy sewing machines, needles, and thread. Some employers shifted the costs of rent, heat, and light onto the workers by hiring them to manufacture clothing, artificial flowers, and other small items in their

" . . . Leaves Me in Poor Circumstances": New Production Methods Affect Workers

In his testimony before a U.S. Senate committee investigating conditions of labor and capital in October 1883, Thomas O'Donnell (who had immigrated to the United States from England eleven years earlier) describes the introduction of ring spinning machines to replace mule spinners at the Fall River, Massachusetts, textile factory where he worked. Ring spinners produced thread with a continuous rather than intermittent motion and could achieve higher speeds. These changes allowed the mill's owners to employ children and reduce wages. O'Donnell describes the sharp decline in his family's living standards that followed.

They are doing away with a great deal of mule-spinning there and putting in ring-spinning, and for that reason it takes a good deal of small help to run this ring work, and it throws the men out of work. . . . There are so many men in the city to work, and whoever has a boy can have work, and whoever has no boy stands no chance. Probably he may have a few months of work in the summer time, but will be discharged in the fall. That is what leaves me in poor circumstances. Our children, of course, are very often sickly from one cause or another, on account of not having sufficient clothes, or shoes, or food, or something. . . .

Q. How much [work] have you had within a year?—A. That would be about fifteen weeks' work . . . I got just $1.50 a day. . . .

Q. That would be somewhere about $133 [in annual wages], if you had not lost any time.—A. Yes, sir.

Q. That is all you have had?—A. Yes, sir.

Q. Do you mean that yourself and wife and two children have had nothing but that for all this time?—A. That is all. I got a couple dollars' worth of coal last winter, and the wood I picked up myself. I goes around with a shovel and picks up clams and wood.

Q. What do you do with the clams?—A. We eat them. I don't get them to sell, but just to eat, for the family. That is the way my brother lives, too, mostly. He lives close by us.

Q. How many live in that way down there?—A. I could not count them, they are so numerous. I suppose there are one thousand down there.

Q. A thousand that live on $150 a year?—A. They live on less. . . .

Q. How long has that been so?—A. Mostly so since I have been married.

Q. How long is that?—A. Six years this month.

Q. Why do you not go West on a farm?—A. How could I go, walk it?

U.S. Congress, Senate Committee on Education and Labor, *Report on the Relations Between Labor and Capital*, vol. 3 (Washington, D.C.: Government Printing Office, 1885), 451–457.

tenement apartments. And mining companies and others often paid in "scrip," or company-issued paper money. This money could be used only at company-owned stores, which charged highly inflated prices. One mining company made $1,000 a month by selling gunpowder—needed by miners to extract coal or ore—at $1.25 above the going rate.

CAUGHT IN THE SHAFTING.

MISS SABINA GOUDETTE WHIRLED AROUND AND HORRIBLY MANGLED IN THE
NORTH GROSVENOR COTTON MILLS, NEAR PUTNAM, CONN.

Caught in the Shafting

The *National Police Gazette* portrayed, in a characteristically lurid fashion, an industrial accident in a North Grosvenor, Connecticut, cotton mill. The *Police Gazette* enthusiastically violated the mores of a genteel culture by focusing on legal and illegal sports, violent crimes and accidents, and sex. Women were often depicted as perpetrators or victims of violence, providing titillation to the male readership. *National Police Gazette*, May 28, 1892—Prints and Photographs Division, Library of Congress.

Most late-nineteenth-century businessmen ignored hazardous working conditions, largely because they had little financial incentive to make the workplace safer. Railroad workers risked being maimed as they ran along the tops of trains to set the brakes for each car or stood on the tracks to drop a coupling pin as the cars crashed together. In 1881 alone, long after safety devices such as automatic coupler systems and the Westinghouse air brake had become widely available, 30,000 railroad workers were killed or injured on the job. "So long as brakes cost more than trainmen," the prominent minister Lyman Abbott predicted, "we may expect the present sacrificial method of car coupling to continue." The courts repeatedly denied damages to injured workers, maintaining that the workers shared the blame for accidents and that by going to work, they accepted the risks of the job. In 1893, Congress narrowly passed the Railroad Safety Appliance Act, which finally made it illegal for trains to operate without automatic couplers and air brakes. The harsh conditions of the emerging industrial capitalist economy were the price that working people paid for the vast industrial transformation of the United States in these years.

Power and Profit

Businessmen stood at the apex of the new system, and many of them argued that they were destined to lead and control. Yet, paradoxically, they viewed the world below their summit with fear and anxiety. How could they tame the ruinous cycle of boom and bust? How could they gain command of the industrial colossus that, at times, seemed unmanageable? Control became their watchword: control of the markets for their raw materials and their products, control of production within their firms, control of the workers who toiled for them, and control of their political environment. A chaotic economic and political environment ultimately crushed their fantasies of total control, but they did attain an unprecedented degree of power and money.

Businessmen Justify Their Rule and Seek Control
In the late nineteenth century, many people worshiped at the altar of capitalist success: "That you have property is proof of industry and foresight on your part or your

father's," one writer asserted, "that you have nothing is a judgment on your laziness and vices, or on your improvidence." Businessmen, politicians, and scholars even attempted to explain capitalist social relations by citing the theory of biological evolution proposed by British scientist Charles Darwin in 1859. According to Darwin, a process of natural selection determines the most adaptable or "fittest" members of a plant or animal species, those best able to survive and reproduce. Social Darwinists distorted this theory to explain "scientifically" the impoverishment of the "unfit" masses and warned that interference on behalf of the "weak" would doom American society. John D. Rockefeller justified brutal economic competition as "a survival of the fittest, the working out of a law of nature and a law of God."

This ideology of Social Darwinism both justified and grew out of the ruthless behavior of business leaders, especially in the railroad industry. In the 1870s, railroad owners and executives organized themselves into cartels (price-fixing rings) that divided up traffic and set freight rates, an approach that seemed preferable to cutthroat competition. But the cartels collapsed when railroad executives slashed freight rates to win customers in hard times. When a cartel member broke ranks, rivals had no recourse but to follow suit; their agreements were not enforceable legal contracts.

A new breed of financial speculators—men who had little interest in running railroads but great interest in profiting from them—also undermined the railroad managers. Financiers led by Jay Gould, Jim Fisk, and Cornelius Vanderbilt rigged the stock market, issuing thousands of shares of new, "watered" stock without increasing the assets they represented. They also launched rate wars to drive down the price of railroad stocks and bonds temporarily so that they could buy distressed railroads at bargain prices.

When the cartels collapsed in the 1880s, railroad managers turned to a simpler method of controlling competition: building huge rail networks to drive smaller lines out of business. Between 1880 and 1893, the big railroads leased more land, bought more equipment, and laid more track, enormously increasing the scale of their operations. Constructed from inferior materials and laid along badly prepared routes, much of this new track had to be rebuilt, at significant expense, within fifteen years.

Large-scale manufacturing enterprises experienced similar boom-and-bust patterns of expansion, competition, and bankruptcy. Industrialists rushed into new markets, overbuilding capacity until initially high prices and profits gave way to sharp competition, falling prices, and declining profits. Like the railroads, manufacturers used size as a competitive weapon. Some grew through horizontal integration, in which several companies producing the same product merged to form a single larger unit that could gain control of prices and markets. Other manufacturers focused on vertical integration, in which one firm coordinated all aspects of production and distribution, rather than buying materials from and selling products to other companies. This strategy insulated firms from competition by enabling them to control their costs of manufacturing. Still others focused on acquiring new technology. By installing a new production process, a firm might cut expenses, lower prices, drive competitors out of business, and then raise prices again.

The most successful firms combined these approaches, as demonstrated by the activities of the two leading industrialists of the period: John D. Rockefeller and Andrew Carnegie. Rockefeller, the son of an itinerant patent-medicine salesman, started as a bookkeeper, earning enough to become a partner in a successful wholesaling firm. In 1863, he invested his money in the fledgling petroleum industry, which primarily produced kerosene for lighting.

Seven years later, Rockefeller and his partners incorporated Standard Oil, a centrally organized combination of oil corporations. Thanks to its close ties with the railroads, which granted discounts or rebates to major shippers, Standard Oil could price its products much lower than those of its competitors and drive them out of business. Dismissing cartels as "ropes of sand," Rockefeller merged competing firms with Standard Oil, pledging willing competitors to secrecy and ruthlessly coercing the unwilling. By 1880, the Standard Oil Trust controlled about 90 percent of the nation's oil-refining capacity; Rockefeller could set the price and virtually control the output of oil. During the next decade, Standard Oil integrated vertically as well, purchasing oil fields, constructing pipelines, establishing a nationwide system of licensed dealers, and building fleets of tankers to serve newly created foreign marketing subsidiaries.

Andrew Carnegie — the wealthiest American capitalist of the period — was an even more potent symbol of individual advancement, although his rags-to-riches rise was actually quite unusual for his day. Carnegie's Scottish father, a linen weaver, lost his job when the power loom was introduced and moved his family to the United States. He and his wife eked out a living in an immigrant neighborhood in Pittsburgh, weaving and taking in laundry. Young Andrew began his working life in factories but eventually became a telegrapher and personal secretary for Thomas A. Scott, the superintendent of the Pennsylvania Railroad's Western Division. When Scott moved up in 1859, Carnegie, at age twenty-four, won Scott's job.

Six years later, Carnegie left the railroad to focus on steel production. He spent the next quarter-century using new technology and techniques of vertical and horizontal integration to ensure his absolute domination over that industry. He built up-to-date mills, acquired companies from competitors, forged alliances with the railroads that both used and hauled his steel, and adapted the management and marketing techniques he had learned at the Pennsylvania Railroad.

Carnegie carried the techniques of vertical integration further than any of his contemporaries. Annoyed by fluctuations in the price and supply of the pig iron that was basic to steelmaking, he began to produce his own supplies. With his partner Henry Clay Frick, Carnegie acquired sources of iron ore, coke, and coal; expanded his iron-making operations; and developed a fleet of steamships and a railroad to transport materials directly to his steel mills. "From the moment these crude stuffs were dug out of the earth until they flowed in a stream of liquid steel in the ladles," trumpeted one admiring observer, "there was never a price, profit, or royalty paid to an outsider."

New Management Systems   Not every late-nineteenth-century businessman tried to dominate his industry as Carnegie and Rockefeller did, but virtually all relentlessly trimmed costs by restructuring their firms and streamlining work processes. Managers of small and large firms alike faced internal and external imperatives to minimize waste and inefficiency. But smaller companies responded more cautiously to the management innovations and production methods that were sweeping corporate America. Most woodworking and metalworking firms, for example, employed fewer than one hundred employees, who turned out relatively small batches of customized products. Such companies opted for limited measures to increase workers' productivity, enhance management control, and increase profits. They might purchase a single new machine, identify a new local or regional market for their products, or modestly (rather than completely) reorganize the work process.

The leaders of gigantic industrial firms, on the other hand, chose a wholly new form of corporate direction. After 1880, big businessmen turned to systematic management, a loose label for various efforts to speed and streamline industrial operations. Initially, unsystematic and decentralized labor-control systems handicapped them. In most nineteenth-century factories, a foreman responsible for achieving production goals supervised each department. But he often had to cajole workers to get the job done or even negotiate with them over output, pay, and other issues. Industrial workers resisted working ceaselessly at peak efficiency, trying instead to set their own pace and give the boss what they considered a fair day of work. Manufacturers complained bitterly about time wasted by workers who stopped to rest, discuss the progress of the work, or wait for machines to be repaired or materials to be delivered.

To increase workers' output, employers began to enforce formal work rules more strictly. A New Hampshire factory headed its list of work rules with "NOTICE! TIME IS MONEY!" One rule stated that washing up "must be done outside of working hours, and not at our expense."

Some manufacturers introduced machinery as part of their campaign to exert control over employees. Fuming at his workers' victory in an 1885 strike, Cyrus McCormick of Chicago's McCormick Harvesting Machine Company vowed, "I do not think we will be troubled by the same thing

***Forty-millionaire Carnegie
in His Great Double Role***

In 1892, this unidentified
cartoonist, along with many
Americans, sharply criticized
the steel baron for his role in
the Homestead strike. Andrew
Carnegie's "Great Double Role"
refers to his accumulation of an
immense personal fortune at
the same time as he endowed
cultural institutions around the
world. "[A]s the tight-fisted employer," ran the caption, "he
reduced wages that he may
play philanthropist and give
away libraries, etc." Utica, New
York, *Saturday Globe*, July 9, 1892—
Prints and Photographs Division,
Library of Congress.

again if we take proper steps to weed out
the bad element among the men."
McCormick installed $500,000 worth of
molding machinery so that he could
"weed out" the skilled workers who had
led the strike, crush their union, and
replace them with low-paid, unskilled
workers. Similarly, John D. Rockefeller
used new barrel-making technology
in his Cleveland plant to break the
power—and lower the wages—of the
company's highly skilled and once-
proud barrel makers.

Andrew Carnegie combined bold
technological innovation and ruthless
employee management to gain control over the work process. For example,
he designed his J. Edgar Thompson steelworks in Braddock, Pennsylvania,
with elevated trains to carry coal overhead throughout the huge mill,
thereby eliminating the jobs of hundreds of shovel-wielding laborers.
Resisting an 1892 strike by workers at his giant plant in Homestead, Pennsylvania, Carnegie managed to lengthen the working day in all of his plants
without raising the daily wage rate. In the mid-1890s, many of his employees worked twelve-hour shifts, seven days a week. "We stop only the time it
takes to oil the engines," said one Homestead worker.

Businessmen Look to Politics   Businessmen saw politics as another
means of boosting profits and consolidating their control of markets and
workers. Business influence pervaded all levels of government in the late
nineteenth century, but as enterprises became national in scope, their owners and managers tried to shape the federal government and nationwide
policies. Managers much preferred to deal with a uniform set of federal laws
or regulations than with a confusing and contradictory assortment of state
and local ones. Big businessmen also found that they could influence the
federal government more easily than state or local governments, which
tended to respond more to local interests. And as journalists and reformers
began demanding that the national government regulate railroads and control monopolies, businessmen sought to influence legislation in their own
behalf.

Corruption and favor buying in government had increased notably
during the Civil War, and they persisted when peace came. Widespread vote
selling led one Ohio politician to call the House of Representatives in 1873
"an auction room." Politicians still embraced "the spoils system" (a term
dating back to the 1830s), in which supporters of the winning party received

" . . . The Duty of the Man of Wealth": Two Perspectives on Men of Wealth

In The Gospel of Wealth and Other Timely Essays, *published in 1889, the industrialist Andrew Carnegie argued that individual capitalists were duty bound to play a broader cultural and social role and thus improve the world. Not everyone viewed Carnegie as the benevolent philanthropist he presented himself to be. His antiunion stance and efforts to get maximum work for the least pay placed him in another light for workers. A "Workman" published a satirical response to Carnegie's book in an 1894 issue of a Pittsburgh labor newspaper.*

Excerpt from Carnegie's *The Gospel of Wealth*:

This then, is held to be the duty of the man of wealth: To set an example of modest, unostentatious living, shunning display or extravagance; to provide moderately for the legitimate wants of those dependent upon him; and, after doing so, to consider all surplus revenues which came to him simply as trust funds, which he is called upon to administer, and strictly bound as a matter of duty to administer in the manner which, in his judgment, is best calculated to produce the most beneficial results for the community—the man of wealth thus becoming the mere trustee and agent for his poorer brethren, bringing to their service his superior wisdom, experience, and ability to administer, doing for them better than they would or could do for themselves. . . .

A Workman's Prayer:

Oh, almighty Andrew Philanthropist Library Carnegie, who art in America when not in Europe spending the money of your slaves and serfs, thou art a good father to the people of Pittsburgh, Homestead and Beaver Falls. We bow before thee in humble obedience of slavery. . . . We have no desire but to serve thee. If you sayest black was white we believe you, and are willing, with the assistance of . . . the Pinkerton's agency, to knock the stuffin[g] out of anyone who thinks different, or to shoot down and imprison serfs who dare say you have been unjust in reducing the wages of your slaves, who call themselves citizens of the land of the free and the home of the brave. . . .

Oh, lord and master, we love thee because you and other great masters of slaves favor combines and trusts to enslave and make paupers of us all. We love thee though our children are clothed in rags. We love thee though our wives . . . are so scantily dressed and look so shabby. But, oh master, thou hast given us one great enjoyment which man has never dreamed of before—a free church organ, so that we can take our shabby families to church to hear your great organ pour forth its melodious strains. . . .

Oh, master, we thank thee for all the free gifts you have given the public at the expense of your slaves. . . . Oh, master, we need no protection, we need no liberty so long as we are under thy care. So we commend ourselves to thy mercy and forevermore sing thy praise.

Amen!

Andrew Carnegie, *The Gospel of Wealth and Other Timely Essays* (1889); "A Workingman's Prayer," *The Coming Nation*, February 10, 1894.

THE LABOR DESPOT.

The Tyranny of the Walking Delegate

The popular image of the trade union official changed as manufacturers attempted to exert greater control over the workplace. In this 1889 engraving, a trade union officer — "the well-fed, well-paid official . . . whose fiat is expected to be obeyed without protest or murmur" — arbitrarily calls a strike. Portrayed as a despotic opponent of business, the official's manner and dress resembled those of the familiar figure of the corrupt political boss. J. Durkin, *Frank Leslie's Illustrated Newspaper*, September 21, 1889 — American Social History Project.

government offices and they in turn paid off the party.

Beginning in 1875, Democrats increasingly challenged Republican dominance in Washington, D.C., as they rebuilt their party from the shambles of the war. The revived Democratic Party united most of the South, and it attracted a growing number of workingmen in northern industrial areas by attacking the increasing concentration of wealth and corruption in politics. In the Compromise of 1877, the Democrats made a deal that gave the presidency to Rutherford B. Hayes but, in return, secured the removal of federal troops from the southern states and African Americans from national and local politics (see the Prologue).

The Compromise of 1877 fed growing disillusionment with political corruption. Against this background, a campaign to clean up politics emerged in the late 1870s and gained momentum in the early 1880s. Some reformers had long advocated replacing the spoils system with a civil service system based on merit and protected against shifts in party power; England, Germany, and other European countries had already embraced such systems. That idea acquired new urgency in the United States in 1881, when Charles Guiteau, a crazed job seeker and member of an opposing faction of Republicans (called the "Stalwarts") assassinated Republican President James A. Garfield. When Guiteau shot Garfield, he announced the succession to a Stalwart supporter: "I am a Stalwart. [Vice President Chester] Arthur is now president." (Actually, Guiteau spoke too soon; Garfield languished for almost three months on his deathbed. In this era when the president and the federal government were much less central to national life, an incapacitated president did not pose a major problem.) Two years later, the Pendleton Civil Service Act created the Civil Service Commission to hire federal workers on the basis of competitive examinations.

Still, politics remained a dirty business. In the particularly grubby 1884 election, Democrats described the Republican candidate, Senator James G. Blaine, as "the continental liar from the State of Maine" to highlight the

THE BOSSES OF THE SENATE.

personal honesty of the Democratic candidate, Grover Cleveland. But Cleveland, the governor of New York, had two skeletons in his own closet. He had hired a substitute to fight for him in the Civil War, as had many better-off northerners, but it was hardly a wise move in retrospect. He had also fathered a child out of wedlock. But Blaine lost ground with Irish Catholic voters after a Protestant minister attacked the Democrats as the party of "Rum, Romanism, and Rebellion," and he offended working-class voters by attending a well-publicized sumptuous feast hosted by Jay Gould and other robber barons in the midst of a depression. Cleveland won narrowly; a shift of six hundred votes in the crucial state of New York would have made Blaine president. The close contest reflected the even balance between the parties in this period. In 1888, Cleveland lost narrowly in electoral votes to Benjamin Harrison, though he had won the popular vote. (Four years later, however, Cleveland won a resounding victory and became the only person to serve two nonconsecutive terms as president.)

Aiding Harrison in 1888 was a lavish campaign chest that department store magnate John Wanamaker systemati-

cally raised from businessmen—the first time that truly large sums of money had been raised from businessmen for a presidential campaign. Ironically, the 1883 Pendleton Civil Service Act had freed political parties from financial dependence on their appointees (who had often provided kickbacks and contributions) only to place them at the mercy of businessmen, who became the alternative source of funds. Industrialists' and financiers' contributions to both the Democratic and Republican parties assured them of support from whichever was in power. As a result, journalist William Allen White argued that senators represented not political but economic entities: "Coal and iron owned a coterie from the Middle and Eastern seaport states. Cotton had half a dozen senators. And so it went."

When popular sentiment demanded that the government regulate business by reining in railroads or curbing monopolies, business-oriented members of Congress could ensure that the resulting laws lacked muscle. Thus, businessmen used their influence to shape the two great measures of federal regulation of business during the late nineteenth century: the Interstate Commerce Act (1887) and the Sherman Antitrust Act (1890). Powerful railroads made the Interstate Commerce Commission—the regulatory agency set up under the 1887 act—their servant instead of their master.

The judiciary provided an even more reliable bulwark of business power in federal circles. Most federal judges began their careers in corporation law, and they served their former business associates from the bench. Court decisions further weakened the already feeble federal laws regulating business. The courts rarely found corporations guilty of violating the Sherman Antitrust Act; instead, they used it to curb labor unions by issuing injunctions—cease-and-desist orders—against strikers and their unions.

The South and West Industrialize

The tentacles of the industrial capitalist goliath gripped not just the railroads and factories of the Northeast and Midwest. It also transformed—albeit less evenly and completely—life in the South, which remained heavily agricultural, and the West, which relied on agriculture and extractive industries. In the post–Civil War era, industrialization—generally under the auspices of northern capitalists—appeared in southern textile factories and coal mines. Meanwhile, railroads brought farmers, even in the remote hill country, under the sway of national and international markets. In the West, capitalist enterprise—manifest in everything from the hard rock mines to the vast corporate ranching spreads to the inevitable railroads—had an even rougher and more brutal edge than in the East. But, as in the East, working people and immigrants (often from Asia or Mexico) generally bore the heaviest brunt of the transforming power of the new profit-driven economy. But so did much longer-standing residents of the land—the

Native Americans—and the land itself, which overgrazing and farming scarred.

The New South   The Compromise of 1877 cemented the rule of southern conservatives and made the region "safe" for northern business, a condition that had not existed during the social and political upheavals of Reconstruction. Consequently, when the depression of the 1870s lifted, northern businessmen began to invest large amounts of money in the South. Men such as Henry Grady, the editor of the *Atlanta Constitution*, envisioned a "New South" filled with cities, immigrants, commerce, and industry financed by northern money, and they courted northern industrial capital. But the New South developed slowly and erratically, because southern dependence on cotton, the domination of northern capital, and the legacy of slavery shaped and sometimes hobbled the growth of industrial capitalism. This meant that the small farmers, black and white, who constituted the vast majority of the southern population, faced even greater insecurity and suffering than did northern workers.

Northern business had easily gained control of southern industry and finance after the Civil War. Emancipation had wiped out the Southern capital invested in slaves. The war's physical destruction caused further losses. Federal action during Reconstruction reinforced the region's dependency. The nation's new financial system tilted toward promoting industry and favored creditors, which did little for the agricultural South, dominated by debtors. Republican banking and currency legislation encouraged northern industry but hampered the operations of southern banks that had not failed outright.

Northern (and to some extent European) investors, who placed their own profits before southern welfare, bankrolled Southern industrial development. They set up low-wage operations to extract raw materials or crudely processed products, such as lumber, coal, cotton, turpentine, and seafood. These industries squeezed profits from the region, depleted resources, and left behind destitute people and a dependent economy. The only major southern-controlled industry was tobacco, which was dominated by North Carolinians such as James B. Duke, who mechanized the industry.

Railroads led the way in southern economic development, as they had in the North. Between 1880 and 1890, laborers laid over 22,000 miles of track, nearly doubling the southern rail network. Twelve large corporations, most of them headquartered in New York City, controlled half of all southern tracks. Aided by state legislators, who provided generous land grants and lenient tax policies to speculators, the railroads helped to develop industries such as the iron industry in Tennessee, Virginia, and Alabama that extracted resources. Birmingham, Alabama, which did not even exist in 1870, became one of the country's largest iron-, steel-, and coal-producing centers by 1900. But such industrialization required northern capital and technical expertise; the South's dependent position circumscribed its ability to act on its own.

The most important southern industry—in fact, the key to southern industrialization—was cotton manufacturing (Map 1.2). Between 1880 and 1890, the number of spindles (rods holding spools of thread) increased ninefold in the four leading textile states (Georgia, Alabama, and the Carolinas), to just under four million. The new southern mills had two unbeatable advantages over their older northern counterparts: the newest, most efficient technology and impoverished and poorly paid workers. White women made up more than half of the mill labor force; black women were almost entirely excluded, and black men were confined to heavy labor outside the main areas of the mill. Southern mills also relied heavily on child labor. In 1896, one in four North Carolina cotton mill workers was a child, compared with one in twenty in Massachusetts. A North Carolina child earned less than four cents for every dime a Massachusetts child earned.

MAP 1.2 The New South at the End of the Nineteenth Century

Despite the promises of its boosters, the New South, like the Old South, remained overwhelmingly agricultural. Still, some industries—wood products, coal, cigarettes, and even iron and steel—had emerged by the end of the century. The most important was textile manufacturing, which spread through the Piedmont, the region of rolling hills that stretched from central Virginia down to Georgia and Alabama.

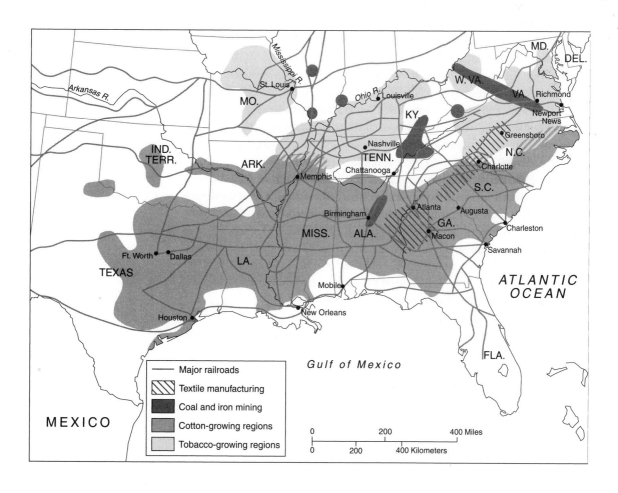

Southern textile workers lived in company towns, where working-class desires for independence and autonomy faced the autocratic and paternalist rule of the corporations. Describing isolated Georgia mill towns in 1891, social investigator Clare de Graffenreid painted a grim picture of "rows of loosely built, weather-stained frame houses" containing only "a shackling bed, tricked out in gaudy patchwork, a few defunct 'split-bottom' chairs, a rickety table, and a jumble of battered crockery." Mill owners, like slave owners before the Civil War, thought of themselves as kindly father figures, but they ruled their company-owned towns with iron fists, refusing to allow them to incorporate and establish local governments. Starvation wages, payment in scrip, and price-gouging company stores eclipsed the advantages of low rent and subsidized schools and churches.

African American Tobacco Workers

In this Richmond, Virginia, factory, women stripped tobacco stems from leaves. As in most southern industries, black workers labored separately from white workers and were relegated to the lowest-paying and least-skilled jobs. Valentine Museum, Richmond, Virginia.

In dramatic contrast to the mostly immigrant workforce of the North, whites born in United States dominated the southern textile mill labor force. Race provided southern employers with a powerful weapon for dividing and controlling workers; white workers tolerated exploitation more willingly if they felt superior to black workers. Women in an Atlanta mill showed their determination to protect textile work as a white "privilege" in 1898, when 1,400 of them struck against the employment of two African American spinners. This pattern of race discrimination was not confined to the textile industry. Cigarette factories hired both black and white workers but separated them.

Even though relatively few foreigners immigrated to the South, immigrants composed a disproportionate part of the urban working class. In 1880, immigrants made up only one in twenty residents of Richmond, Virginia, but one in three of the city's unskilled white laborers.

Outside the cities, southerners employed in factories retained their ties to the soil. In Chatham County, Georgia, black men often stayed on the farms all winter while the women worked in a nearby oyster-processing plant. In Tennessee and Virginia, men of both races toiled in sawmills or coal mines while women worked the farms. Many of the South's major employers — tobacco, seafood, and sugar processors — offered only seasonal employment. In the off-season, their employees returned to farming.

Crop Liens, Debt, and Sharecropping   For Atlanta's Henry Grady, the railroad symbolized the New South, but for many poor white farmers, it stood for exploitation and greed. This was especially true in the hills of the Appalachians, where most white families had never owned slaves and poor farmers had produced food for their own consumption or for trade with local artisans. After the war, these farmers shifted from subsistence agriculture to commercial production, but they paid dearly to get their goods to market. With no competition, hill-country railroad owners could raise rates, even as freight rates elsewhere declined. As railroad lines extended throughout the southern backcountry, farmers were at their mercy.

The crop-lien system exacerbated white farmers' troubles. Cash-poor farmers turned for credit to "furnishing merchants," who used funds borrowed from northern banks to buy seed, tools, and other supplies, which they resold to the farmers in exchange for a lien, or claim, on their next harvest. The merchants not only charged credit customers significantly higher prices than those paid by cash customers, but also added 25 to 50 percent in interest.

Merchants usually insisted that borrowers grow cotton because it was readily marketable. Unfortunately, the widespread shift to commercial agriculture coincided with the beginning of a long-term decline in world prices for cotton. A dramatic increase in Brazilian, Egyptian, and Indian cotton production and — more significantly — a leveling off of international demand for cotton led to a ruinous fall in prices. The record-breaking 1894 cotton crop was more than double that of 1873, but farmers suffered because 1894 prices were only one-third of those paid two decades earlier.

Consequently, white small farmers found themselves trapped in a vicious circle: they could get credit only if they grew cotton; cotton prices kept falling, so they had to plant more; the more cotton they planted, the less food they grew; the less food they grew, the more they had to borrow to buy food. More and more often, their debt surpassed the value of their crops. They had no choice but to commit the following year's crop to the merchants as well. "The furnishing man was the boss, pure and simple," wrote a woman who watched the system work in Alabama. "His word was law." In the end, many white farmers lost their land to these merchants.

On the lowest rung of the southern economic ladder were the tenant farmers, or sharecroppers. In large plantation areas across the South, families — most of them African American — rented small plots of land and paid landowners a large share of the crop at the end of the harvest. While sharecroppers maintained control of their labor and time, the landowners retained the ultimate power of ownership, supplying tools, fertilizer, seed, and land and appropriating most of the crop. Sharecroppers were legally free but economically dependent, drawn into the market system like northern wage laborers. Although they raised crops for the market, African American sharecroppers remained largely outside the cash economy. Each family began the agricultural cycle by securing seed, supplies, and food from the landowner; these items were charged to the family and deducted from its share of the crop at harvest time. Even in the best of times, the family's share was small, but as the price of cotton fell in the 1880s and 1890s, sharecroppers spiraled deeper into debt and dependency. And, although legally free, some sharecroppers lived with the ghosts of slavery. Many white planters still maintained a system of armed "riders" who monitored and disciplined black workers; one woman told of being whipped until her "back was as raw as a piece of raw beef."

Black families scrambled to make a bit of money because every penny earned brought a degree of freedom from dependence on the landowner. Men worked by the day on nearby farms, and women sold chickens, eggs, milk, cheese, and vegetables and did domestic labor. Sharecropper Brown Cobb used his considerable skill as a basket maker to win some concessions from conniving landlords. Still, their poverty was remarkable even in this generally poor region; most black sharecropping women kept house with only a straw broom, a laundry tub, a cooking kettle, and a water pail.

Sharecropping or one of its variants occupied the overwhelming majority of black farming families in the late-nineteenth-century South. Since 90 percent of African Americans still lived in the South and 80 percent of them lived in rural areas, the system touched most of them. Sharecroppers had much in common with the poorest white southerners. Both tilled the cotton fields laboriously by hand, using simple plows and heavy iron hoes. The yoke of debt bore heavily on both. Black or white, poor southern farmers found themselves trapped in a common system, though one divided by race and racism, that made economic independence ever more remote. Even the poorest whites considered themselves superior to blacks, preventing cooperation between the two groups.

The Way They Live

While many white artists dabbled in romantic visions of the rural South, Thomas Anshutz's 1879 painting captured the hardship of subsistence farming in the post-Reconstruction South. Thomas P. Anshutz, 1879, oil on canvas, 24 × 17 inches — Metropolitan Museum of Art, Morris K. Jesup Fund, 1940 (40.40).

"All Must Work Under My Direction": A Sharecropper's Contract

This 1882 contract spells out the terms and conditions under which African American tenant farmers could work small plots of land on the Grimes plantation in Pitt County, North Carolina. Although not a return to conditions of slavery, the contract gives the plantation owner extraordinary control over the conditions of field work and the division of the harvested crop. Sharecroppers were forbidden to keep any cotton seed from the harvest, which would have allowed them to plant their own crop without needing it to be furnished by the plantation owner. Owners could also forbid sharecroppers and their families to work off the plantation, require sharecropping women to work as domestic servants, and physically punish sharecroppers who broke the rules.

To every one applying to rent land upon shares, the following conditions must be read and agreed to.

To every 30 or 35 acres, I agree to furnish the team, plow, and farming implements, except cotton planters, and I do not agree to furnish a cart to every cropper. The croppers are to have half of the cotton, corn and fodder (and peas and pumpkins and potatoes if any are planted) if the following conditions are complied with, but—if not—they are to have only two-fifths. Croppers are to have no part or interest in the cotton seed raised from the crop planted and worked by them. No vine crops of any description, that is no watermelons . . . squashes or anything of that kind . . . are to be planted in the cotton or corn. All must work under my direction. All plantation work to be done by the croppers. . . .

All croppers must clean out stables and fill them with straw, and haul straw in front of stables whenever I direct. All the cotton must be manured, and enough fertilizer must be brought to manure each crop highly, the croppers to pay for one half of all manure bought, the quantity to be purchased for each crop must be left to me.

No cropper to work off the plantation when there is any work to be done on the land he has rented, or when his work is needed by me or other croppers. . . .

Every cropper must be responsible for all gear and farming implements placed in his hands, and if not returned must be paid for unless it is worn out by use.

Croppers must sow and plow in oats and haul them to the crib, but must have no part of them. Nothing to be sold from their crops, nor fodder, nor corn to be carried out of the fields until my rent is all paid, and all amounts they owe me and for which I am responsible are paid in full. . . .

The sale of every cropper's part of the cotton to be made by me when and where I choose to sell, and after deducting all they may owe me and all sums that I may be responsible for on their accounts, to pay them their half of the net proceeds. Work of every description, particularly the work on fences and ditches, to be done to my satisfaction, and must be done over until I am satisfied that it is done as it should be. . . .

Grimes Family Papers, Southern Historical Collection, University of North Carolina, Chapel Hill.

Conflict on the Plains   In the decades after 1870, the workforce was shifting from agriculture to industry at the same time that the number of farms doubled and farmers brought more land under cultivation than in the previous two and a half centuries. The explanation of the seeming contradiction was that agriculture was also industrializing, and fewer workers could produce more food with the help of machinery, irrigation, and drought-resistant grains. The most rapid development occurred on the level, treeless, semiarid Great Plains (Kansas, Nebraska, the Dakotas, and surrounding areas), once dubbed the Great American Desert and written off as unsuitable for farming. Prairie and grassland were easier to bring into production than were forests, which had to be cleared, and the Plains became the heartland of American farming in little more than a generation. White agricultural settlement also extended, although at a slower pace, into California, Nevada, and the huge expanse of land that would become Colorado, Utah, New Mexico, and Arizona.

Until the late 1870s, American Indians had for 250 years so effectively hindered white settlement in the West that white Americans spoke of the "Indian barrier." That barrier was breached when U.S. soldiers responded to the massive Sioux rebellion of 1876. Lakota leaders refused to be restricted to a reservation and defeated U.S. troops led by General Custer in the Battle of Little Big Horn. In response, thousands of U.S. troops flooded the region, suppressed the warriors, and then murdered the Sioux leader, Crazy Horse, after he surrendered in 1877. Although few great battles would follow, Army patrols, starvation, disease, and alcohol would continue to take their toll, devastating the Indians' traditional ways of life.

White settlers and officials and Plains Indians viewed land ownership very differently. Indians on the Plains hunted over a wide range. Tribes, not individuals, owned the land, and all members shared its fruits. The individualistic ways of white settlers mystified these early Americans; as Sitting Bull of the Sioux remarked, "The white man knows how to make everything, but he does not know how to distribute it." The tradition of communal landholding similarly offended white men, who wanted to carve up the West into private pre-

Arriving at the Carlisle Indian School, c. 1879
Federal policy to "Americanize" and assimilate Indians took place off the reservation as well as on the new reservations. Reformers promoted boarding schools to remove Indian youths from their home environments and culture and instill into them white Protestant values. Army officer Richard Henry Pratt modeled the United States Indian Training and Industrial School, founded on an abandoned military base in 1879 in Pennsylvania, after the Hampton Institute, a government boarding school for African American children in Virginia. Carlisle's first students were a group of eighty-four Lakota children, including these three boys. John N. Choate, Negative Collections, Photo Lot 81-12, #125 — National Anthropological Archives, Smithsonian Institution.

Beginning the Deculturalization Process

Richard Henry Pratt's philosophy was "to kill the Indian and save the man." Boys were taught certain skilled trades or modern agricultural techniques; girls learned sewing, cooking, laundry, and housework. The English language was considered key to the "civilizing" process, and Indian languages were forbidden. As this "after" photograph of the three Lakota boys illustrates, traditional dress was replaced by military uniforms. Their hair was also cut, which in Lakota society was a symbol of mourning, therefore causing them much distress. Twenty-four more schools modeled on Carlisle were established outside reservations over the next two decades. John N. Choate, Negative Collections, Photo Lot 81-12, #57, 490—National Anthropological Archives, Smithsonian Institution.

serves. Even those who saw themselves as humanitarians regarded individualism and private property as the highest expressions of human civilization.

These views, backed by federal power, became part of federal reservation policy, a contradictory strategy that was designed to segregate Indians, supposedly to prepare them for future integration. Supporters of the policy claimed that reservations would enforce separation, prevent conflict, and protect Indians from white people who refused to acknowledge Indian rights to the land. It did none of these things. Conflict continued as white settlers and Indians fought over land in some places, over livestock in others. Indians shunned reservations across the West. In eastern Oregon, a band of Nez Percé resisted their eviction from nonreservation lands in 1877. The U.S. Army responded by chasing 200 Nez Percé warriors and their families for 1,700 miles through Idaho, Wyoming, and Montana, making their leader, Chief Joseph, a symbol of Indian resistance. When the Nez Percé finally surrendered, they were taken to Fort Leavenworth, Kansas, then moved from place to place over the next several years as many of them grew sick and died.

Military might alone does not explain the government victories. U.S. troops could communicate by telegraph and travel by railroad, and their force was augmented by the cooperation of white ranchers, homesteaders, and prospectors seeking minerals on Indian lands. Over time, the United States won more by attrition than by victory on the battlefield; Indians could not sustain resistance when their traditional ways of life that relied on access to land were so disrupted that they could not even get food.

That disruption was perhaps most evident in the destruction of the buffalo that had once roamed the plains in huge herds, as many as twenty-five million animals at their peak. Plains tribes—both nomads such as the Blackfeet, Crows, and Comanches, and agricultural groups such as the Pawnees and Wichitas—had depended on the buffalo, not only for meat, but also for hides to make tepees and for robes to keep warm.

The buffalo herds had been dwindling under the impact of commercial hunting since midcentury, but disaster struck after 1870. Philadelphia tanners perfected a new process for turning buffalo hides into cheap leather, and railroads provided a new way to get the hides to market. Hunters took well over four million buffalo between 1872 and 1874, leaving much of the meat to rot. "The buffalo," wrote one army officer who saw the slaughter, "melted away like snow before a summer's sun."

The buffalo slaughter devastated the economy of the Plains Indians, while their white "sympathizers" in the East proposed reforms in government policy that fostered further repression of indigenous cultures. Appalled by decades of atrocity and war, reformers wanted Indians to

"You Should Take Allotments . . .": Responding to the Dawes Act

American Indians were not immune from pressures to accommodate to the new industrial order, as illustrated in this selection from the biography of Edward Goodbird, a member of the Hidatsa tribe in Minnesota. He describes the period immediately following the passage of the Dawes Act in 1887, when Plains Indians were made to give up communal ways of life for individual family farms. Goodbird's experience was exceptional: he prospered under the new system, ultimately becoming an employee of the Bureau of Indian Affairs.

The time came when we had to forsake our village at Like-a-fish-hook Bend, for the government wanted the Indians to become farmers. "You should take allotments," our [Bureau of Indian Affairs] agent would say. "The big game is being killed off, and you must plant bigger fields or starve. The government will give you plows and cattle."

All knew that the agent's words were true, and little by little our village was broken up. In the summer of my sixteenth year nearly a third of my tribe left to take up allotments. . . .

My father left the village, with my mother and me, in June. He had a wagon, given him by the agent. . . . We camped at Independence in a tepee, while we busied ourselves building a cabin. My father cut the logs; they were notched at the ends, to lock into one another at the corners. . . . The floor was of earth, but we had a stove. We were a month putting up our cabin. . . .

Our agent issued to every Indian family having an allotment a plow, and wheat, flax, and oats for seeding. My father and I broke land near our cabin, and in the spring seeded it down. We had a fair harvest in the fall. Threshing was done on the agency machine, and, having sacked our grain, my father and I hauled it, in four trips to Hebron, eighty miles away. Our flax sold for seventy-five cents, our wheat for sixty cents, and our oats for twenty-five cents a bushel. Our four loads brought us about eighty dollars.

I became greatly interested in farming . . . one day the agent sent for me. I went to his office.

"I hear you have become a good farmer," he said, as I came in. "I want to appoint you assistant to our agency farmer. . . . You are to measure off for every able-bodied Indian, ten acres of ground to be plowed and seeded. If an Indian is lazy and will not attend to his plowing, report him to me and I will send a policeman. . . ."

I began my new duties at once. . . .

Edward Goodbird, *Goodbird the Indian: His Story* (1914).

assimilate. To that end, they supported coercion on three fronts: suppressing Indian religion and undercutting tribal authority, educating Indian children in American Protestant values, and replacing communal landholding with private property.

Persuaded that Indians would adapt to white culture, Congress passed the Dawes, or Indian Allotment, Act of 1887, breaking reservation lands into individually owned plots. The act allowed the president to grant American citizenship to Indians who were willing to abandon their communal ways. Families who adopted what the law called "habits of civilized life" would be granted ownership of 160 acres. With tribal consent, the government could sell reservation land to white purchasers, holding the proceeds for the "education and civilization" of Indians. The Dawes Act reaffirmed the right of Congress to grant building rights on Indian lands to railroad and telegraph companies.

The Indian Allotment Act led to a massive transfer of land from Indian to white ownership. When it passed, Indians still held 138 million acres. Within thirteen years, their domain had shrunk to less than 78 million acres, virtually all of it unsuited to the agricultural life the federal government tried to foist on the Indians. Moreover, the Bureau of Indian Affairs destroyed many traditional villages. A few years after allotment, one white observer described the remains of the Hidatsa village at Like-a-fishhook Bend in Minnesota as "rings of dirt where the lodges used to stand, half-filled cache holes all covered with weeds" (Map 1.3).

Over the next decades, white reformers tried relentlessly to stamp out tribal customs. Communal ceremonies, including all kinds of feasts and rituals, were banned. Government-funded boarding schools removed Indian boys and girls from tribal homes—often forcibly—and taught the language and values of the white majority. One young Sioux who was made

Mass Burial

The day after the "battle" of Wounded Knee, the dead Sioux — estimated by the U.S. Army at 84 men, 44 women, and 18 children — were buried in a mass grave at the scene of the massacre on the Pine Ridge Reservation Agency, South Dakota. George Trager, *Burial of the Dead at the Battle of Wounded Knee, [South Dakota]*, 1891, number P1967.103, albumen silver print, 4⅝ × 7⁷⁄₁₆ inches — Amon Carter Museum, Fort Worth, Texas.

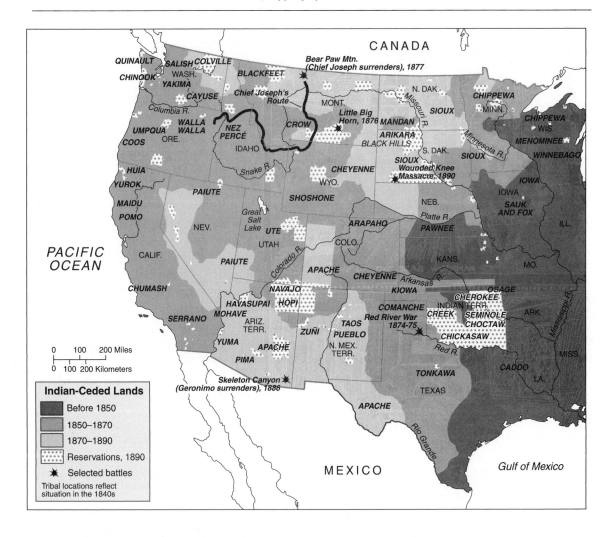

MAP 1.3   Exiling Indians in Their Native Land

to attend a government school at Pine Ridge later recalled how "we looked terrible" in European clothes. "But we had to wear them or be punished."

Although they no longer possessed the means to openly resist this systematic destruction of their way of life, many Plains Indians did not simply accept their fate. In 1888, Wovoka, a young man of the Nevada Paiutes, began preaching his vision of an Indian messiah who would return the American continent to the Indians, bring back the buffalo, and return the dead to life. In a message to a Cheyenne-Arapaho delegation, Wovoka warned "Do not tell the white people" about his prophesies. To prepare for the great day, followers practiced a mystical dance, which white observers dubbed the "Ghost Dance."

Alarmed as the dance swept through Sioux encampments in the fall of 1890, Indian Bureau agents called for U.S. Army assistance. Thousands of

Indians resisted the white settlement that overran the Great Plains after the Civil War. But by 1890, Indians had been forced to cede vast territories that they had once occupied, and they found themselves confined to scattered reservations, almost always on poor-quality land.

"... A Very Sad Sight": The Wounded Knee Massacre

American Horse, a Sioux leader, describes the massacre at Wounded Knee Creek on December 29, 1890.

The men were separated . . . from the women, and they were surrounded by the soldiers. Then came next the village of the Indians and that was entirely surrounded by the soldiers also. When the firing began, of course the people who were standing immediately around the young man who fired the first shot were killed right together, and then they turned their guns, Hotchkiss guns, etc. upon the women who were in the lodges standing there under a flag of truce, and of course as soon as they were fired upon they fled. . . .

[T]he women and children of course were strewn all along the circular village until they were dispatched [killed]. Right near the flag of truce a mother was shot down with her infant; the child not knowing that its mother was dead was still nursing, and that especially was a very sad sight. The women as they were fleeing with their babies were killed together, shot right through, and the women who were very heavy with child were also killed. All the Indians fled . . . and after most all of them had been killed a cry was made that all those who were not killed or wounded should come forth and they would be safe. Little boys who were not wounded came out of their places of refuge, and as soon as they came in sight a number of soldiers surrounded them and butchered them there. . . .

Of course it would have been all right if only the men were killed; we would feel almost grateful for it. But the fact of the killing of the women, and more especially the killing of the young boys and girls who are to go to make up the future strength of the Indian people, is the saddest part of the whole affair and we feel it very sorely.

Robert D. Marcus and David Burner, eds., *America Firsthand* (1989).

Sioux fled to the Dakota Badlands. On December 28, the Seventh Cavalry entered the Sioux encampment at Wounded Knee Creek to search for arms. In the ensuing confrontation, army troops massacred at least 146 people. The Wounded Knee massacre came to signify the violence the white majority was prepared to use to enforce its version of civilization.

Western Farming and Ranching The suppression of American Indians did not quell conflict in the West. Groups with conflicting visions—cattle drovers, sheepherders, farmers, miners, and others—also struggled with one another for domination of the land. Like immigrant factory workers and southern hill farmers, these people found their working lives transformed by the development of industrial capitalism, the expansion of market relationships, and decisions made in eastern boardrooms.

Federal Indian policies and subsidies to build the national railroad network gave a tremendous boost to western settlement and tied the region's farmers into distant markets. Anglo settlers entered New Mexico and Colorado in the 1870s, for example, as the railroad was being completed. The region's economy had been defined for generations by Mexican farm families engaged in subsistence and communal farming and in herding on community-regulated common lands. With the coming of the railroads, this system gave way to commercial farming on private homesteads and to cattle and sheep ranching financed by eastern capital and linked by rail to distant slaughterhouses. By 1889, nearly 72,000 miles of track connected farms west of the Mississippi River to the national and international economies.

Agricultural productivity grew enormously, especially on the Great Plains. Farmers eagerly bought harvesting and threshing machinery on the installment plan, counting on increased output. A single farmer working by hand could reap about seven acres of wheat during the ten days it was in its prime; using automatic binders that cut and tied bundles of wheat, common by 1890, the same farmer could harvest 135 acres. The resulting vast supply enabled the United States to export one-third of its wheat crop by 1900.

But despite rapid productivity gains, the machinery purchases left Plains farmers — already in debt to mortgage holders in the East and in Europe — even more dependent on credit in an agricultural market that was extremely unstable. In the early 1880s, unusually heavy rainfall and temporarily rising wheat prices created boom conditions. But later in the decade, rainfall dropped to its normal level, and drought threatened. Equally important, the price of wheat dropped on the world market. In actual buying power, farmers suffered from seriously fluctuating prices, especially during times of depression: the early and middle 1870s, the late 1880s, and the early and middle 1890s.

Like backcountry southern farmers, Plains farmers were whipsawed by falling prices and rising production costs. They had to produce more just to stay even and pay for their machinery, but the more they produced, the lower prices fell. Developments outside farmers' control further dragged down the price of their crops. Mechanization and the opening of new grain-producing land in Argentina, Canada, and Russia flooded the world market with wheat and corn.

The railroads also contributed to the rising costs of farming. In many areas of the West, as in the South, farmers had access to only one railroad line. Railroads charged as much as the traffic would bear, raising rates to make up for losses from rate cutting on competitive routes elsewhere. Freight rates in the West were often two to three times those in the East.

A Sod House

The Sommers family proudly poses for a photographer in front of their sod house in West Custer County, Nebraska, in 1888. One photographer recalled, "Whenever the traveling photographer came 'round, the sodbusters trotted out all of their possessions. The children were always outfitted in their Sunday best." Families were eager to show friends and relatives back East that their new modest-looking homes were practical adaptations to prairie living and not evidence of poverty. Because cameras could not yet photograph dark interiors, settlers did their best to bring outside whatever prized possessions they owned.
Solomon D. Butcher, 1888—Butcher Collection, Nebraska State Historical Society.

Plains farmers also had to pay high prices to the operators of elevators, the giant grain-storage bins that loomed on western horizons. As with the railroads, large eastern corporations usually owned the elevators. Freight charges for a bushel of wheat could cost more than it could fetch in the marketplace.

While male farmers used expensive machinery for planting, harvesting, and threshing, most Plains farm women churned by hand, carried water in pails, and cooked at open fireplaces. The fortunate had treadle sewing machines to ease the task of making clothing for entire families. Churning butter and collecting eggs were women's work, and they made money selling these items locally or shipping them to points east. Some also sold garden vegetables, sausages, and bread; others took in boarders or earned money washing, ironing, and sewing for local bachelors. Many families set up housekeeping in huts made from large bricks of prairie sod. Though sturdy and warm, many sod houses were dark, dirty, and leaky. Less fortunate Plains families huddled in tarpaper shacks or dugouts—caves with covered openings.

Farm women had to be extremely resourceful in this primitive environment. What Abigail Scott Duniway, who migrated to Oregon in the 1850s, said of a slightly earlier time remained true in this period. The frontier farmer's wife, she observed, "has to be lady, nurse, laundress, seamstress, cook and dairywoman by turns, and . . . attends to all these duties unaided, save by the occasional assistance of an indulgent husband who has cares enough of his own." Exceptional women like Duniway managed to find time to write in the evenings; her writing skills helped to support the family when her husband suffered a crippling accident and lost the farm.

Although more than one million family farms sprang up in the West during the last forty years of the nineteenth century, many agricultural products came from operations that bore little resemblance to the idealized small family farm. In the Red River Valley of North Dakota and Minnesota and in the Central Valley of California, absentee-owned "bonanza farms" of the 1870s and 1880s relied on heavy mechanization and seasonal migrant laborers for large-scale production. By 1880, one 66,000-acre farm along the Sacramento River yielded more than one million bushels of wheat a year. By 1900, the average farm in the Dakotas measured 7,000 acres.

The cattle boom of the early 1880s and rumors of huge profits brought eastern and British investors into ranching. Large corporations dominated the industry, such as the Chicago-owned, three-million-acre XIT Ranch in Texas and the Sparks-Harrell Company in Idaho and Nevada, which grazed 150,000 cattle. Railroads opened even more land for cattle grazing by creating new shipping centers.

Ranching grew heedless of the environmental consequences. Ranchers cared little about the public lands they used for grazing until the mid-1880s, when they faced economic and ecological disaster. The pressure of grazing had led to a decline in grasses and to undernourished cattle. Where it once took five acres to raise a steer, it now took fifty or even more. Bad winters in 1885 and 1886 left hundreds of thousands of cattle dead. Years later, one rancher wrote, "A business that had been fascinating to me before, suddenly became distasteful. I never wanted to own again an animal that I could not feed and shelter." Sheepherders moved into many of the grazing lands after that, because sheep could thrive on nongrass plants that cattle would not eat.

Although westerners who farmed the land, herded animals, and worked in towns were economically interdependent, some clashed fiercely over their different ways of life. Large ranchers fenced public lands; small ones cut the fences. Farmers saw themselves as guardians of settled and sober living in a region rife with lawlessness. They complained that herds trampled crops and that the freewheeling behavior of the cowboys who tended the herds defied law and order. In Kansas, farmers crusaded against saloons, dance halls, and prostitution. Cattle and sheep ranchers feuded with each other, too, although their conflicts were essentially ethnic and religious in origin. In New Mexico, sheep owners were mostly Mexican Americans; in Nevada and southern Idaho, they were Mormons and Basques.

Extractive Industries and Exploited Workers Although grain farming and cattle ranching dominated the western economy, each region developed other specialties, mainly extractive industries that produced massive quantities of raw materials for shipment to other parts of the world. The Pacific Northwest yielded lumber; the Rockies, the Southwest, and California mined metals and coal. The railroad also brought in finished goods of all kinds from the East. Many workers who powered the extractive economy were immigrants like the Irish copper miners of Butte, Montana, and most lived and labored under harsh conditions. But some reaped handsome rewards. Skilled workers in western cities commanded higher wages than their counterparts in the East, and even western farmhands probably had more cash in their pockets than did unskilled industrial workers. But because most regions of the West relied on a single industry, even a slight downturn could bring widespread misery. Boom-and-bust industrial capitalism hit western workers hard.

Large companies had begun shipping lumber to California from the Pacific Northwest in the 1850s and 1860s. Completion of the first railroad linking the Northwest with the East in 1883 created a market for railroad ties and connected the Northwest's small railroads to nationwide systems. As in other industries, technological change increased production in the woods. New saws and axes made it possible to cut trees faster, and the "steam donkey," an engine that pulled logs by cables, took them out of the forest. As a result, the Northwest served markets all over the world.

In other areas, prospecting for metals continued. Miners discovered gold in the Black Hills of South Dakota in the 1870s and in Idaho during the 1880s. Gold and silver mining became even more profitable as copper, lead, and zinc—found in gold and silver deposits—gained importance in industry. European and eastern businessmen poured vast amounts of capital into metal mining and smelting. Many investors ended up with shattered hopes, but others reaped huge profits. After 1879, when Colorado emerged as the nation's leading mining region, eastern capital and western workers unlocked vast stores of mineral wealth.

While Eastern capitalists like the Guggenheims became fabulously rich mining silver, copper, and nitrates, miners labored under horrendous conditions. Fifteen hundred Mexican Americans worked at California's New Almaden Quicksilver Mine, which produced half of the world's supply of mercury, a metal that was essential in the smelting of silver ore. Climbing ladders out of the mine, they hauled 200-pound sacks of ore strapped to their foreheads. Every year, one out of every thirty hard rock miners was disabled and one out of every eighty was killed by an explosion, cave-in, fire, or accident. Many of the rest developed lung diseases.

Western mining towns seemed to mushroom overnight, as Leadville, Colorado, did with the discovery of silver in the Rocky Mountains. From a small cluster of log cabins in 1876, Leadville grew to a sprawling city of 15,000 people four years later. Leadville's experience was repeated across Colorado and Idaho in the 1880s. These towns owed their existence to the mines, but only a minority of their citizens were miners. In Cripple Creek, Colorado, one in four residents worked in the mines; the others provided

Scarred Landscape

Copper deposits were first found in the hills outside Ely, Nevada, in the 1870s. Mining the copper became profitable only around 1900, with the building of railroad lines and investment by eastern capital. After that, large profits were made by the Nevada Consolidated Copper Company and others by digging open-pit mines in which terraces were cut into the landscape. The mining left the landscape scarred, hillsides denuded, and groundwater contaminated. The Copper Flat pit would eventually measure more than a mile across and almost 1,000 feet deep. West Coast Art Company, Copper Flat, Nevada, c. 1909—Prints and Photographs Division, Library of Congress.

services ranging from retailing to prostitution. Western movies recall "parlor houses" with gilt-framed mirrors and brocaded furniture, but most brothels offered plain furnishings and plain sex. The overwhelming majority of women wage-earners on the mining frontier served men in other ways: waitressing and making beds at hotels and restaurants, doing laundry, or cooking and cleaning.

Although mining towns developed a reputation for crudity and lawlessness, they also established stable community institutions. Even Deadwood, South Dakota, known as a sinkhole of gambling, prostitution, and violence, boasted schools, churches, and a theater within months of its founding. As two early residents reminisced, "On one hand could be heard the impassioned call of the itinerant minister of the Gospel, . . . In close proximity would be a loud-voiced gambler calling his game."

The diverse working class of western mining towns included Mexican American miners, Chinese American laborers and launderers, Basque sheepherders, and African American cowboys mixed with European immigrants and white migrants from the East and South. They all participated in an international labor market that helped to populate the West. Indeed, even more of the population of the West than of the East was foreign-born. Between 1860 and 1890, one-third of California's residents were foreign-born, more than twice the proportion of the country as a whole. In 1890, North Dakota had a higher proportion (45 percent) of immigrants than any other state. Immigrants from Scandinavia settled the Great Plains, and many moved on to the Pacific Northwest. Migrants crossed the unregulated Mexican border for short periods to work as field hands or to lay track in Texas, Arizona, and southern California. Also in California, Japanese immigrants and Mexican migrants performed the stoop labor that was required for agriculture. A contract labor system—gangs of workers run by bosses who transported them from abroad and sold their labor—brought Italian workers to California farms and Greek laborers to Utah mining camps.

Of all the western immigrant groups, the Chinese inspired the most hostility. More than 200,000 Chinese, mostly men, had migrated to the United States by 1890. Many had borrowed passage money from labor

Working-class Racism

The cover of the recently founded *Illustrated Wasp,* a West Coast pictorial weekly, offered its support in virulent pictorial terms to white working-class anti-Chinese agitation in San Francisco. San Francisco *Illustrated Wasp,* December 8, 1877—California Section, Negative Number 19,850, California State Library.

"The People Would Always Work Together": Mexican American Homesteaders

In this selection from his handwritten memoir from 1937, Elfido López recalled the communal approach to agriculture that marked his childhood on his family's modest homestead in southern Colorado. The arrival of the railroad in the Southwest in the early 1870s transformed the area's economy and the lives of its residents. Longtime Mexican residents of the area were quickly drawn into the region's expanding wage economy.

When I was 2 years old my father and eleven more men went to Red Rock to file on homesteads. . . . Of the twelve men only six could afford to buy shovels, the other six made shovels out of wood. The shovels were needed to make a irrigation ditch. They had no way to survey the ditch so they just started digging. The men that had good shovels broke the ground and the ones that had wood shovels threw the loose dirt out. . . . They would let the water run behind them and bank it up and dig in front. Then they would let the water run ahead in the ditch to see if they needed to dig the ditch deeper and in this way they made their ditch and it took them four months.

After finishing the irrigation ditch they had to plow their fields. They had no plows, but they made them out of forks of trees. The plows have only one handle, and the points were made out of pieces of iron that the men had sharpened on a rock and nailed to the wood. It was very hard to plow with these plows as they would go every way but straight. They did manage to farm in this way, and they raised good crops of wheat, melons, beans, pumpkins, chili, and almost anything they had to plant. . . .

Each man would not plant more than 3 or 4 acres of wheat as they had no way to cut the wheat except by hand scythes. . . . After they would finish cutting one man's wheat they would go to the next until they had finished the last one. The people would always work together and they never thought that they were doing too much for each other. When a child went to another house the women always gave them something to eat. It was that way with all of them. They did not really have much of anything but they always had something to eat.

Elfido López, "Autobiography," 1937, Elfido López, Sr. Collection. Courtesy, Colorado Historical Society.

brokers, who organized crews to do jobs that most white Americans deemed too dangerous and arduous. Railroad laborers, in particular, were recruited in China in the 1870s through this contract labor system, which was much like indentured servitude. Others found work on their own. Lee Chew was an ambitious young man seeking wealth "in the country of American wizards." In the 1880s, he worked as a domestic servant, learning American ways from his employer, sending money to his family, and saving to open a business. With a partner, he opened a laundry, a typical Chinese American

". . . Indebted to Her Master/Mistress": A Prostitute's Contract

Almost all of the Chinese who immigrated to the United States before 1900 were men. Of the approximately 100,000 Chinese immigrants who resided in the United States between 1880 and 1900, only 5,000 were women. Some found work as laundresses and servants; others arrived as indentured prostitutes. This 1886 contract describes the stringent conditions under which Xin Jin worked as a prostitute in San Francisco in exchange for payment of her fare from China.

The contractee Xin Jin became indebted to her master/mistress for food and passage from China to San Francisco. Since she is without funds, she will voluntarily work as a prostitute at Tan Fu's place for four and one-half years for an advance of 1,205 yuan (U.S. $524) to pay this debt. There shall be no interest on the money and Xin Jin shall receive no wages. At the expiration of the contract, Xin Jin shall be free to do as she pleases. Until then, she shall first secure the master/mistress's permission if a customer asks to take her out. If she has the four loathsome diseases she shall be returned within 100 days; beyond that time the procurer has no responsibility. Menstruation disorder is limited to one month's rest only. If Xin Jin becomes sick at any time for more than 15 days, she shall work one month extra; if she becomes pregnant, she shall work one year extra. Should Xin Jin run away before her term is out, she shall pay whatever expense is incurred in finding and returning her to the brothel. This is a contract to be retained by the master/mistress as evidence of the agreement. Receipt of 1,205 yuan ($524) by Ah Yo. Thumb print of Xin Jin the contractee. Eighth month 11th day of the 12th year of Guang-zu (1886).

_____

Alexander McLeod, *Pigtails and Gold Dust* (1948).

business because it required little capital and demanded grueling labor that white Americans were happy to leave to others.

White workingmen claimed that the Chinese were semislaves who would drive down wages, lower the standard of living, and send American wealth to their families in China. Californians formed anti-Chinese clubs in the 1860s; in 1879, Chinese immigrants were denied the vote and public employment in California. Three years later, the U.S. Congress passed the Chinese Exclusion Act, which suspended Chinese immigration and made resident Chinese ineligible for naturalization.

Legislation did not stem the tide of anti-Chinese mob violence, which peaked in the mid-1880s throughout the West. White mobs torched the Chinatown near the Union Pacific Railroad coal mine in Rock Springs, Wyoming, and gunned down many of its residents. The bodies of twenty-eight victims were found as the ashes cooled the next day.

"All the Houses Were Burned to Ashes": The Rock Springs Riot

The Union Pacific Railroad employed 331 Chinese and 150 whites in its coal mine in Rock Springs, Wyoming. On September 2, 1885, a dispute between Chinese and white miners erupted into violence. The white miners, members of the Knights of Labor, rioted and burned down the Chinese quarter, killing twenty-eight Chinese and causing $150,000 in property damage. The grim story of the riot was given in the Chinese workers' own words in this memorial, or written statement of facts, that they presented to the Chinese Consul at New York.

Whenever the mob met a Chinese they stopped him and, pointing a weapon at him, asked him if he had any revolver, and then approaching him they searched his person, robbing him of his watch or any gold or silver that he might have about him, before letting him go. Some of the rioters would let a Chinese go after depriving him of all his gold and silver, while another Chinese would be beaten with the butt ends of the weapons before being let go. Some of the rioters, when they could not stop a Chinese, would shoot him dead on the spot, and then search and rob him. Some would overtake a Chinese, throw him down and search and rob him before they would let him go. Some of the rioters would not fire their weapons, but would only use the butt ends to beat the Chinese with. Some would not beat a Chinese, but rob him of whatever he had and let him go, yelling to him to go quickly. Some, who took no part either in beating or robbing the Chinese, stood by, shouting loudly and laughing and clapping their hands. . . .

When the Chinese fled to the different hills they intended to come back to "Chinatown" when the riot was over, to dispose of the dead bodies and to take care of the wounded. But to their disappointment, all the houses were burned to ashes, and there was then no place of shelter for them; they were obliged to run blindly from hill to hill. Taking the railroad as their guide, they walked toward the town of Green River. . . . We felt very thankful to the railroad company for having telegraphed to the conductors of all its trains to pick up such of the Chinese as were to be met with along the line of the railroad and carry them to Evanston. . . .

On the ninth of September the United States government instructed the troops to escort the Chinese back to Rock Springs. When they arrived there they saw only a burnt tract of ground to mark the sites of their former habitations. Some of the dead bodies had been buried by the company, while others, mangled and decomposed, were strewn on the ground and were being eaten by dogs and hogs. Some of the bodies were not found until they were dug out of the ruins of the buildings. Some had been burned beyond recognition. It was a sad and painful sight to see the son crying for the father, the brother for the brother, the uncle for the nephew, and friend for friend.

Memorial of Chinese Laborers, Resident at Rock Springs, Wyoming Territory, to the Chinese Consul at New York (1885). Reprinted in Cheng-Tsu Wu, ed., *Chink!* (New York: The World Publishing Company, 1972), 152–164.

Conclusion: Capitalism and the Meaning of Democracy

The United States was the world's richest nation in 1893. Mechanization in both factory production and agriculture had changed forever the way most Americans worked and lived. A vast national and international market linked the miner in the Far West, the tenant farmer in the South, the steelworker in the Midwest, and the garment worker in New York City.

Individuals and families seeking opportunities in industrializing America made new lives for themselves and for their nation. The lure of the "Golden Mountain" brought young men from rural China and Japan. Commercialized agriculture and industrial depression drove millions of young European men and women to the "land of opportunity." Poor Mexican families from agricultural areas were drawn to the expanding economy of the Southwest. And young American-born working-class couples sought their fortunes in the West or set up their own businesses.

Beneath the attractions of individual opportunity and technological progress, however, lay pervasive destitution and discontent. As large industrial and financial institutions secured ever-greater economic and political power, ordinary Americans of all ethnic backgrounds found themselves increasingly subject to forces beyond their control. Lifelong wage earning meant dependence and a betrayal of the longstanding American dream of being beholden to no one, once symbolized by the autonomous farmer and the self-employed artisan. Workers' earnings and the prices they paid for goods were subject to the impersonal mechanisms of world trade and to decisions that were made on behalf of profit in remote corporate boardrooms. Class relations became more stratified. Paupers, multimillionaires, and members of a new middle class all increased in number, but they had little daily contact with one another. What did "democracy" mean in a society with such vast inequalities of economic wealth and political power?

American working people — men and women, wage earners and farmers, American Indians, African Americans, Mexican Americans, European and Chi-

The Street of the Gamblers (by Day)
Arnold Genthe's photographs of San Francisco's Chinatown provide information about the Chinese community at the turn of the century. His characterization of his subjects, however, often conveys a distorted and ominous message. Despite its title, this photograph of Ross Alley, taken some time around New Year's, simply depicts the unusual daytime congestion resulting from the seasonal unemployment of many Chinatown workers after the holiday. Prints and Photographs Division, Library of Congress.

nese immigrants, and descendents of early white settlers—struggled to square the traditional promises of democracy with the realities of a society characterized by economic concentration and previously unimaginable wealth. In communities based on shared ethnic and craft traditions, working people's daily interactions and the organizations they formed fostered support and solidarity for individuals. Those communities and organizations also nourished resistance to employers and to capitalism itself, in a wide spectrum of protest and class conflict that marked the era.

The Years in Review

1873
- The collapse of Jay Cooke & Co. sets off a nationwide financial panic.

1877
- In the Compromise of 1877, a special electoral commission grants the presidential election victory to Republican candidate Rutherford B. Hayes in return for promises to Southern Democrats. These promises include the withdrawal of federal troops from the South, thereby ending Reconstruction.

- The "Indian barrier" to white settlement of the West is removed after the U.S. Army crushes Sioux rebellion and kills Sioux leader Crazy Horse.

- The U.S. Army chases the Nez Percé for 1,700 miles through Idaho, Wyoming, and Montana until they surrender.

1878
- A five-year depression ends, during which over half a million working people were unemployed.

1879
- California denies Chinese immigrants the right to vote and public employment.

- Congress grants women lawyers the right to argue before the Supreme Court.

- Henry George's *Progress and Poverty* blames inequality and corruption on the private ownership of land.

1880
- Republican James Garfield defeats Civil War General Winfield Scott Hancock for the presidency.

1881
- Disappointed job seeker Charles Guiteau assassinates President Garfield; Chester Arthur becomes president.

1882

- Congress passes the Chinese Exclusion Act, suspending Chinese immigration for ten years and declaring resident Chinese ineligible for naturalization.

1883

- The Pendleton Act creates the Civil Service Commission to hire federal workers on the basis of scores on competitive examinations.

- Clocks nationwide are set to a new uniform standard time.

1884

- Democrat Grover Cleveland defeats James B. Blaine for the presidency in a dirty campaign in which Cleveland's sex life and draft dodging are issues.

1885

- A dispute between Chinese and white miners at a coal mine in Rock Springs, Wyoming, erupts in violence as white miners rampage through the town's Chinese quarter, killing twenty-eight Chinese and causing $150,000 in property damage.

1886

- Geronimo surrenders to U.S. forces, ending Apache resistance to federal efforts to resettle them.

- The last remaining nonstandard railroad lines shift to the standard gauge.

1887

- The Interstate Commerce Act establishes a weak federal system of railroad regulation.

- The Dawes Act (Indian Allotment Act) converts communal Indian lands to individual plots in an effort to "civilize" the Indians.

1888

- Republican Benjamin Harrison is elected president in the electoral college, even though Democrat Grover Cleveland, the incumbent president, wins the popular vote.

1889

- The number of states in the Union rapidly expands with the admission of Nevada (1864); Nebraska (1867); Colorado (1876); North Dakota, South Dakota, Washington, and Montana (1889); and Idaho and Wyoming (1890).

- Electric lights are installed in the White House, but President and Mrs. Harrison do not touch them.

1890

- Congress passes the Sherman Antitrust Act, which does little to stop the growth of trusts but is used against labor unions.
- Federal troops massacre 146 Sioux at Wounded Knee.

1892

- Grover Cleveland is elected president for a second term, making him the only person to serve two nonconsecutive terms in that office.
- George Ferris designs the Ferris wheel for the 1893 World's Columbian Exposition in Chicago.
- The "Pledge of Allegiance" is introduced as part of the 400-year celebration of Columbus's "discovery" of America.

1893

- The Federal Railroad Safety Appliance Act makes it illegal for trains to operate without automatic couplers and air brakes.

Additional Readings

For more on the industrialization of America and the transformation of work, see: Susan Porter Benson, *Counter Cultures: Saleswomen, Managers, and Customers in American Department Stores, 1890–1940* (1986); Margery W. Davies, *Woman's Place Is at the Typewriter: Office Work and Office Workers, 1870–1930* (1982); Melvyn Dubofsky, *Industrialism and the American Worker, 1865–1920*, 3rd ed. (1996); Herbert G. Gutman, *Work, Culture, and Society in Industrializing America: Essays in America's Working Class and Social History* (1977); Jacqueline Jones, *Labor of Love, Labor of Sorrow: Black Women, Work, and the Family from Slavery to the Present* (1985); Albro Martin, *Railroads Triumphant: The Growth, Rejection, and Rebirth of a Vital American Force* (1982); David Montgomery, *Workers' Control in America: Studies in the History of Work, Technology, and Labor Struggles* (1979); Michael O'Malley, *Keeping Watch: A History of American Time* (1990); and Olivier Zunz, *Making America Corporate* (1990).

For more on immigration, see: John Bodnar, *The Transplanted: A History of Immigrants in Urban America* (1985); Donna Gabaccia, *From the Other Side: Women, Gender, and Immigrant Life in the U.S., 1820–1990* (1994); Walter D. Kamphoerner, Wolfgang Helbich, and Ulrike Sommer, eds., *News from the Land of Freedom: German Immigrants Write Home* (1991); Stephan Thernstrom, ed., *Harvard Encyclopedia of American Ethnic Groups* (1980); and Xinyang Wang, *Surviving the City: The Chinese Immigrant Experience in New York City, 1890–1970* (2001).

For more on the attempts of business elites to consolidate economic and political control, see: Sven Beckert, *The Monied Metropolis: New York City and the Consolidation of the American Bourgeoisie, 1850–1896* (2001); W. Elliot Brownlee, *Dynamics of Ascent: A History of the American Economy* (1979); Alfred D. Chandler, *The Visible Hand: The Managerial Revolution in American Business* (1977); David Hounshell, *From the American System to Mass Production, 1800–1932: The Development of Manufacturing Technology in the United States* (1984); Morton Keller, *Affairs of State: Public Life in Nineteenth-Century America* (1977); Daniel Nelson, *Managers and Workers: Origins of the New Factory System in the United States, 1880–1920* (1975); Nell Irvin Painter, *Standing at Armageddon: The United States, 1877–1919* (1987); Glenn Porter, *The Rise of Big Business, 1860–1910* (1973); David Rothman, *Politics and Power: The United States Senate, 1869–1901* (1966); Robert H. Wiebe, *The Search for Order, 1877–1920* (1967); and Joanne Yates, *Control Through Communication: The Rise of System in American Management* (1989).

For more on the New South, see: Edward L. Ayers, *The Promise of the New South: Life After Reconstruction* (1992); Pete Daniel, *Breaking the Land: The Transformation of Cotton, Tobacco, and Rice Cultures Since 1880* (1985); Georgina Hickey, *Hope and Danger in the New South City: Working-Class Women and Urban Development in Atlanta, 1890–1940* (2003); Michael Perman, *Struggle for Mastery: Disfranchisement in the South, 1888–1908* (2001); Theodore Rosengarten, *All God's Dangers: The Autobiography of Nate Shaw* (1974); and C. Vann Woodward, *The Origins of the New South, 1877–1913* (1966).

For more on the transformation of the American West, see: William Cronon, *Nature's Metropolis: Chicago and the Great West* (1991); Robert Dykstra, *The Cattle Towns* (1968); David Montejano, *Anglos and Mexicans in the Making of Texas, 1836–1986* (1987); Rodman Wilson Paul, *Mining Frontiers of the Far West, 1848–1880* (1963); William Robbins, *Colony and Empire: The Capitalist Transformation of the American West* (1994); Carlos Arnaldo Schwantes, *Going Places: Transportation Redefines the Twentieth-Century West* (2003); Richard White, *"It's Your Misfortune and None of My Own": A New History of the American West* (1991); and Donald Worster, *Rivers of Empire: Water, Aridity, and the Growth of the American West* (1985).

For more on the encroachment of white settlers on the territory of the Plains Indians, see: David Wallace Adams, *Education for Extinction: American Indians and the Boarding School Experience, 1875–1928* (1995); Dee Brown, *Bury My Heart at Wounded Knee: An Indian History of the American West* (1972); Andrew C. Isenberg, *The Destruction of the Bison: An Environ-*

mental History, 1750–1920 (2000); Robert M. Utley, *The Indian Frontier of the American West, 1846–1890* (1984) and *The Lance and Shield: The Life and Times of Sitting Bull* (1993); and Philip Weeks, *Farewell, My Nation: The American Indian and the United States, 1820–1920* (1990).

For more on women in the frontier West, see: Susan Armitage and Elizabeth Jameson, eds., *The Women's West* (1987); Sarah Deutsch, *No Separate Refuge: Culture, Class, and Gender on an Anglo-Hispanic Frontier in the American Southwest, 1880–1940* (1987); John Mack Faragher, *Women and Men on the Overland Trail* (1979); Julie Roy Jeffrey, *Frontier Women: The Trans-Mississippi West, 1840–1880* (1979); Sandra Myers, *Western Women and the Frontier Experience, 1880–1915* (1982); Virginia Scharff, *Twenty Thousand Roads: Women, Movement, and the West* (2003); Joanna L. Stratton, *Pioneer Women: Voices from the Kansas Frontier* (1981); and Quintard Taylor and Shirley Ann Wilson Moore, eds., *African American Women Confront the West, 1600–2000* (2003).

2

Community and Conflict: Working People Respond to Industrial Capitalism

1877–1893

A S INDUSTRIAL CAPITALISM extended its reach into every corner of the nation's life, Americans differed on the merits of the emerging social order. Among those who deplored the industrial system's callous disregard for human beings was the poet Walt Whitman, who in 1871 had railed against the contemporary "hollowness of heart" and "depravity of the business classes." Humorists Mark Twain and Charles Dudley Warner's novel *The Gilded Age* (1874) satirized the politics and values of the post–Civil War boom years: "Get rich . . . dishonestly if we can, honestly if we must." Historians later adopted their title to describe the materialism and superficiality of the late nineteenth century. Gilded Age America was a society that was dividing along class lines and spoiling for a fight. Industrial capitalists built luxurious mansions and hired private armies to defend their wealth and power; they often enlisted local and national politicians in their cause. Many came to see all working people, in the words of *Century* magazine, as "the vicious and disorderly classes."

Working people, in response, shook their collective fist at the growing visibility of unbridled privilege, especially in the sixteen-year period framed by the railroad strikes of 1877 and the depression of 1893 (Map 2.1). Workers joined together in the Knights of Labor, the eight-hour movement, and the craft unions. They struck not only for higher wages, but also to express solidarity with their fellow workers. They formed independent political parties and debated—and sometimes adopted—radical political ideologies such as socialism and anarchism. And in trying to cope with the impact of industrial capitalism on their daily lives, they drew on shared cultural values—religious, political, ethnic, and craft traditions. In cities, working-class newspapers and debating societies published workers' grievances. Workers

New York Streetcar Workers Strike, March 1886
New York City police drive back striking streetcar workers and their sympathizers as a lone horsecar, operated by company personnel, attempts to make its usual journey along Grand Street. Thure de Thulstrup, *Harper's Weekly*, March 13, 1886 — American Social History Project.

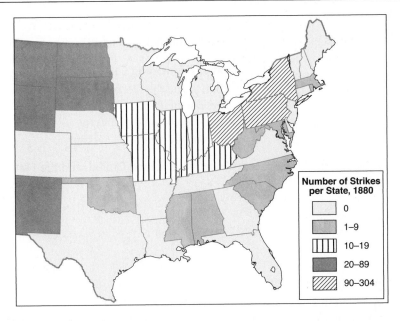

MAP 2.1   A Striking Map: Work Stoppages in 1880

This map, which shows the number of strikes per state in 1880, indicates that strikes were most common in the industrialized regions of the Northeast and Midwest and were rare in the more agricultural South.

inhabited spaces where employers did not go: ethnic, working-class neighborhood stores, saloons, and churches. In rural areas, quilting bees, barn raisings, and outdoor protest meetings provided forums for radical critiques of capitalism's impact on farm families. Resistance—both moderate and militant—flourished in these vibrant labor-reform environments. But large capital would ultimately have the upper hand.

Working People and Their Communities

Working-class life was grounded more in group identity than in ideals of individual effort and initiative. Among native-born workers, collective values stemmed from an abiding belief in independence and liberty spawned by the American Revolution, from religious ideals of equality and justice inherent in evangelical Protestantism, and from community institutions. The cooperative values and traditions brought by immigrants arriving throughout the nineteenth century enriched this mix. Many veterans of fierce social conflicts in Europe remained fervent advocates of egalitarian principles after their arrival in the United States.

The social structures and institutions that underlay working-class life in the late nineteenth century nurtured these collective values. Working people particularly forged bonds of solidarity in their neighborhoods. Not surprisingly, women, who generally did not work outside the home after marriage, were crucial to developing these neighborhood ties. Churches, especially the rural African American churches and the urban immigrant

Catholic parishes, also fostered local community. But religion could be a source of conflict, as when white Protestant moral reformers sought to reshape the manners and morals of working people. Those reformers viewed another crucial working-class institution—the saloon—with particular horror and launched temperance crusades to close it.

Neighborhood Cultures   Immigrants relied on collective traditions and identities to help ease their entry into urban-industrial America. Neighborhoods with names such as German Town, Chinatown, and Little Sweden sprang up across the country, each with its own churches, schools, saloons, and newspapers. Ethnic institutions—foreign-language newspapers, athletic and cultural associations, financial institutions, neighborhood militias, and family-oriented beer halls—helped to soften the worst effects of individual isolation in a new land.

African American neighborhoods, like those of white workers, nurtured solidarity, protest, and resistance. In Washington, Atlanta, and other southern cities, a segregated black culture of mutual aid and self-help eased the afflictions of daily life in a racist society. African Americans fared better—within the severe limitations placed on every aspect of their lives—in large cities, where they could at least secure menial jobs and some small measure of personal freedom.

Working people's neighborhoods nourished collectivity in part because their homes lacked space for socializing. Developers of housing near factories squeezed cheap tenements and wood-frame houses tightly together. In dark apartments, families and boarders shared beds and slept on couches, chairs, and floors. Residents lacked privacy and sought escape on the city streets. Crowds celebrated holidays, neighbors exchanged news and gossip, and activists debated politics, while peddlers sold food and clothing. Mothers socialized on front steps and porches, and children played in streets and alleys.

Immigrant neighborhoods developed an abundant cultural and institutional life. As newcomers arrived, they sought out relatives or people from their villages in the old country. They found housing through the people they worked with and jobs through the people they lived with. Boarding with families from their homelands, they could eat familiar foods, speak their own languages, and discuss their working conditions free from surveillance. Reformers looked askance at the crowding, but revenue from boarders was an essential part of the family economy. An immigrant woman who cooked for four boarders later recalled "that everybody used to do it [at] that time," since "some of the people that came from the other side didn't have no place to stay."

Neighborhood grocery stores, butcher shops, boardinghouses, churches, and saloons sprang up to meet the needs and tastes of particular

"The Workingman's Club": The Saloon as a Social Institution

This description, taken from an article titled "The Saloon in Chicago," conveys a sense of how the late-nineteenth-century saloon met a range of urban workers' social, economic, and cultural needs. The writer, a sociologist, calls the saloon "the working-man's club," comparing it to such institutions as the eating and political clubs that catered to the urban middle and upper classes.

The term "club" applies; for, though unorganized, each saloon has about the same constituency night after night. Its character is determined by the character of the men who, having something in common, make the saloon their rendezvous. . . . The "club-room" is furnished with tables, usually polished and cleaned, with from two to six chairs at each table. As you step in, you find a few men standing at the bar, a few drinking, and farther back men are seated about the tables, reading, playing cards, eating, and discussing, over a glass of beer, subjects varying from the political and sociological problems of the day to the sporting news and the lighter chat of the immediate neighborhood. . . . That general atmosphere of freedom, that spirit of democracy, which men crave, is here realized; that men seek it and that the saloon tries to cultivate it is blazoned forth in such titles as "The Freedom," "The Social," "The Club," etc. Here men "shake out their hearts together." . . .

In many of these discussions, to which I have listened and in which I have joined, there has been revealed a deeper insight into the real causes of present evils than is often manifested from lecture platforms. . . . This is the workingman's school. . . . Here the masses receive their lessons in civil government, learning less of our ideals, but more of the practical workings than the public schools teach. It is the most cosmopolitan institution in the most cosmopolitan of cities . . . Men of all nationalities meet and mingle. . . . It does much to assimilate the heterogeneous crowds that are constantly pouring into our city from foreign shores. But here, too, they learn their lessons in corruption and vice. It is their school for good and evil.

Royal Melendy, "The Saloon in Chicago," *American Journal of Sociology* (November 1900).

ethnic groups, serving as centers of information and communication, connecting neighborhoods with the outside world. In the 1880s, many Czech immigrants to Omaha settled in what became known as "Bohemian Town" or "Praha" (Prague), which was the home to St. Wenceslaus Church, Swoboda's Bakery, Cermak's Pharmacy, and the Bohemian Benevolent Association. But such ethnic labels sometimes hid the mixed and rapid changing nature of immigrant working-class neighborhoods.

In working-class neighborhoods in cities such as Pittsburgh, Milwaukee, and St. Louis, immigrants supported ethnic fraternal organizations — the Sons of Italy, the Polish Union, and the Jewish Landsmanschaft organi-

A Barn Raising

Survival in rural America often relied on community support. Jacob Roher and his neighbors took a break from their construction efforts on his farm near Massillon, Ohio, in 1888 to pose for a photographer. Theodore Teeple, 1888 — Massillon Museum, Massillon, Ohio.

zations — to provide mutual assistance and a familiar cultural milieu. They published newspapers and magazines in dozens of languages, filled with news from the old country and advice to newcomers. Immigrants also created cultural activities, sports teams, and clubs. These institutions nourished a sense of sociability and camaraderie and helped sick, injured, or unemployed community residents.

Networks based on extended families and Old World village ties met many of the immediate needs of immigrant workers, but some problems demanded a broader sense of identity. Antonio Margano, an Italian Protestant engaged in missionary work for his church, complained that New York Italians were "divided into almost as many groups as there are sections of Italy represented" and that "while a man may be known as Italian, he is far better known as a Napoletano, Calabrese, Veneziano, Abruzzese, or Siciliano." But he also observed that the rise of institutions such as Columbus Hospital, the Italian Benevolent Institute, and the Italian Chamber of Commerce pointed to the "development of a larger spirit of co-operation among Italians as a whole." "Italians" and "Germans" were in this sense being invented in America during the same decades when they were created in Europe through political unification.

Immigrant entrepreneurs turned their native languages and knowledge of Old World preferences into business assets. Many acted as intermediaries for individuals dealing with the American legal and financial systems, explaining, translating, and writing letters for a fee. Working-class neighborhoods in cities and small towns provided ready customers for groceries, saloons, barbershops, and variety stores. Although most of the men and women who ran such businesses managed to establish only small, struggling enterprises, the lure of being one's own boss attracted the hopeful.

Like industrial tycoons, some small businesspeople believed that the individual pursuit of wealth was the highest realization of American freedoms. But even the most ambitious local politicians and shopkeepers found that to succeed, they had to collaborate with their families, workmates, and other members of their ethnic and religious groups. Many business owners and professionals who relied on working-class patrons for their livelihoods supported working people's demands and struggles. Local shopkeepers helped strikers by providing food and other necessities on credit.

Similarly, the proprietors of general stores at rural crossroads saw many a farm community through a bad harvest. And although rural "neighborhoods" were not as densely populated as urban ones, they too fostered collective problem solving and socializing. During the 1870s, for example, locusts and drought prompted Kansas women to mount a relief campaign for "families in the country whose only safety from starvation lies in the charity of the people."

The life of William Turner, a skilled ironmolder who in 1880 lived in Troy, New York, with his wife and eight children, illustrates the nature of individual success within the extended family networks and the ethnic, religious, and labor organizations of the late-nineteenth-century neighborhood. Turner emigrated from Ireland in 1850. His father worked as an unskilled laborer at the Albany Iron Works, and by 1860, William and two of his brothers had jobs there as well. The Turners' life revolved around work in the mill — six twelve-hour days per week — and time with the family. William soon became a skilled ironworker. When he married, he found a home in the same row of brick houses where his parents lived.

Turner's rise to the more secure and comfortable position of a skilled worker was the modest success story experienced by millions of Americans — not the "rags to riches" of mythology. Men like Turner dreamed not of riches, but of making a decent life for their families. They found security and solidarity in their ethnic communities, performing the rituals and observing the commandments of their churches and fulfilling their obligations to neighbors and fellow workers.

Working Women at Home Women were central to these working-class communities. Unlike factory workers, women working at home could vary their tasks, laying aside their sewing to stir the soup or comfort a crying baby. For these women, labor was intertwined with family-centered entertainment and neighborhood socializing. They often did certain tasks together while chatting about community events, politics, friends and relations, recipes, and housework techniques. But even running modest households required arduous manual labor and considerable time (Figure 2.1).

More isolated rural women lacked the connections to church, kin, and friends that had sustained them in the more densely populated regions from which they had come, and many women complained of intense loneliness. "As soon as the storms let up, the men could get away from the isolation," wrote Mari Sandoz,

FIGURE 2.1 Out of the Household and into the Household: Women and Work, 1870–1900

Between 1870 and 1900, the number of women in the paid labor force more than tripled, but a majority of women still found employment in the domestic sphere.

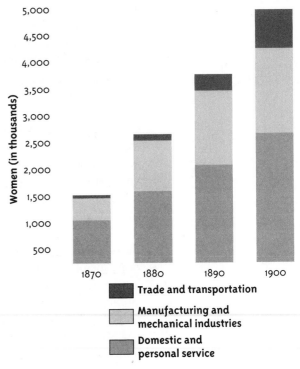

Women (in thousands)

- Trade and transportation
- Manufacturing and mechanical industries
- Domestic and personal service

"Harmony in the Home, in More Ways Than One"
Women bought sewing machines to make clothes for their families but also to provide themselves with incomes. In families such as the Norwegian American Gjevre household in Fairdale, North Dakota, sewing also was a social activity. Companionship could be found at gatherings such as quilting bees or even in the more intimate space of a small parlor. Fred Hulstrand History in Pictures Collection, NDIRS-NDSU, Fargo, North Dakota.

the daughter of a Nebraska homesteader. "But not their women. They had only the wind and the cold and the problems of clothing, shelter, food, and fuel." But rural women's work could have a cooperative dimension. Women helped each other to make quilts, as men shared work to get the harvest in and build houses or barns. Groups of women cooked for the parties associated with both of these kinds of cooperative labor, which featured food, music, and dancing after the work was done.

Before the 1890s, most households were equipped with the same technology that had been used for centuries, with two important exceptions: sewing machines and cast-iron stoves. Sewing machines were quite expensive, but marketed on the installment plan, they became a fixture in both middle-class and poorer households. In many households, men's clothing was purchased, but most women had to produce much of their own clothing and all of their children's, in addition to family linens.

Cast-iron stoves had become common among the middle class in 1870 and spread to people of all classes by 1890. Stoves heated rooms more evenly than did old-fashioned fireplaces. They allowed finer adjustments in cooking temperatures, and cooks no longer had to bend down by open flames to move pots on the hearth. Nevertheless, the stoves were heated by coal and wood, so most women still had to haul fuel and build fires for all of their cooking and heating. Other regular household tasks included hauling pails of water from outside wells and from pumps connected to city water

UNION AGAINST UNION.

THE UNION MAN.—Who Even Put Them Up to that Piece of Impudence?

Union Against Union

A wry comment on the general refusal of working-class men and the trade union movement to consider women's maintenance of the household as work. J. S. Pughe, *Puck*, 1900 — Scott Molloy Labor Archives.

systems, lugging tubs of hot water from the stove for laundry and dishes, and carrying dirty water and bodily wastes back outside.

In some homes, domestic servants did these tasks for pay; this work was the largest source of paid employment for women in the late nineteenth century. In northern cities, most domestic servants were first-generation Irish. Theirs was a life of drudgery and isolation; it was hard, one Irish maid said, "to give up your whole life to somebody else's orders." In the South, domestics were African American women, who rarely had other options and worked for extremely low wages. But domestic servants were not common in workers' homes; most working people hired household help only in emergencies.

Many women earned money by adding to their household work-loads — caring for boarders or taking in laundry or sewing. In western mining towns, women rented or bought large houses and took in workingmen who needed lodgings. One Nevada widow, Mary Mathews, labored until one o'clock every morning to support herself and her small child during the 1870s, running a school, sewing, and taking in laundry. Eventually, she bought a boarding house, where she washed clothes for twenty-six boarders. Many African American married women earned money taking in laundry, which offered considerably more independence than domestic service in white people's houses. These workers sometimes fought to maintain their autonomy, which was especially precious to people who had memories of slavery.

Religion and Community   Of the many institutions that supported community life in working people's neighborhoods, churches were the most important. Most Americans before the Civil War had been Protestants, but many new immigrants were Catholic and Jewish. Still, in 1890, Protestant denominations claimed more than six of every ten church members. All across the country, rural Protestant churches continued to flourish; countless small, often poor, churches sustained and were sustained by the vast majority of the nation's farmers, black and white.

Churches figured centrally in rural African American culture. In Edgefield County, South Carolina, an area that was renowned for lynchings, black tenant farmers and sharecroppers joined some forty small churches established by Alexander Bettis, a leader who urged African Americans to organize their own institutions. The churches engendered Masonic lodges, benevolent societies, burial organizations, and schools, as well as fairs and other social gatherings. This cultural foundation sustained black Americans in "Bloody Edgefield." Many white southerners viewed the networks of black churches and organizations as a threat. "The meanest negroes in the country are those who are members of the churches," declared a writer in the *North Georgia Citizen* in 1879, "and, as a general thing, the more devout and officious they are, the more closely they need watching."

Churches also created community in mining camps and cattle towns. Kansans exaggerated when they proclaimed in the 1870s that there was "no Sunday west of Junction City and no God west of Salina." Protestants sent missionaries west to preach against Mormons, Catholics, and moral decay. Western towns built schools first, but these often served as places of worship on Sunday, uniting different Protestant sects. Josiah Strong, a well-known reformer who began as a young minister in Wyoming, observed that western church meetings brought strangers together as Christians. His church spawned a library, a park, and voluntary organizations that battled liquor and prostitution.

In eastern cities, middle- and upper-class Protestants had moved to the suburbs and abandoned many downtown churches in neighborhoods that were now filled with immigrants. As a result, white Protestant churches lost touch with urban working people and became more oriented toward the well-to-do. Wealthy congregations produced nationally renowned ministers, such as Brooklyn's Henry Ward Beecher, one of the best-known and most influential of these "princes of the pulpit." Beecher's wit and eloquence made him a popular speaker, despite much publicity about his alleged extramarital affairs. Although he had supported the antislavery movement, he viewed the rich with sympathy and the poor with hostility. "No man in this land suffers from poverty unless it be more than his fault—unless it be his sin," Beecher proclaimed.

Nevertheless, a focus on "sin" could lead to broader concerns. Many women started out in church-based antidrink organizations such as the Woman's Christian Temperance Union (WCTU) and then began to take a broader view of the need for social reform. And the Young Men's Christian Association (YMCA) and the Salvation Army did try to bring Protestantism to urban working people. The Salvation Army, an evangelical organization run along military lines, held meetings in the worst slums, even in saloons, and offered "degenerate souls" food, shelter, and low-wage work. The YMCA established gymnasiums, lecture halls, and reading rooms in cities to provide a "wholesome" atmosphere where men could exercise and socialize without the drinking and gambling that prevailed at pool halls, bowling alleys, and saloons. Bible study classes were central to the program. But the predominantly Catholic urban working class did not always warmly receive

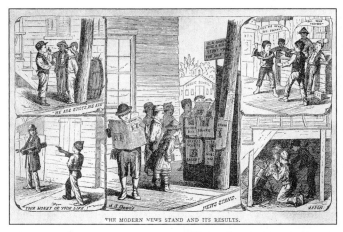

THE MODERN NEWS STAND AND ITS RESULTS.

The Modern News Stand and Its Results

The frontispiece of *Traps for the Young*, an influential 1883 tract by Anthony Comstock, illustrates the threat purportedly posed by "debased" commercial magazines. "They open the way for grossest evils," Comstock wrote. "Foul thoughts are the precursors of foul actions." [A. B. Davis], Anthony Comstock, *Traps for the Young* (1883) — American Social History Project.

missionary work of the Protestant YMCA and Salvation Army.

The YMCA had close ties to the social purity movement, which rejected overt sexual expression and practice. In 1873, Anthony Comstock, a dry goods salesman, YMCA member, and founder of the New York Society for the Suppression of Vice, won passage of an antiobscenity statute (the so-called Comstock Act), which forbade the mailing of obscene, lewd, lascivious, and indecent writing or advertisements as well as contraceptive devices. As an unpaid postal inspector, Comstock personally supervised forty-seven arrests and the destruction of more than twenty-nine thousand photos, leaflets, songs, and contraceptives in 1875 alone. The literature targeted by the law included material on women's reproductive health and descriptions of methods of contraception. Comstock's crusade criminalized social and sexual behavior that deviated from an idealized norm of sobriety, heterosexual monogamy, and piety.

The predominantly urban and working-class Catholic Church took much less interest in the social purity movement than did its Protestant counterparts. It had expanded with the influx of poor Irish and German immigrants in the decades before the Civil War and continued to gain strength as Italians and Poles entered the country after 1880. Parochial schools provided Catholics with educational opportunities that extended through college, and large city parishes offered programs to meet their spiritual, recreational, and charitable needs. The church's hierarchy remained extremely conservative on social issues, as was illustrated by the policy of excommunicating members who were active in socialist organizations. But at the local parish level, priests defended the aspirations of their working-class parishioners.

The Saloon and Its Enemies The saloon was another central institution of working-class culture; one writer called it "the one democratic club in American life." Drinking on the job, prevalent early in the nineteenth century, had generally disappeared by the 1870s. With a shorter workday — usually ten hours for skilled workers — men drank during leisure hours, in popular taverns that were usually located across the street from a factory or down the road from a mine. "Watch the 'dinner pail' brigade," a Worcester, Massachusetts, observer noted in 1891, "and see how many men and boys drop into the saloons along the north end of Main Street" (Map 2.2).

MAP 2.2   A City of Saloons: Boston Bars in 1884

The saloon was ubiquitous in the late-nineteenth-century city. In the area around Boston's Albany and Old Colony railroad terminals, travelers could find 175 different saloons — 80 of them within just 650 feet of the stations. "Every traveler," complained a temperance advocate, "passes through a gauntlet of rum."

Saloons filled tangible needs. Saloon owners cashed workers' checks and lent them money. The beer they served was considered full of nutrients and healthier than the water in working-class neighborhoods, which was drawn from wells and pumps near overused outhouses. Many workingmen ate their meals at saloons. "It is cheaper to live at the barroom than at the poor beaneries," an unemployed Boston man reported in 1889. A visitor to a

Morning Customers

A Chicago saloon, around 1890. Chicago Historical Society.

THE BAR OF DESTRUCTION.

Father, Come Home!

Temperance tracts emphasized the destructive effects of liquor consumption on familial relationships, framing messages in sentimental accounts of little children appealing to drunken parents to forsake the saloon and come home. This Thomas Nast cartoon, *The Bar of Destruction,* repeated motifs that dated back to Timothy Shay Arthur's antebellum bestseller, *Ten Nights in a Bar-room. Harper's Weekly*, March 21, 1874 — American Social History Project.

New Orleans saloon described "a large table . . . [with] trays of cut bread, bowls of butter, salads, and sauces" and "another table . . . [with] a large tureen of soup, a platter of roast beef, a large dish of rice or baked beans."

At the saloon, workingmen could experience mutuality and collectivity, symbolized by "treating" — buying rounds of drinks. They could read newspapers, pick up job leads, enjoy good fellowship, and escape from overcrowded houses and tenements. Popular entertainments — illegal boxing matches, cockfights, and gambling — enlivened the atmosphere. Trade unions and ethnic organizations that lacked their own facilities met in saloons, and local politicians set up unofficial headquarters at the bar, dispensing favors and buying drinks for "the boys." Many saloonkeepers entered local politics; eleven of twenty-four New York City Aldermen ran saloons in 1890.

Except for German family establishments that served beer, most saloons catered only to men. Women who drank generally did so at home. In some places, police regulations aimed at curbing prostitution forbade women from entering barrooms. Even when not legally excluded, women who considered themselves respectable did not go to saloons, so they were effectively prohibited from joining organizations that met there.

Many wealthy people — who did their own drinking at private clubs, at expensive hotels, and at home — crusaded to close saloons. Some of the hardest-fought political battles of the nineteenth century involved efforts to limit drinking. Factory owners led campaigns against licensing individual establishments in an effort to keep their workers sober. They contended that temperance increased efficiency: "the men earn better wages, lose less time, do better work . . . while the relations between employers and workmen are most harmonious." Other temperance crusaders were motivated by religious convictions, a concern about the political threat posed by the independent saloon culture, a distaste for or fear of the (often Catholic) immigrants who gathered at saloons, or a sincere conviction that drinking was the source of working-class poverty.

Indeed, alcohol and alcoholism could create real problems in working-class families. Therefore, labor reformers, too, decried the debilitating

"I Had No Idea of the Inward Appearance of a Saloon . . . ": Frances Willard on Temperance Tactics

Frances Willard was an important leader of the Woman's Christian Temperance Union (WCTU) and its campaign against saloons. She was head of the union's Chicago chapter and became prominent later in the woman suffrage movement. Willard linked her fight against liquor with her desire to protect the home and family against the ravages of the new industrial order. In this selection from her autobiography, Willard describes the WCTU's most widely known tactic: the praying-in-saloons crusade, in this instance in Pittsburgh in 1873.

We paused in front of the saloon that I have mentioned. The ladies ranged themselves along the curbstone, for they had been forbidden in anywise to incommode the passers-by, being dealt with much more strictly than a drunken man or a heap of dry-goods boxes would be.

. . . The leader had already asked the saloon-keeper if we might enter, and he had declined, else the prayer-meeting would have occurred inside his door. A sorrowful old lady whose only son had gone to ruin through that very death-trap, knelt on the cold, moist pavement and offered a broken-hearted prayer, while all our heads were bowed. At a signal we moved on and the next saloon-keeper permitted us to enter. I had no more idea of the inward appearance of a saloon than if there had been no such place on earth. I knew nothing of its high, heavily corniced bar, its barrels with the ends all pointed towards the looker-on, each barrel being furnished with a faucet; its shelves glittering with decanters and cut glass, its floors thickly strewn with saw-dust, and here and there a round table with chairs — nor of its abundant fumes, sickening to healthful nostrils.

The tall, stately lady who led us, placed her Bible on the bar and read a psalm. . . . Then we sang "Rock of Ages" as I thought I had never heard it sung before, with a tender confidence to the height of which one does not rise in the easy-going, regulation prayer-meeting, and then one of the older women whispered to me softly that the leader wished to know if I would pray. It was strange, perhaps, but I felt not the least reluctance, and kneeling on that saw-dust floor, with a group of earnest hearts around me, and behind them, filling every corner and extending out into the street, a crowd of unwashed, unkempt, hard-looking drinking men, I was conscious that perhaps never in my life, save beside my sister Mary's dying bed had I prayed as truly as I did then. This was my Crusade baptism. The next day I went on to the West and within a week had been made president of the Chicago W. C. T. U.

Frances E. Willard, *Glimpses of Fifty Years: The Autobiography of an American Woman* (Chicago: H. J. Smith & Co., 1889), 339–341.

consequences of drink and argued that workers who criticized wage dependency should also shun alcohol dependency. Some unions actively promoted temperance, although it often seemed a losing cause. One prominent labor leader implored workers to "throw strong drink aside as you would an ounce of liquid hell."

Women temperance leaders organized marches on saloons to pray, sing hymns, implore drinkers to pledge abstinence, and shame proprietors. One such group of women, successful in ending the local liquor trade in an Ohio county, formed the Woman's Christian Temperance Union (WCTU) in 1874. Politicizing farm women and women from "respectable" Protestant working-class families, the WCTU recognized the connection between alcoholism and social issues. In the 1890s, it argued that poverty created drinking problems, reversing an earlier stand that excessive drinking caused poverty. The WCTU worked to improve the conditions of the working class, sought power for women inside the home, and endorsed woman suffrage in 1882, decades before any other national group. Its motto, "Do Everything," encouraged women activists to embrace a wide range of social legislation. The WCTU eventually became the largest American women's organization ever.

The Workingman's Hour

As the social and economic gulf separating wage earners and their employers widened, a labor movement of astonishing breadth emerged in the 1880s. Recognizing common interests, workers began to unionize to contest poor working conditions and assert their rights. Labor organization was rooted in the local neighborhoods, institutions, churches, and ethnic societies that structured everyday life for working people.

Despite this pervasive localism, one national labor organization—the Knights of Labor—arose in the 1880s to powerfully challenge the national corporations that increasingly held sway in late-nineteenth-century America. The Knights mobilized unprecedented numbers and won some stunning victories. They fed into a more general "great uprising of labor," which led into nationwide strikes—many of them successful—for shorter workdays. Ultimately, however, an employer counteroffensive that began in the aftermath of the Haymarket bombing of 1886 and had the support of the coercive power of the state halted this onward march of labor by the end of the 1880s.

The Labor Community   With the exception of the Knights of Labor, most unions were local and confined to an individual trade. Cincinnati, an important manufacturing center, boasted thirty-five separate unions in the early 1880s. Here, as elsewhere, most union members were skilled craftsmen in the building trades, foundries, and small consumer-goods industries.

Craft unionists created strong central labor bodies in cities all across the country, from Boston to Chicago, Denver, New Orleans, and San Francisco. In 1882, New York City's Central Labor Union (CLU) brought together a dozen small unions. Within a few years, it functioned as an effective "parliament of labor" for more than two hundred labor organizations. As one printer put it, the CLU constituted an effort to replace the "little-minded, narrow-minded view of the interests of a single occupation" with that of "the general interests of all bodies of wage workers."

Traditional ideas about gender roles and masculinity infused craft unionism. "The craftsmen's ethical code," notes one labor historian, "demanded a 'manly' bearing toward the boss," and "few words enjoyed more popularity in the nineteenth century than this honorific, with all its connotations of dignity, respectability, defiant egalitarianism, and patriarchal male supremacy." Women were barred from most skilled occupations, but unions were hostile even to the women who customarily worked alongside men, as in the cigar industry. Focusing narrowly on "bread and butter" wage goals, craft unions fought for the "family wage" to enable men to support their families "in a manner consistent with their responsibilities as husbands, fathers, men, and citizens." Though the demand for a family wage dignified male workers' struggles at the expense of women's, the two were not entirely separable; higher wages paid to fathers and husbands would benefit most working women.

Although craft unions evinced little interest in women workers, some women organized on their own. During the summer of 1881, African American washerwomen in Atlanta organized a two-week strike, demanding higher fees and recruiting 3,000 supporters by door-to-door canvassing and nightly neighborhood meetings throughout the city. This protest was unusual but not unique. Following the 1877 railroad strike, household workers in Galveston, Texas, had walked off their jobs, and other southern domestics struck from time to time, often led by outspoken washerwomen. More often, however, household workers and independent washerwomen used covert tactics — such as quitting without notice — to resist racism and oppression.

HOME OF THE SCAB WORKMAN

THE HOME OF THE UNION WORKMAN.

Two Homes

These illustrations in the *Boston Labor Leader* compared the homes of a union workman and a scab workman. In this view, strikebreaking was a logical outgrowth of the general moral and physical degradation of the one-room scab household. The "superiority" of the trade unionist was portrayed in the modest but solidly domestic atmosphere of the family's parlor. *Boston Labor Leader*, October 6, 1894 — State Historical Society of Wisconsin.

Boycott Fever

A cartoon in the weekly *Life* satirized the growth of boycotts. "Whereas," reads one boy, representing a committee of disgruntled candy-cart customers, "we find we don't git red color enough in our strawberry cream, nor enough yaller in our wanilla, . . . to say nothin' o' the small measure of peanuts we gits for a cent; therefore, be it resolved . . . that all the stands in the city is boycotted until these things is righted." *Life*, May 27, 1887 — Scott Molloy Labor Archives.

The labor movement offered workers good fellowship and activities that reinforced a working-class consciousness. Unions and their citywide central organizations sponsored social activities: parades, balls, and picnics. More broadly, labor organizations were part of an alternative culture that belonged unmistakably to the producing classes. Many cities had labor reading rooms; Atlanta's Union Hall and Library Association drew 800 people a week during the mid-1880s to read its collection of over 350 newspapers. In Detroit, the labor movement supported a range of daily activities. Workers gathered to read prolabor newspapers in English and German; to argue politics; and to participate in theater groups, singing societies, dances, and educational events. Some joined the Detroit Rifles, a militia that drilled and practiced target shooting on the outskirts of town under cover of darkness. "Every union ought to have its company of sharpshooters," a Detroit worker wrote in the *Labor Leaf*. He urged his compatriots to pick up the gun and "learn to preserve your rights in the same way your forefathers did."

Besides daily fellowship, the labor community offered a spiritual experience of solidarity, a new form of evangelism based on old ideals: the brotherhood of man, divine retribution against injustice, and indignation at human suffering. The labor movement adapted these religious ideals and used spiritual language to reflect and interpret the growing class division. Labor songs drew on hymns, changing the words but not their zealous spirit. Unions, the *United Mine Workers' Journal* suggested, had stepped into the space left when the conservative churches abdicated their true mission. "Jesus Christ is with us outside the church," one worker explained, "and we shall prevail with God."

Righteous belief and a context of community provided the foundation for a wave of boycotts in the mid-1880s. Boycotts, an effort to win concessions from an employer by persuading other workers to stop patronizing the employer's business, proved especially effective in trades serving urban working-class consumers. One business journal reported more than two hundred boycotts in 1884 and 1885 — against newspapers, street railways, and manufacturers of cigars, hats, carpets, clothing, shoes, and brooms. The movement hit its peak in 1886, when countless campaigns touched the South, Far West, Midwest, and eastern seaboard. Denouncing boycotts as "un-American and anti-American," employers turned to the courts. In the spring of 1886, New York courts prohibited boycotts as a form of criminal conspiracy, handing down indictments against more than 100 tailors, bakers, musicians, and waiters. In the most widely publicized of the subsequent trials, five workers who had organized a boycott against Theiss' Music Hall received long prison terms.

"Union for All": The Knights of Labor The Noble and Holy Order of the Knights of Labor, a group founded by nine Philadelphia tailors in 1869, stood at the center of labor activity in the 1880s. In response to employers' use of firings and blacklists to suppress unions, the Knights adopted rigid secrecy for members. Its first leader, Uriah Stephens, had studied for the ministry before apprenticing as a tailor. A man of broad moral vision, he called for an organization that would unite all workers, regardless of race, nationality, occupation, or skill level.

In 1879, the Knights of Labor chose Terence V. Powderly as their "Grand Master Workman." An Irish Catholic machinist and mayor of Scranton, Pennsylvania, Powderly led the Knights for fifteen years. The Order's programs reflected not only Powderly's beliefs in temperance, education, and land reform, but also his conviction that the wage system should be abolished. Under his leadership, the Knights gradually put aside their secrecy, which had hampered their ability to grow, and membership soared.

Under Powderly, the Knights became a stunningly influential national movement composed of hundreds of different local assemblies. Its diversity makes it difficult to generalize about its approaches and policies.

The Great Labor Parade of September 1st

A placard in an 1884 Labor Day march presented the struggle over inequality in the nineteenth century. "Wage-slavery" emerged as an oppressive institution to take the place of racial slavery, defeated in the Civil War. *Frank Leslie's Illustrated Newspaper*, September 13, 1884 — American Social History Project.

"Labor's Catechism": The Knights of Labor's Moral Code

Designed to instruct new recruits on the political and moral principles that guided the Knights of Labor, this manual illustrates the ways in which the Gilded Age labor movement constructed an ideology that was in opposition to the values of acquisitive individualism. The power loom weavers of Rhode Island were the intended audience of this catechism written by labor activists "Bobba Chuttle" and "Betty Reedhook" (pseudonyms evocative of the tools of the textile worker's trade) in 1887. Drawing on church traditions, the pair patterned their educational effort along the lines of a religious catechism's call-and-response format.

Q. What did thy masters promise for thee?

A. They did promise and vow many things in my name: First:— That I should renounce the comforts of life through working for less wages than the weavers in other towns, and starve my wife and hunger my children for the same cause. Second:—That I must not in any way try to better my condition, but be content to work at any price which they think proper to give; neither must I join the Knights of Labor as that is contrary to their by-laws. Third:—That I must bear patiently the insults of all that are put in authority over me, and a host of other things too numerous to mention.

Q. Dost thou not believe that thou art bound to do as they have promised for thee?

A. No, verily; for I have come to the determination to free myself, and to strive to get as much for my work as the weavers in other places for the same kind and quality, and that is the Knights of Labor's duty.

Q. Rehearse the articles of thy belief.

A. I believe in the Golden Rule—do unto others as you would have them do unto you—and in Honesty, his only son, who was conceived by our Common Right, born of the Virgin Truth, suffered under Cotton Treason, was crucified, dead, and buried in Rhode Island, for many years, but is now risen again, and sitteth on the right hand of Justice and Liberty.

Q. What dost thou chiefly learn from these articles of thy belief?

A. I learn to believe that the time has now arrived when I must make a firm stand for a fair share of the profits of my industry, which is nothing less than the Union List, have nine hours' work, seven hours' play, eight hours' sleep, and fair wages every day.

"Labor's Catechism," *The People* (Providence, R.I.), 17 December 1887. Reprinted in Paul Buhle, "The Knights of Labor in Rhode Island," *Radical History Review* (Spring 1978): 39.

For example, although leaders such as Powderly officially opposed strikes and favored good relations with "fair" employers, its members joined and led dozens of work stoppages. And while it preferred "industrial" forms of unionism—that is, organizing all workers regardless of skill—it had locals that were essentially craft-based unions.

In general terms, however, the Knights stood for the twin concepts of "republicanism" and "producerism" that linked the belief in government determined by the people with production determined by the workers. "We declare an inevitable and irresistible conflict between the wage system of labor and republican system of government," they proclaimed. They sought to eliminate both political corruption and the wage system and, thereby, restore independence to American citizens.

With this commitment to republicanism went a deep faith in the "producing classes." If properly mobilized, the Knights believed, this broad social group producing society's wealth—the workers, the farmers, even the honest manufacturers—could rescue America from the hands of monopolists and other social parasites. The Knights excluded "non-producers," such as bankers, speculators, lawyers, and liquor dealers, from their ranks. But they admitted "fair" employers, who respected the "dignity of labor" by employing union workers and selling union-made goods.

Drastic wage cuts accompanying the economic downturn of the early 1880s gave the organization its greatest impetus for growth. Victories against two of the country's most powerful railroads—the giant Union Pacific and financier Jay Gould's Southwestern—brought workers across the nation into the Knights. In the first walkout, they won the restoration of the wage cuts, and in the second, they won an agreement not to discriminate against union members in employment. The victory over Gould, one of the most hated men in America, astonished the nation and brought tens of thousands of new members into the Knights. In Milwaukee, where German American craftsmen had dominated the Order in the early 1880s, less-skilled Polish immigrants streamed into the organization in 1886; nearly a thousand joined on a single day. By 1886, the Order boasted fifteen thousand local assemblies, representing between 700,000 and one million members—nearly 10 percent of the country's nonagricultural workforce. Never had such a great proportion enrolled in unions, although, of course, most workers remained outside the union movement even during this great uprising of labor (Table 2.1).

The Knights' commitment to equality extended beyond healing the split between skilled and unskilled workers and included women, immigrants, Mexican Americans, and African Americans, all previously shut out of the labor movement. The Knights welcomed African Americans from the beginning. Most joined all-black assemblies, but some locals had mixed

TABLE 2.1   One of the Crowd: The Rise and Fall of Union Membership, 1870–1900

In a single remarkable year — July 1885 to July 1886 — membership in the Knights of Labor multiplied at least seven times, probably the most rapid upsurge in union membership in U.S. history. By mid-1886, American trade unions had a combined membership of a million or more people. But the upsurge did not last; by 1890, union membership had dropped by two-thirds.

Union Membership as Percent of Nonagricultural Workforce, 1870–1900

	1870	1880	1886	1890	1900
Union Members (thousands)	300	50	1,010	325	791
Nonagricultural Workforce (thousands)	6,140	8,470	11,404	13,360	17,390
Percent Organized	4.89%	0.59%	8.86%	2.43%	4.55%

Note: All 1886 figures are estimates.

membership, even in the South. Black dockworkers in New Orleans, turpentine workers in Mississippi, tobacco factory workers in Virginia, and coal miners in Alabama, West Virginia, and Tennessee all joined the Knights in the first half of the 1880s. African American workers became the mainstays of many fledgling local assemblies. "The colored people of the South are flocking to us," trumpeted one Knights organizer.

In Fort Worth, Texas, the Knights united European American, African American, and Mexican American workers in the first coalition of its kind in state history. The Central Trades and Labor Assembly in New Orleans represented some 10,000 black and white workers who regularly joined forces in demonstrations and parades. "In view of the prejudice that existed a few years ago against the negro race," a Brooklyn Knight wrote, "who would have thought that negroes could ever be admitted into a labor organization on an equal footing with white men?" (Map 2.3).

The Order's practice of organizing separate black assemblies provoked controversy among African Americans. Some criticized the labor movement's continuing racism, particularly its exclusion of African Americans from skilled trades. A North Carolina mason complained, "The white Knights of Labor prevent me from getting employment because I am a colored man, although I belong to the same organization." But other black

MAP 2.3 Where the Knights Roamed: Knights of Labor Membership by County, 1883

The Noble and Holy Order of the Knights of Labor was the nation's largest labor organization in the 1880s. As this map shows, their influence was spread widely across the Northeast and Midwest.

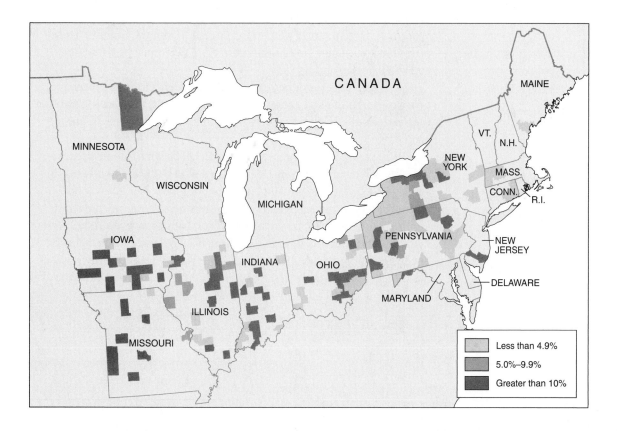

"... Women Should Do Anything They Liked That Was Good": Women in the Knights of Labor

The commitment of the Knights of Labor to equality for women was more than rhetorical, as evidenced by the career of Elizabeth Rodgers, the organization's Master Workman, or head, of the giant Chicago District No. 24. This 1889 portrait of Rodgers, offered by leading national antiliquor activist Frances Willard, underscores the desire on the part of many Knights, both men and women, to connect the struggle for labor reform with a broader vision that included vehement opposition to liquor.

So I went; in an unfamiliar, but reputable, part of the city where the streetcar patrons are evidently wage-workers. I was welcomed to a small, but comfortable, modern house by a woman who came to the door with sleeves rolled up and babe in arms. She was the presiding officer over all the Knights of Labor in Chicago and the suburbs, except the Stock Yards division . . . including fifty thousand or more working men and women. . . . Probably no parallel instance of leadership in a woman's hands, conferred by such peers, can be cited in this country, if indeed in any other.

Mrs. Rodgers is about forty years of age. . . . She has been the mother of twelve children, ten of whom are still living. The youngest was but twelve days old when her mother started for the [1886] Richmond Convention, where the baby was made "Delegate No. 800," and presented by the Knights with a silver cup and spoon, and the mother with a handsome Knights of Labor gold watch.

"My husband always believed that women should do anything they liked that was good and which they could do well," said Mrs. Rodgers, proudly; "but for him, I never could have got on so well as a Master Workman. I was the first woman in Chicago to join the Knights. They offered us the chance, and I said to myself, 'There must be a first one, and so I'll go forward.'"

. . . Mrs. Rodgers got her training as the chief officer of a local board of the Knights of Labor, which office she held four years, and by the death of the District Master Workman became the chief for our great city.

"We take no saloon-keepers," she said, "not even a saloon-keeper's wife. We will have nothing to do with men who have capital invested in a business which is the greatest curse the poor have ever known; but wage-workers connected with the liquor business are not forbidden to join us." I told her I hoped the pledge of total abstinence might be made a test of membership, and she heartily acquiesced in the plan. . . . She seemed to me a sincere Christian, and warmly seconded my statement that "Mr. Powderly [the Knights' national leader] must have the help of God, or he could not speak and act so wisely."

Frances E. Willard, *Glimpses of Fifty Years: The Autobiography of an American Woman* (1889).

leaders believed that the Order's local and national assemblies represented a significant advance, providing a context in which black and white workers could begin to make common cause.

The emergence of the Knights of Labor also moved Irish immigrants to the center of the American labor movement. Irish activism had begun with support for the Land League, an organization of tenant farmers in Ireland that built an enormous following in the late 1870s. In the early years, Powderly claimed, the American labor movement and the Irish land movement were "almost identical," and secret gatherings of the Knights frequently followed public meetings of the Land League. As Patrick Ford, a New York editor, explained, "The cause of the poor in Donegal [Ireland] is the cause of the factory slave in Fall River [Massachusetts]."

Unlike African Americans and Irish immigrants, women had to fight their way into the Knights of Labor. Leaders of the Order spoke vaguely about "equal rights" and embraced the idea of equal pay for women, but equal pay meant little in a gender-segregated workforce. The Knights stopped short of granting membership to women, and Powderly refused to implement a resolution calling for women to be admitted until rules "for the governing of assemblies of women" were prepared. Then Mary Stirling, who had led a successful strike of "lady shoemakers" in Philadelphia, presented herself as a delegate at the Knights' convention in 1881. Forced to take a stand, Powderly finally declared that "women should be admitted on equality with men." Within a few years, one in ten Knights was a woman.

The Knights of Labor provided an unprecedented opportunity for working-class women to join men in the struggle for better lives. The Knights mobilized support for equal pay for women, equal rights for women within all organizations, and respect for women's work, whether unpaid in the home or for wages in the factory or mill. The Order's eclectic reform vision linked women's industrial and domestic concerns to broad social and political issues, giving rise to a kind of "labor feminism" in the 1880s.

The Knights of Labor, did, however, blatantly discriminate against one group: the Chinese. In the early 1880s, the major focus of the Order's political activity was promoting the Chinese Exclusion Act, which closed the nation's gates to Chinese immigrants. The Knights hailed the law as a step forward for "American" workers. Especially on the West Coast, Chinese workers served as convenient scapegoats during hard times.

This persistent racism undercut the Knights' proclaimed commitment to ideals of mutuality and solidarity. Although unwilling to embrace solidarity with Chinese immigrants, the Knights did develop a variety of local institutions that fostered cooperation and mutuality among its members. Many locals maintained cooperative stores on the ground floors of their halls and assembly rooms above, where members could hear labor sermons, read reform papers, or debate politics and economics. Knights also found group expression in balls, picnics, and parades.

MARYLAND.—THE LABOR STRIKE IN THE CUMBERLAND REGION—MERCHANTS IN THE MINING TOWN OF FROSTBURG
CLOSING THEIR STORES BY ORDER OF THE KNIGHTS OF LABOR.—(SEE PAGE 267.)

Closing Stores and Solidarity
A June 1882 cover of *Frank Leslie's Illustrated Newspaper* depicts a scene in the Cumberland region of Maryland during a miners' strike. The boy who is shown ringing a bell in the town of Frostburg was described as an "emissary" conveying a Knights of Labor edict forcing local merchants to close their stores by 7:30 each evening. *Leslie's* professed bewilderment at local businessmen's acceptance of the strikers' "decree." But acquiescence to the new policy was not due to coercion; in the spirit of community cooperation espoused by the Knights, shopkeepers and clerks agreed to experiment with early closing. John N. Hyde, *Frank Leslie's Illustrated Newspaper*, June 17, 1882 — American Social History Project.

The groups that made up the Knights of Labor never achieved total harmony, but for a time, the alliance had enough power and stability to spark widespread fear among industrialists and their friends. During a Cleveland steel strike, employers called on police to intervene. After violent confrontations at the mill gates, the city's daily newspapers launched a torrent of invective against the "un-American" Polish workers, labeling them "foreign devils," "ignorant and degraded whelps," and "Communistic scoundrels." But many members of the Knights reveled in the solidarity. "All I knew then of the principles of the Knights of Labor," the Jewish immigrant Abraham Bisno later remembered, "was that the motto . . . was One for All, and All for One."

1886: The Eight-Hour Movement and Haymarket Square "The year 1886 will be known as the year of the great uprising of labor," proclaimed

George McNeill, a Massachusetts member of the Knights of Labor. "The skilled and the unskilled, the high-paid and the low-paid all joined hands." The Knights' membership drive and the boycott movement peaked that year. Even more important, hundreds of thousands of workers struck, demonstrated, and fought for an eight-hour day.

American workers had been agitating for shorter workdays for decades. In 1884, the demand resurfaced when the Federation of Organized Trades and Labor Unions began a two-year campaign, resolving that "eight hours shall constitute a legal day's work from and after May 1, 1886" and calling for a nationwide strike to begin that day. Local unionists who called for national organizing to deal with employers operating in national markets formed the federation, an alliance of eighteen national unions, in 1881. At its peak in 1886, federation membership totaled as much as 350,000, or 3 percent of the nation's nonagricultural workforce.

From Milwaukee, Chicago, and New York, the eight-hour movement spread to towns and cities throughout the country. "This is the working-man's hour," proclaimed the workers at Boston's Faneuil Hall on the eve of May 1, 1886. Across the nation, about one-third of a million workers demonstrated for the eight-hour day, and 200,000 actually went out on strike. By the end of the year, 400,000 workers had participated in 1,500 strikes, more than in any previous year of American history. Most of the strikers won shorter workdays, and 42,000 won an eight-hour day. These strikes marked an important new phase in the mobilization of unskilled workers, brought many workers into the ranks of the labor movement, and turned thousands of union members into activists.

The national leadership of the Knights of Labor discouraged the demonstrations and strikes for the eight-hour day, but many Knights led local campaigns, working with the unions and with the socialists and anarchists who played a prominent role in the agitation. Although united in their challenge to the concept of private property, socialists and anarchists differed in their views of the role of government. Socialists advocated government ownership of factories and mines, whereas anarchists argued that organized government was by its very nature oppressive.

In Chicago, radicals, most notably Albert Parsons, led the eight-hour movement. The son of a prominent white New England family, Parsons arrived in Chicago after apprenticing as a printer in Waco, Texas, where he had moved before the Civil War. Although he had served in the Confederate Army, Parsons became a Radical Republican during Reconstruction, championing African American rights, addressing meetings, and mobilizing black voters. He met his wife Lucy when she was sixteen and already a passionate labor and antiracist activist. Lucy had probably been born a slave in Texas, but she claimed to be the orphaned child of Mexican and Indian parents. Because Texas laws banned interracial marriage, they moved

"Eight Hours for What We Will!": Rallying Cry for the Eight-Hour Work Day

This poem, titled "Eight Hours," was written by I. G. Blanchard in 1866. Six years later, Blanchard's poem was set to music by the Reverend Jesse H. Jones, who was closely associated with Boston's Eight-Hour League. The song became a rallying cry during the 1886 strike wave that demanded an eight-hour workday.

We mean to make things over,
We're tired of toil for naught,
With bare enough to live upon,
And never an hour for thought;
We want to feel the sunshine,
And we want to smell the flowers,
We're sure that God has willed it,
And we mean to have Eight Hours.
We're summoning our forces
From shipyard, shop and mill;
Eight hours for work, eight hours for rest,
Eight hours for what we will!
From the factories and workshops,
In long and weary lines,
From all the sweltering forges,
From all the sunless mines;
Wherever Toil is wasting
The force of life to live;
Its bent and battered armies
Come to claim what God doth give.
And the blazon on its banner
Doth with hope the nations fill.
Eight hours for work, eight hours for rest,
Eight hours for what we will!
The voice of God within us
Is calling us to stand
Erect, as is becoming
To the work of His right hand.
Should he, to whom the Maker
His glorious image gave,
The meanest of His creatures crouch,
A bread-and-butter slave?
Let the shout ring down the valleys
And echo from ev'ry hill,
Eight hours for work, eight hours for rest,
Eight hours for what we will!

I. G. Blanchard, *Boston Daily Voice*, August 7, 1886.

north in 1873, settling in Chicago, where Albert found employment as a typesetter.

Making contacts among Chicago radicals and hosting socialist study groups in their home, Lucy and Albert Parsons were soon at the center of socialist and anarchist agitation. When Albert lost his job because of speeches he gave during the 1877 railroad strike, Lucy set up a dressmaking shop to support them both. By 1885, as the most famous radical couple in Chicago, they faced regular and vicious attacks in the mainstream press.

On May 1, 1886, Parsons led the 80,000 Chicago marchers in a parade for the eight-hour day. The day passed without incident, but two days later, a clash at the McCormick Reaper Works ended in police beatings and the fatal shooting of two unarmed workers. August Spies, the editor of a prolabor German newspaper witnessed the bloodshed and issued a fiery leaflet, calling Chicago's workers to a protest at Haymarket Square the following evening. Attendance was sparse at the hastily called rally. As the small crowd began to drift away, a bomb exploded, killing a policeman. The police opened fire immediately, killing at least one more person and wounding many more.

The city's antiradical, anti-immigrant civic leaders quickly sought revenge for the policeman's death. Parsons, Spies, and six other anarchist leaders were arrested, charged with conspiracy to commit murder, tried, convicted, and sentenced to death. No evidence ever connected any of the accused with the bomb. Even so, Powderly refused to support Parsons, a member of the Knights, or to criticize the courts. Despite worldwide protest, Spies, Parsons, and two of their comrades went to the gallows in November 1887. One of the remaining anarchists committed suicide. John Peter Altgeld, a German immigrant who had by then become the prolabor governor of Illinois, pardoned the three others in 1893.

The Decline of the Knights Haymarket raised fears among the middle and upper classes—anxiety about aliens, radicals, mobs, and labor organizations and, more broadly, about the prospects for anarchism and revolution. Government responded to these fears by strengthening the police, militia, and the U.S. Army, and vigilante groups proliferated. Capitalists mounted a sustained counteroffensive to destroy the insurgency of the eight-hour movement and other organized labor efforts. Some employers attempted to undercut unionization by hiring workers from different ethnic groups who would have difficulty communicating with one another. Trade association members discharged strikers, locked out workers who joined unions, and circulated blacklists of labor activists. Industrial spies, many of them employees of the rapidly growing Pinkerton Detective Agency, infiltrated labor organizations.

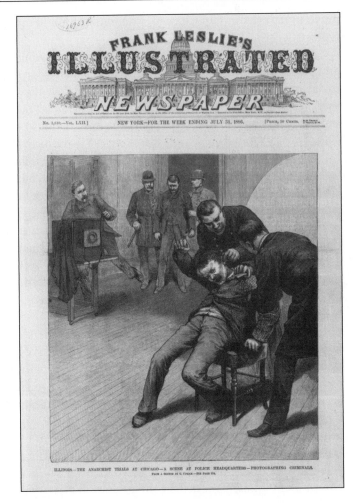

ILLINOIS—THE ANARCHIST TRIALS AT CHICAGO—A SCENE AT POLICE HEADQUARTERS—PHOTOGRAPHING CRIMINALS.

Photographing Criminals
As part of its coverage of the Haymarket incident, one newspaper displayed this scene in Chicago's police headquarters, showing the construction of a criminal identification system based on photographs. The "Rogues' Gallery" would serve as an archive to identify individual criminals (including political dissenters and labor activists) and to discern, according to contemporary scientific beliefs, what "physiognomic" traits (such as skull shape and facial characteristics) indicated innate criminal tendencies. Charles Upham, *Frank Leslie's Illustrated Newspaper*, July 31, 1886 — American Social History Project.

Employers also relied increasingly on the coercive power of the government. During the 1880s, legal charges such as "inciting to riot," "obstructing the streets," "intimidation," and "trespass" were first used extensively against strikers, and court injunctions restricting workers' right to picket became commonplace. One judge, handing down an injunction in a labor dispute, proudly called it a "Gatling [machine] gun on paper."

Weakened by internal disputes, faulty decisions, and disunity of purpose, the Knights of Labor proved especially vulnerable. The most dramatic setback occurred on the same rail lines where the Knights had first become prominent. After a successful strike in 1885, Southwestern Railroad workers struck again in March 1886, demanding wage increases and the reinstatement of a discharged comrade. But railroad executives, realizing that placating workers' organizations fostered militancy and unionization, took a hard

The "Typical" Anarchist
Hairy, disheveled, and perched above the deadly tools of his "trade," he stares out from the cover of an 1886 edition of *The New York Detective Library*, one of the many weekly "dime novels" eagerly read by working people in the late nineteenth century. *The New York Detective Library*, August 7, 1886 — American Social History Project.

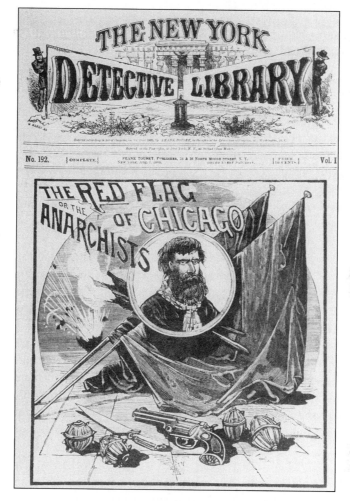

line. In the midst of the eight-hour strikes, the Knights capitulated on May 4, 1886, and called off the walkout.

Across the country, employers who had negotiated with labor in 1884 and 1885 refused to do so in 1886. The Illinois Bureau of Labor reported that of seventy-six attempts to negotiate differences between labor and employers in that year, employers rejected any discussion in thirty-two cases. In the second half of 1886, employers locked out some 100,000 workers. Attempts to improve working conditions — by laundry workers in Troy, New York; packinghouse workers in Chicago; and knitters in Cohoes and Amsterdam, New York — ended in harsh defeats.

All these unsuccessful strikes involved the Knights of Labor, which collapsed, no longer able to protect members' workplace rights. Across the nation, the organization that had boasted perhaps three-quarters of a million members at its peak in 1886 had shrunk to half that size within a year. By 1890, the Knights could claim only 100,000 members.

Labor Politics and Conflict

The decline of the Knights did not, however, mean the end of the working-class challenge to the industrial capitalist order. Working people also mobilized in other arenas and through other organizations in the 1880s and early 1890s. They sought political power, for example, through the mainstream parties and their own labor parties, winning both patronage jobs and some modest legislative gains. Skilled workers mobilized through the American Federation of Labor, which emerged as the dominant labor organization of that era (and subsequent ones as well).

Although the AFL had a narrower social and political vision than the Knights, it proved more adept in winning strikes and making gains for members. The AFL sometimes moved beyond advocating the self-interests of its members, although it never transcended the racism that pervaded American society at this time. The United Mine Workers, however, provided a shining exception and organized coal miners across racial lines. The class struggles that marked urban industrial workplaces also spilled over into the countryside. Across the nation, groups of workers and small farmers struggled against the power of the railroads and the giant corporations. They won some remarkable victories, but as the defeat of steelworkers at Homestead in 1892 indicated, the greater power remained in the hands of the capitalists.

Politics and the Workingman   For much of the nineteenth century, an abiding belief in equality and independence permeated working-class political thought. The Revolutionary-era ideology of republicanism placed on an equal and fair footing all white men who participated in American political and social life. In fact, many election boards required ownership of property in order to vote, but republicanism rested on the assumption that independent producers had skills or access to farmland and could provide adequately for themselves and their families. Women remained outside the bounds of formal political participation, as, in practice, did African Americans, American Indians, and most immigrants. Still, the rhetoric of mainstream American politics promoted the idea that fairness and equal opportunity marked the difference between the United States and the privilege-bound Old World.

By the 1870s, this republican vision of a society of independent citizens was further tarnished. The railroad strikes of 1877 indicated how far the republic had traveled from the egalitarian promise of the eighteenth century; an ugly chasm divided the broad mass of working people from the wealth and political power of industrial capitalists. To Gilded Age labor reformers, the debasement of politics and society rested in part on the capacity of the rich to corrupt governments in their own self-interest. Labor reform undertook the social and moral regeneration not only of the "commonwealth of toil," but also of the nation's political soul. "We stand as the conservators of society," a Vermont labor leader declared in 1887, suggesting that working people sought to cleanse and revive republican government in the new context of economic growth. Observing this effort, labor editor John Swinton gleefully asserted, "There will soon be but two parties in the field, one composed of honest workingmen, lovers of justice and equality; the other . . . composed of kid-gloved, silk-stockinged, aristocratic capitalists and their contemptible toadies."

The Democratic and Republican parties offered workers tangible benefits for participation in mainstream politics, trading municipal jobs for working-class votes. As cogs in well-oiled "machines"—coalitions of ward organizations that controlled politics and jobs in Gilded Age cities—many urban workers, native-born and immigrant alike, took advantage of these economic opportunities. In the West, political machines had ties to the railroads; the Union Pacific, for example, was deeply involved in the politics of Omaha, its eastern terminus. The multilayered state, county, and municipal machines of the South were central to maintaining the Democratic party's power in that region.

Tammany Hall, New York City's powerful Democratic organization and best-known urban machine, attracted working-class families from parishes and social networks all over the city by providing a range of vital social and personal services, including bail, emergency relief, and financial support of neighborhood social and cultural activities. Above all, jobs bound urban workers to political machines; Tammany dispensed some 12,000 patronage positions after its victory in the 1888 elections. With help from machine bosses, young Irish women got jobs in the public schools, their brothers found positions on the police force, and immigrants fresh off the boat went to work constructing city streets, bridges, and buildings. Meanwhile, Tammany bosses got wealthy from bribes and from so-called "honest graft"—profiting from knowledge about a new streetcar line by buying nearby land.

Labor reformers rejected Tammany and other political machines. They championed working-class political activism, which linked the economic struggle to truly oppositional contests in the electoral arena. Declaring in the midst of the 1886 boycotts that it was time to "boycott" the Democratic and Republican parties, New York's Central Labor Union launched an independent labor party to run in the November city election. Their candidate for mayor was reformer and author Henry George, whose *Progress and Poverty* (1879) blamed inequality and corruption on the private ownership

Mary Masquerades as Murray: A Woman in Tammany Hall

In many ways, Murray Hall, a leader of New York City's notorious Tammany Hall, fit the image of the cigar-chomping, whiskey-drinking urban political boss of the early twentieth century. But in one significant way, Hall departed from the stereotype: she was actually a woman (named Mary Anderson) who "passed" as a man for more than a quarter century, including marrying twice. Some lesbians (a term that was not in use at that time) "passed" both to avoid public condemnation and to increase their earnings so that they could live independently. "Passing" also enabled Hall to vote and serve as a political leader in an era when women were denied the franchise.

A peculiar case was brought to light yesterday when Dr. William C. Gallagher of 302 West Twelfth Street reported to the Coroner's office the death of Murray Hall, sixty years old, who kept an employment agency at 145 Sixth Avenue. Death was caused by cancer of the breast. Although Murray Hall had passed for a man for a number of years it now turns out that the person was a woman. . . .

[Hall] was known to hundreds of people in the Thirteenth Senatorial District, where she figured quite prominently as a politician. In a limited circle she even had a reputation as a "man about town," a bon vivant, and all-around "good fellow."

She was a member of the General Committee of Tammany Hall, a member of the Iroquois Club, a personal friend of State Senator "Barney" Martin and other officials, and one of the most active Tammany workers in the district.

She registered and voted at primaries and general elections for many years, and exercised considerable political influence with Tammany Hall, often securing appointments for friends who have proved their fealty to the organization—never exciting the remotest suspicion as to her real sex.

She played poker at the clubs with city and State officials and politicians who flatter themselves on their cleverness and perspicacity, drank whisky and wine and smoked the regulation "big black cigar" with the apparent relish and gusto of the real man-about-town. . . .

"I wouldn't believe it if Dr. Gallagher, whom I know to be a man of undoubted veracity, hadn't said so," said Senator Bernard F. Martin. "Well, truly, it's most wonderful. Why, I knew him well. He was a member of the Tammany district organization, a hard worker for his party, and always had a good argument to put up for any candidate he favored. He used to come to the Iroquois Club to see me and pay his dues, and occasionally he would crack a joke with some of the boys. He was a modest little fellow, but had a peppery temper and could say some cutting things when anyone displeased him. Suspect he was a woman? Never. He dressed like a man and talked like a very sensible one. The only thing I ever thought eccentric about him was his clothing. Now that they say he's a woman, I can see through that. You see, he also wore a coat a size or two too large, but of good material. That was to conceal his form. He had a bushy head of black hair, which he wore long and parted on the left side. His face was always smooth, just as if he had just come from the barber's."

New York Times, January 18, 19, 1901.

"Labor Nowhere Has Its Full and Fair Reward": Henry George Campaigns for Mayor

Author of Progress and Poverty, *Henry George ran for mayor of New York City in 1886. His campaign generated tremendous enthusiasm among working people, particularly trade union members. Although George campaigned for less than a month, he spoke more than one hundred times, sometimes addressing five or more labor unions and church groups in a single evening. This speech, presented to the members of Waiters' Union No. 3 in Manhattan, conveys George's identification with organized labor and his desire to channel the groundswell of working-class activism toward electoral politics.*

When this movement commenced the politicians thought there was nothing in it. . . . The fact of the matter is, that the politicians and newspaper editors — not the newspaper reporters, but the newspaper editors — do not begin to appreciate the strength of this movement; they do not begin to understand the determination with which the workingmen of New York of all classes and all of its occupations have taken hold of this movement. They do not realize that it is not a candidate who is looking for votes; it is the voters who are running the candidate on our side. I am your representative, put in the field by the accredited delegates of organized labor, and as their candidate I propose to run, and as their candidate I feel confident of election. . . .

All men who work for a living, whether by hand or head, are underpaid. Labor nowhere has its full and fair reward. Everywhere the struggle for existence, the difficulty of making a living, is far greater than it ought to be. This cannot be remedied by my election for Mayor; but a start will have been made; we shall at least have begun. From that time forth the questions of work and wages, the questions that concern the earning and the livings of us all, will get such an attention as they never had before. And the men who work for a living will have become conscious of the power of those questions. And the men who in legislatures make the laws, and the men who on judicial benches interpret the laws, and the men who in administrative offices execute the laws — they, too, will become conscious of their power. . . .

If elected Mayor of New York it will be my duty to enforce the law. It will be at all times my duty to preserve order, at all times my duty to protect property; and that I will execute the law. . . . As a class workingmen have nothing to gain from disorder. . . . If the laws do not suit them, let them change the laws. Let there be no appeal to force so long as the ballot remains. That is the safer remedy for American citizens; to that remedy we propose at this election to appeal, and to appeal in tones that will ring through this land. . . .

L. F. Post and F. C. Leubuscher, eds., *Henry George's 1886 Campaign* (1887).

of land. George — with the help of the Knights of Labor, the New York Central Labor Union, and Father Edward McGlynn (a Catholic priest who embraced labor reform) — generated tremendous working-class support. He drew equally intense opposition from the church hierarchy, employers, and the Tammany machine, the last of which fielded iron magnate Abram

TWO GREAT QUESTIONS.

"WHO STOLE THE PEOPLE'S MONEY?" — DO TELL . N.Y.TIMES.

'TWAS HIM.

Who Stole the People's Money?

Critics of the urban political machine were handicapped by a foe that possessed both charitable and corrupt attributes. Thomas Nast's cartoons in *Harper's Weekly* attacking political "boss" William M. Tweed (the portly figure on the left) and his Tammany Hall associates supplied antimachine forces with a powerful weapon. Nast's caricatures, accessible to everyone, succinctly conveyed a negative portrait of the machine that would influence popular perception of the political "boss" into the twenty-first century. Thomas Nast, *Harper's Weekly,* August 19, 1871 — American Social History Project.

Hewitt as the Democratic party's nominee. Although George lost the election, he captured 70,000 votes, one-third of the total and far more than the Republican candidate, Theodore Roosevelt.

The George campaign was the most prominent but not the only labor-reform effort. In almost every town and city with Knights of Labor assemblies, workers discovered their political voice in 1886. Even as the Order itself declined, nearly two hundred Union Labor or Workingmen's parties elected aldermen, mayors, and school board officials. In Rutland, Vermont, the United Labor forces scored a stunning victory, electing a Knights candidate to the state legislature and fifteen justices of the peace. In other places, labor managed to take control of one of the two established political parties.

This political activity produced legislative results. City councils and state legislatures passed laws protecting trade unions and establishing an eight-hour day for public employees. Sometimes simply the threat of third parties provoked concessions from officials, who passed prolabor legislation or put "friends of the workingman" on their slates. In Rochester, New Hampshire, the entry of the Knights of Labor into politics forced the Democratic party to endorse the new labor ticket. The Knights claimed in November 1886 that they had elected a dozen U.S. congressmen, almost all of them members of the established parties who had joined with the labor-reform forces.

Badly shaken by labor's political upsurge, Democratic and Republican urban machines attempted to co-opt many of its issues. In New York,

The Workingman between Two Fires

During the 1886 New York City mayoral campaign, many workingmen faced a dilemma when the Catholic Church hierarchy attacked Henry George, the United Labor Party (ULP) candidate. As this cartoon from the humor weekly *Judge* indicates, although the ULP lost the election, the sizable turnout for George showed that many Catholic voters had ignored Archbishop Michael A. Corrigan's denunciations.

Grant Hamilton, *Judge*, 1886 — American Social History Project.

Tammany endorsed the establishment of a Bureau of Labor Statistics, called for a legal "Labor Day" holiday, and made a variety of other gestures to regain the following it had lost during the George campaign. But what primarily brought trade unionists, like other working people, into the political system was patronage—the provision of municipal jobs to key supporters. By the late 1880s, for example, Chicago's city payroll included more than 400 Knights.

The Rise of the AFL   Many white male skilled workers left the Knights of Labor during the period of legal repression that followed the Haymarket bombing in 1886. Both the Knights and the local and national trade unions organized by craft unions had agitated for the eight-hour day, mounted mass strikes and boycotts, and supported reform legislation. But in the wake of the Haymarket affair, the craft unions, rejecting the Knights' inclusive social and organizational vision, narrowed their focus to issues that were relevant to their own members.

The breach between the Knights and the craft unions widened significantly with the creation of the American Federation of Labor (AFL). In May 1886, Samuel Gompers, a leader of the Cigar Makers' International Union, invited all the national unions to meet and formulate a common position with respect to the Knights. In December, the craft unionists organized a loose alliance of independent national unions. They elected Gompers president, a position that he was to hold for most of the next four decades. Local AFL unions and assemblies of the Knights broke each others' strikes and

TWO ROADS FOR THE WORKINGMAN — ONE LEADS TO PROSPERITY, AND THE OTHER TO VIOLENCE AND RUIN.

Two Roads for the Workingman
No admirer of the labor movement, the satirical weekly magazine *Puck* depicts the warring trade unions and Knights of Labor as essentially the same, taking workers down the "Road of Lawlessness and Disorder." Meanwhile, in the background, P. M. Arthur of the conservative Brotherhood of Locomotive Engineers chugs forward toward prosperity, progress, and — most important — order. Joseph Keppler, *Puck*, August 25, 1886 — Scott Molloy Labor Archives.

invaded each others' territory as the AFL gained strength and the Knights declined.

Most of the unionists who were drawn to the AFL had skills that enabled them to bargain effectively with their employers. These workers could secure concessions from employers as long as they limited their demands to improved wages and working conditions. Disillusioned with the defeats of mass strikes and with broad reform programs that would not win immediate material gains, these skilled craft unionists defined an organizational strategy that they hoped would maximize their power and minimize their vulnerability.

The story of Patrick Henry McCarthy testifies to the extraordinary economic and political power exercised by skilled workers. Born in Ireland on Saint Patrick's Day in 1863, McCarthy arrived in the United States at age seventeen and worked as a carpenter's apprentice. He settled in San Francisco in 1886, where he organized the city's powerful Building Trades Council in 1898 and ran it with an iron hand for twenty-four years.

San Francisco building tradesmen had been in great demand ever since the days of the Gold Rush. When McCarthy arrived, the city was already a center of trade union power, and the building unions exercised tight control of the labor market. No one worked without a union card, everyone worked under union rules at good wages, and union men informally restricted their output so there would be enough work for all. These privileged workers jealously guarded the gates to their trade; some building unions barred all but their members' sons. A black or Asian man had no chance of being admitted. McCarthy, the czar of this labor fiefdom, had little interest in

VIRGINIA.—THE FATAL EXPLOSION AT THE MIDLOTHIAN COAL MINE, FEBRUARY 3D—CARRYING FROM THE SHAFT-CAGE A RESCUE PARTY OVERCOME BY GAS. FROM A SKETCH BY F. C. BURROUGHS.—SEE PAGE 440.

United in Tragedy

Black and white miners and their families gathered outside a mineshaft in Midlothian, Virginia, after a gas explosion in February 1882. This engraving in *Frank Leslie's Illustrated Newspaper* was unusual in portraying an interracial mining scene. F. C. Burroughs, *Frank Leslie's Illustrated Newspaper*, February 18, 1882 — American Social History Project.

unions outside of the building trades and even less concern for the plight of San Francisco's unorganized workers.

With Samuel Gompers as their national spokesman, the leaders of individual trade unions like those in McCarthy's Building Trades Council developed the concept of "business unionism." Their national unions were strong organizations of skilled workers; each had exclusive jurisdiction within a specific craft, charged relatively high dues, and maintained ample funds to finance a strike. Business unionism focused on concrete material goals, to be achieved through collective bargaining with the employer. Willing to use political action if necessary—to fight for protective tariffs or against competition from prison labor—business unionists generally avoided involvement in broad-based political movements.

Although business unionists usually accepted capitalist economic relations and the prevailing social and political order, the AFL and its constituent unions did not lack for militancy, and the rhetoric of the labor movement remained radical. McCarthy's Building Trades Council championed cooperative enterprises and land reform, calling such plans a way to free white workers from wage labor and turn control of the urban-industrial order over to the broad mass of American citizens. The national unions often championed craftsmen's efforts to win an eight-hour day, to defend their organizations, and to protect their traditional control over their jobs.

Strikes became more numerous, better organized, more disciplined, and more successful. Unions won more than 60 percent of the strikes waged in 1889 and 1890. And the strikes of AFL affiliates did not merely express the wage goals of narrow occupational groups. The organization backed sympathy strikes, in which workers demonstrated their support of another striking union by refusing to work. When New York's cabinetmakers struck to preserve their union in 1892, for example, more than eleven other craft groups employed in over one hundred firms joined them. Sympathetic job actions increased nearly fourfold in the early 1890s.

As the AFL gained strength among skilled white workers, the Knights of Labor shifted its sights to rural black workers, western and southern miners, and unskilled immigrants. Although leadership remained in the hands of white English-speaking labor reformers, most new members in the

"... Let Us Prove Ourselves Men": UMWA Organizes African American Miners

In a July 1891 letter written to the National Labor Tribune, *a labor newspaper published in Pittsburgh, Richard L. Davis appealed to his fellow black miners to embrace the banner of unionism and not allow themselves to be used by white coal operators as strikebreakers.*

None of us who toil for our daily bread are free. At one time . . . we were chattel slaves; today we are, one and all, white and black wage slaves, and it is just such [strikebreaking] actions as we have seen taken in the state of Washington that [have] for years been forging the chains of bondage around us more firmly. . . . I think the time has come that the negro should know better than to run from place to place to break down wages, etc. He can plainly see that the money kings of this country are only using him as a tool to fill [their] own coffers with gold. Does any negro think that an operator thinks any more of him than he does of a white man? If you do, you are sadly mistaken, for I remember several instances right here in this valley: whenever the colored men asked for that which was something like right and just, the answer was, whenever you colored men want the same as the whites do then we have no further need for you. This was the answer. Now then I would say to the negro, of which race I am proud to be connected, let us be men; let us demand as much for our labor as any other nationality; let us not suffer ourselves to be trampled upon any more than any other people. We are a people; we are men; we constitute one-sixth of this great country so far as numbers are concerned, consequently it is not a white man's country; it is partly ours as well, so let us prove ourselves men and the equal of any others. We can do it. I want to say that the labor organizations will do more for the negro than any political party can or ever will do. So let us into them and try to make this country what it should be.

R. L. Davis to *National Labor Tribune*, 1891.

southern countryside were African American tenants, miners, rural day laborers, and domestic workers. Long known for advocacy of African American rights, the Knights of Labor increasingly became a black organization in the South. In 1887, for example, 10,000 sugar plantation workers in Louisiana, almost all of them black and members of the Knights, struck for higher wages and an end to payment in scrip. Frightened planters mobilized the state militia and vigilantes, declared martial law, and unleashed a deadly assault that killed more than fifty black strikers in just one confrontation.

The United Mine Workers of America (UMWA) also played an important role in organizing black workers. Founded in 1890 with the support of dozens of local Knights assemblies in coal-mining areas, the UMWA embraced the Knights of Labor's broad, inclusive vision and initially affiliated with both the Knights and the AFL. The UMWA struggled from the outset to build an interracial, industrial union for skilled and unskilled mine workers alike.

One UMWA organizer, Richard L. Davis, traveled all over the South to exhort his fellow black miners to join the union. During the 1890s, he worked as a UMWA organizer throughout Ohio, West Virginia, and Alabama. In 1896 and 1897, he won election to the union's National Executive Board, the only African American to hold a national union office. Repeatedly battling segregation and the distorting influence of "the race question," Davis observed, "I think were we, as workingmen, to turn our attention to fighting monopoly in land and money, we would accomplish a great deal more than we will by fighting among ourselves on account of race, creed, color, or nationality."

Encouraged by the efforts of Davis and other organizers and by the earlier successes of the Knights, the UMWA brought black and white mine workers together in dozens of local unions in the southern West Virginia coalfields. Miners elected a succession of black miners to the West Virginia district vice presidency between 1891 and 1898, and, in turn, black miners provided most stalwart supporters for the UMWA in West Virginia during these years.

Unfortunately, other unions did not follow the same path. Most national unions, reflecting the racism of their members, became narrow organizations of skilled, white male workers. Rejecting the Knights' commitment to interracialism and broad industrial organization and the miners' inclusive approach to organizing, craft unions—notably those in the building trades and the railroad brotherhoods—systematically excluded black workers and the unskilled. The increasingly businesslike and racist policies of AFL craft unionism had overwhelmed the Knights' broader vision of working-class organization.

Class Conflict in the Country   The violence, racial strife, and class conflict that defined industrial life in the 1870s and 1880s found expression not only in industrial towns but also in rural areas, where workers and small farmers opposed powerful economic groups. Here, as in the cities, the power of the wealthy was based on their money, while the power of the poor was grounded in their communities.

By the end of Reconstruction, rural African Americans had created a dense web of churches, fraternal lodges, and educational institutions, and these still served as the basis for political networks even after the white "redemption" of Southern politics. Despite the violent repression that followed the end of Reconstruction, rural African Americans continued to vote in some areas until the end of the century. Most notable was the biracial Readjuster insurgency in Virginia, which successfully challenged white

Democratic rule in the 1880s. Grassroots black political activity was powerful enough in Virginia to send to Congress in 1888 the ex-slave John Mercer Langston, Virginia's first black Congressman — and the last for another 104 years.

White Southern farmers also rooted their political efforts in local communities. Struggling for economic self-sufficiency, the independent white farmers of the South relied on one another for loans of much-needed cash and for assistance with large jobs. Kinship connections reinforced this interdependence, and neighboring farm families swapped work and labored together at parties or "bees," much as their western counterparts did. Farmers' independence and mutuality were thus intimately linked, even as expanding rail lines and the tightening noose of credit drew them beyond their communities into national and even world markets.

In the Georgia hills, farmers called on their community ties to protect their common-law rights to graze animals on unfenced land. Merchants and landlords with interests in protecting crops demanded laws requiring farmers to enclose their livestock and defining the boundaries of their land as legal fences. Railroad companies, liable for damages if locomotives struck wandering animals, welcomed this attack on open grazing. But poor people, landless or with only small holdings, needed open grazing to sustain their herds and remain independent of sharecropping and debt peonage.

"We as poor men and Negroes do not need the law," cried one Georgia farmer in 1885, "but we need a democratic government and independence that will do the common people good." As another farmer argued, the law requiring fencing was "ultimately going to be the ruin of people and especially the poor people that have nowhere to keep their stock [and] . . . are entirely dependent on the landowners for pasture." Battles raged over elections that were called to determine whether land should be fenced. The advocates of fencing won, but they had trouble securing their victory. Outlaws lurking in the Georgia night tore down fences, smashed gates, and threatened proponents of enclosure.

The values expressed in Georgia were mirrored across the country in other conflicts over enclosure. In New Mexico, Juan José Herrerra led a group of Hispanic villagers against powerful cattle ranchers and landowners who had begun fencing the best pasturing and watering lands, which previously had been held in common. Calling themselves Las Gorras Blancas ("the White Caps"), Mexican farmers in 1889 burned fences, cut barbed wire, and generally terrorized cattlemen. At their peak, Las Gorras Blancas claimed more than 1,500 members, garnering the support of the entire Mexican American community and even of some Anglos. They stated their program simply: "Our purpose is to protect the rights and interest of the people in general and especially those of the helpless classes." Among their opponents they listed "land grabbers," political bosses, and monopolizers of water.

Settlers Taking the Law into Their Own Hands

Homesteaders in Custer County, Nebraska, reenacted how they cut down 15 miles of wire fence erected by cattlemen in 1885. Solomon D. Butcher, 1885 — Butcher Collection, Nebraska Historical Society.

Las Gorras Blancas also fought against lumber operations and the railroads. During the building of the Santa Fe Railroad, they burned track, stopped men hauling railroad ties, and sent threatening letters to foremen denouncing unacceptable wage rates. Because they saw themselves as part of a larger collective movement of resistance against industrial capitalism, they applied for membership as an assembly of the Knights of Labor. In the early 1890s, they affiliated with the radical agrarian People's (Populist) Party (discussed in Chapter 3), which won several elections in New Mexico in the 1890s.

At about the same time, neighborhood bands in the Cross Timbers region of Texas were enforcing a similar belief that ownership of the land did not convey the right to restrict free access to grass and water. Many inhabitants were of Scots-Irish and Irish descent, and their deep-seated, traditional dislike of landlords found an outlet in the cry "Land to the cultivator!" Brash fence cutters left taunting notes: "We understand you have plenty of money to spend to build fences. Please put them up again for us to cut them down again. We want the fence guarded with good men so that their mettle can be tested."

The defense of common rights in Texas was linked to a growing opposition to those who monopolized land and credit. Song and story celebrated Sam Bass, a former Indiana farmhand, as "the Robin Hood of Cross Timbers," for stealing from the railroads. Bass may not have considered his crimes symbolic of community resistance to capitalist speculation, but others saw him in that light. Bandits such as Bass and the more infamous Jesse James won the acclaim of farmers and urban workers across the country by taking on railroads and banks, repositories of corporate capital in the Gilded Age.

Bloody Battles at Homestead The same community basis for class struggles against capitalists could also be found in industrial cities and towns. Yet one of the era's most famous strikes — at Andrew Carnegie's Homestead, Pennsylvania, steel mill in 1892 — demonstrated that locally organized workers could not easily defeat new, nationally organized corporations. For their part, urban craft workers seemed to have the upper hand in the campaign to improve their circumstances. The AFL craft unions had consolidated their influence in the late 1880s and early 1890s. Skilled iron and steel workers, in particular, had won high wages based on their knowledge and command of the production process and on their unity in dealing with employers.

At Carnegie's Homestead works, one of the most advanced mills in the world, the Amalgamated Association of Iron and Steel Workers had won an important victory in 1889, securing wages that were one-third higher than those paid to skilled workers at neighboring mills. In addition, the settlement pegged the wages of unorganized unskilled workers to those of the skilled craftsmen. The contract therefore benefited not only skilled unionized workers, but their unskilled nonunion helpers as well.

In Homestead, as elsewhere, community ties reinforced relationships formed on the job. Homestead, with twelve mills, was one of the world's largest industrial complexes in the late nineteenth century. Of its 11,000 residents, 3,800 men worked in the mills — virtually one person from every household. Steelworkers headed the city government and police department and owned most of Homestead's modest homes. Steelworkers saw unionism as a right of citizenship, a bulwark against dependency, and a protector of workers' positions as homeowners in a community they had made their own. As a state militia officer wonderingly remarked, "They believe the works are theirs quite as much as Carnegie's."

Carnegie and his partner, Henry Clay Frick, believed differently, and they decided to break the union's power. Carnegie wanted a cheap and docile labor force, and the Amalgamated Association stood in his way. In June 1892, as Carnegie hid away in Scotland, Frick broke off contract renewal negotiations with union representatives, announcing that the company would in the future bargain only with individual workers. He then prepared for battle, surrounding the mills with 3 miles of twelve-foot steel fence topped with barbed wire; workers dubbed the complex "Fort Frick." He also hired 300 armed Pinkerton agents to protect the scab replacement workers he planned to bring in by boat on the Monongahela River, which ran along company property. On July 2, Frick locked out the workers, shut down the Homestead works, and announced that they would reopen with nonunion labor. The Amalgamated Association responded by mobilizing virtually the entire town, organizing a paramilitary takeover of the local utilities, monitoring all access to Homestead, and closing the saloons.

An Awful Battle at Homestead, Pa.

The *National Police Gazette* portrayed the July 6, 1892, fight between striking steelworkers and Pinkerton strikebreakers on the Monongahela River. Directed to male readers, many of whom were workers, the *Police Gazette* occasionally covered labor conflict, expressing sympathy toward strikers while also exploiting the more sensational aspects of the events. *National Police Gazette*, July 23, 1892 — Prints and Photographs Division, Library of Congress.

On July 6, the heavily armed Pinkertons approached the plant from a barge on the river. Armed with guns, rocks, and a small cannon, an enraged crowd of steelworkers and their wives met the Pinkertons at the river's edge. Nine strikers and seven Pinkertons died during a twelve-hour battle, and many more were wounded. The Pinkertons surrendered to the workers.

In the days that followed, the confrontation spread beyond Homestead as lockouts and sympathy strikes shut down other Carnegie mills. But the Carnegie Company persuaded the governor to send in the Pennsylvania militia, which escorted repairmen, mechanics, and strikebreakers (recruited from as far away as Ohio) into Carnegie's plants. Still, the Amalgamated Association hung on for four more months. Frick wrote Carnegie, "The firmness with which these strikers hold on is surprising to everyone."

The workers believed that they had right on their side, but Carnegie had might. As the company restored production and winter approached, morale faded. On November 20, 1892, the union surrendered; the company fired and blacklisted the Amalgamated leaders. Frick cabled Carnegie: "Our victory is now complete and most gratifying. Do not think we will ever have any serious labor trouble again."

The defeat at Homestead dealt the skilled men of the Amalgamated Association—and craft unionism in general—a stunning blow. It shattered their union and their faith in their powerful craft organization. They had learned about the power of capital and had experienced firsthand the role of government in labor-capital conflict. Technological change had eroded skilled workers' central role in the production process and made them increasingly vulnerable. Gone were the days when skilled craft workers had only to withhold their labor to get bosses to agree to their demands.

Days after the Homestead workers returned to the mills, another violent incident pitted strikers against strikebreakers and company guards, this time in the silver-mining region of Coeur d'Alene, Idaho. Here, too, the owners called on state government for help. The governor of Idaho declared martial law and sent in the state militia, and the striking workers capitulated. Other major labor defeats in 1892 included a strike by switchmen in the Buffalo railway yards, a strike by Knights of Labor in Tennessee coal mines, and a general strike by black and white workers in New Orleans.

Conclusion: Labor, Capital, and the State

Faced with this record of crushing setbacks, AFL president Samuel Gompers asked, "Shall we change our methods?" AFL union membership held steady despite the 1892 losses, and Gompers answered in the negative, believing that trade unions' very survival in the face of employers' all-out attacks proved his policies correct. But he missed the larger meaning of the year's events. In the face of overwhelming defeat, the culture of solidarity that had inspired many skilled craft workers for thirty years was in decline. If Haymarket in 1886 represented the destruction of the Knights' broad vision of labor unity among workers of diverse backgrounds and skills, the narrower but sustaining vision of craft unionism met an equivalent defeat at Homestead and other sites in 1892.

Another lesson of the 1892 strikes was that political power was shifting from the local to the state level. Large corporations could exert greater influence over governors than over mayors and aldermen—especially in communities where the political power of working people remained significant. Fortified by increasing government support, employers made it clear that they would do everything possible to destroy the labor movement.

The Years in Review

1869
- Nine Philadelphia tailors found the Noble and Holy Order of the Knights of Labor.

1872
- Anthony Comstock founds the New York Society for the Suppression of Vice.

1874
- Women activists found the Woman's Christian Temperance Union.

1877
- Great railroad strikes sweep across the nation.

1878

- The Women's Suffrage Amendment to the Constitution is defeated in the Senate by a 34-to-16 vote; supporters will reintroduce it in every succeeding Congress until it is finally passed after World War I.

1880

- The Salvation Army opens its first U.S. mission in New York City, offering food, shelter, and low-wage work to needy people.
- The National Farmers' Alliance, predecessor of the Populist Party, is formed in Chicago.

1881

- African American washerwomen in Atlanta organize a two-week strike to demand higher fees.
- The Knights of Labor admit women members.
- A "Jim Crow" law segregating railroad cars passes in Tennessee, setting a precedent for other southern states.
- Booker T. Washington founds the Normal and Industrial Institute for Negroes (later the Tuskegee Institute) and becomes its president.

1882

- Congress passes the Chinese Exclusion Act.
- The Knights of Labor sponsor the first Labor Day parade.
- The Central Labor Union is founded.

1884

- The Federation of Organized Trades and Labor Unions begins a two-year campaign for an eight-hour workday.

1886

- The American Federation of Labor forms, with Samuel Gompers as its president.
- The Knights of Labor enrolls nearly one million members—about 10 percent of the country's nonagricultural workforce, a much higher proportion than had ever before been enrolled in unions.
- A bomb explodes in Haymarket Square in Chicago; an antiradical crusade follows.
- Reformer Henry George loses the election for mayor of New York City but gets one-third of the votes.
- Weakened by internal disputes, faulty decisions, and disunity of purpose, the Knights of Labor are defeated in the Southwestern Railroad strike.

1888

- New York courts respond to widespread worker actions and criminalize boycotts.

- Tammany Hall, the Democratic organization of New York City, wins city elections and dispenses 12,000 patronage positions.

- African American political strength continues in some areas, and John Mercer Langston is elected, the first black congressman in Virginia.

1889

- Las Gorras Blancas, an organization of Mexican American farmers, burns fences and cuts barbed wire in opposition to the practices of white cattlemen.

- Jane Addams founds Hull House, a settlement house for the urban poor in Chicago.

1890

- The United Mine Workers of America is founded.

1892

- Workers strike but are defeated at Andrew Carnegie's Homestead Steelworks in Pennsylvania.

- The Populist Party is founded.

- Miners are defeated in a violent strike in Coeur d'Alene, Idaho.

Additional Readings

For more on working people and their communities, see: Sydney E. Ahlstrom, *A Religious History of the American People* (1972); Howard Chudacoff and Judith Smith, *The Evolution of American Urban Society* (2000); John D'Emilio and Estelle B. Freedman, *Intimate Matters: A History of Sexuality in America* (1988); Hasia Diner, *Erin's Daughters in America: Irish Immigrant Women in the Nineteenth Century* (1983); Perry R. Duis, *The Saloon: Public Drinking in Chicago and Boston, 1880–1920* (1983); Susan A. Glenn, *Daughters of the Shtetl: Life and Labor in the Immigrant Generation* (1990); Dolores Hayden, *The Grand Domestic Revolution* (1983); Tera Hunter, *To 'Joy My Freedom: Southern Black Women's Lives and Labors After the Civil War* (1997); Kerby A. Miller, *Emigrants and Exiles: Ireland and the Irish Exodus to North America* (1985); Madelon Powers, *Faces Along the Bar: Lore and Order in the Workingman's Saloon, 1870–1920* (1998); Roy Rosenzweig, *Eight Hours for What We Will: Workers and Leisure in an Industrial City, 1870–1920* (1983); Stephan Thernstrom, *Poverty and Progress: Social*

Mobility in a Nineteenth-Century City (1968); and Altina L. Waller, *Reverend Beecher and Mrs. Tilton: Sex and Class in Victorian America* (1982).

For more on the Knights of Labor and community and culture in the labor movement, see: David Bensman, *The Practice of Solidarity* (1985); Francis G. Couvares, *The Remaking of Pittsburgh: Class and Culture in an Industrializing City, 1877–1919* (1984); Leon Fink, *Workingmen's Democracy: The Knights of Labor and American Politics* (1983); Susan Levine, *Labor's True Woman: Carpet Weavers, Industrialization, and Labor Reform in the Gilded Age* (1984); Ronald L. Lewis, *Black Coal Miners in America: Race, Class, and Community Conflict, 1780–1980* (1987); David Montgomery, *Workers' Control in America: Studies in the History of Work* (1982); Richard Oestreicher, *Solidarity and Fragmentation: Working People and Class Consciousness in Detroit, 1875–1900* (1986); and Daniel J. Walkowitz, *Worker City, Company Town: Iron- and Cotton-Worker Protest in Troy and Cohoes, New York, 1855–1884* (1978).

For more on the eight-hour movement and the Haymarket affair, see: Carolyn Ashbaugh, *Lucy Parsons: American Revolutionary* (1976); Paul Avrich, *The Haymarket Tragedy* (1983); James Green, *Death in the Haymarket: A Story of Chicago, the First Labor Movement, and the Bombing That Divided Gilded Age America* (2006); Dave Roediger and Franklin Rosemont, *Haymarket Scrapbook* (1986); and Carl Smith, *Urban Disorder and the Shape of Belief: The Great Chicago Fire, the Haymarket Bomb, and the Model Town of Pullman* (1995).

For more on labor politics, see: Steve Babson, *The Unfinished Struggle: Turning Points in American Labor, 1877–Present* (1999); Walter Bean, *Boss Ruef's San Francisco: The Story of Work, Culture, and Society in Industrializing the Union Labor Party, Big Business, and the Graft Prosecution* (1967); Steven P. Erie, *Rainbow's End: Irish Americans and the Dilemmas of Urban Machine Politics, 1840–1945* (1988); Steven Hahn, *A Nation Under Our Feet: Black Political Struggles in the Rural South from Slavery to the Great Migration* (2003); Michael Kazin, *Barons of Labor: The San Francisco Building Trades and Union Power in the Progressive Era* (1987); David Montgomery, *The Fall of the House of Labor: The Workplace, the State, and American Labor Activism, 1865–1925* (1987); and Michael Nash, *Conflict and Accommodation: Coal Miners, Steel Workers, and Socialism, 1890–1920* (1980).

For more on the Homestead Strike of 1892, see: Arthur G. Burgoyne, *The Homestead Strike of 1892* (1979); William Serrin, *Homestead: The Glory and Tragedy of an American Steel Town* (1992); and Leon Wolff, *Lockout, the Story of the Homestead Strike of 1892* (1965).

3

From Depression to Expansion: Industrial Capitalism Triumphs at Home and Abroad

1893-1900

O N M AY 1, 1893, the World's Columbian Exposition—Chicago's great world's fair commemorating the 400th anniversary of Columbus's arrival in the Americas—opened to the public. Chicago's leading merchants, bankers, and real estate men raised millions of dollars to build a dazzling exhibition that would publicize to the world the cultural and economic achievements of their city and nation and express U.S. businessmen's desire to compete for world markets. Chicago architect Daniel H. Burnham, who oversaw construction of the exposition's "White City," proclaimed that the fair would constitute the third great event in American history, preceded only by the Revolution and the Civil War. The architects and artists who designed the neoclassical buildings of the White City saw themselves as heirs to the Italian Renaissance who would remake and purify American culture through their work. "Look here, old fellow," the sculptor Augustus Saint-Gaudens told Burnham at a planning session, "do you realize that this is the greatest meeting of artists since the fifteenth century?"

But the White City's shining marble edifices were a sham; the "marble" was really just plaster covering wood and steel. An even deeper contradiction lay outside the fairgrounds. At almost the same moment that the fair opened for business, thousands of factory gates swung closed as the nation plunged into one of the worst depressions in its history. "From all the manufacturing and commercial centres," declared the New York City branch of the American Federation of Labor (AFL) just months after the fair's triumphant opening, "there comes the anxious demand for work, soon we fear to be followed by the despairing cry for bread." Alluding directly to the Columbian Exposition, they complained that "a few thousand men and women enjoy the opulence of eastern potentates, while abject millions

Theater at the Brickyard
The workforce of a Massachusetts brick factory proudly posed for a photographer sometime in the late nineteenth century. Ashfield Historical Society, Ashfield, Massachusetts.

grovel in the dust begging for work and bread. This is the industrial and social exhibit of our Columbian year."

Industrial workers and activist farmers responded to the hard times with militant action and with radical electoral campaigns, organizing the most successful political movements outside the major parties in American history—campaigns that built on the solidarity and the cooperative vision of the struggles of the 1880s. But before the century was over, those movements would be sharply defeated. Still worse, immigrants and southern blacks faced a rising tide of nativism and racism. Business interests sought to limit economic depressions by expanding U.S. markets and territories overseas. Recovery from the depression—fostered in part by the expansion of U.S. capitalism abroad (most dramatically evident in the Spanish-Cuban-American War)—improved the material conditions of farmers and working people. Fewer workers could be found "begging for work," but it would be many years before they would regain the political clout they had exerted in the 1880s or 1890s. The triumphant claims of U.S. economic and cultural strength made by the capitalists who planned the White City would ring much more true in 1900 than they had in 1893.

Hard Times and Hard Struggles

The Depression that hit as the White City opened devastated working people and their communities. It also provoked strong reactions. "Industrial armies" set out for Washington to demand public works jobs. And when the Pullman Company responded to hard times with layoffs and wage cuts, its workers launched a massive nationwide boycott and strike against all trains with Pullman cars. But court injunctions and federal troops defeated them.

The Depression of the 1890s The bankruptcy of the Philadelphia and Reading Railroad and the National Cordage Company (a group of rope manufacturers) in the first half of 1893 set off a stock market crash, a run on gold, and a banking "panic." By year's end, about 500 banks and 16,000 businesses were bankrupt. Having led the economy into growth, the railroads now pushed it into depression. By the middle of 1894, more than 150 railroad companies were also bankrupt, stimulating trouble in other industries. Weakness in the agricultural economy suggested the extent to which farming was tied into national and international markets. And when farmers fell on bad times, they in turn dragged down farm machine manufacturers, grain elevator operators, and a variety of rural and small-town businesses.

This was the fifth major depression in American history (the others began in 1819, 1837, 1857, and 1873). Each depression was usually bigger than

"... We Are Starving to Death": The 1893 Depression in Kansas

In this 1894 letter to the governor of Kansas, Susan Orcutt describes the devastation experienced by western Kansas farming communities caught in the iron grip of the depression (spelling and punctuation corrected).

I take my pen in hand to let you know that we are Starving to death. It is Pretty hard to do without anything to Eat here in this God forsaken country. We would of had Plenty to Eat if the hail hadn't cut our rye down and ruined our corn and Potatoes. I had the Prettiest Garden that you Ever seen and the hail ruined It and I have nothing to look at. My Husband went away to find work and came home last night and told me that we would have to Starve. He had been in ten countys and did not Get no work. It is Pretty hard for a woman to do without anything to Eat when She doesn't know what minute She will be confined to bed. If I was in Iowa I would be all right. I was born there and raised there. I haven't had nothing to Eat today and It is three o'clock.

Lewelling Papers, Kansas Historical Society (1894).

the one before, and because the economy and the population kept growing, more people — and a greater proportion of people — were affected each time. More people worked for wages and paid for goods in cash; fewer bartered their labor and the goods they made or the food they grew. The increasingly national economy left Americans progressively more vulnerable to economic forces that they could not control. What happened on Wall Street now affected the lives of Massachusetts railroad workers and Mississippi sharecroppers who would never own stocks or bonds.

The five years of depression brought misery on a scale that had not previously been experienced in industrial America. Plant closings threw Americans out of work in staggering numbers. Although no one bothered to keep track of unemployment in this era, probably more than 15 percent of nonagricultural workers lost their jobs. As in previous depressions, the unemployed and the homeless traveled the country, hopping freight trains to distant places in search of work or handouts.

The statistics mask the depression's devastating impact on individual lives. Consider George A. Smith, laid off by the Boston and Maine and Fitchburg railroads because of the "dull times" in November 1893. Neighbors described Smith, a twenty-seven-year-old father of two, as a "steady, industrious man," but over the next four months, he could pick up only two weeks of work. Having exhausted his savings, he and his family had not even enough money to heat their apartment, buy yeast to bake bread, or pay for a doctor for their ailing son. Facing eviction by an unsympathetic landlord, a desperate Smith sought refuge at the local police station. Smith and his family fared better than some during the hard years of the depression.

"R. N.," a jobless Boston man, shot himself in the head in June 1896. The state medical examiner noted that R. N. "left a letter explaining that he killed himself to save others the trouble of caring for him."

Organized public and private relief efforts did not come close to meeting the needs of unemployed workers like Smith or "R. N." Many middle- and upper-class whites viewed relief with distaste, believing that "getting something for nothing" was a sin. Some described charity as socialistic; others said that it encouraged laziness. Moved by the plight of an unemployed man with five hungry children, a Massachusetts overseer of the poor gave the man some money but carefully covered up his good deed "so that it wouldn't get out." Social Darwinists viewed such charitable acts as wrongheaded, believing that hard times would weed out the "unfit." Local charity organization societies regulated relief efforts to determine who was "worth" helping by prying into the circumstances of poor people's lives. Overall, public assistance and formal charities provided only marginal assistance to the jobless. The down and out more commonly relied on the kindness of family, friends, and neighbors. "The kind that always helps you out," observed one tramp, is "the kind that's in hard luck themselves, and knows what it is."

As millions of families faced starvation, labor organizations demanded that government help by creating jobs. In December 1893, declaring that "the right to work is the right to live," the annual convention of the AFL asked the federal government to issue $500 million in paper money to fund public works. Such demands augured a long-term shift (that would be completed only in the 1930s) in which working people and others gradually came to see the needs of the jobless as more than a local obligation in the manner of charity poor relief.

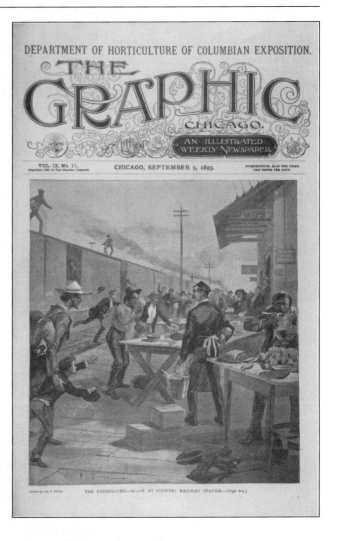

Riding the Rails in Search of Work

At a rural station, free soup and bread drew hungry unemployed people from their hiding places in railroad freight cars. Joseph P. Birren, *The Graphic*, September 9, 1893 — Chicago Historical Society.

Workers on the March   Responding to their own misery and to the contempt of their social "betters," some unemployed workers began to mount protests. In 1894, Ohio businessman Jacob S. Coxey organized a march in

Keep Off the Grass!: Coxey's Army Invades the Nation's Capital

When Jacob Coxey tried to speak at the U.S. Capitol, police arrested him for walking on the grass. Fifty years to the day later, in 1944, Coxey finally delivered this speech from the steps of the U.S. Congress.

We stand here to remind Congress of its promise of returning prosperity should the Sherman act be repealed. We stand here to declare by our march of over 400 miles through difficulties and distress, a march unstained by even the slightest act which would bring the blush of shame to any, that we are law-abiding citizens, and as men our actions speak louder than words We are here to petition for legislation which will furnish employment for every man able and willing to work; for legislation which will bring universal prosperity and emancipate our beloved country from financial bondage to the descendants of King George. We have come to the only source which is competent to aid the people in their day of dire distress. We are here to tell our Representatives, who hold their seats by grace of our ballots, that the struggle for existence has become too fierce and relentless. We come and throw up our defenseless hands, and say, help, or we and our loved ones must perish. We are engaged in a bitter and cruel war with the enemies of all mankind—a war with hunger, wretchedness, and despair, and we ask Congress to heed our petitions and issue for the nation's good a sufficient volume of the same kind of money which carried the country through one awful war and saved the life of the nation.

J. S. COXEY
Commander of the Commonweal of Christ

Congressional Record, 53rd Cong., 2d sess. (9 May 1894): 4512. Reprinted in George Brown Tindall, ed., *A Populist Reader: Selections from the Works of American Populist Leaders* (New York: Harper & Row, 1966), 160–163.

support of his own job creation scheme that emphasized federal spending on public works. To publicize the plan, Coxey recruited an "industrial army" of the unemployed to march on Washington, D.C. "We will send a petition to Washington with boots on," Coxey declared.

Thousands cheered Coxey's band of a few hundred marchers as they moved from one industrial town to another. Thorstein Veblen, a young sociologist, saw the march as more significant than its size suggested. Coxey's appeal to the federal government for relief, Veblen argued, asserted that government had a basic responsibility for the people's welfare, a radical notion at the time—and one that the federal government did not share. Although Coxey's band numbered fewer than 500 when they arrived in Washington on the morning of May 1, 1894, worried national officials had massed 1,500 troops to greet them. Police arrested Coxey and two other

On the Road to Washington, D.C.
Members of Coxey's Army marched into Alleghany, Virginia, their progress marked by a Chicago reporter on horseback. *Frank Leslie's Illustrated Newspaper*, April 19, 1894 — American Social History Project.

leaders for carrying banners on the Capitol grounds, and the marchers disbanded.

Nevertheless, Coxey's movement inspired dozens of industrial armies to set out for Washington that year. In the Far West, their ranks numbered in the thousands. Most traveled on foot, but they sometimes seized trains. The federal government moved as forcefully against them as it had against Coxey. U.S. Attorney General Richard C. Olney, a former railroad lawyer, deployed U.S. marshals and federal troops to end the train seizures. Although troops stopped the hijackings and curtailed the eastward movement of the armies, about 1,200 marchers made the cross-country trek all the way to Washington during 1894.

Olney also fought the protestors on another front: the courts, which stifled protests and especially labor activities by issuing injunctions. Injunctions had begun to be used against the 1877 railroad strikes, and they grew in number and importance in the 1880s. In some of the key struggles of the 1890s, court injunctions would prove to be a powerful antilabor weapon.

Pullman: Solidarity and Defeat   The defeat of Coxey's Army did not end the escalating conflict between the haves and the have-nots. As the depression worsened, Olney used federal troops and injunctions to quell a major strike against the Pullman Palace Car Company, but this time, a violent confrontation erupted.

Contemporaries knew the Pullman Company not only for its famous railroad sleeping cars, but also for its "model" company town: Pullman, Illinois, just south of Chicago. The company charged rents that were 20 to 25 percent higher than rents for similar housing in Chicago and made huge

King Debs

Eugene Debs, president of the American Railway Union, was lambasted by much of the press during the Pullman strike. This *Harper's Weekly* cartoon, like many other published pictures, portrayed Debs as a tyrant paralyzing the country's commerce, but it also made his face familiar to readers across the nation. William A. Rogers, *Harper's Weekly*, July 14, 1894 — Scott Molloy Labor Archives.

profits on utility bills, which, like the rent, they deducted from workers' pay. "We are born in a Pullman house," one employee declared, "fed from the Pullman shop, taught in the Pullman school, catechized in the Pullman church, and when we die we shall be buried in the Pullman cemetery and go to the Pullman hell."

As the depression worsened, George Pullman responded by firing one-third of his employees, cutting the wages of the rest by 25 to 40 percent, and refusing to reduce rents or food prices at the company store. Rebuffed in their efforts at negotiating with the company, Pullman workers walked off the job on May 11, 1894. "Pullman, both the man and the town," the strikers declared, "is an ulcer on the body politic." A local minister put it even more pungently: "George is a bad egg—handle him with care. Should you crack his shell the odor would depopulate Chicago in an hour."

The strikers appealed to the American Railway Union (ARU) for support. Formed in 1893 by charismatic activist Eugene V. Debs and a group of western railroad workers who were still in the Knights of Labor, the ARU was the fastest-growing union in the United States. It had over 150,000 members, more than all the other railroad unions combined. The ARU offered a new model of industrial unionism. It charged low dues and—in contrast to the craft-oriented AFL—accepted all white wage workers employed by railroads, whatever their skill levels or specific jobs. "Even the laundresses who cleaned the sheets from the sleeping compartments" could join, reported Florence Kelley, the chief factory inspector of Illinois. But despite Debs's attempt to admit them, the union excluded African Americans.

"... An Ulcer on the Body Politic": A Pullman Striker Speaks Out

The men and women who labored in George Pullman's "model" town during the 1893 depression endured starvation wages and deplorable living and working conditions. They especially loathed Pullman's paternalistic control over all aspects of their lives. This statement from a Pullman striker, delivered at the June 1894 Chicago convention of the American Railway Union, suggests the depth of the strikers' hatred of their employer and their commitment to the ARU.

We struck at Pullman because we were without hope. We joined the American Railway Union because it gave us a glimmer of hope. Twenty thousand souls, men, women, and little ones, have their eyes turned toward this convention today, straining eagerly through dark despondency for a glimmer of the heaven-sent message you alone can give us on this earth.

In stating to this body our grievances it is hard to tell where to begin. . . . Five reductions in wages, work, and in conditions of employment swept through the shops at Pullman between May and December 1893. The last was the most severe, amounting to nearly 30 percent and our rents had not fallen. . . . No man or woman of us all can ever hope to own one inch of George Pullman's land. Why even the very streets are his. . . .

Pullman, both the man and the town, is an ulcer on the body politic. He owns the houses, the schoolhouses, the churches of God. . . . The revenue he derives from these, the wages he pays out with one hand—the Pullman Palace Car Company, he takes back with the other—the Pullman Land Association. He is able by this to bid under any contract car shop in the country. His competitors in business, to meet this, must reduce the wages of their men. . . . And thus the merry war—the dance of skeletons bathed in human tears—goes on, and it will go on, brothers, forever, unless you, the American Railway Union, stop it; end it; crush it out.

U.S. Strike Commission, *Report on the Chicago Strike of June–July 1894* (1895).

The ARU called for a boycott and a strike against all trains hauling Pullman cars. Because nearly every railroad had Pullmans, this meant a national strike and a far more crippling one than the great railroad strikes of 1877. Unlike the largely spontaneous revolt of 1877, the ARU carefully organized the Pullman strike. Committees across the country coordinated their activities with the strike's headquarters in Chicago. When the boycott started on June 26, the General Managers' Association, an organization of twenty-six railroads operating in Chicago, ordered the discharge of any workers who refused to handle Pullman cars. In response, ARU members around the country brought most of the nation's rail traffic to a halt. Thus, an isolated labor dispute became, in Debs's words, "a contest between the producing classes and the money power of the country." An estimated 260,000 railroad workers joined the battle.

"GIVING THE BUTT"—THE WAY THE "REGULAR" INFANTRY TACKLES A MOB.

"Chicago Under the Mob"
An ardent admirer of the military, artist-reporter Frederic Remington displayed no sympathy for the Pullman strikers in his reports for *Harper's Weekly*. Endorsing suppression, Remington described the strikers as a "malodorous crowd of foreign trash," talking "Hungarian or Polack, or whatever the stuff is." Frederic Remington, *Harper's Weekly*, July 21, 1894 — American Social History Project.

Then railroad managers played their trump card, appealing to Attorney General Olney, who still served on the boards of several railroads, for a sweeping injunction from the federal courts in early July that effectively outlawed the strike. Federal troops and state militia were then dispatched in six states. In Chicago, the arrival of the U.S. Army on the Fourth of July precipitated a violent confrontation with workers that left thirteen dead and more than fifty wounded and caused hundreds of thousands of dollars of damage to railroad property. Almost 3,000 U.S. deputy marshals backed the federal troops. Even the Chicago chief of police later described the deputies as nothing more than "thugs, thieves, and ex-convicts."

During the next week, violence erupted in twenty-six states. Freight cars and other equipment burned in railroad yards, destroying merchandise as well as railroad property. "The strike is now war," screamed a headline in the *Chicago Tribune*. By July 11, an estimated thirty-four people had died. When Debs and other ARU leaders were arrested for disobeying the injunction, the strike began to collapse. In the bitter aftermath, courts convicted Debs and other leaders of civil contempt and sentenced them to prison. The railroads blacklisted many strikers.

Although many prominent citizens criticized the handling of the strike, the notoriously conservative Supreme Court, in a case called *In Re Debs*, upheld the use of injunctions against strikes and unions. It decreed, in effect, that strikes were a conspiracy in restraint of trade. That decision laid the groundwork for the continued use of state militias, federal troops, and injunctions to defend the interests of capital and undercut the strength of the labor movement by preventing communication among striking locals and jailing strike leaders. These new legal tactics would cripple militant unionism for decades.

The Pullman strike sharpened the lines of class struggle. Like Homestead two years earlier, it reminded workers of the combined power of capitalists' private armies and the military force of the federal and state governments. Some labor leaders argued that workers could respond only by creating a labor party that would fight for political power in tandem with the unions' struggle for industrial justice. They viewed the Democrats and Republicans as more interested in party patronage than in the worker's lot. In part because of the defeat of the Pullman strike, ARU leaders joined other labor activists in uniting with a movement that until that time had been mostly agrarian. Urging labor to seek change at the ballot box rather than on the picket line, they joined with the rapidly rising People's Party, one of the largest and most powerful third parties in American history.

The Populist Moment

The People's Party and the larger populist movement shared with the Knights of Labor a communitarian and collective vision that challenged the acquisitive individualism of the Gilded Age. It had roots in the cooperative efforts of the Farmers' Alliance, which spread rapidly across rural America in the 1880s. By 1890, it had moved into politics and created the People's Party, which crafted a bold challenge to the status quo in its Omaha Platform. It won some dramatic victories in 1892 and four years later united behind the eloquent Democratic Party presidential candidate William Jennings Bryan, who powerfully challenged the gold standard. But William McKinley squarely defeated Bryan and quashed the Populist challenge to industrial capitalism.

The Farmers' Alliance and the People's Party   The Populists originated in the cooperative crusade of the Farmers' Alliance, which began in Texas in the late 1870s. This crusade, in turn, built on the efforts of the Grange, or Patrons of Husbandry, which for a decade had been promoting cooperative buying and selling across rural America. These cooperative efforts — stores, warehouses, insurance companies — sought to provide alternatives to the reviled middlemen and "furnishing merchants" who had a stranglehold over rural commerce. (See Chapter 1.) At its peak, the Farmers' Alliance claimed hundreds of thousands of members and supporters nationwide. Local chapters, or "suballiances," not only managed the thousands of cooperative enterprises, or "exchanges," but also helped members to recover stray animals and took vigilante action against thieves and ranchers who were greedy for grazing land. Headed by Charles Macune, the Alliance preached a simple message: "The Alliance is the people and the people are together."

Thousands of paid lecturers communicated this theme at local meetings, larger county gatherings, and massive Fourth of July encampments. Some were dynamic orators, such as "Sockless" Jerry Simpson of Kansas and Mary Elizabeth Lease, an activist in farmer, labor, and Irish nationalist circles and a brilliant speaker. Lease and her husband knew firsthand the difficulties of the farmer from a decade of struggling (and failing) to succeed on Kansas and Texas farms. Ironically, she became best known for declaring that farmers should "raise less corn and more hell" — a phrase that she apparently never uttered. The use of such profanity by a woman would have upset late-nineteenth-century audiences. When Lease spoke once of "the gates of hell," she had to explain to a shocked audience that she

Gift for the Grangers

This chromolithograph visually highlights the benefits of membership in the Grange, or Order of Patrons of Husbandry, an organization that was established in 1867 to assert the vital economic and social contributions of farmers. The movement culture of the Grangers gave pride of place to cultivation and cooperation in the fields and in the household. The celebration of agricultural manual labor at the center of the print is surrounded by scenes depicting the "Farmer's Fireside," a meeting of the "Grange in Session," a "Harvest Dance," and the biblical tale of "Ruth and Boaz" (in which Ruth's selfless harvest labor won the landowner's sympathy). Strobridge Lithography Company, *Gift for the Granger*, chromolithograph, 1873 — Prints and Photographs Division, Library of Congress.

was quoting the Bible. But if she was more decorous than history records, Lease still routinely made fiery speeches denouncing "a system which clothes rascals in robes and honesty in rags."

About one-fourth of Alliance members were women — more in some suballiances. Women gave speeches, wrote for Alliance publications, and ran business affairs. Women's activity in the Alliance reflected their position in the family. Most joined along with their husbands or fathers (and as a result were not required to pay dues). Betty Munn Gay, an activist in the Texas Alliance and a woman's rights advocate, explained that female Alliance members joined as "the companion and helpmeet of man." But she also noted that women had a distinctive interest in the Alliance's reform program since "whenever poverty or misfortune overtakes the family," women "are the chief sufferers." Gay knew this firsthand: her husband's death in 1880 had left her with a mortgaged farm to manage. Still, she found time to participate in the Farmer's Alliance, the Baptist Church, and the Socialist Party.

Spurred by the depression, the Alliance spread like wildfire in the early 1880s. In 1883, the Texas Alliance supported twenty-six lecturers in eleven

"... Monopoly Is the Master": A Populist Speech

The Populist leader Mary Elizabeth Lease held crowds of mid-western and southern farmers spellbound with her fiery oratory. In this selection from one of her many 1890 speeches to large audiences of Kansas farmers, Lease attacked the eastern moneyed interests, accusing them of dominating the lives of southern and western farmers.

This is a nation of inconsistencies. The Puritans fleeing from oppression became oppressors. We fought England for our liberty and put chains on four million of blacks. We wiped out slavery and our tariff laws and national banks began a system of white wage slavery worse than the first.

Wall Street owns the country. It is no longer a government of the people, by the people, and for the people, but a government of Wall Street, by Wall Street, and for Wall Street.

The great common people of this country are slaves, and monopoly is the master. The West and South are bound and prostrate before the manufacturing East.

Money rules, and our Vice-President is a London banker. Our laws are the output of a system which clothes rascals in robes and honesty in rags.

The [political] parties lie to us and the political speakers mislead us. . . . The politicians said we suffered from overproduction. Overproduction, when 10,000 little children, so statistics tell us, starve to death every year in the United States, and over 100,000 shopgirls in New York are forced to sell their virtue for the bread their niggardly wages deny them. . . .

We will stand by our homes and stay by our fireside by force if necessary, and we will not pay our debts to the loan-shark companies until the government pays its debts to us. The people are at bay; let the bloodhounds of money who dogged us thus far beware.

W. E. Connelley, ed., *History of Kansas, State and People* (1928).

counties, and by 1886, Texas membership had swelled to more than 100,000. Meeting in Waco in 1887, the Texas Alliance joined with farmers' groups from Louisiana, Arkansas, and Mississippi and resolved to send lecturers throughout the cotton belt. Farmers greeted them enthusiastically. Texas Alliance lecturer J. B. Barry went back to his native state of North Carolina to organize. "I met the farmers twenty-seven times and twenty-seven times they organized," he wrote back excitedly. "The farmers seem like unto ripe fruit—you can gather them by a gentle shake of the bush."

Though the Alliance merged the interests of dirt farmers and large planters, it spoke primarily to those who owned land and marketed crops. It did not address the problems of the dispossessed, however much its rhetoric appealed to wage earners or landless rural people. Tenant farmers

"... We Are Robbed of Our Means": A Farmer Protests the Railroads' Land Grab

This 1891 letter from a Minnesota farmer to Ignatius Donnelly, the popular author and champion of the agrarian cause, suggests the increasing desperation that drove plains farmers into taking collective action (punctuation and spelling corrected).

In the minds of the forlorn and the unprotected poor people of this and other states, I might say I am one of those poor and unprotected. . . . I settled on this land in good faith; built house and barn, broken up part of the land. Spent years of hard labor grubbing, fencing, and improving. Are they going to drive us out like trespassers . . . and give us away to the Corporations? How can they support them when we are robbed of our means? . . . We must decay and die from woe and sorrow. We are loyal citizens and do not intend to intrude on any Railroad Corporation. We believe and still do believe that the RR Co. has got no legal title to this land in question. We love our wives and children just as dearly as any of you. But how can we protect them, give them education as they should [get] when we are driven from sea to sea? . . .

Ignatius Donnelly Papers, Minnesota Historical Society, 1891.

had little cash for dues or literature and no produce to market cooperatively; what was more, they had to worry about antagonizing their landlords.

Most southern Alliance members opposed efforts to organize black farmers. Deeply racist and committed to the interests of landholders, they disliked sharecroppers and rural laborers. The Alliance therefore used its growing power to insist that other farmers' organizations drop black chapters when the organizations joined the Alliance. These racist attitudes weakened the movement of farmers, as it did that of labor.

Recognizing the potential of the Farmers' Alliance cooperative programs, however, black farmers organized similar groups. The Colored Farmers' National Alliance, which like the white Alliance emerged in Texas, claimed more than one million members by 1890. Its relationship with the white organization was various and changing, on both the national and local levels. Some white Alliance members accepted the black groups as they did black chapters of religious and fraternal organizations; others feared any organized black group and opposed them violently. In some places, black Alliance members created common cause with white ones by trading at Alliance stores, provoking white merchants to accuse the Alliance of stealing their business or of supplying black members with guns.

In 1889, members of the southern Alliance met in St. Louis with the smaller organization from the Great Plains. The groups did not merge, but they agreed on a platform that called for nationalizing the railroads, outlawing large landholding companies, abolishing national banks, and

Going to a Meeting

A rare photograph of a group of Populists near Dickinson City, Kansas, sometime during the 1890s. Kansas State Historical Society.

instituting a graduated income tax. Alliance leader Charles Macune introduced a plan that captured the imagination of farmers across the nation over the next few years. He proposed that the federal government create warehouses, or "subtreasuries," where farmers could store crops until prices climbed to acceptable levels. In return, they would receive loans, paid in certificates that would serve as money. In other words, the government would issue paper money and lend it to farmers, using their stored crops as collateral. The plan would replace and solidify, with government support, the Alliance's own cooperative efforts. If enacted, it would have challenged the control of banks and fostered inflation by helping farmers to pay back debts with cheaper money.

In 1890, the Alliance moved into electoral politics, capturing local Democratic parties in the Southwest. In the Plains states, Alliance members formed independent parties and campaigned extensively. Rural Kansas typically had open-air rallies of 25,000 people. Sixteen hundred wagons gathered for one meeting near Hastings, Nebraska. Such gatherings, in which farmers pulling up in their wagons could look back and see long trains of wagons converging on an encampment, forged the "movement culture" of populism. The movement seemed to transcend old sectional animosities, as it did on July 4, 1890, when North Carolina Alliance leader Leonidas Polk, who had fought with the Confederate Army, journeyed to Kansas, once a hotbed of Unionist sympathy. Speaking at an open-air rally of thousands of farmers, Polk declared, "I tell you that from New York to the Golden Gate the farmers have risen up and inaugurated a movement such as the world has never seen."

November's election results seemed to prove him right. In the South, the Alliance snared four governorships, eight state legislatures, and more than forty seats in the U.S. House of Representatives. In Kansas, Alliance supporters won four-fifths of the seats in the state House of Representatives. In Nebraska, they allied with the Democrats to capture the governorship, and a young Democrat named William Jennings Bryan got himself elected to Congress by courting Populist votes. Buoyed by these successes, Alliance activists began to think seriously about launching a national political party. With a Republican president (Benjamin Harrison) and Senate and a Democratic House of Representatives, the national government seemed mired in stalemate while economic conditions deteriorated.

The Omaha Platform   Although an agricultural depression weakened the Alliance in the South over the next two years, the movement continued to expand in the Midwest and the West. The People's Party held its first convention in July 1892, in Omaha, Nebraska. Thirteen hundred delegates adopted a platform that combined a biting attack on economic and social conditions with a hopeful call to action. "We meet in the midst of a nation brought to the verge of moral, political, and material ruin," declared the preamble. "The fruits of toil of millions are boldly stolen to build up colossal fortunes for a few, unprecedented in the history of mankind; and the possessors of these, in turn, despise the Republic and endanger liberty."

The Omaha Platform, as it was called, embodied a new and bold vision of the power and reach of the federal government. Some planks spoke directly to farmers. They called, for example, for "free" (unrestricted) coinage of silver, a scheme to help cash-poor farmers by increasing the amount of currency in circulation, for government ownership of railroads and telegraph lines, and for Macune's subtreasury system. Other planks had broader appeal: direct election of U.S. senators (who were then still elected by state legislatures); restriction of presidents to a single term; a graduated income tax in which the rich would pay a higher percentage than the poor; and the initiative and referendum, which enabled voters to initiate and enact laws, ensuring democratic participation in decision making on major issues. Calls for an eight-hour workday and for immigration restriction appealed to organized labor.

At its height, the Populists represented the largest and most powerful movement that had ever attempted to transform the American economic and political system and to curb the power of financiers and capitalists. The Populist platform spelled out a radical alternative to corporate capitalism, offering a vision of popular leadership and a democratic "cooperative commonwealth." This new vision sprang directly from the cooperative movement. The opposition that cooperatives had received from furnishing merchants, wholesalers, cotton buyers, grain elevator companies, and bankers had given Alliance members a new understanding of their relationship with commercial elements of American society, spawning a culture of political revolt.

In the 1892 elections, Populists won more than one million votes and elected governors in Kansas and Colorado. Miners helped to put Populist Davis Waite into the Colorado governor's mansion, after which Colorado became one of the most prolabor states in the nation. Presidential candidate James B. Weaver (a former Union general whose presence on the ticket was balanced by running mate James G. Field, a former Confederate major who had lost a leg in battle) became the first third-party candidate since the Civil War to win any electoral votes, capturing Kansas, Colorado, Nevada, and Idaho as well as sharing in the electoral votes of North Dakota and Oregon (Map 3.1).

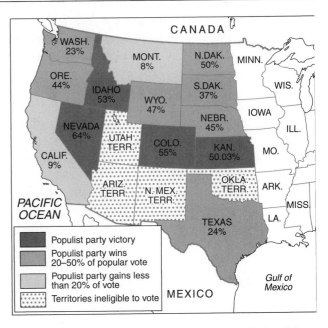

MAP 3.1 The Winning of the West: Populism in 1892

In the 1892 elections, the Populists became the first third party since the 1860s to capture any electoral votes. This map shows the percentage of the popular vote received by Populist presidential candidate James Weaver in the West, where he ran particularly strongly. At the same time, voters elected Populist governors in Kansas and Colorado.

Still, the more dramatic result of the 1892 elections was the triumph of the Democrats, who had already regained control of Congress two years before. Now they defeated incumbent Republican President Benjamin Harrison and returned to that office Grover Cleveland, who had won the presidency in 1884 and then had lost it to Harrison in 1888. Although Republicans dominated the presidency in the late nineteenth century, the nation was actually very closely divided between the two major parties, with small differences in the vote determining the outcome of elections. In these years, Republicans usually controlled the Senate and Democrats controlled the House, with few seats changing hands in any election.

The Cross of Gold   By the time the stock market crashed in 1893, many labor activists were looking to electoral politics for solutions to some of the problems created by the rise of industrial capitalism. Populist successes made such political action look viable, despite a wide spectrum of opinion. While many working people were too angry and desperate to believe in the electoral process, their support for more militant action had diminished with the defeat of the 1892 Homestead steel strike.

Socialists in the labor movement urged the formation of an independent political movement, modeled on socialist parties in industrialized Europe. Calling trade unions "impotent," unable to "cope with the great power of concentrated wealth," socialists had persuaded the 1892 AFL convention to endorse two planks from the Populist platform: the initiative and referendum and federal ownership of telegraph and telephone lines. The next year, in the midst of depression, the convention adopted the entire socialist political program, calling for nationalization of railroads and mines, the eight-hour workday, abolition of sweatshops, government inspection of mines and factories, and municipal ownership of public utilities.

All over the country, labor activists got into politics during 1894. Two hundred trade unionists ran for political office. Populist leaders, too, had concluded that to grow, the party would have to attract urban workers and create an alliance of farmers and laborers. Though Samuel Gompers dismissed such an alliance as "unnatural," AFL members had long supported cooperation between poor workers and farmers. That cooperation emerged in Illinois, when Chicago labor leaders and downstate agrarian activists sought to overcome their ideological differences and launch a united Populist movement in the 1894 congressional elections.

On Election Day, many Illinois coal miners and railroad workers voted Populist. The party did well in Milwaukee, the Ohio Valley coal communities, and the Irish Catholic mining regions of the West. But the Republicans captured the most votes in workers' districts, in part because the Populists drew support away from the Democrats. Appealing to narrow economic interests and ethnic loyalties, Republicans won many workingmen over to the notion that a protective tariff on foreign goods was the key to "a full dinner pail" for all. In the biggest victory in the history of Congress, the Republicans gained 117 seats and became the clear-cut majority party. The 1894 elections had broken through the deadlock of two-party competition and stalemate that had dominated American politics since the Civil War.

Still, Republicans and Democrats had to take the Populists seriously. They had gained more than 1.5 million votes in 1894, half again the number they had received in 1892. To win back supporters, Democrats began selectively to endorse parts of the Populist program. In 1896, facing almost certain defeat, the Democratic rank and file moved to adopt one of the planks in the Populist platform: the call for free coinage of silver. This issue appealingly united the interests of miners (and even mine owners) with those of credit-starved farmers.

The free-silver issue had its roots in the years before 1873, when the U.S. Treasury had made both silver and gold into money, at a fixed ratio: 16 ounces of silver equaled one ounce of gold. The system worked until the price of silver rose on world markets. Then, with silver coins worth more than their face value, people melted them down, and the coins disappeared from circulation. In 1873, the government abandoned silver as a medium of exchange.

After prospectors discovered silver in Nevada and Arizona, its price fell dramatically on world markets in the spring of 1893. Hoping to prop up its value, hard-hit western mining interests pressed to resume the coinage of

The Supreme Court — as It May Hereafter Be Constituted

Puck presented an unabashedly cosmopolitan view of how the Supreme Court might appear if the Populists won the 1896 election. "Gold Bugs and Millionaires" huddle in a "waiting pen," their fate in the hands of nine justices who collectively embody the rustic "old geezer" stereotype: sporting unkempt goatees, their dress severe but informal, their behavior unsophisticated in its lack of ceremony. Frederick B. Opper, *Puck*, September 9, 1896 — New-York Historical Society.

silver at the old 16-to-1 ratio. Bringing silver back into the Treasury would also expand the supply of currency, which was in high demand for industrial and commercial purposes. Farmers joined the campaign to increase the money supply. Strapped with debt and vulnerable to falling cotton and grain prices, they wanted inflation, which would allow them to pay off their debts with cheaper dollars. Their creditors, on the other hand, supported "sound money," by which they meant gold.

The Populists' program went well beyond free silver. Indeed, some of the most prominent Populist leaders had argued against free silver at the 1892 Omaha convention. Congressman and Farmers' Alliance member Tom Watson of Georgia and urban social democrat Henry Demarest Lloyd both maintained that inflation would alienate wage earners and destroy the farmer-labor alliance. But prosilver sentiment ran deep in the country at large, especially after the Panic of 1893 and the sharp deflation that followed.

When silver prices plummeted during the spring of 1893, the American West felt the effect immediately. Mines closed, and owners cut wages in the few that remained open. Hundreds of thousands of people faced destitution in Colorado mining towns such as Aspen, where mine employment dropped from 2,500 to 150 within a week. Some places became ghost towns overnight; discontented idle miners gathered in others.

President Cleveland, a sound-money man, reacted to the crisis by persuading Congress to repeal an 1890 law requiring the government to purchase and coin silver. Meanwhile, gold reserves were being drained, partly by payments for foreign imports and partly because of a rash of redemptions by holders of treasury notes. To replenish the supply, in 1895, the president asked J. P. Morgan and a syndicate of private bankers to finance a purchase of gold. An outraged public saw Cleveland's action as a secret negotiation with Wall Street financiers.

At the 1896 convention, Democrats repudiated Cleveland and instead nominated William Jennings Bryan of Nebraska, the leader of the silver Democrats. The thirty-six-year-old Bryan's brilliant oratory transfixed the convention. Lashing out at Republican sound-money advocates, he declared, "You shall not press down upon the brow of labor this crown of thorns, you shall not crucify mankind on a cross of gold." Meeting soon afterward, the Populists endorsed Bryan, but for vice president they nominated Allianceman Tom Watson.

The Republicans put forth William McKinley of Ohio, an advocate of sound money. McKinley appealed to a middle class that was terrified of violent strikes and gun-toting bankrupt farmers. The campaign, one commentator remarked, "took the form of religious frenzy" as Republicans denounced Bryan as an anarchist and revolutionary. The *New York Times* even wrote an editorial declaring Bryan to be of "unsound mind" and endorsing the view of an "alienist" (as psychiatrists were then called) that the candidate was a "madman" and "paranoic reformer." McKinley won with 52 percent of the popular vote and 61 percent of the electoral college, the most lopsided margin in twenty-five years. Bryan ran strong in the South and the West, especially the silver-mining states (Map 3.2).

Republicans captured support from urban workingmen, especially white Protestant skilled workers in small and medium-sized midwestern cities. These men eyed the Democratic Party, dominated in the North by immigrants, Catholics, and unskilled workers, with growing suspicion and distaste. Many of them blamed the depression on President Cleveland and the Democrats, the party in power when the depression hit. The Republican

MAP 3.2   Crucified on a Cross of Gold? The Republican Triumph in 1896

Republican William McKinley won a decisive victory in 1896 by capturing the populous states of the Northeast and Midwest even while Democrat William Jennings Bryan carried the more rural South and West. The Republican victory in 1896 solidified that party's dominance in national politics, which would last until 1932.

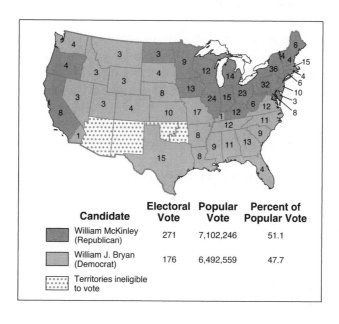

Candidate	Electoral Vote	Popular Vote	Percent of Popular Vote
William McKinley (Republican)	271	7,102,246	51.1
William J. Bryan (Democrat)	176	6,492,559	47.7
Territories ineligible to vote			

program included a high protective tariff that was intended to protect American business and to ease unemployment.

The presidential election of 1896
gave the Republicans control of both the
executive and legislative branches and
marked the end of Populism. Controversy over the decision to emphasize silver and endorse "fusion" with Bryan and
the Democrats soon tore the Populist
movement apart. Some leaders vigorously dissented from what they saw as
a wholesale desertion of the broad re-

"BLOWING" HIMSELF AROUND THE COUNTRY.

forms the Populists had once endorsed. Although the People's Party would
survive for twelve years, Populism and its hope of uniting the producing
classes of town and country had died.

***"Blowing" Himself Around the
Country***

In September 1896, this *Puck*
cartoon derided William
Jennings Bryan's candidacy,
showing him pumping out political promises from a bellows
marked "16 to 1" (the ratio of
silver coinage to gold proposed
by "soft money" reformers to
ease the farm families' economic plight). But the cartoon's
major target appears to be
rank-and-file Populists, portrayed as gullible, whiskered,
and ignorant. J. S. Pughe, *Puck*,
September 16, 1896 — New-York
Historical Society.

Racism Institutionalized and Challenged

Following his defeat in the 1896 election, Populist vice presidential candidate Tom Watson withdrew temporarily from politics. As an Allianceman,
he had urged white southern farmers to unite with black farmers. But Watson soon reemerged as an outspoken white supremacist, blaming African
Americans for the Populists' defeat. In later years, he expanded his attacks to
include Roman Catholics, Jews, and socialists. As Watson's case suggests,
racism became entrenched in American politics and culture as the nineteenth century came to a close.

In the 1880s, Southern states passed numerous segregation laws, a practice that the Supreme Court endorsed. In the 1890s, these states began to systematically disenfranchise black citizens. A horrifying wave of lynchings
swept across the South (Figure 3.1). Some black leaders fought back against
the racist tide, but others preached accommodation. Immigrants, especially
those now coming from Eastern and Southern Europe, also confronted
deep-seated prejudice from white Anglo-Saxon Protestants who viewed the
newcomers as members of an inferior race. These views fueled the rise of
nativist movements and efforts to restrict immigration.

Jim Crow Segregation and the Black Response   A generation of African
Americans had now been born and raised in freedom, with hopes and
expectations appropriate to free people. Nonetheless, de facto segregation
(segregation by social custom) had long dominated the South; schools,
poorhouses, cemeteries, trains, and boats were all segregated. In the late
1880s, a coalition of planters, urban elites, and Populists began to pass state

FIGURE 3.1   In Black and White: Eighty Years of Lynching

This graph illustrates the nearly five thousand deaths by lynching (broken down by race) that were officially recorded in the United States between 1882 and 1965. Lynchings of African Americans were at their worst in the 1890s, but the annual numbers remained high in the early twentieth century.

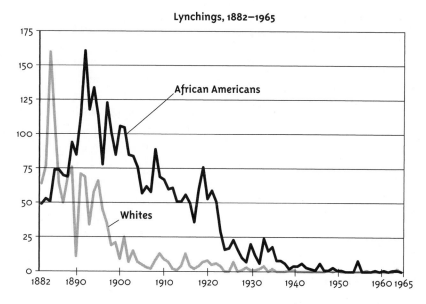

Lynchings, 1882–1965

Justice of the Peace

After the collapse of Reconstruction, some African Americans in the South continued to hold local elective positions, particularly those of sheriffs and judges. This 1889 engraving shows a black justice of the peace presiding over a Jacksonville, Florida, police court. Matthew Somerville Morgan, *Frank Leslie's Illustrated Newspaper*, February 23, 1889 — Prints and Photographs Division, Library of Congress.

and local laws codifying such customs. Thus began de jure segregation (segregation mandated by law).

Black people launched numerous legal challenges. Homer Plessy, who refused to sit in a segregated railroad car, took his case to the U.S. Supreme Court in 1896. In *Plessy v. Ferguson* the justices affirmed segregation, upholding the Louisiana statute that mandated separate railroad cars for white and black passengers and enshrining in law the constitutionality of "separate but equal" public facilities. Only one justice, John Marshall Harlan, dissented. "The thin guise of 'equal' accommodations," Harlan wrote, "will not mislead anyone, or atone for the wrong this day done." The historic decision was not overturned until 1954.

The *Plessy* decision opened the way for even more restrictive racial legislation. It cemented the imposition of "Jim Crow" laws, a system of racial discrimination, segregation of public facilities, and political disfranchisement that was enforced with terror and violence in the 1890s. (The term *Jim Crow* seems to have originated in a song-and-dance routine first performed by a blackface minstrel in the 1830s.) Industrial employers

"... Our Condition Is Precarious in the Extreme": A Plea to Stop Lynchings

The Reverend E. Malcolm Argyle of Arkansas describes the intensity of racist violence against African Americans during the 1890s and cries out for help. This report was printed in Philadelphia's Christian Recorder *on March 24, 1892.*

There is much uneasiness and unrest all over this State among our people, owing to the fact that [black] people all over the State are being lynched upon the slightest provocation. . . . In the last 30 days there have been not less than eight colored persons lynched in this State. At Texarkana a few days ago, a man was burnt at the stake. In Pine Bluff a few days later two men were strung up and shot. . . . At Varner, George Harris was taken from jail and shot for killing a white man, for poisoning his domestic happiness. At Wilmar, a boy was induced to confess to the commission of an outrage, upon promise of his liberty, and when he had confessed, he was strung up and shot. Over in Toneoke County, a whole family consisting of husband, wife and child were shot down like dogs. Verily the situation is alarming in the extreme.

At this writing 500 people are hovering upon wharves in Pine Bluff, awaiting the steamers to take them up the Arkansas River to Oklahoma. . . . What is the outcome of all this? It is evident that the white people of the South have no further use for the Negro. He is being worse treated now, than at any other time, since the [Confederate] surrender. The white press of the South seems to be subsidized by this lawless element, the white pulpits seem to condone lynching. . . . The Northern press seems to care little about the condition of the Negroes [in the] South. The pulpits of the North are passive. Will not some who are not in danger of their lives, speak out against the tyrannical South . . . speak out against these lynchings and mob violence? For God's sake, say or do something, for our condition is precarious in the extreme.

Christian Recorder (Philadelphia), March 24, 1892. Reprinted in Herbert Aptheker, ed., *A Documentary History of the Negro People in the United States*, vol. 2 (1970), 793–794.

extended Jim Crow to the job site, where it undercut the possibilities of labor solidarity by segregating black and white workers, offering privileges to one group and denying them to the other.

Disfranchising black men helped to enact and safeguard segregation. Many social and economic setbacks had followed the end of Reconstruction, but black men still retained their right to participate in politics in much of the South. Some even held elective office. In the 1890s, southern planters, industrialists, and merchants moved decisively to eliminate black

"The Colored Citizens Desire . . . That Some Action Be Taken": Ida B. Wells-Barnett's Antilynching Campaign

Tennessee newspaper editor Ida B. Wells-Barnett was the leader in a national effort to get the federal government to stop lynchings of African Americans. Despite her unstinting efforts, she never succeeded in securing a federal antilynching law before her death in 1931. In the following 1898 petition to President William McKinley, Wells-Barnett, accompanied by the Chicago delegation of Illinois congressmen, protested the lynching of a South Carolina African American postmaster. The federal government took no action.

Mr. President, the colored citizens of this country in general, and Chicago in particular, desire to respectfully urge that some action be taken by you as chief magistrate of this great nation, first for the apprehension and punishment of the lynchers of Postmaster Baker, of Lake City, S.C.; second, we ask indemnity for the widow and children, both for the murder of the husband and father, and for injuries sustained by themselves; third, we most earnestly desire that national legislation be enacted for the suppression of the national crime of lynching.

For nearly twenty years lynching crimes, which stand side by side with Armenian and Cuban outrages, have been committed and permitted by this Christian nation. Nowhere in the civilized world save the United States of America do men, possessing all civil and political power, go out in bands of 50 and 5,000 to hunt down, shoot, hang or burn to death a single individual, unarmed and absolutely powerless. Statistics show that nearly 10,000 American citizens have been lynched in the past 20 years. To our appeals for justice the stereotyped reply has been that the government could not interfere in a state matter. Postmaster Baker's case was a federal matter, pure and simple. He died at his post of duty in defense of his country's honor, as truly as did ever a soldier on the field of battle. We refuse to believe this country, so powerful to defend its citizens abroad, is unable to protect its citizens at home. Italy and China have been indemnified by this government for the lynching of their citizens. We ask that the government do as much for its own.

Cleveland Gazette, April 9, 1898. Reprinted in Herbert Aptheker, ed., A Documentary History of the Negro People in the United States, vol. 2 (1970), 798.

men from the political process. To consolidate their power, these southern leaders also disfranchised the poorest whites, who were prone to agrarian radicalism.

Beginning in Mississippi in 1890, southern governments imposed residency requirements, poll taxes, and literacy tests that disenfranchised black and, to a lesser extent, poor white voters. (Northern states also used literacy tests to disfranchise citizens born abroad.) South Carolina adopted Mississippi's formula in 1895; over the next twelve years, the remaining southern states followed suit. When someone pointed out that Virginia's constitutional convention was engaged in discrimination, future U.S. senator Carter Glass replied bluntly, "Discrimination! Why, that is precisely what we propose; that, exactly, is what this convention was elected for." Cities such as Wilmington, North Carolina, where African Americans and Populists joined forces to win elections, experienced the brutal consequences of resisting the return to white supremacy. A white mob organized by the Democratic Party leaders led a violent coup d'etat in 1898 that replaced the city's elected officials, destroyed the African American newspaper office, and drove hundred of African Americans out of town. Soon, little room remained for black men in the South to exercise the rights they had won a generation earlier (Map 3.3).

Northern political and business leaders acquiesced in these developments. As late as 1889, Republican leaders such as Henry Cabot Lodge, a leader in the anti-immigrant campaign, had supported African American voting rights because black votes sustained the southern GOP. But the sweeping Republican victory of 1896 removed that motivation. The Repub-

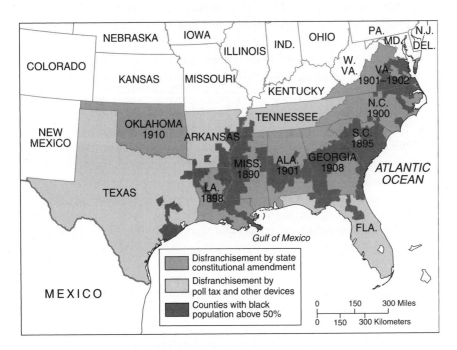

MAP 3.3 Disfranchisement in the New South

From 1890 to 1910, eight states across the South passed amendments to their state constitutions to disfranchise African Americans. These states had significant areas where African Americans were the majority. Texas, Arkansas, Tennessee, and Florida achieved the same ends through prohibitively high poll taxes, effectively denying African Americans in the South the right to vote.

Antilynching Crusader with the Family of a Lynching Victim

In 1892, Memphis, Tennessee, newspaper editor Ida B. Wells-Barnett revealed the role of local white businessmen in the lynching of three black competitors. She is shown here standing with Betsy Moss and her two children, the widow and orphans of Memphis grocer Tom Moss, one of the murdered black businessmen. A white mob destroyed Wells's office, and she was forced to flee north, where her public lectures and writing brought lynchings to national attention. W. F. Griffin — Special Collections, University of Chicago Library.

lican Party, which had been a channel of political activity for African American men for three decades, was effectively closed to them. With the Populists' electoral defeat and retreat into racism, the limited possibilities of Populism also faded.

Racism enhanced the Democrats' strength in the South. Although national elections went to the Republicans, disfranchisement of black southerners had effectively defused the regional Republican and the Populist threats, and by 1900, the South regularly voted Democratic. Racist ideology played an important role in ensuring this outcome, and violence and brutal terrorism reinforced it. Local officials felt no obligation to protect those who could not vote, hold public office, or serve on juries, and the federal government no longer oversaw black southerners' constitutional rights. White mobs, serving as prosecutor, judge, jury, and executioner, tortured and murdered black men for alleged wrongdoings or the "crime" of prospering economically under the reign of Jim Crow. In the 1880s and 1890s, white Southerners lynched more than 100 African Americans each year. They used lynching not only as a ritual of social control, but also as recreation; families brought their children, and mobs dispensed body parts as souvenirs.

Led by journalist and lecturer Ida B. Wells-Barnett, African Americans formed a national antilynching movement to protest the wave of violence. "Nowhere in the civilized world save the United States of America," Wells-Barnett wrote in a petition to President McKinley protesting the lynching of a black South Carolina postmaster, "do men . . . go out in bands of 50 and 5,000 to hunt down, shoot, hang or burn to death a single individual, unarmed and absolutely powerless." She exposed the myth that most lynchings defended white womanhood and instead emphasized white men's fear of economic competition from blacks. Local whites had killed the South Carolina postmaster because his recent appointment to the federal post enraged them; when his wife, their baby in her arms, sought to comfort her dying husband, another bullet crashed through the infant's skull.

Wells-Barnett was the most visible of the many black women who assumed a growing role in the public sphere after black men lost their rights. After their husbands, brothers, and sons were disfranchised, black women whose political skills had been nurtured in churches, temperance organizations, and Republican Party auxiliaries developed the ideology, political strategies, and organizational structure to carry on. African American women emerged as the "diplomats" to the white community.

The single most influential black leader, however, was a man: Booker T. Washington. Born a slave in 1858, Washington had worked as a laborer and domestic servant after the Civil War, eventually fulfilling his dream of attending Virginia's Hampton Institute. In 1881, he founded Tuskegee Institute in Alabama and modeled it on Hampton's industrial education program. The school trained African Americans to work with their hands, on the theory that market economics discriminated between the trained and the untrained rather than between black and white. Tuskegee eventually attracted support from the richest white people in America, including Andrew Carnegie.

Washington asserted that black people should accommodate themselves to white power. "Cast down your buckets where you are," he urged them in his famous 1895 Atlanta Exposition Address. "In all things that are purely social," he reassured white Americans, "we can be as separate as the fingers, yet one as the hand in all things essential to mutual progress." Washington's accommodationist language appealed to white politicians and businessmen eager to roll back black voting rights and secure a docile labor force. His relationships with the white political and economic elite gave him the opportunity to work behind the scenes to influence politics and the power to dispense money and patronage jobs to African Americans—power he preserved ruthlessly and sometimes duplicitously.

Washington's most significant black adversary was W. E. B. DuBois, the preeminent African American intellectual of the twentieth century. The terms of their debate reflected the inherent tension between capitalism and democracy. DuBois attacked Washington's Atlanta speech, accusing Washington of accepting segregation and forsaking political rights to obtain economic goals. But Washington actually supported some direct challenges to segregation and even cooperated secretly with DuBois on a test of Tennessee's Jim Crow law.

The New Immigrants   In the South, segregation and political disfranchisement confined African Americans to the lowest-paying jobs. In the crowded cities of the Northeast and Midwest, newly arrived Slavic and Italian immigrants tended to hold those less-skilled positions. Established immigrants and their American-born children had plenty of opportunity to move into the ranks of foremen and skilled laborers. Because they spoke English, they could also get the new clerical, sales, and managerial jobs. Unskilled and semiskilled workers typically earned less than half what skilled workers received. Skilled and less-skilled workers lived differently, fought separately for their rights, and had distinctly different relationships with their employers.

As in the past, the new immigrants were fleeing economic and political turmoil. Rapid population growth had put tremendous pressure on European peasant economies, and sons were inheriting ever-smaller plots of farmland. New technologies had cheapened shipping, which meant that European farmers faced competition from Canada, the United States, and Argentina. Peasants who lost their farms fell into the ranks of agricultural and urban wage laborers.

Eastern European Jews faced different problems. Living in crowded towns on the western edge of the Russian Empire, they were legally prohibited from owning land; most engaged in trade or artisan labor. Industrialization was undermining their traditional ways of life, and anti-Semitism made them scapegoats for the region's economic problems.

As change swept Eastern and Southern Europe, some displaced farmers and workers responded with protests, but millions of other individuals found emigration a more sensible option. Janos Kovacs, a Hungarian peasant who could "earn only enough for bread and water," concluded

"I Am Obliged to Reside in America": A Gay Immigrant Tells His Story in 1882

The reasons immigrants had for leaving their homelands and coming to America were as diverse as the backgrounds of the immigrants themselves. Although most immigrants came to the United States for economic reasons some sought a new home because of persecution based on their politics, their religious beliefs, or even their sexual orientation. In this 1882 letter sent to medical writer and sexologist Dr. Richard von Krafft-Ebing, a thirty-eight-year-old German-born merchant explained how a homosexual arrest in his homeland forced him to emigrate to the United States.

Until I was twenty-eight years old I had no suspicion that there were others constituted like myself. One evening in the castle garden at X, where, as I subsequently found, those constituted like myself were accustomed to seek and find each other, I met a man who powerfully excited my sexual feelings, so much so that I had a seminal emission. . . .

I know of a case in Geneva where an admirable attachment between two men like myself has existed for seven years. If it were possible to have a pledge of such a love they might well make pretensions to marriage. . . . One thing is true. Our loves bear as fair and noble flowers incite to as praiseworthy efforts as does the love of man for the woman of his affections. There are the same sacrifices, the same joy in abnegation even to the laying down of life, the same pain, the same joy, sorrow, happiness, as with men of ordinary natures. . . .

In consequence of the disgrace which came upon me in my fatherland I am obliged to reside in America. Even now I am in constant anxiety lest what befell me at home should be discovered here and thus deprive me of the respect of my fellow-men.

Richard Von Krafft-Ebing, "Perversion of the Sexual Instinct? Report of Cases," trans. H. M. Jewett, *Alienist and Neurologist* (St. Louis, Missouri), vol. 9, no. 4 (Oct. 1888). Reprinted in *American History: Lesbians and Gay Men in the U.S.A.*, ed. Jonathan Katz (New York: Avon Books, 1976), 59–60.

"there was but one hope, America." Other peasants and workers moved to Canada, Argentina, Australia, and the more prosperous industrial regions of Europe.

The vast majority of emigrants were young. Italian and Slavic men left home without their families, hoping to earn enough money to return to their homelands and marry, buy land, or set up small businesses. Many actually did so, especially Italians. Jews, who were fleeing religious and legal persecution as well as economic adversity, usually came in family groups and seldom returned to their homelands.

Although immigrants' reasons for coming to America in the 1880s and 1890s resembled those of earlier decades, these newcomers faced greater

Mug Shot

A police department arrest record reflects the faith in data and science espoused by some reformers. The reputedly scientific measurements instituted by French anthropologist Alphonse Bertillon claimed to use physical evidence to detect innate criminality and other character flaws, many associated with particular ethnic and racial groups. American Social History Project.

prejudice than had all earlier groups except the Irish and the Chinese. Like the Irish in the 1840s and 1850s, these people were the poorest and least assimilated of the new Americans, and they became targets of nativist, anti-immigrant sentiment. And unlike many earlier immigrants, who were Protestant, most of the new immigrants were Catholic or Jewish, and few spoke English. Because their agricultural and handcraft skills had little value in a rapidly advancing industrial economy, they entered the workforce as unskilled or semiskilled laborers.

The new immigrants also encountered racism. The old elites—white, Protestant, English speaking—regarded them as members of an inferior race and warned that WASPs (White Anglo-Saxon Protestants) were committing "race suicide" by having fewer children than the newcomers. Journalists and politicians equated the physical characteristics of different national groups with mental and moral qualities. Phrases such as "the Hebrew race" or "the Slavic races" appeared routinely in popular journalism. "You don't call . . . an Italian a white man?" a Congressman asked a West Coast construction boss at a hearing. "No, sir," was the reply, "an Italian is a Dago." White Southerners lynched Jews, Italians, and other immigrants, albeit much less frequently than African Americans.

Nativism and Immigration Restriction The 1890s saw a rise in anti-immigrant sentiment, which had many sources. Nativists played on fears of violence and of the diversity of thought, belief, and custom represented by Europeans. Reformers blamed immigrants for municipal corruption. Workingmen's organizations claimed that immigrants kept wages low. Militant Protestants called Catholic immigrants pawns of Romanism. The popular press blamed them for political turmoil. Even those who sympathized with immigrants condemned them for their poverty and their peasant habits.

The perceived threat of foreign-born radicals also fed nativism. Seven of the eight accused conspirators in the Haymarket affair of 1886 were immigrants. In response, the press spouted nativist rhetoric, and anti-immigrant groups formed across the country. Three weeks after Haymarket, a railroad attorney organized the American Party in California, declaring that Americans must exclude "the restless revolutionary horde of foreigners who are now seeking our shores from every part of the world."

The United States had restricted immigration for the first time in 1882, through the Chinese Exclusion Act and a law denying entrance to paupers and convicts. In 1891, a new immigration law gave the federal government complete authority over immigration and created national administrative mechanisms for its control. The law made it illegal for employers to advertise abroad for workers, and it excluded people with contagious diseases. It created provisions for expelling undesirable aliens, requiring that steamship companies return rejected immigrants to Europe. On January 1, 1892, the

Charting the "Undesirable Races"

A publication distributed by the Immigration Restriction League graphically demonstrates the rise in the proportion of immigrants from "less desirable races of Southern and Eastern Europe." The League was alarmed by the ways "new immigrants" differed from previous newcomers in the categories of illiteracy, lack of money and occupation, and the tendency to gather in crowded cities. The League relied on pseudo-scientific evidence to bolster its claims. Publications of the Immigration Restriction League, No. 38 — Prints and Photographs Division, Library of Congress.

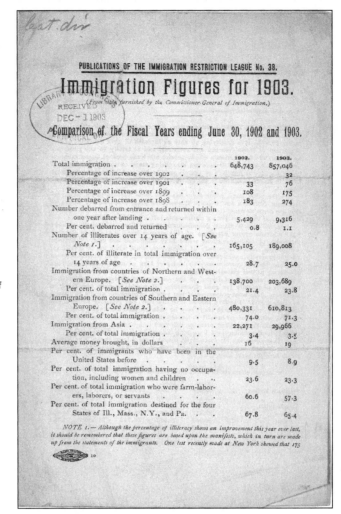

PUBLICATIONS OF THE IMMIGRATION RESTRICTION LEAGUE No. 38.

Immigration Figures for 1903.

(From lists furnished by the Commissioner-General of Immigration.)

Comparison of the Fiscal Years ending June 30, 1902 and 1903.

	1902.	1903.
Total immigration	648,743	857,046
Percentage of increase over 1902		32
Percentage of increase over 1901	33	76
Percentage of increase over 1899	108	175
Percentage of increase over 1898	183	274
Number debarred from entrance and returned within one year after landing	5,429	9,316
Per cent. debarred and returned	0.8	1.1
Number of illiterates over 14 years of age. [See Note 1.]	165,105	189,008
Per cent. of illiterate in total immigration over 14 years of age	28.7	25.0
Immigration from countries of Northern and Western Europe. [See Note 2.]	138,700	203,689
Per cent. of total immigration	21.4	23.8
Immigration from countries of Southern and Eastern Europe. [See Note 2.]	480,331	610,813
Per cent. of total immigration	74.0	71.3
Immigration from Asia	22,271	29,966
Per cent. of total immigration	3.4	3.5
Average money brought, in dollars	16	19
Per cent. of immigrants who have been in the United States before	9.5	8.9
Per cent. of total immigration having no occupation, including women and children	23.6	23.3
Per cent. of total immigration who were farm-laborers, laborers, or servants	60.6	57.3
Per cent. of total immigration destined for the four States of Ill., Mass., N.Y., and Pa.	67.8	65.4

NOTE 1.— *Although the percentage of illiteracy shows an improvement this year over last, it should be remembered that these figures are based upon the manifests, which in turn are made up from the statements of the immigrants. One test recently made at New York showed that 175*

Ellis Island immigration depot opened. Medical inspections were performed there, but only for steerage passengers; those who paid for first- or second-class passage received perfunctory inspections in their cabins.

American nativism often took the form of anti-Catholicism. In 1887, the American Protective Association (APA) organized to drive Irish Catholics out of American politics and soon claimed a half-million members, all of whom took an oath never to vote for a Catholic. The APA explicitly blamed the depression on Catholics, asserting that immigrants had taken the jobs of native-born Americans.

Immigration restriction was one highlight of the Republican platform of 1896, which called for laws to exclude those who could not pass a literacy test in their native language. Such tests would discriminate against peasants

At Bay

A newspaper engraving depicts an attack on an Italian strike-breaker during the 1882 New York freight handlers' strike. Although shown as a victim, the Italian's "exotic" dress and earring marked him as an outsider to contemporary readers. A. B. Shults, *Frank Leslie's Illustrated Newspaper*, August 5, 1882 — American Social History Project.

from Eastern and Southern Europe. Restrictive laws, the platform claimed, would protect the United States by defending American citizenship and "the wages of our workingmen against the fatal competition of low-price labor."

The Immigration Restriction League, a forum for nativism founded in 1893 by a group of Harvard graduates from old Boston families, had advanced the idea of a literacy test. For them, the flood of foreign poor dramatized and symbolized the problems raised by the expanding urban working class. The League drew a line between "old" and "new" foreigners. Like many other native-born Americans, its members regarded the new immigrants from Southern and Eastern Europe as racially distinct from old-stock Anglo-Saxons. This distinction became the linchpin of the anti-immigration crusade.

Most advocates of restriction were Republicans, but nativism and nativist racism permeated all corners of American politics. Populists incorporated anti-Semitism in their rhetoric, and labor activists, seeking an explanation for the sudden sharp drop in their fortunes, embraced anti-immigrant ideas. On the Pacific Coast, labor organizations had long advocated immigration restriction. Building on white workers' fears of competition from Chinese immigrants, they lobbied actively for extension of the Chinese Exclusion Act when it came up for congressional renewal in 1892.

Employers were divided over immigration restriction. Before the depression, many businessmen had supported free immigration, although not necessarily out of tolerance or belief in a free market. New York's *Journal of Commerce* argued nakedly in 1892 that people, like cows, were expensive to produce; immigration represented a gift of a costly commodity. But the belief that immigrants brought labor strife, violence, and radicalism sometimes counterbalanced the desire for a cheap and steady labor supply. The *New York Tribune* called "Huns" (Hungarians and Slavs) the most dangerous of labor unionists and strikers: "They fill up with liquor and cannot be reasoned with."

Territorial and Economic Expansion

Strident nationalism and racism intensified into warmongering in the late 1890s, prompting America's entry into overseas adventures. In 1898, the United States gained its first real overseas empire as the result of the Spanish-Cuban-American War, winning control over Cuba, Puerto Rico, and the Philippines. Filipinos did not, however, acquiesce to American rule and fought a bloody (but unsuccessful) war against the United States. Some American anti-imperialists challenged this expansionist turn in American foreign policy.

But global economic expansion became the order of the day. Some industrialists responded to the 1893 panic by searching for new markets. And as American business recovered from the mid-1890s depression, it became not just more international, but also increasingly organized into giant corporations, the product of a frenzy of mergers. Initially, the AFL-affiliated craft unions also benefited from the economic recovery. But the new century brought a renewed corporate offensive against the labor movement.

The Ideology of Expansion   At the 1893 Columbian Exposition, historian Frederick Jackson Turner had famously proclaimed that the once great American frontier was now closed. Later historians would dispute his influential "frontier thesis," pointing out that the West had never been an empty and uncivilized frontier and that it still had much unoccupied land at the end of the century. But contemporaries embraced his analysis and argued that America would now need to look abroad for natural resources and economic expansion.

Around the same time, patriotism, once linked to egalitarian ideas of republican virtue, grew aggressive and jingoistic. New organizations such as the Daughters of the American Revolution promoted new forms of patriotism, such as a cult of the American flag, now saluted each morning in schools. Some conservatives championed war as the highest form of patriotism and a way of channeling the unrest of the depression years.

Many business, agricultural, and political leaders argued that to secure the nation's economic interests and absorb its surplus production, the United States should expand overseas and win access to international markets as well as resources. "We are raising more than we can consume," avowed Indiana Senator Albert J. Beveridge. "We are making more than we can use. Therefore, we must find new markets for our products, new occupations for our capital, new work for our labor." Recovery from the depression of the 1890s was achieved in part by Americans doing business in other countries, and by 1896, the nation's exports had begun to exceed its imports. American businesses also bought supplies and opened factories abroad. Singer sold sewing machines around the world — machines made in Scotland and Russia as well as New Jersey. International Harvester operated factories in six countries.

American companies attempting to expand abroad did not have some of the advantages of their counterparts in Britain, France, and Germany, which were carving out colonial empires in Asia and Africa. Such overseas empires — composed of countries administered by the mother country — extended the colonizers' political and military clout, giving their businesses special investment and marketing opportunities. Some Americans believed that colonies offered the United States the best chance to enter overseas markets. The nation's previous expansion, they noted, had entailed military conflict on the North American continent — with American Indians and, in the 1840s, with Mexico. Now, idealistic and convinced of their own racial superiority, some Americans were willing to risk further military conflict to follow the example of leading European nations. Such militaristic impulses were fostered by the widespread belief that going to war would bolster American "manhood," a quality that was seen as central to the political system.

The Spanish-Cuban-American War In 1898, proponents of overseas expansion got their chance when the United States entered the Spanish-Cuban-American War, a "splendid little war," in the words of Secretary of State John Hay. The immediate issue was Cuba's ongoing struggle for independence from Spain, 90 miles off the Florida coast. In 1895, Cuban guerrillas resumed their rebellion against Spanish rule and solicited popular sympathy and financial support in the United States. Sensationalized newspaper reports of the brutality of Spanish soldiers toward Cuban civilians fed popular support for U.S. involvement. In New York, William Randolph Hearst's *Journal* and Joseph Pulitzer's *World* competed for circulation by detailing Spanish atrocities. These papers and their imitators —

Competing for Readers

U.S. newspapers headlined stories about Spanish atrocities in Cuba and pressed for U.S. intervention. The papers often reported rumors as facts; the *New York Journal*, for example, distorted an incident involving a search of a Cuban woman by Spanish agents. The illustration showed what amounted to a sexual assault, but the event as pictured never occurred. Frederic Remington, *New York Journal* — Prints and Photographs Division, Library of Congress.

The Spanish Brute Adds Mutilation to Murder

Grant Hamilton's bestial Spaniard, bespattered by American blood, typifies how the U.S. press sensationalized news coverage and exploited patriotic sentiments to support U.S. intervention in Cuba. Grant Hamilton, *Judge*, July 9, 1898 — American Social History Project.

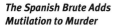

called the "yellow press" after cartoonist Richard Outcault's color comic strip "The Yellow Kid" — offered exaggerated foreign coverage with an unprecedented immediacy, thanks to new telegraph cables and fast printing presses.

On February 15, 1898, an unexplained explosion aboard the U.S. Navy's battleship *Maine*, which the U.S. government had sent into Havana Harbor to protect American citizens and property, killed 266 sailors. Congress blamed Spain and declared war in April, vowing in the Teller Amendment that the United States would guarantee Cuban independence. The public responded enthusiastically. "The newspapers, the theatrical posters, the street conversations for weeks had to do with war and bloodshed," settlement worker Jane Addams wrote of her Chicago neighborhood.

The United States also fought Spain in the Philippine Islands, where guerrillas led by Emilio Aguinaldo had been battling Spanish rule for two years. In 1897, Aguinaldo had gone into exile in Hong Kong. Two days after the U.S. Congress declared war, Commodore George Dewey sailed for Manila, with Aguinaldo on board. On May 1, 1898, the U.S. Navy arrived in Manila Bay, securing the harbor while the Filipino nationalist troops surrounded the capital city. Aguinaldo declared independence on June 12 (Map 3.4).

The U.S. military engagement in Cuba was brief: the U.S. Army and Marines landed in June, and Spanish power was

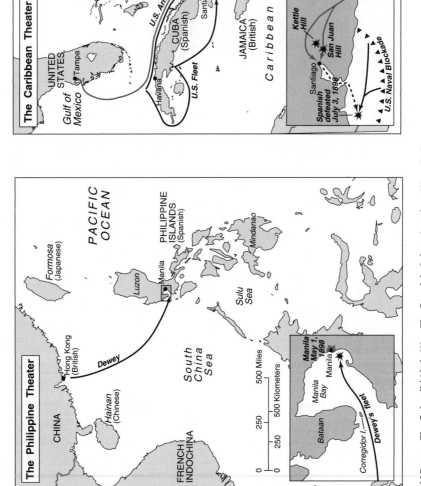

MAP 3.4   The Splendid Little War: The Spanish-Cuban-American War, 1898

In both theaters of the 1898 war against Spain, the United States triumphed quickly, in part because of its naval superiority. In the Philippines, Admiral George Dewey prevailed in a matter of days after the American declaration of war on April 25 and without the loss of a single American life. The Cuban conflict lasted a bit longer, but even there, the fighting was over by August. Before the United States entered the fighting, Cuban rebels had already brought Spain close to defeat.

broken in ten weeks. A young assistant secretary of the navy, Theodore Roosevelt, gained fame by quitting his job and leading a group of cavalry volunteers known as the Rough Riders. (The story of their horseback charge up San Juan Hill has often been retold, but the truth was more mundane than the myth. The Rough Riders were not actually on horseback — the horses had been accidentally left behind — and the hill they charged was nearby Kettle Hill. San Juan Hill sounded more exotic and romantic.) Many black soldiers, who had served in the West, joined the fight in Cuba. More than 10,000 black men, many of them from the North, answered the call for volunteers.

African American leaders, like white ones, divided over the Spanish-Cuban-American war. While Booker T. Washington saw volunteering for the war as an opportunity for black men "to show their loyalty to our land," other black leaders argued that men who were denied the franchise were not obliged to serve in the army. "In the South today," wrote Richmond editor John Mitchell, "exists a system of oppression as barbarous as that which is alleged to exist in Cuba."

An Overseas Empire   In December 1898, the Treaty of Paris ended the war. Spain relinquished its claim to Cuba, sold the Philippines to the United States for $20 million, and transferred the Caribbean island of Puerto Rico and the Pacific island of Guam to the United States without compensation. The United States wanted Puerto Rico as a naval station in the Caribbean and as a market for manufactured goods. U.S. troops had occupied the island in July, meeting little opposition. Not everyone welcomed the terms; Puerto Ricans had little voice in the transfer, and Filipinos were ready to fight for their country's independence.

Although Americans and Filipinos had united to drive the Spanish forces from the islands, their relationship deteriorated after Spain's surrender. Aguinaldo and his broad base of supporters declared independence and established a republic in June 1898, but the United States refused to recognize it. President William McKinley declared that he intended instead to use "every legitimate means for the enlargement of American trade" and that American occupation would "educate, uplift, and Christianize" the Filipinos — ignorant of the fact that many of them already practiced Catholicism. Filipinos were determined to resist; two days before the U.S. Senate ratified the Treaty of Paris in February 1899, Aguinaldo and his forces mounted armed opposition to American occupation.

Nearly 200,000 U.S. troops fought in the Philippine War to suppress the independence movement, killing 16,000 to 20,000 Filipino soldiers between 1899 and 1902. Hundreds of thousands of civilians died from war-related famine and disease. Racism heightened the war's brutality. U.S. newspapers portrayed Filipinos as dark-skinned savages; one report declared that "picking off niggers [Filipinos] in the water" was "more fun than a turkey shoot."

"A Perfect Hailstorm of Bullets": A Black Sergeant Remembers the Battle of San Juan Hill in 1899

The well-known but erroneous image of Teddy Roosevelt charging with his Rough Riders up San Juan Hill in Cuba displaced attention from the role of African American soldiers in Cuba such as Sergeant-Major Frank W. Pullen, Jr. Black soldiers made up almost 25 percent of the U.S. force in Cuba. In this excerpt, Pullen describes how black soldiers almost seemed to have two enemies during the battle of El Caney and the capture of Santiago: the Spaniards and white American soldiers.

No one knows who started the charge; one thing is certain, at the time it was made excitement was running high; each man was a captain for himself and fighting accordingly. Brigadier Generals, Colonels, Lieutenant-Colonels, Majors, etc., were not needed at the time the 25th Infantry made the charge on El Caney, and those officers simply watched the battle from convenient points, as Lieutenants and enlisted men made the charge alone. It has been reported that the 12th U.S. Infantry made the charge, assisted by the 25th Infantry, but it is a recorded fact that the 25th Infantry fought the battle alone, the 12th Infantry coming up after the firing had nearly ceased. Private T. C. Butler, Company H, 25th Infantry, was the first man to enter the blockhouse at El Caney, and took possession of the Spanish flag for his regiment. An officer of the 12th Infantry came up while Butler was in the house and ordered him to give up the flag, which he was compelled to do, but not until he had torn a piece off the flag to substantiate his report to his Colonel of the injustice which had been done to him. Thus, by using the authority given him by his shoulder-straps, this officer took for his regiment that which had been won by the hearts' blood of some of the bravest, though black, soldiers of Shafter's army.

A word more in regard to the charge. It was not the glorious run from the edge of some nearby thicket to the top of a small hill, as many may imagine. This particular charge was a tough, hard climb, over sharp, rising ground, which, were a man in perfect physical strength, he would climb slowly. Part of the charge was made over soft, plowed ground, a part through a lot of prickly pineapple plants and barbed-wire entanglements. It was slow, hard work, under a blazing July sun and a perfect hailstorm of bullets, which, thanks to the poor marksmanship of the Spaniards, "went high."

> Frank W. Pullen, Jr.
> Ex-Sergeant-Major 25th U.S. Infantry. Enfield, N.C., March 23, 1899

Edward A. Johnson, *History of Negro Soldiers in the Spanish-American War* (Raleigh, 1899), 29–32. Reprinted in William Loren Katz, *Eyewitness: The Negro in American History* (New York: Pittman Publishing, 1967), 383–384.

Civilization Begins at Home

A cartoon in the *New York World* derided President McKinley's claim to "uplift and christianize" the Philippines, graphically portraying the racial terrorism occurring in America's own backyard. C. G. Bush, *New York World* — American Social History Project.

Though U.S. troops captured Aguinaldo in 1901 and officially declared peace in 1902, armed conflict continued for another decade.

During the Spanish-Cuban-American war, the United States had also annexed the Hawaiian islands. An American-controlled sugar industry had been developing there for half a century. The sugar interests had established a government favorable to them in 1887, but it was ousted four years later by the new queen, Liliuokalani. In 1893, with the support of the U.S. Marines, a group of planters led by Sanford B. Dole overthrew the queen, and the American ambassador, John L. Stevens, acting on his own authority, proclaimed Hawaii an American protectorate. Dole asked Congress to annex the islands, but an investigation revealed that most Hawaiians opposed it. When the United States sent a special commissioner to restore the queen to her throne under a liberal constitution, Dole refused to step aside. In 1894, he proclaimed Hawaii a republic. After several years of political wrangling, the outbreak of war with Spain convinced politicians of the need for a coaling station in the Pacific by the expanding and steam-powered U.S. Navy. Congress approved Hawaii's annexation in July 1898, and it became a territory, with Dole as governor, in 1900.

Not all Americans endorsed the nation's overseas expansion. In November 1898, a group of prominent citizens founded the Anti-Imperialist League. The writer Mark Twain, former president Grover Cleveland, steel tycoon Andrew Carnegie, activist Jane Addams, and the AFL's Samuel Gompers became national officers or supporters. Addams hated imperialism because of her pacifism and internationalism. Carnegie argued as a capitalist: "Possession of colonies or dependencies is not necessary for trade reasons," he reasoned, pointing out that the United States was leading the world in exports without foreign possessions. Gompers employed the racist language he had long used against Chinese immigration. "If the Philippines are annexed," he asked, "how can we prevent the Chinese coolies from going to the Philippines and from there swarm into the United States and engulf our people and our civilization?"

However prominent, the anti-imperialists did not represent majority opinion. Most businessmen, farmers, and urban working people believed that the United States had the right and duty to extend its influence.

American Soldiers in the Philippines Write Home about the War

The anti-imperialist movement, which rejected annexation by the United States of former Spanish colonies such as Puerto Rico and the Philippines, attempted to build opposition at home to the increasingly brutal war. Although few soldiers joined the anti-imperialist cause, their statements did sometimes provide ammunition for the opponents of annexation and war.

Arthur Minkler, of the Kansas Regiment says:

We advanced four miles and we fought every inch of the way; . . . saw twenty-five dead insurgents in one place and twenty-seven in another, besides a whole lot of them scattered along that I did not count. . . . It was like hunting rabbits; an insurgent would jump out of a hole or the brush and run; he would not get very far. . . . I suppose you are not interested in the way we do the job. We do not take prisoners. At least the Twentieth Kansas do not.

Ellis G. Davis, Company A, 20th Kansas:

They will never surrender until their whole race is exterminated. They are fighting for a good cause, and the Americans should be the last of all nations to transgress upon such rights. Their independence is dearer to them than life, as ours was in years gone by, and is today. They should have their independence, and would have had it if those who make the laws in America had not been so slow in deciding the Philippine question. Of course, we have to fight now to protect the honor of our country but there is not a man who enlisted to fight these people, and should the United States annex these islands, none but the most bloodthirsty will claim himself a hero. This is not a lack of patriotism, but my honest belief.

Soldier's Letters, pamphlet (Anti-Imperialist League, 1899). Reprinted in Philip S. Foner and Richard Winchester, *The Anti-Imperialist Reader: A Documentary History of Anti-Imperialism in the United States,* vol. 1 (New York: Holmes and Meier, 1984), 316–323.

Presidential adviser Mark Hanna explained that the Philippine annexation would allow the United States to "take a large slice of the commerce of Asia. . . . We are bound to share in the commerce of the Far East and it is better to strike for it while the iron is hot." Senator Albert Beveridge of Indiana equated the drive for empire with the near-religious theme of "Manifest Destiny": "Shall the American people continue their march toward commercial supremacy of the world? Shall free institutions broaden their blessed reign . . . until the empire of our principles is established over the hearts of all mankind?" For people like Beveridge, the ostensible closing of the frontier meant that America's "manifest destiny" was now in Asia. Beveridge also echoed the themes of masculine revival that motivated so many advocates of war and manifest destiny. Expansion, he declared, "means opportunity for all the glorious young manhood of the republic—the most virile, ambitious, impatient, militant manhood the world has ever seen."

Politicians and businessmen decided against a policy of European-style colonization; for the most part, the United States would not own territories or administer governments. Instead, American policymakers advocated aggressive economic expansion, which was carried out with a heavy hand in Latin America. Theodore Roosevelt, who became president in 1901 following McKinley's assassination, argued that the U.S. government should exercise "international police power" in the Western Hemisphere, a policy that became known as the Roosevelt Corollary to the Monroe Doctrine. (In 1823, President James Monroe had declared that Latin America should not be subject to European colonization.) Thus, the United States refused to withdraw its troops from Cuba after the war, reserving the right to intervene whenever order seemed to be threatened. The Platt Amendment of 1901, which granted the United States the right to intervene and build naval bases in Cuba, codified this policy. To end U.S. occupation, Cuban legislators meeting to draft a constitution ratified the amendment. Although troops withdrew in 1902, they returned from 1906 to 1909 and again in 1912 and 1917 to prop up governments that were sympathetic to U.S. business interests.

With bases in Cuba and Puerto Rico, American businessmen now focused on building a canal across the Isthmus of Panama, a province of Colombia. In 1902, Colombia rejected a proposed treaty granting the United States the right to build the canal. The next year, a group of Colombian businessmen and politicians, operating with U.S. naval support, declared northern Colombia an independent country and named it Panama. Canal rights and construction quickly followed, and the U.S.-built Panama Canal opened in 1914.

"Benevolent Assimilation"
U.S. troops guard Filipino nationalist prisoners captured in Pasay and Paranque during the Filipino-American War. Prints and Photographs Division, Library of Congress.

In the 1910s and 1920s, the United States placed troops throughout the Caribbean and Central America. It intervened in revolts in Nicaragua in 1910 and 1912, occupied Haiti from 1915 to 1934, and used military power to support economic interests and protect sea routes in Colombia, Honduras, Panama, and the Dominican Republic. This government muscle protected an increased U.S. corporate presence in South and Central America. Exports to Latin America had more than doubled between 1900 and 1914. U.S. corporations treated Latin America as their private preserve and sought to limit competition from European capitalists.

The United States could not pursue such a bold policy in Asia. European powers already had extensive economic interests there, backed by formal colonies or strong ties with local governments (Map 3.5). The United States therefore advocated an "Open Door" policy, hoping to gain new markets and access to raw materials in areas where other nations already dominated. In 1899, Secretary of State John Hay sent notes presenting the new policy to the major occupying powers in China by arguing that all industrialized nations should have equal access to Chinese trade. The European nations and Japan responded evasively, but Hay brashly insisted that they had given "final and definitive" assent.

Almost at the same time, the Chinese launched a rebellion against foreign exploitation. The Boxers, a secret nationalist organization, attacked foreigners and foreign influences throughout China. Five thousand U.S. troops joined an expeditionary force to relieve the siege of the British embassy in Beijing, where the foreign diplomatic corps had taken refuge. The U.S. troops help to break the siege in August 1900 and end the Boxer Rebellion. Hay then successfully used the rebellion to persuade the foreign powers to respond more favorably to a second round of Open Door notes. Hay's Open Door policy did not end foreign (especially Japanese) control of Chinese soil, but it did become the centerpiece of U.S. foreign policy in the new century. American policymakers embraced the dual beliefs that U.S. economic well-being required global expansion and that this expansion would be accomplished by open markets rather than direct imperial conquest.

As business and political leaders had predicted, global expansion and military expenditures increased the nation's wealth and helped to pull it out of depression. For the first time, the United States had an overseas empire, backed by a standing army that had nearly quadrupled in size between 1898 and 1901. U.S. political and military involvement in the internal affairs of other countries would profoundly shape twentieth-century experience.

By 1914, American businessmen had more than $3.5 billion invested abroad, making the United States one of the world's four largest investor nations. Dozens of American companies — Coca Cola, DuPont, Standard Oil, Ford, General Electric, and Gillette among them — operated two or

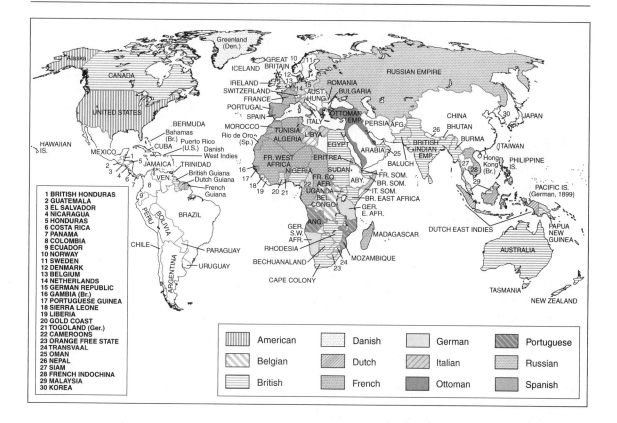

MAP 3.5 The Age of Imperialism: The World in 1900

In 1898, the United States belatedly entered the imperialist race to carve up the globe by acquiring far-flung possessions in the Caribbean and the Pacific. But as this map shows, it lagged behind the established imperial powers such as Britain and France.

more facilities abroad. The United Fruit Company grew bananas for the U.S. market on more than a million acres it owned in Central America; it also owned or controlled Central American railroads, docks, and communications networks. Direct foreign investment in 1914 was 7 percent of gross national product — the same proportion it would be in 1966. U.S. capitalism had truly become international.

Business on the Rebound Supported by global expansion, the U.S. industrial economy began to boom again, growing to astonishing size and strength in the first decade of the new century. The long depression had begun to lift in 1896. The discovery of gold on the Klondike River in the Yukon Territory the next year (and new goldfields in South Africa) suddenly ended both the contentious issue of the gold standard and the deflationary trend that had dominated the economy for the past three decades. The flow of money into the world economy relieved debt-burdened farmers and brought renewed prosperity to industrial workers. With recovery came new talk of cooperation between labor and industry (Figure 3.2).

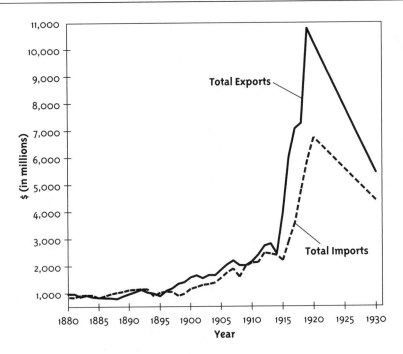

FIGURE 3.2 Going Global: U.S. Imports and Exports, 1880–1930

It was only after 1880 that American involvement in the emerging international economy took off. However, the most rapid growth did not come until the twentieth century.

Big business was the order of the day, and it was carried on in enormous factories. In 1870, only a handful of plants had employed more than 500 workers. By 1900, nearly 1,500 factories had reached that size, and some became truly gigantic. The Cambria Steel factory in Johnstown, Pennsylvania, employed nearly 20,000 people by early in the twentieth century. General Electric employed 15,000 at its factory in Schenectady, New York, and 11,000 at another plant in Lynn, Massachusetts.

As the economy gained strength, businessmen resumed their efforts to reduce competition. Some founded trade associations, organizations that brought competitors together to establish standards or lobby politicians in an industry's interests. Others combined forces more directly; beginning in 1898, American businessmen engaged in a frenzy of merger activity. By the early twentieth century, three hundred giant firms controlled nearly two-fifths of American manufacturing capital. As corporations grew, effective control was concentrated in fewer hands (Figure 3.3).

The financier J. P. Morgan organized the biggest new combination in 1901: U.S. Steel, created from 150 corporations, including Carnegie's, and capitalized at over $1 billion. Competition in the steel industry virtually disappeared. U.S. Steel was large enough to dictate prices, and like Carnegie's earlier company, the giant corporation was vertically integrated, making it invulnerable both to suppliers' price increases and to labor problems.

FIGURE 3.3 Merger Mania, 1895–1905

As the economy rebounded after the 1893–1897 depression, corporations began merging to form larger and often monopolistic companies, a trend that continued into the new century.

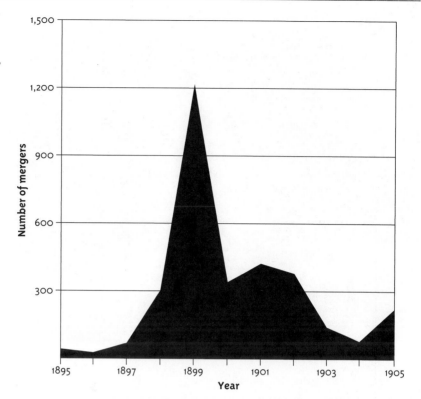

Some attempts at combination failed. Although General Electric and Goodyear became household names, U.S. Leather and United Button did not survive. In industries that did not require large investments in expensive machinery, new competitors could still challenge trusts. By 1910, manufacturing had divided into two distinct sectors. Very large corporations dominated industries that required heavy capital investments, while small firms competed feverishly in industries that did not. Thus, the leather, printing, clothing, and construction industries remained highly competitive, with thousands of firms battling for a slice of the market. Many small manufacturing firms that made clothing, jewelry, and furniture still did batch work, producing many styles, colors, and sizes rather than mass-producing identical items. And small business still dominated retailing. Although Sears and Montgomery Ward had both grown huge through their catalogue sales, and chain stores had emerged in the groceries, drugs, and general merchandise, most retail stores were small and run by individual proprietors.

But big business dominated business-government relationships and business ideology. Only big businesses had the resources to lobby Congress or to create combinations large and powerful enough to ensure dependable

Eat, Drink, and Be Merry
The managers of the nation's competing steel companies gathered together in 1901 to celebrate their merger into the giant U.S. Steel Corporation. The Carnegie Library of Pittsburgh.

supplies, markets, transportation, and banking connections. The problem of how to deal with these huge concentrations of wealth and power and the way their lack of accountability to the people threatened the fabric of democracy became one of the driving issues of the day. Though agitation against big combinations such as Standard Oil had begun in the 1880s, the vaguely worded Sherman Antitrust Act, passed in 1890, did not define either *trust* or *monopoly*. As a result, the courts threw out cases against the sugar and whiskey trusts. Ironically, although the biggest businesses did not suffer from the Sherman Antitrust Act, the labor movement did.

Organized Labor in a Time of Recovery   As the economy expanded following the depression, AFL-affiliated craft unions enjoyed a brief resurgence. Industrial growth created a labor shortage, especially among skilled workers. Knowing that they were in demand, workers became less fearful of the consequences of collective action, and they renewed their struggle to build unions. Between 1897 and 1904, the number of unionized working people more than quadrupled, to over two million.

The resurgence of craft unionism was concentrated in the Northeast and Midwest in basic industries such as railroads, metalworking, construction, and coal mining. Skilled workers—primarily men of Northern and

An Alphabet of Joyous Trusts

A segment of cartoonist Frederick Opper's "Nursery Rhymes for Infant Industries," published in the *New York American* in 1902. Opper closed his primer with these words:

With these alphabet pictures
the artist took pains,
But he's got to stop now, and
with grief nearly busts —
'Cause our language but
twenty-six letters contains,
Though our country contains
twenty-six hundred Trusts.

Frederick Opper, *New York American*, September 1902 — Prints and Photographs Division, Library of Congress.

Western European stock — fought, often with great militancy, to retain and extend shop-floor rights won in earlier scuffles with management. Established craft unions, most of them members of the American Federation of Labor, led these battles.

AFL unions generally excluded less-skilled workers, immigrants, African Americans, and women. Even on occasions when the rank and file showed solidarity with workers of other races and nationalities, AFL leaders typically resisted the integration of nonwhite workers. In Oxnard, California, 1,200 Mexican and Japanese farm laborers won a hard-fought strike against sugar beet growers in 1903. But the AFL refused to charter the group unless they excluded the Japanese workers. Indignant, the beet workers refused to accept a charter under those conditions. "In the past we have counseled, fought and lived on very short rations with our Japanese brothers, and toiled with them in the fields," their Mexican leader wrote to Gompers. "We would be false to them and to ourselves and to the cause of unionism if we now accepted privileges for ourselves which are not accorded to them."

Samuel Gompers thought of unions in more pedestrian terms, as "business organizations of wage-earners." AFL unions were stable, centralized organizations, directed by well-paid professional leaders who held their posts for years. In the building trades, full-time union officials known as "business agents" negotiated with contractors and assigned jobs to union members. These officials, although they helped craft unions to grow more stable and effective, also tended to frame union goals concretely, solely in terms of wages and working conditions.

The upsurge of craft unionism prompted some industrialists to seek peaceful solutions to industrial conflict. In that spirit, corporate leaders, bankrolled by financiers August Belmont and J. P. Morgan, founded the National Civic Federation (NCF) in 1900. Seeking employer acceptance of "responsible" unions, NCF leaders denounced both radicals and antiunion employers. They encouraged mediation as a method for settling disputes and fostered "welfare capitalism"—the pension plans, insurance, and recreational activities that some employers hoped would frustrate union organizers. The NCF urged employers to negotiate industrywide labor agreements through trade associations; such agreements were signed in the metalworking, newspaper, mining, ironmolding, and pottery industries. For a brief moment, the war between owners and skilled workers appeared to be over.

The Labor Question and Its Solution

A two-panel cartoon in a 1902 issue of the satirical weekly *Judge* endorsed the National Civic Federation. The first panel shows British labor relations, "capital and labor fighting to the death, at the same time destroying English commercial life," while the second panel depicts American "labor and capital on friendly terms, aiding each other, and together making the United States the greatest commercial nation in the world." Victor Gilliam, *Judge*, January 25, 1902 — American Social History Project.

That moment soon passed. In one industry after another, rank-and-file skilled workers refused to accept the weakening of their workplace control. Displays of worker militancy, such as a nationwide machinists' strike called in 1900 at the insistence of insurgent locals, convinced most corporate leaders that peace with labor cost too much. They rejected union demands and crushed ensuing strikes. By 1903, many employers had broken with the NCF and reverted to their old union-busting tactics: blacklists to prevent union activists from getting jobs, spies to gather information on organizing efforts, and strikebreakers to keep factories running when strikes did occur.

The National Association of Manufacturers (NAM) led employers in these efforts. Founded in 1895, the NAM united primarily small and medium-size manufacturers. In 1903 it took command of the employers' battle for "the open shop"—a contractual guarantee of the right to work without union membership—and of the employers' right to bar unions from factories. The rhetorical strategy of describing antiunionism as "open" put labor on the defensive.

Together with fluctuations in the economy, the open-shop drive slowed and then halted the spread of craft unionism. After nearly seven years of growth, membership in the AFL dropped by nearly 200,000 in 1905. New technology and the reorganization of factories made it easier for capitalists to replace skilled workers with the less skilled; organizations such as the NAM enhanced businessmen's ability to shape public opinion.

Permanent organizations were more difficult to sustain among workers, where social divisions between the skilled and the less-skilled, immigrant and native-born, black and white, male and female undercut the union movement. More important, the AFL itself helped to undermine the movement through its reluctance to bridge those gaps.

Conclusion: End of a Century, End of an Era

Class conflict defined the final two decades of the nineteenth century as working people confronted, with extraordinary creativity, the profound changes wrought by industrial capitalism. The first truly national working-class movement emerged in these years out of the militant protests and oppositional ideas of workers and farmers across the country. In creating a culture of resistance, the late-nineteenth-century labor movement rejected not only capitalists' growing control over the nation's economic and political life, but also the twin ideologies of acquisitive individualism and Social Darwinism that served to justify that control. While the movement's programs were eclectic, its philosophies diverse, and its outright victories few, it nonetheless succeeded in galvanizing millions of people with an alternative vision of industrial America rooted in mutuality, cooperation, equal justice, and democracy.

But the bitter defeats suffered by the Knights of Labor in 1886, the Homestead workers in 1892, the industrial armies in 1893 and 1894, the Pullman workers in 1894, and the Populists in 1896 eroded the power of this alternative vision and marked the end of an era. As a result, many working people in cities and the countryside retreated into insular cultures that included strong elements of racism and nativism. The nineteenth century closed with the labor and agrarian movements fragmented and their broad, organizing efforts defeated. The return of economic prosperity, the expansion of American corporations abroad, and the wave of mergers that swept through the economy further consolidated the power of giant corporations.

The bitter defeats of the 1880s and 1890s left permanent scars. The United States would never again witness such a broad or fundamental challenge by working people to the claims of capital. Thus, as the new century dawned, neither popular movements nor the government imposed serious constraints on the actions of the nation's capitalists. Working people, African Americans, immigrants, and women would need to find new ways to mitigate their subordinate position in American society.

The Years in Review

1887

- The American Protective Association is formed to drive Catholics out of American politics.

1890

- Mississippi enacts legislation to prevent African Americans from voting, setting a precedent that all southern states will follow over the next two decades.

- Congress passes the Sherman Antitrust Act, the first federal antitrust law, in an effort to regulate big business.

- The Farmers' Alliance moves into politics and captures four governorships and more than forty congressional seats.

1892

- Congress renews the Chinese Exclusion Act.

- The Ellis Island immigration depot opens. Between 1880 and 1900, nine million immigrants arrive in the United States, many from Eastern and Southern Europe. Another fourteen million will arrive between 1900 and 1920.

- The People's (Populist) Party holds its first convention and adopts the Omaha Platform, attacking economic and social conditions and calling for action; Populists win more than one million votes and elect governors in Kansas and Colorado in the fall election.

- Ida B. Wells-Barnett launches an antilynching campaign to stem the growing violence against African Americans in the South.
- Grover Cleveland is elected president for a second term.

1893
- The Chicago's World Fair celebrates the 400th anniversary of Columbus's arrival in the Americas.
- A five-year economic collapse begins as the stock market crashes on May 3.
- The Immigration Restriction League is formed to limit the "new" non-Anglo-Saxon immigrants.
- U.S. sugar planters led by Sanford B. Dole overthrow Hawaii's Queen Liliuokalani with the support of the U.S. Marines. Hawaii is proclaimed an American protectorate.

1894
- Jacob S. Coxey's army of unemployed workers marches on Washington, D.C.
- The Pullman strike ends in defeat for workers.

1895
- Booker T. Washington's "Atlanta Compromise" speech accepts racial separatism.

1896
- Republican William McKinley is elected president over Democratic and Populist candidate William Jennings Bryan.
- The U.S. Supreme Court decision in *Plessy v. Ferguson* sanctions racial segregation.
- Gold is discovered along the Klondike River in Yukon Territory, which leads to the Alaska Gold Rush.

1898
- The United States enters the Spanish-Cuban-American War after the U.S.S. *Maine* explodes in Havana Harbor on February 15, killing 266 sailors.
- The Treaty of Paris ends the war with Spain; Spain relinquishes its claim to Cuba, sells the Philippines to the United States for $20 million, and transfers Puerto Rico and Guam to U.S. control.
- The United States annexes Hawaii.
- Emilio Aguinaldo declares Philippine independence, but the United States refuses to recognize the republic and fights a guerrilla war against the Filipino nationalists.

- The Anti-Imperialist League forms to oppose U.S. annexation of overseas colonies.

1899
- Secretary of State John Hay issues the "Open Door" notes to European powers, arguing that all industrialized nations should be given equal access to Chinese trade.

1900
- Corporate leaders found the National Civic Federation to seek peaceful solutions to industrial conflict and to condemn antiunion employers. By 1903, many employers had broken with the NCF and reverted to union busting.
- The Boxer Rebellion attacks foreigners and foreign influences in China.
- William McKinley is reelected president.

1901
- The Platt Amendment grants the United States the right to intervene and build naval bases in Cuba.
- J. P. Morgan underwrites the creation of U.S. Steel, earning $7 million in the creation of the first billion-dollar corporation.
- Vice President Theodore Roosevelt becomes president after the assassination of William McKinley.

1902
- The Colombian government rejects a U.S. proposal to build a canal across Panama.
- President Theodore Roosevelt declares the end of the war in the Philippines, but fighting continues for another decade.

1903
- Twelve hundred Mexican and Japanese farm laborers win a hard-fought strike against sugar beet growers.
- New leaders declare Panama an independent nation and grant the United States rights to build the Panama Canal.
- W. E. B. DuBois publishes *The Souls of Black Folk* to counter Booker T. Washington's position on segregation.

1904
- The Roosevelt Corollary to the Monroe Doctrine asserts a U.S. right to intervene in Latin America.

1905
- The Niagara Movement demands an end to segregation and racial discrimination in every area of U.S. life; it leads to founding of

National Association for the Advancement of Colored People four years later.

1907
- President Theodore Roosevelt concludes a "gentleman's agreement" with Japan to exclude Japanese workers from the United States.

1909
- U.S. troops are dispatched to Nicaragua.

1914
- The Panama Canal opens.

- U.S. direct foreign investments total $3.5 billion, 7 percent of the U.S. gross national product.

Additional Readings

For more on the 1893 depression and workers' reactions to it, see:
Kevin Boyle, ed., *Organized Labor and American Politics, 1894–1994: The Labor-Liberal Alliance* (1998); Jeremy Brecher, *Strike!* (1972); Stuart B. Kaufman, *Samuel Gompers and the Origin of the American Federation of Labor, 1848–1896* (1973); Alexander Keyssar, *Out of Work: The First Century of Unemployment in Massachusetts* (1986); Altmont Lindsey, *The Pullman Strike: The Story of a Unique Experiment and of a Great Labor Upheaval* (1942); Donald L. McMurray, *Coxey's Army: A Study of the Industrial Army Movement of 1894* (1929); Nick Salvatore, *Eugene V. Debs: Citizen and Socialist* (1982); Richard Schneirov et al., *The Pullman Strike and the Crisis of the 1890s: Essays on Labor and Politics* (1999); Carlos A. Schwantes, *Coxey's Army: An American Odyssey* (1985); and Douglas Steeples and David O. Whitten, *Democracy in Desperation: The Depression of 1893* (1998).

For more on the Populist movement and 1890s electoral politics, see:
Gene Clanton, *Congressional Populism and the Crisis of the 1890s* (1998); Lawrence Goodwyn, *Democratic Promise: The Populist Moment in America* (1976); Steven Hahn, *The Roots of Southern Populism* (1983); Michael Kazin, *The Populist Persuasion: An American History* (1995); Paul Kleppner, *The Third Electoral System, 1853–1892* (1979); Robert C. McMath, *American Populism: A Social History, 1877–1898* (1993); Bruce Palmer, *"Man over Money": The Southern Populist Critique of American Capitalism* (1980); Elizabeth Sanders, *Roots of Reform: Farmers, Workers, and the American State, 1877–1917* (1999); R. Hal Williams, *Years of Decision: American Politics in the 1890s* (1978); C. Vann Woodward, *Tom Watson: Agrarian Rebel* (1963); and James Edward Wright, *The Politics of Populism: Dissent in Colorado* (1974).

For more on the rise of Jim Crow, the spread of white supremacy, and African American responses to it, see: Edward L. Ayers, *The Promise of the New South: Life After Reconstruction* (1992); Gail Bederman, *Manliness and Civilization: A Cultural History of Gender and Race in the United States, 1880–1917* (1996); David S. Cecelski and Timothy B. Tyson, eds., *Democracy Betrayed: The Wilmington Race Riot of 1898 and Its Legacy* (1998); John W. Cell, *The Highest Stage of White Supremacy: The Origins of Segregation in South Africa and the American South* (1982); Glenda Gilmore, *Gender and Jim Crow: Women and the Politics of White Supremacy in North Carolina, 1896–1920* (1996); Grace Elizabeth Hale, *Making Whiteness: The Culture of Segregation in the South, 1890–1940* (1998); Louis R. Harlan, *Booker T. Washington: The Making of a Black Leader* (1972); J. Morgan Kousser, *The Shaping of Southern Politics: Suffrage Restriction and the Establishment of the One-Party South* (1974); Linda O. McMurry, *To Keep the Waters Troubled: The Life of Ida B. Wells* (1999); Michael J. Pfeifer, *Rough Justice: Lynching and American Society, 1874–1947* (2004); Thomas Adams Upchurch, *Legislating Racism: The Billion Dollar Congress and the Birth of Jim Crow* (2004); Joel Williamson, *The Crucible of Race: Black-White Relations in the American South Since Emancipation* (1984); and C. Vann Woodward, *The Strange Career of Jim Crow,* 3rd ed. (1974).

For more on nativism and efforts to restrict immigration, see: Roger Daniels, *Guarding the Golden Door: American Immigration Policy and Immigrants Since 1882* (2004); Andrew Gyory, *Closing the Gate: Race, Politics, and the Chinese Exclusion Act* (1998); John Higham, *Strangers in the Land: Patterns of American Nativism, 1860–1925* (1973); Donald L. Kinzer, *An Episode in Anti-Catholicism: The American Protective Association* (1964); and Alexander Saxton, *The Indisputable Enemy: Labor and the Anti-Chinese Movement in California* (1971).

For more on the ideology of U.S. expansionism, see: Kristin Hoganson, *Fighting for American Manhood: How Gender Politics Provoked the Spanish-American and Philippine-American Wars* (1998); Michael H. Hunt, *Ideology and U.S. Foreign Policy* (1987); Matthew Frye Jacobsen, *Barbarian Virtues: The United States Encounters Foreign Peoples at Home and Abroad* (2000); Desmond King, *Making Americans: Immigration, Race, and the Origins of the Diverse Democracy* (2000); Walter LaFeber, *The Cambridge History of Foreign Relations: The Search for Opportunity, 1865–1913* (1993); David M. Pletcher, *The Diplomacy of Involvement: American Economic Expansion Across the Pacific, 1784–1900* (2001); Emily Rosenberg, *Spreading the American Dream: American Economic and Cultural Expansion, 1890–1945* (1982); John Seelye, *War Games: Richard Harding Davis and the New Imperialism*

(2003); and William Appleman Williams, *The Tragedy of American Diplomacy,* rev. ed. (1972).

For more on the Spanish-Cuban-American War and the Philippine War, see: Ada Ferrer, *Insurgent Cuba: Race, Nation, and Revolution, 1868–1898* (1999); Philip S. Foner, *The Spanish-Cuban-American War and the Birth of American Imperialism,* 2 vols. (1972); John Morton Gates, *Schoolbooks and Krags: The United States Army in the Philippines, 1898–1902* (1973); Brian Linn, *The Philippine War, 1899–1902* (2000); Stuart Creighton Miller, *"Benevolent Assimilation": The American Conquest of the Philippines, 1899–1903* (1979); Thomas Schoonover, *Uncle Sam's War of 1898 and the Origins of Globalization* (2003); and David Trask, *The War with Spain in 1898* (1981).

For more on the changes in business and labor after 1900, see: William E. Forbath, *Law and the Shaping of the American Labor Movement* (1991); Naomi Lamoreaux, *The Great Merger Movement in American Business, 1895–1904* (1985); and Nelson Lichtenstein, *State of the Union: A Century of American Labor* (2002).

4

Change and Continuity in Daily Life

1900–1914

Fashion Sense

This illustration from a 1910 *McClure's Magazine* showed young women employees leaving a New York department store at the end of the workday. Retail sales jobs were more attractive to young women than factory labor was, but wages were usually low and the work was tedious. Wladyslav T. Benda, *McClure's Magazine*, October 1910—American Social History Project.

IN JANUARY 1912, the Procter and Gamble Company (P&G) announced to the readers of the *Ladies' Home Journal* "An Absolutely New Product, A Scientific Discovery Which Will Affect Every Kitchen in America." The "new and heretofore unknown food" was Crisco, a solid vegetable shortening made from cottonseed oil. P&G hoped that the new shortening would replace the pork lard and beef tallow that had long dominated American cooking. If successful, Crisco would not only expand P&G's consumer products offerings, but also assure the company greater control over the market for cottonseed oil, a key raw material in the manufacture of its most famous brand-name product, Ivory Soap. After patenting Crisco in 1910, P&G launched it with the most elaborate and expensive marketing campaign ever seen. The company tested a variety of promotion plans, analyzed the shortening market, sent full-size free samples to every grocer in the United States, and advertised the new product in newspapers and magazines.

Crisco exemplified many of the dramatic changes in America's economy and everyday life at the turn of the century. "Science" and "progressive reform" would dominate the rhetoric of consumer culture. Giant (often global) corporations such as P&G would reorganize factories around new principles of "continuous-process" or "flow" production. Everything from cars and cigarettes to soap and shortening would be produced in massive operations in which abundant and reasonably priced raw materials were a precondition of success. To move these vast quantities of products into the hands and households of millions of Americans, the manufacturers would pioneer new methods of distribution — brand names, advertising, national sales forces, chain stores — to convince people that they "needed" these goods.

But for all the enormous changes that the new century brought, there were clear signs of continuity as well. The factories that pioneered mass production may have been bigger and more efficiently powered by electricity, but the conditions of work remained harsh and demanding. Even if some employers sugar-coated the new regime with lunchrooms and picnics, the scientific management techniques and assembly-line discipline that they imposed on their workers made twentieth-century factory work even more dehumanizing than that in earlier times. The remarkable prosperity of the new century also remained strikingly unequal in its distribution. Mass production and mass leisure made new products and attractions available to a much wider market, but they remained beyond the reach of many people. Rural African Americans, for example, could not afford even cheap consumer products such as Crisco. And although a few women, such as Helen Landsdowne, who wrote the Crisco ads, played leading roles in the consumer economy, the most common job for women remained domestic service.

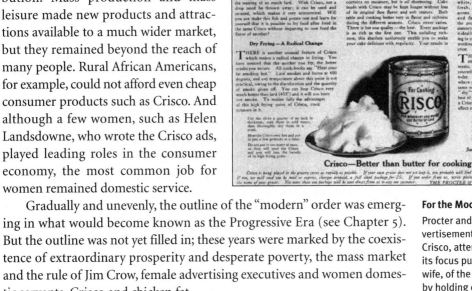

For the Modern Housewife

Procter and Gamble's first advertisement for its new product, Crisco, attempted to persuade its focus purchaser, the housewife, of the shortening's merits by holding out the allure of progress and science. Crisco, the ad claimed, was healthier and more modern than its traditional competitors, lard and butter. *The Ladies' Home Journal*, January 1912—American Social History Project.

Gradually and unevenly, the outline of the "modern" order was emerging in what would become known as the Progressive Era (see Chapter 5). But the outline was not yet filled in; these years were marked by the coexistence of extraordinary prosperity and desperate poverty, the mass market and the rule of Jim Crow, female advertising executives and women domestic servants, Crisco and chicken fat.

The Workplace Transformed

In the aftermath of depression of the 1890s, the United States embarked on an era of remarkable economic growth and prosperity. Between 1896 and 1914, the per capita gross national product increased by almost 50 percent (in constant dollars). By 1910, the United States was the world's greatest industrial power. Underlying this economic growth was an equally remarkable transformation in ways in which American factories produced goods and places in which Americans worked. Increasingly, Americans labored in giant factories organized around assembly lines and structured by techniques of mass production and scientific management. Of course, what employers viewed as a miracle of efficiency and productivity, workers often experienced as a deadening and oppressive regime of surveillance and control.

Some employers recognized that such conditions could as easily produce labor strife as packaged goods, and they attempted to soften the new industrial regime with such benefits as lunchrooms and housing—what came to be called "welfare capitalism." Henry Ford astutely recognized another flaw in the new mass production system: the workers could not afford to buy the goods that they were producing in vast numbers. He began to offer higher wages as a way to both reduce worker turnover and marry mass production and mass consumption. Less often noticed than the "Fordist" regime of mass production and consumption was the way in which industrialization transformed and greatly expanded the world of work for the middle class and for women, not just for industrial workers.

Mass Production   Long before 1913—the year Henry Ford created the first assembly line to manufacture automobiles—other industrialists were isolating the elements and applying the principles of mass production. Manufacturers developed interchangeable parts in making firearms, millers moved grain on conveyor belts, and slaughterhouses set up "disassembly lines" that reduced whole animals to packaged meat. All shared one fundamental idea: mass production would set up systems that would enable materials to flow through the workplace in a continuous process, from the arrival of raw materials at the entrance of the building to the dispatch of finished goods at the exit.

Small flour mills had run a continuous process since the eighteenth century, and soon afterward, the metalworking industries applied some of its principles. During the 1880s, inventors developed new machinery to pack meat, brew beer, and can vegetables. Using conveyer systems, rollers, and gravity slides, these machines automatically sent materials through the production process in a continuous stream. The first automatic canning line opened in 1883, soldering cans at the rate of fifty a minute. Heinz pickles, Campbell's soup, and Borden's milk were among the first products canned in this way. Other companies soon used similar machines to manufacture a variety of products, including soap, cigarettes, matches, and breakfast cereals.

For workers, high-speed machinery brought unremitting and repetitious work. In some industries, the continuous process and the introduction of electric lights meant that factories could operate around the clock. In

A Disassembly Line
As shown here, workers at the Swift and Company meatpacking plant in Chicago performed specialized, repetitive tasks based on many of the same principles that Henry Ford used in the automobile assembly line. Brown Brothers.

1908, the Homestead works of U.S. Steel ran two shifts: a day shift of ten and a half hours and a night shift of thirteen and a half hours. "The men are too tired to take an active part in family life; they are usually ready after smoking a pipe to go to bed," wrote one observer.

The new factories employed huge workforces. The McCormick plant in Chicago had 15,000 workers in 1916; Ford's Highland Park plant employed 16,000. These immense plants had their own railroad terminals, water supplies, energy sources, telephone networks, fire departments, and security forces. As a result, they often operated completely independently of the municipalities and companies that supplied goods and services to households and small businesses.

Of course, some consumer goods were created without mass production. Thousands of small factories and tenement sweatshops manufactured ready-made clothing. Small "batch work" firms produced jewelry, furniture, and other items. But even small factories produced unprecedented quantities of consumer products by relying increasingly on the division of labor.

Scientific Management Despite differences in production methods, nearly all workers experienced new kinds of discipline and control. Time clocks, first patented in 1889, carried an unambiguous message: workers must submit to the machine's — and the boss's — account of their arrival and departure times. Employers continued to perfect the techniques of

Baking a Better Apple Pie

As the principles of scientific management came to play a more significant role in the workplace, some reformers sought to apply standardization and routine to aspects of daily life. Nowhere was this more apparent than in the kitchen. The domestic science movement (or "home economics," as it was later called) attempted to standardize routines and recipes, thereby relieving housewives of the anxieties of inexact cooking and bringing the supposed benefits of efficiency into the home. Fannie Merritt Farmer was a leader in the movement for scientific cooking, helping to entrench the notion of exact measures and procedures designed to produce a uniform product. The following two recipes for apple pie demonstrate the difference between Farmer's precisely measured approach and an earlier, inexact set of instructions.

Starting from Scratch:

Catherine Beecher's Apple Pie

Pare your apples, and cut them from the core. Line your dishes with paste, and put in the apple; cover and bake until the fruit is tender. Then take them from the oven, remove the upper crust, and put in sugar and nutmeg, cinnamon or rose water to your taste; a bit of sweet butter improves them. Also, to put in a little orange peel before they are baked, makes a pleasant variety. Common apple pies are very good to stew, sweeten, and flavor the apple before they are put into the oven. Many prefer the seasoning baked in. All apple pies are much nicer if the apple is grated and then seasoned.

Catherine Beecher, *Domestic Receipt Book* (1846).

Apple Pie by the Book:

Fannie Farmer's Recipe

    4 or 5 sour apples
    1/4 teaspoon grated nutmeg
    1/8 teaspoon salt
    1 teaspoon lemon juice
    1/3 cup sugar
    Few gratings lemon rind
    1 teaspoon butter

Line pie plate with paste. Pare, core, and cut the apples into eighths, put row around plate one-half inch from edge, and work towards the centre until plate is covered; then pile on remainder. Mix sugar, nutmeg, salt, lemon juice, and grated rind, and sprinkle over apples. Dot over with butter. Wet edges of under crust, cover with upper crust, and press edges together. Bake forty to forty-five minutes in moderate oven. A very good pie may be made without butter, lemon juice, and grated rind. Cinnamon may be substituted for nutmeg. Evaporated apples may be used in place of fresh fruit. If used, they should be soaked overnight in cold water.

Fannie Merritt Farmer, *Boston Cooking-School Cook Book* (1905).

"scientific management," also called "Taylorism," after Frederick Winslow Taylor, who pioneered the movement. Taylor insisted there was "one best way" to perform every job and that way could be scientifically determined, planned by managers and taught to workers. In his quest for maximum efficiency, Taylor analyzed how workers performed their jobs, broke the jobs down into steps, and timed workers with a stopwatch. He then set standards for each task, paying a high piece rate for high output and a lower one for substandard results. In 1911, Taylor published *The Principles of Scientific Management*, and Taylorism became all the rage—except among workers.

The Science of Repetition
The small lights attached to this worker's arms and hands enabled efficiency experts to track his movements. The resulting "cyclegraph," a photograph taken by an open-shutter still camera and invented by time-and-motion specialist Frank Gilbreth, was then studied in an attempt to eliminate useless movement and turn mass-production work into a rigid arrangement of "efficient" motions. National Museum of American History, Smithsonian Institution.

Taylorism and mass production went hand in hand. Although efficiency theories were applied to work in many fields—including education and housework—Taylor's program was best suited to large-scale, mechanized production processes. The new system separated manual from mental labor, unskilled from skilled tasks. It broke skilled work into smaller steps that could be done by low-paid semi-skilled or unskilled workers. Taylorites divided the work of a shoemaker, for instance, into forty tasks. Unlike the shoemaker, semiskilled workers knew only how to operate a single machine, but they did not learn to set it up, repair it, or operate similar equipment. Lacking any generalized knowledge of production, these workers had less bargaining power than did the skilled shoemakers they replaced. This strategy not only increased employers' control over the labor force, but also improved their production and profits.

Workers understood this managerial strategy, and they equated Taylorism with diminished autonomy, close supervision, regimentation, and pressure to produce. Some less-skilled workers, new to industrial work, took the new jobs eagerly. But between 1909 and 1913, unskilled immigrant workers in industrial towns throughout the East and Midwest—including Lawrence, Massachusetts; Chicago, Illinois; and Paterson, New Jersey— went on strike against wage cuts, unsafe conditions, and the dehumanizing work patterns required by scientific management and the new mass production methods. For skilled workers, scientific management meant the loss of craft control and the routinization of labor. In 1912, the American Federation of Labor (AFL) came out against Taylor's time-study methods. "We don't want to work as fast as we are able to," one machinist declared in 1914. "We want to work as fast as we think it's comfortable for us to work."

"More Work for Mother?": Scientific Management at Home

While production workers resisted scientific management, middle-class women's magazine writers and editors such as Christine Frederick proposed that women embrace such notions of efficiency and impose them on themselves. Frederick, a major proponent of the new housekeeping, was consulting household editor for Ladies' Home Journal *from 1912 to 1919 and the author of numerous books and pamphlets on scientific management in the home.*

We have had plenty of *invention* for the household, but the great need is now for more science of management, and, above all, for more efficient thinking and analyzing. For in the home, as everywhere else, efficiency *must start in the mind of the directing spirit of the establishment.* Thousands of men are *inefficient,* but are *made* efficient by submitting to the direction of efficient men who stand over them. It is the great misfortune of women as homemakers that each one of them must stand alone as the directing head of a separate establishment, without any trained, efficient mind to guide and direct them. They must apply what efficiency they have or can learn, alone; while men in office and shop can not only be under the guidance of efficient foremen and overseers, but they have in addition the social stimulus of working among other men in competition.

It is therefore *immensely, terribly important* that women get themselves in connection with modern efficiency science, and, most important of all, bring *themselves up to a really efficient attitude of mind.*

Christine Frederick, "New Housekeeping," *Ladies' Home Journal,* September 13, October 20, November 19, and December 16, 1912. Reprinted in *The New Housekeeping. Efficiency Studies in House Management* (Garden City and New York: Doubleday, Page & Co., 1926), 3–22, 181–203.

Welfare Capitalism Taylorism provided the most important new managerial strategy of the early twentieth century, but employers also had other tricks up their sleeves. Haunted by the specter of bitter labor strife, some innovating employers responded by offering incentives to secure greater productivity, higher profits, workers' loyalty, and to discourage unionization. A few large capitalists, such as the Pittsburgh food processor H. J. Heinz, provided lunchrooms, showers, and company-owned housing in an effort to "humanize the business system" and "end the spirit of enmity between capital and labor." Various companies offered a panoply of other programs aimed at promoting workers' "welfare": savings clubs, English classes, company picnics, in-house magazines, and on-site nurses. Many businesses limited these benefits to skilled workers, however.

Some companies provided more direct monetary benefits, profit-sharing plans, pensions, and the opportunity to buy a home. They often introduced these plans—intended to persuade workers to remain loyal to the company and give them a stake in their community—when strikes were brewing and made them available only to workers who took the boss's side.

Amenities
The male employees' bathroom at the National Cash Register (NCR) Company in Dayton, Ohio, in 1900. The facility was part of NCR's extensive welfare program, which also included clubs, sports teams, and landscaping of the company grounds. Courtesy NCR.

Companies frequently promoted themselves as families, modeled on small-town entrepreneurs who prided themselves on their ability to call every employee by name. The "family" of employees sometimes consisted of real families. In New Hampshire's huge Amoskeag Mills, as in California and Colorado agriculture, people often got jobs through family ties, and relatives substituted for one another on the job. When workers knew of an opening, they would bring in their relatives, even after companies established formal employment offices. Working alongside a brother in a factory or picking crops in the same field with a father or daughter sometimes made harsh working conditions easier to bear. But there was also a downside: all working in the same place made families more vulnerable to poverty when employers cut wages, laid off workers, or shut down factories.

Many companies included "Americanization" in their welfare programs—classes that were intended to teach immigrant workers English and acculturate them to American ways. These company programs were part of a broader Americanization movement supported by social workers, civic groups, and government agencies. Some emphasized English and civics and encouraged immigrants to apply for citizenship. Others had a harder edge, emphasizing obedience, discouraging radicalism, and stressing the need to break with Old World customs.

Employers' special interest in Americanization stemmed from two beliefs: that the instruction would help them retain experienced workers in a time of severe labor shortages and that it would instill positive attitudes and values in their workforce. After inaugurating English language classes in 1911 with help from the YMCA, International Harvester took over the program a year later and revised it to stress safety, shop discipline, and welfare work. Lesson One began: "I hear the whistle. I must hurry." As one company spokesman explained, every immigrant employee should simultaneously "learn to speak English correctly and also have impressed upon him the rules he should follow while in and around the works."

"Amoskeag Did All This to Keep Harmony . . ."

The Amoskeag Corporation in Manchester, New Hampshire, operated the world's largest textile mill, employing some 14,000 workers including Joseph Debski who began working at Amoskeag in 1910 when he was fourteen years old. Like a number of large companies during this period, Amoskeag ran a series of welfare programs for workers and their families. In this excerpt Debski describes one company benefit.

The Amoskeag had a textile club; anybody over eighteen who worked there could belong to it. It had a reading room, canteen, billiard and pool tables, and card tables; and they used to have dances, probably once a month in the wintertime. They had a golf course with a clubhouse; and in 1927 they took over the Intervale Country Club. . . . Then they had the Amoskeag Textile Field, which was a baseball field.

There was a general fund to operate things like a Christmas party for employees' children. They'd take all the equipment out of the garage—it was all bare floor—and prepare it for fifteen to twenty-five hundred children from five to fifteen, free of charge. They would try to take the hard cases, people who probably couldn't afford a good Christmas party of their own.

The textile club had an annual meeting at the Jolliet Hall . . . and there'd be fifteen hundred to two thousand people there. They'd have a big dinner and entertainment. We had committees on bowling, athletics, photography. . . . They had about twenty different committees. . . .

Amoskeag did all this to keep harmony amongst its employees. The board of directors established the textile club. . . . During the strike of 1922, the textile club functioned the most because people didn't have anywhere else to go. They would go play cards, play pool. They didn't draw any lines and say people couldn't come in because of the strike. . . . The club kept going . . . until the mid-thirties. . . . It was when the mill was shut down [in 1936] that everything was demolished.

Tamara K. Hareven and Randolph Lagenbach, *Amoskeag: Life and Work in an American Factory-City* (1978).

Of course, many immigrants welcomed the opportunity to learn English, become citizens, and share more fully in American life. Ethnic community leaders often encouraged newcomers to participate in such programs. Many workers also appreciated the fact that company-provided benefits improved their work and home environments. Others, however, viewed the welfare programs as an invasion of their privacy and a poor substitute for higher wages.

"Fordism" Henry Ford proved as much a master of these new techniques of rationalized and mechanized production and welfare capitalism as of innovative automobile production. He also understood that increased production required increased consumption, which in turn required that factory workers be paid well enough to buy what they produced. Therefore, he offered high wages and a high standard of living as the reward for monotonous, repetitive, and alienating labor on the assembly line. This combination of mass production and mass consumption of standardized products has come to be known as Fordism.

Automobiles had been built in America since the 1890s, but only the rich could afford these early models. Henry Ford, a machinist and engineer born on a Michigan farm during the Civil War, was manufacturing medium-price automobiles in 1908 when he introduced his Model T. A simple, low-cost car that could travel even over unpaved roads intended for horses and wagons, the Model T was an instant success. Ford's company grew rapidly, thanks to his constant innovation of the manufacturing processes. By 1914, the Ford Motor Company turned out 250,000 Model Ts a year. When production was finally halted in 1927, 15 million Model Ts had been made.

Making Model Ts

The Ford assembly line in Highland Park, Michigan, was a prime example of continuous-process production. In this photo, taken in 1913, automobile bodies are secured to chassis. Henry Ford Museum and Greenfield Village.

Unlike previous cars, Ford designed the Model T as a standardized product for a mass market. "I will build a motor car for the great multitude," he declared. Ford saw the creation of a complicated product for a mass market as a personal mission. "The way to make automobiles," he explained, "is to make one automobile just like another . . . to make them come through the factory alike—just like one pin is like another pin." For twelve years, he only sold black Model Ts. Having just one model lowered costs and allowed his engineers to scrutinize every phase of the production process.

As in many other industries, mechanization was the key to mass production, and technological innovation was central to success. To produce the Model T, Ford built a state-of-the-art plant for 16,000 workers in Highland Park, Michigan, on the edge of Detroit. The Ford production method centered on the assembly line. Early on, Ford had positioned machines according to their sequence in the production process so that workers hand carried identical parts from one machine workstation to the next. In 1913, Ford's engineers began experimenting with the gravity slides, endless chains, and conveyor belts that were used in the continuous-process production of flour, beer, and other products. Rather than assigning workers numerous tasks on stationary objects, the engineers trained each worker to perform a few simple operations on parts that passed before him. The crowning achievement of their new system was the final assembly of the car by means of a continuous moving chain, to which the car frames were attached. The new continuous-process design reduced assembly time for a Model T from twelve and a half man-hours to less than two.

Although Ford did not acknowledge the influence of Taylorism, his new organization followed its general principles. Separating mental from manual labor and using time studies to plan work were becoming standard practice in many industrial enterprises. Ford went further and applied those principles and the technology of continuous materials handling to a highly complex product. Company after company soon adopted "Fordist" methods. The assembly line transformed the very nature of manufacturing by addressing in a new fashion the old problem of increasing the work pace. Instead of quotas, piecework wages, or foremen who set the pace of production, the machinery itself determined the pace of work.

Fordism meant enormous savings for companies but exhausting, nerve-racking, and alienating labor for workers. Though it alleviated some heavy lifting, the assembly line drained workers. "The weight of a tack," one worker noted, "is insignificant, but if you have to drive eight tacks in every Ford cushion that goes by your station within a certain time, and know that if you fail to do it you are going to tie up the entire platform, and you continue to do this for four years, you are going to break under the strain." Monotony and boredom were severe; as another employee put it, "a man checks his brain and his freedom at the door when he goes to work at Ford's."

Worker discontent increased dramatically, and extraordinarily high worker turnover threatened Ford, like most other employers. With little chance for advancement and few ties to their employers, semiskilled and unskilled workers often quit if they disliked the boss, wanted a vacation, or saw a better opportunity elsewhere. This mobility cost employers money because they constantly had to hire and train new workers. At Ford, the problem was extreme. In 1913, the year the assembly line was developed, Ford had to hire 52,000 workers to maintain a workforce of 13,600. His worries mounted as a number of unions, including the radical Industrial Workers of the World, began organizing in the plants.

To keep out unions and reduce turnover, Ford announced a dramatic scheme, the Five-Dollar Day, in 1914. He reduced the workday from nine hours to eight and offered a profit-sharing plan that brought wages up to a full five dollars a day — double the prevailing pay of laborers and semi-skilled workers in Detroit. Job seekers rioted at the doors to the Highland Park plant. But the wage policy had some catches. Ford fired workers who did not produce. Those who did produce could get the full profit-sharing payment only if they met certain standards both at work and at home. Ford set up a "sociological department" to investigate workers' home lives and administer the plan.

E PLURIBUS UNUM

FORD ENGLISH SCHOOL

After 1914, Henry Ford tied the profit-sharing payments to his Americanization program. He believed that immigrants had to "be taught American ways, the English language, and the right way to live." The program encouraged immigrant workers to move out of ethnic neighborhoods and discouraged them from taking in new immigrant boarders. As at International Harvester, lessons at the Ford English School concerned safety, shop discipline, personal hygiene, and the company's welfare programs, as well as Henry Ford's personal benevolence. The company even taught racism to immigrants; according to one Ford text, black Americans "came from Africa where they lived like other animals in the jungle. White men brought them to America and made them civilized." But despite such statements, the company actually hired more black workers than did other auto manufacturers.

Ford argued that high wages and a forty-hour week would increase consumer demand and bind workers more securely to their jobs, creating both disciplined workers and mass consumers. He believed that mass production would lead nowhere if the masses—the workers—could not afford to buy what they produced. Indeed, Ford made it possible. The price of a Model T—$950 in 1909—dropped to $290 by 1924, boosting sales and allowing Ford to thrive.

Out of the Melting Pot and into . . .
These 1916 graduates of the Ford English School are shown at the finale of commencement exercises. The graduation included a ritual of citizenship in which the graduates, wearing traditional national costumes, disembarked from an immigrant ship and disappeared into a gigantic melting pot (center of photo). Their teachers then vociferously stirred the pot with ladles, and the graduates finally emerged dressed in "American" clothes and waving flags. Henry Ford Museum and Greenfield Village.

White-Collar and Women's Work
While many observers focused on the obvious transformation of the work world of the male industrial laborer—

The Hurry Habit

This 1914 cartoon, which appeared in *Life* magazine, commented on the increasingly frenetic nature of middle-class life in the early twentieth century. M. Fenderson, *Life*, November 1911—American Social History Project.

exemplified by the Ford assembly-line worker—white-collar work and women's work were undergoing equally important changes. The growth of the middle class was as much a by-product of industrialization and mass production factories as was the burgeoning working class.

This explosion of white-collar work—clean work—expanded the white middle class, which had been quite small for most of the nineteenth century. More than factory work, the new jobs required good English-language skills and a willingness to behave according to company rules. Some children of immigrants took such jobs, which their parents could never get, while others followed the older generation to the factories. Immigrants' daughters often entered the white-collar world before their brothers could. Employers barred black Americans from virtually all the new white-collar jobs, although some held professional positions as teachers, doctors, and ministers in their own communities.

Above all, corporations expanded opportunities for people who could sell products and maintain records. At the lowest levels, new entrants to the middle class functioned as clerks. At the highest levels, white-collar workers directed and controlled corporate expansion. Before the turn of the century, many middle-class men had aspired to entrepreneurial independence and had viewed their employee status as temporary. Those views changed as large firms grew and gained control over vital sectors of the economy. Men in salaried jobs ranging from mail boy to chief executive officer now began to think in terms of lifelong employment with corporations.

While most clerical and sales jobs offered workers a lifetime of low-paying, regimented labor, some traveling positions offered opportunities for financial advancement to men who were willing (or eager) to forgo the comforts of a home life and able to adjust to life on the road. Salesmen were central to the developing mass-distribution system. Between 1880 and 1920, the number of commercial travelers increased at least sixfold. With good English and an attractive personality, a small-town boy or an immigrant's

Arts and Crafts for the Working Woman

A popular interest in art pottery emerged at the turn of the century, growing out of middle-class women's interest in employment outside the home and a design reform impulse known as the Arts and Crafts movement. The latter, founded by the English poet, artist, socialist, and reformer William Morris, believed that handmade objects were the answer to the proliferation of low-quality mass-produced goods. The Newcomb Pottery was established in 1894 by Newcomb College (Tulane University's women's college) as part of the school's ambitious program of vocational training for young women artists. Harriet C. Joor, *Chinaberries* Vase, 1902–03, Newcomb Pottery—New Orleans Museum of Art: Gift of Newcomb College, Pierce Butler, Dean, 38.29.

son might dream of expense accounts, good clothes, automobiles, and relative independence from the boss.

A few women worked as commercial travelers for smaller firms, but most companies would not hire women to travel. Instead, women dominated the lowest clerical positions, typing and stenography pools, large bookkeeping staffs, and telephone switchboards. These women generally earned more than other women who worked for wages, but employers subjected them to rigid discrimination and segregation. Bosses defined jobs according to gender: the mail room for men, the telephone switchboard for women. Gender segregation went well beyond job categories; for instance, men and women entered the Metropolitan Life building through different doors and used separate stairways, hallways, and elevators.

Many women found work in department stores, where a few could move up to well-paying jobs as buyers, but most were stuck in tedious and low-paying positions as retail saleswomen. Compared with laundries and factories, stores offered full-time employees steady work without seasonal layoffs. But this security was supported by the insecurity of many part-time workers, who worked only during special sales and heavy seasons, and at a lower pay scale. These women earned very little, but store owners argued that their wages were appropriate because women who worked part time needed only to supplement their families' income. In fact, most part-time saleswomen eked out a meager living for years, hoping to be hired as part

TABLE 4.1 Women's Labor Force Participation Rates
Women's participation in the paid workforce grew steadily before World War II, but the most dramatic increases were among married women.

The Expansion of the Female Labor Force, 1900–1940		
Year	Percentage of All Women Working	Percentage of Married Women Working
1900	20.6%	5.6%
1920	23.7	9.0
1930	24.8	11.7
1940	25.8	15.6

Gibson Girls

In the 1890s, Charles Dana Gibson's magazine illustrations of fashionable young women gained wide popularity. The physical type that he portrayed became the standard of beauty, a romantic ideal that suggested a new independence while also celebrating the privileges and glamour of elite society. Charles Dana Gibson, *Ladies' Home Journal*, April 1895 — American Social History Project.

THE LADIES' HOME JOURNAL

APRIL 1895   TEN CENTS

of the regular staff. Even saleswomen on regular staff were paid roughly half the wages their male counterparts received in departments such as sporting goods and appliances.

Despite discrimination in the workplace, more and more women worked for wages, feeding growing corporate demands for clerical workers to cope with mountains of paperwork and retailers' demands for saleswomen and stock clerks to serve crowds of new customers. The shift from home production to factory and the abolition of child labor also drew increasing numbers of women into manufacturing. As the idea of women working for pay became more acceptable, the prevailing attitude that married women belonged at home faded, and an increasing proportion of wives joined the workforce. In 1890, just under 5 percent of married women worked for wages; thirty years later, twice as many did so. Altogether, the female labor force more than quadrupled between 1880 and 1930 (Table 4.1).

Women's participation in the workforce varied by ethnic and racial group as well as marital status. Unmarried Polish women in Buffalo, New York, often took jobs in factories or as domestic servants, while their counterparts from southern Italy preferred to take in piecework or do seasonal farm labor. Many married African American women worked for wages; few married immigrant women did so. Industrial homework — the piecework manufacture of clothing, artificial flowers, or costume jewelry — enabled women to earn money at home while maintaining family life. In 1902, about 25,000 to 30,000 women did piecework at home in New York City.

Domestic service remained the foremost occupation for single white women in the North

"She Didn't Fire Me — I Fired Myself": Beulah Nelson Protests

African American women were twice as likely as white women to pursue paid employment, but they were more constrained in their choice of occupations. Nonetheless, the shortage of servants gave them some leverage in their jobs. The prospect of migration lent new resolve to black domestic workers as they confronted difficult employers, as revealed in Beulah Nelson's account, told to historian Elizabeth Clark-Lewis.

Before I left, a lady, who was named Miss Addie, and a member of my mother's church — my people all were sanctified — stayed home to have a baby. . . . And I worked [there] . . . three days. Why? Mama sent me, and they was paying a quarter a week! Now, you had to cook the breakfast, you wait on all of them, all the children, and get them ready for school. . . . Fix their lunch and everything. Then you wash up all the dishes. Then you had to go make up all the beds and pick up all the things behind all the children, and then after that you had to go out behind the house, honey, and pick the garden. And pick what kind of vegetables you got to have. You got to wash them and cook them. And they had three meals a day. They would eat they breakfast, and then twelve o'clock they had to have a big dinner. And then they had supper later in the evening.

But they didn't want no nigger to put they hand on their bread. Understand me good now. I set the table up and put the food on the table. But the bread be the last thing. Never bring the bread in until after they say the grace, so the bread would be seeping hot. I wait just as good until they said the grace, and I wouldn't move because I would have had to pick up the bread out of the pan, and I still would have to take knife or fork to lift it to put in the plate to take to the table, and I know she didn't want me to touch it. Right? Well, if she didn't want me to touch it, if I couldn't touch it, I wasn't going to try not to touch it to carry it to the table to give it to them. She said to me, "How long are you going to wait before you bring that bread in here?" I said, "I'm not even going to bring it in there." I said, "You put it in there. You cook it, you don't want me to touch it. If you don't want me to touch it, you don't need me to bring it in there." . . . And that's when she got mad, arguing with me so. She jumped up from table and she said to me, "Beulah, you fired." But she didn't fire me — I fired myself, 'cause I intended to do what I did. . . . I said, "No, if that's the way it's to be — not me!" I said, "For what? Six days a week for twenty-five cents? Not me!" You see, I didn't have to do it — I was leaving.

Elizabeth Clark-Lewis, *Living In, Living Out: African American Domestics in Washington, D.C., 1910–1940* (1994), 65–66.

and for married black women in the South. In 1910, more than 2.5 million women — more than one-third of the female workforce — were servants. African American women who worked as domestics in the South generally lived in their own homes, while northern maids lived in their employers' attics and basements. They found domestic service both physically and

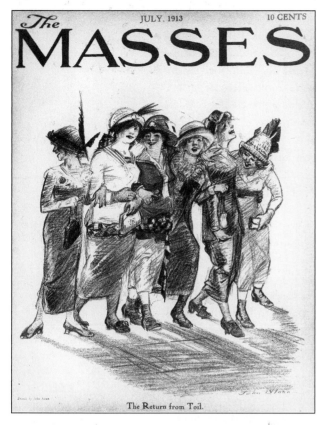

JULY. 1913   10 CENTS

The Return from Toil.

The Return from Toil

John Sloan's cover illustration for the radical magazine *The Masses* presented working women in a new way. *The Masses* often portrayed women as the victims of oppressive working and labor conditions. Here, however, the magazine's artist broke away from the standard sentimental or wretched stereotypes, instead showing working women as strong, independent, and exuberant individuals. John Sloan, *The Masses*, July 1913—Tamiment Institute Library, New York University.

psychologically taxing, involving intimate surveillance by an ever-present employer. Women with other choices abandoned this work in droves; one former servant reported how she happily left behind the "degrading sense of servility."

Even the most desirable of women's jobs had serious drawbacks, reflecting women's second-class position in the labor market. Nursing, a preserve of native-stock Americans, stood at the top of the female job hierarchy. During their apprenticeship in hospital schools, student nurses provided cheap labor. After graduation, most of these women went into private nursing, caring for patients at home or in hospitals and charging a fee for their service. Nurses took pride in their skills, knowledge, and independence, but patients' families viewed nurses as subordinates. Some of their work was disconcertingly similar to that of domestic servants.

Whatever their field—nursing, teaching, domestic service, garment and textile manufacturing, retail sales, or clerical work—women held jobs that usually paid less and carried less prestige than equivalent male positions. With no women in positions of power in either companies or unions, women workers faced widespread sexual harassment. Antonia Bergeron remembered that the bosses at the Amoskeag Company "were very fresh. The boss would chase the girls and slap their behinds, give them kicks in the rear end."

Inequality in Everyday Life

The inequalities of the workplace were mirrored in everyday life. Mass production, urbanization, and new technologies brought new products and services to both rich and poor in the decades after the depression of the 1890s. But not surprisingly, rich and poor did not have equal access to the glittering new goods and services. Although the nation's population became more urbanized, few urban working people had central heating or telephones, and electric lights became a familiar feature in their workplaces, changing many aspects of their jobs, but not in their homes.

New Standards of Living   By the turn of the century, manufacturers mass-produced food products, cleaning supplies, and other grocery store items and promoted them to workers on billboards and streetcar placards and to the middle classes in magazine advertisements. Quaker and Pillsbury now sold prepackaged oats and flour to people who had once been accustomed to scooping them from grocers' barrels. Heinz and Campbell's supplied prepared sauces and soups, while Procter and Gamble offered a variety of brands and grades of factory-made soap—products that had once been made at home. Manufacturers promoted the convenience, cleanliness, and style of throwaway packaging and disposable goods. But they also brought a growing mountain of trash as older habits of reuse and recycling gradually died away.

Only the rich could afford some of these packaged goods. Franco-American, for example, advertised its canned vichyssoise in yachting magazines. But as the firms that put food in cans exploited the economies of mass production, prices began to drop, and these luxuries became more affordable.

Still, there was a huge gap between the lifestyles of the rich and the poor. By the turn of the century, the urban upper classes generally had electricity, natural gas, telephones, central heating, and indoor plumbing. Meanwhile, tenement dwellers fueled their kitchen stoves with scavenged scraps of coal and wood, lit kerosene lamps, and drew water from hydrants located in courtyards near overflowing privies. A new tenement building might include a bathroom and possibly even hot water, but most housing built for workers had no heating or lighting systems.

Within the working class, the levels of comfort enjoyed by skilled and unskilled workers also differed widely. An unskilled worker cobbled together a life for his family on an average of $10 a week. They could barely afford to rent a dilapidated two-room apartment with no running water; buy food, crude furniture, and some ready-made clothing; and purchase the most minimal private insurance—a necessity for workers unprotected by any form of government insurance. A survey done in 1910 concluded that if an unskilled steelworker worked the standard shift—twelve hours a day, 365 days a year—he still could not earn enough to support a family of five (Figure 4.1).

Skilled workers' families, in contrast, lived in relative comfort on an average of $20 a week. The additional income enabled them to rent or buy one- or two-family houses far away from the smoke and stench of the mill and the bright lights of the central city. They shared neighborhoods with families headed by small businessmen and low-level white-collar workers, an occupational group that grew as corporations expanded their managerial ranks. They could eat a varied, healthy diet and take comfort and pride in decent housing and furniture. If they conserved their money, they could afford pianos and hand-operated washing machines and even accumulate some savings.

FIGURE 4.1 The Bottom Line: Family Budgets in Homestead

Standards of living were rising in the early twentieth century. But unskilled workers, many of them immigrants, still spent about half of their meager incomes on food and had very little left over for recreation or the other pleasures of life. This chart is based on family budgets collected in 1908 from twenty-nine Slavic families in the steelmaking community of Homestead, Pennsylvania.

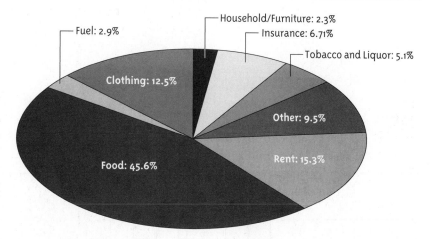

Fuel: 2.9%
Clothing: 12.5%
Food: 45.6%
Household/Furniture: 2.3%
Insurance: 6.71%
Tobacco and Liquor: 5.1%
Other: 9.5%
Rent: 15.3%

Indoor plumbing—like household appliances—indicated higher status. Wealthy homes had indoor plumbing for much of the nineteenth century, but middle-class plumbing systems remained rudimentary until the mass production of pipes and fittings. In Muncie, Indiana, in 1890, no more than two dozen houses had complete bathrooms, and only one family in six or eight had even a hydrant in the yard or a faucet in the kitchen. Even eighteen years later, a study of working families in New York found that although many used indoor toilets, few had full bathrooms.

Plumbing was a godsend to women in all working-class families. Those without this convenience had to carry chamber pots and heavy buckets to and from tenement courtyards, streams, wells, and privies and had to heat washwater on wood- and coal-burning stoves. Leonard Covello's mother cried at the party welcoming her to the United States in 1896, but she smiled through her tears when her husband's landlady, Carmela Accurso, showed her how to bring water into the kitchen with the turn of a handle. "Courage! You'll get used to it here," insisted Accurso. "See. Isn't it wonderful how the water comes out."

Plumbing, gas, and electricity—whether at home or at the commercial laundries that working people patronized when they had no sinks—also enabled higher standards of personal cleanliness. As these conveniences eliminated the work of making fires, cleaning lamps, and hauling wood, coal, and water, people began to keep their bodies, clothes, and houses considerably cleaner. But "labor-saving devices" did not necessarily reduce the amount of time women spent on chores; rather, the innovations simply encouraged them to conform to higher standards of housekeeping.

Residents noticed new levels of cleanliness on city streets, where automobiles and electric streetcars replaced horses and reduced horse droppings. And the new theory that disease was caused by germs—popularized in newspapers and magazines and by home economists in colleges, high

schools, and settlement houses—raised public awareness of the dangers of thoughtless disposal of sewage and garbage.

Wiring a Nation   Electricity created a new landscape of light across the country in the turn-of-the-century decades. Thomas A. Edison had produced his first electric lamp in 1879; even more important, he created a delivery system for generating and transmitting the new form of energy. By 1890, Edison's company manufactured more than one million light bulbs a year. Merchants and city officials used them in shop windows, streetlights, and theater marquees, all of which were electrified during the 1880s. By 1900, advertising signs flashed changing words in blinking lights; New York's Madison Square displayed a forty-five-foot electric pickle promoting Heinz products.

Factories and businesses installed electric lighting in the workplace between 1880 and 1900. In 1893, the Columbia Mills Company of Columbia, South Carolina, became the first textile mill to run on electricity. By 1919, electricity supplied about half of the power used by U.S. factories. Electric light did not flicker or heat up rooms, as did gas lighting. It reduced the danger of fire and made for a less polluted work environment. But workers did not welcome some other changes that electricity brought; for example, it made round-the-clock shifts much more common, and it reduced the number of mechanical breakdowns, which had given workers a much appreciated respite while belts were replaced. "That ruined our playhouse when they got power," one worker recalled.

Cottages for the Working Man
Some workers lived in employer-sponsored cottages located near their industrial employment. These houses were often similar to Daniel Cumming's residence at 1015 Olive Street in Chicago, the middle of the three worker's cottages shown here: one to one-and-a-half stories high with front facing gable roofs and decorative trim. Entrepreneurs and builders combined to supply inexpensive housing, but workers made significant sacrifices to move into the ranks of homeowners. In some cities, immigrants purchased homes at a rate equal to or greater than that of native-born residents. DN-0008602, *Chicago Daily News* negatives collection, Chicago Historical Society.

Privies

Toilet facilities, such as this backyard outhouse, remained minimal in some immigrant urban neighborhoods. Prints and Photographs Division, Library of Congress.

Many workers relied on electricity to get them to their jobs. Electric streetcars—first used in Richmond, Virginia, in 1887—caught on quickly because they were faster, cheaper, and cleaner than horse-drawn cars. Within three years, 15 percent of urban transit was electric-powered, and that figure rose to 94 percent by 1902. Between 1890 and 1902, the amount of track operated by electric railways almost tripled, and the number of

Electricity Comes to Wabash, Indiana

Shortly after Edison developed the incandescent electric light, small towns across the country hired companies to demonstrate electricity to their citizens. In Wabash, Indiana, a local reporter described the scene as four 3,000-candle arc lights were turned on, making Wabash one of the first U.S. cities wholly lit by electric light.

Ringing of the Court House bell announced the exhibition. The city presented a gloomy uninviting appearance. Suddenly from the towering dome of the Court House burst forth a flood of light which, under ordinary circumstances would have caused a shout of rejoicing from the thousands who had been crowding and jostling each other in the deep darkness of the evening. No shout, however, or token of joy disturbed the deep silence which suddenly enveloped the onlookers.

People stood overwhelmed with awe, as if in the presence of the supernatural. The strange weird light exceeded in power only by the sun, rendered the square as light as midday. . . . Men fell on their knees, groans were uttered at the sight, and many were dumb with amazement.

Wabash Plain Dealer, Feb. 7, 14, 21, 28; April 9, 1880, cited in David Nye, Electrifying America: Social Meanings of a New Technology, 1880–1940 (1990), 3.

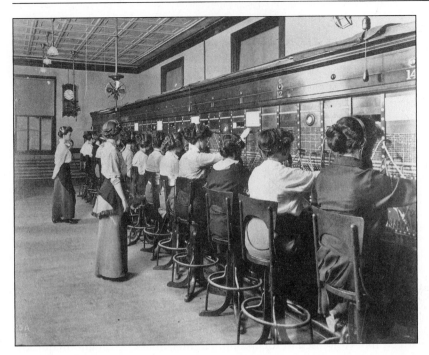

Telephone Operators
The work of telephone operators, such as these women at the New England Telephone Company switchboard in 1915, resembled industrial labor. Closely watched by supervisors, who monitored their speed and enforced rigid work rules, switchboard operators handled up to six hundred calls an hour. Print Department, Boston Public Library.

passengers they carried more than doubled. Electric streetcars offered inexpensive rides all over American cities, giving workers new mobility and creating "streetcar suburbs," residential districts that were separated from industrial centers.

Consumers could not just decide to buy electricity; it had to be made available by private companies and public utilities, which generally served industry and business first. Until 1910, the utilities saw only the wealthy as potential customers. But power companies soon realized that domestic demand, which was high at night, could balance the industrial load, which peaked during the day. After 1918, nationwide home electrification — only 10 percent in 1910 — proceeded rapidly, reaching 70 percent by 1930. Initially, however, most homes used only a few electric lights, and few homes had electric toasters, irons, fans, or other appliances (Figure 4.2).

Working people only belatedly benefited from the telephone wires that crisscrossed the urban sky. The telephone — first shown at the Centennial Exposition in 1876 by Alexander Graham Bell — had become a common tool of business during the 1880s and 1890s. In 1891, the New York and New Jersey Telephone Company had more than five times as many commercial customers as residential ones. Phones would remain too expensive for most urban workers for several decades. Families who needed to call a doctor or a druggist might ask to use the phone of a friendly grocer.

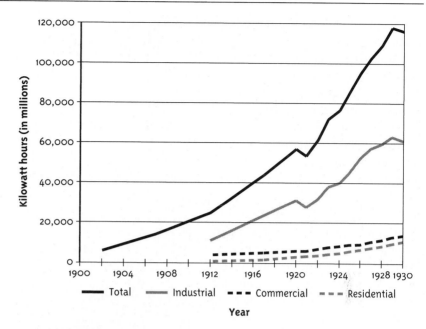

FIGURE 4.2 Uses of Electric Energy, 1902–1930

Use of electricity grew at an incredible clip—almost twenty-fold—between 1900 and 1930. Although industries were by far the heaviest consumers, urban residential use grew at the fastest rate after 1912.

Toward a Consumer Culture

Inequality also marked and shaped the emerging consumer culture. Nationally advertised brands became ubiquitous, as did chain stores. But the rural and urban poor could not afford most of the new products, and the chain stores tended to shy away from working-class districts. Working people did benefit from increased leisure time, and immigrants flocked to moving pictures, with their nickel admission fees and their silent stories that required no knowledge of English. But many Americans lacked access even to the cheap amusements they could afford. Amusement parks did not welcome African Americans, and farm folk lived too far from the bright lights of the city to benefit from urban forms of recreation. The new commercial culture also brought with it class-based cultural conflicts. Middle-class arbiters of morality tried to regulate disorderly amusements and direct working-class audiences into "uplifting" forms of recreation.

Marketing to the Masses As Americans became consumers, linked to the complex distribution network of a national market, their long-standing relationships with local craftspeople and storekeepers weakened. Customers now got information about products not from the people who made or sold them, but from persuasive advertisements. They purchased the mass-produced goods from stores that were conceived on principles similar to those of mass production. These new patterns were by no means universal or complete by the time the United States entered World War I, but they had taken a firm hold on the American way of life.

Advertised brand names gave manufacturers power over wholesalers and storekeepers. Before the 1880s, for example, wholesalers who distributed soap bought it from the manufacturer that offered the best price. But after 1881, when Procter and Gamble accidentally produced a floating soap and started pitching it to the nation, people began to ask for Ivory. Because the product could be obtained only from Procter and Gamble, wholesalers had to buy from that company. Manufacturers that created successful brands and convinced people to trust their advertising rather than the grocer's opinion had other advantages, too. They could charge more for their products and avoid competition and price fluctuations.

The most advanced advertising agencies and the biggest companies conducted sophisticated marketing campaigns that coordinated advertising with market research and other kinds of promotion, such as free samples. By 1911, the large Heinz sales force could coordinate twenty-five thousand store displays with the firm's monthly magazine advertisements. New marketing campaigns took advantage of and contributed to major developments in the advertising media. Newspapers and magazines had published commercial messages for centuries, usually in separate sections full of small, closely packed ads. But the newest periodicals, designed to highlight full-page ads, functioned literally as advertising media and depended on advertising, not subscriptions, for their revenues. Similarly, billboards had been used for many years, but advances in lithographic techniques now enabled the reproduction of huge color images. After 1890, national and regional firms could post thousands of signs at the same time, offering advertisers systematic control over billboards and streetcar placards across the country. And Heinz's pickle in New York and other electric signs kept ads in view around the clock.

Even the foreign-language press came to depend on national advertising. *Il Progresso Italo-Americano* promoted few American brands in 1905,

Picturesque America

Harry Grant Dart's illustration in a 1909 issue of *Life* magazine portrayed the increasingly aggressive and intrusive character of advertising in turn-of-the-century America. Harry Grant Dart, *Life*, 1909—Prints and Photographs Division, Library of Congress.

but in less than a decade, brand advertisements were eclipsing ads by Italian undertakers and dentists and by local merchants selling pasta, olive oil, cheese, and wine. In the Yiddish press, the National Biscuit Company advertised Uneeda Biscuits next to ads for Coca-Cola, Vaseline, Heinz, and Colgate.

Manufacturers were now segmenting their markets by income, producing different versions of a product for different segments. Arbuckle Brothers packaged Yuban coffee for wealthy urbanites and Ariosa for rural and poor city people. The Edison Company offered a range of phonographs in 1910, from the $200 Amberola, with sapphire needle and oak or mahogany cabinet, to a bare-bones model for $12.50.

Similarly, Procter and Gamble realized that to sell Crisco, it needed to accommodate ethnic cooking preferences. To Jews, it pointed out that Crisco was kosher and provided a substitute for nonkosher lard in cooking all-American apple pie. P&G received a New York rabbi's endorsement declaring that "the Hebrew Race had been waiting 4,000 years for Crisco." But in making their appeals to cooks who were accustomed to using chicken fat or olive oil in their recipes, even P&G's clever marketers failed to anticipate some opportunities, as when the Yup'ik and Inupiaq women of Alaska adopted Crisco for use in a berry confection called akutaq, which was traditionally made from caribou fat or seal oil.

In the new century, new kinds of retailing challenged the face-to-face personal relationships that went along with retail credit and delivery. Small merchants felt the competition of new kinds of stores—big city department stores, mail-order houses, and chain stores such as Woolworth's and the Great Atlantic and Pacific Tea Company (A&P)—which differed from traditional retailing not only in size, but also in distribution principles and techniques. Mass merchandising was based on the idea of turnover: moving goods into and out of the store as quickly as possible. Sears, Roebuck and Montgomery Ward honed the principle of turnover to a fine edge. These big Chicago mail-order houses offered a wider range of products than any other stores, and they offered a boon to farmers in remote areas. Montgomery Ward was selling about twenty-four thousand different items in the early 1890s, when Richard Sears and Alvah C. Roebuck began to expand their watch business. By 1900, Sears had surpassed Montgomery Ward, and in 1906, still doing only mail-order business, Sears moved to a forty-acre tract where merchandise was carried, as in mass production, by gravity chutes and conveyor belts. Two thousand employees opened and processed more than nine hundred sacks of mail every day. Sears owned or held a major interest in sixteen manufacturing plants, and it used those facilities to produce its own line of goods.

Chain stores had entered the grocery trade well before 1890, but they remained small until around 1912. In that year, the A&P introduced "economy stores," small operations that did not offer credit and delivery and could be run by two people. By 1915, A&P had twenty-two hundred stores. Consumers were shopping in tobacco, newsstand, variety, and drug chain stores by 1914. A few chains also ran clothing stores, piano stores, bookstores, and lumber yards. Some, like Sears, owned manufacturing plants; others offered low prices on nationally advertised brand merchandise. Local merchants viewed the chains, like the mail-order houses, as a serious threat to their business. And for consumers with cash to spend, the appeal was real; the new retailers offered lower prices and often a better selection. But many industrial workers who lived from paycheck to paycheck remained with the local merchants. They paid higher prices, but the local stores offered credit, and they knew the owners as neighbors or members of the same ethnic group. Moreover, chain stores tended to stay away from working-class neighborhoods. Even as late as the 1920s, two-thirds of Chicago's A&P and National Tea stores were in more affluent neighborhoods.

Leisure Time and Public Recreation Consumer culture of the early twentieth century rested on a new concept: leisure. Free time, an idea that would have mystified most farmers and artisans of a hundred years before, emerged as more people became wage earners, owing employers a certain number of hours a day or week and no more. Eight- and nine-hour days became widespread, the result of decades of dedicated union activity, new technologies, rationalized production, and protective legislation (Figure 4.3).

Like so much else in American life, leisure activities became commercialized. Home-made and local entertainment gave way to dance halls, vaudeville acts that toured the nation, and eventually moving-picture films. Boxing, baseball, and other sports became big business. Designed for profit and engineered by experts in the developing entertainment industry, these diversions turned individuals into audience members. But for all the excitement, there was also a loss, as highly talented paid performers replaced amateurs who had sung, danced, and played music in their homes and neighborhoods.

Public meeting places attracted young people seeking to escape big-city tenements, which offered no place to hold parties and precious little privacy. By the 1910s, greater New York had more than five hundred dance halls. "The town is dance mad," wailed a reformer. Dancing had long been popular in working-class neighborhoods. Workers in cities all over the country had danced not only at weddings and other family celebrations, but also at parties sponsored by unions and fraternal lodges, held in rented halls usually located next door to saloons. As time passed, hall owners opened their ballrooms to the public and made dancing a commercial activity.

FIGURE 4.3 Counting the Hours: The Workday and the Workweek, 1840–1972

As these two graphs indicate, the shorter-hour workweek emerged gradually and, except for the 1930s depression, evenly over the nineteenth and early twentieth centuries. Until 1940, the trend continued steadily downward.

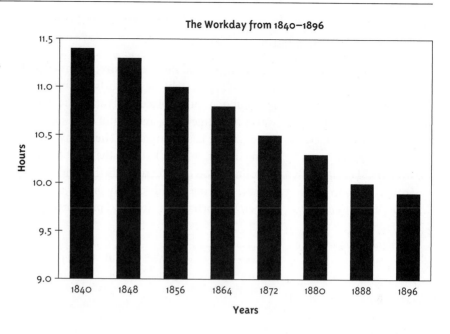

The Workday from 1840–1896

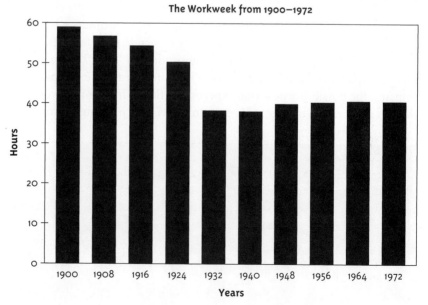

The Workweek from 1900–1972

Dance halls ranged from the respectable to the tawdry. The ones that featured and welcomed female prostitutes and homosexual men were often located in poor areas where residents had little power to object to what went on in neighboring establishments. Gay men and their culture were highly visible in the urban sexual underworld and were more publicly and fully

Coney Island Dance Halls

Coney Island offered eight large dance halls, each with a distinctive culture and customer as catalogued by Beatrice Stevenson for the Women's Municipal League. Reformers often targeted dance halls as a corrupting force for immigrant and working-class women.

At the largest and most exclusive, Saturday night sees an enormous crowd of elaborately dressed girls and men of good appearance and grooming. At other places girls are more plainly dressed, wear shirt-waists and street hats, and at still others the girls are of coarse appearance and are flashily dressed. The forms of dancing and behavior vary at the three grades of halls; in the most fashionable there is a good deal of promiscuous intercourse, flirting and picking up of acquaintances, but the dancing itself is usually proper and conventional; in the most Bohemian, behavior is free and pronouncedly bad forms of dancing are seen.

Beatrice L. Stevenson, "Working Girls' Life at Coney Island," *Yearbook of the Women's Municipal League*, Nov. 1911, p. 19. Cited in Kathy Peiss, *Cheap Amusements: Working Women and Leisure in Turn-of-the-Century New York* (1986, p. 126).

integrated into working-class culture than into that of the middle class. But the mainstays of the dance halls were young working women, who were expected to contribute most of the little they earned to their families. They stretched their pennies by allowing young men to "treat" them to an evening's food, drink, and entertainment in return for female companion-ship and the possibility of sexual experimentation. These young working women pioneered a new mixed-sex realm of leisure; previously, women's

Watch Your Steps

Aware of dancing's popularity, many urban reform organiza-tions arranged alternatives to commercial dance halls. The People's Institute organized this dance on New York's Lower East Side, in a setting in which young men and women's behav-ior could be supervised. People's Institute Papers—General Research Division, New York Public Library, Astor, Lenox and Tilden Foundations.

Summer in the City

Bathers enjoyed the Coney Island surf in 1903. Prints and Photographs Division, Library of Congress.

entertainment had been restricted largely to family outings or activities meant for women only. Dance halls and amusement parks offered young people a place to meet and enjoy each other's company unsupervised. Seeking excitement and independence, young immigrant women and men established the norms of modern romantic companionship.

Commercial amusement parks, which developed during the late 1890s, also featured dancing. By 1919, at least fifteen hundred parks took their place alongside vaudeville shows, movies, and professional sports events, offering diversion to people who were not wealthy. Amusement parks used technology to manufacture pleasure, and they encouraged people to spend money on transitory enjoyment. By 1910, every major city had at least one park that could be reached by trolley. They featured picnic groves, dance halls, skating rinks, pony and boat rides, a penny arcade, a carousel, a Ferris wheel, a roller coaster, and perhaps other rides in addition to nightly entertainment such as fireworks, band concerts, or musical shows. Elaborately decorated and highly mechanized, amusement parks like the Chutes in San Francisco, Pittsburgh's Kennywood Park, Boston's Revere Beach, and Denver's Manhattan Beach offered release from the dullness of the workaday world. "It is just like what I see when I dream of heaven," one young woman exclaimed on her first visit to Brooklyn's Coney Island. The Tunnel of Love had distinctly sexual overtones: "Will she throw her arms around your neck and yell?" advertisements asked.

Coney Island hotels, beaches, and boardwalks catered to a range of pocketbooks; one 1899 guidebook claimed that the area was "divided equally amongst the rich and the poor." Luna Park, a fantasy land of minarets, turrets, and 250,000 electric lights, had a relatively high admission price and was aimed at the respectable middle class. Steeplechase Park, with its fun houses, circuslike sideshows, and rougher rides, attracted working-class youths.

Many individuals crossed class and even race lines in seeking their pleasure — a practice called "slumming." Some frequented bars where prostitutes or gay men spent time and money. On the whole, however, most entertainment was tame enough for the average American, wealthy or not.

The Coney Island guidebook urged guests of the luxury hotels to spend some time at "the great resort for the crowds." People who could not afford Luna Park on a regular basis went as an occasional treat. The park welcomed immigrants if they could afford it; many viewed the diverse crowds as part of the draw. But the amusement parks did not welcome everyone; they generally barred African Americans.

Entertainment for the Masses An outing to an amusement park was an occasional treat, but plenty of everyday entertainment was also available — and at popular prices. Immigrant neighborhoods featured live theater, from participatory, hiss-the-villain melodrama to Shakespeare. By the 1890s, vaudeville competed with other forms of live entertainment by offering something for everybody: shapely women for the men, romantic singers for the women, slapstick comedians for the boys, animal acts for young children. Vaudeville ran almost nonstop — six days a week, from around noon to near midnight — at popular prices, based on the same principle of turnover that was used by department stores. "If I were to sell an orchestra chair for twenty-five cents, four times a day, it would be just as lucrative to me as if sold once for a dollar," declared Benjamin Franklin Keith, the most famous vaudeville impresario.

Over the next decades, nationwide vaudeville circuits emerged, controlled by booking syndicates that promoted big stars. To attract the largest possible audience, vaudeville promoters sought respectability; they sold no liquor, excluded prostitutes, and controlled smoking and drinking. They admitted women free on "Ladies Night" and sometimes courted them with gifts of coal, hams, dress patterns, and bonnets. To attract men, the master of ceremonies announced sports scores, and the boxers John L. Sullivan and Jack Johnson performed song-and-dance routines, told jokes, and sparred onstage. By 1910, more than half the vaudeville audience was middle class, and about one-third of all tickets were sold to women.

Performers at the big vaudeville houses spoke in English, which limited the immigrant audience. But they did feature ethnically oriented acts. Singers, acrobats, and comedians were listed on the program as "Irish," "German," "colored," "Hebrew," or "blackface" acts, each with its typical routine, jokes, and costumes. Many African Americans performed in vaudeville, but in both northern and southern cities, black audience members sat in a segregated balcony that was accessible only from a separate entrance in the alley. Middle-class black Americans refused to patronize vaudeville houses, but they still endured segregation — illegally, in cities such as New York, Chicago, and Los Angeles — in the first-class playhouses they attended.

Vaudeville houses had shown "magic lantern" slide shows before the invention of the movies, and after that invention, they started to include

"Blaybt er Lign Toyt im Hol" ("He Lies Dead in the Hall")

The "new" immigrants at the turn of the twentieth century added to the diversity of American culture by bringing with them the cultural forms and practices of their homelands. Drawing on the Yiddish language and musical traditions of Eastern Europe, Jewish immigrants created expressive musical shows in Lower East Side bars and theaters. This Yiddish song "Di Nyu Yorker Trern" ("New York Tears"), written earlier but first published in 1910, comments on the difficulties and tragedies of immigrant life in urban America.

New York bubbles like a pot
There's constant tumult and hubbub
You see a lot of people rushing around and
Often you see people's tears.
Misfortunes happen here at every step
And yet this hell is called Freeland
They put a family out on the street
Because they can't pay the rent on time
It rains, it pours, the tears flow
And the poor things sit depressed and forlorn

That's the New York tears
Which can never stop
A sob, a scream, a sigh and a woe
That's what you hear all the time
That's nothing new; wherever you go
You see the New York tears

Who hasn't heard of the murder
That took place not long ago on Montgomery Street
They found three people stabbed
A man, a wife, and a mother-in-law in a pool of blood
And there you hear a boy shot his friend
Two children were playing with a pistol
A boy of fourteen, what has he seen of life
The second boy, still younger, aimed at him
When he felt the shot
He screams "mama" loudly
And, running from the third floor
He lies dead in the hall

Mark Slobin, *Tenement Songs: The Popular Music of the Jewish Immigrants* (1982).

one-reel films between live acts. Moving pictures had evolved quickly from the 1893 peep shows that one person viewed by looking into a hand-wound Kinetoscope. Within three years, large-screen projection cinema had been perfected, and vaudeville audiences could watch "the movies" as part of the show. By 1905, entrepreneurs were setting up small storefront theaters featuring continuous shows composed entirely of one-reel films. These "nickelodeons," so named because they cost only a nickel, succeeded instantly. By 1907, there were more than two thousand of them in the United States.

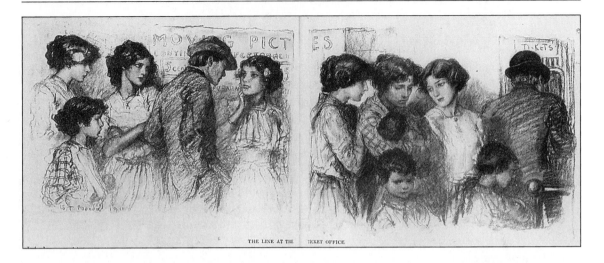

THE LINE AT THE TICKET OFFICE

Three years later, about twenty-six million Americans were attending weekly shows at ten thousand nickelodeons.

At first, as the comedian Milton Berle later remembered, "the movies were something for the lower classes and immigrants. Nice people didn't go to the 'flickers.'" Low admission prices that even children could afford soon made the movies the rage in workers' districts. Silent movies crossed many barriers of language and culture. "It doesn't matter whether a man is from Kamchutka or Stamboul," wrote one movie theater manager, "he can understand pictures." Many early films featured immigrant life, and immigrant producers built the early filmmaking industry. For much of the audience, silent films offered the first sustained contact with mainstream American culture.

Just before World War I, entrepreneurs began to build larger theaters. Equipped with carpets, ushers, and other marks of refinement, these movie halls showed new, longer feature films to the middle classes. Like vaudeville promoters, the most successful theater owners organized nationwide syndicates and circuits. Marcus Loew, who offered combination film and vaudeville shows, owned more than a hundred theaters throughout the United States and Canada.

Entrepreneurial energy also went into sports promotion. Although baseball had been played for decades, it took off as a spectator sport after the turn of the century, as clubs built stadiums along trolley, subway, and railroad lines. But the game was played everywhere, in all kinds of neighborhoods. Sandlot baseball diamonds were sometimes the only open spaces in the smoky, dirty, crowded inner cities. Hard-hitting, slick-fielding sons of immigrants worked their way up from neighborhood pickup games to local semipro teams and even the major leagues. As working people jammed the

The Line at the Ticket Office
This illustration from the reform magazine *Outlook* depicted a scene outside of a moving-picture show in a New York immigrant neighborhood. Wladyslav T. Benda, *Outlook* (June 24, 1911)—American Social History Project.

Moving Day in Hogan's Alley

Richard F. Outcault's color comic, first appearing in the *New York World* in 1896, lovingly portrayed the immigrant, working-class urban neighborhood as energetic and comically chaotic. *Hogan's Alley* (also known as "The Yellow Kid," named after the strange, hairless child in a yellow dress who appeared in each installment) instituted the serialized color comic strip as one of the many features in the new mass-circulation newspapers. Like the movies, newspapers now gained a broad audience by offering a range of features designed to please every taste. Richard F. Outcault, *New York World*, May 3, 1896—Prints and Photographs Division, Library of Congress.

bleachers to see these men, immigrants began to feel that they were part of mainstream American society.

African Americans, however, were again excluded. In the 1880s, as many as two dozen African Americans played professional baseball, but by the turn of the century, the major leagues had a firm whites-only policy. In 1901, Baltimore Orioles manager John McGraw tried (unsuccessfully) to circumvent the color line by claiming that a black second baseman named Charles Grant was actually a Cherokee Indian, "Chief Tokohama." Despite their talents, black players like Grant could play only on all-black traveling clubs such as the Philadelphia Giants.

Uplifting the Masses   The new commercial culture of spectator sports, dance halls, vaudeville theaters, movies, and amusement parks challenged the middle-class ideals and values of thrift, sobriety, moderation, and order. Unlike saloons, these recreations mixed the sexes, providing new arenas for courting; they promised excitement, romance, and adventure and supplanted older, community-organized amusements. An easy escape from the daily stresses of industrial life, these entertainments especially attracted young people, who made them the foundation for a new kind of working-class youth culture.

Commercial entertainment was exuberant, sensual, and irreverent. Genteel reformers considered it exploitative and dangerous. "Looping the loop amid shrieks of stimulated terror or dancing in disorderly saloon halls are perhaps natural reactions to a day spent in noisy factories," one critic admitted, "but the city which permits them to be the acme of pleasure and recreation to its young people commits a grievous mistake." Another reformer called Coney Island "a disgrace," a place where "humanity sheds its civilization and becomes half child, half savage."

Though the genteel wealthy had never successfully controlled the cultural lives of working Americans, they had long held sway over middle-class and mainstream culture. Beginning in the Gilded Age, their spokesmen— ministers, college presidents, political leaders—had sponsored high culture for the masses, seeking to instill in working people the values of thrift, sobriety, moderation, diligence, self-control, and moral uplift. In Pittsburgh, Andrew Carnegie funded a museum, library, and music hall that opened in 1895. It offered free Sunday organ recitals—excluding "all music of low or vulgar character"—to "develop the musical instincts of the people." Working people patronized such "uplift" institutions but turned them to their own ends. In 1891, 80,000 people—more than half of them residents of the Lower East Side—signed a petition to open the Metropolitan Museum of Art on Sundays.

Carnegie's best-known philanthropy supported a new urban institution, the free public library, directed at the reform of working-class reading habits. New paper and printing technologies and distribution networks were bringing reading material to more people than ever before, and literacy was increasing. By 1900, about 95 percent of white native-born Americans, almost 90 percent of white immigrants, and more than half of all African Americans could read and write. And they did read—a flourishing labor and ethnic press for news and political analyses and "dime novels" for romance and adventure. Middle-class critics called the ethnic press subversive and the dime novels cheap and immoral, but they only partially succeeded in directing working-class reading. Most library buildings were forbidding in structure and located outside working-class neighborhoods. Borrowers had to display a respectable demeanor and slog through a considerable amount of red tape to get a library card. As a result, many workers preferred using union reading rooms. In the South, public libraries barred African Americans.

How the Workingman Enjoys the Museum on His Only Day of Liberty
Some advocates of gentility endeavored to create cultural preserves that were sequestered from the taint of "cheap amusements." Prominent among such patrons of high art were the directors of New York's Metropolitan Museum of Art, who until 1891 resisted demands for opening on Sundays—the day when working people could attend. Samuel D. Ehrhart, *Puck*, January 2, 1889— New-York Historical Society.

THE METROPOLITAN MUSEUM.
"It is intended as much for the humblest artisan as for the most refined lover of the fine arts."—*Henry G. Marquand.*
And this is how the workingman enjoys the Museum on his only day of liberty. —*PUCK.*

"The Most Important and Fruitful Discovery . . ."

Literacy was not just for English-speaking workers; for Oscar Ameringer, who spoke and read only German when he first immigrated to the United States, the opportunity to read books in his native language opened up a whole new world. In this selection from his autobiography, Ameringer describes his discovery of American history books, translated into German, at the local public library.

The most important and fruitful discovery I made in the winter of 1887–88 was the public library of Cincinnati, Ohio. I stumbled on the place by sheer accident. . . . The place looked good. It was warm and comfortable. In one of the large rooms of the ground floor people were reading newspapers and other periodicals, some of them in German, and all this was free. So I made myself at home. . . .

I discovered that the Cincinnati Public Library harbored the very place I hankered for. It was the history room up on the third floor, and there I settled down. The few others who patronized it occasionally were bespectacled young men who tended strictly to their own business, never spoke, and usually walked on tiptoe. There was the regular librarian, an elderly maiden lady who was always too busy crocheting to disturb the tranquility of the room. My particular method of reading history was to extract a large volume from the bookshelves, lay it on the table, spread my elbow-cradled face between hands and if there were illustrations, look at the illustrations. If there were no illustrations, I would snooze over the English text. . . .

One day when I passed too close to the elderly maiden lady, she looked up from her crocheting and asked me . . . "If you are so fond of history, would you mind if I selected a course of reading for you? I have noticed your reading is rather indiscriminate. You rarely selected the same book a second time."

I was caught. From now on, it was either read history or keep out.

The first book she handed me was a life of Tom Jefferson. It was written by a [18]48 revolutionist. . . . I should add that this life of Tom Jefferson was printed in German, thereby closing my last avenue of escape from reading it. I didn't snooze over that book. On the contrary, it kept me so wide awake that when "lights out" sounded that night I was still reading, and next morning was first on deck in the history room. This Tom Jefferson was a man after my own heart! His whole crowd belonged to my league. These fellows had no more respect for high priests, princes, kings, and hand-me-down authority than I had. They were rebels from the word go. They . . . had dissolved the unholy partnership between church and state. Declared that one man was as good as the next one and maybe a darned sight better.

Oscar Ameringer, *If You Don't Weaken: The Autobiography of Oscar Ameringer* (1983).

Philanthropists and reformers also tried to lure the "lower orders" to enjoy nature in the parks, away from the debauchery of back alleys, brothels, gaming dens, and saloons. Frederick Law Olmsted, the most influential landscape architect of the nineteenth century, declared that his major work, Central Park in Manhattan, "exercises a distinctly harmonizing and refining influence upon the most unfortunate and lawless classes of the city." Many working people seized the opportunity to get outside. Those who were newly arrived from the countryside or desperate to escape crowded tenements used public parks extensively and with great respect. Unions and fraternal organizations sponsored gatherings in parks. Families spent whole Sundays there, bringing a meal or two along as picnics. Before Adriana Valenti and her family would go to Central Park, she remembered, her mother "would make us all sit on the chair and we all had high shoes at the time—and she would see that they were all buttoned, and if we looked presentable."

But philanthropists and middle-class Americans sometimes differed over the use of parks by working people. In Worcester, Massachusetts, middle-class spokespeople constantly complained about the "unsavory and idle appearance" of the working people who relaxed on the city common. Similar complaints inspired Manhattan's park commissioner to license rental chair businesses in city parks in 1901. After a major public protest and much newspaper publicity, however, free park seats reappeared, and 20,000 people rallied to celebrate victory.

Middle-class people more often entertained themselves at home, considering it the appropriate thing to do. There, they conducted their private lives in quiet, orderly neighborhoods far from the noise and overcrowding of rough-and-tumble working-class districts. They had room to socialize and money to patronize restaurants or private clubs instead of public saloons. In African American communities, too, the people who cared about respectability stayed away from working-class dance halls such as "Funky Butt Hall" in New Orleans; they did their socializing at church-sponsored suppers, fairs, concerts, and excursions, where drinking and often dancing were forbidden.

Conclusion: A New Era Dawns, Old Inequalities Persist

The changes that swept the United States at the turn of the century were evident in the landscape in New York, Pittsburgh, Denver, San Francisco, and other major cities. Public architecture celebrated the dynamic power of urban America. Travelers entered major cities through magnificent new railroad stations built of granite and steel, with vast train sheds and high-ceilinged waiting rooms. Nearby tall office buildings, made possible by new construction techniques, housed the headquarters of large corporations, proclaiming their

Sunday Afternoon in Union Square

At the turn of the century, a group of painters, later termed the Ashcan School, was inspired by the city's diverse population and popular institutions. In particular, John Sloan recorded and celebrated the ways in which New Yorkers dealt with living in a new, heterogeneous environment populated by strangers. In this 1912 painting, for example, he showed how public spaces such as city parks offered people opportunities to watch and assess one another. John Sloan, 1912, oil on canvas, 16 1/4 × 32 inches — Bowdoin College Museum of Art, Brunswick, Maine. Bequest of George Otis Hamlin.

dominant position in the U.S. economy. Downtown department stores competed to present the most opulent displays and the greatest assortment of goods, while expensive restaurants, music halls, and nightclubs offered the middle and upper classes exciting and varied entertainment.

But in individual lives, new ways coexisted with old ones. People bought some new things but not others, and they put their new purchases next to their treasured keepsakes. Farmers ordered from the Sears catalogue but continued to barter eggs and butter for other goods sold by country storekeepers. Urban workers bought some goods from pushcarts and others from department stores. Yet the future was clear: young people insisted on new levels of convenience, leisure, and material comfort. The children of immigrants understood the "land of the dollar" better than their parents ever would. But before immigrants, workers, women, and African Americans could fully share in the bounty, they would have to overcome economic, social, and political barriers that limited their participation. Those inequities and barriers — low wages, dirty streets, unsafe working conditions, racial and gender discrimination — fueled the conflicts of the Progressive era and the decades that followed it.

The Years in Review

1876

- Alexander Graham Bell introduces the telephone at the Centennial Exposition in Philadelphia.

1879

- Thomas A. Edison produces the first electric lamp; by 1890, Edison manufactures more than one million light bulbs a year.

1881

- Procter and Gamble introduces Ivory soap, which becomes the model for nationally distributed brand-name merchandise.

1883

- The first automatic-line canning factory opens, soldering cans at the rate of fifty per minute.

1887

- The first urban electric streetcar system is installed in Richmond, Virginia, by Frank J. Sprague; by 1902, electricity will power 94 percent of all urban transit.

1889

- The first patent is granted for a time clock; many factories will adopt time clocks within the next five years.

1891

- Eighty thousand people, many of them working class, sign a petition to open the Metropolitan Museum of Art on Sundays.

1893

- Columbia Mills Company of Columbia, South Carolina, becomes the first textile mill to run on electricity.
- The first moving pictures are introduced. By 1910, twenty-six million Americans attend weekly shows at ten thousand nickelodeons.

1895

- Andrew Carnegie funds a museum, library, and music hall in Pittsburgh to provide high culture for the masses.

1903

- Luna Park, one of the first amusement parks, opens at Coney Island, New York, with spectacular rides and attractions.
- Wilbur and Orville Wright make the first sustained (852 feet in 59 seconds) manned flight in a gas-powered airplane at Kitty Hawk, North Carolina.

1905

- The first theater dedicated to moving pictures opens in Pittsburgh, Pennsylvania, and charges customers five cents to watch *The Great Train Robbery.*

1906

- Americans hear the nation's first radio broadcast of a voice and music program.

- Sears, Roebuck expands its mail-order business, using manufacturing plants in which the company has a share to produce its own lines of goods.
- San Francisco sets up segregated schools for Japanese immigrants.

1907
- The YMCA offers English language and temperance lessons to immigrant workers.

1910
- White mobs attack African Americans in Boston, New York City, Cincinnati, Houston, and Norfolk after black boxer Jack Johnson's defeat of the "Great White Hope," James Jeffries.
- The United States becomes the world's foremost industrial power.

1911
- Frederick Winslow Taylor publishes *The Principles of Scientific Management.*

1912
- The American Federation of Labor voices opposition to scientific management.
- The S.S. *Titanic* sinks in the North Atlantic with 1,513 people aboard, including streetcar heir Harry Elkins Widener and copper heir Benjamin Guggenheim.
- Procter and Gamble markets Crisco shortening with an innovative advertising and marketing campaign.

1913
- Henry Ford creates the first assembly line to manufacture the Model T; by 1914, 250,000 low-cost Model Ts are produced each year.

1914
- Henry Ford introduces the Five-Dollar Day in an effort to reduce worker turnover and prevent unionization.

Additional Readings

For more on economic growth between 1896 and 1914 and the rise of mass production, scientific management, and welfare capitalism, see: Alfred D. Chandler, *The Visible Hand: The Managerial Revolution in American Business* (1977); Clark Davis, *Company Men: White-Collar Life and Corporate Cultures in Los Angeles, 1892–1941* (2000); Ray Ginger, *Age of Excess: The United States from 1877–1914* (1975); Tamara K. Hareven, *Amoskeag: Life and Work in an American Factory-City* (1978); David Hounshell, *From the American System to Mass Production, 1800–1932: The Development of*

Manufacturing Technology in the United States (1984); Sanford Jacoby, *Employing Bureaucracy: Managers, Unions, and the Transformation of Work in American Industry, 1900–1945* (1985); Nikki Mandell, *The Corporation as Family: The Gendering of Corporate Welfare, 1890–1930* (2002); Stephen Meyer III, *The Five Dollar Day: Labor Management and Social Control in the Ford Motor Company, 1908–1921* (1981); Philip Scranton, *Endless Novelty: Specialty Production and American Industrialization, 1865–1925* (1997); and Olivier Zunz, *Making America Corporate, 1870–1920* (1990).

For more on the transformation of women's work, see: Susan Porter Benson, *Counter Cultures: Saleswomen, Managers, and Customers in American Department Stores, 1890–1940* (1986); Eileen Boris, *Home to Work: Motherhood and the Politics of Industrial Homework in the United States* (1994); Margery Davies, *Woman's Place Is at the Typewriter: Office Work and Office Workers, 1870–1930* (1982); Wendy Gamber, *The Female Economy: The Millinery and Dressmaking Trades, 1860–1930* (1997); Joanne J. Meyerowitz, *Women Adrift: Independent Wage Earners in Chicago, 1880–1930* (1988); Stephen H. Norwood, *Labor's Flaming Youth: Telephone Operators and Worker Militancy, 1878–1923* (1990); Vicki L. Ruiz and Ellen Carol DuBois, eds., *Unequal Sisters: A Multi-Cultural Reader in U.S. History* (1994); and Susan Strasser, *Never Done: A History of American Housework* (1982).

For more on how new technologies changed everyday life, see: Ruth Schwartz Cowan, *More Work for Mother: The Ironies of Household Technology from Open Hearth to Microwave* (1983); Claude S. Fischer, *America Calling: A Social History of the Telephone to 1940* (1992); Suellen Hoy, *Chasing Dirt: The American Pursuit of Cleanliness* (1995); Ronald R. Kline, *Consumers in the Country: Technology and Social Change in Rural America* (2000); David E. Nye, *Electrifying America: Social Meanings of a New Technology* (1991); Michael O'Malley, *Keeping Watch: A History of American Time* (1990); and Linda Simon, *Dark Light: Electricity and Anxiety from the Telegraph to the X-Ray* (2004).

For more on consumer culture and mass marketing, see: Lizabeth Cohen, *A Consumers' Republic: The Politics of Mass Consumption in Postwar America* (2003); Gary Cross, *An All-Consuming Century: Why Commercialism Won in Modern America* (2000); Walter A. Friedman, *Birth of a Salesman: The Transformation of Selling in America* (2004); Lawrence B. Glickman, *A Living Wage: American Workers and the Making of Consumer Society* (1997); Neil Harris, *Cultural Excursions: Marketing Appetites and Cultural Tastes in Modern America* (1990); Carolyn Kitch, *The Girl on the Magazine Cover: The Origins of Visual Stereotypes in American Mass Media* (2001); William Leach, *Land of Desire: Merchants, Power, and the Rise of a*

New American Culture (1993); Roland Marchand, *Advertising the American Dream: Making Way for Modernity, 1920–1940* (1985); Timothy B. Spears, *100 Years on the Road: The Traveling Salesman in American Culture* (1995); Susan Strasser, *Satisfaction Guaranteed: The Making of the American Mass Market* (1989); and Susan Strasser, *Waste and Want: A Social History of Trash* (1999).

For more on the benefits of and social conflicts over increased time for leisure activities and the expansion of mass entertainment, see:
Judith A. Adams, *The American Amusement Park Industry: A History of Technology and Thrills* (1991); Richard Butsch, ed., *For Fun and Profit: The Transformation of Leisure into Consumption* (1990); George Chauncey, *Gay New York: Gender, Urban Culture, and the Making of the Gay Male World, 1890–1940* (1994); Lizabeth Cohen, *Making a New Deal: Industrial Workers in Chicago, 1919–1939* (1990); Francis G. Couvares, *The Remaking of Pittsburgh: Class and Culture in an Industrializing City 1877–1919* (1984); Elizabeth Ewen, *Immigrant Women in the Land of Dollars: Life and Culture on the Lower East Side, 1890–1925* (1985); Steven M. Gelber, *Hobbies: Leisure and the Culture of Work in America* (1999); Andrew R. Heinze, *Adapting to Abundance: Jewish Immigrants, Mass Consumption, and the Search for American Identity* (1990); Lary May, *Screening Out the Past: The Birth of Mass Culture and the Motion Picture Industry* (1980); David Nasaw, *Going Out: The Rise and Fall of Public Amusements* (1993); Kathy Peiss, *Cheap Amusements: Working Women and Leisure in Turn-of-the-Century New York* (1986); Roy Rosenzweig, *Eight Hours for What We Will: Workers and Leisure in an Industrial City, 1870–1920* (1983); Roy Rosenzweig and Elizabeth Blackmar, *The Park and the People: A History of Central Park* (1992); and Shane White and Graham J. White, *Stylin': African American Expressive Culture from the Beginnings to the Zoot Suit* (1998).

5

Radicals and Reformers
in the Progressive Era

1900–1914

Solidarity and Skates
These children were distributing socialist leaflets during a New York streetcar drivers' strike in September 1916. Prints and Photographs Division, Library of Congress.

O N   T H E   W A R M   S P R I N G afternoon of March 25, 1911, a small fire broke out in a bin of rags at the Triangle Shirtwaist Company, a crowded garment factory on New York City's Lower East Side. The factory's fire escapes were poorly designed, and foremen had locked or blocked the exits, fearful that workers would sneak out to rest or would leave with stolen needles and thread. The spreading fire trapped the workers. In less than an hour, 146 people — most of them young Italian and Jewish women recently arrived in America — perished from smoke inhalation or from the desperate ten-story leap to escape the flames. Many more sustained injuries.

The Triangle fire horrified Americans and focused public attention on the human costs of industrialization. In the aftermath of the tragedy, middle-class reformers, socialists, and working people, including survivors of the fire, united to pressure lawmakers for factory regulation. This outpouring of concern was emblematic of the times. By the turn of the century, many Americans — wageworkers, the middle class, and elite humanitarians — sensed that corporate power was out of control and that the industrial order needed fundamental reform. In the first decades of the new century, they expressed this indignation through a growing chorus of public criticism of corporate giants and escalating labor challenges to capital. Running for president in 1912, Woodrow Wilson would declare that in this era of corporate capitalism, "the individual has been submerged" and "people are coming to feel they have no control over their affairs." In that election, three out of four voters agreed that something needed to be done to rein in great wealth and restore individual autonomy, even if they disagreed on who should do the job. Most backed Wilson, who ran as a

Democrat. Others placed their faith in the Progressive Party candidate, Theodore Roosevelt. And 6 percent of the popular vote went to the Socialist Eugene V. Debs. Even the most conservative candidate, Republican President William Howard Taft—who received less than one-quarter of the vote—had taken steps in his previous term to curb the power of giant corporations.

This statement at the polls reflected a wide-ranging set of movements or coalitions that had sprung up to address the cultural, economic, social, and political dislocations and inequities caused by the growth of industrial capitalism. Historians use the term *progressivism* to describe these movements. The term is confusing because it does not refer to a single movement or party; rather, it applies to a network of overlapping and sometimes conflicting organizations and coalitions that campaigned to reform American society between 1890 and the outbreak of World War I in 1914. Millions of Americans from all walks of life marched under the progressive banner— from working people battling for better pay and control over their lives to middle-class urban reformers striving to improve living and working conditions in the slums to black women campaigning against lynching. Some "reformers" had what we might consider conservative goals—to "Americanize" millions of new immigrants, to close working-class saloons, to make city government more businesslike, or to make American society more "orderly." Progressive politicians set goals of "trust busting," regulating corporate activity, and conserving the natural environment. And some parts of the movement addressed issues that were specific to a certain gender, race, or social group, such as women campaigning for the right to vote and African Americans protesting disenfranchisement and lynching.

In retrospect, progressivism accomplished less than it promised. Big business managed to avoid or subvert some of the most significant restrictions on its power, and African Americans actually experienced reversals during this period. Still, the ferment of the Progressive era did bring important improvements in the lives of many ordinary Americans and laid the foundations for the broader reforms of the New Deal era. But if it turned out to be less than promised, progressivism was also more than a series of events in the lives of a few famous men such as presidents Roosevelt and Wilson and their legislative reforms or just middle-class reformers. Middle-class Americans seeking to reorder their society were, of course, prominent in progressive reform. But progressivism was much more than that: it was an insurgency from below. Women of all classes spearheaded major reforms. Another critical influence came, ironically, from radicals who were skeptical of progressivism's potential for effectiveness. Groups who wanted a more thoroughgoing transformation of the system mobilized pressure that would lead to more moderate reforms. As these popular insurgencies moved party politics to the left, national political leaders—for one of the few times in U.S. history—competed to be known as "reformers" and "progressives." Even if feminists, radicals, African Americans, and industrial workers failed to win all of their demands, they succeeded in setting the political agenda to which the more elite progressives such as Roosevelt and Wilson would respond.

Andru Karnegi and Mr. Rucevelt: Simplified Spelling and the Contours of Progressivism

One of the strangest of the many early twentieth-century reform movements was the effort to simplify the spelling of words, led by the Spelling Reform Association. This seemingly peripheral movement was actually a microcosm encompassing the themes and forces found in progressivism in that era: its focus on rationality and technical expertise; its strong support among the middle classes; its disdain for traditional political parties; its optimistic faith in the power of the state; its diverse constituency; its shifting coalitions, depending on the specific social, economic, cultural, and political issue; its international character; and its limited success.

Supporters of the reform complained bitterly that the English language lent itself to innumerable variations in spelling (one obsessive reformer counted 1,690 different spellings of *diarrhea* in Civil War pension applications) and that officially approved spellings were illogical and irrational. *Could*, they argued, should really be spelled *kud* or *cud*, and there were at least twenty ways of spelling the sound of *sh*—as in *ship*, *sure*, *ocean*, *partial*, and *mansion*. *Foolish*, they noted (in what was not the best choice of an example), could be just as logically spelled in 613,975 different ways.

Like many other early twentieth-century reformers, the advocates of simplified spelling engaged in what one historian calls a "search for order." They viewed the lack of standardization in American spelling as chaotic, inefficient, and irrational—hence, badly in need of reform. They complained about the "appalling and incalculable waste of nervous energy" on the teaching of English spelling and calculated that the *Encyclopedia Britannica* could (or kud) be published in twenty volumes instead of twenty-four.

Such searches for order and efficiency relied increasingly on professionals and experts. Progressives differed on many points, but they generally shared an optimistic belief in progress and trust in the ability of professionals to find rational, scientific solutions to social problems. Such ideas appealed particularly to members of the new professional class—physicians, businessmen, engineers, managers, and scholars—who believed that they could build a better society by analyzing social ills and taking intelligent, informed action. As shock troops of the progressive causes, these middle-class professionals and experts were often joined by other young members of the middle class, especially women, who brought a moral and

The Crusaders — Marching Embattled 'Gainst the Saracens of Graft
Using popular stereotypes about Christianity and civilization, this February 1906 *Puck* cartoon celebrated "muckraking" journalists and publications by depicting reformers as the European Crusaders who undertook campaigns during the eleventh, twelfth, and thirteenth centuries to wrest the Holy Land from Muslim control (here termed *Saracens* and representing corruption). Hassman, *Puck*, February 21, 1906 — New-York Historical Society.

sometimes religious fervor to reform. Crusading writers and photographers (dubbed "muckrakers" by Theodore Roosevelt), for example, played a vital role in spreading progressive ideas, linking reform elements, and informing the public about corruption and monopoly. Investigative reporters such as Lincoln Steffens and Ida Tarbell (who wrote for magazines such as *McClure's*) and political novelists such as Upton Sinclair revealed political and corporate wrongdoing, targeting such major institutions as Rockefeller's Standard Oil Company, the stock market, and the meatpacking industry.

These young middle-class progressives tended to distrust political parties. Although the Progressive Party was founded in 1912, most reformers worked outside the political party system; this was particularly true for women, who were still denied the right to vote at the time. While disdaining traditional political parties, however, progressives favored governmental action. Thus, the spelling reformers counted as their greatest success President Theodore Roosevelt's 1906 executive order directing that government publications would henceforth follow such simplified spellings as *kisst* for *kissed* and *thru* for *through*. This use of governmental power reflected the broader progressive conviction that the government should intervene in market relationships on behalf of the poor and of the public.

Despite the prominence of the middle-class experts in simplified spelling and other areas of reform, the progressive movement appealed to a much broader social spectrum. Radical activists worked side by side with more conservative colleagues, endorsing moderate reforms and spreading their more militant ideas at the same time. Black and white women campaigned together for municipal trash collection, bridging the chasm of race. At times (as in the aftermath of the Triangle fire), working-class Americans with their own agendas worked with progressives. And on some issues — spelling reform was one of them — the reform agenda attracted leading industrialists such as Andrew Carnegie or politicians from old-line wealthy families such as Theodore Roosevelt. (Satirists lampooned them as Andru Karnegi and Mr. Rucevelt.) Rather than an internally coherent social movement with an easily definable program, the progressive movement was more of a series of shifting coalitions.

The ideas and values that became part of progressivism in the United States flowed across national boundaries. Factory reformers and public health activists studied the work of their colleagues abroad and met with them despite the expense and time involved in transatlantic travel. Sometimes — as with spelling reform, which the English protested vociferously — the proper nature of reform was debated internationally.

The diversity of participants reflected, in turn, the range of issues that progressives addressed, from seemingly trivial matters such as spelling reform to profound questions about the control of corporate enterprise. Broadly speaking, progressives worked in three areas that all responded in some way to the vast social and economic transformations accompanying industrial capitalism in the United States. Social and economic reformers most directly confronted the inequities of the new order. They crusaded for better housing, cleaner streets, improved sanitation, safer factories, and more humane working conditions, and they challenged the untrammeled

Steelworkers at a Russian Boarding House

Some progressive reformers turned to social science to understand the impact of industrial capitalism on turn-of-the-century America, and photography was one of the new documentary tools available to them. From 1907 to 1908, Lewis Hine was hired to photograph immigrant steelworkers in Homestead, Pennsylvania, for the Pittsburgh Survey, the first extensive study of a major industrial city. In addition to their value as documentary evidence, Hine's photos conveyed a new reform message about the immigrant to the American public. In contrast to the detachment and distaste apparent in Jacob Riis's pictures, Hine constructed a positive view of worthy newcomers, deserving of a role in American society and all the benefits that would bring.
4 1/2 × 6 1/2 inches — Photograph Library, The Metropolitan Museum of Art. Gift of Mr. and Mrs. Wolfgang Pulverman, 1969. Copyright The Metropolitan Museum of Art.

power of giant corporations and trusts. Not surprisingly, such reforms most often had working-class support. Working people were much less likely to share the agenda of the cultural reformers, who campaigned against what they saw as the immorality and vice embodied in prostitution, gambling, and—most especially—drinking. The third group, the political reformers, tried to rein in urban political machines and political corruption. Sometimes, they worked for expanded political franchise (as in the movement for woman's suffrage), but at other times, they actually restricted voting rights (by backing literacy tests that excluded many immigrants and African Americans).

Spelling reform ultimately did not transform the written form of American English. Public protests led Roosevelt to rescind his order, although he vowed to continue it in his private correspondence. But some limited changes stuck—*labour* became *labor*, and *humour* and *rumour* also dropped their second *u* in the United States, although England retains the original forms. Progressivism had a similarly mixed fate. Despite the enormous energy and lofty ideas of progressives, their achievements were limited. But their legacy of an optimistic belief in the positive potential of government marked the beginning of a new relationship between working people and the government.

Women Progressives

Women's activism was central to the development of progressivism. Young middle-class women who created settlement houses in urban neighborhoods played a particularly notable role in pioneering reform causes. Yet even decades before the formation of the Progressive Party in 1912, progressive causes and organizations were identified with women leaders, who—despite or really because of their exclusion from electoral politics—created associations seeking action on issues of pressing concern such as health, child care, and public morality. Such female activism grew significantly at the turn of the century, and it came to focus increasingly on seeking governmental solutions to social problems.

Come, Brothers, You Have Grown So Big You Cannot Afford to Quarrel
William A. Rogers's 1901 *Harper's Weekly* cover depicted capital and labor as evenly matched—with commerce a beleaguered referee. Variations on this theme appeared frequently in the Progressive era's mainstream press. Commerce alternated with other allegorical figures such as "The Nation" or "The Public," suggesting that organized labor now represented a powerful interest, equal to capital and equally oblivious to how its actions affected the well-being of ordinary Americans. William A. Rogers, *Harper's Weekly*, June 1, 1901—American Social History Project.

Not surprisingly, much activism fed into the struggle to win the vote that women had been waging since the middle of the nineteenth century. But some women took a much broader view, calling for the full equality of the sexes, not just the right to vote. They also linked the suffrage cause to efforts to improve laboring conditions, especially by outlawing child labor. Although some support for the rights of working women came from middle- and upper-class female allies, the most important impetus for change came from below, from women who organized themselves into militant unions, particularly in the garment industry.

Social Settlements and Municipal Housekeeping Among the earliest and most dynamic vehicles of progressivism were the settlement houses that were established in working-class neighborhoods, largely by young women from middle- and upper-class homes who sought to ease the transition of immigrants into American life. Beginning in the late 1880s, hundreds of young people moved into immigrant working-class neighborhoods across the United States to live in nonreligious communities devoted to reform. Jane Addams's Hull House in Chicago was the best known, but settlements were to be found in every urban center. In New York, Atlanta, and some smaller southern cities, middle-class African American women ran settlements in poor black neighborhoods. Seeking to provide social services that were otherwise unavailable to their neighbors, black and white settlement workers all over the country organized kindergartens, adult education classes, health programs, and unemployment bureaus. By 1910, hundreds of thousands of working people were using more than four hundred settlement houses nationwide.

For a new generation of college-educated women searching for suitable work, settlement houses offered homes and occupations. These women generally did not have the option of combining careers with family life; instead, they eschewed family in order to forge new careers for women. Living and working in immigrant neighborhoods, settlement workers had a close-up view of the intense emotional bonds and self-sacrifice that sustained the immigrant urban working class. But most middle-class progressives viewed immigrant customs with incomprehension or disdain, and even the most sensitive settlement workers saw their mission as uplifting working-class culture. Lillian Wald, founder of New York's Henry Street Settlement, defended her neighbors fiercely against charges that they were "degraded," encouraged them to form trade unions, and mediated disputes between immigrant women and their Americanized daughters. But she also staged "coming-out" parties for these daughters, modeled on the debutante balls of the elite. In spite of their good intentions, settlement workers and other middle-class progressives often found themselves taking stands against

Settlement Houses and New Immigrants: Places of Caring or Control?

Immigrant men and women had a wide range of experiences with settlement house reformers. As these two documents reveal, some immigrants found the settlement houses to be places of refuge and caring; others encountered reformers who were arrogant and patronizing. The first document, which describes a positive encounter, is drawn from the oral memoirs of Rosa, an Italian immigrant who lived and worked at a Chicago settlement house, Chicago Commons. The second excerpt from "The Free Vacation House," a short story written by Jewish immigrant Anzia Yezierska, illustrates an unpleasant encounter between an immigrant and reformer.

"Then We'd Have Some Cake and Coffee"

In the first beginning we always came in to the club and made two circles in the room. One circle was for those ladies who could talk English and the other was for the ladies who talked German. Mrs. Reuter talked German to the German ladies and Miss Gray talked English to the other ladies. But I guess they both did the same preaching. They used to tell us that it's not nice to drink the beer, and we must not let the baby do this and this. Me, I was the only Italian woman — where were they going to put me? I couldn't talk German, I went in the English Circle. So after we had about an hour or an hour and a half of preaching, they would pull up the circle and we'd play the games together. All together we'd play the games — the Norwegian, the German, the English and me. Then we'd have some cake and coffee and the goodnight song. . . .

Pretty soon they started the classes to teach us poor people to talk and write in English. The talk of the people in the settlement house was different entirely than what I used to hear. I used to love the American people, and I was listening and listening how they talked. That's how I learned to talk such good English. Oh, I was glad when I learned enough English to go by the priest in the Irish church and confess myself and make the priest understand what was the sin! But I never learned to do the writing in English. I all the time used to come to that class so tired and so sleepy after scrubbing and washing the whole day — I went to sleep when they starting the writing. . . .

I have to tell about another good thing the settlement house did for me. That winter my [baby] Leo died we were still living in that little wooden house in the alley. All my walls were thick with frosting from the cold, and I got bronchitis on the lungs, with blood coming up. So one of those good ladies from the Commons, she arranged and sent me to a kind of home in the country where people go to get well. They had the nice nurses in that place and they cured me up good. I had a good time there, too.

Marie Hall Ets, *Rosa: The Life of an Italian Immigrant* (1970).

"For Why Must I Tell You All My Business?"

How came it that I went to the free vacation house was like this:

One day the visiting teacher from the school nursery comes to find out why don't I get the children ready for school in time; for why are they so often late.

I let out on her my whole bitter heart. I told her my head was on wheels from worrying. . . .

"My dear woman," she says, "you are about to have a nervous breakdown. You need to get away to the country for a rest and vacation. . . ."

Later, in a few days, I just finished up with Masha and Mendel and Frieda and Sonya to send them to school, and I was getting Aby ready for kindergarten, when I hear a knock on the door, and a lady comes in. She had a white starched dress like a nurse and carried a black satchel in her hand.

"I am from the Social Betterment Society," she tells me. "You want to go to the country?"

Before I could say something, she goes over to the baby and pulls out the rubber nipple from her mouth, and to me she says, "You must not get the child used to sucking this; it is very unsanitary."

"Gott im Himmel!" I beg the lady. "Please don't begin with that child, or she'll holler my head off. She must have the nipple. I'm too nervous to hear her scream like that."

When I put the nipple back again in the baby's mouth, the lady takes herself a seat, and then takes out a big black book from her satchel. Then she begins to question me. What is my first name? How old I am? From where come I? How long I'm already in this country? Do I keep any boarders? What is my husband's first name? How old is he? How long he is in this country? By what trade he works? How much wages he gets for a week? How much money do I spend out for rent? How old are the children, and everything about them.

"My goodness!" I cry out. "For why is it necessary all this to know? For why must I tell you all my business? What difference does it make already if I keep boarders, or I don't keep boarders? If Masha had the whooping-cough or Sonya had the measles? Or whether I spent out for my rent ten dollars or twenty? Or whether I come from Schnipshnock or Kovner Gubernie?"

"We must make a record of all the applicants, and investigate each case," she tells me. "There are so many who apply to the charities, we can help only those who are most worthy."

"Charities!" I scream out. "Ain't the charities those who help the beggars out? I ain't no beggar. I'm not asking for no charity. My husband, he works. . . ."

"If your application is approved, you will be notified," she says to me, and out she goes.

Anzia Yezierska, "The Free Vacation House," *Hungry Hearts* (1920).

workers' preferences on certain issues, such as banning alcohol. Middle-class progressives tended to view saloons and drinking with horror, whereas most male immigrant workers saw the saloon as a central social and cultural institution.

Settlement houses trained not only immigrants but also an entire generation of reformers. Typically, they spent a few years helping immigrants in the urban slums before moving into better neighborhoods and wider political arenas and campaigning for social justice, improved public health and urban sanitation, and labor reform. Influenced by their experiences in the settlement houses and movements for women's rights, these women became spearheads of reform in a variety of movements, many of them steering middle-class women's clubs toward social and political issues. Although their work was initially humanitarian and nonpolitical, settlement-house workers and their allies ultimately helped to transform U.S. politics and government.

Women working in settlement houses joined forces, for example, with public health reformers to campaign for better sanitation. The Hull House Woman's Club documented more than a thousand violations of Chicago's sanitary ordinances, and Jane Addams became the garbage inspector for her ward. She and her colleagues were among the many women activists who flew the banner of "municipal housekeeping." Describing clean cities as extensions of clean houses, they lobbied municipal officials and volunteered to inspect the work of city contractors charged with picking up the garbage. A common interest in these issues united black and white women's groups, at least temporarily.

Sanitary reformers in government worked closely with activists who were concerned about public health, personal cleanliness, and civic beauty. As cities increased in population and density, the street-cleaning problem alone became cause for alarm. Over three million horses lived in U.S. cities at the turn of the century; Milwaukee's horses alone produced 133 tons of manure every day. City streets everywhere were littered with dead animals. Garbage and sewage disposal was an equally staggering problem. Reformers viewed piles of trash as both a menace to health and an eyesore. But landowners and merchants saw efforts at reform as an infringement of their property rights and a threat of higher property taxes for sanitary improve-

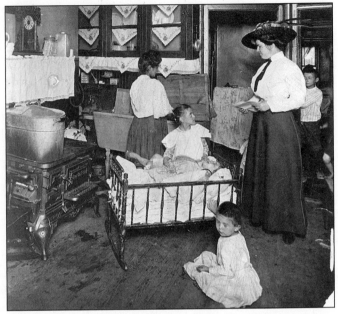

Settlement Worker and Immigrants

This photograph documenting the activities of a settlement-house worker captures the complicated relationship between reformers and the people they "served." The reformers' altruism was offset by their belief in the superiority of middle-class mores, which they imposed on immigrants to get them to relinquish "un-American" customs. People's Institute Papers — General Research Division, New York Public Library, Astor, Lenox and Tilden Foundations.

End of an Era

Around 1900, a photographer captured the unwholesome combination of children's play, open street sewers, and a dead horse in a New York street. Such scenes prompted reformers to campaign for better sanitation in U.S. cities. Prints and Photographs Division, Library of Congress.

ments. To bridge this impasse, sanitary reform in many cities became part of a more general attack on the inadequacies of municipal government and the unchallenged power of the wealthy.

Women's Political Culture Throughout the nineteenth century, women reformers had used the idea of separate spheres for men and women to carve out a public space for themselves. Shut out of party and electoral politics, women had created organizations and movements that transferred their authority from the home to the rest of the world. They sought legislative action on a number of fronts—education, child care, health, public morality, and social welfare—and they did so through private charities, churches, and volunteer groups.

What was new at the end of the nineteenth century was the scale of women's activism and the ability of women's organizations to forge alliances among women of different classes and with powerful men who were interested in reform. Asserting a role that did not depend on the right to vote, women activists represented themselves as the embodiment of civic virtue. New types of women leaders—some with college and graduate school training in the analysis of social problems; some with experience in settlement work; some with backgrounds as activists in labor, suffrage, and temperance struggles—concluded that only the power of government could solve deep-rooted social problems. Undertaking new strategies and alliances based on this understanding, they formed highly organized groups with constitutions, officers, and bylaws, and they called on well-organized local activists in the temperance and woman suffrage movements. Both movements blossomed during the Progressive era, eventually producing the Eighteenth Amendment (Prohibition, 1919) and the Nineteenth Amendment (woman's suffrage, 1920).

A black women's political culture paralleled, and occasionally intersected with, many white women's movements, particularly the Woman's Christian Temperance Union (WCTU), the largest women's organization of the era (see Chapter 2). As Jim Crow laws restricted the political activity of black men, the women of the small but growing black middle class in the South had come to see themselves as leaders of their race and sex. Some supported themselves, primarily as teachers; others could afford to do volunteer work. Many of these women activists came from well-off families,

"Have the Women Organized in Separate Locals"

Women reformers in the Women's Trade Union League, such as Alice Henry, editor of the WTUL newspaper, worked with union organizers during the Progressive era. Many working-class women joined unions, but they often found it difficult to be active members or leaders in the labor movement. In this article, Henry analyzed some of the obstacles to women's participation and proposed a solution.

The commonest complaint of all is that women members of a trade union do not attend their meetings. It is indeed a very serious difficulty to cope with. . . .

At first glance it seems curious that the meetings of a mixed local composed of both men and girls, should have for the girls even less attraction than meetings of their own sex only. But so it is. A business meeting of a local affords none of the lively social intercourse of a gathering for pleasure or even of a class for instruction. The men, mostly the older men, run the meeting and often are the meeting. Their influence may be out of all proportion to their numbers. It is they who decide the place where the local shall meet and the hour at which members shall assemble. The place is therefore often over a saloon, to which many girls naturally and rightly object. Sometimes it is even in a disreputable district. The girls may prefer that the meeting should begin shortly after closing time so that they do no need to go home and return, or have to loiter about for two or three hours. They like meetings to be over early. The men mostly name eight o'clock as the time of beginning, but business often will not start much before nine. Then, too, the men feel that they have come together to talk, and talk they do while they allow the real business to drag. Of course, the girls are not interested in long discussions on matters that they do not understand and in which they have no part and naturally they stay away, and so make matters worse, for the men feel they are doing their best for the interests of the union, resent the women's indifference, and are more sure than ever that women do not make good unionists. . . .

Where the conditions of the trade permit it by far the best plan is to have the women organized in separate locals. The meetings of women and girls only draw better attendances, give far more opportunity for all members to take part in the business, and beyond all question form the finest training ground for the women leaders who in considerable numbers are needed so badly in the women's side of the trade union movement today.

Rosalyn Baxandall, Linda Gordon, and Susan Reverby, eds., *America's Working Women* (1976).

Colored Women's League of Washington, D.C., c. 1894
Founded in 1892 by registered nurse Sara Iredell, the League is pictured here gathered with husbands and supporters on the steps of Cedar Hill, Frederick Douglass's home in Anacostia, Washington, D.C. The League's members, who were dedicated to "racial up-lift," established day nurseries and adult evening schools and worked to improve social conditions in Washington. In 1896, various women's clubs, including the D.C. League, merged into the National Association of Colored Women's Clubs. Luke C. Dilton — Manuscript Division, Library of Congress.

but others, like Julia Sadgwar, a North Carolina teacher and activist, had risen from poverty.

Black women usually moved into community improvement from church organizations. Blending their religious values with activism legitimized their public role: they worked for what they called the "uplift" of their race. Like so many white women, they claimed a distinctly female moral authority. They organized in their communities and went downtown to interact with white officials and bureaucrats. They formed mothers' clubs, built playgrounds, and lobbied for better sanitation. And they campaigned for temperance. In these activities, they adopted white women's political styles, but unlike their white counterparts, black women had to build private institutions — schools, community centers, homes for the aged — to provide services that racist local governments denied to their communities.

Black women activists sometimes prodded white women to recognize their common class and gender across racial lines. Journalist and activist Ida B. Wells-Barnett brought her antilynching campaign to many white groups, including the WCTU, and worked with Jane Addams to block the segregation of Chicago public schools. But relationships between black and white women's organizations were sometimes strained or nonexistent. They were weakened especially by white women whose idea of their own political role was limited to influencing men. The white women believed that since many black men were prevented from voting, black women were politically weak because they would be unable to influence the votes of their fathers, brothers, husbands, and sons. Moreover, white women reformers—like most white Americans—had trouble accepting black women as equals. The national WCTU condemned lynching at its 1893 convention but assigned African American delegates to a separate banquet table. The segregated delegates left the hall in protest before "their sisters had enough good sense and Christianity," reported a black woman teacher in a religious journal, "to call them back and treat them like sisters." But at least some of the time, women created coalitions that transcended race, class, and ethnicity. And although not always radical, women's political culture was inherently dedicated to changing the prevailing order.

Some women activists lived their private lives as well as their public ones in communities of women. In women's colleges, settlement houses, and reform organizations, a growing number of women began to live together as lifelong partners, passionately committed and devoted to each other. Mary Drier of the Women's Trade Union League shared a home with Progressive Party activist Frances Kellor. Countless others forged ties with other women out of the public eye.

Woman Suffrage Women had been campaigning for the right to vote since the middle of the nineteenth century. In 1869, women activists had split into two rival groups, based on differing opinions about the priority that should be given to black male suffrage. The National Woman Suffrage Association, led by Elizabeth Cady Stanton and Susan B. Anthony, opposed the male-only Fifteenth Amendment; the American Woman Suffrage Association, led by Lucy Stone, regarded black male suffrage as a step in the right direction. The development of the broader women's political culture motivated the two factions to unite in 1890, forming a revitalized National American Woman Suffrage Association (NAWSA).

The ultimate strength of the suffrage movement was not in NAWSA, however, but at the local level. Three-quarters of the states had to ratify a constitutional amendment, which meant that suffragists had to win support for the vote state by state. Victories came first in the West. By 1914, women could vote in state, local, and school board elections in ten states west of the Mississippi (including Utah and Wyoming), in the territory of Alaska, and in Illinois. The woman suffrage movement in the West had skilled and articulate leaders, including the editors of women's rights papers in Colorado and Oregon and Jeannette Rankin in Montana, who would become the first woman elected to Congress. Middle-class suffragists and laboring people could sustain coalitions more easily in the West than in the East, where opponents of woman suffrage exploited the divisions between Catholic immigrants and native-born Protestants over issues such as temperance. The coalition that won woman suffrage in Colorado in 1893 mobilized women's clubs, labor union women, and the WCTU to work with male Populists and organized labor. Oregon's Abigail Scott Duniway addressed her women's rights paper to women farmers and working-class women; she called for divorce reform, women's education, and equal responsibility for housework and child care (Map 5.1).

Working-class women saw the vote as only one element in the larger working-class struggle. As one woman wrote to a labor newspaper, "If women have the right of suffrage it will double the number of voices in the hands of the working people." After women reformers rallied to support striking female shirtwaist makers in 1909, young women from the sweatshops began marching in suffrage parades. Settlement-house workers and members of the Women's Trade Union League infused the suffrage movement with their commitment to social justice and the labor movement with

MAP 5.1 Where Women Could Vote, 1890–1918

This map shows the extent of American women's voting rights in the years before passage of the constitutional amendment granting woman suffrage in 1920. The state-level campaign proved successful mainly in western states where low population numbers may have helped suffrage organizers win legislative victories.

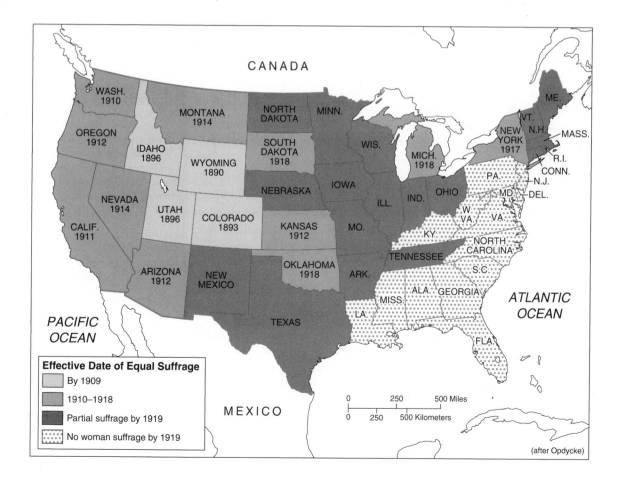

their feminism. It was only in this period that the term *feminism* came into general use to refer to a commitment to the full equality of the sexes and the overall emancipation of women rather than support for woman's suffrage.

Not all suffragists took a broad, feminist view. "All feminists are suffragists, but not all suffragists are feminists," declared one advocate of more sweeping change. Some suffragists, in fact, mobilized conservative arguments that enfranchising women would improve the "quality" of the electorate by increasing the percentage of white and native-born voters. They abandoned earlier demands for suffrage based on "justice" or "equal rights" and instead argued that women voters would bring special "female" qualities to the political process and would defend traditional family life in a time of stress and change.

Nevertheless, by the 1910s, woman suffrage became a mass movement, embracing wealthy socialites and garment workers, local black and white women's clubs, left-wing and conservative women, and increasing numbers of men. As the movement grew, it shifted tactics. Local suffrage organizations with large working-class memberships held open-air meetings and massive parades — organizing techniques that had long been used by socialists and labor groups in both Europe and the United States.

But as support for the movement grew, so did resistance — from liquor interests, machine politicians, the Catholic Church, and some business groups that were concerned that women voters would support other progressive reforms. The battle over a constitutional amendment enfranchising women grew heated during the early 1910s but then stalled, as referenda on woman suffrage were defeated in Pennsylvania, Massachusetts, and New York.

Heavy, Heavy, Hangs o'er Thy Head

A 1911 antisuffrage cartoon published in a satirical weekly (and, unusually, drawn by a woman) presented woman suffrage — and its female proponents — as a threat to conventional family roles. While this idea was foremost in the minds of many women antisuffragists, historians have also argued that they organized to protect gendered class interests, as many of the most vocal antisuffragists were wealthy, educated women who already exercised political influence. Laura Foster, *Life*, September 28, 1911 — American Social History Project.

The Fight to End Child Labor The women of the settlement houses also led the successful drive to improve wages and working conditions in factories and to outlaw child labor. Hull House resident Florence Kelley headed a coalition that in 1893 achieved passage of an Illinois law providing for state investigation of factory conditions. As the state's first chief factory inspector, Kelley campaigned tirelessly for better working hours and conditions and against child labor, in Illinois and elsewhere. Women reformers worked closely with labor activists as they battled for protective legislation — laws that would regulate the hours and conditions of labor for women and children. Many argued that such laws would establish precedents for regulating working conditions for men as well. Progressive politicians, such as Wisconsin's governor Robert La Follette, broadened their concerns to include women's and labor issues, realizing that they would need working people's support to prevail against political machines.

In 1908, the U.S. Supreme Court broke with previous legal doctrine and sanctioned some kinds of protective legislation. The Court's decision in *Muller v. Oregon* upheld an Oregon law limiting women's work in certain kinds of businesses (including the Portland laundry that was involved in the case) to ten hours a day. In its decision, however, the Court observed that women would always depend on men for "protection." This double-edged decision benefited working women but reinforced male domination in its underlying logic. Nevertheless, unlike previous legal doctrine, the decision set limits on employers' control over the terms of workers' employment. In *Muller*, the Court for the first time endorsed "sociological jurisprudence," an argument that was based as much on sociological evidence—such as the reports of factory inspectors—as on abstract legal reasoning.

The approval of state action in *Muller* greatly increased the legislative pace, at least in the North and the West. In 1912 alone, thirty-eight states passed child-labor laws and twenty-eight set maximum hours for women workers. By 1915, thirty-five states had workers' compensation laws. Twenty-five states had passed legislation limiting the working hours of some categories of male workers. Legislators in southern states fought such reforms. They especially resisted child-labor legislation, in deference to textile mill owners. More than one-quarter of the employees of southern cotton mills were children, half of them below the age of twelve years. These children earned less than older workers, but their wages helped to support the family in homes where parents took home too little to pay the bills.

In 1900, more than a quarter of a million children under age fifteen were working in mines, mills, and factories. Other boys (and a few girls) as young as ten sold newspapers, polished shoes, and scavenged for rags and scraps of metal on city streets. The Knights of Labor had advocated the abolition of child labor, but the progressives broadened the coalition of reformers agitating on behalf of children's welfare. Led by professional social workers and educators, activists promoted the building of playgrounds and compulsory school attendance. Settlement-house founder Lillian D. Wald had proposed the creation of a federal Children's Bureau to safeguard children's welfare. In 1912, Julia Lathrop, an Illinois reformer who had lived at Hull House, became the head of the new agency. Under Lathrop's direction, the bureau investigated such topics as infant mortality, juvenile delinquency, and mothers' pensions. The bureau's efforts were an important forerunner of social welfare provisions that emerged fully only during the New Deal years in the 1930s.

Despite the creation of the federal Children's Bureau, the child-labor movement's work was far from finished. The National Child

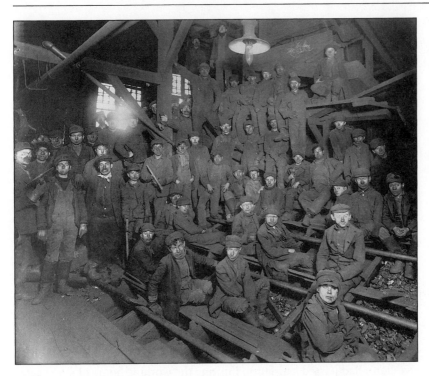

Breaker Boys in Coal Chute, South Pittston, Pennsylvania, January 1911

Lewis Hine took hundreds of pictures as staff photographer for the National Child Labor Committee from 1908 to 1918. Hine traveled across the country, photographing children in textile mills, canneries, glass and shoe factories, mines, and fields to reveal the extent of child labor and the need for enforcement of reform laws. "No anonymous or signed denials can contradict proof given with photographic fidelity," Hine wrote. "These pictures speak for themselves, and prove that the law is being violated." Lewis Hine, January 1911 — International Museum of Photography at George Eastman House, Rochester, New York.

Labor Committee, one of a number of organizations that pioneered nonprofit advocacy by publicizing its cause through pamphlets, mass mailings, and lobbying, stood at the forefront of the movement. The committee sponsored investigations by experts, and it sent its staff photographer Lewis Hine around the country to photograph children working in cotton mills, mines, and canneries and on the streets as newsboys and scavengers. Congress passed federal laws regulating child labor in 1916 and 1918, but a conservative Supreme Court declared them unconstitutional. The movement had greater success at the state level. By 1920, most states forbade the employment of children under fourteen years, set an eight-hour day for workers under sixteen years, and mandated compulsory education.

But simply having laws on the books did not solve fundamental problems. Pauline Newman, a labor activist who had worked as a child in a New York City garment factory, remembered the monotony of cutting threads from 7:30 in the morning until 9:00 at night. "Well, of course, there were [child-labor] laws on the books," she recalled, "but no one bothered to enforce them. The employers were always tipped off if there was going to be an inspection. 'Quick,' they'd say, 'into the boxes!' And we children would climb into the big boxes the finished shirts were stored in. Then some shirts were piled on top of us, and when the inspector came — no children. The factory always got an okay from the inspector, and I suppose someone at City Hall got a little something, too."

The Garment Industry and Working Women's Activism   The Triangle Shirtwaist fire that galvanized activists in 1911 occurred in an industry that was known for its labor militancy. Concentrated in New York City, the ready-made clothing industry was relatively new. For most of the nineteenth century, women had made their own clothing and their children's clothing at home, with or without the help of hired seamstresses, and men with money had used tailors. Consequently, workingmen's clothing dominated the small nineteenth-century ready-made industry. Much of that had changed by the end of the century, as new sewing and cutting machines increased workers' productivity and an organizational innovation—the sweatshop system—developed. Sweatshops employed a handful of workers, almost all of them immigrant Jewish or Italian women. They were supervised by contractors of their own nationality, mostly men, who got materials on credit from manufacturers, bought sewing machines on the installment plan, and rented lofts or tenement apartments for factories.

Thousands of small, marginal firms competed with a few large manufacturers. Workers sweated in steaming shops in summer and shivered in unheated conditions in winter; they had to pay for their own needles and thread. Contractors paid workers by the piece rather than by the hour, and at low piecework rates, workers pushed themselves hard and worked long days to make a living. Many workers participated in short, spontaneous strikes but created few lasting labor organizations.

In the fall of 1909 the industry exploded. Wage cuts and other grievances sparked a wave of small walkouts by workers who produced shirtwaists, the blouses that urban working- and middle-class women wore. The workers were mostly young women whose earnings not only helped to support their families, but also gave them a small measure of independence. In November, they turned out for a huge meeting at New York City's Cooper Union auditorium. The most dramatic and inspiring speaker that night was Clara Lemlich, a young Ukrainian-born activist who called for a general strike against all the companies in the industry. Within two days, between 20,000 and 30,000 workers had walked off their

On the Picket Line
This photograph captures the spirit of the young immigrant women shirtwaist workers who resisted strikebreaker violence and police intimidation during the 1909 Uprising of the Twenty Thousand in New York City.
Prints and Photographs Division, Library of Congress.

"A Pint of Trouble for the Bosses . . ."

The 1909 shirtwaist workers' strike saw young immigrant women step to the forefront of the labor struggle. Shirt-waist worker Clara Lemlich, a young Jewish immigrant, emerged as a key organizer and speaker. A reporter from the New York Sun *witnessed this attack by antiunion thugs on Lemlich and other strikers.*

The girls, headed by teen-age Clara Lemlich, described by union organizers as "a pint of trouble for the bosses," began singing Italian and Russian working-class songs as they paced in twos before the factory door. Of a sudden, around the corner came a dozen tough-looking customers, for whom the union label gorilla seemed well-chosen.

"Stand fast, girls," called Clara, and then the thugs rushed the line, knocking Clara to her knees, striking at the pickets, opening the way for a group of frightened scabs to slip through the broken line. Fancy ladies from the Allen Street red-light district climbed out of cabs to cheer on the gorillas. There was a confused melee of scratching, screaming girls and fist-swinging men and then a patrol wagon arrived. The thugs ran off as the cops pushed Clara and two other badly beaten girls into the wagon.

I followed the rest of the retreating pickets to the union hall, a few blocks away. There a relief station had been set up where one bottle of milk and a loaf of bread were given to strikers with small children in their families. There for the first time in my comfortably sheltered, Upper West Side life, I saw real hunger on the faces of my fellow Americans in the richest city in the world.

McAlister Coleman, "All of Which I Saw," *The Progressive* (May 1950).

---

jobs. A month later, the strike, which became known as "the Uprising of the Twenty Thousand," spread to Philadelphia.

The strikers appealed to the National Women's Trade Union League (WTUL) for help in countering police harassment. Founded in 1903, the WTUL was a coalition of women—some from the working class, some professionals such as Lillian Wald and Jane Addams, and some extremely wealthy women—devoted to bringing women into trade unions as a means of empowerment. League members believed that working women were more oppressed as workers than as women but that women of all classes shared important "bonds of womanhood." The elite WTUL members allied with their working colleagues. They provided funds for strikers, spoke to the press, and arranged for volunteer lawyers, but they also did their share of picket duty and even went to jail. Not everyone trusted them or their financial support. Trade unionist Leonora O'Reilly complained that strikers became reluctant to voice their own opinions because they felt bound to agree with the society women who donated money. Still, despite disputes between women of different classes, the women shared a commitment to making the WTUL a genuine arena for working-class feminism.

The Sun Rises on the Eight-Hour Day

Chicago sculptor Julia Bracken Wendt designed the National Women's Trade Union League seal. The design mixed symbols of both militancy and domesticity, showing a woman in armor holding a shield marked "Victory" while clasping the hand of a mother holding a child in her arms. The sun rises behind and above them, emanating the aims of the League: "The Eight-Hour Day. A Living Wage. To Guard the Home." The design was a great success, appearing on League publications, letterhead, and pins, and even on the wall of Samuel Gompers's office at the American Federation of Labor. National Women's Trade Union Records (54.13) — Manuscript Division, Library of Congress.

The industrywide strikes of garment workers during 1909 and 1910 brought tens of thousands of women into the International Ladies' Garment Workers Union (ILGWU), which had been established a decade earlier. Most of these new members were Jewish, but some were from other ethnic groups. Both in Philadelphia and New York, African American women joined the union and the strike. The conflict dragged on until February 1910, when the ILGWU reached an arbitrated settlement with manufacturers. Employers refused to recognize the union, but they reduced hours and improved working conditions, and at least some agreed to arbitrate future disputes through a board of community and religious leaders.

Within months of the February victory, two other groups of garment workers walked out. At Hart, Schaffner, and Marx, a huge Chicago manufacturer of men's clothing, fourteen young women struck over a cut in their piece rate. They picketed alone for three weeks before coworkers took them seriously, but eventually, 40,000 workers throughout the city's clothing industry joined them. That number was exceeded in New York when 60,000 cloakmakers, mostly male, began a general strike that ended with an agreement devised by Louis Brandeis, who had previously written the brief defending protective legislation in *Muller v. Oregon*. In the strike, Brandeis acted on behalf of Boston department store owner A. Lincoln Filene, who realized that stabilizing wages and working conditions might reduce cutthroat competition and ensure more predictable prices and supplies. By the eve of World War I, unions had made deep inroads into the clothing, fur, and millinery industries. Nearly 400,000 clothing workers became union members between 1909 and 1913.

But as the Triangle fire demonstrated, these partial settlements with garment industry employers did not provide for adequate fire escapes and open doors. By naming American Federation of Labor (AFL) president Samuel Gompers and New York Consumers' League representative Frances Perkins to the Factory Commission that was established after the disaster, politicians acknowledged well-established national reform forces. Crucial to the commission's success were two politicians allied with the Democratic political machine known as Tammany Hall: Robert Wagner and Alfred E. Smith, who served as its chairman and vice chairman. Over the course of

Off to Jail

A garment worker is arrested by the Chicago police during a 1910 strike in which workers protested a cut in their piece rate. Some 40,000 workers throughout the clothing industry eventually walked off the job. Chicago Historical Society [DN-56132].

four years, hundreds of workers testified to the commission about unsafe working conditions. To improve wages and protect the health and safety of New York workers, the commission sponsored fifty-six laws, many of which were passed by Democrats eager not only to wrap themselves in the banner of reform, but also to undercut the growing influence of socialists among working-class constituents.

Democrats felt no pressure to enact reforms to maintain working-class allegiance in the South, however, where a weak trade union movement and virulent racism divided and undermined reform efforts. Two weeks after the Triangle fire, a violent explosion ripped through the Banner coal mine outside Birmingham, Alabama, killing 128 convict miners, mostly African Americans who had been jailed for minor offenses. Although evidence supplied by the federal Bureau of Mines indicated high levels of dangerous methane gas, a state investigating commission declared that the miners' ineptitude had caused the explosion. Middle-class reformers and Alabama's trade union movement called for abolition of the policy of leasing out convicts as laborers, but a coalition of Democratic state legislators and big businessmen outmatched them. Both groups continued to receive substantial profits from convict labor until 1928, when Alabama finally abolished the system, and by the 1930s, every southern state had eliminated the practice.

Radical Challenges to the Status Quo

Radicals, including socialists (who favored public ownership of industries and a more egalitarian distribution of wealth), anarchists (who wanted shared ownership of the means of production but organized voluntarily and without a powerful government), and militant unionists offered a more fundamental critique of the capitalist system than the progressives. Never more than a minority of working people, radicals still influenced politics, society, and culture in the early twentieth century. Although socialist candidates such as Eugene Debs and militant strikes such as the Paterson, New Jersey, silk strike and the miners' strike in Ludlow, Colorado, often met defeat, radicals shifted the terms of debate to the left. Moderate reformers often adopted or adapted radical programs, in part because they sought to defuse the radical appeal and in part because radicals often offered persuasive solutions to the inequities of the day.

Socialists, Marxists, and Anarchists Many garment union activists belonged to or sympathized with the Socialist Party, whose best-known spokesperson was the labor leader Eugene V. Debs. "I am for Socialism," he wrote, "because I am for humanity. We have been cursed with the reign of gold long enough. Money constitutes no proper basis of civilization." American socialism developed from a variety of movements, some home-grown and others imported from abroad. For much of the nineteenth century, religious and secular utopian communities such as the Shakers and Brook Farm in Massachusetts exemplified the possibilities of egalitarian living. Germans who immigrated after the failed European revolutions of 1848 brought with them the radical ideas of Karl Marx, whose writings about the historical inevitability of class struggle had stimulated socialist organizing in industrialized countries everywhere. Although Marxism did not dominate American socialist thought, immigrants who had been influenced by Marx and the international socialist movement had had a major impact on the national railroad strike of 1877 and the eight-hour movement.

The first American socialist political party, the Socialist Labor Party, was formed in 1877, with Daniel De Leon at its head. It and a number of other socialist groups suffered from poor organization and infighting, but the ideal of socialism spread nevertheless. Edward Bellamy's utopian novel *Looking Backward* (1888), for example, sparked considerable interest in the idea of a classless society brought about without bloodshed. Thousands of Americans joined clubs promoting Bellamy's ideas; others devoted their lives to socialist ideals.

Debs joined the Socialist Labor Party in 1897 and helped to foster the merger of several groups into the new Socialist Party in 1901. Within seven years, the party had 41,000 dues-paying members in more than three

"The Red Special"

Eugene Debs, Socialist Party staffers, and the "Red Special" train on which the presidential candidate traveled during his 1908 whistle-stop campaign. Thomas Mooney, 1908 — The Bancroft Library, University of California, Berkeley.

thousand local branches. Running for president on the Socialist ticket in 1908, Debs received more than 400,000 votes. The rapid increase in support for the Socialist Party owed something to Debs's charisma but even more to the social unrest of those years and the party's ability to tap the discontent of workers, farmers, and immigrants. Urban workers formed the core of the party's strength. At first, it was popular mostly with skilled workers, including many German immigrants, but by 1909, it was winning more and more support from newer immigrants from Eastern and Southern Europe. The party also enjoyed substantial rural backing, especially in the Southwest, where many farmers were losing ownership of their land. Middle-class women reformers and Christian socialists added to the mixture of groups and traditions that made the Socialist Party a volatile and exciting organization. Its influence went well beyond its membership; its electoral and legislative successes helped to radicalize the debates about progressive reform. At the time of the presidential election of 1912, for example, party membership peaked at 118,000, but Debs, the Socialist candidate, received 900,000 votes.

Debs Attacks "the Monstrous System" of Capitalism

The 1912 Socialist Party nominee, Eugene V. Debs, called for the abolition of capitalism rather than for its reform. In this speech accepting the party's nomination, he proclaimed the Socialist Party "the party of progress, the party of the future."

The Socialist party is fundamentally different from all other parties. It came in the process of evolution and grows with the growth of the forces which created it. Its spirit is militant and its aim revolutionary. It expresses in political terms the aspiration of the working class to freedom and to a larger and fuller life than they have yet known.

The world's workers have always been and still are the world's slaves. They have borne all the burdens of the race and built all the monuments along the track of civilization; they have produced all the world's wealth and supported all the world's governments. They have conquered all things but their own freedom. They are still the subject class in every nation on earth and the chief function of every government is to keep them at the mercy of their masters.

The workers in the mills and factories, in the mines and on the farms and railways never had a party of their own until the Socialist party was organized. They divided their votes between the parties of their masters. They did not realize that they were using their ballots to forge their own fetters.

But the awakening came. It was bound to come. Class rule became more and more oppressive and wage slavery more and more galling. The eyes of the workers began to open. They began to see the cause of the misery they had dumbly suffered so many years. It dawned upon them that society was divided into two classes—capitalists and workers, exploiters and producers; that the capitalists, while comparatively few, owned the nation and controlled the government; that the courts and the soldiers were at their command, and that the workers, while in a great majority, were in slavish subjection. . . .

The Socialist party's mission is not only to destroy capitalist despotism but to establish industrial and social democracy. To this end the workers are steadily organizing and fitting themselves for the day when they shall take control of the people's industries and when the right to work shall be as inviolate as the right to breathe the breath of life.

Standing as it does for the emancipation of the working class from wage-slavery, for the equal rights and opportunities of all men and all women, for the abolition of child labor and the conservation of all childhood, for social self-rule and the equal freedom of all, the Socialist party is the party of progress, the party of the future, and its triumph will signalize the birth of a new civilization and the dawn of a happier day for all humanity.

Eugene Debs, "Speech of Acceptance," *International Socialist Review* (October, 1912).

Happy Hooligan

Beginning in 1900, Frederick Opper's comic strip featuring the hapless tramp was a major attraction of William Randolph Hearst's *New York Journal*. Unlike Riebe's Mr. Block Happy Hooligan was the undeserving victim of the abuses and insanities of American society, including, in this strip, popular hysteria about anarchists and the police penchant for summary justice. American Social History Project.

Socialists had considerable influence in many unions, including those of the machinists, mineworkers, and garment workers. Many attacked the AFL for neglecting unskilled workers, arguing that organizing unions only of skilled workers along narrow craft lines instead of more broadly by industry had turned the federation into the "American Separation of Labor." Critical of AFL policies, they denounced Samuel Gompers for cooperating with businessmen.

Within the labor movement and in radical organizations, socialists associated with — and sometimes opposed — representatives of another radical force: the anarchists. Anarchists believed that the ideal society must be achieved without increasing the power of governments, which they viewed as inevitably oppressive, and that instead a society based on shared ownership could be organized voluntarily through communes. Resistance to political organizations sometimes inspired solitary acts of violence directed against government, big business, and their leaders. In 1892, Alexander Berkman attempted to assassinate Henry Clay Frick, the manager of the Homestead plant; nine years later, Leon Czolgosz killed President William McKinley. But after the McKinley assassination, most anarchists abandoned this kind of "propaganda of the deed" as counterproductive. The best-known anarchist in the United States was Emma Goldman. After emigrating from Russia in 1885 at age sixteen to avoid an arranged marriage, she worked in the garment industry in Rochester, New York. A charismatic speaker, Goldman lectured on topics ranging from anarchism and the mod-

Mr. Block

Ernest Riebe's comic strip about a willfully ignorant and gullible worker appeared in the IWW's *Industrial Worker*. The strip conveyed the organization's attitude toward workers who lacked class-consciousness or subscribed to the AFL's conservative craft unionism, inspiring IWW songwriter Joe Hill's lyrics: "Oh, Mr. Block, you were born by mistake. / You take the cake. / You make me ache. / Tie a rock to your block and jump in the lake. / Kindly do that for Liberty's sake." The adventures of the beleaguered Mr. Block, as indicated here, also took swipes at the reform wing of the Socialist party. Ernest Riebe — Charles H. Kerr Publishing Co., Chicago, Illinois.

ern theater to birth control and free love, asserting that women had the right to decide not to bear children and to enter into spiritual and sexual unions outside of marriage.

The IWW: Lawrence and Paterson

Although most working people embraced neither anarchism nor socialism, radical ideas about the need for fundamental changes influenced working-class communities in the early twentieth century. The clearest indication of this sentiment was the creation of a new labor organization, the Industrial Workers of the World—popularly known as the IWW, or Wobblies. "An injury to one is an injury to all," the IWW declared. "The working class and the employing class have nothing in common."

The IWW sought to abolish the wage system and to create a society in which workers would own and control the factories, mines, lumber camps, and railroads where they labored. IWW leaders believed that the vehicle for revolutionary change should be a union, not a political party. Organizing all workers into one militant union, they asserted, would lead to a massive general strike. Capitalism would be overthrown, and the people would run industry in a decentralized, democratic fashion.

Socialists, including Eugene V. Debs, together with other radicals and industrial unionists organized the IWW in 1905. Leadership came, in part, from the Western Federation of Miners (WFM), which represented 30,000 hard-rock miners in the Rocky Mountains. During a decade of bitter strikes against some of the largest corporations in America, the WFM's leaders had come to reject capitalism and to embrace unions that spanned an entire industry (steelworkers or railroad workers) rather than a specific craft (carpenters or machinists). The federation's efforts to build alliances with workers in the East culminated in the founding convention of the IWW in Chicago. "Fellow workers," western miner Big Bill Haywood proclaimed, "this is the Continental Congress of the working class." The new movement, he declared, "shall have for its purpose the emancipation of the working class from the slave bondage of capitalism."

Spirited, colorful, and proud in the face of jail sentences and vigilante attacks, the IWW was the most egalitarian labor organization in American history. It believed in organizing all workers—skilled and unskilled, men and women, black and white, Mexican, Chinese, and Japanese. The Wobblies drew on long-standing traditions: the Knights' belief in organizing

"The Lumberjack's Prayer"

Lumberjacks often worked twelve hours a day, seven days a week, faced incredible dangers on the job, and lived under horrendous conditions. The Industrial Workers of the World (IWW) was the only labor organization to pay any attention to workers in the lumber camps of the South and the Pacific Northwest. Although humorous in tone, the poem "The Lumberjack's Prayer" captured the grueling conditions that most lumbermen faced on and off the job.

I pray dear Lord for Jesus' sake,
Give us this day a T-Bone Steak,
Hallowed be thy Holy name,
But don't forget to send the same. . . .
Observe me on my bended legs,
I'm asking you for Ham and Eggs,
And if thou havest custard pies,
I like, dear Lord, the largest size.
Oh, hear my cry, All Mighty Host,
I quite forgot the Quail on Toast,
Let your kindly heart be stirred,
And stuff some oysters in that bird.
Dear Lord, we know your Holy wish,
On Friday we must have a fish,
Our flesh is weak and spirit stale,
You better make that fish a whale.
Oh, hear me Lord, remove these "Dogs,"
These sausages of powder'd logs,
Your bull beef hash and bearded Snouts.
Take them to hell or thereabouts.
With Alum bread and Pressed-Beef butts,
Dear Lord you damn near ruin'd my guts,
Your white-wash milk and Oleorine,
I wish to Christ I'd never seen.
Oh, hear me Lord, I am praying still,
But if you won't, our union will,
Put pork chops on the bill of fare,
And starve no workers anywhere.

I am happy to say this prayer has been answered—by the "old man" himself. He tells me He has furnished—plenty for all—and that if I am not getting mine it's because I am not organized SUFFICIENTLY strong to force the master to loosen up. . . .

He further informs me the Capitalists are children of His—and that He absolutely refuses to participate in any children's squabbles. He believes in letting us fight it out along the lines of Industrial Unionism.

Yours in faith, T-BONE SLIM.

"The Lumberjack's Prayer," Labadie Collection, University of Michigan Library.

across ethnic and racial lines, the shop-floor control enjoyed by skilled craftsmen, and the industrial unionism of coal miners and the American Railway Union.

At first, factionalism, government harassment, and an economic downturn frustrated the IWW. But in 1909, it won nationwide attention by leading a successful strike among unskilled immigrant steelworkers in McKees Rocks, Pennsylvania. In 1909 and 1910, the IWW also led a series of "free speech" fights in western cities, which served as hiring centers for jobs in forests, mines, and fields. But the union's reputation soared in 1912, when it led a massive textile strike in Lawrence, Massachusetts. A new Massachusetts state law requiring employers to cut workers' hours had backfired when employers retaliated by speeding up the looms to compensate for the lost time. The last straw for Lawrence's 30,000 textile workers came when mill owners announced a pay cut. Young women between the ages of fourteen and eighteen, many of whom suffered from malnutrition and overwork, made up half of the mills' labor force. Two days after the pay cut announcement, more than 20,000 workers of forty nationalities went on strike. "We want bread and roses, too," the strikers declared memorably, an indication that they sought not just material gain, but also an acknowledgment of their dignity and their entitlement to some of the finer things in life.

The IWW organized separate strike and relief committees for workers of different nationalities and translated speeches and literature into dozens of languages. Strikers threw up massive picket lines around the mills and paraded through the streets. Mill owners and government officials

"We Want Bread and Roses, Too"
Shouting that slogan, strikers confronted national guardsmen during the Lawrence, Massachusetts, textile strike of 1912. Archives of Labor and Urban Affairs, Wayne State University, Detroit.

responded with a massive show of force, including a declaration of martial law and a ban on public meetings. With an entire town deprived of the workers' meager wages, hunger was widespread. Eventually, New York socialists, concerned about the effects of hunger on the strikers' children, organized to care for them. Margaret Sanger, a nurse who later became famous for promoting birth control, arrived in Lawrence to transport children out of the strife-torn town. "Out of the 119 children, only four had underwear on . . . their outerwear was almost in rags . . . their coats were simply torn to shreds," she later testified.

The departure of the children generated so much sympathy for the strikers that Lawrence authorities decreed that children would no longer be allowed to leave the city. Two days later, a group of Philadelphia socialists arrived to transport 200 children. As a member of the Philadelphia Women's committee testified, "The police closed in on us with their clubs, beating right and left with no thought of the children who were in the most desperate danger of being trampled to death. The mothers and children were thus hurled in a mass and bodily dragged to a military truck, and even then clubbed, irrespective of the cries of the panic-stricken women and children." This turned public opinion across the country against the employers. In March, the mill owners agreed to a settlement that provided raises and overtime pay to workers.

The Lawrence textile strike demonstrated that immigrant workers could unite to win a strike, but the victory did not open the way for widespread industrial organization. A year later, in 1913, the IWW met serious defeat in a silk workers' strike in Paterson, New Jersey, where thousands of immigrant women, men, and children had walked out of the mills. Over the course of seven months, IWW leaders again organized picket lines and called enthusiastic rallies, and again the authorities responded with repression, even arresting socialist Frederick Sumner Boyd for reading the free-speech clause of the New Jersey state constitution at a strike meeting. But Paterson employers, unlike their Lawrence counterparts, exploited divisions within the silk workers' ranks. The skilled, English-speaking workers and their craft unions, put off by the radicalism and anarchism of many of the Italian and Jewish workers, were slow to join the strike. The strike collapsed when the English-speaking mill workers agreed to return to work on a shop-by-shop basis, leaving the unskilled immigrants without support.

The Ludlow Massacre and the Center Shifting to the Left   In mining communities in the Appalachian and Rocky mountains, the United Mine Workers of America (UMWA) overcame the cultural difficulties that defeated the strikers in Paterson. Although highly skilled, coal miners had no tradition of apprenticeship and therefore little control over who entered their trade. Thus, recent immigrants or African Americans could find work as miners more easily than in other trades. Drawing on the legacy of inter-racial unionism inherited from the Knights of Labor and black UMWA activists, the UMWA extended itself to organize all who worked in and around the mines. By 1910, nearly one-third of all coal miners were union-ized, compared with one-tenth of the broader U.S. labor force.

But the mine owners fought back fiercely. In late 1913, John D. Rockefeller's Colorado Fuel and Iron Company led other companies in an open-shop drive—an attempt to guarantee the right to work without union membership—that prompted more than 10,000 miners to strike. The battle was long and bitter. Despite the determination of the miners and their wives, who were active in the struggle, the owners refused to recog-nize the union. They evicted strikers from their company-owned homes and brought in deputies and the state militia to quell the protest. On Easter night in 1914, the troops attacked a strikers' tent camp in Ludlow. Firing machine guns and setting fire to the tents, they killed sixteen people, including twelve children.

In the wake of the Ludlow massacre, the UMWA issued a "call to arms." For ten days, war raged between miners and the state militia, until federal troops finally dis-armed the miners. IWW leader Bill Haywood concluded that the country was gripped by "an irreconcilable class struggle" between workers and capitalists. Most progressives would have avoided those terms, but many of them agreed that in Lawrence, Paterson, and Ludlow, the industrial system had generated a terrifying conflict that threatened the very stability and promise of American society.

Like the electoral challenge by the Social-ist Party, the militant agitation of the Wobblies and mine workers moved the terms of pro-gressive debate to the left. Moderate reformers took up more radical ideas for two reasons. First, they worried about the threat posed by socialists and Wobblies. They sought to counter the appeal of the radicals—and pre-vent the more fundamental changes those groups fa-vored—by offering changes that responded, in part, to the radical critique. When the radicals publicized the inequities and degradations brought by industrial

Class War in Colorado

John Sloan's April 1914 cover illustration for *The Masses* por-trays the devastation and death wrought by the Colorado militia and Rockefeller-hired private police on the miners' tent colony but also emphasizes the strikers' continued resistance.
John Sloan, *The Masses*, June 1914 — Prints and Photographs Division, Library of Congress.

IN THIS ISSUE
CLASS WAR IN COLORADO—Max Eastman
WHAT ABOUT MEXICO?—John Reed

"It Was a Murder and Nothing Less"

The brutal massacre of strikers and their families at Ludlow, Colorado, stunned the nation and led to numerous investigations and reports. Following are two documents about the massacre. The first is an excerpt from a newspaper reporter's account that appeared in the New York World. *The second is a portion of John D. Rockefeller's testimony before the Commission on Industrial Relations, set up by the U.S. government in 1914 to investigate labor conditions. Rockefeller was questioned by Commission chairman Frank Walsh, a noted reformer.*

New York World:

Then came the killing of Louis Tikas, the Greek leader of the strikers. We saw the militiamen parley outside the tent city, and a few minutes later, Tikas came out to meet them. We watched them talking. Suddenly an officer raised his rifle, gripping the barrel, and felled Tikas with the butt.

Tikas fell face downward. As he lay there we saw the militiamen fall back. Then they aimed their rifles and deliberately fired them into the unconscious man's body. It was the first murder I had ever seen, for it was a murder and nothing less. Then the miners ran about in the tent colony and women and children scuttled for safety in the [underground] pits which afterwards trapped them.

We watched from our rock shelter while the militia dragged up their machine guns and poured murderous fire into the arroyo . . . Then came the firing of the tents. . . . The militiamen were thick about the northwest corner of the colony where the fire started and we could see distinctly from our lofty observation place what looked like a blazing torch waved in the midst of militia a few seconds before the general conflagration swept through the place.

Testimony of John D. Rockefeller:

ROCKEFELLER: There is just one thing . . . which can be done, as things are at present, to settle this strike, and that is to unionize the camps; and our interest in labor is so profound . . . that interest demands that the camps shall be open [nonunion].

CHAIRMAN: And you will do that if it costs all your property and kills all your employees?

ROCKEFELLER: It is a great principle.

CHAIRMAN: And you would do that rather than recognize the right of men to collective bargaining? Is that what I understand?

ROCKEFELLER: No, sir. Rather than allow outside people to come in and interfere with employees who are thoroughly satisfied with their labor conditions — it was upon a similar principle that the War of the Revolution was carried on. It is a great national issue of the most vital kind.

New York World, *May 5, 1913; Final Report and Testimony Submitted to Congress on Industrial Relations, 64th Congress, 1st Session (1916).*

capitalism, progressives proposed ways in which reform and regulation could make capitalism more humane while also preserving it.

The second reason moderate reformers incorporated some radical ideas is that they found them attractive. They agreed with the radicals about the threats posed by unregulated big business and great concentrations of wealth. They also adopted the radicals' view that only a strong national state could tame the giant national corporations—an idea that socialist activists had long argued but that broke with deep-seated U.S. traditions of limiting the power of the federal government. Although Democratic and Republican progressives did not endorse as powerful a state as the socialists did, the moderate reformers did come to accept and endorse a new regulatory function for the federal government.

Progressivism and Politics

Women and radicals pressed the mainstream political parties from the outside, whether because they were excluded from the vote or because they sought more far-reaching changes than the conventional parties would contemplate. Still, they succeeded in getting those parties to consider issues (worker safety) and approaches (public ownership of utilities) that were not originally on their agendas. Nevertheless, the actual changes implemented through political reform were often limited and sometimes not even in the interests of poor and working people. For example, some urban reform efforts displaced political machines that had working-class ties in favor of business-oriented city manager or city commission systems. Other "progressives" pushed political reform measures that made it more difficult for immigrants to vote, undercut the efforts of farmer and labor parties, and disenfranchised African Americans.

But if the reform glass was sometimes half (or entirely) empty, the early twentieth century did offer up some remarkably strong reform brews. Indeed, all three presidents of this era served at least a diluted reform elixir. Even the most conservative of the three, William Howard Taft, backed such once-radical measures as the eight-hour workday and the graduated income tax. The high point of progressive sentiment came in the 1912 election when Woodrow Wilson won the presidency and American voters more resoundingly endorsed reform than had occurred at any previous time in U.S. history.

Urban Reform   Reformers on the local and state levels borrowed some ideas from radicals and socialists. Many reformers viewed the corporations that provided municipal services—streetcars, water, gas, and electricity— as rapacious monopolies. The socialist idea of public ownership seemed an

"Give the Property Owner a Fair Show"

Some reformers sought to eliminate from urban government the power and influence of what they thought of as the ignorant working masses. The first document comes from the elite Voters' League of Pittsburgh, which campaigned in 1911 for removing workingmen from local school boards, suggesting that "a man's occupation ought to give a strong indication of his qualifications for membership." In the second document, Rear Admiral F. E. Chadwick, a leader in the municipal reform movement in Newport, Rhode Island, argued for changing local government to ensure a larger voice for "property owners."

Voters' League of Pittsburgh:

Employment as ordinary laborer and in the lowest class of mill work would naturally lead to the conclusion that such men did not have sufficient education or business training to act as school directors. . . . Objection might also be made to small shopkeepers, clerks, workmen at many trades, who by lack of educational advantages and business training, could not, no matter how honest, be expected to administer properly the affairs of an education system . . . where millions of dollars are spent each year.

Rear Admiral F. E. Chadwick:

Our present system has excluded in large degree the representation of those who have the city's well-being most at heart. It has brought in municipalities . . . a government established by the least educated, the least interested class of citizens.

It stands to reason that a man paying $5,000 in taxes in a town is more interested in the well-being and development of his town than the man who pays no taxes. . . . It equally stands to reason that the man of the $5,000 tax should be assured a representation in the committee which lays the tax and spends the money which he contributes. . . . Shall we be truly democratic and give the property owner a fair show or shall we develop a tyranny of ignorance which shall crush him?

Samuel P. Hays, "The Politics of Reform," in Blaine A. Brownell and Warren E. Stickle, eds., *Bosses and Reformers: Urban Politics in America, 1880–1920* (1973).

---

attractive alternative, and many urban reformers, even though they rejected the concept of public ownership of all corporate enterprises, endorsed public ownership of public utilities. The Socialist Party's success in providing clean and efficient government to cities like Milwaukee reinforced the appeal of municipal socialist programs. In elections in 1910 and 1911, Socialist party candidates won more than four hundred public offices, including twenty-eight mayorships, in such communities as Butte, Montana; Schenectady, New York; and Reading, Pennsylvania. In most cases, however, these administrations lasted only one or two terms.

The Boss

The Boss

The standard reform perspective of the urban political machine appeared in *Collier's* in 1906. Graphically, the conception of the Boss had changed very little since Thomas Nast's Tweed Ring caricatures of the 1870s. Walter Appleton Clark, *Collier's*, November 10, 1906 — Prints and Photographs Division, Library of Congress.

Although urban reformers embraced some socialist views and coalitions, the goals of the two groups differed substantially. Where socialists campaigned for social justice, most urban reformers worked for efficient and responsive government. Above all, they wanted to stamp out corruption and curb the power of machines and bosses, some of whom had working-class ties. On the East Coast and in the South, businessmen and other elites seeking more efficient and less costly government dominated local reform efforts. These municipal reformers aimed to destroy corrupt political machines, but they often saw working-class voters—especially immigrants and African Americans—not as allies but as antagonists. Consequently, they sought to strip them of their votes. In the urban East, reformers pushed social programs to "improve" immigrant behavior and immigration reform to reduce the influx of "undesirable" newcomers.

The influence of businessmen and professionals was also evident in new governmental systems that were established in hundreds of small and middle-size cities, especially in the South. These city commission or city manager systems shifted power from popularly elected councilmen to professional administrators. Designed, as John Patterson, president of the National Cash Register Company, put it, to place municipal government "on a strict business basis," such systems took power away from working-class communities. One new form, the commissioner system, originated in Galveston, Texas, in the wake of a 1900 flood that killed 6,000 people. When the local government proved incapable of handling the emergency, a group of businessmen proposed a new charter that gave authority to five commissioners who would serve as both the city council and the city administration. By 1917, more than five hundred cities had adopted the plan. Another system, first tried in Staunton, Virginia, in 1908, combined an elected city council with an appointed city manager, a professional executive. The council set broad policies, and the city manager administered them.

A more democratic type of reform had grown up in midwestern cities such as Milwaukee and St. Louis and in western ones such as San Francisco. In these areas, reformers' attacks on corrupt state and local governments had a strong antibusiness character, and reforms opened up the political system to the influence of working people. One of the leaders of the more democratic reform movement was four-term Detroit mayor Hazen Pingree. First elected in 1889, Pingree increased corporate taxes and provided public services such as electricity and sewers. This program and his support of striking railroad workers won Pingree the backing of immigrants and trade unions. In 1896, he began to draw national attention when he organized a municipal streetcar company. Within a few years, campaigns for public ownership of urban utilities were triumphing throughout the nation.

Pingree, Wisconsin progressive governor Robert La Follette, and others moved to strengthen their reform coalition by opening up the political process to their working-class allies. With the support of unions and some middle-class groups, they pushed for direct primaries, which shifted the power to choose candidates from party bosses to voters. They also established the initiative and the referendum, which put popular issues directly on the ballot, and recall, which allowed voters to remove an official from office before the end of his or her term. Reformers also helped to win passage of the Seventeenth Amendment (1913), which provided for the direct popular election of U.S. senators (instead of election by state legislators, as the Constitution had decreed).

Progressivism and Participation While some reformers worked to open up the political system to working people, others instituted changes that undercut the power and influence of marginal groups. For example, ballot reforms created barriers to voting and to third-party political movements. After decades of promotion, reformers succeeded in having the publicly printed "Australian ballot," which listed all the candidates, replace ballots issued by political parties for voters to carry to the polls. Although the new system discouraged corruption, it made voting more difficult for immigrants who could not read English. It also gave public officials the power to eliminate minor party candidates from the ballot.

"Antifusion" laws further diminished the effectiveness of electoral protests in the South. Throughout the late nineteenth century, disgruntled workers and farmers had organized their own parties and had later thrown their support to major party candidates who backed their demands. The "fusion" of the Populists and Democrats in 1896 was the most powerful example of this tactic. But by the turn of the century, numerous states had passed laws prohibiting two parties from supporting the same candidate, thus making it more difficult for third parties to wield power. In some instances, reformers changed electoral procedures specifically to check the growth of the Socialist Party, which was achieving considerable success on the local level.

Literacy requirements offered a more direct method of limiting workers' political power. Election officials used these requirements to disfran-

"Hammering at the Truth"

Although Progressive era reforms in southern states limited the rights of African Americans, the diverse progressive movement also included individuals who fought for racial justice and equality such as W. E. B. DuBois, an eloquent and insightful African American scholar and activist. In this 1906 speech, he laid out the demands of the Niagara Movement.

The men of the Niagara Movement coming from the toil of the year's hard work and pausing a moment from the earning of their daily bread turn towards the nation and again ask in the name of ten million the privilege of a hearing. In the past year the work of the Negro hater has flourished in the land. Step by step the defenders of the rights of American citizens have retreated. The work of stealing the black man's ballot has progressed and the fifty and more representatives of stolen votes still sit in the nation's capital. Discrimination in travel and public accommodations has so spread that some of our weaker brethren are actually afraid to thunder against color discrimination as such and are simply whispering for ordinary decencies.

Against this the Niagara Movement eternally protests. We will not be satisfied to take one jot or tittle less than our full manhood rights. . . .

In detail our demands are clear and unequivocal.

First, we would vote; with the right to vote goes everything: Freedom, manhood, the honor of your wives, the chastity of your daughters, the right to work, and the chance to rise. . . .

Second. We want discrimination in public accommodation to cease. Separation in railway and street cars, based simply on race and color, is un-American, undemocratic, and silly. . . .

Third. We claim the right of freedmen to walk, talk, and be with them that wish to be with us . . .

Fourth. We want the laws enforced against rich as well as poor; against Capitalist as well as Laborer; against white as well as black. . . .

Fifth. We want our children educated. . . . And when we call for education, we mean real education. . . . Education is the development of power and ideal. We want our children trained as intelligent human beings should be, and we will fight for all time against any proposal to educate black boys and girls simply as servants and underlings. . . .

These are some of the chief things which we want. How shall we get them? By voting where we may vote, by persistent, unceasing agitation, by hammering at the truth, by sacrifice and work. . . .

Courage brothers! The battle for humanity is not lost or losing. All across the skies sit signs of promise. The Slav is rising in his might, the yellow millions are tasting liberty, the black Africans are writhing toward the light, and everywhere the laborer, with ballot in his hand, is voting open the gates of Opportunity and Peace. The morning breaks over the bloodstained hills. We must not falter, we may not shrink. Above are the everlasting stars.

Virginia Hamilton, ed. *The Writings of W. E. B. DuBois* (1975).

Working Against Discrimination

An undated photograph shows editor W. E. B. DuBois and his young staff in the New York City office of *The Crisis*, preparing an edition of the NAACP's publication. The DuSable Museum of African American History, Chicago.

chise African Americans and, in some places, poor whites. By 1920, all southern states and nine states outside the South had adopted such laws. Literacy requirements were one factor in a dramatic decline in voter participation across the country. In an average 1870s election, 80 percent of those who were legally eligible voted; by 1920, the figure had fallen to 60 percent in the northern states and less than 30 percent in the South. The decline in voting also reflected a broader erosion of popular politics — the intense partisanship and heated election campaigns — that had flourished in the nineteenth century. Once-vibrant party loyalties declined, and a new, less participatory style of party politics emerged.

The decline in formal voter participation was in part countered — and possibly generated — by the spread of nonelectoral forms of citizen participation. Large numbers of Americans used other means to confront the problems of the industrial age. Some favored municipal and national commissions, which gave wide publicity to issues and problems. Others joined voluntary associations, such as the National Association for the Advancement of Colored People (NAACP), founded in 1909–1910 by white and black reformers, including the black historian and intellectual W. E. B. DuBois (see Chapter 3), to fight the rise of segregation and the lynching of African Americans. Women reformers, who had never had the option of voting, had pioneered the practice of participating in nonparty organizations in order to influence politicians. Their methods would continue to define the struggle for political and social change well beyond the Progressive era.

Republican Progressivism: Roosevelt and Taft Not all political leaders shared the broad-based impulse for reform that infected so many arenas of American life. But at the end of the nineteenth century, few people would have predicted that such a broad spectrum of national politicians—including all three presidents in the first two decades of the twentieth century—would have backed at least a moderate version of progressive reform. The United States seemed a more conservative place in 1896, when the probusiness Republican William McKinley triumphed decisively over the populist Democrat William Jennings Bryan. The Republicans dominated Congress, led by such Old Guard conservatives as the wealthy Senator Nelson Aldrich of Rhode Island and the autocratic House Speaker Joseph G. Cannon of Illinois.

But then the party regulars made a mistake. Theodore Roosevelt, who had turned himself into a national hero through his role in the Spanish-Cuban-American War, posed a threat to the conservative Republican leadership of the major state of New York as the reform-minded governor. Why not "bury" him in the then-insignificant job of vice president, the regulars cleverly proposed? Their proposal became history, and McKinley and Roosevelt won an easy victory in the 1900 rematch with William Jennings Bryan. Mark Hanna, part of the conservative Republican leadership, was uneasy at the ploy: "Don't you realize that there's only one life between that madman and the White House?" he warned. In September 1901, that one life fell to the bullet of Leon Czolgosz. "Now look," declared an exasperated Hanna, "that damned cowboy is president of the United States."

Roosevelt's path to reform was both implausible and inconsistent. The offspring of an old and established family, he had thrown himself into the rough and tumble of New York politics, becoming a state assemblyman in 1881 at age twenty-three. His energetic opposition to machine politics and his push for civil service reform won him the nickname of "Cyclone Assemblyman." With the same energy and intensity, he threw himself into a series of other careers: cattle rancher in the Dakotas, member of the U.S. Civil Service Commission, president of the New York City Police Board, and assistant secretary of the Navy. Despite his reputation for reform, Roosevelt always described himself as a conservative who supported progressive reform as the best alternative to the radicalism represented by the socialists and Wobblies. "The friends of property, of order, of law," he argued, "must realize that the surest way to provoke an explosion of wrong and injustice is to be shortsighted, narrow-minded, greedy, and arrogant."

As president, Roosevelt followed policies in line with this view of conservative reform. He initially sympathized with mine owners when the UMWA called a major strike in Pennsylvania's anthracite coalfields in 1902, a year after he took office. Then public opinion began to turn against the mine owners after they refused to bargain with the UMWA. Worried that a strike would cripple the economy and leave the nation without fuel for the winter, Roosevelt pressed the operators to settle. By threatening to seize the mines and by calling on the influence of the financier J. P. Morgan, he finally got them to negotiate. The ensuing settlement boosted the cause of the UMWA and of the union movement nationwide.

The coal strike taught Roosevelt that bashing big business could be good politics. That same year, he took the popular step of ordering the Justice Department to prosecute the Northern Securities Company, a monopolistic combine of northwestern railroads organized by J. P. Morgan. This was the first use of 1890 Sherman Antitrust Act against such a powerful corporation — but not the last. The Justice Department filed forty-five cases under the act during Roosevelt's presidency, earning him the nickname "Trustbuster." The most celebrated case was in 1907 against Standard Oil, whose monopoly control of the nation's oil business had been exposed in Ida Tarbell's muckraking articles in *McClure's* and her *History of the Standard Oil Company* (1904). In 1911, the Supreme Court upheld the forced breakup of the company. Roosevelt, a passionate outdoorsman, also restricted businesses such as lumber and mining in the interest of conservation. He brought 125 million acres of public land into the national forest system, doubled the number of national parks, and established numerous national monuments and wildlife refuges (Map 5.2).

But Roosevelt was not a radical and did not oppose all trusts. He dropped many government actions against corporations after industry leaders visited the White House seeking presidential assistance. The president believed, in fact, that "bigness" had become inevitable and rather than challenging that, the federal government needed the power to regulate corporate behavior so that no corporation would be above the law.

This view of an activist federal government seemed an extension of Roosevelt's activist personality and his craving for the limelight. It was once said of him that he wanted to be "the bride at every wedding, the corpse at every funeral." The flamboyant Roosevelt easily won reelection in 1904 over the colorless Democrat Alton B. Parker, a New York judge. Elected on the promise of a "square deal" for all Americans, Roosevelt used his second term to move in more decisively reformist directions and toward expanded government regulation of the economy. In 1906, for example, he won passage of the Hepburn Act, which enabled the previously weak Interstate Commerce Commission (ICC) to regulate railroad rates. The same year, after Upton Sinclair's sensational novel *The Jungle* exposed unhealthy practices in the meatpacking industry and *McClure's* and the *Ladies' Home Journal* exposed fraud in patent medicines, a popular uproar spurred passage of the Meat Inspection Act and the Pure Food and Drug Act.

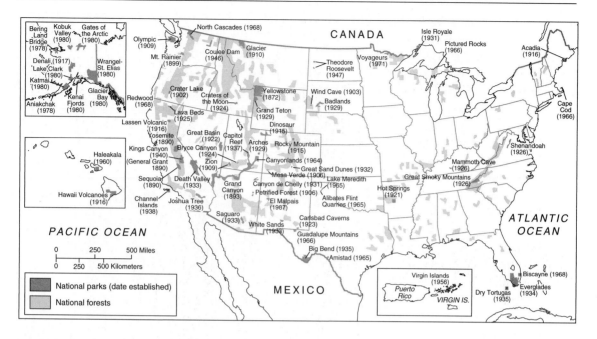

MAP 5.2 Expanding the Public Domain: National Parks and Forests

From 1850 to 1920, as the nation became more urban, a political and cultural conservation movement emerged. Conservationists perceived American "nature" as part of American national identity and promoted the wise and scientific use of natural resources. The movement stressed the importance of nature as an economic, aesthetic, and spiritual resource. The conviction that nature's resources were increasingly imperiled led conservationists during the Progressive era to dramatically expand wilderness and wildlife preservation.

Some big corporations actually supported some of these reforms or turned them to their advantage. The biggest meatpacking companies, for example, supported federal inspections because they would place a burden on smaller competitors. But at the time, most Americans had trouble finding an appropriate label for this president. Many conservatives viewed him as a dangerous radical, but radicals did not recognize him as one of their own. The more aggressive reformer Robert La Follette complained that Roosevelt "filled the air with noise and smoke" but accomplished little. Whatever the label, Roosevelt did take some increasingly progressive stances, supporting an eight-hour day for federal workers, a workers' compensation law, and federal income and inheritance taxes. He also angered conservative defenders of the sanctity of private property by putting his conservation principles ahead of the interests of western cattlemen, lumbermen, and mine owners. In 1907, for example, he delayed signing legislation he had opposed that prohibited new additions to the forest reserve without congressional approval long enough to annex sixteen million acres that the Forest Service had long eyed. "The opponents of the Forest Service turned handsprings in their wrath," Roosevelt later recalled, "and dire were their threats against the Executive; but the threats could not be carried out, and were really only a tribute to the efficiency of our action."

As Roosevelt became bolder in his advocacy of reform, Republican conservatives, who still dominated Congress, became increasingly uncooperative. Some blamed his attacks on big business for the financial panic that hit the nation in 1907. When Roosevelt announced that he would honor his earlier pledge to leave office after one full term, they breathed a sigh of relief. In response to the news that Roosevelt would go on an African safari, conservatives in Congress reportedly raised their glasses in the toast: "Health to the lions!"

Although William Howard Taft, who defeated William Jennings Bryan in the 1908 election, was Roosevelt's handpicked successor, they were a study in contrasts. Where Roosevelt was flamboyant and gregarious, the Cincinnati judge was shy. Where Roosevelt was energetic and physically fit, Taft was slow moving and struggled with a serious weight problem. (In college, he was known as "Big Lub"; while he was president, his weight reached 332 pounds, and he once got stuck in the White House bathtub.) Taft did, however, share some of Roosevelt's reform inclinations, backing the eight-hour workday, mine safety legislation, the graduated income tax (ratified as the Sixteenth Amendment in 1913), and a federal Children's Bureau, as well as helping to strengthen the Interstate Commerce Commission and filing ninety more antitrust suits.

But Taft's conservative judicial temperament made him reluctant to use the office of the presidency as aggressively as Roosevelt had done. He also annoyed progressive reformers by going along with the Payne-Aldrich Tariff, which did not cut tariffs as progressives had hoped. Progressives opposed high tariffs claiming they limited competition and aided trusts, and Taft had campaigned for tariff reform. Then he failed to back progressive efforts to limit the powers of conservative House Speaker Cannon. Taft particularly irritated Roosevelt and other conservationists by firing Chief Forester Gifford Pinchot, a Roosevelt friend and appointee, in an environmental controversy, which progressives saw as capitulation to corporate greed. "For the first time in the history of the country," editorialized the *Louisville Courier-Journal*, "a president of the United States has openly proclaimed himself the friend of thieves and the enemy of honest men."

Teddy the Trustbuster

A critical view of Theodore Roosevelt's reputation as a regulator of corporate abuses appeared in the *Columbus (Ohio) Dispatch* during the 1912 presidential campaign. William A. Ireland, *Columbus (Ohio) Dispatch*, reprinted in *Cartoons Magazine*, November 1912 — Prints and Photographs Division, Library of Congress.

"One of the Little Victims"
An April 1907 article in the *Ladies' Home Journal* featured a young victim of patent medicine, Baltimore toddler John D. Goddard. The article's title succinctly stated the danger posed by patent medicines: "Their Well-Meaning Parents Just 'Gave Them a Little Something' to Soothe Them or Make Them Sleep, — and They Slept!" *The Ladies' Home Journal*, April 1907 — American Social History Project.

Democratic Progressivism: Wilson and the Limits of Reform

Taft's firing of Pinchot, his embarrassment of Roosevelt in a controversy over U.S. Steel, and the Republican's loss of control of the House of Representatives in 1910 led the former president to challenge his successor for the 1912 Republican nomination. Although Roosevelt won most of the primaries, the Republican bosses handed the nomination to Taft. As a result, Roosevelt left the party to run as the nominee of the insurgent Progressive Party. His proposed program, dubbed "the New Nationalism," called for greater government involvement in regulating industrial capitalism, including labor legislation to prevent, in the words of progressive reformer and Roosevelt supporter Jane Addams, "industrial accidents, occupational diseases, overwork, involuntary unemployment, and other injurious effects incident to modern industry." Although Taft had some progressive credentials, he ran — "walked" might be a better description of his lethargic campaign — as the candidate of conservative Republicans.

If the Democrats had also nominated a conservative, Roosevelt might have won a third-party victory. But the Democratic nominee turned out to be Woodrow Wilson, who had established a reform reputation as governor of New Jersey. A stern Presbyterian, Wilson differed sharply from the effervescent Roosevelt in both style and rhetoric. Whereas Roosevelt's New Nationalism called for an expanded national state to regulate capitalism, Wilson trumpeted a "New Freedom," in which antimonopoly policies would restore competition and small-scale business. But the two men shared a fundamental critique of the excesses of industrial capitalism. An even more thoroughgoing critique came from the Socialist candidate, Eugene V. Debs. He dismissed Roosevelt's Progressive Party as "a party of progressive capitalism" and called for "the abolition of this monstrous [capitalist] system" rather than for its reform.

The split in the Republican Party and support from the South, the West, and AFL unions gave Wilson a clear victory (though not a majority of voters). Debs won a surprising 6 percent of the vote (more than any Socialist presidential candidate). Perhaps most startling is that three-quarters of the electorate backed one of the three candidates who had championed the interests of the people over monopoly capitalism, in one of the most resounding endorsements of reform in U.S. history (Map 5.3).

As president, Wilson responded to some, but not all, of the items on the reform agenda. He dragged his feet on the call for woman suffrage and showed almost no sympathy for the problems of immigrants. Wilson—the first southerner elected president since before the Civil War—probably received more black votes than any previous Democratic presidential candidate. African Americans had abandoned Taft, in part because he had appointed or retained only thirty-one black officeholders. But Wilson's record on African American rights proved even more dismal; he ended up making only nine black appointments, eight of them Republican carryovers. Worse still, he extended and defended segregation in the federal civil service. Black federal workers had to use inferior and segregated washrooms and to work behind screens that separated them from white workers. And like his predecessors, Wilson repeatedly ignored both the lynching of hundreds of African Americans by white southerners and the disfranchisement and Jim Crow laws that reversed the modest political and economic gains black Americans had made during Reconstruction.

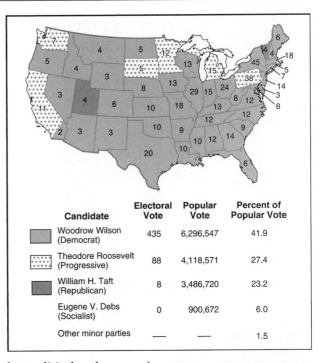

Candidate	Electoral Vote	Popular Vote	Percent of Popular Vote
Woodrow Wilson (Democrat)	435	6,296,547	41.9
Theodore Roosevelt (Progressive)	88	4,118,571	27.4
William H. Taft (Republican)	8	3,486,720	23.2
Eugene V. Debs (Socialist)	0	900,672	6.0
Other minor parties	—	—	1.5

MAP 5.3 The Election of 1912
Few elections in American history produced such a strong endorsement of reform as that of 1912. Three-quarters of the popular vote went to candidates (Woodrow Wilson, Theodore Roosevelt, and Eugene V. Debs) who championed the "people" against monopoly capitalism. William Howard Taft, the one conservative candidate, won the electoral votes only of Utah and Vermont.

Organized labor, which had also backed Wilson, fared much better. Wilson rewarded the labor movement by backing the Clayton Antitrust Act. It replaced the Sherman Act (1890), which had not offered a strong definition of monopolies and trusts and had been used more effectively against labor (especially in the Pullman strike) than against big business. Samuel Gompers called the Clayton Act labor's Magna Carta, or guarantee of basic rights, because not only did it precisely define such prohibited practices as "interlocking directorates" and "discriminatory pricing," but it also specifically stipulated that labor unions and farmers' organizations should not be considered conspiracies in restraint of trade. Wilson also championed a model federal workers' compensation statute, an eight-hour law for railroad workers, and a federal child-labor law. The result of years of pressure from working people and reformers, these bills established, for the first time, the federal government's interest in regulating the conditions of labor.

In one of his first acts as president in 1913, Wilson appointed the Commission on Industrial Relations, authorized by Congress in response to labor radicalism and violence. The commission's chairman, Frank P. Walsh, a Kansas City reformer who was sympathetic to labor, had used a series of public hearings to expose what he called "industrial feudalism." The commission's 1915 report asserted that poor working conditions, autocratic business management, and the concentration of wealth underlay labor violence.

The 'Open Road'

This 1916 cartoon celebrating the insurgent Progressive Party drew its title from a quote by Woodrow Wilson, stating that Americans who were discontented with traditional party politics proposed to "find an open road for themselves." Robert Carter, *American Review of Reviews* (1912) — Prints and Photographs Division, Library of Congress.

It called for an inheritance tax to finance education, social services, and public works; a child-labor law; equal pay for women and men; and protection of the right to join a union and bargain collectively.

Although the Wilson administration ignored most of these recommendations, it did offer some important concessions to labor. The Seamen's Act of 1915 eliminated the oppressive financial arrangements and semimilitary discipline inflicted on merchant sailors. In 1916 came the Keating-Owen bill, which was the first federal child-labor law, and the Adamson Act, which granted railroad workers the eight-hour workday—the first time private workers' hours came under federal regulations. The courts eventually undercut some of labor's legislative victories: they severely weakened the labor provisions of the Clayton Act and declared the child-labor law unconstitutional. Still, Wilson's accommodation of labor was a dramatic step and responded to both the growing power of the AFL and the mass insurgencies represented by the Socialist party, the IWW, and other radical unionists.

Wilson also expanded the government's economic role. He set up the Federal Reserve System (1913), which reestablished a central banking system, and the Federal Trade Commission (1914), which was charged with preventing corporate attempts to inhibit competition. These efforts continued a trend begun a decade earlier under Roosevelt, of concentrating federal power in the executive branch and creating a large administrative bureaucracy to mediate conflicting social and economic pressures. In that sense, Wilson's New Freedom turned out to look a lot like Roosevelt's New Nationalism. As before, however, businessmen were often able to capture control of the regulatory process. Under the Federal Reserve Act of 1913, bankers dominated the regulation of the nation's currency and credit systems, controlling the boards of the regional Federal Reserve banks and shaping the policies of the Federal Reserve Board.

Conclusion: Toward the Modern State

Progressivism responded to the economic, social, and political dislocations that accompanied industrial capitalism's dramatic growth during the Gilded Age: rapid technological change; intense and episodic conflict between capital and labor; the influx of enormous numbers of immigrants from Southern and Eastern Europe, Asia, and Latin America; and the growing national and international reach of American capitalism. Each of these problems posed a special challenge to older American ideals of individual independence and equality.

Progressivism looked to an active government to blunt the worst of capitalism's economic and social problems. Working people, in coalition with socialists, radicals, and feminists, joined in progressive reform struggles, helping to win passage of prolabor legislation, especially the federal Clayton Act. These reforms helped lay the foundation for our modern notion of government and were among progressivism's most lasting contributions to American political life.

But by the time war broke out in Europe in 1914, the central role that many progressives desired for government had been only partially realized: federal, state, and local laws minimally regulated the economy and industrial relations while extending limited protections to consumers and women and children. Assembling the cross-class coalition that made progressive reforms possible had involved significant compromises. Only a relatively small number of working people—those who were organized into skilled-craft unions and those working in industries covered by limited factory reforms—fully benefited from the passage of progressive legislation. Many others—unskilled and manual laborers, domestic servants, agricultural wageworkers, and sharecroppers—remained outside progressivism's protective sphere.

African Americans experienced the Progressive era quite literally as a tightening noose: the federal government repeatedly ignored the wanton lynching of hundreds of African Americans in the South. At the same time, the modest political and economic gains these Americans had made during Reconstruction were rolled back in a flood of Progressive era disfranchisement laws and the purging of African Americans from federal jobs by the Wilson administration. Women had been central to the movements that made up progressivism and had succeeded in expanding their public role in American life. Yet their most important demand—for the right to vote—remained stalled as the United States entered World War I.

Despite these very real limitations, progressivism represented a watershed that marked the beginning of a new relationship between working people and the government. The era's limited

Eight-Hour Victory
Maurice Becker in the radical monthly *The Masses* celebrated the passage of the Adamson Act in 1916, which specified an eight-hour workday (with additional pay for overtime labor) for employees of railroads engaged in interstate commerce. Maurice Becker, *The Masses*, November 1916 — Prints and Photographs Division, Library of Congress.

reforms inaugurated a period of governmental involvement in economic and social affairs that would intensify in coming decades. As a result, working people would look increasingly to government to ameliorate the worst excesses of industrial capitalism. Progressivism set the terms of this new relationship, as working people's experiences in their struggle for a better life were now linked inextricably to national political, economic, and social developments.

The Years in Review

1889

- Jane Addams establishes Hull House.

1890

- Two major factions join to form the National American Woman Suffrage Association.

1901

- The Socialist Party is founded by the merger of several socialist groups; party membership will peak in 1912 at 118,000 members.
- Leon Czolgosz assassinates William McKinley; Theodore Roosevelt becomes president.

1902

- One hundred forty thousand anthracite coal miners strike for an eight-hour day; Roosevelt convinces the mine owners to accept arbitration.

1903

- The Women's Trade Union League is founded by a coalition of working-class and elite women.
- Teddy bears, modeled on Roosevelt's hunting exploits, become popular toys.

1904

- The Republican candidate, Theodore Roosevelt, wins the presidential election, defeating Democrat Alton B. Parker and Socialist Eugene V. Debs.

1905

- The Industrial Workers of the World (IWW) is founded to abolish the wage system.

1906

- The Hepburn Act enables the previously weak Interstate Commerce Commission to regulate railroad rates.
- Congress passes the Pure Food and Drug Act and the Meat Inspection Act following the publication of Upton Sinclair's *The Jungle*.

- Roosevelt issues an executive order calling for "simplified spelling," a typical "scientific" reform of the Progressive era.

1907
- A financial panic, which results from irresponsible speculation and industrial overproduction, brings a minor depression after the general prosperity of the early 1900s.
- The U.S. Justice Department wins an antitrust case against Standard Oil.

1908
- In *Muller v. Oregon,* the U.S. Supreme Court upholds an Oregon law limiting women's work to ten hours a day in certain kinds of businesses.
- The Republican candidate, William Howard Taft, defeats Democrat William Jennings Bryan and Socialist Eugene V. Debs in the presidential election.

1909
- In the Uprising of the Twenty Thousand, garment strikes lead to reduced working hours, improved conditions, and a system for future arbitration.
- The IWW leads a successful strike of immigrant steel workers in McKees, Pennsylvania, and free speech campaigns in western cities.
- President Taft signs the Payne-Aldrich protective tariff, which lowered some tariffs but did not significantly reform protective tariffs.

1910
- Thousands of garment workers strike in New York and Chicago, leading to major union victories in the clothing industry.
- The National Association for the Advancement of Colored People (NAACP) is formally established.
- Socialist Party candidates win hundred of seats in local elections.

1911
- The Triangle Shirtwaist Company fire leaves 146 workers dead because of faulty fire escapes and intentionally blocked exit routes; public outcry leads to factory safety and health reforms.
- A coal mine explosion outside of Birmingham, Alabama, kills 128 convict miners.

1912
- Democrat Woodrow Wilson wins the presidential election, defeating Theodore Roosevelt (candidate of new Progressive Party), Republican William Howard Taft, and Socialist Eugene V. Debs.

- The IWW organizes the successful Lawrence, Massachusetts ("Bread and Roses"), textile strike.
- The IWW meets with defeat in a silk workers' strike in Paterson, New Jersey.
- Thirty-eight states pass child-labor laws, and twenty-eight states set maximum hours for women workers.
- The Department of Labor creates a Children's Bureau to monitor child labor.

1913
- The Sixteenth Amendment (income tax) is adopted.
- The Seventeenth Amendment (direct election of U.S. senators) is adopted.

1914
- Women in eleven states—most in the West—and the territory of Alaska have the right to vote in state, local, and school board elections.
- The Federal Reserve Act is passed—the first comprehensive reorganization of the banking system since the Civil War.
- World War I breaks out in Europe.
- The Clayton Antitrust Act, labor's "Magna Carta," is passed; it exempts unions from antitrust laws and limits the use of injunctions against labor.
- Troops attack a strikers' tent camp in Colorado, killing sixteen people, including twelve children, in what will become known as the Ludlow Massacre.

1915
- The report of the Commission on Industrial Relations asserts that poor working conditions, autocratic business management, and the concentration of wealth led to labor violence.

1916
- Congress passes the first federal child-labor law, the Keating-Owen bill.
- Congress passes the Adamson Act, which grants railroad workers the eight-hour day.

1919
- The Eighteenth Amendment (Prohibition) is adopted.

1920
- The Nineteenth Amendment (woman suffrage) is adopted.

Additional Readings

For more on women in the Progressive era, see: Ruth Bordin, *Women and Temperance: The Quest for Power and Liberty, 1873–1900* (1981); Allen Davis, *Spearheads of Reform: The Settlements and the Progressive Movement, 1890–1914* (1967); Nancy Schrom Dye, *As Equals and as Sisters: Feminism, Unionism, and the Women's Trade Union League of New York* (1980); Jean Bethke Elshtain, *Jane Addams and the Dream of American Democracy: A Life* (2002); Eleanor Flexner, *Century of Struggle: The Woman's Rights Movement in the United States* (1975); Glenda Elizabeth Gilmore, *Gender and Jim Crow: Women and the Politics of White Supremacy in North Carolina, 1896–1920* (1996); Aileen S. Kraditor, *The Ideas of the Woman Suffrage Movement, 1890–1920* (1965); Rebecca J. Mead, *How the Vote Was Won: Woman Suffrage in the Western United States, 1868–1914* (2004); Robyn Muncy, *Creating a Female Dominion in American Reform, 1890–1935* (1991); Annelise Orleck, *Common Sense and a Little Fire: Women and Working Class Politics in the United States, 1900–1965* (1995); Kathryn Kish Sklar, *Florence Kelley and the Nation's Work: The Rise of Women's Political Culture, 1830–1900* (1995); and Meredith Tax, *The Rising of the Women: Feminist Solidarity and Class Conflict, 1880–1917* (1980).

For more on the fight to end child labor, see: Hugh D. Hindman, *Child Labor: An American History* (2002); Kriste Lindenmeyer, *A Right to Childhood: The U.S. Children's Bureau and Child Welfare, 1912–46* (1997); Shelley Sallee, *The Whiteness of Child Labor Reform in the New South* (2004); and Walter Trattner, *Crusade for the Children: A History of the National Child Labor Committee and Child Labor Reform in America* (1970).

For more on radical challenges to the status quo, see: Melvyn Dubofsky, *Hard Work: The Making of Labor History* (2000); Melvyn Dubofsky, *We Shall Be All: A History of the Industrial Workers of the World* (1969); Melvyn Dubofsky, *When Workers Organize: New York in the Progressive Era* (1968); James R. Green, *Grassroots Socialism: Radical Movements in the Southwest, 1895–1943* (1978); Howard Kimeldorf, *Battling for American Labor: Wobblies, Craft Workers, and the Making of the Union Movement* (1999); and Nick Salvatore, *Eugene V. Debs: Citizen and Socialist* (1982).

For more on Progressive era politics and urban reform, see: Paul Boyer, *Urban Masses and Moral Order in America, 1820–1920* (1978); David Brody, *Workers in Industrial America: Essays on the Twentieth-Century Struggle* (1980); John Buenker, *Urban Liberalism and Progressive Reform* (1973); James Chace, *1912: Wilson, Roosevelt, Taft and Debs — The Election That Changed the Country* (2004); John Whiteclay Chambers, II, *The*

Tyranny of Change: America in the Progressive Era, 1900–1917, 2nd ed., (1992); John Milton Cooper, Jr., *The Warrior and the Priest: Woodrow Wilson and Theodore Roosevelt* (1983); Alan Dawley, *Struggles for Justice: Social Responsibility and the Liberal State* (1991); Steven J. Diner, *A Very Different Age: Americans of the Progressive Era* (1998); Louis Filler, *The Muckrakers: Crusaders for American Liberalism* (1968); Lorine Swainston Goodwin, *The Pure Food, Drink, and Drug Crusaders, 1879–1914* (1999); Samuel P. Hays, *The Response to Industrialism, 1885–1914* (1957); Richard Hofstadter, *The Age of Reform* (1955); Melvin Holli, *Reform in Detroit: Hazen Pingree and Urban Politics* (1969); James Kloppenberg, *Uncertain Victory: Social Democracy and Progressivism in European and American Thought, 1870–1920* (1986); Gabriel Kolko, *The Triumph of Conservatism: A Reinterpretation of American History, 1900–1916* (1967); Arthur S. Link and Richard L. McCormick, *Progressivism* (1983); Michael McGerr, *The Decline of Popular Politics: The American North, 1865–1928* (1986); Michael McGerr, *A Fierce Discontent: The Rise and Fall of the Progressive Movement in America, 1870–1920* (2003); Eric Rauchway, *Murdering McKinley: The Making of Theodore Roosevelt's America* (2003); Daniel T. Rodgers, *Atlantic Crossings: Social Politics in a Progressive Age* (1998); David Thelen, *The New Citizenship: The Origins of Progressivism in Wisconsin, 1885–1900* (1972); and Robert H. Wiebe, *The Search for Order* (1967).

For more on the transition to the modern state, see: Robert Harrison, *Congress, Progressive Reform, and the New American State* (2004); Martin J. Sklar, *The Corporate Reconstruction of American Capitalism, 1890–1916: The Market, the Law, and Politics* (1988); Theda Skocpol, *Protecting Soldiers and Mothers: The Political Origins of Social Policy in the United States* (1992); and Stephen Skowronek, *Building a New American State: The Expansion of National Administrative Capacities, 1877–1920* (1982).

Part Two

War, Depression, and Industrial Unionism

1914–1946

*W*HEN THE FIRST U.S. ARMY TROOPS landed in war-ravaged Tokyo early in September 1945, they were commanded by scores of young officers, many born just before World War I. These confident commanders, ex-civilians still in their thirties, had been part of a vast wartime expansion of American power to almost every corner of the globe. But their memories stretched back to the grim Depression years, to high school in the 1920s, and to childhood memories of World War I itself. This generation experienced a transformation in American life that was as dramatic and fundamental as any since the founding of the Republic. When they attended elementary school, the nation's social and political rhythms were still attuned to those of a nineteenth-century agrarian world; by the time they learned that B-29 bombers had dropped atomic bombs on Hiroshima and Nagasaki, U.S. diplomacy, politics, and society had far more in common with the end of the twentieth century than with its start.

In just one-third of a century, from 1914 to 1945, Americans fought two world wars, survived the Great Depression, and saw the emergence of the most powerful trade union movement in the nation's history. As war and revolution convulsed countries around the globe, politics became saturated with debate over the great "isms" of the twentieth century: imperialism, capitalism, socialism, fascism, and communism. The federal government became far more powerful but also more intimately involved with the lives of ordinary Americans. Women got the vote, African Americans demanded their right to vote, and immigrant Americans began to exercise the franchise in huge numbers. New modes of communication, consumption, and transport—movies, radio, chain stores, buses and cars—recast the texture of everyday life.

Four great developments transformed the United States and its place in the world during this third of a century. First, the United States became the world's greatest power, in terms both of its economic infrastructure and its military influence overseas. In 1914, the United States was already the productive equal of Great Britain and Germany; but whereas both world wars sapped the economic vitality of the European combatants—and decimated an entire generation of young men—the American republic emerged from each conflict with ever greater economic and military strength. U.S. industry perfected mass production, put an automobile in the driveway of most families, and developed the kind of technologies—such as aviation, radar, telecommunications, and nuclear fission — that paid off in time of war. Early in 1941, *Life* magazine publisher Henry Luce proclaimed this era "the American Century." Indeed, by the end of World War II, the relative power of the United States recalled the strength of Great Britain at the high noon of its Victorian empire or Rome in the reign of the Caesars.

Second, the federal government became enormously more powerful during these three short decades. In 1914, the post office was perhaps the only agency of the national government that touched the lives of ordinary Americans. But war and depression soon changed all that. U.S. participation in World War I proved a dress rehearsal not just for the next world conflict, but also for the transformative, intrusive impact of the New Deal fifteen years later. During the First World War, the Wilson administration mobilized the American people as never before: government regulated business, took over the railroads, tested and trained millions of military recruits, censored the mail, and sold war bonds in a huge propaganda effort to gain public support for the battles overseas. In the 1920s, Republican presidents tempered the growth of federal power, but even in that more conservative decade, President Herbert Hoover, who had been a highly effective World War I administrator, argued for the kind of nation-state activism that would have surprised his nineteenth-century predecessors.

Many veterans of World War I, including Assistant Secretary of the Navy Franklin D. Roosevelt, would deploy this same kind of organizational energy and ambition when the nation faced its next great crisis, the Great Depression. The Roosevelt administration's New Deal built dams and roads; subsidized millions of farmers; regulated corporations, banks, and the stock market; and established Social Security, which would eventually become the single largest, most expensive, and, for many years, most popular of all government programs. Then came World War II, when the federal government achieved stupendous size and power: it raised an army and navy of sixteen million; it mobilized the nation's leading universities for military research; and it launched the industrialization of previously rural or residential areas, such as southern California, large sections of the agricultural South, and Long Island. By 1944, the military was spending more than 40 percent of the nation's entire gross domestic product.

Third, these were the years during which the labor movement moved to the center ring of American politics and culture. This took place in two stages, during both of which rank-and-file activism and government policy combined to generate an explosive growth in union size and influence. During World War I, the Wilson administration repressed antiwar radicals, but to advance U.S. war aims, the government also linked victory over German autocracy to the spread of an industrial democracy at home. American workers were therefore emboldened to denounce their employers as "Prussian" managers and "Kaiserism" in industry, and they joined unions in a vast wave that crested during the nationwide strikes of 1919, the largest working-class upheaval in the history of the republic.

Fifteen years later, industrial unionism finally won the kind of political support and legislative backing that had been absent during the First World War. The 1935 Wagner Act encouraged trade unionism as a spur to economic recovery and a bulwark of American democracy. But no matter how favorable the law was to labor, the mass unionism of the 1930s required the courageous activism of thousands of women and men. Organizing the biggest industries of their time—automobiles, steel, rubber, and electrical products—they built the new Congress of Industrial Organizations (CIO) and put its power and values close to the heart of a New Deal impulse that stretched well into the post–World War II years.

Fourth, this era of war and depression generated a remarkable transformation in the character of the American people. Although shipping shortages and dangers during the First World War—and the immigration restriction laws that followed—stanched the great transatlantic migrations, the impact of that European diaspora would have a lasting effect on their new country. In the 1930s and 1940s, the sons and daughters of the prewar immigrant wave—the ambitious, assimilationist "second generation"—helped to reestablish the Democratic Party; gave new energy to the labor movement; and poured creativity into science, film, and music. Immigrant daughters figured prominently in the labor upsurge of the 1930s, but women of all backgrounds took advantage of new opportunities in industry and offices. They streamed into jobs that were vacated by men during the two world wars and began to stay in the workforce longer. In 1914, the typical woman worker was an unmarried teenager; after 1945, she was married and in her twenties or thirties.

Southerners both black and white also poured into the industrial workplace. Fleeing a generation-long agricultural depression, many white southerners moved north during the 1920s and 1930s. But the wartime "Great Migration" of African Americans proved even more dramatic. Starting in the First World War and renewing itself in the Second, a huge exodus out of the rural South swelled the African American population of Chicago, New York, Baltimore, Washington, D.C., Detroit, and Oakland, California, moving the aspirations of this community toward the center of U.S. politics. In 1914, African Americans were voiceless and hidden behind a veil of nearly unchallenged white supremacy. Thirty years later, a vigorous civil rights movement, powerfully reinforced by hundreds of thousands of black factory workers, had begun to challenge the old racial order on almost every front.

6

Wars for Democracy

1914–1920

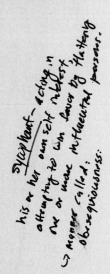

Sycophant — acting in his or her own self interest; attempting to win favor by flattery. I've or more motivated pursues.

↳ manner called: obsequiousness.

No Man's Land

A soldier's corpse, caught on one of the barbed-wire barricades that crisscrossed European battlefields during the First World War, hangs unburied between the trenches of the opposing armies. Imperial War Museum.

IN MID-1918, AS THE CLOUDS of war rolled over the United States, socialist leader Eugene Debs rose from his sickbed to protest the massive government repression that had led to the arrest of thousands of radicals and opponents of U.S. participation in the war. "They tell us that we live in a great free republic," he told a cheering crowd in Canton, Ohio, "that our institutions are democratic, that we are a free and self-governing people. This is too much, even for a joke." Debs knew his own remarks placed him at risk of arrest, but he insisted he "would rather a thousand times . . . be a free soul in jail than . . . be a sycophant and coward in the streets." Rejecting the claim that the United States was fighting "to make democracy safe in the world," Debs believed that wars were waged for conquest and plunder. "The master class," he insisted, "has always declared the wars; the subject class has always fought the battles. The master class has had all to gain and nothing to lose, while the subject class has had nothing to gain and all to lose — especially their lives."

Debs was prophetic. As he perhaps expected, he wound up as a "free soul in jail": this very exercise of free speech led to a ten-year sentence for violating the 1917 Espionage Act. And while munitions makers and a small number of other corporations grew rich from what would later be known as World War I, millions, most of them from the "subject class," died. Ten million people (including 112,000 U.S. soldiers) perished; twice that number died from hunger and disease attributable to the war. Rather than making the world safe for democracy, as President Woodrow Wilson had asserted, the bungled peace enacted at the end of the so-called War to End All Wars would pave the way for a second, even deadlier world war.

But like most political speakers, Debs painted on a broad canvas. In hindsight, we can see that the war years brought vital gains as well as grievous losses for ordinary Americans. Workers benefited from the labor shortage that developed as war production increased. Rural black southerners moved north to fill industrial positions. The flow of immigration from Mexico swelled. Women made their way into traditionally male jobs. With jobs easy to get, workers won better wages and conditions and recognition of their unions. From below, workers, immigrants, women, and African Americans pressed the meaning of a war for democracy beyond the boundaries that President Wilson had intended.

The victory of the United States and its allies in the war seemed to open up further promises not only of a new and fairer social order, but also of greater economic and social democracy. Unions staged massive strikes to redeem the idea of economic democracy; African Americans proclaimed their rights to long-delayed civic equality. But the postwar strikes met defeat at the hands of repressive employers, and a government-sponsored "Red scare" soon crushed most signs of radicalism. Whites beat and killed newly assertive African Americans in a series of brutal race riots. By 1920, many Americans would have agreed with the imprisoned Debs that World War I had neither enshrined democracy around the world nor advanced it more than modestly at home.

World War I Comes to Europe

In the summer of 1914, Europe plunged into a devastating conflict, known then as the Great War and later as World War I. For the next four years, the Allies (France, Great Britain, and Russia) and the Central Powers (Germany, Austria-Hungary, and Italy) faced each other in a horrific standoff. Industrialization provided new weapons of destruction that killed more than nine million people in battle while millions more died from war-related disease and hunger.

From Assassination in the Balkans to War in Europe   On June 28, 1914, Gavrilo Prinčip, a Serbian nationalist, assassinated Archduke Franz Ferdinand, the heir to the Austro-Hungarian throne. Less than three weeks after the assassination, Austria-Hungary declared war on Serbia, and European nations joined in, declaring their loyalty to one side or the other. Russia quickly came to Serbia's aid, and Germany rushed to Austria-Hungary's defense by attacking France, Russia's ally. The next day, Britain joined the conflict on behalf of both France and neutral Belgium, which had come under attack by German troops. Within five weeks, virtually all of Europe was at war.

How did a single shot from an unknown terrorist set in motion a <u>conflagration</u> that would leave millions of people dead? Part of the answer lies in the intense ethnic and nationalist rivalries in the Balkans in southeastern Europe. The nineteenth century had seen the decay of the long-standing Turkish Ottoman Empire and the rise of nationalist sentiment and conflicts among the different ethnic groups living in the Balkan: Serbs, Croatians, Bosnians, Montenegrins, and others. These conflicts would not have led to global war had they not played into larger European tensions. Rising nationalism posed a fundamental threat to Austria-Hungary's already crumbling multicultural empire; Serbian expansionism would further stir up those nationalist aspirations. Even more important, Russia—a fierce defender of the Serbs—and Austria-Hungary sat on opposing sides of two sets of alliances that had emerged in Europe in the previous half-century: the Triple Alliance of Germany, Austria-Hungary, and Italy and the Triple Entente of France, Great Britain, and Russia. These competing alliances fostered an arms race in which each major power feared falling behind its rivals (Map 6.1).

This lethal mix—ethnic tensions, nationalism, global imperial ambitions, escalating militarism, and a convoluted system of alliances and treaties, many of them secret—proved explosive. When Germany decided to back Austria-Hungary against Serbia and Russia, the die was cast. Neither the Allies (Britain, France, and Russia) nor the German-led Central Powers could or would back down. The chain reaction that followed would turn a seemingly obscure incident into a war that was more terrifying and destructive than anything Europe had ever seen.

Total War in Europe   Even though the Allies and the Central Powers each confidently predicted a quick victory, the war turned into a gruesome stalemate. By fall of 1914, the French and British had stopped the German advance toward Paris in northeastern France in a narrow strip of land known as the Western Front, where millions of troops fought from a vast network of parallel trenches filled with mud and rats. Machine guns mowed down soldiers who were ordered "over the top," out of the trenches, in a "no man's land" strung with barbed wire to separate the opposing front lines. During 1915 and 1916, both sides tried to break through enemy lines. The German attack on Verdun, France, in February 1916 involved unprecedented firepower. Ten months and almost 700,000 deaths later, the position of the front had barely changed. The new strategy became one of wearing down the enemy in an intentional war of attrition. In July, the British launched an offensive on the Somme River; 19,000 soldiers died on just the first day. Before the attack ended (and the Allies gained a pathetic 125 miles of mud), casualties on both sides would exceed one million.

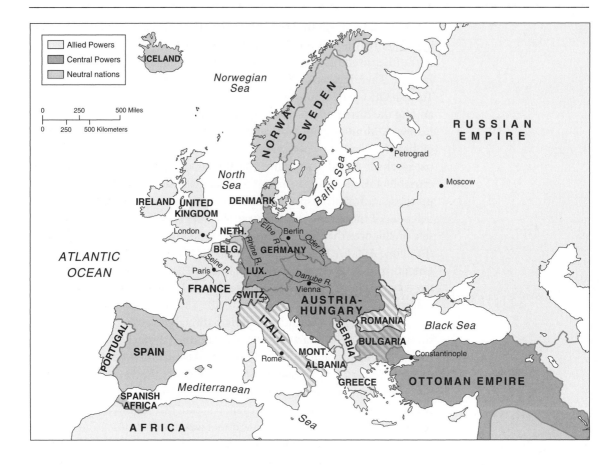

MAP 6.1 Europe at the Beginning of World War I

The Central Powers, or Triple Alliance countries, were bound by the Allied Powers and could barely contain the rising ethnic nationalism within their borders. Although Italy and Romania had been allies of Austria-Hungary in previous years, they initially declared neutrality and later joined the Allied Powers. Bulgaria, originally a neutral nation, joined the Central Powers in 1915.

For the European participants, World War I meant "total war," a phrase suggesting the war's global character, exceptional intensity, and utter destructiveness. The armed forces on each side required huge mountains of supplies and equipment, provided by the new technologies and large-scale production of the industrial age. Well-developed railways and telegraph lines made it possible to move and manage these mass armies; long-range artillery and rapid-fire infantry weapons multiplied their firepower. Machine guns, flamethrowers, tanks, and chemical weapons such as poison gas changed warfare forever. Airplanes and zeppelins dropped bombs from the sky. At sea, submarines altered traditional naval strategy with their stealth, surprise, and capacity for sudden destruction.

Crucial to these operations were the working men and women who labored on the "home front" to produce the materials that were used in this prolonged conflict. These workers and other civilians became, for the first time, "legitimate" military targets. Each side bombed cities from the air and blockaded or shelled ports and seaside resorts. The blockades cut off food supplies, causing widespread malnutrition and vulnerability to disease among civilians, especially the young and the old.

The War in America

Initially, America benefited from the catastrophe engulfing Europe. Its demand for food and weapons proved profitable for the United States, stimulating the economy and pulling it out of recession. But the profits of wartime commerce inevitably drew the United States into the conflict, particularly as Germany viewed the pro-British tilt in American trade and loans as a growing threat. Although Americans were deeply divided in their allegiances and their views of the European conflict, the German use of submarine warfare against "neutral" commerce finally pulled the United States into the war on the side of the Allies. After the American declaration of war in April 1917, the federal government mobilized not just militarily but also ideologically by suppressing dissent and economically by taking a more active hand in the economy than it had in more than half a century.

Neutrality and American Business   In 1914, Wilson's administration urged strict U.S. neutrality. The war seemed to have little to do with the United States, which confined its international activity to the Caribbean, South and Central America, and the Pacific. But the war drew in U.S. citizens who carried goods from the United States to Europe, traveled on American and European ships, and did business with the warring governments and their citizens. Both sides turned to the United States to finance the war: the British sold Americans more than $3.5 billion worth of investments they had in the United States, and the Allies borrowed over $2 billion from American banks and the federal government. By the end of the war, the United States had reversed its historic position as a debtor nation and become a net lender. New York was well on its way toward replacing London as the world's financial capital, and the United States was on the verge of becoming the world's strongest economy.

Much of the money the United States loaned European nations came back immediately in payment for food, raw materials, and manufactured goods. J. P. Morgan & Co., the exclusive purchasing agent for England and France, placed more than $3 billion worth of wartime orders. As the conflict dragged

Won't They Be Edified!
A 1914 cartoon published in the *Chicago Daily News* used racial chauvinism to condemn the European war for undermining the moral supremacy of "Western civilization." *Chicago Daily News*, 1914 — American Social History Project.

WON'T THEY BE EDIFIED!
—*Chicago Daily News.*

Animated Propaganda
Winsor McCay became famous for his comic strips, notably his whimsical and architecturally extravagant *Little Nemo in Slumberland*, and pioneering animated cartoons such as his 1914 *Gertie the Dinosaur*. McCay's 1918 *The Sinking of the Lusitania* was a milestone in the history of animation with its detailed and grim depiction of the event that departed from the simple slapstick standard of contemporary cartoons. It also marked the creation of a new, effective tool for mobilizing popular sentiments in a time of war. American Social History Project.

on, U.S. businesses developed stronger ties to England and France and a greater economic stake in their victory. Between August 1914 and March 1917, the United States sold the Allies about $2.2 billion in armaments—an amount nearly equal to the value of all American exports in 1913. It also shipped iron, steel, copper, and oil to the Allies, paid for by loans from U.S. bankers. By 1917, the nation's gross national product—the sum of all the goods and services the United States produced—rose 20 percent higher than that three years earlier.

But war profits also posed a problem. Under international law, the belligerents could intercept and detain neutral ships, inspect them, confiscate goods they considered contraband, and remove enemy personnel. The United States, which based its foreign policy on freedom of the seas, found neutrality difficult to maintain in this total war. Countless supplies were needed to sustain massive armies and civilians, and each side tried to prevent neutral countries from supplying its enemies. In February 1915, the British navy, the most powerful in the world, began turning back ships carrying war-related goods, including food, to Germany. The Germans retaliated with their new Unterseeboot, or U-boat, launching surprise submarine attacks on Allied ships.

Incidents involving Americans became inevitable, and the clash occurred in May 1915, when 128 Americans died as a German U-boat torpedoed the British passenger ship *Lusitania*, which was rumored to be carrying contraband, off the Irish coast. Responding to a huge public outcry, the United States protested immediately. The Germans, unwilling to push the

United States into the war on the Allied side, expressed regret and agreed to respect international agreements on naval warfare.

Secretary of State William Jennings Bryan urged Wilson to avoid any appearance of taking sides in the European conflict and even recommended breaking commercial ties with the combatants. The president refused, arguing that the United States had to maintain free trade and freedom of the seas and that submarine warfare was immoral, a clear reason to oppose Germany. Bryan—one of the few members of the administration who was genuinely committed to neutrality—resigned over Wilson's reaction to the *Lusitania* affair. The British blockade, Bryan insisted, was equally immoral, because it was starving Germany's civilian population, and he warned that Wilson's actions would lead to war. Bryan's successor, the pro-British Robert Lansing, believed as early as 1915 that the United States "would ultimately become an ally of Great Britain." Lansing's appointment further skewed U.S. policy toward the Allies.

The Debate over American Involvement Increasingly, the war presented Americans with a profound dilemma. Wilson agreed with most business and political leaders that continued U.S. prosperity and tranquility depended on international investment and trade. The main obstacle, in his view, was European-style imperialism—the competitive rush for colonies and exclusive spheres of influence that had secured European domination of world markets and, indeed, the world's people. Wilson opposed high tariffs and advocated an international free-trade system. U.S. producers, Wilson explained in 1912, "have expanded to such a point that they will burst their jackets if they cannot find a free outlet to the markets of the world." Wilson meant his policies not simply to aid industry and raise the standard of living in the United States; a devout Presbyterian, he also saw the spread of free trade and democratic capitalism as a concrete expression of Christian values.

The war that was raging in Europe epitomized the very sort of imperialism Wilson detested, and violations of neutral rights now threatened U.S. peace. The United States faced no immediate military threat. But the president sympathized emotionally and ideologically with Great Britain and feared that an Allied defeat would make Germany a dangerous economic and military rival and an opponent of the U.S. Open Door policy. Furthermore, he worried that a neutral America would be powerless to help shape the postwar world and ensure the openness of world markets to what he called "righteous conquest" by American business.

The public was deeply divided over the war. One in nine Americans had been born in a Central Powers country or had a parent who was born there. German Americans generally favored the Central Powers; those with British

"Let the Capitalists Do Their Own Fighting"

Eugene Debs, industrial union leader and Socialist Party presidential candidate, expressed an intense antiwar attitude in this August 1914 editorial in the working-class newspaper National Rip-Saw. *Radicals and socialists opposed the war believing it resulted from inevitable capitalist rivalry for international markets and raw materials.*

The capitalists tell us it is patriotic to fight for your country and shed your blood for the flag. Very well! Let them set the example.

It is their country; they own it and therefore according to their logic it is their patriotic duty to fight and die for it and be brought home riddled with bullets and covered with flowers as shining examples of patriotic duty to the youth of the nation. . . .

You never had a country to fight for and never will have as much as an inch of one as long as you are fool enough to make a target of your bodies for the profit and glory of your masters.

Let the capitalists do their own fighting and furnish their own corpses and there will never be another war on the face of the earth.

Frederick C. Griffin, *Six Who Protested: Radical Opposition to the First World War* (1977).

---

backgrounds tended to back the Allies. Most Irish Americans, though no special friends of Germany, opposed aid to Britain. Their opposition intensified—as did the struggle for independence in Ireland—after the British crushed the abortive Easter Rebellion of 1916. Nonetheless, when war broke out, the strongest impulse in America was for peace. Peace forces mobilized activists who had previously focused on the domestic reforms favored by progressives.

Across the country, people rallied to oppose U.S. intervention in the conflict. Many radicals and reformers argued that war would suspend domestic reform, endanger civil liberties, and profit big business. Some activists joined an internationalist movement that promoted world order based on international law. Those who opposed the war included the midwestern progressives, such as George Norris and Robert La Follette, and a large bloc of Democratic congressional representatives from the South and the Midwest. William Jennings Bryan, commenting on what he saw as the pro-British, prowar bias of the East Coast, complained to his daughter that "the president does not seem to realize that a great part of America lies on the other side of the Allegheny Mountains." Most feminists and suffragists also opposed the war. Jane Addams and Carrie Chapman Catt, president of the National American Woman Suffrage Association, together founded the Women's Peace Party, which attracted 40,000 members.

Singing Against the War: "I Didn't Raise My Boy to Be a Soldier"

One of the hit songs of 1915, "I Didn't Raise My Boy to Be a Soldier," by lyricist Alfred Bryan and composer Al Piantadosi, captured widespread American skepticism about joining in the European war. In response to the popularity of this antiwar song, Theodore Roosevelt suggested that the place for women who opposed war was "in China—or by preference in a harem—and not in the United States."

Ten million soldiers to the war have gone,
Who may never return again.
Ten million mothers' hearts must break,
For the ones who died in vain.
Head bowed down in sorrow in her lonely years,
I heard a mother murmur thro' her tears:

Chorus:
I didn't raise my boy to be a soldier,
I brought him up to be my pride and joy,
Who dares to put a musket on his shoulder,
To shoot some other mother's darling boy?
Let nations arbitrate their future troubles,
It's time to lay the sword and gun away,
There'd be no war today,
If mothers all would say,
I didn't raise my boy to be a soldier.

What victory can cheer a mother's heart,
When she looks at her blighted home?
What victory can bring her back,
All she cared to call her own?
Let each mother answer in the year to be,
Remember that my boy belongs to me!

(Chorus)

Al Piantadosi and Alfred Bryan, "I Didn't Raise My Boy to Be a Soldier." Recording: Edison Collection, Library of Congress.

Almost all political and labor radicals opposed U.S. intervention. The Industrial Workers of the World (IWW, also known as Wobblies), the Socialist Party, and most anarchists denounced the war as an imperialist conflict—rich men sending poor ones to fight for the cause of empire. "We as members of the industrial army," announced the IWW, "will refuse to fight for any purpose except the realization of industrial freedom." Although relatively few Americans belonged to radical organizations, a growing number were sympathetic to their perspective. In 1914, voters from New York City's Lower East Side elected a Socialist to Congress; two years later,

Milwaukeeans elected a Socialist mayor. Tens of thousands of recent immigrants joined Socialist-sponsored ethnic federations.

Americans urging preparedness—a military buildup that would outfit the United States for war—stood at the other extreme. Many advocates of preparedness had ties to banking and commercial interests and therefore strongly backed Britain and France; they anticipated that they would make more money in war profits than in neutral trade. Conservative businessmen used preparedness as a patriotic cover for antiunion, antiradical, and nativist campaigns. Theodore Roosevelt and other militarists argued that military discipline would restore men's masculinity in the same way as the strenuous life of competitive sports and outdoor activity he had long promoted. When "I Didn't Raise My Boy to Be a Soldier" became a popular song in 1915, Roosevelt found it so antithetical to his notion of manhood that he suggested that it was akin to singing, "I Didn't Raise My Girl to Be a Mother." Preparedness sentiment grew particularly strong in the spring and summer of 1916; in May, 137,000 supporters marched in a thirteen-hour procession in New York City. Even labor leader Samuel Gompers, once a pacifist, endorsed preparedness and won appointment to the Advisory Commission of the Council of National Defense, the group set up by Wilson in the summer of 1916 to develop a mobilization program.

Army Medical Examiner: "At last a perfect soldier!"

A Recruiter's Dream

"At last," an army medical examiner exults, "a perfect soldier!" Robert Minor's cartoon in the July 1916 *The Masses* was published before the United States entered the war. A year later, the magazine's antiwar position would lead to its suppression under the 1917 Espionage Act. Robert Minor, *The Masses*, July 1916 — Tamiment Institute Library, New York University.

Toward Intervention   As the debate over the war raged, President Wilson vacillated. After first supporting neutrality, in the fall of 1915 he recommended a military buildup. A few months later, he again switched positions, this time with an eye on the 1916 presidential election. In 1912, Wilson had won the presidency in a three-way contest, with only a minority vote; to be reelected, he would have to woo a sizable bloc of new supporters.

He therefore launched a liberal campaign that was aimed at attracting progressive, labor, and anti-interventionist voters. In 1916, he appointed the progressive leader Louis Brandeis to the U.S. Supreme Court. Next, he supported important bills to benefit labor and farmers. Once the presidential

BABES ON BAYONETS

Babes on Bayonets

Many American newspapers and magazines featured prowar cartoons depicting German atrocities in Belgium. This cartoon appeared in a 1915 edition of the weekly magazine *Life*. The German slaughter in Belgium did not actually occur. By contrast, tens of thousands of Africans had died in the Belgian Congo by 1915, victims of Belgium's ruthless exploitation of its colony's resources. A. B. Walker, *Life*, 1915 — American Social History Project.

campaign got under way in the summer of 1916, Wilson began to champion the cause of peace. Although his foreign policy positions did not differ much from those of the Republican candidate Charles Evans Hughes, Wilson campaigned on the slogan "He kept us out of war."

This election-year stance won Wilson strong progressive support. Wilson seemed to back everything progressives believed in: an active federal role in upgrading working and living conditions; the settlement of domestic and international conflicts through conciliation rather than war; and, more broadly, the notion of a new world built on principles of rationality and social harmony. Still, Wilson won the popular vote only narrowly, by fewer than 600,000 votes.

Many progressives believed that Wilson's reelection would usher in an era of peace, progress, and social cooperation. Beginning in 1915, Wilson had attempted to play the role of peacemaker, sending his confidant Colonel Edward House on two peace missions to Europe and urging the establishment of an international organization to enforce peace treaties. Operating on the assumption that world peace was linked to domestic stability and the global expansion of American capitalism, Wilson promoted foreign trade. "Go out and sell goods that will make the world comfortable and more happy, and convert them to the principles of America," he told a group of businessmen visiting the White House.

Wilson renewed his peacemaking efforts after the 1916 election, but neutrality became increasingly difficult to sustain. The $10 million a day the Allies were spending in the United States tied Americans ever closer to the British-French alliance. For Wilson, the "moral obligation . . . to keep us out of this war" conflicted with the "moral obligation . . . to keep free the courses of our commerce and finance."

Meanwhile, sensing imminent victory over the Russians on the Eastern Front, the Germans gambled that blocking vital American supplies would bring quick victory on the Western Front. On February 1, 1917, Germany announced the resumption of unrestricted submarine warfare. Two days later, Wilson broke diplomatic relations with Germany. Later that month, British intelligence officers intercepted a telegram from the German foreign secretary, Arthur Zimmermann, to Mexican leaders, proposing that if the United States were to enter the war, Mexico should ally itself with Germany to recover its "lost provinces" in the southwestern United States. Although such an alliance was never a real possibility, the Zimmermann telegram further inflamed U.S. public opinion against Germany, especially since it came at a time of unsettled relations with Mexico in the aftermath of that country's 1910 Revolution (see p. 300).

At the same time that Americans began to look more harshly on the Central Powers, they also began to view the Allies more favorably. In March 1917, when Russians replaced their autocratic tsar with a liberal democratic government, Wilson could argue that the Allied cause was the cause of democracy. But what finally moved the president to action was his belief that he had to defend U.S. commerce and that he could have a hand in the peace only by joining in war.

Still, when the president went before Congress on April 2, 1917, to seek a declaration of war, he spoke in soaring tones of the need to make the world "safe for democracy." "We shall fight," he told an applauding Congress, "for democracy, for the right of those who submit to authority to have a voice in their own Governments, for the rights and liberties of small nations, . . . and [to] make the world itself at last free." Even though commerce and practical politics underlay the decision for war, this democratic rhetoric would inspire many Americans and Europeans during the closing year and a half of the war.

Nevertheless, some Americans remained skeptical. When Congress voted for war four days later, six senators and fifty members of the House of Representatives dissented, including Jeannette Rankin of Montana, the first woman elected to Congress. Some progressives who had supported Wilson joined the antiwar camp, bitterly disillusioned with the president. Ideological opponents of the war included isolationists, internationalists, pacifists, socialists, Wobblies, and agrarian radicals. In local elections held during the summer and fall of 1917, the Socialists did unusually well—an expression, observers felt, of antiwar sentiment. In the Southwest, clandestine tenant farmer groups urged armed resistance to military conscription. "Now is the time to rebel against this war with German boys," read a poster for an abortive antiwar insurrection in eastern Oklahoma, dubbed the Green Corn Rebellion. "Get together, boys, and don't go. Rich man's war. Poor man's fight."

Mobilizing the Home Front   Fearing that dissent would hinder the nation's ability to win the war, the Wilson administration launched a prowar propaganda campaign. A week after the declaration of war, Wilson set up the Committee on Public Information (CPI) to sell it. The CPI distributed 75 million pamphlets explaining government policy, placed slick ads in magazines, produced prowar films, and sent out 75,000 speakers to give short talks before any audience they could find, often in movie theaters. As the war went on, the CPI abandoned the pretense that it was a neutral

JOSEPH PENNELL DEL.

THAT LIBERTY SHALL NOT
PERISH FROM THE EARTH
BUY LIBERTY BONDS
FOURTH   LIBERTY   LOAN

The Power of Pictures

In the mobilization for war, the U.S. government quickly recognized the power of effective, if often fantastic, imagery to shape public opinion. Most illustrators, and especially editorial cartoonists, eagerly produced prowar work. The government even instituted a Bureau of Cartoons, which issued the weekly *Bulletin for Cartoonists* with suggestions about appropriately patriotic themes and, in some cases, instructions for specific pictures. Joseph Pennell, chromolithograph, c. 1918 — Prints and Photographs Division, Library of Congress.

source of information and began to spread exaggerated stories alleging German atrocities.

Employers, civic groups, local governments, and the U.S. Congress eagerly joined the crusade. Steel companies sponsored parades, flag-raising ceremonies, and bond drives. School districts instituted loyalty oaths and offered federally prepared "war study courses." More ominously, Congress passed the Espionage Act (1917) restricting freedom of speech during wartime through harsh penalties for antiwar activity and banning treasonous material from the mails. Congress strengthened the law the next year by adding the Sedition Act, which made it illegal to "utter, print, write or publish any disloyal, profane, scurrilous, or abusive language" about the government or the military. The government arrested thousands of pacifists and radicals who opposed the war—Eugene Debs among them.

The government also moved to mobilize the nation economically. Through agencies such as the War Industries Board, it took greater charge of the nation's economy than it had at any time since the Civil War. Businessmen literally went to work for the government, attempting to rationalize the economy through cooperative agreements. They worked in federal agencies that determined production priorities, fixed prices, and facilitated orderly operations. This system of government-sponsored industrial self-regulation partially fulfilled the progressive vision of the promotion of social well-being through public-private cooperation. The government also took direct control of a few strategic industries: the Railroad Administration ran the nation's entire railroad system as a single unit, while the Shipping Board managed existing merchant ships and launched a massive shipbuilding program. The Bureau of Indian Affairs encouraged Indians to increase food production on reservations, which brought short-term prosperity to some. Yet the same government policies, which aimed at Indian assimilation into white commercial culture, also hastened the breakup of tribal holdings and ultimately led to a dramatic increase in Indian landlessness.

Other wartime agencies increased production by standardizing parts, products, and procedures. Before the war, for example, manufacturers produced typewriter ribbons in 150 different colors; by its end, there were only five. Industrialists expanded their facilities and introduced new production methods, taking advantage of steady wartime demand and "cost-plus" government contracts, which guaranteed a fixed profit plus costs. Thus, the government's military budget subsidized private innovation, laying a foundation for postwar profits.

But the wartime measures with arguably the most lasting significance were the Revenue Acts of 1916 and 1917, which set up a progressive tax on incomes. The Sixteenth Amendment to the Constitution (1913) had sanctioned a federal income tax but had affected few Americans and brought in little money. Now, faced with the necessity of raising $33 billion to underwrite the cost of the war—an enormous sum for a federal government that was then relatively small—Wilson and progressive Democrats turned to taxes on incomes and corporate profits as sources of federal revenue. Their approach was progressive because it placed the largest tax burden on the wealthiest individuals and corporations (in contrast to a national sales tax, which would have applied equally to rich and poor). By the end of the war, a corporate excess profits tax was generating $2.5 billion per year—more than half the federal government's tax revenues.

The Expanding Wartime Economy

The wartime economic boom dramatically benefited working people. Union membership skyrocketed, and workers won higher wages and shorter hours. The labor shortage also drew new workers into industrial employment. Rural migrants from the South and Appalachia—both black and white but especially African Americans participating in what came to be called the Great Migration—headed for the cities, where they found better wages and some relief from the oppressive Jim Crow regime of the South. Meanwhile, in the Southwest, Mexican migrants found employers seeking their labor even as they faced discrimination and segregation. Women's experience was more unambiguously positive; they not only found jobs in industries where they had previously been disdained, but also triumphed in their century-long struggle to win the right to vote.

Labor Gains at Home   Expanded industrial production—and, after May 1917, the draft—created labor shortages, which benefited the organized labor movement. Individually, workers switched jobs and even moved across the country seeking better wages and working conditions. Collectively, they formed new unions and joined established ones. The Amalgamated Clothing Workers' Union doubled in size. The railroad brotherhoods

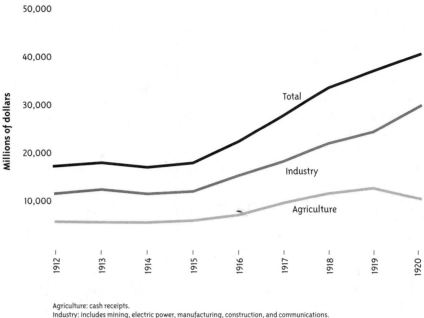

Agriculture: cash receipts.
Industry: includes mining, electric power, manufacturing, construction, and communications.

FIGURE 6.1   Industrial Wages, 1912–1920

The demands of war production and the shortage of workers resulting from the military draft and enlistments helped workers to win higher wages and increased unionization.

mushroomed. Total union membership increased by nearly 70 percent between 1914 and 1920, to over five million. Close to one of every five non-agricultural workers belonged to a union (Figure 6.1).

But even as the number of jobs expanded and companies with steady, highly profitable orders accepted higher labor costs, labor unrest intensified. Consumer prices rose sharply in 1915 as a result of the war; by 1920, they had doubled. Despite steady employment and higher wages, workers found themselves falling behind as inflation cut their purchasing power. Once the United States entered the war, workers had more complaints: state governments suspended safety, hour, and child labor regulations that had been hard won by progressives and unions, and wartime regulations capped workers' wages but not employers' profits.

As the war went on, strikes and threats of strikes became common. Each year from 1916 through 1920, more than one million workers went on strike—a higher proportion of the workforce than during any similar period before or since. And all kinds of workers struck: union and nonunion, skilled and unskilled, male and female, immigrant and native, day laborer and steady worker. Many war era walkouts were huge, involving workers from different companies and different industries striking in support of one another.

During the six months following the U.S. declaration of war in April 1917, union workers in shipbuilding, coal mining, and the metal trades led a massive wave of strikes, collectively withholding more than six million workdays. Most hoped to offset higher prices with increased wages; many sought shorter hours or union recognition. Often, strikers made radical demands for control of their work processes, challenging the scientific management and incentive plans employers had implemented in response to government pressure to increase production. Because the thriving economy required full employment, workers gained enhanced power and won many strikes.

Wartime labor militancy forced the federal government to establish labor relations agencies, which built on the progress labor had made during the first Wilson administration. Labor representatives sat on a number of commissions, along with business and government representatives, a system that was pioneered by the National Civic Federation. Never before had unions secured so extensive a role in determining and administering federal labor policy. Wilson appointed progressives who were sympathetic to unionism, such as Frank Walsh, to key positions in agencies such as the War Labor Board.

The wartime labor bureaucracy generally accepted the then-novel idea that strikes resulted from real grievances and the denial of collective bargaining rights. Hoping to forestall strikes and reduce job turnover, government officials pressured employers to raise pay, shorten working hours, and improve working conditions. Many believed that a strong union movement would channel workers' discontent into orderly contract negotiations and conflict resolution. As President Wilson declared, in a historic reversal of the antiunionism of the federal government, "Our laws and the long-established policy of our government recognize the right of workingmen to organize unions if they so desire." Wilson's support for labor convinced most union leaders to rally behind the war effort. Not only the labor movement, but also working people themselves, benefited. Steady work and higher pay raised their living standard (Figure 6.2).

Industrial Hero

A May 1916 cover of *Collier's* weekly magazine presented a romantic portrait of the industrial worker, reflecting the steel companies' sudden turn to extolling the virtues of their workers in the face of a labor shortage. Herbert Paus, *Collier's,* May 13, 1916 — American Social History Project.

FIGURE 6.2 Creating a National Bureaucracy: Growth in Federal Employment, 1881–1920

As this graph shows, the federal government grew during the Progressive era, but the most rapid growth came during World War I.

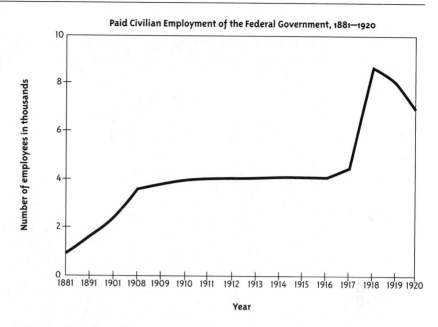

Paid Civilian Employment of the Federal Government, 1881—1920

The Great Migration Even before the United States entered the war, expanding industrial production had dramatically altered patterns of work and residence. Just when mines, factories, and fields needed more workers than ever, the flow of immigrants across the Atlantic dropped sharply because of the war. In 1914, more than one million Europeans had come to America; in 1915, the number fell to less than 200,000, and in 1918, it was only 31,000. That year, the unemployment rate fell to just 2.4 percent, down from over 15 percent just three years earlier. In this context, previously disdained groups—immigrants, African Americans, Appalachian whites, and women—suddenly became desirable employees.

The war also accelerated the movement of Americans from the countryside to the city. The rapidly expanding auto industry, in particular, attracted workers from rural areas in the Midwest, Canada, and the South. Between 1910 and 1920, more than half a million white southerners moved out of their region. The mountainous areas of the Upper South (known as Appalachia) were particularly ripe for an exodus. When the war opened up high-paying jobs in nearby northern cities, an estimated 50,000 West Virginians moved to Akron, Ohio, center of the booming rubber industry.

The "Great Migration" of black southerners offered the most visible example of the shift from country to city. Although African Americans had been moving north in small numbers since the end of Reconstruction, the geographic distribution of the country's black population was much the same in 1910 as it had been half a century earlier. Nine of every ten African Americans lived in the South, chiefly in rural areas. During the next ten years, about 500,000 blacks left the South, most of them after 1916. The

"Such Cases of Outrageous Unspeakable Abuse": A Puerto Rican Migrant Protests Labor Conditions During World War I

Rafael Marchán was one of a group of Puerto Rican workers at Fort Bragg in North Carolina. The high demand for labor spurred the War Department to transport Puerto Rican workers to labor camps in the United States, where they would be housed and fed while working on government contracts at defense plants and military bases. While some U.S. workers experienced gains due to the labor shortage, defense contractors subjected many of the new migrants to harsh conditions and even forced labor. Marchán and others protested to the commissioner of Puerto Rico over the intolerable conditions in the work camp. He gave this deposition in Washington, D.C., in October 1918.

RAFAEL F. MARCHAN, being first duly sworn, deposes and says: That he is a native of Porto Rico, and a citizen of the United States, twenty-seven years old, married, and temporarily residing at Camp Bragg, Fayetteville, North Carolina; that he, and some other 1700 Porto Ricans, were induced and persuaded, . . . to come, and did come, to this country for the purpose of . . . contributing their labor to American industries and works. . . .

The affiant, RAFAEL F. MARCHAN, further deposes and says, that owing to the improper and unsanitary conditions under which the said Porto Ricans labor and live at the said Camp Bragg their health and comfort and even their lives are not only endangered and put in jeopardy but actually broken up and destroyed as it has been the case with some twenty-two of them who have died from utter lack of proper care and medical attention. And the affiant says that at the Hospital the same drinking glass and other utensils are indiscriminately used by all without previous disinfection, with the resulting infection and contagion of such dreaded diseases as influenza, consumption, pneumonia, etc.; and the affiant further says that there have been cases of such utter and inhuman cruelty as to compel sick men under the pretext of their being lazy, to either go to work or be locked up. . . .

And the affiant further deposes and says, that as illustrating the general treatment accorded these Porto Ricans at the Camp, there have been such cases of outrageous unspeakable abuse and degrading ill treatment of the men that some have positively refused to continue at the Camp and announced their intention to leave, but have been prevented to do so by sheer compulsion of force, thus being deprived of their liberty and what is still worse compelled to remain in a state of involuntary servitude; . . . the Fire Chief, who evidently is a regular bully at the Camp has . . . no hesitation in striking men with his fist or brandish his revolver in their faces; and the affiant further says that the acts of cruelty committed daily against these men are too numerous to be cited here in all their repulsive and disgusting details;

(signed) Rafael F. Marchan

Notary Public D.C.

"Rafael Marchan Statement," October 24, 1918, in: Record of the Bureau of Insular Affairs, Record Group 350, File 1493 (Washington, D.C.: National Archives), 123–126.

People We Can Get Along Without

A series of cartoons by Leslie Rogers, published during the 1920s in the African American newspaper *The Chicago Defender*, conveyed everyday tensions between recently arrived southern migrants and longtime residents in the city's black community. Rogers's *Defender* comic strip, *Bungleton Green*, which started in 1920, featured the misadventures of a naïve migrant from the South. Leslie Rogers, *Chicago Defender*, July 9, 1921 — Prints and Photographs Division, Library of Congress.

African American population of Chicago nearly doubled, to more than 100,000. New York, with 150,000 black residents, became the largest African American center in the country.

Black Americans had plenty of reasons to leave the rural South: disfranchisement, segregation, poverty, racial violence, lack of educational opportunities, the drudgery of farm life, and just the daily indignities of living under Jim Crow laws. For Joseph Brown, the turning point came when he was ill and asked an Atlanta druggist for a glass of water. Despite a shelf

"Pass Us Away from Here to a Better Land"

This anonymous letter was typical of the letters from southern African Americans that flooded into the office of the Chicago Defender asking for assistance in coming north. The passes referred to were for free railroad transportation; recruiters looking to hire black workers for jobs in the North sometimes distributed such passes.

Daphne, Ala. 4/20/17
Sir:

I am writing to let you know that there is 15 or 20 familys wants to come up there at once but can't come on account of money. . . . We can't phone you [because] they don't want us to leave here . . . [but] we want to get away if we can. If you send 20 passes there is no doubt that every one of us will come at once. We are not doing any thing here we can get a living out of. . . . Some of these people are farmers and some are cooks, barbers, and blacksmiths. . . . These are nice people and respectable. . . . We all want to leave here out of this hard luck place that does not need this kind of people.

I am a reader of the *Defender* and am delighted to know how times are there & [would be] glad to know if we could get some one to pass us away from here to a better land. . . . Please find someone that need this kind of people and send at once for us. We don't want anything but our wareing and bed clothes and have got no money to get away from here with and begging to get away before we are killed and hope to hear from you at once.

Leslie H. Fishel, Jr., and Benjamin Quarles, eds., *The Black Americans: A Documentary History*, 3rd ed. (1976).

of glasses and a soda fountain, the druggist directed Brown to a bucket of dirty, soapy water out back. "When I left that store and walking back up the hill home, I said, 'God, if you give me strength and give me my health . . . this will never happen to me again.'"

Hard times accelerated the migration of rural black farmers. In 1916, a particularly bad year in the South, the boll weevil attacked the cotton crop, and floods caused extensive damage. Of course, neither the push of southern poverty and racism nor the pull of northern jobs caused most southern blacks to migrate. As late as 1940, three-quarters of all African Americans remained in the South. Leaving, after all, was not always easy. Plantation overseers used violence and threats to prevent an exodus of workers who were crucial to southern agriculture, and state and local governments passed laws designed to put labor recruiters out of business (Map 6.2).

Leaving the South did not mean escaping racism. Kept out of Northern white neighborhoods by law or custom, African Americans migrants crowded into inner-city neighborhoods that became ghettos. Heavy

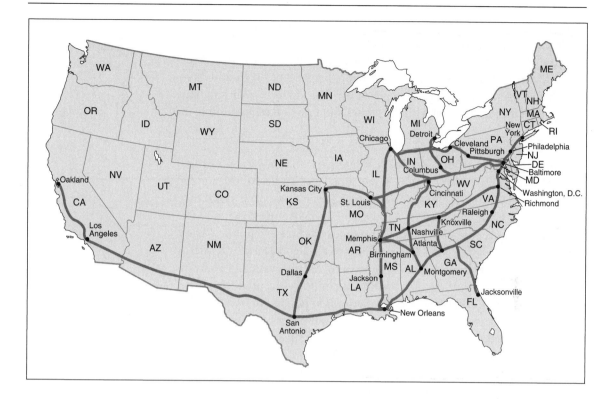

MAP 6.2 Tracking the Great Migration: Routes Followed by Black Migrants

As this map shows, African American migrants to the North chose their destinations based on their state of origin as well as following family and friends: those from Georgia and the Carolinas headed to cities along the eastern seaboard such as New York and Philadelphia; migrants from Alabama and Mississippi headed for the midwestern cities such as Chicago; and those from Texas, Louisiana, and Tennessee often headed west to California.

industries—steel, meatpacking, autos, shipbuilding, and mining—restricted black men to unskilled jobs, which were often the dirtiest and most physically taxing. Employers generally paid black workers less than white workers, though more than they received in the South. Black women usually worked as domestic servants; in 1920, fewer than 7 percent of them worked in industry.

Despite the residential and occupational segregation, racial tensions developed over real or perceived competition for jobs, housing, and political power. White workers, motivated by a deep-seated racism and fearful that black workers would take their jobs or force down wage levels, staged wildcat strikes against employers who hired black workers. Most unions either barred black workers entirely or segregated them in all-black locals with restricted voting and job rights. Black ministers, politicians, and editors often argued, as had Booker T. Washington, that black workers were more likely to find allies among white employers than among white workers. Though the American Federation of Labor (AFL) used black organizers in its wartime campaign to organize Chicago stockyard workers, only 15 percent of African Americans joined, compared with nearly 90 percent of Poles and Slovaks. One southern black migrant expressed a common view:

"Unions ain't no good for a colored man. I've seen too much of what they don't do for him."

In spite of all the problems African Americans encountered, many kept coming north. One former southerner wrote back home: "I should have been here twenty years ago. I just begin to feel like a man. . . . My children are going to the same school with the whites and I don't have to humble to no one."

Tension on the Southern Border   While African Americans headed north, U.S. relations with countries in Central and South America grew tense. Though Wilson supported nonintervention in Europe, he took a different stance toward the Western Hemisphere, using troops to defend U.S. property in Cuba, Haiti, Nicaragua, and the Dominican Republic. "I am going to teach the South American republics to elect good men!" the president declared. American Marines and naval forces intervened in Haiti in 1915, and the next year began an eight-year military occupation of the Dominican Republic. In these places, Americans appointed financial advisers, supervised elections, and maintained law and order by putting down popular insurrections. The United States also became deeply involved in the Mexican Revolution.

The Mexican Revolution had begun in 1910 with an armed revolt against the thirty-five-year dictatorship of Porfirio Diaz. At first a fight over the presidential succession, the conflict broadened into widespread strife that lasted a decade and cost a million lives. Wilson backed first one Mexican faction and then another, hoping to protect U.S.-owned property, especially oil interests. In 1914, U.S. troops occupied the city of Vera Cruz. Two years later, General Pershing led a U.S. expedition into northern Mexico, after Mexican troops loyal to the agrarian radical Francisco "Pancho" Villa raided a town in New Mexico. There was talk of war, but both countries stepped back. Still, U.S. leaders greeted Mexican self-rule warily, in part because Mexico's new constitution gave the state control of that country's mineral resources and restricted foreign ownership of its oil. Samuel Gompers and the AFL supported Mexican workers in their efforts to modernize the country and set up a national labor federation. The AFL's fear of radical unionism and desire to cooperate with economic expansionist policies helped it to align its efforts with U.S. strategic interests in Mexico (Map 6.3).

To avoid the inflation, violence, and social chaos that accompanied the revolution, many Mexicans fled to the United States. In the years before the war, new railroads had opened up the northern part of Mexico, drawing many individuals from the crowded central provinces to the region near the

MAP 6.3   Chasing Pancho Villa: U.S. Intervention in Mexico, 1916–1917

Pancho Villa raided Columbus, New Mexico, to provoke the United States into invading Mexico and thus weaken his opponent, Venustiano Carranza, who was receiving U.S. support. The U.S. Army responded as expected, and U.S. troops spent eleven months unsuccessfully pursuing Villa's army.

U.S. border. Soon, economic opportunities in the rapidly growing American Southwest pulled them across the border. The United States imposed no quota on Mexican immigration, and according to official statistics, more than 185,000 Mexicans entered the United States between 1910 and 1919. Many more crossed the border unofficially. Some estimates indicate that the total number of people of Mexican heritage living in the United States doubled during the decade, to about 750,000 (Map 6.4).

❯❯ Crossing the border was easy. Officials and border patrols understood that the economy of the American Southwest, not legal restrictions, determined Mexican immigration. They were concerned primarily about Chinese immigrants who might try to enter the country through Mexico. As Charles Armijo, who crossed the border between Juárez and El Paso during the Mexican Revolution, explained, "Well, we just came over. . . . Everybody was allowed to go back and forth whenever they wanted. . . . We came over on the streetcar."

Some Mexicans came temporarily, hoping to save money and return home quickly. Others, intending to stay, settled in established Mexican American communities. However long they planned to stay, most worked in agriculture, especially in Texas, California, Arizona, and Colorado. Railroads and mines also hired large numbers of workers; by 1911, about 60 percent of Arizona's smelter workers were Mexicans. Wages were seven to twenty times those paid in Mexico, though still very low by U.S. standards. As the southwestern labor supply swelled, some Mexican Americans, including many with roots in the region that went back to the 1840s, left for better-paying industrial jobs in the Midwest.

World War I created some new opportunities at military bases around San Antonio, especially in construction, transportation, and maintenance work. After the United States entered World War I, many Mexicans working in the United States feared that they would be drafted. But Mexican labor had become vital to the southwestern economy, and employers pushed the federal government to assure Mexican workers that they would be exempt from the draft. To protect agricultural, mine, and railroad workers, the government also suspended a 1917 immigration law that banned contract labor and imposed a literacy test and a head tax on immigrants. Nevertheless, like African Americans in the South, Mexican Americans encountered discrimination all over the Southwest in segregated schools, theaters, restaurants, and neighborhoods. Often, Mexican workers were paid less than the Anglos who worked beside them. Most unions ignored or excluded Mexicans or relegated them to separate locals.

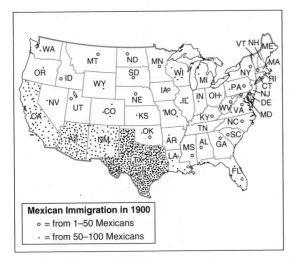

Mexican Immigration in 1900
o = from 1–50 Mexicans
· = from 50–100 Mexicans

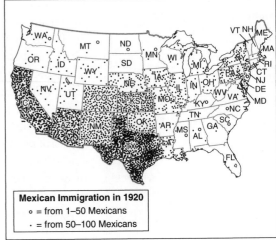

Mexican Immigration in 1920
o = from 1–50 Mexicans
· = from 50–100 Mexicans

Here, as elsewhere in the United States, discrimination sometimes produced violent reactions. In the lower Rio Grande Valley, Mexicans and Mexican Americans fought the Texas Rangers in hundreds of incidents between 1915 and 1917. Anglo farmers often used violence and intimidation to wrest away Mexicans' land. Displaced ranchers fought back by raiding farms and sabotaging trains and irrigation systems. Twenty-one Anglo Americans were killed in these clashes; in reprisal, Texas officials executed 300 Mexican Americans without trial. The sheriff of Cameron County, Texas, attributed the conflict to the "unwillingness of American newcomers to the valley to accept the Mexican" and claimed that the Rangers often shouted, "We have to make this a white man's country!!" In the end, the Mexican ranchers were reduced to being wage laborers.

The Mexican American community contained many radicals, including members of the Socialist Party and the IWW. In New Mexico and Arizona in 1917, the Western Federation of Miners and the United Mine Workers of America brought Anglo and Mexican miners together to cooperate in a series of mine strikes. But their struggle to eliminate unequal wages and win union recognition ended when officials arrested and then deported thousands of Mexican-born strikers.

Other Mexican immigrants avoided political activity, concentrating instead on saving money to buy land or businesses back home. But like many Slavs and Italians before them, many Mexican immigrants gave up plans to return home and settled permanently in the United States. Over time, the long-established Spanish-speaking communities of the West and Southwest became increasingly important in this, the fastest-growing region of the country. Unlike European immigrants, however, Mexican Americans

MAP 6.4   From Mexico to the United States, 1900–1920

These maps, covering the years 1900 and 1920, illustrate the growth of Mexican immigration and the spread of immigrants into the Midwest.

Invading Forces

A 1914 Mexican postcard shows a company of U.S. soldiers marching along the Avenida Independencia in Vera Cruz. Postcards were a popular medium for disseminating photographic images of the war on both sides of the Mexican-U.S. border. Photography Collection, Harry Ransom Humanities Research Center, University of Texas at Austin.

Soldados Norte-Americanos llegando por la Avenida
Independencia

lived not across an ocean from their homeland, but across a nearby border. Many went back and forth to work or to stay with family. In individual lives and in the character of the border towns, two cultures coexisted.

✳ Women Workers and Woman Suffrage

Like Mexicans, women workers found new opportunities in the wartime economy. For the first time, employers offered them traditionally male jobs—for example, as railroad workers and streetcar conductors. Others found metalworking and munitions jobs, often as part of a management decision to hire less-skilled workers. Most of these women moved up from lower-paying jobs they had held before the war in female-dominated occupations, although some had never worked for pay. But the gains women made in traditional blue-collar work proved temporary; once the war ended, most women left or were forced out of their jobs.

The war did, however, hasten the expansion of one area of work that had been open to women since the 1890s: clerical jobs. Women worked in government bureaucracies, which expanded with the U.S. entry into the war. Even more women worked for the growing corporations, which found that achieving and then maintaining horizontal and vertical integration of production and resources demanded considerable paperwork. By 1920, there were nearly eight times as many women clerical workers as there had been in 1900. Despite the loss of blue-collar jobs at the end of the war, there were still 700,000 more women in the labor force in 1920 than in 1910.

"Iron Road"

Many songs composed by Mexican immigrants expressed homesickness, disappointment, and concern over the adoption of "American" values. In the following song, the completion of a railroad line stretching over 600 miles from Victoria, Texas, to central Mexico is portrayed as an occasion for alarm rather than celebration.

El Ferrocarril

La máquina pasajera
No puede hacer cosa buena
Porque "oscurece" en su casa
Y amanece en tierra ajena.

¡Ay! ¡qué dolor!
Tendrían los mexicanos
Al ver el ferrocarril
Que traen los americanos.
La máquina chiquitita
Es la que ha quedado aquí
Y la quieren llegar
Hasta San Luis Potosí.
Oigan y oigan
El ferrocarril bramar
Él que lleva a los hombres
Y nunca los vuelve a traer.

Iron Road

She's like a bird of passage
Who never can do the right thing.
She leaves her home every evening
Just to see what the morning might
   bring.
Oh, what a pain
Will visit those Mexicans
When they hear her steaming down
the track, The train of the Americans.
Just a little bitty steam engine
Is all they left for me
And they really think it'll go from here
To San Luis Potosí.
Listen, listen,
Hear her roar down the track
She's coming for a load of men
That she won't be bringing back.

Manuel Gamio, *Mexican Immigration to the United States* (1930). Reprinted with permission of Dover Publications.

The war also opened up some new opportunities for black women, the least advantaged group in the workforce. Even in Southern cities such as Atlanta, some factories hired black women; between 1910 and 1920, the percentage of black women in domestic service dropped from 84 to 75 percent. Worried employers used legal and illegal coercion to reverse this trend. They took advantage of "Work or Fight" laws, which were ostensibly intended to force unemployed men into military service, to prosecute black women who declined jobs as household workers. A vigilante group in Vicksburg, Mississippi, harassed "idle" black workers, a group that included women who did not want to work as domestics. They tarred and feathered Ethel Barrett while her husband was away fighting in France.

On other fronts, some women war workers were better situated to demand social and political rights and advance the movement for woman suffrage. In New York City, working-class suffragists saw a close link between the vote and the conditions on the job. "Why are you paid less than a man?" asked a leaflet put out by the Wage-Earners' Suffrage League there. "Why are your hours so long?" The answer: "Because you are a woman and have no vote. Votes make the law. . . . The law controls conditions."

Arms and the Woman

Recently hired women operate equipment in a Bloomfield, New Jersey, munitions plant in 1917. Sophia Smith Collection, Smith College.

> The war years saw new divisions within the suffrage movement, particularly over tactical questions. A new militant suffrage group, the National Woman's Party (NWP), formed in 1916. Led by Alice Paul, a social worker who had studied in England, the NWP was founded on the tactics of British suffragists, who held the party in power responsible for the denial of the vote to women. To publicize their grievance, the antiwar NWP began picketing the White House to demand voting rights. Arrested, the imprisoned pickets went on a hunger strike and were brutally force-fed. Meanwhile, more conservative women's groups energetically supported the war by knitting socks, selling war bonds, and preparing Red Cross supplies. They cemented an alliance with Wilson and united local and state suffrage groups in a centrally directed effort.

In different ways, both groups tried to use Wilson's democratic rhetoric to their own advantage. As one historian points out, "Wilson's 'safe for democracy' speech was analogous to Lincoln's Emancipation Proclamation, which did not free any slaves but probably made freeing them inevitable." By asking Americans to fight for "democracy versus autocracy," Wilson put compelling logic behind the drive for universal suffrage.

The combination of the NWP's militant agitation and NAWSA's pragmatic political alliances worked. By 1914, women had acquired the right to vote in the territory of Alaska and in eleven states, all of which, except Illinois, were west of the Mississippi. NAWSA spent the next three years conducting vigorous campaigns throughout the East, while the NWP kept up the pressure in Washington. Three years later, women had won at least

"We Don't Want Other Women Ever to Have to Do This Over Again"

Polish-born suffragist Rose Winslow (her given name was Ruza Wenclawska) started working in a Pennsylvania textile mill at age eleven, quitting eight years later when she developed tuberculosis. In 1917, she was one of five protesters who were sentenced to seven months in prison for obstructing traffic in front of the White House. After she and National Woman's Party founder Alice Paul began a hunger strike, they were transferred to a prison hospital. Winslow smuggled out an account she kept of her stay.

If this thing is necessary we will naturally go through with it. Force is so stupid a weapon. I feel so happy doing my bit for decency—for our war, which is after all, real and fundamental.

The women are all so magnificent, so beautiful. Alice Paul is as thin as ever, pale and large-eyed. We have been in solitary for five weeks. There is nothing to tell but that the days go by somehow. I have felt quite feeble the last few days—faint, so that I could hardly get my hair brushed, my arms ached so. But to-day I am well again. Alice Paul and I talk back and forth though we are at opposite ends of the building and a hall door also shuts us apart. But occasionally—thrills—we escape from behind our iron-barred doors and visit. Great laughter and rejoicing!

My fainting probably means nothing except that I am not strong after these weeks. I know you won't be alarmed. . . .

Alice Paul is in the psychopathetic ward. She dreaded forcible feeding frightfully, and I hate to think how she must be feeling. I had a nervous time of it, gasping a long time afterward, and my stomach rejecting during the process. I spent a bad, restless night, but otherwise I am all right. The poor soul who fed me got liberally besprinkled during the process. I heard myself making the most hideous sounds. . . . One feels so forsaken when one lies prone and people shove a pipe down one's stomach.

This morning but for an astounding tiredness, I am all right. I am waiting to see what happens when the President realizes that brutal bullying isn't quite a statesmanlike method for settling a demand for justice at home. At least, if men are supine enough to endure, women—to their eternal glory—are not. . . .

. . . Don't let them tell you we take this well. Miss Paul vomits much. I do, too. . . . We think of the coming feeding all day. It is horrible. The doctor thinks I take it well. I hate the thought of Alice Paul and the others if I take it well. . . .

All the officers here know we are making this hunger strike that women fighting for liberty may be considered political prisoners; we have told them. God knows we don't want other women ever to have to do this over again.

Doris Stevens, *Jailed for Freedom* (1920).

Hands Across the Water
Demonstrators in front of the White House in July 1917 appealed to representatives of the new Russian government to support American woman suffrage as a condition for Russia's remaining in the Allied camp. The banner roused the ire of patriotic passersby, and soon after this photograph was taken, an angry crowd attacked the suffragists. Harris and Ewing, 1917 — National Archives.

partial voting rights in eight additional states, including New York, long a major battleground, and Arkansas, the first southern state to grant suffrage.

In January 1918, the House of Representatives passed a constitutional amendment giving women the right to vote. Despite Wilson's endorsement of the measure as "vital to the winning of the war," antisuffrage Republicans and southern Democratic senators blocked the amendment. In response, the NWP and NAWSA mobilized a massive outpouring of marches, parades, and meetings to overcome lingering opposition in the Senate and state legislatures, three-quarters of which had to ratify the amendment. On August 18, 1920, Tennessee became the crucial thirty-sixth state to ratify the Nineteenth Amendment, after a twenty-four-year-old legislator changed his vote at his mother's insistence. The Nineteenth Amendment went into effect in time for that year's presidential election. Among the first voters was ninety-one-year-old Charlotte Woodward, who as a teenager had witnessed the start of the women's rights movement at Seneca Falls seventy-two years earlier.

Militancy, Repression, and Nativism

The same radical wartime spirit that infected the most militant suffragists infused some working-class struggles as well, especially those led by the IWW. But radical protesters quickly faced repression, as federal agents (armed with the repressive Espionage and Sedition acts) and local police arrested thousands of Wobblies and critics of the war. Immigrants—especially German Americans—also encountered attacks and suspicions about their loyalty. In the nativist atmosphere, prohibitionists won the banning of alcoholic beverages, in part by associating liquor consumption with immigrants, especially the beer-drinking Germans.

Working-Class Protest and Political Radicalism   In some cases, the new wartime radicalism had foreign sources. Many Europeans who came to America in the decade before World War I had supported socialism, anarchism, and trade unionism in their native lands. As their influence spread through immigrant communities, workers grew increasingly receptive to collective action and political radicalism. The sense of radical possibility—that society could be fundamentally transformed—grew in November 1917, when V. I. Lenin and his Bolshevik Party led a successful Communist revolution in Russia. Other leaders, such as Eugene Debs, drew their radicalism from American sources and insisted that the United States live up to the democratic promises Wilson and others trumpeted.

The new militancy often came from people who had previously seemed indifferent to radicalism and collective action. Among them were many unskilled immigrant workers who had planned to return to their native lands but now were stranded by the wartime disruption of transatlantic travel. Miserable job conditions that had once been seen as temporary became intolerable when viewed as permanent. In Bayonne, New Jersey, Polish refinery workers had long accepted low pay, long hours, and dangerous working conditions. But when they walked off the job in 1915, virtually the entire Polish community supported them. Only police violence and hired thugs broke the strike; five strikers were killed by gunfire. Visiting Bayonne, wrote journalist Mary Heaton Vorse, "you realize that you are in a terrorized city, and that fear is in the very air that you breathe." Still, refinery workers struck again the next year.

Just Before the Firing Started
Moments after these striking workers were photographed confronting guards outside the Bayonne, New Jersey, Standard Oil Works, the private police opened fire, killing five strikers. Prints and Photographs Division, Library of Congress.

Food Riot, 1917
Wartime inflation severely taxed the limited budgets of working-class families. After confronting pushcart peddlers who were charging exorbitant rates for necessities, thousands of women marched to New York's City Hall on February 20, 1917, to demand relief. The "food riot" precipitated a boycott campaign that eventually forced pushcart prices down. National Archives.

Housewives as well as workers took to the streets, protesting high food prices. Wartime inflation had pushed food prices to astonishing levels — for instance, potatoes more than doubled in price during one month in 1916 — and wages, though increasing, could not keep up. In early 1917, a desperate Brooklyn woman overturned a peddler's pushcart. Running after her, the vendor was attacked by hundreds of other women; eventually a thousand rioters battled police. One officer, who refused to arrest rioting women in another Brooklyn neighborhood the next day, explained, "I just didn't have the heart to do it. They were just crazy with hunger, and I don't see how I could blame them."

In this atmosphere of militancy, the IWW found new life. The organization had been in decline when the war started, but during the war years, it shifted its focus from eastern factory towns such as Lawrence, Massachusetts, and Paterson, New Jersey, to the West and the Midwest. There, the Wobblies recruited migratory workers: semiskilled and unskilled farm workers, lumberjacks, railroad men, and miners who moved from job to job, often weathering long bouts of unemployment. Most were single; many were immigrants. The IWW attracted them because they were alienated — literally rootless and terribly exploited, both on the job and in the miserable barracks that employers provided to house them. The IWW organizers understood their needs and offered social networks as well as union leadership.

In 1916, the Wobblies led a strike of 10,000 miners in the Mesabi iron range of northern Minnesota, and they then began an intensive campaign to organize northwestern lumber workers. Around the same time, the IWW signed up thousands of midwestern harvest workers and won better pay and working conditions from wheat farmers who were more eager to take advantage of high grain prices than of cheap labor.

In response to these successes, government at all levels attacked the radical Wobblies, trying to stigmatize them as illegitimate. Police (and hired thugs) beat and shot strikers and repeatedly arrested IWW organizers. In

The Bisbee Deportation, July 12, 1917
All over the country, Wobblies faced coordinated government-employer attacks. In Bisbee, Arizona, a local sheriff, with the aid of the Phelps-Dodge mining company, deputized towns-people to break up an IWW-led strike. Vigilantes arrested 1,200 alleged Wobblies, aliens, and subversives and, as shown in this photograph, loaded them into cattle cars. The cars were towed to the middle of the New Mexico desert and abandoned. Archives of Labor and Urban Affairs, Wayne State University.

Everett, Washington, in 1916, sheriff's deputies removed 40 Wobbly prisoners from jail, took them to a wooded park, stripped them, and made them run a gauntlet of vigilantes, who beat the naked prisoners with guns and whips. The next year, federal agents raided every IWW office in the country and put 2,000 Wobblies in jail, including the entire executive board. Courts convicted most of violating wartime statutes and sentenced them to long jail terms. The IWW would never recover.

Repression and Nativism   The attack on the IWW was only one part of a government effort to end protest and silence dissent. Officials engaged in extensive press censorship. In the summer of 1917, the Post Office Department refused second-class mailing privileges to newspapers and magazines that were critical of the war, the draft, or even the way the war was being conducted. It banned socialist periodicals, which had a combined prewar circulation exceeding half a million, from the mails. The foreign-language press was closely watched; a federal law required that articles discussing the war or the government be submitted in translation for prior approval—a process that was so costly that many papers folded and others adopted a progovernment stance in hopes of winning exemption from the rule.

Critics of the war were also silenced through arrest. The government put 1,500 people on trial for opposing the war or counseling draft resistance. And federal officials detained more than 6,000 German and Austrian

Copyright. H. T. Webster   WEBSTER in New York Globe

The I. W. W. and the Other Features That Go With It

The I.W.W. and the Other Features That Go With It
By using the acronym "I.W.W." in place of the features of Kaiser Wilhelm, this 1917 *New York Globe* cartoon accused the Wobblies of treason. Harold Tucker Webster, *Cartoon Magazine*, September 1917 — Prints and Photographs Division, Library of Congress.

nationals as potential threats to national security. The Wilson administration worried particularly about antiwar sentiment among workers. To counteract the widespread belief that the United States was fighting a businessmen's war, the Department of Labor and the Committee on Public Information deluged factories with posters, slogans, and speakers.

Government repression bred a vigilante spirit. Members of "loyalty" organizations harassed and beat radical opponents of the war and even those who simply refused to buy Liberty Bonds. They also spied on neighbors and coworkers; in the name of patriotism, reactionaries and businessmen used their reports of these organizations to harass radicals and unionists. The Department of Justice granted funding and quasi-official status to the largest loyalty organization, the American Protective League.

Immigrants had a particularly hard time. Even before the United States had joined the conflict, Allied sympathizers questioned the loyalties of "hyphenated" Americans (German Americans, Polish Americans, and so forth). They depicted immigrants as potentially more loyal to their countries of birth than to their adopted land. In fact, the opposite was often true: the experience of war led many immigrants to identify closely with the United States. Tens of thousands of them entered the armed forces, fought in the war, and embraced the rhetoric of democracy and self-determination that Wilson trumpeted.

Even so, fears of divided loyalties lingered. Wilson spoke of the need for "100 percent Americanism," while Theodore Roosevelt called for "America for Americans." Suspicion and hostility focused particularly on German Americans. Mobs attacked German American stores and drove German American performers off the stage. German Americans were harassed, beaten, tarred and feathered, forced to kiss the flag, and, in at least one instance, lynched.

Amid this hysteria, Congress passed several nativist measures. In 1917, a law that was enacted over Wilson's veto imposed a literacy test and other restrictions on immigration. The same year, Congress passed the Eighteenth Amendment to the Constitution, which banned the manufacture or sale of alcoholic beverages; it was ratified in 1919. Though temperance supporters had long advocated Prohibition on moral grounds or as a means of increasing productivity, nativism was involved, too. Many people associated alcohol with immigrants, specifically German Americans, who dominated the brewing industry.

Like many other aspects of the wartime loyalty campaign, Prohibition had little to do with the direct requirements of fighting a war. Rather, the international crisis seemed to validate nativist fears, legitimizing the use of government power to enforce social, political, and cultural orthodoxy. But Prohibition was also a "progressive" measure in its embrace of an activist government, its moralistic impulses, and its promise of a more orderly society and culture. Although many wartime measures were only temporary, the campaign for enforced consensus also had permanent effects: radical groups were severely weakened, and in the next decade, immigration was nearly cut off. The atmosphere of fear and intolerance would persist in the postwar era.

"This Is for Traitors"
The pillory, a device that was used in colonial New England to punish through public ridicule, was resurrected in Cincinnati in 1918. Placed in a public square, this pillory was "a warning to citizens of Cincinnati as to what they may expect in case of disloyalty." Unable to find a convenient dissenter immediately, the photographer of this picture had to make do with an acquiescent volunteer. J. R. Schmidt, 1918 — National Archives.

Winning the War and Losing the Peace

Although American troops entered the war late and suffered only a tiny fraction of the war's casualties, they played a crucial role in the Allied victory in November 1918. Nevertheless, U.S. President Woodrow Wilson could not shape the peace according to the principles of self-determination that he had advocated. Moreover, many Americans, suspicious of foreign entanglements, rejected Wilson's internationalist vision embodied in the League of Nations, and the U.S. Congress refused to ratify the Versailles treaty.

Workers, African Americans, and radicals also, in effect, lost the peace. Most of the immense strikes that shook the nation in 1919 resulted in labor defeats. African Americans found themselves the objects of antiblack riots. And radicals suffered arrest and deportation in a "Red scare" that featured massive violations of civil liberties. Some wartime gains — woman suffrage, for example — persisted into the 1920s, but the soaring promise of a "war to make the world safe for democracy" remained unfulfilled.

American Troops and the Battles They Fought   When the United States declared war in 1917, the Allies had hoped that U.S. troops would quickly be integrated into the French and British combat units that were already fighting in Europe. Instead, Wilson accepted his military staff's recommendation to organized separate American units under U.S. command. To this end, Congress authorized the draft in May 1917. The U.S. Army—about 122,000 strong when war was declared—would grow to 3,623,000 by the time the war ended (Map 6.5).

Proponents of conscription had argued that a draft would strengthen American democracy by bringing young men from different ethnic and class backgrounds into close, cooperative relationships. The reality was

MAP 6.5   Not So Quiet on the Western Front: America in World War I

U.S. troops, commanded by General John J. Pershing, finally arrived on the Western Front in the summer of 1918. They played a crucial role in pushing back the exhausted German troops in battles at Saint-Mihiel, Belleau Wood, Château-Thierry, and especially Meuse-Argonne. Large numbers of American troops saw battle, but the United States suffered many fewer casualties than did the other combatants.

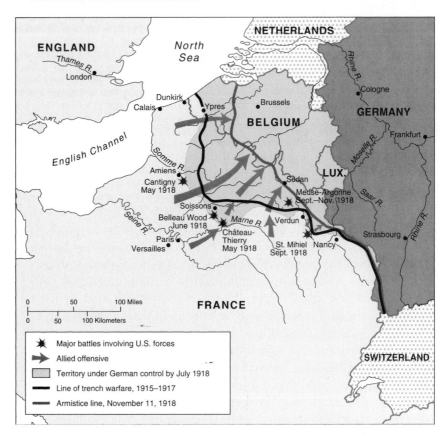

sometimes different. The draft law exempted immigrants who had not filed naturalization papers. And military officials put some foreign-born draftees into ethnically segregated "development battalions," where they were taught English and civics. The army at first declined to take black draftees but eventually established separate units for them. The marines remained exclusively white, and the navy employed African Americans only as cooks and kitchen help.

In the fall of 1917, African Americans began to be drafted in large numbers; eventually nearly 370,000 were inducted. But segregated units and racist harassment (including demeaning insults from white officers) continually reminded them of their second-class citizenship. Under pressure from African Americans, the army put more than half the black soldiers into combat units rather than support groups. But these men remained segregated from white soldiers.

Standardized testing, administered as part of the induction procedure, lent a pseudoscientific gloss to prejudices that lay behind the segregation of troops. The military gave nearly two million soldiers a newly developed "IQ" test, which purported to measure innate intelligence. The psychologists in charge maintained that the tests "proved" that Northern and Western Europeans were more intelligent than Southern and Eastern Europeans, who in turn were thought to be more intelligent than African Americans. In reality, the IQ tests were flawed in both design and administration, and the results were virtually meaningless. The tests actually measured literacy in English and familiarity with mainstream American culture, not intelligence. A typical question read: "Christy Mathewson is famous as a: writer, artist, baseball player, comedian." (Many recent immigrants did not know that the correct answer was "baseball player.") Nonetheless, the army's program legitimized IQ testing, and nativists would use it in the 1920s to justify quotas limiting immigration from Southern and Eastern Europe.

To the colored soldiers of the U. S. Army.

Hallo boys, what are you doing over here? Fighting the Germans? Why? Have they ever done you any harm? Of course, some white folks and the lying English-American papers told you that the Germans ought to be wiped out for the sake of humanity and democracy. What is Democracy? Personal Freedom, all citizens enjoying the same rights socially and before the law! Do you enjoy the same rights as the white people do in America, the land of Freedom and Democracy? Or aren't you rather treated over there as second class citizens? Can you go into a rest urant where white people dine, can you get a seat in a theater where white people sit, can you get a Pullman seat or berth in a railroadcar or can you even ride, in the South, in the same street car with white people? And how about the law? Is lynching and the most horrible cruelties connected therewith a lawful proceeding in a democratic country?

Now, all this is entirely different in Germany, where they do like colored people, where they treat them as Gentlemen and not as second class citizens. They enjoy exactly the same social privileges as every white man, and quite a number of colored people have migthy fine positions in business in Berlin and other big German cities.

Why then fight the Germans only for the benefit of the Wall-street robbers to protect the millions they have lent to the English, French and Italians? You have been made the tool of the egotistic and rapacious rich in England and in America, and there is nothing in the whole game for you but broken bones, horrible wounds, spoiled health or — death. No satisfaction whatever will you get out of this unjust war. You have never seen Germany, so you are fools if you allow ... to teach you to hate it. Come over to see for yourself ... to the fighting who make profit out of this war; do ... em to use you as cannon food. To carry the gun in ... ce is not an honor but a shame. Throw it away and come over to the German lines. You will find friends who help you along.

"To the Colored Soldiers of the U.S. Army"

This propaganda leaflet was dropped by German airplanes behind American lines. By stressing racist conditions in the United States, the leaflets attempted to destroy morale and encourage desertion among African American troops. National Archives.

"You Boys Give 'Em Hell for Me"

The following diary entries by Elmer Sherwood, a corporal from Linton, Indiana, reveal that even a brief experience with front-line combat could be harrowing. Sherwood described fighting on the Western Front near the end of the war.

Oct. 8. . . . Two of our fellows had already been wounded by an explosion near our kitchen this morning, but I was determined to go back for some mess because I was so confounded hungry. . . . I had just got a panful of slum and started eating, when I saw part of the temporary trench I had left, screened by an exploding shell. I thought it had come over the trench, but no — just then Smithy and Netterfield jumped out calling for stretchers.

I dropped my mess and ran to the trench and looked in. Poor Art was dead, one arm completely severed from his body. Danny had a hole in his stomach and we placed him on a stretcher and sent him back to the first aid station. . . . Dan looked at me with a smile on his face as we loaded him into an ambulance. I gave him a word of cheer and he said, "I don't know, Doc, old boy. I've got a pretty bad wound in my stomach. You boys give 'em hell for me." [He died the same day.]

I have seen many die, but none have been so close to me as these fellows. I have worked with them and fought beside them every day since I joined the outfit, and they have been my best pals.

But we must carry on, whatever happens. I ran back to the trench and rescued the battered switch board. . . . We are experiencing a fierce cannonading as I jot down these lines.

Oct. 30. Last night Fritz [the Germans] put on a whale of a bombardment, and I don't see how any of us escaped to tell the story. In the thick of it our communications were knocked out and I was detailed to repair the telephone line. How kind they are to me! Well, I thought of all the mean things I had done in my life, breathed a little prayer.

Flashes of exploding artillery at intervals lighted up the blackness of the night. Explosions of enemy shells on every hand and the scream of big ones going over head to back areas added to the thunderous roar so that I could not have heard my own voice had I dared to speak. Boy! I was glad when I came to that break in the line. I was splicing the wire when — Shriek! Bang! a ton of steel came over me. Just as I finished the job — hell's bells — another hit knocked the line out of place.

For once I lost my cocky self-assurance, for I wasn't so certain that I would ever see home and Mother again. But finally, after stumbling over the body of a dead German, I came upon the next break and spliced it in a hurry. Then I raced back to my hole after reporting communications in order.

William Matthews and Dixon Wecter, *Our Soldiers Speak, 1775–1918* (1943).

Segregated or not, the American troops and the supplies that accompanied them proved crucial to the Allied victory, in part because it undercut German resolve to continue the war. General John Joseph Pershing commanded the American Expeditionary Forces. Between May and September 1918, a million American troops arrived in France; another million came in the next two months. They reinforced French positions in June 1918, and large numbers joined the combat by mid-September.

At the end of September, Pershing launched a drive through France's Argonne forest, pushing the Germans back. German troops, exhausted by an offensive the previous spring and undercut by revolution in Berlin, began to mutiny. One by one, Germany's allies surrendered — Bulgaria in September, Turkey in October, and Austria-Hungary on November 3. Eight days later, the Germans signed an armistice. Argonne was America's major contribution to the war. Though many American soldiers saw battle, few experienced the prolonged trench warfare that ended the lives of 1.8 million Germans, 1.7 million Russians, 1.4 million French, 1.2 million Austro-Hungarians, and over 900,000 British. In contrast, only 112,000 American soldiers and sailors died, over half of them from disease.

At the end of the war, Europe was devastated. Governments had collapsed, and widespread famine had decimated whole populations. In 1918, a worldwide influenza epidemic killed between twenty million and forty million people, as one-fifth of the world's population contracted the virus. A century of optimism and "progress" had been reversed by four years of war.

Wilson and the Shape of the Peace   In promoting the war as a crusade that would make the world "safe for democracy," Wilson argued that all the Allies — including Russia, which had overthrown its tsar in the 1917 revolution — were democracies, battling an autocratic German Kaiser and an

New Faces

This display of plaster casts showed soldiers' mutilated faces (top row) and their reconstructions with the aid of new prosthetic devices (bottom row). In spite of its original purpose, the display now serves as a reminder of the damage inflicted on those who fought in World War I and the imperfect attempts to contend with those gruesome effects. Prints and Photographs Division, Library of Congress.

"Please, Let Me Put Him in a Macaroni Box"

Louise Abruchezze, an Italian immigrant, survived the 1918 and 1919 Spanish influenza epidemic that killed more humans than any other disease in a similar period in the history of the world. In the United States, at least twenty-five million people contracted the flu, and approximately 675,000 died. In this excerpt from an oral history by Charlie Hardy, Abruchezze shares her experience in Philadelphia.

We were the only family saved from the influenza. The rest of the neighbors all were sick. Now I remember so well, very well, directly across the street from us, a boy about 7, 8 years old died and they used to just pick you up and wrap you up in a sheet and put you in a patrol wagon. So the mother and father screaming. "Let me get a macaroni box." Before, macaroni, any kind of pasta used to come in these wooden boxes about this long and that high, that 20 lbs. of macaroni fitted in the box. "Please, please, let me put him in the macaroni box. Let me put him in the box. Don't take him away like that." And that was it. My mother had given birth to my youngest sister at the time and then, thank God, you know, we survived. But they were taking people out left and right. And the undertaker would pile them up and put them in the patrol wagons and take them away.

Interview done by Charles Hardy for WHYY-FM radio program *The Influenza Pandemic of 1918*, Philadelphia, 1984.

Austro-Hungarian emperor. Casting the conflict in this light helped Wilson to win popular support for the war.

But the second phase of the Russian Revolution, which began in November 1917, created a profound crisis for Wilson and the Allies. When Lenin's Bolshevik Party seized control of Russia, it quickly initiated peace talks with Germany and urged European workers and soldiers to stop the war. Lenin also published secret treaties in which Allied governments had agreed to carve up the territory and colonies of the Central Powers at the war's end. This revelation undercut Wilson's claims of a war for democracy. Finally, the Bolsheviks promised a far-reaching social transformation that appealed to downtrodden peoples around the world. For some, the revolutionary Lenin, not the reformist Wilson, seemed the towering figure of the age.

In March 1918, Lenin's new government signed a separate treaty with Germany and withdrew from the war. Within months, the United States, England, and France sent troops to Russia in an ill-fated effort to weaken Bolshevik forces and maintain military pressure on Germany's Eastern Front. Even before the war ended, Wilson seemed to repudiate his principle of national self-determination.

Nonetheless, that principle that each nation had the right to choose its own government became central to Wilson's famous Fourteen Points, which he first proposed in a speech to Congress in 1918. The Fourteen Points called for free trade, freedom of the seas, arms reduction, arbitration of international disputes, and the adjustment of European borders along ethnic lines—all to be achieved through open negotiation of public treaties. To maintain peace, Wilson proposed that a League of Nations be formed to guarantee its members' "political independence and territorial integrity." Although the Allies never formally endorsed the Fourteen Points, they were the main platform on which the war was sold, in both the United States and Europe, during the last year of the war.

Wilson was a popular hero, and when he arrived in Europe late in 1918 to begin peace negotiations, cheering crowds, grateful for American intervention in the war's final months, greeted him. Some diplomats did not share in the popular adulation. French President Georges Clemenceau complained that "Wilson thinks he is another Jesus Christ come upon earth to reform men." And at the peace conference in Paris, Wilson found little support for a treaty based on his Fourteen Points. Italy, France, and Britain had suffered great losses, and their delegates to the conference focused on imposing severe penalties on Germany and promoting their own interests at their enemy's expense. The victors excluded both Germany and Russia from the peace conference.

A number of factors weakened Wilson's bargaining position. First, the United States had contributed least to the war, having declared war last, spent fewer of its national resources, and lost relatively few men. Second, Wilson refused to ally with European socialists, who offered the strongest opposition to the punitive peace treaty the Allied leaders envisioned. Third, Wilson compromised his commitment to self-determination when he agreed to the takeover of German colonies by the Allies. Continued U.S. intervention in the Caribbean, including the occupation of Haiti and the stationing of troops in Cuba in 1917, did not help matters. Irish Americans decried Wilson's acquiescence to the British, who refused to consider granting independence to Ireland. Finally, the president had just suffered political defeat at home; in the 1918 elections, the Republicans captured control of both houses of Congress.

The treaty that was signed at Versailles forced Germany to acknowledge guilt for the war, to cede territory to other countries, and to make huge

Society Note from Moscow

This cartoon, one of a series by Alfred Frueh in the radical weekly *Good Morning*, celebrated the Bolshevik Revolution's impact on Russia's aristocracy: "Count Parasitsky will not occupy his palatial residence in the mountains this summer," reads the caption. "He expects to remain in the city and do uplift work." Alfred Frueh, *Good Morning*, May 15, 1919 — Prints and Photographs Division, Library of Congress.

reparation payments to the Allies for damage to their land and economies. To fulfill the national aspirations of various ethnic groups (and to surround Russia with hostile states), the treaty carved new countries—sometimes illogically—from the old Austro-Hungarian and Russian empires and from parts of Germany. The new nations of Austria, Hungary, Poland, Yugoslavia, Czechoslovakia, Estonia, Latvia, Finland, and Lithuania took their places on the redrawn map of postwar Europe (Map 6.6).

Wilson's major achievement at the conference was persuading the other Allies to include his plan for a League of Nations in the peace treaty. But when the president returned to Washington after months of bargaining, it became clear that Congress disapproved of the plan. Even before he presented the Versailles treaty to the U.S. Senate for ratification, isolationist Republicans, who believed that the United States should avoid foreign entanglements, voiced strong opposition. The treaty empowered the League—which was meant to resolve disputes and guarantee member nations' territorial integrity—to consider collective action in response to aggression. Opponents suggested that the League would restrain U.S.

MAP 6.6　Europe at the End of World War I

World War I dramatically reshaped Europe. Out of the defeated Central Powers — Germany and the Austro-Hungarian Empire — came a host of new nations. Russia, weakened by revolution, also lost territory.

foreign policy and that the treaty restricted congressional authority to declare war. Frustrated by lengthy hearings by the Senate Foreign Relations Committee, Wilson embarked on a speaking tour in September 1919 to arouse popular support for the pact. Late that month, exhausted by the trip, he collapsed from a severe stroke. For the remaining seventeen months of his presidency, Wilson lay in bed, often unable to conduct business. The U.S. Senate twice refused to ratify the Versailles treaty and instead concluded separate peace treaties with the Central Powers. The League of Nations was established without U.S. participation, and it never became an effective force for peace.

Postwar Strikes and Race Riots

While Congress debated the Versailles treaty, strikes and riots erupted across the country. African Americans and workers sought to consolidate and expand gains they had won during the war, to make good on the war's democratic promise. Their opponents sought to roll back wartime advances. A series of titanic clashes rocked the nation. Four million workers — one-fifth of the nation's workforce — struck in 1919. Organized labor and political radicals put forth the most startling and fundamental challenge to the established order that had been seen in the twentieth century; business and government responded with a wave of repression.

In city after city and industry after industry, workers struck in 1919. In the Seattle General Strike, a General Strike Committee, which set up milk delivery for children and laundry service for hospitals and organized some 500 uniformed war veterans to patrol the streets, ran the city for five days. In New York, 50,000 men's clothing workers struck for thirteen weeks, winning a forty-four-hour workweek. Theater workers walked off stage, under the banner of Actors' Equity. In New England and New Jersey, 120,000 textile workers stayed away from their jobs. Striking women telephone operators in New England forced the Post Office Department, which still ran the nation's telephone system under wartime authority, to grant higher wages. Late in the year, 400,000 coal miners walked out, defying a plea from Wilson and a federal court injunction that barred them from striking. Despite determined federal efforts to put down the uprising, the miners

This May Be a Better Goddess Than Liberty — But We'll Have to Be Shown

A cartoon in the *New York Herald*, showing the Statue of Liberty replaced by an exotic statue resembling the Hindu goddess Kali, cast suspicion on the internationalism that the League of Nations espoused. Isolationist politicians and other opponents of the League raised fears that international organizations might restrain U.S. power and autonomy. William A. Rodgers, *New York Herald*, 1919 — American Social History Project.

Feeding the General Strike
These strikers were photographed with groceries that the General Strike Committee had issued to union families. Museum of History and Industry, Puget Sound Maritime Historical Society, Seattle, Washington.

stayed off the job until owners granted them an immediate wage hike of 14 percent and arbitration of their grievances.

In Boston, even the police struck, walking out when the police commissioner suspended nineteen officers who were leading a movement to affiliate with the AFL. During the walkout, the city was hit by a wave of rowdyism, theft, and violence. Massachusetts governor Calvin Coolidge, outraged, established a national reputation by announcing that none of the strikers would be rehired. Coolidge mobilized state troops while he recruited unemployed veterans for an entirely new police force.

Although the demands of these strikes centered on wages, hours, and other traditional issues, the radical spirit that had been evident during the war continued to pervade the labor movement. The war had given railroad workers and miners experience with coordinated bargaining and government administration of industry. In 1919, the railroad unions endorsed a plan for government ownership of all rail lines, and the United Mine Workers debated nationalization of the coal industry. The Bolshevik victory in

BlackSmith

BALLOT

IRON & STEEL WORKERS

The Union Committees are now seeking to get higher wages, shorter hours and better working conditions from the steel companies. Are you willing to back them up to the extent of stopping work should the companies refuse to concede these demands?

TAJNO GLASANJE

Odbor junije sada traži da se dobije bolja plaća, kraći radni satovi i bolji uvjeti za rad od kompanija čelika. Dali ste voljni isti do skrajnosti podupreti da se prestane sa radom ako bi kompanija odbila da udovolji zahtevima?

SZAVAZZON!

Az Union Bizottsága, az Acél Társaságoktól való—magasabb fizetés, rövidebb munka idő és jobb munka feltételek—elnyerése után törekszik. Akar ezek után törekedni? s a végsőkig kitarta—ni? és ha a társaságok ezen kivánalmaknak nem tesznek eleget a munkát beszüntetni?

VOTAZIONE.

I comitati dell'Unione stanno cercando di ottenere paghe piu' alte, ore di lavoro piu' brevi, e migliori condizioni di lavoro. Desiderate voi assecondarli, anche quando dovesse essere necessario di fermare il lavoro se le Compagnie rifiutassero di accettare le domande?

HLÁSOVACI LÍSTOK

Výbor uniový chce dosiahnuť podvyšenie mzdy, menej hodín robiť a lepšie robotnícke položenie od oceliarskych spoločností. Ste vy ochotní ich podporovať do krajnosti, až do zástavenia práce, v páde by spoločnosť odoprela žiadosťučiniť tým požiadavkám.

BALOT

Komitet Unii stara się obecnie o uzyskanie od Stalowych Kompanij większej płacy, krótszych godzin i lepszych warunków pracy. Czy jesteś gotów poprzeć nas aż do możliwości wstrzymania pracy na wypadek, gdyby Kompanie odmówiły naszym żądaniom?

VOTE YES OR NO.   Mark X in square indicating how you vote

 Yes ☒   No ☐

National Committee for Organizing Iron and Steel Workers
WM. Z. FOSTER, Secy-Treas.   303 Magee Bldg., Pittsburgh, Pa.

9

STRIKE BALLOT

How Do You Spell "Strike"?

The strike ballot distributed by the National Committee for Organizing Iron and Steel Workers — printed in English, Croatian, Hungarian, Italian, Slovak, and Polish — indicates the range of nationalities that contributed to the industry's workforce in 1919. William Z. Foster, *The Great Steel Strike and Its Lessons* (1920) — American Social History Project.

Russia and the growing strength of Britain's Labour Party encouraged their fervor. "Messiah is arriving," the Amalgamated Clothing Workers' Sidney Hillman had written to his daughter the year before. "He may be with us any minute. . . . Labor will rule and the world will be free."

The most important strike of 1919 began in September, in the steel industry. Once again, working people took Wilson's democratic rhetoric farther than he intended. As a Hungarian-born steelworker named Frank Smith told a Senate Committee, "this is the United States and we ought to have the right to belong to the union." When the steel companies rejected

"We Ought to Have the Right to Belong to the Union"

The U.S. Senate Committee on Education and Labor set out to investigate the 1919 steel strike while it was still in progress. In his testimony before the committee, Hungarian-born Frank Smith, a Clairton worker, explains why he thought he had the right to a union.

STATEMENT OF FRANK SMITH

The CHAIRMAN. What is your nationality?

Mr. SMITH. I am a Hungarian.

The CHAIRMAN. You are not naturalized.

Mr. SMITH. No, sir.

The CHAIRMAN. How long have you been in this country?

Mr. SMITH. Thirteen years. The reason that I am not naturalized is that I have never stayed long enough in one place; stayed long enough to get my papers.

Senator MCKELLAR. Do you expect to be naturalized?

Mr. SMITH. Yes; I expect to be naturalized, of course, because I've got my family here, my woman, and I have five children; and I have that family, and I would like to know how a man is going to make a living for himself and his wife and five children on $4.73 a day.

The CHAIRMAN. How many hours do you work?

Mr. SMITH. I work 10 hours a day and I get paid for straight 10 hours time.

The CHAIRMAN. And how many days in the week do you work?

Mr. SMITH. Seven days — sometimes six days and sometimes seven days. . . .

The CHAIRMAN. Are you a union man?

Mr. SMITH. Yes, I am a union man.

The CHAIRMAN. Did they treat you in that way because you belonged to the union?

Mr. SMITH. Oh, they won't allow us there if they know that we are union men.

The CHAIRMAN. Are you sure about that?

Mr. SMITH. Yes; I am sure about that.

The CHAIRMAN. And you want the right to belong to the union, too?

Mr. SMITH. Yes, sir; we do. This is the United States and we ought to have the right to belong to the union.

Senator MCKELLAR. Did all of you boys buy Liberty bonds?

Mr. SMITH. Yes, sir; everyone of us. . . . We were all for the United States. We worked day and night for that . . .

Investigation of Strike in Steel Industries, Hearings before the Committee on Education and Labor, U.S. Senate, 66th Congress, 1st Session, vol. 1 (1919).

workers' demands, the unions struck. On September 22, more than 350,000 steelworkers left their jobs, shutting down virtually the entire industry in ten states. The steel companies responded by unleashing a reign of terror. Strikers and their supporters were beaten, arrested, shot, and driven out of steel towns. In Pittsburgh, the sheriff deputized 5,000 loyal U.S. Steel employees and prohibited outdoor meetings. In Clairton and Glassport, Pennsylvania, state troopers clubbed strikers who were attending peaceful gatherings.

The steel companies' refusal to meet with the unions, even at the president's request, won them widespread scorn. To gain popular sympathy, they portrayed the conflict as an attempted revolution by foreign-born radicals. They split the strikers along ethnic and racial lines by bringing in African American and Mexican American strikebreakers. And they launched campaigns to encourage skilled and native-born workers to go back to work. Many native-born skilled workers had joined the strike, but some—reflecting long-standing tensions between unskilled immigrants and skilled "American" workers—stood on the sidelines. Over time, growing numbers of skilled workers fell away from the strike. One Youngstown, Ohio, steelworker, John J. Martin, professed satisfaction at wages and working conditions, maintaining that "the foreigners brought the strike on." Slowly, the strike weakened; in January 1920, the union threw in the towel.

It was a terrible defeat. The immigrant steelworkers had demonstrated a capacity for sustained militancy and discipline, but the steel industry had shown itself capable of crushing even the most massive of walkouts. It would be fifteen years before the next major effort to organize basic industries such as steel, automobile, and electrical equipment manufacturing.

African Americans, too, found 1919 to be a cruel year. A resurgent Ku Klux Klan and other racist organizations urged terrorist attacks on black communities. Meanwhile, African Americans, many of them returning veterans, sought to defend the gains they had won during the war and redeem the war's democratic promise. The resulting tensions—over jobs, housing, and the basic position of black Americans in postwar society—erupted in twenty-five race riots during the second half of 1919. In July, whites attacked blacks in Washington, D.C., in a riot that killed six people and injured a hundred. Perhaps as many as twenty-five African Americans and several white people died in rural Arkansas, where black sharecroppers had begun to organize and arm themselves.

Chicago was the site of the worst riot. Like many racial clashes, it began on a hot summer day at a public facility—a beach—that was being shared uneasily by white and black bathers. When a young black swimmer drifted toward a white section of the beach, someone threw a rock and killed him. Fighting broke out and quickly spread to the city proper, fed by pent-up resentment over housing, job competition, and segregation. In the past, when white rioters had invaded black neighborhoods, the inhabitants had

"We Lost Everything but What We Had On"

The racial tensions in 1919 had begun during the war as working-class whites vented economic frustration against African American migrants taking jobs in war industries. In East St. Louis, Illinois, over several days, white mobs attacked African Americans who defended themselves, resulting in the deaths of thirty-nine African Americans and nine whites. In the following letter to a friend, a victim of the 1917 East St. Louis riot recounted the terror of being caught in the middle of the violence.

3946 W. Belle
St. Louis, Mo.
Dearest Louise:

Was very glad to hear from you. Your letter was forwarded from what used to be my house.

Louise, it was awful. I hardly know where to begin telling you about it. First I will say we lost everything but what we had on and that was very little. . . .

It started early in the afternoon. We kept receiving calls over the phone to pack our trunks and leave, because it was going to be awful. We did not heed the calls, but sent grandma & the baby on to St. Louis & said we would "stick" no matter what happened. At first, when the fire started, we stood on Broadway & watched it. As they neared our house we went in & went to the basement. It was too late to run then. They shot & yelled some thing awful, finally they reached our house. At first, they did not bother us (we watched from the basement window), they remarked that "white people live in that house, this is not a nigger house." Later, someone must have tipped them that it was a "nigger" house, because, after leaving us for about 20 min[utes] they returned & yelling like mad "kill the 'niggers,' burn that house."

It seemed the whole house was falling in on us. Then some one said, they must not be there, if they are they are certainly dead. Then some one shouted "they are in the basement. Surround them and burn it down. . . ." Then they ran down our steps. Only prayer saved us, we were under tubs & any thing we could find praying & keeping as quiet as possible, because if they had seen one face, we would have been shot or burned to death. When they were about to surround the house and burn it, we heard an awful noise & thought they were dynamiting the house. (The Broadway Theater fell in, we learned later.) Sister tipped the door to see if the house was on fire. She saw the reflection of a soldier on the front door—pulled it open quickly & called for help. All of us ran out then & was taken to the city hall for the night—(just as we were). The next morning we . . . were sent on to St. Louis. Had to walk across the bridge with a line of soldiers on each side . . . in the hot sun, no hats, & and scarcely no clothing. . . .

On Tuesday evening . . . our house was burned with two soldiers on guard. . . . We were told that [the crowd] looted the house before burning it. . . .

Robert Asher, "Document of the Race Riot at East St. Louis," *Journal of the Illinois State Historical Society* (1972).

hidden or fled. But in 1919, black Chicagoans fought back, refusing to accept second-class citizenship. Full-scale battles erupted along the borders between black and white neighborhoods. By the time the violence ended five days later, 38 people had died and more than 500 had been injured.

The Red Scare and American Civil Liberties

The mobilization of municipal police forces, state militias, and federal courts against strikers and rioters was part of a larger postwar offensive against radicals and labor militants, which focused on the foreign-born. "Loyalty" organizations intensified their antiradical crusade, even though the worldwide advance of radicalism—often associated with the Bolshevik Revolution—had been largely checked by fall 1919, after an attempted revolution was violently suppressed in Germany and a Soviet government was toppled in Hungary.

UNDER THE STARS AND STRIPES

Under the Stars and Stripes
Daily representations of subversion and menace, such as this Bolshevik serpent in the *Philadelphia Inquirer*, also carried a strong anti-immigrant message, fueling the 1919 Red scare. Morgan, *Philadelphia Inquirer*, March 13, 1919 — American Social History Project.

In the United States, the radical movement had been seriously weakened. The IWW was feeble, its energies drained by defending members who were facing trial on wartime charges. The socialist movement had splintered, weakened by repression, Debs's imprisonment, and internal disagreements. In the summer of 1919, the party split. One faction kept the name Socialist Party and continued to field candidates, believing that they could win enough votes to legislate democratic control of the economy. Debs received nearly a million votes for president in 1920, running from his cell in the Atlanta Federal Penitentiary. A small group modeled on the Bolsheviks went underground to organize a revolutionary movement and eventually established the U.S. Communist Party.

American radicals posed little threat to the status quo, but their opponents were unrelenting. Foremost among the "Red hunters" was Attorney General A. Mitchell Palmer, who led arrests and deportations of thousands of immigrants and radicals. Most had never been charged with a crime. Some, like the well-known anarchist Emma Goldman, had lived in the United States for decades. The largest of the "Palmer raids" took place in January 1920: in one night, federal agents arrested 6,000 alleged radicals in

After the Execution — Boston, August 1927

Thousands of mourners follow behind the funeral carriages of Sacco and Vanzetti. *Labor Defender*, August 1928 — American Social History Project.

Photo *International Newsreel*
THOUSANDS UPON THOUSANDS OF WORKERS MARCHING IN BOSTON BEHIND THE FUNERAL CARRIAGES OF SACCO AND VANZETTI

thirty-three cities. They held many without warrants or formal charges and prevented them from contacting lawyers or relatives. Some of them had no connection to radical activities; others signed coerced confessions. Officials eventually deported 600 of them.

The excesses of the January raids eroded support for the anti-Red campaign. The Labor Department, which had legal jurisdiction over alien deportations, stopped cooperating with the Justice Department. Palmer finally overplayed his hand when he warned that revolutionaries were planning a wave of violence on May Day. Police mobilized to protect buildings and political leaders, but the day passed quietly. Discredited, the anti-Red drive went into decline.

Nevertheless, the Justice Department continued its antilabor, antiradical activities until 1924, working closely with state governments, businesses, and private detective agencies. Military intelligence agents issued an infamous Spider-Web Chart showing connections between activists in national women's organizations, including the American Home Economics Association and the Parent-Teachers Association, as well as political and pacifist groups. The chart implied that they were all part of an international socialist conspiracy.

One case in particular would keep the issue of political repression alive for much of the 1920s. Two Italian-born anarchists, shoemaker Nicola Sacco and fish peddler Bartolomeo Vanzetti, were arrested on May 5, 1920, and charged with killing two men during an armed robbery in South Braintree, Massachusetts. Both men professed their innocence, insisting that they were being persecuted for their political beliefs. Following a trial that was marred by questionable evidence and judicial procedures, the court convicted Sacco and Vanzetti of first-degree murder and sentenced them to death.

For many people in the United States and abroad, Sacco and Vanzetti's case came to symbolize governmental injustice. Protests flared, first among Italian Americans, then among non-Italian radicals, and finally among a broad spectrum of intellectuals and civil libertarians. Under pressure, the governor of Massachusetts appointed a committee of prominent citizens to review the case, but it found no reason to reverse the sentence. On August 23, 1927, as crowds gathered throughout the world to protest, Sacco and Vanzetti were executed. A few months before he died, Vanzetti offered an eloquent summary of his case. His words, as rendered by a New York reporter, were "If it had not been for these thing, I might have live out of my life, talking at street corners to scorning men. I might have died, unmarked, unknown, a failure. Now we are not a failure. This is our career and our triumph. Never in our full life can we hope to do such work for tolerance, for justice, for man's understanding of man, as now we do by an accident."

Conclusion: Toward a Postwar Society

World War I began as the culmination of long-standing European rivalries, but it ended in a political and economic crisis that seemed to threaten the very existence of capitalism. The war undercut the moral, political, and economic bases of all the old European regimes. In Russia, the collapse was complete: a revolutionary socialist government replaced the tsarist regime and in 1924 officially became the Union of Soviet Socialist Republics (USSR). In half a dozen other countries, revolutions were either attempted or threatened. Never before had the foundations of capitalism seemed so shaky.

America's domestic battles in 1919 were part of this larger struggle over the shape of the postwar world. For a brief moment during and just after the war, progressives thought their hopes for domestic reform and international order might be realized, and radicals thought socialism might spread beyond the Soviet Union. But neither of these came to pass. Indeed, U.S. isolationism and the failure of the peace helped to set the stage for another global confrontation twenty years later.

The United States was nevertheless forever changed by the war. The government continued to play a larger role in the economy, in labor relations, and in shaping public opinions. Workers continued to move from the South to the North and West and from Mexico to the southwestern United States. Women gained the vote. Although alien radicals were silenced or deported and wartime suspicion of "foreigners" contributed to the end of open immigration a few years later, most immigrants continued to think of themselves as full-fledged Americans.

When the war ended, so did many of the conditions that favored working-class activism and the development of strong, radical unions. As production levels returned to normal and four million military men reentered the civilian workforce, the labor shortage abated. Intolerance, fear of foreigners, and a dread of radicalism played into employers' hands. Factional bickering and government repression weakened labor and its radical allies, while wartime profits bolstered corporations, enabling them to withstand long interruptions in production. By the early 1920s, businessmen no longer had to deal with a confident, politicized working-class movement. It would be well over a decade before the labor movement would again be able to exert its power nationally.

The Years in Review

1914

- President Woodrow Wilson sends troops to occupy the Mexican port of Vera Cruz in response to a diplomatic slight.
- A Serbian nationalist assassinates the heir to the Austro-Hungarian throne and precipitates World War I; the United States declares neutrality.

1915

- President Wilson endorses military "preparedness."
- Germany begins submarine warfare in February; 128 Americans die when the *Lusitania* is torpedoed in May; a huge public outcry follows.
- U.S. Marines begin a nineteen-year occupation of Haiti.

1916

- Brigadier General John J. Pershing leads 6,000 men into Mexico in an unsuccessful pursuit of General Francisco "Pancho" Villa.
- An estimated 700,000 soldiers die in the German offensive at Verdun.
- U.S. Marines begin an eight-year occupation of the Dominican Republic.
- Running under the slogan "He kept us out of war," Wilson wins reelection, defeating Charles E. Hughes.
- The Industrial Workers of the World finds new life by organizing western migratory workers but also faces sharp government attacks.
- Southern farmers suffer as boll weevils attack their cotton crops and floods cause extensive damage.
- Increasing numbers of African Americans leave the South in the Great Migration, which sends 500,000 north over the course of the decade.

- The Revenue Acts of 1916 and 1917 impose the first substantial income taxes.

1917
- The United States enters World War I in April; the draft begins in May; the first U.S. troops reach France in June.
- Women in New York, Philadelphia, and Boston take to the streets to protest wartime inflationary price hikes for food and other necessities.
- White rioters attack black neighborhoods of East St. Louis for two days in July; 40 African Americans and 9 white people are killed.
- The federal government sets up the Committee on Public Information to disseminate war news and government propaganda.
- The Russian tsar is overthrown in the March revolution; in October, the Bolshevik Party, headed by V. I. Lenin, seizes power.
- The National Woman's Party pickets the White House, demanding that "democracy should begin at home."
- The Espionage Act gives federal authorities wide powers to suppress dissent.

1918
- Wilson issues his statement of war aims, the Fourteen Points.
- U.S. troops push back German troops in France's Argonne forest in America's major contribution to the fighting.
- The German army, exhausted by an offensive the previous spring, collapses, and an armistice is signed in November; more than thirteen million people died in the conflict.
- "Spanish" influenza spreads through Europe, Asia, and America, killing twenty-two million people in the worst epidemic since the Black Death in the Middle Ages.

1919
- The Eighteenth Amendment to the Constitution, banning manufacture and sale of alcoholic beverages, is ratified.
- The Treaty of Versailles, including Wilson's proposed League of Nations, is signed in Paris; the U.S. Senate refuses to ratify it.
- Four million workers—fully one-fifth of the nation's workforce—strike; more than 300,000 steelworkers stage the biggest strike and suffer the worst defeat.
- Attorney General A. Mitchell Palmer begins a campaign to eliminate radicals, or "Reds," from U.S. politics.
- Race riots sweep through the nation, killing 6 people in Washington, D.C., and 38 in Chicago.

1920

- The Nineteenth Amendment is ratified on August 26, granting suffrage to women.

- Italian-born anarchists Sacco and Vanzetti are arrested for murder and convicted in a judicially flawed trial.

- In the largest "Palmer raid," federal agents arrest 6,000 radicals in thirty-three cities, culminating in wholesale violations of civil liberties.

1924

- Soviet Constitution officially forms the Union of Soviet Socialist Republics (USSR).

1927

- Sacco and Vanzetti are executed, despite worldwide protest.

Additional Readings

For more on the first world war in Europe, see: Roger Chickering and Stig Foerster, *Great War, Total War: Combat and Mobilization on the Western Front, 1914–1918* (1991); Modris Eksteins, *Rites of Spring: The Great War and the Birth of the Modern Age* (1989); and Eric Hobsbawm, *The Age of Empire, 1875–1914* (1987).

For more on the war in America and its impact on the economy, see: John W. Chambers, *To Raise an Army: The Draft Comes to Modern America* (1987); Edward M. Coffman, *The War to End All Wars: American Military Experience in World War I* (1968); Valerie Jean Conner, *The National War Labor Board: Stability, Social Justice, and the Voluntary State in World War I* (1983); Frank L. Grubb, *Samuel Gompers and the Great War* (1982); Akira Iriye, *The Cambridge History of American Foreign Relations, vol. 3, The Globalizing of America, 1913–1945* (1993); Jennifer D. Keene, *Doughboys, the Great War, and the Remaking of America* (2001); David M. Kennedy, *Over Here: The First World War and American Society* (1980); Walter LaFebre, *The American Age: United States Foreign Policy at Home and Abroad* (1994); and Ronald Schaffer, *America in the Great War: The Rise of the War Welfare State* (1991).

For more on the African American migration, see: James R. Grossman, *Land of Hope: Chicago, Black Southerners, and the Great Migration* (1989); Carole Mark, *Farewell — We're Good and Gone: The Great Black*

Migration (1989); and Elliott Rudwick, *Race Riot at East St. Louis, July 2, 1917* (1982).

For more on woman suffrage, see: Eleanor Flexner, *Century of Struggle: The Woman's Rights Movement in the United States*, rev. ed., (1975); Maurice W. Greenwald, *Women, War, and Work: The Impact of World War I on Women Workers in the U.S.* (1980); and Rosalyn Terborg-Penn, *African American Women in the Struggle for the Vote, 1850–1920* (1999).

For more on Mexican Americans and U.S. relations with Mexico, see:
John S. D. Eisenhower, *Intervention!: The United States and the Mexican Revolution, 1913–1923* (1993); Lloyd C. Gardner, *Safe for Democracy: The Anglo-American Response to Revolution, 1913–1923* (1984); Manuel G. Gonzales, *Mexicanos: A History of Mexicans in the United States* (1999); James R. Green, *Grassroots Socialism: Radical Movements in the Southwest, 1895–1943* (1978); David G. Gutierrez, *Walls and Mirrors: Mexican Americans, Mexican Immigrants, and the Politics of Ethnicity* (1995); Douglas Monroy, *Rebirth: Mexican Los Angeles from the Great Migration to the Great Depression* (1999); and George J. Sanchez, *Becoming Mexican American: Ethnicity, Culture, and Identity in Chicano Los Angeles, 1900–1945* (1993).

For more on militancy, repression, and nativism, see: William Preston, Jr., *Aliens and Dissenters: Federal Suppression of Radicals 1903–1933* (1963); and David Thelen, *Robert La Follette and the Insurgent Spirit* (1976).

For more on the postwar peace process, see: Robert H. Ferrell, *Woodrow Wilson and World War I, 1917–1921* (1985); Ellis W. Hawley, *The Great War and the Search for Modern Order: A History of the American People and Their Institutions, 1917–1933* (1979); Thomas Knock, *To End All Wars: Woodrow Wilson and the Quest for a New World Order* (1992); Arthur S. Link, *Woodrow Wilson: Revolution, War, and Peace* (1979); and Arno Mayer, *The Politics and Diplomacy of Peacemaking: Containment and Counterrevolution at Versailles, 1918–1919* (1967).

For more on the postwar strikes and race riots, see: David Brody, *Labor in Crisis: The Steel Strike of 1919* (1965); Dana Frank, *Purchasing Power: Consumer Organizing, Gender, and the Seattle Labor Movement, 1919–1929* (1994); David Montgomery, *The Fall of the House of Labor: The Workplace, the State, and American Labor Activism, 1865–1925* (1987); and William M. Tuttle, *Race Riot: Chicago in the Summer of 1919* (1970).

For more on the Red scare, see: Melvyn Dubofsky, *We Shall Be All: A History of the Industrial Workers of the World* (1969); Robert K. Murray, *Red*

Scare: A Study in National Hysteria, 1919–1920, rev. ed., (1980); Kim E. Nielsen, *Un-American Womanhood: Antiradicalism, Antifeminism, and the First Red Scare* (2001); and Regin Schmidt, *Red Scare: The FBI and the Origins of Anticommunism in the United States, 1919–1943* (2000).

7

A New Era

1920–1929

ON JANUARY 1, 1929, the editors of the *Washington Post* prepared a special business supplement to welcome the New Year. "Good Times Are Predicted for 1929," read the banner headline. The *Post* hardly seemed to be going out on a limb with this forecast. After all, two other headlines trumpeted "Record Year Just Ended" and "Gains in Stock Exchange." Further fueling the business community's optimism was the feeling that the federal government took their views to heart. "Hoover's Policies Looked Forward to as Great Aid to Business," still another headline promised.

The *Post* could have made this cheerful prediction almost any time during the 1920s. At least for the wealthiest Americans, these were indeed good times. "The whole upper tenth of a nation," novelist F. Scott Fitzgerald wrote, lived "with the insouciance of a grand duc and the casualness of chorus girls." Fitzgerald, the most celebrated writer of the decade, gave the new era a label that stuck: "The Jazz Age," an invocation of a carefree time of high living, bootleg liquor, and illegal drinking in speakeasies. Fitzgerald himself spent much of the decade in France, drinking and dancing till dawn with his wife Zelda.

More than just the "upper tenth" enjoyed some of the good times. For the first time, substantial numbers of workers lived above bare subsistence levels. Even automobiles and houses became attainable for many. As working hours decreased and incomes rose, leisure time and ways to enjoy it mushroomed, feeding the entertainment industry. Movies and radio promoted consumerism, undermining the traditional ideals and values of the family, community, and ethnic and regional subcultures.

Raids and Refreshment

As wine poured into the streets of a Brooklyn neighborhood after federal agents raided an illegal distillery, local children rushed to catch as much of the illicit drink as they could. *New York Daily News*. Used by permission of the Daily News.

Even so, few Americans lived like grand dukes or like chorus girls. Prosperity was uneven. While the rich got much richer, the average worker saw only a slow rise in income. Workers in some industries suffered falling wages and massive unemployment. On the whole, skilled and white-collar workers did much better than their unskilled counterparts. Farmers suffered for most of the decade. And as usual, African Americans fared worse than whites. A resurgent Ku Klux Klan spewed venom at African Americans as well as at Catholics and Jews. Hostility toward immigrants impelled the nation to shut its doors to foreigners.

But perhaps the most basic problem of the 1920s was the one no one seemed to notice: the unequal distribution of the nation's wealth made its economy fundamentally unsound. Before the year was out, the *Post* would be running very different headlines announcing the crash of the stock market and the early signs of hard times. When a discouraged Fitzgerald, now battling alcoholism, returned to America in 1931, he found a country racked by depression.

Business Conservatism at Home and Abroad

In the 1920s, conservative Republicans with probusiness policies dominated politics. Calvin Coolidge described business as "one of the greatest contributing forces to the moral and spiritual advancement of the race." Such views also shaped American foreign policy, which sought an "open door" for American corporations to operate with a free hand abroad. Ironically, at the same time, the United States decisively closed the "open door" that had long marked its immigration policy and imposed sharp limits on newcomers, especially from Southern and Eastern Europe and Asia.

Conservatism and Corruption in Political Life   The 1920 presidential election set the political tone for the decade. Both major parties nominated middle-of-the-road politicians from Ohio: Republican Senator Warren G. Harding and Democratic Governor James Cox. Since the last election, many Americans had tired of Wilson and his moral righteousness, and they wanted relief from the rampant inflation and social turmoil that had come with the end of World War I — the strikes, race riots, and Red scares of 1919. Harding, capitalizing on this weariness, declared that the country needed "not heroism but healing, not nostrums but normalcy, not revolution but restoration." The election results — a landslide for the Republicans — showed that he had captured the public mood.

Although Harding's vision of "normalcy" embraced generous acts, such as pardoning the imprisoned socialist Eugene Debs, it translated more fundamentally into extraordinary corporate influence on national policy. During the 1920s, the political power of big business climbed to new heights.

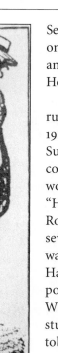

The National Gesture
A 1926 cartoon by Clive Weed in the satirical weekly *Judge* commented on the escalation of governmental corruption during Prohibition. Clive Weed, *Judge*, June 12, 1926 — American Social History Project.

Secretary of the Treasury Andrew Mellon, one of the wealthiest men in the nation, and Secretary of Commerce Herbert Hoover dominated Harding's cabinet.

The discovery of considerable corruption after Harding's sudden death in 1923 destroyed his modest reputation. Subsequent polls of historians have consistently ranked him one of the worst presidents in U.S. history. "Harding was not a bad man," Alice Roosevelt Longworth (Theodore Roosevelt's daughter) later observed. "He was just a slob." She recalled with distaste Harding's drinking and carousing with political buddies in the "Ohio Gang." When she visited the White House study, she found the "air heavy with tobacco smoke . . . every imaginable brand of whisky . . . cards and poker chips ready at hand." Fortunately, she did not open the closet doors, or she might have discovered the president making love to his mistress, Nan Britton.

Whatever his personal failings, Harding himself was never accused of public wrongdoing, but he generally looked the other way when his friends put their hands in the government till — taking kickbacks on government contracts, for example. The most notorious scandal involved the secret leasing, at discount prices, of government-owned oil reserves in California and Wyoming, one of which was called Teapot Dome. The grateful oil companies rewarded Secretary of the Interior Albert Fall, who arranged the deal, with more than $400,000 in bribes.

These gradually unwinding scandals probably contributed to Harding's depression and high blood pressure and finally his death, probably from a stroke. His successor, Vice President Calvin Coolidge, was a very different sort of man — upright, cautious, and introverted. Under Coolidge, Alice Longworth observed, the White House was "as different as a New England front parlor is from a backroom in a speakeasy." But while Coolidge differed in style, he continued the same conservative policies.

The Business of America Is Business   More than most of their predecessors, Harding, Coolidge, and the men who served in their administrations identified the fortunes of America with those of business. "The chief

The Business of America Is Accommodation

In a 1927 ceremony set in front of the Capitol and supervised by President Calvin Coolidge, battle flags that had been captured by northern troops during the Civil War were returned to aged Confederate veterans. Such rites of reconciliation obscured the repressive state of race relations in the South during the 1920s. Prints and Photographs Division, Library of Congress.

business of the American people is business," Coolidge declared. Probusiness conservatives such as Secretary of the Treasury Mellon believed that the government could best aid business by cutting taxes and minimizing federal intervention in the economy. In 1926, Mellon succeeded in persuading Congress to halve the income tax rate for the top bracket of taxpayers and drastically lower the taxes on inherited wealth. Mellon also wanted to return quickly to private hands the businesses that the government had operated during the war. Although the American Federation of Labor (AFL) and the railroad brotherhoods, which had prospered with government control of the trains, wanted the nation to buy the railroads, Congress instead restored them to corporate control in 1920.

Some cabinet officials, however, believed that the government should actively promote and coordinate private economic initiatives. To keep farm prices up, Secretary of Agriculture Henry C. Wallace created cooperative marketing arrangements and voluntary crop reduction programs. Secretary of Commerce Herbert Hoover, the engineer and business executive who had served as head of the Food Administration during the war, sponsored studies of industrial waste and inefficiency, pushed for further standardization in industry, and worked with the State Department to increase exports. Hoover also encouraged state and local governments to use public works to stimulate the economy. But Hoover's modest government activism stayed safely within the bounds of the era's dominant probusiness ideology (Table 7.1).

TABLE 7.1   American Industry in the Global Economy

Three nations — the United States, Great Britain, and Germany — overwhelmingly dominated the world's industrial production in the late nineteenth and early twentieth centuries. By 1881, the United States had overtaken Britain as the leading industrial power, and it increased its lead further in the subsequent years. The Great Depression, however, devastated the two nations' capitalist economies and led to the emergence of the Soviet Union (Russia) as a major industrial power.

Distribution of World's Industrial Production, 1870–1938 (in percentages)

Years	United States	Great Britain	Germany	France	Russia	Japan	Rest of world
1870	23	32	13	10	4	-	17
1881–1885	29	27	14	9	3	-	19
1896–1900	30	20	17	7	5	1	20
1906–1910	35	15	16	6	5	1	21
1913	36	14	16	6	6	1	21
1926–1929	42	9	12	7	4	3	22
1936–1938	32	9	11	5	19	4	21

Source: W.W. Rostow, *The World Economy: History and Prospect, 1978*

The business-government bond became an issue in the 1924 presidential election, when discontented farmers and unionists joined together to back a third-party presidential bid by Wisconsin Senator Robert La Follette. The senator's platform, which harked back to prewar Populism and Progressivism, called for nationalization of railroads and water power, a ban on antilabor injunctions, increased aid for farmers, and a tax system restructured to benefit working people.

The Democrats might have been expected to join La Follette in attacking the business-dominated Republican administration. But deep cultural issues divided the Democrats and deadlocked their 1924 convention. Southern Democrats supported Prohibition and refused to denounce explicitly the racist and anti-Catholic Ku Klux Klan. Meanwhile, the immigrant-led urban political machines opposed Prohibition and wanted to nominate a Catholic, Governor Alfred E. Smith of New York, for president. After a record 103 ballots, the two factions compromised on an obscure and relatively conservative Wall Street lawyer, John W. Davis, who could neither unite his divided party nor offer voters a clear alternative to Coolidge. Although both Davis and Coolidge sharply attacked La Follette as a dangerous radical, he received one-sixth of the popular vote, an extraordinary showing for a third-party candidate. Coolidge, however, won the election easily, and the business-government alliance remained intact.

Capital and Statecraft   The business-government partnership that guided domestic policy also shaped U.S. foreign policy in the 1920s. To open the "door" for American business, Charles Evans Hughes, secretary of state under Harding and Coolidge, used federal power to assist American businesses that wished to expand overseas. Critics charged that Wall Street was dictating American foreign policy, but a State Department official retorted that "in these days of competition . . . capital . . . and statecraft go hand in hand." Working with Herbert Hoover, who as secretary of commerce exercised great influence over American foreign policy, Hughes sought to create a new world order that would bring stability and allow for the expansion of American capitalism—a "Pax Americana," as Hughes put it.

American businesses would have to exercise this global power while the United States stood aloof from the organization that Woodrow Wilson had designed precisely to promote world stability: the League of Nations (see Chapter 6). Without American involvement, the League remained permanently weak. Nevertheless, the U.S. government, American businesses, and American citizens became increasingly active in world affairs during the 1920s. At the Washington Conference of 1921, Hughes, a brilliant diplomat, engineered a halt to the naval arms race, which threatened peace and the ability of American businesses to expand abroad.

American bankers were central to another key diplomatic agreement of the 1920s. By 1924, the Germans could no longer pay the $33 billion in reparations that had been imposed on them at the end of World War I. Hughes sponsored a Washington conference in which American bankers worked out a deal, called the Dawes Plan after Chicago banker Charles Dawes, that sharply reduced German reparations payments and provided massive private loans to restart the German economy. But what looked like a brilliant success ultimately proved a dismal failure. Increasingly, the loans went into speculative ventures or simply propped up the crippled German economy rather than rebuilding it.

Bankers and businessmen were not the only Americans to look overseas in the 1920s. Private voluntary organizations such as the YMCA and Rotary International founded branches in other countries. Like the Coolidge administration, these organizations favored the spread of American business and opposed radical alternatives such as the Socialist and Communist movements that had large numbers of adherents in Europe. Another group of Americans formed a loosely defined peace movement. They won their greatest victory with the Kellogg-Briand Pact of 1928; signed by most of the world's nations, the treaty outlawed war but failed to set up an effective enforcement mechanism.

Business, however, provided the real engine of American internationalism. American companies scrambled to build factories in other countries to take advantage of cheap labor, low tariffs, and easy access to raw materials and markets. By 1929, eight American automakers were running assembly plants abroad. Other companies invested in foreign enterprises; General Electric, for example, held shares in every major electric company in the world. Soon, mass retailers such as Montgomery Ward, Woolworth's, and A&P began to expand into foreign countries. Finally, U.S. companies took an increasingly active hand in exploiting the raw materials of Latin American countries: Venezuelan oil, Chilean copper, Cuban sugar, Argentine beef, and Central American fruit. Direct U.S. investment abroad doubled in the 1920s; by 1930, the United States also led the world in exports.

In selling and investing, American companies received generous assistance from the federal government. Worried about a potential oil shortage, U.S. diplomats helped to identify foreign oil sources that companies might use to satisfy the growing needs of American motorists. Cars also needed rubber tires, so Secretary of Commerce Hoover encouraged Firestone and other tire companies to expand their rubber plantations in West Africa and Southeast Asia to break British dominance of the world rubber market.

The growth of U.S. investment abroad was also facilitated by the government's willingness to "send in the marines." Wilsonian principles of self-determination, Secretary of State Hughes argued, did not apply to poor countries. Over and over, the U.S. military intervened when rebels demanding self-rule threatened American industry. The United States occupied Nicaragua almost continuously from 1912 to 1933 and Haiti from 1915 to 1934. In both countries, the U.S. Marines met resistance in the form of guerrilla warfare, led by Augusto Sandino in Nicaragua and Charlemagne Péralte in Haiti. U.S. Marine Corps General Smedley Butler later gave this blunt summary of his role in U.S. military interventions in Central America: "I helped in the raping of half a dozen Central American republics for the benefit of Wall Street. I spent most of my time being a high-class muscle man for Big Business, for Wall Street and the bankers. In short, I was a racketeer for capitalism" (Map 7.1).

MAP 7.1 Big Stick Diplomacy: U.S. Military Invasions of Central America, 1895–1934

In the first third of the twentieth century, the United States was not reluctant to "send in the marines" to defend what it saw as American interests in Central America. This map shows the locations of U.S. military invasions from 1898 to 1917 and the continuing presence of American troops in the 1920s and 1930s.

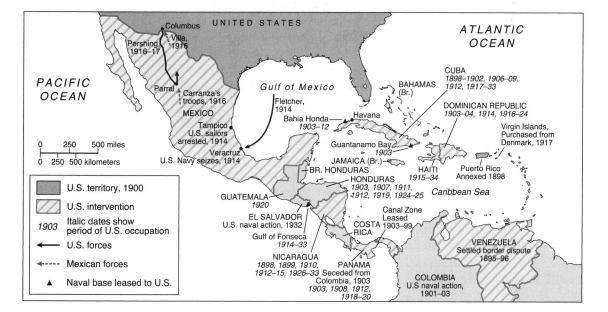

Immigration Restrictions   While the United States stood firmly for the free flow of goods and capital around the globe, it backed away from its earlier commitments to the free flow of people. During World War I, anti-immigrant sentiment had led to a literacy test for immigrants, and wartime conditions had sharply curtailed the influx of foreigners. With the end of the war, immigration returned to previous levels — 800,000 people arrived in 1921 — and anti-immigration sentiment rose with it. Congress passed the Quota Act of 1921 and then, in 1924, the even more restrictive Immigration (Johnson-Reed) Act, which shaped U.S. immigration policy for the next four decades. Initially, the 1924 law limited immigration from all countries to a total of 165,000 a year, less than 20 percent of the pre–World War I average. A 1927 law set even lower limits. Both the 1924 and 1927 laws set quotas by countries, based on the percentage of a

particular nationality in the United States as recorded in the 1890 census. This maneuver was a blatant effort to limit immigration from Southern and Eastern Europe, which occurred primarily after 1890. In the first decade of the twentieth century, an average of 200,000 Italians had entered the United States each year; in 1924, the annual quota for Italians was set at less than 4,000.

Asians fared even worse under the new law, which barred all immigrants who were ineligible for citizenship. That included Asian Indians, Japanese, and Chinese, all of whom were judged ineligible on the basis of past judicial rulings. In 1922, the Supreme Court had ruled Japanese immigrants ineligible for citizenship; the following year another court ruling barred Asian Indians, who had begun immigrating to work in the northwestern lumber mills and on California farms in the early twentieth century. These new immigration restrictions reflected a resurgent nativism and racism. During the Senate debate on the 1924 Johnson-Reed Act, Ellison DuRant Smith of South Carolina urged lawmakers to "shut the door" to preserve "the pure, unadulterated Anglo-Saxon stock" that had made America "the foremost nation in her progress."

Goodwill
The 1928 Havana Pan-American Conference found President Calvin Coolidge defending U.S. intervention in Nicaragua from attacks by Latin American delegates. U.S. press coverage largely ignored the controversy, preferring to herald transatlantic aviator Charles Lindbergh's arrival in Havana with a message of "goodwill." "How sweet it sounds in the ears of the Pan-American delegates," commented the *New Masses* in the caption to this cartoon, "but how different it looks to Sandino and . . . the Nicaraguan patriots." Hugo Gellert, *New Masses*, February 1928 — Prints and Photographs Division, Library of Congress.

Finding the Fittest Family
Many sponsors of immigration restriction believed some ethnic groups possessed superior racial characteristics. The American Eugenics Society was formed to foster the idea that the nation's racial characteristics could be improved by removing inferior racial strains. They promoted Fitter Families for Future Firesides competitions to select eugenically fit families by charting family genealogies and conducting medical examinations at numerous fairs throughout the United States in the 1920s. This was the 1925 "Large Family Winner" in Springfield, Massachusetts. American Philosophical Society.

The new restrictions partially excepted immigration from within the Western Hemisphere. In part because the United States wanted to maintain good relations with its neighbors and in part because farmers (and especially agribusiness) in the Southwest insisted on a ready supply of cheap labor, Mexicans and Canadians could immigrate more freely than Europeans and Asians. Nevertheless, Mexicans faced increased barriers to entry, including a head tax and a visa fee, which were enforced by the new Border Patrol. Still, almost half a million Mexicans entered the United States in the 1920s—double the number in the previous decade.

Mexican immigrants favored the Southwest, but significant numbers headed for jobs in industrial cities of the East and Midwest, such as Bethlehem, Pennsylvania; Detroit and Flint, Michigan; and Chicago, Illinois. The heavily male Mexican population of Chicago forged "Colonias" (Mexican residential enclaves) in industrial areas of the city that the newcomers shared with Eastern and Southern European immigrants. They also began to develop community institutions such as the Chicago Mexican church, Our Lady of Guadalupe, which was formed in 1924.

The New Economy

The U.S. economy experienced a fundamental shift during the 1920s as consumer-oriented industries such as automobile and appliance manufacturing replaced coal and railroads as the leading sectors of the economy. Overall, the 1920s were an era of rising standards of living and economic growth, but the proceeds of that growth were distributed very unevenly. While some industries (automobiles) boomed, others (coal and textiles) declined. While corporate profits skyrocketed, working-class wages grew slowly. While the rich and the middle class enjoyed a dazzling array of new consumer goods, farmers suffered from overexpansion and debt, and unions lost members and influence.

Shifts in Manufacturing   The old economy, based on typical nineteenth-century industries—steel, coal, textiles, railroads, lumber, meatpacking, and shipping—was being replaced by one that was more directly responsive to consumer demand for automobiles, entertainment, processed food, ready-made clothing, petroleum chemicals, home appliances, and other mass-merchandised goods. Demographic changes, in part, drove the change. Americans were having fewer children, and they were moving to cities. In 1920, the urban population had surpassed the rural population for the first time, and it would continue to grow throughout the decade. Households grew more numerous but smaller. In 1890, about one-third of American households had fewer than four people; by 1930, over half did. The increase in the number of households fed the demand for household goods. So did the growth of cities, which meant less time and space for home production.

Consumer goods accounted for more economic activity than ever before and for most of the increase in manufacturing. Yet while manufacturing output nearly doubled between 1921 and 1929, the manufacturing workforce barely grew; almost the same number of workers now produced twice as many goods. During and after the war, manufacturers invested heavily in new machines, which reduced the number of workers needed, especially skilled workers. For example, a machine that painted decorative strips on cars eliminated ten jobs. Many factories also converted from steam to electric power, a more efficient source of energy. Productivity gains (and cuts in employment) also came from speed-ups, the practice of forcing employees to work harder and faster. This was especially prevalent in the southern textile industry. One southern mill hand recalled her nightmares: "I just sweated it out in my dreams just like I did when I was there on the job; wanting to quit but I couldn't afford to."

Service industries, finance, construction, and public utilities all grew more than manufacturing during the 1920s. Construction offered many new jobs (both home and road building boomed), as did commerce, services, and finance. Clerical employment alone increased by nearly a million jobs during the 1920s, while the proportion of workers engaged in manufacturing, mining, agriculture, and railroading declined.

Economic Growth and Social Inequality   Throughout the 1920s, industrialists and bankers hailed what they called "the new capitalism" that had conquered the business cycle and brought prosperity to all. Banker Charles E. Mitchell claimed that this new era was bringing "all classes of the population to a more equal participation in the fruits of industry." But rather than shrinking the gap between the rich and the poor, economic growth increased it. Corporate profits nearly doubled in the 1920s, but factory workers' wages rose only modestly—less than 15 percent, by one estimate. Workers in some industries did considerably better than those in others. Between 1923 and 1929, workers in the automobile, electrical, and printing industries received wage increases of 10 to 28 percent, but those in the shoe, coal, and textile industries watched their wages drop. In general, skilled workers (in construction, for example) and white-collar workers (such as

"They Raised the People's Children"

Cecelia Gaudet, born in Mobile, Alabama, migrated to Chicago in the early 1920s then returned South with her husband. In the South as well as the North, domestic service was one of the few occupations in which African American women could find work. In an interview conducted by author Susan Tucker, Gaudet described her experiences as a housekeeper.

My husband was a boner . . . for Swift's [a Chicago meatpacker]. But he heard from his sister that they were losing some of their property [in Mobile]. So we came back in 1924. I got a job working at housekeeping for a gentleman. He had lost his wife, and he had a sister there. She was an old maid, but they were rich, and she never didn't know nothing about housekeeping.

She and his two children and him, they fell in love with me. He said I was a perfect housekeeper and cook. I was like their mother. I stayed there until I bought me a place in town. They lived too far out, and my husband said it was too hard on me to go out there.

Then, for a good while, I just did work here and there. This family I'd worked for some before, her son got typhoid pneumonia. I nursed him. Then, her daughter she got grown and married, and whenever she wanted something special done, then she'd come around me—for serving parties. And when these babies in white families were born premature, well, I nursed them.

I took a little girl—she wasn't but six years old—and I raised her because I didn't have no children of my own that lived. So I took care of her and sewed at home and sold vegetables, flowers, chickens, eggs. And sometimes I'd go out and serve parties or weddings. . . .

The majority of [black] people here in Mobile worked. And the majority of them made their living working for white people or washing and ironing for them. Everybody couldn't be teachers, and that was the only thing for them to do. They had to work for white people as cooks, housekeepers, maids.

And it's some people that just done it for a lifetime . . . from young people till they got old for the same family. They raised the people's children, and they raised the children's children.

Susan Tucker, *Telling Memories Among Southern Women: Domestic Workers and the Employers in the Segregated South* (1988).

postal clerks) did much better than the unskilled (domestic servants and others).

The ups and downs of the business cycle, which continued despite assertions to the contrary, exacerbated joblessness and insecurity. The initial postwar boom gave way to hard times in late 1920. Prices fell sharply, and 100,000 firms went bankrupt. The economy recovered in 1923, but two more recessions soon followed.

In spite of these fluctuations, the nation as a whole experienced rising standards of living in the 1920s. In the aggregate, the real earnings of all employed wage earners (not just working-class or blue-collar workers) rose about 25 percent. Americans were also getting more schooling; 27 percent of all seventeen-year-olds graduated from high school in 1929, up from 16 percent in 1920. And they were living longer: life expectancy went from age forty-seven in 1900 to fifty-nine in 1930.

Despite the overall prosperity, some people saw signs of deeper economic trouble. Part of the problem lay in the painful and disruptive shift from the old industries that were ailing to the new industries that were not yet mature. But those troubles were compounded by financiers who speculated in new enterprises and engaged in a variety of unsound financial practices, including buying stock on borrowed money and creating dummy corporations that existed only to hold the stocks and bonds of other companies. Stock prices rose steadily throughout the decade, accelerating to speculative heights in 1928 and 1929.

A third sign of trouble came from what analysts of the Great Depression would eventually label "overproduction." By 1928, commercial real estate and consumer-oriented industries such as housing, automobiles, and electrical products were slowing down. Sales lagged, inventories rose, factories cut their output, and unemployment rose. Even before the stock market crash of 1929, many executives thought that their markets were saturated — that is, everybody who was going to buy their products was already doing so. For example, in 1923, new cars outsold used cars three to one; by 1927, that ratio had reversed.

But what the businessman saw as overproduction was underconsumption to the many workers who could not afford to buy the new consumer items the nation's factories were churning out. Workers and farmers were buying all those used cars in the late 1920s because they could not afford new ones. In one Indiana city, almost three-quarters of all families earned less than the Bureau of Labor's minimum cost of living standard. By one estimate, two-fifths of all Americans lived in poverty in the 1920s.

Times Look Pretty Dark to Some

A cartoon in the *Chicago Tribune* prescribed "good old fashioned hard work" as the cure for the depression of 1920 and 1921. Carey Orr, *Chicago Tribune*, 1921 — American Social History Project.

Meanwhile, the rich were getting richer. In 1929, the 36,000 wealthiest families received as much income as did the twelve million poorest. Wealth—in stocks, bonds, and real estate—was concentrated among these fortunate few to an unprecedented degree. This growing social inequality was paralleled by the concentration of productive capacity among a handful of enormous corporations, such as General Motors, General Electric, and AT&T. By 1929, the two hundred largest U.S. corporations controlled half of all corporate assets.

Agriculture in Crisis   While the consumer economy boomed, overproduction, falling prices, and declining income plagued agriculture. Farmers enjoyed modest prosperity until 1920; agricultural prices had risen faster than industrial prices before World War I, and the extraordinarily high wartime demand for farm products further improved farmers' purchasing power. But the economic downturn of 1920 hit agriculture particularly hard. In 1910, a suit of clothes cost the equivalent of twenty-one bushels of wheat; a decade later, that suit was worth thirty-one bushels. A bushel of corn that had sold for $1.22 in 1919 brought just forty-one cents a year later. "'Leven-cent cotton, forty-cent meat, How in the world can a poor man eat?" asked a popular song of the late 1920s.

Overexpansion and debt were at the heart of the farm crisis. During wartime, large European orders for American farm products had prompted farmers to expand, often on borrowed money. When conditions in Europe returned to normal, demand dropped, but output was still increasing, thanks to farmers' investments in new fertilizers, seed strains, and machinery. At the same time, farms in Canada, Australia, Argentina, and Brazil joined in flooding the world market with excess produce. There was no market for all that farmers could grow. Nearly half a million Americans lost their farms, unable to meet their mortgage payments and equipment loans. Many independent farmers, rather than mortgaging their farms or becoming tenants, simply gave up. For the first time in the nation's history, the total number of farms dropped. Thirteen million acres of cultivated land were abandoned between 1920 and 1930.

In these years, a new pattern was emerging in American agriculture. Large, well-financed farms now produced more and more of the country's agricultural output. By 1930, half the nation's farms yielded nearly 90 percent of the cash crop. Large midwestern grain growers prospered by using mechanized equipment. Immense vegetable farms and fruit orchards thrived in California and Florida by shipping fresh produce to colder regions during the winter. Huge farms exploited both impoverished workers and new technologies, and settled farmers without much land or capital could not compete with them.

California's fruit and vegetable industry, for example, depended on migrant labor and huge government-financed irrigation projects. Planting and harvesting an acre of lettuce took ten times as much labor as required for an acre of wheat. As many as 200,000 farm laborers worked in California during the 1920s, three-quarters of them Mexican. Because demand for agricultural labor peaked at harvest time, these workers moved from region to region as the crops ripened. Children and parents worked side by side in the fields, with little opportunity for social life or schooling. Living conditions were atrocious.

Thus, whether within the emerging "agribusiness" of California or on the family farms of the Midwest, economic hard times were a fact of life for rural laborers well before the rest of the country experienced them in 1929. Southern cotton growers particularly faced hard times in years when bumper crops drove prices down. Even worse off were the millions of sharecroppers and tenants. As Alabama sharecropper Ned Cobb put it, "Every time cotton dropped, it hurt the farmer. Had to pay as much rent, had to pay as much for guano [fertilizer], but didn't get as much for his crop." Millions of farmers never recovered from the drastic fall in tobacco, cotton, and wheat prices that followed the giddy expansion of World War I.

The crisis in agriculture revived rural protest and political activism. The Non-Partisan League, founded in North Dakota in 1915 and concentrated in the upper Midwest, campaigned for state ownership of grain elevators, packinghouses, and flour mills; state hail insurance; easy rural credit; and tax exemptions for farm improvements. In North Dakota, the League had elected a state governor and other officials and had instituted much of its program by 1920. But in 1921, League opponents forced a recall election that ousted the governor and attorney general and weakened the League's influence. The American Farm Bureau Federation also promoted farmers' interests but through more conservative channels, stressing cooperative marketing to increase farmers' bargaining power. County agricultural extension agents (appointed in every rural county under the federal Agricultural Educational Extension Act of 1914) encouraged farmers to join the federation rather than more radical farm organizations.

The "Snake Doctor" Invades New Fields

This *New York Evening Mail* cartoon ridiculed the efforts of the Non-Partisan League to spur radical reforms in U.S. agricultural policies. Albert Reid, *New York Evening Mail*, 1921 — American Social History Project.

Many farmers pinned their hopes on the McNary-Haugen bill, which was designed to restore the prewar relationship between farm prices and industrial prices — a balance between farm product prices and expenses that came to be known as *parity*. The bill would have set up a government corporation to purchase the agricultural surplus and sell it abroad; tariffs were to protect domestic prices. Congress passed the bill in 1927 and 1928, but President Coolidge vetoed it. The plan was adopted during the New Deal, however, and became a cornerstone of U.S. farm policy.

Organized Labor in Decline Like farmers, unions suffered in the consumer economy of the 1920s. The once militant labor movement that had led the 1919 strikes virtually disappeared. Conservative labor leaders provided a small elite of craft workers with union representation, but most other workers had to fend for themselves.

Employers used the economic downturn of 1920 and 1921 as an opportunity to reverse labor's wartime gains; they slashed wages and increased hours, often in violation of union contracts. Building on wartime patriotism and the Red scare, they portrayed union shop contracts, which required all employees to join unions, as an infringement on American liberties. They launched a drive for the "open shop," a workplace in which union membership either was not required or was forbidden. By late 1923, union membership had fallen to 3.6 million, from a high of over 5 million in 1920. For the rest of the decade, membership continued to decline despite organizing efforts by radical unions such as the National Textile Workers Union campaign in Southern textile mills. Weakened by membership losses, disheartened by defeat, and confronted by hostile employers and unsympathetic government officials, unions made virtually no progress in organizing the rapidly growing automobile, electrical equipment, and petrochemical industries.

A slightly more encouraging picture emerged initially among the 15,000 sleeping-car porters who worked for the Pullman Company, the manufacturer and administrator of railroad sleeping cars and the country's largest black employer. In 1925, the most important black union in U.S. history, the Brotherhood of Sleeping Car Porters (BSCP), was founded under the leadership of socialist A. Philip Randolph. Thousands of porters soon joined. But the Pullman Company refused to recognize the union, fired several of its leaders, and began hiring Filipino porters to warn African Americans that they could be replaced. Then the AFL, reflecting in part the labor movement's racism in the 1920s, refused to charter the union. By the end of the decade, the BSCP was down to a few hundred members, mirroring the general decline of organized labor in the conservative climate of the 1920s.

In industries that were dominated by a few large companies, employers promoted stable labor relations with relatively high wages, benefits, or

"Let's Stand Together, Workers"

The 1929 Communist-led strike at the Loray Mill in Gastonia, North Carolina, captured national attention, in part because of the violence that accompanied it. These two documents illustrate very different appeals in support of the strikers. The first is a song, "Mill Mother's Lament," written by Ella May Wiggins, a twenty-nine-year-old millworker and mother of five who was killed by vigilantes during the strike. The second is a reporter's description of a strikers' prayer meeting.

"Mill Mother's Lament"

We leave our home in the morning,
We kiss our children goodbye,
While we slave for the bosses,
Our children scream and cry.

And when we draw our money
Our grocery bills to pay,
Not a cent to spend for clothing,
Not a cent to lay away.

And on that very evening,
Our little son will say:
"I need some shoes, dear mother,
And so does sister May."
How it grieves the heart of a mother
You every one must know.
But we can't buy for our children,
Our wages are too low.

It is for our little children
That seem to us so dear,
But for us nor them, dear workers,
The bosses do not care.

But understand, all workers,
Our union they do fear,
Let's stand together, workers,
And have a union here.

———

Jacquelyn Dowd Hall et al. *Like a Family: The Making of a Southern Cotton Mill World* (1987).

"I Call God to Witness"

The strikers today went back to the fundamentals which they brought with them from the mountains. Kneeling on an old store counter salvaged out of the wreckage of the strikers' headquarters, H. J. Crabtree, minister of the Church of God, prayed for divine guidance of the strike. As the old man prayed, a group of strikers stood with bowed heads and as he came to a close fully a dozen joined in the "Amen." . . . Brother Crabtree then preached. His text was "Deliver me, oh Lord, from the evil man; preserve me from the violent man." "I call God to witness who has been the violent man in this strike," the preacher said. "But we must bear it. St. Paul and Silas had to go through with it, and today they sit a-singing around the great white throne. In a few days you'll be a-singing through the streets of Loray with good wages. God's a poor man's God. Jesus Christ himself was born in an old ox-barn in Bethlehem. He was kicked about, speared about, and finally nailed on a cross. And for what? For sin. It's a sin that's causing this trouble. Sin of the rich man, the man who thinks he's rich. . . .

Liston Pope, *Millhands and Preachers* (1942).

Welfare Capitalism and Its Conceits

A 1929 installment of J. R. Williams's popular comic strip *Out Our Way* poked fun at the illusions held by some workers who bought stocks in the companies that employed them. J. R. Williams, *Labor Age*, March 1929 — American Social History Project.

RIDICULING EMPLOYEE STOCK OWNERSHIP

THE STUCK HOLDER.

J.R.WILLIAMS

employee welfare programs. Ford's Five-Dollar Day was only the most generous of a wide range of paternalistic plans that large employers adopted. Some offered stock-purchase plans, pensions, subsidized housing and mortgages, insurance, and sports programs. In southern textile towns, companies built churches and paid ministers' salaries. Some of these programs were aimed specifically at reducing labor turnover, particularly among skilled workers. "Company unions"—created to keep out worker-controlled unions, build employee loyalty, and settle grievances—ran many welfare programs.

Industries with many small, competing producers generally paid lower wages and offered inferior conditions than those that were controlled by a few large firms. In the bituminous, or soft-coal, industry, high wartime prices had prompted the opening of many new mines, particularly in Kentucky and West Virginia. But when demand fell after the war, with competition from oil, natural gas, and hydroelectric power, there were too many mines and miners. Discouraged, many young men left the mining towns for growing industrial cities such as Akron, Ohio, and Flint, Michigan.

In 1922, 600,000 members of the United Mine Workers of America (UMWA), the country's largest and most powerful union, struck for over four months in response to pay cuts. In unionized mines in the North, most operators gave in, but the union failed to win new contracts in nonunion mines. By 1926, two-thirds of the nation's soft coal came from nonunion pits. Hard-pressed owners, determined to compete with new low-priced international competition, broke the unions and slashed workers' pay. Safety standards deteriorated, working hours increased, and wages fell. By 1928, union membership among soft-coal miners had fallen to 80,000 from about half a million in 1920.

Faced with stiff business opposition, a conservative political climate, and declining membership, AFL leaders grew increasingly cautious, especially after 1924, the year of Samuel Gompers's death and the La Follette campaign. Unions confronted new legal barriers after a series of U.S. Supreme Court decisions that upheld "yellow-dog" contracts, in which workers promised when hired that they would never join a union. No charismatic new leader rose to the occasion. Gompers's replacement, UMWA secretary-treasurer William Green, was, a contemporary remarked, "as plain, as plodding, and as undramatic as his name." (The head of the miners' union, John L. Lewis, unkindly reflected: "Explore the mind of Bill Green. . . . I have done a lot of exploring of Bill's mind and I give you my word there is nothing there.") Green reinforced the conservative and conventional direction in which the labor movement was already heading when he took charge. Radicals viewed AFL leaders such as Green as overpaid functionaries who were more interested in feathering their own nests than in organizing the unorganized.

A. F. of L. Delegates

A cartoon by William Gropper that was published in the Communist Yiddish newspaper *Freiheit* (and reprinted in English in the *New Masses*) caricatured delegates to a 1926 American Federation of Labor convention in Atlantic City. "Well, boys," the caption read, "We had a swell convention. Now for the gravy." William Gropper, *New Masses*, November 1926 — Prints and Photographs Division, Library of Congress.

The Expansion of American Consumer Culture

The underlying problems of the economy were not immediately apparent to most contemporary observers. They preferred to focus on the more obvious transformations that the new consumer economy and mass culture were bringing to everyday life: the electric appliances appearing in the nation's homes, the automobiles crowding the streets, the advertisements filling the glossy mass circulation magazines, the radio programs permeating the airwaves, and the ornate movie palaces sprouting up downtown.

The "New Era" brought both continuity and change for women and African Americans. Women, for example, continued to work for considerably lower wages than men even as they ventured into polling places and jury boxes, challenged Victorian restrictions on their behavior, and partook of the new consumer culture. Most black Americans remained mired in poverty in the Jim Crow South, but even some of them were able to acquire the most important symbol of the consumer economy: an automobile. In addition, tens of thousands of African Americans headed north to seek a better life. Although they faced discrimination in the North as well, it did provide greater freedoms, which, in turn, fostered both political militancy and a rich urban culture.

Transformations in Daily Life Across the country, builders scrambled to ease a serious housing shortage. Six million new homes went up between 1922 and 1929, twice as many as in any previous seven-year period. Well over half were single-family dwellings. Although fewer than half of all American families owned their homes and brand-new houses were beyond the means of most working-class families, the growth of mortgage financing allowed more of them than ever before to become homeowners.

Residential patterns remained economically and racially segregated. As cities grew, better-off workers moved outward, while poorer families took over the neighborhoods that were being abandoned. Suburban areas grew twice as rapidly as the center cities did. To keep out African Americans, Asians, Mexicans, and Jews, some suburban towns adopted zoning regulations or "restrictive covenants," special clauses that were written into deeds to regulate the sale of land and houses.

But wherever Americans lived, dramatic changes were taking place inside their homes as well. Oil furnaces, radios, toasters, irons, vacuum cleaners, and wringer washing machines appeared even in working-class homes during the 1920s. Prepared and packaged foods could be found on many working people's tables, and cleaning products were now purchased rather than being made at home, as in the past (Figure 7.1).

Throughout the decade, as appliances multiplied, the use of electricity increased. More than two-thirds of U.S. households were wired by 1930—double the proportion of a decade before. Some electric companies offered wiring services on the installment plan. As new power plants came on line, the price of power dropped by one-third between 1912 and 1930. At first, most homes used only a few electric lights, but as electricity got cheaper, people installed more lights, bought more appliances, and used more current. By 1926, more than half the houses in Zanesville, Ohio, had electric irons and vacuum cleaners, and one-fifth had toasters. Still, the average residential customer in 1930 used only 547 kilowatt hours annually. Customers in the early 2000s would use almost twenty times that much.

Farm homes lagged far behind city ones in household technologies and utilities. Nearly three of every four urban families had bathrooms, but only one in three rural families did. Similarly, only about 10 percent of farms had electricity in 1930, compared with 85 percent of urban and small-town dwellings. Many prosperous farmers bought appliances that ran on gas, but

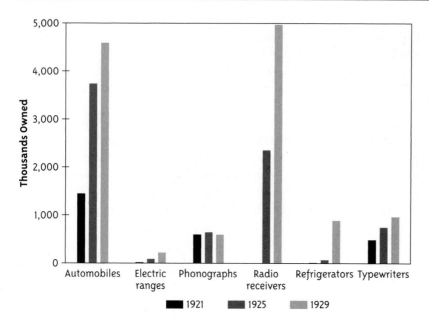

FIGURE 7.1 A Consumer Revolution?: The Production of Consumer Goods, 1920–1930

New consumer goods and appliances spread unevenly across the nation in the 1920s. The most rapid growth came in the production of cars and radios. Labor-saving devices for the home appeared much more slowly. As late as 1930, fewer than one-quarter of American families owned washing machines, and fewer than one-third had vacuum cleaners.

almost three-quarters of the farm homes in the Midwest had no modern household equipment at all, although many had automobiles and tractors.

Still, tens of millions of Americans lived outside the boundaries of the consumer economy, unable to afford new clothes, automobiles, or the many other products that were part of Americans' rising expectations during the 1920s. A third of all families lived in houses that one expert categorized as below "any decent standard." Times of unemployment, seasonal layoffs, or sickness threw blue-collar workers into hard times. "When my husband's working steady," a roofer's wife explained, "I can just manage, but when he's out [of work], things go back." First she stopped sending her wash to the commercial laundry and did it by hand in the kitchen sink. Then she cut back on food. Then, she explained, "the rent goes behind."

Autos for the Masses The single most important product in the new culture of consumption was the automobile, and the number of cars that were manufactured more than tripled during the 1920s. By 1929, almost half the families in the United States owned a car — a level that was not reached in England until 1970. "Why on earth do you need to study what's changing this country?" a Muncie, Indiana, resident asked sociologists Robert and Helen Lynd. "I can tell you what's happening in just four letters: A-U-T-O!"

The automobile transformed not only the way Americans spent their leisure time, but also the economic and physical landscape. The automobile industry in 1929 accounted for nearly 13 percent of the value of all

Model Kitchens

A quarter of a century separated these two "model kitchens" that demonstrate how technology and new consumer products — including washing machines and vacuum cleaners — changed housework. The wood stove in the 1899 kitchen, for example, stands in sharp contrast to the 1924 showcase electric stove. Nevertheless, some innovations were far beyond the means of many American families; over one-third of all U.S. households still had wood or coal stoves in 1940. Anna Leach, "Science in the Modern Kitchen," *Cosmopolitan*, May 1899 — American Social History Project; Prints and Photographs Division, Library of Congress.

manufactured goods; it employed 375,000 workers directly and millions more indirectly. Fifteen percent of the nation's steel went into auto bodies and parts, and 80 percent of its rubber went into tires. Furthermore, the auto industry generated and supported secondary industries and businesses, supplying Americans with tires, new highways, and parking lots. New demands for insurance and consumer credit stimulated financial markets. Whole cities grew up around automobile production. Detroit grew from a population of 285,000 in 1900 to 1.5 million in 1930.

At the beginning of the decade, Henry Ford and the Ford Motor Company dominated the automobile market. Ford was selling transportation, not style, and he emphasized production: the most efficient factories, the lowest price for cars, the largest market. To those ends, during World War I, Ford had developed the huge River Rouge complex in Dearborn, Michigan.

"We Rode the Public a Little Ourselves"

To sell its Model T, the Ford Motor Company established a national network of sales agencies. These were independent businesses, but as one rural dealer recalled, they were forced by Ford to meet sales quotas. To do so, they sometimes used unethical practices.

When I first took the agency I was my own boss like any other business man, selling as many cars as I could and buying more when I needed them. . . . Then one day a representative of the [Ford] Company came to see me . . . and said ten cars a month was not enough for a dealer like me to sell. It seems the Company had made a survey of my territory and decided that the sales possibilities were much greater. Benson [the Ford representative] said my quota had been fixed at twenty cars a month, and from then on that number would be shipped to me.

Naturally, I got a little hot under the collar at this kind of proposition, and I told Benson where he could get off at. . . . Benson was pretty hard boiled. . . . Either I could buy twenty cars a month or the Company would find another agent. . . .

Well, I finally decided to take a chance on twenty cars a month rather than lose the agency. . . . But I sure got it in the neck when the slump of 1920 came on. If anyone wants to know what hard times are he ought to try to do business in a Western farming community during a panic. . . . From September to January of that year I sold exactly four cars. . . .

I am willing to confess that we rode the public a little ourselves while we were getting rid of our big surplus of cars. There are always people that you can sell anything to if you hammer them hard enough. We had a salesman named Nichols who was a humdinger at running down prospects, and one day he told me he had a fellow on the string with a couple of hundred dollars who would buy a car if we would give him a little extra time on the balance. This prospect was a young fellow that had come out West on account of his health and was trying to make a living for his family as an expert accountant. Just at that time the referee in the bankruptcy was doing most of the accounting business around town, and I knew the young fellow wasn't getting on at all. He had about as much use for a car as a jack rabbit. . . .

Well we went ahead and made the sale, but we never got any more payments. The young fellow took to his bed just after that, and the church people had to look out for him and his family until he died. In the final showdown it turned out that the two-hundred dollar equity in the car was everything they had on earth, and by the time we [repossessed] it and sold it as a trade-in there wasn't anything at all. I gave twenty dollars toward his funeral expenses.

"Confessions of a Ford Dealer, as told to Jesse Rainsford Sprague," *Harper's Monthly Magazine*, June 1927.

Assembly Line, 1928

Automobile workers at the end of an assembly line at the Ford River Rouge plant are shown here putting the finishing touches on the stylish new Model A, which replaced the basic black Model T in 1927. Henry Ford Museum and Greenfield Village.

This vertically integrated manufacturing operation had its own port, steel mill, power plant, and railroad, and it operated the world's largest foundry. At its height, the River Rouge complex was the largest factory in the United States, employing more than 75,000 workers. "Fordist" methods — reducing labor costs and increasing output through the use of machinery, keeping prices low and wages high — paid off (see Chapter 4). In 1921, the Ford Motor Company controlled more than half of the U.S. automobile market. The price of a Model T — $950 in 1909 — dropped to $290 by 1924.

Ford's main rival, General Motors (GM), took a different approach. GM president Alfred P. Sloan, Jr., believed that Americans with rising incomes would choose cars not only for their price, but also for their comfort and style. Accordingly, in the late 1920s, GM began to offer a wide range of styles and prices, changing them every year. Sloan called this approach "the 'laws' of Paris dressmakers": "keep the consumer dissatisfied" and eager to buy a new and fancier model. Thus, the company maintained five separate car divisions, ranging from Cadillac, which made the fewest, most expensive automobiles, to Chevrolet, which mass-produced low-priced vehicles.

Increasingly, working people found it easier to afford cars, although perhaps not the models they longed for. For many decades, the installment plan had enabled seamstresses and farmers to buy sewing machines and harvesters. Now three major companies, including GM, financed the postwar auto boom by offering loans to buyers.

Farmers and people in small towns were the first to purchase cars in massive numbers. About three of every ten farm families in the Midwest bought their first cars during the 1920s; by 1930, almost nine of every ten farm families in Iowa, Kansas, Minnesota, Nebraska, and the Dakotas owned cars. For these people, living far from stores and neighbors, automobiles filled a real need and transformed rural social life. One farm woman thought it obvious why her family had bought a Model T before equipping their home with indoor plumbing. "Why, you can't go to town in a bathtub," she told an inquiring government official (Figure 7.2).

Even some poor farmers scrimped and saved to buy secondhand vehicles. About half of white Georgia sharecroppers owned cars by the mid-1930s. Autos weakened the tyrannical grip of southern plantation owners and local merchants because farmers could patronize more distant stores, banks, and cotton gins. Black sharecropper Ned Cobb viewed cars as a work incentive to his sons: "my boys, anyway, they done got big enough to go and correspond girls," he later recalled, and he decided to "buy me a new Ford to please them."

The automobile changed life in the city, too. Cars enabled people to live farther from work. No longer dependent on public transportation, Americans moved away from older working-class neighborhoods and into the suburbs. The new mobility was accompanied by a sense of freedom and control. For young people, the automobile offered the means to socialize away from their parents. For workers in increasingly routinized jobs, it

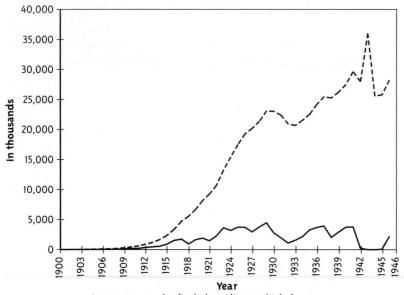

FIGURE 7.2 America Goes Driving: Automobile Sales and Registrations, 1900–1946

This chart documents the rapid increase in car ownership in the first half of the twentieth century. Wartime restrictions on driving and automobile production led to the fall-off in car sales and registrations in the early 1940s.

In thousands

—— Passenger car sales (includes military vehicles)
- - - - Automobile registrations (all cars in use)

Year

Automobiles to Match Milady's Mood

This 1927 advertisement for Paige-Jewett cars suggests how manufacturers and advertising firms used colors and new styles to differentiate their products from those of competitors. Buying became confused with self-expression as consumers were urged to purchase products as a way to display individual taste and distinction. *Ladies' Home Journal,* February 1929 — American Social History Project.

fueled a growing tendency to make recreation a part of everyday life, not just an occasional event. Like other consumer industries, the automobile makers began manufacturing not only products, but also desires. Ultimately, GM's emphasis on marketing proved more effective than Ford's stress on manufacturing. Ford was forced to abandon the Model T, to introduce and advertise new models and colors, and to move toward more flexible manufacturing methods. Henry Ford's vision of extreme standardization and continuous price reduction was on its way out. Replacing it was a more sophisticated form of mass production, based on creating and then fulfilling ever-changing consumer demands.

The Creation of Customers   If manufacturers such as Ford were the captains of industry, advertising men could be seen as the captains of consumerism, charged with manufacturing dreams and creating new wants. Some advertisements associated products with a desirable lifestyle: "Men at the top are apt to be pipe-smokers," read an ad for Edgeworth Pipe Tobacco. Others tried to undermine people's reliance on traditional sources of advice and authority — parents, friends, and neighbors — so that they would trust manufacturers' claims instead. Some pointed out the dire consequences of not purchasing a product: "A single contact with inferior toilet paper," warned a Scott Paper ad, "may start the way for serious infection — and a long, painful illness."

Despite advertisers' suggestion that everybody had to have the latest of everything, most families set their own priorities and purchased the things they wanted most. "It is not uncommon," the Lynds wrote about Muncie, "to observe 1890 and 1924 habits jostling along side by side." A family might have "primitive back-yard water or sewage habits" but own an automobile, an electric iron, or a vacuum cleaner.

Consumption varied from town to town and from region to region but was particularly conspicuous in places such as Flint, Michigan, which was experiencing an economic boom. Flint's auto industry drew large numbers of young workers to the city. Unrestricted by community traditions and family obligations, they eagerly adopted the ethic of consumption, buying cars and clothing on the installment plan. Young single women, too, went into debt to buy stylish clothes. Dressed for a night out, workers flocked to Flint's movie theaters, dance halls, and bowling alleys.

Some businessmen argued that the Flint situation was ideal, that the high wages that were common in the auto industry would not only maintain labor peace, but also enlarge the pool of purchasers for consumer products. Boston reformer and department store owner Edward A. Filene believed that the very idea of mass production was "based upon a clear understanding that increased production demands increased buying, and that the greatest total profits can be obtained only if the masses can and do enjoy a higher and ever higher standard of living. . . . Mass production is . . . production for the masses."

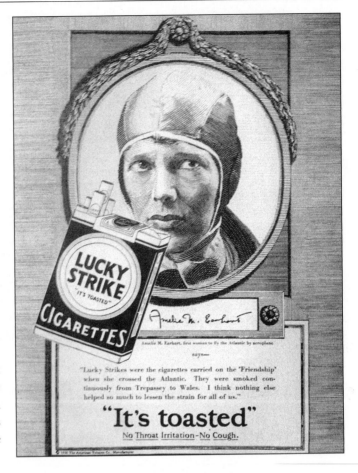

"Smoked Continuously from Trepassey to Wales"
In this 1928 advertisement, aviator Amelia Earhart, the first woman to complete a solo flight across the Atlantic, testifies to the pacifying virtues of Lucky Strikes. American Social History Project.

Mass Culture: Radio, Music, and the Movies The new consumer culture was accompanied by the rise of a truly national popular culture. Popular entertainments such as radio, recorded music, and motion pictures pulled previously isolated social groups into the mainstream. At the same time, however, they divided families by appealing differently to members of different generations. As they reached their wide audiences, these entertainment forms created new desires and aspirations, reinforcing the development of a consumer culture.

By 1926, more than four million radios had made their way into American homes. Families and neighbors gathered in homes and shops to listen to drama, comedy, and crop and weather reports. For the first time, millions of Americans could hear the president's voice, the roaring crowds at the World Series, and the very best professional musicians.

Businesspeople quickly realized that radio offered a wonderful new medium for peddling their wares. Within a few years, companies were sponsoring programs that incorporated commercials featuring "branded

"A Single Maiden, Never Wed"

Graham McNamee was the most popular radio announcer of the 1920s. The flood of mail he received from listeners included many letters, like this one, asking for help in finding a spouse.

Dear Mr. McNamee:

Knowing your great station and its very pleasing official voice reaches into many homes and distant places, it occurred to me that, in view of the fact that I have given the early years of my life to educational advancement by studying nights and working by day, I am now in the thirties, in the best of health, with several degrees and now completing a course in radio Engineering.

I own a farm on the highway to _____, built my own home and garage, but am waiting for a suitable bird to put in the nest. I have partitioned off nothing so far, but want a Protestant girl of settled habits, strong moral fiber, of German, Scotch, or American parentage, of the old school, who can cook the old-fashioned way, loves children, nature, flowers, who will be a real mother and home-maker.

Probably among your many listeners there is a single maiden, never wed, who is looking for such an opportunity, for I am a bachelor self-made in every sense.

Yours,

P.S. You may read my letter to your listeners.

Robert Sklar, ed., *The Plastic Age 1917–1930* (1970).

performers" such as the Ipana (toothpaste) Troubadours, the A&P Gypsies, and "Paul Oliver" and "Olive Palmer," who performed for the Palmolive Company. By 1928, national networks had been established on an explicitly commercial basis to sell expensive radio time. Filling that time were new forms of sponsored programming, such as Pepsodent toothpaste's *Amos 'n' Andy*, an enormously popular comedy show about African Americans (played by white actors), which premiered in 1928.

Even rural Americans listened to radios powered by batteries or windmills. The new medium gave them vital information about commodity prices and weather. Soon, the Department of Agriculture was providing radio stations with scripts for lessons on dairy production, livestock feeding, and cooking. The *National Farm and Home Hour*, which debuted on NBC stations in 1928, provided forty-five minutes of music, weather and crop forecasts, and information on soil improvement and home economics. Just as important, the radio kept farm women company as they churned butter and made beds. As one Missouri farmer wrote to a radio station in 1923: "We hillbillies out in the sticks look upon radio as a blessing direct from God."

Local and ethnic radio broadcasts flourished alongside the emerging national shows. In every city, scores of low-powered stations carried foreign-language programs. Stars of foreign-language radio shows became important figures in the ethnic enclaves.

Ethnic audiences could also buy phonograph records made in foreign languages. By the mid-1920s, phonographs were affordable luxuries for working people. Like radios, they were sold at widely ranging prices, depending on the quality of their cabinets as well as their working parts. "Race records," marketed to black audiences, brought black music to far-flung corners of the United States. In just six months in 1923, blues singer Bessie Smith's first recording, "Downhearted Blues" sold 750,000 copies.

Theater owners also adapted the movies to the needs of ethnic communities by combining films with live entertainment, often directed at a local audience. In the packinghouse district of Chicago, a Polish play accompanied the film; in Little Sicily, Italian music could be heard at the movie house. In "The Stroll," Chicago's African American entertainment district, blues artists played on the same bill as the movie.

Before World War I, moviegoers had been mainly urban, working-class immigrants, but during and after the war, movie theaters sprang up even in remote towns. By the mid-1920s, there were more than twenty thousand movie theaters in the United States. In Carrboro, North Carolina, a small mill town without electricity, the only entertainments had once been baseball, hunting and fishing, music, and conversation. Now, with a movie house equipped with a gasoline-powered generator, mill families could see the latest newsreels and movies. Carrboro was becoming less isolated (Figure 7.3).

At the same time that movies were arriving in small towns, film distributors began building large, ornate movie palaces in the cities. One Baltimore theater featured a 110-person orchestra, a mammoth organ, and fourteen pianos. Workers took the streetcar, and middle-class people drove downtown, to see new kinds of films at these theaters — at first, silent features

Los Madrugadores: Early-Morning Radio Stars

A vibrant musical community for Mexican music emerged in southern California in the 1920s and 1930s with the growth of the Mexican population, the arrival of immigrant musicians, and the rise of radio. Los Angeles commercial radio stations featured many hours of Spanish-language programming, often aired in the "dead" early-morning hours of the radio schedule. Longshoreman Pedro J. Gonzalez (in the center of the photograph) formed Los Madrugadores ("The Early Risers") with other Mexican immigrants. As the group's name suggested, its music reached an audience of working people as they prepared for early-morning work shifts. UCLA Chicano Studies Research Library.

FIGURE 7.3   Take Me Out to the Ballgame . . . and the Movies

New baseball parks, radio broadcasts of games, and the emergence of sport pages in daily newspapers all helped to boost baseball attendance in the 1920s. Movie attendance also grew significantly, reflecting the expansion of movie theaters to small towns across the country, the appeal of Hollywood productions, and the expanding economy.

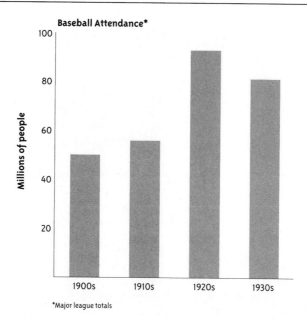

Baseball Attendance*

*Major league totals

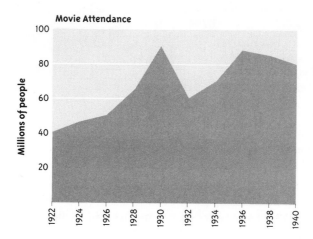

Movie Attendance

running an hour or more and eventually, in the late 1920s, "talking pictures." By 1930, a total of 100 million movie tickets were being sold every week.

The urban movie palaces had their counterpart in what one film historian calls "new palaces of production"—vast studio lots with shooting stages, film labs, and costume shops—centered in southern California, especially "Hollywood," a word that came to describe the movie industry itself, not just its most famous center of production. Starting in 1906 and accelerating thereafter, movie companies headed west to California,

Paradise in the Movie Palace
Designed by renowned architect John Eberson, the Chicago Paradise, which opened in 1928, was one of the grandest of the new movie palaces. Dubbed "the World's Most Beautiful Theater" by Chicago theater entrepreneurs Balaban and Katz, the Paradise had a half-block-long French-inspired Second Empire exterior, featuring a marquee emblazoned with more than 10,000 light bulbs and a seven-story entrance tower. Patrons entered an outer lobby that had a soaring domed ceiling painted with constellations and clouds. In the vast auditorium, a sculpture of three horses pulling a chariot was set above the proscenium arch, appearing to gallop towards the audience. Chicago Architectural Photographing Company Collection, Theatre Historical Society of America, Elmhurst, Illinois.

seeking sunny weather, low taxes, and weak unions. By 1919, more than four-fifths of the world's movies were produced in the Los Angeles area.

Businessmen embraced the new popular culture of Hollywood because it stimulated consumption. People wanted to own the cars and clothes they saw in movies and magazines. Young people and adults began modeling their clothing, speech, and behavior after stars of movies, vaudeville, radio, and professional sports.

Many of the new celebrities came from working-class, immigrant backgrounds. Rudolph Valentino, Hollywood's top male romantic lead, had been born in Castellaneta, Italy. The great magician Harry Houdini was the son of a Jewish tailor. And baseball slugger Babe Ruth, the descendant of German immigrants, came from a poor neighborhood on the Baltimore waterfront. Fans adored these celebrities in part because they spurned the Protestant middle-class values of self-restraint, hard work, and "character." Valentino's erotic portrayal of exotic and passionate characters in movies such as *The Sheik* challenged the Victorian ideal of restrained and decorous

Composograph

When it began publication in 1924, Bernarr Macfadden's *New York Graphic* claimed to inaugurate a new brand of journalism. Its brazen exploitation of the sensational; focus on crime, gossip, sex, and scandals; and utter disregard for the truth set a model that tabloid journalism follows to this day. Its inventiveness extended to publication of "composographs," retouched photographic collages that claimed to show events that were never actually caught on film, such as movie idol Rudolph Valentino's 1926 operation, from which he never recovered. The *Graphic* itself was short-lived, going out of business in 1932. *New York Graphic*, 1926 — Prints and Photographs Division, Library of Congress.

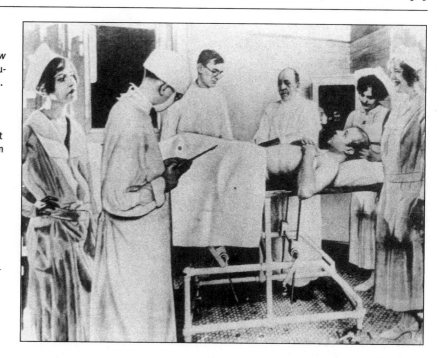

masculinity. Followers celebrated Ruth not only for his extraordinary athletic accomplishments, but also for his oversized appetites for food, clothes, alcohol, and sex.

These icons of mass culture competed with the traditional values of families and local communities in providing the primary channels for children's access to the outside world. Generational conflict often resulted, especially in immigrant homes. Grace Gello, who grew up in an Italian family on New York's Lower East Side, remembered that she and her fiancé would occasionally take the afternoon off from work to go to the movies. "We didn't do this too much because we were afraid of my father. He would say, 'If I catch you, I'll break your neck.'"

For immigrants and their children and for farmers, miners, millworkers, and laborers, movies provided a window on the middle- and upper-class world, with which they had no direct contact. Kate Simon, a writer who grew up among immigrants in the Bronx, New York, recalled that from movies, "we learned how tennis was played and golf, what a swimming pool was and what to wear if you ever got to drive a car . . . and of course we learned about Love, a very foreign country like maybe China or Connecticut."

In a sense, all of America was Americanizing. Mass culture was not only Americanizing immigrants, it was also redefining the nation's values. Such changes proved threatening, particularly to traditional arbiters of public values — ministers, political leaders, police officials, social workers, and academics — who generally opposed change. Although the movie moguls profited from their role as the nation's new cultural brokers, they also worried that if they went too far, they would provoke censorship and attack, a serious concern, since so many of them were themselves immigrants. After a young actress was found dead in the aftermath of a drunken party hosted by "Fatty" Arbuckle, one of the nation's favorite film comedians, the producers realized

Two Celebrities

Catcher Gabby Hartnett was photographed as he exchanged pleasantries with "Scarface" Al Capone (who was known to wield a bat himself on occasion). The Chicago Cubs player was autographing a baseball for the gangster's twelve-year-old son at a charity game in Comiskey Park. UPI/Corbis-Bettmann.

that they needed a frontman. For $150,000 a year, they hired Will Hays, President Harding's postmaster general and an elder of the Presbyterian Church, to set up a system of industry self-policing. Baseball owners had followed a similar strategy a few years earlier, after the scandal when gamblers fixed the 1919 World Series.

Women as Workers and Consumers   "In an age where the emphasis is on consumption," social scientist Lorine Pruette commented in 1929, "women need wages . . . to keep themselves afloat on the tide. . . . The manufacturers need the women as consumers, need the two-wage family and its demands to keep the factories going." Indeed, to help their families survive or simply to live more comfortably, increasing numbers of married women took jobs outside the home during the 1920s. Their numbers were still modest; in 1930, fewer than 12 percent of all married women worked for wages, women who could afford to stay home generally did so. But those who did take jobs were part of a long-term trend; since 1900, the percentage of married working women had doubled. Because poverty remained the most important determinant of whether a woman worked, married black women were five times as likely as married white women to be in the paid labor force.

Although more women entered the workforce in the 1920s, they did not do so on an equal basis with men. In 1929, the average working woman earned only fifty-seven cents to a man's dollar. A key reason for the disparity was that jobs were generally designated as "male" or "female." For example, both men and women, most of them white, could be found in all types of clerical jobs, but bosses preferred women for routine tasks and men for sales and general clerical posts. Employers rarely promoted women to managerial positions.

The Equal Rights Amendment

Suffragist Alice Paul wrote the Equal Rights Amendment. Introduced in every session of Congress since 1923, it passed the House and Senate in 1972 but failed to be ratified by the necessary thirty-eight states.

Section 1. Equality of Rights under the law shall not be denied or abridged by the United States or any state on account of sex.

Section 2. The Congress shall have the power to enforce, by appropriate legislation, the provisions of this article.

Section 3. This amendment shall take effect two years after the date of ratification.

Congressional Record, 1923–1972.

To lower costs, companies introduced a variety of calculating machines and dictaphones (recording machines that eliminated the need for shorthand skills). Following scientific management practices, companies divided the work process into narrow, highly routinized jobs, and the pace of clerical production increased. In large "typing pools," women typed documents for bosses they never saw. These pools more resembled light manufacturing plants than the small company offices of an earlier era.

More satisfying career opportunities opened up in professions that were filled primarily by college-educated women: social work, nursing, teaching, and librarianship. A small but growing number of women found jobs as lawyers, bankers, religious leaders, and editors. Although a handful of these women became well known, most were marginalized, excluded from power even in professions they dominated. Some professions almost entirely excluded women. Most medical schools had quotas of just 5 percent for women students; only a handful of hospitals would hire women interns. The law schools of Columbia and Harvard would not consider admitting women. All told, only 14 percent of wage-earning women occupied professional positions in 1930, while 19 percent held clerical positions and 30 percent worked in domestic service or as waitresses and beauticians.

As women began to gain some economic independence, their legal and social status began to change. Ratification of the Nineteenth Amendment led to the extension of other legal rights; by the early 1920s, women could serve on juries in twenty states. But women did not use the vote to win greater social and economic equality, as suffragists had long hoped. Property, marriage, and divorce laws remained unfavorable to women. Fewer women than men voted throughout the decade, and women voters made choices on bases similar to those of men, shaped less by gender than by class, region, age, race, and religion. As a result, the major political parties

Love and Companionship Came First: Floyd Dell on Modern Marriage

In this mock dialogue from Floyd Dell's Outline of Marriage (1926), a savvy young wife instructed a professor in the ways of modern marriage. She frankly endorsed birth control, simplified housekeeping, shared housework, and paid work for women. At the same time, Dell's dialogue affirmed a romantic view of fundamental sexual differences. Circulated by the American Birth Control League, the tract sought to win support for contraception by portraying its place in respectable, "modern" marriages.

PROFESSOR: "You are married?"

YOUNG WOMAN: "Yes—very much so!" . . .

Q. "How many children have you?"

A. "Two—a boy and a girl. Their names, if you think these people would like to know, are Jack and Jill. Jack is four years, and Jill is ten months old."

Q. "How does it happen that your children have happened along so late in your marriage?"

A. "They didn't 'happen along'—that's the answer! They were planned for just that way."

Q. "But why didn't you have them earlier?"

A. "It would have spoiled everything. We aren't rich—my husband and I. We couldn't afford to be parents any sooner. . . . It's a woman's business to know how not to be caught in that biologic trap—if she wishes to control her own destiny. Knowledge is freedom."

Q. "You kept your job and were a wife at the same time. Didn't that involve a double burden?"

A. "No. We ate at restaurants for the most part—at home only when we especially wanted to. And we both helped get those meals, as if we were on a picnic. We washed the dishes together—it's fun when you do it that way."

Q. "How about his buttons? Did you keep them sewed on for him?"

A. "Not at all. He had managed about his buttons somehow before he married me. He didn't marry me to have his buttons sewed on."

Q. "What *did* he marry you for?"

A. "For love—and companionship."

Q. "Weren't you too tired after your day's work to be a good companion?"

A. "Not a bit of it. Didn't you ever hear of a working girl doing her day's work and then enjoying her evenings with her beau?"

Q. "And you didn't think it your duty to society to start right in producing babies?"

A. "What! as if there weren't enough babies in the world already! It was certainly my duty to society not to burden it with babies that couldn't be properly brought up."

Q. "But you did have babies eventually."

A. "Yes, when we could better afford to."

Floyd Dell. *The Outline of Marriage* (American Birth Control League, 1926), 57–63.

FEB 16 1926

Life

FEBRUARY 18, 1926   Teaching old Dogs new tricks   PRICE 15 CENTS

Teaching Old Dogs New Tricks
The slinky style of the flapper was celebrated in the popular press, most notably in the cartoons of John Held, Jr. Cartoons of high-stepping, bootlegging high society quickly lost their appeal, however, after the stock market crashed in 1929. *Life*, February 18, 1926 — Prints and Photographs Division, Library of Congress.

ignored women voters and women's issues. An Equal Rights Amendment (ERA) to the Constitution repeatedly failed to pass Congress, although it was the focus for many middle- and upper-class women activists. Supporters of hard-won legislation to protect women workers opposed the ERA, fearing that it would invalidate those protections. The only important legislative triumph for the women's movement in the 1920s was the Sheppard-Towner Maternity and Infancy Protection Act of 1921, which for the first time provided federal funds for health care.

Cultural habits may have changed more than politics. The popular 1920s stereotype of the "flapper"—a "new woman" who wore short, loose dresses and used cosmetics, smoked and drank in public, and embraced the sexual revolution—both mirrored and exaggerated the popular rejection of the genteel, corseted Victorian feminine ideal of the late nineteenth century. These changes did not come about overnight or affect all women equally; working-class women had pioneered some of the new attitudes before World War I. And while the 1920s brought much franker and more open discussions of sexuality, sexual behavior had probably begun to change earlier than that. Whatever the date of the change, Americans in the 1920s were waking up to the realization of a sexual revolution. One study found that women who were born after 1900 were twice as likely as those born earlier to have premarital sex. Birth control, more widely available and more reliable in the 1920s, was one force behind the change in behavior. "Rubber has revolutionized morals," declared family court judge Ben Lindsey in 1929.

African American Life in the 1920s and the Harlem Renaissance   The new consumer culture of the 1920s affected black Americans less than most other groups. Most remained poor and in the rural South. Still the Great Migration to the North continued and brought some profound changes as 824,000 African Americans left the South between 1920 and 1930. The black populations of New York, Chicago, and Cleveland more than doubled; that

of Detroit tripled. Some growth came from West Indian immigration; by 1930, 50,000 foreign-born blacks lived in New York alone. Many blacks who remained in the South moved to cities; by the end of the decade, one in five African Americans lived in a southern city, and more African American men held blue-collar jobs than farmed. These growing black communities provided the basis for a relatively prosperous black urban culture, extraordinary for its intellectual and artistic accomplishments and significant for its new political militancy.

The movement into urban and blue-collar jobs did not end discrimination. African Americans could generally get only the least attractive jobs. For example, high-paying jobs in the auto industry went almost exclusively to white workers. Henry Ford, however, pursued a different strategy and had roughly 10,000 African American employees by 1926. Ford's hiring practices were not altruistic. The African American workers his company recruited, generally through local ministers, were unusually loyal—an important consideration, given Ford's fear of unions.

As the northern black working class expanded, opportunities developed for black professionals and businesspeople, and the African American class structure became more complex. Most northern cities had a small black elite that included college-educated lawyers, doctors, and ministers who served black clienteles, along with successful musicians, saloonkeepers, and dressmakers, many of whom catered to whites. A new black middle class emerged to provide services—newspapers, drugstores, insurance, funerals—to their community. For example, Caribbean-born Vollington Bristol used his savings from working as head bellhop at Detroit's Fairfax Hotel to open a successful funeral parlor that catered to the city's booming black population. Black women's clubs, which drew on the new middle class, campaigned for community issues and became a political force in many communities.

These developments fostered a new political militancy and heightened racial pride throughout black America. African Americans who had fought in or supported World War I demanded greater democracy at home. The

"The Shame of America"

During November 1922, the NAACP ran this full-page advertisement in the *New York Times* and other newspapers, pressing for passage of an antilynching bill that had been introduced in the House of Representatives by Leonides Dyer of Missouri in 1918. Although the bill passed in the House by a two-to-one majority in 1922, southern opponents subsequently filibustered and defeated it in the U.S. Senate. *New York Times*, November 23, 1922 — American Social History Project.

"Speak, Garvey, Speak!": A Follower Recalls a Garvey Rally

Marcus Garvey's speeches often drew huge audiences, and stories of Garvey's stubborn resistance in the face of white hostility proliferated among his supporters. In an oral history interview, devotee Audley Moore remembered the Jamaican's defiant behavior at a rally in New Orleans.

Queen Mother Audley Moore: They didn't want Garvey to speak in New Orleans. We had a delegation to go to the mayor, and the next night, they allowed him to come. And we all was armed. Everybody had bags of ammunition, too. So when Garvey came in, we applauded, and the police were lined man to man along the line of each bench. So Mr. Garvey said, "My friends, I want to apologize for not speaking to you last night. But the reason I didn't was because the mayor of the city of New Orleans committed himself to act as a stooge for the police department to prevent me from speaking." And the police jumped up and said, "I'll run you in." When he did this, everybody jumped up on the benches and pulled out their guns and just held the guns up in the air and said, "Speak, Garvey, speak." And Garvey said, "As I was saying," and he went on and repeated what he had said before, and the police filed out the hall like little puppy dogs with their tails behind them. So that was radical enough. I had two guns with me, one in my bosom and one in my pocketbook, little 38 specials.

Interview done by the Oral History of the American Left, Tamiment Library, NYU, for the public radio program *Grandma Was an Activist,* producers Charlie Potter and Beth Friend.

National Association for the Advancement of Colored People (NAACP) benefited from this new spirit; by 1919, it had 91,000 members. The organization worked, largely through lobbying and the courts, for civil rights and an end to lynching. It won some victories, such as a 1927 Supreme Court decision (*Nixon v. Herndon*) that declared unconstitutional a Texas law barring blacks from voting in Democratic Party primaries. But the NAACP failed to win equal voting rights or the allegiance of most poor African Americans, who sometimes viewed it as a club for liberal whites and well-to-do blacks such as Dr. L. A. Nixon, the black El Paso doctor who brought the case against white-only primaries.

In contrast, Marcus Garvey's Universal Negro Improvement Association (UNIA) garnered massive support. Garvey founded the UNIA in his native Jamaica in 1914 and brought it to the United States two years later. The UNIA sought black nationhood and the redemption of Africa from colonialism and promoted self-help and self-respect. Garvey preached pan-Africanism, which viewed black men and women throughout the world as one people and linked the struggle for black rights outside of Africa with the fight to free Africa from colonial rule. Garvey's appeal rested on black pride.

"I Could Not Eat the Poems I Wrote"

Langston Hughes, one of the country's leading twentieth-century poets, came of age during the Harlem Renaissance, a time of great African American creativity. But as Hughes points out in this Freedomways *article, the residents of Harlem did not control the economics behind the art and music of the period.*

When I came back to New York in 1925 the Negro Renaissance was in full swing. Countee Cullen was publishing his early poems, Zora Neale Hurston, Rudolph Fisher, Jean Toomer, and Wallace Thurman were writing, Louis Armstrong was playing, Cora Le Redd was dancing, and the Savoy Ballroom was open with a specially built floor that rocked as the dancers swayed. Alain Locke was putting together *The New Negro* [an anthology of black writing]. Art took heart from Harlem creativity. Jazz filled the night air—but not everywhere—and people came from all around after dark to look upon our city within a city, Black Harlem. Had I not had to earn a living, I might have thought it even more wonderful. But I could not eat the poems I wrote. Unlike the whites who came to spend their money in Harlem, only a few Harlemites seemed to live in even a modest degree of luxury. Most rode the subway downtown every morning to work or look for work. . . .

. . . The famous night clubs were owned by whites, as were the theaters. Almost all the stores were owned by whites, and many at that time did not even (in the very middle of Harlem) employ Negro clerks. . . . Black Harlem really was in white face, economically speaking. So I wrote this poem:

> Because my mouth
> Is wide with laughter
> And my throat
> Is deep with song,
> You do not think
> I suffer after
> I have held my pain
> So long?
>
> Because my mouth
> Is wide with laughter,
> You do not hear
> My inner cry?
> Because my feet
> Are gay with dancing,
> You do not know
> I die?

Langston Hughes, *Freedomways* (1963).

"The New Negro Has No Fear"

Followers of Marcus Garvey paraded at 125th Street and Lenox Avenue in Harlem during an August 1920 Universal Negro Improvement Association (UNIA) convention. Garvey's organization enrolled a million members in hundreds of branches throughout the United States. Numerous UNIA nationalist parades brought out thousands of African Americans in support of the cause of economic and cultural independence. Schomburg Center for Research in Black Culture, New York Public Library, Astor, Lenox and Tilden Foundations.

He publicized black achievements, opposed interracial marriage, and, in a reversal of convention, looked down on light-skinned African Americans. Arguing that blacks should develop their own separate institutions and commercial enterprises, he criticized the NAACP's goal of racial integration.

Under Garvey's charismatic leadership, the UNIA attracted followers from virtually every segment of black America, especially West Indians, recent migrants to the North from the South, and members of the new black middle class. Within a few years, it had a million members in the United States as well as branches in Africa and the Caribbean. But the UNIA's success made it a target of government harassment, and mishandled finances and political infighting devastated the organization. Garvey went to prison for mail fraud in 1925 and was deported to Jamaica two years later. His removal shattered the UNIA, although his ideas remained influential.

Other political groups, including the major political parties, competed for black support. As the northern African American population grew, black votes became significant to the urban machines. Most blacks voted for Republicans, the party of Lincoln. But by maneuvering between the two parties, black political leaders won influence and patronage. In New York

City, police, fire, and other municipal departments began to hire blacks. Soon, black candidates were running for office. Oscar De Priest, the Alabama-born son of ex-slaves who was Chicago's first African American alderman, became, in 1928, the first northern black representative elected to Congress.

Postwar African American political activism was paralleled by a flowering of black culture known as the Harlem Renaissance. Reflecting the racial self-confidence nourished by the growing northern black communities, the writers and artists of the Harlem Renaissance expressed a new pride in black racial identity and heritage. "Negro life," wrote Alain Locke, who coined the phrase "the New Negro" and became the movement's leading philosopher, "is seizing its first chances for group expression and self determination." In music, poetry, novels, plays, dance, painting, sculpture, and photography, black artists and intellectuals celebrated African American spiritual and cultural traditions, rejecting white values and stereotypes.

The Crisis
Heralding the style and substance of the Harlem Renaissance, the NAACP's magazine, edited by W. E. B. DuBois, reached between 60,000 and 100,000 readers monthly. *The Crisis*, May 1929 — Schomburg Center for Research in Black Culture, New York Public Library, Astor, Lenox and Tilden Foundations.

In an era when pan-Africanism was emerging as an intellectual and political movement, some black artists looked to Africa for inspiration. Locke's writings and speeches about black culture echoed Woodrow Wilson's references during World War I to a people's need for self-determination. That theme recurred in black efforts to win liberation for colonized Africans and to identify with them. In "The Negro Speaks of Rivers," Langston Hughes, perhaps the greatest poet of the Harlem Renaissance, tied together the Euphrates, the Nile, and the Mississippi as "ancient, dusky rivers [that] I've known." Other writers, however, such as Zora Neale Hurston and Jean Toomer, concentrated instead on the folk culture of the South.

More popular African American cultural forms flourished too. Singers such as Florence Mills and Ethel Waters and dancers such as Bill Robinson traveled a growing circuit of black nightclubs, theaters, and vaudeville houses. Jazz, an immensely popular and sophisticated musical form, thrived in the developing black communities of the North. By the early 1920s, Louis Armstrong and other important New Orleans jazzmen had moved to

Chicago. Edward "Duke" Ellington moved from Washington, D.C., in 1927 to New York City and began playing at Harlem's Cotton Club.

The Culture Wars of the 1920s

With cultural change came cultural conflicts. Some pitted the city dwellers, who tended to tolerate a wider variety of behaviors (including drinking and a visible gay culture), against country folks. Protestant fundamentalists viewed modern, urban life with particular suspicion and fought against the teaching of modern ideas, including evolution, in the schools. Although associated with the rural South, fundamentalists also won strong support in the growing cities. So did the most vicious opponents of cultural change: the Ku Klux Klan, which spread hatred and spurred violence against African Americans, Jews, immigrants, and Catholics. Probably the bitterest cultural battle was played out over drinking. Antiliquor forces had won their greatest victory with the passage of the Eighteenth Amendment in 1919. But that victory proved their undoing, as widespread evasion of Prohibition increasingly led Americans to question whether "morality" could be legislated or policed.

MAP 7.2 Shift from Rural to Urban Population

The migration of Latinos and whites to areas with agricultural jobs increased population in agricultural areas in the West, Southwest, and Florida. At the same time, African American migrants from the South swelled the populations of northern and western cities.

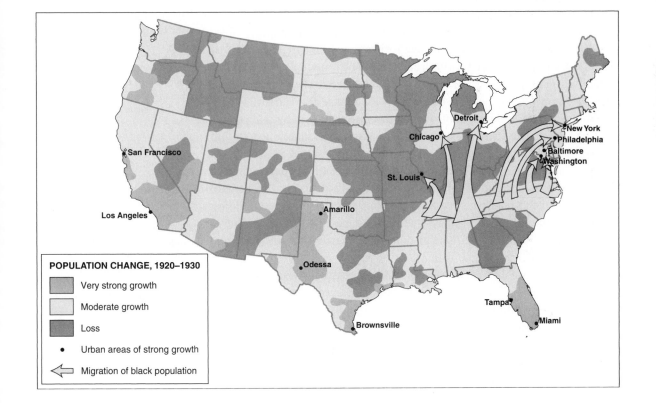

POPULATION CHANGE, 1920–1930

- Very strong growth
- Moderate growth
- Loss
- • Urban areas of strong growth
- ⇐ Migration of black population

The Urban-Rural Divide Ethnic enclaves in large cities continued to preserve old traditions and respect for family obligations. Tens of millions of Americans grew up in homes where only the children spoke English and many went to religious schools that fostered Old World traditions. As late as 1940, New York had 237 foreign-language periodicals. But although their parents bought radios to listen to the foreign-language programs, the children changed the stations and sneaked off to the movies.

Highbrow culture, too, was centered in the large cities. Many of the best-known writers of the 1920s, including Sinclair Lewis, Sherwood Anderson, and H. L. Mencken, portrayed people who lived in small towns as narrow, hypocritical, and spiritually impoverished. *Babbitt*, the title of Lewis's satirical novel about a small-town businessman, entered the language as a synonym for a narrow and self-satisfied conformist (Map 7.2).

Cities permitted behaviors and institutions that were unacceptable in small towns. Major cities such as New York became the center of an increasingly visible homosexual subculture that could be found in certain bars, tearooms, rooming houses, bathhouses, restaurants, and cafeterias, as well as in particular neighborhoods such as Greenwich Village and Harlem. Prohibition pushed gay and lesbian life further out into the open. By criminalizing drinking behavior that even many middle-class people sanctioned, Prohibition undercut conventional moral authority and fostered a set of institutions ("speakeasies") and an amusement district (Times Square) where gay men and lesbians could flaunt social convention. By the late 1920s, New York was in the throes of a "pansy craze," with drag balls that attracted thousands of spectators and Broadway plays that featured gay themes. Gladys Bentley, an openly lesbian African American performer, married her white girlfriend in a well-publicized ceremony in Atlantic City.

Not surprisingly, such transgressions against sexual and gender conventions brought a backlash. In 1927, New York police raided plays such as *The Captive* and *Sex* and arrested their casts, including the flamboyant Mae West. The New York state legislature quickly followed with a ban on plays "depicting or dealing with the subject of sex degeneracy, or sex perversion." Four years earlier, the legislature had lashed out against gay bars and "cruising" by defining homosexual solicitation as a form of disorderly

Pansy Craze

Moving uptown from Greenwich Village and downtown from Harlem, a "pansy craze" gripped New York's Broadway theater district by the close of the 1920s. Nightclubs featuring openly gay performers became the city's hottest entertainment attractions. In 1931, Jean Malin became the master of ceremonies and central attraction at the elegant Club Abbey on West 54th Street. As shown in this drawing from the stylish *Vanity Fair* magazine, the strapping, self-assured Malin (standing beside female impersonator Helen Morgan, Jr.) introduced midtowners and tourists to gay style and humor. Malin's popularity quickly led other clubs to hire imitators: "Before the main stem knew what had happened," *Variety* commented, "there was a hand on a hip for every light on Broadway." Tsugouharu Foujita, *Vanity Fair* (February 1931) — Condé Nast Publications, Inc.

"We Didn't Join American Organizations"

Joe Rudiak, a Polish American steelworker, described growing up in the ethnic enclave of Lyndora, Pennsylvania, where coal miners and steelworkers strove to maintain their cultural traditions and pass them on to their children.

And of the things my mother insisted on, education . . . was one of them. Mother insisted, with a few other families, at least to educate us [in] our own native tongue and [in] writing [at the] language schools. They formed language schools through the churches. And that was a must with most families. . . . Every day—about two hours every day— there was catechism. And during . . . school vacation we had to attend the language schools. The Polish church was a good distance away. There was the problem of shoes, clothing, and weather conditions and all that. And sure we were down a good distance away also from the public school. Mother insisted that we go to the Greek [Orthodox] church; they had the language school. When they had a problem of not having any money, we joined the Ukrainian Orthodox. So I've learned how to speak Ukrainian, but it wasn't my mother's tongue. It meant another language, which came in very handy.

We celebrated various holidays together. We did it as musicians, you see, in our family. And different churches went out caroling, and they gathered money for support of the band and their cultural activities. And this was done during Christmas. We each had costumes of our own native lands. . . . The women would have embroideries of different colors. It was beautiful, beautiful, made out of linen. It was all hand made. . . .

Since we went to the Ukrainian school, [we kids spoke Ukrainian. And] my mother spoke very good Ukrainian and my father spoke good Ukrainian because he spoke it in Europe. So there was no problem as far as learning the language [was concerned], because you got to repeat [it] at home after you came from elementary school. But when the Polish friends would come in, then it was Polish language. It just happened that most of them lived around their own churches, tried to get as close as possible to their social activities. And the church was part of their social activity.

We didn't join American organizations though. There was no drive on among the nationality people, no drive on by the politicians. You've got to understand that they didn't want these people to vote in the first place. The companies controlled the towns. They controlled the courthouse. They controlled the police. They controlled the state police, the coal mine police. There was no encouragement for people to vote up until the Depression.

John Bodnar, ed., *Workers' World* (1982).

conduct—a statute that was often interpreted to mean that all gay and lesbian gathering places were "disorderly." By the 1930s, continued legal harassment and police raids had erased gay life from public view.

Christian Fundamentalism and the Scopes Trial   Culturally conservative Americans saw the growing visibility of urban gay culture as one of many signs that cities were the source of sin, depravity, and irreligion. Many of these Americans supported a Protestant fundamentalist movement that had been gaining strength since the late nineteenth century. The movement reacted against modern urban life, modern science, and liberal Protestants who tolerated both challenges to traditional religion. The term *fundamentalist* came into use in 1909 after publication of a series of pamphlets called *The Fundamentals*, which denounced as corrupt modern scientific theories such as evolution and modern pastimes such as dancing. Intellectuals and urban Americans in the 1920s (as now) saw fundamentalism as a sign of rural backwardness and opposition to change. H. L. Mencken relentlessly mocked "the forlorn pastors who belabor half-wits in the galvanized iron tabernacles behind the railroad yards."

Yet fundamentalist and evangelical Christians had a strong presence in the cities and readily adopted modern means of communication in their proselytizing. The evangelist Aimee Semple McPherson, for example, may have started out preaching at revival meetings in tents, but by the mid-1920s, she was presiding over the spectacular Angelus Temple in Los Angeles, where tens of thousands of people heard her sermons, which were also broadcast over the radio. McPherson's success flowed not just from her message and effective use of the new technology (and her legendary beauty), but also from the incredible growth of the city of Los Angeles, which added 1.3 million new residents in the 1920s.

But if adherents of fundamentalism could be found in cities all over the country, the decade's most famous confrontation over the truth of the Bible erupted in the small southern town of Dayton, Tennessee, in 1925. There, fundamentalists, hostile to any idea that ran counter to a literal reading of the Bible, rallied against the teaching of Charles Darwin's theory that human beings shared an evolutionary link with other primates. The Tennessee legislature had recently passed a law prohibiting teaching that "man has descended from a lower order of animals." When the American Civil Liberties Union chose Dayton high school teacher John T. Scopes to defy the law intentionally as a test of its constitutionality, fundamentalists were outraged. They enlisted former secretary of state and three-time Democratic presidential candidate William Jennings Bryan to aid the prosecution. Clarence Darrow, a prominent liberal lawyer who had defended many political and criminal celebrities, headed Scopes's defense team. The trial was a

Billy Sunday
George Bellows's 1923 lithograph of William Ashley Sunday, the professional baseball player turned evangelical minister, captures the atmosphere of revival meetings during the 1920s. Preaching a return to "old-time religion," traveling evangelists such as Sunday relied on techniques that were inspired by forms of mass entertainment. George Bellows, 1923, lithograph, 9 × 16 1/2 inches — Courtesy of the Boston Public Library, Print Department. Gift of Albert H. Wiggin.

carnival of journalists and onlookers; on the street outside, vendors sold Bibles and toy monkeys.

The most famous moment in the Scopes trial came when the defense — prohibited by the judge from calling scientists to defend evolution — put Bryan on the stand as an expert on the Bible. Darrow ridiculed him before the court and the nation, forcing Bryan to admit that some biblical passages could not be interpreted literally. But Bryan's testimony had no real bearing on the case, and it exaggerated the differences between Darrow and Bryan, both of whom shared a commitment to social justice. In fact, Bryan's fundamentalism was linked to his populism. He had long opposed social Darwinism, or the application of Darwin's principle of "survival of the fittest" to human society — to struggling farmers, laborers, and small businessmen.

Both fundamentalists and scientists emerged from the trial as losers. In the face of the scorn heaped on them by intellectuals, fundamentalists retreated from political life and did not fully reenter politics until the 1980s. Scopes was convicted (although his sentence was later thrown out on a technicality), and Tennessee's antievolution law remained on the books until the 1960s. A few other states passed antievolution laws, and publishers meekly complied by removing discussions of evolution from biology textbooks sold across the nation.

An Upsurge of Racism and Nativism   Like fundamentalism, the Ku Klux Klan is also often associated with southern rural life. Yet in the 1920s, the Klan, too, had a major following in the cities. In its twentieth-century heyday, roughly half of the Klan's three million members lived in metropolitan areas. And although it had considerable support in the South, the Klan had its strongest support in the Midwest and the Southwest. Founded in 1915 and inspired by the Reconstruction-era organization of the same name, the Klan shared with its nineteenth-century namesake a deep racism, a fascination with mystical regalia, and a willingness to use violence to silence its foes. Unlike its predecessor, it professed anti-Catholicism and anti-Semitism as strongly as it affirmed racism (Map 7.3).

The intolerance and vigilantism that were prevalent during World War I had paved the way for the Klan's rise. Farmers going through hard times, underpaid workers facing competition from immigrants and African Americans, and small businessmen who were losing out to national manufacturers and chain stores all lashed out through the Klan against those they believed were threatening their economic well-being. Country dwellers resented the diminishing importance of rural virtues; city dwellers associ-

MAP 7.3   Ku Klux Klan Politics and Violence in the 1920s

Support for the Ku Klux Klan as well as Klan violence spread from the South to the Midwest and North during the 1920s.

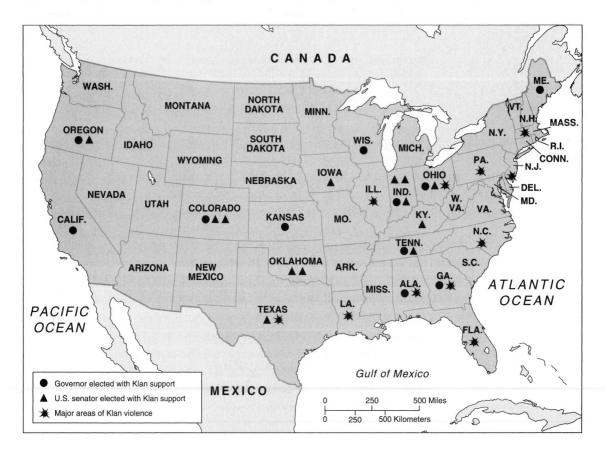

• Governor elected with Klan support
▲ U.S. senator elected with Klan support
✳ Major areas of Klan violence

White Sheets in Washington, D.C.

Forty thousand members of the Ku Klux Klan marched down Pennsylvania Avenue on August 8, 1925. Organized to counter reports of faltering enrollment, the "konklave" succeeded in attracting national attention, but it marked the peak of Klan power in the 1920s. Prints and Photographs Division, Library of Congress.

ated foreigners with gangs and crime. Old-stock urban Protestants felt displaced by Catholics and Jews, and those who remembered the Red scare were left with the suspicion that immigrants were inherently subversive.

Riding on fears of immigrants, Communists, labor unions, African Americans moving north, and Jews and Catholics rising in the economic and social order, the Klan staged parades and cross-burning rallies across the country. Klan leaders gained strong influence over state governments in Texas, Oklahoma, Oregon, Louisiana, Kansas, and especially Indiana. Within a few years, however, a series of sexual, financial, and political scandals had tainted the Klan, and political leaders in several states moved against it.

Although the Klan retreated, the cultural antagonisms that supported it remained strong and surfaced in conflicts over Prohibition. In 1919, the Eighteenth Amendment to the Constitution was ratified, making it illegal to manufacture, sell, transport, import, or export drinking alcohol. Ratification, however, did not reflect a national consensus on drinking. Although the law was not openly flaunted at first, liquor flowed into the country across U.S. borders. Bootlegging and the production of alcohol for medical and religious purposes added to the supply. Alcohol consumption did decline, perhaps by as much as half, but tens of millions of normally law-abiding Americans either broke the law or abetted those who did. Even President Harding had a favorite bootlegger. It became apparent that enforcing Prohibition would require huge police forces.

Opponents of Prohibition argued that because authorities could not enforce the law, it bred crime, corruption, and a disregard for the rule of law in general. Indeed, the vast profits to be made from illegal liquor fed

"There Was Another Unusual Feature of the Flower Shop Basement"

The criminal lawyer George Bieber's first job was in a Chicago bootlegging establishment. Throughout the country, normally law-abiding citizens often disregarded the Prohibition law. The job paid well enough, according to Bieber, to enable him to pay his college tuition.

I was fifteen when the Volstead Act [enforcing prohibition] went into effect, working in the Division Flower Shop. . . . The owners weren't interested in selling flowers. They kept a dozen bunches in the windows, but if some stranger came in and placed a big order, they'd fill it through a genuine florist nearby and send it out under the Division label. That was my job, standing around in the front of the shop and handling people who actually wanted to buy flowers.

The boss was Vincent "Schemer" Drucci. They nicknamed him that because of the wild schemes he was always thinking up to defeat the law. The real business of the Division Flower Shop was converting denatured alcohol into drinkable liquor. Drucci and his partners had first set up a hair tonic plant. This entitled them to buy No. 39B alcohol. . . .

Up to a point, the Cosmo Hair Tonic Company was legitimate. They advertised widely. . . . And they sold quite a few bottles. Not nearly as many as their books showed. To deceive the government inspectors, they would sell a few hundred cases to a friendly wholesale distributor and throw in a few hundred more as a bribe. The books would then show sales of thousands, and on the basis of such a big volume the government would allot the company corresponding amounts of 39B alcohol.

The conversion to drinkable liquor took place in the basement of the flower shop under the direction of the chemist we all called Karl the Dutchman, who was formerly employed by a toothpaste manufacturer. . . . To fake scotch, bourbon, rye, or whatever, Karl would let the rectified alcohol stand for a few weeks in charred barrels in which authentic whiskey had been aged. I would pick up those barrels from a cooperage on Lake Street. They brought enormous prices—as high as $50 or $60 a barrel. The owner's son would help me load them onto a truck, and I remember he wore a diamond ring the shape of a barrel. . . .

Some of Drucci's customers came from out of town, and if he figured a man was a shnook, he would sell him the liquor in a trick 5-gallon can. This can had a tube soldered inside to the top and bottom. Only the tube contained whiskey. The rest of the can was filled with water to give it weight, as the shnook would discover when he got it home.

There was another unusual feature of the flower shop basement— a life-size picture of a cop. The boys used it for target practice. . . .

John Kobler, *Ardent Spirits: The Rise and Fall of Prohibition* (1973).

gangsters who were also involved in prostitution and high-interest loans. With profits rolling in, these types of organized crime provided poor Italians, Jews, Poles, and Irish with a means of upward mobility. Gangster organizations grew in size, sophistication, and power, fighting to establish regional fiefdoms by using the latest technology, from fast automobiles to submachine guns. They also bought off politicians and police wholesale. In some cities, gangs became an integral part of local politics. Al Capone and other flamboyant gangsters became celebrities.

"The very fact that the law is difficult to enforce," an official of the Anti-Saloon League commented in 1926, "is the clearest proof of the need of its existence." But by then, the failure of Prohibition was obvious, especially in urban areas. Organized opposition, once confined to the unions and the liquor interests, mounted. Of nine state referenda that were held in an attempt to modify the law, the "wets" (opponents of Prohibition) won seven. Public opinion polls showed that especially in the large industrial states, wets predominated.

American Indians defended another front in the cultural wars of the 1920s. Backed by Christian missionaries, Hubert Work, secretary of the interior in the mid-1920s, attacked Indian culture and religion, especially the peyote cult, in which worshippers ingested a hallucinogen during a holy rite. Work charged that "gross immorality . . . accompanies native dances." Others lashed out at "Indian paganism" and what they described as "horrible, sadistic, and obscene" heathen practices. Defenders of Indian culture, including both Indians and white supporters, argued for reform of federal Indian policy, based on the Wilsonian principle of self-determination. Conservative critics of Indian culture labeled these defenders "Red Progressives," "anti-American, and subversive . . . agents of Moscow." Over the course of the 1920s, however, Indians won some modest concessions. In 1924, for example, Congress finally passed a law conferring citizenship on all Indians born in the United States. But many states continued to prevent Indians from voting. More far-reaching reform of the nation's Indian policy would not come until the next decade.

Conclusion: Hoover and the Crash

The urban-rural tug of war made its way into the voting booths in the 1928 presidential election. By 1928, the balance of power within the Democratic Party had shifted decisively toward the cities. New York Governor Al Smith easily won the party's presidential nomination. The contrast—at least in image—between Smith and Republican Herbert Hoover could not have been greater. Smith was an anti-Prohibition "wet," a Catholic, a product of urban, ethnic working-class life. Radio coverage of the campaign broadcast his heavy New York accent throughout the nation. Hoover stressed his boyhood in rural Iowa, professing his love for fishing and the simple, small-town life. In fact, he was a sophisticated businessman, the first president to rise to power from the ranks of the managerial elite rather than through party politics.

Prohibition was a powerful issue in the election. Smith was attacked as the candidate of foreigners and drinkers. Because many immigrants had no taboos about alcohol, the "drys" had long identified their crusade with the "100 percent Americanism" ideas of the war era and with the preservation of the American way of life. But it was probably religion, more than anything else, that shaped voting patterns in 1928. Smith

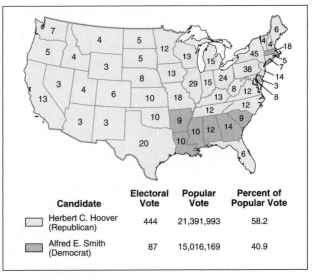

Candidate	Electoral Vote	Popular Vote	Percent of Popular Vote
Herbert C. Hoover (Republican)	444	21,391,993	58.2
Alfred E. Smith (Democrat)	87	15,016,169	40.9

MAP 7.4   Engineering a Victory: The Election of 1928

Republican presidential candidate Herbert Hoover, aided by a strong economy and religious prejudice against his Catholic opponent Al Smith, won a landslide victory in 1928, with twenty-one million votes to Smith's fifteen million. Only the deep South voted Democratic, supporting the party's long commitment to white supremacy.

faced a vicious campaign of anti-Catholic attacks, including rumors that he planned to extend the recently built Holland Tunnel across the Atlantic so that it would connect the White House with the Vatican, and that he would annul all Protestant marriages and declare all the children of these marriages to be bastards. Hoover was not only a Protestant with a rural image, he also had another basic advantage: The Republicans got credit for the nation's prosperity. With both a strong economy and religious prejudice behind him, Hoover won by a landslide, receiving 444 electoral votes to Smith's 87. Thanks to increased participation by immigrant voters, however, Smith won in the nation's twelve largest cities, marking the Democrats as the party of urban America (Map 7.4).

Hoover's victory capped his long successful career in industry, relief work, and government. But he had little time to enjoy it. Within a year, the country was plunged into a devastating depression. Hoover could not remedy the economy's fatal weakness: the tendency of industrial production to far outstrip the American people's ability to consume. The stock market crashed in October 1929. The "motor city" of Detroit — the exemplar of 1920s prosperity — soon had the highest jobless rate in the nation. By August 1931, Ford Motor Company, which employed 128,000 workers in 1929, had only 37,000 workers. By the early 1930s, Hoover's political reputation had been destroyed. The man who, along with Henry Ford, perhaps best symbolized America in the 1920s became one of the most hated men in the country. In a popular joke of the day, Hoover asked Secretary of the Treasury Mellon for a nickel — the price of a pay-phone call — to "call a friend." Mellon replied: "Take a dime; call all your friends."

The shattering of the idols of the vaunted new era — F. Scott Fitzgerald, Henry Ford, Herbert Hoover — suggested to many Americans that they would need to look in very different directions to cope with the hard times ahead.

The Years in Review

1920

- The Eighteenth Amendment is ratified, prohibiting the sale of liquor.
- Republican Warren Harding defeats James Cox for the presidency.
- Commercial radio broadcasting begins.

1921

- Congress enacts the Emergency Quota Act to control the flow of immigrants.
- Opponents of the populist Non-Partisan League oust its state officials in North Dakota.
- The Washington Conference begins negotiations on agreements to reduce naval armaments among leading powers.
- The Sheppard-Towner Maternity and Infancy Protection Act provides the first federal funds for health care.
- Economic recession hits the nation.

1922

- Some 600,000 coal miners strike and win some gains, but unions are in sharp decline.

1923

- The Ku Klux Klan, which was refounded in Atlanta in 1915, reaches its peak membership.
- The U.S. Supreme Court declares Asian Indians ineligible for U.S. citizenship.
- President Warren Harding dies; Teapot Dome and other scandals in his administration are revealed.
- The Equal Rights Amendment is introduced in Congress.
- *Time* magazine publishes its first issue.

1924

- Banker Charles Dawes brokers a plan to reduce German reparations and save the German economy; the plan fails.
- Congress enacts a law that limits new immigration to 2 percent of each nationality present in the United States in 1890; the law totally excludes the Japanese.
- Calvin Coolidge, who had succeeded Harding in 1923, is reelected president. Discontented farmers and unionists back a third-party bid by Wisconsin Senator Robert La Follette.

1925
- Alain Locke's *The New Negro* is published.
- Congress passes the McNary-Haugen bill, designed to restore the prewar relationship between farm prices and industrial prices; Coolidge vetoes it.
- A. Philip Randolph organizes the Brotherhood of Sleeping Car Porters.
- John T. Scopes is arrested in Tennessee and convicted for teaching that "man has descended from a lower order of animals."

1926
- American marines suppress the Nicaraguan nationalist rebellion led by Augusto Sandino and impose a dictatorship under General Anastasio Somoza.
- Secretary of Treasury Andrew Mellon, one of the nation's richest men, pushes through a tax cut for the wealthy.

1927
- The United States deports Marcus Garvey to Jamaica; his departure shatters the Universal Negro Improvement Association, which had won mass support after World War I.
- After making fifteen million Model Ts, Ford ceases their production and switches to the more stylish Model A.
- Charles Lindbergh completes the first nonstop solo transatlantic flight.
- The "talkies" arrive with *The Jazz Singer*.

1928
- Oscar DePriest of Illinois becomes the first black representative elected to Congress from the North.
- More than sixty nations sign the Kellogg-Briand Pact, renouncing war, but it lacks any enforcement mechanisms.
- Herbert Hoover defeats Al Smith for the presidency; Smith's Catholicism is a major factor in his defeat.
- Mickey Mouse debuts in *Plane Crazy* and *Steamboat Willie*.
- NBC premieres *Amos 'n' Andy*, a fifteen-minute comedy show that becomes the most popular program on radio.

1929
- The Agricultural Marketing Act is passed to provide price support for farm products.
- The stock market reaches speculative heights and then crashes on "Black Thursday," October 24.

Additional Readings

For more on business conservatism at home and abroad, see: George Black, *The Good Neighbor: How the United States Wrote the History of Central America and the Caribbean* (1988); Ellis W. Hawley, *The Great War and the Search for a Modern Order* (1979); Lawrence Levine, *Defender of the Faith: William Jennings Bryan: The Last Decade, 1915–1925* (1965); and Emily Rosenberg, *Spreading the American Dream: American Economic and Cultural Expansion 1890–1945* (1982).

For more on immigration restrictions, see: Roger Daniels, *Guarding the Golden Door: American Immigration Policy and Immigrants Since 1882* (2004); John Higham, *Strangers in the Land: Patterns of American Nativism, 1865–1925* (1955); Mae Ngai, *Impossible Subjects: Illegal Aliens and the Making of Modern America* (2004); David M. Reimers, *Unwelcome Strangers: American Identity and the Turn Against Immigration* (1998); and Daniel J. Tichenor, *Dividing Lines: The Politics of Immigration Control in America* (2002).

For more on the new economy and shifts in manufacturing, see: Gregg Andrews, *City of Dust: A Cement Company Town in the Land of Tom Sawyer* (1996); Alfred D. Chandler, Jr., *Scale and Scope: The Dynamics of Industrial Capitalism* (1990); Jacquelyn Dowd Hall et al., *Like a Family: The Making of a Southern Cotton Mill World* (1987); Rick Halpern, *Down on the Killing Floor: Black and White Workers in Chicago's Packinghouses, 1904–1954* (1997); Akira Iriye, *The Globalizing of America, 1914–1945* (1993); Ronald W. Schatz, *The Electrical Workers: A History of Labor at General Electric and Westinghouse, 1923–1960* (1983); and Zaragosa Vargas, *Proletarians of the North: A History of Mexican Industrial Workers in Detroit and the Midwest, 1917–1942* (1993).

For more on the expansion of American consumer culture and transformations in daily life, see: Ronald William Edsforth, *Class Conflict and Cultural Consensus: The Making of a Mass Consumer Society in Flint, Michigan* (1987); Stuart Ewen, *Captains of Consciousness: Advertising and the Social Roots of Consumer Culture* (1976); T. J. Jackson Lears, *Fables of Abundance: A Cultural History of Advertising in America* (1994); Robert Lynd and Helen Lynd, *Middletown: A Study in Modern American Culture* (1929); Roland Marchand, *Advertising the American Dream: Making Way for Modernity, 1920–1940* (1985); and Nathan Miller, *New World Coming: The 1920s and the Making of Modern America* (2003).

For more on mass culture, radio, music, and the movies, see: Lizabeth Cohen, *Making a New Deal: Industrial Workers in Chicago, 1919–1939* (1990);

Tona J. Hangen, *Redeeming the Dial: Radio, Religion, and Popular Culture in America* (2002); David Nasaw, *Going Out: The Rise and Fall of Public Amusements* (1993); Steven J. Ross, *Working-Class Hollywood: Silent Films and the Shaping of Class in America* (2000); Robert Sklar, *Movie-Made America: A Cultural History of American Movies* (1976); and Susan Smulyan, *Selling Radio: The Commercialization of American Broadcasting, 1920–1934* (1994).

For more on women as workers and consumers, see: Susan Porter Benson, *Counter Cultures: Saleswomen, Managers, and Customers in American Department Stores, 1890–1940* (1986); Irving Bernstein, *The Lean Years: A History of the American Worker, 1920–1933* (1960); Julia Kirk Blackwelder, *Now Hiring: The Feminization of Work in the United States, 1900–1995* (1997); William H. Chafe, *The American Woman: Her Changing Social, Economic, and Political Role, 1920–1970* (1972); Nancy F. Cott, *The Grounding of Modern Feminism* (1987); Dana Frank, *Purchasing Power: Consumer Organizing, Gender, and the Seattle Labor Movement, 1919–1929* (1994); David M. Katzman, *Seven Days a Week: Women and Domestic Service in Industrializing America* (1981); Alice Kessler-Harris, *Out to Work: A History of Wage-Earning Women in the United States* (1982); Angel Kwolek-Folland, *Incorporating Women: A History of Women and Business in the United States* (1998); and Leslie Woodcock Tentler, *Wage-Earning Women: Industrial Work and Family Life in the United States, 1900–1930* (1979).

For more on African American life in the 1920s and the Harlem Renaissance, see: Beth Tompkins Bates, *Pullman Porters and the Rise of Protest Politics in Black America, 1925–1945* (2001); Kevin Boyle, *Arc of Justice: A Saga of Race, Civil Rights, and Murder in the Jazz Age* (2004); Genevieve Fabre and Michel Feith, eds., *Temples for Tomorrow: Looking Back at the Harlem Renaissance* (2001); William H. Harris, *The Harder We Run: Black Workers Since the Civil War* (1982); Nathan Huggins, *Harlem Renaissance* (1971); David Krasner, *A Beautiful Pageant: African American Theatre, Drama, and Performance in the Harlem Renaissance, 1910–1927* (2002); David Levering Lewis, *When Harlem Was in Vogue* (1989); Neil McMillan, *Dark Journey: Black Mississippians in the Age of Jim Crow* (1989); Theodore Rosengarten, *All God's Dangers: The Life of Nate Shaw* (1975); and Judith Stein, *The World of Marcus Garvey: Race and Class in Modern Society* (1985).

For more on the culture wars of the 1920s, see: Douglas Carl Abrams, *Selling the Old-Time Religion: American Fundamentalists and Mass Culture, 1920–1940* (2001); Stanley Coben, *Rebellion Against Victorianism: The Impetus for Cultural Change in 1920s America* (1991); Lynn Dumenil, *The Modern*

Temper: American Culture and Society in the 1920s (1995); Edward J. Larson, *Summer for the Gods: The Scopes Trial and America's Continuing Debate over Science and Religion* (1997); Allan J. Lichtman, *Prejudice and the Old Politics: The Presidential Election of 1928* (1979); and George S. Marsden, *Fundamentalism in American Culture* (1980).

8

The Great Depression
and the First New Deal

1929–1935

Detroit, July 1930

During the Depression, unemployment struck the nation's large industrial cities with particular ferocity. In Detroit, automobile production dropped by half. Nearly one-third of all families there had no breadwinner. This unemployed worker took to the streets in search of work. Milton (Pete) Brooks, July 1930, *Detroit News*—Detroit News.

"WE IN AMERICA TODAY are nearer to the final triumph over poverty than ever before in the history of any land. We shall soon . . . be in sight of the day when poverty will be banished from this nation," assured Herbert Hoover as he accepted the Republican nomination for president in 1928. Apparently, the people agreed, for Hoover won by a wide margin that November.

But within a year, the new president would preside over an economic crisis that proved to be the most severe test of the American people and their institutions since the Civil War. On "Black Thursday"—October 24, 1929—the Wall Street stock market crashed. In the next seven days, panicked American investors lost more money than the U.S. government had spent fighting World War I. At the time, many traders and economists considered the market plunge a healthy response to rampant speculation, which had continued despite a decline in industrial production that had begun several months earlier. But none of these experts thought that the 1929 Wall Street crash would signal the onset of a major depression.

They were wrong. The worldwide, decade-long Great Depression struck the United States like a biblical plague, shuttering factories, closing banks, foreclosing on farms, and putting as many as one out of three workers on the street. Mass unemployment and economic insecurity lasted for a full decade, searing the memory and transforming the politics of an entire generation. By 1931, the Depression had spread to Europe and East Asia, where it rocked political institutions and fueled the growth of mass movements that were hostile to liberal capitalism: on the left, communism and socialism; on the right, an even more powerful surge toward militarism, fascism, and ethnocentric nationalism. In the United States, the Depression did not overturn the government or threaten the nation's constitutional democracy, but it did strike a blow at the prestige and power of those who had long considered themselves the nation's elite. The big banks, the big corporations, and the old Protestant upper class had failed to sustain the very prosperity of which they had boasted.

With popular faith in the old laissez-faire order shaken, new ideas and new forces moved to the forefront. Progressive era prescriptions for a new economy, society, and state transformed the United States in the 1930s, making the New Deal the fulcrum on which the history of twentieth-century America turns. This chapter traces the onset of the Depression and the "first" New Deal to 1935. The devastation and experimentation that characterized this five-year period set the stage for the construction of a new political and social order that fundamentally overhauled the United States.

The Onset of the Great Depression

Although the vast majority of Americans owned no stock, few escaped the social impact of the 1929 market crash. Unemployment jumped from fewer than 500,000 workers to more than four million between October and December 1929. Millions more could find only part-time work. Average real wages fell 16 percent in just two years. The effects of the stock market crash spread beyond the borders of the United States. Because New York served as the center of world capitalism, the Wall Street crash sent tremors throughout the shaky system that had emerged after World War I. Banks failed and unemployment soared throughout the industrial world.

As factories and banks closed (Figure 8.1), many politicians and experts still believed that the American economy was sound and the downturn was temporary. "Let the slump liquidate itself," asserted Andrew Mellon, Hoover's ultraconservative secretary of the treasury. Mellon predicted that the economy would right itself if government did not worry too much about the human cost: "Values will be adjusted, and enterprising people will pick up the wrecks from less competent people." But in mid-1931, the economy took another sickening plunge, and by the spring of 1933, fifteen million people—nearly one of every four wage-earners—could not find jobs. Between 1929 and 1933, the gross national product, the sum of all the goods and services produced in the country, fell 29 percent. Many cities went broke. Detroit and Chicago paid their employees in paper scrip—government IOUs. In the West, mining and ranching suffered. Four-fifths of all

FIGURE 8.1 Going Bust: Business Failures, 1929–1945

Bankruptcies, already high in the late 1920s, peaked in 1932, the nadir of the Depression. Although unemployment stayed high, New Deal measures stabilized the business economy. Business failures almost vanished during the prosperous years of World War II.

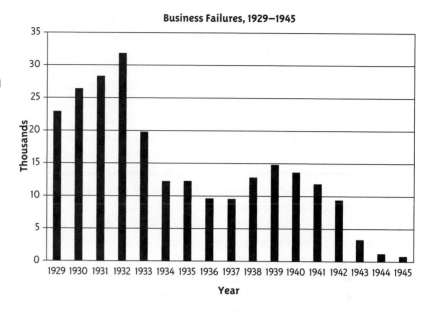

Arizona miners were out of work by 1933. The collapse of the copper industry sent a shock wave across the state, forcing the railroads to lay off 8,000 workers and crippling business in numerous small towns and cities.

The government itself, through the Federal Reserve Board, had fueled Wall Street's frenzied speculation during the late 1920s by keeping interest rates low. Cheap money spurred the building boom of the 1920s, but it also enabled many investors to buy huge amounts of stock "on margin." In effect, they had borrowed against the shares' value and had used that borrowed money to purchase additional shares. While the market soared, investors made tremendous profits; but when it declined, brokerage firms called in their loans, which often amounted to 90 percent of the stock's value at its highest price, and investors lost their entire stake. The Federal Reserve eventually raised interest rates but only after the stock market crash. High rates during the Depression put enormous pressure on the banking system, especially on unstable rural banks and ethnic savings and loans. Uninsured by either state or federal authorities, more than five thousand of these smaller financial institutions failed during the first three years of the Great Depression. Nine million people lost their savings accounts.

Even with all these difficulties, the Great Depression might well have ended in the early 1930s had it not been for the simultaneous collapse of the international economic system. In an atmosphere of spreading panic, nations sought to defend their own economies at the expense of their trading partners. The United States, for example, passed the Smoot-Hawley Tariff in 1930, which raised import duties to the highest levels in our history. The United States sought to protect its farmers from international competition; the result was disaster, as other countries retaliated by increasing their own tariffs. World trade plunged, devastating markets for U.S. farmers and manufacturing jobs for U.S. workers.

The economic ruin of Europe due to World War I made the new economic system particularly vulnerable. Europeans still owed massive war debts to one another and to the United States. They could make payments on those debts only because U.S. banks lent billions of dollars to Germany. That country, in turn, passed the money on to Britain, France, and Belgium in the form of reparations, as stipulated in the Treaty of Versailles (see Chapter 6). These former allies then returned the money to the United States as payments on their war debts. The money flowed back and forth across the Atlantic in a continuous cycle.

The stock market crash halted the American loans. Germany defaulted on its reparation payments to France and Britain, whose governments then stopped paying their American debts. Central European banks, dependent on the American loans, went bankrupt, and an atmosphere of economic crisis spread across Europe. In Germany, as unemployment rolls soared, Adolf Hitler's National Socialist Party (Nazis) grew in power. Hard-pressed European investors sold their American stocks to raise cash, further depressing the U.S. stock market. Some European nations also lowered the value of their currency by abandoning the once sacrosanct gold standard; their paper money could no longer be exchanged for gold at a fixed price. But the United States clung to the gold standard, which made expensive American goods increasingly difficult to sell in world markets.

Hard Times

While the international monetary crisis played itself out, bread lines, soup kitchens, and desperate apple vendors became familiar features of the large cities in the United States. In Colorado, more than half of all schoolchildren were undernourished. With inadequate diets came a rise in dysentery, tuberculosis, pellagra, and typhoid. In the fall of 1930, one New Jerseyite wrote to President Hoover, "Can not you find a quicker way of executing us than to starve us to death?" Joblessness struck hardest in large cities, in single-industry towns, in the Northeast and the Midwest, and among male blue-collar workers, both black and white. As unemployment rose, so did racism and sexism. Mexican Americans, Asian Americans, African Americans, and working women all faced increased joblessness, discrimination, and hostility in the workplace. For rural Americans, a multiyear drought compounded Depression miseries with failed crops and dust storms that forced thousands off their land. Material deprivation was only part of the human cost of the Depression. The psychological strains were severe, too. Almost everyone felt insecure. Those who had jobs feared losing them;

FIGURE 8.2 Depressing the Birthrate

Malnourishment, economic necessity, and declining marriage rates slowed the growth of families during the Depression. Birthrates had been declining throughout the early twentieth century—in part, a continuation of a long-term demographic shift away from the high birthrates that were characteristic of a more rural society. But they fell even further with the onset of the Great Depression, especially in the dark years of the early 1930s. After 1933, families began to have more children as the economy slowly recovered. In 1946, there was a sharp increase—the first sign of the postwar baby boom.

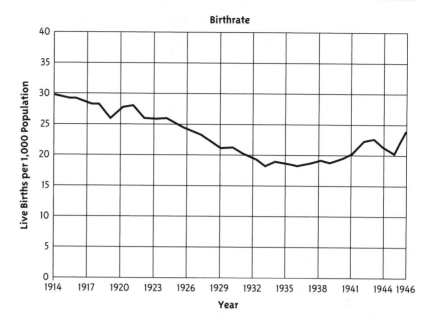

those without work worried about what would become of their families. In the early years of the Depression, people generally blamed themselves for their troubles (Figure 8.2).

The Curse of Unemployment In the months following the stock market crash, joblessness spread across the country. In Detroit and Pittsburgh, mass unemployment followed the collapse in production of automobiles and steel. California escaped the high levels of joblessness until 1932, but in that year, the ripples of distress that had begun in the East finally affected employment in agriculture, food processing, shipping, and real estate in California. Joblessness did not hit the South as hard as the North but only because southern manufacturers slashed wages and prices in a vain effort to capture an even larger slice of the continually shrinking market in textiles, cigarettes, lumber, and other labor-intensive goods. In the nation as a whole, white-collar workers in retail and wholesale trade, communications, banking, and insurance fared somewhat better than blue-collar workers. Fewer government employees than private sector workers lost their jobs (Figure 8.3).

The country's largest manufacturing firms tried to retain their experienced workers by spreading the work around. At General Electric Company, one worker remembered, "They'd just say, 'You come in Monday. Take the rest of the week off.'" Some companies fired unskilled workers and gave skilled workers their jobs, at lower pay rates. By reducing hours and reassigning jobs, Westinghouse Electric Corporation managed to retain almost all employees with more than ten years' seniority at its huge East Pittsburgh plant.

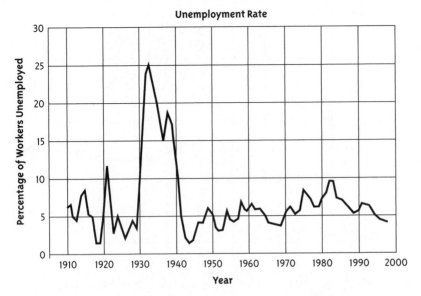

Unemployment Rate

FIGURE 8.3   U.S. Unemployment during the Great Depression

A much higher proportion of all workers were without jobs during the Great Depression than at any other time in the twentieth century. Joblessness declined sharply after 1933, but prospects for an end to the Depression evaporated in 1937 and 1938 as Roosevelt's cuts to public work projects and the promised business recovery failed to maintain jobs.

But most construction companies and smaller manufacturers could not afford to retain excess workers, even part time. Between 1929 and 1933, employment in the construction trades dropped by more than 80 percent. People without money bought neither new houses nor new clothes, further contributing to the downward economic spiral. At one point, only 10 percent of the members of the Amalgamated Clothing Workers' Union in New York City had work.

This great crisis forced Americans onto the road. Many people, employed and unemployed, fell behind on their rent or mortgage payments and lost their homes. By 1932, a quarter of a million youths under age twenty-one (as well as many of their older counterparts) had left home in search of work or shelter, hitching rides or hopping freight trains in what one government agency called a "migration of despair." Kay, an undernourished fifteen-year-old, told an investigator, "Dad hasn't worked steady for four years. Sis, for two. Mother got a job scrubbing—$7 a week, and that's all we had to live on except for some clothes we got from a lodge. . . . There wasn't much else for me to do but go."

The Hardest Hit   As millions of men lost their jobs, working women, especially if they were married, faced some of the greatest wrath. Many people agreed with "A Good Citizen" who wrote to the president: "I know that something can be done about the married women. . . . They have no right taking the jobs and positions of single girls, single men, and married men." People assumed that married women worked only to make "pin money." That was rarely the case, but when layoffs occurred, even progressives thought that married women should be the first to go. Both New

No Laughing Matter

"Mama," runs the caption of this illustration published in the December 12, 1930, issue of *Life* magazine, "it's so nice to have Daddy home all the time now." More than a year after the stock market crash, the situation was too grim a subject to lampoon, even for this magazine that favored arch commentary and collegiate humor. *Life* soon became another victim of the Depression and folded in 1936; Henry Luce quickly adopted its name for his new photojournalism magazine. Victor Anderson, *Life*, December 12, 1930—American Social History Project.

England Telephone and Telegraph and the Northern Pacific Railroad fired all married women in 1931. Most cities banned married women from teaching. Even the American Federation of Labor, which had hundreds of thousands of female members, proposed that "preference of employment" be given to "those upon whom family or dependency rests," by which they meant men.

Millions of women, many the sole support of their children, lived on the edge of destitution. When women could find jobs, employers routinely paid them less than men, even for the same work. Because of irregular employment—for example, women worked an average of only twenty-six to thirty-five weeks a year in the garment, glove, and textile industries— women earned roughly half as much as men. As their household income shrank, women's unpaid work at home greatly expanded. Whereas once they might have bought new clothes, now they darned socks, shortened pants, let out waistlines, and hemmed dresses. Finally, the Depression imposed one more cost on working women: it diminished their opportunity to improve their job status. White women had rapidly entered

"Where Do They Go?"

Meridel LeSueur, poet and journalist, described the plight of unemployed women, of which she was one, in the worst years of the Depression. In the 1930s, women, especially single women with families, experienced some of the greatest difficulties, and resources for the specific needs of women went largely unrecognized by the relief agencies and the public. Jungle was a common term for a homeless encampment.

It's one of the great mysteries of the city where women go when they are out of work and hungry. There are not many women in the bread line. There are no flop houses for women as there are for men, where a bed can be had for a quarter or less. You don't see women lying on the floor at the mission in the free flops. They obviously don't sleep in the jungle or under newspapers in the park. There is no law I suppose against their being in these places but the fact is they rarely are.

Yet there must be as many women out of jobs in cities and suffering extreme poverty as there are men. What happens to them? Where do they go? Try to get into the Y.W.[C.A.] without any money or looking down at the heel. Charities take care of very few and only those that are called "deserving." The lone girl is under suspicion by the virgin women who dispense charity.

I've lived in cities for many months broke, without help, too timid to get in bread lines. I've known many women to live like this until they simply faint on the street from privation, without saying a word to anyone. A woman will shut herself up in a room until it is taken away from her, and eat a cracker a day and be as quiet as a mouse so there are no social statistics concerning her.

Meridel LeSueur, *Women on the Breadlines* (1984).

---

white-collar office and sales work between 1910 and 1930, but in the 1930s, their upward mobility came to a halt.

Women were by no means the only group facing joblessness and discrimination. The deteriorating situation also fed a rise in racial and ethnic tensions at the workplace. Many employers and white workers insisted that native-born white workers receive preference in employment. Mexican Americans were among the foremost victims of this revived racism. In California, joblessness and the migration of white Americans — "Anglos" — from other parts of the country mushroomed at the same time that agricultural production declined, swelling the pool of desperate agricultural workers. By 1933, two people competed for every available job on California farms. In such cases, Anglos routinely got the job, even though growers themselves had recruited many of the Mexicans.

Nearly 500,000 Mexican nationals and their U.S.-born children returned to Mexico either voluntarily or by force during the Depression. Mexicans from agricultural areas emigrated in greater numbers than those

"And Then We Were in California"

Cesar Chavez's father owned a small plot of land in Arizona until a bank foreclosed on his loan. Then he and his family, like thousands of others propelled by the hard times, streamed into California to become migrant farm workers. In the mid-1930s when labor was plentiful, wages were extremely low, and discrimination against Mexican Americans was growing. Many years later, Chavez helped to found the United Farm Workers' Union.

We all of us climbed into an old Chevy that my dad had. And then we were in California, and migratory workers. There were five kids—a small family by those standards. . . . I was about eight. Well, it was a strange life. We had been poor, but we knew every night there was a bed there, and that this was our room. There was a kitchen. It was sort of a settled life, and we had chickens and hogs, eggs, and all those things. But that all of a sudden changed. When you're small you can't figure these things out. . . .

"Following the crops," we missed much school. Trying to get enough money to stay alive the following winter, the whole family picking apricots, walnuts, prunes. We were pretty new, we had never been migratory workers. We were taken advantage of quite a bit by the labor contractor and the crew pusher. . . .

We got hooked on a real scheme once. We were going by Fresno on our way to Delano. We stopped at some service station and this labor contractor saw the car. He offered a lot of money. We went. We worked the first week: the grapes were pretty bad and we couldn't make much. We all stayed off from school in order to make some money. Saturday we were to be paid and we didn't get paid. He came and said the winery hadn't paid him. We'd have money next week. He gave us $10. My dad took the $10 and went to the store and bought $10 worth of groceries. So we worked another week and in the middle of the second week, my father was asking him for his last week's pay, and he had the same excuse. This went on and we'd get $5 or $10 or $7 a week for about four weeks. For the whole family.

So one morning my father made the resolution no more work. If he doesn't pay us, we won't work. We got in a car and went over to see him. The house was empty. He had left. The winery said they had paid him and they showed us where they had paid him. This man had taken it.

Studs Terkel, *Hard Times* (1970).

living in U.S. cities, so by 1940, most Mexican Americans lived in urban areas. Several states encouraged emigration by barring noncitizens from employment on public works projects, and many local governments and private relief agencies offered free rail fare to the Mexican border for those who were willing to leave. In Michigan, Detroit's Mexican population dropped by three-quarters after state officials transported "welfare cases" to

Hooverville, 1933
Homeless Americans built squatter camps, such as this Seattle, Washington, settlement in 1933, and named them after President Herbert Hoover as testimony to his inadequate response to hard times. J. Lee, March 30, 1933—no. 20102, Special Collections Division, University of Washington Libraries.

the Mexican border. In Chicago, relief authorities organized a massive repatriation campaign among Chicano steelworkers.

Economic competition also provoked a new wave of anti-Asian racism. Hard-working Chinese Americans had long dominated the laundry business in New York and other large cities, where such small enterprises provided one of the few opportunities for employment. During the 1920s, other Americans began opening large-scale steam laundries, complete with mechanized washing machines and steam presses. Competition between these large operations and the small hand laundries (usually owned and operated by a single individual or family) increased dramatically during the Depression. When Chinese American launderers in New York refused to abide by a minimum price scheme set by a citywide laundry organization in 1932, the trade association organized a massive boycott of Chinese-owned establishments.

African Americans Face the Depression   Like Chinese Americans, African Americans were poor to begin with, but the Great Depression made their plight worse. African American workers tended to work in the industries that were most affected by the economic downturn: unskilled manufacturing, construction, mining, and lumber. White workers displaced black ones in many of these difficult, low-status jobs, reversing much of the progress African Americans had made in moving into industrial work.

Leaving Los Angeles Involuntarily
The Mexican population of Los Angeles increased from 34,000 to 97,000 over the 1920s. But the mass unemployment and growing discrimination of the 1930s led to the forced repatriation of tens of thousands as Los Angeles officials and federal agencies initiated schemes to return immigrants to Mexico. A highly publicized sweep took place at Los Angeles Plaza in February 1931. The Mexican government also aided the repatriation campaign. Most returnees left by rail, such as these men, women, and children who gathered at Los Angeles's Union Station on May 9, 1932. *Herald Examiner* Collection, Los Angeles Public Library.

Employers sometimes used drastic measures to oust black workers. Atlanta hotels had African American bellhops arrested on trumped-up charges so that their jobs could be given to white men. In Milwaukee, white workers at the Wehr Steel Foundry struck, demanding that their African American coworkers be fired. Depression era joblessness drove hundreds of thousands of African Americans to the brink of starvation. After surveying conditions in Cleveland, where unemployment plagued half the workers in the largest African American ghetto, one observer worried that "the race is standing on a precipice of economic disaster."

In the South, where three-quarters of the African American population still lived, a bitter drought in the summer of 1930 compounded the misery that was engendered by rock-bottom cotton and tobacco prices. Red Cross investigators who were sent to the parched areas reported that both black and white families suffered from hunger, but racist fears prevented a quick response. Community leaders, fearful that African American day laborers would refuse to pick the cotton if there was any other way to put food on the table, refused to start relief programs before the fall harvest. Racial tensions rose, and violence by planters increased. For the first time in a decade, lynchings of African Americans increased; twenty-four were killed in 1932 alone.

The Land That Flew Away

In rural America, a terrible drought compounded Depression miseries. At first, the weather was most severe in the East, but then the dry spell moved to the Great Plains, where temperatures reached 118 degrees Fahrenheit in 1934. Normal rainfall did not return until 1941. Farm income plummeted between 1929 and 1932 as wheat prices sank 50 percent and the price of raw cotton fell by more than two-thirds. Many farmers did not even bother to harvest the crops they had planted. Although farm families could provide some of their own food, they earned too little cash to meet mortgage payments, service loans, or pay their taxes. Hundreds of thousands of families lost their farms. During just two years in Iowa County, Iowa, a once-prosperous corn-growing area, banks auctioned off one of every eight farms. "[We are] worked to death with no income, no leisure, no pleasure, and no hope of anything better," wrote an Indiana farm wife to the secretary of agriculture. "We are a sick and sorry people. . . . My nearest neighbor has turned bootlegger, I can smell the mash brewing in his still."

With the drought came a terrifying series of dust storms. Clouds of dirt reaching to eight thousand feet rolled across the Plains states, sometimes accompanied by thunder, lightning, and powerful winds. A March 1935 storm carried off twice the amount of dirt excavated in building the Panama Canal, in the process destroying half the wheat crop in Kansas and the entire harvest in Nebraska. Some children who were caught outside in the dust storms died of suffocation in the yard-high dirt drifts. Dust made its way into homes, beds, food, and clothes and destroyed crops,

Dust Storm
A wall of dirt and sand descended on Spearman, Texas, on August 14, 1935. Franklin D. Roosevelt Library.

livestock, and a whole way of life. The worst-hit area was dubbed the Dust Bowl (Map 8.1).

Dry weather caused the Dust Bowl, but the destructive way in which farmers had been cultivating the land compounded the weather's effects. When farmers began settling in the southern plains in the 1890s, they plowed up the grasses that had kept the topsoil in place. The region had experienced droughts before, but the dry spell that hit in the 1930s, combined with the new cultivation patterns, generated a human-made ecological catastrophe that coincided with a massive exodus of residents of the southern plains, known as the "Okie" or "Dust Bowl" migration to California.

John Steinbeck's 1939 novel *The Grapes of Wrath* (and the popular film made from it) reinforced the mistaken view that the migrants all fled the dust. While 16,000 farmers did flee the Dust Bowl, about 400,000 people migrated west. They came from a wider area of the Southwest and migrated

MAP 8.1 Dust Bowl

Many people saw the dust storms as a natural disaster, but the more fundamental problem was rooted in destructive farming practices on the Great Plains. When drought hit the region in the early 1930s, farmers from across the plains suffered the loss of crops and their land and homes.

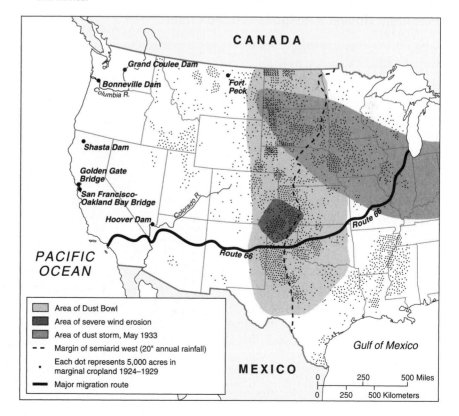

On the Road

Their worldly possessions piled on two rundown vehicles, this migrant family paused en route to California in February 1936. Dorothea Lange, 1936—Prints and Photographs Division, Library of Congress.

for a variety of reasons, including not only drought, but also the drop in agricultural prices and the growing mechanization of midwestern agriculture that eliminated the need for a large rural labor force.

President Hoover's Response to the Crisis

When the Depression struck, few Americans expected the federal government to take dramatic action, for its reach was weak and tenuous. Washington, D.C., was still a sleepy, segregated southern town where, in an era before air-conditioning, offices shut early during the steamy summer months. The government had barely 750,000 civilian and military employees (compared with more than five million today). Only one federal agency touched the lives of most Americans: the Post Office. The federal government had no military draft and no aid for cities, schools, farmers, or the unemployed. The annual national budget was only $4 billion—less than 5 percent of the entire gross domestic product. Only the very rich paid income taxes. Yet President Herbert Hoover seemed to exemplify all that was modern, efficient, and humane in American politics and social thought. Hoover embodied the Horatio Alger

Fundamentally the Ship Was Sound

New Yorker cartoonist Richard Decker commented on the obstinate outlook of conservative business leaders in the face of the nation's mounting economic and social crisis. Richard Decker, *The New Yorker*, March 5, 1932—Copyright 1932, The New Yorker Magazine, Inc.

Of course WE CAN DO IT!

- We dug the Panama Canal, didn't we? And they said we couldn't do that.

- We put an army in France four months after we entered the World War, didn't we? And surprised the world.

- Now we've got a tough one to crack right here in our own back yard.

Men are out of work. Our men. Our neighbors. Our citizens. Honest, hard-working folk.

They want jobs. They're eager to work. But there aren't jobs enough to go 'round. Somebody's got to tide them over.

Who's going to do it? The people who dug that ditch. The people who went to France, or bought Liberty Bonds, or went without sugar—Mr. and Mrs. John K. American.

That means you—and *you*—and Y O U!—every one of us who is lucky enough to have a job.

We're going to share our luck with the folks out of work, aren't we? Remember—there's no National fund they can turn to for relief. It's up to us! And we've got to dig deeper than we did last winter.

But if we all dig deep enough we can keep a roof over every head, food in every pantry, fuel on every fire, and warm clothing on every needy man, woman and child in America.

That will beat Old Man Depression and lead the way to better days. Can we do it? Of course we can do it. Give . . . and give generously.

WHERE TO GIVE: There is no National Agency through which you may contribute. The way for you to give is through your *local* welfare and relief organizations, through your Community Chest or through your emergency unemployment committee if you have one.

THE PRESIDENT'S ORGANIZATION ON UNEMPLOYMENT RELIEF

Walter S. Gifford *Director*
(WALTER S. GIFFORD)

COMMITTEE ON MOBILIZATION OF RELIEF RESOURCES

Owen D. Young *Chairman*
(OWEN D. YOUNG)

● The President's Organization on Unemployment Relief is non-political, and non-sectarian. Its purpose is to aid local welfare and relief agencies everywhere to provide for local needs. All facilities for the nation-wide program, including this advertisement, have been furnished to the Committee without cost.

Stiff Upper Lip

Rather than calling for the creation of federal relief programs, this 1931 advertisement placed by the President's Organization on Unemployment Relief opted for local voluntary charity as a response to the Depression. Hoover firmly believed that relief was a local responsibility. *Literary Digest*, November 21, 1931—American Social History Project.

myth of self-sufficiency and believed in voluntary cooperation and local relief, not federal intervention. But as the Depression years rolled on, the limits of self-help became painfully evident. In response to a growing sense of crisis and mass protests, the federal government would assume new powers and responsibilities that would never be relinquished.

A Small Role for the Federal Government Faced with America's economic collapse, President Hoover thought that the primary role of the federal government should be to coordinate private, state, and local relief and recovery efforts rather than to launch major initiatives. The key to recovery, he believed, was restoring business confidence, which meant keeping the budget in balance and avoiding any direct effort to regulate business or stimulate consumer demand. Hoover assured Americans that the economic crisis in Europe and the breakdown of international trade and monetary relations had caused the nation's dilemma. The U.S. economy itself was "on a sound and prosperous basis" and would soon recover. The president did succeed in winning a one-year moratorium on intergovernmental debt reparations payments, but he failed to achieve the broader agreements that he felt were necessary to restore world trade. In May 1931, he told an Indianapolis audience that the idea that the nation could get out of the Depression through congressional action was no different from the belief that one could "exorcise a Caribbean hurricane by statutory law."

Hoover was an activist in comparison with most of his predecessors, who believed that the federal government had no legitimate role to play when the nation faced a financial panic or economic slump. He set about encouraging the kind of voluntary cooperation among businessmen, farmers, and local governments that he had championed during World War I and his years as commerce secretary in the 1920s. At his request, some major corporations held off wage cuts to maintain consumers' spending power. In cities and towns throughout the nation, local leaders organized a host of presidentially endorsed business committees to promote relief and recovery through voluntary private action. Charitable giving reached record levels, though never enough to alleviate mass unemployment. Hoover responded to the crisis of the agricultural economy, which preceded the stock market crash, by winning passage of the Agricultural Marketing Act of 1929. That legislation made available $500 million for loans to marketing cooperatives, which, in theory, would foster efficiency, limit surpluses, and raise prices. But the unprecedented government effort to bring order to the agricultural sector foundered on Hoover's voluntarist philosophy: The Marketing Act failed to provide the government with the authority to limit production, so farm prices continued to fall.

Hoover also supported other unprecedented, but equally inadequate, measures in answer to the growing economic crisis. He sharply increased spending on public works to $700 million, an unheard-of sum at the time. Government-paid workers began building Boulder Dam and constructing thousands of miles of highway. Hoover set up the Reconstruction Finance Corporation (RFC) to provide billions of dollars in loans to failing banks and businesses. And when drought swept the agricultural South, he authorized direct federal aid to farmers. But Hoover's activism coexisted uneasily with a persistent conservatism that limited his effectiveness. The RFC gave most of its loans to larger and healthier banks and corporations and favored the kind of public works, such as toll bridges, that paid for themselves. And when RFC spending raised the federal deficit, the president won passage of the Revenue Act of 1932, increasing taxes (and hence reducing purchasing power).

Hoover was also a stubborn moralist when it came to the relief of hunger and unemployment. Refusing to commit federal funds to supply basic needs, Hoover argued that local entities should provide relief. Federal involvement, he believed, would strike at "the roots of self-government" and destroy the "character" of its recipients. Such thinking led him to endorse a $45 million appropriation to feed the livestock of Arkansas farmers during a 1930 drought but to reject a congressional grant of $25 million to provide food for the farmers' families. Hogs and bankers, it seemed, were in one category, farmers and the unemployed in another.

The Failure of Local Relief and the Limits of Self-Help   Hoover's program proved clearly inadequate. In 1932, only eight American states had any form of unemployment compensation, and few workers received retirement pensions from their employers. Worse, many relief agencies treated the poor as if personal failings had caused their plight, requiring applicants to submit to humiliating interviews before receiving aid. When provided, relief often took the form of "food orders" that could be used only to

Interviewed on Unemployment

The December 1930 edition of the League for Industrial Democracy's *The Unemployed* presented three business perspectives on the unemployment "problem." Art Young, *The Unemployed*, December 1930—American Social History Project.

Interviewed On Unemployment

J. Egbert Haggle, prominent Chicago packer, is encouraging a movement for the rich to devote two minutes of silent meditation before beginning their Christmas dinners. "This should cheer up the unemployed by letting them know they are being thought about," Mr. Haggle said.

Salomon De Pischer, leading department store owner of New York thinks the trouble with the unemployed is that they are hoarding their money. When asked for his cure for unemployment, the great merchant, without a moment's hesitation, said: "Spend More."

Graves S. Close-Fist, eminent Brooklyn banker, thinks high-living has caused poverty and unemployment. Addressing the exclusive "Four Hours For Lunch Club," Mr. Close-Fist summed up his advice to the unemployed in two words: "Save More."

purchase groceries, with little or no money for rent, clothes, or medical care. Most recipients found this system demeaning. As one Pittsburgh relief recipient put it, "Does a man's status change when he becomes unemployed, so that, while he was perfectly able to handle money while he had a job, he can't be trusted with it when he is out of work?"

In New York, relief agencies granted the average family $2.39 a week (currently equal to about $33), and only half of all qualified families received that tiny sum. By 1931, most local governments and many private agencies were running out of money. In Hamtramck, Michigan, welfare officials cut off relief to all families that had fewer than three children. In Dallas and Houston, government officials denied assistance to African Americans and Mexican Americans. By 1932, only about one-quarter of the jobless received aid, and cities began to take desperate measures. In Detroit, Mayor Frank Murphy, who had been elected in 1930 with strong labor backing, set up municipal feeding stations that served 14,000 people daily. Murphy also opened emergency lodging in empty factories and promoted "thrift gardens" for the jobless on vacant city land. But even Murphy's humanitarianism could not survive the city's deepening financial crisis; within two years, Detroit joined other cities in sharply cutting relief spending.

As the Depression deepened, workers and farmers looked first to the institutions and individuals that had sustained them in earlier crises. They expected a measure of care, sustenance, and protection from their employers, merchants, churches, landlords, and local banks. In what one historian has characterized as a quest for a more "moral capitalism," American workers believed that the chaos and pressures of the market would be tempered by the resources and goodwill of traditional elites. Thus, in many parts of the South, sharecroppers, both black and white, expected landlords and merchants to extend credit, food, and supplies to tide them over the drought and the collapse in cotton prices. And in the mills and factories of the North, many workers expected the company-sponsored welfare programs and work-sharing schemes that had begun in the 1920s to make the economic slump tolerable. In most big cities, working-class families looked to their ethnic associations and religious institutions to help them through the crisis. "Let's have pride enough not to sponge upon public support when Catholic charity is still able to care for its own interests," one Chicago priest urged his flock.

What made the Depression so catastrophic for working-class families was not simply the loss of a job, a home, an insurance policy, or a bank account. Rather, these losses discredited the sustaining institutions of the 1920s, threatening the patterns of loyalty that working people had taken for granted in their families, their communities, and their workplaces. So severe was the Depression that most corporations abandoned the highly touted welfare schemes they had instituted in the prosperous years of the 1920s, slashing wages, hours, and employment. General Electric, for example, stopped paying bonuses to workers with good attendance records, eliminated paid vacations for blue-collar workers, and stopped subsidizing home mortgages. Meanwhile, ethnic benefit societies, churches, and religious charities failed to provide the material support expected of them. In Chicago, more than 80 percent of all neighborhood banks—institutions such as the Italo-American Building and Loan Association and the Lithuanian Dollar Savings—closed their doors, and depositors lost all their money. In a widely read book, *Moral Man and Immoral Society* (1932), theologian Reinhold Niebuhr, then pastor of a working-class congregation in Detroit, declared that capitalism was on its deathbed and that the only remaining question was when it would finally expire.

In this crisis, most working-class people did not initially turn to the state for help. Following the lead of the American Federation of Labor officials, who distrusted the government, many working men and women opposed unemployment insurance, old-age pensions, and government-mandated minimum wages. The unions expected members to look to them for such support. Some leaders of the unemployed shared this preference for self-help over government programs; they developed mechanisms to enable the jobless to produce their own food and other necessities. Nearly two million urban dwellers returned to the farm during the early Depression years. Others formed self-help organizations in the cities. In Seattle, for example, jobless workers founded an Unemployed Citizens' League in 1931, a "republic of the penniless" that arranged for idle fishing boats to be made available to those without regular employment. The league also convinced farmers to allow destitute workers to dig potatoes and pick apples and pears, and it gained permission from landowners for trees to be cut down for firewood. Part of Seattle's economy reverted to barter as league members "traded" their labor, mending clothing, rebuilding furniture, cutting hair, and repairing shoes. By the end of 1932, unemployed workers had formed more than three hundred similar organizations in thirty-seven states. But self-help, no matter how inspiring, could not mend the ills besetting the world's largest capitalist economy. The federal government would have to intervene with new laws, new money, and a new spirit.

Emergence of Radical Protest   Communists and socialists played a large role in mobilizing discontent and turning the attention of the American people to the federal government as a solution to their problems. Radical activists in both groups thought that the inequality and exploitation that were endemic to capitalism had precipitated the Great Depression. The Communists looked to the Russian Revolution and the Soviet Union for inspiration, if not actual guidance, while socialists thought that the overthrow of capitalism might well follow a path that was more in keeping with

"I'm Going to Fight Like Hell": Anna Taffler and the Unemployed Councils of the 1930s

The Communist-led Unemployed Councils mobilized jobless men and women like Anna Taffler in hundreds of local communities to demand jobs and better treatment from relief authorities. In these excerpts from a recorded interview, Taffler, a Communist activist and a Russian Jewish immigrant, described how her own experience of facing eviction pushed her into organizing the unemployed. She also talked about the focus of local councils on issues like fighting for more relief and stopping evictions.

. . . I went to court to answer the dispossess. In walking to court, I really swept the streets with my tears, crying. . . . I can bring my baby home, but I have no home to bring him to because I'm going to be put out. So I went to court to answer the dispossess. And the judge asked me, "Do you owe rent or don't you?" I says, "Yes, Your Honor, but I wish to explain." "Pay the rent or get out!" He didn't give me a chance to explain. So when I walked out of court, I says, "The courts are no good, the system is no good, everything is no good!" And I says, "I'm going to fight like hell!" And I started in. . . .

I still had no home, so I started looking for help, asking around. And I had some friends, and they told me that . . . they're organizing unemployment councils. . . . So I told myself, "You need to be in the organization of the unemployed councils."

Their policy was to give as little relief as possible . . . It was a constant struggle. So we would come to the relief bureau at that time, and we would stay in the auditorium and we would ask people, you know, "We are from the unemployment council. We are from the Workers Alliance. What are your needs?" and so on and so forth. And people were only too glad to get help, you know. I'd go around and sign them up for membership. But if they didn't have the quarter, it was all right, too, you know. But, we would represent them. Some people were denied rent, and they were facing evictions. Some people were cut off of food. And you know how we did it? To open-air meetings, putting up platform right in the front of the relief bureau getting up and letting the people in the whole neighborhood know what's going on.

Interview done by the Oral History of the American Left, Tamiment Library, NYU, for the public radio program *Grandma Was an Activist*, producers Charlie Potter and Beth Friend.

---

the American radical tradition. Neither group had more than a few thousand members, but their influence in such desperate times proved far reaching.

In 1930 and 1931, under banners reading "Work or Wages" and "Fight, Don't Starve!" Communists and socialists organized scores of demonstrations of the unemployed. In Boston and Chicago, 50,000 protesters showed up; in Milwaukee, 40,000; and in Detroit, as many as 100,000. In New York, where demonstrators tried to march on City Hall, the *New York Times* reported that "hundreds of policemen and detectives, swinging nightsticks,

Capturing the Times

The desperation of hard times was mirrored in the modest appearance of the official publication of the Seattle Unemployed Council. *Seattle Unemployed Worker*, April 17, 1932—Scott Molloy Archives.

blackjacks, and bare fists, rushed into the crowd, hitting out at all with whom they came into contact." Clashes with the police also took place when landlords or banks tried to evict families from their apartments or houses. Radicals often led the crowds that moved families and furniture back into their homes, and these disruptive violations of the law forced many landlords to think twice before putting a family on the street. In some black neighborhoods in Chicago, Communist-led Unemployed Councils became so well known that, according to two contemporary observers, when eviction notices went out, "it was not unusual for a mother to shout to the children, 'Run quick and find the Reds!'"

Family farmers took militant direct action as well. By 1932, more than one-third of the farmland in states such as Mississippi and Iowa was scheduled for sale at auction because the farm owners had fallen behind on taxes or mortgage payments. Neighbors often aborted these sales by intimidating potential bidders, buying the farm themselves at a token price, and returning it to its original owner. South Dakota's Emil Loriks remembered that in his county, "farmers would crowd into the courtroom, five or six hundred, and make it impossible for the officers to carry out the sales." In California, too, agriculture was the site of bitter conflicts between landowners and workers. In the Central Valley, desperate Anglo and Mexican American cotton pickers struck the huge agribusiness conglomerations that California writer Carey McWilliams called "factories in the field."

The deadliest conflicts took place in the rural South, where a pervasive climate of repression and racial violence forced almost all radicals to arm themselves and organize in an "underground" fashion. The Communist Party was particularly active in Alabama, where its membership was predominantly black. In Birmingham, the party attracted steelworkers; in the countryside, it attracted black sharecroppers. As organizer Hosea Hudson described it, "we'd tell people—when you join, it's just like the army, but not the army of the bosses, it's the army of the working class, organizing to

"Weren't No Use Under God's Sun to Treat Colored Folks Like We Been Treated"

Ned Cobb, a share-cropper and staunch supporter of the Alabama Sharecroppers' Union, describes how he resisted an attempt by his land-lord, Mr. Taylor, to foreclose on another sharecropper, Clint Webster, in 1932. Cobb ended up spending twelve years in prison for defying the authorities in this incident.

I happened to be at Clint Webster's house one mornin' when Mr. Taylor sent the deputy sheriff [Mr. Woods] over to attach everything the man had and bring it away from there. . . . Well, I knowed I had to take a stand right there because . . . I was going to be next. . . . I stretched out my arms and said, "Mr. Woods, please, sir, don't take what he's got. He's got a wife and children and if you take all his stock and everything else, you'll leave his folks hungry." He told me . . . "I got orders to take it, and I'll be damned if I don't." . . . So I just politely told him that he weren't goin' to do it. . . .

Then the deputy raised sand with me about it. He jumped up and told me, "I'm going to Dadeville to get [Sheriff] Carl Platt and bring him down here. He'll come down here and kill the last damn one of you, shoot you in a bunch."

Now, a organization is a organization, and if I don't mean nothin' by what I say and do, I ought to keep my ass out of it; but if I'm sworn to stand up for myself and stand up for all the poor class of farmers, I have to do it. Weren't no use under God's sun to treat colored folks like we been treated here in the state of Alabama, weren't no sense in it. Work hard and look what's done to me. . . .

Mr. Woods come back that same day . . . with four sheriffs. . . . There were several men in Clint Webster's house when that bunch of sheriffs arrived, five or six of them. But when the sheriffs walked up in the yard, I was standin' outside. . . . I said, "Fellas, here they come, here come the officers." God Almighty, they jumped up and run out of that house goin' out the back way into the field and the forest, clean out of there. . . . Then [Deputy Sheriff] Grant, be standin' in front of me holdin' a shotgun straight on me; wouldn't budge, just standin' there lookin' at me, wouldn't say nothin' . . . just lookin' at me and holdin' that gun, the muzzle part of it. . . .

And bless your soul, I got tired standin' there. . . . So I walked off. I just decided I'd go on in the house. And when I started up the doorstep, [Deputy Sheriff] Meade . . . grabbed me by my right arm and just pressured it, but I absolutely flung him off like you would fling off a leech. . . . I just commenced a steppin' right on in the house. And Mr. Grant shot me three times, in the back. . . . But I didn't stop walkin' when he shot me. Shot me twice more, right quick before I could get in the house. Boom! Boom! Same place, every time he shot me. I just still kept walkin', never did weaken.

Now the door to the north room of that house was open comin' off a hallway. I just walked in that door to the north room and looked back. Mr. Grant still had that gun on me, and I started workin' out with him. He jumped behind a big oak tree and I just kept working' out with my .32 Smith and Wesson. I had that gun on me when I come there that mornin', and they didn't know it. I didn't go there actin' a fool, less'n a person will call me a fool for what I said. My finger was on that trigger all the time and the gun was in my hand. I had on a pair of big overalls, brand new, and the pockets was deep and my hand in the pockets. And I had on a white cowboy hat—that's the way I was dressed and my jumper and a pair of Red Wing boots, about knee-high. . . . And when Mr. Grant shot me—shot me three times, in the same place—my blood came near to fillin' them boots. . . . I was just sloshin' in my blood every step I took.

Well, I shot six times, and when I got done shootin', all of them deputies done cleared out from that house, every one of 'em run away from there.

Dale Rosen and Theodore Rosengarten, "Shoot-Out at Reeltown," *Radical America*, November–December 1972.

make things better." As cotton prices plummeted, the planters cut off food advances to their tenants, reduced the wages for day labor, and forced share-croppers to work off real estate taxes—the landowner's responsibility—by doing roadwork. When the Communists organized the Sharecroppers' Union (SCU) in Tallapoosa County, Alabama, white plantation owners used sheriff's deputies to violently suppress the new organization. In 1931 and 1932, gun battles between lawmen and SCU activists left dozens of share-croppers dead or wounded, and many more were run off their land.

The Scottsboro case focused national attention on the growing terror in the South. In 1931, nine young black males, one only twelve years old, were falsely accused of raping two white women on a freight train near Scotts-boro, Alabama. In a trial that was based on questionable evidence and riddled with prejudice and procedural error, the jury convicted eight of the defendants and sentenced them to death. The defense of the "Scottsboro boys," championed first by the Communist Party and then by the National Association for the Advancement of Colored People, became an interna-tional cause célèbre, much like the Sacco and Vanzetti case during the 1920s. Years of litigation and agitation finally overturned the death sentences, but not before five of the defendants had served long prison terms for a crime that had never occurred.

Eight Face the Electric Chair
One of a series of prints created in 1935 in support of the Scottsboro defendants, this linoleum block shows the influence of the stark, illustrative style of interwar graphic arts in Europe on American political artists. Although designed for publication, the Scottsboro print book was never distributed. Lin Shi Khan and Ralph Austin, *Scottsboro: A Story in Block Prints* (1932)—The Wolfsonian–Florida International University, Miami Beach, Florida, The Mitchell Wolfson, Jr., Collection.

1932: Marching for Our Rights   In the election year of 1932, two great protests demonstrated the potential of the Depression to mobilize people in defense of their rights in a society that they saw still governed by uncaring elites. By 1932, Henry Ford, America's most famous industrialist, had dumped 60,000 workers onto Detroit's relief rolls. On March 7, 1932, more than 3,000 protesters organized by the small, Communist-led Auto Workers' Union marched on Ford's giant River Rouge complex in Dearborn, Michigan. The "hunger marchers" demanded jobs for laid-off workers, a slowdown of the company's assembly line, and a halt to evictions of former Ford workers. As the marchers neared the factory gate, Dearborn police and Ford guards first threw tear gas and then fired their guns at the retreating crowd. Hundreds of shots rang out, killing four marchers and wounding more than sixty others. Within days, hundreds of suspected "Reds" had been arrested throughout the region in a police dragnet.

But Ford's reaction to the march only hardened the participants' determination to effect change. For Dave Moore, who began his political activity fighting evictions in Detroit, the Hunger March was "the turning point in

Anacostia Flats and Flames
The Bonus Marchers' shanty-town burned down within sight of the Capitol on the afternoon of July 28, 1932. Federal troops had set fire to the camp after dispersing the unemployed and homeless World War I veterans who were asking for an early release of their war bonuses. National Archives.

my life. . . . When I saw the blood flowing there on Miller Road, that was the point I became a radical." The following Sunday, an interracial crowd of more than 20,000 people followed the caskets of the slain men and listened to the strains of the "Internationale," the Communist anthem, as the caskets were lowered into the ground. Henry Ford, a hero of the 1920s, became a much-hated man in the city of Detroit.

Four months later, a veterans' march on Washington, D.C., had an even greater impact on the nation. After World War I, Congress had passed a bill promising each veteran a cash bonus to be paid in 1945. But the vets needed the money now, and in May 1932, a group of veterans from Portland, Oregon, set out for Washington to press their case. Twenty thousand ex-servicemen soon set up camp in the capital. But Congress balked as a sizable group of Bonus Marchers took over unoccupied government buildings. In late July, when Hoover evicted the protesters, police killed two veterans. Prodded by Army Chief of Staff General Douglas MacArthur, who considered the Bonus Army a "mob" driven by the "essence of revolution," Hoover called out the regular army, which launched a tank and cavalry assault on the Bonus Army encampment across the Anacostia River from the U.S. Capitol, burning down their temporary shelters. Millions of citizens were horrified by the image, reproduced in newspapers and on newsreels, of a battle-ready army driving off a ragtag collection of men who had faithfully served their country and were now desperately seeking help. "So all the misery and suffering had finally come to this," reported journalist Thomas Stokes, who witnessed the assault, "soldiers marching with their guns against American citizens." Hoover's reputation, like Henry Ford's, collapsed.

Although these conflicts with police and sheriffs, as well as the demonstrations by the unemployed, did not succeed, they had lasting consequences. The stark confrontations of the early 1930s helped to radicalize thousands of impoverished men and women, who later built potent industrial unions and political organizations that played a leading role in transforming the economic status and social expectations of millions of Americans. And despite much heated rhetoric denouncing the government, these early Depression protests helped workers and farmers to turn their attention beyond their neighborhoods and employers and to demand help with their problems from the state. They wanted a "new deal" out of life, and they had the voice and votes to win it.

The Promise of a New Deal

Franklin Delano Roosevelt stands with Abraham Lincoln as a founder of the modern American nation. He was elected president four times and served for more than twelve years, longer than any chief executive in American history. During those years, the United States put in place the social legislation, economic regulations, and governmental apparatus that serves as the foundation for the powerful, politically energetic state that has been a prominent feature of American life ever since. In his inaugural address, Roosevelt responded to mass protests, asserting, "The nation calls for action and action now." Roosevelt did take immediate action with a wide array of programs — collectively known as "the New Deal" — that were designed to restore production and stability in banking, agriculture, and industry.

But Roosevelt was not a radical, nor were the overwhelming majority of his key appointees. Roosevelt drew much of the legislation that was put forward during the famous first hundred days of the New Deal from the program of the most conservative wing of the Democratic Party or from proposals that Herbert Hoover had failed to pass. Even as the government took on new responsibilities, Roosevelt sought to conserve as much of the nation's existing economic and social arrangements as possible. Mistrustful of labor radicals and worried that "the dole," as he referred to cash relief, undermined self-respect, Roosevelt courted business support and strove to balance the budget as soon as possible. And neither Roosevelt nor his principal advisers dared to challenge the power of the southern white landowning elites, especially on issues of race, or to question gender roles in framing emergency relief and social welfare legislation.

Franklin Roosevelt: Experimentation and the Status Quo Roosevelt was born in 1882 into a patrician New York family whose wealth, although substantial, was no match for the spectacular fortunes then being amassed by the Rockefellers and Carnegies. Roosevelt used his charm, money, and social prominence to climb the political ladder. After proceeding from the New York State Senate to the post of assistant secretary of the navy under Woodrow Wilson to the Democratic Party's 1920 vice presidential nomination, Roosevelt contracted polio in 1921 and lost the use of both legs. He would never walk again without heavy braces and much assistance, but Roosevelt's misfortune probably made him more expansive, mature, and socially concerned. He battled his way back into public life with the help of his wife, Eleanor, who displayed a talent for political organization and public speaking that surprised those who had known her as a shy and awkward young wife. Although the Roosevelts became estranged in their marriage, Eleanor proved to be an effective political ally, a woman Franklin often called his "eyes and ears," who also pursued her own political and social causes.

Roosevelt, known simply as FDR, served as governor of New York during the same dark era when Hoover held the White House. He proved to be a more imaginative administrator than Hoover but still had to position himself carefully to win his party's presidential nomination in 1932. He took a laissez-faire approach on the issues of religion and drink (he pledged to repeal Prohibition and did in 1933) but adopted an interventionist policy on the economy and social welfare. In accepting the Democratic nomination, Roosevelt promised "a new deal for the American people."

Between Roosevelt's election in November 1932 and his inauguration in March 1933, the economy dipped to the lowest point of the entire Depression. In mid-February 1933, Michigan's governor ordered all state banks closed to prevent the collapse of the big Detroit institutions. Panic spread in state after state — forty altogether — forcing authorities to declare bank "holidays." Even the New York Stock Exchange shut down.

Not since the days of Lincoln had a president taken office in such dramatic and difficult circumstances. For Roosevelt, it was a golden opportunity. A master of the use of radio, he assured the nation in his inaugural address that "the only thing we have to fear is fear itself." Hoover had made similar appeals on numerous occasions, but Roosevelt's enormous self-confidence, combined with paternal warmth and a plain, friendly manner, gave hope to millions. He later broadcast a radio series of "fireside chats" in which he explained his programs to the public, using easily digestible anecdotes. Within weeks of his election, Roosevelt had come to embody the state as friend and protector. "My mother looks upon the president as someone so immediately concerned with her problems and difficulties that she would not be greatly surprised were he to come to her house some evening and stay to dinner," remarked an insurance salesman.

Unlike Hoover, Roosevelt was an opportunist and an experimentalist

"A Real Mother to the Nation"

Millions of Americans felt a close personal bond not only with Franklin Roosevelt, but also with his wife Eleanor. In letters sent to the White House, people recounted their personal troubles and expressed their gratitude to the president and First Lady. Following are excerpts from letters addressed to Eleanor Roosevelt. The first correspondent begged for a loan to buy baby clothes; the others praised the Roosevelts in strikingly religious terms.

Jan. 2, 1935
Troy, New York
Dear Mrs. Roosevelt,
About a month ago I wrote you asking if you would buy some baby clothes for me with the understanding that I was to repay you as soon as my husband got enough work. Several weeks later I received a reply to apply to a Welfare Association so I might receive the aid I needed. Do you remember?

Please Mrs. Roosevelt, I do not want charity, only a chance from someone who will trust me until we can get enough money to repay the amount spent for the things I need. As a proof that I really am sincere, I am sending you two of my dearest possessions to keep as security, a ring my husband gave me before we were married, and a ring my mother used to wear. Perhaps the actual value of them is not high, but they are worth a lot to me. If you will consider buying the baby clothes, please keep them until I send you the money you spend. It is very hard to face bearing a baby we cannot afford to have, and the fact that it is due to arrive soon, and still there is no money for the hospital or clothing, does not make it any easier. . . .

Ridley Park, Pennsylvania
9/1/34
Dear Mrs. Roosevelt,
I was delighted but I don't believe I was very much surprised when I received your letter. Just to look at your picture and that of our President seems to me like looking at the picture of a saint. So when you answered my letter and promised to have some one help me it only proved you are our own Mrs. Roosevelt. I have told everyone what you done for me. I want them to know you are not too busy to answer our letters and give us what help and advice you can. You hold the highest place any woman can hold still you are not to[o] proud to befriend the poorest class. . . . Thank you and God bless you both.

Nov. 25, 1934
Arkansas City, Kansas
Dear Madam:
I beg to inform you that I have been reading your writings in the Wichita Beacon and I must say that the whole nation should be enthused over them. I was especially carried away with the one on Old

Age Pensions. It brought my mind back to the day of the Chicago Convention, when Mr. Roosevelt was nominated for the presidency.

In our little home in Arkansas City, my family and I were sitting around the radio . . . and when he spoke it seems as though some Moses had come to alleviate us of our sufferings. Strange to say when he was speaking to see the moisten eyes and the deep feeling of emotions that gave vent to every word and when you spoke then we knew that the white house would be filled with a real mother to the nation.

Robert S. McElvaine, *Down and Out in the Great Depression: Letters from the "Forgotten Man"* (1983).

who surrounded himself with politically savvy academics and bold administrators. Many key New Deal officials and advisers, such as Secretary of the Interior Harold Ickes, Felix Frankfurter (whom FDR later appointed to the Supreme Court), and Secretary of Agriculture Henry Wallace, were veterans of the Progressive movement or the home front bureaucracies of World War I. Young men and women just out of Harvard or Columbia filled other vital positions, assuming extraordinary responsibilities. The Protestant world of the big corporate law firms had spurned many of these young Jewish or Catholic law school graduates. And women who had long been active in social reform movements, including Secretary of Labor Frances Perkins, the first female cabinet officer, filled several posts dealing with relief or labor relations.

Rescuing the Banks   Roosevelt's first task was to restore confidence in the financial system. Two days after taking office, he declared a national bank holiday and then called Congress into special session. Although popular anger at the banking system was so great that some in Congress favored outright nationalization of the banking system, the Roosevelt administration pushed through an Emergency Banking Act that regulated the banks instead, empowering the government to lend money to troubled banks, to reorganize failed ones, and to stop the hoarding of gold. Banks that were judged to be solvent were allowed to reopen within a week. Additional laws established the Federal Deposit Insurance Corporation, which guaranteed the security of most family savings, and the Securities and Exchange Commission, which required what FDR called "truth telling" in the stock market. Roosevelt had thus acted decisively, but he nevertheless avoided the most radical solutions. Farmers and others with large debts, for example, urged inflationary policies of the sort favored by the Populists in the late nineteenth century. Roosevelt resisted, insisting on a "sound" dollar, but he still shocked conservatives by taking the nation off the gold standard in April 1933, thus helping to end the deflation that had crippled investment during the depths of the Depression.

Toward National Relief Roosevelt's efforts to save the banks and cut spending differed only slightly from those of Herbert Hoover, but his decision to launch a national relief program introduced a major policy innovation. To provide funds for the unemployed, Congress set up the Federal Emergency Relief Administration (FERA), which immediately began spending $1 billion a year—

Have Faith
Instead of blaring its usual movie advertisement, this theater sound truck toured the streets of Boston in December 1931 to chide citizens who, fearing impending financial failure, had withdrawn their deposits from local banks. Courtesy of the Boston Public Library, Print Department.

roughly 2 percent of the national income. Congress also approved one of Roosevelt's pet projects: the Civilian Conservation Corps (CCC). Like his cousin Theodore Roosevelt, FDR believed that outdoor life was morally and physically curative. During the decade of its existence, the CCC provided temporary work for three million young men, who lived in military-style camps, constructed recreation facilities, and carried out conservation projects under the direction of army officers. Later in 1933, Roosevelt launched the Civil Works Administration (CWA), which quickly hired four million of the unemployed and put them to work on four hundred thousand small-scale projects, mainly road building and repair work.

These emergency work relief programs employed more than ten million Americans. By putting real money in the pockets of the poor, they offered tangible evidence that the New Deal could touch the lives of ordinary Americans. The Roosevelt administration insisted that only public agencies receive federal funds, a policy that undercut the role of private charity, and held state and local officials accountable to government-established federal guidelines. Overnight, the public's expectations of federal officials underwent a dramatic change. "Clients are assuming that the government has a responsibility to provide," reported federal emergency relief administrator Harry Hopkins. "The stigma of relief has almost disappeared except among white-collar groups."

Despite the efforts of Hopkins and other reformers, the distribution of government aid largely replicated the racial, regional, and gender divisions that plagued the nation. Entrenched local elites usually administered the funds and manipulated payments to serve their own economic interests. Monthly FERA payments were ten times higher in New York than in Mississippi because the planter class in the Delta, the backbone of the conservative

"We Can Take It!"

A photograph of a young Civilian Conservation Corps (CCC) worker epitomized the agency's slogan. "Building strong bodies is a major CCC objective," the accompanying caption stated. "More than half of the enrollees who entered CCC during the last year were seventeen years of age. Work, calisthenics, marching drills, good food, and medical care feature the CCC health program." Wilfred J. Mead—National Archives.

southern Democrats, wanted a ready supply of harvest labor. In the West, fruit growers often forced government agencies to cease relief payments when pickers were needed. And in the CCC, black and white workers received equal wages but lived in segregated camps that reflected military practice. Women were largely excluded from work relief. Most New Deal policymakers, working-class radicals, and social service administrators wanted to restore male dignity and livelihood. Roosevelt's New Deal built roads and dams, but it gave lower priority to teaching, child care, and public health. Thus, women, who were a quarter of the unemployed, held fewer than 10 percent of the FERA and CWA jobs.

A Revolution on the Farm To restore prosperity to farmland America, the Roosevelt Administration pushed through an Agricultural Adjustment Act (AAA) that was designed to regulate production and prices in an economic sector from which a quarter of all Americans still derived their livelihood. Within a generation, the AAA did more to transform American farming than had the invention of the mechanical reaper or the enactment of the 1862 Homestead Act.

Agriculture had been in a crisis for years because of low prices and chronic overproduction. In 1931, some states in the South had actually tried to impose a moratorium on that year's cotton crop, and in the Midwest, radical farmers, who had organized into an Iowa-based Farmer's Holiday Association, blocked rural highways to prevent milk, corn, and other farm products from going to market. But in a nation in which rice, wheat, cotton, and tobacco were raised in thousands of counties, such regional efforts were doomed to failure. Passed by Congress in the spring of 1933, the AAA used federal funds to pay farmers who agreed to reduce the size of their crops. New Deal officials argued that, just as major industrial companies manipulated their sales and prices, so a government-mandated reduction in the amount of land under cultivation could force up commodity prices. To finance the payments to farmers, the government taxed food processors, who generally passed the new levy on to consumers in the form of higher costs. Separate government agencies promoted soil conservation and made loans at favorable rates to farmers who reduced their cultivated acreage.

FARMERS'
HOLIDAY

The Spirit of '32
Three striking farmers mimicked Archibald Willard's *The Spirit of '76*, the popular 1876 painting celebrating the American Revolution. When asked by a reporter how he justified Farm Holiday protest actions that broke the law, one elderly man replied, "Seems to me there was a Tea Party in Boston that was illegal, too." August 31, 1932—Scott Molloy Labor Archives.

Since the planting season had already begun by the time the AAA became law, farmers who wanted benefit payments had to destroy crops and livestock. So farmers slaughtered six million baby pigs and plowed under ten million acres of cotton. The destruction of food and fiber in the midst of Depression-bred want created a furor because it highlighted the larger irrationalities that were embedded in the government's market-taming program. But the AAA boosted farm income by 50 percent within four years. Large commercial farmers benefited most, since they could make the greatest reductions in their crops and thereby receive the largest payments. Agribusiness owners used the federal money to retire debts, expand their farms, and purchase new equipment.

Tenant farmers and sharecroppers found themselves worse off under the AAA. Legally, landowners were obligated to share their crop reduction payments with those who rented their land, but they commonly evaded the responsibility, often by taking tenant lands out of production, evicting the occupants, and pocketing the federal payments. The impact of the AAA on these small farmers soon provoked a new wave of protest. In 1934, Arkansas sharecroppers and laborers—both black and white—organized the Southern Tenant Farmers' Union (STFU), which sought to pressure federal officials to stop the evictions and give tenants and sharecroppers their fair share of government price-support payments. The union, which soon grew to 10,000 members, came under attack from planters and local authorities who beat, shot, and arrested hundreds. Although this reign of terror forced the STFU underground, the union still managed to organize cotton pickers'

Organizing in Arkansas

Black and white farmworkers listened to a speaker at a Southern Tenant Farmers' Union meeting. Louise Boyle—Southern Tenant Farmers' Union Papers no. 3472, Southern Historical Collection, Library of the University of North Carolina at Chapel Hill.

strikes in five states in 1936. Black tenant farmers became some of the union's most effective organizers.

At the Department of Agriculture, many of the young New Dealers sympathized deeply with the plight of tenant farmers. But Roosevelt, Secretary of Agriculture Wallace, and other top aides cared more about conciliating the powerful, conservative cohort of southern Democrats they considered vital to New Deal legislative majorities. Wallace therefore fired Agriculture Department radicals in 1935, making clear that the New Deal would do little to threaten the power of planters and agribusiness interests. To provide some help for poor farmers and farm workers, the administration set up a new agency, the Resettlement Administration. But its low budget and marginal administrative clout meant that it could aid only a fraction of the displaced rural poor. Meanwhile, the STFU collapsed; its defeat would prove a harbinger of the massive, decades-long transformation in American agriculture, a mid-twentieth-century development that pushed millions of small farmers off the land and into cities. The New Deal agricultural revolution demonstrated that an intrusive set of government controls and incentives could make American agribusiness the most prosperous and efficient in the world, but policymakers never properly calculated the human costs of that transformation.

Public Investment in the South and West

Many New Dealers believed that the monopolization of capital and manufacturing in the Northeast stifled national economic growth. Indeed, the South and West were virtually undeveloped countries. Because private investment in those regions evaporated so completely, only massive public investment could provide construction jobs and build highways, bridges, and other parts of the infrastructure that were essential to future prosperity.

The $3.3 billion Public Works Administration (PWA), set up in 1933, produced dozens of government-financed dams, airports, courthouses, and bridges. Managed with an incorruptible hand by Interior Secretary Harold Ickes, the PWA proved particularly active on the Pacific Coast. In California alone, the PWA helped to finance the world's largest dam at Shasta; the longest and most expensive suspension bridge, between San Francisco and Oakland; and the nation's first freeway, from downtown Los Angeles to Pasadena. Following the Long Beach earthquake of 1933, the PWA rebuilt the entire school system of Los Angeles County.

In 1933, the New Deal launched its most ambitious and celebrated experiment in regional planning: the Tennessee Valley Authority (TVA). This giant project had its roots in the Progressive era, when many government officials had looked to the development of water resources as a source of inexpensive electric power for booming cities. The TVA was a government-owned corporation that was designed to carry out the comprehensive redevelopment of an entire river watershed spanning seven southern states. With twenty new dams, the authority soon tamed the flood-prone rivers of the Tennessee Valley and, in the process, became the largest producer of electric power in the United States (Map 8.2). Private utility executives thought the TVA socialistic, but the otherwise conservative farmers and manufacturers of the Appalachian South thankfully reaped the benefits of improved navigation, flood control, industrial development, cheap electricity, and new recreational facilities. A separate government entity, the Rural Electrification Administration, brought running water and electric lights to remote farmhouses nationwide by making cheap, government-backed credit available to hundreds of electric power cooperatives.

MAP 8.2 Tennessee Valley Authority

Between 1933 and 1952, the Tennessee Valley Authority improved five dams and built twenty others, taming the flood-prone rivers of the Tennessee Valley and bringing affordable electricity to remote rural areas. The TVA therefore represented social and ecological engineering on a grand scale as well as a major source of employment.

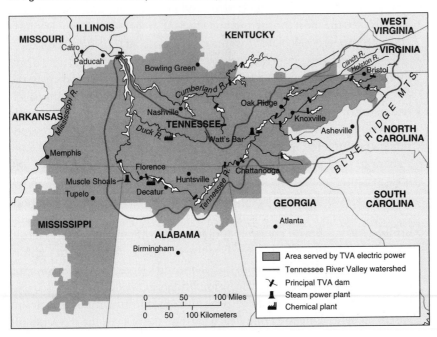

A New Deal for American Indians   At the same time that the New Deal modernized the American South and West, it exhibited more respect for Native American traditions than had the programs of previous administrations. Ever since the adoption of the Dawes Act in 1887, the federal government had tried to force Indians to assimilate into white society by ending communally owned reservations and insisting that they take up "allotments"—individually owned plots of land. This policy proved disastrous for the nation's 300,000 Native Americans, whose tribal land acreage was slashed by more than half. By the 1930s, more than 100,000 Indians lived in abject poverty.

Prodded by John Collier, FDR's reform-minded commissioner of Indian affairs, Congress passed the Indian Reorganization Act of 1934, which ended the allotment of tribal lands to individuals and made possible the restoration of surplus lands to tribes. It allowed the Indians to adopt constitutions giving them self-government, and it opened the way for Indians to seek jobs in the white-dominated Bureau of Indian Affairs. Collier also pushed for the restoration of traditional Native American cultural life, including the revival of ancient dances and religious practices that had been discouraged under the Dawes Act. Collier's "New Deal for Indians" encountered opposition from Protestant missionaries who preferred the assimilationist policy and from some Indian groups that were suspicious of the federal government. Most American Indians remained poor, but the New Deal at least brought them a more sympathetic hearing in Washington.

Transforming American Industry   Industrial recovery was the greatest task confronting the New Deal. How could the downward cycle of falling wages, prices, profits, and employment be stopped? Congress offered one remarkably popular solution by proposing legislation for a thirty-hour workweek to force employers to hire millions of new workers. The Senate actually passed such a bill early in 1933, but business opposed it, and so did the president, who thought that it merely spread the misery around. Instead, Roosevelt pushed through the National Industrial Recovery Act (NIRA), which mandated a government-sanctioned system of business self-regulation, coordinated by a National Recovery Administration (NRA). Like the AAA, the NRA used government power to regulate the market, raise prices, and increase wages. The NRA proved to be far more than another Washington bureaucracy. FDR's flamboyant NRA chief, Hugh Johnson, used many of the propaganda techniques he had learned during his Great War service to turn the recovery effort into a national crusade. Companies that agreed to cooperate with the NRA were allowed to display

Praising and Criticizing the Indian Reorganization Act of 1934

Although John Collier, the commissioner of Indian affairs who was responsible for the new Indian policy, may have viewed Indians with great sympathy, not all Native Americans viewed the Indian New Deal in equally positive terms. In his 1970 oral history interview, Alfred Dubray argued that the act brought positive change, but in the 1968 interview with historian Joseph H. Cash, attorney Ramon Roubideaux, a Brule Sioux, denounced the Indian Reorganization Act as "a white man's idea" of how Indians should live.

Alfred Dubray: It had a lot of advantages that many of the people didn't see, such as making loan funds available, huge amounts of that. Farm programs were developed through this. Cattle-raising programs were initiated. Educational loans were beginning to be made available for Indian youngsters who had never had any opportunities before, hardly, to attend any higher institutions. Unless they just did it by sheer initiative, and if somebody is sponsoring it. So there was a new field there in education, and, of course, mainly the tribal governing body section of it—busy there, and they established their governing body and voted on their representatives and the council members.

I think it was difficult for the people to really recognize what they were doing for probably several years after that, until they got into the change.

Ramon Roubideaux: Well, I might say as far as the Indian Reorganization Act is concerned, I think this is possibly one of the best intentioned but unfortunate happenings that could have possibly taken place as far as the Indian people are concerned. What I am speaking about is that although it did stop the alienation, the sale of Indian lands and did stop the allotment system, it created a socialistic society, and set the Indian people apart from the mainstream of American life and made them a problem. So what this has really done, it has substituted in place of the governing system that the Indians had prior to the Indian Reorganization Act, a white man's idea of how they should live, rather a paternalistic type of government which, had as its object the socializing of all the activities of the Indian people and while the framers of this act and the ones who are responsible for the idea of formulating it probably had the best intentions in the world, I cannot help but think that there was maybe not an overt conspiracy, but one in the back of the mind of these bureaucrats to really perpetuate their own existence. . . . And I think the main thing that was wrong with the whole thing was that the setting of the Indian aside on a different place in the state, designating him as a problem, making him feel he was a problem, beating down rebels, beating down Indians who expressed any independent thinking, rewarding collaborators, rewarding them with positions of importance and completely stifling independent and creative thinking from the Indian people, having, different laws apply to him, setting up a different kind of government. . . . [I]t should have set up a county system exactly like the neighboring counties, with county officials, with municipal officials, with Indians going about their daily political and economic activities in the same way that other people in the state are, so that they could benefit from the intercourse with their white neighbors and the meetings that we have, state-wide meetings of county officials, municipal officials, and in fact, becoming part of the mainstream of American life.

Oral histories courtesy of Institute of American Indian Studies, South Dakota Oral History Center, University of South Dakota.

a blue eagle. Parades, speeches, and posters urged the public to spend money only at businesses that displayed the symbol.

To end the downward cycle of wage cuts and price reductions, NRA codes spelled out permissible production and marketing practices for each industry. Johnson argued that the act would "eliminate eye-gouging and knee-groining and ear-chewing in business." For example, textile companies agreed to limit mills to two forty-hour weekly shifts, to end child labor, and to set minimum wages at $12 to $13 per week. In theory, consumers, labor, and the government would help to write the codes. Such was the case in the coal and garment industries, in which the unions made a spectacular comeback. But in most other industries, the NRA wrote codes at the behest of the largest and most politically influential producers. "The lumber code is not an edict handed us by Congress or the president," bragged a West Coast lumberman to industry associates. "We went to Washington and asked for it."

The NRA generated more than five hundred industry codes, but trade unionists, New Dealers, and some businessmen recognized that industry

"We Do Our Part"

Three unlikely spots for the display of the otherwise ubiquitous NRA eagle. Pare Lorentz, *The Roosevelt Year: A Photographic Record* (1934)—American Social History Project.

self-regulation required a strong labor movement. Unions possessed an intimate, internal knowledge of business conditions, so if labor had enough power, it could ensure that employers complied with the minimum wage standards and maximum hour regulations set out in the codes. But labor power would come only with successful union organizing. Section 7a of the NIRA proved an important and controversial part of each industry code. It gave employees "the right to organize and bargain collectively through representatives of their own choosing . . . free from the interference, restraint, or coercion of employers."

"The Republic Is Imperiled": John L. Lewis Warns of Ignoring Laboring People

John L. Lewis, president of the United Mine Workers of America, was instrumental in the organizing drive that transformed the coal fields in 1933. In February 1933 (before passage of the NRA), Lewis spoke passionately to the Senate Finance Committee about the need for action to protect workers. In his Senate testimony, Lewis called for emergency action, including allowing workers to unionize and replacing corporate autocracy with union democracy. He warned that if action was not forthcoming, the nation might face grave consequences.

The political stability of the republic is imperiled. . . .

We are victims of our own national short-sightedness by failure in the halcyon days of prosperity to intelligently plan for the future. A horde of small-time leaders in industry and finance like the freebooters of old, vied with each other, looted the purse of the population, and diverted the proceeds to their own interests. Now that the day of adversity has come, these same leaders are destitute of competent suggestion to safeguard the present or the future, and they expect the population of this country to remain quiescent while they utter ponderous platitudes about balancing the budget, and the necessity for further wage reductions. . . .

If democracy and corporate participation in industry are to survive in America, labor must have an opportunity to exercise its industrial rights for the protection of itself and our democratic and economic institutions. An emergency now exists which is more critical than would be the case if a fleet of a foreign power were at this moment bombarding the defenses of one of our major ports. The very foundation of democracy and integrity of American institutions is threatened. . . .

A board of emergency control should be created. It should be composed of representatives of industry, labor, agriculture and finance. . . . The board should be instructed to reduce the hours of labor, and the number of days in the work week to a point where the industrial machinery of the nation can substantially take up the slack of unemployment and under conditions where labor is accorded the right of collective bargaining through representatives of its own choosing. This board should also be instructed to stabilize the prices of agricultural products and other commodities . . .

Today the enemy is within the boundaries of the nation, and is stalking through every community and every home, and, obviously, this proposal is the most democratic form of internal regulation that can be devised to deal with our economic and industrial collapse.

United Mine Workers Journal, 44 (March 1, 1933): 3–4.

Employers were forbidden to require their workers to join company-sponsored unions or to make them sign "yellow-dog" contracts promising not to unionize. Labor leaders hailed Section 7a as a Magna Carta for organized labor, but it would take an enormous struggle to transform legislative promise into social reality.

The Revival of Organized Labor

Before the Depression, unions were clustered in a few industries: coal mining, construction, railroads, garment manufacturing, and some specialty crafts. Organizing efforts in other fields had been effectively blocked by management hostility, restrictive court decisions, and corporate sponsorship of tame "company" unions. During the first three years of the Great Depression, high unemployment made workers and their leaders extremely cautious. Strikes were virtually nonexistent as union membership dropped to less than 10 percent of the national workforce. But everything changed in 1933 when workers dramatically embraced collective action. American trade unions tripled their membership during the 1930s and increased their political and economic power in a dramatic fashion. By organizing the great mass production industries of that era—steel, automobiles, electrical products, and rubber—the unions not only raised living standards for millions of families, but also injected an element of popular, democratic control into the heart of American industrial life. Even the agricultural and textile strikes that ended in defeat mobilized thousands of workers and exposed the shortcomings of New Deal legislation.

The Working Class Upsurge of 1933 and 1934 The NIRA's Section 7a, which encouraged industrial workers to organize and bargain collectively, transformed discontent into action. Although Section 7a offered only a vague statement of policy, it had enormous psychological and political impact. The NIRA enabled labor organizers to assert that workers could make a patriotic contribution to the national recovery effort by joining a union. Organizers from the United Mine Workers of America (UMW) toured the coal fields with leaflets that declared, "The President Wants You to Join a Union!" This was a big change from the 1920s, when open-shop employers had sought to brand unions as un-American—an outlook that had frequently been sustained by the use of army and National Guard troops against strikers in the tumultuous years after World War I.

   The sudden rebirth of the UMW demonstrated how quickly unionists seized the opportunities that FDR's programs generated, both to revive their own organizations and, in the process, to transform the very meaning of the entire New Deal. The UMW had languished in the early years of the Depression. In February 1933, a UMW member reported that "as far as West Kentucky is concerned there is no sign of organization . . . you could not organize a baseball team." But once it became clear that the NIRA would be passed, the miners' union gambled its remaining resources on a lightning-quick organizing campaign, throwing 100 organizers into the field. The response was tremendous. By June 17, the day after Roosevelt signed the NIRA, 80 percent of Ohio miners had signed union cards. UMW president John L. Lewis, backed by the swelling membership, pressed mine operators to accept the union's version of a bituminous coal industry code. A series of wildcat (without formal union approval) strikes added to the pressure. In September 1933, the mine operators gave in, accepting a code that raised wages, reduced regional variations in pay, outlawed child labor, established an eight-hour workday, and gave miners the right to select representatives who would ensure that they were properly paid for the weight of the coal they produced. Almost overnight, the UMW had democratized the distribution of power in the coal industry.

NRA codes also aided workers in the garment trades and in trucking; but without an enforcement mechanism, Section 7a proved far less useful to the men and women who labored in the mass production industries of the American heartland. Some frustrated workers began to call the NRA the "National Run Around." The idea that "employees had the right to representatives of their own choosing" was subject to multiple interpretations, so in August 1933, the Roosevelt administration set up a tripartite National Labor Board to resolve labor conflicts. The board established an important precedent when it ruled that employers were obligated to hold secret ballot elections to determine who would represent workers in negotiations. But many employers, especially in the steel and electrical products industries, set up company-dominated unions run by managers and foremen. Others fired union advocates and used proemployer codes to set wages and hours unilaterally. Employers frequently ignored the NRA and the Labor Board, especially when they confronted unions led by radicals, African Americans, or Mexican Americans.

A Wave of Strikes   Under such difficult circumstances, it took courage and political commitment to offer union leadership and even more courage to protest. By the second year of the New Deal, Communists, socialists, and other radical unionists had mobilized whole communities on behalf of labor's organizing drives and work stoppages. While officials of the AFL usually stood on the sidelines, political radicals proved willing and able to assume leadership, notably in the automobile, shipping, and trucking industries, with a series of sometimes violent strikes that put the nation on notice that a new and militant spirit had infused the union rank and file.

By the 1930s, several changes in American life facilitated the task of organizing workers, who had been long divided along ethnic, racial, gender, craft, and political lines. First, the working class had become more

Street Warfare

A Minneapolis truckers' strike turned violent in May 1934 when an alliance of businessmen, backed by the police and city officials, sought to break union picket lines and run scab trucks. But led by a militant, democratically elected set of officers, the Minneapolis Teamsters local sparked a general strike and organized hundreds of workers into paramilitary groups that fought police. By the end of the 1930s, the Teamsters were one of the fastest-growing unions in the United States. UPI/Bettmann.

homogeneous. Immigration had been slowed for nearly two decades; the proportion of foreign-born men and women in the workforce had declined, while the English-speaking children of immigrants had become an increasingly significant presence. Second, the rise of the assembly line and the emergence of giant mass-production factories reduced the tensions that had long existed between skilled craftsmen and less skilled workers. A new category of worker, the semiskilled machine operator, played a particularly important role in the rise of the new unions. Finally, the difficulty of finding employment during the Depression made workers more reluctant than they had been in the past to simply quit their jobs when they were dissatisfied with conditions. Increasingly, they saw the solution not in looking for a better job, but in improving the one they had.

A dramatic confrontation unfolded in Minneapolis when a radical Teamster's Union local, several of whose leaders were followers of the dissident, exiled Russian Communist leader Leon Trotsky, organized among the city's truck drivers and warehousemen during the spring of 1934. When employers balked at recognizing their union, 5,000 truck drivers and warehouse workers walked off their jobs, with the support of thousands of the city's unemployed. Pitched warfare soon broke out between strikers, the police, and a business-funded vigilante group, the Citizen's Alliance. Casualties were heavy on all sides, but the militant union carried the day against employers, police, guardsmen, and timid union officials.

In Minneapolis, unionists had discussed escalating their struggles into a general strike, but in San Francisco, a fierce clash on the city's waterfront actually sparked a mass walkout by every worker in the city. Led by Harry Bridges, an Australian-born longshoreman who was close to the Communists, a new West Coast local of the International Longshoremen's Association (ILA) signed up thousands of longshoremen, who hated the humiliating, early morning "shape-up," in which they scrambled for a day's work on the docks. From the start, Bridges and his colleagues had to battle not only employers, but also the corrupt, conservative national leaders of the ILA, who had long negotiated secret deals with the big waterfront companies.

The San Francisco longshoremen struck in May 1934, and dockworkers from Seattle to San Diego soon joined them. Sailors and waterfront truckers also stopped work in what became the largest maritime strike in the nation's history. The workers maintained a peaceful strike for two months until conservative state officials, backing the shipping companies, decided to retake the waterfront by force. On July 5, "Bloody Thursday," police attacked union picket lines, killing two and injuring scores more.

Outraged longshoremen called for a general strike, soon winning the rest of the Bay Area labor movement to their cause. By July 16, San Francisco was at a virtual standstill, as 130,000 workers — including trolley drivers, construction workers, teamsters, bartenders, and even entertainers — walked off their jobs. For several days, nothing — not even food — moved into or out of Bay Area cities without the approval of the strike committee.

Popeye Versus the Goon

During 1933 and 1934, readers of E. C. Segar's *Popeye* comic strip were introduced to the Goons, powerful, mindless servants of the sailor's nemesis, the horrible Sea Hag. The name was soon applied to violent strikebreakers who patrolled the San Francisco waterfront. Elzie Crisler Segar, *Thimble Theatre*, 1934 — Reprinted with special permission of King Features Syndicate.

The general strike lasted but a few days. Businessmen, newspapers, and government officials maneuvered furiously to split the ranks of labor, denouncing the longshoremen as dangerous radicals while egging on the vigilante groups that destroyed the offices of the Communist Party and several allied organizations. In a compromise, Bridges and his strike committee called off the general strike on July 19 and accepted federal arbitration, which eventually gave the longshoremen most of what they wanted: union recognition, hiring halls controlled by the union, a thirty-hour workweek, and a pay increase.

The Minneapolis and San Francisco strikes followed a pattern that had been set by other union campaigns. In each case, radicals defied conservative AFL leaders and mobilized thousands of working people in concerted, militant strike action. When employers and police launched attacks to break their picket lines, thousands of sympathetic supporters poured out of working-class neighborhoods to aid the embattled unionists. The strikers won only a partial victory, but in each instance, they laid the groundwork for future gains. The leaders of the Minneapolis insurgency went on to organize long-distance truckers throughout the Midwest, contributing to the phenomenal growth of the International Brotherhood of the Teamsters. And the San Francisco strike led to the formation of the International Longshoremen and Warehousemen's Union and to the growth of maritime unionism all along the Pacific Coast.

Organized Labor Meets Defeat in the West and South   In spite of these dramatic union victories, 1934 also witnessed failures, including unsuccess-

"Labor Was in Control"

Mike Quin, a self-described "rank-and-file journalist," reported on the 1934 general strike that effectively shut down San Francisco and Oakland, California. Quin presented a sympathetic picture of the striking workers in The Big Strike, *a collection of his published articles.*

The paralysis was effective beyond all expectations. To all intents and purposes industry was at a complete standstill. The great factories were empty and deserted. No streetcars were running. Virtually all stores were closed. The giant apparatus of commerce was a lifeless, helpless hulk.

Labor had withdrawn its hand. The workers had drained out of the shops and plants like life-blood, leaving only a silent framework embodying millions of dollars worth of invested capital. In the absence of labor, the great machinery loomed as so much idle junk. . . .

Everything was there, all intact as the workers had left it—instruments, equipment, tools, machinery, raw materials and the buildings themselves. When the men walked out, they took only what belonged to them—their labor. And when they took that they might as well have taken everything, because all the elaborate apparatus they left behind was worthless and meaningless without their hand. The machinery was a mere extension of labor, created by and dependent upon labor.

Labor held the life-blood and energy. The owners remained in possession of the corpse.

Highways leading into the city bristled with picket lines. Nothing moved except by permission of the strike committee. Labor was in control.

Mike Quin, *The Big Strike* (1949).

ful efforts to organize unions in California's fruit and vegetable fields and in textile mills throughout the Piedmont region of the Carolinas. California's commercial agriculture depended on a multiethnic workforce. Three of every four of the state's 200,000 farm laborers were Mexican Americans, but workers of Filipino, Armenian, Chinese, and Japanese descent, as well as "Okie" migrants from middle America, also sweated in the cotton fields and fruit orchards. Many Mexican American workers had been influenced by the emancipatory, nationalist ideas that had spread throughout their homeland following the 1910 revolution there. But these workers, many of whom had been born in the United States, were also inspired by the promise of the New Deal and by the presence of Communist Party organizers in their midst.

Nearly 50,000 workers, the vast majority of them Mexican Americans, conducted more than forty agricultural strikes in 1933. In June, 1,500 berry pickers employed by Japanese ranchers in El Monte, a suburb of Los

Angeles, struck for higher wages. Five thousand celery field workers (including a sizable number of Japanese Americans and Filipino Americans) in small towns near Los Angeles soon joined the berry strikers. In October, 12,000 workers left the cotton fields of the San Joaquin Valley, north of Los Angeles. During these bitter conflicts, whole communities organized for a long and bitter struggle. Led by young Communists from the Cannery and Agricultural Workers Industrial Union, these uprisings of the migrant poor continued in 1934, spreading from the Imperial Valley on the Mexican border to the Santa Clara Valley near San Francisco.

Cotton Strike, October 1933
Strikers demanded that local police take action after cotton growers in Pixley and Arvin, California, opened fire on unarmed Mexican pickers, killing three people. Instead, authorities issued additional gun permits to growers and appointed many as deputies. Eventually, several growers in the Pixley incident were prosecuted for murder (and later acquitted by a friendly jury), while a strike leader was charged with criminal syndicalism. The Bancroft Library, University of California, Berkeley.

Almost all these work stoppages ended in violence and defeat. Because of the legislative power wielded by southern planters and western growers, the NIRA's Section 7a excluded agricultural workers from federal labor law. So local elites felt no need to restrain their opposition to agricultural unionism. A San Francisco rabbi who observed the activities of armed Anglo vigilante groups during a 1933 strike wrote to the governor, "Gangsterism has been substituted for law and order in the cotton area." The next year, police tear-gassed union meetings in the Imperial Valley, forcibly evicted more than 2,000 families, and burned workers' homes. Many strike leaders were arrested, tried, and jailed under California's draconian criminal syndicalism act, which made it a crime to belong to a group that sought a change in industrial ownership by force. An entire generation would pass before Cesar Chavez and other unionists sought to improve the lot of California agricultural workers.

The East Coast had its share of bitter strikes, most notably a huge textile walkout that closed mills from Maine to Alabama during the early fall of 1934. The Depression had devastated the textile industry, shortening workweeks and lowering wages to such a degree that malnutrition and disease pervaded the mill villages of the South. Child labor was common, and thousands of families lived in flimsy company-owned houses. But the loudest complaint of the mill workers was of "stretch-outs," the assignment of uncompensated additional tasks to each worker until the pace of their labor became unbearable.

The mill owners wrote and administered the NRA textile code, so the shorter hours and higher wages that were put into effect during the summer of 1933 came at a high price: a vicious stretch-out that taxed workers' minds and bodies for weeks and months on end. "Please do something," wrote thirteen South Carolina mill workers to a federal official. "There is many here that will give you a glad welcome and tell you of the Dirty Deal this eight hour law has given us." But Section 7a proved of little help. Soon after the passage of the NIRA, hundreds of thousands of mill workers flocked to the United Textile Workers' Union (UTW), boosting its membership to more than 300,000. But textile executives, especially in the South, refused to negotiate with the UTW and fired some 4,000 union activists while NRA officials stood aside.

The September 1934 textile strike was therefore a massive protest by almost 400,000 textile workers against the brutality of the mill owners and betrayal by New Deal officials. Whole communities supported the work stoppage, especially in the Piedmont South, where squadrons in automobiles quickly spread the insurgency to the most remote mill villages. In response, the mill owners evicted strikers from company housing, enlisted the support of the police and county sheriffs, and persuaded state officials to call out the National Guard to intimidate workers and arrest thousands of strikers. Violence erupted, and the police killed at least a dozen picketers.

To help settle the strike, President Roosevelt appointed a board of inquiry. The UTW, whose leadership was based in the North, used the federal initiative as an excuse to end the strike, much to the surprise and anger of southern mill workers. The mill owners did not rehire 15,000 strikers and blacklisted many key union activists. Those who did return had to "humble down," acting apologetic and meek to supervisors before they could resume work. In the South, textile unionism collapsed and, with it, the prospect that New Deal liberalism might secure a firm foothold in the region. Textile workers continued to live in misery, and southern labor remained without a voice when industrial unionism swept across the North and West.

Whatever their outcomes, the strike battles of 1934 demonstrated that the New Deal and the new unions had polarized the nation. Progressives, liberal Democrats, and trade unionists demanded new legislation to make the New Deal's promise a social and economic reality. But conservatives were just as alarmed—at labor violence, radical influence, and the growth of government power—and they had just begun to mobilize their forces.

The Counteroffensives Against the New Deal

By the end of 1934, the New Deal had acquired a powerful set of enemies. Since FDR's inauguration, national income had risen by one-quarter, unemployment had dropped by two million, and total factory wages had leapt upward. But the nation's annual output remained only slightly more than half of what it had been in 1929. Ten million workers tried to survive without jobs, and almost twice that many depended, at least partially on relief. The recovery had stalled, and Secretary of the Treasury Henry Morgenthau, Jr., frankly admitted that "we are not making any headway." On the right, many businessmen and bankers had become alarmed with the growth of federal power and the rise of a militant labor movement, while on the left, impatient new voices clamored for the New Deal to do even more to put Americans back to work and ensure a fair distribution of wealth and income.

Resurgence on the Right The NIRA came under particularly fierce attack in part because the process of writing and enforcing industry codes brought to the surface sharp conflicts among competing interests. Many farmers, small businessmen, and consumer groups argued that NRA price and production controls had been written primarily by and for large corporations; their effect was to prop up prices, stifle competition, and retard economic expansion. Even corporate leaders doubted the value of the NIRA. Section 7a, weak as it was, had spurred union organizing, and the NRA codes seemed an open invitation to more government regulation of the corporations.

Business criticism of the NIRA spilled over into a more general conservative criticism of the New Deal. Most businessmen feared that federal jobs programs would lead to higher taxes and a spirit of working-class defiance. "Five negroes on my place in South Carolina refused to work this spring," complained retired DuPont vice president R. R. M. Carpenter. "A cook on my houseboat at Fort Myers," he continued, "quit because the government was paying him a dollar an hour as a painter."

As time went on, more and more business leaders blamed the economy's ills on government functionaries, labor leaders, and individual "chiselers." Government power and budgets, they insisted, should be reduced drastically, and business should be given a greater voice in setting national policy. To promote this view, DuPont executive John J. Raskob, Pierre DuPont, and General Motors chairman Alfred P. Sloan founded the American Liberty League in 1934. Well financed and influential, the league soon

"The Square Deal"
Most nationally syndicated comic strips avoided politics, but a conservative political agenda consistently shaped the characters and stories in the popular *Little Orphan Annie*. Debuting in 1924, the comic strip reached the height of its popularity in the 1930s, even though the adventures of its spunky orphan hero conveyed a faith in self-reliance that was at odds with the cooperative spirit of the New Deal. But it was Annie's benefactor, the industrialist Oliver "Daddy" Warbucks, who epitomized cartoonist Harold Gray's beliefs. Warbucks was a self-made, inventive, and generous millionaire who invariably arrived in the nick of time to save the day. Harold Gray, *New York Daily News*, July 11, 1935 — Copyright Tribune Media Services, Inc. All rights reserved. Reprinted with permission.

came to represent the most reactionary wing of the business community. It campaigned in the courts, the newspapers, and the political arena against the New Deal and its labor-liberal supporters. In California, meanwhile, opponents of Roosevelt and the labor movement organized under the leadership of the Associated Farmers, a powerful statewide organization that provided money, manpower, and influence to all those who were opposed to unions, social reform, and civil liberties in the Golden State.

Populist Critics of the New Deal   Class divisions were also polarizing American politics. While some in business and big agriculture denounced the Roosevelt administration for its intrusive reform of the economy, a majoritarian, populist quest for even more far-reaching reforms became evident in the 1934 congressional elections. The Democrats won a two-thirds majority in the Senate and over three-quarters of the seats in the House. Most of the newly elected Democrats strongly backed the New Deal or stood to its left, seeking to implement an even more radical legislative agenda.

So as the nation moved to the left, the New Deal came under attack from all sides. Its most prominent southern critic, Huey Long of Louisiana, rose to power by attacking corporate interests and portraying himself as a champion of the common man. Elected governor in 1928, he completely dominated Louisiana's government. Under Long, Louisiana built hundreds of schools, hospitals, and bridges; paved thousands of miles of roads; distributed free textbooks; and increased taxes on oil and gas interests.

Long supported Roosevelt in 1932, when he himself won election to the Senate, but he soon criticized the New Deal both for creating huge bureaucracies that interfered in local affairs and for failing to curb the power of the rich. In 1934, Long proposed the "Share Our Wealth Plan," a system of confiscatory taxes on large fortunes and incomes that would enable the government to provide every family with "enough for a home, an automobile, a radio, and the ordinary convenience," plus a guaranteed annual income. Long set up thousands of Share Our Wealth Clubs and developed a large national following.

Other critics of the New Deal took their cues from Charles E. Coughlin, a Catholic priest from the suburbs of Detroit whose weekly radio broadcasts sometimes reached an audience of forty-five million listeners. Like Long, Coughlin at first supported Roosevelt but quickly grew disillusioned. Like so many other Catholic clergymen, Coughlin was a vehement anticommunist, but he nevertheless blamed the Depression on "Wall Street" and "international bankers." Inflationary monetary policy, he believed, would spark a recovery. More broadly, Coughlin promoted "social Catholicism" — a call for class harmony, "living wages," and social legislation to combat the evils of industrialism. Increasingly influenced by European fascists and anti-Semites, Coughlin began to denounce Jews, trade unions, and FDR.

Inauguration
This illustration of Huey Long taking the presidential oath of office appeared in his book *My First Days in the White House.* In his fantasy presidency, Long instituted a range of social and fiscal reforms, aided by a National Share Our Wealth Committee composed of co-operative bankers and industrialists. Long also fantasized about assembling a distinguished cabinet—including Franklin Delano Roosevelt as secretary of the navy. The book was published in 1935, shortly after Long's assassination. Cleanthe, Huey P. Long, *My First Days in the White House* (1935)—American Social History Project.

Coughlin and Long capitalized on popular discontent with the Depression and the unequal distribution of wealth and power. But in spite of their attacks on the rich, they firmly rejected collective ownership of the means of production, the basic tenet of socialism. Instead, they combined nostalgia for an older, community-based way of life with simple plans that they claimed would solve all social ills. The possibility that these populist anti-Roosevelt movements might join forces and enter national politics in 1936 deeply worried Roosevelt and his advisers.

The impressive electoral achievements of left-liberal alliances in several states also concerned the Administration. In California, novelist Upton Sinclair resigned from the Socialist Party in 1933 to form the End-Poverty-in-California (EPIC) movement and run for governor within the Democratic Party. Sinclair proposed that the state turn idle farmland and factories into self-sustaining cooperatives of the unemployed and impose high taxes on corporations and the rich. Attacked as a Communist and a crackpot, Sinclair lost the governorship but received well over one-third of the votes, helping twenty-three EPIC-backed candidates to win election to the state legislature.

In Washington State, EPIC sympathizers helped to elect a U.S. senator and to form the Washington Commonwealth Federation, which became a powerful force in that state's politics. In Minnesota, the labor-backed, left-wing Farmer-Labor Party took control of the state's governorship for most of the 1930s. Behind the scenes, the Communist Party—which in 1935 adopted a "popular front" strategy of building broad alliances with liberals and moderates—gained considerable influence in both organizations. Meanwhile, in Wisconsin, Senator Robert M. La Follette, Jr., and his brother Phil, a former governor, left the Republican Party to revive the old Progressive Party. The possibility that a national, left-leaning third party might form in time for the 1936 presidential election seemed plausible.

Conclusion: Collapse of the First New Deal

By the spring of 1935, the New Deal was in a state of disarray, and its main industrial recovery agency, the NRA, was falling apart. The final blow came on May 27, when, in *Schecter v. United States*, the Supreme Court declared the NIRA unconstitutional. The Court ruled that in allowing the NRA to write legally enforceable codes, Congress had unlawfully delegated its own authority and, by applying the codes to local businesses, had unconstitutionally extended the federal power to regulate interstate commerce. This decision signaled that the Court would strike down much of the New Deal's most far-reaching legislation. Roosevelt, whose first two years in office had raised so many hopes, now faced an uncertain future. The structures of government, politics, and labor relations had proved inadequate, as they had during the Gilded Age, for dealing with profound economic and social crisis. By the middle of the decade, most Americans agreed that basic economic and political changes were necessary. But the questions remained: What sort of changes, and in whose interest?

The Years in Review

1929
- Herbert Hoover is sworn in as president in March, after having decisively defeated Democrat Al Smith in the fall election.
- The stock market crashes on Black Thursday, October 24.

1930
- Communists rally thousands on International Unemployment Day (March 6) to demand government action in the face of mounting joblessness.

- The protectionist Smoot-Hawley Tariff Act sharply raises tariffs on imported goods to the highest levels in U.S. history.

1931

- Nine African American youths are falsely accused of rape in the Scottsboro case, which will attract international attention.

- Japanese troops occupy the Chinese province of Manchuria.

- European banks collapse as the economic crisis spreads internationally.

- Seattle's unemployed create the Unemployed Citizens' League, one of many self-help organizations of the jobless.

1932

- Twenty thousand World War I veterans stage a Bonus March to the Capitol, demanding that their war bonuses be distributed immediately; U.S. troops led by General Douglas MacArthur use force to disperse the protesters.

- More than 3,000 protesters march on the main Ford plant in Dearborn, Michigan, demanding jobs for the unemployed; four marchers are killed, and many more are wounded.

- Hoover establishes the Reconstruction Finance Corporation, which proves an inadequate response to the Depression.

- Franklin Delano Roosevelt is elected president, promising a "New Deal."

- New Yorkers boycott Chinese launderers, who refuse to adhere to a minimum price scheme.

1933

- Nazi leader Adolf Hitler is appointed chancellor of Germany.

- Unemployment peaks at fifteen million; the U.S. gross national product has fallen 29 percent since 1929.

- The Twenty-first Amendment nullifies Prohibition.

- In his first hundred days in office, President Roosevelt declares a bank holiday and establishes the Federal Emergency Relief Administration (FERA), Civilian Conservation Corps (CCC), Tennessee Valley Authority (TVA), Agricultural Adjustment Administration (AAA), and National Recovery Administration (NRA).

- Section 7a of the National Industrial Recovery Act (NIRA), which (on paper) gives workers right to organize, sparks a nationwide upsurge of labor activism.

- The Civil Works Administration puts four million people to work.

1934

- Democrats sweep the fall elections and gain overwhelming dominance in Congress — a sign of the popularity of the New Deal.

- A "New Deal for Indians," centered on the Indian Reorganization Act, alters the relationship between the federal government and Native Americans and ends the allotment of tribal lands to individuals.

- Black and white Arkansas sharecroppers organize the Southern Tenant Farmers' Union to stop evictions of tenants and croppers.

- A wave of militant strikes sweeps the nation, with particularly dramatic confrontations in Toledo, Minneapolis, and San Francisco; strikes in East Coast textile mills and California farm fields have little success.

- Drought hits the Great Plains; terrifying dust storms create the Dust Bowl in Kansas, Oklahoma, Colorado, New Mexico, and Texas.

- Senator Huey Long of Louisiana proposes the "Share Our Wealth Plan," a system of confiscatory taxes on large fortunes and incomes that would enable the government to provide Americans with a guaranteed annual income, old-age pensions, and universal education for children.

- Novelist Upton Sinclair wins one-third of the votes in his run for governor of California as the leader of the radical End Poverty in California movement.

- The Securities Act of 1933 establishes the Securities and Exchange Commission to regulate the nation's stock exchanges.

- Corporate leaders form the American Liberty League to campaign against New Deal reforms.

1935

- The U.S. Supreme Court declares the NIRA unconstitutional, setting off warnings that much of the New Deal legislation will be declared unconstitutional.

Additional Readings

For more on the onset and drastic economic and social impact of the Great Depression, see: Michael Bernstein, *The Great Depression: Delayed Recovery and Economic Change in America, 1929–1939* (1987); John Kenneth Galbraith, *The Great Crash, 1929* (1954); Charles Kindleberger, *The World in Depression*, rev. ed. (1986); David Kyvig, *Daily Life in the United States,*

1920–1940: How Americans Lived During the Roaring Twenties and the Great Depression (2004); Robert S. McElvaine, *The Great Depression* (1984); Studs Terkel, *Hard Times: An Oral History of the Great Depression* (1970); T. H. Watkins, *The Great Depression: America in the 1930s* (1993); and Joan Hoff Wilson, *Herbert Hoover: Forgotten Progressive* (1985).

For more on the Roosevelt administration and New Deal relief, see:
Anthony Badger, *The New Deal: The Depression Years, 1933–1940* (1989); Bernard Bellush, *The Failure of NRA* (1975); James MacGregor Burns, *Roosevelt: The Lion and the Fox* (1956); Blanche Wiesen Cook, *Eleanor Roosevelt, vol. 2, 1933–1938* (1999); Walter Crease, *TVA's Public Planning: The Vision, the Reality* (1990); Linda Gordon, *Pitied but Not Entitled: Single Mothers and the History of Welfare* (1994); David M. Kennedy, *Freedom from Fear: The American People in Depression and War, 1929–1945* (1999); William E. Leuchtenburg, *Franklin D. Roosevelt and the New Deal* (1963); Gail Radford, *Modern Housing for America: Policy Struggles in the New Deal Era* (1996); Lois Scharf, *Eleanor Roosevelt: First Lady of American Liberalism* (1987); Arthur Schlesinger, *The Age of Roosevelt: Crisis of the Old Order* (1957); Jordan A. Schwartz, *The New Dealers* (1993); Harvard Sitkoff, *A New Deal for Blacks* (1978); and Nancy Beck Young, *Franklin D. Roosevelt and the Shaping of American Political Culture* (2001).

For more on the resurgence of organized labor during the early 1930s, see:
Irving Bernstein, *The Lean Years: A History of the American Worker, 1920–1933* (1960); Lizabeth Cohen, *Making a New Deal: Industrial Workers in Chicago, 1919–1939* (1990); Robert Cohen, *When the Old Left Was Young, 1929–1941* (1993); Melvyn Dubofsky, *The State and Labor in Modern America* (1994); Steve Fraser, *Labor Will Rule: Sidney Hillman and the Rise of American Labor* (1991); Gary Gerstle, *Working-Class Americanism: The Politics of Labor in a Textile City, 1914–1960* (1989); and Colin Gordon, *New Deals: Business, Labor, and Politics in America, 1920–1935* (1994).

For more on the Depression and New Deal in the American South and West, see:
Francisco E. Balderrama and Raymond Rodriguez, *Decade of Betrayal: Mexican Repatriation in the 1930s* (1995); James Goodman, *Stories of Scottsboro* (1994); James Gregory, *American Exodus: The Dust Bowl Migration and Okie Culture in California* (1989); Donald Grubbs, *Cry from the Cotton: The Southern Tenant Farmers' Union and the New Deal* (1971); Jacquelyn Dowd Hall et al., *Like a Family: The Making of a Southern Cotton Mill World* (1987); Laurence Hauptman, *The Iroquois and the New Deal* (1981); Robin D. G. Kelley, *Hammer and Hoe: Alabama Communists During the Great Depression* (1990); Greg Mitchell, *The Campaign of the Century: Upton Sinclair's EPIC Race for Governor of California and the Birth of Media*

Politics (1992); Bryant Simon, *A Fabric of Defeat: The Politics of South Carolina Millhands, 1910–1948* (1998); Kevin Starr, *Endangered Dreams: The Great Depression in California* (1996); Graham D. Taylor, *The New Deal and American Tribalism: The Administration of the Indian Reorganization Act, 1934–1945* (2001); and Donald Worster, *Dust Bowl: The Southern Plains in the 1930s* (1979).

For more on critics of the New Deal, see: Alan Brinkley, *Voices of Protest: Huey Long, Father Coughlin, and the Great Depression* (1982); Michael Kazin, *The Populist Persuasion: An American History* (1995); and Leo Ribuffo, *The Old Christian Right* (1983).

9
Labor Democratizes America
1935–1939

IN THE SECOND HALF of the 1930s, America's working people — organized into new industrial unions and allied with President Franklin D. Roosevelt — moved the nation toward a more democratic political and economic order. The roots of that transformation could be seen in the wave of strikes that mobilized so many workers in the summer of 1934 and in the remarkable Democratic congressional victory in the fall elections that year. Many of the new members of Congress stood well to the left of Roosevelt, in favor of an "industrial democracy" that would curb business power, enhance labor's voice, and increase government social spending. "Boys—this is our hour," exulted Harry Hopkins, FDR's top relief official. "We've got to get everything we want . . . now or never."

FDR and his progressive supporters pushed this program though Congress in 1935 and 1936, after which the president won reelection in a massive landslide. Emboldened workers instigated strikes throughout the industrial heartland, establishing a powerful set of new trade unions and putting working-class voters at the heart of the New Deal coalition that dominated American domestic politics for almost half a century. Women and African American workers made great strides in the new activist unions and played vital roles in the surge of cultural activities tied to the New Deal. Although the New Deal would encounter bitter opposition from the late 1930s on, American political and social life and the culture that engaged it had taken a democratic leap forward.

The Second New Deal

Although production had risen by almost 30 percent since early 1933, unemployment remained high in 1935. New Dealers blamed "underconsumption" —

Just Before the Tear Gas
On September 16, 1936, at the height of the Salinas Valley, California, lettuce strike, members of the Fruit and Vegetable Workers' Union blocked a downtown Salinas street. Their intent was to stop a convoy of trucks carrying produce harvested by strikebreakers. California State Police attacked the strikers shortly after this photo was taken. Harold Ellwood, *San Francisco Examiner*, September 17, 1936 — California Section, California State Library. Copyright 1936 San Francisco Examiner. Reprinted with permission.

a chronic weakness in consumer demand caused by low wages, an inequitable distribution of income, and a capitalist system that was no longer growing. Big business and the rich, the New Dealers insisted, would have to give up some of their wealth and power. In a burst of reform that historians have since come to call the "Second New Deal," FDR and most Democrats pushed for measures that would help workers to establish trade unions, find government-paid jobs, and retire with dignity. African Americans and women did not benefit as much as white males did under many of these new social program, yet they continued to support FDR and push for equal rights. New Dealers also sought to break up the giant utility holding companies, raise taxes, and limit the power of banks. Business and commercial interests battled furiously against these measures — they called Roosevelt's tax plan a "soak the rich" scheme — and in the end, New Dealers had to settle for laws that were less sweeping than most wanted. But the conflict made it clear that the nation's politics had tilted to the left.

An Expanded Jobs Program   New Dealers tackled the unemployment issue directly, with a series of programs that were more permanent and substantive than the ones the Civil Works Administration had thrown together so hurriedly two years before. In the spring of 1935, Congress passed a $5 billion Emergency Relief Appropriations Act that funded new agencies designed to provide useful and creative employment to millions. One, the National Youth Administration, initiated work projects for more than 4.5 million students and young workers; another, the Resettlement Administration, aided the rural homeless, agricultural tenants, and owners of small farms.

But Harry Hopkins's Works Progress (later Projects) Administration (WPA) was the most important of these new programs. Unlike the Civil Works Administration, the WPA provided productive jobs, not relief. WPA workers built or improved more than 2,500 hospitals, 5,900 schools, 1,000 airport landing fields, and nearly 13,000 playgrounds. WPA employees saw themselves as workers and citizens, not as welfare cases. They organized unions, demanded higher pay, and lobbied for the continuation of the program when Congress began to cut it back at the end of the 1930s. Roosevelt had insisted that WPA wages be pegged at a level below those in the private sector; even so, the huge jobs program fulfilled a demand that spokespeople for the unemployed had been making for nearly a century. By the time of its demise in 1943, the agency had provided employment for eight million Americans.

The WPA had its greatest impact in the hard-hit industrial centers of the Northeast and Midwest, but it also provided jobs and built schools, bridges, and roads in rural areas of the South and West. The Rural Electrification Administration, which began as part of the WPA, inaugurated a "power revolution" that transformed the lives of rural Americans. It quadrupled the number of farms that had electricity between 1930 and 1945, largely as a result of its support for rural cooperatives.

The Social Security Act   During the first half of the twentieth century, many industrialized Western nations, most notably Great Britain, Germany, and the Scandinavian democracies, built "welfare states" that offered their working populations protection against the hazards of a market economy: unemployment, sickness, old-age insecurity, and the loss of the family breadwinner. American reformers had failed to establish a similar system of universal social insurance during the Progressive era. Veterans of that period, such as Secretary of Labor Frances Perkins, viewed the Second New Deal as an opportunity to compensate for that failure. A women's network of New Dealers and social reformers (including First Lady Eleanor Roosevelt) joined forces to press for the enacting of laws that would protect women as well as male workers from destitution.

The president himself called for legislation that would provide cradle-to-grave security "against the hazards and vicissitudes of life." This was a social, collective insurance program designed to protect the American people from the turmoil that was always present in a capitalist economy. In the late twentieth century, "Social Security" became synonymous with old-age insurance, but the Social Security Act that Congress passed in 1935 embodied a far larger conception of the government's role. In providing social protection to all citizens, including unemployment insurance and aid for poor families, the law represented a fundamental break with traditional elitist notions that the poor and the unemployed were to blame for their condition.

The law contained two types of support for the elderly. Those who were destitute in 1935 could receive a small federal pension: $15 a month in the mid-1930s. But in a longer time frame, many working Americans could look forward to a federal pension that was financed by a payroll tax split evenly between themselves and their employers. Under the new system, an individual's pension check would vary according to marital status and past earnings but not according to state of residence or type of employment. This old-age insurance system accommodated two groups of Americans. On the one side were the clamorous demands of Dr. Francis Townsend's popular old-age movement, which advocated a monthly $200 pension for everyone over age sixty. On the other side were those representing the interests of employers, who sought to limit costly pension expenditures and to standardize benefits across states, regions, and industries.

The Social Security Act also established a federal-state program of unemployment insurance, designed to put cash in the pockets of workers during the periodic layoffs that plagued industries such as automobile,

textile, and clothing manufacturing and construction. A special tax also financed unemployment insurance, but unlike the pension program, the states administered it. Consequently, eligibility and benefits varied widely from state to state; payments were high in the North and low in the South.

Still, the old-age insurance and unemployment programs won nearly universal support. Most Americans saw these entitlements not as relief for the poor, but as insurance that was purchased with taxes deducted from their own paychecks. Both programs redistributed income from the rich to the poor, but their advocates, including Roosevelt, who abhorred "the dole," downplayed this fact. The president saw the Social Security tax largely as a political rather than a fiscal issue. He told his advisers, "We put those payroll contributions there so as to give the contributors a legal, moral, and political right to collect their pensions and their unemployment benefits. With those taxes in there, no damn politician can ever scrap my social security program."

Gender and Race in the New Deal   The New Deal had a decidedly mixed record on issues of concern to women. While the New Deal effort to legitimize social insurance proved enormously successful for workers and recent

Manly Labor and the Security of the Family

New Deal public art often reinforced traditional ideas about the roles of men and women in U.S. society. Seymour Fogel's *Security of the Family*, a mural at the main entrance of the Social Security Building, shows a man seated at a plentiful table reading a newspaper, a symbol of engagement with the public world. A woman stands on the other side of the table, cradling a baby, while children conspicuously play and study nearby. Instead of acknowledging women's work outside the home, in the face of economic and social crisis Fogel's mural heralds men's productive labor as the bulwark of the American family and future of the next generation. Seymour Fogel, *Security of the Family*, 1942, mural, Wilbur J. Cohen Building — National Archives.

retirees, the moral and social biases attached to welfare would become increasingly debilitating for those who could not work. Thus, the Social Security Act provided far less generous and equitable payments for the elderly poor and for dependent children in single-parent families and required far more demeaning applications than the ones for those who had "earned" their benefits. For example, the new social insurance law provided matching funds to the states to finance an Aid to Dependent Children program, but the states did not treat these benefits as a guaranteed entitlement. A woman with dependent children received financial support only if it was approved by a social worker on the basis of the family's degree of need, the mother's adherence to a code of acceptable sexual conduct, and the stability of the home life she provided. In the 1930s, when most eligible women were white and widowed, welfare aid of this sort generated little controversy. But when an increasing number of deserving children began to come from families in which the mother was neither white nor widowed, mainstream Americans developed a negative opinion about what came to be disparaged as "welfare."

Women political activists, led by Eleanor Roosevelt, had a greater role than in any other previous presidential administration. President Roosevelt appointed the first woman cabinet member, Secretary of Labor Frances Perkins; the first woman director of the U.S. Mint; and the first woman judge on the federal Circuit Court of Appeals. But the success of these few individuals translated into only modest gains for women as a whole. Relatively few women found work in the New Deal job-creating agencies, and Social Security coverage failed to include some of the most important categories of female employees, such as waitresses and maids. Women New Dealers, moreover, generally supported an older Progressive agenda of providing "special protection" for female workers rather than demanding equal rights for them.

Many of the New Deal social programs also denied equal benefits to African Americans—in part because of the power of southern Democrats in the New Deal coalition. Southern employers worried that federal Social Security benefits would discourage black workers from taking low-paying jobs in their fields, factories, and kitchens. Thus, old-age insurance covered neither agricultural laborers nor domestic servants—a pool of workers that included at least 60 percent of the nation's black population. Furthermore, unemployment insurance excluded sharecroppers—black or white—and farm laborers (many of whom were of Mexican descent in the West). State administration of the program for dependent children resulted in huge inequities; in the 1930s, monthly payments for a typical family in Arkansas amounted to less than one-eighth those in Massachusetts. Relief programs regularly shortchanged African Americans, and many New Deal work projects assigned blacks to segregated units. The Agricultural Adjustment Act, which sent crop reduction checks to landlords and not their tenants, led to the eviction of thousands of poor farm families from lands that now earned federal dollars by lying fallow.

Nor did FDR throw his support behind an antilynching law that the National Association for the Advancement of Colored People (NAACP) proposed in November 1933. Roosevelt denounced lynching, but he refused to confront the power of the southern racists ensconced within the Democratic party. "The southerners . . . are chairmen or occupy strategic places on most of the Senate and House committees," FDR explained. "If I come

---

"Please Help Us Mr. President": Black Americans Write to FDR

Although Franklin D. Roosevelt never endorsed antilynching legislation and condoned discrimination against African Americans in federally funded relief programs, he still won the hearts and the votes of many African Americans. Yet this support and even veneration for Roosevelt did not blind black Americans to the continuing discrimination that they faced. Indeed, the two views were often combined when they wrote letters to the president asking him to do something about discrimination that they confronted in their daily lives. [Note: This letter is rendered as in original without corrections of spelling errors.]

Reidsville. Ga Oct 19th 1935
Hon. Franklin D. Roosevelt.
President of U. S.
Washington D. C.

Dear Mr. President
Would you please direct the people in charge of the releaf work in Georgia to issue the provisions + other supplies to our suffering colored people. I am sorry to worrie you with this Mr. President but hard as it is to believe the releaf officials here are using up most every thing that you send for them self + their friends. they give out the releaf supplies here on Wednesday of this week and give us black folks, each one, nothing but a few cans of pickle meet and to white folks they give blankets, bolts of cloth and things like that. I dont want to take to mutch of your time Mr president but will give you just one example of how the releaf is work down here the witto Nancy Hendrics own lands, stock holder in the Bank in this town and she is being supplied with Blankets cloth and gets a supply of cans goods regular this is only one case but I could tell you many.

Please help us mr President because we cant help our self and we know you is the president and a good Christian man we is praying for you. Yours truly cant sign my name Mr President they will beat me up and run me away from here and this is my home

[Anonymous]

Federal Emergency Relief Administration Central Files and New Subject Files, National Archives, as published in Robert S. McElvaine, ed., *Down and Out in the Great Depression* (Chapel Hill: University of North Carolina Press, 1983): 83.

out for the antilynching bill now, they will block every bill I ask Congress to pass to keep America from collapsing."

The same racial and regional disparities shaped the last major piece of welfare legislation that was passed during the Second New Deal: the Fair Labor Standards Act (FLSA), passed in 1938. The FLSA banned child labor in manufacturing industries, established the first nationwide minimum wage, and made the forty-hour workweek a national norm by mandating that employers pay time-and-a-half for work over and above that standard. Though those in the labor movement who had sought a thirty-hour work-week to generate new jobs were disappointed, the act did end the traditional half-day of Saturday work, making the "weekend" a two-day affair.

In a concession to the increasingly conservative congressional represen-tatives from the white South, the FLSA pegged the minimum wage to the low pay in the southern textile and lumber industries. Once again, the FLSA denied workers in agriculture, domestic service, and the restaurant trade even those minimal wage standards. But if few workers actually received wage increases under the act in the 1930s, employers and social conservatives had nevertheless conceded the ideological high ground to New Deal liberals.

In the 1930s, African Americans took important steps toward winning the civil rights and economic equality that had long been denied them. Most black leaders did not directly attack racial segregation of schools, jobs, and government programs, but African Americans nevertheless put a new set of demands on the nation's social and political agenda. The legal strategy of the NAACP exemplified this new approach. Lawyers Charles Houston and Thurgood Marshall attacked educational segregation by insisting that southern states abide by the potentially expensive requirements inherent in the Supreme Court's "separate but equal" doctrine (*Plessy v. Ferguson*, 1896).

Evicted

These black sharecroppers were forced off farms by land-lords eager to receive federal crop subsidies. They gathered along Highway 60 in New Madrid County, Missouri, in January 1939. Arthur Rothstein — Prints and Photographs Division, Library of Congress.

"Don't Buy Where You Can't Work"

The women walking this picket line were asking customers to boycott one of the many white-owned stores that refused to hire black employees in West Baltimore, Maryland. Similar demonstrations appeared in New York, Chicago, and other large cities in the early 1930s. Afro-American Newspapers Archives and Research Center.

By demanding actual equality of educational opportunity, NAACP court cases opened border-state professional schools to African Americans and equalized the salaries of many black and white teachers throughout the South.

African American workers demanded economic justice as well as the rights of equal citizenship. In Baltimore, New York, Chicago, and other large cities, they launched "Don't Buy Where You Can't Work" campaigns, insisting that white owners of stores in their communities employ black clerks and salespeople. In the early 1930s, these campaigns had a black nationalist and sometimes anti-Semitic flavor. But they took on an increasingly interracial, prounion character later in the decade, especially under the leadership of Adam Clayton Powell, Jr., a charismatic young minister from Harlem whose talent for oratory would later earn him a career in Congress. By the early 1940s, thousands of African Americans had obtained employment with public utilities, municipal services, and city transit lines in the North.

This strategy had its counterpart in the New Deal, for the administration's accommodation of southern segregationists was balanced in part by the racial liberalism of top government officials. Secretary of the Interior Harold Ickes and First Lady Eleanor Roosevelt helped to recruit Roosevelt's "black cabinet," a group of subcabinet-level officials and outside advisers who fought hard against discrimination in New Deal programs. Members of this group—such as Mary McLeod Bethune, an African American educator and close friend of the First Lady, and William Hastie, the dean of the law school at Howard University—wanted to abolish segregation. But they often had to settle for equal access to government programs, and even that was not always forthcoming.

But activists scored a great symbolic victory for racial equality in 1939, after the Daughters of the American Revolution (DAR) refused to permit the world-famous contralto and African American Marian Anderson to sing in the DAR's Washington concert hall. With the backing of Eleanor Roosevelt, a coalition of black civic leaders and NAACP officials won the Roosevelt administration's approval for Anderson to perform on Easter Sunday at the Lincoln Memorial. The performance established a powerful association between civil rights and a key symbol of American nationalism. "Genius, like justice, is blind," said Ickes, as he introduced Anderson to an audience of 75,000 people.

The Wagner Act   Undoubtedly the most radical and far-reaching piece of legislation that was passed during Roosevelt's "second hundred days" of 1935 was the National Labor Relations Act, known as the Wagner Act, for its sponsor, New York's Senator Robert Wagner. The president was not initially an advocate of Wagner's bill, but he reluctantly put it on his agenda because the legislation would encourage the growth of trade unions, which seemed to offer a solution to two problems confronting the nation. The first was the social turmoil that had been so notable during the New Deal's first two years, especially during the 1934 labor upsurge. "Men versed in the tenets of freedom become restive when not allowed to be free," Senator Wagner had argued. Roosevelt shared Wagner's viewpoint, so in May 1935, when the U.S. Supreme Court struck down the National Industrial Recovery Act that mandated industry self-regulation, the president finally agreed to get behind Wagner's bill. The second problem Roosevelt hoped the proposed act would solve was wage stagnation and underconsumption, which most liberals blamed for the long Depression. American workers had to make more money, and a revived union movement was the only institution that was capable of forcing a big company such as U.S. Steel or General Motors to raise wages for their own employees and then spread the new pay standard to millions of other workers.

But the trade unions did more than raise wages. To the mass of American workers, a huge proportion of whom were immigrants or African Americans, unions represented a doorway into the mainstream of American life. Thus, by encouraging the growth of trade unions, the Wagner Act helped not only to raise incomes, but also to democratize the world of work by giving workers a collective voice with which to settle their grievances and organize themselves to bargain and take political action.

The Wagner Act guaranteed workers the right to freely organize their own unions and to strike, boycott, and picket their employers. It banned "unfair labor practices" by the boss, including the maintenance of

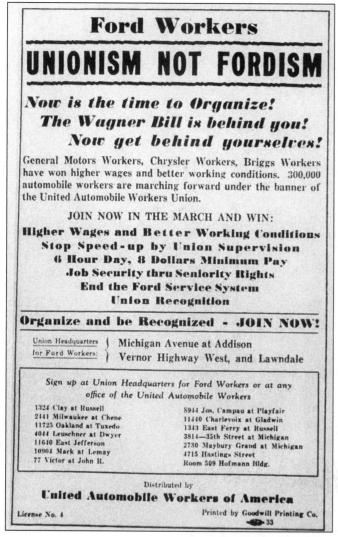

"The Wagner Bill Is Behind You!"

This leaflet distributed by the United Automobile Workers captured the impact of the Wagner Act on union organizing. Scott Molloy Archives.

company-dominated unions, the black-listing of union activists, the intimidation or firing of workers who sought to join an independent union, and the employment of industrial spies. To determine the will of the workers, the new law established a National Labor Relations Board, which would hear employee complaints, determine union jurisdictions, and conduct on-site elections. Whenever a majority of a company's workers chose a union, management had a legal obligation to negotiate with the union over wages, hours, and working conditions. Collective bargaining, wrote a leading economist, was a method of "introducing civil rights into industry, that is, of requiring that management be conducted by rule rather than by arbitrary decision." It was the essence of the industrial democracy that many New Dealers and labor activists sought to build.

The Challenge of Industrial Unionism

A law, however, is not a social movement. To give the Wagner Act real social and political meaning, the nation needed a working-class alliance of explosive power and institutional strength. In June 1935, when Franklin Roosevelt signed the new labor act into law, the obstacles to the creation of such a movement were considerable. Large corporate employers were so certain that the Supreme Court would declare the Wagner Act unconstitutional that they fought the unions and ignored the new statute. Many employers, including General Motors, Goodyear, and Republic Steel, hired labor spies, fired union activists, stocked up on guns and tear gas, and waged a public relations campaign against the act and the unions. Mass industrial unionism would not come easily in the United States, but new people, new ideas, and new organizing tactics mobilized millions of workers throughout the great mass production industries of that era. A fever of organization gripped working-class communities in a huge arc that spread from New

England through New York, Pennsylvania, the upper Midwest, and then on into the Southwestern states, in the process helping to give FDR and other New Deal Democrats a smashing reelection victory in 1936. Working-class empowerment had its impact not only at the work site and the ballot box, but also in the community. Union-sponsored baseball teams and bowling leagues, singing groups, tenant organizations, food cooperatives, and health clinics—all were part of a new participatory culture that gave life and spirit to the industrial unionism of the era. There were few feminists among the men who led the unions or staffed the top New Deal agencies. But the democratic awakening of the 1930s nevertheless had a profound impact on the lives of millions of women and of the men whose skin color had for so long made them something less than full citizens of the republic.

The Committee for Industrial Organization   Most leaders of the American Federation of Labor (AFL) were unwilling to wage the necessary fight. They had no comprehensive strategy for organizing the semiskilled workers who made up the majority of employees in the great mass-production industries. These workers wanted an inclusive form of unionism that incorporated employees of many different skills and trades in a single industrial union. But the AFL adhered to a long-standing philosophy of exclusive jurisdiction, meaning that the various craft unions—carpenters, machinists, electricians, and so forth—would seek to organize only a narrow slice of the skilled workforce in each factory and mill. Equally important, the AFL leadership mistrusted workers who were not of Northern European or U.S. ancestry. William Collins, an AFL official assigned to the auto industry, once joked, "My wife can always tell from the smell of my clothes what breed of foreigners I have been hanging out with."

Such attitudes infuriated unionists such as the United Mine Workers' (UMW) John L. Lewis and the Amalgamated Clothing Workers' Sidney Hillman, both advocates of industrial unionism. In their view, passage of the Wagner Act, the insurgent mood of the working class, and the increasingly antibusiness tenor of the White House meant that there would never be a better time to unionize industrial workers. If unions could seize this opportunity, organized labor would multiply its membership, economic power, and political clout.

By the fall of 1935, Lewis, Hillman, and a few like-minded colleagues had concluded that any mass organizing effort would have to take place outside the AFL framework, under the banner of a new Committee for Industrial Organization, later renamed the Congress of Industrial Organizations (CIO). John L. Lewis proved an inspiring chief of the new industrial union movement, but he was not a radical. The burly, sonorous-voiced UMW leader voted Republican in most elections and had a well-deserved reputation as a union autocrat. But he was determined to organize the labor movement by industry, not by craft. "Great combinations of capital," he argued, "have assembled to themselves tremendous power and influence, and they are almost 100 percent effective in opposing . . . the American Federation of Labor. . . . If you go in there with your craft union they will mow you down."

The success of the CIO's organizing campaign in 1936 and 1937 rested on its ability to tap the energy of thousands of grassroots activists and to provide the national coordination and leadership that would enable the new unions to confront large corporations such as U.S. Steel and General Motors. Lewis hired scores of Communists and socialists because of their exceptional ability as mass organizers, and he backed their efforts with money from the UMW treasury. When reporters probed his decision to hire so many Communists, Lewis replied, "Who gets the bird, the hunter or the dog?" As it turned out, the "dog" got quite a few birds. The leftists with whom Lewis cooperated were energetic, young, and confident. Union radicals, many of whom were Communists or socialists — such as the autoworker Walter Reuther, the longshoremen's leader Harry Bridges, and the Transport Workers' Mike Quill — would soon emerge as the new generation of labor leaders. They were born in the twentieth century. Many were Catholic, some were African Americans and Jews, a few were Mexican Americans, but women were largely absent from the CIO leadership ranks.

The Roosevelt Landslide The CIO organizing drive was closely linked with Roosevelt's 1936 reelection campaign. Lewis wanted "a president who would hold the light for us while we went out and organized," so the nascent industrial union movement broke new ground by making an unprecedented half-million-dollar contribution to the national Democratic Party. As a result, the CIO enjoyed the friendly neutrality of the federal government during the most crucial phase of its organizing work.

To challenge Roosevelt for the presidency, the Republicans nominated Governor Alfred M. Landon of Kansas. Landon's campaign was backed by the conservative Liberty League, the National Association of Manufacturers, and many bitter opponents of the New Deal, but the Kansas governor was not a reactionary; in a tribute to the powerful New Deal coalition, and the ideas that sustained it, Landon endorsed much of Roosevelt's program while promising to administer it more efficiently.

Leaders of the Coughlin, Long, and Townsend movements formed the short-lived Union Party, an uneasy coalition that nominated Congressman William Lemke of North Dakota for the presidency. (Huey Long, who would have been the obvious choice of the new party, had been assassinated in September 1935.) On the left, both the Socialist and Communist parties ran halfhearted campaigns, implicitly backing Roosevelt. Earl Browder, the Communist presidential candidate in 1936, later recalled conducting an "ambiguous campaign in favor of 'my rival,' Roosevelt." Earlier in the decade, the Communists had sharply attacked the New Deal. But now, to fight against big business and the Republicans at home and the rise of fascism abroad, they promoted a "Popular Front" of labor, liberals, New Dealers, and other radicals while proclaiming that "communism is twentieth-century Americanism."

Roosevelt ignored the small parties, directing his fire against the Republicans and the "economic royalists," who, he said, took "other people's money" to "impose a new industrial dictatorship." The forces of "organized money," he charged, "are unanimous in their hate for me—and I welcome their hatred." He concluded, "I should like to have it said of my first Administration that in it the forces of selfishness and of lust for power met their match." Such rhetoric paid off. As one millworker in the South noted, Roosevelt "is the first man in the White House to understand that my boss is a son of a bitch." When the Roosevelt motorcade passed through Michigan's industrial belt, virtually every assembly line ground to a halt as workers, union and nonunion alike, crowded to the windows.

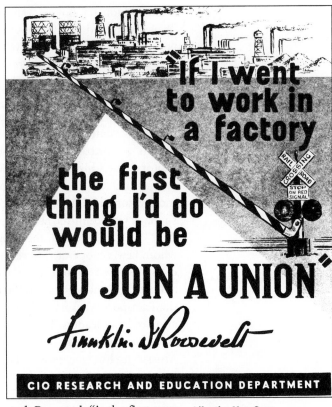

Like the Man Says . . .
A CIO recruiting poster quoted President Franklin Delano Roosevelt's statement supporting unions and collective bargaining. The George Meany Memorial Archives, AFL-CIO.

Roosevelt also benefited from a shift in the loyalties of African American voters. Since the end of the Civil War, African Americans had been steadfast Republicans, but during the 1930s, they moved in massive numbers to the Democratic column. On the surface, this turnaround seemed puzzling. Roosevelt had never added black equality to his legislative agenda, and many of his programs discriminated against African Americans. Nevertheless, African American support for Roosevelt mushroomed during the 1930s (Figure 9.1). His administration responded to the needs of rural African Americans when the disastrous impact of the Agricultural Assistance Act on tenant farmers became apparent. New Deal agencies granted loans to struggling black farmers, helped some tenants to buy land, and created agricultural settlements where displaced farmers could begin anew. Meanwhile, New Deal relief measures and employment projects rescued many African Americans from complete destitution. In Cleveland, for example, the federal government became the largest employer of African Americans, whose job-

FIGURE 9.1 African Americans Vote Democratic

Although the Roosevelt administration never supported civil rights legislation, as it would be defined after World War II, African Americans began to abandon the Republican Party in the 1930s because the New Deal offered them jobs, relief, and a modicum of political power, especially in the urban North. This graph, which was developed by historian Nancy Weiss, shows the dramatic change in black voting patterns between 1932 and 1936. Weiss compiled data on voting in precincts that were predominantly black, which she defined as having a black population of 90 percent or greater in 1940.

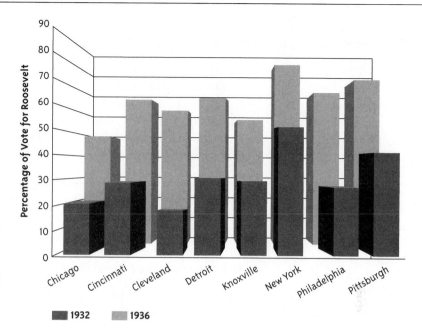

less rate fell from 50 to 30 percent. New Deal agencies also built more than three thousand housing units for the city's minority residents—fully half the public housing built in Cleveland.

On Chicago's South Side, one black resident recalled how "the WPA came along and Roosevelt came to be a god . . . You worked, you got a paycheck, and you had some dignity." Another New Deal agency, the Public Works Administration, spent four times more building African American schools and hospitals than all government agencies combined had done in the previous three decades. In Columbia, South Carolina, a registrar of

Love at First Sight

In an anti-FDR cartoon by James G. Swinnerton published in the *New York American* during the 1936 presidential campaign, a threatening Communist wolf licks the New Deal, represented by a "brain truster" wearing an academic cap and gown and donkey ears. The "Brain Trust" was a group of intellectual FDR advisors who helped construct the New Deal. James G. Swinnerton, *New York American*, 1936 — American Social History Project.

"President Roosevelt Is a Friend to the Laborin' Men"

African Americans wrote and sang many songs during the Depression to acknowledge the debt they felt to President Roosevelt or to tell the story of how joining unions changed their lives. Many of these songs used the rhythms and style of old spirituals or prison work songs. The lyrics of one such song, "Union Dues," were written in a more modern musical idiom, the blues, which became popular in southern African American communities in the 1920s. The folklorist George Korson recorded "Union Dues" during the 1940s.

President Roosevelt is a friend to the laborin' men,
Gives us the right to organize an' be real union men,
Union, union is all over the wide worl',
Back on the farm an' tobacco barns.
I'm glad I'm a union man; long may it live on,
The union will be livin' when I'm dead an' gone.

I got the union blues, don't care where I go,
I got the union blues, don't care where I be,
It's good for you an' good enough for me;
I'm goin' down the road feelin' mighty glad,
I'm goin' down the road feelin' mighty glad,
The union is the best friend that labor ever had.

I'm goin' to write a letter, goin' to mail it in the month o' May.
I'm goin' to write a letter, goin' to mail it this very day.
I'm goin' to thank the President for that seven-hour day.
I'm goin' to close my song, but won't close my mind,
I'm goin' to close my song, but won't close my mind—
That laborin' man was not left behind.

George Korson, *Coal Dust on the Fiddle* (1943).

voters reported that black Americans "say Roosevelt saved them from starvation, gave them aid when they were in distress, and now they were going to vote for him."

Roosevelt garnered 60 percent of the popular vote in 1936 and carried every state but Vermont and Maine. His victory was one of party as well as personality: the Republicans lost twelve more seats in the House of Representatives, giving the Democrats three-quarters of the total. In the Senate, seven new Democrats took office, giving the president's party nearly eight of every ten seats in that body. Democratic gubernatorial candidates won in Michigan, Ohio, Pennsylvania, and New York, four states where battles for union organization were sure to be fought. Urban working people made up the core of the new Democratic electorate. Overwhelming support came from the newly enfranchised children of turn-of-the-century Southern and Eastern European immigrants and from the native-born millions, black and white, who had left the farms for the cities during the 1920s. For them, a vote for Roosevelt and the New Deal was practically a requirement of participatory citizenship, a repudiation of the old industrial order.

Times had changed. In the 1920 election, the Republicans had captured the twelve largest cities, with a plurality of more than 1.5 million votes. In 1936, Roosevelt and the Democrats swamped their opponents in those cities by a margin of more than 3.5 million. In Knoxville, Tennessee, 56 percent of African Americans voted for Roosevelt; 75 percent in Pittsburgh; and 81 percent in New York City. In some midwestern industrial cities, over 90 percent of the Polish American and Italian American vote went to the Democrats. These urban ethnic and African American working-class voters would remain the backbone of the Democratic Party for the next third of a century.

The Flint Sit-Down Strike   Buoyed by Roosevelt's landslide reelection, CIO efforts to organize basic industries—steel, rubber, meatpacking, autos, and electrical products—climaxed during the winter of 1937 in the General Motors sit-down strike at Flint, Michigan, the most consequential work stoppage of the entire twentieth century. During the 1930s and for decades thereafter, General Motors Corporation (GM) was the largest and most profitable corporation in the United States and one of the most sophisticated. *Fortune* magazine called GM "the world's most influential industrial unit in forming the life patterns of the machine age." Not surprisingly, GM managers were increasingly hostile to both the New Deal and the new industrial unions. The CIO's political objectives, reported GM's president Alfred Sloan to stockholders, were an "important step toward an economic and political dictatorship." GM spent more money on labor spies than did any other company.

Autoworkers sought to counter GM's enormous power with a companywide industrial trade union that could defend their dignity on the shop floor, their jobs after layoffs, and their standard of living in the community. The grievances of these relatively well-paid workers did not involve wages so much as arbitrary supervision, economic insecurity, and the dehumanizing speedup that was characteristic of assembly-line production. The foremen "treated us like a bunch of coolies [Chinese peasants]," a Chevrolet employee later remembered. "'Get it out. If you cannot get it out, there are people outside who will get it out.' That was their whole theme." Because of the industry's seasonal production cycle, employees worked long, hard hours during the winter and spring, only to be laid off for up to three months while the company retooled the factories during the off season. "The fear of being laid off," one journalist noted, "hangs over the head of every worker. He does not know when the sword will fall."

After FDR's big victory in November, autoworker strikes began to multiply throughout the industrial Midwest (Figure 9.2). Some were planned

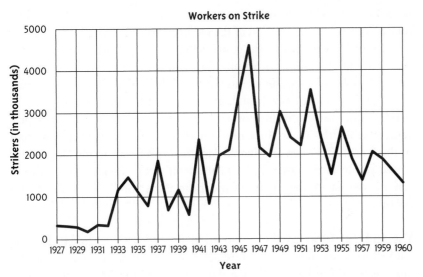

FIGURE 9.2 On Strike!
The number of American workers participating in strikes increased rapidly in the 1930s, reaching a Depression era peak during the sit-down strikes of 1937. But the era immediately after World War II found even more workers on strike. For decades thereafter, the existence of a powerful trade union movement ensured that strike levels remained high.

and authorized by leaders of the fledgling United Auto Workers (UAW), but many were organized by shop militants who understood all too well the impatience and grievances of their workmates. Soon, one General Motors plant after another was shut down, often by workers who remained inside to occupy the factory. These "sit-down" strikes, first attempted in 1935 in Akron's rubber factories, were an innovative tactic that prevented companies from replacing strikers with scabs. It also discouraged the use of violence, because the deployment of police, troops, or other armed groups to oust the men could result in damage to expensive company-owned buildings, machinery, and materials. Occupying corporate property was illegal, but strikers responded that management's failure to abide by the new Wagner Act was a violation of the law as well.

Shortly after Christmas 1936, leaders of the UAW and the CIO authorized a companywide strike at General Motors. Key GM plants had already been occupied in Flint, Michigan, which now became the battleground for the most pivotal labor struggle of the Depression decade. If Flint autoworkers could beat General Motors—the largest producer of automobiles, parts, and accessories in the world—their victory would galvanize workers throughout the basic industries of the United States. Located sixty miles northwest of Detroit, Flint was the corporation's major production center and a near-classic company town. General Motors employed four of every five workers in the city. For the UAW, the burden of conducting the actual confrontation with General Motors rested on a relatively narrow base: a few hundred sit-downers in each plant, an energetic group of radicals (many of whom were Socialist and Communist party members) who ran the strike from day to day, and a few older unionists of national reputation posted to Flint during the conflict. But the UAW also drew on the courage

"We Done It!"

Journalist Ruth McKenney covered the CIO victory in an Akron, Ohio, factory where rubber workers used a new tactic: the sit-down strike. Instead of walking out of the factory and picketing outside, the workers simply occupied the plant. In her novel Industrial Valley, *McKenney drew on her experiences as a journalist to graphically describe the occupation of the Firestone tire plant in January 1936.*

It was 1:57 a.m. January 29, 1936.

The tire builders worked in smooth frenzy, sweat around their necks, under their arms. The belt clattered, the insufferable racket and din and rhythm. The clock on the south wall, a big plain clock, hesitated, its minute hand jumped to two. A tire builder at the end of the line looked up, saw the hand jump. The foreman was sitting quietly staring at the lines of men working under the vast pools of light. . . .

The tire builder at the end of the line gulped. His hands stopped their quick weaving motions. Every man on the line stiffened. All over the vast room, hands hesitated. The foreman saw the falter, felt it instantly. He jumped up . . . his eyes darting quickly from one line to another.

This was it, then. But what was happening? Where was it starting? He stood perfectly still, his heart beating furiously, his throat feeling dry, watching the hesitating hands, watching the broken rhythm.

Then the tire builder at the end of the line walked three steps to the master safety switch and, drawing a deep breath, he pulled up the heavy wooden handle. With this signal in perfect synchronization, with the rhythm they had learned in a great mass-production industry, the tire builders stepped back from their machines.

Instantly, noise stopped. The whole room lay in perfect silence. The tire builders stood in long lines, touching each other, perfectly motionless, deafened by the silence. . . .

Out of the terrifying quiet came the wondering voice of a big tire builder near the window: "Jesus Christ, it's like the end of the world."

He broke the spell, the magic moment of stillness. For now his awed words said the same thing to every man, "We done it! We stopped the belt! By God, we done it!" And men began to cheer hysterically, to shout and howl in the fresh silence. Men wrapped their long sinewy arms around their neighbors' shoulders, screaming, "We done it! We done it!"

Ruth McKenney, *Industrial Valley* (1939).

and determination of thousands of autoworkers and their families who sustained the sit-down strike for more than forty days. During the course of the occupation, sit-downers held frequent meetings, conducted classes on politics and history, put on plays, and scrupulously avoided damaging the factories or their products.

Catching Up on the News
During the sit-down strike, strikers who occupied General Motors' Fisher Body Plant No. 1 avidly followed newspaper coverage of their action. Archives of Labor and Urban Affairs, Wayne State University.

The union's allies in the Democratic Party kept Michigan's powerful state militia at bay, even though the sit-down strike was of questionable legality and Flint police had sought to oust the strikers on more than one occasion. The transformation of the 1936 presidential election into a referendum on industrial unionism convinced key politicians, including Michigan's newly elected governor, Frank Murphy, and President Roosevelt himself, to refrain from using the National Guard or army to evict the strikers.

As in other Depression era industrial conflicts, the unionists organized themselves into paramilitary formations called "flying squadrons" to stop the police from bringing in strikebreakers or dislodging sit-downers. In Flint, a Women's Emergency Brigade, led by the twenty-three-year-old socialist firebrand Genora Johnson, was one of the most effective and celebrated. The red-bereted brigade served as the female shock troops of the solidarity movement; its members carried two-by-fours when they joined in violent confrontations, placing themselves between strikers and police and militia.

With car production at a near standstill, GM finally caved in on February 11, 1937. GM recognized the union as the sole voice of its employees and agreed to negotiate with UAW leaders on a multiplant basis. For the first time, union activists won the right to speak up, recruit other workers, and complain to management without fear of retribution. "Even if we got not one damn thing out of it other than that," declared a GM employee in St. Louis, "we at least had a right to open our mouths without fear." Indeed, an

Meanwhile, Outside . . .
The UAW's Women's Emergency Brigade, along with members of the union local's Women's Auxiliary, marched in front of an occupied Chrysler plant in March 1937. Archives of Labor and Urban Affairs, Wayne State University.

enormous sense of self-confidence, democratic participation, even liberation swept through working-class ranks. Huge crowds thronged the streets of Flint in a celebration that Roy Reuther, an auto union militant, likened to "some description of a country experiencing independence."

Industrial Unionism at High Tide Across industrial America, the GM settlement transformed the expectations of workers and managers alike. In Flint and elsewhere, few workers actively supported the first strikes, picket lines, and demonstrations. Although only a committed minority led the way, their coworkers neither supported the company nor remained neutral in the conflict; most stood back fearfully until the CIO stripped management of its capacity to penalize workers. In the wake of the GM victory, workers in almost every industrial district poured into the new unions, where, for a time, many organized into citywide units that cut across corporate, ethnic, and political boundaries.

In 1937, nearly five million workers took part in some kind of industrial action, and almost three million became union members. In Detroit alone, a rolling wave of sit-down strikes hit dozens of factories. "Somebody would call the office," recalled a UAW organizer, "and say, 'Look, we are sitting down. Send us over some food.'" Workers in Detroit occupied every

Chrysler Corporation facility, twenty-five auto parts plants, four downtown hotels, nine lumberyards, ten meatpacking plants, a dozen industrial laundries, three department stores, and scores of restaurants, shoe stores, and clothing outlets. When the police evicted female strikers from a cigar company and a few stores along lower Woodward Avenue, the labor movement shut down the entire city and put 150,000 protesters in front of City Hall.

Such raw power made the kind of headlines that influenced even the most conservative elite. There were no sit-down strikes at U.S. Steel, but its president, Myron Taylor, read GM's capitulation in Flint as a sign that "complete industrial organization was inevitable." To avoid a violent conflict with steelworkers, Taylor, who presided over the second-largest manufacturing company in the world—the corporation that had smashed the nationwide steel strike in 1919—agreed to raise wages and to recognize the CIO's Steelworkers Organizing Committee as the sole bargaining agent for employees. That was in early March 1937; scores of other major corporations followed suit. In April, the Supreme Court, whose conservative members also recognized the popular impetus behind the Roosevelt landslide and the labor upsurge, surprised almost everyone by declaring the Wagner Act constitutional.

Thus, CIO unionism had a profound impact on the daily lives of millions of ordinary workers. Although the new unions negotiated for higher wages and lobbied for much-needed social legislation, their greatest impact came inside the factory itself, where dramatic changes took place on the shop floor in the relationship between boss and workers. There, shop stewards elected by their workmates gave voice and power to the heretofore inarticulate. "Everybody wants to talk. Leaders are popping up everywhere," reported an organizer from Flint. Shop stewards used their newfound power to argue with the foreman, sometimes backed by employees in their departments, who dropped their tools and gathered around until the grievance was settled. "Before organization came into the plant, foremen were little tin gods in their own departments," declared a 1941 union handbook. "With the coming of the union, the foreman finds his whole world turned

Hello, Mama. We're Makin' History

Denys Wortman's cartoon in the March 25, 1937, *New York World-Telegram* captured the excitement and sense of power felt by many working men and working women when they participated in militant labor action. Denys Wortman, *New York World-Telegram*, March 25, 1937 — American Social History Project.

upside down. His small time dictatorship has been overthrown, and he must be adjusted to a democratic system of shop government."

The AFL, which sharply rejected the call for industrial unionism two years earlier, reaped many benefits from this upsurge. Craft unions, which formerly had organized only skilled machinists, carpenters, and electricians, transformed themselves into industrial organizations so as to compete directly with the CIO. And many antiunion employers, frightened by the CIO success, suddenly appeared eager to negotiate with AFL unions so that they could avoid "Lewis's Reds." Total union membership, both CIO and AFL, rose from three million in 1934 to eight million at the end of the 1930s.

Industrial Democracy   In many company-dominated towns throughout the East and Midwest, old-line Republican officials—white, Protestant, and of Northern European heritage—were either defeated or forced to share power with ethnic Democrats allied with the union movement. CIO industrial unions gave first- and second-generation immigrant workers a collective political voice. In western Pennsylvania steel towns and New England textile centers, the new citizenship and the new unionism were virtually synonymous, linking union membership, New Deal politics, and income stability. "Unionism is the spirit of Americanism," asserted a typical union paper. This working-class Americanism transformed the meaning of citizenship and patriotism. In years past, conservative defenders of the industrial status quo had manipulated patriotic and nationalist sentiment in their own interest. They denounced radicals and unionists as "un-American"; after World War I, police and vigilantes had sometimes forced organizers to kneel and kiss the American flag as a sign of their loyalty to the nation and its institutions.

But during the 1930s, liberals, labor, and the left successfully captured the flag. A telling moment came in 1934 when Secretary of Labor Frances Perkins visited unorganized steelworkers in Homestead, Pennsylvania, to hear their grievances and explain New Deal labor policy. When union militants sought to make their voices heard, the mayor of the town, which was tightly controlled by U.S. Steel, abruptly cut short Perkins's speech and ushered her out of the city hall. Out on the street, amid a crowd of angry steelworkers, she spotted an American flag flying over the local post office. In the lobby of that federal building, under the symbol of national unity, she resumed her speech, detailing, for the largely Catholic, immigrant audience, their rights under federal law.

Soon the Depression era labor movement would deploy huge American flags and other patriotic symbols in all its struggles. In California's San Joaquin Valley, Anglo, Mexican, Filipino, and African American field hands demanded an "American standard of living" and rejected the paltry wage increases offered by the antiunion Associated Farmers. To rally those on

"Made in the U.S.A."

Thomas Bell (born Adalbert Thomas Belejcak) based his 1941 novel Out of This Furnace *on his family's experience as Slovak immigrants who toiled in Pittsburgh's steel mills. The story spans the years from the grandfather's arrival in 1881 to the grandson's participation in the CIO organizing drives of the late 1930s. In the closing pages of the novel, Dobie, the grandson, reflects on the sense of empowerment he and his fellow steelworkers now enjoy, concluding that, despite his ancestry, his participation in the formation of the Steelworkers' Union had made him feel as American as if his family had arrived with the Puritans.*

And he realized now what it was that had once puzzled him about the CIO men. Whatever their ancestry, they had felt the same way about certain things; and because Dobie had been born and raised in a steel town, where the word meant people who were white, Protestant, middle-class Anglo-Saxons, it hadn't occurred to him that the CIO men were thinking and talking like Americans.

"Maybe not the kind of American that came over on the Mayflower," he reflected, "or the kind that's always shooting off their mouths about Americanism and patriotism, including some of the God damndest heels you'd ever want to see, but the kind that's got 'Made in U.S.A.' stamped all over them, from the kind of grub they like to the things they wouldn't do for all the money in the world."

He stared down at the sleeping town without really seeing it.

"Made in the U.S.A.," he thought, "made in the First Ward. Mikie was right; it's too bad a person can't pick their own place to be born in, considering what it does to you. I'm almost as much a product of that mill down there as any rail or ingot they ever turned out. And maybe that's been part of the trouble. If I'm anything at all I'm an American, only I'm not the kind you read about in history books or that they make speeches about on the Fourth of July; anyway, not yet. And a lot of people don't know what to make of it and don't like it. Which is tough on me but is liable to be still tougher on them, because I at least don't have to be told that Braddock [Pennsylvania] ain't Plymouth Rock and this ain't the year 1620."

. . . Made in the U.S.A., he thought, made in the First Ward. But it wasn't where you were born or how you spelled your name or where your father come from. It was the way you thought and felt about certain things. About freedom of speech and the equality of men and the importance of having one law—the same law—for rich and poor, for the people you liked and the people you didn't like. . . . About the uses to which wealth and power could honorably be put. . . . About human dignity, which helped a man live proudly and distinguished his death from an animal's; and, finally, about the value to be put on a human life, one's enemy's no less than one's own.

Thomas Bell, *Out of This Furnace* (1941).

PHOTO-HISTORY

25¢

NUMBER 2

LABOR'S CHALLENGE

Celebration

A May 1937 union demonstration of Aliquippa, Pennsylvania, steelworkers and their supporters was featured on the cover of *Photo-History* (a short-lived, pro-CIO magazine). *Photo-History* (July 1937) — Prints and Photographs Division, Library of Congress.

the picket lines, strikers sang, "Fight for Union recognition, Fight for better pay, Fight to better our condition, In the democratic way, Eighty cents won't feed us, A dollar and a quarter would be fine, Show the farmers that they need us, JOIN THE PICKET LINE."

New Faces in the Union Halls In these union struggles, women workers won their own kind of industrial citizenship, albeit one that was limited by the sexist assumptions of the period. The unions recruited almost a million women in the 1930s, especially in the garment trades, electrical products, clerical and sales work, canning, and tobacco processing. Women sit-down strikers occupied hotels, drugstores, restaurants, and auto parts factories. Women often played an essential role in linking a union's shop activism to the larger community. Most unions organized women's auxiliaries, whose very existence testified to a sense of family solidarity. During the 1934 Firestone strike in Akron, for example, the local newspaper reported, "Shoulder to shoulder with their men, the wives, daughters, and sisters of strikers marched through the business district to strike headquarters in a great victory parade." But such dramatic linkages were far less important than the more subtle ways in which women made the unions present in their neighborhoods and communities. Labor-based tenant organizations, soup kitchens, food cooperatives, recreation halls, singing societies, and education programs drew both women workers and the wives and daughters of male unionists into a dense, supportive social network that strengthened the ties of solidarity inside the factory and out.

The New Deal and the new unions advocated "equal pay for equal work," but the sign carried by one male picketer proved more eloquent and revealing: "Restore Our Manhood," it implored. "We Receive Girls' Wages." Even in industries dominated by women workers, male union activists did not welcome female leadership. Thus, those women who played leading roles in the labor movement were remarkably atypical: divorcees, widows, political radicals, or members of intensely union-conscious households.

Florence Luscomb, for example, earned an architecture degree from MIT in 1909 but soon abandoned architecture (at that time, a very unusual occupation for a woman), first to campaign for woman's suffrage and later to work for prison reform. When the CIO started the United Office and Professional Workers' Union, Luscomb became president of the Boston local. Although she helped to win higher pay, she had trouble building a large union. One problem was that female clerical workers often felt socially superior to factory workers and above trade unionism; another was that stenographers and typists worked in isolated settings and small groups. And as Luscomb later recalled, "the CIO didn't give much assistance in having secretaries organized; they'd be too busy trying to organize the textile workers, and the railroad workers, and large 'important' bodies of the working class."

During the Depression years, the trade union movement became an increasingly important vehicle for the advancement of workers of color, but they overcame the legacy of white working-class racism and official union exclusion only with great effort. Officials of AFL craft unions, who sought to monopolize the labor market for their members, simply excluded African Americans from their trades. In Richmond, Virginia, for example, the AFL Labor Temple prohibited entry to any black worker, union member or not. And when diesel locomotives reduced the number of firemen needed by the railroads, the white railroad brotherhoods waged a virtual war against black workers who remained in the occupation. Therefore, many black organizations, including the Urban League and the NAACP, remained skeptical of the union movement, and many African Americans remained loyal to paternalistic employers.

Attitudes shifted rapidly in the late 1930s, however. First, an inspiring, progressive trade union of African Americans gave a voice to all black workers. Under the leadership of A. Philip Randolph, the Brotherhood of Sleeping Car Porters took advantage of the nation's prolabor mood to win higher wages, shorter hours, and job security for the 35,000 black and Filipino porters and maids who worked for the Pullman Company. Even more important, the protection offered by a signed contract gave these newly empowered people the freedom to press for civil rights in the railroad towns where they lived. Randolph, who was a socialist and a powerful orator, became an important new spokesman for black Americans, relying on his union as a high-profile stage from which to denounce racism where ever he found it, in or outside of unions.

In the tobacco, cannery, longshoremen's, and foundry industries, African Americans often built all-black local unions. But the future of black labor lay with the interracial unions in the industries organized by the CIO.

"It Was a New Idea for Office Workers to Organize . . . A Very Unusual Idea"

In this selection from an oral interview, Florence Luscomb recalls the CIO drive to organize women office workers, an increasingly important occupational category, into industrial unions. Luscomb had a long and distinguished career as a progressive reformer, suffragist, trade unionist, and peace activist. Educated as an architect at MIT, Luscomb was an officer in the NAACP, an organizer for the International Ladies Garment Workers' Union, and, as she recalls, president of the Boston local of the CIO's United Professional and Office Workers of America.

I joined the American Federation of Labor, what they called, the Stenographers, Typewriters, Bookkeepers, and Accountants Union. Not typists, but typewriters. I joined it in the early thirties, because I believed in labor unions, and so I wanted to be a member. And it was really just a fake union. There was just this one public stenographers' office in Boston, and that was a union office. . . . When I became president in 1936, I wanted to put on a big campaign to unionize more office workers. And they [the AFL union] wouldn't do it. . . . When the Congress of Industrial Organizations came along and started to establish a United Office and Professional Workers Union . . . we set up local No. 3 of the UOPWA in the CIO. I was the president for several years, and we did a lot of very active work without getting a very large union.

For example, there was one big firm which had quite a large office staff, and they paid very low wages. We used to go around and find one girl in the office who would think that they ought to be organized, and she'd give us the names and addresses of all the office workers. We'd go and visit them in their homes, and talk union with them. And we got a large group of girls in this office who were very much interested in having the union there. The firm got wind of it, that they were probably going to have a strike on their hands. So they raised their girls' pay, whereupon the girls lost all interest in joining the union! And that happened various times. We got more stenographers with pay raises than we got members of the union, but we did gradually build up the union. It was a new idea for office workers to organize—it was a very unusual idea. They felt themselves socially superior to the person working in a factory, although they might get much less pay than the girls who were working in the factory.

Ellen Cantarow with Susan Gushee O'Malley and Sharon Hartman Strom, *Moving the Mountain: Women Working for Social Change* (1980).

African Americans made up about 25 percent of all packinghouse workers in Chicago, 15 percent of employees in the steel industry, 4 percent of autoworkers (10 percent at Ford), and a large portion of the workers in the lumber and mining camps of the South. Communists and other radicals were particularly active in pushing forward African American rights within the new unions, but all industrial union leaders had to pay at least lip service to the idea of racial equality. As CIO leader Philip Murray, who presided over the organizing drive in steel, forthrightly promised, "there shall be no discrimination under any circumstances, regardless of creed, color, or nationalities."

Such sentiments would be hard to put into practice, but these ideals represented a recognition that the allegiance of African American workers was essential to the success of the new movement. Black workers, for example, often held jobs that were vital to the production process, from the hot and dirty foundries where engine blocks were poured to the stinking and bloody killing floor, where African Americans controlled the flow of carcasses to every department within the great Chicago meatpacking houses.

The CIO's campaign to unionize the steel industry put its egalitarian claims to the test. Black-white conflict had helped to undermine the great steel strike of 1919. Now, the recruitment of black organizers to the Steel Workers Organizing Committee helped to reassure skeptical African American steelworkers that the union would take their interests seriously. The union's success brought an end to some of the most glaringly discriminatory practices in the steel industry. As the lowest-paid laborers won large raises, the enormous wage inequities between high- and low-skilled workers began to shrink. Meanwhile, the CIO's culture of solidarity earned black workers some real social dividends. "Well, you know, I'll tell you what the CIO has done," reported a black worker in Chicago. "Before, everyone used to make remarks about, 'that dirty Jew,' 'that stinkin' black bastard,' 'that low-life Bohunk,' but you know I never hear that kind of stuff anymore. I don't like to brag, but I'm one of the best-liked men in my department. If there is ever any trouble, the men usually come to me."

Others were not so sanguine. Interracial unionism did little to end the social and residential segregation that pervaded working-class America. Although union meetings were integrated—often they were the first integrated event workers of either race had ever attended—activities that even hinted at social equality, such as dances and picnics, remained a flashpoint. Conflict between black and white workers emerged on the shop floor, too, where trade unions tended to reinforce the segregated, hierarchical job structures that had been established in the preunion era. At issue was the seniority system. Unions demanded rigid rules governing promotions and recalls from layoffs. Managers and white workers usually insisted that seniority should be enforced on a departmental, not a plantwide basis, which protected the rights of the well-paid whites who held the best jobs against the claims of black workers who might well have greater overall seniority within the entire factory.

But African American workers did not flinch from a growing loyalty to the new unions. Despite the overt racism of many white workers, the new unionism, with its signed contracts, grievance procedures, and elected shop stewards, generated a kind of industrial citizenship that liberated African Americans from the paternalism, deferential subordination, and overt racism of the old social order. And it provided new organizational weapons with which to fight. The Packinghouse Union would have failed "if it hadn't been for the Negro joining with you," a Kansas City black worker reminded his white brothers and sisters. "We are not asking for favors. We will take what is coming to us."

The Culture of New Deal America

Just as mass production typified American industry in the 1930s, mass culture characterized entertainment, journalism, and the arts during that era. Fifty million Americans went to the movies each week. Radio entered almost every home, and news magazines such as *Time* and *Newsweek* brought East Coast reportage to remote rural areas (Figure 9.3). And for the first time, the federal government employed writers, photographers, actors, and artists on a massive scale.

What was the relationship of this new mass culture to the politics of the era? Almost all newspapers were hostile to labor and the New Deal, and most of the new Hollywood moguls were staunch Republicans.

FIGURE 9.3   The Rise of Radio

By the end of the 1930s, almost every electrified home contained a radio. In 1922, thirty stations broadcast to just 60,000 radio sets. But seventeen years later, over seven hundred stations beamed music, news, drama, and comedy to more than twenty-seven million households.

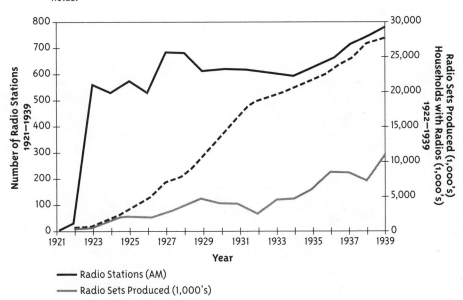

— Radio Stations (AM)
— Radio Sets Produced (1,000's)
- - - Households with Radio Sets (1,000's)

Nevertheless, creative artists who were sympathetic to labor and the left had an unprecedented impact on mass culture in the 1930s. In these Popular Front years, radicals in or close to the Communist Party played a major role in organizations devoted to everything from modern dance to student politics, public housing, and minority rights. The cultural movement had a broad reach, combining a modernist, experimental sensibility in arts and letters with an appreciation of the critical role of workers and farmers in American society. Simultaneously nationalistic and regionally rooted, it celebrated as inherently democratic and creative the folk cultures of the Southwest, the Appalachian South, and small-town New England.

Federal Arts Projects The Roosevelt administration fostered support for New Deal programs by helping artists to create and disseminate works of democratic mass culture. In the early 1930s, the drama, color, and political subjects of the great left-wing Mexican muralists Diego Rivera, José Clemente Orozco, and David Alfaro Siqueiros inspired those who sought to develop socially relevant public art in the United States. Such was the appeal of their work that even the Rockefeller family commissioned them to produce murals for Dartmouth College and Rockefeller Center in New York, while Henry Ford's son Edsel sponsored a Rivera mural with the subject of industrial labor at the Detroit Institute of the Arts. (However, Nelson Rockefeller ordered the removal of the Rockefeller Center mural because Rivera included a portrait of Soviet leader V. I. Lenin.) Late in 1933, New Deal relief and public works agencies began to fund similar works, employing thousands of artists to produce more than fifteen thousand murals, oils, watercolors, and prints. As part of the Works Progress Administration, employees of the Federal Art Project created murals for the walls of federal

The Corn Parade

Few of the post office murals that were commissioned by the Treasury Department Section of Fine Art displayed the humor of Orr C. Fisher's paean to corn. But the Iowa-born Fisher's work suggests the kind of regional boosterism and pride of place that characterized many murals painted by local artists. Orr C. Fisher, *The Corn Parade*, 1941, oil on canvas — National Archives.

Pocahontas Rescuing Captain John Smith

At times, local tastes clashed with individual artists' expressions. In the case of Paul Cadmus's mural for Richmond's Parcel Post Building, it was male nudity that roused concern. Although Pocahontas's breast and the foreground Indian brave's buttocks remained bare, Cadmus had to retouch a suggestive fox head he had mischievously placed over another brave's groin. This was not the first time Cadmus had faced censorship; a Navy admiral demanded the removal of his 1934 painting *The Fleet's In!* from a government-sponsored exhibition, horrified by its depiction of an intoxicated group of sailors flirting with prostitutes and a gay man. Paul Cadmus, *Pocahontas Rescuing Captain John Smith*, 1939, mural — National Archives.

and state buildings and established public art centers in remote communities. The project employed as many as 6,000 painters, sculptors, and muralists, 90 percent of whom were on relief.

New Deal public art embodied the hope of John Dewey, the nation's foremost philosopher, that "our public buildings may become the outward and visible sign of the inward grace which is the democratic spirit." Reflecting the leftist politics of many of the artists, the representational subject matter was often that of ordinary Americans, at work or in struggle, rendered in a heroic, larger-than-life style. Like other elements of New Deal culture, the murals and paintings were overtly masculinist. Women were portrayed as sturdy partners in the American pageant but were not presented as heroines in their own right.

WPA projects for writers and musicians gave important and creative work to thousands of unemployed white-collar workers — not just writers and composers, but also insurance salesmen, librarians, and middle managers. Federal Writers' Project employees published guidebooks, collected folk songs, and recorded interviews with ex-slaves, cowboys, and immigrants. The United States had only eleven symphony orchestras in the early 1930s; the WPA music project created thirty-four more, not just in the biggest cities of the East and West Coasts, but in Oklahoma and Utah as well. Government-paid music teachers gave lessons to 70,000 people in Mississippi and sparked a boom in the sale of secondhand pianos. In New Mexico, amateur musicians collected folk tunes with roots going back to Spain, Cuba, and Mexico; in Oklahoma, they recorded the songs and dances of five Native American tribes. Such cultural work fostered a more democratic vision of the American past, celebrating the "forgotten American" and the "common hero."

The most outstanding contribution to the nation's cultural awareness came from the New Deal photojournalists. To build broad public support for its programs, the Roosevelt administration encouraged the directors of New Deal agencies to document the human suffering caused by the Depression. For this purpose, the WPA, the Department of Agriculture, and the Farm Security Administration (formerly the Resettlement Administration) hired amateur and professional photographers to travel the Depression-ravaged country. Some of the hundreds of thousands of "social-realist" photos they shot—particularly Dorothea Lange's haunting portraits of poor farm women, Arthur Rothstein's shots of dust storms, and Walker Evans's despairing images of sharecroppers—became icons of the Depression. These photos circulated widely in the popular press, including *Time*, *Look*, and *Life* magazines, and they appeared in major museum exhibits and best-selling books.

The Fields Family, Hale County, Alabama, Summer 1936
From 1935 to 1943, photographers working for several government agencies, principally the Farm Security Administration (FSA), produced the most enduring images of the Great Depression. Walker Evans's pictures of the rural poor were part of that massive documentation effort. Wishing to convey both suffering and dignity, FSA photographers searingly presented conditions to the American public, selecting effective compositions and poses that were influenced by advertising and mass-market magazine formats. Walker Evans, 1936 — Prints and Photographs Division, Library of Congress.

Music, Theater, and Hollywood   Folksinger Woody Guthrie and novelist John Steinbeck combined the social realism of the Depression era photojournalists with the populist cultural sensibilities of the left-wing Popular Front. Guthrie, who had taught himself to sing country music and folk ballads in Texas and Oklahoma, wrote songs that celebrated hobos, cowboys, fruit pickers, and New Deal monuments such as the Bonneville Dam on the Columbia River. His best lyrics captured the spirit of America in a style so poetic and direct that one of his songs, "This Land Is Your Land," became a kind of national anthem. John Steinbeck's 1939 novel *The Grapes of Wrath*, a mythic tale of suffering, migration, and redemption, immortalized the Okies who fled the Southwestern Dust Bowl for California. Guthrie's and Steinbeck's work proved powerful and lasting in part because the protagonists were white, rural, and Protestant; their strength and dignity made them icons of the mainstream national culture.

Theater enjoyed a renaissance during the New Deal years as well. In New York, Lee Strasberg and Harold Clurman organized the radical, labor-oriented Group Theatre, which discovered playwrights Clifford Odets, William Saroyan, and Irwin Shaw. Odets's play *Waiting for Lefty*, the story of

"The Yeast Which Makes the Bread Rise": Hallie Flanagan on Drama as Politics

"The theater must grow up," declared Hallie Flanagan, director of the New Deal era Federal Theatre Project (FTP), which provided employment for actors, directors, and technicians during the Depression. By the 1930s, theater was rapidly losing its audiences to movies, and Flanagan sought to win audiences back by revitalizing drama with the excitement and conflict of contemporary life and politics. In this talk on theater as social action, she borrowed the rhetoric of the militant labor movement as she summarized the work of a 1937 summer project that gathered FTP workers from around the country.

Our Federal Theatre, born of an economic need, built by and for people who have faced terrific privation, cannot content itself with easy, pretty or insignificant plays. We are not being given millions of dollars to repeat, however expertly, the type of plays which landed 10,000 theatre people on relief rolls. By a stroke of fortune unprecedented in dramatic history, we have been given a chance to help change America at a time when twenty million unemployed Americans proved it needed changing. And the theatre, when it is any good, can change things.

The theatre can quicken, start things, make things happen. Don't be afraid when people tell you this is a play of protest. Of course it's protest, protest against dirt, disease, human misery. If, in giving great plays of the past as greatly as we can give them, and if, in making people laugh, which we certainly want to do, we can't also protest — as Harry Hopkins is protesting and as President Roosevelt is protesting — against some of the evils of this country of ours, then we do not deserve the chance put into our hands. . . . Here is one necessity for our theatre — that it help reshape our American life. Nor do we work, hereafter, alone. We work not in isolated centers, but in a nationwide Federal Theatre. From that union we should gain tremendous strength. . . .

From it we shall all learn. Through it we shall mutually create a theatre which need not be just the frosting on the cake. It may be the yeast which makes the bread rise.

<hr>

Hallie Flanagan, "Theater as Social Action," in Piere de Roban, ed., "First Federal Summer Theater: A Report," *Federal Theatre*, June–July 1937: 36 (a project newsletter available in the Federal Theatre Project collection, Library of Congress).

a taxi strike, was the most widely performed — and most widely banned — American play of 1935. In the labor movement, skits, plays, and radio dramas became an integral part of union propaganda. In 1935, the International Ladies' Garment Workers Union established the Labor Stage. One of its productions, *Pins and Needles*, became a Broadway hit. Employing actors who were drawn from the garment shops, the show satirized contemporary politics and the lives of ordinary workers.

The government supported dramatic arts through the WPA's Federal Theatre Project, which hired actors, writers, and directors from the relief

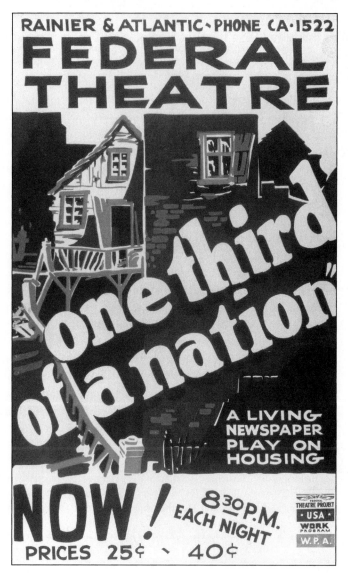

One Third of a Nation
Taking its title from FDR's Second Inaugural Address, the 1938 Federal Theatre Project production played to packed houses in New York and ten other cities. Arthur Arent's "Living Newspaper" play combined documentation and drama — and an imposing four-story tenement set — to convey the causes of and solutions to America's housing crisis. Library of Congress, Federal Theatre Project Collection.

rolls. It produced classics by Shakespeare, Molière, and Marlowe, as well as socially avant-garde works such as the "Living Newspaper" plays and Sinclair Lewis's *It Can't Happen Here*, a drama about fascism coming to America. Many plays were produced in multiple versions, with African American, Spanish, and Yiddish casts. Led by Hallie Flanagan, the exuberant, politically engaged director of Vassar College's Experimental Theatre, the Federal Theatre Project became a lightning rod for conservative criticism of the New Deal, both because it employed so many radicals and bohemians and because many Americans thought that theatrical work was hardly work at all.

I Am a Fugitive from a Chain Gang

Mervyn LeRoy's 1932 film, starring Paul Muni as a wrongly imprisoned World War I veteran, exposed the abuses of the penal system in the South. Museum of Modern Art/Film Stills Archive.

Following the addition of sound to motion pictures in 1927 and the establishment of the major movie studios, Hollywood and its stars had moved to center stage in American mass culture. Though most Depression era films had little social or political content—Busby Berkeley's extravagant production numbers, such as *Gold Diggers of 1933*, were escapist fantasies—there were some exceptions. The dark crime films of the early Depression,

The Ideal Picket

In 1941, trade union activism reached the workplace where some of the nation's favorite fantasies were produced. After Walt Disney fired union organizers on his art staff, his studio cartoonists went on strike. This cartoon from a newspaper report indicated how Disney strikers brought new skills to labor organizing. "There are mighty few labor disputes," the caption stated, "in which just about every striker can make his own picket signs. Consequently, the signs are bright and lively . . . attracting the passerby and winning friends for the Screen Cartoon Guild." *PM*, June 6, 1941 — American Social History Project.

including *Little Caesar* (1930) and *Public Enemy* (1931), explored the gangster underworld, while *I Am a Fugitive from a Chain Gang* (1932) exposed the South's brutal penal institutions. Frank Capra's films, especially those starring Jimmy Stewart, contrasted a populist version of small-town America with the corrupt and self-interested world of powerful politicians and businessmen. And comedians such as the Marx Brothers, Charlie Chaplin, W. C. Fields, and Mae West lampooned the social pretensions of the wealthy.

Many of the film stars of the 1930s, including Eddie Cantor, Joan Crawford, and James Cagney, were partisans of the New Deal. They helped to build the feisty Screen Actors Guild, which not only advanced the economic interests of its membership, but also demonstrated that trade unionism was not just for factory workers. Unionism in Hollywood entered Walt Disney's studios in 1941, when cartoonists successfully struck for higher pay and greater artistic freedom. Such activities generated much controversy if only because they seemed to subvert the hierarchical, celebrity culture promoted by the major studios and the Hollywood media.

Backlash Against Labor and the New Deal

Although the labor movement and the New Deal seemed to sweep all before them in 1936 and 1937, their very success generated resistance and countermobilization from people who had long opposed their progressive goals. By 1937, the U.S. economy was producing as many goods and services as it had in 1929. Businessmen who had been desperate for federal help five years earlier suddenly resented new government initiatives. "The life preserver which is so necessary when the ship is sinking," observed an official of the Chamber of Commerce, "becomes a heavy burden when a man is back on dry land." Thus, conservative businessmen and politicians united to oppose unionizing efforts, FDR's judicial proposal, and the expansion of New Deal programs. In the process, a powerful alliance formed between Southern Democrats and conservative Republicans, and fissures emerged within the working class. As if all these problems were not enough, the economy took a nosedive late in 1937. In a single year, industrial production declined by one-third, manufacturing employment fell by one-quarter, and in the big cities, WPA rolls rose fivefold.

The Conservative Counterattack   In California, a right-wing mobilization began in 1934. The agricultural strikes in the Central Valley, Upton Sinclair's radical campaign for the governorship, and the general strike in San Francisco frightened conservatives. Vigilante groups soon terrorized the state's agricultural districts, kidnapping and beating labor organizers and their supporters. But the Associated Farmers, a statewide interlocking network of packers, shippers, utilities, and employers of migrant labor, emerged as the most powerful new opponent of labor and the New Deal. With strong ties to local sheriffs and police departments, it kept well-organized files on thousands of radicals and union organizers at its San Francisco headquarters. In 1936, urged on by the Associated Farmers, the California Highway Patrol sealed off the state to Okie migrants and crushed a strike by lettuce harvesters in Salinas. The next year, California business interests broke a sit-down strike at Douglas Aircraft, thus helping to keep most of Los Angeles "open-shop" until World War II. Although California voters elected a liberal, Culbert Olson, to the governorship in 1938, the state's economic and political elite would not make peace with the New Deal or with organized labor.

President Roosevelt's ambitious plan to "pack" the Supreme Court with judges who were favorable to the New Deal also generated a furious conservative response. Roosevelt saw his reelection in 1936 as a sweeping mandate, but he feared that the courts, which had invalidated much of the work of the New Deal's first hundred days, would soon strike down the fruits of the second hundred days, including the Wagner Act and the Social Security Act. To preclude this possibility, the president wanted the authority to name up to fifty additional federal judges, including six Supreme Court justices, whenever an incumbent with ten years seniority reached the age of seventy. His plan, made public early in 1937, would have increased the executive power over the judiciary and given him a solid majority of opinion on the Supreme Court.

To many Americans, not just the Republican old guard, the CIO sit-down strikes and the Roosevelt court-packing plan seemed part of the same assault on social order and established property rights. Their fears and resentments exploded on the Senate floor on April 1, 1937, when both Democrats and Republicans denounced the CIO, its sit-down tactic, and what they considered to be Roosevelt's hunger for dictatorial power. On this issue, public opinion turned against the president, and the court-packing plan went down to an embarrassing defeat. But FDR did not come away empty-handed. The Supreme Court itself, perhaps mindful of the public support enjoyed by New Deal initiatives, shifted course and validated most of the legislative initiatives of the Second New Deal, including Social Security and the Wagner Act. Then a series of unexpected retirements gave the president the chance to name several distinguished liberals to the High Court, including Hugo Black, Felix Frankfurter, and William O. Douglas.

The labor movement was not so fortunate. When the Steel Workers Organizing Committee struck the nation's "Little Steel" companies (large corporations such as Bethlehem and Republic that were small only in comparison to U.S. Steel) in May 1937, steel executives were determined to resist, in part because they believed that the upsurge of anti–New Deal sentiment touched off by FDR's court-packing fiasco had also turned the public against the CIO. The strike came to a bloody climax on Memorial Day, May 30, 1937. That afternoon, a crowd of more than 1,000 steelworkers, family members, and supporters marched to the main gate of Republic Steel, on Chicago's South Side. Carrying large American flags, the demonstrators represented a cross-section of the ethnically diverse workforce in Chicago's steel industry, from Southern Europeans, who probably constituted a majority, to smaller groups of African Americans and Mexican Americans. The mood of the crowd was peaceful, but two blocks north of the plant gate, the demonstrators encountered a force of 200 Chicago police, wielding clubs, ax handles, and guns.

When the police refused to give strikers permission to set up a picket line, a few people in the crowd began throwing rocks. The police immediately opened fire. As men, women, and children ran for their lives, police shot at their backs, killing 10 demonstrators and wounding 30 others, including 3 children. Nine people were permanently disabled, and another 28 were hospitalized with injuries inflicted by police clubs and ax handles. The next day, headlines in one of Chicago's newspapers proclaimed, "Reds Riot at Steel Mill," and a coroner's jury pronounced the killings "justifiable homicide."

A matter of months after the CIO's resounding victory in Flint, the 1937 Memorial Day Massacre mobilized antistrike, antilabor forces across the Midwest. Eight more strikers were killed in June, another 160 were seriously wounded, and many more were subjected to police tear gas and arrest. Democratic governors, such as Martin Davey of Ohio ordered the state national guard to jail union organizers, break up picket lines, and escort strikebreakers into Ohio steel plants. Staggered by such unexpected opposition from Democratic officeholders, the CIO's Philip Murray called on President Roosevelt to offer at least a verbal endorsement of union steelworkers who had supported him so loyally during his 1936 election campaign. But Roosevelt, weakened by his Supreme Court defeat, considered the Little Steel strike "a real headache" and spurned Murray's plea for help. "The majority of the people are saying just one thing," FDR declared during a June press conference: "'A plague on both your houses.'" CIO President John L. Lewis offered a rejoinder on Labor Day 1937: "It ill behooves one who has supped at labor's table and who has been sheltered in labor's house

"The Memorial Day Massacre"
This photograph was one of many taken of the May 30, 1937, incident outside the gates of the Republic Steel Company's South Chicago factory. During the subsequent investigation by the U.S. Senate's La Follette Committee, these images — including motion-picture newsreel footage — proved that the brutal attack was unprovoked by the unarmed strikers. Only two words were audible on the newsreel sound track: "God Almighty!" The newsreel was later screened nationally but was never exhibited in Chicago. Negative no. ICHI37116 — Chicago Historical Society.

to curse with equal fervor and fine impartiality both labor and its adversaries when they become locked in deadly embrace." The alliance between labor and the New Deal would not be an easy one.

New Deal Setbacks in the South   Although Roosevelt left the CIO in the lurch during the spring of 1937, he actually stepped up his efforts to make the Democratic Party a more consistently liberal organization. Many New Dealers wanted to industrialize the South, equalize wages there with those in the North, and democratize the political system. In a speech in Georgia in 1938, Roosevelt brought the campaign for an expanded New Deal to the heart of Dixie. He attacked those southerners who were content to maintain a "feudal economic system." "There is little difference between the feudal system and the fascist system," he declared, referring to the rise of reactionary governments in Italy and Germany. "If you believe in one, you lean to the other." Voicing the views of a small but energetic group of southerners who were allied with the New Deal, Roosevelt declared the South "the nation's number one economic problem."

But southern political leaders rejected Roosevelt's gambit. During the court-packing fight and in the debates over relief and the minimum wage, Democratic congressmen and officeholders from the South proved increasingly hostile to New Deal reformism. The white southern oligarchy was more secure in 1938 than it had been in the depths of the Depression. Massive New Deal financial subsidies revived cotton and tobacco cultivation and began a program of farm mechanization that tilted the balance of power still further toward the landed gentry. Especially as the CIO turned its attention to the mills, factories, and refineries of the industrial South, the benefits of federal relief began to pale beside the threat of federal intervention in labor and race relations. As one southern white crudely summed up his fears, "You ask any nigger in the street who's the greatest man in the world. Nine out of ten will tell you Franklin Roosevelt. That's why I think he's so dangerous."

This conservative turn did not reflect the views of the majority of southerners, black and white, who overwhelmingly favored federal regulation of industry and economic aid. But the states of the old Confederacy were not then governed by institutions that would today be considered democratic. Most southern states systematically denied suffrage to African Americans, even as the poll tax made it difficult for poor whites to vote. In Virginia and Mississippi, less than 10 percent of the adult population cast a ballot, in presidential elections. In the long run, New Deal agricultural policies would force millions of rural black Americans off the land and set the stage for the civil rights movement of the 1950s and 1960s. But in the 1930s, such displacement merely depopulated the countryside and intensified racial competition at the bottom of the labor market. As a result, a CIO

effort to organize southern textiles—still the nation's largest industry—collapsed late in 1937.

Roosevelt's effort in 1938 to realign the Democratic Party and
purge opponents of the New Deal also failed. In a series of Democratic primaries, the president supported Democrats who backed the
Second New Deal against conservatives who opposed his program. He
attempted to purge outspoken conservatives such as Senator Walter
George of Georgia, who saw the president's program as "a second
march [by Union General Sherman] through Georgia," and Senator
Ellison ("Cotton Ed") Smith of South Carolina, who had sharply
attacked the Fair Labor Standards Act. But the conservative southern
Democrats held onto their seats in the 1938 elections, and the Republicans won eighty-one new seats in the House and eight in the Senate.

Roosevelt also failed to bring about a liberal realignment in the
West. His defeat there was ironic, for no region had benefited more
from federal generosity in the 1930s. In Montana, for example, federal
agencies spent five times more per capita than they laid out in North
Carolina, largely to help western cattlemen hurt by overgrazing and
falling prices. But these twentieth-century pioneers resented the help. "For
this salvation," one historian observed, "many cattlemen never forgave the
government."

Roosevelt's failure to realign the Democratic Party in 1938 laid the basis
for a generation-long alliance between conservative "Dixiecrats" and Republican opponents of the New Deal, one that effectively frustrated liberal efforts
to expand the welfare state, advance African American civil rights, and
encourage the growth of the labor movement. As a reform movement, the
New Deal was over. For the next quarter century and beyond, the nation
would be governed by a Democratic Party with a split personality. At the
presidential level, the Democrats would make an effective play for the votes
of the northern, urban, working-class majority; once in power, however,
Democratic presidents would be unable fully to deliver real reforms. With
the institutional power their long years of congressional seniority assured
them, southern Democratic legislators and their Republican allies would
block most initiatives that threatened the industrial or racial status quo.

Labor Divided and Besieged   If working-class Americans had been more
politically and socially united, the New Deal and the new unions might well
have parried the conservative assault with greater success. But the enormous
changes that were at work in industry and politics opened up deep cultural
divisions within America's working population. On one side stood the lower
middle class and the old labor aristocracy, largely of Northern European
descent. These men and women had a substantial stake in the existing social
order, be it the comfortable politics of a small midwestern town or the

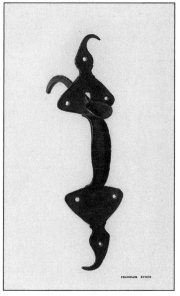

FRANKLIN SYRES

The Art of the Common Man
Some New Deal projects
harbored a conservative perspective. The Index of American
Design, one of the Federal Arts
Projects (FAP), celebrated what
was "American" in the decorative arts by looking back
nostalgically to a preindustrial
past. Between 1935 and 1942,
artists produced 18,000 watercolors of indigenous artifacts,
such as this door latch by an
anonymous Pennsylvania
German blacksmith, a simple
utilitarian farmhouse object
with decorative details, including the curved points on the
cusp. These pictures made up a
pictorial archive that aimed to
connect Americans with their
folk and popular arts — the
"arts of the common man," in
the words of FAP director
Holger Cahill. Franklyn Syres, *Door
Latch*, watercolor, 1943.8.16758 —
National Gallery of Art.

Un-American!

A cartoon published in the *Washington Post* ridiculed the hearings held by Texas congressman Martin Dies's House Committee on Un-American Activities during August 1938. Hollywood darling Shirley Temple is shown holding a hammer and a sickle, the symbol of Communism. Elderman, *Washington Post*, August 24, 1938 — Copyright 1938, Washington Post. Reprinted with permission.

chance to climb a few steps higher on the factory job ladder. Bolstered by organizations such as the Masons, the Knights of Columbus, and the well-established churches, as well as through kinship and friendship, many Protestant workers and some Irish Catholics became hostile to the New Deal and disdainful of the CIO, in which radical Jews, anticlerical Catholics, and cosmopolitan intellectuals held prominent posts. These religious cultural fissures within the working class turned into a political chasm by the late 1930s, generating a revival of the Ku Klux Klan in Indiana, Missouri, and Texas and the appearance of the anti-Semitic, anti-Communist Black Legion in Ohio and Michigan factory towns. Such divisions penetrated the labor movement as well, fueling an intense rivalry between the AFL and the CIO and generating bitter factional conflicts within unions that attempted to consolidate their power in the electrical, farm equipment, newspaper, automobile, and mass transit industries.

In Washington, these conflicts within the labor movement aligned the AFL with some of the bitterest opponents of the New Deal. In 1938, Congress authorized the formation of a House Committee on Un-American Activities (HUAC). Under the leadership of the right-wing congressman Martin Dies of Texas, the committee attacked Popular Front political organizations and exposed left-wing influence in the Federal Theatre Project, ultimately closing it down. The AFL used HUAC's hearings to denounce sit-down strikes and to publicize the role that Communists and other radicals played in the formation of the CIO.

A year later, the National Labor Relations Board came under sharp attack by the House Rules Committee, led by the conservative Virginian Howard Smith. Working closely with Smith and other antiunion southerners, the AFL charged that the National Labor Relations Board (NLRB) favored the CIO. Reeling from his recent defeats, President Roosevelt quickly appointed a new set of NLRB members, who accommodated the AFL's point of view. The new board stressed the importance of stability and the validity of craft union claims. Hence, the NLRB soon proved far less amenable to the industrywide union structures that were favored by the

"The Charge Has Been Made That This Article of Yours Is Entirely Communistic"

The election of a large number of new conservative congressional representatives and senators in 1938 and the subsequent attack on and rollback of federal programs had ominous implications for the New Deal coalition. In 1938, congressional conservatives established the House Committee on Un-American Activities to investigate communist influence both in and out of government. Among those who were called to testify in December was Hallie Flanagan, director of the Federal Theatre Project, who was questioned by Democratic representative Joseph Starnes of Alabama about an article on workers' theater she had written seven years earlier. Despite its ridiculous qualities, the exchange between Starnes and Flanagan reveals the lengths to which conservative Democratic and Republican politicians would go to discredit progressive institutions and individuals and smear them with the taint of Communism.

Mr. Starnes: I want to quote finally from your article "A Theater is Born" . . . "The power of these theaters springing up everywhere throughout the country lies in the fact that they know what they want. Their purpose—restricted, some will call it, though it is open to question whether any theater which attempts to create a class culture can be called restricted—is clear. This is important because there are only two theaters in the country today that are clear as to aim: one is the commercial theater which wants to make money; the other is the workers' theater which wants to make a new social order. The workers' theaters are neither infirm nor divided in purpose. Unlike any art form existing in America today, the workers' theaters intend to shape the life of this country, socially, politically, and industrially. They intend to remake a social structure without the help of money—and this ambition alone invests their undertaking with a certain Marlowesque madness." You are quoting from this Marlowe. Is he a Communist?

Mrs. Flanagan: I am very sorry. I was quoting from Christopher Marlowe.

Mr. Starnes: Tell us who Marlowe is, so we can get the proper reference, because that is all that we want to do.

Mrs. Flanagan: Put in the record that he was the greatest dramatist in the period immediately preceding Shakespeare.

Mr. Starnes: Put that in the record because the charge has been made that this article of yours is entirely Communistic, and we want to help you. . . . Of course, we had what some people call Communists back in the days of the [ancient] Greek theater.

Mrs. Flanagan: Quite true.

Mr. Starnes: And I believe Mr. Euripides was guilty of teaching class consciousness also, wasn't he?

Mrs. Flanagan: I believe that was alleged against all of the Greek dramatists.

Mr. Starnes: So we cannot say when it began.

———

Eric Bentley, *Thirty Years of Treason: Excerpts from Hearings Before the House Committee on Un-American Activities, 1938–1968* (1971).

CIO and by those who saw the labor movement as a regulator of working-class income and purchasing power.

The Roosevelt Recession   In late 1937, the nation seemed close to returning to the conditions of 1933: employed factory workers were cut back to a one- or two-day workweek, and some of the unemployed went hungry once again. The so-called "Roosevelt Recession" was a product both of the president's political blunders and of far-reaching economic problems. By 1937, a remarkable economic recovery convinced administration policymakers that the Depression was nearly over; indeed, rising prices now seemed the real threat. So despite continued high unemployment, FDR cut WPA expenditures, laying off 1.5 million relief workers. This premature effort to balance the federal budget sucked purchasing power out of the economy, as did the $2 billion tax increase required by the new Social Security program (the pension checks would not begin flowing until 1941). But the sharp recession of 1937 and 1938 also had more ominous causes. American capitalism was still an unstable system; none of the New Deal reforms transformed its fundamental character. Instead, Roosevelt's overwhelming victory in 1936, the rise of labor, and the growth of federal regulation might well have inhibited investment by businessmen worried about the effects of these trends on their enterprises.

The administration's response to the recession helped to define the contours of liberal thought and politics for the next generation. After much internal debate, Roosevelt announced two partially complementary initiatives in April 1938. The first was a massive spending bill inspired by the

The Depression Continues
These migrants camped along U.S. Route 99 in Kern County, California, in November 1938. Unemployment rose sharply again during the "Roosevelt Recession." Dorothea Lange, 1938 — Prints and Photographs Division, Library of Congress.

theories of British economist John Maynard Keynes, who argued that in time of economic stagnation, government should "prime the pump" by raising public expenditures. Admitting that he could not avoid a large budget deficit, Roosevelt asked Congress to appropriate $5 billion for public works and relief programs. The government added two million new workers to the payroll, and this soon sparked another tentative recovery.

But Roosevelt and his more radical advisers did not see this strategy as an adequate response to what many considered a stagnant economy. These left-leaning New Dealers believed that the concentration of economic power kept prices high and wages low. To generate significant spending, the nation needed more than budget deficits and public relief; it needed a shift in power from the corporations to workers and consumers. To explore this thesis, Roosevelt appointed Thurmond Arnold as head of the Justice Department's Antitrust Division, and he launched a vigorous attack on business monopolies. Working with Congress, Roosevelt also set up a Temporary National Economic Committee to study corporate power and obstacles to competition. These New Dealers fought business monopolies because they thought that the concentration of power undermined democracy and thwarted the expansion of consumer purchasing power. But this broad vision did not carry the day, even within New Deal circles. It soon lost out to a strategy that focused on manipulation of consumer demand through either tax cuts or spending programs. New Deal liberalism, as a result, became defined by efforts to regulate and stabilize the economy through tax measures and spending policies rather than by an effort to directly redistribute wealth or limit the power of giant corporations.

Part of the reason for the gradual narrowing of New Deal liberalism was a sharp and increasingly effective corporate assault on programs that attacked their power and prerogatives. Businessmen routinely condemned Washington bureaucrats, left-wing New Dealers, and the new "labor bosses." Such rhetoric had its appeal, especially among the affluent, but the major corporations proved more successful when they projected a

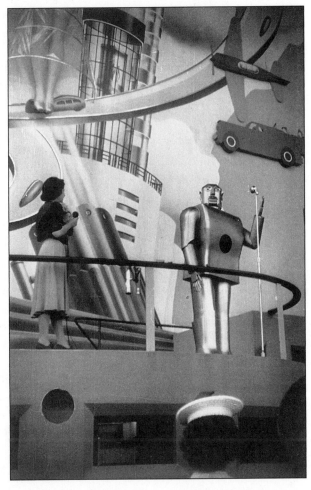

"The World of Tomorrow"

The 1939 New York World's Fair opened in the shadow of approaching war, yet its theme and exhibits optimistically predicted a prosperous, pollution-free future based on the technological expertise provided by American corporations. Among its many attractions was Elektro, a seven-foot "moto-man" in the Westinghouse Corporation's "Singing Tower of Light." Elektro — who "talks, sees, smells, sings, and counts with his fingers" — represented the benefits of electrical power. Queens Museum of Art.

Public Housing

Legislators and real estate lobbyists tried to keep expenditures for public housing low, contributing to the drab uniformity of many government-sponsored projects. But some public housing offered inexpensive homes with the style and amenities of a locality's private residences. With their tall windows and cast-iron balconies, these St. Thomas Houses, for example, fit comfortably into New Orleans's traditional architectural design. *Public Housing: The Work of the Federal Public Housing Authority* (1946) — American Social History Project.

bright future in which they would bring the bounty of new technology and consumer goods to the whole population. Like the New Dealers, executives at companies such as DuPont, General Motors, and Standard Oil of New Jersey looked beyond the Depression to a new era of high-wage consumption. But they celebrated the remarkable technical and organizational innovations that industry had made during the Depression. For example, managers at DuPont transformed a company that was known for the profitability of its munitions business and the paternalism of its labor relations into a modern enterprise that boasted "Better Things for Better Living . . . Through Chemistry." The corporate counteroffensive reached full flower at the 1939 New York World's Fair, where scores of corporations advertised their vision of an abundant future under the guidance of giant conglomerates. GM's Futurama exhibit, which featured an elaborately crafted world of express highways, green suburbs, and well-planned cities, proved the highlight of the fair and offered a corporate alternative to the social democratic vision of New Deal partisans and labor activists.

Conclusion: What the New Deal Accomplished

If the New Deal was stymied at the end of the 1930s, it nevertheless left an enormous legacy that reshaped the nation for more than two generations to come. Economic recovery was actually the least of the New Deal's achievements. It was in many respects an economic failure. None of Roosevelt's recovery programs ended mass unemployment or restored long-term economic growth. At the end of the 1930s, the effort to construct a new mass market for American industry was still incomplete. The labor movement

"I Am Hanging on to the Principles of the New Deal"

In his classic 1941 study of rubberworkers in Akron, Ohio, sociologist Alfred Winslow Jones painted a complex picture of workers' political consciousness at the close of the New Deal era. Jones's study revealed that despite their labor activism a large majority of Akron's unionized rubberworkers continued to accept the basic right of capitalists to use their property as they saw fit. This belief was tempered, however, by a strong sense of social justice. The following interview with James Hunt, a tire-builder, typified the attitudes of many Akron workers and unionists.

All my spare time I devote to the union—to meetings and activities. That's my social enjoyment. I want to see the union eventually a sound and steady organization. I am not at all satisfied with it the way it works at present. . . . Don't get me wrong. I'm a hundred per cent for unions and I think we are twice as well off since the union was organized. . . . Since the union was organized we have had more freedom, security, dependability, and stability in wages. The union has sprung up as a sort of social change in the face of the present fast speed-up system. In the beginning the union grew so fast that . . . anybody and everybody just jumped in and went along. Socialism has crept in and I'm no socialist so I greatly disapprove of that. I want to see majority rule in a union as well as in our government, but that is not true in either at present. . . . We must build a constructive organization instead of a destructive one.

. . . The big trouble with the New Deal is that a few people run the country instead of the majority like they should. Although I have been non-partisan all my life, I am hanging on to the principles of the New Deal, but I really know that it won't solve our problems.

. . . Every worker should make more than just living expenses, but the average one certainly does not. There ought to be a limit on how much the rich can earn and on the profits of any factory or corporation. There ought also to be a minimum for everybody. There is no sense in one man making a dollar an hour and another working twice as hard and making fifty cents. But I don't contend that everyone should make equal wages for that would be wrong too.

Alfred Winslow Jones, *Life, Liberty, and Property* (1941).

was but half-built, commercial investment remained tepid, and trading blocs and war tremors shaking Europe and the Far East threatened the prospect of any revival of overseas trade. Working-class standards of living were no better than those of 1929, and working people still lived in a world of economic insecurity. World War II and half a decade of ultra-Keynesian government spending would be required to eradicate mass unemployment and restore economic growth to the United States.

But if the New Deal failed to make capitalism work, its supporters nevertheless transformed the nation's politics. The Roosevelt electoral coalition would dominate presidential politics until the 1970s. White supremacists from the South belonged to it, but so did progressive farmers from the upper Midwest, urban politicians whose machines had been reinvigorated by the federal relief funds they administered, middle-class liberals anxious for social reform, African Americans who saw the federal government as a new ally, and industrial unions that gave weight and influence to the Democratic Party's left wing. Roosevelt often functioned as a power broker juggling those disparate interests. It was not always a pretty sight, but compared with the far more monolithic power that the pre-Depression Protestant elite had wielded, the Roosevelt coalition had far more legitimacy.

The New Deal and the new unions constituted a cultural triumph because they transformed Americans' vision of themselves and of their nation. With widespread public support, the federal government constructed a welfare state that became an active — even a protective — presence in citizens' lives. The welfare state and the labor laws enacted during the Second New Deal had many flaws, but they held the promise of a new social and political enfranchisement. For at least half of the industrial working class — not only African Americans but also immigrants from Southern and Eastern Europe — citizenship had been merely a formality, underused or unrealized. Despite the power of the coalition of Dixiecrats and Republicans, the new unionism and the New Deal played a decisive role in mobilizing these new Americans into an organized body of citizens whose political power and distinctive outlook gave birth to a new kind of patriotism. In the 1930s, voter participation reached its twentieth century apogee. In the approaching world conflict, the nation would be more unified than ever because its patriotism arose from a pluralism that was far more genuine than that of earlier — or later — times. In the 1930s, America's working people transformed themselves from deferential subjects into self-confident citizens.

The Years in Review

1935

- The Second New Deal, which includes the Works Progress Administration, Social Security Act, and Wagner Act, greatly expands the role of the federal government.

- American Federation of Labor (AFL) dissidents establish the Committee for Industrial Organization (later the Congress of Industrial Organizations, or CIO) under John L. Lewis to back aggressive organizing of industrial unions.

- Populist senator Huey Long of Louisiana is assassinated.

- The Communist Party of the United States proclaims support for a "Popular Front" of labor, liberals, and New Dealers to fight business and the rise of fascism.

1936

- The Supreme Court invalidates the Agricultural Adjustment Act.

- The National Negro Congress is founded to support union organizing drives, agitate for more public housing, and picket discriminatory employers.

- The California's Associated Farmers crush the lettuce harvesters' strike in Salinas.

- Roosevelt is reelected in a huge landslide over Republican Alfred Landon and third-party candidates William Lemke, Norman Thomas, and Earl Browder.

- General Motors employees initiate a massive sit-down strike in Flint, Michigan, which will lead to GM's recognition of the United Autoworkers Union in early 1937.

1937

- Strikes sweep the nation; nearly five million workers take part in some kind of industrial action, and almost three million become union members.

- Roosevelt announces his "court-packing" plan to add six new justices to the U.S. Supreme Court.

- U.S. Steel recognizes the Steel Workers' Organizing Committee, but smaller steel companies resist; workers at Republic Steel in South Chicago stage a strike that turns into a massacre by police.

- A sharp decline in the economy, the "Roosevelt Recession," saps the president's popularity.

- The Brotherhood of Sleeping Car Porters wins union recognition, higher wages, and shorter hours.

1938

- The House Committee on Un-American Activities holds hearings suggesting that many of America's problems are caused by Communist agitators.

- The Fair Labor Standards Act prohibits child labor, sets a minimum wage, and writes the forty-hour workweek into federal law.

- The Democrats lose eighty-one seats in the House and eight seats in the Senate, as Roosevelt's effort to "realign" the Democratic Party fails.

1939

- The New York World's Fair in Flushing Meadows, New York, presents a vision of an abundant future under the guidance of giant corporations.

- African American contralto Marian Anderson gives a concert on the steps of the Lincoln Memorial after the Daughters of the American Revolution bar her from performing in Constitution Hall.

Additional Readings

For more on the Roosevelt administration, Congress, and the Second New Deal, see: Robert Caro, *The Years of Lyndon Johnson: The Path to Power* (1982); Mark Leff, *The Limits of Symbolic Reform: The New Deal and Taxation, 1933–1939* (1984); William Edward Leuchtenburg, *Franklin D. Roosevelt and the New Deal, 1932–1940* (1963); James T. Patterson, *Congressional Conservatism and the New Deal* (1967); and T. H. Watkins, *Righteous Pilgrim: The Life and Times of Harold L. Ickes, 1874–1952* (1990).

For more on the CIO and union organizing, see: Irving Bernstein, *The Turbulent Years: A History of the American Worker, 1933–1941* (1970); Melinda Chateauvert, *Marching Together: Women of the Brotherhood of Sleeping Car Porters* (1997); Dorothy Sue Cobble, *Dishing It Out: Waitresses and Their Unions in the Twentieth Century* (1991); Melvyn Dubofsky and Warren Van Tine, *John L. Lewis: A Biography* (1977); Elizabeth Faue, *Community of Suffering and Struggle: Women, Men, and the Labor Movement in Minneapolis, 1915–1945* (1991); Sidney Fine, *Sit-Down: The General Motors Strike of 1936–37* (1969); Joshua Freeman, *In Transit: The Transport Workers Union in New York City, 1933–1966* (1989); Roger Keeran, *The Communist Party and the Auto Workers' Unions* (1986); Nelson Lichtenstein, *Walter Reuther: The Most Dangerous Man in Detroit* (1997); Vicki Ruiz, *Cannery Women/Cannery Lives: Mexican Women, Unionization, and the California Food Processing Industry, 1930–1950* (1987); Christopher Tomlins, *The State and the Unions: Labor Relations, Law and the Organized Labor Movement in America, 1880–1960* (1985); and Robert Ziegler, *The CIO, 1935–1955* (1995).

For more on gender and race in the New Deal, see: Clayborne Carson et al., *The Struggle for Freedom: A History of African Americans* (2006); Karen Ferguson, *Black Politics in New Deal Atlanta* (2002); Robin D. G. Kelley, *Hammer and Hoe: Alabama Communists During the Great Depression* (1990); Alice Kessler-Harris, *In Pursuit of Equity: Women, Men, and the Quest for Economic Citizenship in 20th-Century America* (2001); George Whitney Martin, *Madam Secretary: Frances Perkins* (1983); George Sanchez, *Becoming Mexican American: Ethnicity, Culture and Identity in Chicano Los Angeles, 1900–1945* (1993); Nikhil Pal Singh, *Black Is a Country: Race and the Unfinished Struggle for Democracy* (2004); Patricia Sullivan, *Days of Hope:*

Race and Democracy in the New Deal Era (1996); Susan Ware, *Beyond Suffrage: Women in the New Deal* (1981); Nancy J. Weiss, *Farewell to the Party of Lincoln: Black Politics in the Age of FDR* (1983); and Howard Zinn, Dana Frank, and Robin D. G. Kelley, *Three Strikes* (2001).

For more on the culture of New Deal America, see: Jane S. De Hart, *The Federal Theatre, 1935–1939: Plays, Relief, and Politics* (1967); Michael Denning, *The Cultural Front: The Laboring of American Culture in the Twentieth Century* (1996); Laurance P. Hurlburt, *The Mexican Muralists in the United States* (1991); Joe Klein, *Woody Guthrie: A Life* (1980); Robbie Lieberman, *My Weapon Is My Song* (1995); Gerald Markowitz and Marlene Park, *Democratic Vistas: Post Offices and Public Art in the New Deal* (1984); Barbara Melosh, *Engendering Culture: Manhood and Womanhood in New Deal Public Art and Theater* (1991); Kathy M. Newman, *Radio Active: Advertising and Consumer Activism, 1935–1947* (2004); Richard Pells, *Radical Visions and American Dreams: Culture and Social Thought in the Depression Years* (1973); and Warren Susman, *Culture as History: The Transformation of American Society in the Twentieth Century* (1984).

For more on U.S. foreign policy during the 1930s, see: Robert Dallek, *Franklin D. Roosevelt and American Foreign Policy, 1932–1945*, 2nd ed. (1995); Frederick Pike, *FDR's Good Neighbor Policy* (1995); and William A. Williams, *The Tragedy of American Diplomacy* (1959).

For more on the lasting legacies of the New Deal, see: Irving Bernstein, *A Caring Society: The New Deal, the Worker, and the Great Depression* (1985); Alan Brinkley, *The End of Reform: New Deal Liberalism in Recession and War* (1995); Steve Fraser and Gary Gerstle, eds., *The Rise and Fall of the New Deal Order, 1930–1980* (1989); and Sanford M. Jacoby, *Modern Manors: Welfare Capitalism Since the New Deal* (1997).

10

A Nation Transformed:
The United States in World War II

1939–1946

Fascism, militarism, Communism, capitalism—these were the world-shaking "isms" that captured the nation's attention both domestically and internationally at the end of the Depression. When Ford Motor Company employees beat up labor organizers in 1937, the unions charged "fascism"; when President Roosevelt increased the budget for the army and navy in 1938, critics cried "militarism." When a recession began in late 1937, critics on the left said that it exemplified the recurring stagnation of "capitalism," and when the Congress of Industrial Organizations (CIO) attempted to organize the aircraft industry, manufacturers branded such tactics as plots to advance "Communism."

Even before the end of the 1930s, then, domestic events were linked to battlefronts and propaganda wars in Europe and Asia. The outbreak of World War II in Europe in 1939 and the U.S. entry into the war two years later further narrowed the gap between life in the United States and events taking place around the world. At home, the U.S. economy doubled in size, ending the Depression era unemployment and turning Detroit, Michigan; Los Angeles, California; Mobile, Alabama; and Portland, Oregon, into boomtowns. By the time the war came to an end in August 1945, those events would transform both American life and the global economy. The United States emerged from World War II as the planet's military and economic powerhouse.

War Production and Victory
Belching defense industry smokestacks, emblazoned with the flags of the Allied nations, resemble cannon fire in this Office of War Information poster, which urged higher industrial production. West Point Museum Collections, United States Military Academy.

The Origins of the Second World War

Just as the Depression of the 1930s had intensified antagonisms within the United States, so too had it bred international conflict. Industrialized nations, including the United States, responded to the widespread decline in consumer buying power by shutting foreign competitors out of their markets and scrambling for additional customers abroad. Such concerns were particularly strong in Germany, Japan, and Italy, whose domestic markets and resources were relatively limited. The militaristic leaders of those countries believed that the existing world order served solely to maintain the international supremacy of Great Britain, France, and the United States. Despite the expansionist policies of Japan and Germany, most Americans remained isolationist, hoping to avoid another world war. But Roosevelt and other American leaders turned their attention to the international situation and away from New Deal reform.

Militarism and Fascism Abroad   In East Asia, the Depression had sharply reduced exports and generated mass unemployment. Japan's authoritarian government moved to eliminate the Asian colonies, of both Europe and the United States, and to create instead an empire—the "Greater East Asia Co-prosperity Sphere"—that was intended to ensure Japan's access to vital raw materials. In 1931, the Japanese Imperial Army took over Manchuria and then gradually extended control over all of northern China. Although the League of Nations condemned the invasion, it imposed no sanctions. In 1937, full-scale war broke out between Japan and China. That year, the Japanese captured the Chinese capital of Nanking, slaughtering close to 300,000 civilians. A civil war between Chinese Communists, led by Mao Zedong, and Chiang Kai-shek's nationalists crippled the Chinese resistance movement.

As the Far Eastern conflict spread, racial animosity and racist imagery quickly surfaced. The Japanese saw the Chinese as an inferior people on whom the Imperial Army could impose their will, and they viewed the United States and Great Britain as decadent and materialistic colonial powers whose strength would crumble when confronted by the pure spirit of Japan. Racial stereotypes also blinded American officials. They often sentimentalized the Chinese as an inherently peaceful peasant people who needed U.S. beneficence to achieve their destiny. In contrast, the Japanese were characterized as a "yellow peril," a devious, rodentlike race that was threatening to bring economic ruin to the West with exports of "cheap Jap goods."

The success of Japan's aggressive actions encouraged European dictators, especially in Italy and Germany, where fascist leaders dreamed of new empires. In Italy, Benito Mussolini's followers had seized power in 1922, ruthlessly suppressing labor unions, parliamentary government, and civil liberties. Mussolini's brand of fascism resembled other authoritarian, right-wing, nationalist movements, all of which opposed liberalism, socialism, and Communism. He appealed to Italian nationalism, trumpeting complaints about Italy's unfair treatment under the 1919 Treaty of Versailles and reminding Italians of their humiliating defeat by Abyssinia (now called

Ethiopia) in 1896—the first time Africans had turned back European imperialists. An aroused Italy invaded Ethiopia in 1935, arraying airplanes, machine guns, and poison gas against the poorly organized riflemen of one of the few independent states left in Africa. When Ethiopia's Emperor Haile Selassie appealed to the League of Nations, the international body condemned Mussolini's act of aggression, but Italy's subjugation of Ethiopia continued apace.

The rise of the German version of fascism—National Socialism, or Nazism—worried Americans more than any other overseas development. Americans had strong cultural ties to Germany, the scientific, literary, and musical traditions of which were influential throughout the Western world. And although Germany's Weimar Republic (the democratic state that was established after the first World War) had become politically unstable by the 1930s, it still seemed to embody much that was cosmopolitan, modern, and democratic in twentieth-century art and culture. Given the advanced character of German science and technology and Germany's enormous economic power, Americans viewed the rise of Nazism with great alarm.

Like the Italian fascists, the Nazis repudiated both the terms of the Treaty of Versailles and also democracy, in all its forms. Nazi leader Adolf Hitler, elected chancellor in 1933, quickly seized dictatorial powers, taking the title of *Der Führer* (the leader), proclaiming a thousand-year Reich (empire), and outlawing all other political parties. Americans were appalled at Hitler's brutal destruction of Germany's democratic institutions, and they recognized that his systematic and aggressive anti-Semitism marked the Nazi regime as something genuinely new and dangerous. When the Nazis burned nearly two hundred synagogues and looted thousands of Jewish shops on November 9–10, 1938, which became known as *Kristallnacht* ("Night of Broken Glass"), a shocked President Roosevelt confided that he "could scarcely believe that such things could occur in a twentieth-century civilization."

Although many people in the West sympathized at first with Hitler's efforts to revise the punitive Versailles Treaty, sympathy soon turned to alarm as it became clear that the Nazis sought to unite all the Germans in Europe in a single German fatherland. In 1933, Hitler withdrew from the League of Nations and began secretly rearming Germany, in violation of the Versailles Treaty. In August 1936, he dispatched part of Germany's new air force to aid Spain's General Francisco Franco and his fascist forces in their attack on that country's democratically elected government. A series of pacts in late 1936 and 1937 united Japan, Italy, and Germany in an alliance that would become known as the Axis, ostensibly to protect themselves against the Soviet Union.

The leaders of Britain and France, hoping to avoid another bloody war, sought to appease the German dictator. In the spring of 1936, when Hitler

Degenerate Art
Beginning in 1937, the Nazis removed more than 16,500 German works of art by leading modern and Jewish artists from public museums and institutions. Six hundred and fifty of the confiscated works were exhibited in a Munich exhibition called *Entartete Kunst* ("Degenerate Art"). "All around us," Adolf Ziegler, president of the Reich chamber of visual arts, exhorted the opening crowd, "you see the monstrous offspring of insanity, impudence, ineptitude, and sheer degeneracy. What this exhibition offers inspires horror and disgust in us all." During its four-month run, the exhibit, an "exorcism of evil," attracted more than two million visitors, exceeding the attendance of any other modern art show, before or since. Suddeutsche Verlag.

violated the Versailles Treaty by sending the German army into the Rhineland, a demilitarized zone in western Germany, neither Britain nor France attempted to force him to withdraw. Within two years, Germany had annexed Austria and then demanded that Czechoslovakia surrender the German-speaking border area known as the Sudetenland. Again, British and French leaders capitulated, agreeing at a conference held in Munich in September 1938 to Hitler's occupation of the Sudetenland. But British Prime Minister Neville Chamberlain's proclamation that the Munich agreement guaranteed "peace for our time" soon came to seem nothing more than shortsighted and cowardly appeasement that fed the dictator's aggressive appetite. By March 1939, Germany had gobbled up all of Czechoslovakia.

Within a year, the Nazis and the Soviets signed a "nonaggression" pact, opening the door to a violent partition of Poland by Germany and the Soviet Union. Many people were stunned by the opportunistic agreement between bitter ideological foes—each of whom saw short-term advantages in a peace treaty. Nine days after signing the pact, Germany invaded Poland on September 1, 1939. Unable to ignore the attack on their Polish ally, Great

Britain and France finally declared war on Germany. World War II had begun.

Germany proved stronger, and the Allies (the term for the nations that fought Germany, Italy, and Japan in World War II) weaker, than most observers expected. Poland surrendered within a month, and the next spring, German troops swept through Denmark, Norway, Belgium, and the Netherlands. In mid-June 1940, the French army collapsed, and the Germans marched into Paris. Hitler continued his offensive, launching a bombing attack on London. In 1940 and 1941, Hungary, Romania, and Bulgaria joined the Axis alliance, and German troops moved into Yugoslavia and Greece. Finally, on June 22, 1941, Hitler broke his nonaggression pact with Josef Stalin and invaded the Soviet Union. The huge German army pushed to the gates of Moscow and Leningrad. Within three months, the Nazis had killed or captured more than three million people inside the Soviet borders.

From Isolationism to Internationalism   President Roosevelt condemned foreign aggression and prepared for war even while the United States remained steadfastly isolationist through much of the 1930s. Fueling this self-contradictory stance was a highly publicized Senate investigation that uncovered evidence that Wall Street bankers, corporate munitions makers, and other "merchants of death" had led America into the Great War and then reaped huge profits from the conflict. Fear of engagements abroad proved so potent that Congress passed a series of Neutrality Acts, mandating an arms embargo against both the victim and aggressor in any military conflict and establishing a "cash-and-carry" trading policy that deprived belligerents of access to American credit, ships, and military goods.

Late in the 1930s, however, the powerful isolationist current gradually ebbed as Americans came to appreciate the threat posed by the rise of fascism abroad. Chinese Americans spearheaded a boycott of Japanese goods; Jews and civil libertarians urged a similar ban on German products. Liberals and leftists who were sympathetic to the Spanish Republic attacked U.S. neutrality laws, which prevented the Spanish Loyalists from securing the military supplies they needed to fend off the fascists in that nation's civil war. Some American radicals supported the Spanish Republican cause directly by enlisting in the Abraham Lincoln Brigade, which fought alongside 35,000 antifascists from fifty-two countries in what some later saw as a dress rehearsal for World War II.

This shift in the public's mood, especially among supporters of the New Deal, enabled Roosevelt to align the nation's diplomacy more closely with that of Britain, France, and China. When Japan renewed its assault on China in 1937, Roosevelt told an audience in Chicago that the United States must help the international community to "quarantine" aggressors and prevent the contagion of war from spreading. After war broke out in Europe in 1939,

Roosevelt began mobilizing public opinion against the Neutrality Acts and even urged "measures short of war" to bolster England, France, and other Allied powers that were engaged in the conflict.

The Nazi conquest of Western Europe in the spring of 1940 pushed the United States toward active engagement in the war. Congress reacted by tripling the War Department's budget, enacting the nation's first peacetime draft, and agreeing in March 1941 to lend or lease war material to enemies of the Axis nations (chiefly Great Britain and later the Soviet Union). Through the lend-lease program, Roosevelt declared, the United States would become "a great arsenal of democracy." White House officials recognized that a Nazi-dominated Europe, combined with Japanese supremacy in East Asia, would permanently bar U.S. trade and business from much of the globe. Most American policymakers saw a world of open capitalist markets as synonymous with U.S. interests.

In August 1941, President Roosevelt and British Prime Minister Winston Churchill issued the Atlantic Charter, a joint declaration of war aims. British and U.S. military officers and war production officials began to coordinate their strategy and planning. In return for this virtual co-belligerency on the part of the United States, Churchill agreed to an increase in U.S. trade and investment in the British empire. The U.S. Navy was soon patrolling the North Atlantic, an action that was just short of outright naval warfare against Germany (Map 10.1).

Meanwhile, Japan's invasion of the French colonies in Indochina provoked Congress to freeze all Japanese assets in the United States. Great Britain and Holland followed suit, preventing Japan from purchasing oil, steel, and other essential materials. Between August and November 1941, U.S. and Japanese diplomats exchanged a series of fruitless peace proposals. When their talks collapsed, Secretary of State Cordell Hull declared, "I have washed my hands of the Japanese situation, and it is now in the hands of . . . the Army and Navy."

A bitter political and ideological debate accompanied the nation's shift from isolationism to rearmament. Even after the fall of France in June 1940, not all Americans shared Roosevelt's predisposition toward intervention in the war. For example, Irish Americans, who hated British imperialism, were leery of an alliance with Britain, and many German Americans were reluctant to go to war against their homeland. A revitalized isolationist movement developed around the America First Committee, led by Sears Roebuck

Volunteers of America

Composed of approximately 3,000 Americans, the Abraham Lincoln Battalion, along with other international volunteers, defended the Spanish Republic against General Francisco Franco's rebel military forces supported by fascist Italy and Germany. It was the first racially integrated U.S. military unit and the first led by a black commander. About 700 of the American volunteers died in Spain. Members of the battalion are pictured here in spring 1938 before crossing the Ebro River near Barcelona and engaging in the largest battle during the 1936–1939 war. The black volunteer in the second row on the right side of the photo is reading a Yiddish newspaper. (He was raised by a Jewish family in New York City.) Abraham Lincoln Brigade Archives, Tamiment Library, New York University.

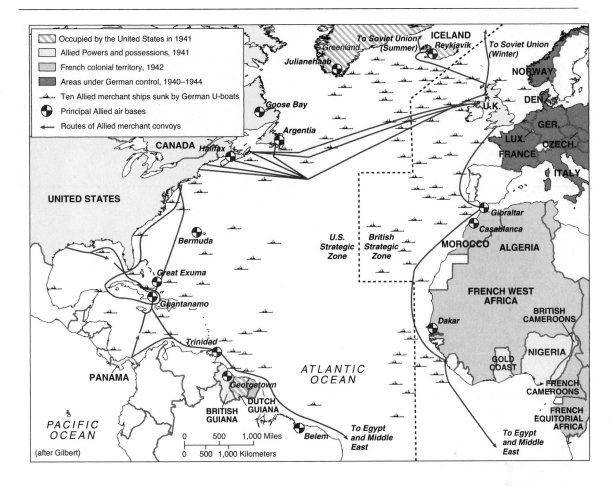

MAP 10.1 World War II in the North Atlantic, 1939–1943

German attacks on Allied and American merchant ships spurred Roosevelt to increase U.S. support for the Allies through the Lend-Lease Act and the Atlantic Charter. In 1941, naval confrontations in the Atlantic increased as the United States shipped supplies to the Allied countries.

Chairman Robert Wood, aviation hero Charles A. Lindbergh, and numerous political and business leaders, most from the Midwest. Although well represented in the Republican Party, the isolationists could find no presidential candidate in 1940. Instead, the GOP nominated Wendell Willkie, a Wall Street utilities executive who was aligned with the internationalist wing of the Republican Party. Willkie's positions differed little from those Roosevelt held in 1940: he would keep the country out of war but would extend generous assistance to the Allies. A magnetic figure, Willkie tried to convince voters that giving the president an unprecedented third term would threaten the nation's democratic traditions. But he was no match for Roosevelt, who won reelection with 55 percent of the popular vote.

The isolationists' political defeat underscored their moral weaknesses. Many isolationists seemed oblivious to the danger of fascism and thought that German domination of Europe was inevitable. Anti-Semitism also tinged isolationist sentiment, even in the face of Hitler's increasingly murderous policies. Charles Lindbergh undercut the isolationists' credibility when he asserted that Jews were among the most active of American groups pressing for the United States to enter the war. Conservative isolationists called the New Deal the "Jew Deal."

Leftist alternatives to internationalism collapsed just as quickly. In the months following Germany's invasion of France, most American trade unionists came to support Roosevelt's program of active U.S. involvement in the conflict. When labor leader John L. Lewis denounced Roosevelt and endorsed Willkie during the 1940 campaign, few workers followed his lead, prompting Lewis to resign as president of the CIO. Unionists such as Philip Murray, the new CIO chief, and Sidney Hillman of the Amalgamated Clothing Workers' Union saw U.S. participation in the war as politically advantageous to labor. Roosevelt, recognizing Hillman as an ally and a sympathetic spokesman in the labor movement, appointed him to important defense mobilization posts. American Communists also lined up behind U.S. intervention. They did so, however, only after alienating many former allies by a rapid about-face, first arguing that the war was merely one of imperialist rivalry and then, after Germany's invasion of the Soviet Union in June 1941, declaring the conflict a great crusade against fascism.

"The Most Interesting Nation in the World Today"
Charles A. Lindbergh was the most popular opponent of American intervention in World War II. The famous aviator, the first pilot to fly solo across the Atlantic, became fascinated by Germany and especially German air power. In the summer of 1936, he accepted the invitation of Luftwaffe head Hermann Göring to visit Germany and inspect its military forces. Charles and Anne Morrow Lindbergh were photographed with Göring during that visit, at which time he made the above observation. Lindbergh returned to Germany in 1937 and 1938. His acceptance of a medal from Göring during the latter visit, at a time when Nazi Germany was increasing its persecution of Jews, provoked great controversy. Heinrich Hoffmann, Time & Life Pictures — Getty Images.

The End of the New Deal

With the approach of war, the era of New Deal social reform came to an end. Roosevelt focused increasingly on the international situation and directed his special adviser and campaign organizer Thomas Corcoran to "cut out this New Deal stuff. It's tough to win a war." In July 1940, Roosevelt filled several influential government posts with conservative advocates of intervention, including Henry Stimson, who had served in President Hoover's cabinet, and Frank Knox, Alfred Landon's running mate in 1936. These men recognized the impossibility of repealing the New Deal and rolling back labor's victories. They aimed instead to block a new round of social reforms and to restore to big business much of its pre–New Deal power and prestige.

Nevertheless, labor leaders managed to take advantage of the defense employment boom to rebuild and expand the industrial union movement. Between June 1940 and December 1941, the unions launched a wave of strikes that boosted wages and enrolled a million and a half new members. Many of these work stoppages won union recognition from the nation's most reactionary employers. The most dramatic occurred at the Ford Motor Company, the only large automaker that had successfully resisted the United Auto Workers' (UAW) organizing drive in 1937. On April 1, 1941, tens of thousands of Ford workers walked out of the gigantic River Rouge complex. Using their own automobiles as a barricade, the strikers formed a mobile picket line that stretched for miles around the Dearborn, Michigan, plant. Within a few weeks, more than 100,000 new workers joined the UAW, under a union shop contract that overnight turned the pioneer auto firm into a bastion of militant unionism.

Despite the UAW's victory, the organizing drive of 1940 and 1941 foundered on the shoals of national politics. In January 1941, Roosevelt declared, "whatever stands in the way of speed and efficiency in defense preparations must give way to the national need." Defense contractors, congressional conservatives, and the military soon demanded an end to industrial disputes. To arbitrate and stop new disputes, the White House set up a National Defense Mediation Board, which included representatives of organized labor, management, and the government. The CIO agreed to cooperate, and its president, Philip Murray, became one of the board's members even as he warned that the government would soon "find its attention directed against labor in order to maintain the status quo as much as possible."

A California aircraft strike in June 1941 demonstrated the extent to which the federal government would use the defense emergency to throw its weight against union militancy and political radicalism. Government authorities did not seek to smash trade unionism outright, only to tame and contain it. The North American Aviation plant in Inglewood, California, which supplied vitally needed training planes to the Army Air Corps paid low wages and earned enormous profits. When a strike erupted in early June, Sidney Hillman and the National Defense Mediation Board joined with the army's top brass to persuade UAW officials to declare the strike a "wildcat," or unauthorized, work stoppage, motivated by Communist opposition to the war. When strike leaders, a few of whom were indeed Communists, resisted orders from UAW officials to return to work, President Roosevelt dispatched 2,500 active-duty troops to disperse the pickets and occupy the factory. Within a few days, the strike had been broken, but the army also pressured the Mediation Board to give workers a big raise, thus helping national UAW leaders to reclaim the loyalty of the workforce. When the plant finally boosted wages in July 1941, a UAW paper greeted news of the award with the triumphant headline "Responsible Unionism Wins at Inglewood."

Fighting the War

The United States was well on its way toward full wartime mobilization by December 7, 1941. The decision to enter the war was made final when the Japanese launched a surprise attack on the U.S. forces in Hawaii and the Philippines. At Hawaii's Pearl Harbor, Japanese planes sank or disabled several of the heaviest ships in the U.S. Pacific fleet, killing 2,400 soldiers and sailors. The next day, Great Britain and the United States declared war on Japan, and Germany declared war on the United States. The Japanese attack—"a date which will live in infamy," Roosevelt called it—swept away nearly all popular resistance to U.S. involvement in the war. American soldiers faced brutal warfare in the Pacific and European fronts that, for many, would shape the rest of their lives. Life in uniform broadened the horizons of almost all soldiers, acquainting millions of provincial Americans with men and women from a kaleidoscope of alien cultures and religions. The draft was egalitarian, touching men from all classes and regions. "The first time I ever heard a New England accent," a Midwesterner recalled, "was at Fort Benning." For many white youths, military service helped to reduce the ethnic and regional differences that had long divided the working class.

War in the Pacific and in Europe   Over the next six months, the Allies took a terrible beating in the Pacific. By May 1942, Japan had seized Indonesia, Indochina, the Philippines, Hong Kong, Malaya, Burma, and most of eastern China. Americans were horrified when they learned three years later of a brutal "death march," in which thousands of American and Filipino prisoners of war perished on a long trek out of the Bataan Peninsula in the Philippines. "If you fell out to the side," recalled Anton Bilek, then a twenty-two-year-old soldier from Illinois, "you were either shot by the guards or you were bayoneted and left there." Most Americans came to hate the Japanese with a passion that was not equally directed at their German or Italian enemies. U.S. propaganda portrayed the Japanese as subhuman apes, insects, rats, and reptiles; Japanese propaganda, in turn, depicted Western leaders as devils, demons, and ogres.

In the Pacific, U.S. strategists successfully contained the Japanese naval advance (Map 10.2). Early in May 1942, relying on a handful of aircraft carriers, Americans turned back the Japanese fleet in the Battle of the Coral Sea. In June, during a four-day carrier battle near Midway Island, the United States regained control of the central Pacific. By mid-1943, the Americans, aided by Australians and New Zealanders, had halted the Japanese advance and regained the initiative in the Pacific war. Under General Douglas MacArthur, the army leapfrogged from the Solomon Islands to New Guinea and on to the Philippines, where they landed in late 1944. Meanwhile, a huge

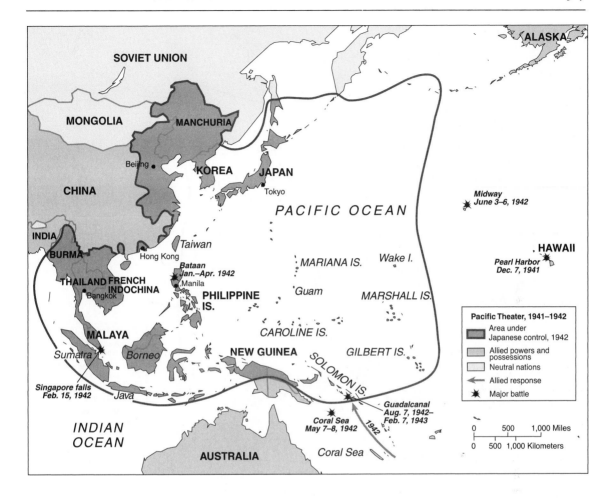

MAP 10.2   The Japanese Advance, 1941–1942

Only five months after the Japanese bombing of Pearl Harbor, Japan controlled the oil of Sumatra, the railroads of Manchuria, the Philippines, parts of New Guinea, and dozens of strategic islands. Many people feared that Australia would fall next.

naval force under the command of Admiral Chester Nimitz used amphibious assault tactics to fight its way through the central Pacific, from Tarawa to the Marianas. Such advances were bathed in blood, with high casualties among the Americans and an even higher toll among the Japanese, who often refused to surrender (Map 10.3).

Determined as Americans were to "Remember Pearl Harbor," the Pacific Theater took second place to Europe, both as a battleground and as a strategic priority. The Soviet Union bore the brunt of the fighting in Europe. Facing almost two hundred German divisions along a huge front, Soviet soldiers and civilians halted, drove back, and then encircled 330,000 troops of the German Sixth Army in the four-month-long Battle of Stalingrad. When the Germans finally surrendered to the Red Army in January 1943, cold, hunger, and constant fighting had decimated their numbers. The Battle of Stalingrad was the turning point in the titanic conflict that

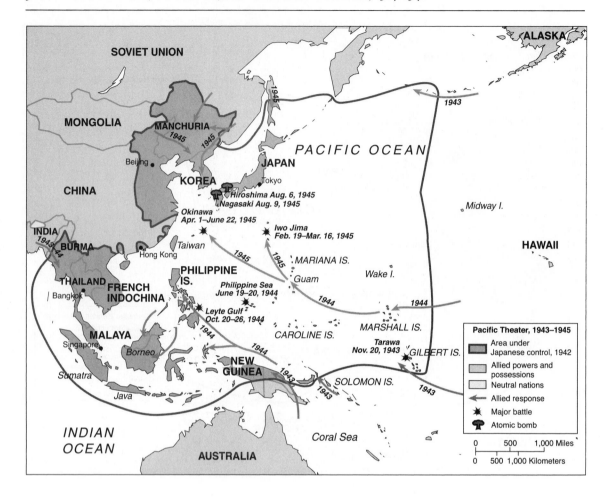

engulfed all of Europe, where military and civilian deaths rose to nearly forty million, including six million Jews murdered by the Nazis. The Soviet Union alone lost twenty-seven million people during the war—the most casualties suffered by any nation.

For British and American planners, debate over a "second front" proved the major strategic issue of the first half of the war. Stalin was desperate for an Anglo-American invasion of France to divert some of Hitler's forces away from the Eastern ("first") Front. Soviet Foreign Minister Vyacheslav Molotov raised the issue repeatedly; he reportedly knew only four English words: *yes*, *no*, and *second front*. But Winston Churchill and the British high command feared enormous battlefield losses in an early invasion across the English Channel. In 1942 and 1943, therefore, the Western allies concentrated their forces on Hitler's Mediterranean periphery, where they confronted only twenty German divisions. Between October 1942 and September 1943, British

MAP 10.3   War in the Pacific, 1943–1945
While Russian forces fought the major land war in Europe, American troops waged slow island by island battles in the Pacific. At Iwo Jima, U.S. troops sustained more than 20,000 casualties, with 6,000 killed, and at Okinawa 7,600 U.S. troops died and another 32,000 were wounded.

The Enemy 1

The cover of a December 1942 issue of *Collier's* magazine commemorated the first anniversary of the Japanese attack on Pearl Harbor. The portrayal of Prime Minister Hideki Tojo as a vampire bat indicates one way in which the Japanese were presented in American popular media and war propaganda. Unlike images of the European enemy, the Japanese were depicted as vicious animals, most often taking the form of apes or parasitic insects. Arthur Szyk, *Collier's*, December 12, 1942 — American Social History Project.

and U.S. forces regained control of North Africa, conquered Sicily, and slowly fought their way up the Italian peninsula toward Rome (Map 10.4).

In lieu of a second front, the British and Americans launched an aerial bombardment of German industry. Flying out of air bases in England, thousands of B-17s, Lancasters, and other four-engine bombers pounded aircraft factories, munitions plants, railroad centers, and oil refineries in Central Europe. Air combat gripped the imagination of both military planners and the public, for it promised to substitute technology and skill for the blood and mud of ground fighting. But the campaign failed. Clouds, wind, darkness, and enemy fighters made a mockery of "precision bombing," so the Germans pushed their aircraft and tank output to new heights in 1943 and 1944. In response, the Allies resorted to area bombing, including tightly packed working-class neighborhoods, an approach that some Americans condemned as a terror tactic.

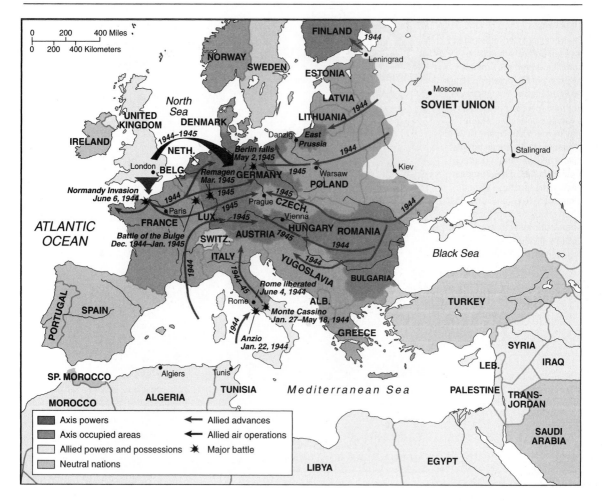

MAP 10.4 Europe at War, 1944–1945

Until June 1944, most fighting in World War II in the European theater took place between the German and Russian armies on a vast Eastern Front. With the British and American invasion at Normandy on June 6, 1944, a Western Front forced the Nazis to divide their forces. Eleven months later, on May 8, 1945, the Germans surrendered.

Life in the Armed Forces   Until the final year of the war, only a small fraction of the sixteen million Americans who served in the armed forces actually saw combat. For most soldiers and sailors, their primary duties entailed training and supplying a vast and complex organization. GIs (so called because their clothing and supplies were "government issue") learned to march, shoot, drive a truck, repair a radio, type, and keep accurate records. Those who were sent to the front entered a nightmarish world of violence and death. Soldiers in World War II possessed far greater firepower than ever before, so it was the first war in which combat deaths outnumbered fatalities from disease or accident. Most of the 405,000 deaths suffered by U.S. forces came in the war's final year, when American armies spearheaded the assault against well-entrenched German and Japanese forces. From the foxholes, war correspondent Ernie Pyle reported, "We see from the worm's-

The Enemy 2

A 1942 poster depicting the Nazi enemy used a stereotype of a monocled Prussian officer that dated back to the propaganda images of World War I. Germans were portrayed as sinister but not as the nonhuman predators that were featured in the anti-Japanese posters. Victor Ancona and Karl Koehler, *This Is the Enemy*, 1942, offset lithograph, 34 1/4 × 23 3/4 inches — Poster Fund, The Museum of Modern Art.

eye view, and our segment of the picture consists only of tired and dirty soldiers who are alive and don't want to die . . . of shocked men wandering back down the hill from battle . . . of smelly bed rolls and C rations . . . and of graves and graves and graves."

Soldiers often formed intense emotional attachments to their unit and to each other. "The reason you storm the beaches is not patriotism or bravery," one ex-GI explained. "It's that sense of not wanting to fail your buddies. That's sort of a special sense of kinship." Such camaraderie became the basis for lifelong friendships and for the veterans' organizations and unit reunions that proved so popular after the war.

Life in the armed services also had a long-lasting impact on America's homosexual population. Many who first expressed their sexual orientation during the war later became pioneers in the gay and lesbian rights movement. Far from home, many gay men and lesbian women felt less social pressure to conform to heterosexual social norms. The military's need for soldiers tended to make it more tolerant, albeit silently, of the homosexual men and women in its ranks. Nevertheless, when the military discovered their sexual orientation, homosexuals received stigmatizing "blue discharges," which denied them GI benefits, adversely affected their employment prospects, and jeopardized their reputations in their hometowns. The military also launched investigations into lesbianism, which coincided, at the end of the war, with the military's decision to discourage female enlistments.

Patterns of discrimination also confronted black soldiers. In 1940, African Americans were excluded from the U.S. Marine Corps, the Coast Guard, and the Army Air Corps. In the U.S. Navy, African American sailors at first served only in the ship's mess, although by the spring of 1942, they were allowed to perform general labor. The army accepted African Americans—more than 700,000 of them by 1944, including 4,000 women in the Women's Army Corps—only on a segregated basis. The new recruits trained in segregated camps such as Camp Shenango in Pennsylvania, where Dempsy Travis was sent: "The troop train was Jim Crow. They had a car for black soldiers and a car for whites. [At the camp] they went to their part and sent us to the ghetto. It seems the army always arranged to have black soldiers back up against the woods someplace. Isolated." The military largely restricted African American GIs to duty in transportation, construction, and

"We Were Fighting and Sleeping in One Vast Cesspool"

The historian William Manchester served as a marine in the Pacific theater. He described the horror of hand-to-hand combat in the Battle of Okinawa in 1945 as U.S. troops neared Japan in the war's final months.

All greenery had vanished; as far as one could see, heavy shellfire had denuded the scene of shrubbery. What was left resembled a cratered moonscape. But the craters were vanishing, because the rain had transformed the earth into a thin porridge—too thin even to dig foxholes. At night you lay on a poncho as a precaution against drowning during the barrages. All night, every night, shells erupted close enough to shake the mud beneath you at the rate of five or six a minute. You could hear the cries of the dying but could do nothing. Japanese infiltration was always imminent, so the order was to stay put. Any man who stood up was cut in half by machine guns manned by fellow Marines.

By day, the mud was hip-deep; no vehicles could reach us. As you moved up the slope of the hill, artillery and mortar shells were bursting all around you, and if you were fortunate enough to reach the top, you encountered the Japanese defenders, almost face to face, a few feet away. To me, they looked like badly wrapped brown paper parcels someone had soaked in a tub. Their eyes seemed glazed. So, I suppose did ours.

Japanese bayonets were fixed; ours weren't. We used the knives, or, in my case, a .45 revolver and MI carbine. The mud beneath our feet was deeply veined with blood. It was slippery. Blood is very slippery. So you skidded around, in deep shock, fighting as best you could until one side outnumbered the other. The outnumbered side would withdraw for reinforcements and then counterattack.

During those 10 days I ate half a candy bar. I couldn't keep anything down. Everyone had dysentery, and this brings up an aspect of war even Robert Graves, Siegfried Sassoon, Edmund Blunden and Ernest Hemingway avoided. If you put more than a quarter million men in a line for three weeks, with no facilities for disposal of human waste, you are going to confront a disgusting problem. We were fighting and sleeping in one vast cesspool. Mingled with that stench was another—the corrupt and corrupting odor of rotting human flesh. . . .

After my evacuation from Okinawa, I had the enormous pleasure of seeing [John] Wayne humiliated in person at Aiea Heights Naval Hospital in Hawaii. Only the most gravely wounded, the litter cases, were sent there. . . . Each evening Navy corpsmen would carry litters down to the hospital theater so the men could watch a movie. One night they had a surprise for us. Before the film the curtains parted and out stepped John Wayne, wearing a cowboy outfit—and 10-gallon hat, bandanna, checkered shirt, two pistols, chaps, boots and spurs. He grinned his aw-shucks grin, passed a hand over his face and said, "Hi ya, guys!" He was greeted by a stony silence. Then somebody booed. Suddenly everyone was booing.

This man was a symbol of the fake machismo we had come to hate, and we weren't going to listen to him. He tried and tried to make himself heard, but we drowned him out, and eventually he quit and left. If you liked [John Wayne's film] *Sands of Iwo Jima*, I suggest you be careful. Don't tell it to the Marines.

William Manchester, "The Bloodiest Battle of All," *New York Times, Sunday Magazine*, 14 June 1987. Reprinted by permission of Don Congdon Associates, Inc. Copyright © 1987 by William Manchester.

other support units. As one ex-sergeant in the Quartermaster Corps recalled bitterly, "We serviced the service. We handled food, clothing, equipage. We loaded ammunition, too. We were really stevedores and servants."

The military's rising need for manpower eventually lowered some racial barriers. The all-black 99th Fighter Squadron known as the Tuskegee Airmen won accolades in Italy early in 1944 when its crack pilots shot down twelve German fighters on two successive days. Another racial barrier fell January 1945, after the Germans smashed through the Allied lines in Belgium, killing or capturing thousands of Americans at the Battle of the Bulge. The 2,500 African Americans who volunteered to replace those who had been lost fought side by side with white troops to repel the final Nazi counteroffensive.

An American Soldier of the Antitank Co., 34th Regiment, Who Was Killed by Mortar Fire

Until September 1943, government censors blocked the publication of all photographs showing dead American soldiers. After that, censors continued to withhold many pictures — such as this photograph taken on Leyte Island in the Philippines on October 31, 1944 — that did not, even in death, conform to the heroic image of the American fighting man. National Archives.

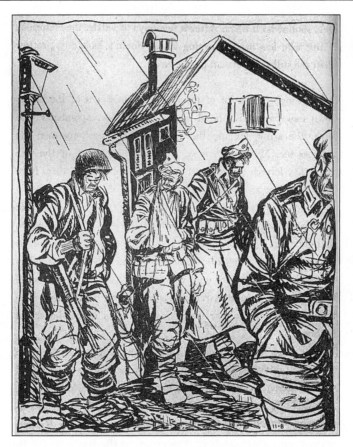

"Fresh, Spirited American Troops, Flushed with Victory, Are Bringing in Thousands of Hungry, Ragged, Battle-Weary Prisoners"

Sergeant Bill Mauldin's cartoons in *Stars and Stripes*, the Army newspaper that was distributed to troops, contradicted the American press's upbeat and sanitized coverage of the war. Mauldin's unromantic and biting cartoons, which often celebrated the insubordinate spirit of American soldiers, were reviled by officers such as General George S. Patton (who personally reprimanded the cartoonist for "undermining the morale of the army"). But the troops eagerly read Mauldin's work, featuring the weary and cynical archetypal GIs Willie and Joe. Bill Mauldin, *Up Front* (1945) — Copyright 1944 Bill Mauldin. Reprinted with permission of the Estate of Bill Mauldin.

The Home of One of Our Distinguished Personnel

A March 1944 sketch by twenty-year-old Corporal Ben Hurwitz of the U.S. Army 351st Regiment, 88th Infantry Division, First Battalion, shows a GI in front of his makeshift "home away from home" in Tufo, Italy. Used with permission of Joshua Brown.

"True Towel Tales . . . As Told Us by a Soldier"
One of a series of towel advertisements published during 1943 and 1944 that framed its sales pitch in homoerotic imagery inspired by purported testimony from GIs overseas. The ads, which are sexually ambiguous, suggest how the same-sex environment in the military afforded young men, both gay and straight, opportunities for sexual self-discovery. *McCall's*, June 1944 — Prints and Photographs Division, Library of Congress.

The military experience of Mexican Americans contrasted sharply with that of black Americans, in large part because the army never officially segregated Latino soldiers. Nearly three million Hispanic people lived in the United States at the outbreak of the war. Most resided in California, Texas, and the Southwest. About 350,000 went into the armed forces, nearly all of them as draftees. Combat units welcomed most Mexican Americans, and the army encouraged publicity about their outstanding records under fire. Most often assigned to the infantry, Mexican American soldiers

"You Can't Fight All of Them"

The African American novelist, photographer, and filmmaker Gordon Parks served as a reporter-writer assigned to an all-black air force unit during the war. He recalls a small but telling racial incident that occurred in Virginia.

Our plane took off in a blinding rainstorm—and it landed in another one at Norfolk, Virginia. A taxi took me to the ferry landing where I would cross over into Newport News. I sat there in the waiting room for an hour on top of my battle gear among a boisterous group of white enlisted men. Four Negro soldiers were huddled in a nearby corner. Two of them were propped against each other, sleeping. . . .

We filed out when the ferry whistled. It was still raining and we stood near the edge of the dock watching the boat fasten into the slip. Through the wetness I noticed a sign reading COLORED PASSENGERS and another one reading WHITES ONLY. The four black soldiers moved automatically to the colored side, and so did I. How ironic, I thought; such nonsense would not stop until we were in enemy territory.

After all the outgoing passengers were off and the trucks and cars had rumbled past, we started forward. Then I saw a Negro girl step from the ferry. She . . . was in the direct line of the white enlisted men, who stampeded to the boat screaming at the tops of their voices. I saw the girl fall beneath them into the mud and water. The four Negro soldiers also saw her go down. The five of us rushed to her rescue. She was knocked down several times before we could get to her and pull her out of the scrambling mob.

"You lousy white bastards!" one of the Negro soldiers yelled. "If I only had a gun!" Tears were in his eyes, hysteria in his voice. A long knife was glistening in his hand.

"Soldier!" I shouted above the noise, letting him get a look at my officer's cap. "Put that knife away!"

He glared at me fiercely for a second. "But you saw what they did!"

"Yes, I saw, but we're outnumbered ten to one! You can't fight all of them. Get on the boat!" He looked at me sullenly for another moment, then moved off. We cleaned the mud from the girl's coat and she walked away without a word. Only proud anger glistened on her black face. Then the four of us joined the soldier I had ordered away. He was standing still tense beneath the sign reading COLORED PASSENGERS.

"Sorry soldier," I said. "We wouldn't have had a chance against a mob like that. You realize that, don't you?"

"If I gotta die, I'd just as soon do it where I got real cause to." His tone was resolute. I had to answer. I was tempted to hand him the bit about the future and all that, but the future was too uncertain. The yelling was even louder now on the other side of the boat. "Sons-of-bitches," he muttered under his breath.

Gordon Parks, *A Choice of Weapons* (1966).

suffered casualties that were disproportionate to their numbers in the general population.

American Indians could not vote in three states, but they could be—and were—drafted. Many resisted the draft, but about 25,000 Indians served in the military; among them were 300 Navajo "code talkers" who baffled Japanese electronic eavesdroppers by transmitting radio messages in their little-known language. They confused some Americans as well: fellow marines temporarily took a few Navajos prisoner, thinking they were Japanese spies.

Mobilizing the Home Front

World War II ended the Depression with a massive dose of government-stimulated demand, doubling the gross national product within four years. At the peak of the war, the military commanded about 47 percent of all production and services. But because of chronic shortages in machinery, raw materials, and labor, the government could not let the cost and pace of either military or civilian production be determined by the free market. Government officials concluded that the whole economy would have to be centrally planned, with controls placed on the distribution and cost of virtually everything, from steel and machine tools to chickens, chocolate, and clothing. The war brought an enormous industrial boom; unemployment, which had been 14 percent in 1940, virtually disappeared by early 1943. World War II era arms production factories were gigantic, which helped to make a higher proportion of Americans blue-collar industrial workers than at any other time in U.S. history. The war also changed the relationship between labor and capital, both at the workplace and in the corridors of power in Washington.

Government-Business Partnership   Roosevelt assigned the primary responsibility for mobilizing industry to the military and to corporate executives. The armed services set overall production requirements, and executives took the key posts in the mobilization agencies in Washington, D.C., serving as "dollar-a-year-men" while remaining on their company payrolls. They established what Sears vice president Donald Nelson, who became chairman of the War Production Board, called "a set of rules under which the game could be played the way industry said it had to be played." The government suspended antitrust laws, paid most of the cost of constructing new defense plants, and lent much of the rest at low interest rates. Cost-plus contracts guaranteed a profit on the production of military goods.

To fight inflation, other government agencies regulated wages, prices, and the kinds of jobs people could take. Following Pearl Harbor, the president set up the War Labor Board to arbitrate labor-management disputes and set wage rates for all workers. The Office of Price Administration began the complicated and controversial task of setting price ceilings for almost all consumer goods and of distributing ration books for items that were in short supply. Finally, the Selective Service and the War Manpower Commission determined who would serve in the military, whose work was vital to the war production effort, and when a worker could transfer from one job to another. These federal agencies were highly political institutions. By the end of the war, labor, capital, consumers, and government policymakers disagreed constantly over the administration and enforcement of programs and policies.

Government planning of this sort fostered further concentration of the U.S. economy. In 1940, the top one hundred companies turned out 30 percent of the nation's total manufactured goods. By the end of the war, the same one hundred companies held 70 percent of all civilian and military manufacturing contracts. Executives used their connections to key military procurement officers to obtain prime contracts as well as the material and labor needed to meet production requirements. Coca-Cola accompanied the troops overseas, where bottling plants followed the battle lines; a piece of Wrigley gum went into each soldier's "K-rations" or field meals. Small businesses were pushed aside; if they went under, one War Production Board official explained, they could blame "the process of natural selection in the business world."

Not unexpectedly, military officials and dollar-a-year men came to have similar political and economic visions. Lieutenant General Brehon Somervell, the chief of supply for the U.S. Army, established an elite school at Fort Leavenworth, Kansas, where business leaders attended seminars and classes on the military's new role in U.S. economic life. General Electric's president, Charles E. Wilson, the powerful second in command of the War Production Board, proposed that business executives receive reserve commissions so that close cooperation between defense contractors and the military might continue after the war ended. This relationship came to be known as the military-industrial complex.

To Buy Is Patriotic

From smoking to skin care, advertisers rushed to identify their products with the war effort after the United States entered the conflict. *McCall's*, August 1942 — American Social History Project.

The Wartime Industrial Boom   World War II was a metal-turning, engine-building, multiyear conflict that required an enormous amount of manual labor. In the aircraft industry, for example, 100,000 Americans worked at the Douglas Aviation plants in El Segundo and Long Beach, California; 50,000 at a Curtiss-Wright plant in New Jersey; and 40,000 at Ford's bomber plant in Ypsilanti, Michigan. Forty-three percent of all nonagricultural workers became blue-collar workers, the highest proportion in U.S. history.

The war proved especially beneficial to the American West, whose Pacific ports, favorable climate, and huge federal landholdings, suitable for testing new airplanes and weapons, attracted military procurement contracts. The big winner was California, which received one-eighth of all war orders. Aircraft worker Don McFadden remembered that Los Angeles "was just like a beehive. . . . The defense plants were moving full-time. . . . Downtown movies were staying open twenty-four hours a day." The University of California, California Institute of Technology, and Stanford University became key links in the military's weapons development program. "It was as if someone had tilted the country," noted one observer. "People, money, and soldiers all spilled west."

Full employment had a radical impact on the lives of ordinary Americans. Fifteen million workers—one-third of the prewar workforce—used their new labor power to change and upgrade their jobs. Some shifted from one factory department or office to another; at least four million—triple the prewar total—crossed state lines to find better jobs. The rural South experienced the largest exodus, California and Michigan the greatest influx. As factory work, especially in defense facilities, grew in prestige and earning power, office and service employment declined in status and pay. "For the majority of workers the war was an experience of opportunity rather than limitation," observed Katherine Archibald of her fellow shipyard workers in Oakland, California. "It was like a social," Peggy Terry of Paducah, Kentucky, said, remembering her first months in a defense plant. "Now we'd have money to buy shoes and a dress and pay rent and get some food on the table. We were just happy to have work" (Figure 10.1).

Most servicemen and urban workers enjoyed an unprecedented rise in their standard of living. Between 1939 and 1945, real (controlled for inflation) wages grew 27 percent. Indeed, the wages of those at the bottom of the social scale grew more rapidly than did the highly taxed incomes of those at the top; the war generated the most progressive redistribution of American wealth in the twentieth century. The military provided medical and educational benefits for a substantial portion of the male population, while a larger proportion of the working class could afford to take advantage of schools, hospitals, and clinics. Life expectancy, after remaining stagnant for a decade, increased by three years for the white population and five years for African Americans. Infant mortality declined by more than one-third between 1939 and 1945.

White workers from immigrant backgrounds gained an added benefit. Unlike the anti-immigrant Americanization campaigns of World War I, the propaganda that was used in this war attempted to unify the American people around a vision of cultural pluralism that included white ethnics. The *Detroit News* praised the nearly spotless attendance records of six workers at GM's Ternstedt Division in Detroit, whose names were Kowalski, Netowski, Bugai, Lugari, Bauer, and Pavolik. "Look at the names . . . the sort of names one finds on an All-American football team . . . and at Ternstedt's, management and workers alike are hailing them as the plant's All-American production team." In many factories and mills, new opportunities for promotion, combined with vigilance by the industrial unions, enabled "ethnics" to break into the skilled trades or the ranks of first-line supervisors. These wartime developments accelerated the decline of immigrant working-class institutions, such as foreign-language radio programs and newspapers and immigrant fraternal organizations, that had begun in the previous decade.

Labor's War at Home At the outset of the conflict, most labor leaders had quickly agreed to a no-strike pledge. The resulting decline in shop floor strife pleased the Roosevelt administration and business leaders alike. But patriotic unionism created other problems. In arbitrating the wages of millions of workers, the War Labor Board gave priority to increasing production and resisting inflation, not raising wages or settling workers' grievances. Even some employers recognized the dilemma this created for trade union leaders. If unions could not strike or bargain for higher wages, then why should workers join them?

The War Labor Board therefore put in place a "maintenance of membership" policy, which virtually mandated that any employee at a unionized workplace must join and pay dues to the union. Thus, the expansion of war production led automatically to an expansion of union membership,

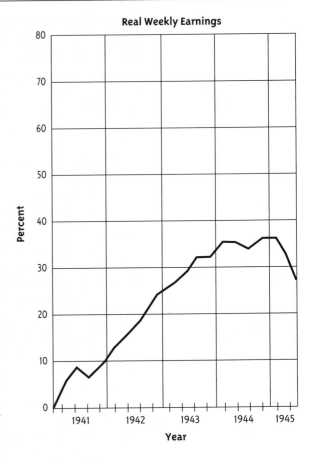

Real Weekly Earnings

FIGURE 10.1 We're in the Money: Wartime Pay

Despite wage controls and inflation, real weekly income increased by more than 30 percent during World War II. This was because millions of workers migrated to higher-paying jobs and put in long hours of overtime. Weekly pay dropped sharply when the opportunity to earn overtime shrank at the end of the war.

Guns Make Butter

July 1941 listings of available industrial jobs cluttered a Detroit labor-exchange blackboard, showing the dramatic effect that the war in Europe had on the U.S. economy. Scott Molloy Labor Archives.

which jumped from fewer than ten million to nearly fifteen million. An organizer in the electrical industry recalled: "We'd circulate membership cards in front of the management. . . . I remember a two-year period, 1942–43, where we went through some sixty-six or sixty-eight plants, organized them, and held elections. We lost one!"

But the growth of unions hardly eliminated workers' grievances. Foremen and managers often took advantage of labor's no-strike pledge to regain some of the power unions had wrested from them in the turbulent prewar years. And the wartime demand for more and more production also generated conflicts over speed-ups and safety. Edward Osberg, who made airplane engines for Chrysler during the war, remembered, "whenever engineers and general superintendents devised a new process to make something faster or better, they went ahead and did it. They didn't care if it killed someone or if the fumes and dust were dangerous." Workers challenged management over the right to set production standards and piece rates, assign work, and discipline employees. Unauthorized strikes over such issues mounted steadily from 1942 until the end of the war. Government officials denounced these stoppages as "unpatriotic," but rank-and-file pressures kept many unions in turmoil.

The largest wartime labor confrontation took place in the coal industry. John L. Lewis, head of the United Mine Workers, never thought the War

"Is That Giving Labor a Square Deal?"

In 1942, the Michigan CIO Council formally endorsed the no-strike pledge, but the employer attack on wages the following year caused the council to reconsider its actions. At the 1943 annual meeting, delegates debated a resolution recommending that "unless the assurances that were made to labor at the time we gave up our right to strike" were honored, the pledge should be nullified.

Delegate Washington (Local 600, UAW): We are hurting ourselves. We are taking things away from our boys who are on the battle lines the products of labor that they need to protect themselves and win this war. And I want to urge all of you who are Americans, who are with the allied nations, who are sincere in wanting to see this war won that you vote down this resolution and continue to give your support to the administration.

Delegate Lucas: Some time ago labor made a very noble gesture. That was a matter of giving a no-strike pledge. Arguments to the contrary notwithstanding, there were certain commitments that were made to labor at that particular time. Does anyone in the hall question that these commitments have not been lived up to by the administration? . . .

When it comes to the question of giving labor its just due, it seems that the administration seems to not be able to find any money to do anything with but when it comes to the question of building plants for corporations who have already more than they need, they can find billions of dollars to do that with. Is that giving labor a square deal? I don't think so. My personal sentiments are on this question that the no-strike pledge should be revoked here and now.

Richard Polenberg, ed., *America at War: The Home Front, 1941–1945* (1968).

Labor Board's wage freeze equitable, and during 1942, he came under increasing pressure from dissatisfied miners to obtain pay increases for them. To force the War Labor Board to reconsider, Lewis called 500,000 miners out on strike four times in 1943 alone. These strikes generated a storm of protest. All the major newspapers denounced Lewis, and public opinion polls condemned the strikes. In June 1943, Congress passed (over Roosevelt's veto) the Smith-Connally War Labor Disputes Act, which gave the president the power to seize strikebound mines and factories. The legislation made it a crime to advocate wartime work stoppages and prohibited unions from using membership dues money to contribute to electoral campaigns. This bill was the first antiunion measure passed by Congress since the early 1930s, and it foreshadowed the more conservative legislative climate of the postwar years.

But that did not stop Lewis. On November 1, 1943, the miners struck again. Roosevelt seized the coal mines and threatened to end the miners' draft defer-

Zero Hour

A cartoon in the March 29, 1943, issue of *Time* magazine interpreted John L. Lewis's challenge to the War Labor Board's wage formula in military terms. Lewis, arguing that "bayonets cannot mine coal," extracted a wage increase for miners in spite of the wartime wage ceiling. James Cutter, *Time*, March 29, 1943 — American Social History Project.

ments. At the same time, however, the president understood that the nation and the war effort ran on coal and that, as Lewis had always maintained, "bayonets cannot mine coal." Roosevelt ordered Secretary of the Interior Harold Ickes to negotiate a contract that was acceptable to the miners, even though it punched a big hole through the wartime wage ceiling.

Economic Citizenship for All?

During World War II, those who had long been on the margins of American life had their best opportunity in years to become first-class citizens. Full employment gave them the chance to improve their livelihoods, while the ideology that sustained the war effort — antifascist, inclusive, and democratic — legitimized the economic and civic aspirations that were held by African Americans, Latinos, and those women who wanted to participate more fully in the world of work and politics. Yet limits on pluralism and tolerance persisted for many, especially for Japanese Americans.

Women in the Workforce The wartime mobilization transformed the roles women held in the workplace. Shortly after the nation entered the war, the War Manpower Commission mounted a special campaign to recruit women, especially married housewives, into the defense industries. Government propaganda sounded a patriotic — if hardly feminist — trumpet: women workers were backing their men at the front, not pioneering a pathway out of the kitchen. As *Glamour Girls of '43*, a government-produced newsreel, announced, "Instead of cutting the lines of a dress, this woman cuts the pattern of aircraft parts. Instead of baking a cake, this woman is 'cooking' gears to reduce the tension in the gears after use."

Work in a factory was an enormous transition from the kitchen, one that enhanced the self-confidence and expanded the horizons of millions of American women. War worker Delle Hahne remembered a meal at a friend's house at which "his mother and grandmother talk[ed] about which drill would bite into a piece of metal at the factory. . . . My God, this was Sunday dinner in Middle America . . . it was a marvelous thing." Soon a popular song was being heard frequently on the radio, celebrating a young

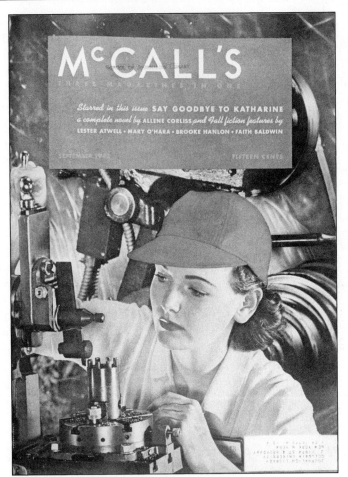

Industrial Chic

She now operates a drill press, but her lipstick is still unsmeared. Once women were mobilized for the war effort, magazines found it opportune to confer some romance on work that had previously been construed as neither romantic nor appropriate for women. The September 1942 cover of *McCall's* magazine imbued the new female industrial worker with the same kind of clean, unruffled glamour that the magazine had applied to women's household work before the war. *McCall's*, September 1942 — General Research Division, Library of Congress.

defense factory worker named "Rosie the Riveter," who could "do more than a male can do." The number of working women rose from eleven million to nearly twenty million during the war. In 1940, one of every twenty production workers in the auto industry was a woman; by 1944, the number of women had grown to one in five. In a dramatic — and in some cases bitterly resisted — move, African American women, who had been confined largely to agricultural labor and domestic work before the war, entered higher-paying and more dignified factory, clerical, and sales jobs.

The growth of female employment during the war did not generate a radical transformation in the way most Americans defined the rights and proper role of women. Many male workers were profoundly prejudiced against working women, greeting them with a barrage of hisses and whistles as they made their way through formerly all-male workplaces. And most employers, unions, and government officials agreed that "Rosie" would be "the Riveter" only for the duration of the war, after which she would gratefully turn over her job to a returning veteran. Virtually all factories segregated jobs by sex and denied women workers specialized training. Although the War Labor Board insisted on "equal pay for equal work," employers frequently assigned women to inspection or small assembly jobs or simply reclassified jobs to escape equal pay provisions. Most women remained segregated in a low-wage ghetto.

A large proportion of the female workforce was married with children. Working wives and mothers therefore bore a double burden of homework and wage work. Housing was cramped, and rationed foods were often more difficult to prepare. The government did build hundreds of child-care facilities during the war—far more than ever before—and more than 50,000 children attended such centers by 1943. But federal day-care programs were inadequate, and many women refused to use them because of their high cost, low quality, and restricted hours. By 1944, social agencies and mass media blamed working mothers for a new social phenomenon, the "juvenile delinquency" of unsupervised children.

By war's end, women made up 20 percent of all unionists, but the response of organized labor to their needs was mixed. Trade unions staunchly supported equal pay for equal work, if only to protect male members who might otherwise lose their jobs or their high pay to the tide of women workers. But most unions provided little or no support for the idea of maternity leave or government-funded child care. A 1944 UAW conference of women

After Work

Men and women workers begin to unwind as they finish their shift in a Richmond, California, shipyard. Dorothea Lange, September 1943 — Prints and Photographs Division, Library of Congress.

"We Were Determined to Stay"

Celia Saparsteen Yanish worked as a machinist in New York City during the war. In this oral history interview from 1980, she recalls the trials and tribulations of breaking into "men's work" during the war.

Before the war I worked in metal shops, assembling locks and doing other assembly work, until 1941 when the government set up a defense training school where they taught you to operate a bench lathe and drill press. . . . I was one of three girls in the school.

When the class was over we were sent to the machine shop. I was very happy. For the first time in my life I was going to be able to do skilled work. . . . I didn't know what it was, but I knew that until then only men had done this work.

[The men] were afraid we women were taking away jobs and they resented us. They complained they wouldn't be able to undress in the shop and work half nude like they did before. They said the women would interfere with their work, would distract them. . . .

I was about 24 at the time and I knew how to handle myself. I didn't laugh at the men's dirty jokes. But another girl who was only 17 did laugh and so the men got more and more brazen. They would be looking up her skirt until she would start to cry.

We worked on a competitive system. You had to keep up with the man standing next to you because he made more money if he could increase his production. If you slowed down, they would say, "we knew these women would be no damn good." We were exhausted all the time. The men would go home and sit down to a prepared meal, but when the women came home they had to get the meal ready for their family. . . .

It was very rough for a while, but we were determined to stay, and eventually the majority of the men learned to accept us and respect us as co-workers and union sisters.

Miriam Frank, Marilyn Ziebarth, and Connie Field, *The Life and Times of Rosie the Riveter* (1982).

workers endorsed such demands, but as Millie Jeffrey, the first head of the auto union's Women's Bureau, recalled, "The policies of the UAW were always very good. Getting them implemented was another story." When the automakers began to fire women workers at the end of the war, unions such as the UAW raised few objections — perhaps not surprisingly, given the union's overwhelmingly male leadership.

Origins of the Modern African American Civil Rights Movement

Although a widespread women's movement failed to materialize during the war years, the early 1940s did see the flowering of the modern civil rights movement. For the first time since Reconstruction, African Americans possessed the collective resources to inaugurate a nationwide liberation movement. Almost 10 percent of the southern black population moved to northern cities during the war, while an approximately equal number migrated from farm to city within the South. The number of African Americans who held industrial jobs almost doubled, and earnings—although still below par—soared from 40 percent of the average white wage in 1939 to nearly 60 percent after the war. This movement of black southerners from rural marginality to urban empowerment, one of the most important social and political transformations in American history, accelerated dramatically during World War II and continued for decades afterward.

African Americans joined together in unprecedented fashion to make their aspirations known. Membership in the National Association for the Advancement of Colored People (NAACP) increased nearly tenfold during World War II, and with the CIO, the NAACP campaigned against Southern state poll taxes, which discouraged voting by poor people of all races. Under the leadership of a talented legal team led by Charles Houston, dean of Howard University Law School, and future Supreme Court Justice Thurgood Marshall, the NAACP won a crucial Supreme Court decision in 1944 that outlawed "whites-only" primaries. (Because victory in the Democratic primary was equivalent to winning elections in the one-party South, these primaries effectively disenfranchised African Americans.) Well-organized voter registration campaigns encouraged blacks to vote, even in the South, where the proportion of African Americans who were registered to vote jumped from 3 percent to 12 percent during the war years.

The egalitarian and democratic values for which the United States claimed to be fighting legitimized African American demands for a better life and equal citizenship. African Americans worked and fought under the popular "Double V" symbol, which stood for victory over fascism abroad and over discrimination at home. And the government took notice. In 1943, the War Labor Board ordered an end to wage differentials based on race, explaining that "whether as vigorous fighting men or for production of food and munitions, America needs the Negro." Removal of racial barriers at home, the board added, "is a test of our sincerity in the cause for which we are fighting."

The CIO's wartime organizing efforts also transformed African Americans' consciousness. Despite continuing racism among white workers and corporate managers, the CIO's campaign to organize a multiracial workforce into plantwide industrial unions gave black workers enormous leverage to press their grievances. Calling the CIO a "lamp of democracy," an NAACP journalist wrote, "The South has not known such a force since the historic Union Leagues in the great days of the Reconstruction era."

Although wartime conditions made African American advancement possible, it required forceful and well-organized protests by black workers to persuade unions and the federal government to root out discrimination in jobs, housing, and politics. The first, and in many ways the most dramatic, protest movement began in 1940, when A. Philip Randolph and other leaders of the Brotherhood of Sleeping Car Porters announced plans for a march on Washington to win African Americans access to good jobs in the new defense plants. Randolph wanted thousands of African Americans to descend on the still-segregated capital city in July 1941 unless the federal government took vigorous steps to end racial discrimination in war industries and in the military. The prospect of such a peaceful march frightened even the Roosevelt administration liberals, so just one week before the assemblage, the president issued Executive Order 8802, creating a Fair Employment Practices Committee (FEPC) and directing government agencies, job-training programs, and contractors to end racial and religious discrimination. In return for this remarkable advance, Randolph canceled the march.

The FEPC had far-reaching implications because it opened hundreds of thousands of high-paying jobs to African American war workers. As the Urban League's Lester Granger put it, "Employment is a civil right." But the FEPC was pitifully weak as a legal and administrative entity. FEPC officials could do nothing to modify segregation in the armed forces; and in the South, federal policy was little more than a legal fiction. In Baltimore, the Maryland State Employment Service systematically discriminated against African Americans who sought work. "Even if you had a graduate degree in electronics," remembered Alexander Allen, who worked for the Baltimore Urban League, "you would still be sent to the black entrance (for common labor and unskilled work)."

In the North, however, the federal government acted more forcefully, especially if war-related production or services were at stake. Well-publicized FEPC hearings legitimized racial progressivism and engendered a new sense of citizenship, which soon turned into a wave of direct, forceful action by black workers and their allies. "I am for this thing called Rights," a disgruntled woman wrote to the FEPC. Another asked President Roosevelt to help her find a job because "we are citizens and we pay taxes." Government action soon followed. In Philadelphia, which was second only to Detroit as a center of defense manufacture, the FEPC and the War Manpower Commission ordered the city's transit system to promote eight African Americans to positions as streetcar drivers. When the system's white employees responded with a protest strike in 1944, the federal government sent in 8,000 armed soldiers to end the stoppage. Afterward, Philadelphia employers opened more good jobs to the city's African Americans.

Detroit was an even more impressive center of rights-conscious activism. African American workers at Chrysler, Ford, and other companies staged their own work stoppages to protest racial discrimination on the job. African American women, who had long been excluded from factory work, occupied the personnel office at Ford's new Willow Run factory in 1942, leading to the opening of hundreds of war plant jobs to women who had been maids and domestics. Racial conflicts over housing became equally tense. When African Americans moved into Detroit's federally financed Sojourner Truth housing project early in 1942, a crowd of rock-throwing, working-class whites blocked the way. City and federal officials caved into the pressure, barring occupancy by African Americans, but a coalition of black civic groups and CIO activists forced Detroit officials to reverse themselves again, this time opening the apartments to black and white occupants alike. CIO and NAACP leaders told a rally the next year that "full and equal participation of all citizens is fair, just, and necessary for victory and an enduring peace."

Such assertiveness generated white resistance. Southern segregationists such as Mississippi's Democratic senator James Eastland denounced the FEPC as a "Communist program for racial amalgamation." And white resistance often exploded in urban factories and neighborhoods where the two races competed for jobs, housing, and political power. As black workers broke out of their job ghettos and moved into formerly all-white departments, a spectacular wave of racist strikes shut down scores of factories and shipyards. In many factories and mills, newly empowered white workers came to see the seniority system and the local union leader as protectors of their racially exclusive job rights, which they defended with almost as much steadfastness as they did their segregated neighborhoods. Racial violence

The Detroit Riot, June 21, 1943
While police stood by, white crowds terrorized African Americans on Detroit's Woodward Avenue. As shown here, African American motorists were pursued and beaten, and their cars were destroyed. Shortly after this photo was taken, the victim's car (halted in front of the bus) was overturned and set on fire. *Detroit News.*

peaked in 1943, with 250 incidents in forty-seven cities. The worst riot erupted in Detroit, where a fight at the Belle Isle amusement park ignited thirty hours of violence and left 25 blacks and 9 whites dead and almost 700 people seriously injured.

Race riots flared in wartime Los Angeles, too, but with a difference: this time the violence targeted Mexican American males. Resentment against Mexican Americans—especially those who defied mainstream society by wearing the distinctive, loose-fitting "zoot suits" favored by young Chicanos—mushroomed as discriminatory barriers to employment fell. In

"We're Looking for Zoot-Suits to Burn"

Al Waxman, editor of the Eastside Journal, *an East Los Angeles community newspaper, describes the brutality of soldiers and the Los Angeles police during the 1943 anti-Mexican riot.*

At Twelfth and Central I came upon a scene that will long live in my memory. Police were swinging clubs and servicemen were fighting with civilians. Wholesale arrests were being made by the officers.

Four boys came out of a pool hall. They were wearing the zoot-suits that have become a symbol of the fighting flag. Police ordered them into arrest cars. One refused. He asked: "Why am I being arrested?" The police officer answered with three swift blows of the night-stick across the boy's head and he went down. As he sprawled, he was kicked in the face. Police had difficulty loading his body into the vehicle because he was one-legged and wore a wooden limb. Maybe the officer didn't know he was attacking a cripple.

At the next corner a Mexican mother cried out, "Don't take my boy, he did nothing. He's only fifteen years old. Don't take him." She was struck across the jaw with a night-stick and almost dropped the two and a half year old baby that was clinging in her arms. . . .

Rushing back to the east side to make sure that things were quiet here, I came upon a band of servicemen making a systematic tour of East First Street. They had just come out of a cocktail bar where four men were nursing bruises. Three autos loaded with Los Angeles policemen were on the scene but the soldiers were not molested. Farther down the street the men stopped a streetcar, forcing the motorman to open the door and proceeded to inspect the clothing of the male passengers. "We're looking for zoot-suits to burn," they shouted. Again the police did not interfere. . . . Half a block away . . . I pleaded with the men of the local police sub-station to put a stop to these activities. "It is a matter for the military police," they said.

Carey McWilliams, *North from Mexico* (1968).

Zoot-Suit Riot

In the weeks preceding the riots, a nationally syndicated comic strip satirically skewered the zoot-suiters. Li'l Abner Yokum, cartoonist Al Capp's good-natured and dull-witted hero, became the pawn of zoot-suit manufacturers. As "Zoot-Suit Yokum," he performed heroic deeds that prompted a nationwide fashion fad — much to the horror, as this panel shows, of more levelheaded citizens. Capp's treatment reflected general hostility toward the defiant style favored by many young Mexican Americans. After the riots, the Los Angeles City Council passed a law that made wearing a zoot suit a misdemeanor. *Mercury Herald and News*, April 25, 1943 — Copyright Capp Enterprises, Inc. 1997. All rights reserved.

June 1943, local newspapers played up a story about Mexican youths who had been arrested for assaulting a group of Anglo sailors. In response, thousands of marines, sailors, soldiers, and civilians visited a reign of terror on Mexican American neighborhoods in Los Angeles, beating up young zoot-suiters, stripping off their clothes, and cutting their long hair. More than 100 people were injured in the riots, which inspired anti-Mexican activity in seven other cities as well. Only when the Mexican ambassador interceded — and fear grew that the Axis countries would make effective propaganda of the riots — did the U.S. government declare downtown Los Angeles off-limits to naval personnel.

The Limits of Pluralism   Although World War II enlarged the compass and definition of American citizenship, American pluralism and tolerance had distinct limits. While the United States was fighting anti-Semitic Nazi Germany on the battlefield, perceptible anti-Semitism existed at home. As millions of Jews perished in concentration camps in Europe, the U.S. State Department and other government officials opened America's doors to only a handful of refugees. In 1939, the ship *St. Louis*, filled with more than 900 Jews fleeing Nazi Germany, sailed from one closed U.S. port to another, seeking to disembark its desperate passengers. But U.S. immigration laws were harshly enforced, forcing the ship to return to Europe where most of the passengers ended up in Nazi death camps.

Conscientious objectors to the draft — especially Jehovah's Witnesses — had an extremely difficult time in World War II. At least 6,000 objectors went to prison, sentenced to an average of five years; beatings by guards and other prisoners were common. Many Jehovah's Witnesses, who refused to salute the flag because of their religious beliefs, were kept in solitary confinement for months, often on rations of bread and water.

But U.S. treatment of Japanese Americans proved to be the government's most egregious wartime abridgment of civil liberties. While the U.S.

"I'm as Loyal as Anyone in This Country"

In July 1943, government investigator Morris Opler interviewed a Japanese man, identified only as "an Older Nisei" (the first generation of Japanese Americans born in the United States), who was interned at Camp Manzanar. The man was indignant at having to sign a formal declaration of loyalty to the United States.

If this country doesn't want me they can throw me out. What do they know about loyalty? I'm as loyal as anyone in this country. Maybe I'm as loyal as President Roosevelt. What business did they have asking me a question like that?

I was born in Hawaii. I worked most of my life on the west coast. I have never been to Japan. We would have done anything to show our loyalty. All we wanted to do was to be left alone on the coast. . . . My wife and I lost $10,000 in that evacuation. She had a beauty parlor and had to give that up. I had a good position worked up as a gardener, and was taken away from that. We had a little home and that's gone now. . . .

What kind of Americanism do you call that? That's not democracy. That's not the American way, taking everything away from people. . . . Where are the Germans? Where are the Italians? Do they ask them questions about loyalty? . . .

Nobody had to ask us about our loyalty when we lived on the coast. You didn't find us on relief. . . . We were first when there was any civic drive. We were first with the money for the Red Cross and the Community Chest or whatever it was. Why didn't that kind of loyalty count? Now they're trying to push us to the east. It's always "further inland, further inland." I say, "To hell with it!" Either they let me go to the coast and prove my loyalty there or they can do what they want with me. If they don't want me in this country, they can throw me out. . . .

Evacuation was a mistake, there was no need for it. The government knows this. Why don't they have enough courage to come out and say so, so that these people won't be pushed around? . . .

I've tried to cooperate. Last year I went out on furlough and worked on the beet fields in Idaho. There was a contract which said that we would be brought back here at the end of the work. Instead we just sat there. . . . We had to spend our own money. The farmers won't do anything for you. They treat you all right while you're working hard for them but as soon as your time is up, you can starve. . . . When I got back to Manzanar, nearly all my money that I had earned was gone. . . .

Michi Weglyn, *Years of Infamy: The Untold Story of America's Concentration Camps* (1976).

government detained some German Americans and Italian Americans and confiscated their property, all Americans of Japanese descent were presumed to be disloyal simply by virtue of their national origin. General John L. DeWitt, chief of the West Coast Defense Command, charged that "the Japanese race is an enemy race. It makes no difference whether he is an American citizen or not."

Starting in March 1942, the government rounded up all Japanese Americans on the West Coast, citizens and noncitizens alike, transporting them to specially constructed "relocation" camps. In California, nativists and racists who had long resented successful Japanese American merchants, fishermen, and fruit and vegetable farmers supported the detention campaign By the end of 1942, the U.S. government forced more than 100,000 Japanese to abandon their jobs, businesses, and homes for a life in one of ten camps scattered throughout the West. Conditions in the remote and desolate detention camps were spare at best, deplorable at worst. Families crowded into long, wooden barracks with a minimal amount of privacy and furnished only with cots, blankets, and bare light bulbs. Internees had to fend for themselves, making their own furniture and tending their own meager vegetable gardens (Map 10.5).

Japanese Americans, like other first- and second-generation Americans, were overwhelmingly loyal to the United States. But among a sizable minority, detention bred precisely the hostility and resistance that government officials feared. In 1943, more than one out of every four Japanese American males born in the United States refused to pledge "unqualified

MAP 10.5   Geography of Shame

The U.S. government forced more than 100,000 Japanese Americans to leave their homes and businesses on the West Coast and report to one of fifteen assembly centers. At these centers they were first processed and then transported by train to one of ten permanent relocation centers, or camps, hundreds or even thousands of miles from their homes. A much smaller number of Japanese Americans who were not citizens (about 17,000), most of whom were considered "enemy aliens," were placed in internment camps, while those labeled as troublemakers who were U.S. citizens were sent to citizen isolation camps.

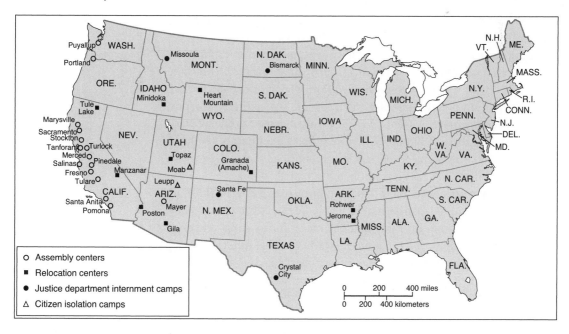

- ○ Assembly centers
- ■ Relocation centers
- ● Justice department internment camps
- △ Citizen isolation camps

Manzanar Relocation Center, April 1942
These Japanese Americans in the newly opened California internment camp had gathered to watch the arrival of fellow internees. War Relocation Authority Photo 210-GID-B3, from Edward H. Spicer, Asael T. Hansen, Katherine Luomala, and Marvin R. Opler, *Impounded People* (1969) — Used by permission of Rosamond B. Spicer.

allegiance" to the nation. Still, when the military drafted young Japanese American internees in 1944, only a minority resisted. Some 3,600 of these young Americans served in the segregated 442nd Regimental Combat Team, the most decorated unit in the U.S. Army. In 1945, the 442nd helped to liberate the Nazis' infamous Dachau concentration camp, even as the parents of many of these same soldiers lived behind barbed wire.

The Supreme Court affirmed the legality of Japanese American internment in 1943 (*Hirabayashi v. United States*) and again in 1944 (*Korematsu v. United States*). By the time of the second decision, a few justices had doubts about the detention policy. The internment order, Justice Frank Murphy wrote in a dissenting opinion, went "over the brink of constitutional power" and into "the ugly abyss of racism." But only in 1988, after decades of legal action and public protest, did the U.S. government finally offer the surviving detainees modest financial restitution and a formal apology.

Chinese Americans, who had often been lumped together with other Asians, worried that anti-Japanese hatred would be directed at them. They put up signs in their stores explaining that "This is a Chinese shop" and even wore buttons proclaiming "I am Chinese." Many Chinese Americans also proved their patriotism by joining the military. Charlie Leong, a resident of San Francisco's large Chinatown, later recalled that "to men of my generation, World War II was the most important historic event of our times. For

How to Tell a Chinese from a "Jap"

These three panels appeared in the *Pocket Guide to China*, a U.S. Army pamphlet illustrated by cartoonist Milton Caniff (best known for the comic strips *Terry and the Pirates* and, after the war, *Steve Canyon*). This pamphlet and other official wartime publications that were distributed to American soldiers used outrageous racial stereotypes to distinguish between Asian friends and foes. American Social History Project.

the first time we felt we could make it in American society." Almost one-quarter of all Chinese adult males were drafted or enlisted.

Many other Chinese men and women broke out of their employment ghetto in laundries and restaurants as labor shortages opened up new opportunities. In the San Francisco Bay Area, Chinese Americans filled 15 percent of the shipyard jobs. A further breakthrough came in 1943, when Congress finally repealed the hated Chinese Exclusion Act. Although the new law set a token immigration quota of only 105 people per year, it allowed Chinese permanent residents to apply for citizenship. Asian Indians, who had also been excluded, sought similar naturalization rights, finally securing them in 1947.

The End of the War

American arms production far outstripped that of any other nation, and by 1944, the United States was producing nearly half of all the world's goods. In the same year, American armies, for the first time, confronted large numbers of German and Japanese troops. Hundreds of thousands clashed in northern France and the Philippines. With a continuous supply of American-made planes, tanks, ships, and guns, the Allied war effort soon ground down the German, Italian, and Japanese forces. The defeat of Hitler in Europe and the use of atomic weapons against Japan ended the war but raised questions about how the United States would transition to a peacetime economy.

Victory in Europe　On June 6, 1944 (D-Day), the long-awaited British-American invasion of Western Europe began. In the largest amphibious landing in military history, 156,000 troops jumped from their boats onto the beaches of Normandy in France. Reinforcements soon swelled Allied ranks to two million, who served under the overall command of an American general, Dwight Eisenhower. By September, the Allies had retaken most of France and Belgium; by the fall, they were fighting just inside German territory. But in December, the German army staged a desperate counterattack—the Battle of the Bulge—pushing deep into Belgium and France. The fierceness of the attack surprised U.S. strategists, and German soldiers initially outgunned and outmanned several U.S. infantry divisions. But in the largest single battle ever fought by the U.S. Army, more than 100,000 defiant soldiers halted the German offensive and made an Allied victory in the spring all but inevitable.

Eisenhower's army crossed the Rhine in March 1945 and soon encountered horrifying evidence that the Nazis had been starving and executing millions of Jews, Gypsies, Poles, Russians, and German political opponents in a string of concentration camps that stretched from Buchenwald in Germany to Auschwitz in Poland. "As we entered the camp, the living skeletons still able to walk crowded around us," recalled J. D. Pletcher, a captain in the 71st Division Headquarters, of his encounter with Dachau. "It is not an exaggeration to say that almost every inmate was insane with hunger." Much later, the world would discover that the leaders of the Roosevelt administration had known about the genocide but had done little to stop the slaughter.

Roosevelt, whose physical condition had deteriorated rapidly following his reelection to a fourth term in November 1944, died on April 12, 1945. Vice President Harry Truman, a former senator from Missouri, later said that he

"The Walking Dead"

Leon Bass, an African American soldier, recalls what he felt as a nineteen-year-old with the 183rd Combat Engineers when he helped to liberate the Buchenwald concentration camp in 1945.

We had gone through the Bulge, we had seen the horrors of war: death, people who were wounded. Many of us came very close to losing our lives during that period. But we had no knowledge, and our first encounter came one day when we were asked to go to a place outside of Weimar, Germany. It wasn't a mission of battle, it was just to go. And we came to this place, which was somewhat like a security place, a place you might see in any urban center that was a prison. But we were totally unprepared—at least I was, for what I encountered when I went into Buchenwald. The outside was very beautiful. . . . all the grass was well-manicured and cared for. And then you go inside, and then all of a sudden the stark horror of it all strikes you. And that's the way I encountered it at the age of 19. When I walked in I saw what should be considered to be human beings that had been reduced to the point where they were just merely surviving. I called them the walking dead, because I felt they had reached the point of no return. The malnutrition had set in and it was just a matter of time. . . .

I didn't speak to anyone else that day. The shock was just too much. . . . No I didn't encounter anyone to share feelings with at that time. I only know that after I got there it became a part of me; and as much as I didn't want to deal with it, I couldn't get rid of it.

Yaff Eliach and Brana Gurewitsch, eds., *The Liberators: Eyewitness Accounts of the Liberation of Concentration Camps,* vol. 1 (1981).

Death Camp

When British soldiers liberated the concentration camp in Bergen-Belsen, Germany, in April 1945, they found thousands of unburied dead. Of the 60,000 camp survivors, almost half would die in the next few weeks, most succumbing to typhus. In an attempt to quell the epidemic, the British liberators buried the dead in mass graves and eventually burned the camp to the ground. The systematic extermination of almost six million European Jews during World War II was part of an overall death toll that claimed at least fifty-five million lives. Imperial War Museum.

felt as if "the moon and all the planets" had fallen on his ill-prepared shoulders. Truman had spent his youth as a dirt farmer and unsuccessful investor and businessman. In the 1920s and 1930s, he served as the protégé of Tom Pendergast, Kansas City's powerful political boss. Truman won national stature early in the war when he presided over a Senate investigation into corruption and inefficiency in the mobilization effort. In 1944, when Roosevelt allowed Democratic conservatives to cut the liberal Henry Wallace from the ticket, Truman proved to be the perfect compromise candidate for vice president.

Truman had none of Roosevelt's great self-confidence; nor did he inspire the same public loyalty or hatred as had the man who had been elected four times to the White House. But in foreign affairs, Truman did not deviate from Roosevelt's strategy: the war would be concluded with an unconditional surrender, in both Europe and the Far East. In the days after Truman took office, the mighty Soviet, American, and British armies blasted their way into the heart of Germany. On April 30, with Soviet troops encircling Berlin, Hitler committed suicide. In the next few days, American troops swept through Munich and on into Czechoslovakia, the Soviets captured Berlin, the British took Hamburg, and German troops finally gave up fighting in Italy. On May 7, 1945, Germany surrendered unconditionally. The war in Europe was over.

Japan's Surrender   In Asia, the Allies generally avoided direct confrontation with the main body of the Japanese army on the mainland. Instead, U.S. forces closed in on Japan by island-hopping across the Pacific. Savage hand-to-hand combat on the islands of Tarawa, Saipan, and Guam allowed the United States to put long-range B-29 bombers within striking distance of the Japanese home islands by 1944. In October of that year, American troops began the reconquest of the Philippines with a devastating defeat of the Japanese Navy at the Battle of Leyte Gulf. The next spring, after ferocious fighting, the United States took the islands of Iwo Jima and Okinawa, near the Japanese homeland. In early May 1945, British, Indian, and Nationalist Chinese troops retook Burma in South Asia. The Japanese army remained in control of Korea, Manchuria, and much of China and Southeast Asia. But massive and continuous bombing raids on Japanese civilian and military targets terrorized and de-

The Battle of Peleliu Island, September 1944
Oppressed by 115-degree heat and trapped by withering Japanese fire, U.S. Marines took cover in the sandy terrain of the small Central Pacific island. The battle was part of the U.S. strategy for the reconquest of the Philippines. After more than two months, 2,336 deaths, and 8,450 casualties, American forces prevailed (10,695 Japanese were killed). National Archives.

Miyuki Bridge, Hiroshima, August 6, 1945
Three hours after the United States detonated an atomic bomb over Hiroshima, shocked and wounded survivors wandered near a bridge a little over a mile from ground zero. Yoshito Matsushige — Hiroshima Peace Culture Foundation.

moralized Japan's population, smashed its industry, and further isolated its forces on the Asian mainland from those on the home islands.

After Germany surrendered in May, British and American intelligence agencies expected that Japan would also stop fighting—especially if the Soviet Union entered the war in the Far East. Therefore, Great Britain and the United States pushed for the earliest possible Soviet attack on Japanese-held Manchuria. Stalin agreed to open hostilities against Japan on or about August 8, three months after Germany's surrender. "Fini Japs when that comes about," President Truman wrote in his diary.

But Truman did not wait for a Soviet declaration of war. On August 6 and 8, U.S. planes dropped atomic bombs on the Japanese cities of Hiroshima and Nagasaki. The Hiroshima blast leveled nearly five square miles and instantly burned to death nearly 80,000 people. Tens of thousands more died soon afterward from injuries, burns, and radiation. In Nagasaki, where poor visibility reduced the accuracy of the bombing, about one and a half square miles were destroyed; 35,000 people were killed immediately, and another 60,000 were injured. In less than a week, Japan agreed to surrender. The war in Asia formally ended on September 2, 1945 (V-J Day).

Americans soon learned that the atomic bombs that had been dropped on Japan were the products of an enormous wartime mobilization of scientific talent and engineering skill called the Manhattan Project. The project inaugurated not just a new age of weaponry, but an era of bureaucratically organized and government-funded big science. News reports of the enormous effort that had been required to build the bomb raised the prestige of atomic physicists, radar engineers, military planners, and other technical experts to extraordinary heights. Vannevar Bush, an architect of the Manhattan Project, declared science "the endless frontier," the quest that would sustain American power, purpose, and democracy now that the era of westward pioneer migrations was over.

President Truman persuaded most Americans that the bombings of Hiroshima and Nagasaki had been necessary to compel Japan's surrender without the enormous loss of life that would have resulted if Allied forces had invaded Japan. After the devastating bombing raids by both sides on civilian targets, two more bombs, even though they were atomic bombs, did

"Why Do You Have to End the War Twice?"

Bernard Feld was a graduate student working with the Manhattan Project in the 1940s. Those who built the atomic bomb understood very well its potential for destruction and death. In this excerpt from a 1980 interview, Feld recalled his dismay not at the bomb's development and its first use at Hiroshima, but at using the second bomb against Nagasaki.

So on August 6th, when the bomb was dropped, everybody was elated. When we got the information on August 7th that it had gone off and that apparently had, as a bomb, worked extremely well. Well, people were used to killing a lot of people. Strategic bombing was an aspect of World War II, and people didn't think much about that aspect.

To me, actually, the important event was not the first bomb, but the second. . . . [W]hen they announced the second bomb . . . , that came as a shock to me. I said, "But the war is over." In fact, the headlines at that time were "Japanese Surrender." And then bang, there was the bomb in Nagasaki. And that hit me like a glass of cold water thrown at you. I suddenly said, "Now, wait a second. What for?" I mean, great, we ended the war—but why do you have to end the war twice?" . . . and that really started me thinking about what it was all about.

The Reminiscences of Bernard Feld, Columbia Oral History Research Office, Columbia University, 1980, 19–20.

---

not seem particularly excessive to some Americans. "We're sitting on the pier in Seattle," one GI remembered, "sharpening our bayonets, when Harry [Truman] dropped that beautiful bomb. The greatest thing that ever happened."

But others raised pointed questions about Truman's decision. Why was Truman in such a rush? The Americans had no major military operations planned until November 1945, and in any case, the projected full-scale invasion of Japan was not to occur before spring 1946. Why couldn't Truman have waited for the Soviet Union to enter the war or explore the peace feelers that a divided Japanese government had begun to send during the summer of 1945? Such questions led General Eisenhower to conclude, "it wasn't necessary to hit them with that awful thing." Admiral William Leahy, head of the U.S. joint chiefs of staff, concurred: "The use of this barbarous weapon at Hiroshima and Nagasaki was of no material assistance in our war against Japan. The Japanese were already defeated and ready to surrender."

Why, then, did the United States drop the atomic bombs? It was less for military than for political reasons, it seems, because these weapons offered the United States a means not only to win the war against Japan, but also to give American diplomacy the upper hand over the Soviets. By 1945, a fundamental conflict over the shape of the postwar world had begun to divide the Soviets and their Western allies. When Churchill, Stalin, and Roosevelt, the leaders of the "Grand Alliance," met together for the last time in February

1945 at the Russian resort city of Yalta, those tensions started coming to a head. The leaders did reach agreements on contentious issues such as the military division of Germany and plans for a new international organization (the United Nations), but the fate of Eastern Europe, now occupied by the Red Army, remained unresolved. Roosevelt won a fence-straddling compromise between Stalin and Churchill that gave the Soviets part of eastern Poland and promised free elections to determine the economic character—Communist or capitalist—of a postwar Polish state. Stalin interpreted the agreement as tacit Western acceptance that Poland and the rest of Eastern Europe would fall within the Soviet sphere of influence.

But in July, when Truman met at Potsdam, Germany, with Stalin and the new British Prime Minister, Clement Attlee, to complete the work begun in Yalta, the end of the Pacific war was in sight, and jockeying for postwar position replaced wartime cooperation. Truman later described the conference as a "brawl." As World War II wound down, a new conflict loomed on the horizon: a Cold War that would pit the United States and Western Europe against the Soviet Union. In that context, the United States viewed the atomic bomb as a diplomatic weapon. Just before the first atomic test in July 1945, Truman noted that "if it explodes, as I think it will, I'll certainly have a hammer on those boys"—and he meant the Soviets, not the Japanese. The White House wanted to ensure America's supremacy in postwar Asia and curb Soviet ambitions in Eastern Europe. Secretary of State James F. Byrnes later recalled the hope, widely shared in Washington at the time, that the bomb's use would enable the United States "to dictate our own terms at the end of the war."

Conversion to a Peacetime Economy   On the home front, Americans celebrated the end of the war but also searched for signs that the United States could avoid a postwar depression and sustain the wartime prosperity that had pulled so many people out of poverty and fear (Figure 10.2). In 1944, President Roosevelt had outlined a "second bill of rights" that included the right to a job, medical care, education, housing, food, clothing, and recreation, and Congress had passed the G.I. Bill of Rights to provide returning veterans with access to education and job training. But the transition to a peacetime economy would take place in an atmosphere charged with the fearful memories of an earlier peace: the economic collapse after World War I, the bitter industrial conflicts that followed, and the bread lines and Hoovervilles of the Great Depression. World War II generated millions of new jobs, but what would happen when the defense plants shut down and twelve million GIs came home? Could a free-market economy successfully reemploy these workers, keep inflation under control, and raise the real incomes of a vastly expanded labor force?

Most business leaders wanted to dismantle wartime controls as soon as possible and undercut the public support that had sustained New Deal liberalism. While their companies had profited handsomely from the wartime alliance with the government, U.S. capitalists had little interest in the state-sponsored economic planning and labor-management collaboration they saw in postwar Western Europe. They remained intensely suspicious of the kind of New Deal social engineering that organized labor favored, and they wanted to be free of government or union interference in determining wages and prices. As GM's Alfred P. Sloan put it, "It took fourteen years to rid this country of prohibition. It is going to take a good while to rid the country of the New Deal, but sooner or later the ax falls and we get a change."

Unions, together with their liberal and consumer allies, put forth their own ambitious postwar planning agenda. Few labor leaders, especially in the CIO, believed that the welfare of the working class would be advanced only, or even primarily, by postwar collective bargaining. Instead, they hoped that labor would continue to exert an influence on economic and business decisions, both public and private. Thus, in the early years of the war, the CIO's Philip Murray had urged the creation of a series of industry councils that would fuse economic and political bargaining—"a program for democratic economic planning and for

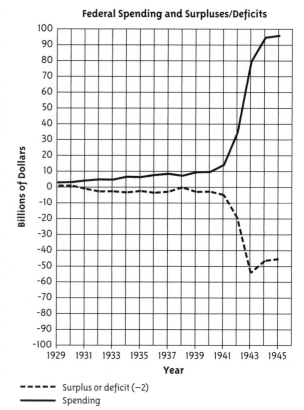

Federal Spending and Surpluses/Deficits

- - - - Surplus or deficit (−2)
——— Spending

FIGURE 10.2 Federal Spending in Depression and War

Although the New Deal doubled federal spending, budget deficits remained modest in the 1930s. A vast expansion in military spending during World War II pushed expenditures upward tenfold and generated massive deficits. During the war, the federal debt jumped fivefold, to $260 billion.

Welcome Back

During the war, housing construction came to a virtual standstill. The return of millions of servicemen to civilian life in 1945 set off a national housing crisis. American Social History Project.

Add Post-War Adjustments

Reflecting male fears rather than postwar reality, this cartoon suggested that returning veterans would confront a job market in which prewar gender roles were now reversed. In fact, few women workers kept their jobs at war's end. Jay N. ("Ding") Darling — Courtesy of the "Ding" Darling Wildlife Society.

participation by the people in the key decision of the big corporations." Labor played a key role in reelecting Roosevelt to a fourth term in 1944, and nine months later, liberals and progressives in the United States took heart from the smashing victory of the Labour Party in Great Britain's first postwar election. As one observer put it, "Union leaders no longer regard themselves as a force merely reacting to managerial decision . . . but as a force which itself can influence the whole range of industrial economic activity."

The UAW's Walter Reuther embodied this ambition. A trade unionist who was equally at ease among the shop floor militants of Detroit and the policymaking bureaucrats of Washington, Reuther called on the government to convert taxpayer-financed war plants to the mass production of badly needed housing and railroad equipment. Most strikingly, he demanded a 30 percent increase in autoworkers' wages, which would just about make up for the income those workers lost when the postwar workweek shrank to forty hours. But Reuther did not limit his argument to a narrow consideration of wages. A believer in Keynesian economics, he wanted to boost working-class "purchasing power." He challenged management to keep car prices at prewar levels to stave off an inflationary surge, raise working-class living standards, and win labor support from middle-class consumers. Reuther demanded that General Motors "open the books" to show that its profits and productivity made an inflation-proof wage increase possible.

Few issues were more contentious than the Office of Price Administration (OPA), whose fate was central to an orderly and progressive conversion of the war economy to a peacetime footing. In 1945, this popular and effective government agency helped to sustain working-class living standards by enforcing price and quality standards for hundreds of different hard-to-find products. Bolstered by the voluntary efforts of almost 300,000 OPA "price checkers," the agency's leverage over business pricing policies gave millions of consumers a stake in the outcome of the labor-liberal effort to sustain a postwar New Deal. OPA chief Chester Bowles, a spirited liberal, called the agency's housewife volunteers "as American as baseball," even as some merchants denounced them as a "kitchen Gestapo" that diligently enforced government price controls.

These tensions erupted in a massive postwar strike wave. Beginning late in the fall of 1945, a five-month wave of strikes, the largest such action since 1919, put three million workers on the street. These stoppages had a twofold purpose: to win substantial wage increases that would set the pattern for all American workers in the postwar years and to preserve government-mandated price ceilings so that inflation would not erode working-class living standards. Strikes shut down the steel, electrical, oil, coal, and meatpacking industries. Union efforts to stop production went largely uncontested, so most of the strikes were peaceful and effective. When the police did intervene against the unions, labor responded with mass picket lines or with a general strike of the sort that brought commerce to a complete halt in Stamford and Hartford, Connecticut; Lancaster, Pennsylvania; Houston, Texas; Rochester, New York; Camden, New Jersey; and Oakland, California.

The wave of strikes in 1945 and 1946 marked the height of union strength and social solidarity during the twentieth century. It was the final episode in the great cycle of industrial confrontations that had begun with the railroad strikes of the 1870s and erupted again every decade, reminding the nation of the seemingly insolvable conflict between labor and capital.

"People Were Literally Dancing in the Streets"

Autoworker Stan Weir, an enthusiastic participant in the 1946 general strike in Oakland, California, described the workers' jubilant mood in the early hours of the strike and the way they took control of the city for more than two days.

The Oakland general strike was called by no leader. It was unique, I think, in general strikes in this country. There was a strike of women who were the clerks at Kahn's and Hastings' department stores and it had been going on for months. The Teamsters had begun to refuse to make deliveries to those department stores and the department stores needed commodities badly.

Not many people had cars right after the war and you took public transportation to work in the morning. You had to go downtown to the center of Oakland and then out in the direction of your workplace. So thousands and thousands of people traveled through the heart of town every morning on the way to work, on public transportation. Very early one morning, here were the policemen of Oakland herding in a string of trucks, operated by a scab trucking firm in Los Angeles, with supplies for these department stores. Some truck driver or some bus driver or street car conductor asked some policeman about the trucks. . . . Well, that truck driver, that bus driver, or that street car conductor didn't get back on his vehicle . . . and that increased till those trucks and those buses and those street cars just piled up and thousands of people were stranded in town.

In a small way it was a holiday. The normal criteria for what was acceptable conduct disappeared. No one knew what to do and there were no leaders. No one called it. Pretty soon the strikers began forming into committees on the street corners. Certain shopkeepers were told to shut down and drug stores to stay open. Bars could stay open if they didn't serve hard liquor, and they had to put their juke boxes out on the sidewalk. People were literally dancing in the streets in anticipation of some kind of new day. Soon the strikers began to direct traffic and only let union people into town and keep out those who it was feared might be against the strike. It lasted fifty-four hours.

Stan Weir, "The Informal Work Group," in Alice Lynd and Staughton Lynd, eds., *Rank and File: Personal Histories by Working Class Organizers* (1973).

Union workers claimed, and much of the public agreed, that their struggle embodied the hopes and aspirations of all Americans. The assertion ex-tended even to military veterans and active service personnel. After V-J Day, U.S. troops in Asia organized a "bring the troops home" movement, demanding rapid demobilization of U.S. troops from North China, the

Philippines, and Indonesia. Savvy unionists and radicals in uniform led this effort, which often resembled a labor protest. In December 1945, when 4,000 troops marched on an army headquarters depot in Manila, their commander quipped, "You men forget you're not working for General Motors. You're still in the Army."

The big strikes of early 1946 were as much political as economic contests. Although presidential fact-finding boards in both the auto and steel industries had recommended substantial wage hikes with no corresponding rise in OPA price guide-

"Tests Have Shown . . . That Our Three Average Men Are Equal"

A frame from *Brotherhood of Man*, an animated short produced by United Productions of America, a studio created by former Walt Disney animators, for the United Automobile Workers' 1946 interracial organizing drive. *Ammunition*, February 1947 — United Automobile Workers of America.

lines, corporate leaders remained intransigent, vowing that "until [the Office of Price Administration] authorizes fair prices, nothing can be settled through collective bargaining." In the end, President Truman caved in, announcing that in return for a wage increase of about eighteen cents per hour, he would allow the steel corporations to raise the price of steel five dollars a ton.

Labor leaders soon concluded that the political winds had shifted against them and they would have to settle for Truman's offer. Indeed, the great strikes of 1946 proved a costly victory for organized labor. True, every major corporation agreed to negotiate with the union that represented its employees, thus demonstrating the permanence of the industrial unions that had been built during the 1930s and expanded during the war. But businessmen also insisted that postwar contracts include a "management security" clause giving them more power to set production standards and to limit the authority of shop stewards and union officials. More important, the wage increases that had been won during the walkouts evaporated quickly under the galloping inflation that was let loose when government price controls were lifted in the summer and fall of 1946.

With inflation running at more than 12 percent, most of the big unions had to return to the bargaining table for another round of wage hikes in 1946. Although the unions reached settlements without strikes, most manufacturers again raised their prices, blaming "Big Labor" for the inflationary spiral that gripped the economy. Middle-class consumers and industrial workers alike turned against the unions, and the entire country soon grew hostile toward the labor movement. The incapacity of either the Truman administration or the unions to stop the inflationary surge discredited the Rooseveltian state and demoralized millions of working-class voters. Responding to the Republican campaign slogan, "Had Enough?," voters in

1946 deprived the Democrats of control of Congress for the first time since 1930. Democrats sustained their greatest losses in the industrial regions stretching from Connecticut to Illinois — precisely the area with a heavy urban-labor constituency.

Conclusion: A New Order at Home and Abroad

With the end of World War II, the New Deal also ended and, with it, the cycle of union growth and working-class recomposition that had transformed the structure of American society. The labor movement was now an established part of the American political and social order. And the federal government continued to exercise far greater power than it had a generation earlier. But perhaps the most profound transformation of all was the evolution of the United States into the preeminent global power, with immense influence over the economic and political affairs of a world that was divided along economic and ideological lines. Within that context, America would have to confront a host of issues that had been raised, but not always resolved, by the Depression, the New Deal, and World War II. For the next half-century, the nation would puzzle over the extent to which the government should regulate the economy, expand the welfare state, restrain union growth, endorse the nascent civil rights insurgency, and recognize the claims made by the still small movement for women's equality.

The Years in Review

1922
- Benito Mussolini's fascists seize power in Italy.

1924
- With the death of V. I. Lenin, Joseph Stalin outmaneuvers rivals and consolidates his power within the Soviet Union.

1931
- The Japanese army captures Manchuria and then gradually extends control over all of northern China.

1933
- In Germany, Nazi leader Adolf Hitler seizes dictatorial powers.
- President Franklin D. Roosevelt proclaims the Good Neighbor Policy toward Latin America.

1935
- Italy conquers Abyssinia (Ethiopia).
- Congress passes the Neutrality Act; two more such acts pass in the next two years and limit U.S. action in world crises.

1936

- Hitler takes and rearms the Rhineland.

- Japan, Italy, and Germany sign pacts with one another, giving birth to the Axis military alliance.

- The Spanish Civil War begins; Congress prohibits the United States from sending arms to either side, but individual Americans join the International Brigades of volunteers defending the Republic, which is defeated by Francisco Franco in 1939.

1937

- Japan launches a new invasion of China.

1938

- Nazis smash Jewish shops and loot homes and synagogues in Germany in a wave of destruction known as *Kristallnacht*.

- France and Britain sign the Munich Pact, hoping to appease Germany and limit its expansion; British Prime Minister Neville Chamberlain heralds the pact as ensuring "peace in our time."

1939

- The Soviet Union signs a nonaggression pact with Germany.

- Germany invades Poland; Britain and France declare war; World War II begins.

1940

- Germans sweep through Western Europe in blitzkrieg attacks, launching simultaneous air and land campaigns.

- President Roosevelt defeats Wendell Willkie to win an unprecedented third term as president.

1941

- Germany invades the Soviet Union.

- Japan launches a surprise attack on U.S. forces at Pearl Harbor, Hawaii, bringing the United States into the war.

- A. Philip Randolph, in conjunction with civil rights and labor groups, threatens a march on Washington, D.C., to protest racial discrimination; Roosevelt heads it off by issuing Executive Order 8802, creating the Fair Employment Practices Commission.

1942

- Roosevelt issues Executive Order 9066, which results in 100,000 Japanese Americans being forced to abandon their homes and jobs and live in concentration camps throughout the western states.

- Japanese troops capture the Philippines; more than 5,000 captured U.S. servicemen die during the Bataan death march.

- Allied troops invade North Africa.
- The United States wins crucial battles at Guadalcanal and Midway.
- Civil rights activists found the Congress for Racial Equality.

1943
- Congress repeals the Chinese Exclusion Act but sets a new quota of only 105 Chinese immigrants per year.
- White Americans attack Mexican Americans in the "zoot-suit riots."
- Racial violence peaks in 1943, with 250 incidents in forty-seven cities; the worst riot is in Detroit, where 34 people die.

1944
- On D-Day (June 6), 156,000 Allied troops land on the beaches of Normandy, France.
- President Roosevelt defeats Republican challenger Thomas Dewey for a fourth term in the White House.

1945
- The last meeting of the Big Three — Churchill, Roosevelt, and Stalin — takes place at the Yalta Conference.
- Franklin D. Roosevelt dies on April 12; Harry Truman becomes president.
- Germany surrenders unconditionally on May 4, ending the war in Europe.
- On August 6 and 8, U.S. planes drop atomic bombs on the Japanese cities of Hiroshima and Nagasaki; Japan surrenders, ending World War II.
- Truman meets with Churchill and Stalin at the Potsdam Conference to decide the shape of the postwar world.
- At war's end, an outbreak of strikes occurs; five million workers go on strike, losing 120 million days of work over the next twelve months.

1946
- Frustrated by postwar inflation, voters put Republicans in control of Congress for the first time since 1930. Democrats lose many of the urban labor votes that sustained them throughout the Roosevelt administration.

Additional Readings

For more on the origins of World War II and the U.S. shift from isolation to internationalism, see: Akira Iriye, *Origins of the Second World War in Asia and the Pacific (Origins of the Modern War)* (1987); Maurice Isserman,

Which Side Were You On?: The American Communist Party During the Second World War (1993); Warren F. Kimball, *The Juggler: Franklin Roosevelt as Wartime Statesman* (1994); Clayton R. Koppes and Gregory D. Black, *Hollywood Goes to War* (1987); Walter LaFeber, *The American Age: United States Policy at Home and Abroad 1750–Present* (1994); and David Wyman, *The Abandonment of the Jews: America and the Holocaust, 1941–1945* (1998).

For more on the experience of soldiers fighting the war, see: Stephen E. Ambrose, *Citizen Soldiers: The U.S. Army from the Normandy Beaches to the Bulge to the Surrender of Germany, June 7, 1944 to May 7, 1945* (1998); Alison R. Bernstein, *American Indians and World War II: Toward a New Era in Indian Affairs* (1991); Allan Berube, *Coming Out Under Fire: The History of Gay Men and Women in World War Two* (1990); John Dower, *War Without Mercy: Race and Power in the Pacific War* (1986); Jere Bishop Franco, *Crossing the Pond: The Native American Effort in World War II* (1999); Herbert Garfinkel, *When Negroes March* (1959); Peter S. Kindsvatter, *American Soldiers: Ground Combat in the World Wars, Korea, and Vietnam* (2003); Leisa D. Meyer, *Creating GI Jane: Sexuality and Power in the Women's Army Corps During World War II* (1996); Williamson Murray and Allan R. Millett, *A War to Be Won: Fighting the Second World War* (2000); Michael S. Sherry, *The Rise of American Air Power: The Creation of Armageddon* (1989); Ronald H. Spector, *Eagle Against the Sun: The American War with Japan* (1985); and Studs Terkel, ed., *"The Good War": An Oral History of World War II* (1997).

For more on economic, industrial, and political changes on the home front during the war, see: James Baughman, *Henry R. Luce and the Rise of the American News Media* (1987); John Morton Blum, *V Was for Victory: Politics and American Culture During World War II* (1977); Paul Fussell, *Wartime: Understanding and Behavior in the Second World War* (1989); Alan Gropman, *Mobilizing U.S. Industry in World War II* (1996); Howell John Harris, *The Right to Manage: Industrial Relations Policies of American Business in the 1940s* (1982); Nelson Lichtenstein, *Labor's War at Home: The CIO in World War II* (1984); Geoffrey Perrett, *Days of Sadness, Years of Triumph: The American People, 1939–1945* (1985); Richard Polenberg, *War and Society: The United States, 1941–1945* (1972); Brian Waddlee, *The War Against the New Deal: World War II and American Democracy,* (2001); Margaret Weir, Ann Shola Orloff, and Theda Skocpol, eds., *The Politics of Social Policy in the United States* (1988); and Allan Winkler, *The Politics of Propaganda: The Office of War Information, 1942–1945* (1978).

For more on the war's impact on women, African Americans, and Japanese Americans, see: Beth Bailey and David Farber, *First Strange Place: The Alchemy of Race and Sex in World War II Hawaii* (1994); Roger Daniels,

Concentration Camps, North America: Japanese in the United States and Canada During World War II (1981); Susan E. Hirsch and Lewis A. Erenberg, eds., *The War in American Culture: Society and Consciousness During War World II* (1996); Maureen Honey, *Creating Rosie the Riveter: Class, Gender, and Propaganda During World War II* (1985); Michael K. Honey, *Southern Labor and Black Civil Rights: Organizing Memphis Workers* (1993); Roger Horowitz, *Negro and White, Unite and Fight: A Social History of Industrial Unionism in Meatpacking, 1930–90* (1997); Peter H. Irons, *Justice at War* (1993); Daniel Kryder, *Divided Arsenal: Race and the American State During World War II* (2000); Ruth Milkman, *Gender at Work: The Dynamics of Job Segregation by Sex During World War II* (1987); Franklin Odo, *No Sword to Bury: Japanese Americans in Hawai'i During World War II* (2004); Greg Robinson, *By Order of the President: FDR and the Internment of Japanese Americans* (2001); Kenneth William Townsend, *World War II and the American Indian* (2000); and Emily Yellin, *Our Mothers' War: American Women at Home and at the Front during World War II* (2004).

For more on the end of the war, the development and use of the atomic bomb, and postwar activism, see: Gar Alperovitz, *Atomic Diplomacy: Hiroshima and Potsdam*, rev. ed. (1995); George Lipsitz, *Rainbow at Midnight: Labor and Culture in the 1940s* (1994); J. Robert Moskin, *Mr. Truman's War: The Final Victories of World War II and the Birth of the Postwar World* (2002); Richard Rhodes, *The Making of the Atomic Bomb* (1995); and Martin J. Sherwin, *A World Destroyed: The Atomic Bomb and the Grand Alliance* (1975).

Part Three

Cold War America— And After

1946–2007

O N JANUARY 7, 1946, 20,000 American servicemen held a mass meeting in Manila, at which they listened to sergeants, corporals, and other veteran GIs demand that the Army ship them home. They were homesick, but many also protested U.S. plans to station troops in North China, Indonesia, and the rest of the Philippines, where Communist insurgencies and nationalist revolts challenged old oppressors. This "Bring the Boys Home" movement quickly spread throughout the Far East and won widespread support back in the United States. Bowing to the popular pressure, the War Department soon accelerated troop demobilization to fill every available ship with veterans who were eager to return home.

The revolt of the overseas servicemen dissipated within weeks, but it encapsulated much of the tension that would govern U.S. diplomacy and politics during the post–World War II years. The United States became the world's preeminent military and economic power, with millions of troops spread all over the globe. Much of Europe and Asia lay in ruins, while the U.S. industrial machine remained untouched by the ravages of war. But the deployment of American strength — and the purposes for which it would be used — generated unexpected controversy both at home and abroad.

For all their prosperity, Americans did not feel secure in 1946. The planet was dividing into two armed and hostile camps, embodying different social and economic systems: one composed of nations that were allied to or occupied by the Soviet Union, the other a slightly looser network of states led by the United States. This military and ideological rivalry — dubbed the "Cold War" by American financier and presidential adviser Bernard Baruch — generated an expensive and dangerous arms race and bloody conflicts over the next three decades in China, Greece, Korea, Vietnam, and Central America.

America's protracted struggle with the Soviets gave rise to a dual set of containments: abroad, the U.S. helped erect a worldwide set of anti-Communist alliances; at home, the Cold War generated a sharp turn to the right, containing within well-policed boundaries the ideas and activities that were considered politically acceptable. The unions recruited new members and conducted frequent strikes early in the postwar era, but government regulations forced radical anticapitalist ideas out of the house of labor. "McCarthyism," which first took its name from the inquisitorial investigations conducted by Wisconsin senator Joseph McCarthy, provided a convenient label for the repressive atmosphere created by the political obsession with the American Communist Party.

Since the 1950s, American politics and society have been transformed in two fundamental ways. First, an amazingly creative mass movement of black and white citizens swept aside the structures of legal segregation and discrimination that for almost one hundred years had mocked the Union victory in the Civil War. The civil rights revolution gave enormous energy to the reforming impulse that culminated in the 1960s in President Lyndon Johnson's "Great Society." Medical care for the poor and elderly, greater access to education, a more liberal and less racist immigration law, and a highly touted "War on Poverty" seemed but a continuation of the New Deal social agenda. The movement for African American liberation made all Americans more rights conscious, raising the expectations and aspirations of young people, women, gays, the disabled, American Indians, and all those who felt marginal to the mainstream of American life. The women's movement that began late in the 1960s offered a particularly potent political and cultural challenge to the gender inequalities that were so thoroughly embedded within the very structure of marriage, work, and public life.

The rights revolution of the 1960s also transformed working-class America. The typical worker of the 1950s—a male breadwinner in a blue-collar union job supporting a family—had virtually ceased to exist. The massive entry of women into the paid labor force has radically altered the character of American family life. Moreover, since 1965, a wave of immigrants from Asia, Latin America, and Eastern Europe has made the working class of most cities even more cosmopolitan than it had been in the years of transatlantic immigration before World War I.

But these great social and ideological changes shifted American politics to the right, not the left. Indeed, the second signpost to the history of the last half century has been the unexpected rise of a powerful conservative current in American politics. Liberalism had but a brief flowering in the 1960s because the polarization generated by the war in Vietnam, the revival of feminism, and the upheaval in race relations fractured the coalition that had long sustained the majority status of the Democratic Party. Then, just a decade later, the unexpected stagnation in U.S. living standards brought into question the even older New Deal linkage between economic prosperity and activist government. In the 1970s and early 1980s, a sharp decline in the productivity and profitability of American business ended the great postwar boom that had doubled Americans' living standards in just a generation. As high-paying industrial jobs vanished and the unions shrank in size, white working-class loyalty to the Democrats declined as well.

The collapse of liberalism in the 1970s helped to pave the way for the presidency of a conservative Republican, Ronald Reagan, whose successful efforts to roll back taxes, cut social spending, curb union power, and expand the military represented a decisive postwar break with the political legacy of the New Deal. The influence of Reaganite Republicanism proved as great as that of any twentieth-century president. The Democratic Party itself became much more conservative. And even with the end of the Cold War and the improved economy under the two-term presidency of Democrat Bill Clinton, efforts to expand the welfare state and legitimize a socially activist government proved largely unsuccessful.

At the beginning of the twenty-first century, issues of international security, increasing economic inequality, and cultural divisions defined the election and presidency of George W. Bush. The terrorist attacks on September 11, 2001, generated a wave of patriotic nationalism that the Bush administration leveraged to declare a virtually unlimited "war on terror." In addition to a military invasion of Afghanistan, which destroyed much of the al-Qaeda infrastructure there, President Bush inaugurated a far-reaching expansion of the federal government's authority to investigate and detain suspected terrorists, both at home and abroad. In the spring of 2003, the Bush administration launched an unprovoked invasion of Iraq that easily toppled dictator Saddam Hussein but then led to a protracted and increasingly unpopular war against a well-armed and highly motivated insurgency.

11

The Cold War Boom

1946–1960

Smile When You Say That
Despite the calm demeanor of this anti-Rosenberg picketer at a 1953 demonstration in Washington, D.C., the message on his sign suggests the intensity of anti-Communist hysteria in the postwar period. Elliott Erwitt/Magnum.

"AMERICA AT THIS MOMENT stands at the summit of the world," announced Winston Churchill in August 1945. That same month, Walter Lippmann wrote, "What Rome was to the ancient world, what Great Britain has been to the modern world, America is to be to the world of tomorrow." The former British prime minister and America's most respected newspaper columnist stood in awe for good reason. During World War II, the United States had mobilized an army of twelve million and had bankrolled or equipped an equal number of Allied troops. It had assembled the world's largest navy and air force and had built the atomic bombs that wiped out two Japanese cities. But friend and foe alike found the great size and vibrancy of the U.S. economy most impressive. In the four wartime years, U.S. income, wealth, and industrial production all doubled or more than doubled. By 1947, the United States produced roughly half the world's manufactures: 57 percent of the steel, 43 percent of the electricity, and 62 percent of the oil. America now dominated in precisely those industries — aviation, chemical engineering, and electronics — that spelled victory in modern war.

This enormous military and industrial power enabled the United States to become the guardian of a postwar Pax Americana, a restructuring of international politics and finance in a way that made them more responsive to U.S. interests. The United States now indissolubly linked its interests to a global order that depended on American economic strength and political will. This melding of foreign and economic policy created tensions with the other great world power, the Soviet Union. The resulting "cold war" pitted East against West and served as a backdrop to the impressive midcentury U.S. economic growth. In the immediate postwar years, more than ever before, international developments shaped the everyday lives of American women and men while New Deal pension, wage, and home loan guarantees provided the economic security that enabled many Americans to enjoy the fruits of the postwar economic boom.

The Cold War in a Global Context

Economic growth and political stability in the United States stood in stark contrast to the radical transformations that swept the rest of the globe in the years immediately following World War II. In 1947, Churchill described Europe as "a rubble-heap, a charnel house, a breeding ground of pestilence and hate." There, depression and war so discredited the old elites that many people doubted that capitalism could long survive. Although the Soviet dictator Joseph Stalin had betrayed the ideals of the Russian Revolution to establish a brutal and despotic regime, millions of people throughout the world still looked to the Soviet Union as an alternative to capitalism, which they identified with the chaos of the Great Depression and World War II. In France, the Communists and Socialists, who had led the anti-Nazi resistance, were far more popular than business leaders were, and even many conservatives there supported the postwar nationalization of the country's most important banks and manufacturing firms. In Britain, the Labour Party swept Churchill and the Conservatives out of power, raising the possibility that America's closest ally might embrace socialism. In Greece, Italy, and Yugoslavia, Communist parties seemed on the verge of assuming power. Meanwhile, powerful independence movements emerged in Asia and Africa, shaking the colonial empires that France, Britain, and the Netherlands had built. After the 1949 revolution in China, American policymakers became more hostile to nationalist and reform movements in the colonial world and turned the Cold War "hot" by responding militarily to the North Korean invasion on that Asian peninsula and supporting the French armies in Indochina.

Origins of the Cold War   Nothing is inevitable in history or politics, but the Cold War antagonism that soon divided "East" and "West" would have been exceedingly hard to avoid. The Soviets sought to dominate a buffer zone of satellite states along Russia's historic borders to prevent invasion from the west while at the same time probing for political and social weaknesses in Western Europe. In wartime conferences, American policymakers seemed to accept the idea of a Soviet sphere of influence in Eastern Europe. At a meeting in the Ukrainian resort city of Yalta in February 1945, Roosevelt and Churchill thought it fruitless to oppose Soviet dominance in Poland once the Red Army had fought its way across that nation. After mid-1945, however, President Harry Truman grew uncomfortable with these arrangements. Although Stalin showed no interest in an invasion of Western Europe, the Soviet Union's suppression of nationalist aspirations in Eastern Europe, combined with its encouragement of anticapitalist and anticolonial movements worldwide, led Western leaders to view the Soviet Union as an inherently expansionist power.

The intensity of the Cold War—the costly and dangerous militarization of the rivalry; the all-encompassing, global character of the antagonism; and its protracted, half-century length—might have been mitigated or ameliorated through careful statesmanship. U.S. leaders believed that they had a duty to create a new economic order. Henry Luce, an influential spokesman for American internationalism and the publisher of *Time* and *Life*, urged readers of those magazines to "go over the earth, as investors and managers and engineers, as makers of mutual prosperity, as missionaries of capitalism and democracy." Although the Soviets desperately needed assistance in rebuilding their country, President Truman canceled lend-lease aid to the Soviet Union almost immediately after Germany's surrender, convinced that the United States had to "stop babying the Soviets." In Poland, where Americans wanted elections, the Soviets suppressed opposition parties to keep that buffer state firmly under their control. And much haggling took place over the international control of atomic energy. Although some in the United States were willing to give the newly formed United Nations a role in this area, President Truman and military leaders insisted on a system of mandatory international inspections that would preserve U.S. atomic supremacy. The Soviets, rejecting this U.S. plan, forged ahead with a secret program to build their own atom bomb, which they would test in 1949.

Containing the Soviets and Dividing Europe

Two influential individuals, George F. Kennan and Winston Churchill, helped to codify and globalize the meaning of these growing tensions, which ultimately led to a divided Europe. Early in 1946, Kennan, the highest-ranking U.S. diplomat in Moscow, cabled an explosive 8,000-word assessment of Soviet intensions to State Department officials in Washington. Kennan's "long telegram" quickly circulated throughout the federal government. The influential journal *Foreign Affairs* published an even more ideological, anti-Communist version, under the pseudonym "Mr. X." Both traditional Russian insecurities and Marxist-

Number 1, 1948
The postwar movement of Abstract Expressionism, exemplified in Jackson Pollock's work, marked a sharp break from earlier representative painting. Unlike the previous generation of artists, the Abstract Expressionists rejected political themes, developing techniques that reflected the irrationality of Cold War hostilities and potential nuclear annihilation. But the obscurity of these paintings made them malleable propaganda tools in U.S. government–sponsored cultural festivals and exhibits. Ironically, Abstract Expressionism became a symbol of America's postwar power.
Jackson Pollock, 1948, oil on canvas, 68 inches × 8 feet 8 inches — The Museum of Modern Art.

Leninist dogma motivated Soviet leaders, wrote Kennan. These leaders based their totalitarian rule in the Soviet Union on an irrational fear of capitalist encirclement and of foreign hostility. To counter the Soviets, Kennan wrote, the United States should pursue a policy of "firm containment, designed to confront the Russians with unalterable counterforce at every point." Kennan's strategy of containment came to characterize the Cold War posture that the West adopted toward the Soviets for more than a generation. Although Kennan construed containment largely in economic and diplomatic terms, the strategy soon took on a decidedly military cast as Cold War antagonisms deepened.

In March 1946, Winston Churchill gave the idea of containment a powerful rhetorical flourish. In one of the most famous speeches of the twentieth century, Churchill warned that an "Iron Curtain" of Soviet domination had descended across central Europe, and he called for a new Anglo-American military alliance to oppose it. Many Americans, including some within the policymaking elite, thought Churchill's harsh speech unnecessarily provocative, given that in early 1946, the Soviets tolerated some pluralism and multiparty competition in Finland, Austria, Hungary, and Czechoslovakia. But Churchill's Iron Curtain speech bolstered arguments that compromise or negotiation with the Soviet Union would prove fruitless.

Thus, the ideological confrontation with the Soviets soon turned into a military and economic projection of U.S. power, first in the Eastern Mediterranean and then throughout all of Western Europe. In Greece, President Truman faced a crisis early in 1947. There, as in so many other Eastern European societies, business and landowning elites had been discredited by their collaboration with the fascists during World War II. Local Communists, emerging from the anti-Nazi resistance, took up arms; soon, civil war engulfed the nation. The British government backed conservative Greek monarchists with troops and financial aid, but in February 1947, officials of Britain's new Labour government informed Truman that Britain could no longer afford to assist anti-Communist forces.

President Truman and his advisers decided the United States should fill the political and military breach left by the British. However, they faced a skeptical American public and a fiscally conservative Republican Congress. Truman resolved this difficulty by announcing what came to be known as the Truman Doctrine. Requesting $400 million in economic and military aid for Greece and Turkey, America's new ally in Asia Minor, the president framed his goals in sweeping terms: "At the present moment in world history, nearly every nation must choose between alternative ways of life." To win popular support for this open-ended initiative, Truman took the advice of Republican senator Arthur Vandenberg "to scare [the] hell out of the country." Whatever the merits of the particular conflict, Truman argued, "I believe that it must be the policy of the United States to support free peoples who are resisting attempted subjugation by armed minorities or by outside pressures." Truman defined political upheaval as inherently undemocratic. With money and arms, America would guarantee the political status quo in Greece and defend friendly regimes elsewhere in the world.

The administration followed the Truman Doctrine within a few months by an even more ambitious program, the $16 billion Marshall Plan for the reconstruction of Europe ($150 billion in current U.S. dollars). Secretary of State George Marshall proposed the plan in a June 1947 speech. It offered aid even to the Communist regimes of Eastern Europe, but only under conditions that would link their economies to the West, thus threatening their role as buffer states for the Soviet Union. When the Soviet Union forced those nations to reject Marshall Plan assistance, the economic partition of Europe was confirmed. And when Czech Communists seized control of Prague's coalition government in what became known as the "coup" of February 1948, Congress overwhelmingly approved funding for the Marshall Plan.

A tangible symbol of American wealth and generosity, the Marshall Plan scored a twofold victory in much of Europe. It strengthened the hand of conservatives in countries such as France, Italy, Greece, and Belgium, where Communist movements had strong support. And it sparked a powerful economic recovery in countries with an educated workforce, a well-built infrastructure, and a social democratic tradition, such as Germany, Norway, the Netherlands, Great Britain, and France. Those countries were able to take advantage of Marshall Plan aid and to share its fruits relatively equitably. But in other parts of Europe — such as Italy, Portugal, Greece, and Spain — the Marshall Plan proved less successful. There, foreign aid merely reinforced existing inequalities and inefficiencies, lending support to corrupt or authoritarian governments for more than two decades.

The economic and political division of Europe led inexorably to a military divide as well. The central issue remained the revival of German power, feared both by the Soviets and by many in the West. In June 1948, U.S.-led efforts to link the currency in Berlin's western sector to that of West Germany alarmed the Soviets: Berlin lay deep within the Soviet zone of occupation. They responded with a blockade of all Western European goods into the former German capital.

Peace Banished from Paradise
The Soviet satirical weekly magazine *Krokodil* ("Crocodile") portrayed the Marshall Plan as a bulwark preserving the power and privilege of business, military, and religious elites in the West. Y. Ganf, *Krokodil*, June 20, 1950 — General Research Division, Library of Congress.

President Truman ordered a spectacular airlift, which triumphantly supplied the city's residents with coal, food, and clothing for nearly a year. By May 1949, when Stalin lifted the blockade, Berlin had become an international symbol of resistance to Soviet intimidation.

Against this contentious backdrop, the United States pushed for the creation of a Western European military alliance, called the North Atlantic Treaty Organization (NATO), and the eventual rearmament of West Germany. Policymakers and analysts saw NATO as part of a strategy of "double containment," in which the revival of Germany, contained by a military alliance that was sensitive to French fear of German economic and military power, would in turn help to contain the Soviet Union. The Soviets replied with their own military alliance, the Warsaw Pact, thereby polarizing Europe further into two mutually hostile camps. In Eastern Europe, Communist governments suppressed all opposition political parties and institutions; in Western Europe, NATO froze the Communists out of the governments of France and Italy, halting the political and economic experimentation that was under way there (Map 11.1).

MAP 11.1   Cold War Europe, 1955

By the mid-1950s, most of Europe was sharply divided into two opposing camps. In 1949, the North Atlantic Treaty Organization (NATO), which was led by the United States, brought together twelve Western nations in an anti-Communist alliance. Responding to the addition of West Germany to NATO in 1955, the Soviet Union created an opposing alliance, known as the Warsaw Pact.

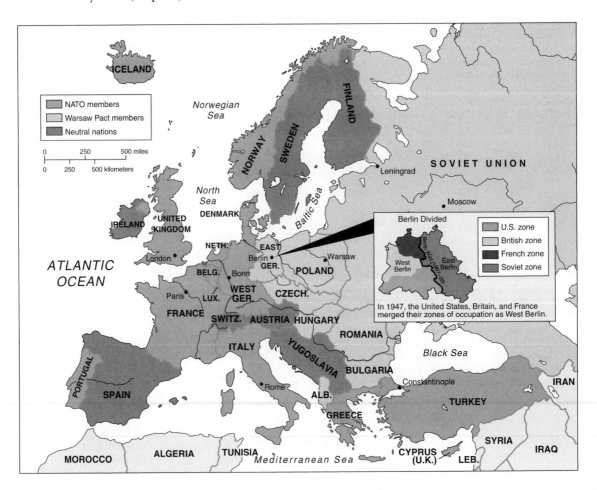

Cold War Showdowns Outside Europe   While the Cold War solidified European political allegiances, upheaval continued in much of the rest of the world. From Africa to Iran, from India to Southeast Asia and China, World War II had undermined Western colonial powers, unleashing a great wave of nationalism. Burma, Indonesia, India, and the Philippines soon achieved independence, followed a decade later by most of the Western colonies in Africa. Anticolonial nationalists often allied themselves with revolutionary social movements. In Vietnam and China, Communists under the leadership of Ho Chi Minh and Mao Zedong created powerful military insurgencies that championed the peasants' need for land as well as the nationalism of most urban workers and intellectuals. In India, the British imprisoned Mohandas Gandhi, Jawaharlal Nehru, and other nationalists during World War II, but jail merely enhanced their political and moral stature. In 1947, India was partitioned into two independent nations: Muslim Pakistan and predominantly Hindu India.

During the war, the United States looked with some favor on anticolonial movements in Asia, especially those that fought against the Japanese occupying forces. American foreign service officers who met with Chinese Communists during the war praised them as patriots and "land reformers," even as U.S. military advisers grew increasingly frustrated with the corrupt rule of the pro-Western Chinese dictator Chiang Kai-shek, who preferred to deploy his army against the Communists rather than the Japanese. In September 1945, before honored guests from the U.S. Intelligence service, the Vietnamese Communist Ho Chi Minh declared his nation's freedom from France in a speech that borrowed much language from the American Declaration of Independence.

But Cold War tensions transformed U.S. attitudes toward these left-wing, anticolonial movements. Although the United States provided Chiang Kai-shek with billions in military aid, Mao's Communist army took power in October 1949, forcing the Nationalists to flee to the island of Taiwan. Many Americans soon asked, "Who lost China?" Truman's new secretary of state, Dean Acheson, argued that the civil war there "was the product of internal Chinese forces, forces which this government tried to influence but could not." But Republicans and other conservatives, many with prewar missionary experience on the Asian mainland, accused the State Department of being "soft" on the Red Chinese. American policymakers became more hostile to nationalist and reform movements in the colonial world. In 1950, the United States began to send military aid to the French, who were fighting Ho Chi Minh's forces in Indochina.

The Soviet explosion of an atomic bomb in August 1949 combined with the "loss" of China accelerated both the arms race and the militarization of U.S. diplomacy. In January 1950, President Truman gave the go-ahead for the development of a controversial new "super" bomb, a thermonuclear weapon that was hundreds of times more powerful than the 10,000-kiloton

Better Safe Than Sorry

An advertisement in a 1951 edition of the professional periodical *School Executive* sells "dog-tag" necklaces for children to help identify their presumably mutilated remains after nuclear war. New York City's public school system issued tags during that year. *School Executive*, August 1951 — American Social History Project.

device that destroyed Hiroshima. First tested late in 1952, the new hydrogen bomb threw off a fireball — five miles high and four miles wide — that vaporized Eniwetok Atoll in the Marshall Islands. Within a year, the Soviets began their own H-bomb tests, eventually exploding a monster weapon with the power of fifty million tons of TNT.

The United States accompanied this new stage in the nuclear arms race with a plan for tripling the nation's arms budget. A secret report by the National Security Council, NSC-68, assumed that the Soviets were preparing a military assault on one or more of the "Free World's" outposts. "We must realize that we are now in a mortal conflict; that we are now in a war worse than any we have experienced," argued Robert Lovett, one of the report's influential authors. "It is not a cold war; it is a hot war. The only difference between this and previous wars is that death comes more slowly."

The "hot war" fears of NSC-68 seemed fulfilled on June 25, 1950, when a Communist North Korean army crossed the 38th parallel into South Korea, where American troops had once been stationed. Although Stalin approved of the invasion, the driving force behind his agreement was the North Korean revolutionary Kim Il Sung, who maneuvered Stalin into supporting reunification and ousting the American-backed conservatives who ruled the South. American policymakers instantly imposed a global, strategic template on what was essentially a regional struggle. Truman quickly won United Nations' backing for the dispatch of U.S. Army troops to South Korea. (The Soviets, who might have vetoed this U.N. action, had absented themselves from meetings of the U.N. Security Council in protest over the United Nations' failure to admit Communist-led China.) Despite early victories under General Douglas MacArthur, the invasion of Chinese troops across the Korean-Chinese border turned the war into a bloody, three-year stalemate. Korean casualties mounted to more than a million killed and wounded, and the United States lost 34,000 men before signing a July 1953 truce that left the Communists still in control of North Korea (Map 11.2).

The Korean War made it politically possible for the Truman administration to triple defense spending to nearly $50 billion a year. By 1955, the United States had hundreds of military bases in thirty-six countries. New alliance systems, such as the Southeast Asia Treaty Organization (SEATO) and the Rio Pact, kept Asian and Latin American states friendly

Cold War Illusions
The September 26, 1950, issue of *The Reporter*, an influential liberal weekly, featured an article by a Russian colonel who had defected to the United States in 1949. Kyril Kalinov's "How Russia Built the North Korean Army" was presented as proof of Soviet treachery. Kalinov, however, did not exist; the article was written by a Central Intelligence Agency operative. *The Reporter*, September 26, 1950 — American Social History Project.

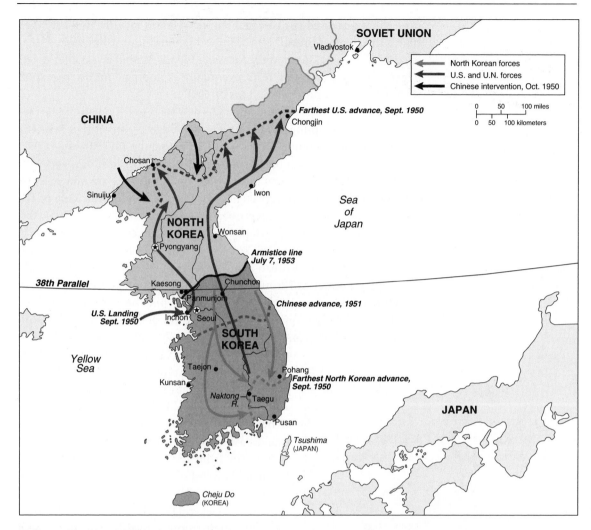

MAP 11.2   The Korean War, 1950–1953

In an effort to reunify the peninsula, North Koreans invaded South Korea. With United Nations approval, the United States sent troops and forced the North Koreans back, but the conflict ended in a stalemate. U.S. military troops remained stationed along the Korean border for fifty years.

to the United States through a combination of diplomacy, foreign aid, and covert manipulation of their newspapers, politicians, and trade unions. In Korea, Spain, and the Philippines, the mere presence of large U.S. military bases bolstered authoritarian governments. But clandestine operations, often orchestrated by the newly formed Central Intelligence Agency, sometimes supported pro-U.S. military coups d'états. In Iran (1953) and Guatemala (1954) and later in Brazil (1964) and Chile (1973), the CIA cooperated closely with right-wing military officers in removing popularly elected liberal or leftist leaders that threatened U.S. business interests. U.S. troops also intervened directly in Vietnam, the Congo, and the Dominican Republic.

The New Deal Under Attack

Although the Great Depression had discredited business leaders, the successful wartime production effort seemed to prove that American capitalism worked and that in government and outside it, corporate managers should once again be trusted public figures. As H. W. Prentis, a prominent spokesman for the National Association of Manufacturers, asserted during the war, "it is not government that has wrought the miracle that is being accomplished today in the production of war materials but the initiative, ingenuity and organizing genius of private enterprise." Business leaders knew that they might have to pay higher wages to organized workers, but they rejected the idea of democratic power sharing in shops and offices. Industrial unions, executives complained, deprived them of the power to assign work as they saw fit, to fire unsuitable employees, and to speed up production. A larger conservative effort to dismantle the Roosevelt electoral coalition accompanied this corporate counterattack against labor. Together, they sought to repulse the Truman administration's efforts to advance New Deal style legislation, including more public housing and a system of national health insurance. Southern Democrats became increasingly reactionary at the same time that Republicans discovered the usefulness of anti-Communism as an issue they could use to discredit New Deal liberals and trade union officials. In the 1950s, President Dwight D. Eisenhower's "Modern Republicanism" marginalized the most virulent forms of anti-Communism and, for a time, created the appearance of an accord between labor and management.

Capitalism Regains the Initiative   In their postwar campaign to regain "the right to manage," employers enlisted the state as an ally. By 1947, more than seventy antilabor bills had been introduced in the House of Representatives. Companies in construction, transport, and retail sales wanted to outlaw the secondary boycott, which the Teamsters and Longshoremen used to pressure antiunion employers whose goods they handled. Employers in the South and West simply wanted to stop the spread of unionism, and Republicans especially feared the CIO, whose Political Action Committee had helped to ensure Roosevelt's reelection in 1944. Finally, conservatives and some liberals wanted to force the Communists out of the union movement. The Republican-dominated Congress that took power in 1947 lent a sympathetic ear to such antiunion interests; by June, a coalition of Republicans and southern Democrats had achieved a landmark revision of the New Deal labor law by overriding Truman's veto of the Taft-Hartley Act.

The Taft-Hartley Act, named for its two principal sponsors, Fred Hartley of New Jersey and the GOP stalwart, Senator Robert Taft of Ohio, signaled a major shift in the tenor of class relations in the United States. The new law deprived foremen of the protection that the Wagner Act afforded workers, made sympathy strikes and boycotts more difficult to carry out, and allowed states (in practice, those in the South and mountain West with weak union movements) to ban the union shop. The act also legalized employer "free speech" during union organizing campaigns, which gave managers a greater opportunity to intimidate workers before a National Labor Relations Board (NLRB) election. And it gave the federal government considerable veto power over union politics and strikes. Labor leaders had to declare themselves to be non-Communist if they wanted their unions to participate in NLRB elections. And if they headed large unions, they had to bargain knowing that the president could postpone for eighty days any strike that was deemed a "national emergency"—a power that Truman used thirty-seven

Don't Go Daft with Taft
Ohio Republican Senator Robert Taft, cosponsor of the Taft-Hartley Act, is confronted by trade union demonstrators in Seattle, Washington, in August 1947. Corbis/Bettmann-UPI.

"You Couldn't Have Elections": Leon Sverdlove on the Taft-Hartley Act

Although many union members, like Leon Sverdlove of the Jewelry Workers union in New York, resented having to divulge their political views, they accepted the Taft-Hartley Act's requirement that labor leaders declare themselves to be non-Communist if they wanted to participate in NLRB supervised elections. As Sverdlove found, however, even accepting the act's dictates did not protect unions and their members from accusations of Communism, and many union leaders and workers suspected of being Communist sympathizers were forced out of organized labor.

SVERDLOVE: If you didn't sign the Taft-Hartley Act, you couldn't have elections, you couldn't present grievances against the employer for unfair labor practices. And a lot of unions, with people like myself, who felt the way we did, were heroic about it. "We'll never sign. Why should we have to? Asking us our politics under the American constitution . . ." It all sounded good, but it wasn't for real; it just wasn't for real. So, if we don't sign, we're going to leave ourselves wide open to charges by the International that we're not protecting the interests of the members of the union, which would be very true. And it would make us subject to charges and possible expulsion and then what? So we'd have a group, a few of us left-thinking, progressive-thinking people who would be bounced out, after all the years of work. . . . And then what? And that's exactly what happened to so many left-wing unions. It's as if somebody had just a few firecrackers to shoot off, and he shot 'em off before the Fourth of July, and on the Fourth of July he had nothing. That's the way we felt about it. So we signed the Taft-Hartley Act, you know, we signed whatever the document was to be signed that could resort to the Labor Board. How could you exist? We would say, "How can we get along without the Labor Board?" You just couldn't do it.

We made the turn, and we became, what shall I say—more moderate. But that didn't prevent us from continuing to sponsor, to participate in anything that was progressive. I would say that the connection that was severed was one of a specific left-wing policy sponsored by the Communists at that time. That's what we broke with. I'm not ready to dump that whole period, and flush it down the drain. I don't think so. For me, it was a real developmental thing and I have to admit, depending on what you want to call it, any education that I had, was during the course of the years that I spent in the left-wing movement, closely associated and related to the Communist Party. There's no question about it, that whatever inherent abilities I might have had were sharpened and developed in that period.

Debra E. Bernhardt and Rachel Bernstein, *Ordinary People, Extraordinary Lives*, New York University Press, 2000.

times in the remainder of his term. None of these restrictions made the Taft-Hartley Act the "slave labor law" unionists called it, but together they helped to deradicalize the union movement, curb interunion solidarity, and keep the movement from organizing new regions and new workers.

The Failure of Interracial Solidarity   Though the tides of public sentiment, congressional votes, and administration policy were all shifting against unions, the labor movement and its liberal allies were not without resources to mount a counterattack. The unions' postwar political strategy was two-pronged: (1) a concerted campaign to organize the South, called Operation Dixie and (2) a political comeback in 1948, based on the reform and realignment of the Democratic party.

In Operation Dixie, the CIO sought to built a counterweight to the political power of the racist landlords and reactionary employers who dominated the postwar South. During World War II, labor shortages and government wage guidelines pushed wages upward more rapidly in the South than in any other region, and the unions had organized more than 800,000 southern workers, one-third of them black. In the Deep South, black veterans, many in uniform, marched boldly into rural courthouses to demand the right to register and vote. Such patriotic, labor-based civil rights initiatives helped to double African American voting registration during the 1940s. Starting in 1946, northern unions, especially those in the CIO, hired hundreds of organizers, opened scores of offices, and began vigorous organizing campaigns in textiles, lumber, tobacco processing, and other southern industries. "When Georgia is organized," predicted a leader of the union drive, "you will find our old friend Gene Talmadge [the conservative governor of Georgia] trying to break into the doors of the CIO conventions and tell our people that he has always been misunderstood."

But Operation Dixie failed. Resistance from the political and industrial leadership of the white South proved overwhelming: during the next few years, the proportion of unionized southern workers actually declined. City officials, churches, and police bitterly opposed "outside" organizers in the employer-dominated textile towns and lumber mill villages across the South. And although black workers proved exceptionally union-conscious, many southern whites rejected interracial solidarity. Union organizers found that "mixed" meetings could be held only outdoors, that interracial handshakes were taboo, and that African American participation had to be downplayed. Facing physical intimidation from vigilantes and lawmen alike, Operation Dixie organizers were often beaten and run out of town. Organizing the South in the late 1940s would have required a massive interracial campaign by a militant CIO leadership that enjoyed backing in the northern Democratic Party and throughout the labor movement. But President Truman was ambivalent, and labor's ranks were increasingly divided over the role of Communists and other radicals.

The 1948 Election The failure of Operation Dixie meant that unions would not transform southern politics. But labor leaders still hoped to "realign" the American political system, either by building the power of labor, small farmers, and African Americans within the Democratic party (and thereby pushing most of the conservatives into the GOP) or by creating an entirely new third party based on a liberal-labor coalition. Until the spring of 1948, most union leaders therefore opposed Harry Truman as the Democratic presidential candidate. Many, including more than half of all CIO officials, expressed interest in forming a third party.

In 1948, the Communists, supported by a slice of the old New Deal coalition, formed a new Progressive Party, nominating former vice president Henry Wallace for president. Wallace's vision of an expanded New Deal, of racial egalitarianism, and of peaceful coexistence with the Soviet Union differed sharply from the outlook of policymakers in the

'Jim Crow Must Go'

WALLACE SHOWS IT CAN BE DONE

HENRY WALLACE

Wins Battle Against Segregation

See story on page 3

Picture and caption courtesy Pittsburgh Courier

KKK "SCARE" FAILED! — Crowds gathered to hear former Vice President Henry Wallace speak to non-segregated audiences in the deep South. This definitely mixed audience reflects the keen feeling and interest aroused by Mr. Wallace's words. In Atlanta, despite KKK threats, never in the city's history did so many white photographers and writers seek entry to an affair at a Negro institution. The rally was held in the Wheat Street Baptist Church. Above, the New Orleans' audience was typical of the mixed crowds which came from far and near to hear Wallace.

The Wallace Campaign

A Progressive Party flyer promotes integration in the Deep South. Tamiment Institute Library, New York University.

Truman administration: late in 1946, Truman dismissed Wallace as secretary of commerce after he made a speech critical of the administration's tough line toward the Soviets.

But rather than realigning American politics, the Wallace effort put an end to political experimentation and wed labor even more closely to the Democrats. Anti-Communist liberals, including Eleanor Roosevelt and Walter Reuther, denounced Wallace as politically naive, called for the elimination of Communist influence in all liberal and labor organizations, and supported Truman's tough stance toward the Soviet Union. The CIO and the AFL rejected the Progressive Party and endorsed Harry Truman's candidacy.

In the 1948 election, most observers assumed that voters would put Republican Thomas Dewey, the financially well-connected governor of New York, into the White House. But Truman surprised everyone. A Missouri politician with traditional racial attitudes, Truman knew that his reelection would hinge, in the words of his adviser Clark Clifford, on winning the support of "labor and the urban minorities." His administration therefore shifted leftward. Fearful that Wallace's Progressive Party would appeal to liberal Democrats in the North, Truman made civil rights a major presidential priority for the first time in seventy-five years. He called on Congress to pass a new Fair Employment Practices Act that would end job discrimination, and in July 1948, Truman signed an executive order that desegregated the armed forces. He thereby capitulated to the antidiscrimination protest campaign led by the African American union leader, A. Philip Randolph. Truman pushed for national health insurance and a big public housing program and promised to work with a new Democratic Congress to repeal the Taft-Hartley Act. Denouncing "Wall Street Republicans" on a frenetic whistle-stop campaign across the country, he thwarted Wallace and Dewey by galvanizing midwestern farmers and urban workers who had been part of the old Roosevelt coalition. When Truman won in November, he excitedly told the press, "Labor did it!"

Truman's victory in 1948 put the Democrats back in control of Congress, but conservatives retained a working majority there. Many Southern Democrats, who mounted their own "States' Rights" presidential campaign in 1948, with Strom Thurmond of South Carolina heading the ticket, no longer saw the Democratic Party as a reliable bulwark of white supremacy. Over the next third of a century, they would abandon their old party and shift to either the Republicans or an even more conservative third party. When Truman sought to pass his liberal "Fair Deal" legislative program, a coalition of Republicans and Southern "Dixiecrats" blocked his initiatives at every turn. Congress did pass a National Housing Act in 1949, but it led primarily to the building of low-cost urban housing projects, which soon turned into slums.

The drive toward civil rights stalled as well. After Truman partisans marginalized the Progressive Party, most Democratic leaders sought to regain the loyalty of the white South. Truman's commitment to black equality flagged during his second term, and in 1952, the Democratic presidential nominee, Adlai Stevenson, downplayed civil rights even further, choosing for his running mate an Alabama senator who stood for the maintenance of the status quo. Southern politicians and business leaders soon mobilized against the extension of federal power, the spread of unions, and the push for civil rights. The growth in African American voting strength came to a halt in the early 1950s. Thereafter, xenophobic anti-Communism and outright appeals to racism increasingly characterized southern election campaigns. "Northern political labor leaders have recently ordered that all doors be opened to Negroes on union property," declared one election flyer.

"This will lead to whites and Negroes working and living together. . . . Do you want that?"

The Weapon of Anti-Communism   America's encounter with the specter of domestic Communism proved a crucial contribution to the political stalemate and cultural conservatism of the early postwar years. Scores of Americans, perhaps as many as 300, did indeed provide information to Soviet agents, largely during the era of the Popular Front and World War II, when the politics of a fervent antifascism generated an apparent common bond among liberals, Communists, and the Soviet Union. Some of the people who provided information held high office, including Harry Dexter White, an assistant secretary of the Treasury, and Alger Hiss, a State Department official who participated in the Yalta conference with Roosevelt. But the actions of a few motivated post–World War II anti-Communism far less than a pervasive antiradicalism that now merged with a postwar hostility to the New Deal and its partisans.

Anti-Communism was both a partisan strategy that was exploited by top politicians and a popular grassroots movement. In 1947, fearing that he might be outflanked on "internal security" issues by the Republicans, Truman boosted funding for the FBI, set up a loyalty program for federal employees, and asked the attorney general to draw up a list of subversive organizations. And between 1945 and 1952, congressional committees conducted eighty-four hearings on Communist subversion, and the House Committee on Un-American Activities (HUAC) held the most infamous to investigate Hollywood, higher education, unions, and the federal government. In the well-publicized HUAC hearings, investigators demanded that witnesses not only affirm their loyalty to the government but also prove it by naming former Communist associates. "Don't present me with the choice of either being in contempt of this committee and going to jail," pleaded the Hollywood actor Larry Parks, "or forcing me to really crawl through the mud to be an informer." Though Parks did name his former left-wing friends and associates, his career, like those of many others, was ruined when film studios and other large employers blacklisted suspect employees. By one estimate, 13.5 million Americans fell within the scope of various federal, state, and private loyalty programs. Roughly one of every five working people had to take an oath or receive a security clearance as a condition of employment.

The most relentless interrogator, Republican senator Joseph McCarthy of Wisconsin, cast himself as the ultimate patriot, directing his inquisitorial skills against "respectable" targets in the State Department, Ivy League universities, and the U.S. Army. McCarthy achieved national stature early in 1950 by exploiting public frustration over the "loss" of China and the

"Asking for No Favors": Anna Gordon Speaks for Working Mothers

In testimony to a U.S. Senate subcommittee in 1953, Mrs. Anna Gordon, an officer in the U.S. Navy Women's Reserves, argued for women's right to combine motherhood and careers, a point of view that had seemed viable during the war years but changed soon afterward. Along with the integration of African Americans in the military, the Women's Armed Services Integration Act of 1948 had established a permanent presence for women in all branches of the armed forces. In October 1949 an Army regulation required the discharge of female servicewomen who had children under the age of eighteen.

Statement of Mrs. Anna Gordon, East Orange, N.J.

First of all, it would seem to me that forcing the resignation of women with minor children is in this day and age an anachronism.

The choice between marriage or a career or children or a career is no longer a problem. A woman who has spent years in preparation for a career and has a living interest in what she is doing does not nowadays give it up with a sigh of resignation when she is preparing for the role of motherhood; nor does she usually give up thoughts of motherhood for a career; the modern woman finds that both are compatible, except for a temporary withdrawal from professional life—and I think we have heard how temporary sometimes that may be. . . .

In this day and age homemaking hardly takes up all of a woman's time and many a mother who is not forced to work because of economic pressure still does much more than a routine job even if at considerable inconvenience to herself, rather than retire. . . .

Can the services afford to discard these women? They are asking for no favors, merely for the opportunity to remain available if needed. In the event of an emergency, would these women be content to stay at home and await the return of the children from school, do you suppose, when they are not even spending their days in this fashion when there is no emergency? And I hardly think that these women are not representative of others all over the country.

Appointment or Retention of Certain Female Reserve Personnel with Minor Children, Hearings before a Subcommittee of the Committee on Armed Services, United States Senate, 83rd Congress, 1st Session, on S. 1492, May 14 and 15, 1953 (Washington, DC: U.S. Government Printing Office, 1953).

consolidation of Soviet power in Eastern Europe. To McCarthy and his followers, these events represented more than just diplomatic setbacks. At one point, McCarthy claimed to have a list of 205 Communists employed in the State Department. In his eyes, Secretary of State Dean Acheson was the "Red Dean . . . Russian as to heart, British as to manner"; the years of Roosevelt and Truman he called "twenty years of treason." Using his chairmanship of a minor Senate subcommittee to launch wide-ranging and often crudely partisan investigations, McCarthy charged that Communist sympathizers in the highest reaches of government shielded Soviet spies. Although such charges were nonsense, McCarthy's manipulation of the press and the

"White People Wake Up"

Conservatives played on southern whites' racist fears in battling postwar efforts to end Jim Crow and unionize workers. Propaganda such as this 1950 North Carolina election flyer for the Willis Smith campaign helped to defeat southern liberals such as Frank Graham, a former member of President Harry Truman's Civil Rights Commission.

WHITE PEOPLE
WAKE UP
Before it's too late
You may not have another chance

DO YOU WANT?

NEGROES	working beside you, your wife and daughters in your mills and factories?
NEGROES	eating beside you in public eating places?
NEGROES	riding beside you, your wife and your daughters in buses, cabs, and trains?
NEGROES	sleeping in the same hotels and rooming houses?
NEGROES	teaching and disciplining your children in school?
NEGROES	sitting with you and your family at all public meetings?
NEGROES	going to white schools and white children going to Negro schools?
NEGROES	to occupy the same hospital rooms with you and your wife and daughters?
NEGROES	as your foremen and overseers in the mills?
NEGROES	using your toilet facilities?

Northern political labor leaders have recently ordered that all doors be opened to Negroes on union property. This will lead to whites and Negroes working and living together in the South as they do in the North. So you want that?

FRANK GRAHAM FAVORS MINGLING OF THE RACES

He admits that he favors mixing Negroes and whites—he says so in the report he signed (For proof of this read page 167, Civil Rights Report)

DO YOU FAVOR THIS—WANT SOME MORE OF IT?
IF YOU DO, VOTE FOR FRANK GRAHAM
But if you don't
VOTE FOR AND HELP ELECT
WILLIS SMITH FOR SENATOR

He will uphold the traditions of the South

****

Know the truth committee

Samuel Lubell, *The Future of American Politics* (1951).

The Enemy Within

Hollywood producers, cowed by the House Committee on Un-American Activities' witch-hunts, strove to prove their loyalty. *The Red Menace* (1949) was but one of a flurry of films that melodramatically "exposed" a gangsterlike network of Communists subverting America. Audiences, however, seemed to prefer science fiction fantasies that portrayed malevolent intergalactic creatures infiltrating American society, such as the 1953 film *Invaders from Mars*. Michael Barson Collection.

new medium of television (which broadcast many of the hearings) proved so masterful that he became one of the most feared political figures of the early 1950s.

Liberals, non-Communist radicals, labor activists, and others who questioned the direction of postwar society were often the real target of anti-Communist probes. As the head of one government loyalty board noted, "The fact that a person believes in racial equality doesn't prove he's a Communist, but it certainly makes you look twice, doesn't it?" Many businessmen found Communist subversion to be a convenient explanation for labor conflict. "Whoever stirs up needless strife in American trade unions advances the cause of Communism," asserted the *Nation's Business* late in 1946. Such employers worked closely with congressional investigators and state officials, who were happy to "Red-bait" union officials when a strike or NLRB certification election was imminent. Nongovernmental groups such as the American Legion, with 17,000 posts, also played a powerful role in the anti-Communist movement. Feature articles in the Legion's magazine asked such questions as "Does Your Movie Money Go to Commies?" and "Do Colleges Have to Hire Red Professors?"

Not surprisingly, anti-Communism polarized the labor movement. In the 1930s and 1940s, Communists and other radicals played an indispensable role in building the new unions; now anti-Communists accused them of "infiltrating" these organizations. Ironically, the Communists had been among the most zealous patriots of World War II. But after the war, this resurgent nationalism turned against the Communists. Millions of workers were still first- or second-generation immigrants, whose sense of "Americanism" had only re-cently been affirmed by the patriotism that surged through their communities during the New Deal and the wartime years.

Although many immigrants had once sought to combine socialist politics with patriotic Americanism, the Cold War forced them to choose. To be a radical, let alone a Communist, seemed now to be un-American.

Religious, ethnic, and racial loyalties often determined the ways in which working Americans responded to the anti-Communist impulse. Catholics, especially those of Irish or Eastern European extraction, who had themselves been the subject of nativist prejudice in the 1920s, were among the most ardent anti-Communists. The Red Army's occupation of Eastern Europe had an

Are You Now or Have You Ever Been a Member of the Communist Party?

Autoworker Basil Gordon kneels on the sidewalk outside a Los Angeles Chrysler Corporation plant in July 1950 after receiving a beating from fellow workers. Gordon and two other workers were attacked when they refused to say whether they belonged to the Communist Party. AP/Wide World Photos.

electrifying impact on millions of Americans of Slavic and Hungarian origin, who constituted perhaps half of the CIO's membership. When the Soviets arrested Church leaders in Poland, the Catholic Church in America mobilized tens of thousands of adherents to protest the "Satan-inspired Communist crimes." Priests from working-class parishes played an aggressive part in the effort to oust Communists from the leadership of unions such as the United Electrical Workers.

In contrast, relatively few African Americans joined in the anti-Communist crusade. Their lack of enthusiasm reflected the Communist Party's long commitment to civil rights and its active recruitment of black workers as members. But more important, the discrimination that African Americans endured made them skeptical of white efforts to define "Americanism." Coleman Young, who would later become the first African American mayor of Detroit, denounced a congressional investigating committee that questioned his loyalty:

> I fought in the last war and . . . I am now in process of fighting against what I consider to be attacks and discrimination against my people. I am fighting against un-American activities such as lynchings and denial of the vote. I am dedicated to that fight, and I don't have to apologize or explain it to anybody.

McCarthyism divided American Jews more sharply than any of the nation's other ethnic groups. By the late 1940s, anti-Semitism had begun to wane in the United States, and prospects for assimilation seemed good. Therefore, second- and third-generation Jewish Americans entered the middle class more rapidly than any other ethnic group. Yet American Jews, who had been solid Roosevelt partisans, were often victims of the anti-Communist impulse. In New York City, 90 percent of all teachers who were fired by the Board of Education were Jewish; in Detroit and Flint, Michigan, Communists who were "run out" of the auto plants were often taunted with anti-Semitic epithets.

A notorious espionage case accentuated Jewish fear of renewed anti-Semitism. In 1950, the U.S. government tried and convicted Julius and Ethel Rosenberg, both active Communists and the children of Jewish immigrants, for conspiracy to commit espionage and delivering atomic secrets to the Soviet Union. In June 1953, they were executed. Julius clearly had given the Soviets information provided to him by his brother-in-law, a machinist at the Los Alamos weapons laboratory, but little evidence implicated Ethel. They were the first American citizens ever to be executed for treason in time of peace, and their deaths frightened Jewish progressives, causing many to abandon their longtime participation in radical causes.

Eisenhower's "Modern Republicanism"   McCarthyism's hold on American politics lost some of its power once the Republicans regained control of the White House and both houses of Congress in the 1952 elections. For Republicans like the new president, Dwight D. Eisenhower, Joseph McCarthy's strident brand of anti-Communism paid few political dividends; meanwhile, the death of Joseph Stalin in March 1953, followed three months later by armistice in the Korean War, eased Cold War tensions and national anxieties. McCarthy still made headlines, but he became an object of growing criticism. In November 1954, the U.S. Senate voted to censure him. Thereafter he quickly lost influence, though the political and ideological constraints imposed by the anti-Communist impulse did not fully ebb until well into the 1960s.

Eisenhower called himself a "modern Republican"; he ran for president in 1952 as an internationalist who was determined to keep the right wing of his party in check. Born in Abilene, Kansas, in 1890, Eisenhower had made the Army his career, rising through the ranks as the consummate planner and military diplomat. During World War II, he used these skills to organize the Normandy landings on D-Day and to coordinate the Anglo-American push into Germany.

Known to the public as "Ike," Eisenhower and his vice presidential candidate, Richard Nixon, won 55 percent of the popular vote. An admirer of businessmen, Eisenhower put eight millionaires in his first cabinet. He pushed for private development of offshore oil and hydroelectric power, which the old New Dealers wanted to keep in federal hands. And he favored balanced budgets, even when the two recessions that took place during his administration cut federal income and generated high levels of unemployment. The corporate spirit of his administration became apparent early in 1953 when a Democratic congressman asked Eisenhower's nominee for secretary of defense, Charles E. Wilson, the former head of General Motors, whether he foresaw a conflict between his new governmental responsibilities and his old employer. Wilson confidently, and controversially, responded, "What is good for our country is good for General Motors, and vice versa."

Eisenhower was hardly a reactionary. Although most of the leading figures in his administration had fought New Deal labor and social welfare reforms, once in power they did little to undermine them. Indeed, the Eisenhower administration locked the New Deal in place, creating a new cabinet office (Health, Education, and Welfare), raising the minimum wage, and broadening Social Security coverage. After the Soviet Union launched the first earth-orbiting satellite, Sputnik, in 1957, Eisenhower endorsed the liberal view that federal funds should be used to improve American education in science, technology, and languages. Eisenhower had no enthusiasm for school integration, but neither did he pander to white racism in the South. Indeed, African Americans gave him more of their votes in 1956 than any Republican presidential candidate had received in twenty years.

On international policy, Eisenhower and his secretary of state, John Foster Dulles, were Cold Warriors who believed the Communist bloc an implacable foe of Western civilization. But as fiscal conservatives who feared high taxes and an intrusive "garrison" state, they also sought to limit the size of the military. Eisenhower and Dulles therefore relied on relatively inexpensive nuclear weapons and a worldwide aerospace delivery system. Dulles, a master of provocative speech and imagery, condemned the Truman era's containment doctrine as "appeasement" and instead declared that the United States would employ "massive retaliation" to protect Free World interests. Critics called Dulles's policy nuclear "brinksmanship" because it involved repeatedly taking the nation to the verge of war. But nuclear brinkmanship proved virtually useless in the real world. When Vietnamese nationalists came close to defeating the French in May 1954, Eisenhower refused to order a nuclear air strike to stop them. When Hungarians revolted against Communist rule two years later, the United States failed to intervene, fearing a larger confrontation with the Soviets. By the time he left office in 1961, Eisenhower himself criticized what he called the "military-industrial complex" and advocated vigorous U.S. diplomacy as a means of reducing Cold War tensions.

Progress of Science in the U.S.A.

A cartoon in the *Baltimore Sun* captured the consternation in the United States that greeted news of the Soviet Union's successful launch of Sputnik I in October 1957. The first artificial satellite to orbit the earth undermined widespread assumptions about U.S. technological superiority and sparked anxiety that the Soviet Union would win the "space race." The cartoon also chastised the government for postwar policies that inhibited scientific research. Richard Q. Yardley, *Baltimore Sun*, October 18, 1957 — Baltimore Sun.

The Affluent Society and Its Discontents

From 1947 until the early 1970s, the United States enjoyed an unprecedented era of sustained economic growth. Even with five short recessions, real wages and the overall production of goods and services doubled, while unemployment and inflation remained low. This newfound material affluence deeply affected Americans on the job and at home, reshaping the way they thought about themselves and their society. In the 1930s, many New Deal theorists assumed that the U.S. economy was permanently crippled. Its strength, they believed, could be restored only by breaking up big corporations and redistributing wealth and income. But the postwar boom made that political agenda irrelevant. It eased class and ethnic tensions and seemed to create a kind of truce between capital and labor that limited the appeal of unionism and fostered a workforce that identified with the middle class. Inequalities of race, gender, and skill remained stark. In the 1950s, segregation by race remained pervasive; employers assigned women, white and black, to clerical or domestic tasks; and only those with a college degree could obtain many of the better jobs. Despite these problems, one working-class youth likened the new prosperity to "a teenager's first kiss. Not much, but never to be forgotten."

The Postwar Economic Boom Postwar affluence was no accident; it arose out of New Deal politics, the experience of World War II, and America's new role in the world. From World War II, many Americans learned the great lesson that federal money and political will power could vanquish unemployment. Congress passed the Employment Act of 1946, which committed the federal government to promote "maximum employment, production, and purchasing power" and set up a Council of Economic Advisers that was charged with developing "national economic policies." During the next quarter-century, government fiscal policymakers based their work largely on theories developed by the British economist John Maynard Keynes. Keynes argued that in modern capitalist societies, governments could combat business slumps by using its power to tax and spend in order to regulate consumer demand for goods and services. Liberals wanted to sustain consumer purchasing power through government spending on public works, schools, housing, Social Security, and unemployment insurance. Conservatives, who feared such programs would erode market incentives and open the door to government planning, favored tax reductions for business instead. Throughout the 1950s, liberals and conservatives fought to a standoff on these issues. Though business taxes remained at the high levels established during World War II, government spending on social programs grew slowly.

Two new forces dominated the nation's economy in this era: a strong union movement and an enormous peacetime military establishment (Figure 11.1). Though the Taft-Hartley Act (1947) and the failure of Operation Dixie signaled the end of labor's expansive phase, large unions still negotiated higher wages and pushed for increased government spending. The labor movement enrolled more workers than at any other time in U.S. history, reaching a high point of nearly 35 percent of the labor force in 1953. Sophisticated corporate executives realized that disruptive strikes and

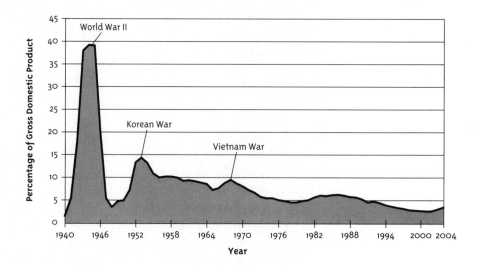

FIGURE 11.1 **The Military-Industrial Complex: Defense Spending as a Percentage of U.S. Output, 1940–2004**

Military spending has been central to the American economy in the post–World War II era. After the end of the war, defense spending as a percentage of the entire economy defined as gross domestic product dropped sharply. But the Cold War — and the hot wars of Korea and Vietnam — pushed it much higher. It gradually dropped as the United States became less actively engaged in Vietnam; a further decline came with the end of the Cold War.

contentious wage negotiations—especially if they were part of a broad offensive against corporate power—would embitter relations on the shop floor and hamper the company's long-range planning. In 1948, therefore, General Motors offered the UAW a contract that included two pillars of the postwar accord: an automatic Cost of Living Adjustment (COLA) clause keyed to the consumer price index and an unconditional 2 percent "annual improvement factor," designed to give workers a share of GM's substantial productivity gains. The GM idea soon spread, and by the end of the 1950s, more than 50 percent of all major union contracts included the COLA principle. Nonunion firms such as IBM and DuPont, anxious to keep unions out, copied the pattern, paying top wages, matching union benefits, and establishing employee grievance systems.

The second pillar of the postwar boom was military spending. By 1950, about half of the federal budget, or more than 10 percent of all goods and services consumed in the United States, went to the armed services. Because of the Cold War, most citizens accepted massive government spending for the military. Arms production helped to fuel the growth of key sectors of the economy, such as aircraft manufacturing and electronics. It fostered economic growth and urbanization in the South, where the military built many new bases, and in southern California, Seattle, and Long Island, where the growing aviation industry contributed to a vibrant postwar sprawl (Map 11.3). The political consensus on military spending allowed the federal government to fund social programs that otherwise would have been controversial. Educational, medical, housing, and pension benefits for veterans grew rapidly, and in 1956, Congress voted to fund a multiyear, multibillion-dollar Interstate and Defense Highway Program, the largest public works project in the nation's history.

MAP 11.3   The Military-Industrial Complex in Los Angeles

During the Cold War, massive military spending helped to expand the economy and the population of Southern California. In the 1960s, approximately one in seven Americans owed their jobs to the military-industrial complex.

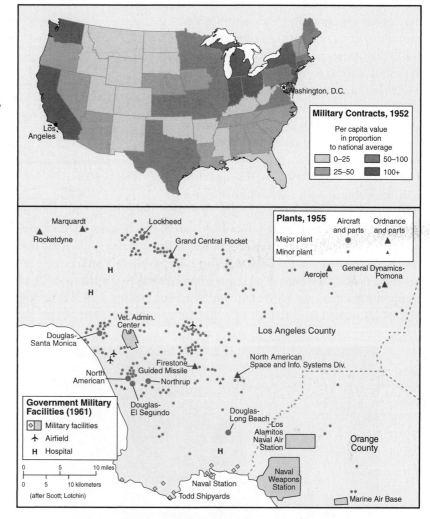

The nation's prosperity put real money into the average citizen's pocket. Between 1941 and 1969, family income almost doubled. Because Americans felt more secure economically, they went ahead with marriages and pregnancies they had postponed during the Depression and World War II. The birthrate leaped by 25 percent after 1945 and remained high throughout the 1950s. "It seems to me," wrote a British visitor in 1958, "that every other young housewife I see is pregnant." Americans ate better, lived in more spacious homes, and could afford to see the doctor more often. During the full employment 1940s, the life expectancy of white Americans rose from sixty-three years to sixty-seven years, while that of African Americans increased from fifty-three to sixty-one (Figure 11.2).

The whole system seemed a never-ending spiral of growth and abundance, prompting contemporary observers to conclude that American capitalism had found the solution to all economic problems. "The world revolution of our times is 'Made in the USA,'" wrote the business consultant Peter Drucker in 1949. "The true revolutionary principle is the idea of mass production."

The Service Economy In the quarter-century after the war, corporations added staff, governments hired more teachers and policemen, and unions upgraded many jobs that had once been casual or low paid, such as telephone repair, warehousing, and seafaring. For the first time in U.S. history, white-collar workers outnumbered blue-collar workers. Workers who sat behind a desk, stood behind a counter, or presided over a classroom had composed less than one-third of the workforce in 1940 but swelled to almost half of all those employed by 1970. In the two decades after 1950, the

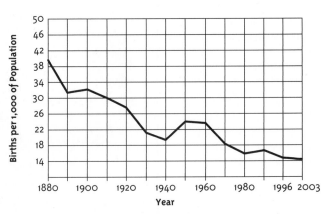

FIGURE 11.2 Baby Booms and Busts: The U.S. Birthrate, 1880–2003
The birthrate had been declining in the United States for more than a century. The one exception was the post–World War II "baby boom." In the 1950s, families grew larger, and the American rate of population growth approached that of India.

The Last of the Red Cars
The federal highway program shifted resources away from public transportation and toward the construction of a massive interstate highway system. Dating back to the start of the twentieth century, Southern California's Pacific Electric Railway, known as the Red Car system, used streetcars, light rail, and buses to carry passengers throughout the greater Los Angeles metropolitan area. But plans to modernize the Red Cars were overwhelmed by automobile lobbyists and public officials who envisioned a web of freeways throughout the region. Federal subsidies for the highway system tolled the death knell for the Red Car, which ceased operation in 1961. While most of the old cars were consigned to the scrap yard on the city's Terminal Island, as shown here, some of them were shipped overseas for use in other countries' public transportation systems. Electric Railway Historical Society.

"If You Had a Fast Car . . . You Were a Big Man"

Interviewed in the late 1970s, Ed Schafer and Boyd Pennington of St. Louis recalled their teenage passion for "hot rods." In the 1950s, tens of thousands of Americans, most of them white working-class men, transformed the standardized consumer automobiles coming out of Detroit into personalized masterpieces.

Ed Schafer: I had my first car when I was 14 in 1953. I was the only guy in the 8th grade that drove to school. I lived in the country and drove to school on the back roads. I had a 1940 Chevrolet that you had to tie the doors shut, but I could tear the engine down and put it back together. I bought it for $25, a piece of junk, but it ran and I could keep it running. . . . You had to have fender skirts and you had to have the rear end of the car dropped almost to the axle. . . . I think what we tried to do was make it as different as possible to what Detroit put out and it was neat to watch Detroit follow us; decking, cleaning the chrome and the ornaments off, lowering the silhouette, lowering the entire car.

Boyd Pennington: If two guys had exactly the same color car within two days somebody had something different. There was quite a lot of rivalry between cars even though they were old cars, of course some of it was show; terrycloth seat covers and mud flaps.

Ed Schafer: Our interest was stimulated by California, by the news we got from there and by the movies and songs that were prevalent then.

Boyd Pennington: The West Coast always led. You could travel out to California and it would take a year for that trend to move to the Midwest. In the early 1950s there was *Honk, Hot Rod, Rod and Custom, Car and Custom,* just a whole stack of West Coast magazines. . . . There are some things I'm not too proud of. We did steal from other people; we did make regular trips into South St. Louis because it was so easy to steal fender skirts, hubcaps, tail-lights or whatever was big at the time. . . . People knew what we were doing, I mean it's hard to conceal from your parents that you have, probably four, five thousand dollars of equipment in your garage. . . .

Ed Schafer: We had a fairly large group of people, 15, 16 guys, and the camaraderie was unbelievable. There was no way one guy would rat on another. . . . Your importance in the club increased by your performance on the dragstrip. It didn't matter if you were a nerd; if you had a fast car and could make it down a quarter mile faster than anyone else, you were a big man.

George Lipsitz, "They Knew Who We Were: Drag Racing and Customizing," *Cultural Correspondence* (Summer–Fall 1977).

growing demand for consumer goods spurred the creation of new department stores and supermarkets, staffed by three million additional employees. And in almost every large corporation, thousands of managers and supervisors manipulated paper, people, and products. The sociologist C. Wright Mills captured the new world of work in his influential study *White Collar* (1951): "What must be grasped is the picture of society as a great salesroom, an enormous file, an incorporated brain, a new universe of management and manipulation."

The growth of the service industry reinforced the popular, but misleading, notion that the United States had become a classless, "postindustrial" society. Despite the deployment of much highly touted automated machinery, factory work still required an army of manual workers. Although blue-collar employment declined steadily as a proportion of the workforce, to 35 percent by 1970, manufacturing workers actually increased in number from twenty-two million to twenty-six million between 1950 and 1970. Moreover, half of all service jobs involved manual labor — trash collection, maintenance, and food preparation, for example. The greatest growth in so-called white-collar employment came in sales and clerical work — jobs that might be considered white-collar, in the sense that a typist did not spot-weld body joints, but that involved little creativity or autonomy. "My job doesn't have prestige," bank teller Nancy Rogers noted. "It's a service job. Whether you're a waitress, salesperson, anything like that . . . you are there to serve them. They are not there to serve you."

The postwar shift to service and clerical work would have been impossible without the influx of twenty million women into the workforce. In 1950, a total of 31 percent of all women were employed outside the home; twenty years later, the figure was 42 percent. Unlike the war years, the postwar job market confined women to a female labor ghetto. Ninety-five percent of them worked in just four job categories: light manufacturing (home appliances and clothing), the retail trade, clerical work, and health and education. And within those categories, men took the high-status work while the routine jobs went to women. In 1960, for example, males held 90 percent of high school principal positions, while 85 percent of elementary school teachers were women (Figure 11.3).

Such job segregation helped to keep women's work low-paid and dead-end. In Baltimore, for example, employers kept women who were clerical employees on the job after World War II but forced women who worked in high-wage aircraft assembly to take lower-paying jobs as waitresses or service workers. Women's average weekly wages in that city therefore fell from $50 to $37. The same process of exclusion took place among professionals as well. Because many graduate schools discouraged women from enrolling and because World War II veterans took so many seats at the nation's

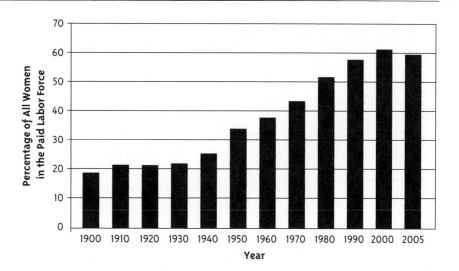

FIGURE 11.3 Women in the Workforce, 1900–2005
Since 1940, the percentage of women employed outside the home has more than doubled. In 2005, there were 69.3 million women in the labor force, compared to 12.8 million in 1940. From Information Please database, www.infoplease.com/ipa/A0104673.html.

colleges and universities, there were actually fewer women doctors and lawyers in the 1950s than there had been two decades before.

The New Sexual Orthodoxy   The sexual ideology of the early postwar years relegated women to the secondary labor market. All too quickly the wartime self-confidence of "Rosie the Riveter" gave way to a rigid definition of gender roles that was reminiscent of mid-nineteenth-century social spheres. Experts celebrated women's submissiveness and domesticity, branding sexual freedom as potentially subversive, even pro-Communist. The popular media portrayed women largely as incompetent and vulnerable, fulfilled only in the context of a stable and secure marriage. By the late 1940s, women's magazines such as *Ladies' Home Journal* and *Redbook* filled their pages with articles such as "What's Wrong with American Women?" and "Isn't a Woman's Place in the Home?" Author Betty Friedan labeled all this the "feminine mystique" in her 1963 best-selling book of the same name.

The new sexual orthodoxy also applied to American men and equated masculinity with rationality and control over one's emotions. Men, too, were expected to marry. To attain maturity and respectability required being a "family man," even in late adolescence. Employers shunned men who were still single in their thirties. Homosexuality was a criminal offense that was thought to sap the moral fiber of both the individual and the nation. Indeed, the anti-Communist movement engendered a wave of homophobia,

"Women Without Men": *Look* Magazine Surveys Single Women

The 1950s saw an ideal perpetuated in books, magazines, movies, television, songs, and ads, that portrayed the white, middle-class woman who could be fulfilled only by a happy marriage. In the following article from a popular magazine of 1960, Eleanor Harris, a journalist, offered a sociological survey of the more than one-third of adult American women whose lives did not fit the domestic norm. Harris details the "frenzied" mating efforts of women who have tried, but failed, to marry, as well as the adverse psychological effects of being single.

. . . a little more than one third of the 62,827,000 women in the United States are getting along without steady male companionship. How do they adjust to this fact of life? How do they like their manless lot? What do they do about changing it? Do they want to change it?

To find the answers to these questions, I have interviewed scores of widows, divorced women, bachelor girls, men, gynecologists, psychologists, psychiatrists, managers of women's hotels, executives of women's organizations and Government statisticians.

1. Despite the assumption by many males that women cease looking for sex, men and marriage after the age of 50, the fact is that, as one gynecologist put it, "they remain interested in all these things until cremation."

2. Many unattached women of "nice" background are as much drawn to sexual relations with men as married women are, or perhaps more so; relentlessly, they go about most of their lives trying to find sexual fulfillment. . . .

Almost to a woman, those I interviewed said the same thing: "I have only one problem. I would like to be married, but I find it impossible to meet eligible men no matter how I try—and nobody can say I don't try. . . . "

In general, the married women are dissatisfied with their marriages. "The problems of the single, divorced and widowed women are more difficult," an experienced psychiatrist says. "But probably a common denominator in this group is that they feel they are not getting much out of life—not accomplishing as much as they are capable of. This holds for their jobs, studies, social activities, any area of their lives—a general dissatisfaction applies to all of them." He adds, "In the younger age group, the dominating symptom among the unmarried is likely to be anxiety; in later years, it's depression."

However depressed they may be, most of them continue the frenzied man hunt.

Eleanor Harris, "Women Without Men," *Look*, 5 July 1960, 43–46.

intensifying the persecution of male and female "perverts." When the FBI mounted an all-out effort to discover the sexual habits of those who were suspected of subversive political behavior, gay-baiting rivaled Red-baiting in its ferocity, destroying careers, encouraging harassment, and forcing those who "confessed their guilt" to name their lovers and friends.

CIVIL DEFENSE GROUPS

Men

- FIRE-FIGHTING
- RESCUE WORK
- MEDICAL TEAMS
- GEIGER CREW
- STREET CLEARING
- POLICE AUXILIARY
- AIR-RAID WARDEN
- REBUILDING

Women

- MEDICAL TEAMS
- CAR-DRIVING
- AIR-RAID WARDEN
- GEIGER CREW
- CHILD CARE
- HOSPITAL WORK
- SOCIAL WORK
- EMERGENCY FEEDING

Here are some of the civil-defense jobs open to men and women.

Holocaust or No Holocaust, A Woman's Place Is in . . .

An illustration in the widely circulated 1950 book, *How to Survive an Atomic Bomb*, designates "appropriate" civil-defense jobs for men and women. Richard Gestell, *How to Survive an Atomic Bomb* (1950) — American Social History Project.

Despite the heavy emphasis on marriage and the family, or perhaps because of it, Americans indulged an appetite for vicarious sex. The postwar era gave birth to the cosmopolitan, sexually permissive, and hugely successful *Playboy* magazine in 1953. Filled with advertisements for liquor, stereo equipment, and cars, the magazine demonstrated that lust itself was a consumer commodity that was eminently suitable to the upwardly mobile. Although *Playboy* had a predominantly male audience, publishers marketed sexuality to women, too. *Peyton Place*, the steamy story of a town in rural New England, became the best-selling novel of the century. Published in 1956, it sold ten million copies, largely to women.

These rigid gender roles made the lives of midcentury working women particularly difficult. Most American men saw cooking, cleaning, and changing the baby's diapers as "women's work." Consequently, women who did work outside the home carried the burden of housework and child rearing as well. And though American families acquired dishwashers, vacuum cleaners, and other labor-saving appliances, housework still demanded as much time as it had thirty years earlier for the average woman. According to one survey taken during the 1950s, half of all working women said that they had no leisure time at all.

Race and Ethnicity at Work Millions of other workers—perhaps as many as 40 percent—found work outside the industrial and service sectors as poorly paid farm laborers, cabdrivers, cannery workers, and dime store clerks with little job security. Such jobs are often thought of as belonging to a distinct "secondary" labor market—segregated from the more secure work in the core economy, but still essential to the functioning of the system. Although casual employment has long been part of the working-class experience in America, in the postwar era this secondary labor market, once comprising mostly manual labor, evolved to include clerical and service employment. Workers in those fields tended to come from marginal groups: racial minorities, teenagers, and women.

The flight from farming expanded the ranks of casual laborers. Mining and agriculture together supported one in four American families before the war, but consolidation and mechanization eliminated fifteen million of

"We Just Stood Up for Our Own Self"

Jim Justen grew up in Kenosha, Wisconsin, during the 1950s, a time when homosexuality was considered a criminal offense. Gays were subjected to the same hysteria and persecution that was engendered by anti-Communism and were pressured to conform to mainstream cultural and gender norms. Yet many individuals did not try to hide or suppress their sexual preferences.

I knew that I was gay, had been closeted of course in high school, but there was a small minority of gay people around us in school, and we knew who was and who wasn't. And a few tricks that we were going to bed with occasionally and that was about it in high school. In fact I had my first lover in high school. I ran with a pretty rough bunch of people, regrettably. My ex-lover used to fight golden gloves and I got my butt kicked at one time, and made up my mind I was going to learn to fight. And I spent a year learning how to fight. He taught me how to fight and defend myself. And if a problem developed it was going to be solved real fast. We just stood up for our own self and that was it. I guess we made up for the fact that we were gay by being strong enough to handle any situation that would come up.

I notified my mother and father somewhere around the time I was nineteen years old or so that I was gay. I told my mother first and she accepted it although she would rather see grandchildren on my side. My father's only attitude when I told him was, "you are the way you are and you better do one thing—accept yourself for what you are and don't try to change or you will be a screwed-up person." He did know some gay women that he worked [with], some lesbians on the railroad, he was close to and friends to. My father was a very bright shrewd person; he was my best friend as well as my father.

Interviewed by Miriam Frank, June 28, 1996. Courtesy of Miriam Frank.

these jobs in one generation. The nation's agricultural population fell from one in five to one in twenty. In Midwestern states such as Iowa and Ohio, the factories and offices of the region's cities readily absorbed rural migrants, mainly whites with some education. But in the rural South, Puerto Rico, and the Mexican borderlands, the process of depopulation was far more traumatic.

In the South, mechanization of the plowing, weeding, and picking of cotton displaced more than four million farmers and farm laborers. Mechanization hit African Americans the hardest; by 1960, fewer than 10 percent worked on the land. Between 1940 and 1970, more than five million African Americans moved from the South to the North, most of them to the largest cities. At one point in the 1950s, the black population of Chicago swelled by more than 2,200 new arrivals each week. The South Side of America's second city now rivaled Harlem as the cultural capital of black America (Map 11.4).

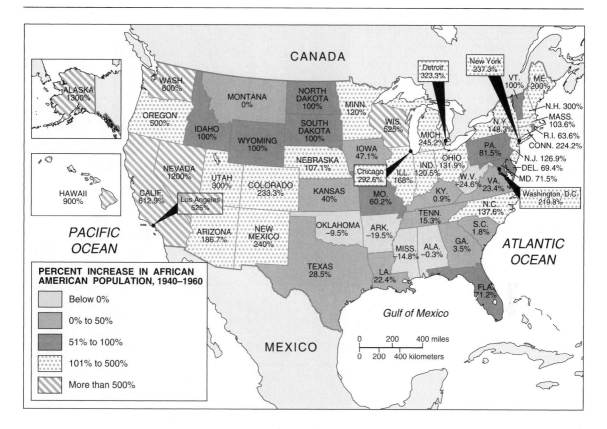

MAP 11.4 Great Migrations: African Americans Move North and West, 1940–1960

African Americans followed migration patterns that were similar to those of the 1910s as they moved out of the South in far greater numbers during and after World War II. The mechanization of cotton farming decreased the need for a large rural black population at the same time that urban areas in the North and West beckoned with industrial and service jobs.

The same economic transformation that drove African Americans north also drove Puerto Ricans from their island farms and into the mainland cities. During the 1940s, a U.S. government program, "Operation Bootstrap," encouraged the mechanization of the island's sugarcane plantations and the growth of low-wage, tax-free industries in cities such as San Juan. Rural employment plunged, and the island's urban population tripled. Yet Puerto Rico's unemployment rate remained among the highest in the Caribbean.

These conditions prompted a large migration to the mainland. Since the 1920s, a small but steady stream of Puerto Ricans had moved to New York and other eastern cities. In the postwar years, cheap airfares, family connections, and the hope of steady employment lured 40 percent of all islanders to make the move. By the end of the 1960s, New York City had a larger Puerto Rican population than San Juan did. El Barrio in East Harlem became the center of Puerto Rican life in New York, the home of salsa music, scores of social clubs, and hundreds of small Puerto Rican grocery stores, or bodegas, which served as the center of social and economic life for many immigrants.

Mexican immigrants fleeing the poverty of their homeland also poured into American cities. Though many crossed the border illegally, some 4.5

million Mexicans came to the Southwest between 1942 and 1964 through a government-sponsored bracero work program, although such workers were still often cheated out of wages and savings. Some of the new immigrants found employment on the vast factory farms that dominated California and Arizona agriculture, but many went to the growing cities of California and the Southwest. From 1950 to 1960, the Chicano (Mexican American) population in Los Angeles County more than doubled, growing from 300,000 to more than 600,000. By 1968, the Chicano community in East Los Angeles approached one million. In that year, 85 percent of the nation's Chicano population lived in urban areas.

This economic revolution also marked a watershed in the history of American cities. The arrival of millions of Mexican Americans, African Americans, and Puerto Ricans reshaped the character of the nation's urban centers. In some ways, the lives of these postwar migrants and immigrants resembled those of earlier immigrants, such as the Irish in the 1850s or the Jews, Italians, and Eastern Europeans of the early twentieth century. They, too, had to make the change from rural to urban life, figure out the city's ways, and in some cases learn a new language. Much like earlier immigrants, Chicanos, Puerto Ricans, and African Americans drew on their traditional cultures while adapting to the new world of the city.

In other ways, however, the postwar arrivals confronted a very different economic landscape. Although the U.S. economy boomed, it no longer generated the urban construction and manufacturing jobs, which had provided employment for so many early-twentieth century-immigrants. In Chicago and Detroit, a decline in meatpacking, auto parts manufacturing, and steelmaking permanently eliminated hundreds of thousands of high-wage, unionized jobs, thus forcing many of the new migrants and immigrants into insecure, low-wage positions at the bottom of the job ladder.

Puerto Ricans, Chicanos, and African Americans faced discrimination not only in hiring, but also in housing, schooling, and social services. When they tried to move into traditionally white neighborhoods, they faced discrimination by realtors and landlords and, in some instances, violence at the

Young Mother
Documentary photographer Elliott Erwitt captured the incessant demands of housework and child care in one New Rochelle, New York, home in 1955. Elliott Erwitt/Magnum.

"Hard, Dirty Work Should Be Paid For"

In her testimony to a Senate subcommittee, Ruth Green, a worker in an interstate laundry company, argued that despite union efforts to raise wages, a federal law mandating a minimum wage of at least 75 cents an hour was needed. On October 26, 1949, President Truman signed into law an amendment to the Fair Labor Standards Act of 1938 to establish a new minimum wage of 75 cents an hour. Some groups, however, remained excluded from the act's protection.

My name is Ruth Green. I am at present working in a laundry in Richmond, Va. I have worked in this same laundry 13 years, starting at a wage of $8 a week. During all this time, I, a widow, had one daughter to support and have raised a cousin, a girl now 17 years of age and in school.

Wages were raised at the rate of $1 or sometimes $2 a year. We organized into a union 3 years ago — now my wages are $24 a week; after deductions for old age, I have a check of $23.76, for 40 hours work at 60 cents an hour. . . .

Laundry work is hard work; it is unhealthy work. We work in heat and steam. Often, in bitter cold weather, the piece workers have to keep their windows open because of the steam and hot air from the pressing machines. This causes all of us to be in the draft. None of our laundries under contract carry insurance for inside workers. If workers become ill, they must bear the total expense.

Hard, dirty work should be paid for. Laundry workers need a minimum wage of at least 75 cents an hour.

Congress, *House Committee on Labor and Public Welfare, Fair Labor Standards Act Amendments of 1949*, 81st Congress, 1st Session, April 1949 (Washington, DC: U.S. Government Printing Office, 1949).

---

hands of angry white homeowners. Urban police forces, virtually all white in the 1950s, clashed repeatedly with the new urban migrants. The trouble was a product not only of white racism, but also of the aggressive professionalism with which urban police departments now did their jobs. Police in Oakland and Los Angeles were then among the most innovative and corruption-free in the nation, but they were also among the most brutal and insensitive when it came to arrests and interrogations.

The new arrivals could not easily achieve political remedies for such problems without U.S. citizenship. Since many Chicanos could not vote, they had few political representatives. And though Puerto Ricans had been granted full U.S. citizenship in 1917, most Puerto Ricans found mainland literacy tests an obstacle to voter registration. Urbanized African Americans could and did vote in the 1950s, which gave them some political leverage. But urban political machines, such as the one headed by Richard Daley in Chicago, managed to contain and channel African American demands. Throughout the 1950s, then, these urban minorities lived in a segregated and culturally isolated world, even in the most cosmopolitan of cities.

Symbolic changes, such as the integration of major league baseball after Jackie Robinson joined the Brooklyn Dodgers in 1947, did not change the realities of everyday life. Although many African Americans organized protests against job discrimination and police brutality, such campaigns did not generate mass involvement or much media attention until the dramatic boycotts and sit-ins in the South captured national attention (Chapter 12). For the most part, these minority communities in the North remained inwardly focused, sustained by their own institutions and cultural traditions.

Bodega

More than 40,000 *puertorriqueños* arrived in the United States each year between 1946 and 1956. Most settled in New York City, where *bodegas*, or family-owned grocery stores, were the first Puerto Rican–owned businesses and mainstay of the immigrant community — the place to get Caribbean and Spanish American delicacies, locate information about official and informal services, and catch up on news about the community as well as friends and relatives back home. Justo A. Marti — Center for Puerto Rican Studies, Hunter College, CUNY.

Unity and Division Within the Working Class   Although postwar trade unions helped to create the economic conditions that greatly reduced divisions within the industrial working class, they had increasingly limited capacity to transform the work lives of racial minorities and those who labored in the service economy. Since the 1930s, unions had greatly reduced wage differences between skilled and unskilled blue-collar workers; by 1958, tool and die makers in an auto plant made only 20 percent more than unskilled assembly-line workers. Through grievance and seniority systems, organized labor had also reduced the influence of personal or ethnic favoritism in the workplace. In many steel mills, Catholic workers of Eastern European extraction, who had labored for three generations at heavy, sweaty jobs, finally got a chance to do skilled work. And with a definite set of rules to govern the authority of supervisors to assign work, the old saying "It's not what you know, but who you know" became obsolete in many workplaces.

During the 1950s and 1960s, workers wanted both higher pay and the rights of conscious dignity that they believed their unions had been established to defend. They rejected the idea that one could be traded off for the other, which many managers and some union officials favored. One-third of all strikes in the 1950s were wildcat stoppages that arose when workers balked at speedups or contested management efforts to erode what they saw as their hard-earned work rights. In 1959, rank-and-file steelworkers pressured union officials into calling a 119-day strike that forestalled the elimination of work rules and safety standards that labor had won in the 1930s and 1940s.

Such massive stoppages did not have the political impact of the strikes that had made headlines in 1937 or 1946, however. After 1950, most company-

"We Consider This Part of the City to Be Ours": Latino Life in Manhattan

When Puerto Ricans began arriving in New York City in massive numbers in the late 1940s, they found already established Latino communities. In this excerpt from Guillermo Cotto-Thorner's autobiographical novel, Trópico en Manhattan *("Tropic in Manhattan"), Juan Marcos, a new arrival, travels with his friend Antonio, a seasoned New Yorker, from the airport to El Barrio, the Puerto Rican community in uptown Manhattan.*

The plane prepared for a graceful landing in the mysterious city of hope. Off in the distance, Juan Marcos saw the vertical zig-zag of the Manhattan skyline. The streets seemed so wide to him; he hadn't yet adapted to the dimensions of the metropolis. . . .

In a few minutes he found himself "walking underground" for the first time in his life. The subway captivated him. He began to feel that sensation of mystery and splendor that the city instills. . . . Their car of the subway filled up at the first stop, and the newly arrived greenhorn saw a beautiful blonde balanced before him clinging to one of the stiff, enameled handles that hung from the ceiling. Juan Marcos thought he was in Puerto Rico where courtesy hasn't suffered the sad fate that it has in New York. He stood up and in broken English said to the woman: "Lady, dis is a sit for yu." The girl looked him up and down and said in a rude, contemptuous tone, "Don't be a sucker."

Juan Marcos felt as though he'd been slapped across the face. . . . Juan Marcos thought: "What a shameless girl. Are all the women here like that?" He was extremely agitated. He felt like giving the girl a piece of his mind, but how, if his English wasn't even good enough to sell a bag of tomatoes? . . .

Juan Marcos had read and heard so much about El Barrio, the Puerto Rican colony in Manhattan scattered all over lower Harlem. Leaving the subway station, he stopped instinctively to look it over, while Antonio carried his suitcase as a gesture of courtesy. . . . On both sides of the wide street, the newly arrived friend could only distinguish two large buildings which stretched from corner to corner. Parallel windows, identical stairs reaching down to the sidewalk from six floors above the street. No, they weren't two buildings: they were many apartment buildings stuck together. . . . Hundreds, thousands of fellow Puerto Ricans lived there who, like him, had left the island to try their luck in New York. . . .

"This," [said] Antonio, "is our neighborhood, El Barrio. It's said that we Latins run things here. And that's how we see ourselves. While the Americans take most of the money that circulates around here, we consider this part of the city to be ours."

Juan Flores, ed., *Divided Arrival: Narratives of the Puerto Rican Migration, 1920–1950* (1987).

wide strikes were aimed at adjusting wage and benefit packages, not at changing the distribution of power in the workplace. And wildcat strikes had little long-range effect, even when they were temporarily successful. "We're moving rapidly away from the crusading spirit of the thirties," admitted a shop steward in an aircraft union at the end of the decade. "In 1953 we had one of the most militant unions in the labor movement. We had wildcat strikes, direct job action. . . . Today there is much less of this. People no longer file grievances because they think it is no use."

The merger of the AFL and the CIO in 1955 ratified these changes in the union movement. With the CIO's expulsion of Communist-dominated unions, few substantial differences remained between the two federations. The AFL, dominated by the construction trades and other "business" unionists, was almost twice the size of the CIO. It was therefore fitting that the AFL-CIO did not choose the CIO's visionary president, Walter Reuther, as their new leader but George Meany, a Bronx plumber who had risen to leadership in the AFL during the 1930s and 1940s. Meany, who would later boast that he had never led a strike, won high wages for union members by adapting the labor movement to the contours of American capitalism. In the years after the 1955 merger, the amount of energy and money unions devoted to organizing new workers declined, as did the unions' relative independence from the Democratic Party. "We do not seek to recast American society in any particular doctrinaire or ideological image," Meany asserted. "We seek an ever rising standard of living."

Because both labor law and management practice encouraged an insular, depoliticized form of collective bargaining, some trade union leaders became little better than corrupt businessmen, who undercut the price of labor they "sold" for kickbacks and payoffs from employers. Union corruption, exposed in a series of congressional hearings presided over by Senator John McClellan in 1957 and 1958, proved to be especially prevalent in decentralized, highly competitive industries, such as trucking, the restaurant business, and dock work, in which autocratic union leaders could cut "sweetheart" deals with employers and ignore rank-and-file sentiment. Gangsters actually ran some locals; nepotistic families presided in many

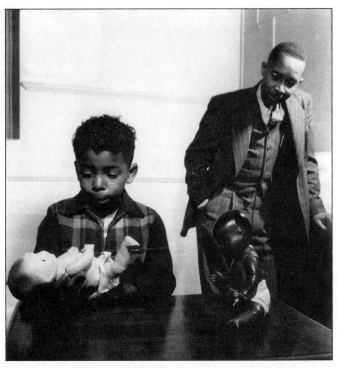

Dolls and Discrimination
Studies conducted by sociologists Kenneth Clark (right) and Mamie Phipps Clark at their Northside Center for Child Development in Harlem demonstrated the detrimental impact of segregation on African American children. For example, when asked to choose between a white and a black doll, African American children from segregated environments preferred and identified with the white one. These studies were instrumental in convincing the Supreme Court in its 1954 *Brown v. Board of Education* decision that racial segregation in public schools was unconstitutional. Gordon Parks — Prints and Photographs Division, Library of Congress. Courtesy of Gordon Parks Foundation.

"Sweetheart Deal": Corruption in the Teamsters Union

Allen Friedman, a Teamster strong-arm man in Cleveland in the 1950s, describes how he worked with a local attorney to "organize" the workers at local Italian restaurants while "shaking down" the restaurant owners. Trade union corruption became big news in the 1950s, after Senate investigating committees found Mafia influence at the highest levels of the Teamsters, the International Longshoremen's Association, and the Hotel and Restaurant Workers.

The attorney's idea was for me to go to each of the restaurants he represented, signing up the members so that he would have to be called in to negotiate the contracts. In exchange for his giving me the list of names of the restaurants involved, I would negotiate a "sweetheart deal" which wouldn't cost the restaurant owners very much more than they were already paying. It was a good arrangement for everyone. . . .

The idea that unions organize workers isn't always true. With big places we had to work hard to sign people to pledge cards, then present enough pledge cards to the boss to show that the workers were behind us. . . . With smaller places we didn't always bother to organize. We'd just tell the boss we had the members pledged to join, flashing phony cards, not all of which were even filled out by the employees. Sometimes we'd have two or three signatures. Sometimes we'd have none. It didn't matter. If we could bluff our way through, we would. . . .

John Felice, an acquaintance of mine, headed the local that controlled the beer truck drivers. When the beer arrived, I'd tell the driver that he wasn't supposed to deliver the beer that day because John Felice sanctioned the strike. The driver would go on to his next stop. . . . It was easy to organize those places. Stop the supplying of essential services and they're out of business.

Generally the meetings would be similar. The restaurant owner would start yelling, the attorney talking with him in his native language, quieting him. He then would explain that the owner should slip me a few hundred dollars and I would give him a sweetheart contract. The owner understood the bribe, paid it, and got a good deal. The employees didn't care because they kept their jobs and got a little better deal than they had had.

Allen Friedman and Ted Schwarz, *Power and Greed: Inside the Teamsters Empire of Corruption* (1989).

others. The moral standing of the union movement plummeted—one reason for the decline in the proportion of American workers who were AFL-CIO members, from about 33 percent of the workforce in 1955 to little more than 20 percent two decades later.

The stagnation of the union movement also fostered increasingly sharp divisions within the working class. Race and gender prejudice always separated American workers, but the inability of the unions to organize white women, African Americans, and others in the growing secondary labor force hardened these divisions in the working class. Meanwhile, union policy on two key issues of the period, automation and employee fringe benefits, further divided workers. In the 1930s, unions sought to spread the burden of unemployment by reducing the length of the workweek, even if that meant smaller paychecks for everyone. In the 1950s, with unemployment far less of a problem, workers faced rapid technological change—then called automation—that eliminated many of the best blue-collar jobs. But the unions had no effective response. On unionized West Coast docks, the "containerization" of most cargo generated a two-tier workforce: a small group of well-paid, steadily employed machine operators and a large group of casual workers who did the dangerous work of lifting and hauling.

Mobbed Up

Inspired by the notoriously corrupt leadership of the International Longshoremen's Association, the 1954 film *On the Waterfront* portrayed trade union officials as gangsters. Everett Collection.

An even more pervasive division within the working class took place when unions focused their energy on bargaining over health and pension plans, which came to constitute a semiprivate welfare state for union members. In the late 1940s, the labor-liberal effort to expand Social Security and inaugurate national health insurance had stalled, so unionists turned to the bargaining table to secure pensions and medical care for their members, so-called fringe benefits. By the end of the 1960s, almost all unionized workers had some sort of employer-paid health insurance, and two-thirds were covered by pensions. But the hefty benefit packages that unionized workers won made their lives and expectations very different from those of insecure workers who labored in poorly paid service and clerical occupations. The relatively egalitarian wage pattern of the mid-1940s eroded, and soon high-wage workers came to resent the taxes they paid for state-supported welfare. Thus, the weakness of the postwar welfare state and the resulting creation of a privatized substitute helped to split the American working class into two segments, one relatively secure and the other—predominantly young, minority, and female—left out in the cold.

The Ethos of a Classless Society

During the 1950s, many Americans thought that the nation's "labor problem" had been solved. Although the distribution of income did not change in the postwar years—the top tenth of the population consistently took home almost 40 percent of the national income—the economic pie was getting bigger, so there seemed no need to redivide it. "The union," wrote the editors of *Fortune*, "has made the worker, to an amazing degree, a middle class member of a middle class society." Many

Americans, especially those who enjoyed a measure of economic security, had always wanted to believe that the United States was a nation in which social class was unimportant, wealth was widely shared, and social conflict was muted. In the postwar era, however, this vision became pervasive, not only among conservatives, but also on college campuses and in union halls, newsrooms, and television studios. One fantasy of a classless society—achieving instantaneous fame and fortune—gained widespread popularity on television quiz shows in the 1950s. As even Philip Murray, the president of the CIO, asserted to a union audience, "We have no classes in this country."

At the same time that many people denied the existence of class differences, ethnic and religious divisions were growing less important to white Americans. Almost two generations had passed since the end of mass European immigration. With only half as many foreign-born residents in the United States as there had been during the Depression, mass institutions such as the military, the public schools, and the big corporations downgraded ethnicity as a social marker. Although churches and synagogues benefited from increased attendance in the 1950s, many worshipers came to see their faith as part of a homogenized "civic religion" that validated the "American way of life." Perhaps President Eisenhower put it best when he affirmed, "Our government makes no sense unless it is founded in a deeply religious faith—and I don't care what it is."

The growth of the comprehensive high school had the same homogenizing effect. After the war, secondary school enrollment rose to 80 percent of its potential constituency. Virtually all white Americans spent three or four formative years in a public institution that offered classless homogeneity as part of its official ideology. Elaborate sports contests and the emergence of a distinct teen culture in the 1950s soon eclipsed the ethnic antagonisms that had bitterly divided white youths since the late nineteenth century. For millions of working-class young men, for whom service in the military provided a rite of passage from adolescence to adulthood, the postwar draft, which lasted from 1948 until 1971, further diluted ethnic, religious, and regional parochialism.

The explosive growth of college and university enrollments also contributed to the process. The enactment of the G.I. Bill (officially known as the Servicemen's Readjustment Act) in 1944 had democratized higher education by making it broadly available to those who had

Television Dreams

Columbia University English instructor Charles Van Doren (left) was the most renowned quiz show celebrity, going on from his triumph on NBC's *Twenty-One* to become one of the stars of the network's *Today* show. However, a 1959 congressional investigation revealed that many of the big-money game shows were rigged. Van Doren was implicated in the scandal, which led to fraud indictments and his disappearance from television. Everett Collection.

served in the armed forces. World War II veterans took advantage of generous government payments. "Everybody went to college," remembered a Sicilian-born architect who had spent his childhood in the Bronx. "Suddenly we looked up, we owned property. Italians could buy. The G.I. Bill, the American dream. Guys my age had really become Americanized."

Still, class and racial divisions clearly structured upward mobility. The "tracking" of high school students into academic or vocational courses usually replicated social class divisions in the local community, and many of the white working-class youths who found higher education suddenly within reach enrolled in community colleges and technical schools rather than in the prestigious liberal arts colleges. Until the late 1960s, African Americans and Mexican Americans found managerial and professional jobs largely closed to them.

Suburban America   The New Deal, the new unions, and the new sense of citizenship held by ethnic Americans laid the basis for the proliferation of suburban housing tracts that spread outward from the urban fringe during the early postwar decades. New Deal planners believed in cheap credit, which they extended to farmers, hospitals, homeowners, and veterans. After the war, the government continued to guarantee low-interest loans through the Veterans Administration and other government agencies. For the first time in their lives, huge numbers of working people could afford better housing. And their demand was desperate. The Depression and war virtually halted residential construction; now millions of veterans and workers needed homes for their growing families. The demand was so great that in 1945, the city of Chicago had put 250 old streetcars up for sale as potential homes.

Before World War II, the suburbs had been reserved largely for the well-to-do. Working-class Americans lived near their work, often in apartments or cramped row houses in ethnic neighborhoods. Except in the Midwest, most workers rented, because purchasing a house required a down payment of 50 percent on a ten- or fifteen-year mortgage. In the postwar era, inexpensive single-family suburban homes, best symbolized by the three huge Levittowns that sprouted in potato fields outside New York City and Philadelphia, seemed to reverse this trend. William Levitt's wartime experience in constructing family quarters on a navy base convinced him that if financing were available, contractors could make millions of dollars housing veterans and their families. With other builders, he prodded officials of the Veterans Administration and the Federal Housing Administration (FHA) to guarantee low-interest loans that would make suburban homes cheaper than rental apartments. Assured of a mass market, Levitt used assembly-line methods to erect thousands of identical homes, complete with white picket fence, green lawn, and a well-equipped kitchen. Buyers snapped up 1,400 houses in the first three hours after sales began in March 1949.

Suburban Development, 1957
An aerial view of Levittown, Pennsylvania, under construction. Margaret Bourke-White, *Life* magazine, Copyright Time, Inc.

By 1960, three out of every five families owned their own dwelling. Some thought the new suburbs would transform feisty urban white ethnics into conservative homeowners concerned chiefly with keeping the crabgrass at bay. "No man who owns his own house and lot can be a Communist," Levitt asserted. "He has too much to do." The sociologist David Riesman compared life in suburbia to "a fraternity house at a small college in which like-mindedness reverberates upon itself."

But suburbanization itself did little to ameliorate social class divisions. Although workers might own homes that were nearly identical to those of their middle-class neighbors, they were unlikely to vote Republican, repudiate their union, or join the Rotary Club. Urban autoworkers who followed a relocated Ford plant to exurban Milpitas, California, liked the spaciousness of their new tract homes, but most did not believe that they had left the working class. More than mobility, blue-collar families valued security. In a suburban community, one sociologist reported, "the people of working-class culture stay close to home and make the house a haven against a hostile, outside world."

Many women had mixed feelings about their new suburban surroundings. Suburban housewives loved the spaciousness and convenience of their new homes, the safety of the neighborhood, and the access to good public schools. But at a time when millions of married women were entering the labor market, most suburban housing developments were designed for families in which Mom stayed home, Dad worked in the city, and relatives remained at a distance. The early housing tracts contained few of the social institutions—the corner grocery store, the nearby grandparent, the convenient streetcar—on which women had long relied to ease their burden of shopping, housework, and child rearing. By making work outside the home more difficult for women and cutting them off from traditional support networks, the insular suburban neighborhood enforced conformity to postwar gender roles.

As the suburbs grew, government housing policies actually deepened racial and class divisions across metropolitan America. The Federal Housing Administration (FHA), which financed about 30 percent of all new homes in the 1950s, advised developers to concentrate on a particular housing market based on age, income, and race. To ensure neighborhood homogeneity and preserve property values, the agency endorsed "restrictive covenants" that barred Jews and African Americans from buying homes. (William Levitt permitted neither black families nor single women to sign a mortgage.) And because federal housing agencies followed private lenders in "redlining"—refusing to write mortgage loans—in the inner city, housing stock there deteriorated in the 1950s. Such neglect quickly turned many neighborhoods into slums. In cities such as Chicago, Philadelphia, and Buffalo, white families typically moved to the suburbs a few years after the appearance of the first African Americans on their block. Northern housing soon became more rigidly segregated than it had been at any time since the Civil War.

The nation's public housing failure exacerbated urban apartheid. Because of resistance from realtors, mortgage bankers, and home builders, the government funded only 320,000 units of public housing in the decade after Congress passed President Truman's housing act in 1949. To minimize land costs, developers built most of the new "projects" in massive blocks. Unlike the tax subsidies for single-family suburban homes, public housing was thought of as welfare, so local governments usually imposed income restrictions on project residents. Families with rising incomes had to leave, ensuring the economic segregation of those who remained. In the end, no one liked American-style public housing—not the taxpayers, not the housing industry, not the politicians, not even the people who lived there.

Massive expressways added insult to injury as they slashed through urban neighborhoods in the late 1950s. The new superhighways, which replaced more accessible trolleys and interurban trams, often disrupted stable working-class communities. When residents protested, policymakers told them, "You can't stop progress." Like low mortgage rates for single-family homes, the government-sponsored freeway boom represented a massive subsidy for suburban commuters and a tax, both fiscal and social, on city dwellers (Map 11.5).

Public Housing

In the years following World War II, as many middle-class families moved to the suburbs, inner-city public housing increasingly became identified with poor Americans. Living in public housing was viewed by many as a stigma, and new high-rise projects took on a harsh and regimented appearance. Prints and Photographs Division, Library of Congress.

The World of *Father Knows Best* Television reinforced the family-oriented privatization of American society in the postwar era. By 1960, TV was a fixture in 90 percent of all homes, and TV programming mirrored the nation's social and cultural landscape, if often in an exaggerated form. In the early days of television, radio-inspired situation comedies offered TV viewers a sympathetic glimpse of urban working-class families enmeshed in a world of tenements, street-corner stickball, and manual labor. During the 1950s, shows such as *The Honeymooners*, starring Jackie Gleason as a New York City bus driver, offered a comic but sometimes realistic portrait of working-class dreams and aspirations. But the television networks soon replaced urban farces of this sort with situation comedies and westerns that bleached ethnicity, class, and social commentary out of their story lines. *Father Knows Best*, introduced in 1953, exemplified the new world of

MAP 11.5 The Interstate Highway System in 1930 and 1970

The 1956 Interstate Highway Act funded an extensive system of highways that allowed cars and trucks to replace trains as the major form of transportation and shipping. The highway expenditures also benefited the postwar expansion of suburban development.

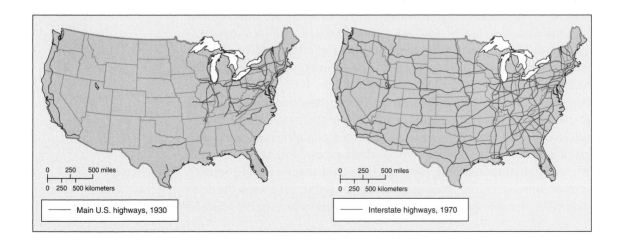

0 250 500 miles	0 250 500 miles
0 250 500 kilometers	0 250 500 kilometers
—— Main U.S. highways, 1930	—— Interstate highways, 1970

suburban respectability: the Andersons lived in a large house on Maple Street in "Springfield," U.S.A. Jim Anderson, the father (played by Robert Young) had no politics, held few strong opinions, and never had a bad day at the office. All the action in *Father Knows Best* took place at home, where the middle-class father exercised a benevolent despotism over three not particularly rebellious children. Jane Wyatt, who played the mother, maintained perfect order in her house and kept her opinions to herself.

Although small-town domesticity permeated the dominant cultural ideal, some unexpected cultural works challenged the placid world of *Father Knows Best*. In the mid-1950s, the "beat" writers, led by Allen Ginsberg and Jack Kerouac, denounced what they saw as the materialism, sexual repression, and spiritual emptiness of middle-class American life. "These have been years of conformity and depression," wrote Norman Mailer in 1957, voicing a critique that was common among intellectuals who were sympathetic to the beats. "A stench of fear has come out of every pore of American life, and we suffer from a collective failure of nerve." Though the beats attracted only a small following, they stirred widespread controversy and comment. Newspaper and magazine reporters sneered at the "beatnik" style of dress and speech, hinting darkly about "racial mixing" and sexual immorality at their parties.

Rock-and-roll, which exploded onto the American cultural scene in the mid-1950s, originated in the music that dominated black working-class communities during and after World War II. Many of the leading artists were newly urbanized migrants from the rural South; among the most important was the blues singer Muddy Waters, who moved from rural Mississippi to Chicago in 1941. Waters and his band brought the pulse and energy of the electric guitar to the traditional country blues form. By the mid-1950s, he and other black singers, such as Chuck Berry and Ray Charles, had created and refined a new musical genre, rhythm-and-blues. Charles's gospel-inspired piano playing in "I Got a Woman" launched the rock-and-roll revolution in 1954. Elvis Presley, a white Memphis teen, made rock-and-roll a national craze when he combined the energy and beat of African American rhythm-and-blues with the lyrics and sentiments of southern white "country music." Flaunting his sexuality and his working-class demeanor, Presley scandalized an older generation of viewers when he

Beats — By Way of Hollywood
A publicity still from the 1959 film *The Rebel Set* displays some of the stereotyped characteristics that were ascribed to "beatniks." Dressed in black, wearing sandals, and sporting distinctive hairstyles (goatees for men, severe yet flamboyant ponytails for women), the two beats crouch on a bare mattress and "groove" on poetry. The paintings in the background display drug-induced nightmare themes. Everett Collection.

"Beboppers Were by No Means Fools"

In the late 1940s the modernist sound of bop reached a creative and popular peak in the work of musicians such as Dizzy (John Birks) Gillespie and Charlie "Yardbird" Parker. This new form of jazz expressed the spirit of the African American communities out of which it emerged. In his 1979 autobiography, Dizzy Gillespie explained the social context of his music and challenged the myths of the bebop culture.

We never wished to be restricted to just an American context, for we were creators in an art form which grew from universal roots and which had proved it possessed universal appeal. Damn right! We refused to accept racism, poverty, or economic exploitation, nor would we live out uncreative humdrum lives merely for the sake of survival. . . .

Within society, we did the same thing we did with the music. First we learned the proper way and then we improvised on that. It seemed the natural thing to do because the style or mode of life among black folks went the same way as the direction of the music. Yes, sometimes the music comes first and the life-style reflects the music because music is some very strong stuff, though life in itself is bigger. Artists are always in the vanguard of social change, but we didn't go out and make speeches or say "Let's play eight bars of protest." We just played our music and let it go at that. The music proclaimed our identity; it made every statement we truly wanted to make. . . .

A "square" and a "lame" were synonymous, and they accepted the complete life-style, including the music, dictated by the establishment. They rejected the concept of creative alternatives, and they were just the opposite of "hip," which meant "in the know," "wise," or one with "knowledge" of life and how to live. . . .

Beboppers were by no means fools. For a generation of Americans and young people around the world, who reached maturity during the 1940s, bebop symbolized a rebellion against the rigidities of the old order, an outcry for change in almost every field, especially in music. The bopper wanted to impress the world with a new stamp, the uniquely modern design of a new generation coming of age.

Dizzy Gillespie with Al Fraser, *To Be, Or Not . . . To Bop* (New York: Doubleday, 1979), excerpted from pp. 278–302 and p. 483. Used by permission of Doubleday, a division of Bantam Doubleday Dell Publishing Group

appeared on the normally staid *Ed Sullivan Show* in 1956. But he immediately became a teenage idol, and his songs became rock-and-roll anthems.

While some parents and conservative social critics denounced rock-and-roll as an evil influence on the young, Hollywood quickly discovered that money could be made from the rebellious youth culture. Films such as *The Wild One*, *Rebel Without a Cause*, and *The Blackboard Jungle* offered sympathetic portraits of teenage "delinquents" trapped in a crass adult society that neither cared about nor understood them. Marlon Brando's and

James Dean's brilliant acting perform-
ances communicated the personal alienation of a generation. Partly as a result of
the popularization of such attitudes,
millions of Americans would, within a
decade, come to see the rejection of
bourgeois values not as a semicriminal
impulse but as a "counterculture"—an
alternative way of looking at, and perhaps changing, an unhappy world.

Conclusion: New Challenges for the Postwar Order

During the great boom that began after
World War II, the real income of
working-class Americans, blue-collar
and white-collar, began the advance that
would double the standard of living of
the majority of families within a single
generation. Cold War arms spending
helped to boost the economy, but the
New Deal legacy—strong unions and a
state-regulated business system—generated the stability and security that
enabled postwar capitalism to flourish.
Americans bought cars, houses, vacations, and TV sets, but they also began
a quest for a more expansive and plastic sense of life. Some urban youths
chafed at the ideological and social constraints that a claustrophobic Cold
War culture imposed, and a few middle-class women reassessed the virtues
of suburban family life. But the largest measure of frustration, as well as
hope, arose among those whose skin color had denied them full access to
the opportunities that the New Deal and the postwar prosperity had opened
for so many white Americans. Even before the 1960s had begun, black
Americans would demand that American citizenship, both legal and social,
was their birthright as well.

The Pulp Threat

A 1954 montage that appeared
in newspapers presents what
many Americans saw as a new
danger threatening the nation's
youth. In Senate committee
hearings and other forums, parents, social scientists, and
public officials called for censorship laws, claiming that
crime and horror comic books,
along with other salacious and
sensational publications, contributed to the growing problem
of juvenile delinquency. Prints
and Photographs Division, Library of
Congress.

The Years in Review

1944

- The Bretton Woods Conference makes the dollar the basis for
  international financial transactions.

"They Behave as If Drugged"

Many middle-class American adults were disturbed by the nature of the adolescent culture that emerged in the 1950s. Some parents sought advice from "experts" such as the psychiatrist Fredric Wertham, who gained fame as a critic of comic books. This letter from a middle-class mother expresses a range of common concerns reflecting Cold War anxieties.

Dear Dr. Wertham:

We have two boys, 7 and 13, with unusually high intelligence and excellent ability in school and in sports. . . . They have a library of fine books of their own, and read library books almost daily, yet in the presence of comic books they behave as if drugged, and will not lift their eyes or speak when spoken to. . . . What we would like to know is, what can be done about it before it is too late? My boys fight with each other in a manner that is unbelievable in a home where both parents are university graduates and perfectly mated. We attribute the so-called "hatred" that they profess for each other to be harmful influence of these books plus movies and radio. . . .

We consider the situation to be as serious as an invasion of the enemy in war time, with as far reaching consequences as the atom bomb. If we cannot stop the wicked men who are poisoning our children's minds, what chance is there for mankind to survive longer than one generation, or half of one?

James Gilbert, *A Cycle of Outrage: America's Reaction to the Juvenile Delinquent in the 1950s* (1986).

- Democrat Franklin Roosevelt wins a fourth presidential term with Harry S. Truman as vice president.

1945
- Harry S. Truman becomes president following the death of Franklin Roosevelt.
- Atomic bombs are dropped on Hiroshima and Nagasaki, Japan. World War II ends.
- The United Nations is formed.

1946
- George F. Kennan lays out "containment" doctrine.
- In Operation Dixie, unions attempt to organize southern workers; the effort ultimately fails.
- Dr. Benjamin Spock's *Baby and Child Care*, a radically different approach to child rearing that focuses on the needs of the child, is first published.

- A massive postwar strike wave raises wages but also sparks rapid inflation.

1947

- The Taft-Hartley Act, which undercuts unions, passes over President Truman's veto.
- Truman boosts funding for the FBI, sets up a loyalty program for federal employees, and asks the attorney general to draw up a list of subversive organizations.
- Jackie Robinson integrates major league baseball.
- The United Mine Workers of America wins the first health and pension fund package in labor history from mine owners.
- The Truman Doctrine commits the United States to assisting countries in fighting Soviet expansion or internal Communist threats.
- Secretary of State George Marshall announces a $16 billion plan for the reconstruction and integration of Europe; it becomes known as the Marshall Plan.

1948

- The Soviets blockade Berlin; the United States responds with an airlift.
- Truman is elected in a four-way presidential race, defeating Republican Thomas Dewey, Progressive Party candidate Henry Wallace, and Dixiecrat Strom Thurmond.
- The United Nations approves the partition of Palestine to create the new state of Israel.

1949

- The CIO expels nine unions for refusing to purge themselves of Communist leaders and support government policies.
- Congress passes Truman's public housing bill. Only 320,000 units are built in the first decade because of resistance from realtors, mortgage bankers, and home builders.
- Pro-Western Chinese dictator Chiang Kai-shek is overthrown by Mao Zedong's Communist army.

Robots

During the 1950s, science fiction stories and films became increasingly popular, although their vision of the future was often pessimistic. Besides alien invasions and atomic disasters (including devastating destruction wrought by gigantic monsters that were created or awakened by nuclear experiments), another favorite theme was the mixed blessing of automation: the robot as a labor-saving device that could all too easily turn against humankind. Virgil Finlay, *Amazing Stories*, October–November 1953.

- The North Atlantic Treaty Organization (NATO) is formed. In response, the Soviets later created the Warsaw Pact alliance of Eastern European nations.
- The Soviets explode their first nuclear bomb.

1950
- Communist North Korea invades South Korea, and U.N.-backed American troops enter conflict; a truce leaving the Communists in control of North Korea is reached in 1953 after a three-year stalemate that results in 34,000 American deaths.
- Communists Julius and Ethel Rosenberg are charged with delivering atomic secrets to the Soviet Union; convicted in 1951, they are executed in June 1953 despite worldwide protests.
- The Truman administration announces a new foreign policy plan, NSC-68, which commits the United States to an expensive military buildup in the fight against Communism.

1952
- Republican Dwight D. Eisenhower defeats Democrat Adlai Stevenson for the presidency.

1953
- The CIA supports a military coup in Iran, restoring the Shah to power.
- *Playboy* magazine is first published.
- Soviet premier Joseph Stalin dies, temporarily encouraging hope for a new U.S.-Soviet relationship.
- Labor union membership in the United States reaches a peak of 32.5 percent of the labor force.

1954
- The Senate votes to censure Joseph McCarthy, who had led an anti-Communist crusade.
- The United States organizes the South East Asian Treaty Organization to stem Communism in Asia after the French are defeated in Vietnam.
- The CIA supports a military coup in Guatemala, ousting the elected leader Jacobo Arbenz.
- Black singers Ray Charles and Chuck Berry launch rhythm-and-blues, which leads to rock-and-roll.

1955
- The AFL and the CIO merge.

1956
- Congress funds the multibillion-dollar Interstate and Defense Highway Program, the largest public works project in U.S. history.

- Rock-and-roll star Elvis Presley creates a national scandal when he dances suggestively during an appearance on *The Ed Sullivan Show*.

- Capturing 57 percent of the popular vote, President Eisenhower easily defeats Adlai Stevenson in the presidential election.

1957
- The Soviet Union launches the Sputnik satellite into orbit.

1958
- The United States launches its first space satellite.

- A major recession temporarily ends the postwar boom.

1959
- More than half a million steelworkers strike for 119 days to successfully defend union work rules and safety standards.

Additional Readings

For more on the Cold War in a global context, see: Norman Friedman, *The Fifty-Year War: Conflict and Strategy in the Cold War* (2000); John Lewis Gaddis, *We Now Know: Rethinking Cold War History* (1997); Jon Halliday and Bruce Cumings, *Korea: The Unknown War* (1988); Akira Iriye, *Cultural Internationalism and World Order* (1997); Michael Kort, *The Columbia Guide to the Cold War* (1998); Walter LaFeber, *America, Russia, and the Cold War* (1985); Melvyn P. Leffler, *A Preponderance of Power: National Security, the Truman Administration, and the Cold War* (1992); Thomas J. McCormick, *America's Half-Century: United States Foreign Policy in the Cold War* (1989); Ronald McGlothen, *Controlling the Waves: Dean Acheson and U.S. Foreign Policy in Asia* (1993); and Brenda Gayle Plummer, *Rising Wind: Black Americans and U.S. Foreign Affairs, 1935–1960* (1996).

For more on the decline of the New Deal, the economic boom, and the shifts in the labor movement, see: Ely Chinoy, *Automobile Workers and the American Dream* (1992); Robert M. Collins, *More: The Politics of Economic Growth in Postwar America* (2000); John M. Findlay, *Magic Lands: Western Cityscapes and American Culture After 1940* (1992); Joshua Freeman, *Working-Class New York: Life and Labor Since World War II* (2000); Barbara S. Griffith, *The Crisis of American Labor: Operation Dixie and the Defeat of the CIO* (1988); Martin Halpern, *UAW Politics in the Cold War Era* (1988); Nelson Lichtenstein, *Walter Reuther: The Most Dangerous Man in Detroit* (1997); Richard H. Pells, *The Liberal Mind in a Conservative Age: American Intellectuals in the 1940s and 1950s* (1994); and David Stebenne, *Arthur J. Goldberg: New Deal Liberal* (1996).

For more on presidential politics in the late 1940s and 1950s, see:
Stephen E. Ambrose, *Eisenhower* (1987); Alonzo L. Hamby, *Man of the People: A Life of Harry S. Truman* (1998); Michael J. Hogan, *A Cross of Iron: Harry S. Truman and the Origins of the National Security State, 1945–1954* (1998); David K. Johnson, *The Lavender Scare: The Cold War Persecution of Gays and Lesbians in the Federal Government* (2004); Zachary Karabell, *The Last Campaign: How Harry Truman Won the 1948 Election* (2000); Michael J. Lacey, ed., *The Truman Presidency* (1989); and Arnold Offner, *Another Such Victory: President Truman and the Cold War* (2002).

For more on the domestic anti-Communist campaigns, see: Peter Biskind, *Seeing Is Believing: How Hollywood Taught Us to Stop Worrying and Love the Fifties* (1983); Paul Buhle and Dave Wagner, *Hide in Plain Sight: The Hollywood Blacklistees in Film and Television, 1950–2002* (2003); Ronald Radosh and Joyce Milton, *The Rosenberg File: A Search for the Truth* (1997); Ellen Schrecker, *Many Are the Crimes: McCarthyism in America* (1998); and Allen Weinstein, *Perjury: The Hiss-Chambers Case* (1977).

For more on women and gender politics during the 1950s, see:
Stephanie Coontz, *The Way We Never Were: American Families and the Nostalgia Trap* (1992); Susan J. Douglas, *Where the Girls Are: Growing Up Female with the Mass Media* (1994); Barbara Ehrenreich, *The Hearts of Men: American Dreams and the Flight from Commitment* (1983); Daniel Horowitz, *Betty Friedan and the Making of the Feminine Mystique: The American Left, the Cold War, and Modern Feminism* (1998); Eugenia Kaledin, *Mothers and More: American Women in the 1950s* (1984); Helen Laville, *Cold War Women: The International Activities of American Women's Organizations* (2002); Elaine Tyler May, *Homeward Bound: American Families in the Cold War Era* (1999); Joanne Meyerowitz, ed., *Not June Clever: Women and Gender in Postwar America, 1945–1960* (1994); Kate Weigand, *Red Feminism: American Communism and the Making of Women's Liberation* (2000).

For more on race, ethnicity, and division within the working class, see:
Michelle Brattain, *The Politics of Whiteness: Race, Workers, and Culture in the Modern South* (2001); Elizabeth A. Fones-Wolf, *Selling Free Enterprise: The Business Assault on Labor and Liberalism, 1945–1960* (1994); David Halle, *America's Working Man: Work, Home, and Politics Among Blue-Collar Property Owners* (1987), Jack Metzgar, *Striking Steel: Solidarity Remembered* (2000); Stephen Grant Meyer, *As Long as They Don't Move Next Door: Segregation and Racial Conflict in American Neighborhoods* (2000); Thomas J. Sugrue, *The Origins of the Urban Crisis: Race and Inequality in Postwar*

Detroit (1998); and Heather Ann Thompson, *Whose Detroit?: Politics, Labor, and Race in a Modern American City* (2001).

For more on the rise of suburban America and popular culture during the 1950s, see: Rosalyn Baxandall and Elizabeth Ewen, *Picture Windows: How the Suburbs Happened* (2000); Tom Engelhardt, *The End of Victory Culture: Cold War America and the Disillusioning of a Generation* (1998); Herbert J. Gans, *The Levittowners: Ways of Life and Politics in a New Suburban Community* (1982); James B. Gilbert, *A Cycle of Outrage: America's Reaction to the Juvenile Delinquent in the 1950s* (1988); Peter Guralnick, *Last Train to Memphis: The Rise of Elvis Presley* (1994); David Halberstam, *The Fifties* (1993); Dolores Hayden, *Building Suburbia: Green Fields and Urban Growth, 1820–2000* (2003); Kenneth T. Jackson, *Crabgrass Frontier: The Suburbanization of the United States* (1985); Lisa McGirr, *Suburban Warriors: The Origins of the New American Right* (2001); Rickie Solinger, *Wake Up Little Susie: Single Pregnancy and Race Before* Roe v. Wade (1992); Ed Ward, Geoffrey Stokes, and Ken Tucker, *Rock of Ages: The Rolling Stone History of Rock & Roll* (1986).

12

The Rights-Conscious Sixties

1960–1973

Attack

A Greyhound bus carrying both black and white "Freedom Riders" was attacked and destroyed by more than 200 whites outside of Anniston, Alabama, in May 1961. It had been chartered by the Congress of Racial Equality as part of a campaign to challenge racial segregation along interstate bus routes in the South. The mob firebombed the bus and savagely beat the civil rights protesters as they tried to escape, leaving one paralyzed and another brain damaged. Bettmann/Corbis.

A T T H E I N A U G U R A T I O N of President John F. Kennedy in January 1961, poet Robert Frost forecast a new age of "poetry and power," matching the nation's influence abroad with a new surge of self-confidence and harmony at home. The "Sixties" did renew the nation's great postwar boom, but that era, stretching all the way from the late 1950s into the early 1970s, saw a higher degree of ideological and social polarization than any time since the Civil War. Millions of ordinary Americans came to feel that they could make their collective weight felt on issues that had once been handled behind the closed doors of the county courthouse or the corporate board room. A growing sense of "rights consciousness" encompassed the aspirations not only of African Americans, Latinos, or American Indians, but also of groups that were defined by age, gender, income, and sexual orientation. By the early 1970s, the spread of new social values had begun to transform the workplace as well, creating demands for equity in hiring and promotion, for a healthy and safe environment, and for personal recognition and dignity where none had existed before. The social movements of the 1960s revived for a time the workplace militancy that had once been part of the culture of an insurgent, rights-conscious working class.

The Civil Rights Movement

Most Americans think of the modern civil rights movement as beginning in May 1954 when attorneys from the National Association for the Advancement of Colored People (NAACP), led by Thurgood Marshall, won a U.S. Supreme Court decision, *Brown v. Board of Education*, which decreed that in education, the old "separate but equal" standard was inherently discriminatory. In a unanimous decision skillfully orchestrated by the new Chief Justice, Earl Warren, the high court declared segregated public schools unconstitutional. The court based its opinion on the Reconstruction era "equal protection" clause of the Fourteenth Amendment as well as psychological and sociological research findings that segregation itself was harmful to black children.

As moral symbol and settled law, the *Brown* decision would prove enormously important, but at the time, its influence was but one strand in a complex set of social movements and political transformations that made the early postwar years so crucial to the civil rights impulse. The modern black liberation movement emerged from the World War II "Double V" campaign against fascism abroad and racism at home (see Chapter 10) and took the form of countless local struggles by local activists. After the war, this small-scale civil rights movement, with allies in labor, religious, and community organizations, continued to secure employment, housing, and political rights, especially in Northern cities. It was joined by a rising tide of civil rights activists from the South, including many longtime NAACP organizers, to form a national movement for racial equality.

Continuing the Fight in the North Local struggles for racial equality took place in the 1940s and early 1950s in cities across the North, Midwest, and West. In New York City, the leaders of this upsurge were black communists and their allies who had cut their teeth on the CIO organizing campaigns of the 1930s and 1940s. Linking the fight for racial equality to the recent successful battle against international fascism, this urban movement demanded not integration per se, but immediate equality from city officials, local merchants, landlords, and employers. Although city unions were crucial to the 1945 passage of the first state-level Fair Employment Practices Commission, a broad coalition of clubs, lodges, churches, and synagogues created a powerful interracial network that stretched across the five boroughs.

Jewish New Yorkers were among the key allies in this fight. Rabbi Stephen Wise, the nationally prominent leader of reform Judaism, argued that "our work is based on the premise that anti-Semitism, like all other forms of ignorance and discrimination, is a product not primarily of ignorance and misunderstanding but of complex political, social, and economic forces." This Jewish-black alliance was particularly effective in the late 1940s in overturning "restrictive covenants" that barred both Jews and African Americans from desirable neighborhoods and city housing projects, such as the New York City apartment complex Stuyvesant Town, which was the largest urban redevelopment project of its time, and later in Levittown, a huge new suburban housing tract in Pennsylvania and on Long Island.

Black Chicagoans also made their city a frontline in the continuing struggle for justice. In 1955, a murder in Mississippi galvanized the attention of African Americans around the country, a grim reminder of how much was at stake in the struggle for racial equality. Fourteen-year-old Emmett Till, a black Chicago native who was visiting relatives in the Mississippi Delta, whistled at a white woman in the ramshackle country store where he and some friends had gone to buy bubble gum. Four days later, the woman's husband and his half-brother kidnapped Till, beat him, shot him in the head, and tied his body with barbed wire to a metal fan, which they dumped into the Tallahatchie River.

Till was not the only black person Mississippi white racists murdered that summer, but when his mutilated body was returned to Chicago, 250,000 outraged African Americans viewed the coffin, which was kept open at the insistence of Till's mother. Millions more saw photographs of the boy's mutilated body in *Jet*, a national African American magazine; Mrs. Till wanted everyone to see the kind of sadism that went unpunished in the postwar South. All the institutions of black Chicago stood by her determined quest for justice. The Packinghouse Workers, an interracial union then at the height of its power, lent crucial support to Till's family. The *Chicago Defender*, the largest African American newspaper in the country, put the Till murder and subsequent trial on its front page for weeks on end. Congressman Charles Diggs of Michigan, one of only three African American members of the House of Representatives, attended the Mississippi trial, determined that southern white violence would no longer escape the critical gaze of the northern African American community. An all-white, all-male jury acquitted Till's assassins, but the case proved to be a landmark in the emerging civil rights movement.

Southern Clashes in the 1950s After Till's funeral, the most dramatic events in the American civil rights story would take place largely in the South. For more than a decade, the *Brown* decision proved a hollow victory for African Americans because neither the courts nor the government took decisive action

Emmett Till

The terror that African Americans faced in the South was starkly revealed in the August 1955 mutilation and murder of fourteen-year-old Emmett Till in rural Tallahatchie County, Mississippi. The murderers, Roy Bryant (center left) and J. W. Milam (center right), are shown here posing with their wives for news photographers after they were brought to trial and acquitted by an all-white jury. Ed Clark, September 1, 1955 — Time Life Pictures/Getty Images.

to force school desegregation. In 1955, for example, the Supreme Court accommodated the anti-integrationists by ruling that desegregation need only take place with "all deliberate speed," a confusing and cautious approach that President Eisenhower endorsed because "It's all very well to talk about school integration — if you remember that we may also be talking about social disintegration."

Federal ambivalence encouraged white segregationists to test *Brown*'s limits. Although Little Rock, Arkansas, school officials were prepared to desegregate in 1957, Governor Orville Faubus produced a violent crisis by sending National Guardsmen to block the entry of black students, ostensibly to preserve "order" at Central High School. When a shrieking crowd chased six black teenagers from the school, President Eisenhower reluctantly federalized the Arkansas Guard and sent 1,000 U.S. Army paratroopers to Little Rock. In response, Faubus shut Little Rock public high schools for the entire year. Across the South, the number of school districts that engaged in even token desegregation fell from 712 in the first three years after the *Brown* decision to just 49 between 1957 and 1960.

A reborn civil rights movement broke the stalemate and captured the imagination of millions of Americans, both white and black. This upsurge was not based in the unions, as it had been just after World War II (see Chapter 10), but rather found much of its visible leadership in African American churches and the NAACP, whose attorneys' long march through the courts had begun to dismantle the legal foundations of America's Jim Crow laws.

The new movement was born in the heart of Dixie: Montgomery, Alabama, where the Confederate flag still flew over the state capitol building. Nothing rankled Montgomery's black community more than the segregated bus system. In an act of daily humiliation, African Americans had to pay their fare in the front, then get off the bus and reenter in the back. If the bus began to fill with whites, white drivers would often shout, "Niggers get back!" and blacks would have to move farther back on the bus, giving up their seats to whites. On a cold December afternoon in 1955, Rosa Parks, a longtime NAACP activist, refused to cooperate with this degrading ritual. As whites crowded into the bus, she kept her seat. She was arrested, and the city charged her with violating the bus segregation ordinance.

Female activists in the Montgomery's Women's Political Council and the local

Back of the Bus
Segregated seating on a southern streetcar in 1951. Schomburg Center for Research in Black Culture, New York Public Library, Astor, Lenox and Tilden Foundations.

"We Were Prepared"

Jo Ann Robinson, president of the Women's Political Council (WPC) and an English teacher at the all-black Alabama State College, describes what her organization did to help organize the Montgomery, Alabama, bus boycott. The WPC, a group of black working-class and middle-class women formed in 1946, had vigorously protested Montgomery's segregated bus system for many years before Rosa Parks refused to give up her seat on the bus.

Fred Gray told me Rosa Parks was arrested. Her case would be on Monday. He said to me, "Jo Ann, if you have ever planned to do anything with the council, now is your time." I called all the officers of the three chapters, I called as many of the men who had supported us as I could reach, and I told them that Rosa Parks had been arrested and she would be tried. They said, "You have the plans, put them into operation." We had worked for at least three years getting that thing organized.

The Women's Political Council had begun in 1946, after just dozens of black people had been arrested on the buses for segregation purposes. By 1955, we had members in every elementary, junior high, and senior high school, and in federal, state, and local jobs. Wherever there were more than ten blacks employed, we had a member there. We were prepared to the point that we knew that in a matter of hours, we could corral the whole city.

I didn't go to bed that night. I cut stencils and took them to the college. . . . We ran off thirty-five thousand copies. After I had talked with every WPC member in the elementary, junior high, and senior high schools to have somebody on the campus during the day so I could deliver them, I took them to school with me in my car.

Monday morning, December the fifth, 1955, I shall never forget because many of us had not gone to bed that night. It was the day of the boycott. We had been up waiting for the first buses to pass to see if any riders were on them. It was a cold morning, cloudy, there was a threat of rain, and we were afraid that if it rained the people would get on the bus. But as the buses began to roll, and there were one or two on some of them, none on some of them, then we began to realize that the people were cooperating and that they were going to stay off the bus that first day.

Henry Hampton and Steve Fayer, with Sarah Flynn, *Voices of Freedom: An Oral History of the Civil Rights Movement* (1990).

NAACP were ready when Parks, an ideal test case, was arrested. The Women's Political Council, founded in 1946, had long been involved with voter registration efforts in the black community and had previously lobbied the city government for better treatment of African Americans on city buses. With the established connections, these firebrands were able to spread word of Parks's arrest through the black community; within hours, African American leaders decided to boycott the city bus system in protest.

"I Just Have To!"

In this oral history excerpt, Carla Hayes reveals the economic impact of the civil rights movement. Civil rights organizing and protests were not confined to the South during the 1950s and 1960s; boycotts and picketing of stores in New York's Harlem had taken place since the 1930s, and school desegregation activists in New York City had been protesting and facing arrest throughout the 1950s.

Negroes regularly shopped at Woolworth's on 125th Street in Harlem. You could find everything there, from needles and thread to buttons and bows. The only thing you could not find was a Negro working there. The Negroes in Harlem were cordially invited into the store, and their money was accepted enthusiastically; however, they could not apply for employment.

This caused the civil rights leaders in the Harlem community to protest. They marched to the store and picketed out front for months. This was in the late '50s or perhaps early '60s. I recall snowy and cold days of February. My own dear mother was a protester.

My mother was a vital woman in those days. She was strong and determined. She also believed in fair play. None of her six children, including me, ever felt put upon or denied. It was her sense of fair play that compelled her to march against Woolworth's. She would say, "If the store is in Harlem and takes Harlem's money, it should give back to Harlem by giving jobs to the people of Harlem."

She felt this way wholeheartedly. I could tell by the way she would get dressed. She was determined to spend the entire day on the picket line and therefore would dress warmly and comfortably. More important were the shoes she would wear: "I have to be able to walk comfortably," she would stress each morning.

I recall my mother practicing her march in the living room of our apartment. She would almost appear to be proud. I remember being proud of her. She would march all day. Then she would return home with different emotions. She was quiet and a little broken. My sisters and I would hurriedly get a large bucket and fill it with hot water. My mother would soak her feet and sigh.

We would ask her, "Mama, are you all right?" "Sure, sugar," would be her reply. "Mama, why are you doing this to yourself?" we would inquire. "I have to," she would answer. "I just have to!" The next day, she would find good-fitting shoes, practice her march, and come home tired. Day after day this went on.

My mother's walking was not in vain, because I obtained a sales-clerk job at Woolworth's in May 1970. I recall going to work with pride because my own dear mother had walked a way for me.

Carla Hayes, *2004 Voices of Civil Rights*, http://www.voicesofcivilrights.org.

The thirteen-month-long boycott demonstrated how a social movement both builds on the previous work of local activists and organizations and creates its own momentum. African American demands were initially modest: greater courtesy toward black passengers, employment of African American drivers in black neighborhoods, and an easing of—but not an end to—segregated seating on the buses. As week after week passed, Montgomery's black citizens grew more confident of their ability to stick together and resist white intimidation. And they found an inspiring public spokesman in the Reverend Dr. Martin Luther King, Jr., an Atlanta-born, twenty-six-year-old minister who was then in his first pulpit. King skillfully linked Old Testament prophecy and the legacy of African American suffering to inspire a new generation of civil rights activists. By the time the U.S. Supreme Court ruled that Montgomery buses must integrate, in December 1956, a new civil rights activism had spread through the South and the North.

Although the nonviolent approach that King preached would soon gain a national following, civil rights activists in the South privately debated and sometimes publicly rejected nonviolence as a useful strategy in the face of unrelenting violence and a legal system that was unwilling to protect African Americans. Local resistance by African Americans to racist violence throughout the South (a region with long traditions of both rural gun ownership and defending family honor) often relied on armed self-defense. As one black women's newsletter from Jackson, Mississippi, argued, since "no law enforcement body in ignorant Mississippi will protect any Negro who has membership in the NAACP . . . the Negro must protect himself." Robert F. Williams, a NAACP chapter leader in Monroe, North Carolina, gained local renown by organizing armed defense against Klan harassment; he rose to national prominence in 1958 when Monroe police arrested two African American boys, eight and ten years old, for kissing a white girl while playing a game and sentenced them to a juvenile detention school. Williams shamed the United States by drawing international attention to the case and using the government's Cold War rhetoric to support civil rights for African Americans. Although censured by the NAACP in 1959 for publicly advocating armed self-reliance, Williams continued his activism and gained broader attention within the civil rights movement through widely published debates with Martin Luther King, Jr., over the principle of self-defense. Williams also helped to bridge northern and southern activism as he traveled to Harlem to speak before groups of black nationalists.

Freedom Now!　In February 1960, black college students initiated a series of nonviolent "sit-ins," which swept through the South and captured national attention. The protests started when four neatly dressed African American students from North Carolina A&T College violated a Greensboro segregation ordinance by taking seats at a Woolworth's lunch counter to demand service that had traditionally been denied them. "All of us were afraid," recalled David Richmond, "but we went and did it." When a nervous waitress refused them service, the four pulled out their books and prepared for a long stay. The sit-in galvanized thousands of black students, who led sit-ins throughout the upper South. "I felt at the time it was like a crusade," Nashville sit-in leader John Lewis remembered. Although gangs of white youths often taunted and abused the African American students, at least 70,000 people participated in sit-ins in more than one hundred cities during the winter and spring of 1960.

The sit-ins demonstrated that mass civil disobedience and nonviolent confrontation were effective tactics. Activists soon organized the Student Nonviolent Coordinating Committee (SNCC), which served as a vanguard within the civil rights movement. SNCC was never a large organization, but its members, predominantly young African Americans, were creative and dedicated — "commando raiders," one observer called them, "on the more dangerous and exposed fronts of the racial struggle." Television broadcasts and magazines put the students' message before millions of Americans, focusing the eyes of the nation on southern racial injustice, thus prompting federal intervention.

In May 1961, the Congress of Racial Equality (CORE), a civil rights group that was based primarily in the North, organized a series of "Freedom Rides" to test recent court orders mandating the integration of southern bus

Woolworth's Sit-In, May 28, 1963
White youths shower abuse and food on a Tougaloo College professor and students who are staging a sit-in at a segregated lunch counter in Jackson, Mississippi. After soda, ketchup, mustard, and sugar failed to deter them, the civil rights demonstrators were doused with spray paint and beaten. State Historical Society of Wisconsin.

"They Shot the Tires Out"

Hank Thomas, a "Freedom Rider," recalls the destruction of an integrated bus by a white mob in Anniston, Alabama, on May 14, 1961. Volunteers from all over the country, organized by the Congress of Racial Equality, arrived in the South to integrate the segregated southern buses in a series of Freedom Rides.

The Freedom Ride didn't really get rough until we got down in the Deep South. Needless to say, Anniston, Alabama, I'm never gonna forget that. When I was on the bus they [whites] threw some kind of incendiary device on. I got real scared then. You know, I was thinking—I'm looking out the window there, and people are out there yelling and screaming. They [whites] just about broke every window out of the bus. . . . I really thought that that was going to be the end of me. They shot the tires out, and the bus driver was forced to stop. . . . And we were trapped on the bus.

It wasn't until the thing [smoke bomb] was shot on the bus and the bus caught afire that everything got out of control. . . . First they [whites] closed the doors and wouldn't let us off. But then I'm pretty sure . . . that somebody said, "Hey, the bus is gonna explode . . ." and so they started scattering, and I guess that's the way we got off the bus. Otherwise, we probably all would have been succumbed by the smoke. . . . I got whacked over the head with a rock or I think a stick as I was coming off the bus.

The bus started exploding, and a lot of people were cut by flying glass. . . . Took us to the hospital, and it was incredible. The people at the hospital would not do anything for us. They would not. And I was saying "You're doctors, you're medical personnel." They wouldn't. . . . But strangely enough, even those bad things don't stick in my mind that much. Not that I'm full of love and goodwill for everybody in my heart, but I chalk it off to part of the things that I'm going to be able to sit on my front porch in my rocking chair and tell my young'uns about, my grandchildren about.

Milton Meltzer, ed., *The American Promise* (1990).

terminals. "Our intention," CORE leader James Farmer later explained, "was to provoke the southern authorities into arresting us and thereby prod the Justice Department into enforcing the law." When the integrated group of Freedom Riders reached Alabama, white mobs burned one of their buses and, with the tacit approval of local police, savagely attacked the riders. But SNCC bolstered the Freedom Riders with new volunteers, who quickly filled Mississippi's jails.

Movement activists also created grassroots organizations to serve as vehicles of empowerment within African American communities. The sit-ins, Freedom Rides, and marches opened the way for a new sense of citizenship and participation, putting African American maids, tenant farmers, laborers, and students in the vanguard of the civil rights movement. This change became clear during a year-long series of demonstrations in Albany, Georgia, in 1961 and 1962. There, SNCC activists mobilized the entire community for a precedent-setting civil disobedience campaign. Demanding integration of stores, restaurants, bus stations, and schools, African American high schoolers, farm laborers, and churchwomen filled Albany's jails week after week. Children as young as eleven and twelve years of age were prominent in these demonstrations. Going to jail, ordinarily a shameful as well as a dangerous experience, now became a badge of courage.

The battle to desegregate Birmingham, Alabama, which began in April 1963, fully nationalized the impact of the civil rights movement. Birmingham African Americans held mass meetings for sixty-five consecutive nights, often followed by marches to the downtown business district that ended in arrest or attacks by police. City police, under the command of a reactionary segregationist, Eugene "Bull" Connor, used fire hoses and police dogs to disperse marchers. Thousands of high school students singing "freedom songs" joined the protests, as did hundreds of African American workers from the city's steel mills and coke ovens. Televised images of Birmingham police dogs attacking defenseless marchers helped to swing northern public opinion massively against segregation. During the summer of 1963, there were 758 demonstrations and marches, more above the Mason-Dixon line than below it, representing a diverse movement. Many of the protesters fought for economic justice as well as civil rights as they demanded more jobs for minority youths, increased funding for inner-city schools, and an end to police brutality. More than half of all African Americans who were polled by a national newsmagazine reported a sense of "personal obligation" to get involved.

A. Philip Randolph, the African American trade unionist whose threat of a 1941 march on Washington had helped to integrate World War II defense plants (see Chapter 10), now unveiled plans for a new mass demonstration in the capital to demand jobs, housing, and higher wages for blacks. Backed by the United Auto Workers and other liberal trade unions, the August 1963 "March on Washington for Jobs and Freedom" brought to the capital a crowd of almost a quarter-million people, at that time the largest political gathering in U.S. history. Dr. King delivered a speech that articulated a broad moral vision of the civil rights movement, a synthesis of Christian idealism and appeals to America's highest principles of freedom and equality. "I have a dream," he declared, "that one day this nation will rise up and live out the true meaning of its creed . . . when the sons of former slaves and the sons of former slave owners will be able to sit together at the table of brotherhood."

When Washington Steps In Civil rights activity put federal officials on the spot. In 1960, Massachusetts Senator John F. Kennedy had defeated Vice President Richard Nixon in the closest presidential race of the twentieth century. Kennedy's paper-thin victory was a product of a lingering recession, which hurt the Republicans, as well as substantial support from the white South, which still maintained a traditional loyalty to the Democrats. Kennedy, the first Catholic president, was not a passionate liberal; he wanted to boost economic growth and contain Communism abroad. He once remarked to Nixon, "who gives a shit if the minimum wage is $1.15 or $1.25, compared to something like Cuba."

Kennedy found civil rights issues divisive and embarrassing. By exposing America's racism, the movement seemed to give the Soviets a propaganda tool and made it more difficult for Kennedy to woo the newly independent nations of Africa and Asia. And in Congress, he needed the support of southern Democrats, who held near-veto power over all legislation. Although the president supported integration, he also sought political stability, working closely with his brother Robert, the new attorney general, to this end. During the Freedom Rides, the Kennedys called on southern governors to suppress white violence, but they also urged CORE and SNCC to end the rides and focus their energies on activities that the White House saw as less disruptive: voter education and registration.

President Kennedy finally put his administration behind a sweeping desegregation bill after the Birmingham demonstrations forced civil rights issues to the top of the nation's agenda. In a nationally televised speech on June 11, 1963, the president declared the denial of civil rights not only a constitutional problem, but also a powerful "moral issue" that required tough new laws outlawing segregation in public accommodations, integrating public schools, and prohibiting discrimination in programs receiving federal funds. That very night, the necessity for such federal law was again made clear when a sniper assassinated Mississippi's NAACP field secretary, Medgar Evers, in his driveway.

The next year, all eyes were on Mississippi, where SNCC and CORE brought hundreds of northern white students to teach in "Freedom Schools" and conduct voter registration drives in the black community. In mid-June, three civil rights workers were reported missing: James Chaney, an African American civil rights worker from Meridian, Mississippi; Michael Schwerner, a white CORE activist from New York City; and Andrew Goodman, a white summer volunteer from Queens College in New York City. Federal agents eventually uncovered their mangled bodies. Klansmen and Mississippi police had kidnapped the activists and beaten them to death with clubs and chains. At the Democratic convention that summer, Mississippi civil rights forces challenged the credentials of the segregationist white Democrats who composed the state's convention delegation. The

Mississippi Freedom Democratic Party lost the credentials battle but won a well-publicized moral victory as delegate Fannie Lou Hamer mesmerized the convention and a national television audience with her account of the violence and intimidation suffered by black voters across the state.

The Liberal Hour

The civil rights movement reopened the door to reform in American politics, a door that had been shut tight since the waning years of the Great Depression. For more than a generation, the conservative alliance between the white South and northern business for the most part successfully resisted extension of the liberal social legislation that was pioneered during Franklin Roosevelt's presidency. The civil rights movement broke this stalemate by isolating southern conservatives and breathing new life into the liberal-labor coalition that had backed New Deal reforms a generation earlier.

Missing

The notice issued by the FBI in June 1964 for missing civil rights workers Andrew Goodman, James Chaney, and Michael Schwerner. Agents found their bodies buried in an earthen dam near Philadelphia, Mississippi, weeks later. Only in 2005 was Edgar Ray Killen, a Ku Klux Klan organizer, convicted of manslaughter. Federal Bureau of Investigation.

Lyndon Johnson and Reform Politics

Lyndon Baines Johnson, a Texas-born president, presided over the nation's liberal hour. Johnson had been an ardent New Dealer when elected to Congress during the 1930s, but as a senator and then as majority leader of the Democrats during the 1950s, he became far more cautious. For this reason, among others, Kennedy chose Johnson as his vice presidential running mate in 1960 to keep Texas in the Democratic column and reassure southern conservatives.

Johnson took the presidential oath of office inside Air Force One, at Love Field in Dallas, on the afternoon of November 22, 1963, just hours after John F. Kennedy was murdered as his motorcade drove through Dallas. The assassin, Lee Harvey Oswald, struck the forty-three-year-old president with two shots from a high-powered rifle. His precise motivation remains unknown because just two days later, Jack Ruby, a Dallas strip-club owner who was well known to the local police, killed Oswald.

Kennedy's assassination had two great consequences for American politics: it put a dark question mark over the legitimacy of the nation's institutions and the motivations of its highest officials. Although a high-profile commission chaired by U.S. Supreme Court Chief Justice Earl Warren concluded that Oswald was not part of an assassination conspiracy, an increasingly large proportion of the American people came to think otherwise. Many saw the Kennedy years as a mythic "Camelot," a luminous, hopeful moment in U.S. history that was transformed on November 22, 1963, into a turbulent era of social upheaval, domestic violence, and unpredictable politics. However, Kennedy's assassination also advanced the liberal agenda. President Johnson championed the nation's reform impulse as a way both to legitimate his unexpected assumption of presidential power and to accommodate the remarkable pressure that arose from the African American community. Johnson was determined to demonstrate to Kennedy loyalists and skeptical liberals that he had outgrown his conservative Texas roots. In January 1964, the new president declared an "unconditional war on poverty" in his State of the Union address; then, in the spring and summer, he added his considerable legislative and lobbying clout to the movement that won long-delayed passage of Kennedy's Civil Rights Act in June of that year.

In a highly polarized contest, Johnson won the presidency in a landslide in November 1964, thereby opening the door to a brief but heady era of liberal politics during which almost every piece of Lyndon Johnson's "Great Society" legislation was written into law. With running mate Hubert Humphrey, a staunch liberal from Minnesota, Johnson won 61 percent of the popular vote, defeating Republican Barry Goldwater, the ideologically conservative senator from Arizona. Riding on Johnson's coattails, the Democrats won staggering majorities in both the House (295 to 140) and Senate (68 to 32).

The Great Society   At the heart of the Great Society was the legal revolution in civil rights. For the first time since Reconstruction, the federal government used the full extent of its power to dismantle the racial hierarchies that local white elites had long presided over in education, business, and government. These elites were now expected to conform to a national standard mandating legal equality for minorities and women. The 1964 Civil Rights Act ended segregation in all public accommodations, including theaters, restaurants, and swimming pools. Under Title VII, an Equal Employment Opportunity Commission championed demands for equitable hiring and promotion practices in private employment. The long-prevailing practice of listing jobs in newspaper help-wanted ads for "white" and "colored," as well as for "men" and "women," was soon abolished.

In a similar fashion, the Voting Rights Act of 1965 gave the U.S. attorney general the right to intervene in counties where fewer than half of all eligible voters were registered. The new law sent hundreds of federal voter registrars into the "Black Belt" counties of the South; within a decade, two million additional African Americans were on the voting rolls. An equally large

number of whites registered for the first time. As a result, the South underwent its greatest political transformation since the end of Reconstruction.
By the 1970s, a biracial, two-party system emerged as voters elected thousands of black officials in the South, from mayors and sheriffs to state legislators and congressional representatives (Map 12.1).

Liberal majorities in the House and Senate allowed President Johnson
to secure enactment of his broader program of social reform, which he
called "The Great Society." Since the 1930s, the benefits of New Deal era

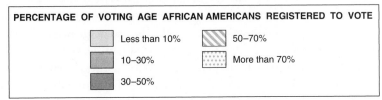

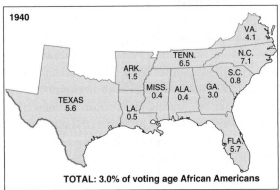
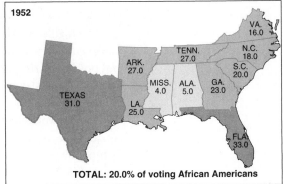
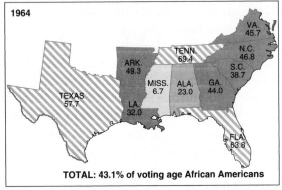
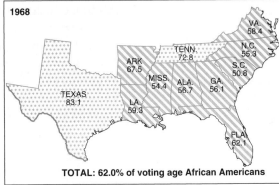

**MAP 12.1   The Reenfranchisement of African Americans: Black Voter Registration,
in the South, 1940–1968**

Black voter registration leapt forward in two stages. During World War II and the years immediately afterward, the first wave of the modern civil rights movement generated widespread
interest in voting, which multiplied by seven times the proportion of blacks voting in the
South. White resistance in the 1950s slowed further increases until the Civil Rights Act of
1965 generated another dramatic increase in black voter registration.

Prescribing Legislation

Retired Americans picketed outside the annual convention of the American Medical Association (AMA) in 1965 to protest the organization's opposition to Medicare. The AMA denounced the health insurance plan as a step toward the imposition of "socialized medicine," a term that was coined by conservatives who were opposed to the expansion of government health services, which suggested totalitarian control, decreased patient care, and greater financial cost. *New York World-Telegram and Sun* Newspaper Photograph Collection, Prints and Photographs Division, Library of Congress.

social programs and legislative reforms had been limited largely to white urban wage earners, for whom Social Security, state unemployment benefits, hospital subsidies, and the federal labor law had all been tailored. But now the sense of social citizenship that was inherent in these reforms expanded to include millions of additional Americans, those who were black, brown, poor, aged, or employed in agriculture and service industries.

The most important and far-reaching of the Great Society programs extended government-financed medical care to the aged and the poor. Medicare, which provided health insurance as part of the Social Security program, was enacted in 1965. The next year, Congress again broadened the social safety net by passing Medicaid, which offered federal medical assistance to welfare recipients of all ages. Both programs proved popular, especially Medicare, whose beneficiaries were almost all solidly middle-class retirees. But without effective cost controls, these social programs stoked the fire of inflation in the health care system, leaving employers and individuals who were still excluded from these government programs to bear these spiraling costs. Although one-quarter of all Americans now held some kind of government-financed medical insurance, fiscal and administrative problems blocked the extension of this system to the remainder of the population.

Congress also overcame the racial and religious impasse that had long stymied a federal program of aid to schools. In the South, conservatives no longer feared that federal dollars would be used to advance racial integration, because desegregation of the schools was rapidly becoming an accomplished fact. And in the North, President Johnson accommodated Catholic advocates of federal aid to parochial schools through a school aid bill that distributed aid on the basis not of the needs of the schools themselves but of the poverty of their student populations. Total federal expenditures for education and technical training tripled in the decade after 1964.

Finally, a dramatic liberalization of America's immigration policy proved one of the Great Society's lasting legacies. The Immigration Act of 1965 eliminated the quota system that had favored northern European immigrants since the 1920s (see Chapter 7). In its place, the new bill opened the door to many more immigrants from Asia, the Middle East, and Africa, whose ranks would swell in the 1970s and 1980s when political instability and economic crisis swept those regions.

The War on Poverty   Even though Great Society programs doubled federal spending for social welfare, these initiatives were largely uncontroversial because both the poor and the middle class could take advantage of them. Johnson's War on Poverty, launched in early 1964, proved far more divisive.

The War on Poverty increased some direct income support to poor people, but most of the new funding went to programs that were designed to help the poor get an education and secure a job. Head Start, the most popular of these programs, provided nutritious food and intellectual stimulation to preschoolers. Upward Bound sought to aid disadvantaged teenagers. The Job Corps retrained unskilled adults and those who had dropped out of school. VISTA (Volunteers in Service to America) offered a vehicle for college-trained young people to help residents in Appalachia and other pockets of rural poverty. Such educational programs cost far less than the relief and public works projects of the New Deal. Indeed, antipoverty expenditures amounted to less than 1 percent of the federal budget during the 1960s.

Despite its relatively small budget and its emphasis on motivation, the War on Poverty proved to be highly controversial because it was linked to a rights-conscious mobilization of the poor. To encourage a new self-help attitude among the poor, the administration's antipoverty agency, the Office of Economic Opportunity (OEO), established the Community Action Program to encourage "maximum feasible participation" by residents of impoverished areas in programs that affected their communities. Within two years, more than one thousand Community Action Agencies had sprung up across the nation, many infused with the spirit of the civil rights movement. The new agencies challenged the way in which local officials used federal antipoverty funds, put protesters in the streets, and filed lawsuits. Such activism outraged governors and mayors, who had long controlled federal largess. "We are experiencing a class struggle in the traditional Karl Marx style," asserted one city official in Syracuse, New York. This assessment was an exaggeration, but when these officials demanded an end to this federally sponsored challenge to their power, the White House and the OEO flinched. After 1966, funding for experimental antipoverty programs declined, and state officials assumed the right to take over any community-based agency they did not like.

Was the War on Poverty a failure or a success? Poverty rates fell in the 1960s, even if the expanding economy and low overall unemployment deserved the lion's share of the credit. The proportion of poor people in the United States decreased from 23 percent in 1962 to 11 percent in 1973. There was a 30 percent reduction in infant mortality, a three-year increase in life expectancy, and a leap in school attendance for African Americans, Hispanics, and low-income whites. Unemployment among African Americans

"We Are Poor but We Know What We Want"

The Reverend Lynward Stevenson was president of the Woodlawn Organization, a community group representing a poor Chicago neighborhood that helped shape local War on Poverty policy. The Johnson administration instructed that the War on Poverty be conducted locally with "maximum feasible participation" on the part of the poor communities that were being served. But people who tried to act on this mandate often came into conflict with established social service bureaucracies and the political machines that controlled them, as evidenced by Reverend Stevenson's testimony before Congress in April 1965.

Why haven't we, the Woodlawn Organization, a grassroots neighborhood community organization representing the Greater Woodlawn Community, been allowed to fight the War on Poverty? Is it that we are too stupid, that we are poor, that we are Negroes, that we are like children who must be planned for? . . .

The Organization which elected me its President has said to the city of Chicago. "All right, we are poor, but we know what we want and we will fight in the great American tradition to get it." We have told the city of Chicago we will fight for jobs, for an end of slumlord exploitation, for an end to dead-end ghetto schools, for security from "Negro removal" via the bulldozer. This is SELF-DETERMINATION. That is what drove this nation into its birth, and brought forth every historical advance since.

. . . We took hope when Congress and President Johnson proposed to the nation a War on Poverty. It meant to us that this can be our great leap forward into an open, integrated, equal country. In Chicago, [however] there is no War on Poverty. There is only more of the ancient, galling war against the poor.

It is a war against the poor when only the rich benefit from public funds. It is a war against the poor when the white-shirted social workers, the bankers who run the powerful charities, the ward committeemen get fat off money appropriated to help the poor lift themselves off the bottom.

It is a war against the poor when we are told by the President and Congress that we can plan for ourselves, but then find that we can only stand in the waiting rooms of Chicago's city hall, while plans are made for us. It is a war against the poor when the Chicago Committee deals out its money to people whose knowledge of the poor comes from the television set. Oh, it is not a war of guns and explosives. It is an undeclared war by the rich and by the local politicians. What they want to do is to destroy our dignity. That is why they insist on planning for us.

I am here to tell you that we want the Federal law on maximum feasible local participation enforced in Chicago. My people want it. The 40,000 poor of Greater Woodlawn who make up the Woodlawn Organization want it. . . .

Before we will be shorn of our dignity we will go into the streets. For the rich of this land must understand this is our dignity, our place in America that we are struggling for. And our dignity can no longer be bought off for a pittance, or decided by others.

Lynward Stevenson, Woodlawn Organization *Newsletter*, April 14, 1965.

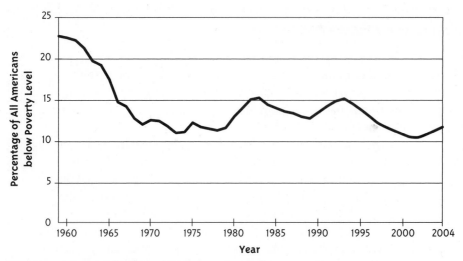

FIGURE 12.1 Poverty's Decline and Persistence: Poverty Rates, 1959–2004

Full employment, a rise in real wages, and government antipoverty programs sharply decreased the proportion of Americans — both black and white — living in poverty during the 1960s and early 1970s. Thereafter, economic stagnation as well as a loss of government interest in the problem of poverty halted the dramatic gains that had been won in the 1960s.
U.S. Census Bureau, "Persons Below Poverty Level and Below 125 Percent of Poverty Level," http://www.census.gov/hhes/povery/histpov/histpov3/html.

remained at double the level for whites; and among inner-city youths, crime, poverty, and unemployment increased to three times the rate among their white suburban counterparts. All such comparative social indexes would worsen in the 1970s, when economic growth dropped sharply (Figure 12.1).

The problem was that Johnson administration officials ignored the structural changes in the economy that made it increasingly difficult for poor people to earn a decent living. The decline of the Appalachian coal industry threw more than half a million miners out of work. The mechanization of southern cotton production pushed millions of African Americans off the land. Economic changes in both Puerto Rico and Mexico crippled labor-intensive agriculture, forcing millions of Latinos with few economic resources to migrate to northern cities. These massive population movements took place at precisely the time when industry was fleeing to the suburbs, stripping central cities of more than one million blue-collar jobs. Therefore, whatever the usefulness inherent in the War on Poverty's education and job-training programs, these structural changes sentenced millions of Americans, disproportionately people of color, to a secondary labor market that was characterized by high turnover and low pay.

Racial Violence and Black Power   By the mid-1960s, some civil rights activists chafed at the pace of change and questioned the political compro-

Prime-Time Poverty

By the early 1960s, television news programs regularly reported on poverty in the nation's cities. But most prime-time dramatic programs ignored life in the inner city. One exception was the 1963 CBS series *Eastside/Westside*, featuring George C. Scott (right) and Cicely Tyson as idealistic New York City social workers. Although the series' characters won small victories against discrimination and inequality — as in the episode pictured here, with Ruby Dee and Earle Hyman portraying a black couple living in a previously all-white neighborhood — *Eastside/Westside*'s view of urban poverty as an insurmountable problem was unusually pessimistic. The program lasted only one season. The Everett Collection.

mises and alliances with white liberals that mainstream movement leaders had made. In 1963, the year of the March on Washington, the civil rights movement had seemed to be the culminating affirmation of a liberal faith in the harmonious perfectibility of American institutions. But in the years that followed, the battle against racial injustice took on an increasingly bitter tone. Beginning in the summer of 1965, looting, fires, and police gunfire swept Los Angeles, Cleveland, Newark, Detroit, and other cities as African American riots focused the national spotlight on racial tensions in the North. Hundreds of people were killed, thousands were injured, and millions of dollars' worth of property was destroyed as violent upheavals scarred more than two hundred American cities.

Newspaper headlines blamed the violence and bloodshed on small groups of radical agitators and heavily armed black snipers. Later investigations revealed that the vast majority of casualties were African Americans who had been shot by government forces. Many of those who were injured held steady jobs and supported families, but researchers also spotlighted the social problems that lay behind the upheavals. Detroit, for example, had long been a Mecca for black migrants; but in the 1950s and early 1960s, the auto companies built new manufacturing plants in all-white suburbs such as Livonia and Wyandotte. Although manufacturing boomed in Michigan during most of the 1960s, Detroit's unemployment rate rarely dropped below 10 percent. As a result, the median income of African Americans remained at about 55 percent that of whites. As the city's tax base dwindled, schools were poorly maintained, and social services began to unravel.

In the Watts ghetto of Los Angeles, the situation was even worse: unemployment remained stuck at 20 percent, and three of every five Watts residents depended on some sort of welfare benefit. On the street, teenagers bitterly resented the treatment the nearly all-white Los Angeles Police Department (LAPD) meted out. The LAPD seemed to make arrests less to enforce the law than to intimidate young African Americans. One study showed that 90 percent of juveniles who were arrested never had charges filed against them. Meanwhile, Watts residents confronted other reminders that they lived in a racist society. In 1964, a huge majority of white

Californians voted to repeal a state law banning racial discrimination in the sale and rental of housing. In 1965, when the Watts riot erupted, involving as many as 80,000 people, one Los Angeles resident explained that it was as if the community were saying, "We're hungry. Our schools stink. . . . It's obvious the integration route ain't going to work. Now we've got to go another way."

Across the North, African American activists had been advocating economic self-reliance and black nationalism since the 1930s. The most inspiring figure was a charismatic Black Muslim named Malcolm X. A drug dealer and pimp in his teenage years, Malcolm Little converted to Elijah Muhammad's separatist Nation of Islam early in the 1950s while serving time in a Massachusetts prison. With other Black Muslims, Malcolm X adopted a new last name and saw integration with the "white devil" as an illusory solution to black problems; instead, he advocated self-reliance, black pride, and unity. "The worst crime of the white man has been to teach us to hate ourselves," Malcolm X declared to the ghetto youths who were his most devoted following. "We hated our head, we hated the shape of our nose. . . . Yeah we hated the color of our skin." By the mid-1960s, Malcolm X searched for an accommodation between his nationalist ideology and the cosmopolitan spirit of the mainstream civil rights movement, but in early 1965, he was assassinated, probably by followers of Elijah Muhammad who were jealous of Malcolm's popularity. His ideas became even more widely popular after his death, however, especially after the publication of Alex Haley's best-selling *Autobiography of Malcolm X* in 1966.

This new brand of racial assertiveness won other articulate spokesmen. The young SNCC leader Stokely Carmichael popularized the slogan "Black Power" during civil rights marches in the summer of 1966. Insisting that African Americans must control their own institutions, Carmichael stirred African American crowds with the impatient declaration "It's time we stand up and take over; move on over, or we'll move on over you." The California-based Black Panther Party combined grassroots organizing and social programs, such as free breakfasts, with a firm stance on self-defense. These urban militants argued that African Americans were the vanguard of the socialist revolution they forecast for the United States. By 1969, their inflammatory rhetoric—"Off the pig" was a favorite insult hurled at the police—drew heavy media attention. The FBI targeted the Panthers as dangerous revolutionaries and infiltrated the organization, provoking greater violence and shootouts with the police.

Bayonets on Linwood and Hazelwood

African American residents gaze at a National Guard patrol on the second day of the 1967 Detroit riot. Copyright 1967 The Detroit News.

"Fight Them and You'll Get Your Freedom"

In December 1964, less than two months before his assassination, Malcolm X spoke with a group of African American teenagers from McComb, Mississippi. The young activists had come to New York City under the auspices of the Student Nonviolent Coordinating Committee. When they visited Malcolm X, he applauded their efforts and urged them to take an even bolder stance.

One of the first things I think young people, especially nowadays, should learn, is how to see for yourself and listen for yourself and think for yourself. Then you can come to an intelligent decision for yourself. This generation, especially of our people, has a burden, more so than any other time in history. The most important thing that we can learn to do today is think for ourselves. . . .

My experience has been that in many instances where you find Negroes talking about nonviolence, they are not nonviolent with each other, and they're not loving with each other, or forgiving with each other. Usually when they say they're nonviolent, they mean they're nonviolent with somebody else. I think you understand what I mean. They are nonviolent with the enemy. A person can come to your home, and if he's white and wants to heap some kind of brutality on you, you're nonviolent; or he can come to take your father and put a rope around his neck, and you're nonviolent. But if another Negro just stomps his foot, you'll rumble with him in a minute. Which shows you that there's an inconsistency there.

I myself would go for nonviolence if it was consistent, if everybody was going to be nonviolent all the time. I'd say, okay, let's get with it, we'll all be nonviolent. But I don't go along with any kind of nonviolent unless everybody's going to be nonviolent. If they make the Ku Klux Klan nonviolent, I'll be nonviolent. If they make the White Citizens' Council nonviolent, I'll be nonviolent. But as long as you've got somebody else not being nonviolent, I don't want anybody coming to me talking any nonviolent talk. . . .

So don't you run around here trying to make friends with somebody who's depriving you of your rights. They're not your friends, no, they're your enemies. Treat them like that and fight them, and you'll get your freedom; and after you get your freedom, your enemy will respect you. And we'll respect you. And I say that with no hate. I don't have any hate in me. I have no hate at all. I don't have any hate. I've got some sense. I'm not going to let somebody who hates me tell me to love him. I'm not that way-out. And you, young as you are, and because you start thinking, are not going to do it either.

George Breitman, ed., *Malcolm X Speaks* (1966).

Whatever its limitations as a political strategy, Black Power encouraged African Americans to take increased pride and interest in their African roots and in their history of struggle and cultural innovation. Many blacks began to celebrate African American food, fashion, poetry, prose, theater, dance, and music. And within little more than a decade, black voters had united to elect a score of black mayors in cities such as Newark, Detroit, and Oakland. Although the movement could not dismantle the structural inequality in the larger society, African American activists won a certain degree of local political power and an even larger sense of self-confidence within the worlds of fashion, entertainment, and literature.

Rights Consciousness in the Workplace

An assertive rights consciousness also took hold in the workplace. Title VII of the 1964 Civil Rights Act forbade employment discrimination on the basis of race, creed, sex, or national origin and established an Equal Employment Opportunity Commission to investigate and litigate such bias. As with the Wagner Act thirty years earlier, the government put its moral and administrative weight behind a new set of employee rights, which soon had a profound impact on the U.S. workplace. Newly conscious of their rights, black and Latino workers stiffened the backbone of union drives in janitorial services, government employment, and the garment and textile industries. "Back in the late 1960s," remembered one union organizer, "whenever you went into one plant the first thing you looked to was how many blacks are there working. . . . And if there were forty blacks you could count on forty votes."

Some unions linked themselves directly to the civil rights struggle. Seeking to organize New York City's hospital service workers, such as orderlies and cafeteria workers, the leaders of Local 1199, the Drug and Hospital Employees' Union, proclaimed that their campaign ran on "union power plus soul power." To black hospital workers such as Doris Turner, their own workplace activism was but an extension of the civil rights movement in the South. "Really and truthfully, they were one [struggle], just being waged in different places." By the early 1970s, Local 1199 began to transform the very character of hospital work in many big cities by providing a living wage for a workforce that was predominantly African American, Puerto Rican, and female.

XIXth Olympiad Protest
As "The Star-Spangled Banner" is played during the 1968 Mexico City Olympics, the American gold and bronze medalists in the 200-meter dash raise their fists in the Black Power salute. Outraged by this silent tribute to black dignity and protest against racial discrimination in sports, the International Olympics Committee ejected Tommie Smith (center) and John Carlos (right) from the Olympic Village. UPI/Corbis-Bettmann.

Union Rights and Civil Rights
Malcolm X and trade union leader A. Philip Randolph share a platform during a 1962 rally celebrating a successful hospital workers' strike organized by Local 1199 of the Drug and Hospital Employees' Union.
1199 News, Local 1199, Health Care Employees Union, New York City.

Two thousand miles away, in California's Central Valley, a farm labor workforce that was composed largely of Mexican and Filipino immigrants also adopted the tactics and ideas the civil rights movement pioneered. Unlike the Birmingham civil rights activists, farm labors continued to look to unions to fight discrimination. Led by Dolores Huerta and Cesar Chavez, a charismatic organizer who had spent his childhood as a migrant laborer, California farmworkers struck the Delano vineyards early in 1965. Had these desperately poor workers relied only on their own resources, their union would have been smashed like other agricultural labor unions before them. Federal labor laws did not cover farmworkers, and the growers easily imported thousands of strikebreakers from Mexico. But the United Farm Workers (UFW) held on for five years by presenting their strike not as a simple union-management conflict, but rather as La Causa, an awakening of the Mexican American community to both its ethnic heritage and its full citizenship rights. UFW rallies, marches, and picket lines featured huge, blood-red banners imprinted with the black Aztec eagle that symbolized Mexican pride and power. When UFW strikers marched three hundred miles to the state capital at Sacramento to call attention to their working conditions, they sang "We Shall Overcome" in Spanish and English.

With the help of thousands of students and hundreds of priests and nuns, the UFW mounted a national boycott against California grape growers who refused to recognize the union. "We got to the point where we could track a grape shipment from California to Appleton, Wisconsin, and have pickets waiting for them at the loading docks at two o'clock in the morning," remembered one organizer. The UFW had modest success as a union but won great influence as a political and cultural force in the West. By the 1970s, the UFW could mobilize more campaign workers than all the other unions in California combined, and in Arizona, the union registered 100,000 new Mexican American voters. As a result, Mexican Americans in the Southwest gained new respect and increased political clout.

The Vietnam Experience

If the burgeoning social movements of the 1960s revealed the domestic problems of post–World War II society, the Vietnam War brought to the surface the tensions that were inherent in the U.S. effort to manage the

"The Women Have to Be Involved"

Jessie Lopez De La Cruz came from a family of migrant farmworkers living in California's San Joaquin Valley. Her experiences as a farm- worker and a mother of six children helped her to organize effectively for the UFW. Her ability to relate to the workers in the fields and to involve the women in the union- ization struggle proved to be important contri- butions to the battle for farmworkers' rights.

Growing up, I could see all the injustices and I would think, "If only I could do something about it! If only there was somebody who could do something about it!" That was always in the back of my mind. And after I was married, I cared about what was going on, but felt I couldn't do anything. So I went to work, and I came home to clean the house, and I fixed the food for the next day, took care of the children and the next day went back to work. The whole thing over and over again. Poli- tics to me was something foreign, something I didn't know about. I didn't even listen to the news. I didn't read newspapers hardly at all. True Romance was my thing!

But then late one night in 1962, there was a knock at the door and there were three men. One of them was Cesar Chavez. And the next thing I knew, they were sitting around our table talking about a union. I made coffee. Arnold had already told me about a union for the farm- workers. He was attending their meetings in Fresno, but I didn't. I'd either stay home or stay outside in the car. But then Cesar said, "The women have to be involved. They're the ones working out in the fields with their husbands. If you can take the women out to the fields, you can certainly take them to meetings." So I sat up straight and said to myself, "That's what I want!"

It was very hard being a woman organizer. Many of our people my age and older were raised with the old customs in Mexico: where the husband rules, he is king of his house. The wife obeys, and the chil- dren, too. So when we first started it was very, very hard. Men gave us the most trouble. . . . They were for the union, but they were not taking orders from women, they said. When [the union] formed the ranch committee [to represent workers' grievances to management] at Chris- tian Brothers [a large wine company], the ranch committee was all men. . . .

When the first contract was up, we talked about there being no women on the ranch committee. I suggested they be on it, and the men went along with this. And so women were elected.

Ellen Cantarow, et al., *Moving the Mountain: Women Working for Social Change* (1980).

Viva La Causa!

When the National Farmworkers Association (the predecessor of the United Farm Workers of America) was founded in 1962, Cesar and Richard Chavez adopted a symbol for the organization that had great meaning for the Mexican American community. "A symbol is an important thing," Cesar Chavez explained. "That is why we chose an Aztec eagle. It gives pride. When people see it they know it means dignity." It was also a practical selection: the eagle's wings were squared off so that it would be easier for farm workers to draw on the handmade flags they carried. American Social History Project.

global political economy. The road to Vietnam was paved with the arrogance of American Cold War statecraft. Like Presidents Truman and Eisenhower before them, Kennedy and Johnson wanted the United States to appear strong and command respect from foe and friend to keep world markets open, maintain the international balance of power, and carefully orchestrate the pace of social and economic change, even at the expense of democracy and development. As U.S troops poured into Southeast Asia, opposition grew at home, at first among university students, but later among middle-class professionals and working-class youths. Debate over the Vietnam War polarized the nation and, in 1968, generated a political and social crisis that destroyed Lyndon Johnson's hopes for a second term and ushered into office conservative Richard Nixon, who nevertheless promised "peace with honor."

The Road to Vietnam During his first months in office, President Kennedy faced three reversals that seemed to demonstrate a systemic weakness in the Western camp. In April 1961, a CIA-organized invasion of Cuba, at the Bay of Pigs on the island's southern coast, failed to overthrow Fidel Castro's young revolutionary regime. Five months later, East German Communists erected an ugly concrete wall across Berlin to halt the flow of refugees to the increasingly prosperous West. Then a pro-Western government in the Southeast Asian kingdom of Laos collapsed. These setbacks were all manageable, but they nevertheless suggested that vigilance and determination would be necessary to maintain U.S. credibility in a dangerous world.

Toughness seemed to pay off in the fall of 1962, when the Soviets installed intermediate-range ballistic missiles in Cuba. Kennedy responded with a U.S. naval blockade of the island. For a moment, the world seemed poised on the brink of a nuclear confrontation, but the crisis ended when the Soviet Union agreed to remove the missiles. Kennedy's victory won him much support at home and gave him the political strength to negotiate in 1963 a treaty with the Soviet Union banning the above-ground testing of nuclear weapons. But the long-term consequences of the Cuban missile crisis were ambiguous. The Kremlin was determined that the United States would not outgun them again, so the Soviets began building up their naval and long-range missile forces and ended a five-year period of internal reforms. Meanwhile, Kennedy, Johnson, and their key aides concluded that they could use military force, or its threat, as an effective tool of statecraft.

This reasoning led the United States into a tragic war in Vietnam. There, an independence movement led by the Communist and nationalist Ho Chi Minh had won substantial support among Vietnamese peasants, students, intellectuals, and urban workers. In 1954, Ho's forces defeated the French colonial army at Dien Bien Phu and won independence for the

Operation Barrel Roll, 1982
The Plain of Jars in northern Laos, pockmarked with bomb craters, nine years after the United States ended its aerial campaign. Hiroji Kubota/Magnum.

northern half of Vietnam. The United States quickly stepped in to replace France as the dominant power in South Vietnam, backing the authoritarian regime of Ngo Dinh Diem, a Catholic aristocrat, who sought to build a viable political alternative to Communism in the south. But Diem's support never spread beyond the army and a narrow circle of landlords and urban Catholics. Although aware of Diem's weaknesses, Kennedy wanted to prove, in the words of one Pentagon analyst, that the United States was "willing to keep promises to its allies, to be tough, to take risks, get bloodied, and hurt the enemy badly." So the United States steadily increased the number of its military advisers in Vietnam; at the time of Kennedy's death in November 1963, they numbered more than 16,000.

Johnson also saw Vietnam as a proving ground for U.S. global power. On August 2, 1964, North Vietnamese torpedo boats skirmished with the American destroyer *Maddox* in the Gulf of Tonkin; two days later, radar operators on the *Maddox* and another destroyer, the *C. Turner Joy*, reported another attack (though the Navy soon concluded that, as a result of stormy seas, the nervous sailors had probably generated a false report). Johnson labeled this attack an "open aggression on the high seas against the United States," enabling him to secure congressional passage of the Gulf of Tonkin Resolution mandating the president "to take all necessary steps, including the use of armed force" to aid South Vietnam. In February 1965, the U.S. Air Force began a sustained bombing campaign against North Vietnam, after which the United States sent an ever-increasing number of ground combat troops to Southeast Asia—more than half a million by the middle of 1968.

Fighting the War As troop levels in Vietnam rose, the military swept in to its ranks hundreds of thousands of teenagers. At first, few young men gave much thought to the politics of the war. "I didn't have any feelings one way or the other," one draftee remembered. "I figured it was more or less right, because why would I be going if it wasn't right?" The military draft, or Selective Service System, was indeed selective. Because college students initially were entitled to deferments, most escaped the first years of the draft. If they ended up in the Army, they usually served as officers or in noncombat posts. In contrast, poor Americans, white as well as black and Latino, were far more likely to be drafted and assigned to combat. Draftees, only about one-quarter of the army, represented 88 percent of infantry riflemen in 1970 and two-thirds of all battle deaths. The Veterans Administration concluded that the disproportionate casualties suffered by American minorities was the product not of direct racial bias, "but of discrimination against the poor, the uneducated, and the young." This represented a major change from World War II. Then, the draft had reached deep into the middle class and to men who were already established in jobs and careers (Figure 12.2).

Politics and new technology helped to shape U.S. military strategy in Vietnam. The military initially assumed that expensive technology and sophisticated organization would substitute for much of the blood and sweat of ground combat. But a massive, carefully orchestrated campaign of aerial bombing proved ineffective against the rifles and booby traps of the enemy foot soldiers who usually fought in small combat units. U.S. bombing of Vietnam, Laos, and Cambodia after 1970 could not stop the infiltration of personnel and supplies from North Vietnam or destroy the southern bases of the insurgent National Liberation Front (NLF). This failure led to the massive deployment of U.S. troops, who sought out the enemy in a series of search-and-destroy operations that began in 1965. But the NLF and the North Vietnamese Army avoided pitched battles with U.S. forces. U.S. military leaders therefore came to define victory not by the seizure of enemy territory or the defeat of hostile battalions but by the physical annihilation of individual enemy soldiers.

This war of attrition led to a bureaucratic fixation

FIGURE 12.2   Escalation and De-escalation: U.S. Troops in Vietnam, 1962–1972

Although President Kennedy sent more than 16,000 military "advisers" to Vietnam in the early 1960s, the dramatic expansion of American troops did not begin until the spring of 1965. Antiwar protests and disillusionment with the war effort grew along with the escalating commitment of troops. In 1969, President Nixon began a "Vietnamization effort" that was designed to reduce the number of American soldiers in Vietnam and quiet the furor at home.

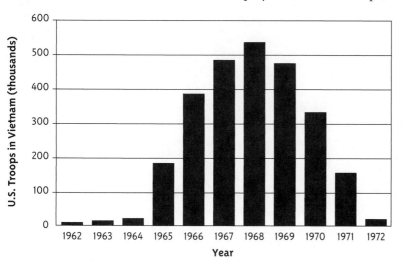

"A Relative Thing"

This poem, written by Corporal William Ehrhart in the early 1970s expresses the sense of futility that many American foot soldiers experienced during the Vietnam War. VC and ARVN are abbreviations, respectively, for "Viet-cong," or guerrilla forces of the National Liberation Front, and the "Army of the Republic of Vietnam," the South Vietnamese military.

We are the ones you sent to fight a war
you didn't know a thing about.

It didn't take us long to realize
the only land that we controlled
was covered by the bottoms of our boots.

When the newsmen said that naval ships
had shelled a VC staging point,
we saw a breastless woman
and her still born child.

We laughed at old men stumbling
in the dust in frenzied terror
to avoid our three-ton trucks.

We fought outnumbered in Hue City
while the ARVN soldiers looted bodies
in the safety of the rear.
The cookies from the wives of Local 104
did not soften our awareness.

We have seen the pacified supporters
of the Saigon government
sitting in their jampacked cardboard towns,
their wasted hands placed limply in their laps,
their empty bellies waiting for the rice
some district chief has sold
for profit to the Viet Cong.

We have been Democracy on Zippo raids,
burning houses to the ground,
driving eager amtracs through new-sown fields.

We are the ones who have to live
with the memory that we were the instruments
of your pigeon-breasted fantasies.

We are inextricable accomplices
in this travesty of dreams:
but we are not alone.

We are the ones you sent to fight a war
you did not know a thing about—
those of us that lived
have tried to tell you what went wrong.
Now you think you do not have to listen.

Just because we will not fit
into the uniforms of photographs
of you at twenty-one
does not mean you can disown us.

We are your sons, America,
and you cannot change that.
When you awake,
we will still be here.

"A Relative Thing" by W. D. Ehrhart is reprinted from *Beautiful Wreckage: New and Selected Poems*, Adastra Press (1999); by permission of the author.

with the daily "body count." Because the distinction between civilians and NLF combatants became hopelessly confused, American soldiers were soon reporting as an enemy fatality any Vietnamese who was killed by U.S. firepower. A T-shirt worn by some U.S. soldiers expressed the GIs' frustration: "KILL THEM ALL! LET GOD SORT THEM OUT!" The consequence of such attitudes came in the village of My Lai, where an American platoon landed one morning in 1968. "When the attack started," one sergeant recalled, "We were mad and had been told that the enemy was there and we were going in there to give them a fight for what they had done to our dead buddies." The U.S. platoon took no enemy fire, but within a matter of minutes, the village exploded with American grenades and machine gun bursts. Soldiers murdered more than 350 Vietnamese villagers. There was one American casualty: a GI who shot himself in the foot out of disgust at what he was witnessing.

The Antiwar Movement and the New Left   The Vietnam War was fought at home as well as abroad. Until the end of the 1960s, most Americans supported the war. But its length, cost, and character generated a growing opposition—or, rather, two kinds of antiwar sentiment. A highly ideological antiwar movement emerged out of the New Left radicalism that was present on many college campuses. But this student opposition to the Johnson administration's Vietnam policies was accompanied by a late-blooming, far more conservative rejection of the war with the position "Win Now or Get Out." Conservative opponents of the war considered themselves traditional patriots, and they had nothing but contempt for the New Left, but they were unwilling to bear the costs of what seemed an endless struggle. By 1968, antiwar sentiment on both the left and the right had become so great that continued escalation of the war was no longer tenable.

The My Lai Massacre
This picture was one of several taken in Quang Ngai province on March 16, 1968, by an Army photographer that appeared in *Life* magazine in late 1969; until that fall, the massacre had been covered up by Army personnel. The incident played a role in turning Americans against the war in Vietnam. Ron Haeberle, *Life* magazine.

The New Left came to life on college and university campuses in the early 1960s, when many contemporary observers still bemoaned a "silent generation" of youthful, career-minded conformists. Early New Left activists identified with the civil rights movement, which promised to restore moral vision to American life, and with the university, which seemed to be a place where ideas could have immediate and beneficial consequences. Unlike the "Old Left" of the Depression era, most Sixties leftists rejected Marxist ideology and the need for well-structured political organizations. And unlike most working-class students, whose urgent desire to find a secure job often shaped their social outlook, middle-class students in the prosperous 1960s were "free" for a few crucial years to reflect skeptically on the gap between the liberal promise of American life and social reality.

The 1962 Port Huron Statement, a founding manifesto of the leading New Left organization Students for a Democratic Society (SDS), called on America to live up to its highest democratic ideals. SDS urged activists to respond not only to issues of poverty, but also to the problems of modern life, from alienation and bureaucratic impersonality to the threat of nuclear war. "A new left," SDS proclaimed, "must give form to the feelings of helplessness and indifference, so that people may see the political, social, and economic source of their personal troubles and organize to change society." Early New Leftists saw the civil rights movement as proof that students, intellectuals, and racial minorities in the United States could spark a transformation of the society. "SDS seemed hip and bold," recalled Jeremy Brecher, an Oregon student in the early 1960s. "It had an enthusiasm for direct action, an attitude of defiance towards the establishment, and a con-

From Protest to Resistance
Confronted by a phalanx of soldiers, federal marshals, and police, antiwar demonstrators block the Pentagon on October 21, 1967. Marc Riboud/Magnum.

stant looking for points where change could be stimulated and supported." From 1963 to 1966, SDS sent groups of students to Chicago, Newark, and elsewhere to organize "interracial movements of the poor."

The early New Left adopted radical tactics to advance a set of classically liberal ideals. At the University of California, Berkeley, students formed a Free-Speech Movement (FSM) in 1964 when conservative politicians and businessmen persuaded university officials to crack down on campus civil rights activism. Students were outraged when campus police prohibited the collection of funds for civil rights work or the distribution of political literature on campus. In response, FSM activists waged a nonviolent, disruptive, and, in the end, largely successful struggle against paternalistic university officials. FSM leader Mario Savio, who had worked for civil rights in Mississippi, asserted that in Berkeley and the Deep South, "[t]he same rights are at stake in both places, the right to participate as citizens in democratic society and the right to due process of law."

Conflicts over university governance spread to hundreds of schools, but a fierce debate over the politics and morality of the Vietnam War soon overshadowed campus reform issues. After President Johnson ordered massive air strikes and troop deployments in 1965, a generation of radical students moved into the forefront of the antiwar movement. A few were pacifists who opposed the use of organized violence for any purpose. Others came to sympathize with, and even glorify, the NLF as heroic nationalists. Most agreed that the war — and America's role as global policeman — violated the ideals of democracy and freedom. Antiwar marches, which had drawn only a few thousand in 1965, rapidly grew in size; by 1967, a million protesters marched in the streets of New York, San Francisco, and Washington, D.C.

For young Americans, the draft stood as a prime symbol of the war. Millions of young men tried to evade it. Some fled to Canada; many feigned physical or psychological problems in hopes of winning deferments; others, on the left and right, used family connections to gain safe berths in the National Guard. A few thousand took public stands as draft resisters, burning their draft cards and challenging the government to imprison them. Catholic priests Philip and Daniel Berrigan inspired a wave of clandestine attacks against local

draft boards, in which files were burned or drenched with blood. By the late 1960s, draft resistance—organized and unorganized, overt and covert— was so widespread that the nation's legal system could no longer effectively handle the flood of cases.

The antiwar movement won thousands of working-class recruits after 1968. By then, nonelite universities such as Wayne State in Detroit, Kent State in Ohio, and all-black Southern University in Baton Rouge, Louisiana, had become centers of movement activity. Long hair, marijuana, and rock music spread to factory night shifts, construction sites, and mail rooms staffed by young workers. The radicalization of working-class youths had a direct effect on the military. After 1967, drug use among soldiers and sailors soared, desertions quadrupled, and hostility toward officers took on a political coloration. Anti-war sentiments escalated in the U.S. military, culminating in the founding of the Vietnam Veterans Against the War in 1967, which grew to number 30,000 GIs at its peak. Peace symbols and Black Power fists appeared on GIs' helmets. "Almost to a man, the members of my platoon oppose the war," explained one sergeant in 1971.

The American labor movement was an ideological casualty of the Vietnam War. Leaders of the AFL-CIO were staunch anti-Communists, so they backed the war. But to many student activists, the white working class itself seemed to have bargained away its radical potential. "The next time some $3.90-an-hour AFL–type workers go on strike for a 50-cent raise," exploded Berkeley activist Marvin Garson in 1967, "I'll remember the day they chanted 'Burn Hanoi, not our flag,' and so help me, I'll cross their picket line." Instead, many activists looked to the Black Power movement or to the Cuban and Vietnamese revolutions for models of how social change might be instigated in the United States.

Repressive police activity advanced the hothouse radicalism that was becoming characteristic of the late 1960s New Left. While state and local

Operation Dewey Canyon III
Facing a barricade that had been erected to keep them off the steps of the Capitol, hundreds of veterans — many in wheelchairs or on crutches — return medals that they had received during tours of duty in Vietnam. Perhaps the most moving of all antiwar demonstrations, this ceremony was the culmination of a week-long campaign during April 1971 that was organized by the Vietnam Veterans Against the War (VVAW) to dramatically publicize atrocities that had been committed by the United States. The VVAW named the protest after secret American invasions of Laos in 1969 and early 1971. Leonard Freed/ Magnum.

police attacked marchers and harassed demonstrators, an FBI counterintelligence program spearheaded a nationwide effort to "expose, disrupt, and otherwise neutralize" civil rights, black power, and antiwar activity. Government intelligence agents joined some radical groups as agents provocateurs whose faux militancy discredited antiwar activism and individual radicals.

The New Left self-destructed in 1969 and 1970. One SDS splinter group known as the Weathermen identified themselves as urban guerrillas waging underground warfare as part of the global struggle against the "Amerikkkan" empire. Between September 1969 and May 1970, police recorded at least 250 bombings that were linked to U.S. radical groups. Campus Reserve Office Training Corps buildings and draft board headquarters were favorite targets. The spate of bombings slowed in 1970 after three Weathermen accidentally killed themselves when a homemade bomb exploded in their Greenwich Village townhouse. Although hundreds of thousands of people, adults as well as students, still turned out for antiwar protests, the New Left fragmented at the very moment when broad layers of the American people might have been most receptive to its political and moral arguments.

The Rise of the Counterculture The impact of the New Left was cultural as well as political. Millions of Americans sought new forms of community, questioning traditional forms of monogamy and family, suburban life, the headlong pursuit of material possessions, and the value that society placed on scientific rationality and emotional repression. The rise of rock music, the end of many sexual taboos, and the growing use of marijuana and psychedelic drugs represented only the most obvious indications that American culture was in the midst of a great change.

Music was central to the 1960s counterculture. Early in the decade, folk musicians such as Bob Dylan set the tone for the era's political idealism by reviving such songs as Woody Guthrie's "This Land Is Your Land," which celebrated a democratic, populist America. By 1963, however, the year of the Birmingham demonstrations and President Kennedy's assassination, Dylan's "Blowin' in the Wind" reflected impatience with a liberalism that was turning sour. About the same time, soul singers such as Otis Redding and Aretha Franklin, Motown stars such as Marvin Gaye, and British rock-and-roll groups such as the Beatles and the Rolling Stones were renewing rock-and-roll's connection to its African American roots. After 1965, San Francisco bands such as the Grateful Dead, which performed routinely at protest rallies, enlivened the robust Bay Area radical culture. Popular music now seemed to spread the messages of social criticism and possibility. "The music and the world it created," recalled one former activist, "helped give us a sense that we were defining the culture, and the whole society was following."

If You Can't Beat 'em, Absorb 'em

Columbia Records denounces the "Establishment" in an advertisement that was placed in underground newspapers in December 1968. Abbie Hoffman, a leader of the antiestablishment Yippies, later commented that such corporations "were taking the energy from the streets and using it for a commercial value, saying, 'If you are in the revolution, what you got to do is buy our records,' while we were saying, 'You got to burn your draft card, you can't go to Vietnam, you have to come to the demonstrations and the protests.' It was a conflict and we called their process cooptation: . . . They were able to turn a historic civil clash in our society into a fad, then the fad could be sold." *Rolling Stone*, December 7, 1968 — American Social History Project.

The counterculture pioneered a new form of journalism as well. Hundreds of "underground" community newspapers celebrated rock music and the drug scene, publicized movement protests, and experimented with a journalistic style that was intensely personal and highly critical of established institutions. Many of these papers flourished only briefly, but they

Comix!

In the spirit of the counterculture, underground cartoonists rejected the style and substance of commercial comics and newspaper comic strips and enthusiastically embraced every taboo. The starched suburban antics of *Archie* were replaced by the slovenly inner-city iconoclasm of Gilbert Shelton's *Fabulous Furry Freak Brothers* (represented here by brother Fat Freddy). The standard paternal and patriotic superheroes were rearranged into Shelton's sadistic and superpatriotic *Wonder Wart Hog*, Spain Rodriguez's vengeful guerrilla-fighter *Trashman*, and others. Meanwhile, Robert Crumb and S. Clay Wilson delved into the darker recesses of consciousness, producing a range of characters who reveled in the violent excesses of "sex, drugs, and rock-'n'-roll." Gilbert Shelton, *Gothic Blimp Works*, 1969 — Copyright Rip Off Press, Inc.

had a lasting influence on the mainstream news media, redefining the meaning of "news" and helping to open the door for a new generation of investigative journalists.

The impact of the counterculture spread to almost every segment of society. American Catholicism, for instance, underwent a surprising transformation, in response both to the reformist Second Vatican Council of 1962 and to the new social movements of the era. Among the laity, obedience to church authority declined, and as popular mores changed, millions of Catholics came to ignore church teachings on sexual matters. By the mid-1970s, three-quarters of all Catholics who were polled said that if necessary, they would have an abortion or advise their wives to do so; and in Chicago, two-thirds of Catholics under age thirty who considered themselves pious approved of premarital sex.

1968: A Watershed Year The year 1968 played host to a number of dramatic and unexpected events as the nation's Cold War consensus seemed to break apart. Although the Vietnam War would drag on for seven more years, it had become clear by the end of 1968 that Americans were no longer willing to pay the price of "winning" that bloody conflict. Lyndon Johnson's presidency disintegrated, Richard Nixon succeeded him in the White House, and modern American liberalism went into sharp decline.

Late in January, during Tet, the Vietnamese New Year, the NLF launched a massive offensive that put its combatants inside almost every Vietnamese town and city. Nightly news broadcasts brought graphic, painful pictures to the American public, including scenes of a gun battle inside the American embassy compound in Saigon. The bitter fighting, which raged through February and March, killed thousands of NLF soldiers. American generals claimed victory, but the Tet offensive actually dealt President Lyndon Johnson's Vietnam policy a political deathblow. Until then, most newspaper and the television network coverage had favored U.S. government policy. The Tet offensive shattered that optimistic story line. "To say that we are mired in a stalemate seems the only realistic, if unsatisfactory, conclusion," reported respected news anchor Walter Cronkite. Thereafter, the news media greeted official government pronouncements with skepticism and gave antiwar activity increased coverage and respect (Map 12.2).

The NLF offensive also shook the Democratic Party. Until Tet, party liberals had hesitated to criticize President Johnson; in late 1967, when antiwar Minnesota senator Eugene McCarthy announced that he would challenge

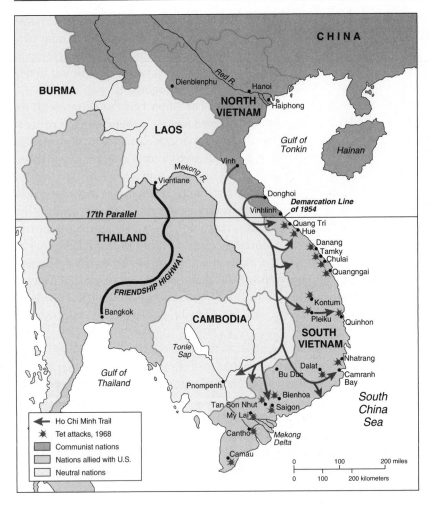

MAP 12.2   The Tet Offensive of 1968: Turning Point in the Vietnam War

On January 31, 1968, North Vietnamese troops and supporters of the National Liberation Front attacked scores of sites throughout South Vietnam. Although they were routed by U.S. and South Vietnamese forces, the surprise attack demonstrated that the United States was not close to victory and turned U.S. public opinion against the war. Soon afterward, President Johnson announced that he would not run for reelection and partially halted bombings of North Vietnam.

the incumbent president for the 1968 Democratic nomination, his prospects seemed marginal. After Tet, however, the news media spotlighted McCarthy's effort, student volunteers poured into his campaign, and he startled Johnson with a near-upset in the New Hampshire primary. New York senator Robert Kennedy, the former U.S. attorney general, sensed Johnson's vulnerability and declared his own presidential candidacy, calling for a halt to the bombing and a revival of the War on Poverty. In a series of hard-fought primaries during the spring of 1968, McCarthy and Kennedy battled each other and the Democratic Party establishment, demonstrating the breadth of public sentiment that was committed to a de-escalation of the war.

Meanwhile, Tet precipitated a reevaluation of the war by the elite lawyers, bankers, and State Department officials who had presided over U.S. foreign policy since World War II. The war generated disquiet on Wall Street and complaints from America's allies in Europe. By 1968, the costs of the war had spiraled well beyond those that had been forecast just two years before, superheating the economy, generating inflationary pressures at home, and weakening the value of the dollar abroad. To men such as Dean Acheson, a corporate lawyer and Truman's secretary of state, the war was an open wound that sapped America's global strength. Acheson told Lyndon Johnson: "We need to stand back and get our priorities right. Enemy number one is Russia. . . . The vital strategic areas in their proper order are Western Europe particularly Germany, Japan, the Middle East, Latin America—and only then Southeast Asia."

President Johnson caved in. On March 31, he announced that he would stop bombing North Vietnam, cancel a planned troop increase, and end his reelection campaign. The antiwar movement had split the Democratic Party and forced a powerful president to repudiate his own foreign policy and renounce another term in office. These dramatic developments might well have opened the way for America to make a decisive turn to the left, toward a new foreign policy and a more radical program of social reform at home. Yet 1968 proved to be a turning point that did not turn. Within little more than two months of Johnson's announcement, the two most visible opposition figures in American politics, Robert Kennedy and Martin Luther King, Jr., lay dead.

King was the first to fall. Convinced that the black movement had to take up the demand for economic as well as political justice, King had gone to Tennessee to help organize support for striking Memphis sanitation workers. Marches, demonstrations, and arrests gave this sixty-day municipal sanitation strike much of the flavor of the early civil rights movement; the slogan boldly printed on their picket signs, "I AM A MAN," spoke as clearly about the real meaning of the conflict as did the union's demand for higher wages and a contract. On April 4, hours before King was to lead another mass march on City Hall, a white ex-convict named James Earl Ray shot him from ambush. After King's death, African American neighborhoods across the United States exploded in riots, signaling a bitter end to the once-hopeful civil rights era.

After helping to lead the mourning for King, Robert Kennedy returned to the primary campaign. On June 4, with enthusiastic support from California Latinos and African Americans, he won the Democratic primary in that crucial state. But after Kennedy made a triumphant speech to California campaign workers in Los Angeles in the early morning hours of June 5, Palestinian nationalist Sirhan Sirhan shot him as Kennedy returned to his hotel room. "I won't vote," one black New Yorker later told a pollster. "Every good man we get they kill."

The murders of King and Kennedy eroded the sense of legitimacy and democratic fairness that were the prerequisite for the nation's political

CHICAGO'S AMERICAN, THURSDAY, AUGUST 22, 1968

Here's Cast of Characters in Drama of Streets

CLEAN GENES   THE MOB   OPEN CONVENTIONERS   HIPPIES   YIPPIES   GREASERS   BIKERS

"Identify Them by Their Garb"
As Democratic National Convention delegates and protestors arrived in Chicago in late August 1968, the *Chicago American* published a guide to the "cast of characters" converging on the city. Illustrating student supporters of Eugene McCarthy, activists identified with the National Mobilization Against the War ("the Mobe"), liberal Democrats opposed to the Johnson administration, hippies, Yippies (who nominated a pig as their presidential candidate), apolitical greasers, and outlaw bikers, the guide identified political attitudes through stereotypes of dress and hair style. The *American* failed to notice any African Americans among the dissenting delegates and demonstrators.
Bruce Darrow, *Chicago American*, August 22, 1968 — Chicago Historical Society [ICHI27492].

institutions to work. They were brought into question yet again at the Democratic National Convention in Chicago, where liberals within the Democratic Party felt deprived of an antiwar standard-bearer and resentful of party rules that unfairly limited the representation of dissident views. Meanwhile, outside the convention center, Mayor Richard J. Daley encouraged police officers to harass and beat antiwar radicals who were protesting in the streets. Inside, with solid backing from Lyndon Johnson, conservative Democrats, and organized labor, Vice President Hubert H. Humphrey captured the Democratic presidential nomination, leaving his party still bitterly divided.

Humphrey's Republican opponent was Richard Nixon, the former vice president. Nixon was a Republican centrist, an opportunist who was remarkably adept at manipulating the political passions of his era. In a carefully scripted campaign, Nixon denounced the campus upheavals, the ghetto riots, and many Great Society reforms, aiming his message at what he called the "silent majority" of "forgotten Americans, the non-shouters, the non-demonstrators." But Nixon also went after the peace vote, declaring that he had formulated a plan — never spelled out during the campaign — to bring "peace with honor" in Vietnam.

Third-party candidate George Wallace compounded Humphrey's difficulties by stepping into the void that liberalism's disarray had created. Wallace, a former governor of Alabama, was a Vietnam hawk and a racist who had learned to substitute new code words, such as "law and order," for the old segregationist cant. At the end of September, polls gave Wallace 21 percent of the national vote; his greatest strength was among Democratic voters in the white South, in the lower middle class, and among blue-collar workers in the industrial Midwest. Wallace attracted many supporters by tapping a deep vein of alienation and social resentment among working-class Americans. He appealed, in his own words, to the "average

"There Were Police Chasing Them with Billy Clubs"

Barry Edmonds, a prize-winning photographer for the Booth Newspaper chain, covered the August 1968 demonstrations by a few thousand antiwar activists and Yippies (the Youth International Party)—a flamboyant group led by Abbie Hoffman and Jerry Rubin—who gathered in Chicago to protest the Democratic National Convention. The Chicago police broke up protests with tear gas and billy clubs, beating hundreds of activists, bystanders, and reporters. Vivid reports of the battle fed a widespread sense that American society was being torn apart. Here, Edmonds describes what he saw in Chicago.

After about two blocks, a running mob of people—about fifty—burst out of an alley in front of our station wagon. I stopped to avoid running over them. There were police chasing them with billy clubs.

A young man in a tan summer suit—he was well-dressed and carried one camera—ran in front of our vehicle. A cop yelled, "Get out of here with that camera." The man ran to the sidewalk, but one cop circled a parked car to cut him off, and another cop was just five feet behind him with a raised club.

The young man raised his hands when he saw the cop in front, like he was surrendering, but both cops grabbed him, one on each side. A third cop came up behind him with a billy club and made a running swing at the man's head. It didn't knock him out. He began screaming in a high pitched voice, like a girl, it sounded. He dropped to the sidewalk, and the two cops turned away, but the cop who had clubbed him from behind—he was a short, stocky man—was still clubbing the man, who lay on the pavement, still screaming. Then the cop left, and "Yippie medics" came up, wearing white smocks. . . .

I drove on, slowly. . . . Some more "Yippies" in their white smocks with crude red crosses sewn on the sleeves were kneeling by another man down on the sidewalk. The man's face was bloody. . . . I heard somebody ask, "Can you take this man to the hospital? . . ." They laid the man across the back seat of our station wagon. He had a bandage around the crown of his head. . . .

There were police all over, and we told the man to stay down. He kept saying, "I'm sorry. I'm sorry. Gee, my wife is really going to be worried." He didn't look like a Yippie or a hippie or a newsman—he was just a person.

Ann Arbor News, August 28, 1968.

man," who was "sick and tired of theoreticians in both national parties and in some of our colleges and some of our courts telling us how to go to bed at night and get up in the morning."

Frightened by the Wallace phenomenon, the AFL-CIO and other unions deluged their members with leaflets and pamphlets pointing out Wallace's antiunion, proemployer record. This appeal worked, and Humphrey won the votes of many northern workers who had once favored Wallace. In the end, the Alabamian took only 13.5 percent of the national vote, mostly in the South. Humphrey also won back the support of some on the antiwar left when he belatedly broke with Johnson's war policy and pledged to halt the bombing of North Vietnam. But Nixon and his vice presidential running mate Spiro Agnew, the governor of Maryland, squeaked through in November 1968, capturing the White House with but 43.4 percent of the popular vote and 56 percent of the electoral college vote (Map 12.3).

Nixon, Vietnam, and Détente

Richard Nixon sought to diffuse Vietnam as a domestic political issue to give his administration more political space in which to maneuver, both at home and abroad. Like Johnson, Nixon believed that rapid, unilateral withdrawal of American support from South Vietnam would lead to the domino-like fall of all the countries of Southeast Asia to the Communists. His "peace plan" therefore turned out to mean a "Vietnamization" of the war: a slow reduction in the combat role played by U.S. troops, accompanied by the more active engagement of the South Vietnamese military, an intensification of the U.S. air war, and dramatic incursions into neighboring Cambodia and Laos.

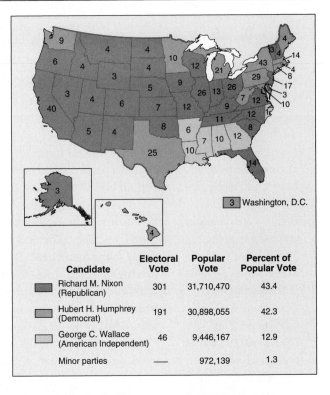

Candidate	Electoral Vote	Popular Vote	Percent of Popular Vote
Richard M. Nixon (Republican)	301	31,710,470	43.4
Hubert H. Humphrey (Democrat)	191	30,898,055	42.3
George C. Wallace (American Independent)	46	9,446,167	12.9
Minor parties	—	972,139	1.3

MAP 12.3 Presidential Election of 1968

The 1968 election reflected the country's social and political polarization. Johnson's withdrawal from the election, Robert Kennedy's assassination, and George Wallace's vigorous third-party campaign left the Democratic Party in shambles. Nixon won the election with only 43 percent of the popular vote.

The political contradictions that were inherent in this policy were demonstrated in May 1970, when U.S. troops invaded Cambodia. In response to this unexpected escalation, hundreds of American college campuses erupted in the most massive, disruptive set of antiwar demonstrations of the entire Vietnam era. At Kent State University in Ohio, four undergraduates were killed when the National Guard troops fired rifles into a crowd at an antiwar rally; and at Jackson State University in Mississippi, police killed two more students. As hundreds of thousands of antiwar demonstrators converged on Washington, the Nixon administration was forced to announce that U.S. ground troops would be withdrawn from Cambodia within a few weeks. Shortly thereafter, an angry Democrat-controlled Senate repealed the Gulf of Tonkin Resolution and forbade the further use of American troops in Laos or Cambodia.

U.S. troop levels and battle deaths thereafter declined. From a peak of 540,000 in 1969, the number of U.S. soldiers stationed in Vietnam dwindled to about 60,000 three years later. A new lottery system made the draft more equitable, and the emergence of a smaller, all-volunteer military ended conscription outright. Meanwhile, many high-profile political figures, inside and outside the Democratic Party, began to demand an immediate U.S. withdrawal, a sentiment that had once been associated only with the most radical New Leftists. After 1971, there were no major antiwar demonstrations in the United States.

Nixon's search for a politically acceptable end to the Vietnam War led his administration to seek the cooperation of China and the Soviet Union in brokering a peace settlement and in reducing tensions among the great powers. Advised by the brilliant but devious Henry Kissinger, who headed Nixon's National Security Council and later became secretary of state, the president sought a balance-of-power "détente" with these erstwhile enemies. When he visited "Red" China in February 1972, Nixon seemed to repudiate twenty-five years of Cold War invective against the mainland Communists. The U.S. rapprochement with China soon led to a new set of arms and trade agreements with the Soviet Union, which feared a Chinese-American alliance. The Strategic Arms Limitation Treaty, signed by Nixon and Soviet premier Leonid Brezhnev in a May 1972 Moscow ceremony, did little to slow the qualitative escalation of the arms race, but the agreement itself, which limited the total number of missiles and bombers, ratified elite accommodation, on both sides of the Iron Curtain, to the geopolitical status quo.

Despite the cordiality in Beijing and Moscow, Nixon could not find "peace with honor" in Vietnam, even after years of negotiations in Paris. When Henry Kissinger announced that "peace is at hand" in a 1972 election eve press conference, America's Vietnamese allies in Saigon objected to any agreement that left Communist troops in the South. Nixon and Kissinger sought to break this stalemate in December with a massive B-52 bombing campaign that, for the first time, targeted Hanoi itself; but little changed, and when the Paris peace accords were finally signed early in 1973, the North Vietnamese military advantage remained intact. The United States won the release of several hundred airmen who had spent years in North Vietnamese prison camps, and the Hanoi government waited two years before launching its war-winning military offensive in the South. By that time, the South Vietnamese no longer had the will to fight, and Congress refused to authorize further bombing or funding for the Vietnamese war effort. As Communist tanks rumbled into Saigon late in April 1975, U.S. officials and their Vietnamese civilian supporters left in humiliating disarray.

Beyond Vietnam: Nixon's Domestic Agenda   Richard Nixon had one overriding goal at home: to build a Republican majority based on a new conservative coalition that accommodated the racial and cultural interests of the heretofore staunchly Democratic white South. His administration therefore pursued a "southern strategy" that downplayed desegregation of schools and jobs, sought a more conservative tilt to the Supreme Court, cut back Great Society social programs, and demonized both the New Left and Democratic Party liberals. Nixon appealed to what he called "the silent majority," seeking a curb on government activism and a return of spending power to the business and political elites that were so influential at the state and local level.

Nixon's strategy would eventually prove to be a political success, but during most of his first term, it was a policy failure. The Senate refused to confirm Nixon's first two nominees to the Supreme Court; both Clement Haynsworth and G. Harold Carswell were southern conservatives with a segregationist past. Nixon also could not stop the rapid, court-ordered desegregation of southern schools. The president succeeded in abolishing the Johnson era Office of Economic Opportunity, but Democrats saved many other Great Society social programs. The Nixon administration escalated the government's clandestine war against New Left activists, but government prosecution of prominent radicals such as Benjamin Spock, Jerry Rubin, and Tom Hayden ended in acquittal or mistrial.

Nixon appointed four mainstream conservatives to the Supreme Court, including Warren Burger, who replaced Earl Warren in 1969. But the Burger Court continued much of Warren's activist tradition, especially on racial matters. In *Alexander v. Holmes* (1969), the Supreme Court unanimously decreed that it was "the obligation of every school district to terminate dual school systems at once." It strengthened this ruling in *Swann v. Charlotte-Mecklenburg Board of Education* (1971) by ruling in favor of the use of busing to achieve racial balance in the schools. Thus, fifteen years after *Brown v. Board of Education*, integration was finally becoming a reality for a majority of African American schoolchildren in the South. The Burger Court also struck a blow against discrimination in hiring and promotions when it decreed, in *Griggs v. Duke Power* (1971), that employment tests and standards that had a "disparate impact" on blacks and other minorities were inherently racist. Finally, in *Roe v. Wade* (1973), the Burger Court helped to push forward a social revolution by declaring that a woman's right to privacy invalidated most state laws forbidding abortions.

Because social and economic liberalism remained powerful during the early 1970s, Nixon often accommodated himself to this ideological current if he thought it politically advantageous. He approved congressional efforts to boost spending for Medicaid, food stamps, and Aid to Families with Dependent Children; he also signed the costly legislation that indexed Social Security to inflation and brought the indigent aged, blind, and disabled into the system. Nixon even tried to link the interests of the Republican Party to the urban civil rights community when, in 1969, he endorsed the "Philadelphia Plan," which required construction unions in Philadelphia to set "goals and timetables" for the hiring of black apprentices when they were employed on government contracts. Within a year, this controversial affirmative action idea was incorporated into regulations governing all federal hiring and contracting, thereby covering more than one-third of the entire national labor force. Affirmative action programs were politically advantageous to Nixon. They appealed to middle-class African Americans, cost practically nothing, and exacerbated tensions between unions and blacks, both of which were core constituencies of the Democratic Party.

Extending and Ending the Long Sixties

Whatever the merits of Nixon's clever statecraft, American politics, culture, and social expectations still bore the democratic imprint of "the Sixties." The giant Woodstock rock festival in August 1969 and massive antiwar protests in November 1969, May 1970, and April and May 1971 demonstrated that a self-conscious youth culture and a new capacity for political mobilization had spread far beyond the campuses that had first spawned radical thought and action. In the early 1970s, both middle-class environmentalists and blue-collar workers demanded that the country take notice of their concerns. Chicanos, Native Americans, and a new women's movement expanded the definition of full citizenship. The Watergate crisis brought the growing polarization of American politics into sharp relief, making that scandal the last act of the Sixties drama.

The Environmental Movement   The environmental movement, which overnight became a major political force in the 1970s, was an offspring of the nation's new participatory political culture. Ecological awareness had its roots in the early-twentieth-century conservation impulse that had helped to establish the national park system. However, this movement had dwindled during the midcentury decades when depression, war, and the rush to suburbia absorbed so much energy and imagination. By the 1960s, however, the growth of America's high-consumption, "throwaway" economy had begun to generate a new environmental awareness, especially among many affluent suburban whites. During the 1950s and 1960s, the California-based Sierra Club transformed itself from a hiking group into an influential national organization that blocked the construction of new dams on several western rivers; and in 1962, Rachel Carson's book *Silent Spring* aroused widespread public concern about the effect of insecticides, such as DDT, on the everyday environment. Then, in early 1969, a major oil spill off the coast of Santa Barbara, California hit the evening news, with dramatic film of thousands of dead seabirds and blackened coastal beaches. President Nixon signed legislation setting up the Environmental Protection Agency early in 1970. But environmental consciousness truly became a national preoccupation three months later, on April 22, 1970, when hundreds of thousands of Americans participated in a set of "Earth Day" demonstrations.

The environmental movement borrowed direct action tactics from the New Left and resonated with the back-to-nature ethic of the counterculture. Ecology groups held sit-ins and demonstrations but also became effective participants in local politics and Washington lobbying. In the 1970s, environmentalists blocked a new round of urban freeways, stopped development of a noisy supersonic transport plane, and slowed the spread of nuclear power. For many people, this new movement rechanneled some of the passions that had been aroused by opposition to the Vietnam War. "Our life-styles, our industries, and our population growth are leading to the extinction of more and more species, to the poisoning of our air, water, and food," asserted one group of activists, "This growing destruction threatens the continued existence of the human species."

The Occupational Health and Safety Movement

Although environmentalists and unionists often clashed over industrial regulation and infrastructure construction in the 1970s, millions of workers also became increasingly conscious of their right to a safe and healthy workplace. The industrial boom of the 1960s and early 1970s pushed industrial accident rates and health problems up nearly 50 percent, and in 1970, the Labor Department estimated that 2.2 million workers were disabled each year from job-related health problems, proportionately far more than in Western Europe or Japan.

Before the early 1970s, neither workers nor their unions had made health and safety top issues. "In the past," noted one labor official, "the union practice . . . was to trade and barter its safety and health demands for a couple of cents an hour in wages." "When it came to safety, the older guys would say 'If you die, you die,'" recalled one construction worker. For other workers, including utility linemen and hard rock miners, the dangers of the work sustained their pride in the skill that was needed to do the job. But these sentiments changed in the 1960s, as male workers could find little "manliness" in being exposed to lead and mercury poisoning, asbestos, cotton and coal dust, pesticides, and radiation. Unions in steel, coal, and oil pressured Congress for health and safety laws.

In response, Congress passed the 1970 Occupational Safety and Health Act

. . . And the Breathing Isn't Easy

A cloud of dust containing harmful crystalline silica envelops a plumber sawing a concrete floor. Silicosis, a progressively debilitating, incurable disease of the lungs caused by inhaling silica dust, is common among workers in mining, foundries, shipyards, and construction. Mine Safety and Health Administration.

(OSHA), which created a new set of workplace rights and, like the U.S. Supreme Court's 1954 *Brown v. Board of Education* decision, helped to legitimize a grassroots struggle. Although OSHA had many limitations, including a cumbersome regulatory mandate, it did offer union activists a new tool with which to assert employees' rights to a healthy workplace. At the Olin Corporation's Film Division works in North Carolina, unionist James Reese used his chairmanship of the plant safety committee to confront management over the safe use of many chemicals. Proudly, he memorized the OSHA standards for each. "For once," he explained, "I had something that they had to listen to. I finally had a law to back me up."

Passage of the OSHA law caught industrialists unaware, but once they saw how it empowered workers, they lobbied Congress for cuts in inspection funds, exemptions for small firms, and delays in implementation of health standards. Governmental action to ensure safe working conditions proved to be dependent on the extent to which workers in each industry forcefully pressed their claims. In the coal fields, where the respiratory disease known as black lung disabled thousands of miners each year, a dynamic movement led by miners, antipoverty activists, and liberal doctors forced Congress to establish the Mine Safety and Health Administration, which was better funded and more sympathetic to workers than OSHA was; accident rates in the coal fields declined sharply. In contrast, workers in the largely nonunion textile industry gained little from OSHA. There, employers dominated the debate over the extent to which factory cotton dust generated the respiratory malady known as "brown lung," so disabled textile operatives went largely uncompensated by insurance companies and local workers' compensation boards.

Hispanics and Native Americans Demand Equal Rights Since the New Deal era, cultural pluralism in the United States had been an important element of the country's unofficial creed, but in the early 1970s, a multicultural sense of the nation's ethnic and racial diversity took on a far more tangible reality. Hispanic Americans were the fastest-growing minority group in the United States, about 5 percent of the population. Miami was home to more Cubans than any other city except Havana, and more Mexicans lived in Los Angeles than in any other urban place except Mexico City. The Miami Cubans—middle-class, entrepreneurial, and intensely anti-Communist— were among the most politically and culturally conservative of all Americans, but many Puerto Ricans and Mexican Americans, especially the youth, had been inspired by the American civil rights movement and the farmworkers' struggle.

In the spring of 1968, Chicano students in Los Angeles and other cities held a series of school boycotts, or "blowouts." Poor-quality education was a key issue for the whole community, according to participant Carlos

Vasquez. "Chicano students became radicalized," he recalled, "when they asked, 'Why are our schools the way they are?'" The student protests spurred a broader movement that sought increased power for the Mexican American community. Meanwhile, the same dynamic unfolded across the continent as Puerto Ricans flexed their activist muscles. In Chicago and New York City, the Young Lords, an organization that drew members from urban street gangs as well as from college campuses, proved to be an important catalyst. According to Pablo Guzman, a Young Lords leader in New York, "We tapped an intense nationalistic fervor among Puerto Rican people. In this way we were able to cut across all ages and types and reach a broad segment of the population."

The pluralistic effervescence of this era also encouraged a movement among American Indians. By the 1960s, Indian life had reached a crisis: life expectancy was twenty years below the national average, unemployment was ten times higher, and suicide among Indian youths had reached epidemic proportions. But in the rights-conscious spirit of the 1960s, Indians sought not only federal antipoverty aid, but also recognition that Native Americans constituted a separate people with a distinctive cultural and legal claim to their heritage and land.

In 1964, the Puyallup in the state of Washington held "fish-ins" to protest state court decisions that denied them their treaty-guaranteed fishing rights. Then in the spring of 1969, the Navajo and Hopi attacked Peabody Coal Company mining operations in the Southwest, complaining, as one Navajo tribal elder put it, that "Peabody's monsters are digging up the heart of the earth, our sacred mountain, and we also feel the pain." Later that year, a group of 78 Indians, calling themselves "Indians of All Tribes," occupied Alcatraz Island in San Francisco Bay, turning the site of a notorious federal prison into "liberated" territory for some eighteen months.

An even more dramatic confrontation came in 1973, when 300 Oglala Sioux seized the town of Wounded Knee in South Dakota, where the U.S. cavalry had massacred hundreds of Indians in 1890. These militant, youthful American Indian Movement activists demanded a democratization of reservation governance and U.S. adherence to long-forgotten treaty obligations. Scores of heavily armed FBI agents laid siege, but Indian activists held out for seventy-one days before agreeing to a cease-fire and a court trial of the principal leaders. The occupations at Alcatraz and Wounded Knee provided an ideologically charged

Wounded Knee, South Dakota, 1973

An American Indian Movement (AIM) activist rejoices after hearing that the federal government has agreed to a cease-fire and negotiations at the Pine Ridge Reservation in South Dakota. The three-month confrontation between AIM and federal marshals began in February 1973 when AIM seized hostages at a reservation trading post to dramatize their protest against Bureau of Indian Affairs policy and conservative tribal leadership. UPI/Corbis-Bettmann.

backdrop to a wave of Indian lawsuits that reestablished land claims and tribal institutions from Maine to Alaska. By the 1980s, Indian poverty was still widespread, but no one doubted the Indians' claim to cultural and political recognition in a multicultural America.

The Women's Movement   The women's movement was by far the largest and most influential of all the social movements of the early 1970s, for it touched almost every fiber of American life. The stunning rebirth of American feminism emerged in part from the New Left's probing of the political dimension of personal life. As an ideology and a social movement, feminism flourished in the years before World War II. It was reborn in the late 1960s as a result of the merger between the self-emancipatory impulse of the New Left and the political agenda that had long been put forward by an older generation of women reformers.

Beginning in the late 1950s, a small group of well-placed American women sought to achieve equality between the sexes in much the same way that the NAACP used the courts and Congress to fight racial discrimination. Prodded by such veteran liberals as Eleanor Roosevelt, President Kennedy appointed a Commission on the Status of Women in 1961, but women's issues won popular notice only with the 1963 publication of Betty Friedan's best-selling book *The Feminine Mystique*.

Friedan's commitment to women's rights had been shaped during her decade of left-wing union activism in the 1940s, but now she offered an even broader critique of women's status at home and at work. According to Friedan, a "feminine mystique" stifled millions of women whose suburban imprisonment unnaturally deprived them of creativity, careers, and their very humanity. In 1966, Friedan and 27 other professional women established the National Organization for Women (NOW) "to take action to bring American women into full participation in the mainstream of American society now." NOW prodded the federal government to enforce the ban on sex discrimination in employment and public accommodations included in the 1964 Civil Rights Act.

The feminist impulse might have remained confined to these relatively elite women had their ideas not been given a dynamic moral vision and intense personal meaning by the explosion of feminist consciousness within the New Left. Young women joined the political movements of the 1960s with fervor and dedication. But many were dismayed to discover that their male comrades did not think of them as equals. At SDS meetings, remembered one participant, "Women made peanut butter sandwiches, waited on tables, cleaned up, got laid. That was their role." This gap between radical vision and discriminatory practice drove tens of thousands of young women out of the antiwar and student movements. Bringing with them skills, networks, tactics, and a language for describing their oppression,

"Personal Problems Are Political Problems"

Consciousness-raising groups, a common feature of the women's liberation movement, helped women to discover the social roots of their individual problems. These quotations suggest the diverse ways in which different consciousness-raising groups grappled with the link between the personal and the political. The first quotation is from a woman talking in 1970 about her ongoing group. The other statements were made by women in the 1980s, recalling their experiences in the late 1960s and early 1970s.

Carol H.: So the reason I participate in these meetings is not to solve any personal problem. One of the first things we discover in these groups is that personal problems are political problems. There are no personal solutions at this time. There is only collective action for a collective solution. I went, and I continue to go to these meetings because I have gotten a political understanding which all my reading, all my "political discussions," all my "political action," all my four-odd years in the movement never gave me. . . . I believe at this point, and maybe for a long time to come, that these analytical sessions are a form of political action. . . .

Arlene S.: Our group was very different, nonpolitical. Other groups seemed to have a harshness to them. The message was you had to move forward, you had to deal with issues. There was a sense of confrontation and judgment. Our group, I feel, accomplished so much more, but in a different way. We just talked about ourselves, and it was very warm.

Phyllis F.: We perpetuate sexism until we become conscious of the part that we play. That's what women's groups were meant to do because they were really well thought out. They were actually political groups. They really got me. You know, if you said politics to me back then, I would have left the room. I came from the dead 1950s, and I didn't know from radical politics. But in the group, they just said, well, the personal is political. Just work on yourself, that's politics. Okay, I could deal with that. And you know, it works. Not immediately that minute, maybe, but over time. There are battered women's shelters and rape crisis services across the state of New York that did not exist in the early 1970s. These came out of CR.

Abby T.: When I first joined consciousness-raising, I was aware of its being part of large political ferment. There were the civil rights movement, the assassinations, the antiwar stuff, the SDS organizations on campus. The Women's Movement just seemed to flow out of all of this, and so right from the beginning I thought of it as political.

Anita Shreve, *Women Together, Women Alone: The Legacy of the Consciousness-Raising Movement* (1989).

"Welfare Is a Woman's Issue"

In this Ms. *magazine article, Johnnie Tillmon, one of the founders of the National Welfare Rights Organization (NWRO), illustrates the connections between welfare rights and women's liberation. Welfare recipients, largely female, adopted much of the outlook that was sparked by the civil rights movement and the women's movement. Since the 1930s, Aid to Families with Dependent Children (AFDC) often had been doled out in a discriminatory, condescending manner, especially toward women of color. Led by groups like the NWRO, poor people challenged the system's long-standing paternalism and proclaimed welfare to be a right of citizenship. NWRO chapters sprouted in forty-five cities; welfare recipients led demonstrations for better treatment and fought for special grants for housing, food, and children's school clothing.*

I'm a woman. I'm a black woman. I'm a poor woman. I'm a fat woman. I'm a middle-aged woman. And I'm on welfare.

In this country, if you're any one of these things — poor, black, fat, female, middle-aged, on welfare — you count less as a human being. If you're all those things, you don't count at all. Except as a statistic.

I am a statistic.

I am 45 years old. I have raised six children.

I grew up in Arkansas, and I worked there for fifteen years in a laundry, making about $20 or $30 a week, picking cotton on the side for carfare. I moved to California in 1959 and worked in a laundry there for nearly four years. In 1963 I got too sick to work anymore. Friends helped me to go on welfare. . . .

Welfare's like a traffic accident. It can happen to anybody, but especially it happens to women.

And that is why welfare is a women's issue. For a lot of middle-class women in the country, Women's Liberation is a matter of concern. For women on welfare, it's a matter of survival.

The truth is that A.F.D.C. is like a supersexist marriage. You trade in *a* man for *the* man. But you can't divorce him if he treats you bad. He can divorce you, of course, cut you off anytime he wants. But in that case, *he* keeps the kids, not you.

The man runs everything. In ordinary marriage, sex is suppose to be for your husband. On A.F.D.C. you're not suppose to have any sex at all. You give up control of your own body. It's a condition of aid. You may even have to agree to get your tubes tied so you can never have more children just to avoid being cut off welfare.

The man, the welfare system, controls your money. He tells you what to buy, what not to buy, where to buy it, and how much things cost. If things — rent for instance — really cost more than he says they do, it's just too bad for you. . . .

Maybe it is we poor welfare women who will really liberate women in this country. . . .

———————————

Rosalyn Baxandall, Linda Gordon, and Susan Reverby, eds., *America's Working Women: A Documentary History — 1600 to the Present* (1976).

these young women built an explosive and ultimately massive movement for women's liberation. As one woman remembered, "In the black movement I had been fighting someone else's oppression. Now there was a way I could fight for my own freedom, and I was going to be much stronger than I ever was."

Flowering in the early 1970s and continuing to grow throughout the decade, the women's movement sent shock waves into every recess of American society. Hundreds of thousands of women took part in consciousness-raising groups, where they discussed every aspect of their lives, ranging from discrimination on the job to the destructive results of competition over men to failed sexual relationships. Feminists argued not only that men should share in the responsibilities of child rearing, but also that government should fund a universal system of child-care centers. Feminists used petitions, picketing, and legal action to demand wage parity with men and opportunities to advance in professions, such as law, medicine, academia, journalism, and architecture, in which women had been systematically marginalized. The Women's Equity Action League brought class-action suits against nearly three hundred colleges and universities, forcing them to agree to change their employment and admission policies.

Feminists also sought to change the ways in which women were represented in the larger culture. In August 1968, a group of women startled the nation by disrupting the Miss America pageant, charging that beauty contests encouraged the notion that women were merely objects for men's sexual pleasure. Believing that language was crucial to the formation of attitudes, feminists attacked the use of such demeaning labels as "chicks" and "girls" and urged women who married to keep their own surnames as symbols of their individuality. Feminists challenged television producers and newspaper editors to portray women in a more diverse and realistic fashion. Arguing that traditional scholarship ignored women, feminist authors wrote women back into American history and demanded an end to gender stereotyping in educational materials.

Feminists frequently linked the transformation of U.S. health care to the campaign for the legalization of abortion. Before 1970, this procedure was illegal in virtually every state. Women who wanted to end unwanted pregnancies were forced to seek out illegal abortions or to self-induce miscarriages; thousands of women died each year as the result of botched operations. Arguing that a woman had a right to "control her own body," feminists joined population control advocates in lobbying state legislatures for legislation that would

Our Bodies, Ourselves

Growing out of a workshop at a 1969 women's conference in Boston, a 193-page booklet called *Women and Their Bodies* and later *Our Bodies, Ourselves* was a groundbreaking popular manual on women's health. Written in accessible language and providing information that challenged contemporary medical practice that limited women's knowledge about their own bodies, the book became an underground sensation, selling 250,000 copies. Starting in 1973, *Our Bodies, Ourselves* was published in a commercial edition that, to the present, has sold more than three million copies. *Our Bodies, Ourselves* (Simon and Schuster, 1973).

legalize abortion. They made slow, state-by-state progress until 1973, when the U.S. Supreme Court's landmark *Roe v. Wade* decision guaranteed women access to abortions in the early stages of pregnancy.

The women's movement proved highly controversial, and many Americans resisted both the concrete reforms its activists demanded and the feminist ideology that stood behind them. But most polls in the early 1970s recorded a steady shift in public opinion toward feminist positions on such issues as pay equity, child care, and abortion. The movement spread from the white middle class as African American and poor women made links between racism, sexism, and economic injustices. Even those who rejected feminism embraced the transformations that it wrought. As one secretary put it, "I'm no women's libber, but I believe women should get equal pay." Millions of women office workers helped to transform the work culture: they refused to serve coffee to male coworkers, wore pants to work, insisted on being addressed as adults, and demanded the right to promotions and better pay.

The Gay and Lesbian Rights Movement   The feminist challenge to traditional sex roles also encouraged the growth of the gay and lesbian rights

After Stonewall I

In the months following the June 1969 Stonewall Rebellion, New York police continued to raid bars where lesbians and gay men gathered. In the early morning hours of March 9, 1970, police raided the Snake Pit, a Greenwich Village bar, arresting all 167 employees and patrons. After the "suspects" were taken to a local station house, Alfredo Vinales, an illegal alien who was afraid of being deported if his homosexuality was discovered, tried to escape. After leaping from a second-floor window, he was impaled on an iron picket fence. Frank Giorandino, *New York Daily News*, March 9, 1970.

After Stonewall II

Vinales's act of desperation graphically articulated the oppression of gays. "No matter how you look at it," as one gay activist slogan went, "Vinales was pushed." The horror of the Snake Pit incident helped to mobilize hundreds of gays to join the new movement. In June 1970, the first march commemorating the anniversary of the Stonewall Rebellion was organized, an event that is now observed every June by hundreds of thousands of gays and lesbians around the world. Peter Keegan, June 29, 1975 — Getty Images.

"We Are Inside You"

Fran Winant wrote this poem, entitled "Christopher Street Liberation Day, June 28, 1970," to commemorate the first anniversary of the Stonewall riot, which the newly formed Gay Liberation Movement celebrated with a march in New York City.

With banners and our smiles
we're being photographed
by tourists police and leering men
we fill their cameras
with 10,000 faces
bearing witness
to our own existence
in sunlight
from Washington Maryland
Massachusetts Pennsylvania
Connecticut Ohio
Iowa Minnesota
from Harlem and the suburbs
the universities
and the world
we are women who love women

we are men who love men
we are lesbians and homosexuals
we cannot apologize
for knowing
what others refuse to know
for affirming
what they deny
we might have been
the women and men
who watched us and waved
and made fists
and gave us victory signs
and stood there after we had passed
thinking of all they had to lose
and of how society punishes
its victims
who are all of us
in the end
but we are sisters and sisters
brothers and brothers
workers and lovers
we are together
we are marching
past the crumbling old world
that leans toward us
in anguish from the pavement
our banners are sails
pulling us through the streets
where we have always been
as ghosts
now we are shouting our own words
we are a community
we are a society
we are everyone
we are inside you
remember
all you were taught to forget
we are part of the new world . . .

Karla Jay and Allen Young, eds., *Out of the Closets: Voices of Gay Liberation* (1972).

movement. Throughout the postwar years, most gay men and women had kept their sexual orientation secret, fearful of job loss or public humiliation if they openly acknowledged it. But a dramatic change took place after a riot involving New York City police and gay patrons of the Stonewall Inn in June 1969. The Stonewall Rebellion sparked a wide range of political and cultural gay organizations and publications. Homosexual men raised the demand for "Gay Power," consciously linking their struggle for dignity and sexual freedom with that of African Americans and other "oppressed minorities."

Much the same dynamic took hold among lesbians. Many lesbians who had long hidden or denied their sexual orientation found that the women's movement provided them with a broader community in which they could openly profess their sexuality and fight for their rights. Gay men and women denied that homosexuality was a crime or a sickness and publicly "came out," holding marches, pushing for legislation to end decades of bias and discrimination, and calling for "gay liberation." The effort paid off: in 1973, the American Psychiatric Association ended its classification of homosexuality as a mental disorder, and by the mid-1970s, a slight majority of Americans opposed job discrimination based on sexual orientation.

Militancy and Dissension in the Labor Movement   American unions had many things going for them in the 1960s. The AFL-CIO had a cordial relationship with presidents Kennedy and Johnson, and its leaders supported the Great Society programs of the mid-1960s and the occupational health and safety legislation of the early 1970s. The unions enjoyed the longest era of sustained high employment since World War II. Because of cost-of-living adjustments, many blue-collar workers won real wage increases even in the inflationary years after 1966. Most big unions won employer-funded health insurance, higher pensions, and increased vacation pay.

At the same time, a democratic sensibility surged through the nation's factories. Workers sought respect, equality, and a sense of workplace citizenship from their employers. "The worker wants the same rights he has on the street after he walks in the plant door," asserted Jim Babbs, a twenty-four-year-old white worker at a Ford plant outside Detroit. "This is a general feeling of this generation, whether it's a guy in a plant or a student on campus, not wanting to be an IBM number."

Union leaders faced a rebellious rank and file. Contract rejections, a rarity before 1962, soared after 1965; wildcat strikes reached a postwar high. In the steelworkers', miners', teachers', and postal employees' unions, top union leaders who seemed too complacent were not reelected. Between 1961 and 1973, every national autoworkers' contract the UAW signed pushed at least a score of local workers to strike to humanize conditions.

This new working-class mood had its greatest impact among public employees, especially those who worked for the 80,000 units of state and local government. Before World War II, public employment meant secure, high-status jobs, which were often reserved for those with close ties to the city machine or the local ethnic political club. But by the 1960s, civil service employees' wages had fallen well behind those of organized labor, while overcrowded classrooms, deteriorating public transit systems, and teeming welfare offices reduced the quality of public employees' work life. Public employees therefore unionized rapidly and sometimes struck. Their work stoppages grew nearly tenfold in the decade after 1965. Because many of these strikes were illegal, public sector unionism had the feel of an underground movement, a consciousness-changing social crusade. In Hamtramck, Michigan, in 1965, junior high school teachers defied state law and staged a twenty-four-hour-a-day "prolonged teachers' meeting" to force the local school board to recognize their union. Leaders of the American Federation of Teachers (AFT) frequently courted arrest and jail during their still-illegal strikes in the 1960s.

The most startling expression of the new militancy erupted in the postal system in March 1970, when 200,000 workers struck urban post offices across the North and West. Postal employees had once been mostly older white males, but by the late 1960s, the workforce in this huge bureaucracy resembled that of the nation. As the Post Office Department mechanized, many of the half-million postal workers bridled under the factorylike discipline. Their strike amounted to a revolt—not only against their employer, the federal government, but also against their own union leaders, who had long functioned largely as Capitol Hill lobbyists. President Nixon countered by sending troops to sort the mail, but the strike succeeded in forcing Congress to raise wages and reorganize the postal system.

Despite growing worker militancy, the labor movement did not hold its own in the 1960s. Unions recruited two million additional members in the decade, largely in public sector employment, but the proportion of all workers who belonged to unions declined from 29 percent in 1960 to 23 percent fifteen years later. Organized labor failed to grow because it failed to link itself to the dynamic social movements that had emerged in those years. On the two great issues of the 1960s—race and Vietnam—unions stood divided and hesitant. While some organizations, such as Hospital Workers Local 1199 and the United Farm Workers, took advantage of the idealism and energy of the New Left and the civil rights movement, no major trade union leader was prepared to give 1960s era radicals the kind of backing Communists and Socialists had briefly enjoyed in the 1930s.

When it came to civil rights, unions were as much a part of the problem as they were part of the solution. Since the 1940s, the trade union movement had been the most integrated major institution in American life, and in the early 1960s, black and minority workers made up about one-quarter of total union membership. But the AFL-CIO lacked the will to combat racial discrimination within its own affiliates. George Meany, labor's top officer, disliked socially disruptive civil rights demonstrations, including the 1963 March on Washington.

Throughout the civil rights era, craft unions in the construction trades, which limited membership tightly, remained almost all white. "We don't take any new members, regardless of color," asserted one building trades leader. When apprenticeships did open up, many construction workers believed that union cards should go to their sons and relatives as a sort of patrimony, much as in a family-run business. Such exclusionary practices naturally offended urban African Americans, who often saw white workers from the suburbs earning good pay on construction projects just a few blocks from the ghetto. Although the Nixon administration's Philadelphia Plan targeted discriminatory recruitment patterns among these craft unions, it proved relatively ineffective because a recession in the early 1970s cut employment and intensified job competition between whites and blacks.

Racial tensions were not confined just to the traditionally conservative wing of the union movement. An even more ominous conflict emerged in 1968 as the New York City AFT local fought a decentralization plan that offered parents a limited form of community control of the schools. The AFT claimed that black nationalists who were hostile to Jewish teachers dominated some local school boards, and the new plan would give these activists the power to ignore seniority rights and grievance procedures. Community-control advocates, on the other hand, argued that the AFT was unwilling to share power with African American and Puerto Rican parents and their increasingly assertive leaders. This bitter conflict, which began in the Ocean Hill–Brownsville school district in Brooklyn, generated four strikes in the fall of 1968 and drove a wedge between groups that had long been allies in the fight against discrimination.

Even the UAW, whose progressive leaders put money and muscle behind the civil rights movement, found itself at odds with black activists. By the early 1960s, 200,000 African American workers made up more than one-fifth of the total UAW membership. They were confined largely to the most grueling work in the most dangerous and dirty departments. Black activists, many veteran union organizers from the 1930s and

School's Open, But . . .

A Brooklyn public school classroom during the 1968 New York City teachers' strike. AP/Wide World Photos.

1940s, fought Walter Reuther and other white UAW leaders for more African Americans in high union office, a more vigorous union fight against workplace racism, and political power in Detroit. But the explosion of black nationalism and workplace militancy that swept Detroit factories in the aftermath of the city's 1967 riot surprised UAW pioneers of both races. Tension declined only after the auto corporations rushed hundreds of African Americans into the supervisory ranks, the UAW hired more black staff, and the recessionary layoffs of the early 1970s purged Detroit factories of some of their most militant workers.

Vietnam proved just as problematic an issue for the labor movement as race. Under the leadership of George Meany, the AFL-CIO steadfastly defended U.S. conduct of the war, even after business leaders had begun to waver. Meany called opponents of the war a "coalition of retreat," even though leaders of a number of traditionally liberal unions, such as the UAW, the Packinghouse Workers' Union, Local 1199, and the American Federation of State, County and Municipal Employees, criticized the war and Meany's hawkish politics. In New York, San Francisco, and Los Angeles, local unions participated in mass antiwar marches; and in 1968, Walter Reuther, who had grown frustrated with Meany's knee-jerk anti-Communism, pulled the UAW out of the AFL-CIO. With the Teamsters, the UAW formed the Alliance for Labor Action (ALA), which Reuther hoped would revitalize the labor movement. But the ALA disintegrated in the early 1970s, after the Teamsters raided the United Farm Workers in California and endorsed President Nixon for reelection in 1972.

Political Polarization   Conflict between the social movements of the 1960s and organized labor was not confined to top-level disputes over foreign policy or civil rights legislation. In his 1968 campaign, George Wallace demonstrated the extent to which white working-class discontent with high taxes, declining neighborhoods, black militancy, and student radicalism could be turned toward a populism of the Right. In the years that followed, most workers remained liberals when it came to such welfare-state programs as Social Security, unemployment compensation, and job training, and they grew increasingly hostile to the Vietnam War. But on other social issues of the era—affirmative action, school busing to achieve racial balance, a woman's right to an abortion, and a defense of the symbols of American patriotism—white working-class men grew increasingly attracted to a new kind of politicized social conservatism.

This became clear in New York City on May 8, 1970. Antiwar demonstrators had gathered at a federal building near Wall Street to protest the U.S. invasion of Cambodia. Suddenly, a shining wave of yellow and orange surged through the crowd. A contingent of 200 construction workers wearing bright plastic hard hats and armed with pliers and hammers pounced on the "longhairs." To the chant of "All the way with the USA," the "hard hats" roughly elbowed the young protesters aside and returned the building's flag, which had been lowered to half mast in homage to the four antiwar students just slain at Kent State University, back to full height.

The White House and the conservative leaders of the New York building trades had actually orchestrated the hard-hat demonstration, but a new social stereotype was born: the tough, prowar, blue-collar worker; a hardworking taxpayer who was hostile to African Americans on welfare; a family man who spurned marijuana and the liberation of women. The hard hats seemed to stand for working-class anger and resentment against all the social changes and political innovations of the 1960s. Although white blue-collar workers increasingly opposed the war, they also resented the college students who led antiwar protests and publicly denounced the draft. At issue was not a difference over foreign policy, but class antagonism. Working-class opponents of the Vietnam War hated antiwar demonstrators even more than they disliked the Southeast Asian conflict. One worker whose son was serving in Vietnam lamented the inability of poorer boys to "get the same breaks as the college kids. We can't understand how all of those rich kids . . . get off when my son has to go over there and maybe get his head shot off."

The women's liberation movement sparked similar patterns of reaction and resentment. Many Americans, male and female, felt threatened by the renewal of the women's movement and its challenge to cherished traditional values. Although increasing numbers of women were entering the paid labor force, most held routine jobs that offered few psychic or emotional rewards. To many such women, the role of mother in the traditional family seemed more likely to provide a sense of security and dignity. Seeing "women's libbers" as privileged professionals, many working-class women interpreted feminist criticism of traditional women's roles as a threat to their own sense of self-worth. President Nixon appealed to this antifeminist reaction in 1971 when he vetoed federal support for day-care centers, arguing that they would undermine the nation's "family centered traditions."

This new attack on social liberalism and New Left radicalism bolstered support for a conservative movement that had been growing for several years. Although the 1960s are generally remembered as a decade in which left-wing activism characterized the political commitments of a whole generation, ultraconservative groups such as Young Americans for Freedom (YAF) and the John Birch Society had begun to recruit many ardent followers well before the rise of the New Left. They directed their hostility toward the entire legacy of the New Deal and thought even John F. Kennedy and Richard Nixon insufficiently anti-Communist. As early as 1961, for example, the YAF drew more than 3,000 people to a New York rally that celebrated antiunion employers, conservative intellectuals, and congressmen whose efforts to eliminate Communist influence in government and the professions had never flagged. Despite his loss in the 1964 presidential election, Barry Goldwater remained a conservative icon, but many conservative activists transferred their loyalty to actor Ronald Reagan, who was elected governor of California in 1966. His denunciations of New Left students and environmental activists won him an enthusiastic following.

President Nixon drew on the energy of all streams of conservatism in his 1972 reelection campaign. His acerbic vice president, Spiro Agnew, targeted radicals, hippies, black activists, and welfare mothers as the causes of America's problems. Nixon himself conducted a "Rose Garden" campaign, staying mostly in the White House instead of going out on the campaign trail, to emphasize his personal commitment to world peace and stability. Nixon's opponent was Senator George McGovern of South Dakota, a staunch liberal who urged the nation to "come home" from Vietnam. But the Democratic campaign proved inept and disorganized, and because of his dovish stance on the war in Indochina, the AFL-CIO refused to endorse McGovern. Meanwhile, Nixon won the allegiance of many former supporters of George Wallace, whose candidacy ended when a would-be assassin's bullet paralyzed and nearly killed him in May 1972. Nixon easily won reelection with more than 60 percent of the popular vote, including many southerners and blue-collar workers who normally voted Democratic.

The Watergate Crisis   Nixon's reelection seemed to mark the consolidation of conservative power. But his second term unraveled quickly as the constitutional crisis known as "Watergate" ignited public passion and consumed the administration's energy. The origins of the crisis, which forced a sitting president from office for the first time in American history, were threefold: the rapid growth of unfettered presidential power during the Cold War era; the polarization of the political process that arose out of the debate over the Vietnam War; and the secretive, resentful character of Nixon himself.

Like so many presidents before him, Nixon claimed that in the interest of national security, the White House had the right to take extraordinary action against its opponents. Thus, during his first term, Nixon not only had escalated covert police activity against black power and antiwar activists, but also had begun using government spies against an "enemies list" of elite journalists, Democrats, and even some dovish Republicans. This mentality soon saturated Nixon's own Committee to Reelect the President, which took in millions of dollars in illegal contributions and funded a variety of "dirty tricks" that were designed to sabotage the election efforts of their Democratic opponents.

The June 1972 break-in at the offices of the Democratic National Committee in the Watergate complex was one of many such actions; this time, however, a security guard caught the intruders, two of whom had been White House security consultants. Nixon's press secretary dismissed the break-in as a "third-rate burglary attempt," but the White House's effort to cover up these illegal activities proved to be Nixon's undoing. "Play it tough," Nixon ordered his top aide H. R. Haldeman right after news of the Watergate break-in became public. Nixon arranged to pay the burglars almost $500,000 in hush money from secret reelection committee funds. The president also tried to get the CIA to stop an FBI investigation of the affair, a deliberate obstruction of justice.

The Nixon White House successfully managed the Watergate scandal all through the 1972 campaign, but the cover-up unwound rapidly in 1973. John Sirica, a tough federal judge, was unwilling to let justice stop with jail terms for a handful of low-level operatives, and two young *Washington Post* reporters, Bob Woodward and Carl Bernstein, doggedly pursued the Watergate money trail back to Nixon's reelection committee and his top White House aides. Mark Felt, second-in-command at the FBI, secretly aided the reporters in this effort.

In the spring and summer of 1973, televised hearings by a select Senate investigating committee revealed the White House's role in an ever-expanding network of deceit and unconstitutional governance. Nixon fired Haldeman and other top Oval Office aides in a vain effort to purge officials whom the Watergate cover-up had tainted. Nixon's own criminality soon became the central focus of the Senate probe, especially after the stunning news, in July 1973, that the president himself had ordered the secret taping of all conversations that took place in the Oval Office. The White House lost even more

"I Am Not a Crook"
In 1973, as the Watergate scandal grew, political cartoonist Edward Sorel likened the Nixon administration to a band of trapped gangsters. *Ramparts*, August–September 1973 — Edward Sorel.

credibility in October 1973, when Vice President Agnew abruptly resigned after evidence surfaced that he had accepted bribes and kickbacks while serving as governor of Maryland and as vice president. Meanwhile, an investigation of Nixon's own financial affairs revealed a set of criminal irregularities in his tax returns. Then, on the night of October 20, after the president's own two top Justice Department appointees had resigned in protest, Nixon fired Archibald Cox, the Harvard Law School professor he had appointed as an independent special prosecutor in the Watergate matter. This generated a firestorm of public indignation, forcing Nixon to appoint a new independent prosecutor.

Congressional sentiment, public opinion, and the federal courts now turned decisively against Nixon. When the president himself released a heavily edited version of the White House tapes late in April 1974, they proved embarrassing, incomplete, and self-serving. In July, a unanimous Supreme Court forced the release of all the tapes, including a devastating conversation of June 23, 1972, in which Nixon ordered his aides to obstruct an FBI investigation of the break-in. Faced with certain congressional impeachment for "high crimes and misdemeanors," Nixon resigned the presidency on August 7, 1974. Although President Gerald Ford, whom Nixon had appointed vice president to replace Agnew, soon pardoned Nixon, twenty-five other members of his administration, including several top advisers and the attorney general, served time in prison.

Conclusion: An Increasing Rights Consciousness

Nixon's downfall marked an end to the long "Sixties." The nation's drift toward what historian Arthur Schlesinger called an "imperial presidency" moderated because the memory of Watergate put in place a set of sturdy warning signals against greater centralization of executive power. Likewise, even after the fragmentation of the civil rights movement and the New Left, the experience of the 1960s left in place a far greater sense of rights consciousness than had existed at any time during the previous century. In law and in practice, at work and at play, for women and men, and among white, brown, and black Americans, the United States could never go back to the unexamined assumptions that had governed social intercourse and workplace hierarchy in the 1950s and the years before. A new freedom had been enshrined not only in the civil rights laws of the 1960s, but also in the pervasive transformation of American political culture itself. But rights consciousness is not an abstraction; it must have a very concrete social and economic foundation. In the coming decades, the greatest threat to American liberties would come not from an overweening executive or racial bigots, but from an economic earthquake that was reshaping the world of work, both at home and around the globe.

The Years in Review

1954

- In *Brown v. Board of Education*, the U.S. Supreme Court declares segregated public schools unconstitutional.

1955

- By refusing to give up her seat to a white rider, Rosa Parks sparks a thirteen-month-long bus boycott in Montgomery, Alabama.

- Emmett Till, a fourteen-year-old Chicago resident, is kidnapped, brutally beaten, and murdered in Mississippi.

1956

- Martin Luther King, Jr., and other African American leaders (most of them ministers) found the Southern Christian Leadership Council.

1957

- U.S. Army paratroopers are sent to Little Rock, Arkansas, to enforce the desegregation of Central High School.

1958

- Liberal Democrats win big in the congressional elections.

1959

- Fidel Castro leads revolution that takes control of Cuba from corrupt U.S.-supported dictator Fulgencio Batista.

1960

- Four black college students demand service at a Woolworth's lunch counter in Greensboro, North Carolina, and initiate a wave of sit-ins across the South.

- Democrat John F. Kennedy defeats Vice President Richard Nixon in the presidential election.

1961

- The Congress of Racial Equality organizes a series of "Freedom Rides" to test the legal desegregation of southern bus terminals.

- The CIA organizes an invasion of Cuba in an attempt to overthrow Fidel Castro.

- East German Communists erect a concrete wall across Berlin in an effort to stop the flow of refugees to the West.

1962

- In the Cuban missile crisis, after the U.S. blockade of Cuba and threatened air attack, Soviet Premier Nikita Khrushchev agrees to remove Soviet missiles.

- The New Left organization Students for a Democratic Society issues the Port Huron Statement.

- Cesar Chavez and Delores Huerta found the United Farm Workers to gain union rights for farm workers.
- Publication of Rachel Carson's *Silent Spring* arouses widespread concern about the use of insecticides.

1963
- Betty Friedan's *The Feminine Mystique* becomes a best-seller and brings women's issues to public notice.
- Medgar Evers, a NAACP leader in Mississippi, is assassinated.
- The "March on Washington for Jobs and Freedom" mobilizes nearly a quarter of a million people; there, Martin Luther King, Jr. delivers "I have a dream" speech.
- John F. Kennedy is assassinated in Dallas, Texas. Lyndon Johnson becomes president.

1964
- The Freedom Summer campaign mobilizes hundreds of northern student volunteers to help register black voters in Mississippi; three civil rights workers are murdered.
- Lyndon Johnson defeats conservative Republican Barry Goldwater by a record margin in the presidential election. Democrats sweep the congressional elections.
- The Civil Rights Act passes, ending segregation in all public accommodations.
- Congress passes the Gulf of Tonkin Resolution, giving President Johnson the freedom to expand the war in Vietnam.
- The Free-Speech Movement is organized at the University of California campus in Berkeley.
- The Beatles, the English rock-and-roll sensation, tour the United States.
- President Lyndon Johnson declares a War on Poverty.

1965
- The Voting Rights Act passes Congress, ending most barriers to African American voting in the southern states.
- Congress enacts Medicare and, the following year, establishes Medicaid.
- The New Immigration Act eliminates the racist quota system that had favored Northern European immigrants since the 1920s.
- Malcolm X is assassinated.
- The United Farm Workers organize a five-year protest and boycott against California grape growers.

- U.S. troops are sent to the Dominican Republic to block the leftist government.

1966

- Betty Friedan and other feminists found the National Organization for Women.

1968

- U.S. troops murder more than 350 Vietnamese villagers in My Lai.
- The NLF's Tet offensive convinces Americans that the Vietnam War is at a stalemate.
- President Johnson announces that he will stop bombing North Vietnam, cancel a planned troop increase, and end his reelection campaign.
- James Earl Ray assassinates Martin Luther King, Jr.
- Sirhan Sirhan assassinates Robert Kennedy.
- Republican Richard Nixon defeats Vice President Hubert Humphrey and third-party candidate George Wallace to become president.
- Young Indian activists found the American Indian Movement.

1969

- The Woodstock rock festival draws over 400,000 spectators.
- The Stonewall Riot launches the gay liberation movement.
- Nixon orders the secret bombing of Cambodia.

1970

- U.S. troops invade Cambodia, sparking massive antiwar demonstrations, which result in deaths of students at Kent State and Jackson State universities.
- Environmental activists organize the first "Earth Day."
- Congress passes the Occupational Safety and Health Act to protect workers.
- President Nixon creates the Environmental Protection Agency.

1971

- President Nixon imposes wage and price controls to staunch accelerating inflation.

1972

- President Nixon visits Communist China.
- A security guard apprehends intruders at the Democratic National Committee offices in the Watergate complex in Washington, D.C. President Nixon and other White House officials attempt to cover up the burglary and other illegal activities.

1973

- The Paris peace accords are signed, ending much direct U.S. involvement in Vietnam War. American POWs return home.

- In *Roe v. Wade*, the U.S. Supreme Court rules that women have a right to abortion in some circumstances.

- Three hundred Oglala Sioux seize the town of Wounded Knee, South Dakota, and resist an FBI siege for seventy-one days.

1974

- Richard Nixon resigns the presidency.

- Gerald Ford pardons Nixon of any crimes he may have committed while in office.

1975

- North Vietnamese regular troops capture Saigon; U.S. officials and Vietnamese civilian supporters flee in helicopters from the roof of the U.S. embassy.

- Led by Pol Pot, the Khmer Rouge seize all of Cambodia.

Additional Readings

For more on the civil rights movement, see: Raymond Arsenault, *Freedom Riders: 1961 and the Struggle for Racial Justice* (2006); Taylor Branch, *Parting the Waters: America in the King Years, 1954–1963* (1989); Clayborne Carson, *In Struggle: SNCC and the Black Awakening of the 1960s* (1995); William H. Chafe, *Civilities and Civil Rights: Greensboro, North Carolina, and the Black Struggle for Equality* (1980); John D'Emilio, *Lost Prophet: The Life and Times of Bayard Rustin* (2003); John Dittmer, *Local People: The Struggle for Civil Rights in Mississippi* (1994); David Garrow, *Bearing the Cross: Martin Luther King, Jr., and the Southern Christian Leadership Conference* (1999); Peter Louis Goldman, *The Death and Life of Malcolm X* (1979); Hugh Davis Graham, *The Civil Rights Era: Origins and Development of National Policy, 1960–1972* (1990); Michael J. Klarman, *From Jim Crow to Civil Rights: The Supreme Court and the Struggle for Racial Equality* (2004); Steven F. Lawson, *Running for Freedom: Civil Rights and Black Politics in America Since 1941* (1990); Chana Kai Lee, *For Freedom's Sake: The Life of Fanny Lou Hamer* (1999); Manning Marable, *Race, Reform, and Rebellion: The Second Reconstruction in Black America, 1945–1990* (1991); Doug McAdam, *Freedom Summer* (1990); James T. Patterson, *Brown v. Board of Education: A Civil Rights Milestone and Its Troubled Legacy* (2001); Charles M. Payne, *I've Got the Light of Freedom: The Organizing Tradition and the Mississippi Freedom Struggle* (1995); Timothy B. Tyson, *Radio Free Dixie: Robert F. Williams and the Roots of Black Power* (1999); and J. Harvie Wilkinson, *From "Brown" to "Bakke": The Supreme Court and School Integration, 1954–1978* (1979).

For more on policies of the Kennedy and Johnson administrations, see:
James G. Blight and David A. Welch, *On the Brink: Americans and Soviets Reexamine the Cuban Missile Crisis* (1990); Robert Caro, *The Years of Lyndon Johnson: The Path to Power* (1982); Robert Dallek, *Flawed Giant: Lyndon Johnson and His Times, 1961–1973* (1998); Robert Dallek, *An Unfinished Life: John F. Kennedy, 1917–1963* (2003); Michael B. Katz, *The Undeserving Poor: From the War on Poverty to the War on Welfare* (1989); Alice Kessler-Harris, *In Pursuit of Equity: Women, Men, and the Quest for Economic Citizenship in 20th-Century America* (2001); Michael E. Latham, *Modernization as Ideology: American Social Science and "Nation Building" in the Kennedy Era* (2000); James T. Patterson, *America's Struggle Against Poverty 1900–1994* (1995); Gerald Posner, *Case Closed: Lee Harvey Oswald and the Assassination of JFK* (1994); Richard Reeves, *President Kennedy: Profile of Power* (1994); Arthur Meier Schlesinger, Jr., *Robert Kennedy and His Times* (1996); and Robert Weisbrot, *Maximum Danger: Kennedy, the Missiles, and the Crisis of American Confidence* (2001).

For more on rights consciousness in the workplace, see: Peter B. Levy, *The New Left and Labor in the 1960s* (1994); and Nelson Lichtenstein, *Walter Reuther: The Most Dangerous Man in Detroit* (1997).

For more on the Vietnam War, see: Christian G. Appy, *Patriots: The Vietnam War Remembered from All Sides* (2003); Christian G. Appy, *Working-Class War: American Combat Soldiers in Vietnam* (1993); Loren Baritz, *Backfire: A History of How American Culture Led Us into Vietnam and Made Us Fight the Way We Did* (1998); Larry Berman, *No Peace, No Honor: Nixon, Kissinger, and Betrayal in Vietnam* (2001); David Kaiser, *American Tragedy: Kennedy, Johnson, and the Origins of the Vietnam War* (2000); David W. Levy, *The Debate over Vietnam* (1995); Thomas Powers, *The War at Home: Vietnam and the American People, 1964–1968* (1973); Herbert Schandler, *The Unmaking of a President: Lyndon Johnson and Vietnam* (1977); William Shawcross, *Sideshow: Kissinger, Nixon, and the Destruction of Cambodia* (1987); Neil Sheehan, *A Bright Shining Lie: John Paul Vann and America in Vietnam* (1989); Terry Wallace, ed., *Bloods: An Oral History of the Vietnam War by Black Veterans* (1992); and Marilyn B. Young, *The Vietnam Wars, 1945–1990* (1991).

For more on the antiwar movement, the New Left, and the counterculture, see: Wini Brenes, *Community and Organization in the New Left, 1962–1968: The Great Refusal* (1989); Howard Brick, *Age of Contradiction: American Thought and Culture in the 1960s* (1998); Charles DeBenedetti, *An American Ordeal: The Antiwar Movement of the Vietnam Era* (1990); Morris Dickstein, *Gates of Eden: American Culture in the Sixties* (1997); Max Elbaum, *Revolution in the Air: Sixties Radicals Turn to Lenin, Mao and Che*

(2002); Michael S. Foley, *Confronting the War Machine: Draft Resistance During the Vietnam War* (2003); Todd Gitlin, *The Sixties: Years of Hope, Days of Rage* (1993); Maurice Isserman and Michael Kazin, *America Divided: The Civil War of the 1960s* (1999); Allen J. Matusow, *The Unraveling of America: A History of Liberalism in the 1960s* (1984); James Miller, *"Democracy Is in the Streets": From Port Huron to the Siege of Chicago* (1994); and Timothy Miller, *The 60s Communes: Hippies and Beyond* (1999).

For more on 1968 as a watershed year, see: Dan T. Carter, *The Politics of Rage: George Wallace, the Origins of the New Conservatism, and the Transformation of American Politics* (1996); and Lewis Chester, Godfrey Hodgson, and Bruce Page, *An American Melodrama: The Presidential Campaign of 1968* (1969).

For more on the women's movement, see: Alice Echols, *Daring to Be Bad: Radical Feminism in America 1967–1975* (1990); Sara Evans, *Personal Politics: The Roots of Women's Liberation in the Civil Rights Movement and the New Left* (1980); Sara Evans, *Tidal Wave: How Women Changed America at Century's End* (2003); David J. Garrow, *Liberty and Sexuality: The Right to Privacy and the Making of Roe v. Wade* (1998); Cynthia Harrison, *On Account of Sex: The Politics of Women's Issues, 1945–1968* (1989); Ruth Rosen, *The World Split Open: How the Modern Women's Movement Changed America* (2000); Benita Roth, *Separate Roads to Feminism: Black, Chicana, and White Feminist Movements in America's Second Wave* (2004); and Vicki L. Ruiz, *From Out of the Shadows: Mexican Women in Twentieth-Century America* (1998).

For more on other 1960s movements and labor organizing, see: John D'Emilio, *Sexual Politics, Sexual Communities: The Making of a Homosexual Minority in the United States, 1940–1970* (1998); Melvyn Dubovsky, *The State and Labor in Modern America* (1994); Leon Fink and Brian Greenberg, *Upheaval in the Quiet Zone: A History of Hospital Workers' Union, Local 1199* (1989); Martin Halpern, *Unions, Radicals, and Democratic Presidents: Seeking Social Change in the Twentieth Century* (2003); Samuel P. Hays, *Beauty, Health, and Permanence: Environmental Politics in the United States, 1955–1985* (1989); and Judith Stein, *Running Steel, Running America: Race, Economic Policy, and the Decline of Liberalism* (1998).

For more on President Nixon and political polarization, see: John A. Andrew, *The Other Side of the Sixties: Young Americans for Freedom and the Rise of Conservative Politics* (1997); Dan T. Carter, *From George Wallace to Newt Gingrich: Race in the Conservative Counterrevolution, 1963–1994* (1996); Joan Hoff, *Nixon Reconsidered* (1995); and Stanley I. Kutler, *Wars of Watergate: The Last Crisis of Richard Nixon* (1992).

13

Economic Adversity
Transforms the Nation

1973–1989

Plant Closing
A northern California lumber company auctions off its works and equipment in the fall of 1988. A wave of California mill closings occurred during the 1980s as giant building material and paper corporations, such as Louisiana Pacific and Georgia Pacific, moved their operations abroad. Evan Johnson.

LIKE HIS FATHER before him, Steve Szumilyas worked at Wisconsin Steel on Chicago's Southeast Side. At 4:00 P.M. on Friday, March 28, 1980, he was checking steel slabs before they went into the reheating furnace when his foreman came by with news that would shatter his world. The company would lock the gates at the end of the shift; the mill was closing, and 3,400 steelworkers were out of a job. Szumilyas was on the street. Had it not been for his wife's new job, his family would have lost their suburban home. Steve Szumilyas would be employed again, but at only half the wages he earned in basic steel production.

Szumilyas's layoff would prove symptomatic of the era. "Nobody," wrote *Time* magazine, "is apt to look back on the 1970s as the good old days." After a quarter-century of rapid growth, wages, productivity, and output dropped sharply in all of the great industrial nations. Recessions became more severe and more frequent, while unemployment rose to double the average level of the immediate postwar years. Many Americans connected this economic turmoil to liberal foreign and civil rights policies. Throughout the 1970s, the radical right gained more notoriety and support for attacking government activism and traditional liberalism. Thus, these conservative men and women, who decried the developments in the rights-conscious sixties and the pillars of the New Deal social and political order, paved the way for conservative Ronald Reagan's election to the presidency in 1980.

The Shifting World Economy

The economies of all the major industrial powers became more integrated in the 1970s and afterward. Oil, food, manufactured goods, money, and people circulated at a much higher level throughout the global economy. But globalization did not generate stability or prosperity. In the United States, the growth in the efficiency of the economy — what economists call "productivity" — dropped like a stone. Over the next quarter-century, economic growth would continue, but at an annual rate of about 2 percent — far lower than the rate during the twenty-five years after World War II. Meanwhile, West Germany and Japan, which had been bested on the military battlefield, would forge ahead in peacetime, competing successfully for the American market in steel, autos, machine tools, and electrical products. Inflation combined with low economic growth reduced corporate profits. In response, most businesses sought to drive down their costs by cutting wages, lowering their tax burden, and attempting to end the governmental regulations they found most burdensome. Many U.S. corporations moved production to low wage, nonunion regions of the South or to "offshore" sites in Latin America or Asia.

As corporate concerns moved to the center of American politics, the liberal statecraft that had animated the New Deal and the Great Society became unworkable. The Nixon and Carter administrations' efforts to apply the fiscal remedies of economist John Maynard Keynes — increasing taxes and government spending to dampen inflation, boost employment, and encourage business investment — proved increasingly ineffective in the years after 1973. The policy of spending to end an economic slump, which liberal economists of the 1960s had seen as a remedy for high unemployment, proved politically unattractive a decade later when federal budget deficits also stoked the inflationary fires.

The End of the Postwar Boom   With inflation levels soaring — reaching a high of more than 18 percent in one year — and the unemployment rate rarely below 7 percent, the decade after 1973 brought the postwar boom in the United States to an unsettling end. For two full decades, from the early 1970s to the early 1990s, real wages stagnated for most Americans, and for young males, they actually dropped by 25 percent. At the end of these two decades, a freshly minted male college graduate could look forward to earning only slightly more each year than a typical high school graduate of the previous generation. Family income increased during these decades of slow growth, but largely because many women and teenagers took paying jobs and because all Americans worked longer hours (Figure 13.1). Meanwhile, income inequalities widened dramatically. Top corporate executives earned about 20 times as much as ordinary workers did in the 1960s; thirty years later, the multiplier was an astounding 115 times.

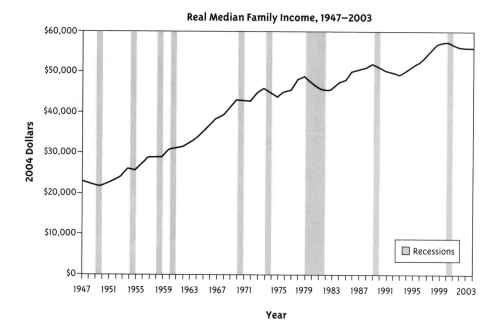

Real Median Family Income, 1947–2003

FIGURE 13.1 The Postwar Boom Slows: Median Family Income, 1947–2003

Family income increased dramatically in the first quarter-century after World War II. Thereafter, family income grew much more slowly and would actually have declined had not more wives and teenagers entered the workforce. Lawrence Mishel, Jared Benstein, and John Schmitt, *The State of Working America, 2004–05* (2005).

What accounted for this new era of economic hard times and social inequality? To begin with, the Vietnam War's spiraling costs set off the first of several great waves of inflation, which soon made U.S. products more expensive than those of other countries. In 1971, the amount that was paid to foreign producers for imported goods exceeded that paid for U.S. exports; for the first time in the twentieth century, the United States registered a balance-of-payments deficit. Consequently, the United States could no longer maintain the dollar as the world's currency standard, so in August 1971, President Nixon allowed the value of a dollar to "float"—to go up or down in relation to the price of gold and to other currencies according to the world's shifting economic and political currents. In effect, Nixon had devalued the dollar, which made U.S. exports cheaper but imports more expensive. Soon, imported oil became much more costly. In October 1973, in the midst of a war between Israel and its Arab neighbors, Arab oil producers declared an embargo on oil shipments to the United States and Western Europe. The Organization of Petroleum Exporting Countries (OPEC) manipulated the resulting shortage to raise prices from $3 to $12 a barrel. Just five years later, after a revolution in Iran toppled the pro-Western monarchy there, oil prices reached $34 a barrel.

Although many economists and pundits thought that the oil shortage signaled the onset of a worldwide drop in the production of fossil fuels, the energy crisis of the 1970s was actually a political phenomenon. The marketplace reflected the U.S. defeat in Vietnam and the subsequent shift in power from Western consumer countries to the Latin American and Middle

Eastern states that controlled OPEC and other producer cartels. In 1974, the disruption of energy supplies
and the dramatic rise in the price of oil led to federally
mandated gasoline rationing. Panicky motorists lined
up at gas stations to buy a commodity that most had
taken for granted only weeks before; in the Northeast,
thousands of truckers blocked interstates demanding a
price rollback. Conservation measures, the discovery of
new oil fields, and a reassertion of Western economic
power would end the worldwide energy crisis about a
decade later, but while the oil shortage lasted, Americans began to feel increasingly insecure, hostage to economic forces well beyond their control.

As the oil shock reverberated through the U.S.
economy, the rising price of gas and oil forced many
energy-reliant industries to close. In 1974 alone, factory
output fell 10 percent, and unemployment nearly
doubled. Inflation rose into the double digits, eroding
the value of pensions and paychecks. Economists coined a new term —
"stagflation" — to describe this unusual mix of economic problems: low levels of economic growth, high unemployment, and persistent inflation (Figure 13.2). Overnight, Americans became far more pessimistic. "You always
used to think in this country that there would be bad times followed by
good times," commented a Chicago housewife. "Now, maybe it's bad times
followed by hard times followed by harder times."

Higher oil prices and growing competition from foreign producers
would have been less of a problem had not thirty years of Cold War militarization distorted key sectors of the U.S. economy. Encouraged by huge government procurement contracts, American businesses — especially
electronics and aviation — had focused their capital resources and technological know-how on producing armaments. Such massive spending provided employment for large numbers of defense workers in the postwar
years. But ultimately, the nation's huge military budget — on a proportion-
ate basis twice as great as Germany's and seven times that of Japan — sapped
America's productive strength, diverting resources from the development of
commercially competitive products.

Worse, the expertise that developed sophisticated, high-tech military
products was not readily transferable to the increasingly competitive consumer market. For example, during the 1960s, managers at the venerable
Singer Sewing Machine Company, whose product stood for Yankee ingenuity in every hamlet from Spain to Surinam, focused corporate research
efforts on missile and warplane guidance systems. Singer's share of the
world sewing machine market spiraled downward when the company failed

**You're like a bunch of . . . of . . .
of . . . CAPITALISTS!**
A 1974 cartoon suggests that
the oil crisis was linked to
the profit motive, the use of
economic power by the Organization of Petroleum Exporting
Countries echoing American
business tactics. Dennis Renault,
Sacramento Bee, 1974 — Sacramento Bee.

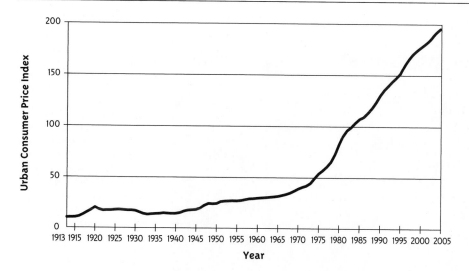

FIGURE 13.2 The Higher Cost of Living: Twentieth-Century Inflation

In the twentieth century, prices leapt upward during and after major wars — World War I, World War II, and Vietnam. Post-Vietnam inflation was made worse by a worldwide increase in the price of oil, wheat, and other major commodities.

to retool its U.S. factories and lost its reputation for high-quality production. Sewing machines from Sweden and Korea took over the American market, forcing Singer to close its flagship New Jersey factory in 1979. By the 1980s, Singer manufactured sewing machines only in Hong Kong.

Finally, a legacy of the 1960s, the growing rights consciousness in the workplace, created legal and regulatory difficulties for many U.S. companies. Workplace safety and health as well as the equitable treatment of women and African Americans became inflammatory issues during the 1970s. A new feminist consciousness in the workplace helped to generate laws and court decisions covering areas of interpersonal relations and employer-employee contact that had once been considered exclusively private. The Equal Employment Opportunity Commission received more than one hundred thousand complaints per year. Only later, after much debate and protest throughout the 1970s and 1980s, did Congress enact the Americans with Disabilities Act in 1990 and the Family and Medical Leave Act in 1993, both of which prohibited employers from discriminating against their employees because of physical incapacity or absence from work because of childbirth or family emergency. Thus, the hiring, pay, promotion, and layoff of employees became subject to governmental review and private litigation to an extent that was unmatched even during the heyday of the industrial union movement three decades earlier.

The ecological consciousness that emerged after 1970 also demonstrated the extent to which a sense of democratic empowerment had transformed the corporate economy. Until the early 1970s, nuclear power seemed the embodiment of technological progress, national security, and economic efficiency. Powerful, authoritative supporters in Congress, industry, and science argued that the "mighty atom" would end U.S. dependence on foreign

No Nukes

Many activists who opposed the proliferation of nuclear weapons and nuclear power facilities used direct-action tactics to forestall the building of reactors. On May Day 1977, thousands of demonstrators affiliated with the Clamshell Alliance blocked construction of a nuclear plant in Seabrook, New Hampshire. Almost 1,500 were arrested and jailed in armories around the state. After two weeks, the armories were still filled because many demonstrators refused to leave until all "clams" were unconditionally released. Governor Meldrin Thompson, who had hoped to stem protest with mass arrests, relented, releasing them all. Ellen Shub.

oil and dirty coal. But commercial nuclear power proved neither as safe nor as cheap as its advocates claimed, and some "experts," radicalized by the Vietnam War, defected from the pronuclear consensus. When thousands of antinuclear protestors took to the streets in the late 1970s, numerous engineers and scientists bolstered the credibility of this new social movement. Dramatic confirmation of such fears came in 1979 when a near-meltdown at Pennsylvania's Three Mile Island utility near Harrisburg forced the evacuation of 100,000 people. Radioactive contamination outside the facility seemed slight, but the actual cleanup of the reactor proved a time-consuming, billion-dollar project. Soon after the incident at Three Mile Island, thirty energy companies canceled plans to build nuclear reactors.

The New Shape of American Business

With economic hard times in the offing, many conservatives in the business community and in politics argued that the nation would have to shift resources from labor to capital and cut back the environmental programs and regulatory laws that investors and industrialists thought burdensome. Thus, *Business Week* editorialized in 1974, right after the first oil shock: "it will be a hard pill for many Americans to swallow—the idea of doing with less so that big business can have more." Earnings dropped one-third from the previous two decades; in manufacturing, workers earned only about one-half of their earlier pay. Although an excess of managers, the growth in foreign competition, and the rise in energy prices accounted for the lion's share of the difficulties, the new rights-conscious activism proved highly visible and vexing. In the decade before 1975, Congress passed more than twenty-five major pieces of regula-

"They Have Largely Destroyed the Pride of Craft"

The introduction of new technologies has always altered the relationship between managers and workers, often by eliminating the need for skilled laborers. Helen Zalph and her colleagues in the printing division of the New York Daily News *discovered this fact for themselves when computers revolutionized the way in which they put together the paper during the 1970s. What management gained in efficiency, workers lost in terms of their control over the production process, a sense of community and teamwork, and the sense of pride that comes with skilled craft work.*

ZALPH: The old time print shop was vastly different from what you see here now. It was one huge room and you could stand at one end and see everyone working, which is very nice in terms of having a sense of unity and knowing who is doing what and what's going on and who's where. That's all gone now and we have these little cubby holes and pathways to here and pathways to there. We're very separated from each other now and you don't have the same sense of being one union and one group of people. It's the people in the laser room, and the people in the computer room, and the VDT operators and everybody separate from everybody else. I think that that's kind of sad, I liked the old print shop much better. And certainly in terms of the work, printers were really craftspeople. They really had to know what they were doing to get a professional looking printing job done. They have largely destroyed the pride of craft, and the need for that kind of expertise with the elimination of many of the requirements that come with the new procedure. You let the computer do it all. You don't have to know typeface, you don't have to know a type size, the computer knows it. . . .

BERNHARDT: What has the introduction of computers meant in terms of how many printers are needed to put out the paper?

ZALPH: The number has dropped vastly. In this composing room the machinery isn't even working properly, it's really not as efficient as it should be, and yet we're down to half the printers we had when we started this new system. We've been able to do almost double the work or more and could probably do much more than that if there were call for it. In terms of printers we recognize that there really is not a need for the numbers.

Interviewed by Debra Bernhardt, September 6, 1981, Courtesy Wagner Labor Archives/Tamiment Library.

tory legislation that required 40,000 new federal workers to administer. In response, corporations stepped up their efforts to influence government decisions, increasing fivefold their lobbying operations in the nation's capital.

For generations, American firms had periodically moved their factories from one state to another to take advantage of low wages and cheap land. In the 1970s, this trend accelerated as firms moved out of the Northeast and into the Sunbelt, a broad crescent stretching south from Virginia to Florida and west through Texas and southern California. Federally funded superhighways and more efficient telecommunications linked this vast region to the population centers of the North and enabled firms to build small, highly efficient factories and warehouses. Generous tax incentives encouraged the move, and the introduction of air-conditioning made the region more suitable to office work. Finally, the massive influx of Latin American and Southeast Asian workers into Florida, Texas, and California offered corporations an even larger pool of cheap Sunbelt labor. By the 1980s, formerly rural North Carolina had the highest percentage of manufacturing workers of any state as well as the lowest blue-collar wages and unionization rates in the country. The North lost more than manufacturing jobs. The computerization of clerical work allowed large financial service firms such as Merrill Lynch, American Express, and Citibank to shift many operations to the South and the West.

Give Me a "$"!

Using the crowd-pleasing tactics of a high school pep rally, Sam Walton exhorts employees at the opening of a new Wal-Mart "Hypermart." Eli Reichman/TimeLife Pictures/Getty Images.

If jobs could be moved to Texas, they could also be shifted to Mexico, Taiwan, and Indonesia. Until the 1960s, U.S. investment in Latin America and the Pacific basin focused largely on the extraction and processing of raw materials mined or grown in those regions. But beginning in the 1970s, a number of American firms produced some of their most sophisticated components in low-wage foreign factories. Between 1971 and 1976, manufacturers of color TVs shifted more than 90 percent of their subassembly production to Asia. Such foreign "outsourcing" of high-value goods and parts sustained the profitability of many "American" product lines. But in the long run, such policies eroded the U.S. manufacturing base and the technical expertise of its workers, managers, and engineers.

Such trends reshaped the business landscape in general and the fates of two great companies in particular. Until the 1970s, General Motors was the largest manufacturing company in the world. But the corporation's failure to build fuel-efficient or stylish cars cost it more than 15 percent of the entire U.S. automobile market in a single decade. Because of its cumbersome, hierarchical bureaucracy, GM, which had once been the most cost-efficient of all automobile firms, now lagged behind both foreign rivals and U.S. competitors. In response, GM managers closed more than twenty factories and outsourced billions of dollars in parts production to low-wage firms in the American South and Mexico. The corporation's blue-collar payroll fell by half, devastating once bustling centers of GM production such as Flint and Pontiac in Michigan.

The rise of the retailing giant Wal-Mart foretold which type of companies would survive the postboom economy. At the end of the 1980s, Wal-Mart was the nation's leading retailer, with a payroll that was second in size only to that of the U.S. Postal Service. When Sam Walton founded Wal-Mart early in the 1960s, Sears, Woolworth's, and other long-established chains that dominated the big cities and their nearby suburbs dwarfed this pint-sized, Arkansas-based retailer. But with the completion of the interstate highway system and the growth of exurban communities in the Sunbelt, the big shopping centers lost much of their convenience and appeal. Walton therefore located his stores in the once-neglected small-town hinterlands, especially in the South and Midwest, where land was cheap, labor was nonunion, and competition was limited. Although Walton gave his firm a "just folks," small-town image, Wal-Mart was among the most sophisticated of global corporations, importing huge quantities of clothing and household goods from fifty countries. Managers used the latest computer technology to track sales, minimize inventory expenses, and squeeze suppliers. Wal-Mart's success made the Walton family the richest in the nation, but the company's rapid growth bankrupted thousands of independent merchants whose viability sustained Main Street life throughout small-town America.

Stagflation Politics: From Nixon to Carter   Of the three presidents who sought to revive the fortunes of American capitalism during the 1970s, Republican Richard Nixon actually presided over the most "liberal" administration. During his tenure, Congress passed, and the president signed, laws indexing Social Security payments to inflation, extending unemployment benefits, and regulating oil and gas prices during the first energy crunch. Declaring himself a "Keynesian," Nixon also used government power to directly attack both inflation and the growing trade imbalance. In August 1971, for example, when the Nixon administration devalued the dollar, it also froze wages and prices and raised the tariff on foreign cars. The administration designed this "New Economic Policy" (NEP) to keep a lid on pay increases and rein in organized labor but also to avoid the kind of massive unemployment and high interest rates that a later generation of more conservative policymakers would routinely adopt as the orthodox anti-inflation remedy.

President Nixon's economic activism gave him enough inflation-free breathing space to win the 1972 election, but his NEP proved unequal to the profound shifts that were transforming the world economy. When U.S. price controls were eliminated in 1973, the cost of living rocketed upward, fueled by sharp increases in the prices of grain, oil, lumber, and other internationally traded commodities. Vice President Gerald Ford had the misfortune to move into the Oval Office in August 1974, just weeks before the nation plunged into the deepest recession since the Great Depression. In an October 8, 1974, televised speech, he announced a voluntary anti-inflation campaign that he called "Whip Inflation Now" (WIN), exhorting Americans to sign pledge forms to save energy and reduce waste, but the program ultimately proved unsuccessful. As production declined by more than 10 percent in 1974 and 1975, nearly one-tenth of the workforce became unemployed. Ford's unimaginative, passive response reminded many people of the kind of economic conservatism that had prevailed in the White House during the 1920s. Ford vetoed most congressional efforts to increase countercyclical spending on education, jobs, and infrastructure construction.

Gerald Ford's ineffectual domestic leadership gave James Earl Carter, a little-known former governor of Georgia, the opportunity to win the Democratic presidential nomination in 1976 and then edge his way into the White House. Carter, a technocrat who had been trained in nuclear engineering in the U.S. Navy and a Christian moralist, argued that his lack of experience in Washington gave him a fresh, honest perspective. "I will never lie to you," he told campaign audiences in a not-so-subtle reference to the Watergate scandal. Although he was one of the more conservative Democrats who campaigned for the presidency that year, Carter had broken with the tradition of southern racism. Andrew Young, a Georgia-based civil rights leader, served as his confidant, and Carter appointed numerous veterans of the 1960s civil rights movement to posts in his administration.

Jimmy Carter's single-term presidency failed because he never managed to tame the double-digit inflation that frightened so many Americans. With few ties to organized labor or to traditional liberals, Carter won the White House by appealing to the anti-incumbent mood that dominated political life in the years following Watergate and President Ford's unpopular 1974 pardon of ex-president Richard Nixon. Carter advocated energy conservation, but he had neither the will nor the political leverage to impose Nixon-style price controls. Carter also rejected most efforts to restart Great Society–like social welfare initiatives, including Democratic proposals for national health insurance and federal programs to promote full employment and fund abortion services for poor women. And he gave only tepid support to the labor movement's 1978 effort to reform the National Labor Relations Board. An increasingly well-organized and outspoken business community successfully lobbied against the bill, which would have reduced employers' ability to resist union-organizing drives.

Instead, Carter turned to a radical deregulation of the airline, trucking, railroad, and telephone industries to curb wages and prices. New Deal era liberals thought that enterprises in these industries required close government supervision, either because of the vital services they rendered or because of their inherent instability. But Carter Democrats had come to see such price and market regulation as economically inefficient and hostile to consumer interests. Administration officials believed that prices would fall

Winning with a Button
President Gerald Ford's "Whip Inflation Now" campaign, which involved distributing tens of thousands of WIN buttons, was aimed at combating the problems of rising inflation and energy costs through voluntary efforts. When the program failed, the buttons quickly became the object of ridicule and a symbol of Ford's ineffectual administration. American Social History Project.

and service would improve if they took a laissez-faire approach.

The Carter administration's conservative tilt became apparent in its rescue of the Chrysler Corporation, which in 1979 stood at the brink of bankruptcy. Chrysler maintained factories that were aging and inefficient compared to those of Japan, resulting in equally outmoded automobiles. The financially troubled corporation needed billions of dollars to retool, but the big banks would not extend credit. Chrysler executives argued that only a government loan guarantee—a federal bailout—could save the company and thousands of well-paid jobs. Such loan guarantees were not new; in 1971, the Lockheed Corporation, one of the nation's major defense contractors, had secured this type of federal help. But the conditions under which Washington guaranteed the Chrysler loan opened the door to a further decline in the standard of living of millions of American workers. Together with the big banks, federal officials demanded that Chrysler's workers make hundreds of millions of dollars in wage concessions as part of the bailout package. As Chrysler's president, Lee Iacocca, explained in the midst of the crisis, "It's freeze time, boys. I've got plenty of jobs at seventeen dollars an hour; I don't have any at twenty." The leadership of the United Auto Workers convinced autoworkers that such concessions were the only way to save their jobs. Chrysler went on to earn record profits in the mid-1980s, but the Chrysler bailout proved to be the first in a long wave of concession contracts and wage rollbacks that swept through almost every unionized industry.

Carter broke with traditional economic liberalism again when he appointed Paul Volcker, a conservative Wall Street banker, as the chairman of the powerful Federal Reserve Board in 1979. Volcker's appointment signaled the death of Keynesianism as a government policy tool. The president abdicated stewardship of the economy in favor of Volcker, who instituted a set of "monetarist" policies that severely restricted the growth of the money supply and thereby pushed interest rates toward 20 percent—their highest level since the Civil War. By the early 1980s, his program had cut the annual inflation rate from 12 percent to 4 percent.

Volcker's monetarism had a huge impact, especially on the goods-producing sectors of the economy. Big-ticket consumer items became far more expensive. "Those interest rates have killed me and my business," complained Bruno Pasquinelli, whose Illinois homebuilding firm faced

"Carter and the Killer Rabbit"
A sketch by political cartoonist Pat Oliphant comments on a peculiar incident that occurred when President Carter was on vacation in Georgia during the summer of 1979. Carter was fishing when a swimming rabbit "attacked" his rowboat. The president managed to fend off the animal with one of his oars. The story, which was widely disseminated by the press, epitomized for many Americans the weakness of the Carter administration. Pat Oliphant, 1982, pencil on paper (sketchbook), 4 × 6 inches. Reproduction courtesy of Susan Conway Gallery, Washington, D.C.

"I Have Very Little Hope"

Mary Morgan, an African American steel-worker who was laid off from U.S. Steel's South Works in Chicago in early 1983, and Carl Stezco, who worked at the Wisconsin Steel mill in Chicago for thirty years until the plant shut down in 1980, describe what it is like to lose a job and be unable to find another one. The decline of the steel industry in the 1970s left unemployed steelworkers with few options.

MARY MORGAN: I started at South Works in 1973. I had two kids still at home and was just separated from my husband. He died a few months later.

I really liked that job. By me being a widow, I could support myself. I didn't have to go out and ask somebody for money. I didn't have to go on Aid [Family Assistance]. I could support my own self. That's very important to me.

I've been off work [for one and one-half years]. I haven't been able to find anything else. And all my benefits is ran out, even my little savings. My children help a little. I have six — all grown now. They're all unemployed. Three of them worked at one company that was sort of like the mill. It's all but closed down now. . . . I have my youngest son, my oldest daughter and one little grandchild living with me. . . .

I've been looking for other jobs. I've been to Sweetheart, Tootsie Roll. Sure-Plus, Libby's, Soft Sheen. . . . Most of them just say they're not hiring. It gets discouraging.

I have very little hope — very, very little. I'm praying that I can find me a job somewhere. But if they don't open up something where people can get a job, it don't look very good at all. I guess they just want us all to dig a hole and get in it.

CARL STEZCO: I've been every place [to] look for a job. . . . I went to Jay's Potato Chips. They gave me a test and said, "You're overqualified." I said, "I'll tell you what, you said you're paying $5 an hour, well I'll work for $3." They still wouldn't take me. I'm a skilled electrician, plumber, pipe fitter. But they ain't gonna hire a guy like me. I still go out every day and look.

My wife isn't healthy. She can't work. We have a two-flat, but the mortgage isn't paid off. I get $160 in rent on the other apartment. I'm paying $200 on the mortgage and $160 in gas bills. So you can't make ends meet. I only eat one meal a day. Food stamps turned me down. I don't know where to turn. I'm ashamed to ask for anything. I always swore I'd never go on pension — I'd work till the day I died. . . .

. . . I pray every day. That's all I have faith in anymore.

David Bensman and Roberta Lynch, *Rusted Dreams: Hard Times in a Steel Community* (1987), pp. 93–94.

near-bankruptcy. High interest rates also pushed up the value of the dollar against foreign currencies, making American cars, steel, and electronic products even less competitive overseas. Wave after wave of plant closings swept through the Midwest and Middle Atlantic states. In 1982 alone, 2,700 mass layoffs eliminated more than 1.25 million industrial jobs. Cities such as Youngstown, Buffalo, Cleveland, Gary, Milwaukee, and Detroit, once the industrial crown jewels of the nation, now exemplified a declining "Rust Belt." Almost 11 percent of the U.S. workforce was unemployed, the highest proportion since 1940.

This blue-collar depression struck older male breadwinners with particular force. When plants closed, many of these workers experienced a deep sense of loss and a feeling that their inability to "bring home the bacon" reflected on their masculinity. "I've had to change my life-style completely," reported Pete Jefferson, an African American who lost his job when his steel mill closed its doors. "I come from a Southern family. They always looked up to me because I'd done so well financially. I used to be head of the family; now I'm just a member." Alcoholism, depression, and divorce grew more frequent in the months and years that followed a factory shutdown. Few blue-collar men over age forty were able to retrain; most would find new work, but rarely at the same high levels of pay or with the same pension and health care benefits.

The Nation Moves to the Right

Many of these blue-collar workers would turn to the Republican Party, helping to push American politics to the right in the late 1970s. The multiple traumas of that decade — Vietnam, Watergate, the oil shocks, and the Iranian hostage crisis — generated a pervasive sense of cynicism and alienation. In the quarter-century after 1973, the percentage of Americans who agreed with the statement "The best government is the government that governs the least" nearly doubled, to 56 percent. Not unexpectedly, electoral participation dropped sharply; many Americans who had traditionally supported an activist, governmental solution to the nation's problems now stayed home on election day. Among those who did vote, conflicts over race, gender, and sexuality offered many working-class whites the opportunity to vote for conservative politicians, who promised not to bus children outside their neighborhoods in the name of desegregation or raise taxes to benefit "welfare queens." In what seemed to be an increasingly unstable geopolitical environment, American foreign policy also moved to the right. Beginning even before Ronald Reagan took office, top policymakers abandoned détente and projected a more aggressive posture in the Cold War conflict.

The Rise of the New Right   After 1968, barely half of all potential voters cast ballots in presidential elections—about one-third fewer than voted in the New Deal era or the early 1960s. This withdrawal from the electoral process was concentrated among working people and the poor, whose disappearance from the voting rolls pushed all American politics to the right. The decline in voter turnout had many sources, but two stand out. First, institutions that traditionally linked individual voters to national politics, such as trade unions and urban political machines, had become far less influential. The professionally crafted thirty-second television spots and computer-generated direct-mail fund-raising letters that replaced these grassroots institutions proved to be ineffective in mobilizing those at the bottom of the social ladder. Second, political participation declined among poor and working-class voters because the Democratic Party failed to offer alternative policies around which these voters, once its most loyal supporters, might be mobilized. Between the end of the 1960s and the end of the 1970s, the number of Americans who agreed with the polling statement that the "people running the country don't really care what happens to you" shot up from 26 to 60 percent.

Political demobilization among once-stalwart supporters of the Democratic Party was soon matched by the rise of a "New Right," which made a powerful bid for the allegiance of many of these same voters. For most of the twentieth century, political conservatism in the United States had been closely linked to the views of affluent white Anglo-Saxon Protestants, who looked with some disdain on blacks, Catholics, Jews, unionists, and immigrants. This brand of "Old Right" conservatism mistrusted activist government, denounced international Communism, and defended laissez-faire economics. Although traditional conservatism did not disappear in the 1970s, its elite spokesmen lost much of their influence to a New Right, dedicated to mobilizing the body politic against secular culture, feminist ideas, and the government social programs that had first been launched during Lyndon Johnson's presidency.

The New Right grew in response both to the decline in popular confidence in the nation's institutions and to the transformations that were taking place in American culture. Social and ideological changes during the 1960s challenged what many people saw as their traditional values and proper place in the social hierarchy: the father-centered family, the Christian character of American public life, and an unproblematic patriotism. Thus, the New Right appealed to millions of Americans who had once been stalwart Democrats: white southerners, urban Catholics, and disaffected unionists.

But the New Right was not simply a backlash against "the Sixties"; a militant brand of conservatism had begun to flourish long before the end of

Yellow Ribbon

Inspired by the 1973 pop song "Tie a Yellow Ribbon Round the Ole Oak Tree," many U.S. communities displayed yellow ribbons during the Iran hostage crisis. The song was inspired by a real incident involving a released prison inmate's return home. As a sign of her continuing faith in him, his wife had tied a yellow ribbon around the oak tree in their town square. Wally McNamee, January 1981 — Corbis.

that decade. Barry Goldwater's 1964 presidential campaign was a crystallizing event, transforming the nascent New Right from a circle of collegiate intellectuals into something of a broad political movement. Key conservative leaders of the 1970s and 1980s, including columnist George Will, Chief Justice William Rehnquist, Equal Rights Amendment opponent Phyllis Schlafly, radio and TV pundit Pat Buchanan, and direct-mail entrepreneur Richard Viguerie had all been passionate Goldwater partisans. Raising millions of dollars for New Right initiatives, Viguerie proved a particularly imaginative organizer, who combined the Goldwater campaign donor list with that of the George Wallace partisans. Soon, he gained power in the Republican Party. "Direct mail," asserted Viguerie, "is like having a water moccasin for a watchdog. Silent but deadly."

Conflicts abroad also helped conservatives at the polls. For decades, Iran's monarch Reza Shah Pahlavi had been a bulwark of U.S. influence in the Persian Gulf. But the billions of dollars in oil revenue that washed over his nation of thirty-five million had set off explosive tensions among both secular radicals, who fought for a constitutional democracy, and Islamic fundamentalists, who sought to impose an anti-Western theocracy. As the Shah's army disintegrated, Islamic religious leaders (ayatollahs) led by the exiled Ayatollah Ruhollah Khomeini consolidated their power. The 1979 Iranian revolution precipitated a second oil shock, which tripled world oil prices and further strained the already weak American economy. Islamic militants added to U.S. woes when they seized the U.S. embassy in November 1979 and held fifty-two embassy personnel hostage for 444 days. A long-running American Broadcasting Company TV news show, *The Iran Crisis — America Held Hostage* (which ultimately became *Nightline*), reflected a widespread sense of U.S. impotence and frustration, which was exacerbated by a failed rescue mission during which eight U.S. commandos died.

Events in Afghanistan compounded the situation. A pro-Soviet faction had gained power there, but Communist rule was tenuous, especially after Islamic radicals seized power in neighboring Iran. To forestall the collapse of their Afghan clients, the Soviets airlifted thousands of troops into the capital, Kabul, in December 1979. President Carter called the invasion the "gravest threat to peace since 1945" and demanded an increase in the military budget, the reinstatement of draft registration for eighteen-year-old men, and the speedy development of a new generation of medium-range missiles for deployment in Europe. In Afghanistan itself, the Central Intelligence Agency shipped sophisticated arms to Muslim guerrillas, who soon stalemated more than 100,000 Soviet troops.

The Iranian hostage situation and the Soviet presence in Afghanistan humiliated Carter. He had come into office promising to deepen détente (see Chapter 12), but such foreign relations disasters convinced many conservatives and some liberals that détente was a poor bargain for the United States. Senator Henry Jackson of Washington led a faction within the Democratic Party that opposed both trade liberalization with the Soviets and a new arms agreement until the Kremlin respected the human rights of Jews and other minorities within the Soviet Union. Among Republicans, a powerful nationalist current also opened a breach within party ranks. Therefore, when President Carter sent to the Senate a treaty relinquishing U.S. sovereignty over the Panama Canal, ratification proved contentious, even though diplomats of the Nixon-Ford State Department had negotiated most of the agreement. The treaty was ultimately ratified, but by the last year of his presidency, Carter's foreign policy lay in ruins.

Revolt Against Taxes and Busing   The civil rights revolution had a huge impact on the urban white working class in many Northern cities, among them Irish Americans in Boston, Slavic Americans in South Chicago, and Italian Americans in Brooklyn. Many of them now lived in cities that were presided over by black mayors such as Cleveland's Carl Stokes, elected in 1967, and Detroit's Coleman Young, who began a twenty-year tenure in 1973. As long as cities were prosperous and schools were well funded, it seemed possible that a multiracial set of urban institutions might emerge with relatively little social tension. But economic hard times in the 1970s, combined with the decline of the cities and their school systems, made it virtually certain that racial conflict would erupt and that white working-class voters would shift rightward in response.

Tensions exploded over court-ordered busing to achieve racial balance in the schools. By the early 1970s, racial integration of public schools in the rural South had largely ended the state-supported dual system there, but in most large urban areas, segregated schools continued to mirror the racial divide that persisted in residential neighborhoods. To remedy such de facto segregation, courts often ordered local school boards to institute cross-neighborhood busing. Despite the loss of familiar neighborhood schools, African American parents supported these plans, hoping that their children's attendance at resource-rich, formerly all-white schools would enhance their educational opportunity and performance. But in Pontiac, Michigan; Louisville, Kentucky; and Kansas City, Missouri, busing

South Boston Backlash

The Boston busing controversy turned violent in the spring of 1976. On April 5, a group of white high school students from South Boston and Charlestown who were opposed to busing visited City Hall to meet with a councilwoman who supported their boycott of classes. Outside the building, the teenagers encountered and then assaulted labor lawyer Theodore Landsmark. The attack sparked a series of violent racial incidents that extended into the summer. Stanley Forman.

programs quickly generated white opposition, sometimes leading to school boycotts and violence.

The most spectacular clash over school busing came in Boston, the city that had spawned nineteenth-century movements for free public education and the abolition of slavery. For years, the Irish American–dominated Boston school board had kept the city's schools racially segregated. In 1975, after a long, NAACP-initiated legal battle, a federal district court issued a sweeping integration order that mandated, among other remedies, the busing of pupils from all-black Roxbury to South Boston, an economically declining Irish section of the city. Federal courts in Massachusetts, as elsewhere, excluded from integration plans the white, middle-class suburbs, so the burden of the busing plan fell almost entirely on the children of the urban working class, both black and white.

The stage was set for an ugly confrontation when the first black students were bused across town. For three years, Boston police struggled to protect black children from angry white parents screaming, "Nigger go home!" More than 20,000 white students left the Boston public schools, many to escape desegregation. Boston's inflamed racial climate finally subsided in the 1980s when a new generation of politicians, both black and white, launched a set of biracial electoral campaigns to defuse urban tensions. The busing controversy also faded from the news, both because a new cohort of conservative judges backed away from the tactic and because the racial integration of most big-city school systems had become unworkable. White flight and the growth in immigrant and minority populations gave most urban school systems a substantial African American and Latino majority enrollment.

Because of the enfranchisement of millions of African American voters, direct appeals to racial intolerance largely vanished from public political discourse during the 1970s and 1980s. High public officials who used words such as "nigger," "Jap," or "kike" invariably apologized for their gaffes. But American political discourse remained saturated with an array of code words, phrases, and substitute issues that indirectly expressed white racial prejudice. Urban crime, escalating drug use, and the growth of public assistance programs were real issues, but much of the rhetorical denunciation of "welfare queens" (women who grew wealthy by taking advantage of the welfare system), "drug lords," and "forced busing" gave the public debate a thinly disguised racial edge.

All this helped to discredit many government functions and fuel a series of an antigovernment tax revolts. In 1978, passage of California's Proposition 13, a ballot initiative limiting property taxes and slashing local government revenues, signaled the ability of New Right conservatives to turn the tax issue against liberal governance itself. As one state legislator put it, Proposition 13 was "a bullet from a loaded gun that went off in California on its way to its ultimate target — the high level of Federal spending." Soon conservative activists were mounting antitax campaigns in Michigan, Idaho, Nevada, Massachusetts, Oregon, and Arizona. They argued that at issue was not only the fairness of the tax system, but also wasteful government expenditures for education, welfare, and other social programs. Most of the tax savings went to business, not to ordinary taxpayers, but the antitax agitation of these years had a profound impact on civic life. Combined with the stale taste left by Watergate, it helped to mobilize public sentiment against the government's assuming responsibility for pressing social and economic problems.

Gender Politics   School busing and taxes were not the only issues that mobilized conservatives in the 1970s. Explosive moral and cultural questions about the role of women and the status of homosexuals proved just as powerful. Before the 1970s, most evangelical Protestants avoided politics, which they saw as hopelessly corrupt. But court rulings that legalized abortion, curbed school prayer, and deprived segregated Christian academies of their tax-exempt status unleashed a wave of activism. In the South, the Carter administration's efforts to eliminate tax breaks for hundreds of new religious academies mobilized thousands of Protestant conservatives to participate in Republican Party politics, the Moral Majority, and other Christian political groups.

"Liberate Us from the Liberators"

Teddi Holt, a full-time homemaker from Georgia with three sons, helped to found Mothers on the March (MOM) in the late 1970s, a New Right organization dedicated to "preserv[ing] and strengthen[ing] the home."

I am pleased that God blessed me with the privilege of being a woman. I have never been envious of the role of men but have had respect for both sexes. There's no doubt that there has been discrimination against women, but that is past history, just as discrimination against blacks is past history in the US. . . .

NOW's [The National Organization for Women's] primary goal was to pass the Equal Rights Amendment (ERA) without amendment. Second, it included as a secondary goal—"right to abortion on demand." And third, it supported "a woman's right to . . . express her own sexuality and to choose her lifestyle. . . ." Such goals were foreign to me. I could not imagine any woman with my background having such goals, because they did not hold to traditional values and/or Judeo-Christian ethics on which the Constitution and our laws are based. . . .

It was obvious to me that ERA was certainly not a protection of women's rights. In fact, it would remove many protections and exemptions that were specifically placed in our laws, recognizing the fact that our Creator had most certainly created us male and female: two separate, very different, equally important human beings. . . .

Just what were we women to be liberated from? These women [feminists] were calling for liberation from the things women like me love most—our husbands, our children, our homes. My cry became: "God, liberate us from the Liberators!" . . .

We believe that the mothers of this and other nations must stand up for the protection of our homes and our children. In no way are we extremists, unless we be guilty of extreme devotion to our husbands, our children, and our homes. It is our sincere belief that if we do not unite against the threats to the home, if we retire to the convenience and security of our houses and do not speak out, then it will not be long until we, the "keepers at home" (Titus 2:5) will not have a home to keep!

Robyn Rowland, ed., *Women Who Do and Women Who Don't Join the Women's Movement* (1984).

For Protestant fundamentalists, gender issues took on the air of a religious war. In these conflicts, denominational lines had less meaning than did the split between theological liberals and conservatives. The former had little quarrel with the nation's pluralist, secular culture; the latter, regardless of denomination, saw the United States as an increasingly amoral nation in which the difficulties that it faced at home and abroad were but the outward sign of an inner debasement. Perhaps for this reason, evangelical Christianity enjoyed an extraordinary renaissance in the 1970s among both black and white Americans. Between 1965 and 1985, membership in liberal Protestant churches declined, but the conservative Southern Baptists, America's largest Protestant denomination, gained three million members. By the start of the 1980s, more than forty-five million Americans considered themselves fundamentalists. Scores of congregations moved to the suburbs and built huge new churches, often with money donated by the Sunbelt's energy, real estate, and banking entrepreneurs. Evangelical ministers, such as Virginians Jerry Falwell, founder of the politically influential Moral Majority, and Pat Robertson, used the latest in television technology and programming to spread their conservative message well beyond the traditional southern Bible Belt.

Pro-Life Prop

An antiabortion demonstrator brandishes a plastic replica of a fetus during a protest outside a New Jersey abortion clinic in February 1990. Pictures played a significant role in promotion of the "pro-life" cause, reducing a complex debate over women's rights and the development of life into a single figure, "the unborn child." Ignoring developmental stages in the womb, they presented images that either depicted full-term, baby-like "fetuses" (such as the plastic doll shown here) or focused on the most developed parts of the fetal anatomy (such as the head, hands, and feet) while avoiding those that were less identifiably "human." Donna Binder.

Three gender issues served as New Right cultural and religious lightning rods: the U.S. Supreme Court's 1973 decision in *Roe v. Wade*, which legalized abortions; the feminist-backed effort to pass the Equal Rights Amendment (ERA) to the U.S. Constitution; and the increasing rights consciousness and public visibility of gay Americans.

Before 1973, abortion was legal in some localities but not in every state. Feminists and civil libertarians argued, and the Supreme Court came to agree, that governmental prohibitions against a medical abortion were not only unenforceable, but also a violation of a woman's right to privacy, especially during the first trimester of pregnancy. Most women who sought abortions were not vocal feminists, but conservatives linked the exercise of the new abortion rights to what they perceived as the sexual licentiousness of the 1960s. They denounced legalized abortion as murder of the unborn, a spur to sexual promiscuity, and, as one activist put it, an attack on "the right of a husband to protect the life of the child he has fathered in his wife's womb."

Antiabortion forces across the country rallied quickly after the *Roe v. Wade* decision. In the North, Catholic Church leaders organized the first antiabortion demonstrations. Among many Catholics, as among most evangelical Protestants, the degree of opposition to abortion and the defense of what many saw as the sanctity of "God-given" gender roles within the family determined the depth of one's religious commitment. In state and local jurisdictions, "pro-life" groups waged a vigorous legal and legislative campaign to restrict abortion rights when they could not eliminate them outright. Activists often picketed abortion clinics and courted arrest in order to stigmatize this medical procedure and the doctors who performed it. But across the picket lines, they faced an equally fervent "prochoice" movement, whose members argued that the right of a woman to choose an abortion was fundamental to her dignity and citizenship.

The ERA, which both houses of Congress approved in 1972, also proved to be a controversial issue in the 1970s and early 1980s. The proposed amendment simply stated that "equality of rights under the law shall not be denied or abridged by the United States or by any State on account of sex." It thus ratified, in symbolic and legal terms, the new roles that women were exploring and the new gender egalitarianism that was reshaping so many aspects of American life. In education, for example, coeducation came to scores of all-male colleges and universities, including Yale, Dartmouth, Princeton, the University of Virginia, and the military academies. And when Congress amended the Civil Rights Act in 1972 to require equal expenditure of federal funds on male and female students, the skill and visibility of women in competitive sports leapt forward.

Although many Republicans had once been staunch supporters of the ERA, a new generation of social conservatives attacked it as little more than a proxy for the entire feminist agenda. As debate on the proposed constitutional amendment rolled through key state legislatures, New Right leaders such as Phyllis Schlafly and Jerry Falwell organized thousands of activists against it. Falwell told his large television audience, "In families and in nations where the Bible is believed, Christian women are honored above men. . . . The Equal Rights Amendment strikes at the foundation of our entire social structure." Twenty-eight state legislatures approved the ERA by the end of 1973, but public opinion turned against the amendment during the remainder of the decade—so much so that five states eventually rescinded approval. It never became part of the U.S. Constitution because supporters could not win passage in the three-quarters of all state legislatures (thirty-eight) necessary for final ratification (Map 13.1).

The key to the New Right's victory in this battle lay in the very different meaning the idea of women's equality held for men and women depending on age, class, and economic expectations. Many working-class men feared that passage of the ERA would undercut whatever control they still possessed over their work and family lives. For their part, many working-class women, especially those in the South and Middle West, defended a home-centered "separate sphere" as the key to their sense of dignity and self-worth. Many of them did not identify with the feminist leaders who had

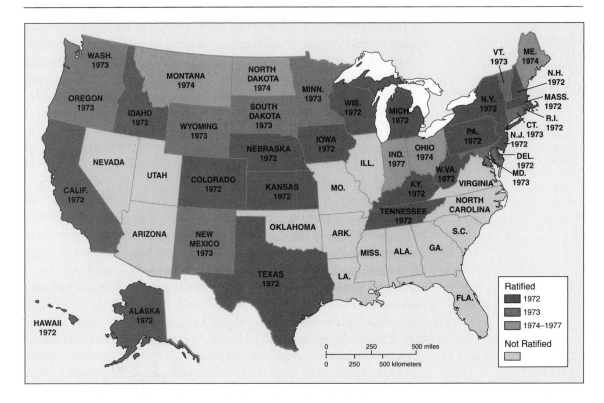

MAP 13.1 States That Ratified the Equal Rights Amendment
The Equal Rights Amendment passed Congress in 1972 and was quickly ratified by a majority of states but not the three-quarters required. By the mid-1970s, conservative and religious groups opposed the amendment as too feminist, and it never became part of the U.S. Constitution. Idaho, Kentucky, Nebraska, Tennessee, and South Dakota later rescinded their ratifications.

injected the ERA into national politics. One otherwise liberal trade unionist explained that she distrusted *Ms.* magazine publisher Gloria Steinem because "I think maybe she looks above us. I feel she's fighting for women like herself, professional women. . . . So I don't consider myself part of her movement."

The new visibility and rights consciousness projected by gay Americans also polarized American politics and culture. In the surge of "gay pride" that followed the 1969 Stonewall Inn riot in New York City, many homosexuals expressed their sexual orientation with an openness that had been denied to previous generations. They built a new kind of urban counterculture, which included gay and lesbian bars, newspapers, and magazines, as well as numerous social and political groups. The once-buried history of gay Americans came alive in an outpouring of books and movies. For the first time, local politicians acknowledged a definable gay vote. In the 1970s, the victorious mayoral campaigns of George Moscone in San Francisco and Edward Koch in New York City benefited from the support of a mobilized gay electorate.

Horrified, fundamentalist Christians attacked the public display of homosexuality as blasphemous. In 1977, Anita Bryant, a popular singer and

Anti-ERA

Carrying signs that warned of ways in which the Equal Rights Amendment would purportedly victimize women and that referred to President Carter's daughter Amy and his wife Rosalynn (both ERA supporters), opponents of the amendment demonstrate in front of the White House in February 1977. Warren K. Leffler, Prints and Photographs Division, Library of Congress.

News-Breaking

An ACT-UP protestor, shouting, "Fight AIDS, not Arabs," interrupts anchor Dan Rather during the January 22, 1991, broadcast of the *CBS Evening News*. Mario Suriani, AP/Wide World Photos.

advertising celebrity, won national attention when she campaigned against the specter of "militant" homosexuals corrupting young students in Florida's public schools. Bryant spearheaded the successful movement to repeal a Dade County ordinance that protected homosexuals from employment discrimination. Physical attacks on gays increased, including attacks against high-profile leaders. In 1978, Dan White, a conservative former San Francisco politician, assassinated Mayor Moscone and Harvey Milk, the city's first openly gay member of its board of aldermen. When White was found not guilty of the crime by reason of insanity, San Francisco's gay community erupted in a night of street violence.

The New Right's hostility toward homosexuals intensified in the early 1980s when AIDS, the deadly acquired immune deficiency syndrome, began to ravage the male homosexual communities of San Francisco, New York, Los Angeles, and other big cities. Within a decade, more than 100,000 people had died, while another two million (both gay and straight) were infected with HIV (human immunodeficiency virus), the

"This Is Not a Gay Issue. This Is a Human Issue": AIDS Patient Roger Lyon Speaks Out

In the following testimony before a 1983 congressional committee, Roger Lyon, an AIDS patient, described his personal experience with the disease and expressed his hope for increased government involvement to combat the AIDS crisis. When AIDS struck the gay community during the early 1980s, many gay people who had not previously been politically active began to take action. Demands for rights and recognition by the gay and lesbian community had been growing throughout the postwar period, and the burst of community health activism in response to the AIDS epidemic built on these earlier expressions of "gay pride" and activism.

STATEMENT OF ROGER LYON, SAN FRANCISCO, CALIF.

I was diagnosed with Kaposi's sarcoma [a cancer of the connective tissue causing red and purple skin lesions] on February 3 of this year. Prior to that time I was having absolutely no AIDS-related symptoms whatsoever. On physical exam at that time three lesions were found internally. . . .

February 4 I entered UC, I went to University of California without an appointment, at the suggestion of my doctor, and started what is called their staging process—a battery of tests to determine the extent of this disease. At that time I was basically numb. I had no feeling. I was just moving. UC has been—they have been very kind and helpful. . . .

However, it is a matter of day-to-day waiting, waiting for something to happen, living in constant fear that I am going to wake up one morning to find lesions, waking up finding that I have some other opportunistic infection, cryptospordiosis, possibly pneumocystis pneumonia.

At this time I am basically living in fear of what is to come. . . .

I came here today with the hope that this administration would do everything possible, make every resource available—there is no reason this disease cannot be conquered. We do not need in-fighting, this is not a political issue. This is a health issue. This is not a gay issue. This is a human issue. And I do not intend to be defeated by it. I came here today in the hope that my epitaph would not read that I died of red tape.

Congress, House Committee on Government Operations, *Federal Response to AIDS: Hearings before a Subcommittee of the Committee on Government Operations, House of Representatives*, 98th Cong., 1st Sess., August 1 and 2, 1983 (Washington, DC: U.S. Government Printing Office, 1983).

virus that causes AIDS. To many heterosexual Americans, not only those in the New Right, AIDS seemed less a disease than a moral judgment on the gay lifestyle. But the AIDS epidemic soon spread well beyond the gay community, first to intravenous drug users and then to heterosexuals, the latter reminding moralists that gay people had no monopoly on promiscuity. A burst of gay community health care activism late in the 1980s won homosexual Americans respect within the public health community and greater awareness of gay issues and rights. By the mid-1990s, the promotion of safe sex, along with the deployment of new medicines, had limited the devastating impact of the AIDS epidemic within the United States.

The Reagan Revolution and Economic Disparity

The rise of the New Right, the demise of détente, and the persistence of stagflation doomed the presidency of Jimmy Carter and opened the door to Republican Ronald Reagan's sweeping victory in the 1980 presidential contest. Born in Illinois, Reagan achieved modest fame as a Hollywood actor in the 1930s and 1940s. He was then a prolabor, New Deal liberal who was active in the Screen Actors Guild. But after World War II, Reagan sided with conservative anti-Communists during a violent set of film industry strikes. In the 1950s, as a corporate spokesperson for General Electric, one of the nation's most aggressively antiunion firms, Reagan became an active Republican. Elected governor of California in 1966, he served two terms, during which he fought to slow the growth in state spending for health, education, and welfare. He won national attention as a bitter opponent of the student movement on California campuses and as a strong supporter of the Vietnam War. By the time he left the governor's mansion in 1975, he was the de facto leader of the resurgent Republican right. The movie star turned political superstar won the presidency with a promise of a new economic program to end the stagflation of the 1970s. Under Reagan, tax cuts and defense spending boosted some regional economies. But tax breaks for corporations and the wealthiest Americans increased the overall disparity between the rich and poor, as unions continued to struggle against foreign competition and domestic hostility to the labor movement.

Reagan's Presidency   Reagan was by far the most conservative figure in the 1980 presidential race. He easily defeated the mainstream Republican candidate, ex-CIA director George H. W. Bush, for the Republican nomination; and in the general election, he marginalized support for the GOP moderate John Anderson, who ran as an independent. Reagan attacked détente, emphasizing the need to increase the military budget and project American power abroad. He took skillful advantage of the nation's economic difficulties to denounce government efforts to manage the economy and regulate business. Reagan opposed outright corporate taxation and advocated sharply lower personal tax rates for the rich. In rhetoric, if not always in practice, he supported the New Right's conservative social agenda. "Government is not the solution to our problem," he asserted in his first inaugural address, "government is the problem."

The Republicans won the election by retaking the white South from the Democrats and increasing their victory margin among middle-class, suburban voters. Most strikingly, Reagan captured the votes of half of all blue-collar workers and more than 40 percent of union households. These "Reagan Democrats," who had once been core supporters of the New Deal and the welfare state, now helped to tilt American politics against new taxes and social spending initiatives. Only African Americans voted solidly Democratic. On Reagan's coattails, the Republicans gained twelve Senate seats, giving them a majority in that body for the first time since the early 1950s. The House maintained a slim but dispirited Democratic majority (Map 13.2).

Reagan and the Republicans promised to transform American politics in a fashion just as sweeping as that inaugurated by Roosevelt's New Deal nearly fifty years earlier. Declaring the Soviet Union an "evil empire," Reagan won a 40 percent increase in arms spending, including expensive new weapons systems, such as the "Star Wars" antimissile shield. Reaganite intellectuals, such as U.N. ambassador Jeane Kirkpatrick and State Department official Elliot Abrams, defined most insurgencies in developing countries as Soviet-inspired, Soviet-supported terrorism. The Reagan administration therefore adopted a "rollback" strategy that targeted revolutionary movements in Africa and Latin America. The administration also sought to overcome what some pundits called the "Vietnam syndrome," which was defined as a lingering reluctance to commit U.S. military forces abroad. To this end, the administration increased military aid to the Afghan rebels, organized and armed a group of counterrevolutionary Nicaraguans, sent the Marines into the Lebanese civil war, and in 1983 launched a military invasion of the tiny Caribbean island of Grenada, where pro-Cuban radicals had taken power.

By "getting the government off our backs," Reagan hoped to unleash a tide of entrepreneurial energy that would restore economic growth and pay for the military buildup by cutting taxes, government regulations, and social spending. In 1981, with the cooperation of many conservative Democrats in Congress, the new administration cut business and income taxes by 25 percent and pared $25 billion from domestic social programs. Meanwhile, Reagan's new secretary of

MAP 13.2 Presidential Election of 1980

Ronald Reagan won all but six states and the District of Columbia, ending up with an electoral count of 489 to 49. Taking 51 percent of the popular vote, he captured many traditional Democratic voters in the South and urban centers. Reagan's popularity also helped Republican candidates to win a majority in the Senate for the first time in twenty-five years.

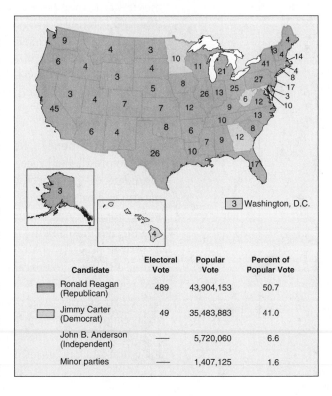

Candidate	Electoral Vote	Popular Vote	Percent of Popular Vote
Ronald Reagan (Republican)	489	43,904,153	50.7
Jimmy Carter (Democrat)	49	35,483,883	41.0
John B. Anderson (Independent)	—	5,720,060	6.6
Minor parties	—	1,407,125	1.6

Invasion Fantasies

Hollywood exploited the new Cold War in John Milius's *Red Dawn*, a 1984 film about a Soviet takeover of the United States. Such fantasies failed to anticipate the direction that invasion would actually take: six years later, McDonald's opened its first fast-food franchise in Moscow. Everett Collection.

the interior, James Watt, worked to open federally controlled land, coastal waters, and wetlands to exploitation by mining, lumber, oil, and gas companies. Both the Environmental Protection Agency and the Occupational Safety and Health Administration became much more solicitous of the business point of view. Commentators called Reagan's program of tax cuts and regulatory reforms "supply-side economics" or just "Reaganomics." Its partisans argued that business profits, sales, investment, employment and even tax revenues would soar in an economic environment that was so much more favorable to entrepreneurship.

Such was the theory. Reaganomics did cut taxes sharply for corporations and the wealthy, reducing the top individual tax rate from 70 percent in the 1970s to 28 percent in 1986. A family with an income between $100,000 and $200,000 gained an average of $8,400 in extra income from the Reagan tax cuts. But the taxes that most working-class Americans paid actually rose during the 1980s because state and local taxes increased to make up for reductions in federal aid and because Social Security deductions increased almost every year.

The Reagan tax policy had an additional consequence, which many of its architects were unwilling to advertise. Between 1981 and 1986, federal income tax receipts plummeted by $750 billion. This loss of income, combined with huge increases in military spending, generated staggering federal budget deficits of some $150 billion to $200 billion a year (Figure 13.3). Thus, Reaganomics ensured that regardless of which party controlled Congress or the White House—and however great the social need—the federal government would find it virtually impossible to initiate new programs. Moreover, because the government had to borrow so much to cover the tax shortfall, interest rates remained at double-digit levels. The strong dollar drove down the cost of imported Japanese cars and German machine tools, but it also ensured that domestic manufacturing would continue to struggle and blue-collar unemployment would remain at near-depression levels.

Reaganomics also forced deep cuts in welfare spending. The social programs that were inaugurated or expanded in the late 1960s had helped to reduce poverty in the United States, but in the 1970s, inflation and recession began to undermine this progress. During the 1980s, conservative ideologues such as Charles Murray and George Gilder argued that liberal social

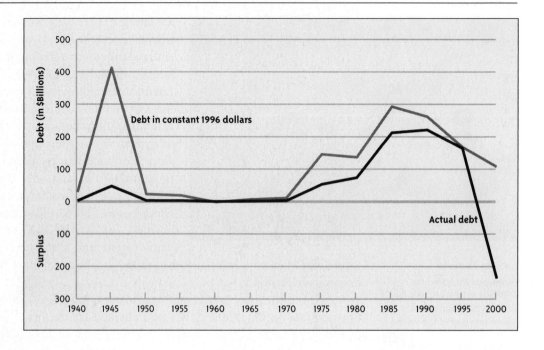

policy itself produced poverty and generated a self-perpetuating "under-class" that was dependent on government handouts. Declaring such social programs a failure, the Reagan administration's policymakers set out to destroy them. Large cuts in food stamp, child nutrition, and job-training programs followed; Aid to Families with Dependent Children, public service employment programs, and low-income housing projects also suffered.

Not all welfare programs were cut so drastically — only those that assisted the poor. The administration spared the social programs and tax policies that benefited people who had a solid attachment to paid work — Social Security, Medicare, and the tax deduction for interest on home mortgages. These middle-income entitlement programs bore no stigma; most Americans considered them a right rather than a handout. Thus, in the 1980s, even conservative Republicans considered Social Security, by far the nation's most expensive income-transfer program, the "third rail" of American politics: touch it and you die.

The Reagan Boom   The same economic policies that devastated the country's industrial heartland generated regional booms in the Sun Belt and in high-tech New England. Defense spending, foreign investment, and the maturation of the baby boom generation sent real estate values soaring on the coasts. In financial centers such as New York, Dallas, Los Angeles, and Miami, Reagan administration policies that deregulated the banking industry and the stock market set off a wave of speculation, much of it vis-

FIGURE 13.3   The Rising Federal Deficit Under Reagan

Reagan's tax cuts and increased military spending tripled the federal debt to $2.8 trillion by 1989.

Photo Op

Press photographers are shown here taking pictures of Ronald Reagan during a "photo opportunity." Formal photography sessions, scheduled by the White House staff, dated back to the 1930s, when FDR's press secretary instructed photographers to avoid showing the polio-afflicted president in a wheelchair. During the Reagan administration, however, photographic access to the president was controlled and orchestrated to virtually guarantee that no unflattering or negative picture would be recorded. Believing that the look was more important than the meaning of an event, White House staff dictated the time, the place, and even the angle of vision of "photo ops." The resulting pictures helped to shape a positive, upbeat image of Reagan for the public. National Archives.

ible in the suburban and exurban centers whose overnight growth often eclipsed that of the downtown office districts. Tysons Corner, Virginia; the Route 1 corridor to Princeton, New Jersey; Clayton, Missouri; Newport Beach, California; Rockville Pike, Maryland; and the Route 580 corridor just east of the Oakland hills in northern California—these were not the bedroom suburbs of the 1950s, but entirely new towns complete with gleaming office parks, huge shopping malls, and high-priced homes and condominiums. In them lived a workforce that was segregated by race, class, and personal expectations from the people who were still struggling in the nation's older, urban manufacturing and service sectors. In the 1980s and afterward, these "edge cities" represented a physical manifestation of the great social divisions that Reaganite capitalism generated.

Income distribution in the United States, though far less egalitarian than that in most other industrial democracies, had remained fairly stable for a quarter-century after the end of World War II. But in the early 1980s, the United States, in the words of economists Barry Bluestone and Bennett Harrison, took a "Great U-Turn" that widened the distance between the well and poorly paid to an extent greater "than at any point in the life-times of all but our most senior citizens, the veterans of the Great Depression." Between 1977 and 1990, the income of the richest fifth of the population rose by one-third; that of the top 1 percent almost doubled, even as the total income of the bottom 60 percent actually fell, the income of those who lived below the poverty line dropping most sharply (Figure 13.4).

There were critics aplenty, but much of American popular culture celebrated the new rich. Greed and extravagance became the stuff of

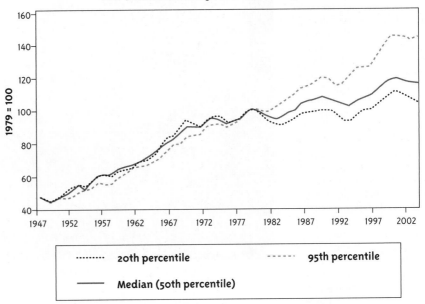

Low-, Middle-, and High-Income Growth, 1947–2003

television dramas such as *Dallas* and *Dynasty*, whose ruthless but stylish characters owned the hot stocks, luxury homes, and designer clothes that most viewers coveted. Their real-life counterparts paraded across the fashion and society pages of glossy magazines, daily newspapers, and the aptly named television series *Lifestyles of the Rich and Famous*. Young lawyers, bankers, stockbrokers, and businessmen—the young urban professionals sometimes mocked as "yuppies"—flocked to the thriving financial districts, where they sought to win their share of the vast fortunes created by corporate consolidations and leveraged buyouts. The films *Wall Street* and *Working Girl* captured the lure of this new era of deal-making wealth, while Tom Wolfe's novel *Bonfire of the Vanities* revealed its darker, amoral side.

Millions of white-collar professionals, managers, and small business-people stood well below these high rollers on the American income pyramid. Constituting perhaps 25 percent of the working population, this slice of the middle class also seemed to bask in the glow of the Reagan revolution; their salary increases kept pace with inflation, their income taxes were lower, and they voted Republican in overwhelming numbers. But this seemingly prosperous middle stratum was not immune to the economic and social difficulties of the 1980s. Since the end of World War II, white-collar workers had enjoyed job stability in return for their loyalty to corporate employers. Corporations in the United States employed three or four times as many managers and supervisors as those in Japan and Europe. These people were a costly burden—too costly in an era of corporate mergers and rising

FIGURE 13.4 Low-, Middle-, and High-Income Growth, 1947–2003

After World War II, the average income of the wealthiest Americans declined relative to the average income of the poorest. But in the 1970s and 1980s, higher unemployment and more favorable tax treatment of the rich reversed this trend and increased income inequality dramatically. Both rich and poor doubled their income in the first twenty-five years after World War II. But in the next quarter-century, the incomes of the poor stagnated while those of the rich continued to grow substantially. Lawrence Mishel, Jared Benstein, and John Schmitt, *The State of Working America, 2004–05* (2005).

Haves

The ostentatious display of self and wealth became a hallmark of 1980s America. In this case, a young, upwardly mobile professional couple poses in their high-rise apartment for a magazine photograph — unself-consciously displaying the nanny as one of their possessions. Patricia Morrisroe, "The Yupper West Side: The New Class," *New York*, May 13, 1985 — Diego Goldberg/SYGMA.

international competition. Therefore, when top executives began reorganizing their enterprises to make them "lean and mean," many long-serving middle managers found themselves unemployed for the first time in their lives. "I was hurt," remembered a middle manager who had been nudged into retirement by a large pharmaceutical company. "After thirty-four years with the company, I was surprised that it came down to an economic relationship. . . . I thought I was in — a family kind of thing."

Downsizing, a polite term for mass dismissals, intensified during the recession that began in 1989, when a new wave of reorganizations and layoffs swept through the banking, stock brokerage, and real estate sectors. These sweeping white-collar layoffs became a routine management practice and continued well into the boom of the 1990s. Of course, total professional and managerial employment increased during the 1980s and 1990s, even in some newly restructured companies, but this churning of the white-collar labor force generated widespread middle-class insecurity, even among people who kept their jobs.

Despite the erosion in the job security of many male breadwinners, family incomes rose modestly in this era because more members of the family went to work. The most important additions to the workforce were women, primarily wives, whose labor-force participation increased from 40 to 60 percent in the quarter-century following 1970. By the 1990s, paid work was virtually universal among middle-class and working-class women under age forty. Indeed, their labor represented the difference between comfort and hardship. Virtually all of the income gain among white two-parent families in the years after 1967 can be accounted for by the wages of wives and daughters.

The American middle class sustained its relative affluence by what can only be called family speedup. To the surprise of an earlier generation of optimistic social forecasters, the growth of office automation and the deployment of a wide array of technological gadgets — from personal computers to faxes and mobile phones — did not reduce the working hours of professionals and office workers. Global commerce lengthened the workday, often right at home. For Motorola executive Sheila Griffin, a cell phone and voice mail started the workday during her early morning commute. "I get to the office and check the faxes. I get Europe out of the way and then work on things in our own time zone." By 6:30 P.M., thirteen hours after leaving

"It's the Freon"

As more Americans used computerized systems to increase production, the workers who manufactured computer chips and circuit boards began to see the downside of the digital revolution. Silicon Valley production workers not only labored in tedious and low-paying jobs, often at or just above the minimum wage; they were also frequently exposed to an array of toxic chemicals. At Q.E.S., where journalist Diana Hembree worked undercover in the early 1980s, production workers were exposed to Freon 113, which caused skin rashes, drowsiness, nausea, giddiness, and nervous system depression.

From the outside, the plant looked more like a real estate office than a factory. Along with hundreds of other "board shops" in the area, it makes printed circuit boards—the brains and memory banks of computers—for other high-tech firms. . . .

At first I was so pleased to have persuaded Q.E.S. to hire me that I clipped the tiny wires with unfeigned enthusiasm. But as the morning wore on, my neck and shoulders ached from craning over the boards, my eyes smarted, and I felt drowsy. After what seemed like interminable hours clipping boards, I stole a glance at the clock: only 9:45. I could smell a peculiar odor, but had no idea what it was.

"Sleepy?" asked the older woman beside me when I tried to stifle a yawn. "It's the freon," she said confidentially, nodding at a machine a few feet away. "Go to the bathroom and splash cold water on your face and arms; that helps a little. Or, if you can't keep your eyes open a second longer, drop something on the floor and take your time picking it up. That's what I do. . . ."

Since [Angel, a coworker had] been working with the freon, he had broken out in a rash and he had painful, recurring stomach aches. . . . Richard, a friendly, awkward twenty-year-old who was clipping beside Angel, said he didn't know if freon could actually hurt him, but washing circuit boards made him feel dizzy and disoriented. "The last time I did it," Richard said, "I felt like I was in a white cloud. . . ."

[The] new floor supervisor, Ray Burks, told me . . . : "Worrying about chemicals is fine if you have money and options, but compared to being evicted tomorrow if you can't pay the rent, chemical fumes and skin rashes seem pretty minor. . . ."

At the back of the assembly room stands a large machine in which circuit boards are coated with molten tin-and-lead solder. For the past three weeks, the machine has blanketed the room with noxious fumes, causing dizziness among the work force and sending several women to the bathroom to vomit. . . .

At least three other employees have called OSHA to ask for an investigation of the foul-smelling fumes; they talk about it daily in excited whispers. But so far, no inspectors have shown up.

Diana Hembree, "Dead End in Silicon Valley," *The Progressive*, October 1985.

home in the predawn darkness, Griffin is back with her family. "Then at about 9:30 P.M. the phone rings, and it's Japan."

In the two decades after 1969, the average employed American worked an extra month a year—about two and a half weeks more for men, seven and a half weeks more for women. Vacation time declined, overtime rose, and moonlighting soared. Women bore the brunt of this family speedup. Columnist Ann Landers pronounced herself "awestruck at the number of women who work at their jobs and go home to another full time job." One study found that employed mothers averaged more than eighty hours a week of employment, housework, and child care. "These women talked about sleep the way a hungry person talks about food," reported a California sociologist. Teenage employment also increased, even among middle-class families. Teenagers helped to pay for college, cars, and clothing, and they proved essential labor in the nation's burgeoning service economy. Wal-Mart, McDonald's, and Foot Locker could hardly have remained open without a vast adolescent workforce.

The Ranks of the Poor At the very bottom of the American social hierarchy stood the one in eight Americans whose incomes fell below the U.S. government's poverty line during the 1980s. The proportion of all Americans who were considered poor reached its postwar low in 1973, but stagflation drove this number upward until it peaked at 15 percent in the early 1980s. Increasingly low levels of unemployment, especially in the 1990s, decreased the number of people who were living in poverty, but even during the most prosperous times, about one-tenth of all whites lived in poverty, as did one-third of the nation's African Americans and one-quarter of all Latinos.

Low pay, structural changes in the economy, and institutional racism caused most poverty in late-twentieth-century America. During the 1980s and into the early 1990s, American business generated some thirty million new jobs, but most of them were in the service sector, which paid on average about 20 percent less than did jobs in manufacturing or transportation. The most rapidly growing occupations—home health care attendant, sales clerk, food server, janitor, and office clerk—were low-paid and part time, offering few pension or health care benefits and affording little opportunity for promotion. McDonald's, the largest employer of black youths in the nation, hired almost all its workers on a part-time, minimum-wage basis, which ensured a turnover rate of more than 100 percent per year. "You make minimum wage," complained one Baltimore resident, "and there are so many people applying that the jobs are snapped right up."

During the Reagan era, the government cut back or abandoned welfare programs and wage standards that had been designed to compensate for the economy's inability to generate enough high-paying jobs. By 1989, state and

"You Don't Have to Know How to Cook"

An anonymous teenager describes cooking hamburgers at McDonald's on a computerized grill in the allotted ninety seconds. Over the years, more than ten million Americans have found work at McDonald's; most are paid the minimum wage. In the name of efficiency and profitability, McDonald's has reduced formerly semiskilled jobs such as short-order cook to unskilled and mindless grill-tending.

They called us the Green Machine 'cause the crew had green uniforms then. And that's what it is, a machine. You don't have to know how to cook, you don't have to know how to think. There's a procedure for everything and you just follow the procedures. . . .

You're on the ten-in-one grill, ten patties in a pound. Your basic burger. The guy on the bin calls, "Six hamburgers." So you lay your six pieces of meat on the grill and set the timer. Beep-beep, beep-beep, beep-beep. That's the beeper to sear 'em. It goes off in twenty seconds. [Then press the patties down with a spatula.] Sup, sup, sup, sup, sup, sup. Now you turn off the sear beeper, put the buns in the oven, set the oven timer and then the next beeper is to turn the meat. This one goes beep-beep-beep, beep-beep-beep. So you turn your patties, and then you drop your re-cons [handfuls of reconstituted onions] on the meat, t-con, t-con, t-con. Now the bun oven buzzes. This one turns itself off when you open the oven door so you just take out your crowns [tops of buns], line 'em up and give 'em each a squirt of mustard and a squirt of ketchup.

Now, you get to put on the pickles. Two if they're regular, three if they're small. That's the creative part. Then the lettuce, then you ask for a cheese count ("cheese on four please"). Finally the last beep goes off and you lay your burger on the crowns. . . .

Then scoop up the heels [the bun bottoms] which are on top of the bun warmer, take the heels with one hand and push the tray out from underneath and they land (plip) one on each burger, right on top of the re-cons, neat and perfect. It's like I told you. The procedures makes the burgers. You don't have to know a thing. . . .

You follow the beepers, you follow the buzzers and you turn your meat as fast as you can. . . . To work at McDonald's you don't need a face, you don't need a brain. You need to have two hands and two legs and move 'em as fast as you can. That's the whole system. I wouldn't go back there again for anything.

Barbara Garson, *The Electronic Sweatshop: How Computers Are Transforming the Office of the Future into the Factory of the Past* (1988).

local welfare payments dropped by an average of 40 percent from their 1973 level. Job-training programs received drastic cuts, and the minimum wage, which the Reagan administration froze at 1981 levels, lost some 44 percent of its value through inflation. A full-time minimum wage worker could not keep a family of four out of poverty.

Have-Nots

In November 1989, a homeless woman finds meager shelter outside of Filene's department store in downtown Boston. Ellen Shub.

A significant number of Americans fell out of the world of work. The decline in the value of unemployment compensation and welfare, coupled with sharp hikes in urban rents, generated a new, or at least a vastly more visible, phenomenon: homeless Americans, between one million and three million of them during the 1980s. When homeless people first appeared in large numbers in the late 1970s, many Americans labeled them as "bag ladies," "winos," and "junkies" or assumed that they had just been released from mental hospitals. But within a few years, it became clear that for millions of working Americans, homelessness was only a layoff or a family crisis away. One of every five homeless people held a job but still could not afford housing. On cold winter nights, whole families, not just single men, searched for food and warmth at the crowded, squalid shelters that opened in almost every American city.

A fearful wave of criminality and drug addiction washed over inner-city neighborhoods during the 1980s. The importation of hard drugs, especially inexpensive "crack" cocaine, generated a violent world of well-armed drug lords and street-corner salesmen. Homicide became the leading cause of death among urban black males aged fifteen to twenty-four, a rate that was six times greater than that of other Americans. In many large metropolitan areas such as New York City, one of every four African American men in their twenties and one of every eight Latino men of the same age were in prison, on probation, or on parole.

Prisons, in fact, became one of the great growth industries of the 1980s and 1990s. For most of the twentieth century, the United States maintained an incarceration rate that was comparable to that in other industrialized nations — about one per thousand. But as the idea of rehabilitation faded during the 1970s, government at all levels began to jail criminals simply to keep them off the street. Fueled by a set of stiff drug laws that hit African Americans the hardest, the prison population tripled to two million between 1980 and 2000, giving the United States both the most prisoners and the highest incarceration rate of any nation in the world. The United States was also one of the few Western nations to retain the death penalty. After the Supreme Court affirmed its legality in 1975, southern and western states carried out executions with increasing frequency. And like the drug laws, states applied the death penalty disproportionately to African Americans, who made up half of all inmates on death row.

"I Fear for My Children"

Deborah M., a homeless single mother in New York City, describes trying to raise her children while shifting from one dormitory-style public shelter to another. Early in 1991, after spending time in a temporary apartment, a city agency finally placed her and her children in their own apartment.

This could happen to anyone. As for me, I finished high school, I've done a year and a half of college, I'm a certified nurse's aide and a bank teller, and I'm homeless. . . . I have four children: fourteen, thirteen, nine, and the baby was two. . . . I had teenage girls so we had to sleep in [our] clothes. . . . You don't have locks on your doors. . . . The worst part of being there is that I fear for my children. . . . Whatever place we moved, I took them to [school in] Queens. We had to get up at five. It took us in traveling time an hour and a half to an hour and forty-five minutes. . . .

From the little timid children that they were, they're not that anymore. . . . My oldest daughter had to stop her cheerleading, swim meets, her gymnastics because we didn't know where we would be living day by day. I have a lot of problems with her now. . . . There is a lot of bad kids in the shelter. I don't blame the mothers or nothing. A year from now I see her not in school, pregnant. . . . She thinks that she's so much older and wiser now . . . like nobody can tell her anything.

My son said that he is tired of moving around, he's sleepy: "Do we have to move tomorrow again?" We moved to six different shelters, most of them was overnight. My children changed drastically, they got hostile, disrespectful, angry, they just got the attitude that they just didn't care anymore. . . . Like they lost their self-identity. . . . My children lost all sense of security.

When they just saw the place [temporary apartment-style shelter] they ran through the whole apartment. "This is going to be my room. Oh, we have a bathroom!" The first thing my daughter said is, "I'm just going to love it here, I'm so glad that we're not in the shelters anymore." My children have improved greatly since we moved here. They have found me an apartment back in Queens, it's a whole house, and hopefully in the next two or three weeks, we'll be out of here.

Homeless with Children, WNYC-TV, June 1991.

Struggling Against the Conservative Tide

The organized working class was on the ideological and economic defensive throughout the 1980s. In almost every strike and negotiation, unions sought to defend the status quo: to save jobs and maintain their existing wage levels and health benefits in the face of the concessions, or givebacks, that employers demanded. A bitter and divisive "culture war" reinforced this corporate offensive against the unions, putting on the defensive the secular values and cultural pluralism that had long undergirded the political and ideological hegemony of the New Deal and its reform successors. In addition, there were challenges to the right's efforts to remake American culture. Throughout these years, Americans could, with equal ease, watch a televangelist preach the gospel or a pop music star challenge sexual mores. After 1986, Reagan's political star began to dim when foreign policy scandals and the waning of the Cold War sapped his conservative influence both at home and abroad.

The Labor Movement Under Fire   Reaganomics proved to be disastrous for American trade unions. In the 1970s, the unions represented almost one in four working Americans, but during the 1980s, this proportion dropped sharply, so in the private sector, organized labor represented only 8 percent of all workers—a huge decline from the early postwar years, when trade unions were pervasive in manufacturing, utilities, transport, mining, and the telephone industry. Moreover, unions became weak, and their leaders became fearful; from the 1980s onward, strikes were rare, even when management cut wages, pensions, and health care benefits (Figure 13.5).

What accounted for this debacle? The plant closings and layoffs that swept through many heavily unionized industries provided one answer. U.S. Steel, which had once employed a unionized workforce of 200,000, transformed itself into USX Corporation, shut down a dozen steel mills, and acquired Marathon Oil, from which it soon derived the bulk of its sales and profits. The United Steelworkers of America, which proved to be incapable of organizing nonunion "mini-mills" in the South, lost almost half its members in little more than a decade. The United Auto Workers lost even more

FIGURE 13.5   The Decline of American Unionism: Union Membership, 1930–2005

Unions grew rapidly in the 1930s and 1940s and maintained their strength for most of the next three decades. But because they were unable to organize white-collar and service workers who were employed by firms such as Wal-Mart, McDonald's, and Microsoft, unionism remained confined to public employment and the declining manufacturing sector. Therefore, the proportion of all Americans who were members of a trade union declined sharply in the 1980s, 1990s, and early 2000s.

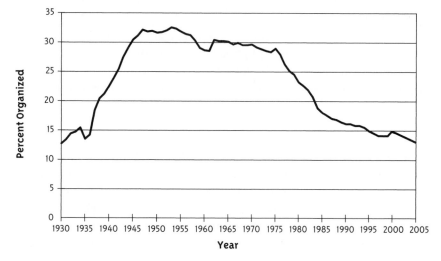

members—half a million after 1978—when Japanese auto sales captured one-quarter of the U.S. market. The Big Three automakers shut down dozens of plants, and auto parts makers fled the unionized North for low-wage Tennessee, Alabama, and Mexico.

Beginning in the 1970s, many employers became much more aggressive in their efforts to avoid or break trade unions, even in the once labor-friendly North. Their tactics skillfully combined both a paternalistic carrot and an antiunion stick. Corporations in such growing fields as finance, information technology, and health care offered workers an attractive menu of new benefits, often including on-site health clubs and child care. But most of these same companies remained bitterly antiunion. Management consultants advised executives of a group of New Jersey hospitals to figure out "who is going to be most vulnerable if the union knocks," then "weed 'em out. Get rid of anyone who's not going to be a team player." By 1984, companies fired prounion workers at a rate four times higher than in 1960.

Hardball antiunion tactics went hand in hand with another old-fashioned management strategy: cutting wages. In unionized industries, this was called "concession bargaining." Instead of negotiating a wage boost in each new contract, workers now faced corporate demands for a wage cutback—and not only in firms facing stiff foreign competition (Figure 13.6). As a business spokesperson summed up the situation, "An abundant supply of labor makes it more possible than ever before to operate during a strike. This possibility constrains union demands." During the first half of the 1980s, American workers lost about $500 billion in wage givebacks and other concessions.

In the midst of this wave of concession bargaining, President Reagan's destruction of a trade union of government employees, the Professional Air Traffic Controllers Organization (PATCO), immeasurably strengthened capital's hand against organized labor. These well-educated, well-paid controllers, many of them politically conservative Air Force veterans, complained of the intense mental stress and physical strain that were inherent in their work. The union wanted Reagan to increase the staff and reform the management of the federal government's Federal Aviation Administration, which employed most PATCO members. When the air traffic controllers struck in August 1981, Reagan waited only three days to fire more than 10,000 of these federal employees and fill their jobs with supervisors and hastily trained replacements. Not since Massachusetts governor Calvin

Die American

Many Americans believed that the end of the postwar boom in U.S. industry was caused by Asian competition and blamed the Japanese in particular for "stealing" American jobs. Anti-Asian sentiments were expressed in U.S. trade union publicity campaigns urging consumers to "buy American," and some frustrated workers resorted to violence against Asian Americans. One of the most prominent cases occurred in 1982 in Highland Park, Michigan, when Vincent Chin, a Chinese American, was beaten to death with a baseball bat. Chin's autoworker assailants were sentenced to probation and mild fines. *Detroit News.*

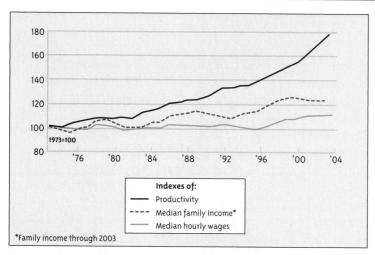

*Family income through 2003

FIGURE 13.6 The Gap Between Productivity and Wages

Productivity, or the quantity of goods and services produced in the nation, increased sharply in the 1980s and 1990s. While corporate profits increased, decreased union membership and increased use of technology meant that workers did not benefit from their increased productivity.

Coolidge broke the Boston police strike in 1919 had the government so thoroughly smashed a union of its own employees.

Reagan's destruction of PATCO transformed every strike into a union-busting opportunity. In both private companies and public agencies, managers had little trouble finding unemployed or underpaid workers who were willing to replace union strikers. Most "scabs," or strikebreakers, were motivated by sheer economic necessity, given the wage stagnation and high unemployment of the late twentieth century. But worker solidarity could hardly be expected to flourish in an era that celebrated entrepreneurial freedom, wage inequality, and the virtue of corporate downsizing. In almost every long strike during the 1980s, management found it relatively easy to recruit replacement workers who were eager to keep their enterprise afloat. A strike of professional football players in 1984 graphically revealed this shift in sentiment and public perception. Thousands of fans flocked to the stadiums, jeering picket lines manned by players they considered too well paid, to cheer on football teams that were composed entirely of third-string replacements.

Corporations that had been deregulated during the late 1970s mounted especially vicious attacks on unions. Nonunion upstart companies grabbed market share from industry stalwarts, but in the new, competitive environment, some firms went bankrupt, while others cut wages, broke their unions, and even skimped on safety precautions. In 1983, after selling hundreds of millions of dollars' worth of high-interest "junk bonds," Frank Lorenzo bought Continental Airlines, declared it bankrupt, and then slashed the pay of thousands of pilots, machinists, and flight attendants. When the workers struck, Lorenzo broke their unions by hiring replacement workers from the tens of thousands of unemployed pilots and machinists who had been laid off during the recession of the early 1980s. He then moved on to Eastern Airlines, which he added to his empire in 1986. Using similar tactics, Lorenzo again demanded massive wage concessions that were certain to precipitate a strike. But this time, well-paid airline pilots joined machinists and flight attendants in a highly effective work stoppage that won sympathy from passengers, solidarity from the labor movement, and even grudging admiration from Wall Street. Their lengthy

"A War Against Working People"

In a July 1978 letter, United Auto Workers president Douglas Fraser resigned from the Labor-Management Group, a nongovernmental committee composed of eight corporate executives and eight labor leaders, arguing that business leaders sought confrontation, not cooperation, in their dealing with working people. The group met regularly in the late 1970s to discuss cooperative approaches to resolving labor-management conflicts.

I believe leaders of the business community, with few exceptions, have chosen to wage a one-sided class war today in this country—a war against working people, the unemployed, the poor, the minorities, the very young and the very old, and even many in the middle class of our society. The leaders of industry, commerce and finance in the United States have broken and discarded the fragile unwritten compact previously existing during the past period of growth and progress.

For considerable time, the leaders of business and labor have sat at the Labor-Management Group's table—recognizing differences, but seeking consensus where it existed. That worked because the business community in the U.S. succeeded in advocating a general loyalty to an allegedly benign capitalism that emphasized private property, independence and self-regulation along with an allegiance to free democratic politics.

That system has worked best, of course, for the "haves" in our society rather than the "have-nots." Yet it survived in part because of an unspoken foundation that when things got bad enough for a segment of society, the business elite "gave" a little bit—enabling government or interest groups to better conditions somewhat for that segment. That give usually came only after sustained struggle, such as that waged by the labor movement in the 1930s and the civil rights movement in the 1960s. . . .

But today, I am convinced there has been a shift on the part of the business community toward confrontation, rather than cooperation. Now, business groups are tightening their control over American society. . . . The rise of multinational corporations that know neither patriotism nor morality but only self-interest, has made accountability almost non-existent. At virtually every level, I discern a demand by business for docile government and unrestrained corporate individualism. Where industry once yearned for subservient unions, it now wants no unions at all. . . .

I have concluded there is no point to continue sitting down at Labor-Management Group meetings and philosophizing about the future of the country and the world when we on the labor side have so little in common with those across the table. I cannot sit there seeking unity with leaders of American industry, while they try to destroy us and ruin the lives of the people I represent.

Radical History Review, Fall 1978.

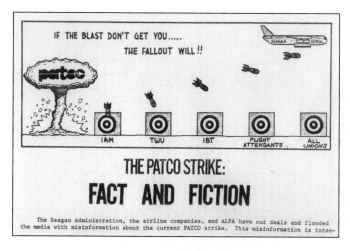

A Warning

This illustration is from a leaflet that was distributed during the summer and fall of 1981 by the Los Angeles local of the Professional Air Traffic Controllers Organization (PATCO). The leaflet urged other airline and airport workers to support PATCO and warned that the Reagan administration's suppression of the union would permit the airline companies to force layoffs and contract concessions from all workers in the industry. Los Angeles Professional Air Traffic Controllers Organization, 1981.

strike threw the airline into bankruptcy, forced Lorenzo out of the airline business, and put the brakes on deregulation of the airline industry.

The battle to maintain wages and benefits often took place in a single factory, company, or community where embattled unionists tried to mobilize families, neighbors, and community activists in defense of an entire way of life. In the coal fields of Appalachia, in the Arizona copper mines, on California factory farms, and in midwestern manufacturing towns, unionists demonstrated that they could still organize for long, bitter social struggles that were reminiscent of those that had been waged during the last quarter of the nineteenth century.

In Austin, Minnesota, for example, Local P-9 organized retirees, high school students, family members, and sympathetic unionists in a battle against wage concessions at the venerable Hormel Meatpacking Company. Throughout the bone-chilling winter of 1985–1986, the Austin working-class community, "P-9 Proud," mobilized tens of thousands of supporters throughout the upper Midwest. But strikers could gain little support from the Democrats or even from many liberals. A Democratic governor sent in National Guard troops to prevent mass picketing, while the leadership of United Food and Commercial Workers Union urged the Hormel workers to accept another round of wage concessions. The Austin strike ended late in 1986 with the community divided, P-9 defeated, and Hormel victorious.

Reaganism Reaches an Impasse As fiscal austerity and the liberal-labor retreat shifted American politics to the right, the long recession of the early 1980s began to lift. Thus, Ronald Reagan and his party entered the 1984 campaign season at the height of their popularity. The Democrats were deeply divided. Jesse Jackson, an African American minister whose Rainbow Coalition aspired to represent a multiracial alliance of the poor and working class, proved a dynamic spokesman for the party's social democratic wing. In contrast, Senator Gary Hart represented a growing neoliberal current, progressive on social issues but increasingly cool toward the labor movement and the welfare state. Former vice president Walter Mondale bested both of these candidates and injected some excitement into the campaign by selecting New York City congresswoman Geraldine Ferraro as his running mate. Ronald Reagan won the election in a landslide, taking

P-9 Proud
P-9 strikers and supporters in Austin, Minnesota, confront the Minnesota National Guard outside the Hormel plant on a cold January morning in 1986. Hardy Green.

59 percent of the popular vote and every state except Minnesota, Mondale's home state. Although African Americans and Jews voted solidly Democratic once again, Republicans kept the allegiance of blue-collar "Reagan Democrats," swept the white South, and won a majority of votes even among white women and union members.

But Reaganism reached an impasse after the start of the new term, both as an economic doctrine and as a foreign policy prescription. Although unemployment began to fall and the stock market began to boom, supply-side economics had little to do with it. Rather, the surge in military spending, combined with lower interest rates and a large federal budget deficit, pulled the U.S. economy out of the recession. Indeed, Congress repudiated much of Reagan's supply-side tax program early in his second term; by closing numerous tax loopholes and subjecting capital gains to the same tax rate as ordinary income, it raised the effective tax rate on corporations and the rich.

Reagan's aggressively anti-Communist foreign policy also ran into trouble. Outraged by the administration's policy of "constructive engagement" with white South Africa, U.S. college students spearheaded a broad national movement demanding that universities and companies divest themselves of investments in the strictly segregated apartheid regime. Early in 1985, thousands of protesters were arrested at South African embassies and consulates. This activism spurred Congress to pass, over President Reagan's veto, a law banning new investments in South Africa or loans to the South African regime, an important step in the peaceful revolution that brought multiracial democracy to that nation in the early 1990s.

Symbols Speak Louder than Words

On December 9, 1986, Oliver North appeared before the House Foreign Affairs Committee, which had called him to testify about his role in the Iran-Contra scandal. Dressed in his Marine uniform, North presented himself as a symbol of American patriotism in an effort to counterbalance his refusal (citing his Fifth Amendment rights) to discuss his illegal activities in the basement of the White House. Many news photographers angled their cameras to shoot North from below, casting him as the hero looking down on his interrogators. (North did eventually testify before the committee in July 1987.) Mark Leighton/Corbis-Bettmann.

Opposition to U.S. intervention in the civil wars in Nicaragua and El Salvador and increased military spending also grew in the 1980s. Although Reagan hailed the Nicaraguan counterrevolutionaries (known as Contras) as "freedom fighters," Congress remained skeptical; in 1984, it passed the Boland Amendment banning U.S. military aid to the Contras. Finally, Reagan's support for a new round of Cold War military spending encountered stiff resistance, especially after reformer Mikhail Gorbachev assumed power in the Soviet Union.

Crisis engulfed the Reagan presidency in 1986 when the public learned that officials from the Central Intelligence Agency (CIA), the National Security Council (NSC), and the State Department had conspired to organize a covert and illegal government operation to aid the Contras in violation of the Boland Amendment. At the instigation of CIA director William Casey and national security adviser Robert McFarlane, the United States secretly sold millions of dollars worth of military equipment to Iran, a regime that the United States publicly denounced for supporting terrorism. The profits from this illegal arms trade, along with other money that was raised secretly from foreign governments, were then used to fund the Contras in their war against Nicaragua's radical Sandinista government. Several NSC officials went to jail, and much evidence suggested that Reagan had condoned the illegal acts. Although Democratic lawmakers shied away from any effort to impeach the still-popular president, the Iran-Contra affair nonetheless deprived Reagan of his ability to set the national political agenda for the remainder of his term. In the 1986 congressional elections, the Democrats recaptured control of the U.S. Senate, and the next year, a liberal coalition generated sufficient pressure to persuade the Senate to reject Robert Bork, Reagan's highly conservative U.S. Supreme Court nominee. In his place, the Senate easily approved Anthony M. Kennedy, who with Sandra Day O'Connor, a 1981 Reagan appointment and the first women to serve on the high court, became the core of a centrist bloc on the Supreme Court.

Culture Wars   Reaganism proved to be far more of a political than an economic success. If at the end of the 1980s, the Reagan administration stood at a policy impasse, its eight years of governance had nevertheless shifted the nation's politics well to the right. The Republican Party no longer had room for a liberal, pro-welfare-state wing. The Democrats still controlled Congress, though they had neither the votes nor the will to propose legislation of the sort that Lyndon Johnson and Hubert Humphrey had once championed. Reagan Republicans set the nation's political agenda, even if they could not always carry the day on any particular issue. If the culture of the university and the old-line philanthropies remained largely liberal, conservative intellectuals' presence grew on television talk shows, on news-

paper opinion pages, and in such influential, well-funded think tanks as the Heritage Foundation and the Cato, Hudson, and American Enterprise institutes.

But Reaganite political power was not matched by a conservative capacity to transform the nation's social mores or restrain the increasingly adventuresome character of U.S. culture, entertainment, and social thought. This caused enormous frustration to many intellectuals and politicians on the right, who saw Reaganism not merely as a political or economic doctrine, but also as a movement to reverse some of the dramatic cultural changes that had transformed American society since the 1960s. William Bennett, Reagan's secretary of education, denounced "relativism" and "multiculturalism" in university curricula, arguing instead for a return to the study and celebration of what he called the "Judeo-Christian tradition." Allan Bloom, a neoconservative political theorist, briefly soared to prominence with publication of *The Closing of the American Mind*, a 1986 best-seller that assaulted student activism, cultural relativism, academic Marxism, and rock-and-roll.

But American culture remained pluralistic. Evangelical Protestantism continued to grow in numbers, and in 1986, allies of the conservative televangelist Pat Robertson won control of the Southern Baptist Convention, the nation's largest religious denomination. But the influence of the Religious Right remained limited. Several states did impose some restrictions on the right of women to secure an abortion, especially for teenagers or for women in the last trimester of pregnancy, but this medical practice remained legal and widely available in the United States. Women's participation in the workforce continued to increase, and at the end of the 1980s, affirmative action programs still benefited members of racial minorities who sought employment, job promotions, or admission to college. Meanwhile, several well-known fundamentalist ministers, including Jimmy

Pornography Hearings
Attorney General Edwin Meese's Commission on Pornography was appointed during Ronald Reagan's second presidential term to appease conservative and fundamentalist supporters who thought that the "Reagan Revolution" had not sufficiently altered the nation's social agenda. During 1985 and 1986, public hearings were held in six U.S. cities, featuring testimony of anonymous witnesses who claimed to be "victims" of pornography as well as displays of sexually explicit pictures and films. The hearings focused on visual images to support otherwise unsubstantiated arguments about the harmful effects of pornography — and sexual behavior in general. U.S. Department of Justice.

Heritage USA

A scene in the Baptism Pool in Jim and Tammy Bakker's 2,300-acre revivalist theme park and campground, located on the border between North Carolina and South Carolina. By 1986, Heritage USA was one of the nation's top tourist attractions, drawing more than six million visitors a year to its rides, water park, petting zoo, hotel, and shopping mall. But in 1989, Jim Bakker was convicted of defrauding investors of hundreds of millions of dollars, and Heritage USA folded. He subsequently served five years in federal prison. Jerry Valente/Sipa Press.

Swaggart and Jim Bakker, became embroiled in embarrassing sex and financial scandals.

Popular music defined a technological and aesthetic frontier. Cassettes replaced vinyl records as the Sony Walkman and the portable boom box made listening both more all-pervasive and more private. Country music still held the greatest radio audience, but rock-and-roll, which dominated record and cassette sales, continued to showcase the nation's cultural avant garde. Two of the biggest pop stars of the 1980s, Michael Jackson and Madonna, were not only fabulously successful entertainers, but also racial and gender experimentalists. Jackson, whose 1982 album *Thriller* sold more copies than any other record in history, transformed himself into a racially and sexually ambiguous icon. Madonna, an indefatigable exhibitionist, redefined a modern sexuality that deployed an earthy postfeminist sensibility, exemplified in her "Material Girl" and other best-selling songs.

Music television, a genuinely new art form, burst onto the scene in 1981 with the appearance of the MTV cable television network, about the same time that rap, or hip-hop, emerged out of the African American ghettos. Combining rhythmic verse with a driving beat derived from scratching the surface of a record and sampling the music of other rhythm-and-blues and rock-and-roll performers, rap spoke to the daily experiences of black inner-city youth facing gang violence, the crack epidemic, police brutality, and economic strain. By the end of the decade, many Latinos, who introduced bilingual lyrics, and white suburban teenagers had enthusiastically embraced the music, the accompanying hip-hop style in fashion, and rap's outlaw image. Groups such as Public Enemy, whose "Fight the Power" was an openly Afrocentric anthem, moved the music onto political terrain.

Conclusion: The Reagan Legacy

In the 1970s and 1980s, the United States entered an era of post–New Deal politics and political economy. The globalization of trade, finance, and manufacturing put enormous pressure on American firms and made far less efficient and effective the kind of liberal interventionist economic policies that had worked so well when the North American continent coincided with U.S. labor and product markets. But politics still trumped market forces. Thus, the price of oil, which seemed to rise inexorably during the

Fight the Power

Organized politics had failed to engage many young and underemployed African Americans; instead, they opted for explicit, angry, often Afrocentric lyrics as the vehicle for their protest. A strain of "political rap" evolved that took on issues of racism, police brutality, apartheid, and media exploitation. Public Enemy's "Fight the Power," which took its title and sampled beats from the Isley Brothers' 1975 R&B classic, gained national exposure in Spike Lee's 1989 movie Do the Right Thing.

Elvis was a hero to most
But he never meant — — to me you see
Straight up racist that sucker was
Simple and plain
Mother — — him and John Wayne
Cause I'm Black and I'm proud
I'm ready and hyped plus I'm amped
Most of my heroes don't appear on no stamps
Sample a look back you look and find
Nothing but rednecks for 400 years if you check
Don't worry be happy
Was a number one jam
Damn if I say it you can slap me right here
(Get it) let's get this party started right
Right on, c'mon
What we got to say
Power to the people no delay
To make everybody see
In order to fight the powers that be
(Fight the Power)

—————————

"Fight the Power," from *Fear of a Black Planet*, Public Enemy, Def Jam Records, 1990.

1970s, plunged after 1984, largely because of political disarray among the oil-producing nations in the Middle East, government-mandated conservation measures, and slower economic growth.

Likewise, the stagnation in the American standard of living was not a product of what some politicians of the 1970s liked to call "an era of limits"; it reflected instead an increasingly successful effort to make American workers pay for the return of U.S. business to a more profitable and competitive status. Reagan's massive tax cut in 1981 slashed social spending and offered the wealthy billions in tax relief. And his destruction of the air traffic controllers' union later that same year inaugurated a generation-long assault on the organized working class that was as debilitating as the defeat of the Homestead strikers in 1892 and the immigrant steelworkers in 1919.

Reaganism began a realignment in American politics and political economy that would take a full generation to complete. The new conservatism

won recruits in the white South and among northern blue-collar Democrats. It eroded labor's strength, legitimized business's power and prestige, and checked the headway the civil rights, women's, and gay rights movements had made. But anti-Communism still constituted much of the glue that held together the Reaganite majority, so the end of the Cold War would open the door to a new configuration of politics and ideology on the home front as well as abroad.

Scratching

DJs work out "scratch" rhythms on records at a Bronx playground party in 1984. "Hip-hop" culture emerged out of black inner-city neighborhoods in the 1980s, appropriating fragments of previous musical forms to construct a new genre of popular music. By the end of the decade, hip-hop style and rap music had spread to the suburban mall. Yet while young Americans embraced hip-hop and businesses packaged youth-oriented products in hip-hop style, the African American reality continued to be dominated by unemployment, the crack epidemic, and "black-on-black" violence. Henry Chalfant/City Lore.

The Years in Review

1972
- Congress approves the Equal Rights Amendment, but it fails to win ratification by states after the New Right mobilizes against it.
- Title IX of the Civil Rights Act of 1964 prohibits gender discrimination in schools that receive federal funding, resulting in major gains for women's athletics.

1973
- The Organization of Petroleum Exporting Countries raises oil prices from $3 to $12 a barrel. The resultant energy crisis leads to federally mandated gasoline rationing in 1974 and a nationwide speed limit of 55 miles per hour.

1974
- In September, President Ford pardons Richard Nixon, who resigned in August to avoid impeachment.

1975
- New York City narrowly averts bankruptcy; President Ford refuses to provide federal assistance.
- Boston plunges into crisis when working-class whites oppose school busing.
- The Strategic Arms Limitation Treaty puts a ceiling on nuclear missile development.

1976
- Georgia Democrat Jimmy Carter defeats Gerald Ford to become president.

1977

- A new climate of homophobia grows when singer Anita Bryant spearheads a successful movement to repeal a Florida antidiscrimination ordinance.

1978

- California voters pass Proposition 13, capping property taxes.
- Iran's Reza Shah Pahlavi is deposed; the next year, Islamic militants take over the U.S. embassy and hold fifty-two Americans hostage for 444 days.

1979

- A near-meltdown occurs at Pennsylvania's Three Mile Island nuclear power plant.
- President Carter appoints conservative Paul Volcker as chairman of the Federal Reserve Board; interest rates climb to 20 percent, and the U.S. economy plunges into a recession.
- The U.S. government officially recognizes Communist China.
- Sandinistas topple the Somoza family dictatorship in Nicaragua.

1980

- The United States boycotts the Moscow Olympics in response to the Soviet invasion of Afghanistan, signaling the breakdown of détente.
- Easily defeating Jimmy Carter, Republican Ronald Reagan is elected president; the Republicans gain control of the Senate for the first time in almost thirty years.

1981

- The Reagan administration and Congress cut taxes and domestic social programs and raise military spending.
- President Reagan fires more than 10,000 air traffic controllers for striking against the Federal Aviation Administration.
- Reagan appoints Sandra Day O'Connor, first woman justice, to the U.S. Supreme Court.
- MTV first appears on cable television.

1982

- The first case of AIDS is reported in the United States.

1984

- Ronald Reagan captures 59 percent of the popular vote, defeating Democrat Walter Mondale and the first female vice presidential candidate, Geraldine Ferraro.
- Congress bans U.S. military aid to the Nicaraguan Contras, but the Reagan administration secretly sells arms to Iran and uses the profits to support the Contras.

1985

- The local packinghouse union in Austin, Minnesota, wages an unsuccessful strike against Hormel.

- In response to ballooning federal debt, Congress passes the Gramm-Rudman-Hollings Act requiring a balanced budget.

- Congress bans new investment in South Africa or loans to its apartheid regime.

1987

- Enthusiasm for televangelism wanes after Jimmy Swaggart and Jim Bakker are involved in sex and money scandals.

- A half-million people assemble for a gay pride march in Washington, D.C.

Additional Readings

For more on the end of the postwar boom, see: Donald L. Barlett and James B. Steele, *America: Who Stole the Dream?* (1996); David Bensman and Roberta Lynch, *Rusted Dreams: Hard Times in a Steel Community* (1988); William Greider, *Secrets of the Temple: How the Federal Reserve Runs the Country* (1989); Max Holland, *When the Machine Stopped: A Cautionary Tale from Industrial America* (1990); and Robert B. Reich, *The Work of Nations: Preparing Ourselves for 21st Century Capitalism* (1992).

For more on the changes to U.S. business in the 1970s and the rise of globalization, see: William Greider, *One World, Ready or Not: The Manic Logic of Global Capitalism* (1997); Bennett Harrison and Barry Bluestone, *The Great U-Turn: Corporate Restructuring and the Polarizing of America* (1998); Robert B. Reich and John D. Donahue, *New Deals: The Chrysler Revival and the American System* (1986); and Susan J. Tolchin and Martin Tolchin, *Dismantling America: The Rush to Deregulate* (1985).

For more on presidential policies under Gerald Ford and Jimmy Carter, see: James M. Cannon, *Time and Chance: Gerald Ford's Appointment with History* (1998); Peter N. Carroll, *It Seemed Like Nothing Happened: America in the 1970s* (1990); Burton I. Kaufman, *The Presidency of James Earl Carter, Jr.* (1993); Kenneth E. Morris, *Jimmy Carter: American Moralist* (1996); and Robert A. Strong, *Working in the World: Jimmy Carter and the Making of American Foreign Policy* (2000).

For more on the rise of the New Right, see: William C. Berman, *America's Right Turn: From Nixon to Clinton (The American Movement)* (1998); Thomas Ferguson and Joel Rogers, *Right Turn: The Decline of the*

Democrats and the Future of American Politics (1987); Godfrey Hodgson, *The World Turned Right Side Up: A History of the Conservative Ascendancy in America* (1996); John B. Judis, *William F. Buckley, Jr.: Patron Saint of the Conservatives* (1990); Rebecca E. Klatch, *Women of the New Right* (1988); Matthew Lassiter, *Silent Majority: Suburban Politics in the Sunbelt South* (2005); William Martin, *With God on Our Side: The Rise of the Religious Right in America* (1996); Bruce J. Schulman, *The Seventies: The Great Shift in American Culture, Society, and Politics* (2001); and Judith Stein, *Running Steel, Running America: Race, Economic Policy and the Decline of Liberalism* (1998).

For more on the revolt against taxes and busing in the 1970s and 1980s, see: Robert Kuttner, *Revolt of the Haves: Taxpayer Revolts and the Politics of Austerity* (1980); and J. Anthony Lukas, *Common Ground: A Turbulent Decade in the Lives of Three American Families* (1986).

For more on gender politics during the 1970s and 1980s, see: Susan M. Hartmann, *From Margin to Mainstream: American Women and Politics since 1960* (1989); Susan M. Hartmann, *The Other Feminists: Activists in the Liberal Establishment* (1998); Alice Kessler-Harris, *In Pursuit of Equity: Women, Men, and the Quest for Economic Citizenship in 20th-Century America* (2001); Jane J. Mansbridge, *Why We Lost the ERA* (1986); Rosalind Pollack Petchesky, *Abortion and Woman's Choice: The State, Sexuality, and Reproductive Freedom* (1990); Judith Stacey, *Brave New Families: Stories of Domestic Upheaval in Late Twentieth Century America* (1998); and Winifred D. Wandersee, *On the Move: American Women in the 1970s* (1988).

For more on the growing economic disparity and issues among the poor, see: Paul Blumberg, *Inequality in an Age of Decline* (1980); Thomas Byrne Edsall, *The New Politics of Inequality* (1985); Arlie Hochschild, *The Second Shift: Working Parents and the Revolution at Home* (1989); Katherine S. Newman, *Falling from Grace: Downward Mobility in the Age of Affluence* (1999); Juliet B. Schor, *The Overworked American: The Unexpected Decline of Leisure* (1993); Ruth Sidel, *Women and Children Last: The Plight of Poor Women in Affluent America* (1992); and William Julius Wilson, *The Truly Disadvantaged: The Inner City, the Underclass, and Public Policy* (1990).

For more on labor struggles in the 1970s and 1980s, see: Jefferson R. Cowie, *Capital Moves: RCA's Seventy-Year Quest for Cheap Labor* (1999); Thomas Geoghegan, *Which Side Are You On?: Trying to Be for Labor When It's Flat on Its Back* (1992); Barbara Kingsolver, *Holding the Line: Women in the Great Arizona Mine Strike of 1983* (1997); and Kim Moody, *An Injury to All: The Decline of American Unionism* (1997).

For more on President Reagan and his policies, see: W. Elliot Brownlee and Hugh Davis Graham, eds., *The Reagan Presidency: Pragmatic Conservatism and Its Legacies* (2003); Sidney Blumenthal and Thomas Byrne Edsall, eds., *The Reagan Legacy* (1988); Matthew Dallek, *The Right Moment: Ronald Reagan's First Victory and the Decisive Turning Point in American Politics* (2000); E. J. Dionne, Jr., *Why Americans Hate Politics* (1992); Frances FitzGerald, *Way Out There in the Blue: Reagan, Star Wars, and the End of the Cold War* (2000); Fred Halliday, *From Kabul to Managua: Soviet-American Relations in the 1980s* (1989); Joel Krieger, *Reagan, Thatcher, and the Politics of Decline* (1986); Edmund Morris, *Dutch: A Memoir of Ronald Reagan* (1999); and David Thelen, *Becoming Citizens in the Age of Television: How Americans Challenged the Media and Seized Political Initiative During the Iran-Contra Debate* (1996).

14

The American People in an Age of Global Capitalism

1989–2001

Sweatshop

Asian workers labor in a garment shop in lower Manhattan in 1991, in a setting reminiscent of sweatshop working conditions in the clothing industry earlier in the twentieth century. Andrea Ades Vásquez — American Social History Project.

FOR TWENTY-EIGHT YEARS, the Berlin Wall symbolized the Cold War division of Europe and the power of political ideology to shape the economic and social lives of millions of people in the alliance systems that enfolded most of the globe. Then, early on the evening of November 9, 1989, a young East German couple — we do not know their names — walked to the Invalidenstrasse gate to find out whether the political upheavals in their homeland had opened the barrier to ordinary Berliners. To their amazement, the once fearsome Volkspolizei, who were now the demoralized agents of a rapidly crumbling system, let them pass to the bright lights of the West. Within hours, men and women from both sides of the Wall were attacking the edifice with hammers, picks, and any other instruments they could find. Communism was in collapse, and the Cold War would soon be history.

The startlingly abrupt end of European Communism revolutionized international politics. For the first time in nearly half a century, the United States faced no superpower rival. Indeed, for the first time since the end of World War I, capitalism was once again truly a world system, unchallenged on any continent, including Asia, where even the hard-line Communist rulers of China and Vietnam now welcomed foreign investment and encouraged a new class of entrepreneurs.

An increasingly unfettered system of global trade and finance undermined national sovereignty and economic autonomy, not only in Europe and North America, where barrier-free markets were being put in place, but also throughout East Asia and Latin America, where the International Monetary Fund and other supranational bodies came to play a highly prominent role. McDonald's, Nike, Toshiba, and the other transnational corporations actively sought to shed their old national attachments. But the power and pervasiveness of capitalist consumer culture hardly eliminated the search for ethnic, racial, and linguistic identity in the years leading up to the turn of the millennium. In the United States, the debate over cultural values and racial identity continued, though never in as tragic and bloody a form as the warfare that erupted over similar issues in the Caucasus region of the former Soviet Union, the Balkan region of Southeastern Europe, and Central Africa.

A New Geopolitical Order

The Cold War cost more than $11 trillion. But such enormous military expenditures did not bring about the collapse of the Soviet Union and its satellites. No NATO tank fired a shot. No bomb fell on the Kremlin. Instead, a massive, home-grown insurgency, led by workers, dissident intellectuals, and advocates of national self-determination, and fueled by the brittle nature of the Soviet economic system, cracked the Communist bloc regimes, thereby leaving the United States as the world's sole nuclear super-power. During the presidency of George Herbert Walker Bush, the United States took advantage of this new configuration of international power to end the "Vietnam syndrome," send half a million troops to the Persian Gulf, and inaugurate an era in which the United States saw few obstacles to the direct application of its military power abroad.

The End of the Cold War   The downfall of Soviet power began in 1980 when striking Polish workers organized Solidarność ("Solidarity"), an independent trade union with nearly ten million members. Solidarity, which had strong support from the powerful Polish Catholic Church, demonstrated how a working-class movement could offer an entire nation moral and political leadership. The Polish military drove Solidarity under-ground late in 1981, but when it reemerged later in the decade, it won a smashing electoral victory. Lech Walesa, a shipyard unionist, was soon installed as the first freely elected president of the Polish nation in more than sixty years.

Solidarity's example had an impact throughout Eastern Europe. Under a relatively youthful party secretary, Mikhail Gorbachev, the Soviet Union in the late 1980s undertook a series of reforms: *perestroika*, which was designed to restructure the production system, and *glasnost*, which was meant to open the society to political and artistic debate. Gorbachev knew that in a world of increasing technical complexity and communications, Soviet-style authoritarianism had become economically dysfunctional. No regime could keep track of all the computers, copiers, and communication devices that were necessary to modern production in the information age. Gorbachev

Collectibles

News photographs and footage of the dismantling of the Berlin Wall in November 1989 powerfully symbolized the end of the Cold War. Less noted was the subsequent commercialization of that symbol, including the sale of pieces of the notorious wall to souvenir-hunting Germans and foreign tourists. Wolfgang Kaehler/Corbis.

therefore wanted to liberalize Communist rule. But strikes and demonstrations soon erupted throughout the Soviet Union. Coal miners, railroad workers, Baltic nationalists, and urban intellectuals all formed independent organizations that called on Gorbachev to quicken the pace of political and economic reform. In Hungary and Poland, like-minded officials lifted most of the old restrictions on travel and emigration beyond the Iron Curtain.

Beginning in September 1989, a wave of huge demonstrations shook Communist regimes across Eastern Europe. A massive tide of East German emigrants surged through Czechoslovakia and Hungary to the West, undermining the authority of the Communist hard-liners who still clung to power in the German Democratic Republic (GDR). Finally, ordinary Germans poured through the Berlin Wall. The GDR quickly disintegrated, and by the end of 1990, all of East Germany had been incorporated into the wealthy, powerful Federal Republic of Germany. The Communist government in Czechoslovakia also tumbled, and reformers strengthened their hand in Hungary and Bulgaria. In Romania, the Communist dictatorship fell only after a week of bloody street battles between ordinary citizens and police, who defended the old order to the bitter end.

Radical change finally reached the Soviet heartland in August 1991, when thousands of Russian citizens poured into the streets to defeat a reactionary coup d'état. The Communist Party quickly collapsed, and the Soviet Union began the painful and uncertain process of reorganizing itself as a loose confederation of independent republics (Map 14.1). Boris Yeltsin, who headed the Russian Republic, replaced Gorbachev as president of a much-diminished state.

The collective courage and willpower of ordinary men and women ended the Cold War. Most insurgents had sought civil rights and political democracy, not a capitalist revolution, but they got one nonetheless. New governments in the Soviet Union and Eastern Europe began opening their

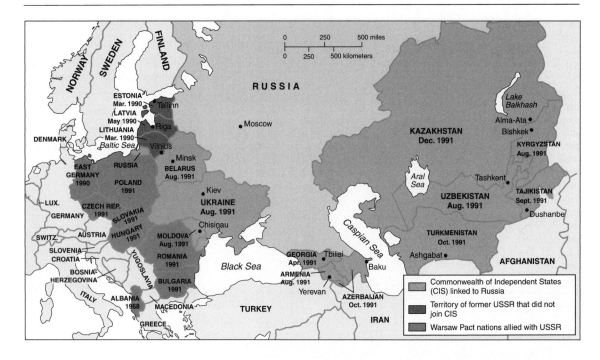

MAP 14.1   New States and New Conflicts: The Post–Cold War Map of Europe and Asia

The decline of Soviet power and the breakup of the Soviet Union enabled Eastern European nationalism to flourish once again. A series of stable states emerged in central and northern Europe. But in the former Yugoslavia and the Caucasus (between Russia and Turkey), upheaval and civil war proved to be endemic.

economies to Japan and the West, selling off state-owned enterprises and even establishing stock markets. In Poland, Hungary, Estonia, Latvia, and the Czech Republic, the process generated relatively successful economic systems that were oriented toward the West; but in Ukraine, Russia, Romania, Slovakia, and Bulgaria, the standard of living plunged amid political instability and plummeting production. Cuba, China, Vietnam, and North Korea remained authoritarian regimes, but almost all the Asian Communist countries abandoned state planning and encouraged capitalist trade and enterprise.

In the United States, partisans of Ronald Reagan claimed much of the credit for ending the Cold War, greeting the demise of European Communism as a political and ideological triumph. Reagan's forthright denunciation of the Soviet Union as an "evil empire," along with his administration's military buildup, were said to have heartened eastern bloc dissidents at the same time that the arms race exhausted the productive capacity of the Soviet Union and other inefficient Communist regimes. But the Cold War doves held that the West's militarized posture had long helped the Communists to rationalize their authoritarian rule. As the historian and diplomat George Kennan put it, the more U.S. policies had followed a hard line, "the greater was the tendency in Moscow to tighten the controls . . . and the greater the braking effect on all liberalizing tendencies in the regime."

George Bush's "New World Order"
George Herbert Walker Bush, who was elected president in 1988, did not embody the New Right fervor of the

Confrontation

In the immediate aftermath of the June 1989 Tiananmen Square massacre, when Chinese troops killed hundreds of students as they crushed a democratic protest in Beijing, one image that symbolized the spirit of the demonstrators was published and broadcast around the world. A lone Chinese citizen blocked a convoy of tanks on Beijing's Avenue of Eternal Peace. After a tense standoff, in contrast to the government's earlier bloody suppression, the tanks did not harm the protester but instead drove around him. Corbis/ Reuters.

Reaganites. He was a traditional upper-class conservative whose father, Prescott Bush, had been a New York investment banker and Connecticut senator. Unlike Reagan, Bush had easily weathered the Great Depression, though he faced real danger as a naval flier in World War II. After he graduated from Yale University, his father staked him to a business career in Texas, where Bush adapted himself both to the entrepreneurial unpredictability of panhandle oil operations and to the hard-edged politics of southwestern Republicanism. After serving two terms in the House of Representatives, he held a series of high-profile appointments under presidents Nixon and Ford, including U.S. ambassador to the United Nations and director of the Central Intelligence Agency.

Bush stood for Reaganite continuity during the 1988 presidential campaign, even as he implicitly criticized the Reagan presidency by calling, in his acceptance speech at the Republican National Convention, for a "kinder, gentler" society. But such moderation would have to wait until after the campaign. Bush chose a brashly conservative Indiana senator, J. Danforth Quayle, for his running mate to appease conservative Republicans. During the fall, his campaign slandered his opponent, Massachusetts governor Michael J. Dukakis, calling him unpatriotic and soft on crime. In an infamous commercial, the GOP touched a racist nerve when it charged Governor Dukakis with responsibility for rapes committed by a black convict named Willie Horton during a work furlough from a Massachusetts prison.

President Bush felt sufficiently emboldened by the collapse of Communism to announce an American-dominated "new world order." During his administration, several of the most troublesome proxy wars that had been energized by the larger East-West conflict rapidly wound down. The Soviets withdrew from Afghanistan in the late 1980s (see Chapter 13), after which the CIA stopped supplying the Afghan rebels with advanced weapons. The brutal war there, waged among rival Islamic religious factions, did not stop, but it no longer played a role in superpower politics. Likewise, in Central America, the Bush administration ended U.S. support for the antigovernment Contra forces in Nicaragua in return for a pledge that the Soviets and Cubans would stop supplying arms and aid to the ruling Sandinista party. The deal paid off handsomely for Bush when free elections gave the Nicaraguan presidency to a pro-U.S. candidate in 1990. And in neighboring El Salvador, a peace treaty signed in 1992 ended the civil war there, allowing left-wing rebels to participate in electoral politics.

Finally, the end of the Cold War created a far more advantageous atmosphere for the liberation of South Africa. There, the apartheid regime headed by F. W. de Klerk released from prison the African National Congress (ANC) leader Nelson Mandela, who had spent twenty-seven years in confinement. The ANC had long maintained an alliance with the Communists, which kept U.S. governments wary, especially during the Reagan presidency, when administration policy favored a "constructive engagement" with the racist white South African government. But as Mandela and the ANC swept to power in the early 1990s, even conservative U.S. diplomats applauded. The disintegration of South Africa's all-white regime quickly reduced the level of violence throughout southern Africa.

The end of the Cold War left the United States as the world's only superpower, so even as international tensions declined, U.S. leaders had a relatively free hand to deploy American military might abroad, unhampered by a countervailing Soviet response. This new state of affairs became clear in December 1989, when President Bush dispatched thousands of troops to Panama to oust a corrupt dictator, Manuel Noriega, in an overt display of U.S. military power that echoed early-twentieth-century interventions in Latin America. A short, bloody war ended with Noriega's capture and extradition to the United States, where he was convicted in a Miami courtroom of drug-related offenses. Little actually changed in Panama, which remained one of the major transshipment points for illegal drugs in the Western Hemisphere.

About a year later, in an even more massive deployment of its military might, the United States confronted the troops of the Iraqi dictator Saddam Hussein, whose invasion and annexation of the oil-rich emirate of Kuwait threatened to destabilize U.S. allies in the Persian Gulf. The Bush administration assembled an international coalition, including the Soviets, Germany, Japan, and most Arab states, to endorse the dispatch of nearly 500,000 U.S. troops to the region by the end of 1990. Britain, France, and Saudi Arabia committed an additional 200,000 troops. Although many Americans, including most congressional Democrats, believed that economic sanctions imposed by the United Nations might force Iraq to with-

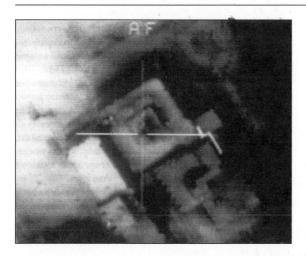

High-Tech War

Americans glimpsed the Persian Gulf War largely through television, often seeing images that were in fact composed of other video images. In this case, a video display aboard a Stealth F-117 bomber locks a Glide "smart" bomb's infrared guidance camera onto a target in Baghdad. The accuracy and glamour of such high-tech weapons were highlighted in news coverage that was heavily censored by the military. Only after the war did the military reveal that "smart" weapons made up only 7 percent of the 81,980 tons of bombs dropped on Iraq and Kuwait — and of that total figure, 70 percent, or 62,137 tons, missed their targets. Prints and Photographs Division, Library of Congress.

draw from Kuwait, Bush administration officials argued that economic pressure alone would prove ineffective.

On January 15, 1991, U.S. forces launched a massive, high-tech bombing campaign against Iraq called Operation Desert Storm that paved the way for the tank-led ground assault a month later. Mobilizing hundreds of thousands of U.S. and British armored troops, the February campaign took but one hundred hours to reclaim Kuwait and enter southern Iraq. Antiwar demonstrations filled the streets of Washington and San Francisco briefly, but light casualties and a swift victory soon generated a wave of patriotic fervor and soaring approval ratings for the president.

But the Gulf War left a mixed legacy. President Bush hoped that the successful, massive use of military power against Iraq would shatter the nation's "Vietnam syndrome" by confirming a renewed U.S. willingness to intervene abroad as the world's unchallenged superpower. But U.S. public opinion remained skittish when it came to the deployment of U.S. troops, especially when diplomatic interventions or humanitarian missions turned violent, as they would in Somalia in East Africa and the former Yugoslavia in Eastern Europe. In the Persian Gulf itself, Kuwait was once again an independent nation, but the Bush administration chose to end the war with Saddam Hussein still in power, largely because the Bush administration saw his regime as a regional counterweight to Iran. However, this meant that the Iraqi dictator would likely seek to rebuild his army and suppress domestic opposition, which he did in brutal fashion immediately following the withdrawal of American troops. The United Nations therefore continued an economically debilitating trade boycott, while the United States maintained an active military presence in the region, periodically bombing Iraqi targets.

A New Economic Order

The U.S. military victory in the Persian Gulf was not matched by a sense of economic well-being at home. By the fall of 1990, the U.S. economy had plunged once again into recession. The Iraqi invasion of Kuwait generated a huge spike in the price of oil, which shook consumer confidence and depressed corporate profits and investment. Although oil prices soon moderated, the recession did not lift for a full two years, after which unemployment declined slowly, and real wages remained stagnant. White-collar workers and professionals, like factory workers in earlier decades, found their income and status subject to the ebb and flow of global economic forces. Economic instability also intensified traditional class and racial divisions and tensions in the country, which flared throughout the 1990s. Although the U.S. economy would ultimately boom by decade's end, the rapid growth of the World Wide Web and other elements of the telecommunications revolution put all labor for sale within an increasingly integrated global marketplace. Millions of new immigrants flocked across U.S. borders seeking better jobs and a secure future. These new arrivals, along with a new generation of labor leaders who had been groomed in the 1960s, became a decisive force in pushing labor back to the left.

The Postwar Economy Unlike the early 1980s, when blue-collar workers received most of the pink slips, a decade later professional, managerial, and other white-collar workers were just as likely as factory workers to become victims of corporate "downsizing." Nearly two million people lost their jobs in the three years that followed the Persian Gulf War; 63 percent of American corporations cut their staffs during that time. Post–Cold War layoffs in the high-paying defense industries hit the California economy, which had sailed through the 1980s, particularly hard. Although the national economy produced millions of new jobs, the threat of layoffs generated a pervasive insecurity at all levels of the workforce. As AT&T's vice president of human resources explained: "People need to recognize that we are all contingent workers in one form or another." No wonder some called the downturn of the early 1990s the "silent depression."

But U.S. corporations staged a remarkable turnaround once the recession began to lift. In contrast to the 1970s and 1980s, American businesses again competed successfully at home and abroad. Productivity growth finally rebounded to levels that had not been seen since the late 1960s, profits leaped upward, and the stock market soared more than fourfold between 1991 and 1999 in one of the great Wall Street booms of all time (Figure 14.1).

FIGURE 14.1 Stock Mania: The Stock Market, 1985–2006

The collapse of the dot-com boom in 1999–2000 and a series of corporate bankruptcies in 2000–2001 brought a sharp decline in the stock market that continued after the 9/11 terrorist attacks.

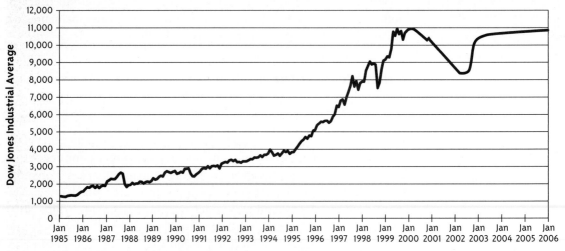

Key industries—steel, automobiles, telecommunications, microchip manufacturing, computer software, entertainment, aircraft, and finance—were once again creative, innovative, and profitable. By the late 1990s, unemployment, inflation, mortgage rates, and oil prices had fallen to their lowest levels in three decades. Most experts once again counted the United States the most competitive industrial nation in the world. *Time* magazine captured the ambiguity of this accomplishment in a 1994 cover story headlined "We're Number 1. And It Hurts."

What accounted for this simultaneous sense of productive accomplishment and economic insecurity? The two phenomena were closely linked, because corporations benefited enormously from the wage stagnation, de-unionization, low taxes, and deregulatory business climate that characterized this era. The virtual abandonment of antitrust action during the 1980s and 1990s led to a massive wave of corporate mergers and reorganizations, which opened the door to both cost-cutting layoffs and speculative stock market recapitalizations. "There is no job security anymore," reported Karen Tarlow, a Wall Street bank officer in her late forties. "It's very insidious how the rich get richer." In oil, telecommunications, health care, and finance, a new set of powerfully competitive firms emerged almost overnight. Exxon bought Mobil, Bell Atlantic acquired GTE, WorldCom bought MCI, and Daimler-Benz merged with Chrysler. Between 1992 and 1998, the value of all corporate mergers advanced nearly tenfold to more than one trillion dollars. In real dollar terms, this was the biggest merger wave in nearly a century.

The U.S. government also spurred the competitiveness of corporations that were headquartered in North America by devaluing the dollar against the currencies of other industrial nations. Suddenly, U.S. corporations that traded abroad, such as Boeing, or faced import competition, such as General Electric and the automotive giants, found that they could sell their products more cheaply than those of many foreign competitors. Further easing the competitive pressure on U.S. firms, wages had risen far more rapidly in Europe and Asia than in the United States during the 1980s. Additionally, foreign nations faced some unique challenges in this period. The German government had to raise taxes to pay the huge costs of reunification, while Japan struggled with a decade-long recession brought on by the near-collapse of its overheated banking and real estate sectors. Thus, after decades of decline, the U.S. share of world manufacturing exports began to rise in the years after 1986.

U.S. firms also benefited in the 1990s from adopting the most advanced organizational techniques and technological innovation. In the steel industry, the introduction of German-style mini-mills slashed by more than half the number of hours required to produce a ton of steel. In autos, Japanese inventory and production scheduling methods and new levels of automation enhanced quality, cut labor costs, and shortened the engineering time for

"You Work Your Hardest, Then the Next Thing You Know, You're on the Streets Looking"

In 1994, Mother Jones, a socially progressive journal named for the early-twentieth-century labor organizer Mary Harris Jones, interviewed working Americans in different parts of the country on their views about their jobs, economic opportunities, and their hopes for the future. Their opinions were as diverse as their occupations.

Charlie Seda, 26
Construction worker
$10/hour
High school graduate
Married, 2 kids

I've worked a lot of temporary jobs. They aren't reliable. The agencies tell you, "OK, we got you a job. It's up to you to keep it." You work your hardest, then the next thing you know, you're on the streets looking.

I didn't want to work at minimum wage anymore. I had a hard time getting union work, but with a union, the pay's more reliable. I've had the job I'm on now two months. It's only the second job I've had that I feel confident when I wake up in the morning that I still have a job.

Ana Nolasco, 26
Garment worker
$5.50/hour
High school graduate
Single, 1 kid

I came to the United States to find honest work. I had done hand embroidery for my family in El Salvador—hearts and birds mostly. One day I read in the paper they were hiring people to run embroidery machines. . . .

Even with jobs moving to Latin America, the living in America is still better than in El Salvador. The wages they earn in a week, I earn in a day here.

Most factories are closing down or moving away. I worry about it. I take English lessons on Saturdays because I want to do something besides factory work. That way, if the factory closes down, I could do something else. I'd like a job in an office—something that was more intellectual, less physical.

Karen Tarlow, 47
Asst. vice president
Wall Street bank
$65,000/year
MBA in finance
Divorced

I always thought, "If I get more credentials, I'll get what's due me." So I went for my MBA at night. I still have not gotten the raises and promotions I should have. It's not that I didn't work hard; it's not that I didn't give things up. I gave up an awful lot. But I didn't get rewarded properly. I hit the glass ceiling hard. . . .

I'm 47, I've had all this education, and I find myself asking, "Where do I go now?" There is no job security anymore. The dream is gone; it's not going to get better. As we export jobs, other places will get better, but look at all the people here who aren't buying goods and services. We're becoming a Third World country.

It's very insidious how the rich get richer. They do it beyond the government, no matter what the government tries to do. Insider trading is the norm.

Marie Dupuy, 43
Day care center owner
$25,000–$30,000/year
Bachelor's degree
2 kids
In Haiti I was from a privileged family. When I came to the United States, I stayed as a legal alien for 10 years. It's a big decision for a black, foreign-born person to become a citizen. Now I make sure I fulfill my civic duties.

I taught French in public schools for four years. I don't think teachers are paid what they're worth. They get frustrated, they hate the kids, hate their jobs. But teachers need to be more conscientious about their responsibilities. All children deserve better. I looked for a better way to help. I opened a day care center, and now I'm satisfied in my work.

My children are going to be successful Americans. Their names will be known all over. I'm not talking about how much money they make; I hope they will make a difference.

Ashley Craddock, "American Workers Talk About Their Jobs and the Future," *Mother Jones*, March/April 1994 (http://www.motherjones.com/mother_jones/MA94/craddock.html).

new models, enabling Chrysler and Ford to earn record profits. And the telecommunications revolution, which made fax machines, e-mail, cellular telephones, and overnight package delivery pervasive, enhanced productivity in factories, offices, and hospitals.

Perhaps most important, the computer revolution finally began to pay off. Despite the fanfare that accompanied dramatic advances in digital technology, computerization had been slow to boost white-collar service sector productivity, whose growth lagged far behind that of even run-of-the-mill factories during the 1970s and 1980s. But by the early 1990s, a generation of employees had been trained on the new machines, which sat on the desks of more than six out of ten workers (compared to fewer than two out of ten in Japan). As *BusinessWeek* put it, "Networking [the linking together of large numbers of desktop computers] finally united all the systems, and voila! Productivity began to take off."

But a rising economic tide—including the powerful surge flowing out of the computer industry in Silicon Valley in Northern California—could not lift all boats or solve all problems. The reconfiguration of the American economy brought real social and psychological costs, which were borne not only by the unemployed and the Rust Belt factory workers, but also by millions of suburban families and college-educated "knowledge workers" who might otherwise seem to be the beneficiaries of the new economy. Real family income continued to drop throughout the first half of the 1990s, even as record numbers of women, teenagers, and new immigrants entered the workforce. Health care expenses rose inexorably, twice as fast as the overall consumer price index. In response, insurance companies and corporations restricted coverage and demanded copayments. By 1992, more than thirty-seven million Americans did not have medical insurance.

On Trial: Race, Gender, and National Identity   The decade of the 1990s was not only a period of growing economic inequality. It was also a period of high-profile investigations, hearings, and trials in which the new politics of race, gender, and American identity played out before a media-savvy audience of millions. The courtroom and the hearing room now served as sites of furious contention. These televised spectacles were not, in fact, well suited to resolving the nation's deep-seated cultural and social divisions. But a fascinated citizenry focused its gaze on these events because no new election and no new statute could fully represent the complicated and contradictory values that Americans brought to their understanding of race, sex, and nationhood.

President Bush's decision in 1991 to nominate Clarence Thomas to fill the U.S. Supreme Court seat that had been vacated by the death of civil rights pioneer Thurgood Marshall would have been controversial in any event. Although Thomas had been born into southern poverty, the Yale-educated black conservative criticized civil rights leaders and had helped to undermine affirmative action litigation as chairman of the Equal Employment Opportunity Commission (EEOC) during the Reagan administration. Republicans backed Thomas, while leaders of the civil rights community, who wanted to keep an African American on the Supreme Court, were split as to whether such a conservative black figure could properly fill Marshall's slot on the bench.

Thomas's confirmation battle before the Senate Judiciary Committee became red hot in October 1991 after Anita Hill, a black law professor who

Caught on Tape

A frame from the amateur video of the March 3, 1991, beating of Rodney King by Los Angeles police officers. George Holliday shot the video from his apartment across the street. 2002 Getty Images.

had been an aide to Thomas, testified that the nominee had frequently made lurid remarks to her and repeatedly pressured her for dates. Feminists and liberals who were hostile to the Thomas nomination immediately championed Hill's charges. The nominee charged that his accusers were turning the confirmation proceedings into a "high-tech lynching." The nation watched in stunned amazement as a panel of white male senators subjected Hill's motives and veracity to fierce personal attack. The Senate confirmed Thomas by a vote of fifty-two to forty-eight, even as Americans became far more sensitive to issues of sexual harassment in the workplace. In 1992, the EEOC recorded a 50 percent jump in official complaints on the issue.

Television played a key role in another racial spectacle that transfixed the nation. On the evening of March 3, 1991, a black motorist, Rodney King, became a symbol of white racism and police brutality when a nearby resident captured on videotape the beating that King suffered at the hands of four Los Angeles policemen after a traffic stop. Millions of people saw King take more than fifty blows from club, foot, and flashlight as he lay on the ground. Sympathy for King turned to violent outrage in April 1992 when a white suburban jury acquitted his police assailants. Black and Latino rioters burned hundreds of houses and stores in the South Central section of Los Angeles, particularly those occupied by Korean immigrant shopkeepers who, despite their recent arrival in Los Angeles, enjoyed more economic success than the rioters. The city called in police and National Guard, but the violence killed 53 people and injured thousands. Property damage amounted to a billion dollars, making the riot the most costly in U.S. history.

A Digital Revolution   Television was not the only powerful cultural and political force that transformed American society in these years. The deployment of millions of easy-to-use computers began to replicate the productivity breakthrough brought on by the birth of the mass-production assembly line early in the twentieth century. Then, skilled tool and die craftsmen built the precision metal-cutting machinery that would be operated by so many untutored farmhands and immigrants. In the 1990s, skilled programmers churned out thousands of different computer programs ("software") that allowed clerical workers and managers to perform tasks

"No Police, No Help": Violence Against Koreans in Los Angeles

Ishle Yi Park, a young Korean woman living in Los Angeles, wrote this poem in June 2002 reflecting on the Korean experience as targets of black and Latino rage a decade earlier. "Sa-I-Gu, 4-29" refers to April 29, 1992, when anger over the acquittal of the four white police officers, who had been accused of beating black motorist Rodney King in March 1991, spilled over into resentment against recent immigrants in South Central Los Angeles. Korean shop owners became targets for many of the working-class African Americans and Latinos who were denied access to economic opportunities.

Sa-I-Gu

"We are our first and last line of defense. Me. You."
K. W. Lee

koreans mark disaster
with numbers — 4-29 — Sa-I-Gu.
no police. no help. . . .

*

we see grainy reels of a black
fish flopping on concrete
arched, kicked, nightsticked,

flopping not fish but black man —
here I rub my own tender
wrists, ask unanswerable questions —

why are the cops doing this?
my mother will answer simply,
wisely, because they are bad.

of the looters, because they are mad.
and why hurt us she chokes
because we are close   enough.

I moan, slip under the fold
of her arm. she strokes my hair

and keeps me protected
as I must one day protect her. . . .

mile high cameras hover,
zoom in, dub it:
war of blacks & koreans

watch us ripped
to red tendon
for scraps in the lot
they abandoned

show latasha shot on 50 channels,
not 200 shot korean grocers
whose names & deaths
were always kept local

"No Police, No Help": Violence Against Koreans in Los Angeles (*cont.*)

silence white as white silence

we have no jesse
no martin no malcolm
no al, no eloquent, rapid tongue

just fathers, thick-tongued
and children, too young to carry more
than straw broomstick and hefty bag.

all the women cry
and hurl what is not already shattered.

*

who returns with
straw broomstick?

cooks rice that steams
untouched on the kitchen table,

slips off a mother's
devastated keds, slips her into bed?
two mornings after,
they march over ashes

dust licking proud ankles
30,000 koreans

sing in a language
most will never master:

we shall overcome. someday.
peace.

Ishle Yi Park, http://www.inthefray.com/la10/imagine/park15/park15.html.

once restricted to well-trained professionals. "Up until the early 1980s, the only people able to use personal computers were a very tiny elite," reported a Princeton economist. "Now, a lot of software is for numskulls."

Soon the Internet and the World Wide Web linked together millions of computers all across the globe. The Internet had its origins in Pentagon efforts, begun in the 1960s, to build a communications network that would be capable of surviving a nuclear war and to share expensive computer resources. But imaginative scientists and clever hackers soon spread this digital network well beyond the military laboratories and university research facilities of its inception. By the late 1980s, e-mail was becoming commonplace, and in the mid-1990s, the development of graphical, interactive Web pages generated an explosive new stage in the growth of this medium. The number of Web pages doubled every eighteen months thereafter, transforming the locus of commerce, entertainment, and information retrieval (Figure 14.2).

The imaginative hold of this vast digital network approached that of other great world-transforming technologies: steam power and the railroad in the early nineteenth century, electricity fifty years later, and the

FIGURE 14.2 Web Mania: Internet Hosts, 1999–2006

The appearance in 1993 of Mosaic, the first graphical browser for the World Wide Web (and the predecessor to Netscape Navigator), led to the explosive growth of the Internet. Between 1999 and 2006, the number of Web "hosts" (basically, computers housing Web sites) grew more than nine times. From the Internet Systems Consortium Domain Survey, www.isc.org.

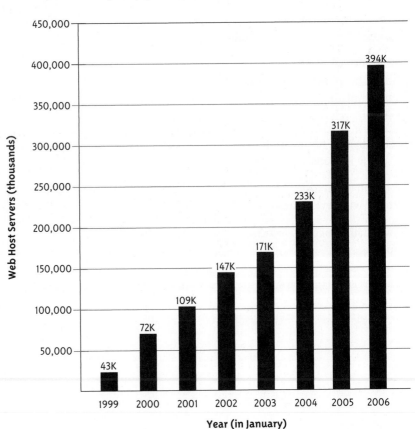

"These Workers Were in Tears"

The U.S. government allows American companies to recruit high-tech workers from abroad through the H-1B visa program. As David Bacon reveals in his article, "Immigrants Find High-Tech Servitude in Silicon Valley," their temporary status limits workplace organizing in these industries and results in poor conditions for and abuse of these white-collar workers.

When Kim Singh left India to become a contract worker in Silicon Valley, he thought he would find a good job in the electronics industry. Instead, he found a high-tech sweatshop.

Singh worked for three different companies. Each got him an H1-B immigration visa, allowing him to work in the U.S. as a software engineer. The first company, he says, withheld 25 percent of the salary from each of its immigrant engineers. "After each of us left, none of us received the money," Singh alleges.

At the second company, "I worked seven days a week, with no overtime compensation. And the only ones required to work on weekends were the H1-B immigrants," he says.

The third company rented an apartment for four H1-B engineers in San Jose, charging each $1,450 a month, while holding onto their passports. This company "threatened to send some back to India if they didn't get contracts. These workers were in tears. They were nervous wrecks, ashamed to ask for money or help from their families back home. . . ."

For India and the Philippines, the source countries for most H1-B workers, the continued loss of highly-skilled engineers recruited by Silicon Valley contributes to brain drain.

"Our educational system produces highly-skilled workers, who then leave to become the working poor in America, while breaking down our ability to industrialize our own country," says Anuradha Mittal, Indian-born co-director of Oakland, California's Food First. "We wind up subsidizing U.S. industry."

High tech lobbyists reply that the industry faces a crippling labor shortage, threatening U.S. economic growth. The problem isn't an absolute scarcity of labor, however, but a shortage of people willing to provide high skills at the salary industry wants to pay.

AFL-CIO executive vice president Linda Chavez-Thompson asks why companies themselves don't train workers for vacant jobs. "They use this program to keep workers in a position of dependence," she charges. "And because these workers are often hired under individual contracts, U.S. labor law says they don't even have the right to organize."

David Bacon, *Labor Notes*, No. 258, September 2000. Reprinted with permission of *Labor Notes*, www.labornotes.org.

internal combustion engine during the first third of the twentieth century. Like these technologies, computerization promised a revolutionary transformation in the structure of production, the organization of society, and the meaning of work. And for the people who were in the right place at the right time, it generated enormous wealth.

Like Rockefeller and Ford before him, Microsoft president Bill Gates combined technical expertise and business savvy to make himself the richest man of his era. Born to a wealthy Seattle family in 1955, Gates dropped out of Harvard to join the wave of youthful West Coast computer "hackers" who refounded the computer industry in the late 1970s. Like Steve Jobs and Steve Wozniak, creators of Apple Computer Corporation and pioneers in personal computing, Gates put his entrepreneurial faith in the proliferation of millions of inexpensive desktop computers. But rather than building the hardware, his firm purchased, rewrote, and copyrighted DOS, the essential operating system for the machines. Within a decade, Microsoft programs had become the de facto software standard for more than 80 percent of all the personal computers that were sold in the world. The growth requirements of the software industry meshed seamlessly with many of the characteristics that were peculiar to late-twentieth-century U.S. capitalism: entrepreneurial flexibility, a close partnership with a large number of commercially oriented universities, a cosmopolitan and multiethnic workforce, and "ownership" of the cyberworld's lingua franca: American English.

The craft workers of this cyber-revolution were the driven, youthful programmers, whose workaday roles actually resembled those of the skilled machinists, technicians, and draftsmen who had been crucial to the industrial transformation of the nation nearly a century before. Like the proud craft workers of Bridgeport and Cincinnati, college-educated programmers stood at the very nexus of production. "It is their skill in coding, in turning strings of numbers into life-altering software, that is Microsoft's lifeblood," observed a computer-savvy journalist. But for most programmers and other skilled workers, 35 percent of whom were immigrants, loyalty lay with the craft, not with any single company. Job-hopping was endemic in the software industry. Indeed, a growing proportion of these skilled technical workers were "temps," temporary workers who received few benefits other than a paycheck from the companies in whose offices they spent their many hours, months, and years.

The Internet made the world smaller. Employing digital technology, firms could now farm out highly skilled jobs across the globe, not just manufacturing jobs. This phenomenon, what many companies called "outsourcing," included both technology and service sector jobs. For example, in the 1990s, Dell Computers began setting up call centers in India to handle customer support. This move proved to be so successful that roughly 44 per-

cent of Dell's workforce toiled outside the United States by 2003. Dell then slashed almost 6,000 U.S. jobs, most of them in central Texas near the firm's headquarters.

The New Immigration   Globalization did not just send goods, technology, and jobs abroad, it also made possible, even necessary, the massive immigration that transformed U.S. politics and economic life in the decades after 1970. Throughout the late twentieth century, huge numbers of Asian and Latino immigrants flocked to U.S. shores to fill millions of new service, retail, clerical, and light manufacturing jobs. This new wave of immigrants rivaled in sheer numbers the great trans-Atlantic flows of a century earlier. In the 1960s, annual immigration had totaled only a quarter-million; by the 1990s, the United States was admitting more than 800,000 legal immigrants a year and perhaps half again as many illegal immigrants, mainly from Mexico. More than 40 percent of the newcomers were from Asia, especially the Philippines, China, South Korea, and Vietnam; about 35 percent came from Latin America and the Caribbean.

One of every three new immigrants entered the United States through California, making the nation's most populous state its unofficial Ellis Island as well. By the 1990s, one-third of the population of Los Angeles, the nation's second-largest city, was foreign-born; on the North American continent, only Mexico City had more Spanish-speaking residents. As hundreds of thousands of Mexicans and Central Americans streamed into poor neighborhoods and communities in East Los Angeles and the San Gabriel Valley, tens of thousands of Koreans settled in an old working-class neighborhood just west of downtown

Roundup

U.S. Border Patrol agents arrest a group of Mexicans who illegally entered the United States near San Diego, California. More than one million undocumented migrants cross the border between Mexico and the United States yearly. U.S. Border Patrol.

Los Angeles. At the same time, equally large numbers of immigrants from Taiwan, Hong Kong, and Vietnam transformed the old Chinatown neighborhood near City Hall. Asians and Latinos would shortly make up more than half the workforce in southern California (Map 14.2).

New York's foreign-born population, like that of Los Angeles, also approached 35 percent of its total populace in the 1990s — a level that the city had last reached in 1910, at the height of Southern and Eastern European immigration. Long-established immigrant communities, including those composed of Puerto Ricans, Irish, and Poles, grew rapidly during the 1970s and 1980s, even as hundreds of thousands of Haitian, Dominican, Colombian, East Indian, Chinese, and Russian immigrants settled into the city's poorer neighborhoods. Nearly 200,000 Mexican immigrants arrived after the peso was devalued in 1986. Mostly undocumented, they traveled thousands of miles by truck and car from some of the poorest rural regions of Mexico in search of work. "We came because we are poor farmers and our parents did not have enough to send us to school," explained a young food deliverer.

Newcomers also transformed Miami; by the 1980s, it had the highest percentage of foreign-born residents of any U.S. city. First came an influx of nearly 600,000 Cubans, many of them well-to-do exiles from the Cuban Revolution of 1959. Then, in the late 1970s and early 1980s, tens of thousands of political and economic refugees arrived from Haiti, Guatemala, El Salvador, and Nicaragua. The huge number of Latino immigrants changed the face of the city; as Spanish became the language of foreign trade, Miami became the commercial "capital of Latin America," a politically stable, financially well-regulated marketplace that was hospitable to businesspeople from a dozen countries. Latin businesses flourished in the North as well. In old industrial cities such as Passaic, Paterson, and Union City, New Jersey, Latino-owned businesses, including restaurants, nightclubs, cigar shops, fruit stands, and clothing stores, transformed the look, sound, and smell of the main shopping areas. As one Union City resident noted, a few years earlier, many shops "used to [have] signs saying, 'We speak Spanish.' Now the signs say, 'We speak English.'"

In the United States, immigrants with skills, family connections, and an entrepreneurial outlook could do very well. In Los Angeles, New York, and other cities, many Korean families owned and managed fruit and vegetable markets. Vietnamese, Chinese, Thais, Mexicans, and Iranians opened tens of thousands of new restaurants, making the American dining experience far more cosmopolitan. Indian, Pakistani, and Chinese immigrants with English-language, engineering, and computer electronics skills won a solid beachhead in Silicon Valley and other high-tech enclaves. And a small number of wealthy individuals from Hong Kong, Saudi Arabia, and Japan took

MAP 14.2   New Immigration of Latinos and Asians, 2000

According to the 2000 Census, 11 percent of the U.S. population was foreign born, and the majority of those recent immigrants (51 percent) came from Latin America. Asians made up the second largest group of immigrants. While still concentrated on the two coasts, Asian and Latino communities have spread across the country.

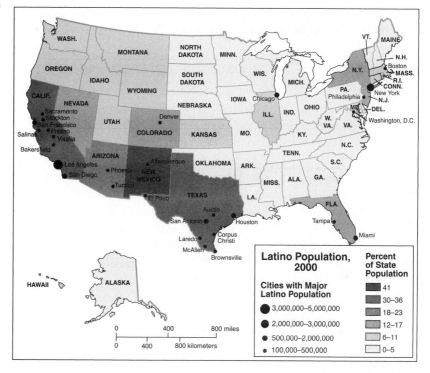

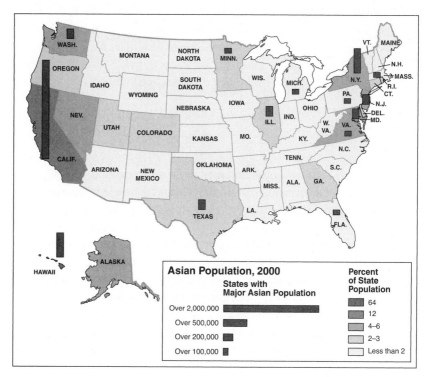

"There Is Blood in Every Dollar I Make"

Mr. Ji (not his real name) was a quality control officer in a pharmaceutical factory in Canton, China; his wife worked in a factory day-care center. The Jis decided to come to the United States in the early 1980s to get better medical care for their twelve-year-old daughter. The Ji family bags and tags garments in a New York City sweatshop, working long hours at below minimum wage. Mr. Ji, age sixty-two, recounts the difficulties he and his family have had to endure in coming to America.

I don't understand America's policy. They let you come. But once you are here, they don't care at all. They don't care if you can get a job or what you do. You are all on your own. It's one thing to let immigrants in. But once they are here, you have to digest them. We get below minimum wages. This is the tenth factory we worked in. It's all the same. Finally we decided to stop hopping around. There is no labor law here. The government is acting like an idiot who doesn't know what's going on. The minimum wages are not for real. . . . In China, I just do desk work, giving people ideas. Now I'm doing this totally meaningless work. America is a world where the strong devours the meek.

I am at a point of no return. If I go back, I'll be looked down on by everybody. They'll think I'm such a failure. . . . I can't go back empty-handed. It'll be so embarrassing. . . . I want to learn English, I felt handicapped. I feel I'm without my limbs. I don't want to be dependent on other people. But I don't have any time at all. . . . Now I'm so tired when I get home, sometimes I don't even cook, just make some instant noodles. . . .

We have to work so hard for so little money. Last Saturday we worked from 9 A.M. until 10:30 p.m. Between us we made eighty dollars. It's the best day since I came to the U.S. . . . I am tied down to my job. I feel like a slave. I can't go anywhere. Even if there is gold out there, I won't have time to pick them up. . . . There is blood in every dollar I make. . . . We all thought U.S. is such an advanced country. I don't see too much personal freedom here. You are free if you have money.

Interview conducted by Ying Chan, New York City, 1990.

advantage of the undervalued dollar to make substantial investments in commercial real estate, residential properties, and stateside industries.

Most of the new immigrants were solidly working class, however. They came because even minimum-wage work in the United States paid five or ten times more than they could earn in the cities, barrios, and villages of their homelands. Like the Italians and Irish who arrived in the nineteenth century, many of the new immigrants hoped to return to their native countries to buy a farm, build a house, or open a business. But like their predecessors, most did not succeed. In New York and Los Angeles, Latino and Asian immigrants labored in hundreds of sweatshops of the sort that progressive reformers had once condemned. Likewise, in Nebraska, Colorado, and South Dakota, a new generation of immigrants labored in slaughterhouses, under conditions similar to those portrayed in Upton Sinclair's 1906 novel *The Jungle*. "We came with illusions of earning a little money, investing it, and doing something in Mexico," noted one undocumented immigrant in New York City. "But those who get $180 for working seven days, what can they do? They return defeated to Mexico." Even where the work was technology-based and legal (as in many of California's most successful new computer firms), English-speaking clerical, sales, and research and development employees worked in the front office; in the back shop, scores of Asian and Latino women built chips, stuffed circuit boards, or moved inventory. Their work remained as routine and insecure as that of sweatshop garment workers a hundred years before.

Labor's Leftward Movement   By the early 1990s, American trade unions were in decline. Unionized labor represented only 16 percent of all American workers; each year, the proportion dropped. Trade unions no longer set the wage standard in any major industry — not even in automaking or steel, in which nonunion factories and mills represented an increasingly large production sector. Perhaps most threatening, the idea of unions seemed stale and antiquated. "'Organized Labor.' Say those words, and your heart sinks," wrote Thomas Geoghegan, an embattled prounion attorney. "Dumb, stupid organized labor." Under the leadership of Lane Kirkland, whose politics had been molded by the conservative labor chieftain George Meany, the AFL-CIO devoted few resources to organizing and had little presence on television or in other media. Kirkland and the generation of unionists who came of age during the administrations of Franklin Roosevelt and Harry Truman thought that labor's revival depended on the election of a prolabor president and Congress, which would pass laws to liberalize U.S. labor law to make organizing easier. But growing Republican control of both the Senate and the House in the 1990s foreclosed any expectation that the unions would find much help from the federal government.

In this crisis, an insurgent group of top union officials, mostly representing workers in public employment, the service trades, and manufacturing, overthrew Kirkland and took control of the AFL-CIO. It was the first successful challenge to a sitting AFL or AFL-CIO president in more than one hundred years. The new AFL-CIO chose John Sweeney as president. As the former president of the Service Employees International Union (SEIU), Sweeney recruited a multiracial organizing corps numbering in the hundreds, some with New Left backgrounds. SEIU had spent a sizable proportion of its dues to successfully organize thousands of janitors, health care workers, and public employees. Its organizers sometimes employed the tactics of the civil rights movement — sit-ins, civil disobedience, and public marches — to organize low-wage African American, Asian, and Latino workers in the fast-growing service sector of the economy.

"Queremos Justicia! We Want Justice!"

In this article for a labor newsletter, Marcy Rein, communications coordinator for Service Employees International Union Local 1877, describes the "rolling strike" strategy that striking janitors used in northern California to win higher wages.

"In the beginning the [janitorial] contractors said, 'I'm the boss, you do what I say,'" recalls Reyna Alferez of Service Employees Local 1877's bargaining committee. Softly she continues, "I told them, 'You pay a little to us and you take a lot from us. You have Volvos and BMW's. Who makes the money to buy them?'

"The employers said we're paying just a little because those people are just minority people. We got mad, and we understood that when we want something, we have to fight for it."

And fight they did. Local 1877 blindsided the contractors with a month-long rolling strike in June. The bosses never knew where trouble would visit next or how long it would stay. . . .

Local 1877 represents 5,000 janitors in four Northern California counties: Alameda, Contra Costa, San Mateo, and Santa Clara. More than 80 percent are Latino, most of the rest are African American and Asian. Under the old contract, two-thirds earned less than the federal poverty wage—$7.28 per hour for a family of four. . . .

At a special convention . . . , some 700 janitors set their contract goals: one master agreement, wages above poverty level, family health insurance, and protections for immigrant workers.

Then they hit the streets, demonstrating at work, marching on San Jose Airport, and doing civil disobedience in Oakland and Palo Alto. Each action sent the same emphatic message: "Queremos justicia! We want justice!"

Local 1877 organizers decided on the "rolling strike" to maximize disruption for the contractors—making it harder to hire permanent replacements—and minimize hardship for members who, living paycheck to paycheck, couldn't weather a continuous strike.

In the first week, workers struck in a different county each night, taking out three to five work sites. But in the second week the strike overran the organizers' careful plans. Workers hit in every county every night, walking out and staying out. Altogether about 70 sites were struck. . . .

After four weeks, the contractors gave in to most of the union's demands.

The new master contract, approved 6-1, brings all members above the current poverty wage. Annual increases average four percent. Members on the bottom of the scale get 5.5 percent, and everyone stays ahead of inflation.

Marcy Rein, "Aggressive Tactics Help Janitors Clean Up on Contract," *Labor Notes*, September 1996. Reprinted with permission of *Labor Notes*, www.labornotes.org.

Sweeney and his allies moved the labor movement to the left in hopes of revitalizing it. They reached out to feminists, civil rights leaders, ecologists, left-wing academics, and liberal clergy in an effort to build a prounion coalition. The AFL-CIO also recruited thousands of students for a high-profile "union summer" organizing experience. "Labor must organize without the law," asserted the new AFL-CIO president, "so that we can later organize under the law." It had taken a quarter-century, but the Sixties generation had finally made its voice heard at the union movement's leadership level.

For a time, it seemed that this initiative might work. The SEIU, the largest union in the country, organized hundreds of thousands of poorly paid home health care workers in California, Illinois, and other states. Workers in textile mills in Martinsdale, Virginia, and Kannapolis, North Carolina, whose unionization efforts had been thwarted for decades, finally won National Labor Relations Board elections. And in Las Vegas and Los Angeles, citywide labor movements led by New Left veterans successfully leveraged the organization of thousands of Latino immigrants to build the kind of labor political power that shifted politics in both Nevada and California in a more liberal direction. In almost every national election that was held in the late 1990s and into the new century, organized labor proved to be effective in mobilizing its own members and their families, and they became increasingly reliable Democratic voters.

The powerful International Brotherhood of Teamsters underwent a remarkable transformation during these years as well. For decades, the top leadership of the Teamsters seemed to be synonymous with corruption and criminality, but in the 1990s, a vigorous reform movement, the Teamsters for a Democratic Union, helped to elevate Ron Carey and a rank-and-file slate to top union posts. Carey and other reformers battled old-guard unionists to democratize and energize the Teamsters. Their efforts paid off in the spectacular strike victory of 185,000 Teamsters against the United Parcel Service (UPS) in August 1997. The first successful nationwide strike in nearly two decades, the UPS strike won widespread public support for labor's demand that UPS upgrade thousands of low-wage, part-time jobs to permanent, full-time positions. "The rank and file felt like, yes, we do make a difference," said Barb Joyce, a Des Moines truck driver. "The day after the strike when we went back to work everybody on the road was waving and blowing kisses to us."

But Carey's success was short-lived. In a bitter reelection contest, Carey relied on Washington consultants who, unknown to him, illegally laundered contributions to bolster his campaign. When this scheme became known, a federal judge overturned the election and threw Carey out of the union. Carey's fall (he was ultimately replaced by James P. Hoffa, son of the legendary Teamster leader) hurt union reform, but for the first time since the 1940s, the unions maintained a firm alliance with other liberal

Protesting the WTO

When a march of trade unionists protesting against the World Trade Organization (WTO) arrived in downtown Seattle, many labor activists joined youth and environmental protesters who were already blocking access to the WTO meeting. Visible among the banners and placards carried by demonstrators were those of the International Longshore and Warehouse Union, which shut down all Pacific coast ports for a day. David Bacon, November 30, 1999.

organizations. The Seattle meeting of the World Trade Organization in November 1999 graphically illustrated this alliance when unionists and ecological activists united to demand that the WTO enforce worldwide labor and environmental standards. A protest banner proclaimed: "Teamsters and Turtles: Together at Last!"

Historically low levels of unemployment in the last half of the 1990s raised wages and emboldened workers (Figure 14.3). By the end of the decade, the official jobless rate stood just above 4 percent, the lowest level in three decades. Low-paid service workers, especially Latinos and African Americans, who had not shared in the 1980s boom, now began to find jobs at wages that were rising smartly for the first time in a generation. Full employment, sustained for several years, had a radically beneficial impact on the lives of the poorest Americans. Faced with a labor shortage, companies began to offer jobs to people who had been described as unemployable just a few years before. In the cities, crime rates began to fall, the drug culture dissipated, and some young black men began to find steady employment. Campaigns to institute citywide "living wages" (sufficient income to put workers above the poverty line) proliferated across the country.

But organized labor failed to take real advantage of these more favorable circumstances. Employers such as Wal-Mart, Kmart, FedEx, and the Japanese auto factories that had been transplanted to the United States remained uncompromisingly hostile to unionism. Union membership rose in the public sector, but when the imports and recession devastated industrial employment in the early 2000s, union ranks again dropped dramatically, such that organized labor represented just one in

FIGURE 14.3 Declining Unemployment

During the economic boom that began in 1991, African American and Hispanic workers were able to take advantage of the growing job market (as evidenced by their unemployment rates), a benefit that had largely eluded both groups during the previous expansion in the 1980s. Unemployment began increasing in 2000 with the economic dip following the market drop and accelerated under the Bush administration. U.S. Bureau of Labor Statistics, Employment and Earnings, Unemployed and Unemployment Rates by Educational Attainment, Sex, Race, and Hispanic Origin, 1992–2005.

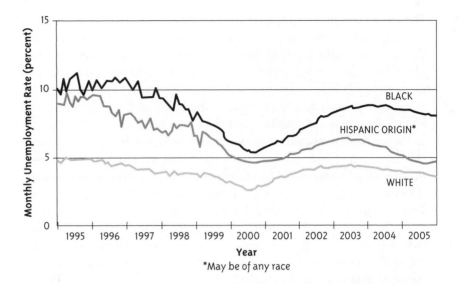

ten American workers. A sense of crisis once again gripped sections of the AFL-CIO top leadership, precipitating the formation in 2005 of a rival labor federation called Change to Win. Determined to organize the unorganized, the SEIU-led group hoped to recapture the insurgent spirit that had been sparked by the old Congress of Industrial Unions seventy years before.

The Rise and Fall of Clintonian Liberalism

Labor was hopeful in the 1990s because the political winds shifted, if briefly, in its favor. President Bush had been a caretaker executive who saw his domestic policy goals in largely negative terms—avoiding, as he once put it, "stupid mistakes" in order to "see that the government doesn't get in the way." He once told his chief of staff, John Sununu, "We don't need to remake society." William Jefferson Clinton came into office in 1992 with ambitious plans for social reforms, especially in the area of health care. But he also promised to recast American liberalism so as to make it acceptable to the generation who had voted for Ronald Reagan and George Bush. No matter how much the Democratic Party's agenda shifted toward issues of middle-class social and economic concern, Clinton partisans could not appease the rightward-tilting Republicans, who gained control of Congress in 1994 and impeached the president in 1998 for lying about a sexual escapade with a White House intern. Despite the labor movement's bold effort at revitalization, such intractable ideological conflicts, along with Clinton's own personal and political blunders, constrained the rebirth of liberal politics and social policy in the 1990s.

The 1992 Election   In the recession that followed the Gulf War, the Bush administration's passivity in the face of economic hardship cost the president virtually all the goodwill the U.S. military victory had generated. President Bush did sign legislation that raised the minimum wage, stiffened clean-air regulations, and protected disabled Americans against discrimination, but Bush championed one piece of legislation with the greatest consistency: a reduction in the capital gains tax, whose benefits would flow largely to the wealthy. Democratic prospects therefore looked bright in 1992 when Bill Clinton, the forty-six-year-old governor of Arkansas, emerged from the crowded primary field to become the party's presidential nominee. Clinton called himself a "New Democrat," and he was anything but a conventional liberal. He supported the death penalty, favored a work requirement for parents receiving welfare support for their children, and proved to be indifferent to organized labor. As the five-term governor of a conservative southern state, he accommodated himself to the interests of the region's economic elite. Within the Democratic Party, he allied himself with prodefense, free-trade conservatives. His wife, Hillary, was a partner in Arkansas's most powerful law firm and for a time a member of Wal-Mart's board of directors.

Although his political career had tilted toward the center, Clinton was in many ways a product of the 1960s. The son of a widowed nurse growing up in a small Arkansas town, he became a consummately ambitious student-politician. He identified with the civil rights movement in high school, and as a Rhodes Scholar at Oxford University, he took part in anti–Vietnam War demonstrations. Though not as radical as some activists in his generation, Clinton avoided the draft, experimented with marijuana (though he claimed he "never inhaled"), and campaigned for left-liberal Democrats, including George McGovern in 1972. After graduating from Yale Law School, he returned to Arkansas, where his large circle of friends helped him to win the governorship in 1978. He was just thirty-two, the youngest U.S. governor in four decades.

The 1992 campaign was intensely ideological and the first election contest since 1964 in which domestic political issues held center stage. George H. W. Bush stood for the status quo, but he faced a determined challenge from the Republican Party's right wing. In 1988, when he accepted the Republican nomination for president, Bush had pledged to the convention delegates, "Read my lips: no new taxes." But two years later, Bush broke that pledge to reach a budget deal with the Democrats that sought a much-needed reduction in the federal budget deficit, which had climbed to more than 3 percent of the entire gross domestic product. His pact with the Democrats infuriated conservative Republicans and sparked a primary challenge from Pat Buchanan, a former high-level aide to presidents Nixon

Time on His Mind

Although television viewers who watched the October 15, 1992, presidential debate might not have remembered the positions taken by the three major candidates on issues, many noted that George Bush twice consulted his watch during the proceedings. Some voters interpreted the gesture as an indication of President Bush's detachment from issues affecting Americans. Ron Edmonds/Associated Press.

and Reagan. A prominent New Right warrior, Buchanan was hostile to abortion and gay rights. He also exemplified a new strain of post–Cold War conservatism that rejected Wilsonian internationalism and trade liberalization. Buchanan therefore campaigned against the highly controversial North American Free Trade Agreement (NAFTA), which was supported by most multinational corporations and the leadership of both major political parties.

Billionaire computer services entrepreneur Ross Perot proved to be an even more significant political outsider. Although Perot had once been a conservative Republican and a right-wing backer of the Vietnam War, he spent $60 million of his own money to run an independent campaign for president as a commonsense "populist." Perot argued for more education and training and a kind of hands-on economic governance that was at odds with laissez-faire doctrine. "It's time to take out the trash and clean up the barn," he told TV audiences in his folksy, down-home manner. Perot therefore struck a nerve among both liberals and conservatives.

Bill Clinton and his running mate, Al Gore, an environmentally conscious senator from Tennessee, promised to break the budget gridlock in Washington and raise living standards by rebuilding the nation's infrastructure, restoring higher taxes on the rich, launching a federally funded jobs program for welfare recipients, and, perhaps most important, reorganizing the nation's entire health care system. Clinton saw himself in the tradition of Franklin Roosevelt and the New Deal. As the candidate promised to focus "like a laser" on the work-related anxieties of ordinary Americans, campaign strategist James Carville tacked a soon-to-be-famous note above his desk: "It's the economy, stupid!"

Clinton and Perot crushed Bush in the 1992 election. The Republican took only 37 percent of the popular vote, while the mercurial Texas businessman garnered a remarkable 19 percent — the best third-party showing since Theodore Roosevelt's Progressive Party campaign of 1912. Clinton and Gore won 43 percent, which translated into 370 electoral college votes, 100 more than they needed to win (Map 14.3). As usual, African Americans voted for the Democratic ticket by almost nine to one. And the proportion of women who voted for Clinton and Gore was some eight points higher than that of men. Poll after poll demonstrated that women were particularly likely to favor and benefit from the kind of social programs that Clinton and most Democrats advocated. Fewer women than men enjoyed employer-funded health insurance; conversely, children and their mothers were the prime beneficiaries of food stamps and Medicare. Because of their child-care needs and employment status, many women endorsed the programs to aid women and children that conservatives derisively called "the Nanny State." Liberals and feminists therefore labeled 1992 "the Year of the Woman." Female representation in the House of Representatives nearly doubled— from twenty-eight to forty-seven—and the number of women in the Senate tripled, from two to six. African Americans increased their number in the House to forty-one, an all-time record.

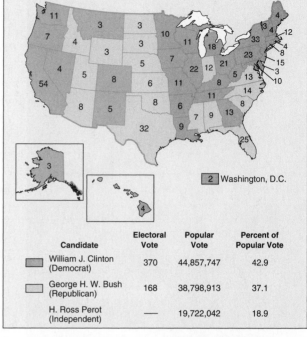

Candidate	Electoral Vote	Popular Vote	Percent of Popular Vote
William J. Clinton (Democrat)	370	44,857,747	42.9
George H. W. Bush (Republican)	168	38,798,913	37.1
H. Ross Perot (Independent)	—	19,722,042	18.9

MAP 14.3 Presidential Election of 1992

As a conservative Democrat, Bill Clinton and his running mate Al Gore won support in many Republican strongholds in the South and West to soundly defeat incumbent George H. W. Bush. H. Ross Perot won an impressive 19 percent of the popular vote but no electoral college votes.

The Clinton Administration   The political trajectory of the Clinton administration can be divided into two phases. Between late 1992 and the fall of 1994, Clinton and his advisers sought to implement an ambitious program of social reform that harked back to issues that had last been debated during the liberal heyday of the mid-1960s. But Clinton's failures, both personal and political, led to a sweeping Republican victory in the 1994 congressional elections, after which his administration sought little more than survival in office, even at the cost of a programmatic accommodation to congressional conservatives.

Clinton appointed an unusually diverse cabinet. He put African Americans in charge of the departments of Agriculture, Commerce, and Energy, heretofore the reserve of conservative white businessmen; and he made Janet Reno, a Florida law enforcement official, the first female attorney general. Hispanic politicians from Colorado and Texas took over stewardship of the Department of Transportation and the Department of Housing and Urban Development. Clinton named the liberal economist Laura Tyson as head of the Council of Economic Advisers and Robert Reich, a well-known critic of the nation's growing inequality of wealth, education, and wages, as secretary of labor. Not long after his inauguration, Clinton had the chance to appoint to the U.S. Supreme Court Ruth Bader Ginsberg, a pioneer in the legal fight against gender discrimination. And in 1994, he nominated

Stephen Breyer, an economic conservative whose social views tended toward liberalism, to the Supreme Court.

Early in 1993, Clinton signed social legislation that Bush would have vetoed: the Family and Medical Leave Act, which guaranteed workers their jobs when they returned from childbirth or a family medical emergency; the Brady bill, which regulated the sale of handguns; and the "Motor-Voter" bill, which made voter registration available through many state agencies, including those that issued driver's licenses. Clinton ended the Reagan era ban on abortion counseling in family-planning clinics and won new funding for more police and prisons, as well as a youth-oriented job corps.

But on the big economic issues, the Clinton administration demonstrated substantial continuity with the policies of his Republican predecessors. In his presidential campaign, Clinton emphasized the need for new social investment: in infrastructure, education, environmental technology, and health care. Once in office, however, he dropped the fight for large-scale infrastructure spending—and the jobs it would have created—when his more conservative advisers warned that the federal government needed to sacrifice social spending and emphasize deficit reduction. Clinton did push through Congress a substantial tax increase on wealthy individuals, which restored some of the tax progressivity that had been lost during the Reagan era. Otherwise, his administration remained fiscally conservative, which mollified Wall Street bond traders and generated the lower interest rates that Clinton's more orthodox advisers thought necessary for business investment and economic recovery.

Despite this accommodation of the fiscal conservatives within his own administration, Clinton proved to be a polarizing figure whose person and presidency evoked social and cultural controversies that had been smoldering since the Vietnam era. To many Americans, Clinton never seemed to be an entirely legitimate president, especially with regard to military issues. Although they maintained a facade of apolitical neutrality, many military officers were contemptuous of their commander-in-chief, who had avoided the draft during the Vietnam War. Therefore, Clinton's early effort to support gay rights within the armed services generated a storm of criticism, forcing his administration to promulgate a confusing "Don't Ask, Don't Tell" doctrine regarding the homosexual orientation of enlisted personnel.

When it came to the use of American military forces abroad, the Clinton administration was hesitant and inconsistent. For the first time in more than half a century, a powerful, isolationist current emerged within the ranks of both political parties. Clinton and his key advisers continued to support United Nations peacekeeping missions and NATO military interventions in unstable regions, but they sought to avoid, at almost all costs, the death of American troops in foreign combat. This first became clear in Somalia, where a U.N. humanitarian effort to end political anarchy and provide food and relief supplies had turned into a military conflict with regional warlords. When a firefight cost the lives of 17 U.S. servicemen in Somalia in October 1993, Clinton responded by withdrawing all American troops. In the former Yugoslavia, where Serbian and Croatian nationalists battled each other and the Serbs instigated a series of bloody "ethnic cleansing" campaigns against Bosnian Muslims, the Clinton administration refused to use sufficient military force to actually stop the massive bloodshed. In Bosnia, therefore, the United States and other Western powers stood aside while Serbian nationalists shelled Muslim Sarajevo for more than two years. Finally, in late 1995, after NATO bombed Serbian gun emplacements and tank units, the United States brokered a settlement that sent American and other U.N. troops to Bosnia as peacekeepers for a set of new, ethnically based mini-states. Three years later, the same dynamic played itself out in Kosovo, a Serbian province that was inhabited largely by ethnic Albanians.

Clinton considered his economic diplomacy of even greater importance than these skittish military interventions. His administration backed U.S. membership in NAFTA over the adamant opposition of organized labor and most Democratic liberals. NAFTA made it far easier for Canadian and U.S. corporations to buy low-cost goods from Mexico, sometimes produced by the American subsidiaries that had fled south to take advantage of the low wages there. Although the movement of jobs to Latin America did not amount to the "giant sucking sound" Ross Perot had predicted in the 1992 presidential campaign, NAFTA proved a powerful weapon in the hands of employers, who used the specter of a factory shutdown to forestall employee drives for higher pay and unionization. Some economists estimated that nearly one-quarter of all the recent growth in wage inequality derived from this downward pressure on U.S. wages.

Remnant of a Mass Murder The decision of the Clinton administration not to intervene in the genocide in Rwanda marked one of the worst foreign policy and moral failures of the administration. Here, the remains of a refugee mark the murder of more than 1,000 Tutsi victims by Hutu extremists in a parish church where they had taken shelter in Nyarubuye, Rwanda. The extermination of 800,000 Rwandans, mostly of Tutsi descent (10 percent of the African nation's population) during one hundred days in 1994 has the dubious distinction of being the fastest instance of mass murder in the twentieth century. Gilles Peress/Magnum.

Health Care Reform   In the most important legislative battle of his administration, Clinton fought to establish a system of universal health care. More than 20 percent of all Americans under the age of sixty-five had no insured access to a doctor. Moreover, health care costs were rising at twice the level of inflation, and the United States was spending more of its total income, 14 percent, on medical care than any other nation. America's fragmented, employment-based commercial health insurance system created a paperwork nightmare. A Toronto hospital administrator who was familiar with Canada's "single-payer" system of universal coverage (the government paid doctors and hospitals from tax revenues) found U.S. health care costs bloated by "overwhelming duplication of bureaucracies working in dozens of insurance companies, no two of which have the same forms or even the same coverage."

The U.S. health insurance system raised contentious political and social issues. During the 1980s, management efforts to trim health insurance costs precipitated more than 80 percent of all strikes that took place in the United States. The United Mine Workers (UMW) of America fought the most spectacular of these struggles in 1989 — an eleven-month siege of the Pittston Coal Company — in defense of miners' health care benefits and pension rights. Police arrested some 3,000 miners and UMW supporters during a campaign that resurrected the sit-down tactics and mass demonstrations that had been characteristic of the industrial union movement during the Great Depression.

President Clinton and his wife, Hillary, whom he put in charge of the health care project, rejected a Canadian-style single-payer system. Although recognizing its economic efficiency and political popularity, they argued that health care reform had to be built on the existing system of employer-paid benefits and private insurance. The Clinton plan would have regulated insurance costs, allowing the government to mandate employers to provide health insurance for all their employees.

But the Clintons miscalculated. American capitalism had transformed itself dramatically since the last era of health care reform in the 1960s (when Medicaid and Medicare became law), and low-wage, low-benefit companies in the expanding service sector, especially restaurants and retailers, bitterly resisted employer health care mandates. In addition, almost all the smaller insurance companies, which sought the youngest and least risky clients, assailed the plan. These companies bankrolled a widely viewed set of television commercials that pointed to the complexity and regulatory burden that were inherent in the Clinton plan. Trade unions strongly backed the Clinton plan, but after more than two decades of waning strength, organized labor commanded far less political influence than it had when Congress had enacted Medicare three decades earlier.

Indeed, the fate of the Clintons' plan turned into a referendum on the capacity of the state to resolve social problems. Their proposed reforms would have instituted a new level of social citizenship, but conservatives feared such an entitlement, both because of the expense and because of the legitimacy it conferred on governmental activism. The crisis of confidence in all levels of government greatly strengthened the right-wing critique. In the 1960s, more than 60 percent of all Americans trusted the federal

"I'm a Daughter of Mother Jones #14"

The active participation of the wives and daughters of striking miners was crucial in the United Mine Workers' 1990 victory over the Pittston Coal Company. When strikers were forced by a court-ordered injunction to stop picketing, a new organization, the Daughters of Mother Jones, took up the challenge. In a television documentary on the strike, several of the organization's members described their tactics and why they embraced Mother Jones, the fiery labor organizer who stood with the West Virginia miners during their epic struggles to unionize earlier in the century.

DELLA MULINS: . . . I joined the [UMW's] Ladies Auxiliary and we got out and we let the community be aware of what was coming. We delivered posters to stores saying "This Establishment Supports the UMW." We went to churches and got them involved. We went to the stores, we even went to doctors and clinics. So when the strike came down the community already knew what they were up against.

SHIRLEY JOHNSON: I was a housewife. I didn't get out and get into nothin' until this. You learn a lot about different things if you're in a union—all the injustice and causes there are in this world. I say get out and get involved in 'em.

COSBY TOTTEN: I used to work in the coalmines and I got laid off and I heard that Pittson Coal Company had taken its health care away from the elderly workers. My first reaction was: they can't do that, can they? But they did and it made me angry so I got involved in this struggle. . . . Besides bein' on up there in front of the office picketing, we did take over the corporation office for 32 hours—we had fun.

BRENDA WALLACE: We went in at 9:00 one morning and didn't come out till 4:00 the next evening. When one of the women from the office came in and said, "Is this a sit-in?" we didn't say anything, we just started singin'.

EDNA SAULS: We didn't tell our names when we went into the Pittston building, 'Cause we had in mind that if we were arrested we'd tell 'em we were Daughters of Mother Jones. There were 39 women who went in there and we had numbers. I was #14. Reporters would ask me, "What's your name?" and I'd say, "I'm Daughter of Mother Jones #14." Lots of reporters didn't even know who she was. . . .

CATHERINE TOMPA: I truly believe in fightin' for what you believe in. If it's right fight for it, 'cause that's the only way you're gonna win anymore, is to fight. And I believe this old sayin' of Mother Jones, "Pray for the dead and fight like hell for the living."

Kathy Scott et al., producer, *Drawing the Line at Pittston*, Paper Tiger TV, 1990.

Swearing-in on Smoking

In the 1990s, new evidence about cigarette smoking's contribution to rising rates of lung cancer prompted a public outcry against American tobacco companies. In particular, anti-smoking advocates protested their manipulation of nicotine levels to keep smokers addicted and their targeting of young adults in advertising. Despite incontrovertible scientific evidence to the contrary, the CEOs of the nation's seven largest cigarette companies, at an April 1994 House Energy and Commerce Subcommittee hearing, testified under oath that they did not believe nicotine was addictive. In 1998, in the face of class-action suits lodged by 46 state attorneys-general to cover increased smoking-related health care costs, tobacco companies agreed to restrict marketing, reveal previously secret trade documents, and pay state governments $206 billion to cover medical costs and finance education campaigns to deter tobacco use. John Duricka, Associated Press.

government. Thirty years later, after Vietnam, Watergate, and three severe recessions, fewer than half that many thought as well of their national governing institutions.

By August 1994, when the Clinton health plan died in Congress, even many Democrats had abandoned the ambitious effort to restructure one-seventh of the nation's economy. Health care inflation did moderate in the mid-1990s, both because of the regulatory scare and because of the rapid rise of health maintenance organizations, which had eclipsed hospitals and individual physicians as primary providers of medical services. But health insurance remained linked primarily to employment, which meant that the twenty-first-century rise in unemployment and health care inflation would strand millions of additional citizens without medical insurance.

Congressional Conservatives Go to Battle   The collapse of the Clinton health care initiative generated a large vacuum in American politics, which a reinvigorated Republican Party promptly filled. With a Democrat as president for the first time in twelve years, the leading conservative media and political spokesmen became more strident and more ideological. In a 1994 election manifesto, Georgia congressman Newt Gingrich codified the broad right-wing militant attacks on "feminazis," "Washington insiders," and "political correctness" into the "Contract with America," which sought to unify ideologically scores of Republican congressional campaigns. Gingrich and other GOP conservatives avoided divisive cultural issues such as abortion rights and school prayer, calling instead for large reductions in federal social spending, congressional term limits, partial privatization of Medicare

and public education, the elimination of five cabinet departments, and a new set of tax cuts.

Although many voters were apparently unaware of Gingrich's Contract with America during the 1994 elections, liberals were nonetheless dispirited during the campaign. Labor did not mobilize its troops, and among women, turnout was the lowest it had been in twenty years. The Republicans captured control of both the House and Senate for the first time in forty years, won several governorships, and gained ground in most state legislatures. In the House of Representatives, the elections sent to Washington a large, unified class of ideologically right-wing GOP freshmen. As the newly chosen speaker, Gingrich embodied a dramatic transformation within the Republican Party, whose legislative leadership now shifted from the old Midwest to the Deep South.

The resurgence of the Republican Party was made possible in large measure by the dramatic resurgence of conservative, evangelical religious sentiment and organization across America. Most members of the Religious Right simply advocated their beliefs and values while continuing to participate in civic life, but some fundamentalist sects sought to remove themselves entirely from the temptations, corruptions, and regulations of contemporary American society. One such Christian group, the Branch Davidian cult and their charismatic leader, David Koresh, occupied a compound near Waco, Texas, in the early 1990s. When U.S. Bureau of Alcohol, Tobacco, and Firearms (ATF) agents sought, in early 1993, to arrest the Branch Davidians, who, they suspected, possessed illegal firearms, at their Waco compound, the Branch Davidians offered armed resistance. In the battle that followed, four ATF agents were shot and killed. After a fifty-one-

Massacre
Students flee Columbine High School in Littleton, Colorado, after two teenagers armed with automatic weapons and explosives murdered twelve of their classmates and a teacher before committing suicide. The April 1999 incident highlighted the fearful toll of the estimated two hundred million guns in circulation in the United States, particularly their impact as a major "health problem" for young Americans. According to the Centers for Disease Control and Prevention, 4,643 children and teenagers were killed with guns in 1996 (including 1,309 suicides and 468 unintentional shootings). The *Journal of the American Medical Association* estimated that the cost of medical care for gun-related injuries amounted to $4 billion in 1995 alone. Since 1960, a million people have died from gunshots in the United States. Corbis/AFP.

"Contract with America"

In the 1994 elections, conservative Republican Congressman Newt Gingrich, who would subsequently become speaker of the U.S. House of Representatives, sought to unify the Republicans around an election manifesto, "the Contract with America," that aimed to dismantle the New Deal and the Great Society. His efforts produced government gridlock but not the sweeping right-wing change that he had forecast. In this speech, Gingrich provides the ideological framework for the Republican program.

Once you accept the premise we're going to go in this direction—we're going to replace the welfare state, we're going to reassert American civilization, we're going to develop the opportunity society, we're going to move into the information age, we're going to compete in the world market, and we're going to reassert civic responsibility—then anybody who's willing to work within that framework is someone we want to have a total dialogue with, and we want to accept good ideas from everybody who agrees on the general direction. But we don't particularly want to have a single ounce of compromise with those who still believe that they can somehow improve and prop up and make work a bureaucratic welfare state and a counterculture set of values which are literally killing the poor. . . .

I believe we should have a conscious strategy of dramatically increasing private charities. I believe that private charities are more effective, are less expensive, and are better for the people they're helping. I want to make the following case, and I'm prepared to fight this out in virtually any arena that we can arrange. There is an enormous moral burden, but not on those of us who would replace the welfare state. There is an enormous moral burden on those who would keep the poor trapped in public systems that are destroying them. The burden of destroying the poor is on the left. It is the left which traps the poor in public housing projects where no one goes to work. It is the left which traps the poor in public school buildings in the inner city where virtually no one educates. It is the left which keeps the poor in neighborhoods where they insist on putting violent criminals back on the street to prey upon the innocent. And it is the left which has designed a tax code and a welfare code which destroy families. . . .

[T]he pursuit of happiness implies active engagement. Pursuit comes from an active verb, to pursue. It doesn't suggest pursuit stamps, a Department of Happiness, or happiness therapy; nor does it guarantee final result. It doesn't say the achievement of happiness; it says the pursuit. And, of course, it was intimately bound up in freedom and private property because in the original wording, it was the right to possess, the pursuit of possession of property, not the pursuit of happiness.

"What the Elections Mean to Conservatives" by Newt Gingrich, Heritage Foundation Lecture #510, December 14, 1994 (http://www.heritage.org/Research/GovernmentReform/HL510.cfm).

day standoff, Attorney General Janet Reno approved a new assault on the compound. But instead of a firefight, government agents triggered a conflagration and mass suicide that killed 86 people in the compound, including 25 children.

For many Americans on the extreme right, the fiasco at Waco transformed Koresh into a martyr who had defended both gun ownership and Christian separatism. An anti-Semitic, antiblack militia movement that was intensely hostile to the authority of the federal government emerged in some economically hard-pressed rural areas. The nation became acutely aware of such widespread sentiment on April 19, 1995, precisely two years after the Waco tragedy, when Timothy McVeigh and Terry Nichols, who had contact with right-wing militias, exploded a fertilizer truck bomb in front of the Murrah Federal Building in Oklahoma City, killing 168 people. At the time, it was the most costly terrorist attack on U.S. soil.

Clinton's hopes at the outset of his presidency for carefully orchestrated reform were over. He managed a successful rearguard defense of his presidency after 1994, but only by shifting his politics to accommodate Republican conservatives. The president quickly distanced himself from the remaining liberals in Congress, later announcing, in his 1996 State of the Union address, "The era of big government is over." He signed into law a drastic revision of U.S. welfare law that ended the federal government's sixty-year commitment to families with dependent children. Henceforth, caregivers—most of whom were young mothers—would be eligible during their entire lifetime for only five years of federal benefits. Many states

Male Bonding
A Promise Keepers gathering in June 1996 attracted 60,000 men to the Charlotte Motor Speedway in Concord, North Carolina. During the 1990s, the predominantly white male evangelical Protestant organization filled scores of raceways and stadiums to preach the return of male authority and responsibility within the Christian family.
Peter A. Harris/Associated Press.

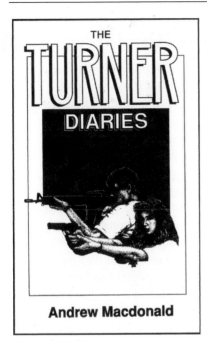

Andrew Macdonald

Instruction Manual

A novel called *The Turner Diaries* was reputed to be the inspiration for the Oklahoma City bombing. Written by American Nazi Andrew Macdonald in 1978 and widely distributed via mail order and sales at gun shows, the book depicted in gruesome detail a white supremacist insurrection against the U.S. government — including the bombing of federal buildings in Washington, D.C., and Houston — and the extermination of the nation's Jews and people of color. Barricade Books, Inc.

soon enacted even more restrictive guidelines. The government provided no new monies for child care or job training yet expected most welfare recipients to get a job in the private sector, a task that the boom in fast-food and other service-sector employment eased in the late 1990s. Conservatives claimed that this reform would break the welfare "cycle of dependency."

Gingrich Republicanism had its echo in California, where voters enacted a state ballot initiative in 1994 curbing the rights of illegal immigrants to access vital social services. Proposition 187 denied unlawful residents of the United States access to prenatal and childbirth services, child welfare, public education, and non-emergency health care. Its passage, which reflected the severity of the economic downturn in California, was a belated effect of a 1978 ballot proposition that had frozen most property taxes, costing local government more than $200 billion in badly needed revenue. (California schools, once among the best funded in the country, had deteriorated sharply, to quality levels that had historically been characteristic of the far poorer South.) In a pattern reaching back to the anti-Asian movements of the late nineteenth and early twentieth centuries, conservatives laid the blame for economic insecurity on nonwhite immigrants. An infamous TV spot that was broadcast during the 1994 campaign showed Mexican illegal immigrants rushing through a San Diego border checkpoint, with the ominous voiceover: "They keep coming." Although federal courts overturned the statute, the controversy over immigration would continue to polarize California, and eventually national, politics.

Persistence of Racial Divisions   America's political divisions were matched by growing racial tensions that flared anew in the second half of the decade. The wall of mutual distrust that had long existed between black city dwellers and the police, revealed so starkly during the Rodney King beating and the bloody Los Angeles riot that followed, grew throughout the 1990s. These tensions became visible to tens of millions of Americans in 1995 when police arrested the black former football star and sports commentator O. J. Simpson after the stabbing murder of his ex-wife Nicole and her friend Ronald Goldman, both of whom were white. Simpson's televised trial, which saturated the airwaves and print media and dominated everyday conversation for nine months, turned into an international media extravaganza. His high-powered defense team exploited America's racial divide, charging detectives who investigated the murder with racism and portraying their client as the victim of a biased system of justice. Sixty percent of all African Americans thought Simpson innocent, while 75 percent of

"Working for My Benefits": Brenda Steward Describes the Work Experience Program

During the 1960s and 1970s, welfare reform movements from the left sought to increase benefits and expand community power, but in 1996, critics from the right passed the federal Welfare Reform Act, restricting welfare benefits. Brenda Steward, a New York City Work Experience Program (WEP) worker, helped to organize her fellow welfare recipients to demand improvements to the "workfare" program. Workfare required welfare recipients to "pay off" their welfare benefits by working menial jobs for the city at well below minimum wage. Participants in the program did not receive wages, only their welfare benefits. In some cases, they did the work of full-time civil servant workers but without basic rights such as the right to unionize.

STEWARD: I've been involved in the WEP Program for a little over two years. . . . I was laid off from my former job. I was working with a community-based organization with teenagers and young adults, getting them work experience and also allowing them to obtain their GED. And through budget cuts they were forced to lay me off. I was forced to go onto the public assistance roll and through that they said it was mandatory that we work for our benefits.

They placed me in the Department of Social Services, in one of the IS Centers which is the Income Support Center. And I was doing clerical work there. . . . The majority of the people were on staff being paid a full salary and I worked alongside of those staff people. But after I was there for a few months, the director of the center was very pleased with the work that I was doing. I worked with a group of social workers doing filing, answering phones and what they called the Winro Report, which is a statistical report of recertification. Because there was such a backlog in our Income Support Center, they asked me to take on the role of doing just the Winro Report. In a normal setting, if I were on staff, they would have considered that a promotion, something that is generally handled by a supervisor or maybe an office manager. In my case I was just working for my benefits.

No change in salary, no change in my position. When I went into the WEP Program I already had the skills that I was doing there, so they didn't really give me that particular job skill. I brought the skill with me. After being there for two years, we were told that our names would be submitted to personnel so that we could possibly be hired in those positions since we were already working. Rather than train somebody else for that position, let us work in those positions and put us on staff for full salary. Well my name was submitted over a year ago and I haven't had a response from anybody as of yet.

Interviewed by Janine Jackson, 1996. Courtesy of *Labor at the Crossroads*.

Digital Manipulation

The avalanche of news coverage of the O. J. Simpson case provoked criticism of the press's preoccupation with celebrity and sensation. The case also sparked controversy over the news media's manipulation of visual information, abetted by the new tool of digital imaging. The June 27, 1994, cover of *Time* magazine featured Simpson's police "mug shot." The *Time* picture seemed unremarkable until it was compared to the same week's cover of *Newsweek*, which also displayed the police photograph. In contrast to *Newsweek*'s unretouched cover (shown here), *Time* had digitally darkened Simpson's face to lend the image greater drama and, some commentators suggested, menace. Los Angeles Police Department/ *Newsweek*, June 27, 1994. Used by permission.

whites believed him to be guilty. His acquittal in October 1995 by a jury of nine blacks, two whites, and one Hispanic revealed once again the pervasive racial attitudes that constitute the diverging social and legal realities of white and black Americans.

The success of the 1996 "Million Man March" seemed to confirm the continuing centrality of race and gender—as opposed to class or politics—as a defining identity for huge numbers of African Americans. Answering the call of the Black Muslim leader Louis Farrakhan, hundreds of thousands of African American men assembled peacefully on the Mall in Washington, D.C., to affirm their solidarity and dignity. Leaders of the march, the largest convocation of African Americans since the 1963 March on Washington headed by Dr. Martin Luther King, Jr., made no demands on the government but implored black men to reclaim the moral and economic leadership of the black community and black family.

In the same year as the Million Man March, however, voters in the nation's largest state enacted the California Civil Rights Initiative, which banned affirmative action at the University of California and in state agencies, further intensifying racial divisions and hostilities between white and black Americans. Most university administrators and corporate executives strongly backed affirmative action guidelines. They saw diversity as essential to the legitimacy and effectiveness of their businesses in a multiracial society. An exhaustive study by two former Ivy League college presidents demonstrated that African American students who were admitted under affirmative action guidelines graduated as readily as any other group of students. They then went on to careers in the professions, government, and business in proportions even greater than that of their white peers. But affirmative action remained highly controversial in the United States in the mid-1990s. Most conservatives argued that it contravened the idea of a color-blind society, of a social order based on merit, and that the civil rights laws of the 1960s had successfully ended most racism, eliminating the necessity for such policies. Indeed, the conflict over affirmative action turned into an argument over the degree to which racism remained a reality within American politics and society.

Polarization and Stalemate

In the years just before and immediately after the turn of the millennium, American politics became highly polarized. A plurality of all Americans supported President Clinton, sought a separation of church and state, favored abortion rights, and looked to the government to regulate business and tax the wealthy. But free trade, affirmative action, and foreign policy issues, especially those involving the rights of Palestinians and Israel's settlement policy on the West Bank of the Jordan River, divided the Democrats. In contrast, the Republicans formed an increasingly unified political, cultural, and religious identity. By the late 1990s, with a "new economy" boom in full swing, big corporations became increasingly hostile to government taxes and regulations. Their agenda won the support of a politicized and rapidly growing evangelical Protestant community, which now conflated liberalism, secularism, progressive taxes, and federal interest in social welfare with gay rights, out-of-wedlock children, hostility to Christianity, and a subversion of patriotic values. Bitter division over such issues characterized both the impeachment of President Clinton late in 1998 and the presidential campaign and disputed election of 2000.

Impeachment Politics   In the 1996 election, Clinton and Gore ran a relatively muted, apolitical campaign. Running against Robert Dole, a veteran GOP senator from Kansas, they had little trouble winning reelection, albeit with only 49 percent of the popular vote. (Ross Perot took only 8 percent this time.) Voter turnout fell to its lowest level since 1924. But the election provided a political coming of age for one group of voters. The Latino electorate, which had increased substantially, swung sharply to the Democrats. Although this rapidly growing population had given Ronald Reagan more than 40 percent of their vote, many Latinos were furious with the GOP's anti-immigrant politics. In both 1996 and 1998, their wholesale shift into the Democratic column locked up California for Clinton and his party.

Clinton's reelection did nothing to ameliorate conservative hostility to his presidency and his person. The U.S. Constitution provides for the removal of a sitting president if the House of Representatives, by a majority vote, impeaches (charges) and the U.S. Senate, by a two-thirds vote, convicts the president of "high crimes and misdemeanors." Three presidents have faced such a quasi-judicial drama. In 1867, the politics of Reconstruction stood at the heart of Andrew Johnson's Senate trial; in 1974, Richard Nixon resigned when the House seemed certain to impeach him for abuse of presidential power during Watergate; and in December 1998, the House impeached Bill Clinton on charges of perjury and obstruction of justice. The constitutional crisis that enveloped Clinton hinged not on his public statecraft, but on his character and the consequences of his personal

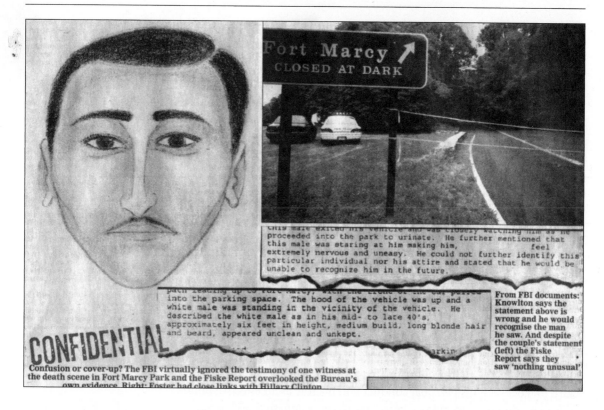

Fort Marcy
CLOSED AT DARK

...this male exited his vehicle and was closely watching him as he proceeded into the park to urinate. He further mentioned that this male was staring at him making him,   feel extremely nervous and uneasy. He could not further identify this particular individual nor his attire and stated that he would be unable to recognize him in the future.

...path leading up to Fort Marcy, when the bottom of the car parked into the parking space. The hood of the vehicle was up and a white male was standing in the vicinity of the vehicle. He described the white male as in his mid- to late 40's, approximately six feet in height, medium build, long blonde hair and beard, appeared unclean and unkept.

From FBI documents: Knowlton says the statement above is wrong and he would recognise the man he saw. And despite the couple's statement (left) the Fiske Report says they saw 'nothing unusual'

CONFIDENTIAL

Confusion or cover-up? The FBI virtually ignored the testimony of one witness at the death scene in Fort Marcy Park and the Fiske Report overlooked the Bureau's own evidence. Right: Foster had close links with Hillary Clinton

Assassin Fantasies

In an effort to undermine Clinton's credibility, some critics indulged in outlandish attacks against the administration, even accusing it of conspiracy and assassination. The 1993 death of Deputy White House Counsel Vincent Foster in Fort Marcy Park, Virginia, for example, was ruled a suicide by independent counsel Robert Fiske, but the tabloid press and right-wing print and Internet publications almost immediately began issuing reports of an official coverup to suppress evidence of foul play deriving from Foster's knowledge about Whitewater. *London Sunday Telegraph*, October 23, 1995. Used by permission.

conduct. To conservatives, President Clinton was an intensely polarizing figure. He had appropriated many Republican issues, such as a balanced budget, welfare reform, and tough-on-crime measures to expand the death penalty and put more police on the street. At the same time, he seemed to embody the conservative's view of the lax social and cultural values of the 1960s, including an unconstrained sexuality and freewheeling capacity to spin the truth in his personal and business affairs.

Clinton's legal and political troubles began in 1994, when Attorney General Reno appointed an independent counsel to investigate questionable real estate investments that Bill and Hillary Clinton had made in 1978 in what became known as "Whitewater." Although several of the president's earlier associates were eventually jailed in connection with these Arkansas land dealings, Clinton and his wife never faced criminal charges. However, four years later, another independent counsel, Kenneth Starr, an aggressive conservative former judge, transformed the Whitewater investigation into a probe of Clinton's sexual conduct and the truthfulness of his testimony on this subject.

In 1995 and 1996, President Clinton had an affair with Monica Lewinsky, a twenty-two-year-old White House intern. This episodic sexual relationship was not itself illegal, but lying about it under oath or attempting to convince others to do so would constitute perjury and obstruction of justice. Clinton might well have done so when Lewinsky and he gave depositions in a sexual harassment suit. Clinton damaged his credibility when, in January 1998, he publicly and vehemently denied having had sex with Lewinsky and then, six months later, admitted to an "inappropriate relationship" with Lewinsky before a grand jury.

The furor over the Lewinsky affair revealed deep national divisions and revived the culture wars that had characterized public debate in the late 1980s and early 1990s. To those who sought the president's impeachment and removal from office, Clinton's mendacity about the affair spoke for itself. His recklessness shamed the nation, subverted its legal institutions, and proved him unfit for office. Clinton seemed to embody all that conservative moralists found intolerable in contemporary American life. Representative Tom DeLay of Texas, one of the most militant of the conservative Republicans, thought the impeachment fight "a debate about relativism versus absolute truth." House Judiciary Committee chairman Henry Hyde wondered whether, "after this culture war is over that we are engaged in, an America will survive that's worth fighting to defend."

Clinton's supporters did not defend his sexual escapades or the lies he told about them. But they thought impeachment and removal from office a punishment that was disproportionate to his transgressions. They drew a sharp line between his personal conduct and his role as an effective political leader. Moreover, to many Clinton partisans, Kenneth Starr's massive, intrusive investigative effort was, in the words of Hillary Clinton, part of "a vast right-wing conspiracy" that represented an attempt by the Republican Right to persecute Clinton and "criminalize" normal political debate.

Nearly two-thirds of all Americans solidly backed Clinton's continuation in the White House, even as they repudiated his private conduct. The president's strong approval ratings were bolstered by steady economic growth, low unemployment, and his popularity as a defender of Social Security, public education, and racial reconciliation. African Americans, white women, and liberal Democrats fervently supported Clinton, in part because they found nothing particularly dreadful in lying about extramarital relationships and in part because of the prominent role played by conservative white southerners in the impeachment investigation. Therefore, Clinton partisans applauded when the Democrats recaptured the California statehouse and gained five congressional seats during the 1998 midterm elections, a remarkable showing for the party that held the White House. Taking responsibility for the GOP setback, Newt Gingrich resigned both his speakership and his seat in the House. (Ironically, it was later revealed that Gingrich was having an extramarital affair with a young assistant while actively criticizing Clinton's similar behavior in the midst of the impeachment crisis.)

But conservative Republicans still controlled both houses of Congress, and they doggedly persisted in their effort to oust the president. By a narrow partisan majority, the House of Representatives approved four articles of impeachment against Clinton on December 18, 1998. But the House impeachment managers could not convince two-thirds of the Senate to follow suit; they acquitted the president on February 12, 1999. For conservative Republicans, the abortive prosecution of the president constituted a sharp political setback, but their success in tarnishing the Clinton persona was sufficient to sideline him during the presidential election season that was about to unfold.

The 2000 Election   Despite Clinton's difficulties, the Democrats had a lot going for them in 2000. A seven-year economic boom had pushed the stock market to new highs and lowered unemployment to levels that had not been seen since the prosperous 1960s. The nation was at peace, and the federal budget actually ran a surplus for the first time in three decades. Vice President Al Gore, whom the Democrats chose at their Los Angeles convention, represented continuity—perhaps too much so given Clinton's tarnished persona. Gore therefore selected as his running mate Senator Joseph Lieberman, a centrist Democrat from Connecticut, who had been one of the few Democrats to publicly chastise Clinton during the Lewinsky affair.

Most Republican leaders threw their support behind Texas Governor George W. Bush, the oldest son of the former president. Bush had avoided going to Vietnam by serving in the Texas Air National Guard. He had then followed his father into the Texas oil business but proved to be most successful as the politically well-connected owner of the Texas Rangers baseball team. He was more authentically Texan than his patrician father had been, and in the late 1970s, he had experienced a religious conversion that put him at ease and at one with evangelical Christians.

Surrounding himself with advisers from his father's administration, candidate Bush represented a kind of restoration: he would rescind the Clinton tax increases, restore a traditional sense of honor to the White House, and avoid humanitarian interventions abroad. Although he had to fight his way through the early primaries against Vietnam War hero John McCain, who represented Arizona in the U.S. Senate, Bush captured the Republican nomination because of staunch support from two key constituencies. He had the overwhelming support of corporate America, in particular the oil industry, whose allegiance he confirmed by selecting as his running mate Richard Cheney, the former Reagan era defense secretary and Wyoming congressman, who had most recently been CEO of Halliburton, an international oil services and construction conglomerate. And Bush had the passionate endorsement of Protestant evangelicals, whose social and cultural infrastructure—a growing set of radio and television networks;

huge megachurches that functioned as social and educational centers for busy suburbanites; and a vigorous, well-funded network of think tanks and advocacy groups—made them a potent and organic part of the Republican political universe.

But George Bush could not win a majority of American voters for his program. Late in the 2000 election season, Al Gore's adoption of a rhetorical populism revitalized his labor and liberal base, while on the left, the consumer advocate Ralph Nader, running as an independent, denounced corporate influence in both parties, thereby winning 2.7 percent of the national vote. Bush accommodated this Democratic and liberal majority by showcasing African American and Latino speakers at the Republican convention and then by asserting a Republican "compassionate conservatism" that endorsed higher educational standards in the public schools and favored subsidizing the cost, but not controlling the price, of medicine for the elderly.

On November 4, 2000, Gore won the national popular ballot by more than half a million votes, but the electoral college count—and the presidency—would be determined by who won Florida, with its crucial twenty-five electoral votes (Map 14.4). The television networks mistakenly gave Florida to Bush on election night, but the GOP margin, fewer than one thousand votes out of some six million ballots cast, was far too close to be decisive. As all eyes focused on a required recount, it became clear that the electoral process, in Florida and elsewhere, was deeply flawed. The highly partisan and constitutionally questionable set of politics that had been on display during the impeachment crisis now spilled over into bitter wrangling that engulfed the election outcome. Even before the election, the Florida Republicans who controlled most state offices purged tens of thousands of likely Democratic voters from the rolls. In Palm Beach County, a poorly designed ballot led several thousand Gore supporters to vote inadvertently for the right-winger, Pat Buchanan, who was also running for president. In other Florida counties, especially those with lots of poor and African American voters, antiquated vote-counting machines threw out thousands of ballots on which the paper tabs, called "chads," were not fully punched out.

Gore's lawyers demanded a hand count of these rejected ballots, but an even more determined set of Bush attorneys filed suit to halt the recounts. For thirty-seven days, no one knew who would be the next president. Florida secretary of state Katherine Harris, who had cochaired Bush's Florida campaign, certified a Bush victory in the state ballot, but on December 8, the Florida Supreme Court ordered a recount of all ballots that the state's voting machines had thrown out. The issue finally went to the U.S. Supreme Court, which ruled in a partisan five-to-four decision on December 12 that the recounts should stop. George W. Bush was made president by court decision.

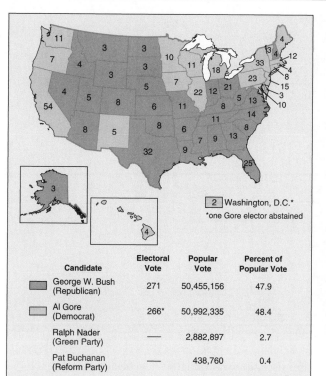

Candidate	Electoral Vote	Popular Vote	Percent of Popular Vote
George W. Bush (Republican)	271	50,455,156	47.9
Al Gore (Democrat)	266*	50,992,335	48.4
Ralph Nader (Green Party)	—	2,882,897	2.7
Pat Buchanan (Reform Party)	—	438,760	0.4

2 Washington, D.C.*
*one Gore elector abstained

MAP 14.4 Presidential Election of 2000

Al Gore won the popular vote and, as this map reveals, had strong support across the country. The election was decided only after the Supreme Court ruled against a recount in Florida, thus awarding that state's twenty-five electoral votes to George Bush and giving him a four-vote lead in the electoral college.

The Early Days of the George W. Bush Administration Although the Republicans had hardly won a mandate either in the general election or in Congress, where the Senate was divided 50-50, the Bush administration quickly signaled that it would govern from the right in order to push forward its ambitious program of tax reductions and regulatory reform at home, combined with nationalist unilateralism abroad. Bush appointed Colin Powell, the widely respected former head of the Joint Chiefs of Staff, as the nation's first African American secretary of state and put a traditional business conservative, Paul O'Neill, at the Treasury. But other appointments tilted much farther to the right. His national security adviser, Condoleezza Rice of Stanford University, also an African American, was a tough nationalist conservative who had served under Ronald Reagan. Secretary of Defense Donald Rumsfeld, who had held the same post under President Ford, surrounded himself with foreign policy hawks. Attorney General John Ashcroft and chief political adviser Karl Rove, both highly politicized evangelicals, sought to enhance and expand the linkages between the GOP and conservative Protestants and Catholics.

President Bush used all his powers to push social and economic policy to the right. Early in 2001, he rescinded regulations that had been approved by President Clinton that would have better protected workers from repetitive motion injuries. He set up a White House office to funnel federal funds to religious organizations that provided social services, and he greatly restricted government-funded medical research that used the stem cells that were produced during an early stage of human embryo development. And he supported a voucher program by which the federal government would pay a part of the tuition of students who wanted to attend private or religious schools.

While these ideologically charged initiatives served to consolidate Bush's evangelical base, the president placed a massive tax reduction for business and the wealthy at the top of his domestic agenda. In 2001, he asked for a package of tax breaks for the wealthy, totaling $1.6 trillion over ten years. The Senate balked, but Congress gave the president $1.35 billion nevertheless.

Butterfly Ballot

The confusing design of the punch-card ballot used in Florida's Palm Beach County on Election Day, 2000, led many voters to mistakenly choose conservative Reform Party candidate Patrick Buchanan when they intended to vote for Democratic candidate Al Gore. Gary I. Rothstein/Associated Press.

When it came to foreign policy, the Bush administration was unilateralist to a far greater degree than that of any recent president, including his father and Ronald Reagan. The new administration revived work on the "Star Wars" antimissile system that had first been proposed by Reagan; it requested funds for a new generation of tactical nuclear weapons; and it allowed the U.S.-Russian Anti-Ballistic Missile Treaty to lapse. In the Middle East, Bush administration hawks tacitly endorsed the Israeli settlement program on the West Bank and stepped up pressure against Iran, which had inaugurated its own nuclear program. The Bush administration was suspicious of the United Nations and refused to join its International Criminal Court.

The president rejected the view, endorsed by most nations and almost all scientists, that carbon dioxide emissions from power plants and motor vehicles were responsible for the global "greenhouse effect" that was warming the earth's atmosphere. The administration therefore rejected domestic conservation measures and worked closely with oil and chemical companies to reduce costly environmental regulations. Vice President Cheney dismissed conservation measures as but a "sign of personal virtue" that had no serious role in "a sound comprehensive energy policy." Alone among 178 nations, the United States refused to sign the Kyoto Treaty that addressed global warming by setting emission standards for industrialized nations. Then the Bush administration boycotted a conference in Bonn that had been called specifically to meet U.S. objections.

Cover-Up

Conservative Attorney General John Ashcroft, unhappy with press photographs showing him in front of the seminude *Spirit of Justice*, one of two statues adorning the podium in the Department of Justice's Great Hall, allocated $8,000 for the purchase of curtains to hang over the offending aluminum Art Deco sculpture. Kamenko Pajic/Associated Press.

Conclusion: America's Political Rift

The boldness and early success of the Bush agenda reflected the ideological and political coherence of American conservatism at the dawn of the twenty-first century. But it had not won over a majority of Americans; nor was it popular abroad. By the late summer of 2001, the stalemate that had gripped U.S. politics in the late Clinton years seemed pervasive once again. The Republicans lost their control of the Senate when a maverick GOP Vermonter declared himself an independent. Bush's approval rating in the polls stood at a remarkably low 50 percent; indeed, the very legitimacy of his presidency remained in question as the bright early days of September 2001 unfolded. But all that was about to change — and in the most dramatic and tragic fashion.

The Years in Review

1980
- Striking workers in Poland organize Solidarity, which challenges Communist rule.

1981
- IBM licenses the MS-DOS operating system, owned by a small Seattle company called Microsoft, for its line of personal computers.

1988
- Soviet leader Mikhail Gorbachev introduces *perestroika* and *glasnost* reforms. Three years later, the Communist Party collapses.
- Republican vice president George H. W. Bush defeats Michael Dukakis for the presidency.

1989
- Germans pour through the Berlin Wall, signaling the end of Communism in Eastern Europe.

- The Chinese regime crushes a student demonstration in Beijing's Tiananmen Square.
- The United Mine Workers of America launches an eleven-month strike against the Pittston Coal Company, winning a new contract the following year.

1990
- President Bush breaks his "no new taxes" pledge.

1991
- In Operation Desert Storm, U.S. forces launch a massive air assault against Iraq in response to its invasion of Kuwait.
- The Senate confirms the nomination of Clarence Thomas to the U.S. Supreme Court despite a former aide's charges of sexual harassment.
- Four Los Angeles policemen beat motorist Rodney King; their acquittal in April 1992 leads to riots in South Central Los Angeles.

1992
- Democratic Arkansas governor Bill Clinton defeats President Bush and third-party candidate Ross Perot to become president.
- The number of women jumps from twenty-eight to forty-seven in the House of Representatives and from two to six in the Senate.
- The national debt hits $3 trillion, having more than quadrupled since 1981.

1993
- Congress enacts the employer-friendly North American Free Trade Agreement legislation.
- Clinton unveils a complex universal health care plan; Congress rejects it a year later.
- Eighty-six members of the Branch Davidian cult die in a fire and suicide when federal agents assault their Waco, Texas, headquarters.

1994
- U.S. troops intervene in Haiti in an effort to restore democracy.
- Nelson Mandela is elected president of South Africa in the nation's first multiracial elections.
- The Republicans debut their Contract with America, which calls for reductions in federal social spending and taxes; they capture control of both the House and Senate for the first time in forty years.

- California voters approve Proposition 187 denying illegal aliens access to educational and health services.
- Former football star O. J. Simpson is arrested for the murder of his wife after a ninety-minute chase that is watched by millions on television; his trial the following year ends in acquittal.
- Attorney General Janet Reno appoints an independent counsel to investigate President Clinton's questionable real estate investments in the 1980s—known as Whitewater.
- Baseball players strike over salary caps; the season is canceled, and there is no World Series for the first time in ninety years.

1995
- Reformer John Sweeney is elected AFL-CIO president.
- The Internet becomes part of everyday life with the growing popularity of the World Wide Web.
- Timothy McVeigh and Terry Nichols explode a truck bomb in front of the Murrah Federal Building in Oklahoma City, killing 168 people.
- President Clinton has a sexual affair with White House intern Monica Lewinsky; when news of the affair surfaces in 1998, he initially denies it.

1996
- President Clinton signs into law a major revision of the welfare law that ends the sixty-year commitment to poor families with dependent children.
- California voters approve the California Civil Rights Initiative, which bans affirmative action at the University of California and in state agencies.
- President Clinton is reelected, easily defeating Republican Bob Dole and third-party candidate Ross Perot.

1997
- One hundred eight-five thousand Teamsters wage a successful strike against the United Parcel Service, the first successful nationwide strike in nearly two decades.

1998
- Economic growth and new tax revenues combine to turn the federal budget deficit into a surplus for the first time in years.

1999

- The Senate acquits Clinton in the second impeachment trial of a president in the nation's history.

2000

- Nation faces thirty-seven days of uncertainty following contested presidential election between George W. Bush and Al Gore in which the U.S. Supreme Court, in a 5-to-4 decision, decides in Bush's favor.

2001

- George W. Bush is inaugurated as the forty-third president.

Additional Readings

For more on the post–Cold War world, see: Michael R. Beschloss and Strobe Talbott, *At the Highest Levels: The Inside Story of the End of the Cold War* (1993); and Colin L. Powell (with Joseph E. Persico), *My American Journey* (1995).

For more on the new global economic order, see: Benjamin R. Barber, *Jihad vs. McWorld: How Globalism and Tribalism Are Re-Shaping the World* (1996); James K. Galbraith, *Created Unequal: The Crisis in American Pay* (1998); Doug Henwood, *Wall Street: How It Works and for Whom* (1997); Arlie Russell Hochschild, *The Time Bind: When Work Becomes Home and Home Becomes Work* (1997); Chalmers Johnson, *Blowback: The Costs and Consequences of American Empire* (2000); Michael T. Klare, *Resource Wars: The New Landscape of Global Conflict* (2001); Robert Kuttner, *Everything for Sale: The Virtues and Limits of Markets* (1999); Richard K. Lester, *The Productive Edge: How U.S. Industries Are Pointing the Way to a New Era of Economic Growth* (1998); Peter Schrag, *Paradise Lost: California's Experience, America's Future* (1999); and Tom Vanderbilt, *The Sneaker Book: Anatomy of an Industry and an Icon* (1998).

For more on the computer revolution, see: Steven Levy, *Hackers: Heroes of the Computer Revolution* (1994); Steven Manes and Paul Andrews, *Gates: How Microsoft's Mogul Reinvented an Industry — And Made Himself the Richest Man in America* (1994); and Dan Schiller, *Digital Capitalism: Networking the Global Market System* (1999).

For more on the labor movement in the 1990s, see: Kim Moody, *Workers in a Lean World: Unions in the International Economy* (1997); Jo-Ann Mort, ed., *Not Your Father's Union Movement: Inside the AFL-CIO* (1998);

Bob Ortega, *In Sam We Trust: The Untold Story of Sam Walton and How Wal-Mart Is Devouring America* (1998); and Ray M. Tillman and Michael S. Cummings, eds., *The Transformation of U.S. Unions: Voices, Visions, and Strategies from the Grassroots* (1999).

For more on the Clinton administration, see: Kenneth Baer, *Reinventing Democrats: The Politics of Liberalism from Reagan to Clinton* (2000); James Macgregor Burns and Georgia J. Sorenson, *Dead Center: Clinton-Gore Leadership and the Perils of Moderation* (1999); E. J. Dionne, Jr., *They Only Look Dead: Why Progressives Will Dominate the Next Political Era* (1997); David Maranis, *The First in His Class: The Biography of Bill Clinton* (1996); Michael Meeropol, *Surrender: How the Clinton Administration Completed the Reagan Revolution* (1998); Theda Skocpol, *Boomerang: Clinton's Health Security Effort and the Turn Against Government in U.S. Politics* (1996); and Bob Woodward, *The Agenda: Inside the Clinton White House* (1995).

For more on the new immigration, see: Elliott Robert Barkan, *And Still They Come: Immigrants and American Society, 1920 to the 1990s* (1996); Nancy Foner, *From Ellis Island to JFK: New York's Two Great Waves of Immigration* (2000); David M. Reimers, *Still the Golden Door: The Third World Comes to America* (1985); and Reed Ueda, *Postwar Immigrant America: A Social History* (1994).

For more on race in the 1990s, see: Lani Guinier, *Lift Every Voice: Turning a Civil Rights Setback into a New Vision of Social Justice* (1998); George Lipsitz, *The Possessive Investment in Whiteness: How White People Profit from Identity Politics,* rev. ed., (2006); and DeWayne Wickham, *Bill Clinton and Black America* (2002).

15

America's World After 9/11

2001–2007

ON THE MORNING OF September 11, 2001, the skyscrapers of Manhattan were cleanly etched against a bright blue sky. Few New Yorkers actually saw American Airlines Flight 11 crash into the north tower of the 110-story World Trade Center at 8:45 A.M., but images of the tragedy unfolding above the seventy-eighth floor were soon broadcast to a worldwide audience. When a second airliner plowed into the south tower at 9:02 A.M., everyone began to realize that a well-planned and executed assault was underway. An engineer who was working in the basement of the World Trade Center recalls that after the first plane hit, he struggled to reach the ground floor:

> Catching my breath, when I reached the top . . . I noticed debris coming down. [A]s I got closer I realized there were people hitting the ground[,] exploding on impact among office furniture and luggage[.] I was sickened by the sight. I waited for a lull and ran for it out the doors to the open air [. I]t was chaos[:] fire engines; all over people screaming. [I] looked up and saw both towers on fire[. I] couldn't believe my eyes. [P]eople were jumping[.] I saw a couple holding hands freefalling from at least the 90–95th floors. I ran to [B]roadway and watched from there[. I] still was in shock.

Hijackers flew a third plane into the west side of the Pentagon in northern Virginia just fifteen minutes later, killing 125 military and civilian employees, and at 10:00 A.M., a fourth aircraft, possibly headed for the U.S. Capitol building or the White House, crashed in a southwestern Pennsylvania field after passengers struggled with the hijackers who had commandeered the aircraft. By then, both World Trade Center towers had collapsed in a swirling cloud of smoke and dust that transformed the lower third of

Toxic Cloud

The second World Trade Center tower collapses, photographed from across the Hudson River in Jersey City. The thick cloud of toxic dust and debris that emanated from the destruction of the two buildings spread over downtown Manhattan. Ray Stubblebine — Reuters/Corbis.

Manhattan Island into something resembling the aftermath of a nuclear attack. In all, 2,813 people died in the attacks, making September 11 the bloodiest day on U.S. soil since the 1862 battle of Antietam during the Civil War.

The 9/11 attacks reverberated around the world. As residents of New York City, Washington, D.C., and Pennsylvania responded to the local destruction, the Bush administration consolidated domestic national security agencies and launched an open-ended international war against terrorism. This "war on terror" came to include invasions and occupations of Afghanistan in 2002 and Iraq in 2003.

But Americans also worried about a faltering economy. Even before the stock market shut down after September 11, the economy had been reeling from a series of major corporate bankruptcies in 2000 and 2001. It would take time for an economic recovery after 9/11 because fear ravaged the airline and tourism industries. Meanwhile, giant retailers such as Wal-Mart were reshaping the global economy even as their employment practices drew increasing scrutiny at home. As cogs in a new global assembly line, working Americans continued to experience a decline in their standard of living as wages remained stagnant, living costs rose, and tax cuts increased the divide between the wealthy and the poor and middle classes.

The economy and the war created even more divisions in the nation. In the 2004 presidential election, George W. Bush rallied 51 percent of voters behind the war and against abortion and gay marriage. Once reelected, Bush tried to privatize Social Security, but solid Democratic opposition, combined with the government's failure to provide prompt relief for the victims of Hurricane Katrina in 2005, further eroded support for the Bush administration. By 2006, the Republican Party was itself divided and demoralized. In November of that year, voters returned a Democratic majority to Congress for the first time since 1994.

The Shock of 9/11

The September 11 terrorist attacks shut down the nation and left people around the world in a state of confusion, fear, disbelief, and helplessness. The federal government grounded all commercial airliners for several days, stranding tens of thousands of travelers in Europe, Asia, and throughout the United States. The White House and the U.S. Capitol were evacuated, and tall buildings throughout the country emptied. The New York stock exchanges closed for a week. Meanwhile, Americans struggled to understand Osama bin Laden and the brand of Islamic extremism that he and his followers espoused. A wave of patriotism swept the nation as many Americans put aside political and cultural differences in favor of a unified patriotic front. But when the identities and origins of the terrorists became public knowledge, Arab Americans became the target of much discrimination and some violence.

New York City: The Social Ecology of Disaster   In the hours and days following the 9/11 attack, New York City's leaders and its citizenry began a grim vigil. When city officials shut down the public transportation system on the day of the attack, hundreds of thousands of New Yorkers could be found walking the streets, many in confusion and despair. Those with relatives or friends who had worked in the twin towers quickly plastered lamp posts, telephone booths, and bus shelters with flyers and pictures of their loved ones in the hopes (usually unrealized) of getting word of their whereabouts. A worker at a downtown hospital spent September 11 and 12 answering phone calls from people who were desperately looking for their loved ones. "I had the late shift on the 12th, and that was the heaviest and hardest. Only one out of 200 names could be confirmed as treated and released. The unique grief of the hospitals in the area was that we stood ready for massive casualties, and there were none."

First responders — police, fire, and emergency medical personnel — and construction workers rushed to lower Manhattan to claw through the smoldering mountain of debris of the collapsed twin towers in the hope of pulling out survivors and then, when the hours and days passed and few were found alive, to recover the remains of those who had been killed. A New York City firefighter, who had rushed to the World Trade Center site after the towers collapsed, recalled that as he ran toward the grim scene,

> The air and soot was getting thicker, and with each step we took, the mountain of destruction was becoming surreal. Twisted I-beams formed an interwoven web that looked like a huge roller-coaster track. Emergency vehicles were torn in half. City buses appeared to be the victims of their own bomb blasts. I prayed that I would wake up from this nightmare. We reached what is known as "Ground Zero." Time stood still as we began digging for survivors.

The stench of death and toxic dust permeated the air over Manhattan, spreading to the city's outer boroughs of Brooklyn and Staten Island.

The sense of uncertainty and fear among New Yorkers continued for weeks after the attack. Heavily armed National Guard troops and police officers required citizens who lived below 14th Street in lower Manhattan to show identification before being granted entry into their own neighborhoods. The Herculean efforts of emergency personnel and construction workers to find the bodies of victims slowly gave way to a growing sense of despair among those who were digging in "the pile"; the horror of finding body parts was made worse by the growing legions of workers who became physically ill from hours and days spent breathing unfiltered dust while they dug.

The federal Environmental Protection Agency quickly declared the air in lower Manhattan safe to breathe, although the cloud of toxic pollution

Global Warming
Scientists are concerned about the accelerated melting of Greenland's 700,000-square-mile ice sheet due to the rise in worldwide temperatures caused largely by carbon dioxide emissions (the "greenhouse effect"). Climatologists predict that even the slow melting of the ice sheet, which contains one-tenth of the world's fresh-water reserves, will severely affect coastal sea levels and contribute to the extinction of species and increasingly cata-strophic storms. Meanwhile, the United States, the larg-est producer of greenhouse emissions, refuses to sign inter-national treaties restricting airborne pollution. John McCon-nico/Associated Press.

that followed the collapse of the towers coated the lower third of Manhat-tan, inside and outside, for weeks after the attack. (One of the first priorities of the federal and city leaders was the rapid reopening of the city's stock exchanges.) Epidemiological studies later revealed a host of health and envi-ronmental problems, especially for many of the people who had had direct contact with the site.

Initial estimates of 5,000 to 10,000 deaths dropped sharply as the grim effort to count the victims continued in the weeks after September 11. What emerged from the tally of those who died in the twin towers, a total of 2,600 people, including 343 firefighters, provides a demographic cross section of the international, ethnically diverse World Trade Center workforce that labored in the finance, insurance, and service sectors of the global economy. More than eight of every ten people who died (2,106) were U.S. born; 53 were born in the United Kingdom, 46 in the Caribbean, 34 in India, and 20 in Japan. Of those who were killed, nearly 76 percent were white, 9.4 per-

"I Cannot Compromise When It Comes to My Beliefs"

In the weeks after the 9/11 attacks, many Arab Americans experienced harassment and fear of reprisal. Debbie Almontaser describes her personal experiences in this excerpt from an article she wrote for the Gotham Gazette. *Ms. Almontaser had come to the United States from Yemen when she was three years old. As a child, she wore the* hijab, *a headscarf that was a sign of modesty, but after being taunted at school, she did not wear it again until she moved to New York City as an adult. In September 2001, Ms. Almontaser worked as a teacher in a public school in Brooklyn in a neighborhood where there were many Arab Americans.*

Arab-American and Muslim women have become very limited in their daily routines. I for one was a prisoner in my own home for almost a month after September 11th. I was afraid to go out in public alone because I wear the hijab. My husband became my escort; he drove me to work and drove me home. He did everything that I needed to get done outside because I feared for my safety, if not my life. . . . There have been many attacks in the city. Women wearing the hijab have been chased and had their hijabs pulled off. Many have been spat on. Gangs of teenagers beat three women in Brooklyn. One woman walking down the street with her child in a stroller was stoned with cans, bottles and trash. An Islamic school in Brooklyn was vandalized with eggs and dog droppings. Local businesses had their windows or awnings destroyed. . . . Many Arabs, Muslims and South Asian[s] do not know enough English, or know enough about their civil rights, to make reports. Some fear being detained by police or discovered by their attackers. . . . Many feel guilt and shame for what has happened, even though they had no involvement whatsoever in the hideous acts of terrorism.

Many of my friends at work . . . have asked me to take off the hijab in public and wear it when I get to work or class. I very much appreciated their concern and told them not to worry. But taking off the hijab was not something I would do. I cannot compromise when it comes to my beliefs. I would rather die than take it off. For me, it would almost be like asking me to walk around topless.

Gotham Gazette, an online publication about New York City (http://www.gothamgazette.com/commentary/107.almontaser.shtml).

cent were Hispanic, 7.9 percent were black, and 6.3 percent were Asian. Most who died were in their thirties and forties, and the vast majority (three in four) were male.

In the weeks following the attacks, Americans of all ethnic groups and political and religious beliefs were caught up in a national wave of patriotism. American flags flew from homes, buildings, and car antennas. Fund-raising efforts around the country raised millions to aid the victims' families. However, Americans of Middle Eastern descent and practicing Muslims did not necessarily share in this show of togetherness. They faced discrimination and injury from people who blamed them for the attacks, despite the fact that the hijackers' extreme beliefs were shared by very few.

Islamic Extremism   Who *was* responsible for the attacks? All of the 19 hijackers were from the Middle East; 16 of them were from Saudi Arabia. They were trained and financed by al-Qaeda (a name that means "the base" in Arabic), a theocratic, militarized Islamic network that had conducted an increasingly bold set of bombings and attacks during the previous decade that were designed to rid the Middle East of both Western influence and the corrupt, authoritarian regimes that dominated the region. Al-Qaeda's leader was Osama bin Laden, whose own political and religious trajectory mirrored that of thousands of other Islamic extremists. Raised in a wealthy Saudi family and influenced by radical Islamic scholars while at the university, bin Laden became a militant when he volunteered to fight the Soviets in Afghanistan during the 1980s. In this guerrilla war, the CIA provided money, arms, and training to a variety of Islamic warlords and Arab fighters who were conducting a *jihad*, or holy war, against a secular, imperial enemy. The Soviet defeat in 1989 emboldened these Islamic warriors, who now turned their ire against the West and the Saudi regime, especially after the United States established a permanent military presence there during and after the first Gulf War (see Chapter 14). Al-Qaeda wanted to destroy Israel, eliminate Western influence, and replace most Arab regimes with an authoritarian theocracy. Islamic militants were responsible for bombing the basement of the World Trade Center in 1993, attacking U.S. embassies in Kenya and Tanzania in 1998, and killing 19 crew members of the U.S.S. *Cole* in early 2000, when a small boat laden with explosives detonated next to the destroyer's hull in a Yemeni port.

The United States responded ineffectively to al-Qaeda during the years and months leading up to September 11. Although bin Laden was harbored by the Afghan regime, whose Taliban leadership shared his reactionary ideology, al-Qaeda remained a largely stateless formation that enjoyed support in a number of countries, including Pakistan, Egypt, and Saudi Arabia itself. Episodic military retaliation against al-Qaeda during the Clinton administration therefore proved largely fruitless, especially when the stalemated Israel-Palestine peace process increased Middle East tensions in the late 1990s. The Bush administration actually downgraded its assessment of the threat posed by al-Qaeda in the months before 9/11 because the new Republican administration thought that "rogue" states such as Iran, North Korea, and Iraq were primarily responsible for the growing terrorist incidents around the world.

The War on Terror

The September 11 attacks transformed U.S. politics and its military posture internationally. Although nearly half of all Americans questioned the very legitimacy of his presidency during the first months of 2001, George W. Bush finally assumed the moral and emotive presidential cloak after a stirring September 20 speech before a joint session of Congress. Declaring a "war on terror," Bush asserted that the United States would use its military might to crush not only the terrorists who were responsible for the attacks, but also any government that supported those groups or individuals. He attributed the rise of Islamic terrorism not to the vexing politics of the Middle East, but to "the murderous ideologies of the twentieth century; by sacrificing human life to serve their radical visions, by abandoning every value except the will to power, they follow in the path of fascism, Nazism, and totalitarianism."

President Bush claimed expansive federal authority to fight the "war on terror." Republican majorities in both houses of Congress, with the support of many Democrats, passed legislation that centralized domestic security agencies into a cabinet-level Department of Homeland Security and dramatically increased the federal government's power to monitor and prosecute citizens and noncitizens alike in the pursuit of national security. In the spring of 2003, the U.S. defied much of world opinion and invaded Iraq, insistent that Iraq's development of chemical, biological, and nuclear weapons posed a worldwide threat. Although the president famously declared, "Mission Accomplished" after six weeks of fighting, the occupation of Iraq proved far more difficult, dangerous, and costly to both the United States and Iraq.

Homeland Security   In the fall of 2001, when the Taliban regime in Afghanistan refused to shut down al-Qaeda training camps or expel bin Laden, the U.S. government began military operations in that remote central Asian nation. From new air bases in the former Soviet Union, American bombers and fighter planes roamed Afghani skies at will, supporting an insurgent and Afghani-led Northern Alliance that occupied Kabul, the capital, in early November 2001 (Map 15.1). The Taliban regime disintegrated shortly thereafter, but not before bin Laden and many of his fighters had escaped to the remote tribal provinces of northwest Pakistan, from where he periodically denounced on video and audiotape the United States and its Middle East allies. Although a multinational force stayed in Kabul and other cities to sustain the moderate Islamic regime, headed by Hamid Karzai, that replaced the Taliban, the influence of regional warlords subverted the growth of Western-style constitutional government in Afghanistan.

The war in Afghanistan enjoyed broad support at home, but the Bush administration's effort to open a front against potential domestic terrorism proved far more controversial. Unlike many European and Latin American nations, the United States had never had an "interior ministry" that centralized all of the state's police and border security functions within one high-profile bureaucracy. Post-9/11 investigators blamed the attacks on the

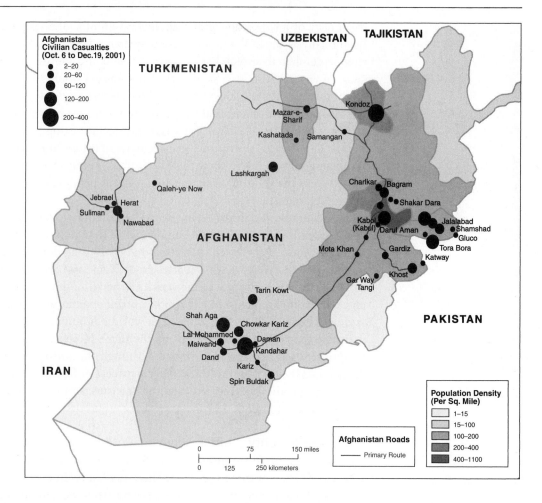

Afghanistan Civilian Casualties (Oct. 6 to Dec.19, 2001)
- 2–20
- 20–60
- 60–120
- 120–200
- 200–400

Population Density (Per Sq. Mile)
- 1–15
- 15–100
- 100–200
- 200–400
- 400–1100

Afghanistan Roads
— Primary Route

0   75   150 miles
0   125   250 kilometers

failure of the FBI and the Immigration and Naturalization Service (INS) to detect the hijackers and on the poorly paid and privately employed airport screeners who had not stopped the terrorists at the boarding ramps. Oversights and miscommunications convinced many members of Congress, as well as many other Americans, that a more systematic and centralized approach to internal security was now necessary.

Within a month of 9/11, Bush created a new White House office of "homeland security," initially headed by Pennsylvania governor Tom Ridge. Fourteen months later, Congress passed a Homeland Security Act, establishing a new cabinet post that was the largest reorganization of government functions since the creation of the Defense Department a half century before. The new Department of Homeland Security absorbed twenty-two government agencies, including the INS, Coast Guard, Border Patrol, Customs Service, and Federal Emergency Management Administration (FEMA). The new law placed airport security screeners on the government

MAP 15.1   Operation Enduring Freedom

Citing Afghanistan's support for al-Qaeda and the presence of terrorist training camps, the U.S and British military began intensive bombing of Afghanistan within a month of the 9/11 attacks. The initial military campaign removed the Taliban government, but Taliban forces continued to recruit and resist U.S.-led coalition forces through 2006. Steve Carter, scarter72@hotmail.com.

Rambo III

The fictional character John Rambo, played by a well-oiled Sylvester Stallone, is shown here allied with Afghanistan's anti-Soviet Mujahedin in the third film in the action hero series. The 1988 film, said to be one of the most violent ever made, lionized the Mujahedin resistance in Afghanistan, among whom Osama bin Laden was a major organizer and financier. Everett Collection.

payroll as part of a new Transportation Security Administration (TSA). Conservative Republicans, who controlled Congress, chafed at this dramatic expansion of government power. They stripped TSA personnel of their collective bargaining rights and weakened union and civil service protections for the 170,000 other federal workers who had been incorporated into the new Department of Homeland Security.

With a compliant Congress, the administration also pushed through a sweeping expansion of federal prosecutorial power called the USA Patriot Act. This law extended government power to monitor telephone and e-mail communications and authorized federal officials to seize, without search warrants, financial, medical, computer, and library records. It created a new crime category called "domestic terrorism" that many civil libertarians considered far too expansive and administratively pliable. Indeed, public sentiment, including that of many conservatives who were suspicious of overweening federal power, soon turned cool toward the Patriot Act. By 2005, seven states—Alaska, Colorado, Hawaii, Idaho, Maine, Montana, and Vermont—and 389 cities and counties had passed resolutions condemning the new law for undermining civil liberties.

The War in Iraq   The Bush administration made Iraq the next target of the "war on terror." For more than a quarter of a century, Saddam Hussein had ruled Iraq in a brutal and dictatorial fashion. Hussein instigated wars against neighboring Iran and Kuwait and used chemical weapons against his own internal enemies, including the restive Shiites in the south and the independence-seeking Kurds in the northern part of Iraq. But Hussein and the fascist Baath Party apparatus with which he ruled Iraq were secular nationalists. No credible evidence existed linking Hussein with al-Qaeda, bin Laden, or the September 11 attacks.

Many in the Republican Party, especially the influential group of neoconservatives who now occupied high-level positions in the National Security Council and at the Pentagon, wanted "regime change" in Baghdad. In his 2002 State of the Union address, President Bush declared Iraq, along with Iran and North Korea, part of an "axis of evil," not because they were allied or worked in tandem, but because they were hostile, authoritarian "rogue" states that were said to be building "weapons of mass destruction"—atomic, chemical, or biological—for use against their neighbors or the West. Although North Korea and Iran were indeed on their way toward becoming nuclear powers, Iraq stood at the top of the Bush administration's military agenda. Hussein, despite his 1991 defeat in Kuwait in the first Gulf War, remained a symbol of Arab defiance toward American power in the Middle East. He barred United Nations inspectors from Iraqi territory in 1998 and won increasing international support to lift the economic sanctions that had been imposed on his nation after the first Gulf War. Key policymakers in the White House and Pentagon, especially Vice President Dick Cheney, who had been secretary of defense during that conflict, now thought that the U.S. decision to leave Hussein in power had been

Color Me Terrified

Homeland Security chief Tom Ridge introduces a color-coded threat advisory system in March 2002. The five alert levels, escalating from green for a low-level warning to "severe risk" red, was supposed to inform the public about imminent terrorist threats and prompt appropriate preventive measures on the part of federal and local government agencies. But critics noted that the criteria for subsequent alerts were confusing and possibly motivated by partisan political aims. Joshua Roberts — AFP/Getty Images.

an embarrassing mistake. Indeed, in an interview with CBS correspondent Katie Couric in September 2006, Bush let slip the administration's thinking, telling her, "You know one of the hardest parts of my job is connecting Iraq to the war on terror."

To rationalize their war policy, Bush, Cheney, and Secretary of Defense Donald Rumsfeld artfully conflated the 9/11 attacks with the anti-Americanism of the Iraqi regime, declaring both Hussein and the hijackers enemies in an increasingly ill-defined war on terror. To this end, the administration emphasized the threat posed by Iraqi weapons of mass destruction (WMD), in particular by a nuclear weapons program that war advocates asserted was well under way. However, the Bush administration faced a dilemma in making WMD the justification for a new Iraq war. If Hussein still held threatening WMD stockpiles, a new round of United Nations inspections, which got under way in late 2002, might well find and destroy them. Most U.S. allies, especially France and Germany, wanted to give U.N. inspectors time to do their work. So too did millions of ordinary people, who poured into the streets of London, Madrid, New York, Rome, and Barcelona on February 15, 2003, in the largest set of coordinated mass anti-war demonstrations in world history.

But the Bush administration would not be deterred. Democrats in Congress remained skeptical but were afraid to seem unpatriotic, especially after the 2002 midterm elections strengthened Republican control of in both houses of Congress. Meanwhile, the American military had already begun to position an invasion force in the Persian Gulf region, so top U.S.

officials came to see the United Nations as an obstacle that might delay or derail the war. With the possible exception of Secretary of State Colin Powell, all of these officials thought that a military showdown was vital and imminent. The United States had the military and diplomatic support of Great Britain, but when the invasion of Iraq began on March 19, 2003, after Hussein failed to comply with a U.S. ultimatum to leave Iraq, the U.S. government found little support in the United Nations or among most of its traditional European allies. In contrast to the 1991 Gulf War, no Muslim nation publicly supported the United States. Over 90 percent of the troops were American; the rest were British.

The invasion was a military success. With fewer than 100,000 active combat troops, highly mobile U.S. Army and Marine forces shot forward to Baghdad, annihilating those few Iraqi tanks that sought battle. Baghdad was captured on April 5, 2003, and organized resistance ceased a few days later. President Bush declared the end of major hostilities on May 1, after he had flown by helicopter and landed on the deck of the aircraft carrier U.S.S. *Abraham Lincoln*, anchored off San Diego. Behind him stood a huge banner that read "Mission Accomplished." Hussein eluded capture until December 2003, when he was found hiding near Tikrit, his birthplace and center of power. He was convicted of numerous crimes against humanity and was hanged in Iraq at the end of 2006.

The Failure of the Occupation   It soon became clear that the U.S. mission in Iraq was far from accomplished, and it would become increasingly difficult and contentious with each passing month. The United States and Britain conquered Iraq with fewer than 150,000 troops, enough to defeat Hussein's army but not enough to establish order in a country with a population and territory the size of California. U.S. and British diplomats called on other nations to provide additional troops and resources, but aside from token forces sent by Spain, Italy, and Holland, they found few takers. In April, widespread looting destroyed what remained of the old governing apparatus in Baghdad and other big cities. Unemployment soared, and the restoration of public services moved slowly, in part because American occupation policy barred many Baath Party members from their former jobs as managers and technicians. Although the United States appropriated $87 billion for the occupation and reconstruction of Iraq, it paid much of this money to large U.S. and British corporations, such as Bechtel and Halliburton, in part because the new American administrator of Iraq, L. Paul Bremer III, sought a rapid, free-market transformation of the Iraqi economy. The United States was unwilling to give the United Nations a substantial role in the reconstruction process; meanwhile, the failure of the Americans to find even a handful of WMD further delegitimized the American project in Iraq.

Although the United States sought to enlist prominent Iraqis in an advisory governing council, the occupation authorities faced a growing insurgency by the summer of 2003. Bombings and land mines planted on roadways took a steady toll of GIs and noncombatant Iraqis. By November 2006, nearly 3,000 U.S. military personnel had died in Iraq, and more than 20,000 had been gravely wounded. Civilian Iraqi causalities, both from insurgent bombs and from U.S. retaliation, were at least ten times as great. No one quite knew who these insurgents were. U.S. occupation authorities claimed that the insurgents were Hussein loyalists, criminal elements, and al-Qaeda fighters who had traveled to Iraq to kill Americans. A more likely view held that the essential motivation for the insurgency was Iraqi nationalism, especially that of the Sunni minority that was concentrated in and around Baghdad, Fallujah, and Mosel. The five-million-strong Sunni community had long provided the ruling elite in Iraq. But now the Sunnis were being marginalized, not only by the Americans, but also by the two other key groups in Iraq: the Shiites in southern Iraq, who wanted to establish an orthodox Islamic regime not dissimilar from that of neighboring Iran, and the Kurds in the north, also Muslims, who tolerated inclusion within an Iraqi state only as long as it did nothing to curb the de facto independence they had achieved under U.S. military protection (Map 15.2).

As in Vietnam, U.S. firepower easily overwhelmed military resistance when insurgents sought to wage pitched battles. In Fallujah, where the death and public mutilation of the bodies of four American private contract employees inflamed American sensibilities in April 2004, Marines battled their way to the city center, killed hundreds of insurgents, and threw a cordon around the city of 300,000. But such battles were rare in Iraq, in part because coalition forces lacked on-the-ground intelligence about enemy movements and personnel. This intelligence deficit lay at the heart of the humiliating and inhumane treatment that was meted out to Iraqi prisoners being held at the huge Abu Ghraib prison just outside Baghdad. U.S. military and CIA interrogators sought to "soften" up Iraqi suspects in the hopes of extracting information about the insurgency, but when digital photographs of the physically and sexually humiliating interrogation techniques became public during spring 2004, the U.S. military effort in Iraqi lost much legitimacy, both at home and throughout the Middle East. Only low-level military personnel were punished for the brutality that clearly contravened the Geneva Conventions that are intended to ensure humane treatment of prisoners of war.

If U.S. military efforts to defeat the insurgency proved costly and futile, a political solution also eluded Bush administration policymakers. The capture of Saddam Hussein in December 2003 and his subsequent trial for crimes against his own people merely inflamed Sunni sensibilities and

MAP 15.2 Major Ethnic and Religious Divisions in Iraq, 2006

Religion and ethnicity divide the Iraq nation. Although 97 percent of the population is Muslim, they are divided between two sects: Shiites, who make up 65 percent, and Sunni, who make up 32 percent. Three-quarters of the population is ethnically Arab, and 20 percent is Kurdish. The Kurdish population is mainly Sunni but has a strong secular government.

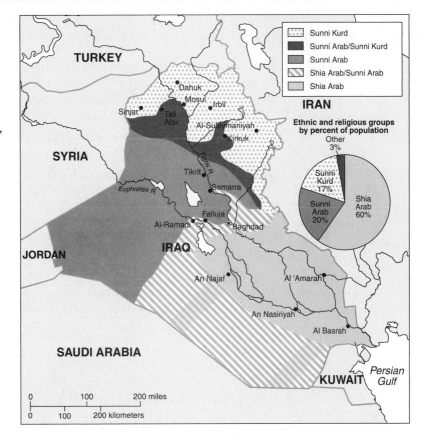

threatened to turn the former dictator into a national martyr. In June 2004, the United States transferred "sovereignty" to an interim Iraqi government, and in January 2005, Iraqis participated in their first multiparty election in a generation, choosing representatives for a 275-member Constitutional Assembly. Because the Sunnis had boycotted these elections, the Shiite majority and Kurdish separatists largely shaped in their own interests the constitution that emerged. Although ratified in October 2005, the new constitution lacked legitimacy, especially in Sunni eyes. Indeed, by early 2006, it was becoming increasingly difficult to distinguish the U.S.-Shiite fight against the insurgency from an increasingly brutal civil war that Sunnis and Shiites waged against each other.

New Business and Conservative Agendas

The 9/11 attacks shook the American economy just as the nation was beginning to emerge from a recession that had begun the year before. A series of scandals involving major corporations, most notably the energy company

"Regaining My Humanity"

Camilo Mejia, a Nicaraguan and Costa Rican citizen living in the United States, joined the U.S. Army in 1995 as a way to fund his education. He served as an infantryman from 1995 until 1998, then continued as a reservist in the Florida National Guard. His National Guard contract was to end in May 2003 but was extended because of the war in Iraq. After serving one tour in Iraq, Sergeant Mejia filed an application for conscientious objector status. Although most military personnel continued to support the war in Iraq, Sergeant Mejia decided that he could no longer participate in it. He was sentenced to one year in prison for refusing to return to combat. He was released from prison on February 15, 2005.

I realized that none of the reasons we were told about why we were in Iraq turned out to be true. There were no weapons of mass destruction. There was no link between Saddam Hussein and al Qaeda. We weren't helping the Iraqi people and the Iraqi people didn't want us there. We weren't preventing terrorism or making Americans safer. I couldn't find a single good reason for having been there, for having shot at people and been shot at.

Coming home gave me the clarity to see the line between military duty and moral obligation. I realized that I was part of a war that I believed was immoral and criminal, a war of aggression, a war of imperial domination. I realized that acting upon my principles became incompatible with my role in the military, and I decided that I could not return to Iraq.

By putting my weapon down, I chose to reassert myself as a human being. I have not deserted the military or been disloyal to the men and women of the military. I have not been disloyal to a country. I have only been loyal to my principles. . . .

Many have called me a coward, others have called me a hero. I believe I can be found somewhere in the middle. To those who have called me a hero, I say that I don't believe in heroes, but I believe that ordinary people can do extraordinary things.

To those who have called me a coward I say that they are wrong, and that without knowing it, they are also right. They are wrong when they think that I left the war for fear of being killed. I admit that fear was there, but there was also the fear of killing innocent people, the fear of putting myself in a position where to survive means to kill, there was the fear of losing my soul in the process of saving my body, the fear of losing myself to my daughter, to the people who love me, to the man I used to be, the man I wanted to be. I was afraid of waking up one morning to realize my humanity had abandoned me. . . .

From *Stop the War Now.* Copyright © 2005 by Medea Benjamin and Jodie Evans. Reprinted with permission of Inner Ocean/New World Library, Novato, CA. www.newworldlibrary.com.

Enron, exposed the dangers of unregulated free-market capitalism and eroded public support for corporate America. Although the economy appeared to improve beginning in 2004, declines in real wages and soaring health care costs meant that most Americans found themselves on a contin-

Presidential Action Figure
Reflecting the seeming early success of the Iraq invasion, Blue Box Toys' "Elite Force Aviator Action Figure" went on the market in Spring 2003. The doll sported the naval flight uniform that President George W. Bush wore when he emerged from the jet fighter that carried him to the May 1, 2003, ceremony on the aircraft carrier U.S.S. *Abraham Lincoln*. Blue Box Toys/Getty Images.

ued downward economic spiral. That same year, the presidential election broke a decades-old pattern of declining public interest in presidential campaigns. The Republican and Democratic parties spent far more money than they had in any previous election, and voter interest, turnout, and mobilization exceeded those of any contest since 1968. George Bush again won a narrow and sharply polarizing electoral victory over the Democratic nominee, John Kerry, confirming the profound social and ideological divisions that characterized American politics in the early twenty-first century.

Corporate Corruption in an Unbalanced Economy   The booming 1990s ended when the deflation of the high-flying "dot-com" stocks in March 2000 resulted in massive bankruptcies and layoffs in the high-technology sector. By one calculation, nearly 250 Web-based businesses collapsed in a few months' time. In the San Francisco Bay Area, Boston, Seattle, and Denver, salaries and stock portfolios all came crashing down. In March 2001, the overall stock market recorded its worst week since 1989. Consumer confidence fell, corporate profits plunged, and layoffs spread throughout the manufacturing economy. The recession might have remained confined to the financial and high-tech sectors of the economy, but the terrorist attacks had a devastating impact on airlines, hotels, restaurants, and tourism in general. Despite congressional appropriation of more than $15 billion in emergency funds for the airlines, every major carrier was in or near bankruptcy within months of the 9/11 attacks. Four hundred thousand hotel and restaurant workers lost their jobs when Americans slashed their travel and shopping plans. Service sector employment fell faster in the last quarter of 2001 than in any three-month period since World War II.

The spectacular and shameful series of corporate scandals that came to light early in the new century did nothing to sustain confidence in the nation's financial and business structures or their leaders. Executive misconduct, speculation, and sudden bankruptcy were rife among the energy and telecommunications companies that had benefited from Clinton era deregulation and political and financial connections to powerful Republican politicians, including key Bush administration officials. Houston's Enron Corporation had once been a staid oil and gas pipeline company, but in the 1990s, it purchased a far-flung set of utility companies and established a highly profitable and managed market supplying electricity. Hailed as a pioneering model of free-market economics and high-tech forecasting, Enron claimed assets of $62 billion in 2000, making it the sixth largest corporation in the United States. But the company was corrupt. In 2000, it manipulated its West Coast electricity supply to generate rolling blackouts in California and panic the state into signing ultra-profitable long-term service contracts. Meanwhile, Enron executives sustained its high-flying stock price only by an increasingly convoluted and desperate series of illegal financing schemes. When the inevitable crash arrived, the company cheated thousands of employees out of their retirement savings even as they lost their jobs.

"Statue of Liberty"
One of the most widely distributed of the photographs of abuse in Abu Ghraib prison showed an Iraqi hooded and forcibly maintaining a "stress position," an interrogation technique that had been approved by the Pentagon. An interrogator told the prisoner that he would be electrocuted if he relaxed. Like many of the tortured prisoners, he was not a terrorist; jailed for a carjacking, he had no valuable information to divulge. Iraqis later dubbed the photograph "Statue of Liberty." American Social History Project.

The Enron collapse was followed by bankruptcies and huge layoffs in the telecommunications industry, which had borrowed enormous sums to overbuild revenue-losing fiber-optic networks in the 1990s. Lucent Technologies, the telecommunications giant that had once been a pillar of U.S. manufacturing as the supplier of millions of prosaic telephone receivers, cut nearly one hundred thousand jobs in 2001. Global Crossing, a high-speed voice and data carrier, and WorldCom, the nation's second-largest long-distance carrier, both declared bankruptcy the next year amid accusations of executive looting and self-dealing. Also charged with financial criminality were the top executives of Adelphia Communications, who had looted the family-owned TV-cable business of a billion dollars. In all, these corporate criminals squandered a combined $460 billion in shareholder value and destroyed hundreds of thousands of jobs and pensions.

In the wake of these scandals there was much finger pointing from the business press and from Democratic critics of "crony capitalism." The chairman of Goldman Sachs, a major Wall Street investment bank, declared, "I cannot think of a time when business . . . has been held in less repute." But few thought that anything more than a beefed-up regulatory apparatus was necessary to resolve these problems. This regulation came in the form of the 2002 Sarbanes-Oxley Act, which made top corporate executives take more responsibility for the financial dealings of their underlings and forced the

"We Had Our Goose Cooked"

Deborah Perrotta, a for-mer Enron employee who was involuntarily laid off on December 5, 2001, along with nearly 6,000 others, described the loss of her company pension at a congressional hear-ing. When Enron's corrupt accounting prac-tices forced the company into bankruptcy, thou-sands of workers, including Ms. Perrotta, lost their retirement funds, which consisted mostly of Enron stock.

Due to the accounting practices, lack of ethics and weak legislation coupled with Enron's freezing of our 401k plans, I and thousands of others lost our jobs and the resources we had to fund our retirements. Because I was contemplating retiring at the age of 58, I increased my deductions because I believed Enron was secure, since Arthur Anderson, analysts, management and the investment community routinely validated it.

I chose the stock award plan because I believed it was in my fam-ily's best interests to reinvest in Enron stock based upon the continued confidence of Wall Street and management's projections of future growth and profitability. . . .

Little did we know that they were inflating revenues and the stock price to increase their bonuses and that our board lacked the integrity to ask the right questions and protect the shareholders, employees and investors from fraud. By September of 2001, my 401k funds went from $39,000 to a little over $6,000.

In September we were notified that the company was changing saving plan administrators, and the last date for any investment fund balance changes would be October 26, 2001. . . .

During this period of the lockout Enron's stock price fell by more than 50%—from $15.40 at the close on October 26 to $7.00 at the close on November 20. However, while we had to wait during the blackout period, our leadership had the ability to move their stock. This is ter-rible, what is good for the goose should be good for the gander. How-ever at Enron the gander got rich and we had our goose cooked.

Five of my friends' total losses combined exceeded $6 million. This may sound like these were rich people, but this was money that they were planning to live off in retirement. For my friends in their fifties, this money simply cannot be replaced. . . .

It seems to me that at every turn the way the law works and the decisions Enron executives made combined to see that a handful of people got millions and thousands of people who worked to build Enron lost everything.

U.S. House, *Testimony Before the Subcommittee on Oversight of the House Commit-tee on Ways and Means, Hearing on Employee and Employer Views on Retirement Security,* March 5, 2002 (http://waysandmeans.house.gov/legacy.asp?file=legacy/oversite/107cong/3-5-02/3-5perro.htm).

big accounting firms to maintain an arms-length relationship with the companies that they audited. The Bush administration initially opposed even this mild reform, and its officials actually congratulated themselves for doing little to avert the corporate meltdowns, asserting instead that the disappearance of Enron and the others vindicated the free market. Bush's first Treasury Secretary, Paul O'Neill, saw the bankruptcies as more of a validation than an indictment of contemporary capitalism. "Companies come and go," he said. "Part of the genius of capitalism is people get to make good decisions or bad decisions and they get to pay the consequences. . . . That's the way the system works."

Stabbed in the Back

Enron's streamlined logo became a symbol for corporate corruption and a focus of political cartoon commentary on the bankrupt company's treatment of its employees and investors. J. D. Crowe, *Mobile Register*.

But the system was misshapen and dysfunctional for most Americans. By 2004 and 2005, the media and the government had largely turned their attention away from corporate scandals. In 2004, the economy grew over 4 percent, its best performance since 1999. Yet most families actually fell behind economically, the average middle-class family losing real income for the fifth year in a row. Behind the disconnect between economic growth and family incomes lay the extremely lopsided nature of the economic recovery that began in 2001. Corporate profits leaped forward by 50 percent, but real wage and salary income was up less than 7 percent (Figure 15.1). This imbalance was partly a function of government policy: Bush's tax cuts favored corporations and the wealthy; the evaporation of the minimum wage, and the increase in trade with low-wage Asian nations cut the real wages of millions of U.S. workers; and the soaring cost and decreasing availability of employer-funded health insurance battered the disposable income of white- and blue-collar workers alike.

America in a Global Assembly Line

One company seemed to symbolize the new realities of work in twenty-first-century America. By 2006, Wal-Mart was the largest company in the world, employing 1.6 million women and men in more than six thousand "big box" stores, 80 percent of which were in the United States. An oil price spike in the first half decade of the new century temporarily gave Exxon-Mobil more revenue than Wal-Mart, but few observers doubted that the retail giant had a far greater impact on international trade, on domestic living standards, and on the very fabric of modern capitalism. Wal-Mart was important not just because it was big, but because its hyperefficient combination of sophisticated telecommunications, centralized distribution, ruthless price cutting, and close supplier

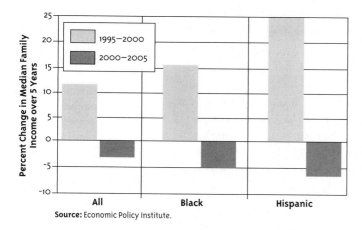

FIGURE 15.1 Where Has the Increase Gone?

During the economic boom of the late 1990s, the median family income increased for most sectors of society. Between 2000 and 2005, the U.S. economy grew 14 percent and corporate profits increased by 18 to 21 percent per year. But median family income dropped by almost 3 percent, resulting in an ever-growing economic disparity between the wealthiest 1 percent and the lower 95 percent of the population.

links generated a productivity surge that was comparable only to results of the Ford Motor Company's invention of the assembly line at the start of the twentieth century or IBM's mass deployment of the mainframe computer in the 1950s. The Reaganite evisceration of labor law (see Chapter 13), combined with a precipitous drop in the real value of the minimum wage, had also helped to create the social context that enabled Wal-Mart, Kmart, Home Depot, and other huge discounters to build retail empires that transformed the very structure of world capitalism.

The mass retailers were now king. For more than a century, from about 1880 to 1980, the manufacturing enterprise stood at the center of the American economy's production-distribution nexus. Big firms such as U.S. Steel and General Motors, as well as a host of consumer goods manufacturers that included Procter & Gamble and Kraft Foods, set the prices, established the distribution networks, and dominated the market for their product, both at home and abroad. By the early years of the twenty-first century, however, the big box retailers stood at the apex of the world's supply chains, leveraging their enormous buying power to squeeze their suppliers, bankrupt less efficient and smaller competitors, and move into new markets, such as groceries and pharmaceuticals, that had once sustained a higher-wage, unionized workforce. These companies became manufacturing giants in all but name, tracking consumer behavior with meticulous care and then transmitting buying preferences down the supply chain.

This marketing system shifted the worldwide production of most consumer goods to East Asia—to China above all. Wal-Mart located its world buying headquarters in Shenzhen, a booming city of seven million located just north of Hong Kong in Guangdong Province. With more than forty million migrant workers and 130,000 garment factories Guangdong produced one-third of China's total exports in the early twenty-first century, most transported to the West Coast ports of North America by a trans-Pacific conveyor system that relied on huge containerships. Wal-Mart and the other U.S. retailers owned no factories in China, but their demands for rock-bottom prices and on-time delivery created a world of industrial sweatshops, usually staffed by tens of thousands of young women, that mirrored the chaotic industrialization of early nineteenth-century England or turn of the twentieth-century New York City. Not unexpectedly, strikes and protests have mushroomed in coastal China since the 1980s.

Wal-Mart's rapid expansion also generated a wide range of social conflicts in the United States, extending from the small towns of rural America to Los Angeles, New York, and Chicago. In the 1980s, Wal-Mart located most of its big box stores in southern and midwestern small towns, generating howls of protest from Main Street merchants and neighborhood groups. These protests proved largely ineffectual, but a decade later, when Wal-Mart moved into metropolitan America with its grocery-selling "supercenters," the company's antiunion, low-wage, low-benefit policies came under intense scrutiny and increasingly vocal opposition. Indeed, Wal-Mart's prospective entry into the Southern California supermarket industry precipitated a bitter, four-month strike in 2003–2004, when executives at several grocery firms locked out almost 70,000 unionized workers in order to negotiate a new contract that would bring the wage and benefit standards of their own labor force down to the Wal-Mart level. The strike ended in a union defeat, which sent a jolt through the entire labor movement and its liberal and Democratic Party allies. Thereafter, the reform of Wal-Mart's employment policies, especially the company's inadequate health care benefits, became a political flashpoint within American politics. Labor and community mobilizations stopped Wal-Mart from building stores in some large cities, even as city councils and state legislatures, angry that so many Wal-Mart employees were forced to rely on state-funded programs for routine medical care, debated ordinances and laws that would force the big box retailers to pay higher wages and offer better health insurance. In national politics, where Republican control of the government stifled social reform,

Welcome to Wal-Mart

In 2004, protests greeted Wal-Mart's plans to build a Mexico City store near the Teotihuacán pyramids, one of the country's major archaeological sites. Despite demonstrations, the store opened. With 657 stores in Mexico, Wal-Mart is now that country's largest private employer. Andrew Winning/ Reuters/Corbis.

labor unions and the Democrats kept Wal-Mart, whose executives had contributed heavily to the Bush reelection effort in 2004, under a steady drum beat of criticism.

The 2004 Election   In his campaign for reelection, President Bush attracted intense support from just over half of the American voters. The extremely high approval ratings he enjoyed immediately following the 9/11 attacks dwindled in subsequent months, peaking only during combat operations in Iraq in spring 2003 and again following the capture of Saddam Hussein in December of the same year. But these fluctuations hardly mattered, because as Bush confidant and political strategist Karl Rove once put it, "We have cement under our base." Republicans campaigned as the party that was most determined to wage a "war on terror," reinvigorating the national security issues that had served conservatives so well during the Cold War. Throughout the campaign, Bush did not emphasize the actual conflicts that were being waged by American troops in Iraq, Afghanistan, or other parts of the world. He appealed instead to the generalized insecurity that many Americans felt in the aftermath of September 11. Thus, the Republicans held their 2004 nominating convention in New York City, where, despite massive street demonstrations attacking the president and his Iraq war policy, Bush sought to recapture the sense of unity, crisis, and fearfulness that had made him seem such a strong and steadfast leader in the immediate aftermath of 9/11.

Bush buttressed his claims to patriotic leadership with a strong appeal to the conservative, evangelical, and increasingly politicized Christians who were the vaunted base of the Republican electoral coalition. To large campaign audiences mobilized through the new mega-churches that were becoming so popular in exurban America, the president asserted his belief in a "culture of life," which implied opposition to abortion. President Bush also made clear his opposition to civil marriages for gay people, which had become a legal reform of increasing viability in some northern and western communities, and he made frequent public references to his Christian beliefs. As one Ohio campaign brochure put it, "George W. Bush shares your values. Marriage. Life. Faith." In 2004, 78 percent of white evangelical Christians voted for the president.

President Bush and Vice President Cheney faced a Democratic ticket composed of two senators, John Kerry of Massachusetts and John Edwards of North Carolina. Edwards had made millions as an attorney who sued large corporations and insurance companies in personal injury cases. In North Carolina, where unions were almost nonexistent and the civil rights movement had faded, such a career was one of the few venues in which a high-profile resistance to corporate hegemony might find expression. John Kerry was also a millionaire. Like Bush, Kerry had been a member of Yale's exclusive Skull and Bones secret society as an undergraduate, but now he was one of the more liberal members of the Senate and a genuine war hero who had commanded a combat patrol boat in Vietnam. Indeed, Democrats mistakenly thought that Kerry's valorous Vietnam service would insulate the Kerry-Edwards ticket from Republican insinuations about military weakness and lack of patriotism that had dogged President Clinton.

With a huge mobilization of money and people on behalf of Kerry and Edwards, Democrats were determined to reverse what they saw as the illegitimate verdict that Florida election officials had rendered and the U.S. Supreme Court had upheld in December 2000, giving Bush the presidency (see Chapter 14). Kerry enjoyed overwhelming support from those Americans who opposed the Iraq war, even though he failed to fully repudiate his 2002 Senate vote granting Bush authority to launch an attack. Kerry's equivocation gave Bush the opportunity to denounce him as someone who "flip-flopped" on the issues.

Derision
A Texas delegate at the Republic National Convention displayed an adhesive bandage with a purple heart, mocking the combat decorations received by Democratic presidential candidate John Kerry during the Vietnam War. While not officially endorsed by the Republican Party, a strategy of misrepresentation and distortion about Kerry's military service pervaded the 2004 election campaign. Robert Galbraith/Reuters/Corbis.

Although Bush won by 51 percent of the popular vote, largely in the same states that he had captured in 2000, an astonishing eleven million additional people voted for him than had done so in the last election. The conservative support enabled the Republicans to pick up four additional seats in both the House and the Senate. But John Kerry did extremely well too, eclipsing Al Gore's 2000 total by more than seven million votes, largely because of an unprecedented mobilization of core Democratic constituencies, chiefly union families and African Americans. Indeed, the labor movement was the backbone of the Democratic turnout. In Ohio, whose electoral votes were essential to both candidates, the unions put more volunteers on the street than at any time since the heyday of the CIO. But the Republicans mobilized even more Ohio campaign workers, some 85,000, who spurred to action a wave of religiously motivated voters that had never before been seen in Ohio politics.

President Bush's Right-Wing Agenda   President Bush was determined to "spend the political capital" he believed his victory had earned. With this self-proclaimed "mandate," he attempted to pass an ambitious political agenda at the start of his second term in 2005. He planned to appoint more conservative jurists to the federal bench, especially the U.S. Supreme Court, should the long-expected vacancies finally open up there. He wanted to make permanent the tax reductions Congress had passed in the early years of his first term, and he hoped to transform Social Security, a public pension system that had long been thought of as an untouchable "third rail" of American politics. And, of course, Bush sought to pursue the continuing war in Iraq until the insurgency there was defeated and a regime that was amenable to American influence was firmly in place.

President Bush proved successful in moving the U.S. Supreme Court decisively to the right on social and civil liberty issues. When Justice Sandra Day O'Connor announced her retirement in July 2005, followed shortly thereafter by the death of Chief Justice William Rehnquist, Bush nominated, and the Congress confirmed, two conservative jurists who seemed certain to align themselves with justices Antonin Scalia and Clarence Thomas, the aggressive judicial radicals who had long endorsed the most expansive exercise of presidential power. A fifty-year-old appellate jurist, John Roberts, who had once worked in the Reagan Justice Department, took over for Rehnquist as Chief Justice. After unexpected opposition among congressional Republicans and right-wing pundits to his first nominee Harriet Miers, his White House counsel, Bush nominated in her place Samuel Alito, a staunch judicial conservative, who was confirmed in early 2006 after a hard-fought Senate battle.

But the rest of the president's political agenda faced far greater difficulties. Claiming that Social Security would soon face serious funding difficulties, Bush sought to transform the retirement system by creating private investment accounts that would be paid for with money diverted from the Social Security trust fund itself. Conservatives disliked Social Security for both practical and ideological reasons. It was an efficient government-run program that redistributed funds from the young to the old and from the affluent to the poor. And it represented a huge source of potential capital and new investment that many Wall Street firms hoped to manage directly. Over time, Bush's plan would have drained trillions of dollars from the system and stripped it of its "social" character. The president barnstormed the nation in 2005, but as most Americans came to understand the implications of this effort to privatize Social Security, they turned decisively against this "reform," dooming, for the moment at least, any large-scale effort to dismantle the highly successful retirement system.

The Unraveling of the Bush Regime

As the trauma of 9/11 faded over time, Americans once again turned their attention to the conflicts and controversies that were an inescapable

"Like We Was All Fugitives"

Cory Delany, a twenty-four-year-old resident of Waggerman, Louisiana, was in New Orleans with his family during and after Hurricane Katrina. In an interview for a Minnesota newspaper, he described the five days his family spent trying to get his wheelchair-bound mother to safety. His experiences starkly reveal the dearth of emergency assistance for many of the city's poor residents who were stranded for days without food or water and treated as criminals by police.

I was on the roof trying to flag down helicopters. Nobody would stop. They would give us a thumbs-up and keep on going. . . . On the third day, I just got tired of sitting in this house. I had to get my mama and them out of here. So I went outside. I got three pieces of plywood and like 12 two-by-sixes and [I] built a raft. I tried to get my mama out that house. When I finished building the raft, that's when the boat came and got us. . . .

When we got out of the boat [at a staging area], we meet a police officer. He had a M-16 in his hand telling everybody, "They're coming to get you, walk up to the top of the bridge. The buses are coming to get you, they'll be here in like two hours. . . . " We was all in this one little spot, like 2,000 people in this one little spot. Elderly people, infant babies, handicapped people, sitting in this one little spot waiting on these buses that was supposed to come get us in an hour or two. . . . The second day, 50 buses was riding past us. All the police officers rode by. Nobody stopped to tell us nothing, all they did was show us their guns and stick them out the window. . . . They just kept going. We went three days with the buses just passing by us, everybody getting frustrated. . . .

So the police came back, got out of their cars with their M-16s and their AK-47s ready to shoot somebody. They told us to back up like we was all fugitives. They pointed their guns at us and told us, they not coming for ya'll. Ya'll got to fend for yourself. Try to walk to the Superdome. . . . So we walked down and my people just got tired of walking, so we put up a little camp. There was like 25 of us at that time, 'cause all of us was sticking together. . . . We stayed out there two more nights sleeping on the interstate, this is like five nights now. . . . People was out there barbecuing. You know why? 'Cause black people are not just going to go out like that. They're not going to just die off like that. It's like they just expected us to die. The National Guard finally says, ya'll get ya'll family and ya'll come with me. . . .

So they took my mama to some place in Texas I've never heard of. We couldn't get in touch with them for like three more days. They made us stay out there for three more days, sitting on the interstate waiting on another bus to come and bring us to Dallas. . . . We ended up in this concentration-like camp with barbed wire fences and snipers, like we did something wrong.

City Pages, Volume 26, Issue 1294, September 20, 2005. Interview by Darryl Thibodeaux (http://citypages.com/databank/26/1294/article13694.asp?page=8).

consequence of the dramatic spread of the twenty-first-century global market in goods, labor, and ideas. The unending, disastrous war on terror and the conflict in Iraq generated a new wave of antiwar sentiment and greater popular mistrust of the Bush administration and the GOP-controlled Congress. But the everyday lives of most Americans remained structured by the ever-shifting shape of a capitalist economy that was now inextricably bound to a worldwide market. Social inequality became front-page news in 2005 when Hurricane Katrina ravaged New Orleans, Louisiana. The citizens who were left in the city to weather the storm were largely poor, black, and working class. Images of the destitution and destruction of a major American metropolis pushed many Americans to wonder why the U.S. government was promising so much abroad but could deliver so little at home. Many blamed the growing presence of illegal immigrants, but such xenophobia generated a countermobilization on the part of millions of Latino immigrants and their allies, who took to the streets during the spring of 2006 in protest. With outrage over the war, economic inequality, and bigotry, the Democrats finally retook Congress in the 2006 midterm elections.

Hurricane Katrina   Although President Bush won reelection by asserting that his administration could best provide for and protect American citizens, a crisis at the end of the summer of 2005 put such claims in jeopardy even as the nation came to see that homeland security entailed far more than the projection of military power abroad. When Hurricane Katrina slammed into the Gulf Coast on the morning of August 29, it destroyed tens of billions of dollars in property from the Florida panhandle to the Texas state line. The greatest damage came in New Orleans, where the municipal levees, built and maintained by the U.S. Army Corps of Engineers, failed to hold back the storm's surging water, subjecting the city to massive flooding that had not been seen since the early nineteenth century. The rapidly rising water trapped more than 100,000 residents, most of whom were black, poor, or without cars, in their homes without electricity, water, or food. When tens of thousands of them fled to the Superdome sports arena and the city's convention center downtown, they found themselves literally on their own for more than three days, even as television crews broadcast images of the squalor and chaos that had engulfed these bewildered refugees. At least 1,300 people died during and after Hurricane Katrina made landfall, most of them residents of low-income New Orleans neighborhoods. They fell victim not only to high water, but also to sickness, heat, and thirst because of an inadequate evacuation plan and an excruciatingly slow response from National Guard units and FEMA, now a subunit of the Department of Homeland Security. With much of New Orleans, Biloxi, Mississippi, and other Gulf Coast cities and towns destroyed, more than 1.5 million people were displaced, eventually finding shelter in schools, sports arenas, hotels, and trailers in Houston, Baton Rouge, Memphis, and other outlying southern and even northern cities. Hurricane Katrina was the most expensive and one of the most deadly disasters in U.S. history.

The Katrina debacle had two long-range consequences. First, it once again put environmental issues on the national agenda. Most scientists thought that the destruction of Gulf Coast wetlands that had been going on for decades had exacerbated the impact of the hurricane's storm surge, and some meteorologists hypothesized that global warming was increasing the frequency and intensity of Atlantic hurricanes. Second, and more immediate, the disparate and highly graphic racial and class consequences of the storm seemed to discredit the Bush administration's militarized ideology of homeland security and minimal government activism. FEMA head Michael Brown resigned in disgrace on September 12, and Congress quickly appropriated at least $70 billion for reconstruction aid. Conservative efforts to make the Bush tax cuts permanent were put on hold. Opinion polls recorded a sharp drop in the number of Americans who approved of the president and the way he was doing his job (Figure 15.2). A year after Hurricane Katrina, corruption and mismanagement were key words in all government reports and newspaper stories: less than half the money that had been appropriated to assist victims had been spent, $2 billion had been lost through fraud and waste, mobile homes costing $900 million went unused because they were unsuitable in a flood plain, and only 35 percent of New Orleans residents returned to the Crescent City.

The Politics of Immigrant Citizenship
The public's anger at the neglect of New Orleans during and after Hurricane Katrina turned to active hostility when it came to immigration politics during the first decade of the

Looters vs. Finders
The predicament of tens of thousands of poor and mainly African American New Orleans residents in the wake of Hurricane Katrina plainly revealed continuing racial and economic inequality. Unequal treatment also characterized some news coverage of the disaster. For example, a number of photographs showing flood survivors' search for supplies were accompanied by descriptive captions that relied on racial stereotypes to interpret events. The caption to the photograph on the left described a young man wading "through chest deep flood water after looting a grocery store," while the photograph on the right was described as showing two residents "after finding bread and soda from a local grocery store." Associated Press/Dave Martin; Agence France-Presse/Chris Graythen.

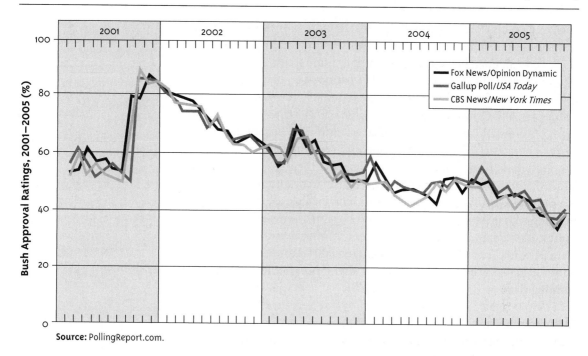

Source: PollingReport.com.

FIGURE 15.2   Sinking Popularity

Although the 9/11 attacks provided President Bush with a significant increase in public support, his approval ratings have declined steadily since. The growing dissatisfaction with the war in Iraq, the mishandling of aid for victims of Hurricane Katrina, and the economy resulted in an all-time low rating of 34 percent in early 2006.

twenty-first century. Economically hard-pressed Americans had long seen immigrants, especially those whose legal status was questionable, as competitors for jobs and a burden on schools, hospitals, and the welfare system. Many business leaders, the Bush administration, and the Democratic Party favored an expanded guest worker program and a path toward regular citizenship for undocumented immigrants, estimated at more than twelve million, who already lived inside U.S. borders. But passionate opposition was expressed by opponents of mass immigration and legalization. Encouraged by some conservative politicians and television commentators, much of this animosity turned against the recent wave of Latino immigrants. These immigrants had recently transformed the workforce in cities across the country, including Memphis, Cincinnati, and Pittsburgh, not just those in the Southwest, the traditional locus of the nation's Mexican American population. "I tell you that the area where I grew up now resembles Tijuana more than the U.S.," one Nashville resident proclaimed. "My neighborhood is gone. . . . I can't read the signs because I don't speak Spanish — in my native country!" A vigilante group calling itself the "Minutemen" made highly publicized visits to the U.S.-Mexican border, while in Congress, many politicians backed highly restrictive measures that would criminalize illegal aliens and appropriate billions for a "Berlin Wall"–style fence between the two nations.

This debate divided both major political parties, but it also energized millions of Latinos, both citizens and noncitizens. Beginning in early spring

2006 and cresting on May Day of that year, hundreds of thousands of Latinos marched in demonstrations all across the country. Vowing to boycott work and shopping, the May 1 "Day Without Immigrants" had its epicenter in Los Angeles, but tens of thousands of Latinos also marched in Denver, Phoenix, and New York as well as in such unlikely towns as Santa Maria, California, and Omaha, Nebraska. In Chicago, marchers chanted, "USA! USA!," "Amnistia!," and "Bush, escucha, estamos en la lucha ["Bush, listen, we're fighting back"]!" As one participant put it, immigrants deserved "not just green cards, not just visas, but citizenship." Because their nonunion, largely Latino workforce participated in these marches, numerous Midwestern pork- and poultry-processing plants remained closed on May Day. For the moment, these demonstrations and boycotts returned the American protest tradition to its early twentieth-century ethnic-proletarian origins, a time when the quest for citizenship and equal rights was inherent in the fight for higher wages, stronger unions, and more political power for the working class.

Bush Republicans Divided and Defeated　　After the May 2006 demonstrations, the legacy of the Iraq war continued to fester, helping to drain the Bush presidency of the remaining power and legitimacy it had won after 9/11. Continuing corruption and scandal fed into the rising criticism of the Bush administration, which was evident both inside and outside the Republican Party. Just two years after the 2004 election, voters dealt the president and his party a devastating blow, delivering majorities in both the U.S. House and Senate to the Democrats for the first time since 1994.

Although the midterm elections were focused on Iraq, scandals and legal trouble plagued the Bush administration. Tom DeLay, the powerful House majority leader, was forced to resign his seat in April after he was indicted on campaign finance corruption charges. Other Republican congressmen also resigned their seats, failed to stand for reelection in November, or were tarnished by the jailing of Jack Abramoff, a notorious influence peddler and staunch Republican partisan. Sexual impropriety scared the Republican base as well, as Florida Congressman Mark Foley abruptly resigned in September when it became known that he had solicited former congressional pages for homosexual companionship. And a two-year-long investigation into Bush administration officials' disclosure of the identity of a covert CIA operative, Valerie Plame, resulted in the indictment and ultimate conviction for perjury and obstruction of justice of I. Lewis "Scooter" Libby, top aide to Vice President Dick Cheney. Libby was sentenced to thirty months in prison in June 2007, though he did not have to serve a single day in jail because President Bush commuted his jail sentence two weeks later.

Meanwhile, the death toll of U.S. servicemen and servicewomen killed in Iraq continued its relentless climb, and by 2006, public opinion polls reported that more than two-thirds of Americans considered the Bush administration's conduct of the war misguided. Among the chief critics were a sizable number from within the military itself—recently retired officers who now publicly attacked Defense Secretary Donald Rumsfeld, whom they charged with not having an effective "exit strategy" for U.S. troops in Iraq.

The Bush administration's efforts to enhance presidential power in the larger "war on terror" also generated enormous controversy. In 2006, the U.S. Supreme Court declared that "unlawful combatants" who were being held at the U.S. military base in Guantanamo Bay, Cuba, and other secret prisons must be given access to U.S. courts and must be treated in accordance with Common Article 3 of the Geneva Conventions, which forbids torture. When the U.S. Congress sought legislation respecting these rights, the Bush administration insisted on highly restrictive military tribunals that denied many prisoners the right of access to a formally constituted court of law. When the Bush administration sought to redefine the Geneva Conventions in a way that would dramatically weaken accepted prohibitions against torture, prominent Republicans with close ties to the military objected. Former Secretary of State Colin Powell, who had resigned right after the 2004 elections, thought that any tampering with these international agreements would undermine the "moral basis" of the American war against terrorism. The president eventually got most of what he wanted but exposed the fissures within his own party.

Concerns about the Bush administration's handling of the war turned the 2006 midterm elections into a referendum on Iraq. President Bush and other Republicans declared that they would "stay the course" until the insurgency within Iraq had been defeated. Anything less, they said, was tantamount to surrender in the battle against al-Qaeda. But most Americans now made a sharp distinction between the "war on terror" and the conflict in Iraq, which a report from the CIA and other intelligence agencies concluded had contributed to instability and insurgency throughout the Middle East. Within the Democratic Party, grassroots sentiment moved decisively toward a rapid withdrawal of American troops from Iraq. The Democratic victory in the 2006 elections had immediate political consequences: Defense Secretary Rumsfeld resigned from his post, and it seemed that President Bush might have to reconsider his strategy in Iraq.

The December 2006 report of the bipartisan Iraq Study Group—co-chaired by James Baker, former secretary of state in the George H. W. Bush administration and trusted Bush family adviser, and Lee Hamilton, vice chairman of the 9/11 Commission and a former Democratic congressman from Indiana—called for major changes in U.S. military and diplomatic policy in Iraq and the Middle East. However, despite the moderate nature of the report's recommendations and the broad bipartisan support it generated, the Bush administration stubbornly refused to consider changes in its

Iraq policy. The president opted instead for a "troop surge," which began in January 2007 and involved the insertion of nearly 30,000 additional U.S. military forces in and around Baghdad, the Iraqi capital, intended to quell sectarian violence and prop up the weak civilian government. Not surprisingly, U.S. military casualties dramatically increased during the surge, with no discernable decrease in the sectarian violence that continued to wrack the country. By the summer of 2007, more than 3,600 U.S. troops had been killed and nearly 30,000 wounded, many of them gravely, in the almost five years since the U.S. military led the invasion to overthrow Saddam Hussein.

Despite the president's repeated calls for "patience," support for the Iraq war and America's continued presence there weakened considerably during 2007. Democrats, while strongly opposed to the war, had trouble agreeing on a strategy to extricate American troops from the quagmire that Iraq had become. A number of Republican senators and representatives broke ranks with the president, calling for a firm date for withdrawal of U.S. military forces from Iraq or for implementation of the Iraq Study Group's recommendations. Soon the president had great difficulty holding together his own party, many of whose elected officials were concerned that continued failure to end the war seriously jeopardized the Republican Party's electoral chances in 2008. George W. Bush, like Richard Nixon before him during the Vietnam War, had become increasingly isolated, seemingly impervious to the growing political crisis his actions in Iraq had engendered within the United States and throughout the world. And like Nixon, Bush's overall public approval ratings sank to historic lows for a sitting president, reaching 26 percent in several opinion polls—a powerful measure of how isolated and unpopular the president and his war in Iraq had become.

Conclusion: Looking Forward

Controversies over Katrina, immigrant rights, the war, and the conservative social and cultural agenda gave hope to many people that the conservative political ascendancy was at an end and that reinvigorated popular social movements, including the labor movement, would now take the lead in fighting for economic security and social justice for all Americans. History offers no clear blueprint for change, but it does suggest that fundamental transformation comes in sudden and dramatic fashion. The liberation of African Americans came in two great forward leaps: the first during and immediately following the Civil War, the second a hundred years later, in the civil rights revolution of the 1950s and 1960s. Likewise, American women twice thrust onto the national agenda issues involving their own political and social liberation: first during the decades before World War I and then again a half-century later in an even more profound exploration of their personal and political consciousness. Latino, Asian, and Native Americans and gay Americans have fought their own unfinished battles. And the growth of American citizenship for women, people of color, and all those who trade their labor for bread cannot be divorced from the activism of the working class itself. American workers, including very recent immigrants, have repeatedly discovered their voice and their power in a series of unexpectedly major popular insurgencies that have invigorated the republic over the course of the last two centuries.

We cannot foretell the future. But we can be certain that in a globally integrated workplace, where men and women must still labor for their livelihoods, people who see their identity as workers will play a central role in shaping the new world. In new immigrant communities, in old factory towns, in urban ghettos and suburban office parks, and all across the new retail archipelago, the working class, in all its twenty-first-century diversity, is certain to press forward its claim to dignity and social justice.

The Years in Review

2001

- George W. Bush is inaugurated as the forty-third president.
- Two hijacked jetliners strike the World Trade Center in a terrorist attack against United States; a third hijacked plane flies into the Pentagon; a fourth crashes in rural Pennsylvania.
- In response to the September 11 terrorist attacks, U.S. and British forces launch daily bombing of Taliban government and al-Qaeda camps in Afghanistan.
- Following the bombing campaign, Afghani opposition troops oust the Taliban regime; the search for Osama bin Laden and other leaders of al-Qaeda continues.
- Congress passes the Uniting and Strengthening America by Providing Appropriate Tools Required to Intercept and Obstruct Terrorism Act, known as the USA Patriot Act, which extends government surveillance powers.

2002

- Enron chairman Kenneth L. Lay resigns as the company declares bankruptcy; the federal government begins an investigation of company fraud for hiding debt and misrepresenting earnings.
- In his first State of the Union address, President Bush labels Iran, Iraq, and North Korea an "axis of evil" and declares that the United States will wage war against states that develop weapons of mass destruction.
- President Bush signs legislation creating a new cabinet-level Department of Homeland Security.

2003

- The United States and Britain invade Iraq.

- Bush signs a $350 billion tax cut package, the third-largest tax cut in U.S. history.

- In one of the most important rulings on the issue of affirmative action in twenty-five years, the Supreme Court upholds the right of affirmative action in higher education.

- The Recording Industry Association of America cracks down on the illegal downloading and swapping of songs over the Internet, filing lawsuits against hundreds of people.

2004

- Graphic photos of American soldiers abusing and sexually humiliating Iraqi prisoners at Abu Ghraib prison spark outrage around the world.

- Massachusetts is the first state to legalize gay marriages.

- The United States returns sovereignty to an interim government in Iraq but maintains more than 130,000 troops in the country to fight a growing insurgency.

- The 9/11 Commission harshly criticizes the government's handling of terrorist attacks.

- The final U.S. report on Iraq's weapons finds no weapons of mass destruction.

- George W. Bush is reelected president, defeating Massachusetts Senator John Kerry.

2005

- Hurricane Katrina wreaks catastrophic damage on Mississippi and Louisiana, and 80 percent of New Orleans is flooded; all levels of government are criticized for the delayed and inadequate response to the disaster.

2006

- The midterm elections give the Democrats a majority in the House of Representatives for the first time since 1994 and reflect a growing opposition to the war in Iraq among the American people.

- The bipartisan Iraq Study Group issues a report calling for broad changes in U.S. military and diplomatic policy in Iraq; the Bush administration ignores the recommendations in favor of its "stay the course" military strategy.

2007

- After a federal investigation of the leaked identity of covert CIA operative Valerie Plame, I. Lewis "Scooter" Libby is convicted of perjury, obstruction of justice, and making false statements to a federal investigator and is sentenced to thirty months in prison. President Bush subsequently commutes his sentence before Libby serves jail time.

- Bush administration announces new "troop surge," deploying nearly 30,000 additional U.S. troops in and around Baghdad to quell growing sectarian violence in Iraqi capital.

- Bush's opinion poll numbers continue to drop throughout the year; in June, only 26 percent of Americans approve of the president's performance in office.

Additional Readings

For more on the September 11 attacks and the domestic aftermath, see: Geneive Abdo, *Mecca and Main Street: Muslim Life in America After 9/11* (2006); Phyllis Bennis and Edward Said, *Before and After: US Foreign Policy and the September 11th Crisis* (2002); Nancy Chang and Howard Zinn, *Silencing Political Dissent: How Post-September 11 Anti-Terrorism Measures Threaten Our Civil Liberties* (2002); Mary L. Dudziak, *September 11 in History: A Watershed Moment?* (2003); and David Rosner and Gerald Markowitz, *Are We Ready? Public Health Since 9/11* (2006).

For more on the war on terror in Afghanistan and Iraq, see: Andrew J. Bacevich, *New American Militarism: How Americans Are Seduced by War* (2006); George Packard, *Assassins Gate: America in Iraq* (2006); Frances Fox Piven, *The War at Home: The Domestic Costs of Bush's Militarism* (2004); John Prados, *America Confronts Terrorism: Understanding the Danger and How to Think About It* (2002); Ahmed Rashid, *Taliban: Militant Islam, Oil, and Fundamentalism in Central Asia* (2001); James Risen, *State of War: The Secret History of the CIA and the Bush Administration* (2006); Zachary Shore, *Breeding Bin Ladens: America, Islam, and the Future of Europe* (2006); and Steven Strasser, ed., *The Abu Ghraib Investigations: The Official Independent Panel and Pentagon Reports on the Shocking Prisoner Abuse in Iraq* (2004).

For more on the new business and conservative agendas, see: Benjamin Barber, *Jihad vs. McWorld: How Globalism and Tribalism Are Reshaping the World* (2001); E. J. Dionne and William Kristol, eds., *Bush v. Gore: The Court Cases and the Commentary* (2001); William Greider, *One*

World, Ready or Not: The Manic Logic of Global Capitalism (1998); Akira Iriye, *Cultural Internationalism and World Order* (2001); Walter LaFeber, *Michael Jordan and the New Global Capitalism* (2002); Nelson Lichtenstein, *Wal-Mart: The Face of Twenty-First-Century Capitalism* (2006); and Joseph Stiglitz, *Globalization and Its Discontents* (2003).

For more on Hurricane Katrina, see: Douglas Brinkley, *The Great Deluge: Hurricane Katrina, New Orleans, and the Mississippi Gulf Coast* (2006); and Michael Eric Dyson, *Come Hell or High Water: Hurricane Katrina and the Color of Disaster* (2006).

For more on immigration, see: Alejandro Portes and Ruben G. Rumbaut, *Immigrant America: A Portrait* (2006).

Appendix 1
The Declaration of Independence

IN CONGRESS, July 4, 1776.

The unanimous Declaration of the thirteen united States of America,

When in the Course of human events, it becomes necessary for one people to dissolve the political bands which have connected them with another, and to assume among the powers of the earth, the separate and equal station to which the Laws of Nature and of Nature's God entitle them, a decent respect to the opinions of mankind requires that they should declare the causes which impel them to the separation.

We hold these truths to be self-evident, that all men are created equal, that they are endowed by their Creator with certain unalienable Rights, that among these are Life, Liberty and the pursuit of Happiness. — That to secure these rights, Governments are instituted among Men, deriving their just powers from the consent of the governed, — That whenever any Form of Government becomes destructive of these ends, it is the Right of the People to alter or to abolish it, and to institute new Government, laying its foundation on such principles and organizing its powers in such form, as to them shall seem most likely to effect their Safety and Happiness. Prudence, indeed, will dictate that Governments long established should not be changed for light and transient causes; and accordingly all experience hath shewn, that mankind are more disposed to suffer, while evils are sufferable, than to right themselves by abolishing the forms to which they are accustomed. But when a long train of abuses and usurpations, pursuing invariably the same Object evinces a design to reduce them under absolute Despotism, it is their right, it is their duty, to throw off such Government, and to provide new Guards for their future security.—Such has been the patient sufferance of these Colonies; and such is now the necessity which constrains them to alter their former Systems of Government. The history of the present King of Great Britain is a history of repeated injuries and usurpations, all having in direct object the establishment of an absolute Tyranny over these States. To prove this, let Facts be submitted to a candid world.

He has refused his Assent to Laws, the most wholesome and necessary for the public good.

He has forbidden his Governors to pass Laws of immediate and pressing importance, unless suspended in their operation till his Assent should be obtained; and when so suspended, he has utterly neglected to attend to them.

He has refused to pass other Laws for the accommodation of large districts of people, unless those people would relinquish the right of Representation in the Legislature, a right inestimable to them and formidable to tyrants only.

He has called together legislative bodies at places unusual, uncomfortable, and distant from the depository of their public Records, for the sole purpose of fatiguing them into compliance with his measures.

He has dissolved Representative Houses repeatedly, for opposing with manly firmness his invasions on the rights of the people.

He has refused for a long time, after such dissolutions, to cause others to be elected; whereby the Legislative powers, incapable of Annihilation, have returned to the People at large for their exercise; the State remaining in the mean time exposed to all the dangers of invasion from without, and convulsions within.

He has endeavoured to prevent the population of these States; for that purpose obstructing the Laws for Naturalization of Foreigners; refusing to pass others to encourage their migrations hither, and raising the conditions of new Appropriations of Lands.

He has obstructed the Administration of Justice, by refusing his Assent to Laws for establishing Judiciary powers.

He has made Judges dependent on his Will alone, for the tenure of their offices, and the amount and payment of their salaries.

He has erected a multitude of New Offices, and sent hither swarms of Officers to harrass our people, and eat out their substance.

He has kept among us, in times of peace, Standing Armies without the Consent of our legislatures.

He has affected to render the Military independent of and superior to the Civil power.

He has combined with others to subject us to a jurisdiction foreign to our constitution, and unacknowledged by our laws; giving his Assent to their Acts of pretended Legislation:

For Quartering large bodies of armed troops among us:

For protecting them, by a mock Trial, from punishment for any Murders which they should commit on the Inhabitants of these States:

For cutting off our Trade with all parts of the world:

For imposing Taxes on us without our Consent:

For depriving us in many cases, of the benefits of Trial by Jury:

For transporting us beyond Seas to be tried for pretended offences

For abolishing the free System of English Laws in a neighbouring Province, establishing therein an Arbitrary government, and enlarging its Boundaries so as to render it at once an example and fit instrument for introducing the same absolute rule into these Colonies:

For taking away our Charters, abolishing our most valuable Laws, and altering fundamentally the Forms of our Governments:

For suspending our own Legislatures, and declaring themselves invested with power to legislate for us in all cases whatsoever.

He has abdicated Government here, by declaring us out of his Protection and waging War against us.

He has plundered our seas, ravaged our Coasts, burnt our towns, and destroyed the lives of our people.

He is at this time transporting large Armies of foreign Mercenaries to compleat the works of death, desolation and tyranny, already begun with circumstances of Cruelty & perfidy scarcely paralleled in the most barbarous ages, and totally unworthy the Head of a civilized nation.

He has constrained our fellow Citizens taken Captive on the high Seas to bear Arms against their Country, to become the executioners of their friends and Brethren, or to fall themselves by their Hands.

He has excited domestic insurrections amongst us, and has endeavoured to bring on the inhabitants of our frontiers, the merciless Indian Savages, whose known rule of warfare, is an undistinguished destruction of all ages, sexes and conditions.

In every stage of these Oppressions We have Petitioned for Redress in the most humble terms: Our repeated Petitions have been answered only by repeated injury. A Prince whose character is thus marked by every act which may define a Tyrant, is unfit to be the ruler of a free people.

Nor have We been wanting in attentions to our Brittish brethren. We have warned them from time to time of attempts by their legislature to extend an unwarrantable jurisdiction over us. We have reminded them of the circumstances of our emigration and settlement here. We have appealed to their native justice and magnanimity, and we have conjured them by the ties of our common kindred to disavow these usurpations, which, would inevitably interrupt our connections and correspondence. They too have been deaf to the voice of justice and of consanguinity. We must, therefore, acquiesce in the necessity, which denounces our Separation, and hold them, as we hold the rest of mankind, Enemies in War, in Peace Friends.

We, therefore, the Representatives of the united States of America, in General Congress, Assembled, appealing to the Supreme Judge of the world for the rectitude of our intentions, do, in the Name, and by Authority of the good People of these Colonies, solemnly publish and declare, That these United Colonies are, and of Right ought to be Free and Independent States; that they are Absolved from all Allegiance to the British Crown, and that all political connection between them and the State of Great Britain, is and ought to be totally dissolved; and that as Free and Independent States, they have full Power to levy War, conclude Peace, contract Alliances, establish Commerce, and to do all other Acts and Things which Independent States may of right do. And for the support of this Declaration, with a firm reliance on the protection of divine Providence, we mutually pledge to each other our Lives, our Fortunes and our sacred Honor.

Georgia
Button Gwinnett
Lyman Hall
George Walton

North Carolina
William Hooper
Joseph Hewes
John Penn

South Carolina
Edward Rutledge
Thomas Heyward, Jr.
Thomas Lynch, Jr.
Arthur Middleton

Maryland
Samuel Chase
William Paca
Thomas Stone
Charles Carroll of
   Carrollton

Virginia
George Wythe
Richard Henry Lee
Thomas Jefferson
Benjamin Harrison
Thomas Nelson, Jr.
Francis Lightfoot Lee
Carter Braxton

Pennsylvania
Robert Morris
Benjamin Rush
Benjamin Franklin
John Morton
George Clymer
James Smith
George Taylor
James Wilson
George Ross

Massachusetts
John Hancock

Delaware
Caesar Rodney
George Read
Thomas McKean

New York
William Floyd
Philip Livingston
Francis Lewis
Lewis Morris

New Jersey
Richard Stockton
John Witherspoon
Francis Hopkinson
John Hart
Abraham Clark

New Hampshire
Josiah Bartlett
William Whipple

Massachusetts
Samuel Adams
John Adams
Robert Treat Paine
Elbridge Gerry

Rhode Island
Stephen Hopkins
William Ellery

Connecticut
Roger Sherman
Samuel Huntington
William Williams
Oliver Wolcott

New Hampshire
Matthew Thornton

Appendix 2
Constitution of the United States of America

Note: The following text is a transcription of the Constitution in its original form.

We the People of the United

States, in Order to form a more perfect Union, establish Justice, insure domestic Tranquility, provide for the common defence, promote the general Welfare, and secure the Blessings of Liberty to ourselves and our Posterity, do ordain and establish this Constitution for the United States of America.

Article I

Section 1
All legislative Powers herein granted shall be vested in a Congress of the United States, which shall consist of a Senate and House of Representatives.

Section 2
The House of Representatives shall be composed of Members chosen every second Year by the People of the several States, and the Electors in each State shall have the Qualifications requisite for Electors of the most numerous Branch of the State Legislature.

No Person shall be a Representative who shall not have attained to the Age of twenty five Years, and been seven Years a Citizen of the United States, and who shall not, when elected, be an Inhabitant of that State in which he shall be chosen.

Representatives and direct Taxes shall be apportioned among the several States which may be included within this Union, according to their respective Numbers, which shall be determined by adding to the whole Number of free Persons, including those bound to Service for a Term of Years, and excluding Indians not taxed, three fifths of all other Persons. The actual Enumeration shall be made within three Years after the first Meeting of the Congress of the United States, and within every subsequent Term of ten Years, in such Manner as they shall by Law direct. The Number of Representatives shall not exceed one for every thirty Thousand, but each State shall have at Least one Representative; and until such enumeration shall be made, the State of New Hampshire shall be entitled to chuse three, Massachusetts eight, Rhode-Island and Providence Plantations one, Connecticut five, New-York six, New Jersey four, Pennsylvania eight, Delaware one, Maryland six, Virginia ten, North Carolina five, South Carolina five, and Georgia three.

When vacancies happen in the Representation from any State, the Executive Authority thereof shall issue Writs of Election to fill such Vacancies.

The House of Representatives shall chuse their Speaker and other Officers; and shall have the sole Power of Impeachment.

Section 3
The Senate of the United States shall be composed of two Senators from each State, chosen by the Legislature thereof for six Years; and each Senator shall have one Vote.

Immediately after they shall be assembled in Consequence of the first Election, they shall be divided as equally as may be into three Classes. The Seats of the Senators of the first Class shall be vacated at the Expiration of the second Year, of the second Class at the Expiration of the fourth Year, and of the third Class at the Expiration of the sixth Year, so that one third may be chosen every second Year; and if Vacancies happen by Resignation, or otherwise, during the Recess of the Legislature of any State, the Executive thereof may make temporary Appointments until the next Meeting of the Legislature, which shall then fill such Vacancies.

No Person shall be a Senator who shall not have attained to the Age of thirty Years, and been nine Years a Citizen of the United States, and who shall not, when elected, be an Inhabitant of that State for which he shall be chosen.

The Vice President of the United States shall be President of the Senate, but shall have no Vote, unless they be equally divided.

The Senate shall chuse their other Officers, and also a President pro tempore, in the Absence of the Vice President, or when he shall exercise the Office of President of the United States.

The Senate shall have the sole Power to try all Impeachments. When sitting for that Purpose, they shall be on Oath or Affirmation. When the President of the United States is tried, the Chief Justice shall preside: And no Person shall be convicted without the Concurrence of two thirds of the Members present.

Judgment in Cases of Impeachment shall not extend further than to removal from Office, and disqualification to hold and enjoy any Office of honor, Trust or Profit under the United States: but the Party convicted shall nevertheless be liable and subject to Indictment, Trial, Judgment and Punishment, according to Law.

Section 4

The Times, Places and Manner of holding Elections for Senators and Representatives, shall be prescribed in each State by the Legislature thereof; but the Congress may at any time by Law make or alter such Regulations, except as to the Places of chusing Senators.

The Congress shall assemble at least once in every Year, and such Meeting shall be on the first Monday in December, unless they shall by Law appoint a different Day.

Section 5

Each House shall be the Judge of the Elections, Returns and Qualifications of its own Members, and a Majority of each shall constitute a Quorum to do Business; but a smaller Number may adjourn from day to day, and may be authorized to compel the Attendance of absent Members, in such Manner, and under such Penalties as each House may provide.

Each House may determine the Rules of its Proceedings, punish its Members for disorderly Behaviour, and, with the Concurrence of two thirds, expel a Member.

Each House shall keep a Journal of its Proceedings, and from time to time publish the same, excepting such Parts as may in their Judgment require Secrecy; and the Yeas and Nays of the Members of either House on any question shall, at the Desire of one fifth of those Present, be entered on the Journal.

Neither House, during the Session of Congress, shall, without the Consent of the other, adjourn for more than three days, nor to any other Place than that in which the two Houses shall be sitting.

Section 6

The Senators and Representatives shall receive a Compensation for their Services, to be ascertained by Law, and paid out of the Treasury of the United States. They shall in all Cases, except Treason, Felony and Breach of the Peace, be privileged from Arrest during their Attendance at the Session of their respective Houses, and in going to and returning from the same; and for any Speech or Debate in either House, they shall not be questioned in any other Place.

No Senator or Representative shall, during the Time for which he was elected, be appointed to any civil Office under the Authority of the United States, which shall have been created, or the Emoluments whereof shall have been encreased during such time; and no Person holding any Office under the United States, shall be a Member of either House during his Continuance in Office.

Section 7

All Bills for raising Revenue shall originate in the House of Representatives; but the Senate may propose or concur with Amendments as on other Bills.

Every Bill which shall have passed the House of Representatives and the Senate, shall, before it become a Law, be presented to the President of the United States: If he approve he shall sign it, but if not he shall return it, with his Objections to that House in which it shall have originated, who shall enter the Objections at large on their Journal, and proceed to reconsider it. If after such Reconsideration two thirds of that House shall agree to pass the Bill, it shall be sent, together with the Objections, to the other House, by which it shall likewise be reconsidered, and if approved by two thirds of that House, it shall become a Law. But in all such Cases the Votes of both Houses shall be determined by yeas and Nays, and the Names of the Persons voting for and against the Bill shall be entered on the Journal of each House respectively. If any Bill shall not be returned by the President within ten Days (Sundays excepted) after it shall have been presented to him, the Same shall be a Law, in like Manner as if he had signed it, unless the Congress by their Adjournment prevent its Return, in which Case it shall not be a Law.

Every Order, Resolution, or Vote to which the Concurrence of the Senate and House of Representatives may be necessary (except on a question of Adjournment) shall be presented to the President of the United States; and before the Same shall take Effect, shall be approved by him, or being disapproved by him, shall be repassed by two thirds of the Senate and House of Representatives, according to the Rules and Limitations prescribed in the Case of a Bill.

Section 8

The Congress shall have Power To lay and collect Taxes, Duties, Imposts and Excises, to pay the Debts and provide for the common Defence and general Welfare of the United States; but all Duties, Imposts and Excises shall be uniform throughout the United States;

To borrow Money on the credit of the United States;

To regulate Commerce with foreign Nations, and among the several States, and with the Indian Tribes;

To establish an uniform Rule of Naturalization, and uniform Laws on the subject of Bankruptcies throughout the United States;

To coin Money, regulate the Value thereof, and of foreign Coin, and fix the Standard of Weights and Measures;

To provide for the Punishment of counterfeiting the Securities and current Coin of the United States;

To establish Post Offices and post Roads; To promote the Progress of Science and useful Arts, by securing for limited Times to Authors and Inventors the exclusive Right to their respective Writings and Discoveries;

To constitute Tribunals inferior to the supreme Court;

To define and punish Piracies and Felonies committed on the high Seas, and Offences against the Law of Nations;

To declare War, grant Letters of Marque and Reprisal, and make Rules concerning Captures on Land and Water;

To raise and support Armies, but no Appropriation of Money to that Use shall be for a longer Term than two Years;

To provide and maintain a Navy;

To make Rules for the Government and Regulation of the land and naval Forces;

To provide for calling forth the Militia to execute the Laws of the Union, suppress Insurrections and repel Invasions;

To provide for organizing, arming, and disciplining, the Militia, and for governing such Part of them as may be employed in the Service of the United States, reserving to the States respectively, the Appointment of the Officers, and the Authority of training the Militia according to the discipline prescribed by Congress;

To exercise exclusive Legislation in all Cases whatsoever, over such District (not exceeding ten Miles square) as may, by Cession of particular States, and the Acceptance of Congress, become the Seat of the Government of the United States, and to exercise like Authority over all Places purchased by the Consent of the Legislature of the State in which the Same shall be, for the Erection of Forts, Magazines, Arsenals, dock-Yards, and other needful Buildings;—And

To make all Laws which shall be necessary and proper for carrying into Execution the foregoing Powers, and all other Powers vested by this Constitution in the Government of the United States, or in any Department or Officer thereof.

Section 9

The Migration or Importation of such Persons as any of the States now existing shall think proper to admit, shall not be prohibited by the Congress prior to the Year one thousand eight hundred and eight, but a Tax or duty may be imposed on such Importation, not exceeding ten dollars for each Person.

The Privilege of the Writ of Habeas Corpus shall not be suspended, unless when in Cases of Rebellion or Invasion the public Safety may require it.

No Bill of Attainder or ex post facto Law shall be passed.

No Capitation, or other direct, Tax shall be laid, unless in Proportion to the Census or enumeration herein before directed to be taken.

No Tax or Duty shall be laid on Articles exported from any State.

No Preference shall be given by any Regulation of Commerce or Revenue to the Ports of one State over those of another; nor shall Vessels bound to, or from, one State, be obliged to enter, clear, or pay Duties in another.

No Money shall be drawn from the Treasury, but in Consequence of Appropriations made by Law; and a regular Statement and Account of the Receipts and Expenditures of all public Money shall be published from time to time.

No Title of Nobility shall be granted by the United States: And no Person holding any Office of Profit or Trust under them, shall, without the Consent of the Congress, accept of any present, Emolument, Office, or Title, of any kind whatever, from any King, Prince, or foreign State.

Section 10

No State shall enter into any Treaty, Alliance, or Confederation; grant Letters of Marque and Reprisal; coin Money; emit Bills of Credit; make any Thing but gold and silver Coin a Tender in Payment of Debts; pass any Bill of Attainder, ex post facto Law, or Law impairing the Obligation of Contracts, or grant any Title of Nobility.

No State shall, without the Consent of the Congress, lay any Imposts or Duties on Imports or Exports, except what may be absolutely necessary for executing it's inspection Laws: and the net Produce of all Duties and Imposts, laid by any State on Imports or Exports, shall be for the Use of the Treasury of the United States; and all such Laws shall be subject to the Revision and Controul of the Congress.

No State shall, without the Consent of Congress, lay any Duty of Tonnage, keep Troops, or Ships of War in time of Peace, enter into any Agreement or Compact with another State, or with a foreign Power, or engage in War, unless actually invaded, or in such imminent Danger as will not admit of delay.

Article II

Section 1

The executive Power shall be vested in a President of the United States of America. He shall hold his Office during the Term of four Years, and, together with the Vice President, chosen for the same Term, be elected, as follows:

Each State shall appoint, in such Manner as the Legislature thereof may direct, a Number of Electors, equal to the whole Number of Senators and Representatives to which the State may be entitled in the Congress: but no Senator or Representative, or Person holding an Office of Trust or Profit under the United States, shall be appointed an Elector.

The Electors shall meet in their respective States, and vote by Ballot for two Persons, of whom one at least shall not be an Inhabitant of the same State with themselves. And they shall make a List of all the Persons voted for, and of the Number of Votes for each; which List they shall sign and certify, and transmit sealed to the Seat of the Government of the United States, directed to the President of the Senate. The President of the Senate shall, in the Presence of the Senate and House of Representatives, open all the Certificates, and the Votes shall then be counted.

The Person having the greatest Number of Votes shall be the President, if such Number be a Majority of the whole Number of Electors appointed; and if there be more than one who have such Majority, and have an equal Number of Votes, then the House of Representatives shall immediately chuse by Ballot one of them for President; and if no Person have a Majority, then from the five highest on the List the said House shall in like Manner chuse the President. But in chusing the President, the Votes shall be taken by States, the Representation from each State having one Vote; A quorum for this purpose shall consist of a Member or Members from two thirds of the States, and a Majority of all the States shall be necessary to a Choice. In every Case, after the Choice of the President, the Person having the greatest Number of Votes of the Electors shall be the Vice President. But if there should remain two or more who have equal Votes, the Senate shall chuse from them by Ballot the Vice President.

The Congress may determine the Time of chusing the Electors, and the Day on which they shall give their Votes; which Day shall be the same throughout the United States.

No Person except a natural born Citizen, or a Citizen of the United States, at the time of the Adoption of this Constitution, shall be eligible to the Office of President; neither shall any Person be eligible to that Office who shall not have attained to the Age of thirty five Years, and been fourteen Years a Resident within the United States.

In Case of the Removal of the President from Office, or of his Death, Resignation, or Inability to discharge the Powers and Duties of the said Office, the Same shall devolve on the Vice President, and the Congress may by Law provide for the Case of Removal, Death, Resignation or Inability, both of the President and Vice President, declaring what Officer shall then act as President, and such Officer shall act accordingly, until the Disability be removed, or a President shall be elected.

The President shall, at stated Times, receive for his Services, a Compensation, which shall neither be increased nor diminished during the Period for which he shall have been elected, and he shall not receive within that Period any other Emolument from the United States, or any of them.

Before he enter on the Execution of his Office, he shall take the following Oath or Affirmation:—"I do solemnly swear (or affirm) that I will faithfully execute the Office of President of the United States, and will to the best of my Ability, preserve, protect and defend the Constitution of the United States."

Section 2

The President shall be Commander in Chief of the Army and Navy of the United States, and of the Militia of the several States, when called into the actual Service of the United States; he may require the Opinion, in writing, of the principal Officer in each of the executive Departments, upon any Subject relating to the Duties of their respective Offices, and he shall have Power to grant Reprieves and Pardons for Offences against the United States, except in Cases of Impeachment.

He shall have Power, by and with the Advice and Consent of the Senate, to make Treaties, provided two thirds of the Senators present concur; and he shall nominate, and by and with the Advice and Consent of the Senate, shall appoint Ambassadors,

other public Ministers and Consuls, Judges of the supreme Court, and all other Officers of the United States, whose Appointments are not herein otherwise provided for, and which shall be established by Law: but the Congress may by Law vest the Appointment of such inferior Officers, as they think proper, in the President alone, in the Courts of Law, or in the Heads of Departments.

The President shall have Power to fill up all Vacancies that may happen during the Recess of the Senate, by granting Commissions which shall expire at the End of their next Session.

Section 3

He shall from time to time give to the Congress Information of the State of the Union, and recommend to their Consideration such Measures as he shall judge necessary and expedient; he may, on extraordinary Occasions, convene both Houses, or either of them, and in Case of Disagreement between them, with Respect to the Time of Adjournment, he may adjourn them to such Time as he shall think proper; he shall receive Ambassadors and other public Ministers; he shall take Care that the Laws be faithfully executed, and shall Commission all the Officers of the United States.

Section 4

The President, Vice President and all civil Officers of the United States, shall be removed from Office on Impeachment for, and Conviction of, Treason, Bribery, or other high Crimes and Misdemeanors.

Article III

Section 1

The judicial Power of the United States shall be vested in one supreme Court, and in such inferior Courts as the Congress may from time to time ordain and establish. The Judges, both of the supreme and inferior Courts, shall hold their Offices during good Behaviour, and shall, at stated Times, receive for their Services a Compensation, which shall not be diminished during their Continuance in Office.

Section 2

The judicial Power shall extend to all Cases, in Law and Equity, arising under this Constitution, the Laws of the United States, and Treaties made, or which shall be made, under their Authority;—to all Cases affecting Ambassadors, other public Ministers and Consuls;—to all Cases of admiralty and maritime Jurisdiction;—to Controversies to which the United States shall be a Party;—to Controversies between two or more States;—between a State and Citizens of another State;—between Citizens of different States;—between Citizens of the same State claiming Lands under Grants of different States, and between a State, or the Citizens thereof, and foreign States, Citizens or Subjects.

In all Cases affecting Ambassadors, other public Ministers and Consuls, and those in which a State shall be Party, the supreme Court shall have original Jurisdiction. In all the other Cases before mentioned, the supreme Court shall have appellate Jurisdiction, both as to Law and Fact, with such Exceptions, and under such Regulations as the Congress shall make.

The Trial of all Crimes, except in Cases of Impeachment, shall be by Jury; and such Trial shall be held in the State where the said Crimes shall have been committed; but when not committed within any State, the Trial shall be at such Place or Places as the Congress may by Law have directed.

Section 3

Treason against the United States, shall consist only in levying War against them, or in adhering to their Enemies, giving them Aid and Comfort. No Person shall be convicted of Treason unless on the Testimony of two Witnesses to the same overt Act, or on Confession in open Court.

The Congress shall have Power to declare the Punishment of Treason, but no Attainder of Treason shall work Corruption of Blood, or Forfeiture except during the Life of the Person attainted.

Article IV

Section 1

Full Faith and Credit shall be given in each State to the public Acts, Records, and judicial Proceedings of every other State. And the Congress may by general Laws prescribe the Manner in which such Acts, Records and Proceedings shall be proved, and the Effect thereof.

Section 2

The Citizens of each State shall be entitled to all Privileges and Immunities of Citizens in the several States.

A Person charged in any State with Treason, Felony, or other Crime, who shall flee from Justice, and be found in another State, shall on Demand of the executive Authority of the State from which he fled, be delivered up, to be removed to the State having Jurisdiction of the Crime.

No Person held to Service or Labour in one State, under the Laws thereof, escaping into another, shall, in Consequence of any Law or Regulation therein, be discharged from such Service or Labour, but shall be delivered up on Claim of the Party to whom such Service or Labour may be due.

Section 3

New States may be admitted by the Congress into this Union; but no new State shall be formed or erected within the Jurisdiction of any other State; nor any State be formed by the Junction of two or more States, or Parts of States, without the Consent of the Legislatures of the States concerned as well as of the Congress.

The Congress shall have Power to dispose of and make all needful Rules and Regulations respecting the Territory or other Property belonging to the United States; and nothing in this Constitution shall be so construed as to Prejudice any Claims of the United States, or of any particular State.

Section 4

The United States shall guarantee to every State in this Union a Republican Form of Government, and shall protect each of them against Invasion; and on Application of the Legislature, or of the Executive (when the Legislature cannot be convened), against domestic Violence.

Article V

The Congress, whenever two thirds of both Houses shall deem it necessary, shall propose Amendments to this Constitution, or, on the Application of the Legislatures of two thirds of the several States, shall call a Convention for proposing Amendments, which, in either Case, shall be valid to all Intents and

Purposes, as Part of this Constitution, when ratified by the Legislatures of three fourths of the several States, or by Conventions in three fourths thereof, as the one or the other Mode of Ratification may be proposed by the Congress; Provided that no Amendment which may be made prior to the Year One thousand eight hundred and eight shall in any Manner affect the first and fourth Clauses in the Ninth Section of the first Article; and that no State, without its Consent, shall be deprived of its equal Suffrage in the Senate.

Article VI

All Debts contracted and Engagements entered into, before the Adoption of this Constitution, shall be as valid against the United States under this Constitution, as under the Confederation.

This Constitution, and the Laws of the United States which shall be made in Pursuance thereof; and all Treaties made, or which shall be made, under the Authority of the United States, shall be the supreme Law of the Land; and the Judges in every State shall be bound thereby, any Thing in the Constitution or Laws of any State to the Contrary notwithstanding.

The Senators and Representatives before mentioned, and the Members of the several State Legislatures, and all executive and judicial Officers, both of the United States and of the several States, shall be bound by Oath or Affirmation, to support this Constitution; but no religious Test shall ever be required as a Qualification to any Office or public Trust under the United States.

Article VII

The Ratification of the Conventions of nine States, shall be sufficient for the Establishment of this Constitution between the States so ratifying the Same.

The Word, "the," being interlined between the seventh and eighth Lines of the first Page, the Word "Thirty" being partly written on an Erazure in the fifteenth Line of the first Page, The Words "is tried" being interlined between the thirty second and thirty third Lines of the first Page and the Word "the" being interlined between the forty third and forty fourth Lines of the second Page.

Attest William Jackson Secretary

Done in Convention by the Unanimous Consent of the States present the Seventeenth Day of September in the Year of our Lord one thousand seven hundred and Eighty seven and of the Independence of the United States of America the Twelfth In witness whereof We have hereunto subscribed our Names,

G°. Washington
Presidt and deputy from Virginia

Delaware
  Geo: Read
  Gunning Bedford jun
  John Dickinson
  Richard Bassett
  Jaco: Broom

Maryland
  James McHenry
  Dan of St Thos. Jenifer
  Danl. Carroll

Virginia
  John Blair
  James Madison Jr.

North Carolina
  Wm. Blount
  Richd. Dobbs Spaight
  Hu Williamson

South Carolina
  J. Rutledge
  Charles Cotesworth Pinckney
  Charles Pinckney
  Pierce Butler

Georgia
  William Few
  Abr Baldwin

New Hampshire
  John Langdon
  Nicholas Gilman

Massachusetts
  Nathaniel Gorham
  Rufus King

Connecticut
  Wm. Saml. Johnson
  Roger Sherman

New York
  Alexander Hamilton

New Jersey
  Wil: Livingston
  David Brearley
  Wm. Paterson
  Jona: Dayton

Pennsylvania
  B Franklin
  Thomas Mifflin
  Robt. Morris
  Geo. Clymer
  Thos. FitzSimons
  Jared Ingersoll
  James Wilson
  Gouv Morris

The Preamble to The Bill of Rights

Congress of the United States
begun and held at the City of New-York, on Wednesday the fourth of March, one thousand seven hundred and eighty nine.

The Conventions of a number of the States, having at the time of their adopting the Constitution, expressed a desire, in order to prevent misconstruction or abuse of its powers, that further declaratory and restrictive clauses should be added: And as extending the ground of public confidence in the Government, will best ensure the beneficent ends of its institution.

Resolved by the Senate and House of Representatives of the United States of America, in Congress assembled, two thirds of both Houses concurring, that the following Articles be proposed to the Legislatures of the several States, as amendments to the Constitution of the United States, all, or any of which Articles, when ratified by three fourths of the said Legislatures, to be valid to all intents and purposes, as part of the said Constitution; viz.

Articles in addition to, and Amendment of the Constitution of the United States of America, proposed by Congress, and ratified by the Legislatures of the several States, pursuant to the fifth Article of the original Constitution.

The First Ten Amendments to the Constitution as Ratified by the States

Amendment I
Congress shall make no law respecting an establishment of religion, or prohibiting the free exercise thereof; or abridging the freedom of speech, or of the press; or the right of the people peaceably to assemble, and to petition the Government for a redress of grievances.

Amendment II
A well regulated Militia, being necessary to the security of a free State, the right of the people to keep and bear Arms, shall not be infringed.

Note: The following text is a transcription of the first ten amendments to the Constitution in their original form. These amendments were ratified December 15, 1791, and form what is known as the "Bill of Rights."

Amendment III

No Soldier shall, in time of peace be quartered in any house, without the consent of the Owner, nor in time of war, but in a manner to be prescribed by law.

Amendment IV

The right of the people to be secure in their persons, houses, papers, and effects, against unreasonable searches and seizures, shall not be violated, and no Warrants shall issue, but upon probable cause, supported by Oath or affirmation, and particularly describing the place to be searched, and the persons or things to be seized.

Amendment V

No person shall be held to answer for a capital, or otherwise infamous crime, unless on a presentment or indictment of a Grand Jury, except in cases arising in the land or naval forces, or in the Militia, when in actual service in time of War or public danger; nor shall any person be subject for the same offence to be twice put in jeopardy of life or limb; nor shall be compelled in any criminal case to be a witness against himself, nor be deprived of life, liberty, or property, without due process of law; nor shall private property be taken for public use, without just compensation.

Amendment VI

In all criminal prosecutions, the accused shall enjoy the right to a speedy and public trial, by an impartial jury of the State and district wherein the crime shall have been committed, which district shall have been previously ascertained by law, and to be informed of the nature and cause of the accusation; to be confronted with the witnesses against him; to have compulsory process for obtaining witnesses in his favor, and to have the Assistance of Counsel for his defence.

Amendment VII

In Suits at common law, where the value in controversy shall exceed twenty dollars, the right of trial by jury shall be preserved, and no fact tried by a jury, shall be otherwise re-examined in any Court of the United States, than according to the rules of the common law.

Amendment VIII

Excessive bail shall not be required, nor excessive fines imposed, nor cruel and unusual punishments inflicted.

Amendment IX

The enumeration in the Constitution, of certain rights, shall not be construed to deny or disparage others retained by the people.

Amendment X

The powers not delegated to the United States by the Constitution, nor prohibited by it to the States, are reserved to the States respectively, or to the people.

Index

Page numbers in *italics* refer to illustrations or sidebar documents.

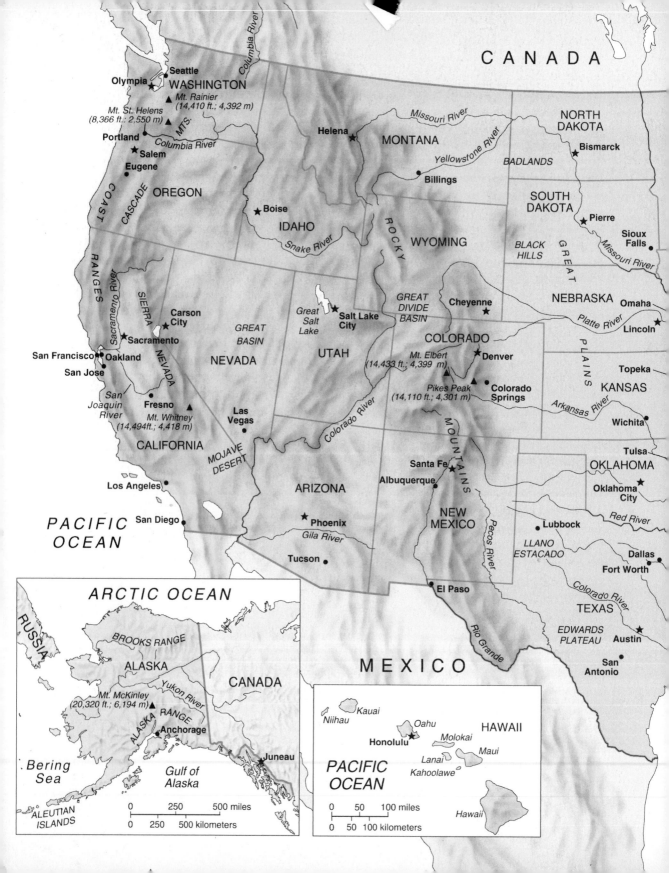

CANADA

WASHINGTON
Seattle
Olympia ★
▲ Mt. Rainier (14,410 ft.; 4,392 m)
Mt. St. Helens (8,366 ft.; 2,550 m) ▲ MTS.
Portland
Salem ★
Eugene •
Columbia River
COAST
CASCADE
OREGON

Boise ★
IDAHO
Snake River

Helena ★
Missouri River
MONTANA
Yellowstone River
Billings •

ROCKY
WYOMING

NORTH DAKOTA
Bismarck ★
BADLANDS

SOUTH DAKOTA
Pierre ★
BLACK HILLS
Sioux Falls
Missouri River
GREAT

Carson City ★
Sacramento River
SIERRA
Sacramento ★
San Francisco
Oakland
San Jose
San Joaquin River
NEVADA
Fresno •
Mt. Whitney (14,494ft.; 4,418 m) ▲
CALIFORNIA
MOJAVE DESERT
Los Angeles •
San Diego •

GREAT BASIN
Great Salt Lake
Salt Lake City ★
UTAH
Las Vegas •

GREAT DIVIDE BASIN
Cheyenne ★
COLORADO
Mt. Elbert (14,433 ft.; 4,399 m) ▲ Denver •
Pikes Peak (14,110 ft.; 4,301 m) ▲ Colorado Springs •
Colorado River

NEBRASKA
Omaha •
Platte River
Lincoln •
PLAINS
Topeka •
KANSAS
Arkansas River
Wichita •
Tulsa •

Santa Fe ★
Albuquerque •
MOUNTAINS
NEW MEXICO
ARIZONA
Phoenix ★
Gila River
Tucson •
Pecos River
El Paso •
Rio Grande

OKLAHOMA
Oklahoma City ★
Red River
Lubbock •
LLANO ESTACADO
Dallas •
Fort Worth •
Colorado River
TEXAS
EDWARDS PLATEAU
Austin ★
San Antonio •

PACIFIC OCEAN

MEXICO

ARCTIC OCEAN
RUSSIA
BROOKS RANGE
ALASKA
CANADA
Yukon River
Mt. McKinley (20,320 ft.; 6,194 m) ▲
ALASKA RANGE
Anchorage •
Juneau •
Bering Sea
Gulf of Alaska
ALEUTIAN ISLANDS

0   250   500 miles
0   250   500 kilometers

HAWAII
Kauai
Niihau
Oahu
Honolulu ★
Molokai
Maui
Lanai
Kahoolawe
PACIFIC OCEAN
Hawaii

0   50   100 miles
0   50   100 kilometers